Christian Home Educators'

CURRICULUM MANUAL: JUNIOR/SENIOR HIGH

by Cathy Duffy

Published by
Grove Publishing
16172 Huxley Circle
Westminster, California 92683

ISBN 0-929320-10-7

ACKNOWLEDGMENTS

My thanks to all the home educators who have shared their experience and expertise. I always appreciate hearing about different families' experiences with materials, because the true test of anything is how well it works in practical usage, rather than how good it looks in the brochure. Thus, this book is a reflection of the experience of many, many home educators.

Many people have helped substantially beyond sharing their experiences, some with earlier editions, and some with the present edition. It would be too time and space consuming to name all those who have helped in one way or another, but you can identify some of my "assistants" who helped with reviews since their names follow their reviews in brackets. If you see someone's name followed by my initials, that means that the review is a combination of both that reviewer's and my own input.

My husband has been infinitely patient as I have devoted endless hours to research and writing. My sons have also been an encouragement to spend that time because of the growth in Christian character that I see in their lives, which I attribute largely to the privilege that God has given us in home education.

- Cathy Duffy

Table Of Contents

Junior High Science: Preparing for High School/Junior High, Recommended Texts and Resources/ High School Level/Recommended Texts and Resources/For Lab Work/Health/Creation Science

INTRODUCTION

In our critical thinking class, we discussed an example of how appearances influence our thinking. If we read the local newspaper from Town A, noting that three-fourths of the articles had to do with criminal activity, and compared this to a similar newspaper from Town B, which devoted only one-fourth of its articles to crime, could we rightly conclude that there is much more crime in Town A than Town B? Definitely not! Each newspaper's policy and purposes would need to be examined. We would have to consider how many reporters were assigned to cover crime rather than society, sports, and business news. Numerous other factors could be important.

A nagging concern I have felt all through the writing of this book has been the overall impression which it leaves with the reader. I fear that by devoting so much space to college preparation and traditional educational materials, people will assume that both are always the avenues of first choice.

One of my goals has been to provide the necessary information for whatever approach people choose, while providing some ideas about why we might choose one alternative over another. The description of traditional record keeping and course requirements simply takes up more space than creative alternatives.

In truth, many home educated teens have been educated in very unconventional ways. College entry has not been dependent upon traditional documentation and courses of study.

My concern is that we have conscious goals rather than that we "do things properly" or follow any particular road to reach those goals.

As I consider all of the information going into this book, I realize that it can easily seem overwhelming. The abundance of information to consider is more than enough to cause us to have second thoughts about this home education venture.

Many of us chose home education for our teens based upon negative reasons such as avoidance of bad situations, school failure, or lack of money for private school. Negative motivation is not enough to carry us through for very long. We need to come up with some positive reasons for going to all this trouble or we are likely to feel resentful and give up easily when the going gets rough.

Here are some positive reasons for home educating teenagers that I have come up with both from our experience and that of others.

Spiritual growth - home educated teens are not constantly weighing their spiritual walk against what is acceptable in the eyes of their peers. There is time and opportunity for spiritual growth.

The ability to stand alone - because they do not have to spend the majority of their time with peers, they are much less concerned about fitting in. (There are exceptions to this among home schooled teens!) They tend to develop their own convictions and stick by them.

Confidence - schools are competitive environments that cause many students to lose confidence in their ability to do anything well. At home we can develop individual strengths and provide encouragement as needed without having to combat the destructive criticism some teens endure in school.

Responsibility - teens at home usually have a significant amount of responsibility. Some help teach and care for younger brothers and sisters. Some help in family businesses. Some are involved with other activities that encourage mature and responsible behavior.

Self-government - most teens are doing much of their work independently. They learn to schedule themselves. Many of them discover that learning is something that they are doing for themselves rather than for someone else, and some of them design their own courses of study based upon their own goals.

Stewardship - they learn that they can make wise and foolish choices in using their time. Most find that they have time to pursue other interests if they wisely use study time.

Pursuit of special interests - home educated teens generally have time to pursue hobbies or sports, develop talents, or work on projects of their own design.

Socialization - most home educated teens are able to interact well with people of different ages since they are not restricted to peer interaction the majority of the time. Most of them can carry on an interesting conversation.

Consideration for special learning needs - teens with learning disabilities can be successful at home because of the one-on-one teaching and use of special resources that fit their needs.

Exposure - teens have opportunities to see more of "real life" than when restricted to classrooms. They are better prepared to make career choices.

Work experience - many home educated teens work for family businesses, other employers, or themselves. They have flexibility in their school schedules that makes working easier.

Family unity - this is one of the most important "byproducts" of home education we and others have experienced. Our teens are not ashamed to be part of our families. We are all working together toward common goals. Each of us has a necessary role in the family to support and encourage each other. Instead of trials, our teenagers are blessings!

These are some of the positive goals upon which we should be focusing. We realize that home educating some teenagers will be a constant battle. Home education does not automatically change personalities and family relationships. These things take time, energy, and much prayer. There are no guarantees for particular results, but we certainly can influence the situation. When we feel discouraged, tired, and overwhelmed, as we all do from time to time, it helps to examine the fruit of our labors. Is it worth all of the trouble? Definitely yes!

Planning

First Things First

Why

"Daddy, why do you put gas in the car?"

"Because the car needs gas to make it go."

"But, Daddy, why do you need the car to go?"

"So I can go to work, Sweetheart."

"But why do you need to go to work? Why can't you stay home with us?"

"Because we need the money that I get from working to pay for our food. If I don't go to work, we will need to stop eating."

"Oh."

Conversations with three-year-olds can be very frustrating, but we ought to listen closely to the kinds of questions they ask. A three-year-old is concerned about fundamental reasons for why things are as they are. As we grow older, we still sometimes wonder, but we often cease asking questions, frequently because we are embarrassed that we do not know the answers in the first place. We become accustomed to doing things simply because we see others doing them, and these things then become habit or custom. It is not long before we lose sight of our fundamental reasons for our actions, even if we knew what they were in the beginning.

Our educational plans are easy prey for the forces of custom and habit, partly because it is so rare that anyone dares to do anything radically different educationally. Now, here we are, choosing to educate our teenagers at home—a radical decision. Yet, even having taken that radical step, we still tend either ignorantly or gullibly to accept traditional goals and methods. We accept statements such as, "You can't get into college without a high school diploma," as gospel truth, especially when they come from professionals in the education field. We are just too accustomed to accepting what we read and what we are told (especially by authorities) about education and other topics without asking questions. We also find it more comfortable to do things as we remember them being done in our own educational experience.

Home education is by its nature at least a step or two away from the established trail, so if we have made that initial commitment to home educate a teenager, we have already shown a willingness to consider and choose alternatives. But we need to maintain that questioning attitude. We often get caught up in traps of custom and habit when we choose the methods and materials that we will use. We do not really know what we are getting into, so it usually seems best to rely upon course work laid out by someone who has more educational experience than us. That may not be a bad choice, but, at the same time, it may not be the best choice.

If we are home educating a child who had difficulty with typical school curriculum, more of the same is unlikely to work at home. If we have a child with stronger mechanical skills than academic skills, we should be providing opportunities for development of those mechanical skills rather than concentrating solely on the academic. When honestly evaluating educational choices, how willing are we to choose for ourselves a path that is quite different from everyone else's? Are we willing to ask the fundamental questions, "What should my child learn?; Why should my child learn this?"; and, "How and when will he best learn it?"

We then face questions that take us back to our basic philosophy of life. Why do we do anything? Our thoughts, words, and actions ultimately reflect our basic beliefs—at least they should.

Let us apply this to education. If we believe that man exists to serve the State, then his education should be structured to produce a good servant for the State. The student will learn not to question the authority and wisdom of his master. He will learn the skills deemed useful by the State and look to it for approval for his actions. He will strive to be what the State desires—a productive, uncomplaining, unquestioning servant to further the State's goals. If the State decides that it knows best how to raise young children and mandates state day care centers for all preschool age children, a good citizen will gladly enroll his or her children. If the State decides, as it has done in California, that creation science is false and evolution is true, we are not to question its authority and wisdom.

A more common, although unacknowledged, philosophy that influences education is that of self as the center of one's existence. If we believe that man exists to serve himself ("Looking out for number one!"), then we cannot expect him to do anything beyond that which brings him pleasure and satisfaction. Education might or might not do this. What educational goals are valid for a person who wants to meet only his personal needs? Academic skills are valid only insofar as they serve as a barter item that can be traded for money to spend on personal fulfillment or utilized to impress people. If those personal desires and needs are already taken care of, what remaining motivation is there for education?

Alternatively, if we believe that man exists to serve God, our allegiance shifts from the State or the self to God. The kind of education given to a servant of the Almighty God should differ drastically from that given to a servant of the State or the self because the purposes are vastly different. A servant of God desires to learn the skills that will help him to serve God's purposes, and he looks to the unchangeable God for wisdom and direction. Meanwhile, a servant of the State wants to do that which pleases other men, and a person who plans to serve only himself, will be asking, "What's in it for me?"

So, before beginning, we need to ask ourselves, "What do we believe—about God, about life, about man's purpose in life?" If we have a strong spiritual foundation, the task is easier. But we need to apply our spiritual beliefs to every area of life, not just those with which we are comfortable. Those beliefs should influence everything we do, including educational choices. We should choose among educational alternatives with God's purposes in mind.

The state you live in may have exceeded its authority in limiting your educational options. It may require that you cover specific course work or that you use specific books or that you have a State certified teacher supervising your work. It has its own purposes in mind. Check carefully before accepting their assertions of authority over you. If they are within the law, try to work with them as much as possible in good conscience without sacrificing the education that your child should receive or the convictions you hold. (Hebrews 13:17) If necessary, choose as Peter did to obey God rather than man. (Acts 4:19)

How

We should now have at least the beginnings of a philosophical foundation upon which to build. If thinking about the "whys" of life is new to you, you will likely need several years for your ideas to develop. You will probably be adjusting your philosophy periodically as fresh insights find their way into your thinking. We can't wait until we have it all together to begin home education—it will never happen. But at the least, make sure you have a starting perspective, be it even so undeveloped as a new Christian's statement of faith in the saving work of Jesus Christ. Salvation itself brings us into the knowledge that we belong to Him, not to ourselves. This is an important perspective to have when approaching education.

While it is possible that you and I might not be in agreement about our basic philosophy of life, that is not the point. The point

is that we must have a philosophy as a guide to point us in a direction. If we give little or no thought to life or man's purpose here, we have no underpinnings for our educational choices. The State is all too ready to take over the education of our child, filling our purposeless void with its own agenda. Without philosophic direction for our child's education, we might as well relinquish that responsibility to the State.

As we begin to choose how we will proceed to educate our children, our philosophy should be close at hand dictating which choices are appropriate—in fact helping us to form a philosophy of education. That philosophy of education will be the beliefs we have about how education, as we view it, can best be accomplished.

Let us look at three different philosophies of education and some of the outcomes that result.

Public schools, in spite of classes on self-esteem and self-actualization, follow an underlying philosophy that places society above the individual. Their purpose is to produce citizens who will be productive rather than a drain on society, and who will help to support the State in perpetuating the public school system. Their purposes have to do with saving welfare costs, providing the business sector with employees, and producing citizens who are properly socialized—able to interact with others according to accepted custom. Obviously they are having serious trouble meeting these goals. But, based on their philosophical objectives, the public schools have developed an educational philosophy that includes assuming the task of being substitute parents, teaching children about sex, drugs, alcohol, self-esteem, and other subjects that they feel will help to produce adults fitted for our society. Traditional educational courses are still taught, but traditional courses are often overshadowed by these State-mandated courses that go far beyond what many of us feel are appropriate to the role of schools.

Christian Liberty Academy is an education provider with a different educational philosophy. Christian Liberty Academy offers a home education correspondence program. Its goals are overtly religious. It says, "Our educational system is religious in that all education is inescapably religious. It is impossible to train a child in an ideological vacuum that is morally, ethically, and religiously neutral. To attempt to do so is to make the child a practical, if not a professing atheist. Education will either be Christian or it will not be Christian. It will either tend to produce Christians or it will produce the opposite." (*Christian Liberty Press Catalog*, 1988-89.) Because of its educational philosophy, the Academy stresses the traditional basic subjects, loyalty and patriotism, the free enterprise system, the strength and importance of the family, and the importance of diligence and hard work—the old Puritan work ethic, along with strong Christian course content.

David and Micki Colfax are a non-Christian couple living on a remote ranch in northern California who have gained national recognition home schooling their four sons.[1] Three of their sons have received scholarships to Harvard University. The Colfaxes developed their educational philosophy through their experience. They saw that each boy had special interests and talents, so they provided plenty of books, materials, and equipment and let them explore their interests, rather than trying to cover every standard subject. They did believe in and provide a foundation in the basics of math and English, but provided little structure beyond that. Within their educational philosophy is room for developing individual talents and using a wide variety of methods, including some that are very untraditional, to accomplish goals.

These three examples show how diverse philosophies of education and their outcomes can be. The way we proceed with our home education should be an outgrowth of our philosophy.

Diversity in Approach

Just because we are Christians does not mean that we must duplicate Christian Liberty Academy in our approach. All Christians do not have to follow a "party line" when it comes to education. We have to decide what we feel is true about education. Consider questions such as these: Do we feel that our children learn best by repetition and memorization or by experience? Should our teenagers be allowed to work independently and assume responsibility for either learning or not, or should there be constant enforcement? How much say should teenagers have in choosing which subjects to study? Should vocational subjects be valued as highly as traditional school subjects?

How we approach education should be an individual decision based upon our philosophy or beliefs. If our philosophy is still in the formative stages, we might rely on the example or directions of others as to how to proceed with home education. But, as we develop our philosophy, we will also be developing our own specific ideas about how to best educate our children. In a group of even a small number of veteran home educators, the discussions are sure to get hot and heavy. Each of them has had time to think and work through her (or his) ideas about education. They are bound to have some different and even contradictory ideas.

Since we are talking about teaching teenagers, it is important to remember that these young people are at an age when they too have ideas and opinions and want to understand why they are doing things. If we cannot provide a good rationale, we might find ourselves battling over the validity of daily assignments or else imposing arbitrary authority. Then the issue becomes one of control rather than what is appropriate for study. Enforcement, when not backed up by sound reasons, can lead to serious problems in our relationships with our teenagers.

Be Prepared

Do not casually dismiss the need for personally developing your own ideas about education. At some point you will probably be required to defend your ideas about home education to authorities, relatives, friends, or your children.

What

Our basic philosophy of life tells us WHY we are doing what we are doing. Our educational philosophy takes our philosophy to a deeper, more practical level by telling us HOW we plan to go about accomplishing our goals. By combining the WHY and the HOW we should arrive at the WHAT—the subjects or courses to study. Sometimes we are bound by the restraints of state requirements and must teach a very specific list of subjects. But, in most states, we have quite a bit of leeway in interpreting requirements. The constriction is more likely to come from our own (parents' and teen's) plans for the future.

One of the primary concerns is college entry. Colleges usually require that high school students complete specific courses to qualify for entry. However, even though colleges list specific requirements, it is good to keep in mind families like the Colfaxes who trusted their own instincts about what was most important for their sons without trying to meet all the specific requirements. Other home schoolers have also been accepted by colleges without the traditional educational background and paperwork. Many colleges are willing to individually evaluate potential students, so the need to plan a course of study to meet college entry requirements is debatable.

Laying aside our old ideas of what high school students need to learn is difficult. We may have done just fine with the courses we had. What worked for us should work for our children. Right? It might work, but it might not be best. And then again, it might not work. Consider: Should all children learn algebra and geometry? Is diagramming essential to a good knowledge of English grammar? Are biology and chemistry the best choices for high school science? If a child already has an excellent foundation in United States history, must he study it again at high school level, or would he do better to specialize in a single area of U.S. history? Does health education need to be taught as a class? Should all high school students write research papers? These are examples of the kinds of questions we must consider when we discuss individual subject areas.

We should each examine carefully our preconceptions and decide what we consider essential and what is open to discussion. Our conclusions will likely be influenced by the weight of state laws, future educational goals, and our accountability to others whether it be a correspondence course, independent study program, or other authority.

Methods and Materials

Most of us are free to choose whatever materials we want to use. At this time no state has a prescribed curriculum for home educators, although it is possible that state Departments of Education will try to impose curriculum restrictions in the future. (Fox, Linda P., "Home School Curricula," *Home School Re-*

---

1   You can read about the Colfax family in their book, *Homeschooling for Excellence* (Warner Books) [$11.99].

searcher, Vol.4, No. 4, Dec., 1988, p. 12.) The present limitations on curriculum choices are likely to come from correspondence courses or independent study programs. Students enrolled in correspondence courses are required to use materials that come with the course. Of course, other materials could be used as supplements, but there is seldom time left for extras. Some independent study programs prescribe a curriculum to be followed, but usually these programs allow home educators to make their own choices.

I expect that many people reading this book will be planning their own curriculum, since those enrolling in correspondence courses are generally provided with the basic information they need within that structure.

I have tried to research a fairly broad range of options since I realize that home educators are an extremely diverse group. Some feel that all curriculum materials must be Christian, while others do not. Some feel that the spiritual principle of accountability requires that we enroll under some authority other than that of our own household. Some want to follow a traditional approach to high school education, using typical textbooks, while others want to experiment with more creative, unstructured methods. Many choose a combination of traditional and experimental methods. There are good reasons for choosing any of the above or other options.

A decision does not have to be made as to who is right or wrong about educational philosophy. Usually each person's philosophy of education grows out of his own personal experience. If our children respond to certain methods, then we will be convinced that those are the best methods, even though those same methods might not work well with other children. Our personality and style of teaching will also have a lot to do with our preferences. A warm, gregarious teacher might prefer personal educational methods—discussion, activities, and interaction. An introspective, introverted person might prefer that her children work independently as much as possible. What is right for someone else may not be right for you!

Putting Ideas to Work

After we have dealt with these philosophical issues and come up with our own ideas about what education should be, we must bring all of our conclusions back into the real world and figure out how we can make all of this work with <u>our children</u> in <u>our circumstances</u>—a sometimes uncomfortable encounter with reality.

Where the Rubber Meets the Road

In this corner—The Home Schooling Parent! In the other corner, Reality! Now shake hands, go to your corners, and come out fighting!

It's fine to read descriptions of correspondence high school programs or browse through A Beka's brochure on their high school video program. They make teaching teenagers at home sound like a breeze. But they are only dealing with a part of the puzzle. We parents must also deal with a thing called reality. Reality is the younger child who needs to be taught how to read; endless meals that need preparing; medical and dental appointments; chauffeuring to soccer, gymnastics, and little league; pregnancy; ministry; grocery shopping; mounds of laundry; and children who would rather be doing anything but school. If we had nothing else to occupy us besides teaching our children, it would certainly be much easier. But I do not know of any home schooling parent who is free from life's routines.

When we begin to plan how to teach our teenagers at home, we must first look at our situation. Do we have any experience? Do we have any confidence in our ability to teach our teenagers? How much time do we have available? How many interruptions are we likely to have? Can we expect any support from Dad or from others? Can we survive without support? Are we able to make compromises between our ideal concept of how it should be and reality, then live with those compromises without guilt?

Experience and Confidence

Those of us who have been home educating through elementary school and are making the transition into junior or senior high school will obviously find the task less overwhelming than someone just beginning to home educate. Even though there are changes as we move into the high school years, we have already learned the basics of running a home school—organization, record keeping, purchasing materials, establishing a routine that prevents the house from decaying while school is in session. Those of you who are just beginning might consider enrolling in a correspondence course, independent study program, or other home school service that will help you with these basics so that you can concentrate on the actual schooling. You might want to jump ahead to Chapter Eight to learn more about these options before reading on.

Experience, confidence, and finances are probably three of the most important factors to consider when making the choice of whether to enroll in a program or go it alone. Experience and confidence also have much to do with the methods and materials we choose to use. If we have confidence in our ability to tackle

new challenges, then we are more likely to fare well working independently. "Going it alone" means we will have to dig for information, take responsibility for keeping our own records, plan course work without help, and rely on ourselves for recognition of a job well done. If you lack confidence, you are with the majority, so do not be discouraged by your doubts. By realizing ahead of time that you need more support, you can make choices with which you will be more comfortable.

Experience goes a long way toward building our confidence. If we have already done some sort of teaching in Sunday school, traditional school, informal classes, or home school, it is not such a mysterious process to us. The educational establishment has tried to create a mystique about the teaching process to add prestige to their jobs and, sometimes, to keep parents from interfering. But, once you have taught, you KNOW what is involved. Any positive experience will give you the reassurance that YOU CAN DO IT! You realize that it is often a process of trial and error with each child to find out what produces the desired results.

Most people suffer some doubts before beginning, but just making it through one year of home education will give you a tremendous boost in confidence (unless you make a total mess of it, which rarely happens). But we all have different personalities, some more confident than others, some needing more encouragement. That's all right. Just make sure that you are involved with someone who will provide you with the feedback you need, whether it be a support group, a correspondence school, independent study program, school service, or an experienced home schooler.

Support groups, as small as two families, are essential for most of us. I have met many, many home educating moms with tremendous doubts about what they have been doing. Ninety percent of the time they are doing a great job and just need to have someone objective tell them so.

At the same time, we do not want to tell someone they are doing a wonderful job if it is not true. We render no one a favor by praising him falsely when he needs someone to confront him with the truth. Some home educators pull their children out of school to protect them from harmful situations or failure but lack any positive goals for accomplishment. They feel that avoiding the negative is sufficient. Yet they harm their children in other ways by not providing for their educational needs. Such people are doing a disservice to their children and to the reputation of all home educators. We need the kind of support that encourages us to do a good job, that holds us accountable, and that urges us to keep on trying when things get discouraging.

Suggested Background Reading About Home Educating Teens

Catholic Education: Homeward Bound by Kimberly Hahn and Mary Hasson (Ignatius Press) [$14.95] reflects the growing popularity of home education among Catholic families. Hahn and Hasson present the rationale for home education but spend most of their time on what to do and how to do it. As you might expect, they strongly stress spiritual purpose and focus throughout our educational endeavors. The book deals with teaching all ages, with one chapter particularly focused on teaching teens.

Countdown to Consistency: A Workbook for Home Educators by Mary Hood, Ph.D. (The Relaxed Homeschooler) [$8.95], is subtitled "Understanding and Clarifying Your Educational Philosophy." Hood proposes four philosophical categories of home educators, of course allowing for much overlap. She does a superb job of describing philosophies so that novices can understand basic differences, then she ties in related areas—assumptions about life and learning; educational goals; teacher/student roles and relationships; curriculum design; methods of planning, instructing, and evaluating; and selection of materials. She includes worksheets to help us think through different areas and record our conclusions. At only forty-five pages, with much blank space for our own notes, this book offers a quick jumpstart for developing a philosophy of education.

In *The Relaxed Home School* (The Relaxed Homeschooler) [$10.95], author Mary Hood Ph.D., (who is also the author of *Countdown to Consistency)* describes her own philosophy of education. She covers some of the background territory such as I do in the first few sections of my book. Then she goes on to "demonstrate" her philosophy in action in her own family by telling us how they tackle each subject. Mary's approach is, as the title indicates, relaxed. She is a Christian home educator, but does not rely on a Christian-textbook approach to learning. She stresses the need for goals, coupled with an openness to many ways of attaining them. Her children have significant input into goal and strategy decisions, reflecting their own personal goals, talents, and interests. Since my own philosophy of education is very similar to Mary's, I highly recommend her book so that you get the "real life" side of applying the curriculum decisions you might make based on my own book. Another of Mary's books, *Onto the Yellow School Bus and through the Gates of Hell* [$10.95] is a very personal, thought-provoking examination of government schools that will reinforce your commitment to home education.

Effective Parenting of Teens: What the Bible Says About Raising Teenagers (Family Ministries) [$13] is a seminar presentation consisting of two audio cassettes and detailed notes in book form. Pastor Reb Bradley presents biblical strategies for raising teens that are full of wisdom and common sense. He presents his ideas in a clearly-structured manner so it is easy to walk away with specific "to-do's" for your family. He believes that the teen years should be a blessing rather than a "curse" as so many people expect. He rejects typical youth group activities and encourages teens to take on adult responsibilities. Through-

out his presentation, he also teaches parents how to encourage and uplift their teens.

Hearth and Home by Karey Swan (Singing Springs Productions) [$17] needs mention here even though it receives a more complete review under "Homemaking" in Chapter Eighteen. In numerous places, Karey addresses child raising and education, but especially in Chapter Fourteen, "Thought Food for the Future," she addresses life preparation issues in regard to education and the choices we make for our children. She promotes a "mentorial" approach to higher education, not as an exclusive answer, but as a primary way of meeting the right goals. Thought provoking ideas here!

The Home School Manual by Ted Wade (Gazelle Publications) [approx. $30], seventh edition due early 1998, is one of the most comprehensive books available. Ted covers all of the basics of home schooling and offers the most balanced presentation of the pros and cons of home schooling that I know of. Special sections by guest authors add extra depth. There is much help here for both beginning and veteran home schoolers. Since the book is a massive 560 or so pages, Ted provides six "guided tour" options, which list pertinent chapters to read depending upon your situation—investigating home education, teaching young or preschool children, just beginning to teach elementary grades, continuing elementary grades (veterans), high school at home, and teaching children with handicaps. Chapters reviewing resources have been expanded, and they should be helpful to compare with those in this book and Mary Pride's *Big Books of Home Learning*. Addresses are listed for home schooling organizations and government education offices for all states, for Canadian provinces, and for a few overseas countries. Ted also enlisted the skills of organizing expert, Marilyn Rockett, to create a number of reproducible charts and forms for this edition. A new CD-ROM version is planned for summer of 1998. I suggest putting *The Home School Manual* in one form or another on your home school library basics list.

Homeschooling for Excellence by David and Micki Colfax (Warner Books) describes their home school experience. A fuller description of this book appears in Chapter One.

HotHouse Transplants (Grove Publishing) [$11.95] is a compilation of stories written by Christian home schoolers who have graduated and moved on to college and careers. The focus in many of the stories is on the question, "How is your life different in terms of purpose and direction as a result of homeschooling?" This is an encouraging book to read for parents who wonder if home schooling through high school is worth the effort.

No Regrets by Alexandra Swann (Cygnet Press) [$16.95] describes the homeschooling experience of the Swann family, a tremendous contrast to the Colfax family in the approach they took. A more complete description of this book and the Swann's experience appears in Chapter Six.

The National Home Education Research Institute produces quality research on home education that might be very reassuring to parents who wonder if this is really a safe or good thing to do. NHERI provides research reports and a quarterly journal addressing topics such as the academic achievement of the home educated, their success in college and adulthood, and their success in terms of "socialization" [$25 per year for individuals or $40 for libraries or organizations]. The newest, most thorough presentation of home school research can be found in Dr. Ray's book *Strengths of Their Own* [$12.95] (available through NHERI). Founded by Dr. Brian Ray, NHERI serves as a clearinghouse for research to the public, policy makers, and other researchers. Write for information about specific research, subscriptions to the journal, or to order the book.

Reaching the Heart of Your Teen by Gary and Anne Marie Ezzo (Questar) [$9.99] is the best book I have yet found on parent teen relationships. While I can't give a blanket endorsement of everything the Ezzos teach in their seminars and other books, their ideas presented in this book are full of Godly wisdom and common sense. They challenge parents to put forth the effort necessary to develop the kind of relationships with their teens that grow into lifelong bonds of friendship rather than rebellion and a desire for separation and independence. Rejecting the common belief in the inevitability of teenage rebellion, they promote a healthy interdependence rather than unhealthy codependence. They include practical strategies on a just about every issue that arises between parents and teens, including communication, discipline, and restoring "lost" relationships.

The Simplicity of Homeschooling by Jack and Vicky Goodchild (HIS Publishing Company) [$20] is a book and audio tape set by homeschooling pioneers that reflects the conclusions that many pioneer families have come to share about what home schooling and the home school lifestyle ought to be. The book, by Vicky, is for both beginners and veterans. It addresses some of the beginner's questions with encouragement and reassurance. Vicky then describes seven primary homeschool methods, mentioning resources for more information and/or curriculum for each. Obviously, she prefers unit study approaches the most, but, like many experienced home educators, she also believes that the best home schooling pulls in elements of a number of different approaches to tailor what we do to fit our own families. Vicky also covers the question of what to do with preschoolers, homeschooling high schoolers (with lots of specific helps), curriculum suggestions, goals, scheduling, support organizations, and resource and curriculum suppliers (selective lists). A theme throughout the book is the importance of developing a "learning lifestyle," of creating a home where education is encouraged and enjoyed rather than enforced. The audio tape by Jack Goodchild is totally different

presentation addressing some of the same ideas, but directed to dads who might be more likely to listen than to read the book. It summarizes the importance and value of home schooling with some practical suggestions for dads, then ends with a beautiful song by Monte and Karey Swan.

In *The Teenage Liberation Handbook: How to Quit School and Get a Real Life and Education*, Grace Llewellyn (Lowry House) [$14.95] speaks directly to teens, encouraging them to consider the unschooling option. Philosophically, Llewellyn comes from a very different place than most Christian home schoolers. Because of this foundational divergence, we might find ourselves disagreeing with some of her logic, however, she has exceptional insight into much of the flawed logic of compulsory education and its incarnation in traditional high schools.

Rather than bore us with a recitation of philosophy, Llewellyn writes in a friendly, big sister style, using lots of stories and examples. She does not reject the idea of learning, but suggests better ways to learn than attending school. She even has sections with suggestions for covering basic subject areas for students who either are college bound or want to study those subjects for personal reasons. She gets into work, apprenticeship, entrepreneurships, and all sorts of other real-life options, all the time encouraging teens that they can do things differently.

Although the book is written to teens (there is an introductory chapter written to parents), because Llewellyn's philosophy is a major part of the book, I would encourage parents to also read the entire book and discuss differences of opinion with their teens. In spite of philosophical conflicts, I recommend this book to challenge and expand our thinking about how we "do" high school. (An expanded, revised edition is due in 1998.)

Real Lives: Eleven Teenagers Who Don't Go to School by Grace Llewellyn (Lowry House) [$17] is a thought provoking journey through the lives of eleven teenage homeschoolers. These teens tell their own stories in their own words, which heightens the impact. They come from a variety of philosophical backgrounds, many of them following a self-determined approach to education, similar to that recommended by Llewellyn in *The Teenage Liberation Handbook*. This is a book for teens to read themselves, although some parents might feel uncomfortable having their teens read this book independently because of language and lifestyle references. However, it is valuable as proof that nontraditional approaches can work as well or better than traditional approaches.(SE)

Also check out the how-to resources in Chapter Six under the heading "For More Detailed Help," many of which also discuss philosophy of education.

Qualifications

When we set out to educate young children at home, our educational background was not a major factor. Most of us had the fundamental knowledge to instruct our children in the basics, and we could easily learn what we did not know already or refresh our knowledge as we went along. Such is not the case when

we teach teenagers. Beyond sixth grade, the subject matter becomes increasingly complicated and requires more knowledgeable input from the teacher. This does not necessarily mean that we need a strong educational background to educate our teens at home. But we need to know our strengths and weaknesses, and we need to be willing to seek help if necessary.

If our math skills and background are weak, we need to have someone else available on whom we can rely for assistance. Our choice might be Dad, a correspondence course, a tutor, or another home schooling parent. If we did fairly well in high school math, we might do fine just reviewing as our children learn, keeping current on what they are learning so that we can lend a hand as needed.

Writing is an essential part of our teen's education. If we are weak in the area of writing, we have no means of evaluating our child's written work. We need to have someone else available to assess writing assignments and advise us on problem areas.

A correspondence course can be very useful for those of us with poor educational backgrounds, but it is not a total solution. Correspondence courses take time for paper work to travel between teacher and pupil. Quite often, the student needs immediate help which is not available. Sometimes, correspondence teachers are available for telephone consultation, but that can get quite expensive.

Some parents have hired tutors to help with individual classes. Other parents have banded together for mutual benefit, trading skills and talents. (See Chapter Eight for possible options to consider.)

Before you begin, honestly evaluate your capabilities. Make sure that you do not take on more than you can handle. If your child "graduates" from high school without the ability to write a decent paper or solve basic algebraic or geometric problems, his future choices might be seriously limited. At the same time, do not underestimate your own potential or ignore the wealth of resources which can help you overcome your limitations.

Logistics

Have you ever tried to explain an algebra concept with constant interruptions? It is impossible! Teaching teens becomes even more challenging when you also have your hands full trying to educate or care for your younger children. I often found it frustrating trying to work with two teenagers and just one younger child. My youngest still needed quite a bit of assistance with his work—often just a brief question. But all it took was one brief question to derail my train of thought when I was explaining a difficult concept. Younger children cannot always tell when you are occupied or when it is the appropriate time to ask questions. And, of course, babies have no concept of proper timing. On the other hand, teenagers generally are able to study much more independently than younger children, so overall you should be spending much less time with them individually. You might be able to time classes so that interruptions are not a problem. Consider saving subjects that cannot be interrupted until evening when Dad can either teach or hold down the fort and run interference for you.

Some families have found it helpful to have older children tutor younger children. This is a great idea since it reinforces the knowledge of the older child while freeing Mom from having to be everything for everyone. However, all older siblings do not make good tutors, and sometimes the friction between older and younger children created in tutorial situations is worse to live with than the pressure of Mom doing it in the first place.

Be realistic in assessing the personalities and relationships in your family for tutoring and working together. Our children do not automatically develop wonderful personality characteristics when we home school. That is often one of our long-term goals. More commonly, our children irritate each other from constant togetherness.

Shared Responsibility

Housework is an important topic when we discuss the logistics of home education. It can be very difficult to maintain a home school if the schoolhouse is rotting beneath our feet. Between lesson planning, research, teaching, checking work, field trips, music lessons, Scout activities, sports, and friends, we somehow must find time to maintain the homestead. I am not talking about "House Beautiful" but about keeping the health department from investigating. Some families are fortunate enough to be able to hire someone to come in every week or two to clean. It costs less than visits to the psychiatrist, so consider stretching the budget to cover the cost.

Much better is the situation where home maintenance is every family member's responsibility. Time is set aside for housework. Even the youngest children can help dust or pick up. Older children can mop floors, launder the clothes, prepare meals, wash windows, and mow the lawns.

In our society we have grown used to the idea that children should be involved in "activities" and parents are responsible for providing everything else to allow their children to participate in the activities. We end up shipping our children off elsewhere hoping they will acquire all the skills they need for life. We provide athletics to get them in shape, and then we hire gardeners to do the physical labor in our yards. We sign them up for "culinary arts" while Mom struggles to do all the cooking at home alone. We sign them up for activities to rescue them from boredom and to help them burn up their excess energy while we work ourselves into physical exhaustion.

Home schoolers are making radical changes in educational approaches. It is only right that those changes should extend to the way we view our family life and activities for children. If we have our children take on important roles in maintaining the home they will learn far more than by participating in all manner of outside classes. Beyond that, it is important that children realize that the home belongs to the family, not to mom. My family knows not to say, "I cleaned the floor for you, Mom." They clean for the whole family! Every family member wears clothing and can see if the laundry basket is full. Any child older than ten should be able to sort and run a load of laundry with minimal help. Our son or daughter should never be blaming Mom because his favorite shirt or her favorite blouse is still in the laundry. Teenagers, especially boys, have a vital interest in food. They are entirely capable of fixing meals, and what better way for them to realize how much work is involved? The point is, to make home education successful, it has to be a joint venture for all family members. One person (Mom) cannot be all things to all people.

Help and Support

Physical help and emotional support are both important to home schooling parents to varying degrees. Interestingly, the two often come together. If another person is heavily involved in helping us teach our children, they are most likely also emotionally involved with us and our children.

In some families, fathers provide both physical and emotional support. However, many families have unrealistic expectations about father's participation. When families first begin home schooling, they often plan on father teaching one or two classes in the evenings along with acting as principal of the school. After Dad has been at work nine or ten hours, he still has his share of home maintenance. Then there are the nights set aside for Bible study, Awana, Scouts, and sports. Dad is lucky if he has a free evening or two a week. Despite good intentions, such plans often do not work out. Even so, some fathers still manage to provide much needed emotional support even though they do not have time to teach classes.

In some cases, unfortunately, fathers might not even be interested in the educational process. Sure, they are concerned that their children are doing well, but they do not want to get into discussions of whether or not John is ready to handle algebra. Count yourself fortunate if your husband is really involved with home education, but, if not, keep in mind that he has other priorities such as providing for his family. Do not try to use guilt to manipulate him into a more active role—it rarely works.

If Dad is not a terrific help when it comes to support or assistance, where do we go? Trading teaching talents with other home schoolers or taking advantage of some of the options discussed in Chapter Eight can help us with physical support in the actual teaching. Emotional support can be more difficult to come by. I have met home educators who have providentially found just the person they need to be a friend and confidante about home schooling, yet I also know of veteran home educators who are still praying that God will supply them with a supportive friend. All it takes is one other person. Emotional support (or lack of it) is a crucial factor for many home schooling mothers deciding whether to stick with it or not. We need another adult with whom we can discuss discipline and motivation problems. We need input from other home schoolers about ideas for methods and materials. And, most of all we need some encouragement that what we are doing is worthwhile.

Many home educating mothers are surrounded with skeptics. At the merest mention of frustration or fatigue, friends and relatives quickly chime in, "Why don't you put them back in school?" Even experienced home educators occasionally consider what it would be like to put their children into school. (Especially on bad days!) Mothers without anyone supportive to turn to do not dare voice such thoughts because the reaction they know they will get is, "Well, it's about time you came to your senses." It can be quite daunting when dealing with self-doubts to have everyone else reinforcing your fears.

Some home schooling moms have sought support from church or Bible study groups. However, it is rare to get the kind of feedback we need from someone who is not home schooling, even though it may be possible. I do know of many supportive grandmothers helping their daughters or daughters-in-law, who wish that they had known about home education when their own children were young. All of us are not fortunate enough to have helpful mothers in the wings. The most practical source of support is usually another home schooling mom—just one person with whom we can compare notes and share frustrations.

It takes time to develop a relationship to the point where we can be honest and open about our experiences, sharing both our triumphs and our struggles. Finding such relationships can be difficult if you live in an isolated area. But, even if you can establish a friendship that involves long distance calls, it can be justified like the housekeeping expense. It might be the vital ingredient you need to maintain your sanity and keep on going.

Enrolling in a program or joining a group is great as long as you can afford the time and cost, and if there is something available for you to join. Since many more families are educating teens at home than in the past, there are more possibilities than there used to be. In years past it was a rarity to run into a parent educating a teen at home. Now support groups specifically for home educated teens are springing up across the country.

Independent study programs and school services are better able to advise us about teaching teens as they gather more experience each year. We might find the support we need through such a program, but we need to carefully check a program's knowledge of and experience with teens. It is possible that we might end up paying to be their guinea pig. That in itself might not be bad if they are willing to do the research for us and ensure that we get the service we are paying for.

When We Need Some Part-Time Income

Whatever our family's reasons for home schooling, many home schooling mom's must supplement (or even provide) the family income. This adds a tremendous burden to the already challenging task of home education. However, many moms have discovered opportunities for working from or in their homes enabling them to be available for their children while also earning money. Certainly, it is easy to let the work take precedence and end up abandoning our children to their own devices, a pitfall that I strongly caution you to guard against. While some home school moms do work part-time away from home, that situation is even more difficult. I suggest avoiding it if at all possible.

The Art of Compromise

Most of us have our idealized goals for home education. The reality is that we will have to make some compromises between our ideals and what we can physically accomplish in the time we have with the resources available to us.

I love really digging into literature, analyzing plots and characterizations. I wanted to have two days a week for literature discussions, but we were also studying government and economics that year, which absolutely required discussion. There just was not enough time to have literary discussions more often than once every week or two. I could have given up on literature and saved it for the next year, but that would have interfered with important goals for the following year. I could have felt guilty and inadequate, but instead, I compromised. The boys would read the background information provided in the literature texts on their own, and we would have discussions as time allowed. It was not the best approach, but my sons still had the experience of reading many types of literature, and they gleaned some background information on their own.

We can always take the view, "What would they be learning if they were in a traditional school?" Although there are some excellent teachers and classes in schools, there is no guarantee that any child is going to absorb all that wonderful class content listed in the course outline. Often students drift through classes just marking time and completing minimal requirements. We should be able to provide more than the bare minimum even if all we do is choose quality texts and make sure our child reads them.

All this is not to say that just anything will suffice. I believe that we should set high (but realistic) standards and hold our children to them. But we need to be careful of aiming so high that satisfaction is always just out of reach, while guilt and inadequacy stare us in the face.

Blessed are the Flexible for They Shall Not be Broken

Flexibility is a mandatory characteristic of successful home schools. I can guarantee that you will encounter many situations where you will have to alter course, put something on hold, or deal with unanticipated problems. If you are set in your mind that

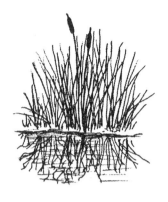

NOTHING is going to interrupt your plan for home education, you are setting yourself up for a nervous breakdown.

We will need to deal with household problems from time to time. If the plumbing is backed up, school will be interrupted for a trip through the yellow pages, several telephone calls, and a visit by the Roto-Rooter man. If mom is sick, we are allowed to declare a school holiday. Planning some "floating holidays" helps alleviate the guilt of taking time off to stay in bed when we have a 103 degree temperature. Flexibility might have to extend to the planned course of study. We might have to change course in midstream if our teen is just not able to learn a certain subject with the materials we bought or if he needs an extra three or four months to complete Algebra I. If we can bend with these situations, accepting them as normal, we will not find ourselves surrendering in frustration because things are not going the way we planned.

While most of us tend to strive too hard and judge ourselves too harshly, there are those among us who need less flexibility and more accountability and discipline. Some of us drop all planned academic work every time a field trip comes up—whether or not the field trip is worthwhile for our child. Emergencies and sudden changes in schedule are a way of life rather than an occasional occurrence. Priorities shift according to our latest interest. Challenging subjects are easily abandoned and rarely replaced. We justify lack of progress with excuses such as, "We'll make it up later."

Those of us who suffer from too much flexibility might do better under the guidance of an independent study program, correspondence course, or other overseer who will help keep us on track. If it seems like too much trouble to either hold ourselves accountable or work under someone else, perhaps we should put our children back in school.

Living with Our Choices

We begin by deciding what we really wish to accomplish. Next we look hard and long at our situation. Then we decide what we realistically can expect to achieve, while maintaining some flexibility. We must then do what we can to the best of our ability, and trust God to cover our deficiencies.

CHAPTER THREE

Getting Things Done

If we cannot convince our teenager to clean his room, how on earth can we hope to get him to cooperate with his education?

The teen years are sometimes the most trying for parent-child relationships aside from educational issues. We have to realize that we are dealing with young adults, not just larger children. Teenagers are developing (we hope) minds of their own. They want to have more control over themselves and their environment. We should worry if this is not happening. A certain amount of conflict is normal with teenagers since they are trying to become independent from their parents. This situation does not mean that we should expect rebellion from our teenagers! There is a clear distinction between differences of opinion and rebellion. Differences of opinion are normal and should be expected. Rebellion or deliberate disobedience should not be allowed.

Our teenagers will be forming their own opinions about how their lives should be organized and how much freedom or responsibility they should have. Although they are forming their own ideas, it does not mean that they should be able to act upon them at will. As long as teens are living at home under parental authority, parents have the final say. However, parents should increasingly consider the views of their teenagers, gradually allowing more self-government and independence as teens show they deserve it.

Both Gregg Harris, in his seminars on the family and home education, and Dr. James Dobson, the well known Christian child-psychologist and author, paint a balanced picture of carefully shifting privileges and restrictions as teenagers exhibit increased responsibility and maturity or their opposites. If a teen finishes household chores without reminders, takes responsibility for his school work, and is otherwise acting reliably and maturely, then he deserves to have more freedom such as an increase in free time and less parental supervision. If a teen never gets his chores finished and does poorly with his studies, then the reverse should apply—he should have less freedom and more parental supervision.

Unfortunately, it is not quite so simple as it sounds. Friction arises when parents and teen disagree over how much privilege should be allowed and what restrictions are reasonable. The potential parent/teenager problems multiply when home schooling is added to the picture. If our teens were in school, we might not have needed to be involved beyond making sure they completed their homework. Now, we might be contending with them over every aspect of their schooling, especially if the home school choice is the parents' rather than the teenager's. Yet, even though the situation is more complicated, the same principle applies. As teens exhibit responsibility in getting work finished thoroughly and on time, we should give them more freedom in determining their own schedule. As they make wise decisions in choosing courses, we allow them more leeway in those choices. As they

show that they do not need to be directed to make wise ethical and moral choices, they can be trusted to make those decisions on their own, and we need to give them opportunities to do so.

We face a challenge in motivating our teenagers to care about education for their own sake. What's in it for them? All they can see is more of the same through high school and, possibly, for four or more years beyond. Meanwhile, some of them feel that life is passing them by. Some of our teens want to go to "real" schools for the social happenings and sports, but rarely for the educational opportunities there. They want friends, activities, and recognition and sometimes feel deprived of those because of home schooling. Rarely does a teen ask to return to school solely for educational reasons. Our entire culture belittles learning. The television/movie/entertainment industry that so heavily influences attitudes, places no value on learning. Instead it advocates concern about appearance, material goods, entertainment, and self-indulgence.

In addition, American teenagers face an identity crisis of sorts. In other cultures and in our country's past history, teens are and were already well along the path of future careers, accepting much adult responsibility that our teenagers often do not have until their mid-twenties.

For American young people, the teen years are often a wasted period, a time of waiting to get on with life. During the teen years, when many are trying to figure out who they are and what they want to do with their lives, society gives them few alternatives. In school, they can aspire to be cheerleaders or sports jocks, nerds or part of the "in" group. At home we can expand their choices some, but legal restrictions limit their options. They are required to be "in school," whether at home or elsewhere. Outside work hours are restricted. Employers rarely hire high school students younger than 16, and most of our families do not rely on the help of our teens for survival. It is no wonder that many teens feel useless and worthless.

Ideally, we prefer that our teens derive meaning and purpose for their lives from their spiritual walk. Yet, few of our teens are truly mature spiritually. They are often very emotionally confused. Some teenagers will find their self-confidence in their academic work. But others will use their failures in school to convince themselves of their worthlessness. Many parents of teens decide to home educate, hoping to restore their child's self-esteem which has been severely battered by repeated failures. However, to transform educational failure into success, things have to be done differently than they have been in the past.

Many teenagers have never developed good study habits. Whether our children were not taught or refused to learn does not really matter. If our teens do not have the necessary study skills and habits, we end up force feeding school lessons—a very poor way of providing an education.

There are three areas that we need to address regarding study habits: motivation, learning styles, and study skills. All of these are crucial to successfully teaching our teenagers at home.

Motivation

This issue is probably the one we fear most. We already are aware of difficulties in motivating our teens. Is it worth the hassle to add school to the list of areas of potential conflict? There is an underlying assumption parents make that teenagers would rather avoid school work, and that we will have to force them to do it anyway. Yet, this assumption might or might not be valid.

Whether a teenager has been in a conventional, traditional school or a home school, if he has not developed self-motivation, he has a problem. Some children discover the value of education at an early age and understand that they are working for themselves more than for teachers or parents. Some children love to learn, and even better, see education as the means of preparing themselves for God's purposes in their lives. That love of learning most often sprouts when a child has been given room to explore areas of learning that interest him in ways that are enjoyable to him. If a child has been regimented through the educational process with little regard for his personal interests and abilities, he is much less likely to develop a love for learning. In fact, many children develop an attitude toward education that asks only, "What am I supposed to do to make the teacher happy?"

Our first task is to enlist our child's interest in learning for his own sake. One important step is to allow our teenagers some say about their course of study. They might have some interests or preferences that can be incorporated into their course of study without any problem. Why arbitrarily force them to take French rather than Spanish? Also, in choosing a course of study, we have a chance to sit down together with our teens, discuss and agree upon goals, examine the requirements, and jointly figure out how best to meet those goals and requirements. Let's not underestimate our teens. Most of them really do care about their futures, but many of our battles originate from their feelings of powerlessness. They have little control over what happens in their lives at a time when they need experience in developing independence. Granted, some of our teenagers might not be very interested or helpful with planning courses. Yet, if they have a voice in the planning, they are likely to take more interest in the outcome.

The average child is going to complain about having to work hard, a normal human reaction to which we can all relate. Yet learning requires work in one form or another. Forcing our teens to work is one solution, but a poor one. If we can shift our teenager's motivation away from performing for us or performing to avoid punishment, and instead focus it upon performing to meet self-imposed goals, we will have made our job infinitely easier.

Our goal should be to have our teen function as a partner in his schooling rather than as a reluctant participant. He should be actively involved in planning course work and in following through to completion. He should be performing for himself, not for us! If we rely primarily on strategies like rewarding our children for completing school work, we are sending the message that they are performing for our benefit. Their only benefit is the reward they receive from us—poor motivation to become a life-long learner.

At the same time, if our teen is performing for himself, we have to be willing to allow him more room for decision making. Are we willing to allow him five years to finish high school if he wants to spread out his workload? Is there some tradeoff agreement we can make? (e.g., He agrees to work at a part-time job and contribute financially to the family, since he will be dependent for a longer time.) Are we willing to allow him the freedom to decide whether or not to prepare for college? Can we set aside our own egos enough to let him choose a future that is not particularly ambitious?

Like many teenagers, our child might feel that school is just something to get through. By about age fifteen, our teenagers are aware of their academic inclination or its lack. If academics are not their strong suit, the specter of two or three years more of the same might seem like torture. We might need to take a radically different approach to learning to arouse their interest. Independent study, self-designed projects, a vocational apprenticeship, part-time school (see Chapter Eight), or another nontraditional approach might provide the turning point in their education. For some teens, a part-time job that convinces them of the need for academic skills might be necessary before they can make any significant progress.

Programs such as 4-H, Boy Scouts, and Girl Scouts (check your phone book for such organizations in your area) can often provide educational incentive as well as valuable help for parent-teachers. These programs are available to even those who live in isolated rural areas, since members can work either as part of a group or independently. (You should investigate the philosophy of these organizations; the most obvious problem is the Girl Scouts adoption of some New Age philosophy.)

In 4-H, members work on specific projects of their choosing. Sharing what they have learned is an important part of the process—sometimes through exhibits at state fairs or through individual presentations. Scouting programs have children work toward merit badges and skill awards with advancement in rank.

A wonderful benefit (and one of the goals) of all of these programs is to expose children to a wide variety of careers. For example, Boy Scouts can work on merit badges in aviation, metalwork, electronics, first aid, cooking, communications, dentistry, home repairs, nature, veterinary science, and many other areas. Scouts can choose whatever topic interests them and pursue it further than the merit badge if they so choose. Counselors are available through the Scout programs to help with the various badges, so we are not dependent upon the limited skills of two parents. 4-H leaders serve as teachers in a similar way. In our family, we have used Boy Scout merit badge work as part of our school course work. The added incentive of completing a merit badge does wonders for motivation.

The most difficult type of child to teach will be the one who just does not seem to care about anything. He does not mind if life passes him by. Somehow we need to find what I call "the magic button" that will turn him on.

The magic button might be a specialized study area, athletics, or any one thing in which he can excel. Often the unmotivated teen feels worthless—that everyone does everything better than he. It usually takes persistence and trial-and-error on our part to help him discover a talent or skill that is his special gift, but it is interesting to see how skill in one area translates into increased confidence in other areas.

Responsibility may be the key for others. Some teens have been treated like young children for too long, and have not had opportunity or inclination to develop self-motivation. Granting them more responsibility might encourage them to take charge of themselves.

Others need to be challenged. What does he want to do with himself? If he had to get a job tomorrow, what kind of job would he want? I have heard of a situation where the child was so lacking in motivation that the parents had to literally put him out on his own for survival to arouse any kind of response. A less drastic alternative would be to follow the Biblical injunction that those who don't work don't eat (Proverbs 19:15). If you have an anorexic child this would be an unwise approach, but for most normal teens, especially boys, it works. For others it might be total social isolation or no money or no new clothes. We hope we will not need to take drastic steps, but if necessary, we are better off taking them sooner rather than later.

Although we might sometimes have to resort to negative motivation such as restricting food, money, clothing, or free time, positive motivation is the preferred choice. Try all the positive ideas you can find before resorting to "take-aways."

A change in our tactics might also be in order. Instead of ordering our teenager to do things, we should set up "if-then" situations. We tell our child, "If you complete your paper by three o'clock, then you may spend time at your friend's home." Avoid negatively phrased statements such as, "If you do not finish your paper, then you cannot visit your friend." The first sounds more like a privilege, the second more like a threat.

Contractual agreements might also be useful. We are obligated to provide our children with food, clothing, shelter, and love. Everything beyond that is open to negotiation—use of the radio, television, telephone, computer, skateboards, bicycles, cars (even if they paid for them). Such agreements can be difficult to keep track of, so keep this idea for truly challenging situations.

A teen just beginning home school, having spent the rest of his educational years in conventional schools, often relies on external motivation such as that used by schools. Some teens have become apathetic or even rebellious over years of unfulfilling and unproductive schooling. To develop inner motivation and discipline to learn is a long, difficult process of undoing past damage and instilling a fresh perspective. Sometimes a firm, possibly even a heavy hand might be necessary at first (accompanied with heaps of love and encouragement). We might not have enough years of home education available to us to undo the damage! The only solution is prayer that God will intervene and restore a love of learning in our child's heart.

Physical Changes

Another factor that can make home educating teens more challenging is emotional instability. We might feel sometimes that our teenagers are purposely acting irrationally just to bug us. Psychologist James Dobson says of the early adolescent period, "Human chemistry apparently goes haywire for a few years, affecting mind as much as body. ...[U]nderstanding this glandular upheaval makes it easier to tolerate and cope with the emotional reverberations that are occurring. For several years, some kids are not entirely rational! Just as a severely menopausal woman may accuse her innocent and bewildered husband of infidelity, a hormonally depressed teenager may not interpret his world accurately, either....He is going through a metamorphosis that has turned everything upside down." (*Parenting Isn't for Cowards*, by Dr. James Dobson, p.144.)

Teenagers often do not know what they really want, and they are often reluctant to communicate their uncertainties to anyone else. This situation seems to be at its worst when teens are going through the greatest physical changes. Their tempers flare for no apparent cause; they are reluctant to get out of bed; they are unable to concentrate on schoolwork; and, they often are easily depressed. A common feeling is one of being overwhelmed—particularly by school work.

The answer is not to remove all pressure by eliminating everything that feels overwhelming, but sometimes a little grace and mercy go a long way in conveying the fact that we are aware they are struggling. If we cut back in just one area temporarily, it might be enough to encourage them to tackle the rest.

After my experience with my sons and observations of many other teenagers, I can see why school officials formed junior high schools. Many kids bottom out when they hit puberty. There is no point pushing some of them ahead academically when they are barely functioning. A holding pattern is sometimes more appropriate. At the same time, there are a few who breeze through early adolescence and are ready and able to accelerate their school work. Trying to teach to both extremes in one classroom is almost impossible.

Because of the struggles that many junior high teens are undergoing, they can often be difficult to teach. In schools, the social atmosphere often brings out the worst in them. However, at home we can deal with the spiritual implications of their actions. Hormonal imbalance is not an excuse to become totally self-centered!

Contrary to common expectations the teen years do not have to be a time of confrontation and rebellion. If we expect our teens to be polite, considerate, and responsible, they are as likely to live up to those expectations as they are to live up to the more common expectations of rebelliousness, laziness, and rudeness.

The choice is often ours. In fact, many families with positive expectations feel that the teen years are the best of all. Obviously all home educated teenagers are not paragons, but we have the opportunity to create an atmosphere that will encourage growth in Christian character. We just have to be realistic, reasonable, and optimistic in our expectations.

For parents just entering the teen years with their oldest child, it helps tremendously to be forewarned about what to expect and equipped with advice on how to handle the challenges. Too much advice targeted at parents of teens assumes that children are attending regular day schools and are unable to avoid peer pressure, gangs, dating, and other fallout of the school milieu. An exception is Inge Cannon's teaching in her *Growing in Wisdom and Stature* audio tape series (Education PLUS+) [$39 for complete set; $17 for volume 3]. The series is presented in three volumes, directed toward parents. The third volume is of particular interest here since it deals with the teen years. There are three tapes in this volume addressing the three age groups of adolescents (11-14), teenagers (14-18), and young adults (18-24). Inge addresses physical developments as well as topics such as spiritual growth, relationships, activities, work attitudes, dating, and careers.

Socialization

In the elementary grade years we dismiss school socialization as generally more negative than positive. While socialization at junior and senior high levels can be even more negative, teens do have growing needs for social interaction. Teens who feel like they are missing out in the social arena cannot be ignored. Some of them need to interact with more people, stretching themselves in new situations. Some are seeking close friendships. Others are looking for responses from others that let them know that they are "acceptable," while others need to have a chance to excel in one area or another. In schools, the avenues for meeting these needs have been acceptance by cliques; participation in drill team, band, or cheerleading; membership in clubs; sports participation; and academic awards. Since we usually cannot provide all of these opportunities in home schools, many of us jump at any convenient opportunities that come along, good or bad.

We must be conscious of the underlying needs prompting pleas to be allowed to go to school, yet we must recognize that school is not the only place to meet them. If we identify our son's or daughter's need, we can better determine what to do.

Besides school, there are other avenues for helping teens develop feelings of competence and self-worth, many of which are mentioned throughout this manual for other purposes.

For friendships, the best place to look is other home schooling teenagers. Church youth groups might or might not have members who would be suitable friends. Having no friend is better than having a friend who is a bad spiritual influence, a difficult fact for many teens to accept. (Refer them to the book of Proverbs if they doubt you.) Friends need not be same-age peers, but might be younger or older.

A sense of purpose and accomplishment might be achieved through volunteer work or a job. Considering that many teens feel unneeded, purposeful accomplishment that helps others seems like one of the best ways of meeting teenagers' needs while motivating them to extend themselves.

With a little imagination we can come up with ideas for academic recognition. Pizza Hut's program of free pizza prizes for book readers comes to mind. Recognition in the local newsletter is another idea.

Sports are a more challenging problem. I deal with physical education and the bigger sports questions in Chapter Eighteen, but many teens like to participate in sports activities for social reasons. More and more such opportunities are being developed by local home school groups. They are contracting with YMCAs to run programs during school hours for home schooled students. Home School groups are creating their own programs. Some groups are putting together teams which compete in organized competitions with other schools. Now, there's even a national home school basketball tournament every year! Opportunities are multiplying quickly in response to the exponential growth in the number of home schooled children. There certainly will be some barriers and limitations for sports participation, but we need to keep in mind what is most important. Sports participation cannot be the primary purpose for returning our children to school.

We cannot let teenagers pressure us into allowing them to attend school for the wrong reasons, but at the same time we must be sensitive and do our best to provide for legitimate needs.

If your teens are resistant to the idea of home schooling, I recommend that you have them read two books. The first, *A School To Come Home To*, is written by a home school graduate, Lisa Dunlop (DBLM Publications) [$8.95]. Unlike the multitude of books written by adults, telling what home schooling is like, Lisa's book tells it from a teen's point of view in story form. Actually, the book itself is a testimonial to home schooling. It is well-written, has an interesting story line, and uses dialogue that sounds like real teenagers talking rather than someone's idea of what teenagers might say.

The second book was put together by my youngest son, Matt. He compiled stories by a number of young adults who have graduated from home school (including himself) in a book called *HotHouse Transplants* (Grove Publishing) [$11.95]. These young people share personal experiences relating to home schooling as well as their transitions to college and the work-world. Both teens and parents can read about the struggles and pressures teens encounter, the challenges they have faced, the lessons they've learned, and the encouragement they have to offer to those considering home education through the teen years.

For parents still concerned about the socialization question, I recommend *Will My Child Fit?* by June B. Whatley (June Whatley) [$9.95]. June Whatley subtitles her book, "An answer to the question: 'What about socialization?'" While not narrowed to teen concerns, the book does a great job of handling socialization questions from both biblical and practical perspectives. Whatley backs up her defense of homeschooling with research documentation that proves the benefits of the right kind of socialization.

Learning Styles

I believe that most children prefer to be successful in whatever they attempt, including school work. Unfortunately, many of them have such miserable educational experiences that they abandon all hope of excelling in academics. After a few years of repeated failure and frustration, they balk at each additional opportunity to find out how "dumb" they are. No wonder so many children hate school. But problems rarely have to do with basic intelligence. More often they are related to the way material is presented to the student.

We each perceive information well and process it efficiently in unique ways. Some learn best by interacting with other people; some by studying books in quiet solitude; some by physically handling materials; and, some by working in a typical classroom. Reading books is a treat to one child and a chore to another. Learning by building representational models and other types of hands-on activity stimulates academic learning in one student while it bores another. These individual preferences reflect our different personalities and learning styles.

One of the most important advantages to home education is that we can design our home school program in a way that suits each person's learning style, using methods and materials best for each. We can adjust our methods and materials in a way that schools cannot.

I have gone through periods of extreme frustration in our home schooling when I felt like I was simply not communicating at all with one of my sons when it came to school subjects. No matter how much work I put into coming up with great lesson plans, I found it difficult to stimulate his interest and motivate him. Then I read *Learning Patterns and Temperament Styles*, by Dr. Keith Golay (Manas Systems) [$12]. So many things that had been reverberating in my brain fell into place. By examining the situation from a learning styles perspective, I saw that we were communicating on two different wave lengths. What I thought would be an enjoyable way to learn did not coincide with what my son perceived as enjoyable.

I originally made this discovery when my son was about ten years old. Although I had been aware of his need for hands-on work at earlier ages, I assumed that he had outgrown such things. Not so! Like most children, he had changed and matured, yet his underlying learning style was still alive and well and in need of some attention. In high school, I tended to slip back into teaching styles more comfortable to me and again reached a point (although not as serious) where we needed to make adjustments to accommodate his learning style needs. Changing methods to coincide with his learning style has more than once made a significant difference in his attitude and his school work.

Identifying my son's learning style was only part of the puzzle. Another part was my own learning style. Unless we first recognize our own strengths and weaknesses, we cannot know how we are communicating or miscommunicating with others. When we find that our strengths and weaknesses are opposite those of our child, we need to be cautious in our choice of teaching methods. However, since teens should be doing a large percentage of their work independently, our learning style as the teacher is not as crucial as at younger grade levels. It becomes more important to choose texts and materials appropriate for each child, since these will be the primary learning tools.

I have included information to help you identify learning styles for yourself and your teenager. But before we try to identify learning styles we must add a few cautions. This theory is only one of many that have been used. I feel that this approach is the most workable since it is neither oversimplified nor too complicated.[1]

Reflective Educational Perspectives offers another learning style approach in a format that is easy for home schoolers to use. They use a system of five learning styles, four of which correspond to those used in this book (Wiggly Willy = Performer, Perfect Paula = Producer, Competent Carl = Inventor, Sociable Sue = Relator). It further breaks each style down by disposition, preferred modality, best study environment, interests, and talents. They have *Self-Portrait* profiles or assessment instruments for identifying learning styles—Level 1 for elementary grades, Level 2 for junior high, and Level 3 for senior high and adults. (The dividing age between Levels 2 and 3 is about age 15.) Instructions and analysis information are included. You can purchase the *Learning Styles System* which includes a 95-page manual, two adult profiles, and up to four children's profiles [$45; additional profiles are $3.25 each]. The *System* walks us through the process of using the profiles, then applying what we discover in areas of curriculum and methodology, environment, motivation, time, and areas for growth for all family members. It suggests ways to overcome learning style conflicts in situations where there are significant differences between parent(s) and child(ren). Lists of resources for various modalities and styles take the recommendations to the practical level. [Note: Many of the recommended items are reviewed in the *Christian Home*

---

[1] For further reading see *Please Understand Me: Character and Temperament Types* by David Keirsey and Marilyn Bates [$11.95] (Golay elaborates on some of Keirsey's work. Keirsey discusses sexual and relationship personality characteristics—read it with cautious discernment.); and *People Types and Tiger Stripes: A Practical Guide to Learning Styles* by Gordon D. Lawrence [$7.95]. (Both *Please Understand Me* and *People Types and Tiger Stripes* are available from the Center for Applications of Psychological Type.) All of the above along with Golay's book are based upon the work of Isabel Briggs Myers. For a different approach read *In Their Own Way* by Thomas Armstrong (Jeremy P. Tarcher, Inc.) [$10.95]. All are non-Christian in philosophy. For a comprehensive yet easy-to-read examination of five different learning style models, read Cynthia Tobias' *The Way They Learn* [$10.99]. This book is published by Focus on the Family, and Tobias is a Christian, so it avoids problems we find in books such as Keirsey's.

ADULT LEARNING STYLES

Wiggly Willy

- Has trouble organizing and following through
- Would rather play and have fun than work
- Tends to do things impulsively
- Probably did poorly in school (often due to lack of interest or boredom
- Looks for creative and efficient solutions to tasks
- Dislikes paperwork and record keeping
- Prefers activity over reading books
- Prefers to teach the fine arts, physical education, and activity-oriented classes

Competent Carl

- Likes to be in control
- Thinks and acts logically
- Likes to understand reasoning and logic behind ideas
- Is selectively organized
- Likes to work alone and be independent
- Is impatient with those who are slow to grasp concepts and those who are disorganized
- Is often uncomfortable in social situations and has trouble understanding others' feelings and emotions
- Tends to avoid difficult social situations
- Likes to make long-term plans
- Prefers to teach math, science, and other logic-related subjects rather than language arts and social studies

Perfect Paula

- Likes everything neatly planned ahead of time
- Likes to follow a schedule
- Is not very good at coming up with creative ideas
- Is comfortable with memorization and drill
- Gets upset easily when children don't cooperate
- Worries about meeting requirements
- Often prefers to work under an umbrella program for home educators
- Prefers to teach with pre-planned curricula
- Is more comfortable with "cut and dry" subjects than those which require exploration with no clear answers

Sociable Sue

- Enjoys social interaction
- Likes to belong to groups, especially for activities
- Worries about what other people think
- Tends to be insecure about how well he/she is doing with home education
- Is idealistic about expectations and goals
- May or may not be organized, depending upon accountability
- Is more interested in general concepts than details
- Prefers to teach subjects related to language arts, social studies, and, possibly, the fine arts

Educators' Curriculum Manuals, and you should read complete descriptions of as many of these products as possible before making choices.]

A Self-Portrait for Mac makes the assessments available on Macintosh computers. Most home educators would purchase the home use version for $45. The computer program scores and prints out the results and also includes the 95-page manual. Reflective Educational Perspectives offers other related materials. *A Self-Portrait Interactive Styles for Parents and Teachers* includes 2 *Interactive Styles* profiles and a follow-up booklet for $12.50. In addition they have materials on relationships, teachers in the classroom, and on the workplace.

Whatever we do with learning styles, we must remember that God did not create people to fit neatly into little boxes. People tend to be untidy mixtures of all kinds of character traits that defy classification more often than not.

Ideally, we like to have a reasonable balance of personality characteristics with no strongly dominant style, although this is rarely the way we are. A person without extremes usually finds it easier to teach or work with people of all other learning styles.

First, let us look at typical adult characteristics of the four learning styles within the methodology I use in this book. (See the chart of Adult Learning Styles on this page.) Do not be sidetracked by the names. Women can be Wiggly Willys and men can be Perfect Paulas. Look at the four learning styles and try to determine which has the most characteristics that are like you. You will likely find some of your characteristics in two or more different learning styles, but try to identify which is most like you, which is next closest to you, working down to the learning style that is least like you. Consider these characteristics as your own strengths and weaknesses that you will keep in mind as you work with your children.[2]

Next, we will see that there are differences between the adult learning style descriptions and the child's. This takes into account the fact that as we grow older, we learn to control our immature tendencies and develop splinter skills (skills for accomplishing specific tasks or acting in certain situations) as needed. As you look at the chart of Teen's Learning Styles on the next page, you will notice that a Wiggly Willy child tends to be carefree, living for the moment. Adults might also feel that way, but they are seldom free to act out their lives that way. As we

---

2   I have a two-tape audio presentation of *Learning Styles* available that comes with the adult learning styles separated onto four sheets which you can rearrange to better identify your own learning style strengths and weaknesses. It also includes a booklet of the overheads and handouts for the session (GrovePublishing) [$9.95].

TEEN PREFERRED LEARNING STYLES

Wiggly Willy

- Does not like deep thinking or intellectual discussions
- Is impulsive—likes to be free to act spontaneously without restraint
- Learns best by doing; a hands-on person
- Dislikes planning ahead and organizing
- Prefers to figure our his own way to accomplish tasks
- Has a short attention span with tasks or situations he finds uninteresting
- Gets bored easily in large group meetings or classes
- Is not motivated by long-range rewards
- Likes to be creative
- Generally dislikes traditional school methods

Competent Carl

- Likes to be in control of himself and his surroundings
- Likes to analyze things
- Is a problem solver
- Self-motivated
- Likes long-term, independent projects
- Values intelligence and wisdom
- Has poor social skills and difficulty relating to peers
- Enjoys solitary activity (sometimes because it is too uncomfortable or too difficult to understand other people, or sometimes because he just doesn't notice other people)
- Often interested in logical subjects like math and science
- Wants efficient schooling; resists busywork and unnecessary repetition

Perfect Paula

- Responsible; oriented toward duty and "what should be done"
- Follows the rules, respects authority
- Likes things clearly structured, planned, and organized and is good at those type tasks
- Seldom acts spontaneously or impulsively, but is more cautious and certain before acting
- Reliable
- Likes to belong to groups
- Wants approval and affirmation
- Usually works well with typical school curriculum

Sociable Sue

- Social person—warm and responsive
- Wants to understand "Why?"
- Interested in people, ideas, principles, and values
- Not a detail or technical person; more interested in concepts
- Likes to be known, recognized, or acknowledged, and might be an (over) achiever because of her desire to please and impress people
- Vulnerable to conflict and criticism
- Dislikes competition, preferring cooperation because of her sensitivity to others
- Gets excited about new projects, but loses enthusiasm once the novelty wears off
- Curriculum preferences are highly unpredictable

grow older, we learn to adapt to those around us and to act in ways which are socially acceptable. Some of the changes also reflect spiritual growth. For instance, a Competent Carl personality usually has difficulty relating to other people, yet, because of a desire to develop friendships or share the Lord with others, he might stretch to develop the interpersonal skills that were originally lacking.

Keep in mind that children's learning style characteristics are not set from the time they are young. Typically, very young children are more like Wiggly Willys. As they mature, their true learning style becomes more evident, although when this occurs varies from child to child. Often we notice what appear to be learning style changes as children hit their teen years. Our middle son, Josh, appeared to have some Perfect Paula leanings in the elementary grades, but around age twelve there was a dramatic shift toward Competent Carl characteristics. Our oldest son, Chris, seemed to be a classic Wiggly Willy in younger years, but exhibits more Sociable Sue characteristics as he gets older. Do not "identify" a child's style and always expect him to respond according to your classification. Be wary of mentally and academically "boxing them in" and missing the changes as they mature. Use learning styles as indications rather than as definitions. Ideally, we would like to see at least some characteristics from all four learning styles in each child instead of characteris-

tics of only one style. If our children are not limited to the confines of a single learning style, they can learn from a broader array of methods.

If there are seeming contradictions in learning styles this might indicate that our child has a learning disability, and he is operating in an unnatural (for him) learning style because he is unable to function in his natural style. We most often see learning disabilities appear as Wiggly Willy characteristics. The short attention span, inability to concentrate or do paper and pencil tasks, and other problems might be the result of frustration over difficulties with those tasks. Teenagers should be able to adapt to different learning styles with increasing ease. If they have significant difficulty, consider having them tested for learning disabilities.

We also should be working on Christian character formation, which means that we are overcoming personality weaknesses. We cannot excuse character weaknesses that are linked to learning styles—problems such as carelessness, inattention, lack of consideration for others, etc.—as learning style faults. These are the areas that need extra attention. The teen who has trouble paying attention to detail needs gentle help to encourage him to spend the needed time reviewing difficult material. Teens who are oblivious of the needs of others need gentle reminders to take the time to exhibit concern and consideration.

PREFERRED METHODS

Wiggly Willy	Perfect Paula	Competent Carl	Sociable Sue
– variety in methods and materials – games – competition – audiovisual aids – short, dynamic presentation – construction activity – freedom to work independently on projects of his own choosing	– workbooks – consistent structure – routine – lectures following outlines – repetition and memorization – drill and review – time to prepare for any discussion	– student/teacher discussions and question/answer sessions when he can do a lot of the talking – logically organized lectures – long-term projects – independent work – problem solving – debate – brainstorming	– small group discussion – social interaction – enthusiastic presentation – creative writing – role playing – situations where she is personally recognized and valued – (needs but does not necessarily enjoy) repetition for technical detail

Each learning style also has typical methods that they do not like:

Wiggly Willy	Perfect Paula	Competent Carl	Sociable Sue
– long-range goal setting – complicated projects – planning – paper and pencil tasks – workbooks	– creative activities such as role playing, dramatization, and imaginative writing – changes in a planned schedule – constant changes in the curriculum	– listening to peer group discussion – wasting time on previously mastered material – repetition	– drill done in a boring manner – competition – being ignored – isolated work

Learning styles apply directly to the choices we make in course work for our teens. We generally assume that all teenagers should be able to work out of textbooks on their own, but this is not necessarily so. A strong Sociable Sue will suffer from the isolation of working totally independently. She needs more interaction, either with her parents or with other people. Many Wiggly Willys in high school still need to work with hands-on materials to help them tackle academic assignments. Many of our high school dropouts are simply Wiggly Willys who were handed materials that suited other learners, although many certainly suffer from learning disabilities.

The way to use learning style information is to identify subjects which pose the most problems for our child. We then look to learning styles to direct us to teaching/learning methods that best reach our child in that subject area.

For instance, a Wiggly Willy who struggles with math might need a math program with lots of practical application and even some hands-on work in real life situations, or with math manipulatives such as *Cuisenaire® Rods* or *Mortensen* materials. (See the Mathematics section for more information.) Perfect Paula might need a more clearly structured program with definite objectives that she can achieve. Competent Carl might need more independence and control over his studies. He might also need materials which have less busy work and repetition. Sociable Sue might prefer discussion and oral work over workbooks designed for independent study.

I address learning style needs in each subject area chapter, but meanwhile, the charts on this page show preferred and disliked learning methods typical of each learning style.

Even though you will undoubtedly discover exceptions to the "Preferred Methods" chart, these suggestions should give some starting places when you need alternative teaching methods.

The second chart here reflects least-preferred learning methods for each type of learner. These are often the weaknesses that we will be working to overcome.

While we can concede that God makes each one of us individually for His purposes, we do not have to submit to the inherent weaknesses of particular personality/temperament styles. Each style has its weaknesses. Wiggly Willys tend to have poor study habits and be irresponsible. They need to learn diligence, and they need to learn that irresponsibility is a selfish character trait that says, "I don't care about anyone except myself!" Perfect Paulas have trouble with new situations or new ways of doing things. They are often too rigid. They need to learn that life will not always be neatly organized to keep them safe in their narrow comfort zone. Competent Carls often lack social skills, yet they must learn to relate to others to develop relationships and share Christian love and fellowship with others. They also must realize that they will not be allowed to live out their lives in isolation, but that sooner or later they must learn how to work with other people. Sociable Sues need to learn how to pay attention to detail and follow through. They also need to recognize that we are not to look to men for approval and direction, but to God. They must let go of their reliance upon what other people think.

Motivation and Learning Styles

Motivating teenagers is difficult, yet understanding learning styles might make the task a bit easier. The key is recognizing that what motivates one person might do nothing for another.

Wiggly Willys tend to live in the here and now. Grades are poor motivators unless there is some immediate effect. With teens, the reward can be a little more delayed than for younger children, yet it must be immediate enough for them to keep it in mind as a realistic possibility. Wiggly Willys rarely are concerned with consequences, good or bad, a month or two down the road. Special trips are good motivators, yet they must happen right away. Prizes, time off, and food are more immediate motivators that work well. (Overeating or undereating can be problems for some teens, so use food as a motivator with care.) We do not want our children to be motivated simply by rewards, but until they reach a point of maturity where they are choosing to do things for worthy reasons on their own, we will probably use some form of rewards to enlist their cooperation.

Perfect Paulas are anxious to follow the rules and do what is right, so motivation is less of a problem. Good grades are often sufficient motivation. We do have to watch that our Perfect Paulas do not become gullible "slaves" to authority—doing whatever is requested of them unquestioningly. This personality type can too easily be manipulated by those with a political agenda or persons in positions of responsibility who mean well but lack wisdom.

Competent Carl likes to be in control. Allowing him to design his own course of study or work under "learning contracts" approved by his parents works well. He can usually be motivated by money since he plans ahead and might have goals, or even business ideas, for which he is saving. Free time to pursue his own interests is another effective motivator. Sometimes Competent Carl's desire to be in control causes him to overstep the boundaries. He has a tendency to want to do things his way, without regard for the wishes of others. Clear boundaries of authority need to be defined for these learners.

Sociable Sue is motivated by personal recognition and affirmation. A pat on the back goes a long way. She is concerned about what other people think, so she will usually try to please people if she can. There is a danger, though, in whom she decides to please. Sociable Sues easily fall under the influence of their peers in preference to the influence of God and parents. They need to seek approval from God first; next, from their parents; then from others with authority over them; and after that, from their peers.

Perhaps you thought that you were simply covering the school subjects at home. After studying learning styles, you can see that character training is just as important, perhaps more so, than anything else we hope to accomplish at home.

Study Skills

While all these changes—physical, spiritual, mental, and emotional—are taking place, we sometimes overlook another shift that should have taken place between elementary and high school. Teenagers should be assuming much more responsibility for their own learning. The burden of teaching is shared between parent and teen. Some of us have been spoon feeding our children because it has seemed too large a battle to get them to take personal responsibility for their education. I have seen some parents home schooling their teenagers, providing everything but the air to vocalize answers for their children. They pre-read all texts and explain them to their children. They help them through written assignments. They never hold them accountable for deadlines, independent assignments, or studying on their own. Some of us, perhaps, worry that our children might fail if we do not push them along every inch of the way.

This dependency may have been acceptable in early elementary school, but, unless there is a serious learning disability, our teenagers should increasingly be teaching themselves to a great extent. We need to risk letting them fail or fall short! In traditional public and private schools and college, students are expected to take personal responsibility for homework assignments, term papers, etc. No one follows them around with daily reminders. Home schooling parents have a strong tendency (maybe because we have too much opportunity) to nag about assignments. It would be much better to make sure that our child has the assignment and due date recorded in a notebook that is unlikely to be misplaced, then leave it to him to assume responsibility for remembering. We can use the energy we save on nagging to figure out rewards for meeting assignment deadlines and work well done, or appropriate consequences for late or inadequate assignments.

We are assuming that there has been some mutual agreement about goals and deadlines at the beginning. If we want our children to be independent learners, we need to give them a significant voice in setting those goals. However, many teens lack the maturity to follow through to meet those goals without some established schedules and deadlines. For students who need help with scheduling, create a master schedule so they can see how they should be spending their time. You should probably also use a daily assi gnment form (possibly in calendar format like most planning books) for students who have difficulty pacing themselves. Self-disciplined learners, who know how to set their own priorities and schedules, might be able to work without daily deadlines. You might want to use the Daily Activity Log—Independent Study (Chart B) for these students, by writing out a week's worth of assignments but allowing them to decide how to schedule the work. Another option is to allow self-directed teens to fill out this form as their record of completed work.

One helpful resource is Castle Heights Press' *The Homework Assignment Book*, an individual student assignment book which has preassigned subject headings and dates. (We need a new book for each school year, just like the planner books.) It allows for an extended school year, with dates beginning in August and ending in late June. Subject areas listed are Bible, English, Foreign Language, History, Math, Science, and Other. Because of the subject headings, and also since writing space is limited, this book will work better with older students than with younger.

I hear occasional reports that home schoolers entering or reentering the school system in junior or senior high typically have trouble finishing their work on time. They are not used to working under the time restrictions to which other students have become accustomed. Home school schedules are of necessity less rigid than regular school schedules. That is not bad in itself, but we need to teach our teens how to use their time efficiently. Most teens are great at stretching a fifteen-minute assignment out for three hours so that they can complain about being overworked. I know that there are some families demanding too much of their children, but there are those who excuse too readily and expect too little. Even in the public schools, teachers are having students do much more work than some home schoolers, since some of our children have learned how to tug on our heartstrings and elicit sympathy very well by the time they reach high school.

On the other hand, our children might be doing the best that they can. They might simply need practice with such things as math computation and handwriting to acquire speed.

Note Taking

In school, students are expected to know how to take notes from lectures and textbooks and for assignments. They are tested on the information contained in those notes. Many home schooled students are <u>never</u> taking notes! There are many situations in life, other than school, where note taking is essential. There are meetings where we need to take notes about our responsibilities; seminars and church services where we want to record what the speaker is sharing; situations where we want to record information on how to make something; and so on. It is a skill that our teens will need whether or not they go on to college. We can develop the skill little by little. We should not start by reading *War and Peace* and requiring a plot summary. Instead, begin with a paragraph concerning only one topic. Teach them how to summarize in their own words rather than trying to record the paragraph word for word. Help them practice identifying important points.

Alternatively, they might begin with note taking from a textbook. They can outline and take notes from the chapter they are studying in history. This is an excellent way for them to study, in addition to providing practice in note taking. Sunday sermons (if your pastor does not ramble) are also good for practice.

Studying

I will discuss grading and testing later in this book, but we need to realize that children must know how to study properly before they will be equipped to take tests. Some students retain information well on their first encounter. Others need to go back and review to cement information into their memories. Either way, they need to be able to sort out what they are learning, determining the key points and what is merely interesting background. For some students this is very difficult and requires much practice and maybe some help. Yet, the more they practice, the better they are able to do it.

Do not suddenly introduce studying and tests for every subject at junior or senior high school level when students have been practicing neither. Begin the transition in upper elementary grades. Junior high is a good time to push the transition unless your child is already struggling through this developmental period.

A number of resources are designed to help boost study skills. *Getting Smarter* (Good Apple) [$12.99] helps students ex-

amine and improve their study habits, set goals and priorities, organize, learn how to study and how to schedule their time, take notes, and take tests. The student book is a reproducible workbook. Students can work independently through most of it, but good teaching suggestions are included in a brief teacher's guide. Recommended for grades 6-12.(S)[3]

Efficient Study Skills (Educators Publishing Service) [$5.95] is a workbook for high schoolers that will help them learn to read various kinds of writing for different purposes, develop listening skills, take notes, and concentrate. The teachers' edition contains the entire student text with commentary and presentation ideas so you probably need purchase only the teacher's edition.(S)

What Smart Students Know (Random House) [$16] (ISBN#51788085-7)is by Adam Robinson, author of the excellent book about SAT strategies, *Cracking the System*. In this book, Robinson broadens his outlook to include learning strategies that will improve student success in traditional school skills—notetaking, reading textbooks, classwork, tests, participation, etc. Even in homeschools, many students are using traditional texts, correspondence courses, or other approaches that closely resemble the classroom methodology. Even those who are using more creative learning methods might find themselves in the college classroom or other setting where these skills will be useful. Robinson tells us that attitude is a major factor in success, then he goes on to contrast the attitudes of successful and unsuccessful students, leaving us with tips on how to cultivate an orientation toward success. (This is practical, not just positive thinking platitudes.) One of Robinson's key contributions is his list of twelve questions that he claims all smart students ask themselves, either consciously or unconsciously, when they are learning a subject. These are strategies which Robinson pulls together under his term for successful learning—CyberLearning. The word "cyber," from the Greek and meaning "to pilot" or "to be in control," reflects a key Robinson theme—that the successful learner must take control of his own learning. Even though Robinson assumes that most learners are more restricted than are home educators in their learning options, home educated students can learn a great deal about how to "play the school game" well.(S)

How to Be a Superstar Student is a video course designed to both teach and motivate students (The Teaching Company) [$49.95]. It includes two extended-play video tapes for a total of 8 lessons. Our extremely animated master teacher host for this series, Mr. Tim McGee, addresses attitudes such as honesty, courage, and perseverance throughout the series. In specific lessons he shares tips to enhance learning—how to mark texts as you read, how to properly use a math text, how to improve essay writing skills, organizing your time, preparing for college, how to study for exams, and more. McGee does not promote cheap tricks just to get through. Instead, he stresses diligence, hard work, and efficient organization. Interspersed video clips of successful students reinforce and enhance McGee's message. While

---

3   Throughout this book, I use (S) to indicate that a resource is secular in nature rather than Christian.

younger teens can benefit from much of this, I think the best audience will be older, self-motivated students who are preparing for college or even already attending college. These will be the students who have matured to the point where they desire to do their best and want to improve their skills because THEY want to, not because parents think they should.(S)

The Skills Bank Home Tutor (SkillsBank Corporation) is a computer program for IBM compatible and Apple II machines which includes a module called "Study Skills." (See lengthy review of the program under math resources for junior high.) This module covers a number of study skill areas: using dictionaries and books, using references and recording information, using consumer information, and using graphic information. Of particular interest to junior and senior high students should be the sections on using reference materials, taking notes, and developing outlines, as well as the consumer information helps such as warranties and guarantees, leases and contracts, and filling out forms.(S)

Organization

"I couldn't find the paper," is not an acceptable excuse for missing assignments. Some children are extremely disorganized by nature. They "stuff" or "toss" rather than neatly put away. Things disappear into their room, never to be seen again. They are always missing books, papers, pens, and pencils or whatever else is crucial to the task at hand. It makes one wonder if these are no more than disguised attempts to evade schoolwork.

Such habits can create tension and ill feeling. We can waste time arguing about messes and lost items or we can provide some negative reinforcement to improve the situation by requiring that missing assignments be redone from scratch. If a book is missing, give a substitute assignment that is more difficult than the original assignment. If all pencils are missing, charge a premium price and sell him one of yours.

We should expect our children to be at least somewhat organized, and we should provide them with tools to make it easier—shelves for school books, containers for pens and pencils, notebooks for specific purposes.

We also need to set a good example. Are our record books always where they belong? Do we keep our teachers' manuals put away properly? Do we file important papers so we won't lose them? I find it a constant battle to stay organized myself. My desk is always five inches deep with "work in process." It is in a neat stack unless someone brushes the desk. Then disaster strikes. Nevertheless, there is an organizational system of sorts in effect.

What looks like disorganization to some may not be to others. Do not be too hasty in judging by appearance only. As long as our teen can find what he needs in a reasonable amount of time, we should not get too uptight about it, but if he cannot, consider some corrective strategies.

Research Papers

I am certain that many of you question the value of research papers and will decide that they are not worth the trouble. However, I believe that research papers are useful tools for learning how to integrate writing, thinking, organizing, and research skills with knowledge. Research papers can also be used by teens to investigate topics or subjects that interest them. This will help them become better informed and, possibly, provide glimpses into future career paths. I personally think that every child of normal ability should complete at least one research paper, and that a goal of one lengthy research paper per school year is practical.

Some of us parents have never written a research paper, and the prospect of requiring one from our child is daunting, but it can be relatively simple. Many books are available that break the process down into manageable steps. The process is not overwhelming, just time consuming. Computers are wonderful for saving time on rewriting! Some word processing programs automatically insert footnotes or endnotes in the proper places, a tedious and challenging task on a typewriter.

For a first research paper, it is best to start simply. Have your child use only two or three sources, preferably short books that are easy to read and summarize. Have them take brief notes. Do not hold them accountable to footnote every single statement they make in their paper. Rather than footnotes, they could simply include a bibliography. As they gain experience, require more sources, use of periodicals, interviews, or a wider variety of sources. Hold them increasingly accountable to footnote any information that is not general knowledge. If you feel inadequate evaluating the paper, enlist another parent to help you.

Resources are available for both the research and report writing aspects.

➲ **Information, Please!** (D.P. & K. Productions) $15 per volume except for Getting Started - $18

Designed particularly for home educating families, the *Information, Please!* books are the perfect tool for helping our children become proficient information seekers. There are four books: Getting Started, Beginning, Intermediate, and Advanced. Reading skills are prerequisite, but most third graders should be able to do most of the questions from the Getting Started level. Getting Started is an introduction to the use of reference materials, appropriate for almost any student who is just beginning to work with such tools. It also has 12 practice pages similar to the content of each of the other three books (four pages per book). These will give you a better idea of how the books work and also help you pinpoint the appropriate level for students. Beginning is best for grades 1-5. Intermediate should be appropriate for grades 6-8. Advanced should be best for grades 9 and up.

Each book has forty pages with ten questions per page. Many children need some assistance initially as they learn where to look for answers, but soon they will be able to identify the correct sources and find it for themselves. The research, especially once we are past the Beginning level, goes beyond the standard dictionary/thesaurus/encyclopedia/globe approach found in most other classroom designed materials. Some of the information can be found at home, but you will probably want to plan a weekly trip to the library to "do research." A child can work alone or with a parent's assistance. We can photocopy these pages for children in our family so they can compete to see who can find all the answers first. We might give different sheets to different students if we prefer to avoid competition. Questions are extremely eclectic. Examples from the upper level books: "What causes the blackness under an injured fingernail?", "Which two countries had the highest casualties during WWII?", "What does 'P.S.' stand for at the end of a letter?", "What is the English translation of the Japanese word judo?", "*What* is the gestation period of deer?", and "From which country did Israel capture the east side of Jerusalem?" Upper levels include life-application questions concerning etiquette, wages, careers, etc., appropriate for each age group. Even better, the author is a Christian home schooling parent, so we also encounter Scripture-related questions. Answers will vary from single word to lengthier explanations, and answer keys are included. *Information, Please!* seems more like a game than a part of the curriculum, yet it accomplishes a major educational goal in equipping our children to do their own research.

⊃ Report Writing: Formula for Success (Continental Press) $6.75

Beginning report writers will find this small book an unintimidating step-by-step guide through each of the steps. They begin with note-taking and developing an outline, then move on to writing and editing, ending with footnotes and bibliographies. This is not an exhaustive guide to research papers, but it is an excellent starting place that will be helpful to most students.(S)

⊃ Research Skills Projects

by Phil Schlemmer (Prentice Hall) $21.95

This book is the first of a series of five books (called "Learning on Your Own!) written for "gifted and motivated" students in the upper elementary and junior high grades, although it also works well for high school students who have not yet learned how to do research. Since the goal of the series is to teach independent-learning skills, the first book teaches students how to do their own research. Lessons are labeled at three levels of "independence"—basic, intermediate, and advanced. Students who have already done some independent work might be able to skip some of the basic lessons. Although it was designed for the classroom, *Research Skills Projects* can be adapted for homeschooling. The major elements you might have to omit are "oral reports to the class" and discussions. (Substitute the rest of the family or mom and dad for the class in these instances.) Students practice researching various subjects, building library skills, and learning how to make proper note and bibliography cards. Students also learn how to use business letters and the telephone as research tools. Lessons are set up as a series of ten projects with a number of activities within each. This approach breaks the research steps into manageable chunks so that students don't get overwhelmed. This book is far more comprehensive than resources like *Report Writing* and *Write Source* since it works with specified research topics in a number of lessons, teaching students how to narrow their focus by walking them through the process. Numerous reproducible student worksheets help students plan, organize, and record the results of their learn-

ing. Evaluation sheets are provided for teachers, a big help to home school parents unfamiliar with research themselves. The other four books in the series focus on subject areas. Titles are *Writing Projects, Science Projects, Mathematics Projects*, and *Social Studies Projects*.(SE)

⊃ The Write Source

See the reviews of *Write Source 2000* and *Writers Inc* handbooks. These are the most comprehensive yet appealingly designed and easy-to-use handbooks covering both grammar skills and research report writing. They have excellent examples and instructions for footnoting and creating bibliographies.(S)

Projects

Projects are not nearly as debatable as research papers. Every teen should complete at least one project (preferably more than one) that requires independent work. It might be for a science fair or another school assignment, but it is even better when the project is designed to fulfill the student's personal interest in a topic. For instance, if a person becomes interested in model railroading he reads books, visits hobby stores, talks to others who have built model railroads, collects and makes his modeling materials, and, finally, builds the model railroad.

These types of projects are what are more commonly called hobbies. I recently read a newspaper article written by a gentleman (probably a child psychologist) who presented seminars on parenting skills. In his seminars he asked parents how many of them had hobbies when they were growing up. Most of them raised their hands. He next asked, "How many of your children have hobbies?" A very small percentage of the hands went up.

Hobbies were a means for many of us to explore and develop interests and talents as we were growing up, even though we were not aware of it. Today, we schedule our children's time so tightly that they seldom have enough free time to develop hobbies, yet hobbies are often the door to future career interests.

In our home schools I would love to see us allow our children time to develop worthwhile hobbies. However, I doubt that playing Nintendo games or riding skateboards should qualify as hobbies. A hobby should be a learning experience rather than a form of entertainment. In my mind, qualifying hobbies would be such things as animal care, electronic projects, robotics, computer programming, carpentry or woodworking, stamp collecting, cooking, sewing, painting, and playing a musical instrument. Hobbies should not replace more school-like projects, and they should not be turned into mandatory performance subjects, but they certainly do need some space of their own.

Tools For Success

Remember that motivation, learning styles, and study habits are three tools for success in home education. We need to gain our children's cooperation, address their learning style needs, and help them develop independent learning skills, all of which are important if we wish our teenagers to become lifelong learners.

Goals - Purposeful Planning

In this "Me" generation, the popular philosophy is that everyone deserves whatever they want out of life. We should "go for it" no matter the cost to anyone else. Self-fulfillment has top priority. Sometimes, as Christians, we overreact to the self-centered emptiness of this philosophy by taking the laid-back attitude, "We'll just do whatever the Lord leads." Years can pass while Christians are waiting for the Lord to lead them into doing something with their lives. Meanwhile, everything is on hold. Waiting on the Lord turns into parasitical dependence on others until something "spiritually meaningful" comes along.

God gives each person talents, abilities, and interests, and I believe that He expects us to develop and use them to the best of our abilities without waiting for special revelation.

We have to discern the difference between selfishness and Godly personal fulfillment. Selfishness is a desire for whatever serves our purposes, without regard to others. Godly personal fulfillment means following a path that brings fulfillment as we follow God's designs for our lives. Personal fulfillment may come through service to others, preparation for a career, or other choices, but the key is our motivation. Is our desire for our own purposes or God's? If we are in tune with God, His purposes usually become the desires of our heart, so the choice to serve God usually means that we will find personal fulfillment, rather than the unhappiness and frustration so many fear.

Sometimes God takes us on circuitous routes in preparing us for His purposes. We may not see the outcome of it all, but that does not give us an excuse to sit back and wait for things to fall into our laps. God uses every experience in our lives, whether it be education, our first job, a service project, or whatever, to teach and train us. We need to make ourselves available for all of those experiences, not just the "biggie" at the end. Without each of the little steps, we will never reach the end. Whether or not we see the end goal clearly is not really important. Following God's direction for our lives, as best we understand His will, is the true goal—for ourselves and for our teenagers.

Discovering God's direction is not necessarily easy. Some teens have a close walk with God and are comfortable with following His direction, while others are not. Quite often decisions are in the hands of us parents, and it is up to us to discern God's will. The ideal situation is for parents and teens to pray together for the Lord's leading. No matter who does the praying and deciding, the decisions to be made during the teen years are often very significant and should be bathed in much prayer.

Career Goals

Even though we are boggled by the idea of teaching high school at home, we have to be thinking even further down the line and asking ourselves, "Are we preparing our children to attend college?" There is no right or wrong answer to this question. It all depends upon career and personal goals.

How many teenagers actually know what career lies ahead for them? Certainly, some have strong ideas about what they would like to do, but how many will actually end up in careers they now envision? Ask a group of adults two questions: "What (if any) career did they wish to follow when they were in high school?" and, "Did they end up in that career?" It is amazing to see how few people do find themselves in a career they envisioned for themselves in high school. After all, how many of us planned that we would be home educating our children? How many of us had even heard of the idea?

Teens who haven't a clue about what they might wish to do in the future should examine their interests, talents, and abilities for possible choices. If a person likes to be in control with everything well organized, and enjoys tackling difficult tasks and problem solving, he will probably want to pursue a career that includes these challenges, such as business management or entrepreneurship. A person who loves creative activity and solitude for dreaming up ideas should consider careers that allow space and time for creativity, such as freelance art, writing, or a self-created job. A person who loves to tinker with machinery and figure out how to make things work should be looking at careers in mechanical fields.

Academic aptitude is an important factor in career choices. A teenager who hates to read and study is unlikely to want to spend an additional four years or more in college preparing for a career. Whether we like to admit it or not, all home educated children are not cut out for college level work, some because they see no point and others because they lack the academic aptitude. As with any other cross section of the population, there are those in homeschooling who are below average in their academic ability. Pushing such students toward college for career preparation might be cruel and misdirected.

Vocational training or other options are perfectly legitimate and sometimes better choices. Some teenagers wish to pursue careers that require vocational training that they cannot obtain at a college. College might be a waste of time for them. It makes more sense for them to spend that four years and the college tuition fees to set themselves up in business or learn a trade.

But What If I Don't Want to Go to College?: A Guide to Successful Careers through Alternative Education by Harlow G. Unger (Facts on File) [paperback ISBN 0-8160-3498-2 - 10.95; hardcover ISBN 08160-3497-4 - $22.95] is a useful book for those exploring career possibilities that do not require college. Unger discusses many types of careers in terms of both broad categories and specific jobs. He assesses the demand within the various occupations and likely earning potential. While the careers he discusses do not require college degrees, some do require further education of some kind. Charts in the back of the book compare hundreds of career possibilities (including those requiring college degrees) by the number of workers and average earnings. Checklists entitled "Identification of Essential Employability Skills" help students determine whether they are even ready for the job market or what skills they need to develop. Addresses for career related organizations or alternative education providers are listed throughout the book. Even though I can think of a few promising career options that are not included in the book, there is a great deal of helpful information for those who have no idea what direction they want to go. (ISBN #

Other popular books on career choices are easily available through libraries and bookstores. One such well-known book is Richard N. Bolles' *What Color is Your Parachute?* I found an earlier book by Bolles especially interesting for home schoolers. His book, *The Three Boxes of Life And How To Get Out of Them*, (Ten Speed Press) [$18.95] discusses the balance of learning, work, and play that we create in our lives. He shows how unbalanced most people become with excessive time spent on learning in comparison to work and play during college years, then work crowding out learning and play in the middle years, and, finally, play taking precedence over work and learning in the retirement years. As I read his book, I realized that homeschoolers tend to create a healthier balance through the teen years, often including more work than is typical for most teens. We also see more home school families creating balanced lives with fathers creating their own businesses that allow time to learn and play with their families. It would be wise for teens to read this book as they make college and career decisions; it will help them keep the long view in mind.(S)

For an overview of career possibilities check out *The Occupational Outlook Handbook* for 1996-97, published by the U.S. Department of Labor (U.S. Government Printing Office) [$32 paperback; $38 hardcover]. It contains information on over 300 occupations within fifteen main groups, including descriptions, occupational outlook (how much demand there is for people trained in each field), training or education required, and sources and reference materials for more occupational information.

Books such as these need to be updated frequently, so it is often best to look for them in the library rather than invest money in something with limited usefulness.

One older, out-of-print book that I thought very useful in determining the next step after high school is *College Yes or No: The High School Student's Career Decision-Making Handbook*, (by William F. Shanahan, Arco Publishing, Inc., 1980 edition, out of print, but possibly available through your library. The library call number is 650.14.) The author includes helpful tools such as a "self-profile" work sheet to help identify strengths, weaknesses, interests, and personality characteristics. He honestly points out pros and cons of college, vocational training, apprenticeships, enlistment in the armed services, and federal government careers. Unfortunately, he ignores entrepreneurial options, assuming that all high school graduates will end up working for someone else. Mr. Shanahan provides much concrete information that will get students through the fundamentals

of the planning process. He also directs them to many other sources for more information on specific areas of interest.

While doing career research, remember that some of the best career possibilities are never mentioned in books. I recall a gentleman we met who traveled around the world designing rides for theme parks. I never have seen such a career listed in a book, but it sounds intriguing. There is always room for new inventions, new services, and new ideas that are the foundations for new careers. So keep an open mind about possibilities.

Unfortunately, choosing careers is not based solely upon what we would like. It is also based upon what talents and physical abilities God has given us. My son wanted to be a pilot, but he has poor eyesight. We discovered that poor eyesight is one of the factors used to screen the many applicants who want to be commercial pilots. Maybe he could still be a pilot, but he has selected more realistic options. Many young men would love to play major league sports as a career, but only a fraction of them actually do, and even those who make the cut frequently find their careers abruptly terminated by injuries. Many young women plan to marry and remain at home with their children, but what if circumstances force them into the work force? They need to have other possibilities in mind.

Quite naturally, teens first look at career choices from the personal end—what do they most enjoy? However, the world might not respond to their interests by providing jobs that are just what they want. They have to look at career opportunities in their field of interest. How many jobs are available in a specific career? (We cannot have thirty presidents of the United States at one time.) What sorts of prerequisites are there for a career? Are the prerequisites possible for them to attain? (Can they make it through all the years of medical school and internship to be a doctor?) Does the career provide a living wage or would it have to be a hobby? (Many artists have to find another type of job to earn a living while they pursue art in their spare time.) Is it a dead-end job—one that if terminated would leave a person in the position of starting all over again? (Remember what happened to the buggy whip manufacturers after Henry Ford started producing Model T's on the assembly line?)

No matter how much career planning a person does, it still remains likely that he or she will have more than one career. Career counselors generally agree that the average American adult probably has four or five different careers in his lifetime. So, while career planning is useful in the short run, our teens must also prepare broadly enough to be able to switch careers if necessary.

"Only about ten percent of people end up in occupations they envisioned for themselves as teen-agers," according to George Schenk, a career advisor for colleges and businesses. (*The Register*, Orange County, California, February 9, 1989.) He goes on to say that a U.S. Labor Department survey discovered that "forty to seventy percent of all employees are unhappy in their work." From Mr. Schenk's perspective, finding a career that is satisfying is a happy accident that happens too infrequently.

For now we will put aside the spiritual implications of each person choosing his or her career without reliance on God's direction, but we will come back to it later. From a secular viewpoint, the chances of choosing the "right" career can be improved with exposure and testing.

Exposure means letting our teens see, hear, and experience as much as possible of potential careers—the more exposure, the better (assuming that we are excluding unacceptable choices). Teens who wonder what it would be like to own a restaurant can arrange a behind-the-scenes tour and an interview with a restaurant owner. Potential computer programmers can visit a programmer at work and find out what he really does. Exposure can also mean part-time work at a variety of jobs. In fact, the greater the variety of job experience the better. The more firsthand experience that our teens have with different careers, the more information they will have for making realistic judgments about their future choices. They discover that standing at a cash register for five hours straight can be more physically demanding than it appears. They discover that customers do not always come to the salesperson, but that the salesperson quite often has to travel and search out customers on his own. They learn that veterinarians receive emergency calls at all hours just like family doctors, and that policemen rarely use their guns, but spend a lot of time intervening in family quarrels—not very glamorous. They discover that there are almost always dreary, mundane tasks that go hand-in-hand with any job. While some teens learn which careers to avoid, others are fortunate enough to discover the career of their dreams through such exposure.

Even if our teenagers do not have time to work at many different jobs, interviewing people in different types of careers is an excellent experience both for information gained and for the interview experience itself.

A Special Resource for Extra Help

Mentoring Your Teen (Education PLUS+) by Inge and Ronald Cannon [$69] covers so many topics that it needs special space. *Mentoring Your Teen* consists of six audio cassettes and a 220-page syllabus. It is divided into six topics:
– How to determine if college or apprenticeship is best
– How to select curriculum to maximize preparation
– How to keep records that will open doors of opportunity
– How to assess interests, talents, and options
– How to write a resume that will earn a hearing
– How to be the best mentor a young person could have

As you can see, it delves into topics that are covered here and elsewhere in this manual. Even though I am not addressing some of these topics until later, I will provide the complete description of *Mentoring Your Teen* here.

As the title indicates, apprenticeship receives major attention in the first session. Inge Cannon defines apprenticeship, and suggests both traditional and nontraditional apprenticeship options. She tells us how to tie an apprenticeship in with other academic preparation, as well as how to set up a unique one for our son or daughter. Apprenticeship is not offered as the only viable option, but as an alternative or adjunct to college. In fact, even if our son or daughter absolutely is not interested in an apprenticeship, this seminar will still be extremely valuable no matter what life-preparation options they choose.

When it comes to selecting curriculum, Inge lays out the traditional Carnegie unit approach in detail, but she also cautions us to make sure that the goals of man do not supplant God's. She suggests various methods and resources for tackling subjects to illustrate her point.

The section on records, particularly the part dealing with transcripts, is the most thorough I know of. If you want to create a credible, professional transcript, you will benefit from Inge's step-by-step instructions. (A blank transcript form is located in the pocket of the binder.) This session on transcripts is also available by itself.

The next section helps with assessment of interests, talents, spiritual gifts, and career possibilities. Some charts and assessment tools are included. Inge is a fan of Life Pathways (reviewed in this chapter), so she recommends their program and refers to some of their materials in this discussion.

Resumés are next. Both older and young adults can learn how to prepare impressive resumés by working through this section, following the instructions and suggestions. Do not wait until the end of high school to listen to this section! According to Inge, we should be recording resumé information much earlier.

In the last session, Inge tells us that the idea that parents should be mentors to their children is both scriptural and largely neglected. This section is motivational and instructional for both parents and children.

The seminar as a whole is directed primarily to parents, probably because they look at the long range planning more than do their children. However, teens should start by listening in on the sections about apprenticeship and assessment of interests/talents/options. I think that most teens would also benefit from the discussion of curriculum and goals, although I know that most of them will not be terribly interested in listening through the entire discussion. Resumés and mentoring sections will spark interest at different stages for each person, so you might find it appropriate to pull out one of those sections for your teens to use at a later date. Probably, the only section of the seminar teens should be able to skip altogether is the section on record keeping.

The entire *Mentoring Your Teen* seminar is ultra-professional from the content through the quality of the tapes and syllabus. *Mentoring Your Teen* is strongly focused on the limited number of topics it addresses. Even though it covers some topics that I do within this manual, it offers more depth or more step-by-step help on the selected topics (aside from curriculum). Highly recommended.

Career Tests

Schools commonly use tests to help identify interests and aptitudes for career planning. While results of such tests are rarely accurate in predicting what career a person will actually pursue, they are useful in helping us examine our strengths and weaknesses, and to cause us to look at various possibilities that we perhaps would not otherwise consider.

Career assessments are becoming increasingly available to home educators. One of the most widely used career assessment publishers is EdITS.

The general name for their series of assessments is the *Career Occupational Preference System*. There are three types of tests: interests, ability, and values. Only one level of each of the ability (*Career Ability Placement Survey-CAPS*) and values (*Career Orientation Placement and Evaluation Survey-COPES*) tests is offered. However, there are three levels for interest testing (*Career Occupational Preference System-COPS*): *COPS II* for grades 6-12 (4th grade reading level); *COPS-R* for grades 6-12 (6th grade reading level); and, *COPS-P* for college students and adults. The first two *COPS* tests are simple and rather fun for junior or senior high students. Mature high schoolers could choose the *COPS-P* if desired. [The *COPS-PIC* (COPS Picture Inventory) is now available and is appropriate for nonreaders or those with language difficulties.] After scores are tabulated, the student turns to the "career clusters" at the back of the test booklets. Here are listed fourteen major career areas, with many possible specific careers within each area. It also lists suggested courses of study and activities or experiences for further career exploration or preparation. A work sheet instructs students to list skills required for preferred careers, encouraging them to look realistically at their aptitude for careers that interest them. The *CAPS* test helps students to be realistic in assessing their abilities for careers that interest them by testing such skills as numerical ability, verbal reasoning, mechanical reasoning, and manual speed and dexterity. The *COPES* test helps to evaluate personality traits and personal values such as practicality, independence, leadership, orderliness, and conformity in terms of careers.

The package available for home educators is the MATCH. This contains one copy each of the *COPS, CAPS,* and *COPES*. These can be easily administered by home educators. Check their catalog for prices.

JIST Works, Inc. is another source for tests as well as for a wide array of books and materials on career planning and job searching. They offer a number of testing tools, many selected from other publishers. *The Self-Directed Search* (SDS) is written at a low reading level so that virtually anyone can use it. It takes less than an hour and the test-taker can score it himself. Results are used to identify cross-referenced occupations in the accompanying *Occupations Finder* booklet. Results can also be used with *The College Majors Finder*.

The Career Exploration Inventory: A Guide for Exploring Work, Leisure, and Learning (or CEI) is an easy-to-use assessment instrument which takes into account hobbies, leisure activities, and interests which might not immediately be considered when discussing careers. After results are compiled, the Inventory suggests possible careers which might tie in with activities that people most enjoy. (JIST Works has samples available of the CEI, The World of Work and You, The Employability Development Plan, SDS, and six other assessment instruments.)

Among the many other useful resources from JIST Works is a 32-page workbook entitled *Exploring Careers: The World of Work and You*. Ideal for high school students, it pulls together information, assessment tools, job matching charts, and interpretive assistance all within the one book, although JIST Works considers it primarily an assessment tool. For more extensive career descriptions, personal characteristics, training, and education required, they can refer to the 462-page book *Exploring Careers* [$19.95] from which *The World of Work and You* is derived. An *Instructor's Guide* [$14.95] is available that describes activities and includes some reproducible work sheets. A *Preview Kit* containing all three items is available for $19.95.

JIST Works sells many other resources useful for career and college planning. Request their free catalog for complete descriptions.

Christian Career Planning

As Christians, our perspective about career planning should be different from non-Christians since we believe that God has a plan for each of our lives. He can lead each of us into the career that He has for us. The catch is that we must be walking in God's will, following His leading, and listening to counsel from those He has put in authority over us. Unfortunately, many of our teenagers do not maintain a close walk with God, and they fall back on their own limited wisdom in making their choices.

We now have available to us a few guides to career planning written from a biblical perspective.

Alpha Omega has one LifePac in their Social Studies series that focuses on career planning (LifePac number 904.) It stresses God's role in career choices, discusses career selection according to interests and abilities (self-tests included), then concludes with instruction on how to apply for a job.

School of Tomorrow also covers career planning throughout various levels of their Social Studies PACE's.

Christians seeking comprehensive help in career planning and/or choosing a college major will be interested in *Life Pathways*. This is a Christian ministry which is a division of Larry Burkett's financial planning ministry.

Life Pathways provides career assessments based upon interests, skills, work priorities, and personality. We order the assessment booklet and instructions, complete the assessment, then return it to *Life Pathways* for scoring and evaluation. We then receive an in-depth, personal report along with a helpful manual. The goal is not job placement, but to identify career areas that are most likely to fit each person, which in turn, helps with placement. This is one of the rare career planning or testing services which takes into account the believer's responsibility to and reliance upon God. This service is useful for older teens and adults. The price for one assessment is $99. Quantity discounts are available. Although we can get assessment instruments to use on our own fairly inexpensively, *Life Pathways'* in-depth analysis and Christian perspective will be worth the extra cost to many.

Bob Jones University Press Testing and Evaluation Service offers the *Career Guidance Spectrum* [$82]. This career/vocational guidance program provides biblically-based direction to career and vocational planning. It uses survey, assessment, and career guidance materials to provide feedback and relevant data in areas essential to wise career decision-making. The results of this evaluation provide over 25 pages of personal reports along with a 180-page guide to college majors and several other supplementary materials. This evaluation is great for senior high school students, but might also be used by high school graduates.

Those looking for a do-it-yourself approach to comprehensive Christian career planning should check out *Finding the Career That Fits You* by Lee Ellis and Larry Burkett (Moody Press) [$21.99]. Drawing upon some of what is included in *Life Pathways*, they walk you through personality and skill assessments with the DISC survey for personality and their own survey of workplace related skills. Next, you complete a "Work Priorities Evaluation" to identify personal priorities in terms of work. Then, you examine seven broad categories of occupational groups and specific careers within each group. In the "Action Plan Summary" section, you put all of this together. At this point you are ready to start identifying the particular job/career you desire. A career investigation worksheet helps you line up your personal assessments with actual jobs. The next chapter helps you create a resumé. Final chapters cover job searches, managing your finances, and starting your own business. *Finding the Career That Fits You* is easy to read, easy to use, comprehensive, and Christian in focus. The surveys and numerous check-off lists, and fill-in-the-blank sections make this a consumable book, so buy separate copies for each person who needs to use it.

A companion book to *Finding the Career That Fits You* by the same two authors is *Your Career in Changing Times* (Moody Press) [$18.99]. This hard cover book offers some of the same analysis we encounter in *Finding the Career That Fits You,* but without the actual surveys. There's a lot more here on the changing workplace, economic realities, and real life stories. While many non-Christian authors have dealt with economics and the workplace, Burkett's Christian perspective makes this more valuable and practical in many ways.

Homeschoolers might choose either book, but they don't need both. I suggest *Finding the Career That Fits You* for average teens. *Your Career in Changing Times* is great for both adults and mature teens who want a better understanding of the work "marketplace" and the unsettling economic changes we are experiencing in our country.

A new resource more specifically oriented toward Christian home educators is *Heading in The Right Direction: Seven Steps to Biblically-Based Career Planning for Young Adults* by Becky Preble (Career Directions) [$58]. A 90-minute audio cassette walks the young person through a seven-step process for identifying possible careers. Unlike most other resources, this one focuses on two key concepts: 1.) that our lives are to be of service to God and 2.) the use of a "talents" approach to identifying possible careers. *Heading in The Right Direction* includes the *Talent Discovery Guide*, a talent-based career identification instrument. With this instrument, young people are guided to first review activities in which they have participated (hobbies, sports, community/school/church activities, and work), identifying those which were most enjoyable. Then they work through the instrument noting which particular skills and personality traits within each activity reflects an aptitude. This approach takes students immediately beyond mere interests into the realm of aptitude and enjoyment, two features that are crucial for identifying appropriate career choices. The binder includes very simple to follow instructions, outlines of the audio presentations, additional case story readings, and an appendix of additional steps for researching careers. Reflecting the paths being chosen by home educators, it treats with equal esteem college, apprenticeships, full-time careers, homemaking, and entrepreneurship.

If a young person is not yet ready to make a career decision, but wants to begin identifying and developing his or her gifts and talents, *LifeKeys* (Bethany House Publishers) by Kise, Stark and Hirsh might be very useful. See the complete description under "Personal Development" in Chapter Eighteen.

Career Research

If your teen has narrowed career interests down to a selected range of possibilities, he can conduct further research by talking to people already in those career fields or reading books such as the following:[1]

➲ **Careers for.... series** (VGM Career Horizons) prices range from $9.95-$14.95

25 books in this series will help young people who have identified personality characteristics or avocations, but who have trouble figuring out what career will fit. Examples of titles (which all begin with *Careers for...*) are: *Animal Lovers and Other Zoological Types, Bookworms and Other Literary Types, Foreign Language Aficionados and Other Multilingual Types, Good Samaritans and Other Humanitarian Types, Travel Buffs and Other Restless Types, Writers and Others Who Have a Way with Words,* and *Sports Nuts and Other Athletic Types.*(S)

➲ **Career Opportunities for Writers** by Rosemary Guiley (Facts on File) paperback - $18.95; hardcover - $29.95(S)

➲ **Career Opportunities in Art** by Haubenstock and Joselit (Facts on File) $15.95(S)

➲ **Career Opportunities in the Music Industry** by Shelly Field (Facts on File) paperback - $18.95; hardcover - $29.95(S)

➲ **Careers in.... series** (VGM Career Horizons) prices range from $10-$17

This series is advertised as VGM's professional careers series. It includes books on careers in accounting, advertising, business (includes consulting and owning your own business), communications, computers, education, engineering, health care, marketing, science, and others.(S)

---

1   Throughout this book, I use (S) to indicate that a resource is secular in nature rather than Christian.

➲ Considering a Church Career? by Philip Bickel and Curtis Deterding (Concordia Publishing House) $3

This 64-page book is aimed at those within the Lutheran church (Missouri Synod) considering a church career. However, most everything discussed applies to most churches. The first part of the book covers background questions about purpose, calling, "the right reasons," fears, and other topics. The second section discusses specific careers, necessary qualifications and education, and possible careers within broader categories. A chart at the end of the book shows which Concordia College campus offers programs for the various careers.

➲ Opportunities in.... series (VGM Career Horizons) prices range from $11-$14

There are well over 150 titles in this series. These books cover all areas. The catalog lists them under groupings: building, industrial, and mechanical services; business and management; office and computer; communication; health care; fitness; art and design; scientific and technical; public and social service; travel and leisure; ecology and environmental; and service occupations. There are about a half dozen books in each category. For instance, Communication includes books about magazine publishing, newspaper publishing, public relations, technical communications, telecommunications, television and video, and writing.(S)

Look for titles on other specific careers in the library, secular book stores, or the VGM Career Horizons or JIST Works catalogs.

Vocational/Trade School Preparation

"A craft is described as 'an art or skill,' and a craftsman as 'one who practices some trade or manual occupation.' Contrary to what many believe, the need for qualified craftsmen continues to grow throughout the world....never before have craftsmen been so much in demand" (*College Yes or No*, p.49). Training as a craftsman might start with adult education classes and progress into vocational or trade schools or through apprenticeships. We will deal with apprenticeships separately a little later. Educational institutions for trade or vocational training might be called trade, technical, vocational, or proprietary schools.

Some students might wish to begin vocational training while still in high school. They might be able to do this through work experience or apprenticeship, or they might be able to learn about a trade from a knowledgeable adult. Some school systems offer a combination of both classroom and practical experience. This used to be structured as a separate vocational arm of the

school district, but it is increasingly incorporated into the regular high school program. Such programs are often open to home educated teens although usually with a minimum age of sixteen. In California it is called the Regional Occupational Program or ROP. The idea is very practical. However, potential dropouts and underachieving students are often shunted into ROP programs to keep them in school, so the general atmosphere in some classes can be less than ambitious. On the other hand, much of the ROP training is excellent and diligent students graduate with skills that allow them to find immediate employment.

Such programs are slated for dramatic changes because of Goals 2000. The goal will be to increase on-the-job training through the high school years.

Students without access to vocational classes can study on their own with appropriate textbooks. Glencoe/McGraw-Hill has an entire *Technology Education* catalog of vocational textbooks and resources under headings such as architecture, auto body, carpentry, electricity, electronics, entrepreneurship, manufacturing, photography, and welding. If students want to study through any such texts it would help greatly to have a knowledgeable adult to consult.

One publisher, Education Associates, offers a program called *Project Discovery* which can be used for do-it-yourself ROP type training. The program is packaged in units for specific trades/vocations including such topics as: accounting and bookkeeping, advertising and editorial design, dental care, drafting, electricity, food technology, greenhouse work, masonry, medical records, plumbing, retailing, shorthand, small engine repair, upholstery, and many more (40 kits in all). They are designed to be used as self-contained units. Each includes detailed instructor notes, student instructions, work performance benchmarks, tools, equipment and materials needed by student and instructor. These courses do not provide complete training but serve as introductory experience and training appropriate for junior and senior high students. Many of the units were designed for "special needs" students by using high interest/low reading level materials and hands-on work. Prices range from $335 to $1930 for each unit. Parents without background should be able to help their teens through some of the units, while others such as plumbing would require a teacher with at least some familiarity with the subject.

For further training after high school, students need to consider various available options. Vocational schools are not all the same in the way they are set up. Most common are "on campus"[2] study, correspondence, or a combination of both. Courses offered by campus and correspondence schools are similar to each other, however some courses, such as truck driving and diesel mechanics, require at least some time at a "campus" for hands-on instruction. Some courses are set up for the book work to be completed through correspondence, then a residency or "on campus" period arranged for the rest of the instruction. Admission re-

---

2   Campuses may be located near home, in which case, students can live at home while going to school. In many cases, the campus will be at too great a distance for students to remain at home.

quirements are generally either a high school diploma or an equivalency (GED) certificate.

For some students, it might be too abrupt a change to move from home school to a full-time vocational school far from home. An interim choice might be for teens to take a related course at a local college or through adult education for a semester or two. This transition can help them learn how to function in a classroom environment without the added cost and adjustment of living away from home.

The Distance Education and Training Council, a council of national organizations for adult education, will send you a free brochure listing accredited correspondence schools for vocational training.

Apprenticeships

Apprenticeship programs have been around since Adam began training his sons in farming. Apprenticeships can be formally set up by contract or agreement, or they may be informal situations where an older or more skilled person (mentor) shares his skill or knowledge with another person who acts as an assistant while he is learning. The term mentorships include both apprenticeships and less formal relationships that might be as simple as an older, wiser person providing advice to a younger.

Apprenticeships are most prevalent in the craft trades such as construction work. Usually unions are in control of both craftsmen and apprentices. Sometimes there are long waiting lists for apprentice openings. There are pages of apprenticeship information sources in *College Yes or No* (pages 56-60). A beginning point for more information would be your regional Bureau of Apprenticeship and Training (BAT) Office.

Home schoolers are looking at more innovative approaches to the apprenticeship idea. Bill Gothard of the Institute in Basic Life Principles has been a prime mover in encouraging businessmen, judges, physicians, etc. to offer apprenticeships under Godly men to young people. They have set up a home education program called the Advanced Training Institute International. Enrollment in that program by the entire family is required for any students interested in any of their apprenticeship opportunities. Applicants for apprenticeships must show individual initiative and diligence in their learning. Faith and character growth are both expected to continue while under apprenticeship. The Institute is preparing a series of *Life Purpose Journals* to lead students through the learning sequence of II Peter 1:5-10 in preparation for apprenticeship assignments.

Rather than advertising a list of apprenticeships to choose from, the Institute relies on the Lord to open up opportunities according to individual needs.

Developing Other Apprenticeship Opportunities

Apprenticeships do not have to be set up through recognized organizations. Anyone can arrange an apprenticeship or mentor-

ship, but we must know if there are legal requirements that might prevent recognition of proficiency. For instance, some states do not require that prospective lawyers graduate from law school but only that they pass the state bar examination.

In the National Homeschool Association's newsletter appeared a discussion of mentorships with some guidelines on mentoring relationships quoted from an article by Sharon B. Bruce in *Nonprofit Times*, September, 1988. Bruce identifies seven steps to follow in making a mentor/mentee selection:

1. Identify what you need from the relationship; carefully spell it out.
2. Identify what you are willing to contribute to the relationship.
3. Be willing to share your needs, expectations, and limits.
4. Identify the qualities you are looking for.
5. Consider several candidates.
6. Make a tentative choice; carefully discuss all aspects of the relationship with your choice.
7. Put everything in writing; agreement will guarantee a good start.
(*National Homeschool Association Newsletter*, Summer, 1989, p.5.)

These guidelines for mentors should be useful in most apprenticeship opportunities. It is important that expectations are clearly understood by both parties.

Sometimes mentoring situations arise on their own; a child meets an adult and forms a relationship that grows into one of mentoring without any plan or decision. While we should be on guard that this does not happen with adults we would not want influencing our children, it is often a blessing and a sign of God's provision for our needs even before we recognize them.

Military

The military services sometimes have different requirements from everyone else. At this time, the military services are categorizing students who either have diplomas from unaccredited schools or have graduated with a GED certificate in a less desirable category of applicants. It does not matter to them that home schooled students who are in the military already function well above the level of average recruits.

This means that young people who want to join a branch of the armed services must plan more carefully. They can do their high school work through an accredited correspondence school or under an accredited Independent Study Program. The other alternative is to attend junior college for one semester (completing 15 units) after completing high school, which will qualify them for a higher category.

We are hoping to see a change in this policy, and the National Center for Home Education is actively pursuing that end as I write.

Meanwhile, it would be wise to consult a military recruiter as soon as we realize that our child is considering entering one of the services.

There are placement tests given by the various armed services, and applicants can prepare with books such as *Practice for the Armed Forces Test-ASVAB* [$12], *ASVAB Basics* [$11], *Practice for Army Placement Tests* [$10], and *Practice for Air Force Placement Tests* [$10.95] (Arco).

On the Job Training

Whether or not students are college bound, there is nothing like a dose of reality in the form of a job to help them plan for the future. Work experience helps teens to understand the realities and responsibilities of being an employee, provides them with an income so they can begin to assume responsibility for their own needs, helps them to explore different job opportunities or careers, and helps them learn and develop skills.

When teens are working for someone other than Mom and Dad, they realize that they have to act without waiting for parental reminders. It is now their responsibility to do what they are told or what is needed, or they lose both job and income. The income is often the incentive that prompts teens to seek employment. While we do not want to encourage our teens to earn money to spend foolishly, or possibly sinfully, it is good to encourage them to buy their own clothing (especially if they want the expensive fad items), pay for their own entertainment, build a savings account, etc. Teens need some experience managing their own finances, and it is better to gain that experience on a smaller scale while still under their parents' influence than to suddenly have to figure it all out when they get married and move out.

The last two reasons I have listed for gaining work experience—career exploration and development of skills—relate most closely to the purposes of this book. It would be ideal if our teens could all find beginning jobs in the areas of their potential career interest, but, unfortunately, there are many more fast food jobs than engineering jobs available to unskilled teens. Even if that first job is less than ideal, it will help our son or daughter develop basic job skills and possibly alert them to the type of job that they will not want. On the other hand they might find themselves in a job which leads to a career. It is often true that we never know whether or not we like something until we try it.

Getting a Job

Some home educated teens have found jobs in their desired career fields simply by making themselves available. One teen helped a veterinarian with animal care, first as a volunteer, later as a hired assistant. Some teens volunteered to help do the "dirty work" on construction jobs, then later went on to more rewarding careers in the construction field. Being willing to fill in for an employer on short notice or at minimum pay might not be very rewarding at the time, but it often opens doors in the future.

Some teens are fortunate to stumble across a job without having to go through the application process. Maintaining relationships with adults involved in areas of the teenager's own personal interest will help teens to be in the right place at the right time for such jobs.

Actually, it might be better if they have to go through the application process, because it is a good learning experience for the future. A teenager is practicing applying for jobs at a time in his life when his livelihood does not depend upon it. If a teen blows an interview at Jack-In-The-Box, all is not lost, and he has gained valuable experience. Better to undergo the learning process under these conditions, than when he is interviewing with IBM or Bank of America.

I highly recommend that you pick up one or two job applications from businesses for your teen to practice filling out. It is amazing to read articles about how poorly many job applicants fill out such forms. The application is the first impression a person makes upon his potential employer. Blank spaces, erasures, cross-outs, or inadequate information are certain to hurt an applicant's chances of being hired. Practice ahead of time might make a crucial difference in getting a job.

Want to Work? The Teen's Guide to Successful Job Hunting (Royal Fireworks Press) [$9.99] helps teens get that first, part-time job while they are still in school. A lot of information is packed into this 44-page book. Part I deals with talents, skills, interests, and abilities, but balances those issues with the short-term nature of most teen jobs. Unlike some "getting a job" guides, this one also suggests considering entrepreneurships as an alternative to be being an employee. Part II covers the actual job hunt-where to look, how to dress, the application, and the interview. Part III helps teens once they have the job, with chapters on ethics, responsibility, communication, performance, learning from mistakes, evaluation, and how to leave a job. Since the book is written for typical teens (which usually does not include home educated teens), some of the ideas will seem overly obvious. For instance, there is a self-quiz on ethics that will seem ridiculously obvious to most home educated teens, but it still serves to enlighten them about the ethical (or unethical) mindsets of other teens.

Education Associates, Inc. sells many items designed to help job seekers, especially those who are looking for something more permanent. *Seven Steps to Employment* tells how to develop a resume, find and act upon job openings, fill out applications, interview, and follow up the interview. Individual booklets from Education Associates cover some of that same territory and more. Representative booklet titles are: *Filling Out the Forms, Keeping a Job: Now That You Have It, Face to Face: Making a Good Impression, Your Attitudes Make a Difference, Grooming for Job Success*, and more.

Job seekers with below average reading skills need special help that can be found in *Get That Job!* (Globe Fearon Educational Publisher) [$8.25]. This book, written at second grade reading level, tells how to complete a social security card application, helps them to understand vocabulary they will encounter on job applications, and discusses the importance of appearance, language, and attitude for a successful interview.

Entrepreneurs

Because they are learning at home, most of our teens have already been exposed to the do-it-yourself approach. Many of them approach the job issue the same way—by creating their own businesses. This approach is certainly more difficult, especially if teens are planning to create a business that will be viable enough to support a family in future years. Nevertheless, many home educated teens are well on their way to doing so. Josh Harris, son of Gregg Harris, published a top-quality magazine for teens and young adults, which he has, unfortunately for us, discontinued so that he can pursue other ventures and training. I have met a number of young men who have developed computer-related businesses. Some home school graduates have created businesses which provide music and entertainment at parties and other events.

Many home schooling families are beginning to look at entrepreneurship in a whole new light, largely due to leaders like Gregg Harris who have shown that family business is far more than just another way of making a living. Family businesses can be the launching pads for our children—both a training ground and an early start as they prepare to take on adult responsibilities. A family business can be the means by which fathers ensure that their sons are equipped to provide for their own families. For some families and teens it simply makes more sense to pool the parents' wisdom and funding capital with the teen's energy, rather than leaving their teens on their own to succeed or fail. As the job market becomes more and more insecure and unpredictable, family businesses might be rare islands of stability, providing "employment" for family members, while growing and expanding to employ others outside the family. Such businesses are usually small enough to respond fairly rapidly to changes in the marketplace, something impossible for most large businesses.

All of this is not intended to disguise the potential difficulties and problems. But the importance of having control, of being employers rather than employees in a world of government mandates and political correctness is becoming increasingly obvious.

Just as home schooling families each have their own way of home schooling, we find that they also each have their own way of doing family businesses. However, very few seem to be mom and pop operations with children only marginally involved. Most assign important tasks to children with mom and dad involved to varying degrees, depending largely upon whether or not dad has another primary job. Many families find themselves starting from scratch to create their family business. Often mom and the kids run the business in its early stages, with dad "coming home to work" once the business is profitable. Some families even consider building businesses to "hand-off" to their children when they become adults.

As I mentioned before, some teens start businesses on their own, but some choose to serve apprenticeships to gain knowledge and experience under someone who already "knows the ropes" so that they can prepare for future business ventures.

Those who want to find out what it takes to start their own business need to read books such as *Capitalism for Kids: Growing Up To Be Your Own Boss* [$9.95] and *The E-Myth Revisited* (about why businesses fail and what to do about it) by Michael E. Gerber [$15], both available from Bluestocking Press. Another helpful resource is the bi-monthly newsletter, *Young Entrepreneur* (KidsWay, Inc.) [$16 a year], which is full of money-making business venture suggestions, how-to's, resources, and contacts. You will get two free back issues when you subscribe. (They offer a 30-day money-back guarantee.)(S)

Those who want to understand the biblical principles behind entrepreneurship should listen to Jonathan Lindvall's tape, *Self-Employment, Preparing Our Children for Financial Freedom* (Bold Parenting) [$5.95]. (Self-Employment is reviewed as part of a two-part *Financial Freedom* tape set under "Economics.")

Volunteerism

Volunteer work might well be of equal or greater benefit than getting a job. Often the work required by volunteer organizations teaches teens skills that surpass what they might learn in the fast food business or cashiering for a small store. Volunteer organizations tend to hand out job assignments according to what needs to be done rather than according to job descriptions, so teens usually receive much broader training in the volunteer arena. They also have the opportunity to build both personal and professional relationships with adults. Check with your pastor for suggestions, or contact your city hall for a list of volunteer organizations in your area.

Family Life

In our modern society, "liberated" women are free to work full time, raise children, and do the bulk of the housework. We are sure to reap criticism if we offer our young women the option of preparing themselves for careers as homemakers rather than "career-persons." While people say that women who choose to be homemakers are not second-class citizens, the reality is that almost everything in our society (government, taxes, public opinion, and education to name a few) gives us the opposite message.

We cannot rely on our daughters marrying men who will be able to provide sufficient income to allow their wives to remain at home. Yet, it is still possible to live on one income, especially when both husband and wife are willing to make sacrifices. If our daughters wish to be homemakers they will need to know how to budget carefully and make wise use of their resources. We should encourage and help them by providing the skills and knowledge they will need to operate on a limited budget.

Instead of textbooks, life situations can be the teacher. Our daughters can learn to sew, cook, maintain a home, and raise children by practicing those things at home. This is experience that many other young women seldom get since they are not in the home very many hours of the day.

Young women might want to study about child development, learn how to sew, or in other ways develop their skills as homemakers as part of their high school curriculum. Refer to the home economics recommendations in Chapter 16 for possible resources.

Because of the changes being wrought in our society, our young women might not have the option of choosing to be homemakers to the exclusion of any other employment. They might need to work off and on throughout their lifetimes, or they might need or want to supplement their husbands' incomes with work done from their homes. These are the realities that we must keep in mind. Because of them, we should simultaneously prepare our daughters so they are able to do other things beyond the range of homemaking if required.

Choosing a basic skill to develop for such contingencies is wise. Offering music or dance lessons, providing bookkeeping services for small businesses, and typing/word processing services are examples of skills that homemakers can call upon at short notice.

No matter what our young women choose as their desired careers, we cannot know what God has in store for each of them. We cannot neglect academic skills because our daughters wish to be homemakers. They might unexpectedly need to support their families in emergency situations, or they might choose to educate their own children. In either case a lack of academic skills might be a terrific handicap to overcome.

We should not neglect our boys when it comes to instruction in household skills. They should know how to maintain their own household. It is a sad situation when Mom is ill and Dad and the children (girls or boys) cannot figure out how to do a load of laundry. The same goes for meal preparation, grocery shopping, and basic housecleaning. I am not advocating role reversal, but survival skills. Our boys might live on their own. We do not want them to bring home their laundry for us to do every Saturday, or drop in every evening for dinner. We need to think in terms of equipping our sons to survive without mothers, not send them out searching for a wife who will become a substitute mother.

Summary

Whether or not our teens have clear ideas of what they wish to do in the future, we should try to provide them with as broad an education as we reasonably can. We must provide materials and experiences that will enlarge the possibilities for their futures. Meanwhile, we should keep the doors to various possibilities open by providing broad and thorough coverage of academics until it is obvious that goals can and should be narrowed.

We will certainly run into limitations in what we are able to provide for our children, yet that really is not a crucial factor in our success or failure. If we provide the basic tools of learning, our children can apply those in any situation. The ability to acquire knowledge and skill, along with flexibility—the ability to change old or habitual ways of thinking and acting—might be more important than any specialized training that our teens receive in our rapidly changing society.

A Christian Foundation

Building on a Solid Foundation

We have discussed goals and various ideas which shape them, but before we go on to plan our course of study, we must make sure that we are not "building on sand." Without spiritual foundations, our children are gaining knowledge, but without wisdom.

By the time our children reach high school, we hope they will have a solid foundation in Scripture and God's principles. Even more important, but often lacking, is a personal relationship with God. While we have neither the time nor the space to deal with spiritual fundamentals here, do not overlook the priority that should be placed upon them. Because each of us has a free will, some of our teens will not yet have accepted Jesus as their Savior. Even some of those who have might not be allowing Him to be Lord of their lives. This lack of commitment will definitely hinder our educational efforts. The shared vision of serving God's purposes is missing, and the guidance and strength of the Holy Spirit is missing in each day's activities.

Fortunately, many of our teens do have a personal relationship with God and can build upon it. Upon a solid foundation we can build a Christian view of life and the world, including our place in it. There are many, many excellent books and resources which will help teens begin to evaluate themselves and the world around them in light of God's Word. I will recommend a few to you which can be helpful in beginning or building upon a spiritual foundation.

A thought-provoking book for unsaved, questioning, or doubting teens to begin with is *How To Be Your Own Selfish Pig*, by Susan Schaeffer Macaulay (Chariot Victor Publishing) [$9.99]. Macaulay speaks to the essential questions without sermonizing. The book has interesting pictures and photographs that help reinforce the ideas presented.

Josh McDowell has also written many books that speak to the thinker who wants to intellectually "see" that Christianity makes sense. *Evidence that Demands a Verdict* (Thomas Nelson Publishing) [$14.99] is one of the most well known. Josh set out to debunk Christianity and the Bible but ended up doing the opposite. The evidence he found is presented here. *Don't Check Your Brains at the Door* by Josh McDowell and Bob Hostetler (Word Publishing) [$9.99] presents much of that same evidence but in a version that is great for teens. Chapters are short with more dialogue and stories to make it interesting. Short "Workouts" activities end each chapter, taking teens directly to Scripture to learn for themselves. This book actually goes beyond

Evidence into topics such as the New Age movement, lifestyle choices, sex, televangelists gone astray, and peer pressure. Chapter titles accurately reflect the style of the content. For instance, "The Luke Skywalker God: Exposing the Impersonal Force Myth," "If You're OK, Then I *Must* Be OK: Exposing the God-Will-Grade-on-a-Curve-Myth," and "Stars in Your Eyes: Exposing the Love-at-First-Sight Myth." A four-session, interactive video course, based on the book, is also available. (These resources are typically recommended for junior or senior high Sunday School classes, but they will be useful in some homeschooling situations.) Check your local Christian book store for other titles by McDowell.

Jonathan Lindvall directly challenges home schooled young people in his six-audio tape *Bold Christian Youth Seminar* [$34] (Bold Christian Living). Lindvall encourages students to seek God first in their lives, then to make "bold" decisions regarding dating, honesty, relationships, career, etc., based upon biblical direction. He also encourages students to go to their parents for support and advice in making major decisions. He covers topics like spiritual commitment, future ministry, faithfulness in present commitments, honor, humility, dating, career preparation, higher education, preparation for parenthood, and preparing for financial freedom. Lindvall discusses his experiences both as a youth pastor and as a school principal, using anecdotes and stories, so the presentations are fairly entertaining. The tapes are appropriate for both junior and senior high students, although the younger students might have difficulty staying tuned in for so long. (Complementary tapes addressing parents on some of the topics from this seminar are available. See the Bold Parenting catalog for titles.) [Judy Eastman/C.D.]

A set of three videos, with six different presentations from American Portrait Films addresses basic spiritual issues. The series is called *Making a Decision That Lasts Forever: A Traveler's Guide to the Ultimate Destination*. Each video can stand alone, so it is not necessary to purchase the entire set. Videos feature two dynamic speakers, Rice Broocks and Jacob Aranza, each doing three of the presentations. Titles are "The Power of a Changed Life" (Broocks) and "The Deadliest Three Letter Word" (Aranza) on the first tape; "Repent and Believe" (Broocks) and "Sin's Greatest Price" (Aranza) on the second tape; and "The Power of the Cross" (Broocks) and "Finishing The Race" (Aranza) on the third tape. The intro of the first tape (first 5-7 minutes) is very different from the main part of the video. It uses some very flashy, graphic footage that will bother some viewers. You can simply skip that part and start with Broock's presentation if you wish. Both Broocks and Aranza present strong Scriptural messages with lots of humor. They incorporate other video footage that holds your attention. These videos are great for junior high through adult audiences. [Tapes are $19.95 each or $49.95 for the set of three.]

You will find other helpful faith-building resources listed under "General Resources" and under "Philosophy, Religion, and Apologetics" in this chapter. Also check Chapter Nine for Bible study resources.

Developing a Christian Worldview

Christians often interpret the term "worldview" to mean viewing mankind with God's eyes and recognizing that all men are in the same sinful, needy state. Developing an understanding of other cultures, often through "missions" education, is one of the educational tools we use to implement this idea of worldview.

In recent years "worldview" has taken on a broader, slightly different meaning. The term is now used to identify the type of philosophical framework through which we interpret all areas of life. Thus, a person might have a Secular Humanist worldview, a Marxist worldview, a Biblical Christian worldview, etc.

When I discuss worldview education for high school, I am generally referring to the second, broader definition, which encompasses the first definition.

For children below the ages of fourteen or fifteen, worldview education should be narrower in scope. Providing our children with a strong foundation of Bible knowledge is the most important thing we should do. We can add to that a good foundation in all subject areas which includes the influence of ideas and beliefs, however, with a narrow focus. For example, when we learn about scientists we can study how their religious beliefs influenced their scientific outlook. Missions education also is very appropriate in the foundational years.

Because older students are better able to make connections and relate ideas to one another, worldview education should change to the broader definition in the latter years of high school. In those years, students can tie information together, tracing patterns of philosophical thought and their results. We should then encourage them to consider their responsibility as Christians to live a life that reflects a biblical Christian worldview—a suiting culmination to our years of home schooling.

World Views in Action

A 1989 Gallup poll found that "...cheating is rampant in high school and college....about 75% of high school students admit to cheating, while about 50% of college students do."

In 1990, in our neighboring city of Anaheim, California, AIDS activists handed out condoms to eager teens in front of their high school. School officials, observing what was occurring, were only concerned that "activists stayed on the sidewalk and didn't block traffic...." One recipient remarked, "They know

The PEERS Test

(Nehemiah Institute)

The PEERS Test "World View Opinion Survey" is a great tool for identifying where anyone stands in relation to a biblical worldview. The letters in PEERS stand for Politics, Economics, Education, Religion, and Social Issues, the areas addressed by questions within the survey. Questions are answered on a scale stretching from strongly agree to strongly disagree, addressing issues such as free enterprise, government-run entitlement programs, premarital sex, and academic freedom. Tests can be given by anyone, then they are sent to Nehemiah for machine scoring. Scoring reports include scores for the five PEERS categories, character traits (degree of conviction, consistency), view of civil government, likelihood of a person's impact on society, agreement with biblical position on each question, and a summary of results. This test is illuminating! It can be used by older teens and adults, and they offer a separate test designed for junior high students along the same lines. The test authors clearly advocate particular views of government, economics, and social policy, some of which are not universally accepted by Bible-believing Christians. So keep in mind, that there is an element of "political correctness" present, even though it is likely to be agreeable to most who might use such a test.

The cost per test ($12 for the older level, $9 for the junior high level), which includes scoring and reporting, is high for a single test, but drops dramatically as the number of tests purchased increases. Consider getting together a group to do the test. This is a great tool for Sunday School classes or other church or Christian school groups. Contact Nehemiah for price information.

Nehemiah Institute also publishes a *Worldview Curriculum* [student book - $22.50; teachers' guide - $7.50] in a self-paced, independent-study format. Since the course takes about 22 hours to complete, it is obviously less comprehensive than other options described in this chapter. It covers the five key areas addressed by the test, the Christian history of the U.S., an overview of key people of God since the Flood, and a call to Christian "action." The course includes a student workbook and teacher's guide with a copy of the PEERS test included in the student workbook.

we're going to do it anyway, so why not give us some protection?"

Most Christian home educators still find such attitudes shocking or dismaying because they so clearly violate God's law. But there has been such a turnaround in attitudes toward ethics and morality in the United States that basing our judgments on God's law is often considered a backwards, ignorant way of looking at things. The Judeo-Christian worldview that prevailed in our country two centuries ago has been discarded or perverted so drastically that few even recognize what that worldview might be. Unfortunately, many Bible-believing Christians have become so confused by popular psychology, the media, government, and others with influence that their worldviews suffer from distortion and inconsistency. A worldview should provide a coherent and consistent foundation for life. From that worldview we should be able to develop beliefs, positions, and attitudes about all areas of life.

The Bible provides the guidelines by which we form our worldview. It is vital that we study Scripture in relation to ethics, government, science, the arts, and all other areas of life so that we have solid reasoning to back up our biblical Christian worldview. Those who reject the Bible use other sources to validate their belief systems. If we want to convince others of the correctness of our position, we will be much more effective if we first understand the worldview which is influencing them as well as its sources. In fact, part of developing a biblical Christian worldview should be examination of other possibilities.

We like to think that the truth should be obvious to others, but we overlook the fact that people do not purposely choose to believe something they think is stupid or unbelievable. They have good reasons for what they believe (although those reasons will usually reveal contradictions or faulty reasoning on some level of examination). When we discuss an issue with someone on the other side of the fence, the bottom line is usually not the issue itself, but the worldview that informs each of our opinions. For instance, many people believe that man is nothing more than a highly developed animal. Each man is answerable only to himself. Since they do not believe in an afterlife, they must do all they can to make their "stay on earth" as enjoyable as possible. So, of course, it makes sense to abort babies who will cramp their lifestyles or interfere with their developing careers or irritate (and possibly scare off) their live-in lovers. The bottom-line issue is the purpose and sanctity of life, while abortion rights and choice are side issues.

What Does This Have To Do with Education?

I believe that ideas result in actions; generally speaking, bad ideas result in bad actions, and good ideas produce good actions. The mess facing our society is the natural consequence of belief in and action based upon bad ideas about God, man, man's relationship to God, the family, government and all other areas. For instance, Adolph Hitler believed the Aryan race to be superior to all others. He believed that inferior races and "damaged" Aryans such as the retarded, the ill, and the elderly were a drain on society. It was then his duty to eliminate those problems. His actions were a natural outworking of his belief system. Handing out condoms to teenagers and giving them the message that we know that it is just too difficult for them to restrain themselves is an action based upon the belief that men are no more morally responsible than animals. Cheating follows a slightly different line of logic. The usual excuse is, "It doesn't hurt anyone else, so it's up to me," which denies man's subjection to God's authority and places morality on a relativistic plane.

What ideas do our children truly believe about God and man? Have they begun to develop a biblical Christian worldview that will guide them through life? While the media has certainly played a vital role in the advancement of false ideas, schools bear

equal or greater responsibility. We recognize the obvious distortions such as the idea that homosexuality is merely another, equally valid, lifestyle choice. We have more trouble recognizing the truth twisting behind ideas such as, "All teenagers go through a period of rebellion," and "If we all pay enough taxes, government can solve all of the problems of hunger and homelessness," and "God probably created the world, but he used evolution to accomplish His goal."

While we can and should begin to help our children develop a biblical worldview from the time they are young, the teen years are a crucial time for focusing on its importance. This means looking beyond the typical course of study for high school. Most of us have simply adapted the typical course of study which has been followed by most schools for many years. We assume that by using Christian textbooks and including a Bible study course, we will have taken care of any philosophical problems. Unfortunately, if our goal is to help our child develop a biblical worldview, it's not enough.

What will our teens face when they complete high school? Some will be able to continue their education at good Christian colleges, although a "Christian" label is no guarantee that a college or university teaches biblical truth. Others will continue their education at secular colleges and universities where they will encounter both obvious and subtle challenges to their faith every day. Still others will be working with people who follow all types of non-Christian belief systems.

Are They Properly Equipped?

We must ask ourselves if we are equipping our children to, first of all, be able to stand firm in explaining their belief in Jesus Christ as Savior, and, secondly, to be able to bring the precepts of Christianity back into positions of influence in all areas of life. Unless they understand how those areas of life are dominated by other belief systems, they obviously will not have any idea what changes are needed.

One of our family's goals in home education has been to raise our children to do more than just hang on to their own personal faith. We want them to be used by God. To equip them, an important part of their education is developing a biblical Christian worldview, and within that, teaching them how to examine all areas of life.

At the same time, we also teach them how those holding other worldviews interpret those same areas. Unless they understand the presuppositions that form opinions, they are like gardeners trimming branches off a tree that is suffering from root disease.

Defining Your Course

While we should be laying the background for worldview studies in the elementary grades, our students need to be mature enough to wrestle with challenging ideas before really delving into serious worldview studies. Usually, this should be reserved for the upper high school level.

How we choose to approach worldview education at high school level will vary from person to person, depending upon our interest in and knowledge of different subject areas. Francis

Schaeffer was very interested in the arts, so he developed his discussion of worldview based upon historical analysis of changes in the arts. David Noebel has developed the Summit program with more emphasis on history and political systems, although he addresses many other subject areas.

In these and other in-depth worldview studies, history stands out as the common unifying subject. The flow of events and their results provide obvious evidence with which we can begin our study. From history we can build in any direction we choose—art, literature, philosophy, politics, etc.—going as far as we feel is practical.

How We Did It

We began worldview education as a specific study with our two oldest sons (at ages 14 and 16) with a do-it-yourself approach, worked within that framework for a year, then added Summit Ministries' "Understanding the Times" curriculum the second year.

I want to share some of what we have done to give you some possibilities to consider. The book that prompted my thinking in this direction and provided the rationale for the course was Francis Schaeffer's *How Should We Then Live?* (Crossway). Although I read the book many years ago, I still used it with my sons after we had studied a time period and the related topics. It served as an excellent way to review and tie everything together. (Schaeffer presents too many ideas in each chapter for teens to read without preparation. They need background first or else they are overwhelmed with unfamiliar ideas. You might use the book *Turning Point* or another of the resources I recommend as an easier-to-understand introduction.)

Choose A History Text

A good history book which discusses philosophical ideas and their impact on events is crucial. Excellent texts trace those ideas beyond their immediate time period down through following generations. The text that I have found to be most useful is the Bob Jones University Press's *World History for Christian Schools*. It covers art, philosophy, world religions, literature, science, law, and politics fairly well for a high school text. The discussion questions are the outstanding feature. Questions such as, "What motivated European rulers to either support or oppose the Reformation?", "What influence did Christians have on nineteenth-century Europe?", and "What impact did European society have on Christians?", extend thinking beyond the facts into the realm of belief systems.

Developing Units of Study

Next, I developed unit studies with a worldview emphasis by expanding on content in chapters or units in the history book. I also used a comprehensive time line, *The World History Factfinder*. (A similar book, *The Timetables of History* by Bernard Grun [Simon and Schuster] [softbound edition, ISBN 0-671-74271-X - $20], is more commonly available to home educators.) I looked through the time line for particular people, places,

or events that would be helpful in developing worldview themes. I was also looking for relationships between ideas and events that are easy to miss in history books. For instance, events on the "religious front" often had dramatic impact upon politics, the French revolution being a good example.

I spent more or less time on each academic area according to the topics and the time period being studied. For instance, when we began with creation and early history, biology (theories of origins) received more attention than it did in the Middle Ages.

Once I determined which topics to teach, I chose a variety of resources to use for each.

Art

Because of my experience with Schaeffer's book, I incorporated art, music, and architecture at the beginning of our studies. Our primary source for the arts was *History of Art* by H.W. Janson (Harry N. Abrams, Inc.) [present edition ISBN 0810934426 - $65]. This very large book is the best resource to use because Janson follows a historical outline, tying in information from other subject areas where appropriate. The abundant illustrations include most paintings, sculptures, and buildings referred to by Schaeffer in *How Should We Then Live?* A less expensive, slightly abridged version entitled *The History of Art for Young People* is available from Harry N. Abrams, Inc. [$49.50]. In spite of its level, this is for older teens and adults, and it will work just as well as the original book.

Cornerstone Curriculum Project's *Adventures in Art* by David Quine can be used for a more thorough study of paintings described by Schaeffer. The first two levels in the *Adventures in Art* series help children to learn to observe art. The third level moves into worldview applications via the teacher guide which quotes frequently from Schaeffer and follows his line of thought. (See the review in Chapter Seventeen.) David Quine's *World Views of the Western World* includes use of *Adventures in Art*, although you might be able to substitute either of Janson's books.

For those who are intimidated by Schaeffer and prefer not to spend the time or money to use some of the mentioned resources, I suggest Dr. R.C. Sproul's message on Art which is part of the *Christian Worldview* audio tape series from Ligonier Ministries. This provides a much briefer overview of the connection between art and worldviews.

Literature

Literature is a wonderful revealer of worldviews, so I incorporated literature throughout our studies. I chose a few of the influential authors from each historical period and read either excerpts or entire books. The selected readings were not all by Christians. Part of our goal is understanding opposing belief systems, and that can best be done by reading what their proponents have to say for themselves rather than always reading a Christian's interpretation of what they say. Reading an excerpt from Machiavelli's *The Prince* helped us understand the pragmatic attitudes of rulers of the Renaissance and after. (We probably see more pragmatism today than was evident four and five centuries ago!) We discussed Machiavelli's worldview and the conclusions he formed because of it. Sir Thomas More's *Utopia*, written twenty years before his conflict with King Henry VIII, described his vision for a perfect world. We watched the movie *A Man for All Seasons* about the later period of More's life and contrasted the evident changes in his philosophy. *Luther on Education* (a translation of two of Martin Luther's educational treatises) provided interesting reading. From his perspective, it seemed a good thing for government to establish state schools to ensure that children learned to read and become industrious. This led into a discussion of government's responsibility to its citizens and imposition of philosophical views through law.

Sources for literature were often old editions from thrift stores[1] or library books, but I have found A Beka's *Masterpieces from World Literature* an excellent source for representative reading.

Another useful resource for tackling literature from a Christian worldview is *Reading Between the Lines: A Christian Guide to Literature* by Gene Edward Veith, Jr., (Crossway Books). Also consider the literature program, *Learning to Love Literature* (The Weaver), which incorporates Veith's book. See the reviews of both in Chapter Thirteen.

Philosophy

Philosophy certainly is evident within other subjects like history, religion, and literature, but I chose to spend even more time studying other philosophical/religious systems. Philosophy can be overwhelming for many teens, but we don't need to jump into "deep" philosophy to begin with. We can pique their interest by starting with Greek and Roman mythology. Various books on mythology are easily available, although one that seems to be most easy to find is *Mythology* by Edith Hamilton (New American Library) [available in a number of editions]. From there, we can move into the broad philosophical questions at an introductory level with resources such as *Between Heaven and Hell* and *The Universe Upstairs*. A next step might be R.C. Sproul's six-audio tape series on *Christian Worldview* [$18 for the set] which addresses philosophy in the first seven of twelve messages contained on the tapes. These messages address the topics of secularism, existentialism, humanism, pragmatism, positivism, pluralism and relativism, and hedonism. Each message is thirty minutes long, so this is introductory level, appropriate for most older teens.

Philosophy is inevitably religious, and the study of various religions focuses philosophy a little more narrowly. While most history books address various religions and their origins, it helps to devote extra study to belief systems that have persisted through the centuries such as Hinduism, Buddhism, and Islam. Many of these ancient religions, particularly Hinduism, are becoming increasingly popular in the United States but go unrecognized under various New Age disguises.

The teaching that there are many roads to God, characteristic of some of these religions, is symptomatic of the relativistic post-

modernism that is growing to dominate American culture. Postmodernism essentially tells us that we cannot know truth, all is relative, so whatever you choose to believe is fine for you. Islam and other such religions propone "truth" that is contrary to the gospel. Such philosophical/religious issues are really at the heart of our worldview study.

Often, it is only after we have gone through other subject areas and raised questions that lead back to the origins of beliefs that students are ready to examine such fundamentals of philosophy. So don't be in a rush to get into heavy philosophy.

Understanding the Times

Although we had already been working through our own worldview studies the first year, the second year we incorporated the "Understanding the Times" (UTT) curriculum. We continued with history, art, and architecture, and expanded our literature studies, while UTT filled in other areas, saving me much preparation time.

"Understanding the Times" is a video-based version of their one- and two-week programs offered by Summit Ministries at their Colorado headquarters and other sites. The purpose of UTT is to enable Christians to obey two particular Scriptural commands. The first is Colossians 2:8, "See to it that no one takes you captive through philosophy and empty deception according to the tradition of men, according to the elementary principles of the world, rather than according to Christ." The second is 1 Peter 3:15, "But sanctify Christ as Lord in your hearts, always being ready to make a defense to everyone who asks you to give an account for the hope that is in you, yet with gentleness and reverence."

"Understanding the Times" divides worldviews under three headings: Secular Humanism, Marxism/Leninism, and Biblical Christianity. (An appendix addresses New Age worldviews in the original book, but the new abridged edition of the book uses a framework of four worldviews which includes New Age.) UTT then examines ten areas or topics within each of the three worldviews. The ten areas are theology, philosophy, ethics, biology, psychology, sociology, law, politics, economics, and history. There are over thirty tapes, most having two lessons per tape. Some topics such as creation/evolution and modern history receive much more attention than others.

Students each have a binder containing outlines for the videos which they fill in as they watch. The two-volume teacher's manual (in binders) provides lesson outlines, previews of the next video lessons, project instructions, scheduling options, tests, answers for weekly "notes" sheets and tests, suggestions for using the course in church and community settings, and much more. Supplemental books and readings also come with the course. Discussion of the videos and readings is a vital and exciting part of the course (the best part according to the first group I worked with).

---

1   The various Norton anthologies (W.W. Norton and Company), often available at thrift or used book stores, make valuable additions to your home library.

Understanding the Times is also the title of a 912-page book by Dr. David Noebel of Summit Ministries [$36.95 retail; $18.50 for classes]. The book is designed to be used as part of the course, although it can be used on its own with no problem. The book addresses the same ten subject areas listed above, with an entire chapter addressing each area from each of the three major worldviews. (This is a very large book!) Unlike the video series, the book balances time spent in each area. The text is very useful in conjunction with the videos. It is written at an adult reading level, and the content is challenging. So it is not a book to assign blindly for teen reading. It is intended to serve as a reference tool to which we can refer when confronted in one of the topical areas. Because of this, there is repetition of content in some chapters, allowing pertinent information to be available where needed.

A 402-page, abridged version of *Understanding the Times* [$19.95 retail; $14.95 for classes] (co-published by Association of Christian Schools International and Summit Ministries) condenses the information contained in the original. It follows the same format, although each of the ten areas is addressed in four chapters instead of three. The three chapters from the original book that discuss Biblical Christian, Marxist/Leninist, and Secular Humanist worldviews are abridged. A fourth chapter has been added addressing each topic from the Cosmic Humanist or New Age worldview. You'll find fewer quotes in the abridged edition, but it still covers the information fully enough for a survey class or an introductory study on the topic. Students who will be using the book for research purposes will find the unabridged edition more useful, and those headed for college will find the unabridged a better resource because of its comprehensiveness. However, the abridged edition is more readable than the original, and it also serves as the foundation for the ACSI course, which might dictate it as our choice. (See the review of the ACSI course below.)

Although we began our worldview studies with only our family, when we began the UTT course we included five other teenagers. I have seen the effectiveness of the course in meeting its Scriptural goals. In fact, I am so impressed with the course that I think it or a similar course should be offered to all Christian teens <u>and</u> parents. I strongly recommend using the course with two or more students because of the learning that takes place through discussion and interaction.

The catch is the cost—$995 plus textbook and notebook costs, about $35 per student at class prices. (Notebook pages can be duplicated for class use to save money, but students will definitely need a binder and tabs to organize and keep them together.) Summit has tried to make the course more easily available by offering it in two separate packages. The Basic Teaching Package ($570) contains all teaching materials and selected videos. Those teaching the course only once a week for a year will find this to be sufficient for their course. Others might start with the Basic Teaching Package, then add the Daily Video Package when they are able ($425). This includes the remaining videos.

Consider these possible solutions. Those who really want to use the entire course, videos and all, might form group classes,

encourage your church or church school to invest in the videos for their library, or solicit donations. (The CSA Creation Resource Lending Library has purchased the *Understanding the Times* videos and makes them available for a freewill offering. See CSA Creation Resource Lending Library under "Sources.") Sometimes a few groups are formed and they trade videos back and forth. Summit Ministries is trying to make the course more easily available by offering some course components separately, although there are restrictions about how they may be purchased.

Comprehensive Worldview Courses

➲ ACSI's Understanding the Times

Those who cannot use Summit's complete UTT for whatever reason can still pursue biblical worldview studies. ACSI's version of "Understanding the Times" is much less expensive since it centers around the abridged book, relying on discussion and activities rather than videos [abridged edition - $19.95; teacher edition - $24.95; student workbook - $7.50]. The teacher edition for this course comes in a three-ring binder, and there is a companion student workbook. This is an excellent alternative designed for use in Christian schools for a single semester. Daily lesson plans guide students through reading, discussion, and activities centered around the ten topics of the book instead of the organization structure used by the Summit video course which emphasizes more current issues. The course is definitely designed for an interactive group rather than an independent student, so gather one or more teens to participate with you. The teacher edition includes masters for overheads for classroom use, but the overhead masters can be used directly from the teacher edition rather than reproducing them on transparencies. You might spread the course out over a full school year, using two or three days per week instead of five. Unlike the Summit course, students in the ACSI course read almost all of the book. The course also requires a significant amount of writing.

The lessons are well designed, even for the teacher unfamiliar with these topics. However, teachers must read the chapters and familiarize themselves with the material ahead of each lesson. Most teachers will probably need to do additional reading and research to prepare themselves to teach this course. We can still supplement with videos and other resources, but the lessons rely on teacher presentation far more than in the Summit course.

The lessons themselves are excellent. They incorporate a significant amount of direct Bible study, something lacking in Summit's course. The variety of classroom activities—constructing charts, reading, completing lecture notes, brainstorming, role playing, etc.—should be very effective at engaging students at a deeper level than in the video course. This ACSI course makes teaching worldviews more practical than ever for those on a tight budget. All I would change would be to supplement with a few videos and require a research paper.

➲ Lightbearer's Christian Worldview Curriculum (Summit Ministries) $795; student workbook - $14.95; textbook (*UTT*) - $14.95

Students in grades 7 through 9, most of whom are too young for the other courses reviewed here, can be introduced to the study of worldviews through Summit's new video-based program. This is a full-year course that incorporates the abridged version of *Understanding the Times* and Susan Schaeffer Macaulay's *How to Be Your Own Selfish Pig*. It follows the order of the *UTT* book, working through the areas of theology, philosophy, ethics, biology, psychology, sociology, law, politics, economics and history, all from a biblical Christian perspective. The teacher manual contains detailed instructional guidelines. The course itself uses more than twenty integrated video presentations as students discuss, write, role play, read, and research each topic. The variety of activities should make the course appealing to most junior high students, although it is a challenging course that requires a good deal of work. Scripture memory is also integrated throughout the course. Field trips to see or apply worldviews in action are encouraged throughout the school year. Articles from Focus on the Family's magazines *Brio* and *Breakaway* or from *God's World* are supposed to be selected for discussion, so you will need access to one or more of these if you intend to do this. Each section ends with a quiz, and answers are provided in the teacher manual.

The entire course consists of the videos, a teacher manual, student workbook(s), the above-mentioned books, plus several other supplementary books such as *The Light and the Glory*. Each student will need a student workbook plus copies of *Understanding the Times* (abridged) and *How to be Your Own Selfish Pig*. Videos in this course are less of the "talking head" variety most typical of the older level *Understanding the Times* course; they include *The Crossing, Christy*, David Barton's *Keys to Good Government, William Wilberforce, The Chickenomics* series, *Incredible Creatures That Defy Evolution*, and other such titles. The course must be taught and requires teacher planning and preparation. It works best in a group (it is definitely designed for a classroom), although that group might be quite small.

➲ Understanding the Times

See descriptions of the video course, book, and "camp" above.

➲ World Views of the Western World by David Quine (Cornerstone Curriculum Project) $125 for first student; $75 for each additional student in the same family

This is a three-volume, comprehensive worldview curriculum which draws heavily upon the works and ideas of Dr. Francis Schaeffer. Each volume is published in an easy-to-handle, lay-flat binding; each of these books serves as a course resource-teaching syllabus for students. It is designed so that students can work independently, although this would not preclude group discussion and interaction. In fact, the course best lends itself to a combination of independent and group work. The course is arranged chronologically: the first volume covers Ancient Rome and Greece and the Middle Ages; the second covers the Renais-

sance, the Reformation, the Revolutionary Age, and the Rise of Modern Science; the third volume covers the Age of Reason, the Age of Fragmentation up through the present. Rather than aiming for comprehensive coverage of history it focuses instead upon the key ideas that dominated each period. Following the lead of Francis Schaeffer in *How Should We Then Live?* (both the book and the video series), Quine centers study primarily around the areas of philosophy/religion, literature, music, and the fine arts. He also ventures beyond Schaeffer into economics, law and government, and science. In addition, extensive writing is required, and basic paragraph and essay writing skills are taught for the lengthier assignments. A chart at the beginning of Volume One shows subject area unit equivalencies; the entire three volumes are equivalent to 15 Carnegie units, so this is a major part of a student's high school course work. It includes enough units for requirements in English, history, government, and fine arts, with the equivalent of 2 units of philosophy/theology, 1 unit of science history, and surplus units in government, political theory, and economics (which looks great on a transcript). You will need to add math, lab science, and foreign language classes (plus health, p.e., driver's ed and other such extras) to complete high school requirements.

Following through the weekly lesson plans, students read from the research-teaching syllabus and answer questions and write essays directly in it. They are also directed to view videos, listen to audio cassettes, and read from other sources. For the first volume, you will need to purchase or borrow a number of other resources such as *The Aeneid* by Virgil, *Affliction* by Edith Schaeffer, *The City of God* by Augustine, *How Should We Then Live?* by Francis Schaeffer, *The Republic* by Plato, *The Universe Next Door* by James Sire, the *How Should We Then Live?* video series, Cornerstone's *Adventures in Art* and *Classical Composers and the Christian World View*, audio tapes by Francis Schaeffer, and audio tapes from the Knowledge Products series on figures such as Aristotle and Plato. All of these resources are valuable additions to a library rather than resources to be used only for school.

Volume One begins with an introduction to the course and covers the basics of defining worldviews. From there it moves on to a comparison/contrast study of the biblical Christian worldview and Greco-Roman worldviews. In-depth studies of the Book of Job, *The Iliad*, and *City of God* are representative of Quine's strategy of using significant pieces of literature as "springboards" for integrated study in each area. The second half of Volume One shifts to the Middle Ages, examining the changes in philosophical and theological ideas and their consequences through this era and beyond. The other two volumes continue with the same format, following the time periods described above. Volume One is available at this time, with Volume Two partially complete.

While students can do the entire study independently, there are no built in mechanisms for accountability—no tests or quizzes. However, there are numerous essay questions and writing assignments. Parents should be looking over this work and discussing the course content with students. However, most parents are not familiar with the course content themselves which makes this rather difficult. Ideally, parents should also participate in the study, at least reading through the material, watching videos, and listening to the tapes. If this is not possible, having a student narrate lesson content to the parent, summarizing what they have learned, might be adequate although less than ideal. Consider having a few students who are working through the study (simultaneously but independently) meet with a knowledgeable adult periodically to discuss course content. If none of these ideas are practical, all is not lost. We might leave accountability at the student's doorstep: they get out of it what they put into it. When you consider how little students retain of what they "learn" under the most stringent accountability systems, there is something to be said for allowing them to absorb as much as they can without outside coercion. After all, this is most often how adults function when they want to learn something. The key here is student motivation. I have found in teaching worldviews that once most students grasp the idea of worldviews and how important it is, learning follows naturally. They easily understand that this is learning that matters!

This course parallels what I did with worldview education with my own sons more closely than any of the other programs. (*Understanding the Times* can still fit in as an adjunct to this course as it did with ours.) It is far more comprehensive in scope and depth than anything else available. Keep in mind that it is a new course, so it is bound to have a few bugs and rough spots. But those looking for a serious worldview course that is the primary focus of the high school years need look no further.

Note: Each volume contains a consumable course and is intended for use by only one student. No photocopying or resale is allowed. Thus, you need to purchase a separate book for each student, although additional books are purchased at discounted prices.

➲ Worldview Academy

Worldview Academy offers week-long camp experiences centered around worldview study for students ages 13 and up plus weekend-long presentations for both teens and adults. Worldview Weekends typically run Friday evening and all day Saturday, covering worldview basics and some key issues. Worldview Academy, since it runs an entire week, focuses on three primary areas: worldviews, apologetics/evangelism, and leadership. Ten hours are devoted to each of the first two areas, and seven hours are devoted to leadership. Examples of topics covered within these three primary areas are creation and evolution, the preeminence of Scripture, cults, communication, government, economics, and the arts. A review and mini debates take up two more hours of camp time.

At Worldview Academy, sessions are presented by different teachers who interact with the young people throughout the day (classes, meals, games, etc.). While Summit Ministries describes itself as a seminar, Worldview Academy describes itself as a camp, with greater emphasis on relationships and interaction. Attendees are encouraged to maintain contact with camp "counselors" as they take what they learn out into the real world. Camps scheduled thus far for 1998 are to be held in California, Florida, Illinois, Pennsylvania, Missouri, Minnesota, Texas, and Washington. Cost ranges from $345 to $355 depending upon location. Dates, locations, and costs change each year, so contact Worldview Academy for current information. Worldview Weekends are scheduled for other locations so also check for those opportunities. Seventy percent of WVA students are home educated, so our teens should feel "right at home."

Worldview Academy presentations have been taped, and those tapes, together with a notebook and teaching materials, will soon be available so that those who cannot attend will still have the opportunity to learn and be inspired. Contact them for more details about price and availability.

Design Your Own Course

Some parents will want to design their own worldview study since they have their own ideas about how comprehensive they wish it to be and which topics to include. Many of the resources reviewed next under "General Resources" might serve as beginning points for do-it-yourselfers.

From there, you might consider some of the other resources recommended not only under the "General" heading but also under the specific topic headings. These resources are either ones that we have used or ones that others have recommended to me.[2]

You should also check out the resources available from the *Christian Worldview Library* which lends a huge assortment of books, cassettes, and videos on Bible study, American history, world history, economics, business, ethics, abortion, current events, home education, plus many more topics. We can select materials to use as either foundations or supplements for worldview studies. Resources are available for both adults and children. Family memberships are $30 per year.

General Resources

➲ Battle for Our Minds [audio or video series and booklet]
by R.C. Sproul (Ligonier Ministries) video - $15; audio - $8; booklet - $4

This presentation consists of three 30-minute messages available on either video or audio tapes. A Study Guide booklet contains summaries, outlines, illustrations, and questions for comprehension and discussion. The presentation is divided into the three topics Classical/Biblical Worldview, Age of Enlightenment, and Secularism. On the first tape Sproul discusses the nature of God and His relationship with man. On the second and

---

2   The *Understanding the Times* course incorporates a number of the books and videos reviewed in this chapter. I have marked those that are used with the course with an asterisk "*".

third tapes he traces the shifts in philosophy through the Enlightenment and into secularism. Like Summit Ministries' *Understanding the Times*, Sproul uses a chart to identify how each worldview addresses ten major areas of life, here identified as God, religion, church, science, government, law, nature, life, the arts, and work. Since the presentation deals with abstract ideas, I recommend the video rather than the audio presentation because the visual mode holds attention better than auditory. Also, it helps to see the visual diagrams on the video rather than having to consult the booklet. Either way, we still need the booklet because it includes information not on the tapes such as comparison charts and explanations.

⊃ **The Battle for the 21st Century** by Marshall Foster (Mayflower Institute) book - $14; audio cassettes - $20

Marshall Foster presents "The Battle for the 21st Century: The Family Dynasty Strategy" as a seminar. If we cannot attend, next best is to get the four audio cassette tapes and seminar book and do it on our own or with a group. It lays the foundation for understanding basic principles in relation to God, government, families, and education. The seminar is designed for teens and adults. Marshall's writing style is much like his speaking style—colorful, illustrated with anecdotes, loaded with information, and motivating. The book is less than 100 pages, so it is quick reading. The point Foster makes is that we need to understand and adopt a biblical plan of action for our families as we march into the 21st century. Parents who want to teach their children about worldviews will find that this book makes a great starting place for understanding worldviews since it traces back through ideas and philosophies, showing their impact on subsequent events.

⊃ **Biblical Worldview magazine** (American Vision) free to supporters of American Vision, $20 suggested donation

Gary DeMar, author of *God and Government* and leading spokesman for the Christian Reconstruction movement, edits this monthly magazine. It tackles history, theology, current events, and other topics that relate to worldviews. In sampling topics from a single issue (June 1994) I found articles concerning Christian schools and certification and accreditation; the Olympics and the gay agenda; Christians taking visible stands on issues such as abortion and gay rights; commentary on Kurt Cobain's suicide and worldviews; and a reprint of Patrick's Henry's "give me liberty or give me death!" speech headed by the question of whether or not such a speech would be "tolerated" today. Even with an insert on ministry activities, the magazine is modest in size. However, many of the articles are extremely thought provoking, especially for those who want to understand the Reconstructionist position or compare it to the ideas of other Christians.

⊃ **Brave New Schools** by Berit Kjos (Harvest House) $11.99

Berit Kjos is an expert on the pagan agenda that has invaded our government schools. But, unlike many critics of government schools, she also understands Goals 2000 and the big picture of societal restructuring in which that pagan agenda plays a signifi-

cant role. In *Brave New Schools*, she demonstrates how leading children through occult Indian ceremonies, warping the way children view environmental issues, and negating the influence of parents are leading children to reject Christianity in favor of a global, New Age vision for the future. She also reveals the totalitarian aspects of that future, drawing parallels particularly with Nazi Germany. The book is thoroughly researched and footnoted, and it includes a chronology of crucial turning points in education and a glossary of terms that help us understand the true meaning of the restructuring process. By including many real-life stories, Kjos easily holds the attention of both teen and adult readers.

⊃ **Building A Biblical World View** [video] by David Quine (Cornerstone Curriculum Project) $20

David Quine draws heavily from Francis Schaeffer, author of *How Should We Then Live?*, as he presents this introduction to worldviews. Quine helps us define and identify worldviews, then shows why it is vital that we teach a biblical Christian worldview. After laying the foundation, he answers the question, "How do I teach the various subjects from a biblical worldview?" He primarily uses his own products—*Making Math Meaningful, Adventures in Art, Science: The Search, Music and Moments with the Masters*, and *Classical Composers and the Christian World View*—to explain how we do this since he created them for that very purpose. This 65-minute video is professionally produced, but it is essentially Quine presenting before a small audience. While David Quine often speaks very passionately on this subject, he seems a bit conscious of the video and is consequently a little "stiffer" than he usually is in his presentations. This is the first in a projected series of videos.

⊃ **Children at Risk*** by Dr. James Dobson and Gary Bauer (Word Publishing) $12.99

Changing views about families are some of the most visible evidences of worldviews which have shifted away from a dependence upon Judeo-Christian values. Dr. Dobson and Gary Bauer, president of the Family Research Council, pile up the evidence showing that forces destructive to families are growing in strength. They trace the disintegration through all areas that touch our children—education, families, moral codes, the media, politics, child care, and art. They call for a return to Judeo-Christian values and outline a strategy for achieving that goal. While I challenge their recommendation of a voucher system to solve our educational woes, other suggestions are helpful.

⊃ **Christian Action for the 1990s** [audio tape seminar] by John Eidsmoe (John Eidsmoe) $30

Constitutional lawyer and scholar, John Eidsmoe presents an 8-hour seminar addressing major issues facing Christians in the United States. Topics presented include Christianity and Government, Religious Freedom, the Constitution, Evolution, Humanism and the New Age, Child Abuse, and Abortion. A binder holds the eight, one-hour cassette tapes.

Another audio seminar by Eidsmoe, *Current Issues in Biblical Perspective* [$30], complements *Christian Action for the*

1990s. It covers Communism, War and Military, Economics, Education, Pornography, Gambling, a Constitutional Convention, Crime and Punishment, Juvenile Law, and Dispensationalism and Reconstructionism. These tapes should work well if you choose to approach worldviews topically; use the first few from Christian *Action as* part of your introductory studies, then bring in the others when you discuss those topics.

➔ Christian Home Learning Guides by Marshall Foster and
Ron Ball (Mayflower Institute or Zane Publishing, Inc.) $45

This is actually a single very large book (almost 500 pages) divided up into numerous sections, many of which correspond to the educational CD-ROMs from the Zane Home Library. The book can stand alone as a history-oriented biblical worldview curriculum guide. Foster and Ball explore philosophy and beliefs as they impact all the different subject areas, presenting the rationale for a biblical Christian view. Elements of the Principle Approach are incorporated; making this a sort of "Principle Approach made simple" course. Marshall Foster's background as a history researcher tilts the entire book more toward history than any other subject. A huge appendix includes important historical documents and writings such as the *Mayflower Compact* and *Declaration of Independence*. An interesting feature is the inclusion of critiques of the Zane CD-ROM programs. Foster and Ball deal with the humanistic, evolutionary assumptions evident in the programs, using them as a way of teaching the alternative biblical Christian worldview. If you purchase the Zane programs, you really need this book. If you don't have the programs, you can still benefit from the information presented here. Note: the Zane Home Library CD-ROMs are being marketed through Amway distributors who will also be selling this book. They did not supply any of their programs for review.

➔ Christian Worldview [audio tapes] by Dr. R.C. Sproul
(Ligonier Ministries) $18 for the set

See the review of the entire series under "Philosophy, Religion, and Apologetics." The message on Science within this series introduces the topic in relation to a biblical Christian worldview.

➔ Citizen newsletter (Focus on the Family) donation requested
for subscription

Focus on the Family's *Citizen* informs Christians about current issues that affect the family. It stresses the importance of involvement and political action. In each issue of the newsletter, they focus on hot topics with at least one in-depth article. They follow such articles with resource lists for more information and groups to contact. Although *Citizen* advocates educational vouchers for private schools which many home educators oppose, it is still an excellent source of information on current events for both teens and parents.

➔ Community Impact Seminar Series [videos] (Gospel
Light) $79.96 for all four or $19.99 each

Co-produced with Focus on the Family, this series of four high-quality videos was designed primarily for churches. However, it also is a great tool for answering the natural question, "If

we learn all of this about worldviews, what do we do with it?" The goal of the series is to encourage Christians to be involved in society and the political arena, to bring the Christian worldview "into the marketplace." Assuming a typical church audience, the first video begins by answering the question posed as its title: *Why Christians Need to Get Involved (#8511601120)*. The second video, *Winning the War of Ideas* (#8511601139), tells us that we are involved in a battle, but one that operates at the idea level to shape hearts, minds, and society. It addresses the vital issue of right and wrong, subjectivity and objectivity. The third video, titled *How to Speak Out for Truth* (#8511601147), promotes a strategy of principled persuasion that addresses our audiences where they're at. It includes practical tips such as narrowing our focus when talking to someone of a different persuasion; i.e., don't try to explain the fundamental differences between secular humanism and biblical Christianity when the issue is whether or not to have a pornography store in the neighborhood. The fourth video, *How to Make a Difference in Your Community* (#8511601155), explains how one person or a small group can make a huge difference. Host John Eldredge uses stories and practical application throughout the videos in a very engaging presentation. Eldredge occasionally introduces other speakers to expand on particular issues via interspersed tape interviews. Chuck Colson, Gary Bauer, John Stott, Dennis Prager, Dallas Willard, R.C. Sproul, and Vernon Grounds all make appearances in this series. Each video is 30 minutes long and comes with an outline and discussion guide intended to take about another 30 minutes.

➔ Culture Wars/Current Issues, course H155 (Landmark's
Freedom Baptist Curriculum) $35

This course deals with many of the moral issues facing us today. It begins by acknowledging the Christian foundations of our country, then it addresses the cultural warfare that has developed as pagan worldviews have vied with Christianity for the hearts and souls of men. It covers such issues as Christians and public policy, the death penalty, Christian education, abortion, abstinence, rock music, and many others. Each issue is defined and addressed from a biblical point of view. (I was pleasantly surprised to find one of the strongest defenses for separation of *school* and state I have encountered; the book clearly teaches that government should not be involved in education.) Each chapter expresses strong opinions and encourages political involvement. At the end of each chapter are a number of questions, both short answer and essay, and Bible verse memorization. The course is intended for tenth grade students and it includes a worktext, quizzes, exams, and answer keys.

➔ A Dance with Deception by Charles Colson (Word
Publishing) $5.99

Charles Colson has presented hundreds of social and political commentaries on his *BreakPoint* radio program. Many of those commentaries are brought together in this book. You can find just about any important issue addressed here; among them are issues such as condom distribution, civil rights, education, health care, welfare, the big bang theory, abortion, films, and court decisions. Drawing upon current events, Colson's commentaries make lively and informative reading that will challenge the way you think about the issues. Each commentary is only a few pages long, so if teens have a tight schedule they can select one or two to read in a short period of time.

◆ **Deadline** by Randy Alcorn (Questar) $10.99

This is a fictional story of one man's struggle to find peace. He is caught between two ideologies represented by two close friends. When these friends die in an auto accident, he begins to search for the truth, and, in the process, he discovers more than he was looking for. This is not an action story like *This Present Darkness* because the heart of it addresses life issues. However, there is a strong, interesting story line. It will appeal mostly to teens or adults who enjoy thinking and discussion. Alcorn tackles most of the "hot" political and moral topics of today—the press, abortion, gay rights, sex ed, divorce, adultery, parental involvement in children's upbringing, euthanasia], etc. There is hardly an issue that he misses. This is an excellent book, although Alcorn tidies things up too neatly at the end with a number of late-breaking revelations. The purpose of the book seems to be to show how a Christian worldview should affect all areas of life—worldviews in action. Alcorn accomplishes this purpose in a format that should be very appealing to teens. [Josh Duffy]

◆ **Defeating Darwinism by Opening Minds** by Phillip E. Johnson (InterVarsity Press) hardcover - $15.99; paperback - $9.99

You should first read my reviews of two of Johnson's other books, *Darwin on Trial* and *Reason in the Balance*. This book is a condensed, easier-to-read version of both. Johnson deals with the ideas of truth, reason, and intelligent design as primary arguments against Darwinism. He also addresses the battle between relativism (postmodern thought) and Christianity (which denies relativism), the real conflict we face. Johnson believes that as scientific evidence disproving evolution continues to build, evolutionists will be forced to confront the fact that empirical evidence and their theories are in direct conflict. As Christians, we can encourage the opening of minds to confront the real issues involved in the battle over evolution.

In aiming for a younger, less-informed audience than he did with his other books, Johnson uses an e-mail letter from Emilio, a European university student, to draw out three key mistakes Christians and other theists make when discussing evolution. He also uses the context of the screenplay version of the Scopes Trial in the movie *Inherit the Wind* as a backdrop for his arguments throughout the book, exploring the use of media to control the message, the distortion of truth by the media, the arguments presented in the movie versus the true situation, the reversal of the Scopes trial situation that occurs today (schools being challenged for teaching evolution and creationists on the defensive side), and the arguments the public perceives and believes without logical analysis. This approach makes *Defeating Darwinism* an excellent introduction to Johnson's works for our teens.

◆ **Discover Your Children's Gifts** by Don and Katie Fortune (Revell/Chosen Books) $14.99

Subtitled "A parent's handbook to recognize and develop your children's God-given gifts," this book has many applications for home educating families. I list it here to help answer the "So what do *I* do?" question that naturally arises from worldview studies. This book includes a test for identifying spiritual gifts using seven key words or categories to describe each type of person. Those seven categories are perceiver, server, teacher, exhorter, giver, administrator, and compassion person. Many worldview courses such as Summit's urge us to political action, yet that is an area where some people feel they have absolutely no aptitude. This test will encourage our young people (and maybe ourselves also) to discover for which areas of service God has equipped them. Then they can make realistic plans for action reflecting their personal spiritual gifts. (See complete review under "Bible.")

◆ **Evaluating Books: What Would Thomas Jefferson Think About This?** by Richard J. Maybury (Bluestocking Press)

See the review under "Evaluating Books" in Chapter Fourteen. Many of the principles in Maybury's book will assist us in selecting reading material to better understand worldviews.

◆ **Foundations of Liberty** (Liberty Bookstore/East Moline Christian School) 1-4 titles - $2 each; 5-9 titles - $1.80 each; 10 or more titles - $1.50 each

See the complete review in the "Foundations" section of Chapter 13. These topical booklets cover government, law, economics, the judicial system, history, and philosophy either under topics specifically related to one of these areas or a current issue. Writings from some of the best conservative Christian thinkers develop students' understanding of issues such as biblical Law, limited constitutional government, the right of private property, and the free market system.

I envision these booklets being used in a number of ways. Reading through one of them, then writing an original paper based upon those readings, would be an excellent assignment for a high school student. Incorporating appropriate articles into a history, government, economics, health, or more general worldview course would also be valuable. Parents might read these to expand their knowledge of subjects, and if you have self-motivated students, they too might want to read these just for their own information.

◆ **Getting Off the Textbook Interstate, History Via the Scenic Route** [audio tape seminar]

See the review under "History" in this chapter. This tape series also serves as a wonderful introduction for creating your own worldview studies.

◆ **Government Nannies** by Cathy Duffy (Noble Publishing Associates) $13

I have to include my own book here since it grew out of my concern for the proper role of government from both Christian and Constitutional perspectives. It addresses the fundamental questions, "Who owns the children?" and "Do citizens serve the State or does the State serve the citizens?" Christians have been confused and inconsistent in the ways that they address these issues; so it is important to examine what is happening in the arenas of family life, parenting, education, preparation for employment, and personal privacy with these questions in mind. High schoolers find the book very readable. However, I would recommend it for those at least fifteen and older because it is usually around this age that teens begin to be concerned about issues outside their personal domain. This book is also available directly through us at Grove Publishing. We also have an audio tape with a booklet titled *Goals 2000 and School -to-Work* which includes an overview of some key issues addressed in the book. [$5.95])

⮑ **The Great Evangelical Disaster** by Francis Schaeffer (Crossway) $13.99

Francis Schaeffer is an author who concentrated on the application of Christianity in our lives. While some of his philosophical works are heavy reading for most high schoolers, some of his books are quite appropriate. An example is his last book, *The Great Evangelical Disaster*, which I highly recommend.

⮑ **How Should We Then Live?** by Francis Schaeffer (Crossway) $14.99

In what is probably his most well-known book, *How Should We Then Live?*, Francis Schaeffer uses history, religion, philosophy, art, music, literature, and culture as a background for a discussion of society and how we should be living if we are under God's direction. Personally, I would like to see all of our children study this book before they graduate from high school. I recognize that many of them will find the range of information and ideas presented overwhelming, so I would not recommend such a study until junior or senior level. Before then, teens are unlikely to have acquired the cultural literacy necessary to understand ideas Schaeffer speaks about in this book. A video series by the same title is a little easier to understand than the book, so you might consider it as an alternative. (Videos are available through Great Christian Books, Christian Book Distributors, and other sources.)

Also check out other books by Francis Schaeffer such as *The Christian Manifesto*.

⮑ **Idols and Ideas** [video/study guide set] (The Constitutional Coalition) $25 for all three components

This set includes a video tape, study guide, and the book, *Seven Men Who Rule the World from the Grave* by Dave Breese. The video and study guide can stand on their own or you can read the book before or along with the video. (See the review of the book below.) The video is divided into seven, 18-20 minute long segments; you will probably want to watch one per "sitting." Each segment is presented by an authority on the pertinent area of study. For example, John Stormer, author of *None Dare Call It Treason*, covers Karl Marx and Jim Drexler, headmaster of Westminster Christian Academy, presents the overview of John Dewey. The quality of presentations varies greatly; John

Stormer, William Coulson, and Andrew Southwell are excellent, but Dr. John McGowen's presentation on Keynes is not nearly as good in either content or presentation. (You might even skip the video on Keynes and use only the chapter from *Seven Men* and the discussion questions from the study guide.) The study guide follows a different arrangement for each section; most sections highlight key points addressed and all of them include discussion questions and suggested answers. Discussion questions are very good, although many times they require viewers to stretch beyond the content of the tape to answer questions. The study leader might, in some cases, choose to share information from the suggested answers if that seems helpful. You will need only one study guide for the leader/teacher. Ideally, you should go through the video and discussion for one key person, then assign reading from the book before tackling the next person. *Idols and Ideas* is an excellent way to introduce a study of worldviews. It will work well for home educators as well as for Sunday School classes or other groups. And the price makes this a real bargain.

⮑ **The Index of Leading Spiritual Indicators** by George Barna (Word Publishing) $10.99

George Barna is well known for his statistical reports and analyses relating society and spiritual/moral issues, published in the *Barna Report* newsletter. This book pulls together results of surveys conducted by the Barna Research Group from 1982 up through the present. Results are presented in the context of the entire time period, describing changes that have occurred such as the temporary rise in church attendance in the mid '80s. Frequently, commentary is included which helps explain the data. Among the many topics addressed are religious beliefs, religious activity, church attendance, morality, religious knowledge, religious influence, and religious leadership. Sometimes home schoolers spend most of their lives around like-minded people and have little understanding of what others really believe. Here we find a window onto the "collective mind" of modern American society so that we can better minister to our fallen nation. Teens will also find this a terrific resource for research paper data.

⮑ **Intellectuals** by Paul Johnson (HarperCollins Publishers) $15

What people say or teach and what they actually do are often at odds with each other. This is a common failing of man, which rarely attracts much attention. However, many philosophers who have claimed to have answers to life problems or issues need to be held to a higher level of accountability in this area. Consequently, author Paul Johnson examined the lives of a number of major philosophers and authors, comparing what they taught with how they lived. The results are interesting revelations of sometimes rather extreme worldviews at work. The primary philosopher/authors chosen for this study are Rousseau, Shelley, Marx, Ibsen, Tolstoy, Hemingway, Brecht, Russell, Sartre, Edmund Wilson, Gollancz, Lillian Hellman, George Orwell, Evelyn Waugh, Cyril Connolly, and Norman Mailer. Other historical figures who were friends, compatriots, or acquaintances of those listed also undergo some lifestyle dissection. The common thread is the all too common discrepancy between beliefs and actions. For example, Rousseau, who claimed to love all of mankind, relegated his own children to an orphanage (to die) rather than be bothered with the responsibility of parenting.

The various sections of this book are written such that they can be read independently of each other. This feature makes it easy to tie in studies of the featured individuals with periods of history or with literary studies. The reading level is high, so either digest information yourself and pass it on to your children, or assign reading to mature students in reasonably-sized doses.

Johnson states in his conclusion: "One of the principal lessons of our tragic century, which has seen so many millions of innocent lives sacrificed in schemes to improve the lot of humanity, is-beware intellectuals. Not merely should they be kept away from the levers of power, they should also be objects of particular suspicion when they seek to offer collective advice."

As a resource for proving the link between false worldviews and their negative consequences, this book is invaluable.

➲ Jeremiah Films

Jeremiah Films has made a number of films that are useful for studying worldviews. (*The Pagan Invasion* series and *Gods of the New Age* from Jeremiah films are described elsewhere in this section, *The Evolution Conspiracy** is described under "Creation Science," and *AIDS: What You Haven't Been Told* is reviewed under "Sex Education.") They divide their films into four categories: Cult/Occult, New Age/Apologetics, Contemporary Issues/Prophecy, and Pro-Life/Motivational. The films vary in length from 25 to 104 minutes. One video that targets worldviews in particular is *False Gods of Our Time*, a "docu-drama providing Biblical evidence for a Christian world view." Send for a brochure listing all of their titles to choose those appropriate for your studies.

➲ L'Abri Fellowship Foundation

With many branches around the world, the L'Abri Fellowship Foundation offers newsletters on numerous worldview related topics, cassettes, seminars, videos, lecture reprints, and referrals for materials. Some L'Abri branches offer opportunities for individuals to come and pursue personally tailored study for up to two or three months, using tapes, books, lectures, and discussions with a tutor's supervision. Older teens especially might be interested in pursuing such an opportunity.

➲ Let Us Highly Resolve by David and Shirley Quine (Cornerstone Curriculum Project) $10

David Quine has developed an entire line of math, science, art, and music curriculum all based upon a biblical Christian worldview and reflecting the ideas of Francis Schaeffer. In *Let Us Highly Resolve*, David and his wife Shirley give us a "handbook" for raising our children according to that worldview. From building upon the biblical foundation and teaching our children absolutes and proper reasoning, we can build our families up in faith, truth, and knowledge, equipping them to carry the message of the gospel to the world. The Quines show us how we can raise our children to "challenge our culture with the truth of Christian-

ity." You might consider this sort of a foundational book on the philosophy of raising families and of education. Some of the ideas are very profound and challenging, but the Quines translate those ideas into real life with many stories from their own lives and experiences. If you are interested in doing more than just "getting through school" with your children, this is a must read.

➲ Liberating the Nations: Biblical Principles of Government, Education, Economics, & Politics by Stephen K. McDowell and Mark A. Beliles (Providence Foundation) $12.95

As the title suggests, this is a far-ranging book. It uses the Principle Approach to demonstrate how a thoroughly Christian worldview should work itself out in various areas of life. The principles themselves are described in the first chapter. Chapter headings give you a fair idea of the rest of the book: God's Plan for the Nations, Origins & Development of Government & Liberty, The Protestant Reformation in Europe, The United States & Liberty in Modern Times, Christ's Teachings on Public Affairs, The Principle Approach to Education, The Home and the School, The Church, The Arts, Media, and the Press, The Framework of Godly Government, Principles of Christian Economics, Biblical Principles of International Relations & War, and A Practical Agenda for Discipling a Nation. The authors offer us an overview of these topics rather than thorough coverage of each. However, those unfamiliar with the ideas presented will find this a good place to begin to examine the Principle Approach. It is primarily for parents, but if you wish to have teens read it, I suggest selecting appropriate sections rather than requiring that they read the entire book.

➲ Men of Faith series (Bethany House Publishers) $4.99 each

Bethany publishes a line of what they describe as "readable and concise" biographies on men who were living testimonials to a biblical Christian worldview. Examples of the featured men of faith are Martin Luther, Charles Finney, Jim Elliot, John Wesley, Samuel Morris, William Carey, and Terry Waite. A parallel series, *Women of Faith series*, tells the stories of women such as Amy Carmichael, Corrie ten Boom, Mary Slessor, and Florence Nightingale. Since these biographies are quick-reading, students can become acquainted with more "godly heroes" than if they tackle more challenging and time-consuming biographies.

➲ National Public-policy Resource Theme-packets by C. Bernard Schriver

Read the complete description under "Current Events." Many of the *Theme-packets* help to expand study on worldview topics. Packets related to the Constitution, separation of Church and State, family issues, education, the free market, elections, and environmentalism would all be useful, as would many others.

➲ The New Absolutes: How They Are Being Imposed on Us and How They Are Eroding Our Moral Landscape by William Watkins (Bethany House) hardcover - $19.99; paperback - $11.99

In his discussion of relativity versus absolutes, Watkins cogently observes that while many Americans claim to be relativists (i.e., what's right for you isn't necessarily right for me; there are no unchangeable values), they live like absolutists. However, they follow a new set of absolutes which are in direct conflict with a Judeo-Christian worldview. He draws upon polls and current events to make his case, then examines new and old absolutes in the areas of public religious expression, the sanctity of life, marriage, family, sexual relationships, feminism, race, and history/cultures. Watkins calls for "intolerance" of the new absolutes—challenging false ideas that are destroying our culture. The book is fully documented with footnotes and a lengthy bibliography which makes it very useful for teens working on research papers or topical studies. The reading level and content is adult level, but mature teens should find the book very useful both in its basic premise and as it deals with each of the issues it addresses.

➲ Postmodern Times: A Christian Guide to Contemporary Thought and Culture by Gene Edward Veith, Jr. (Crossway Books) $13.99

We have passed from the modern age into an era commonly referred to as the "postmodern age." Postmodernism is largely defined by its philosophy, a philosophy that denies absolute truth and values a type of spirituality that revolves around "self." It essentially says that man cannot truly know anything, a philosophy that leaves man in a hopeless position. Veith traces the philosophical background leading up to postmodernism in a survey fashion. He examines contemporary evidences of postmodernism in the arts, architecture, literature, politics, and religion. He addresses the problems within the Christian church using as an example a young man "who says that he believes in the inerrancy of Scripture, Reformed theology, and reincarnation" (p. 211). Veith ends with a call for the Church to renew its commitment to Truth and to sharing that Truth within our postmodern culture in a way that addresses the confusion that prevails.

Although *Postmodern Times* is definitely written for an adult audience, I would encourage mature teens (as well as adults) to read it.

➲ Reason in the Balance, The Case Against Naturalism in Science, Law & Education by Phillip E. Johnson (InterVarsity Press) $19.99

Phillip Johnson, author of *Darwin on Trial,* takes the issue of evolution versus creationism to a deeper level in this book where he contrasts the truth claims of naturalism (the worldview behind Darwinism) and theistic realism (Johnson's term for his own worldview which says that "God is objectively real"). Johnson brilliantly makes a case against naturalism, along the way demonstrating the validity of theistic realism. He draws on current events, legal decisions, science, and common sense to make his case. He builds a strong case proving that naturalism is the estab-

lished religion in America. He then also shows how Christianity, and even theism in general, is now viewed with contempt. He delves into the concept of natural law based upon a belief in God as the law maker and the rejection of natural law based upon naturalistic assumptions that there are no eternal truths or absolutes.

Reason in the Balance is a must read for parents, but I also highly recommend it for teens. However, this is a challenging book, so save it for the final years of high school. Read it in sections, followed by discussion. Johnson includes research notes on each chapter at the end of the book. Most of them are enlightening, so check them out as you read each chapter.

It is helpful to have read *Darwin on Trial* prior to reading this book so that you understand his occasional references to debates between Johnson and eminent evolutionists, but it is not essential. Johnson's *Defeating Darwinism by Opening Minds* (InterVarsity Press) is an easier-to-read book covering some of the key issues of both of these books.

➲ Seven Men Who Rule the World from the Grave* by Dave Breese (Moody Press) $11.99

One of the supplemental books for UTT impresses me as being an excellent resource for anyone studying worldviews. In *Seven Men Who Rule from the Grave,* Breese identifies seven key players in recent world history—Marx, Wellhausen, Keynes, Darwin, Dewey, Freud, and Kierkegaard—who have had tremendous impact (often for evil), even though it frequently goes unrecognized. He traces their influence from their lives up through the present. Within this biographical framework, Breese provides deeper studies of law, philosophy, and economics. This is written at a reasonable level for most teens to read, with only a few exceptions such as in the discussion of existensialism/Kierkegaard. I recommend this book as the best starting place to introduce teens to the idea of worldviews. The book is also part of the *Idols and Ideas* video/study guide set reviewed previously.

➲ Symposium on the Christian Worldview [Audio Tapes] (Christian Liberty Academy)

This 1989 conference specifically addressed worldviews. There are fifteen tapes covering a wide array of worldview issues, but with a number of them specifically addressing curriculum. Examples of titles are "Conflicting Worldviews: the Dilemma of Double-Mindedness," "A Christian Worldview of Language," "A Christian Worldview of Mathematics," and "Christian Worldview of the Media."

Other tapes from conferences sponsored by Christian Liberty Academy also relate to worldview issues. All are listed in their *Christian Liberty Conference Series Audio Cassette Tape Catalog.*

➲ Teaching World Views [audio tape with booklet] by Cathy Duffy (Home Run Enterprises) $5.95

In this audio presentation, I show the effect of ideas on events—that what people believe can radically influence what happens. We see that Christian beliefs seem to be having little effect in our present day and the problems we have as a consequence. Then I discuss how we parents can educate ourselves to understand worldviews—basic books to read, tape sets to listen to—so that we can understand ideas ourselves, then pass this on to our children. The last section is a discussion of resources to use with our children to address worldviews within the different parts of our curriculum. The booklet includes reproductions of the overheads used in the presentation and the resource recommendations list.

◗ Turning Point; A Christian Worldview Declaration by

Herbert Schlossberg and Marvin Olasky (Crossway) $12.99

Turning Point is the introductory book to an entire worldview series published by Crossway. It is a foundational book similar to *How Should We Then Live?*, but it is much easier to read. The authors use stories to illustrate worldview disagreements which are either confusing Christians or setting Christianity in opposition to conflicting worldviews. They give us some historical and philosophical background, although they spend much less time in these areas than does Schaeffer. Instead they offer more "connections" between worldviews and current events. Story illustrations make it easy to read and understand the weighty ideas presented. *Turning Point* strives to motivate Christians to move out of a narrow religious arena to influence the world.

"Turning Point" is also the title of a series of topic-specific books from Crossway, each of which offers an in-depth study of a different topic. Books in the series cover the media, international politics, the press, popular culture, national politics, population issues, compassion for the poor, use of resources and scarcity, literature, crisis childbearing, the arts, and education. Series titles reviewed elsewhere in this book are *Reading Between the Lines* (literature), *Recovering the Lost Tools of Learning* (education), *Freedom, Justice, and Hope* (the poor), *The Soul of Science* (history of science), and *Postmodern Times*. All of the reviewed books are outstanding, and I assume that the others are similar in quality.

◗ Ultimate Issues: Right Answers to Wrong Thinking

[video] (Ligonier Ministries) video - $15; audio - $8;
discussion guide - $1.50

R.C. Sproul presents four, 30-minute segments that address basic worldview questions. The first presentation, "There Are Only Two Worldviews," contrasts atheism and theism as being on opposite ends of a spectrum. Beliefs based on fundamental presuppositions about God are shown to result in continual conflicts, especially in regard to ethics. The second segment, "The God Who is There," deals with the existence of God. Sproul examines philosophical beliefs about reason and our knowledge of God that get into some fairly deep territory. "His Word is Truth," the third presentation, explores the reliability and authority of Scripture, considering its role as a source of truth. The last segment, "Christ the Only Way," covers the basics of salvation, while delving into topics like "forensic justification" and the role of forgiveness in salvation.

The first segment is one of the best introductions to worldviews I have seen or heard. The third segment does a good job of

explaining the vital role of Scripture in a Christian worldview. The final segment is a strong presentation of the reformed Protestant understanding of salvation and justification, the value of which will depend upon the audience, their spiritual maturity, and personal theological beliefs. The second segment is the most challenging for teens—it is heavy on philosophy and harder to understand than the other three. Students need not watch all four segments. While the entire tape is of value, you might decide that some segments are more appropriate or useful at this time than others.

Filmed interviews (man-on-the-street style) with young people are interspersed throughout all of the segments. The contrasting answers coming from a wide variety of worldviews beautifully illustrates each topic. Sproul speaks with passion and body language which also enhances the "watchability" factor.

A Discussion Guide folder comes with the video. For each segment, it lists the learning objective, a four-point outline, and ten discussion questions. The questions are excellent, challenging students to go beyond the content of the presentation to stretch their thinking and apologetic skills. These presentations are also available on audio tape, but the video is so well done, so visually engaging, and so reasonably priced, that you really should get the video.

◗ Why So Many Christians Are Going Home to School by

Llewellyn B. Davis (Elijah Company) $12.95

This is a good book to start with if you feel fuzzy about what all this worldview stuff is that I'm talking about. Even though education is the primary topic of the book, Mrs. Davis concentrates on worldviews in chapters one, five, six, and seven, and the Christian worldview underlies the discussion throughout the rest of the book. The pertinent chapter titles give us a good idea of the contents: Education, Worldview, and Culture; Education's Hidden Curriculum: The Belief System; Presuppositions of American Education; and The Biblical Perspective of Education. Mrs. Davis does an excellent job of outlining the major worldview contrasts in an easy-to-understand way. She identifies key questions for us to ask ourselves in developing our own worldview. She also uses charts to contrast worldviews of secular humanists, cosmic humanists, and Christians about the crucial themes of God, man, the world, authority, truth, ethics, and values. Other resources do similar comparisons, but Davis gives us some well-written background and neatly ties it all together with educational issues.

◗ WORLD magazine (God's World Publications) $49.95 per year

World brings us a Christian perspective on news and issues in a colorful, weekly magazine. Each issue features a mix of articles of varying length and depth. From political cartoons, quotes, and short takes to lengthy analysis and research articles, *World* tries to keep us up to date on the most important happenings. They don't limit their coverage to strictly Christian topics, but instead address timely political and social happenings. The flavor is conservative and Protestant. Over the past few years the editorial positions have become stronger and almost always consistent in applying a biblical Christian worldview and a belief in limited government. This makes *World* far more trustworthy as a source than *U.S. News and World Report* or other such magazines. *World* makes great reading for both parents and teens.

⮑ World Proofing Your Kids by Lael F. Arrington (Crossway Books) $12.99

The subtitle of this book is misleading. It reads: "Helping Moms Prepare Their Kids to Navigate Today's Turbulent Times." While the author does direct some of her comments directly to moms, the message is just as important and applicable for dads. The book is really about introducing children to worldview thinking and application. It lays a background for parents who are new to the subject, then shows us how to translate that knowledge to our children through practical and fun family activities. She shows parents how to have family devotion time that children will look forward to as a key to developing worldview understanding. She tackles current issues from a worldview perspective—abortion, the media and entertainment, feminism, politics, etc.—highlighting current events that make the issues real. Full of practical suggestions, the book includes resource suggestions for books and videos that appeal to different age levels to be used as jumping-off points for family discussion on issues and ideas. This is a great introductory book for parents (both moms and dads!) just getting into worldviews.

Topical Resources

Absolutes: Right and Wrong

One of the most crucial aspects of our worldview is our belief in absolutes, unchanging standards of right and wrong. Josh McDowell relates that in researching his book *Right From Wrong*, pollsters discovered that 57% of supposedly committed Christian young people do not believe that an objective standard of truth exists. They fail to realize that without that standard everything else is meaningless. Consequently, this is an area that deserves special attention.

⮑ Right From Wrong by Josh McDowell and Bob Hostetler (Word Publishing) $14.99

McDowell and Hostetler base this book on surveys of young people, particularly "churched youth" who claim to be saved, attend church regularly, and otherwise seem to have their acts together. Yet, these surveys reveal that the foundation for their beliefs and actions is woefully lacking. It seems that when push comes to shove, they act no different than unchurched youth because they don't understand the principles behind right and wrong. This book is written for parents, laying the blame and responsibility on those of us who fail to live what we claim to believe and those of us who fail to pass the "baton of faith" on to our young people. Older teens can also read the book, but parents need to be aware that they are setting themselves up for judgment. The book is full of stories and examples that make it exceptionally readable. For those who like to see the data, the last

four chapters analyze the primary survey upon which the book is based. There are some really great sections in this book that parents might excerpt to use with their teens even if they don't have them read the entire book. For example, the section on "Pretzel Logic" is a fantastic, two-page treatment of the question, "When is killing acceptable or unacceptable?" under a relativistic worldview. The book goes beyond the "look how awful things are" analysis to offer "what should we do" suggestions. The authors miss many of the strategies that home schooling families have already discovered since they seem to be unfamiliar with them, but this is nevertheless a very valuable book.

Philosophy, Religion, and Apologetics

⮑ Another Gospel by Ruth A. Tucker (Zondervan Publishing House) $25.99

Ruth Tucker exposes twelve major cultic belief systems, the New Age movement, and other minor cults in this fully documented book. She presents the historical research on the origins and founders of the movements, their theology/philosophy, their present operation and influence, and points of contrast with biblical Christianity. Since Tucker relies heavily on the historical approach, much of this reads like interesting storytelling rather than dry theological analysis. Teens should find it very readable. Major cults covered are Mormonism, Seventh-Day Adventism (which she presents with the caution that many Christian theologians do not consider this denomination cultic), Jehovah's Witnesses, Christian Science, New Thought and Unity, The Worldwide Church of God, The Way International, The Children of God, The Unification Church, Hare Krishnas, Baha'i, and Scientology. At the back of the book are the major tenets of orthodox Christianity as well as those of ten of the cults (as written by the organizations themselves). This book might function as the basis of an intensive study of cults or as a reference book.

⮑ Between Heaven & Hell by Peter Kreeft (InterVarsity Press) $9.99

The subtitle of this book is "A Dialog Somewhere Beyond Death with John F. Kennedy, C.S. Lewis, and Aldous Huxley." All three of these men died on the same day, and Kreeft takes advantage of that historical fact to position the three together, meeting at some point before they reach their final destiny. A debate ensues with Kennedy representing the "modernist Christian" (essentially humanist) viewpoint that Jesus was just a good man and that the Bible cannot be interpreted literally; Huxley presents an Eastern pantheistic view; and Lewis champions Christian theism. Since the book is essentially an apologetic for the Christian faith, Lewis dominates, first dealing with the nature of God and the person of Jesus Christ. The debate begins between Kennedy and Lewis, then shifts to Huxley and Lewis. Kreeft concentrates on the logical arguments for orthodoxy as he presents the case for Christianity through Lewis. They are easy enough to follow through the Kennedy-Lewis debate (with a few complex digressions), but the logic shifts to a more challenging level in the Huxley-Lewis debate. All teens can deal with the first half, and if that is all they read it is worth every bit of it. Those who are tuned in to logical arguments (and philosophy) and enjoy the mental challenge will get the most out of the second half. Like a number of Lewis' writings, this book takes deep philosophical ideas and puts them into a more accessible format. It forces the reader to think through each of the crucial issues in relation to his or her faith.

⊃ A Blueprint for Thinking [video/audio tapes] by R.C. Sproul (Ligonier Ministries) video - $30; audio - $12; study guide - $4

See the complete review in Chapter Eleven. This is an excellent series for introducing the study of worldviews, since it deals with the foundational questions from a Christian viewpoint.

⊃ Can Man Live Without God by Ravi Zacharias (Word Publishing) $12.99

Ravi Zacharias, through his speaking ministry, carries the gospel into major secular universities around the world, a place where the message of Christianity is seldom welcome. Using stories, quotations, anecdotes, and logic he challenges his listeners to examine their worldview and compare it to the biblical worldview. This book seems to draw heavily from those presentations, identifying the key issues and supplying the answers. It is divided into three main sections. The first, "Antitheism is Alive—and Deadly," deals with issues such as God's existence, ethics, evil, and death. The second section, "What Gives Life Meaning?", investigates man's relationship to God, and the nature of truth, knowledge, and love. The third section, "Who Is Jesus (and Why Does It Matter?)," compares Jesus' truth claims with those of other religions. Two appendices also make for interesting reading. The first consists of questions and answers recorded at lectures given at Harvard University. The second offers brief biographies of "mentors to the skeptic," key philosophers (Descartes, Hume, Kant, Kierkegaard, Nietzshe, Russell, and Sartre) who have contributed to modern day skepticism. Yes, the content is deep, but Zacharias' presentation is so compelling and logical that older teens should be able to handle it. This is one of the very best books for addressing worldview questions posed by analytical, logical thinkers (Competent Carls).

⊃ Christian Research Institute

Christian Research Institute (CRI) was founded by Dr. Walter Martin and is now headed by Hank Hanegraaff. "While CRI is concerned with and involved in the general defense of the faith (apologetics), its area of research specialization is limited to those elements within the modern religious scene that compete with, assault, or undermine biblical Christianity." Consequently, they offer a range of books, pamphlets, audio tapes, and video tapes on subjects such as apologetics, astrology, Charismatic issues, Christian doctrine, cults, eschatology, Freemasonry, Jehovah's Witnesses, Mormonism, New Age movement, and Scientology. Tapes and books are from speakers and authors such as Walter Martin, Billy Graham, Ron Rhodes, Hank Hanegraaff, Ken Ham, A.E. Wilder-Smith, F.F. Bruce, and Ravi

Zacharias. Request their resource listing of all titles that they offer.

CRI also publishes the *Christian Research Journal* [$20 a year], a scholarly, quarterly magazine on topics such as the above as well as current events in the "Christian world." Articles are thoroughly researched and documented, so they serve as excellent research sources.

⊃ Christian Worldview [audio tapes] by Dr. R.C. Sproul (Ligonier Ministries) $18 for the set

Six tapes contain twelve 30-minute messages that begin by analyzing various philosophical viewpoints in light of biblical Christianity. The first seven messages address secularism, existentialism, humanism, pragmatism, positivism, pluralism and relativism, and hedonism. The remaining five focus on science, economics, government, art, and literature. These latter five messages are excellent for introducing students to a biblical Christian view of these areas which are rarely considered as having any philosophical viewpoint. Use each tape to begin the discussion for each area, then use other resources to expand the study. Even if you do not use the first seven tapes, it is worth purchasing the set for these last five messages. They can be used along with other courses in science, government, etc. or they can be used as the introductions for your own unit studies on worldviews. (Dr. Sproul's theological background is reformed Protestantism.)

⊃ Comparing World Views by Roy Hanson (Family Protection Ministries) $4.50 (postpaid)

For those who have little understanding of the major philosophies shaping today's society, I recommend *Comparing World Views*. This booklet gives a concise summary of what a Christian worldview is and compares this with secular humanistic and cosmic humanistic (New Age fits in here) worldviews in chart form. The implications of how our worldviews shape our lives are also shown.

⊃ Every Thought Captive: A Study Manual for the Defense of Christian Truth by Richard L. Pratt, Jr. P & R Publishing Co. $7.99

Recommended for older teens, this book about apologetics is based upon the methods of the theologian, Cornelius Van Til.

⊃ Exploring Ethics, Exploring Apologetics, and Exploring Faith and Discipleship (Christian Schools International)

See reviews under "Other Resources for Bible Study and Spiritual Growth." This series was written for to instruct students in worldview issues.

⊃ The Giants of Philosophy [audio cassettes] (Knowledge Products) $17.95 per two-tape set

These cassette tapes assume no prior knowledge, so they are excellent for a basic education in philosophy. However, they are geared towards adults, so save them for mature high schoolers who have developed their analytical thinking to the point where they can grasp the abstract ideas presented. Thirteen, two-tape sets cover Plato, Aristotle, St. Augustine, St. Thomas Aquinas, Spinoza, Hume, Kant, Hegel, Schopenhauer, Kierkegaard, Nietzsche, Dewey, and Sarte. Tapes are not intended to represent a Christian point of view, so use discretion about when to share them with students. These are very challenging, but they are an excellent tool for introducing philosophy and philosophers to those who would find it extremely difficult to wade through philosophy texts or translations of the original writings. Some tapes from this series are used in Cornerstone Curriculum's *Worldviews of the Western World*. (S)[3]

⮕ Gods of the New Age [video] (Jeremiah Films) $19.95

Caryl Matrisciana lived in India for twenty years and speaks from experience when she explores the New Age movement's Hindu roots and the dramatic increase in the numbers of people holding such beliefs. However, this is not just her personal story, but a presentation of factual information about topics such as meditation, yoga, chanting, visualization, and gurus. It helps us recognize that New Age ideas, which recognize an anti-God spiritual force, are increasingly replacing or incorporating atheistic secular humanist ideas. Information is presented through interviews and startling film footage. This video exposes the growing impact of New Age worldviews on all of our culture.

⮕ The Islamic Invasion by Robert Morey (Harvest House Publishers) $8.99

Robert Morey is a respected scholar and one of the most well-known figures in the field of apologetics. He has written other "apologetic" books such as *How to Answer a Jehovah's Witness, How to Answer a Mormon, Reincarnation and Christianity*, and *Battle of the Gods*. In *The Islamic Invasion*, he confronts the teachings of the second largest religion in the world (second only to Christianity). Rather than working, as Geisler does, through the logical fallacies, Morey first presents background and teachings of Islam, then examines problems and contradictions within the belief system. He also shows factual contradictions between the Bible and the Quran (or Koran), although Islam claims that Allah is the same God as the God of the Bible. Morey's writing style in this book is very easy for teens to read. While the table of contents offers general guidelines to the book's content, the lack of an index is an irritation. For information about other books by Morey, write to the Research and Education Foundation of which Morey is the Executive Director.

⮕ The Kingdom of the Cults by Walter Martin (Bethany House) $29.99

This is the classic book on cultic religions. Historical and theological information is included, documenting the origins and teachings of most cult beliefs we will encounter. This is one of the most helpful books available. As I write, it is being updated and expanded under the direction of Hank Hanegraaff and the Christian Research Institute. The new edition, due December 1997, will add about 50% new material and will also include a CD-ROM.

⮕ Library of the Future, Third Edition [CD-ROM] (World Library)

See the review in Chapter Eleven under "Literature." Many of the major philosophers are represented here. This is an easy way to access what various philosophers have to say.

⮕ Mere Christianity by C.S. Lewis (Simon and Schuster) $6

C.S. Lewis was a brilliant thinker with a gift for translating difficult concepts into language understandable to the man on the street. In *Mere Christianity*, he addresses the basic issues of God, Jesus, salvation, faith, and the trinity. He does so with analogies and illustrations, raising and answering the most challenging questions confronted by those who would defend the Christian faith. This book is profound yet easy-to-read. Some might quibble about Lewis' acceptance of some doctrines of the Church of England—holdovers from its Catholic origins. But these instances are so few, that they should not deter anyone who seeks a greater understanding of Christianity. Possibly more disturbing is his seeming acceptance of evolution, particularly in the last chapter. In that same chapter, some of the expressions he uses sound "New Age." If we recognize that the book was written in 1943 when Christians were scarcely dealing with evolution and its conflicts with Christianity, and Eastern philosophies were largely unfamiliar, we can grant Lewis more leeway in his phraseology and interpretation. You can skip the last chapter if you must, but there are some golden nuggets in there that make it worth working through the problems. This is a book for everyone—it presents the message of salvation to the unsaved while at the same time it provides food for thought for the longtime Christian. (ISBN 0684823780)

⮕ Operation World by P. J. Johnstone (Zondervan Publishing House) $14.99

Operation World is a handbook of information on most countries, including their spiritual status. It gives economic and geographical information to help us understand the situations of various peoples, but the emphasis is on religious views and spiritual needs. It tells what percentages of each country's population belong to which religions. Combined with other background information, this helps us better understand various cultures.

⮕ The Pagan Invasion video series (Jeremiah Films) $19.95 each

There are thirteen videos in this series, each 48 minutes long. They combine interviews, narration, and location film footage in fast-paced, visually-engaging presentations. Titles of the thirteen tapes are: *Halloween: Trick or Treat* (pagan roots); *Invasion*

---

3   (S) is used throughout this book to indicate resources that are secular rather than Christian in nature. (SE) indicates that a resource is secular and includes controversial material or other content that some Christians might find objectionable.

of the Godmen (eastern mysticism); *Meditation: Pathway to Deception?*; *The East Seduces the West*; *Dawning of the New Age*; *Evolution: Hoax of the Century?*; *Evolution: From Physics to Metaphysics*; *Preview of the Anti-Christ*; *Secrets of Mind Control*; *The Latter Day Empire* (Mormonism); *Joseph Smith's Temple of Doom*; *Religion vs. Christianity*; and *Doorways to Satan* (the media).

Many of the titles are helpful for studying new age philosophy, evolution, the occult, and Mormonism. Jeremiah Films uses some of the same footage in these films that appears in some of their others such as *Gods of the New Age*.

⊃ The Search [video] (Inter-Varsity Christian Fellowship of the U.S.A.) $24.95

This 26-minute video is an excellent introduction to New Age beliefs. It clearly contrasts New Age beliefs on key spiritual issues (God, the value of man, the future, definition of truth, and authority) with biblical Christian beliefs. The video comes with a great little discussion guide so that we can develop ideas even further.

⊃ The Universe Next Door: A Basic World View Catalog by James W. Sire (InterVarsity Press) $13.99

Sire's book is an overview of the major worldviews, each dealt with in a separate chapter. The first chapter defines what a worldview is, then outlines seven basic questions whose answers will tell us what worldview a person holds. The second chapter describes the Christian Theistic worldview. The following chapters tackle the conflicting worldviews of deism, naturalism, nihilism, existentialism, Eastern pantheistic monism, and New Age. Sire presents an orthodox Christian view, although staunch Calvinists might feel that he strays from their philosophy. Sire notes, "While it is not the purpose of this description of theism to take sides in a famous family squabble within Christian theism (predestination vs. free will), we must note that Christians disagree on precisely what role God takes and what role he leaves us. Still, most would agree that God is the primary agent in salvation" (p 38).

While Sire delves rather deeply into philosophy and logic, he uses a multitude of examples and life applications. He quotes frequently from literature and philosophy, actually teaching us much about a number of major philosophers along the way. He makes no attempt to be nonjudgmental, but clearly shows where each of the non-Christian worldviews either fails to provide answers or contradicts itself.

[Note for those who have already studied worldviews: While various authors often use different classifications in describing worldview categories, Sire uses a few differentiations that I found very interesting: he subdivides existentialism into either atheistic or theistic existentialism, and he separates Eastern pantheistic monism from New Age beliefs because of the latter's emphasis upon the value of the individual unlike the Eastern pantheist's idea of losing one's individual consciousness.]

This is heavy reading, appropriate for mature, motivated teens and for parents. Those who need something a little lighter should read *The Universe Upstairs* (InterVarsity Press), a cartoon version of this book.

⊃ The Universe Upstairs by Merve Jones (InterVarsity Press) $5.99

"Guess what mom? I have a new religion. This kid at school told me about it. It's just like Christianity, only not as complicated."

What happens to you as a parent if you hear this kind of statement from your teens? You could refuse them dinner and yell at them day and night to "repent." Or you can make sure your teens are ready when faced with a theological discussion. The best way to do this is to teach them about worldviews. However, the problem you probably will find is that it can be boring and hard to understand. *The Universe Upstairs* by Merve Jones, leaves no room for complaining. The book is basically a comic book. It is definitely not boring and it is fairly easy for a junior high student to understand. It presents different questions that your teens might be asked about their religion and discusses them thoroughly. The discussions are in chapters covering Christianity, deism, naturalism, nihilism, existentialism, New Age beliefs, and others. The book equips teens to witness effectively because they know their faith thoroughly. So now instead of worrying about your teen being converted to false religions, they will be converting others to Christianity.[Matt Duffy]

⊃ What Is Truth? [video] by R.C. Sproul (Ligonier Ministries) $15

This is a great starting place for both parents and teens for teaching worldviews. R.C. Sproul addresses the ultimate question, "What is truth?", as the foundation for all the other questions of life. He discusses the dominance of relativistic thinking and the absurdity it produces. He deals with the crucial issue of Jesus and His "truth" claims, demonstrating that He has to be either who and what He claims or else a colossal liar. A biblical Christian worldview has to be based on Jesus and His Word or else it is no more valid than any other worldview. Beginning with a video such as this sets the stage for further study. The next topic should probably be the inerrancy of Scripture. (Sproul has an audio tape series of ten 30-minute messages titled *Explaining Inerrancy* and another series of either audio or video tapes as well as a paperback book titled *Knowing Scripture*.)

The video is 50 minutes long, so it is necessarily limited to an introduction of the topic. Actually, this is a very appropriate level of introduction for teens and most adults. R.C. Sproul is an engaging speaker and the video was professionally filmed on a set, so the high quality makes it easy to watch, another plus.

⊃ When Skeptics Ask: A Handbook on Christian Evidences

by Geisler and Brooks (Baker Book House) $23.99

Study of worldviews almost inevitably leads us into discussions with others about faith issues. This book addresses the common and not so common questions unbelievers raise to challenge our claim that salvation is through faith in the work of Jesus Christ. It begins with questions about God, His existence, and His nature. Examples of questions and challenges addressed: "If God created all things, then how did He create Himself?" and "God is nothing but a psychological crutch, a wish, a projection of what we hope is true." Following chapters deal with other gods, evil, miracles, Jesus Christ, the Bible, Bible difficulties, archaeology, science and evolution, the afterlife, truth, and morals.

Geisler and Brooks cover the major issues, although they cannot possibly address every challenge within this one book. They steer us to other sources when necessary. For example, in the chapter on Bible difficulties they recommend Gleason Archer's *Encyclopedia of Bible Difficulties* (Zondervan Publishing House) for those who want to study further.

I find this book particularly useful because of its topical arrangement and the logical layout. It frequently follows the common progression of questions into which such discussions fall. This means that it will be more useful than an encyclopedic book where we have to jump around to follow a particular topic.

I also appreciate the fact that opposing arguments are treated with respect rather than ridicule, even while the authors are exposing their fallacies.

While many of Geisler's books are very challenging reading (lots of logic employed to present arguments), this one should be understandable to most high school students, especially if they read it in sections as they confront the various issues. See also the review of the follow-up book, *When Critics Ask* (Victor Books) by Norman Geisler and Thomas Howe, which expands the same type of discussion into the beliefs of cults.

History

Read the sections in Chapter Thirteen on "America's Christian History" and in Chapter Eight on the "Principle Approach" for many resources that broaden our students' understanding of history beyond textbook content.

➲ Getting Off the Textbook Interstate: History Via the Scenic Route [audio tape seminar] by Diana Waring (Diana Waring - History Alive!) $20.95

Diana Waring is a dynamic and entertaining speaker with a mission and a message. Her goal is to help us teach our children a Christian worldview. In this four-tape seminar, she recommends using history as the primary vehicle. On the first tape, she urges us to reject the dry textbooks that rush through factoids without bringing history to life in favor of real books and other resources and experiences. The other three tapes in the seminar use history as the backdrop for teaching other subject areas from a worldview perspective. Tape two, "Making History Come Alive through Literature," presents both the rationale and a reading list for literature at all different learning levels. Tape three, "Making History Come Alive through Art and Music," draws on such sources as Francis Schaeffer's *How Should We Then Live?*, David Quine's *Adventures in Art*, and Diana's own background in music to show how the arts are primary vehicles for worldviews. The fourth tape, "Making History Come Alive through Math and Science," exposes the beliefs and motivations of

mathematicians and scientists through history, particularly those who were Christian.

Diana shows how to translate some of what I discuss in this chapter into courses of study, making the task sound eminently practical and worthwhile. She also describes numerous resources for the various subject areas, covering all age levels. You will want to keep pen and paper handy to take notes as you listen.

➲ Modern Times: From the Twenties to the Nineties by Paul Johnson (HarperCollins Publishers)

See the review in Chapter Thirteen under "World History." The theme of this book, that the rejection of moral absolutes results in a decline in societies, makes this an especially apropos book for worldview studies.

➲ What in the World's Going on Here? [audio tapes] Diana Waring (Diana Waring - History Alive!) $20.95

Since this is a new way of studying history which many of us have not experienced, I highly recommend to you Diana Waring's tape series, *What in the World's Going on Here?, Volumes One* and *Two*. In each volume, on four, 60-minute audio cassettes, Diana teaches us "how to re-evaluate world history from an eternal perspective: God sovereignly ruling over the affairs of men and nations." Volume One covers four time spans: creation to the destruction of Assyria, the rise of Babylon to Jesus Christ, destruction of Jerusalem to the fall of Constantinople, and the Renaissance/Reformation to Queen Victoria. Volume Two covers Napoleon through World War II, which roughly corresponds to the nineteenth and twentieth centuries. Volume Two also discusses the modern missions movement. This is sort of a whirlwind tour through history, summarizing and relating key events in chronological order, to show how all of history relates to God purposes. Diana directs her dynamic presentations to parents, although teens should listen along with parents as we relearn history together.

To make the audio tapes even more effective, use Diana's *Ancient Civilizations and The Bible* [$19.95], a unit study guide that serves as a companion to the first two tapes of Volume One of the tapes. (This is the first in a planned series.) It can be used with children about fourth grade and up, and many of the books and activities lend themselves to participation by the entire family. Study is broken down into twelve units, arranged chronologically as on the tapes. For each unit, there is a list of recommended reading with age designations. Most books are available through libraries, although there is a good mix of secular and Christian resources. Combined with the audio tapes and discussion questions provided in the book, this list forms the core of our study. We can choose what topics to emphasize, which activities to do, and which resources to use. Timeline, research, and reporting activities followed by a vocabulary list shift students into more "school like" activities. For hands-on learners, Diana includes projects and activities relating to geography, art, music, and cooking. The final section for each unit features suggestions for creative writing, drama, and art. It should take about twelve months to complete the studies in this book.

If you have the time to cover world history at this pace, studying through this book and succeeding volumes can be sufficient for world history course credit. You might also be able to develop your language arts study from it sufficient for high school credit. It will work especially well if you can begin at junior high level, taking the time to fully develop your studies. Supplement with the *Maps and Timeline Pack* [$19.95] and the *Pictorial Timechart Set One: Ancient and Bible History* and/or the *Pictorial Timechart Set Two: European and American History* [$7.95 each].

Parents interested in teaching worldviews should find this a valuable resource since that theme pervades both the audio tapes and unit studies.

See also the review of Waring's *Getting Off the Textbook Interstate: History Via the Scenic Route.*

Science

➲ CSA Creation Resource Lending Library

This lending library offers quite a few creation science resources on a freewill offering basis. A sampling of their offerings includes videos by Dr. A.E. Wilder-Smith, *The Evolution Conspiracy*, the *Understanding Genesis* series with Ken Ham and Dr. Gary Parker, *The Genesis Solution, The Case Against Evolution/Case for Creation* (MacKay), and titles from Moody Science. Audio cassettes include presentations on a range of creation/evolution-related topics by presenters such as Ken Ham, Tom Willis, John Mackay, Dave and Mary Jo Nutting, Dr. Duane Gish, and Dr. Henry Morris. We can order by mail or in person. They ask a minimum of $1.50 for videos and $1 for audio tapes to cover postage costs. Additional contributions help them maintain the library and expand their offerings. Request a current catalog for complete listings.

➲ Darwin on Trial by Phillip E. Johnson (InterVarsity Press) $11.99

I recommend this book primarily to parents, although bright teens who are interested in science, philosophy, or logic should find it illuminating. Johnson tackles Darwinism head on rather than simply defend the creation model. His purpose is to prove that Darwin's ideas have no foundation in fact but are a faith position with little evidence to support them. He bolsters his arguments with scientific evidence. Because Johnson's discussion often centers around science, this book will appeal most to those with a scientific "bent." However, non-scientists can skip the chapter on molecular evidence (the heaviest chapter, scientifically) if they get overwhelmed. Johnson studiously avoids arguments from the Bible, demonstrating that even on the evolutionists' terms and from their own philosophical perspective, the theory of evolution is insupportable. The first edition of this book challenged the staunchest supporters of evolution to respond. A number of them have done so, although without offering irrefutable arguments. Those challenges are addressed at the end of this second edition. Some Christians will be annoyed at Johnson's dismissal of "young earth" creationism, but he does a tremendous job of addressing both scientific and philosophic is-

sues at an understandable level. (Note: This is a book that you can give to non-Christian science teachers!)

➲ The Evolution Conspiracy* [video]

See "Science" for a complete description. This video is excellent for a study of worldviews. It demonstrates how fundamental evolution is in the belief systems of those who reject the God of the Bible.

➲ Facts and Bias: Creation vs. Evolution—Two World Views in Conflict video (Master Books) $19.95

This video is part of the *Answers in Genesis* series featuring Ken Ham and Gary Parker. On this particular video, Ken Ham addresses the creation vs. evolution debate from the point of view which asks, "How should we think about this?" rather than "What should we think about this?" This approach gives us the tools to analyze the so-called data presented by evolutionists. Ham talks about the world-view-biased presuppositions that both creationists and evolutionists bring to the debate, then challenges both views with questions such as, "Were you there?", "Did anyone see it?", "Can you do it again?", and "How do you know?" He shows how evolutionists have built their theories on beliefs rather than facts, and that those beliefs contradict the evidence. He shows how creationism is also based upon beliefs, but that it also has explanations in Scripture that claim to be the witness of the only one who was present—God. He also demonstrates how the facts that we do have support creation rather than evolution as an explanation. He emphasizes how foundational the belief in creation is for supporting the Christian worldview. Ham is an entertaining, oftentimes humorous speaker, who moves quickly through his presentations. The video was professionally filmed at a church presentation, and color graphics were very effectively inserted in the video for the overheads Ham used throughout his talk. This is a great video to use with teens since it holds the audience's attention and effectively conveys a vital message. (If you like this video, check out the other eleven in the *Answers in Genesis* series.)

➲ Facts, Not Fear: A Parent's Guide to Teaching Children About the Environment by Michael Sanera and Jane Shaw (Regnery Publishing, Inc.) $14.95

See the review in Chapter Fifteen. Students challenging the environmental-extremists' worldview will find this book very helpful for debunking pseudo-science masked as environmentalism.

➲ The Genesis Solution video (Films for Christ) $29

See the complete description under "Science." If you have to pick just one film on creation and evolution, the choice might be between this film, *Facts and Bias*, and *The Evolution Conspiracy.*

➲ Men of Science, Men of God (Master Books) $6.95

This small, easy-reading book is a wonderful introduction to famous scientists who operated from a Christian worldview—men like Isaac Newton, Michael Faraday, Johannes Kepler, and Louis Pasteur. We can learn, as did these scientists, that the Bible and science do not contradict one another, and that science can be analyzed and understood because it reflects a God of order. We can select readings from this book to tie in chronologically with history studies or read the book straight through.

⮞ **A Scientist Looks at Creation** (American Portrait Films) $19.95

See the complete description under "Creation Science." This video offers a simplistic look at worldviews from a scientific perspective. It concentrates much more on science than on religious implications, but it opens the door for discussions about the evolution/creation debate as well as questions about the age of the earth.

⮞ **The Soul of Science**
by Nancy Pearcey and Charles Thaxton (Crossway) $14.99

This book is foundational for understanding science from a worldview perspective. It explores history, philosophy, and science, demonstrating how the Christian worldview and belief in a God of order motivated scientific inquiry, experimentation, and exploration. A major purpose of the book is to disprove the modern belief that science and religion are contradictory. The authors reveal the thoughts and actions of famous scientists, not as reported in recent years, but through their own works and those of their contemporaries—a more accurate portrayal of who they were and what they believed. The book itself is fairly challenging reading, but if you can read through even the first few chapters with your teens, you are likely to experience a radical change in thinking about science and religion. (If the reading is too heavy for teens, parents should read it and discuss the main points with them.)

Economics

⮞ **Christian Worldview** [audio tapes] by Dr. R.C. Sproul (Ligonier Ministries) $18 for the set

See the review of the entire series under "Philosophy, Religion, and Apologetics." In the Economics message within this series, Dr. Sproul addresses the question of how various economic systems support or conflict with biblical principles. He briefly covers the essential questions.

⮞ **Economics in One Lesson** by Henry Hazlitt (Random House)

See the review in Chapter Thirteen under "More Challenging Resources for Economics."

⮞ **The Great Economic Thinkers** [audio cassettes]
(Knowledge Products, available through Bluestocking Press) $17.95 per two-tape set

This is heavy-duty economic education, geared toward adults. While mature, interested high school students can understand the information, most likely adults will use the tapes to educate themselves. Rather than a limited view of economic philosophy, these tapes present the various schools of thought from

classical economics to monetarism and supply-side. However, the tapes, narrated by Louis Rukeyser, are slanted toward supply-side, free market economic ideas. The thirteen sets cover The Classical Economists, Karl Marx: Das Kapital, Early Austrian Economics, Alfred Marshall and Neoclassicism, Welfare Capitalism Begins, Walras: Markets in Equilibrium, Institutionalism, Schumpeter and Dynamic Economic Change, The Chicago School, The Free Market Process, The Keynesian Revolution, The Keynesian Heritage, and Monetarism and Supply Side Economics. Single sets can be selected since they are not dependent on one another. However, a balanced overview requires familiarity with the variety of ideas.(S)

⮞ **Whatever Happened to Penny Candy?** by Richard Maybury (Bluestocking Press) $8.95

See the review under "Economics." This book serves as an introduction to basic principles of economics.

Psychology

⮞ **Dr. William Coulson on Education** [video] (Ken Fast Productions) $21.95

In this 35-minute interview, filmed in Canada, Dr. William Coulson condemns the psychological manipulation in which he was involved through the 1960s and 1970s along with Carl Rogers and Abraham Maslow. He discusses present-day violence and sexual permissiveness that has resulted from failed psychological theories. He also targets the educational system as a culprit. Coulson forthrightly rejects even his own work as he reveals the path of destruction that has followed in the wake of many experimental psychological programs with children. Coulson is an advocate of home and private education as well as voucher programs. His support for vouchers is my one objection to this video, but I suspect that he, like many other Christians, simply does not realize the long range effect of vouchers. Although Coulson is speaking to a Canadian audience, the problems he addresses are the same as those we face in the U.S. This is a great video to share with those outside the home school community.

⮞ **Psychoheresy: The Psychological Seduction of Christianity** by Martin and Deidre Bobgan (Eastgate Publishers) $10.95

The Bobgan's have stirred up a great deal of controversy with their criticism of Christian reliance on psychology. They have not limited their attacks to non-Christians, but have challenged Christian psychologists who "...[treat] problems of living by the use of psychological rather than or in addition to biblical means." They see a dangerously increasing reliance on psychological answers which deters people from seeking Scriptural solutions to their problems. They are basically in line with Kilpatrick, whose book is also reviewed here, but they go further in identifying and criticizing well-known Christian psychologists.

➲ Psychological Seduction: The Failure of Modern Psychology by William Kirk Kilpatrick (formerly published by Thomas Nelson Publishing; now out of print)

This is an excellent expose of the failure of man's wisdom. Kilpatrick examines different ideas about the nature of man and how even Christians have come to interpret behavior based on false psychological presuppositions. The reading level is easy enough to make this book one of the few on psychology that is accessible to teens. Although the book is now out of print, it is well worth tracking down a copy if you can.

Literature/Reading

➲ Christian Worldview [audio tapes] by Dr. R.C. Sproul (Ligonier Ministries) $18 for the set

See the review of the entire series under "Philosophy, Religion, and Apologetics." The last message in this series addresses literature.

➲ Read for Your Life by Gladys Hunt and Barbara Hampton (Zondervan Publishing House) $12.99

Subtitled, "Turning Teens into Readers," this book does much more than stimulate reading interest. It includes valuable discussions about fantasy and imagination, choosing books, reading skills, and worldview interpretation. One chapter challenges students to read the entire Bible for both personal and literary reasons. The value of this book is that it deals with literature in relation to the Christian teen's life in all its dimensions. The worldview section stresses the importance of recognizing authors' worldviews, then reviews basic definitions of various worldviews. The second half of the book is annotated descriptions of over 300 books with recommendations that often include cautions or philosophical observations.

Law and Government

➲ The Challenge of Godly Government (The Committee for Biblical Principles in Government) $5.95; leader's guide - $3

This 80-page book serves a number of purposes. It is a Bible study; a study of the principles of government, particularly our U.S. government; and a practical course about Christian political involvement and activity. Divided into 12 lessons, it can be used with groups or for individual study. However, for teens, I highly recommend that it be used for study followed by discussion. This would be a great vehicle for dad's involvement. Each lesson is introduced with an article by a noted Christian author such as John Eidsmoe, Chuck Colson, Gary DeMar, David Barton, and Rus Walton. Following the article are a number of Bible readings with questions, all related to a particular theme for each lesson. Questions are thought provoking. For example, following reading of Philipians 2:9-11 and Galatians 3:24, the questions are "Comment on the statement: 'Today America is a pluralistic society, with citizens of many differing religious views, including humanism'," and "Do Christians have the duty to declare the preeminence of the principles of the Bible? Explain your answer." The book is not reproducible so purchase a separate one for each person involved in the study. The Leader's Guide is es-

sentially a "suggested answer" key. It is very helpful, but keep in mind that those coming from various theological perspectives might answer questions differently.

You might also want to check out their new publication which I haven't had time to review thoroughly. It is entitled The Challenge of Godly Justice: Applying Biblical principles to justice. It addresses such topics as the purpose of government, the nature of justice, the duty of Christians to civil officials, civil disobedience, crimes and punishments, and church justice. The content is certain to be controversial and thought-provoking. It follows the same discussion with study guide format as the first book and prices are the same.

➲ Christian Worldview [audio tapes] by Dr. R.C. Sproul (Ligonier Ministries) $18 for the set

See the review of the entire series under "Philosophy, Religion, and Apologetics." The message on Government is excellent, addressing the questions of the Christian's position in relation to government and to what extent he should be involved.

➲ Constitutional Law for Christian Students by Michael P. Farris, Esq. (Home School Legal Defense Association)

This book will help students understand important court decisions that have changed the way our government functions. There are many good examples of worldviews in action if we closely examine some of these court cases. (See the full review under "Studying the U.S. Constitution and Law.")

➲ Electing America's Leaders: Participating in the Political Process to Elect Quality Leaders by Jessica Hulcy (KONOS) $15

More than a book to encourage political involvement, this 45-page guide is a fantastic study in government. Use it along with other resources for a government class; it can be your primary resource or a supplement depending upon which of the hundreds of suggested activities you choose to use and what grade levels you are addressing. It follows the KONOS format in that it is divided under themes: leadership, government, election, the two-party system, and campaigning. Under each thematic section are activities related to history, language arts, Bible, government, practical living, geography, reasoning skills, art/crafts, character training, drama, research skills, math, and current events. However, not all of these areas are addressed under every theme. Activities are appropriate for a wide age span, elementary grades through high school. Some are great for groups, whether it's your family or another group. Others require individual reading, research, and writing that must be done individually. The flexibility makes this book a terrific resource for all sorts of situations. You will need reference resources and other materials besides this book. While a reference list of books available through most local libraries is provided at the back of the book, we are often left on our own to figure out where to locate information. While we might love to have our teens doing this sort of research, it does require more time from both mom and student(s) for research, reading, and planning.

The first section on leadership supplies an important introduction to elections and government from the biblical perspective, so we should use that section first. From there we can select sections depending upon current political happenings. If an election is coming up soon, then use the sections on the two-party system, elections, and campaigning first, filling in with the section on government, and some of the section on leadership as you choose. Jessica Hulcy clearly promotes a limited, Constitutional government, biblical principles, and political activism, with no pretenses of neutrality as we find in most books on government. For example, in a discussion about wise and unwise decisions, Bill Clinton's decisions on a number of issues are listed for consideration. Only a few activities reflect current events that will date this book; almost all will still be useful ten years from now.

➲ The Giants of Political Thought [audio cassettes]
(Knowledge Products) $17.95 per two-tape set

Ideas have tremendous influence in the political realm; in fact, politics might be the major battlefield for attempts to put ideas into action. Thus, it becomes vital to understand some of the most influential figures in the political thought arena. The historical figures we learn about in these twelve audio tape sets are Paine, Jefferson, Thoreau, William Lloyd Garrison, Adam Smith, J.S. Mill, Wollstonecraft, Machiavelli, Boetie, Marx and Engels, Rousseau, Burke, Hamilton/Madison/Jay, Hobbes, Locke, and Tocqueville. Tape sets are not dependent upon each other, so select one or more. Because this is heavy thinking material, they will appeal to adults more than teens. However, students with a strong history background should enjoy them. I reviewed the tapes on John Locke (*Two Treatises of Government*) and found them to be easier to understand than were tapes from the philosophy series. They often include storytelling illustrations that are very engaging. Some tapes from this series, including those on Locke, are used in Cornerstone Curriculum's *Worldviews of the Western World.*(S)

➲ God, Man, and Law: The Biblical Principles by Herbert W. Titus (Advanced Training Institute International) $55

Students (or adults) with an interest in law and government really should read this book to understand the background and philosophy of both areas from a Christian perspective. It is written at a high level, quoting lengthy passages from court cases, writings by law professors, and others addressing academically sophisticated audiences. The book is footnoted and indexed, and it features a glossary at the back. It is divided into eight chapters with significant subheadings under each. The eight chapter titles give us a sense of the content: God, Man, Legal Education, and Law; Law: The Biblical Foundations; Jurisdiction; Equality; Fault; Vow; Dominion; and Restitution. As an example of the subheadings, the chapter on "Vow" has the subheadings Vows, Oaths and Promises; The Law of Contracts; The Sanctity of Promise; Liberty of Contract; and Agreement and Consideration. While reading straight through the book is the recommended approach, it can also be used more selectively to research particular topics. While this book is not for everyone, I highly recommend it to those pursuing careers in law and gov-

ernment. See the review of the companion audio tape series below.

➲ God, Man, and Law: The Biblical Principles [audio tape set] by Herbert W. Titus (Landmark Distributors) $30

This series of eight audio tapes serves as a companion to the book of the same title, reviewed above. The eight tapes each accompany a chapter of the book, explaining the basic principles and outlining the "big picture." They are not dependent upon the book; you might listen to these without ever reading the book, although they certainly do not cover nearly as much material. On the other hand, the tapes also lay a foundation that makes the book much easier to read. The ideal would be to use both, listening to each tape before reading the correlating chapter.

➲ In His Majesty's Service: Christians in Politics by Robert A. Peterson (Huntington House) $9

Inspiring stories of nine men who made a major impact on government demonstrate the power that godly men can have in politics. These "political heroes" are Edward VI of England, William Bradford, John Winthrop, Nathaniel Ward, John Witherspoon, Richard Bassett, William Wilberforce, Sir Robert Anderson, and Abraham Kuyper. Great for high school students and adults.

➲ An Overview of Constitutional Law by Paul Jehle
(Landmark Distributors)

See the review in Chapter Fourteen.

➲ Politics for the People by Bruce Barron InterVarsity Press
$9.99

If you want to understand the nuts and bolts of political involvement, this is the book for you. I highly recommend it to parents and teens who have any interest in politics. Find out how your local representative's office functions, how you can make government work for you, how you can most effectively convey your opinions, how you can get involved in elections and issues and work with others to accomplish political goals. and much more. Although written for an adult audience, I recommend that teens considering political involvement read at least parts of it to better understand the political process. The book is nonpartisan but Christian in its viewpoint.

➲ The Second American Revolution* by John W. Whitehead
(Crossway Books) $11.99

Constitutional attorney, John Whitehead, has been on the front lines in the battle to defend First Amendment rights for Christians as well as for those of other religious beliefs. In this book, he traces the history of law in the United States from its original theological underpinnings to its present shifting, humanistic foundations. He shows how the change in our view of law has resulted in the undermining of our Constitution. This book should shake our faith in the ability of our Constitution to withstand the onslaughts of secular humanists. Instead of leaving us with a dismal outlook, he offers challenging strategies for restoring our nation, which help to answer the question posed by Schaeffer, "How should we then live?"

Whatever Happened to Justice? by Richard J. Maybury (Bluestocking Press)

For a very easy-to-understand treatment of law systems, this is the book. It very well depicts the changes that have taken place in our legal system. Highly Recommended. (See complete review under "Studying the U.S. Constitution and Law.")(S)

Social Issues

Abortion

Note: I review a number of anti-abortion tapes here. Notice that different tapes are more appropriate for different audiences.

The Hidden Holocaust [video] (American Portrait Films) $19.95

Students who truly want to understand how abortion proponents think will appreciate this video. Jane Chastain interviews key people on both sides of the issue—congressmen, doctors, philosophers, feminists, an ACLU spokeswoman, a priest, etc. We get insight into their logic (or lack of logic, depending upon your viewpoint), which is exactly what we need to see abortion as a worldview issue. A sonogram suction abortion and aborted babies are shown, although this is not as graphic a presentation as *The Silent Scream* or *The Massacre of Innocence*. This video is not as emotionally manipulative as others, but instead lines up the arguments for consideration while maintaining a pro-life stance. It uses the Bible, particularly at the end, to further strengthen the pro-life position, which limits the potential audience to those who honor Scripture. High school students will benefit from this video more than younger students, since they will recognize more of the names and faces and their influence in the battle.

In Defense of Life by Keith A. Fournier and William D. Watkins (NavPress) $8

The authors tell us we face a societal choice between "the way of life" and "the way of death." "The way of life upholds the intrinsic worth of all human beings. The way of death degrades humanity, turning the strong against the weak..... The way of life leads to a just, moral society. The way of death turns justice and morality on their heads, calling evil good, and good evil." This book is researched and footnoted, which makes it very useful for students exploring such issues for research papers or presentations. The authors offer strategies for promoting the way of life at the end of the book.

Killer Angel: A Biography of Planned Parenthood's Founder Margaret Sanger by George Grant (The Reformer Library) $7.95

The roots of the abortion movement are steeped in eugenics and racism. Margaret Sanger, founder of Planned Parenthood, was a Socialist who rejected marriage for a promiscuous and immoral lifestyle. She advocated elimination of "the lower classes" and "the unfit" and was a supporter of Hitler's early efforts to purify the Aryan race. Her background has been buried from public view, and most people perceive her legacy, Planned Parenthood, as an altruistic organization. This book reveals the truth with footnoted documentation. At 116 pages, this is a brief treatment of the subject. You will want to keep your dictionary handy since George Grant is a "wordsmith" who likes to use interesting words that are unfamiliar to many of us. Still, this is a book for teens to read as well as for parents.

The Massacre of Innocence [video] (American Portrait Films) $19.95

This powerful video is for Christian audiences. The first part describes what abortion is, using graphic footage of the process and the results. (Fast forward or skip parts that are too overwhelming.) The next part is unusual among anti-abortion films. It presents the historical context of abortion, its link to pagan worship, and how it fits with modern worldviews. The biblical stand is very well presented, tying together all of this information. The second part does not have the graphic footage of the first part, and you might want to use only the second half with viewers who are against abortion but need more background in terms of worldviews. It also calls on Christians to be active in any number of suggested ways against the American Holocaust.

At the end of the video is a separate segment with host Eric Holmberg who speaks very compassionately from his own experience to those who have had or been involved with an abortion.

No Alibis [video] (American Portrait Films) $19.95

A pregnant reporter is assigned to write a story on the abortion issue. Part of her research includes a visit to the classroom of a high school teacher with unpopular pro-life views. Within this top-quality drama, there is also a background story about a pregnant girl who has been jilted by her irresponsible boyfriend. The video manages to convey a great deal of factual information about abortion within the story context. It is emotionally charged and engages the audience in the lives of the characters. The lack of graphic abortion footage that we see in many other anti-abortion videos make this video much easier to recommend to groups of all types. Because much of the drama revolves around a high school setting, it is especially appropriate for teens. (It is produced by Pat Boone and stars one of his daughters.)

The Silent Scream [video] (American Portrait Films) $19.95

Dr. Bernard Nathanson, former abortionist, now a pro-life spokesman, documents the physical reality of what takes place in abortions. He used models and film to show human development. He shows the instruments with which abortions are performed and describes the procedure. The most disturbing parts of this video are footage of an actual abortion and pictures of aborted babies. The abortion is a suction abortion seen via ultrasound images, accompanied by Dr. Nathanson's explanation. Because the video is so graphic, it is not recommended for everyone. I personally would recommend it to those who are considering abortion or who are counseling women who are. There are no emotional arguments, simply a presentation of the truth. The video is so strongly persuasive that I suspect that the numbers of pro-abortionists would drop dramatically if everyone were required to watch it.

⮑ **Who Broke the Baby?** [video] (American Portrait Films) $19.95

This video is good for teenage girls. It does not contain graphic footage of abortions, although it does describe what is involved. Instead of impressing the audience with the horrors of abortion, it emphasizes the value of life. It addresses the key arguments used in favor of abortion with answers that will reach any audience. There are no religious arguments presented.

Euthanasia

With the 1996 Ninth Circuit Court decision supporting a "right to die," the euthanasia issue appears to moving on a course similar to that of Roe v. Wade. This might be the most explosive issue we face even in the next decade because of our aging population coupled with the bankruptcy of Medicaid and Social Security. Economic factors will make euthanasia popular among many of those who see their earnings disappear to support an increasingly nonproductive, aging group of baby boomers. As Derek Humphry, president of the pro-euthanasia Hemlock Society says, this might be the last major "social issue" for liberals to conquer. I urge you to give this issue as much attention as the abortion issue.

⮑ **Not Worth Living? A Look at Euthanasia** [video] (Gospel Light) $19.99

Focus on the Family's John Eldridge hosts this presentation on euthanasia. The video was not available for review before we went to press, but they tell me it will be about a half hour long and include a study/discussion guide.

⮑ **The Right to Kill** [video] (American Portrait Films) $19.95

William F. Buckley, Jr., hosts this educational documentary on euthanasia. Interviews with both advocates and opponents bring out issues on both sides, although arguments are weighted against euthanasia. Some of the most powerful messages are inferred from interviews with Dutch physicians describing the attitudes of doctors in the Netherlands where active euthanasia has become quite common, even without the permission of patients. Interviews with activists in the United States who are promoting liberal euthanasia laws alert us to the critical nature of the issue. The video ends with a strong message affirming the value of life. The video is suitable for all junior and senior high students as well as adults.

⮑ **A Christian Response to Euthanasia** (Crusade for Life) $30

This unit study on euthanasia includes the video, *The Right to Kill*, within a three ring binder containing the rest of the study. It can be used in any type of Christian group where the audience is old enough to deal with the issue—Sunday School classes, youth and college groups, Christian high schools, and home schools. The study is divided into four parts, although, depending upon

the time you have each session, you might be able to present it in fewer than four sessions. Each of the sections includes a lesson plan, discussion suggestions, worksheets, and handout masters. Every lesson includes looking up a number of Scriptures to investigate God's opinion on the purpose and sacredness of life as well as the issue of who has the right to determine when each of us lives or dies. The first lesson is an introduction to euthanasia. The second provides a background on decision making. The third lesson includes three case histories which are used for discussion about the ethics of medical treatment in difficult situations. The lesson ends with study of the Scholl Institute of Bioethics' paper "Principles Governing Medical Treatment Decisions" so students are not left with the feeling that there are just too many gray areas. The fourth lesson concerns the Christian response to those who are suffering. Practical suggestions and addresses for more information are included. Extra helps are included: a Bible study centered around biblical answers to the key issues surrounding euthanasia, a glossary, an annotated bibliography, and helpful articles. In addition, we get *The Mercy Killers,* a glossy "tabloid" format paper that actually is substantial enough to be a book in itself. *The Mercy Killers* covers just about every aspect of the issue: court decisions, the legal situation, "Suicide in the Greek Tradition," "The Judeo-Christian Tradition," the relationship between abortion and euthanasia, euthanasia's history in America, "The True Face of Euthanasia," non-religious aspects, Germany's experience, and the present situation. A descriptive timeline takes us through the slide down the slippery slope that has taken place through the 1980s and 1990s.

The study requires some preparation time, particularly to read through some of the material and possibly to preview the video. While the study actually skips a section of the video, I recommend that you use the entire tape if you have time. Also notice the extremely reasonable price which includes the study for only $10 more than the cost of the video alone.

Feminism

⮑ **The Feminist Gospel: The Movement to Unite Feminism With the Church** by Mary Kassian (Crossway) $12.99

Feminism plays a major role in attempts to reshape society, not just in the workplace but in such diverse areas as education, the definition of the family, child care, politics, and religion. Many of us are at least somewhat familiar with the radical, anti-God feminists, but few Christians really understand the impact of feminism on the Church. Kassian examines both ends of the feminist movement, examining the driving ideas which are implicit in the movement. She looks at the various facets of the movement generally bringing the discussion back to philosophical issues. Ultimately, it appears that feminists have tried to reinterpret the Gospel so that it affirms feminist dogma, rather than judging feminist ideas and accepting or rejecting them in light of Scripture. This is a comprehensive work, not light reading, but a crucial book for those who really desire to understand and evaluate the feminist movement.

Pornography

➲ Fatal Addiction* [video] (Focus on the Family)

Dr. James Dobson's historic interview with convicted murderer Ted Bundy is a powerful message against pornography. Bundy frankly shares how pornography first influenced then drove him to uncontrollable evil. The message is very heavy, but the video is strictly of the interview, so there are no problems with visual content. This is an especially important message to share with teenage boys. The video is only available when we make a donation to Focus on the Family and receive it as a gift in return. Check with Focus for further details.

Compassion and The Poor

➲ Bringing in the Sheaves by George Grant (The Reformer Library) $11.95

George Grant offers practical solutions to society's problems, basing those solutions on Scriptural directives and principles. In *Bringing in the Sheaves* he describes the exacerbated problems created by government attempts to fix societal ills such as unemployment, poverty, homelessness, and hunger. Grant offers suggestions for solving these problems and examples of Christian compassion in action which we can use as models. Recommended for mature teens and adults.

➲ Freedom, Justice, and Hope: Toward a Strategy for the Poor and the Oppressed by Olasky, Schlossberg, Berthoud, and Pinnock (Crossway) $12.99

This is one of the books in Crossway's "Turning Point Christian Worldview Series." It is very broad, encompassing compassion issues, government, economics, Marxist ideology, and many related topics. Each chapter is written by one of the authors, making it easy to read selectively. This means that if we are studying a topic covered within this book, we can pull out one chapter to supplement study of that issue. However, chapters do relate to each other, building a total picture in order to provide a framework for Christian action. Reliance on the Bible as the ultimate source for the answers to society's needs provides solid backing for the ideas presented here.

Current Events

Current events are marvelous for identifying and studying worldviews; they represent worldviews in action. Look for articles in newspapers, newsletters, and magazines. One of the most useful tools for teaching worldviews has been my collection of such articles. I began with a three-ring binder and manila envelopes which I hole-punched for the binder. I labeled the envelopes with worldview area headings such as religion and philosophy, family issues, education, government, science, abortion/euthanasia, etc. I began collecting articles on these topics well in advance of the time I would teach on the topics, so that by the time I needed them I had a substantial collection. Sharing such articles with teens adds an immediacy to the issues. They can see that worldviews are very much a part of society, for good

and for evil. In addition to newspapers and popular news magazines check out *World* magazine (God's World Publications), *Current Events for Christian Schools*, *National Public-policy Resource Theme-packets*, and other such resources. (The aforementioned resources are reviewed in Chapter Thirteen under "Current Events.")

Books in General

Books such as those reviewed in this chapter will shape and influence attitudes in a way that textbooks rarely do. Our teens need access to good libraries that carry books representing all points of view, including that of Christians. Church libraries might be more valuable than public libraries. If libraries cannot provide what you need, Christian bookstores or mail order sources such as those listed in this book (Chapter 20) can certainly help you. An important point to remember is the value of example. If we are reading such books and discussing some of the key issues with our teenagers, later when they are interested in or mature enough to understand more about issues, it is more likely that they will follow our example and read such books on their own.

Serious Consequences

Studying worldviews certainly involves extra effort, but consider the consequences if we ignore it. Our children will be easy prey for those who can defend their worldviews. They will lack the knowledge to identify falsehoods and inconsistencies. True Christians are in the minority when it comes to influencing popular opinion in America. We arrived at this state of affairs because almost everything members of our society have learned has been filtered through non-Christian lenses, distorting truth in such a way that we Christians have become unable to even recognize some of the distortions. How can our children turn things around if they cannot identify the problems and their causes?

Ignorance might even be deadly. As Christians become a smaller percentage of the population while Relativists increase, we face the danger of persecution for our beliefs. The "exclusivity" of Christian absolutists who "practice intolerance" is already creating major conflict. Believing in absolutes and unchangeable values might well be labeled as "hate crimes" in the near future.

A number of non-Christian belief systems battle for dominance in our culture. The Christian belief system right now has the status of an "also ran." It is time for Christians to again make their voices heard, but before we do, we have to make sure we understand our own message.

Putting World View Studies on a Transcript

"World view education overlaps many basic high school subjects, sometimes making it a challenge to translate course content onto a standard transcript. What will most likely occur will be that many topics are covered, but it will take two years (or more) of study to accumulate enough study within each area to equal a course in that area.

The end result might even be different than the standard high school course of study. We might list a course in philosophy, ethics, and law—a course unlikely to show up on the typical transcript. However, this should be an asset rather than a liability in terms of college admission.

Even if it means creating a nontraditional course of study, I feel that it is vital that the study of worldviews be included. As far as I am concerned, developing our sons and daughters into educated Christians who can readily see and explain the validity of their belief in God is at least as important as any other aspect of education.

Stepping Out

Taking this spiritual foundation one step further—that we might be both hearers and doers of the Word—we need to help our teenagers become involved in the world around them through social action and community service.

They can begin by involvement with their church, not just in the youth group fun activities, but in helpful ways such as assisting in Sunday School, visitations, or with jobs related to church upkeep. They can get involved with "adopt a grandparent" programs, meals on wheels, or a myriad of other volunteer organizations. They can do it on their own or as part of a family or group ministry. There are always hundreds of opportunities for service available to us—as simple as taking cookies to a shut-in, reading to someone who is ill, or helping to collect items for the needy. Everyone can do something!

Short term mission programs are fantastic opportunities for our teenagers. Many organizations train groups of teens and take them to foreign countries to minister with both physical assistance and the gospel. Highly recommended is **Youth With A Mission** (YWAM) with bases for outreach around the world. (For missions training and opportunities contact Youth With A Mission, North American Office.) YWAM Publishing offers a book called *The GO Manual: Global Opportunities in Youth With A Mission*, which describes both long and short term mission outreaches as well as schools and training opportunities [$2.99]. Reading this book will save you from having to play "twenty questions" on the telephone or by mail.

One of the most popular ministries offering worldwide, summer missionary opportunities is **Teen Missions**. Write to Teen Missions Recruitment at the address in the Appendix.

Both YWAM and Teen Missions offer a wide variety of opportunities since they minister in many ways to people in many different countries. For other ideas, check out the book *Stepping Out: A Guide to Short Term Missions* (YWAM Publishing) [$8.99]. It describes some possible options as well as the reality of mission work so that young people are prepared for the practical aspects as well as the spiritual opportunities. Whatever they choose, a summer spent in volunteer ministry work can be truly life changing.

Obviously, these suggestions for building spiritual foundations are just scratching the surface. Each teenager's spiritual needs will be different. Knowing that God has a plan for each of our children, the most important recommendations that I can give are that we be in constant contact with Him to know what choices He would have us make, and that we encourage our teens to do the same.

Course of Study

Junior High

The course of study for junior high is fairly easy to deal with. Students should be developing basic study skills and foundational knowledge for the more specialized learning they will encounter in high school. It is a time for reviewing, consolidating, remediating, and learning according to each student's needs. Consequently, the course of study might be different for each student. There is no set list of courses they must take, although typically they should study Bible, math, history, science, language arts, and sometimes foreign language. They should also participate in physical education and electives, including the arts.

If our teens plan to enroll in a traditional high school, we should make sure that courses typically taught in junior high school have been covered. It will be even more important to make sure students have the necessary learning skills and work habits to be successful in high school. Read the section on Study Skills in Chapter Three for ideas for improving these areas.

High School

We have talked about philosophies and goals, yet we still need to figure out what subjects our high schooler should study to start him along the road to these goals. These subjects will be the high school course of study.

Before getting into details, we face the personal question of how much confidence we have in defending unusual courses of study or alternative methods of learning. Do we feel safer sticking with a traditional course of study, or are we confident enough to incorporate informal learning situations or unusual subjects? Confident parents can present a unique course of study to a college admissions officer, assuring him that their student has received a fantastic education. An insecure parent is more likely to present such a transcript or portfolio with apologies, implying that it was an inferior education. For our child's sake, we must be honest about the strengths and limitations of our own personalities, because we might be the ones who have to "sell" others on our educational program.

Our confidence in persevering through all of high school is probably even more crucial. Some parents who home educated teenagers for the first year or two of high school, then tried to enroll them in regular day schools (public and private) in the middle of high school, have been told that no credits would be allowed for work done at home. Their students would have to begin high school again as freshmen. Schools have the right to refuse to recognize course work from unaccredited schools, and some do. This means that once we begin high school at home, our only choice might be to continue for the entire four years. If we suffer serious doubts about sticking with it through high school, we should do one of two things. We can make sure there is a high school willing to allow credit from home education so we will have somewhere to turn if things do not go well. (Get this in writing!) The alternative is to work through an <u>accredited</u> school or correspondence course.

The Swann family members were early pioneers in home schooling who chose to use accredited correspondence courses so they could be certain their children would be able to go on to college. Their eldest daughter, Alexandra, relates the story of her parents' educational choices for the family in her book *No Regrets* [Cygnet Press] ($16.95). The Swanns began with Calvert for the elementary years, then enrolled in American School for high school. From there, Alexandra and some of her brothers and sisters went on to college correspondence courses through Brigham Young University and masters degree programs through California State College at Dominguez Hills. With ten children, all accelerated learners blazing their own educational trail through home schooling, these choices provided a solid, widely-accepted educational foundation. Choosing correspondence courses provides security and assistance with the teaching load, although we lose a certain amount of control over the curriculum. However, in many situations (e.g., new home schoolers, large families, uncertain future) such choices are wise.

If there is a possibility that our teen will enter a regular high school sometime after his freshman year, ensuring that course work parallels that done in the school becomes important. Accredited correspondence courses are more likely to be accepted than our own self-designed courses, but we can still put together courses with widely-recognized textbooks covering the typical course content.

Confidence will definitely influence the decisions we make about the choices confronting us. There are many different ways of planning a high school course of study. The more confident we are, the more freedom we are likely to exercise in determining how we will proceed.

For both philosophical and practical reasons, home educators will have diverse ideas about what they consider essential course content. Let us look at some of the ideas that might shape our course of study.

Types of Courses of Study

Cultural Literacy

In his book, *Cultural Literacy, What Every American Needs to Know* (Houghton Mifflin/McDougal Littell) [$19.95], E.D. Hirsch, Jr. states that people must practice effective communication to function effectively, that effective communication requires shared culture, and that shared culture requires transmission of specific information to children (Hirsch, p. xvii). That specific information comes primarily from books which have been widely recognized as having had a significant impact upon society's thoughts—books such as the *Bible*, Plato's *Republic*, and other great literary and philosophic works. It also comes from the arts and languages. Hirsch says, "...to understand what somebody is saying, we must understand more than the surface meanings of words; we have to understand the context as well" (p.3). In defining cultural literacy, Hirsch says, "It is the background information, stored in their minds, that enables them to take up a newspaper and read it with an adequate level of comprehension, getting the point, grasping the implications, relating what they read to the unstated context which alone gives meaning to what they read" (Hirsch, p.2). He concludes that general cultural literacy is necessary for people to learn about new ideas, develop new technology, and deal with events and challenges. Hirsch believes that people trained in narrow vocational educational pursuits rather than with broader tools of learning will have difficulty expanding their learning or dealing with new situations (Hirsch, p.11).

Charlotte Mason

Charlotte Mason, a proponent of home education more than sixty-five years ago, promoted ideas similar to those of Hirsch. Her reasoning differed only slightly. Mason's description of a liberal education is in close accord with what Hirsch promotes—an education that consists largely of reading acknowledged, influential literary works. She says, "...one of the main purposes of a 'liberal education for all' is to form links between high and low, rich and poor, the classes and the masses, in the strong sympathy of common knowledge" (*The Home Schooling Series: A Philosophy of Education*, p.78 [Charlotte Mason Research and Supply Co.]). Mason further believed that a liberal arts education (as she proposed it be taught) would enhance each person's intellectual ability, attention, and power of recollection—boons to both the intellectual and business worlds. Mason also believed, unlike Hirsch, that education is the "necessary handmaid to religion"—meaning education provides Bible reading skills and also goes far beyond into shaping moral and character training.

For more information about Charlotte Mason's educational philosophy you can read the entire original *Home Schooling* series in six volumes [$58.95] and/or subscribe to *The Parents Review Magazine for Home Training and Culture* [6 years of back issues available - $5 for sample issue].

Liberal Arts or Classical Education

In centuries past, education for older levels consisted largely of reading and discussing great books—the liberal arts (sometimes called classical) education similar to ideas of both Hirsch and Mason. The idea of using workbooks would have seemed ridiculous. Children were expected to have accumulated a great deal of factual information through study and memorization at younger levels. When children reached their teens, it was time to begin the real thinking and application of knowledge.

Many people have been promoting a return to some form of classical education. Proponents would have students concentrate on a liberal arts education in high school and college, learning additional skills in college and after graduation, but there is by no means universal agreement about what specifically constitutes a classical education. Generally speaking, it would include literary studies of recognized classical authors from most periods of recorded history. Some think specifically of Greek and Roman writings and their pagan civilizations as the source for classical education, but few, if any, modern-day proponents concentrate solely, or even primarily, on these roots. Classical education in its popular revival stresses writing and communication skills, and, generally, a foreign language (preferably Latin). Study of history, philosophy, world religions, and the fine arts are incorporated for the light they shed on other subjects.

In *Recovering the Lost Tools of Learning: An Approach to Distinctively Christian Education* (Crossway) [$13.49], Douglas Wilson discusses various approaches to education, but ultimately promotes a classical form of education based on Dorothy Sayers' *The Lost Tools of Learning*. Sayers divided education into two parts: the Trivium and the Quadrivium. The Trivium consists of three parts: grammar, dialectic and rhetoric. (For easy-to-understand explanations of these terms, I refer you to Wilson's book.) These three areas provide foundational information as well as learning skills for children through high school. The Quadrivium is concentration on specific subjects (which might begin in high school). The idea is that after children have learned how to think and express themselves, then is the proper time for them to begin in-depth study of particular subjects, particularly for future career or educational goals.

Wilson generally has a favorable attitude toward home education, yet he has difficulty believing that a home school can provide as excellent an education as a good Christian school (which follows Sayers' plan). If we overlook his misgivings, we find that he does a superb job of explaining the need for an education which is both Christian and classical, as well as how to provide it.

Douglas Wilson has also collaborated with Wesley Callihan and Douglas Jones to write a related book entitled *Classical Education and the Home School* (Canon Press). This 60-page book contains none of Wilson's reservations about home education. It summarizes the philosophy behind the classical approach, describes the component parts with tips on how to teach each, generally addresses the question, "What curriculum should we use?", and offers a suggested reading list. One three-page section, "A Brief Definition of Classical and Christian Education," brilliantly explains the three key elements of a classical education: the "pattern of conducting the student through the three stages of grammar, dialectic, and rhetoric;" the content; and "the importance of the historical and cultural position of the teacher and student [Western civilization]." It makes the distinction between a Christian classical education and the pagan revival of classical education that glorified the Greeks and Romans. And, finally, it underlines the importance of a Christian worldview. This is a great little book for those investigating the idea of classical education.

Harvey and Laurie Bluedorn of Trivium Pursuit publish *Teaching The Trivium*, an excellent newsletter with articles that explain the classical method and its application. They write much of the content themselves but include occasional pieces by others as well as correspondence and questions they receive. Reading through these newsletters or republished articles from older editions (available from Trivium Pursuit) will acquaint you with the nuts and bolts of resources and methods for the classical approach that have been "field-tested" and work for home schooling families.

A classical education can easily encompass instruction in worldviews; in fact, it almost always will because of the nature of the reading material used. Alternatively, you might find it easy to incorporate some ideas from the classical approach into your own eclectic curriculum. You might find yourself (as I have) borrowing some ideas, but not the complete curriculum from the classical camp.

One excellent resource for a classical education is the CD ROM *Library of the Future, 3rd edition,* from World Library. This single CD features more than 3500 entries including more than 1750 complete, unabridged literary works. Books, stories, plays, children's classics, poetry, historical documents, and scientific works comprise a fairly complete classical library. Because it is a secular library we will not find works such as Calvin's *Institutes*, although we do find the *Confessions* of St. Augustine. A few other examples from the Library are numerous works by authors such as Aesop, Hans Christian Anderson, Aristotle, William Cullen Bryant, Lewis Carroll, Chaucer, Cicero, Demosthenes, Arthur Conan Doyle, the brothers Grimm, Hawthorne, Irving, Keats, Kipling, Milton, Plutarch, Poe, Shakespeare, Twain, and Wilde. There are also selected works from such notables as Francis Bacon, Frederic Bastiat, Emily Bronte, Edmund Burke, Coleridge, Confucius, Darwin, Descartes, Dickens, Freud, Goethe, Karl Marx, and Thomas Paine. One curious entry is the contemporary book by Phillip E. Johnson, *Darwin on Trial*. This is an easy-to-use way to access literature. Think of both the space you save plus fewer trips to the library with all this at your fingertips. Even better, there are search features that allow us to search by word, subject, phrase, date (century or era), country, and category. We can read and compare works simultaneously, print hard copies, save text in ASCII format, read on-screen information about authors, and view related video clips. The program can run on IBM compatible machines (386 or higher) under DOS (3.3 or higher) or Windows (3.1 or higher), although, features are somewhat limited under the DOS

platform. You'll also need a sound card to hear the audio accompaniment to the video clips, although I don't see this as a major feature. Earlier editions of the Library are available, but they have fewer entries. Highly recommended.(S)

Another useful resource for those pursuing the classical approach might be the *Robinson Self-Teaching Home School Curriculum* since it features many of the reading selections you might want to use. (See the complete review for more details.)

A specialized resource of particular appeal to Catholics is *Designing Your Own Classical Curriculum: A Guide to Catholic Home Education* by Laura M. Berquist (Bethlehem Books) [$11.95]. This book reviews the foundations of a classical education, although not as thoroughly as does Wilson in *Recovering the Lost Tools of Learning*. However, Laura Berquist devotes much more attention to outlining a recommended course of study for grades K-12. She divides studies according to her "translation" of the Trivium, then shares specific recommendations for each grade level. Drawing on her experience in actually constructing and teaching this curriculum, she adds personal comments explaining her preferences and how they might work for other families. She recommends a broad mixture of resources from Catholic publishers and distributors, Seton's correspondence program, BJUP, Saxon math, *Learning Language Arts through Literature*, and other highly-regarded resources as well as "real" books. She includes recommended reading lists for each level, and she uses a helpful key to show us where we might obtain almost all of the resources. Even those who are not particularly enthusiastic about the classical approach but who prefer a truly Catholic education will find this book an invaluable source for locating resources.

Principle Approach

The Principle Approach provides a solid, well-developed philosophy of Christian education, although the methodology is challenging. The Principle Approach can encompass a classical education, Charlotte Mason's ideas, cultural literacy, and other ideas described here, because it outlines a foundation that answers the questions about why we do what we do in education. It operates at a more fundamental level than do most of the others.

In its full implementation, the Principle Approach requires much study and planning on the part of the teacher/parent, but the results are worth the effort. Most people using the Principle Approach have children keep a notebook for recording information which has been researched and studied. The application of concepts is also recorded in the notebook.

The principles are described slightly differently by various persons using this approach, but the following list from Rus Walton's *Fundamentals for American Christians* is typical. The principles are identified, studied, and used as a foundation for further learning. The principles are based on the following ideas:

– God's sovereignty

– Individuality

– Personal property

– Self government

– Family government

– Stewardship
– Local autonomy
– Voluntary Association

History is an important aspect of the Principle Approach—primarily America's Christian history—but the Principle Approach can be applied to all subject areas as explained in Mr. Rose's book listed below.

If the Principle Approach appeals to us, junior high and high school would seem to me the ideal time to pursue this with our children since they are now able to deal with abstract ideas better than at elementary levels (although many families are implementing this method very successfully at younger levels.)

Below are listed books based upon the Principle Approach. Contact Foundation for American Christian Education (F.A.C.E.), the American Christian History Institute (or check ACHI's website), or Landmark Distributors for more information. These organizations have authored, inspired, or distributed much of the available material. Landmark Distributors has an extensive catalog of Principle Approach resources.

F.A.C.E.'s catalog features a comprehensive list of Principle Approach resources. They also sponsor an "Apprenticeship" program several times a year, providing hands-on experience in applying the Principle Approach. Contact F.A.C.E. for details.

Seminars on the Principle Approach take place from time to time. James Rose, president of the American Christian History Institute, heads an outstanding list of presenters at annual seminars sponsored by the Institute. These seminars are geared for a range of needs including day schools, youth, and home educators. Contact the American Christian History Institute for details on upcoming seminars as well as smaller-scale presentations. Tapes of individual sessions as well as complete seminars are available through the Institute.

Heritage Ministries has an extensive catalog of tapes and resources, most of them by Paul Jehle, but they also feature others from speakers such as Rus Walton, Belinda Beth Ballenger, Archie Jones, John Eidsmoe, and John Stormer.

Ben Gilmore also presents seminars for teens through adults once a year in Morgan Hill, California and Columbus, Georgia. Ben Gilmore tells me that these seminars "are designed to separate the serious student from the casual observer." The seminars draw political leaders, grass roots activists, homeschool, government school, and church leaders. These four-day seminars cover the principles of Biblical government, illustrations of God's hand in history, and an understanding of the logic of good government and the principle of self-government. Tapes of the seminar are available [$100 a set] for those unable to attend. Contact ACH Study Groups for more information.

There are numerous resources written about and based upon the Principle Approach. Reviews of some of the more general resources follow, while others can be found in chapters on specific subject areas. The majority of those will be found in the areas of history, government, and the Constitution. There are a few Principle Approach resources for language arts and science. Tapes from seminars on the Principle Approach often include sessions focused on various subject areas. Check with the American

Christian History Institute, ACH Study Groups, and Heritage Ministries to see what they offer.

Noah Webster's Dictionary plays a vital role in the Principle Approach, so it heads the list of resources.

⊃ **The American Dictionary of the English Language, a facsimile 1828 edition** by Noah Webster (Foundation for American Christian Education) $60

Webster's 1828 Dictionary is a vital part of the Principle Approach since one of the first steps in studying a subject is to properly define it. This dictionary, in contrast to modern dictionaries, provides biblical references within many definitions to clarify the meaning and usage of words. Definitions of many words have changed since 1828, and this dictionary also helps us properly interpret source documents from America's beginnings by defining words as their original writers intended. See the description of the computer version listed as *Noah Webster's 1828 Dictionary.*

⊃ **Noah Webster's 1828 Dictionary [computer program]** (Christian Technologies Inc.) $30

This computer version of Webster's 1828 Dictionary is available only for Windows on either 3.5" disks (13 high density disks) or CD-ROM. I highly recommend the CD-ROM version rather than the disks because the CD-ROM will be much easier to install and load, and it offers you the option of minimal installation requiring minimal hard drive space. Almost all of the text of the original is here, but enhanced with search features. (Missing are the preface, the history of the English language, and the foreign fonts, none of which are crucial.) We can search only for words that are defined, not words within those definitions. However, we can click on each defined word and a side column shows all other defined words that contain the original word as part of their definitions. It's not a synonym finder, although synonyms will appear within that list. It should be especially helpful for those using the Principle Approach researching the meanings and applications of words. The Dictionary is also contained on the *American Student's Package* CD-ROM. See the review under Bible resources.

⊃ **Building a Biblical Philosophy of Education and Building a Biblical Worldview Curriculum** by Paul Jehle (Landmark Distributors) $55 each set

This is a 12-tape set about developing a biblical philosophy of education, followed by another 12-tape set on developing a biblical world view curriculum. According to Lori Harris, who is familiar with just about everything on the Principle Approach, the first set is the best introduction to the Principle approach available on audio tape.

⊃ **Come Let Us Reason** by Kris Scribante Bayer (Libertatis Causa) $9.95

Thinking Biblically about Education or An Explanation of the Principle Approach is the subtitle of this book. In 112 pages, Kris Bayer concisely describes the Principle Approach and offers beginning steps in the 4R process for history, literature, geography, government, Bible study, reading, writing, grammar, science, and math. While this book combines philosophy with how-to, it focuses more on principles of teaching rather than the details of what to do when. Occasionally, the author recommends resources, and she includes a ten-page annotated resource list at the end of the book. This book is an excellent, unintimidating introduction to the Principle Approach for home educators—great starting place.

Libertatis Causa also publishes a companion journal, *Come Let Us Reason Journal* [$5].

➲ The Education of James Madison
by Mary-Elaine Swanson (The Hoffman Center) $21.95

Swanson outlines the education of James Madison from home education, tutoring, and a small local school, on to college and his own self-education. Many of Madison's contemporaries received similar educations, and the results were outstanding. After reading this book, we can then judge whether a return to this caliber of education is an answer to the failed education system which has produced 23 million illiterates. This is a thought-provoking book for parents, educators, and mature teens. In essence it lays out the Principle Approach method of teaching and learning in a biographical fashion through the life of Madison. It gives parents a vision for what can be accomplished in home education.[Diane Wheeler]

➲ A Family Program for Reading Aloud by Rosalie June
Slater (Foundation for American Christian Education) $16

Now in an updated, expanded 1997 edition, this helpful guide for parents is more than just recommended reading lists, although those are included. It outlines the Principle Approach as applied to literature and a study of American history. Although books and themes from American history receive the most attention a few other authors such as Sir Walter Scott and Charles Dickens are included. Most recommendations focus on younger children, but guidelines in the new material in the second half of the book expand into topics and recommendations for junior and senior high students. Most of these recommendations are presented within particular topics such as "Reading about the Pioneers" and "Reading about the French Revolution." The purpose of this book is to urge and inspire us to study literature from the Principle Approach rather than attempting to read "everything out there." Fewer books are recommended, but information on the books and authors included is far more extensive than what we find in other reading "guides."

➲ George Washington Study Guide (Noah Webster
Educational Foundation)

"A family study on the Life of George Washington" by Belinda Beth Ballenger is designed to prepare parents and classroom teachers to teach Washington's life from the "Principle Approach." Historically, George Washington was called The Moses of America. The study looks at Washington in the light of that Biblical and historical perspective. The study includes Ballenger's guide plus "The Making of George Washington" by

William Wilbur. While it is ideal for students ages 10-15, it can also be used with younger children.

➲ A Guide to American Christian Education for the Home and School, The Principle Approach, second edition by
James B. Rose (American Christian History Institute) $35

This is THE book about how to teach the various subjects by the Principle Approach. It is a beautifully bound, very large book—550 pages, requiring a significant study effort. However, it attempts to answer all the questions that arise over implementation of the Principle Approach. It defines the Principle Approach and the Seven Principles. It discusses application of the Principle Approach in both the school at home and the Christian school. Some of the most valuable information in this book is that which tells how to use the Principle Approach to teach literature, geography, history, economics, science, mathematics, and typing.

➲ Homeschool Teaching Packets by Daniel R. Eby (Patria
Ministries) $12 each

Each packet in this series is a 36-week outline for both parent and student(s) for a liberal arts and science curriculum using the Principle Approach. Two packets are available thus far. Other topics are in development for junior and senior high students. These packets should make it easier for parents to teach the Principle Approach since some of the work has already been done for us.

Rudiments of America's Christian History and Government Home School Teaching Packet teaches the founding principles of America's Christian history. It aids the student in understanding the relationship of individual character and responsibility, and the strength and character of a nation. It must be used in conjunction with the Bible and some of the resources from The Foundation for American Christian Education, including *Rudiments of America's Christian History and Government* by Slater and Hall. This is challenging course work designed for grades 7-10. Students research various topics and record their findings in notebooks along with their weekly outlines, definitions, at least one essay per week, quizzes, and tests. The primary emphasis is upon study of the Bible, history, and government. Grading and record-keeping pages plus reproducible map masters are included for this specific study.

The second packet, *Providential Geography: A Stage for Men and Nations - Year One*, is the first-year course of a two-year study in geography. It teaches mathematical and physical geography primarily from Lt. Matthew Maury's outline on geography. The second packet will continue the study based on Maury's outline, also covering political geography. Each of these packets advances a Christian worldview of geography. As in the *Rudiments* packet, there are outlines for lessons, goalsheets (which are, essentially, detailed lesson plans), quizzes, exams, and maps. These *Providential Geography* packets are used as a companion to two historic texts: the first is Maury's *Manual of Geography*, written in 1888 (revised and updated to be available by summer 1998), and the second is Guyot's *Physical Geography* (reviewed elsewhere in this manual). A third text, Bob

Jones University Press' *Geography for Christian Schools,* is used to supplement these texts. A facsimile portion of Maury's text needed for the first year packet is included with each *Year One* packet at no charge until the updated Maury text is complete.

➲ **The Noah Plan: An Educational Program in the Principle Approach** (Foundation for American Christian Education) $60; subject guides - $25 each

See the complete review under "Unit Studies and Comprehensive Programs." Coupled with the subject area *Subject Guides,* this is the most complete Principle Approach curriculum available.

➲ **The Rudiments of America's Christian History and Government: Student Handbook** by Rosalie J. Slater and Verna M. Hall (Foundation for American Christian Education) $13

The purpose of this book is to introduce students to the reasoning and writing of biblical principles applied in *The Christian History* volumes and *Teaching and Learning America's Christian History.* If you intend to use the "red books" published by F.A.C.E., I strongly recommend that you also get this book so that you will know what to do with the others. At the back of the book is a section that concisely instructs us as to how to apply the Principle Approach, including the creation of notebooks. The bulk of the book consists of two separate but closely related studies. The first study is of Noah Webster's *Letters to a Young Gentleman Commencing His Education.* Obviously aimed at a young person, probably in the teen years, the letters address issues of character including character in relation to government. Students are directed to create their own notebooks as they work through questions and assignments for various sections of *Letters.* Frequently, assignments refer students to *Christian History of the Constitution, Teaching and Learning America's Christian History,* and *Webster's 1828 American Dictionary.* The second study traces the "Chain of Christianity Moving Westward," narrowly focusing on the principle of individuality. Within that framework, students investigate topics such as Old Testament law, Greece, Rome, the Reformation, English law, constitutional government, and America. Students can work through most of this on their own, but they should have a good grounding in history before tackling it. I highly recommend that parents do the study along with children for their own benefit and so that they can participate in and direct discussions. If you want more assistance in using this study, consider also using *Rudiments of America's Christian History and Government Home School Teaching Packet* by Daniel Eby (reviewed above).

➲ **Teaching and Learning America's Christian History: The Principle Approach,** by Rosalie Slater (Foundation for American Christian Education) $35

This volume outlines the seven basic principles of the Principle Approach with lesson plans and background information. Each topic is frequently cross referenced to the *Christian History Volumes* by Verna Hall (reviewed in Chapter Fourteen). This

book will get you started but will not carry you through into all subject areas as does the book by James Rose.

Unschooling

The idea of letting children follow their own inclinations in their education has been called "unschooling." The philosophic ideas behind this approach are most often associated with John Holt, author of numerous books such as *How Children Learn, How Children Fail, Instead of Education,* and *Teach Your Own.* Holt's books are available from libraries and bookstores, especially from John Holt's Book and Music Store, an arm of Holt Associates, a home-school organization that he began many years ago. Further support for moving away from traditional ideas of schooling ironically comes from New York State Teacher of the Year, John Taylor Gatto. In his book, *Dumbing Us Down* (New Society Publishers) [$9.95], he strikes at the heart of the system, demonstrating how the methods of compulsory state education are doomed to failure.

Many home educators support these philosophic ideas to varying degrees and have allowed their teens to follow their interests in putting together a course of study to fit their career goals. In general, those following an unschooling approach allow teens to choose what, when, and how to study, according to their need for knowledge or proficiency in different areas. For instance, a person interested in becoming a veterinarian can work part time with a veterinarian, similar to an apprentice. On his own he can read books related to the subject. If the intent is to go on to college for further training, the student would study whatever subjects he needs to pass college entrance exams. (See the descriptions of Grace Llewellyn's books *The Teenage Liberation Handbook: How to Quit School and Get a Real Life and Education,* and *Real Lives: Eleven Teenagers Who Don't Go to School* under "Suggested Reading About Home Educating Teens" in Chapter Two.

The unschooling approach advocated by the above authors obviously is dependent upon our teenager being self motivated. It certainly is easier on us parents if our student takes responsibility for his own education, but we have to watch that we are not expecting more maturity from our child than is realistic. Even the most independent learner might need a guiding hand or occasional prod to keep him from descending into slothfulness.

Unit Study

Although I devote all of Chapter Ten to unit study, I must mention it here also since this, too, is an approach to developing your course of study. While many families feel comfortable with unit study in the elementary grades, they often turn to more traditional approaches in junior and senior high. However, with the advent of some of the comprehensive unit study packages being developed and marketed in recent years, unit study for the teen years is becoming increasingly popular and practical.

Practical

Some home educated teens want to work in construction, farming, plumbing, or another trade that will not require college education. They want a practical course of study that will prepare

SAMPLE STUDENT SCHEDULES/ JAMES MADISON HIGH SCHOOL

Student A

9th Grade	10th Grade	11th Grade	12th Grade
Introduction to Literature	American Literature	British Literature	Introduction to World Literature
Western Civilization	American History	Principles of American Democracy (1 sem.)	Algebra II and Trig.
Algebra I	Astronomy/Geology	Amer. Democracy and the World (1 sem.)	Principles of Technology
Spanish I	Spanish II	Plane/Solid Geometry	Art History/Music History
P.E./Health	P.E./Health	Biology	Technical Writing (elective)
Typing/Word Processing (elective)	Bookkeeping (elective)	P.E./Health (elective)	Graphic Arts (elective)
		Psychology (elective)	

Student B

9th Grade	10th Grade	11th Grade	12th Grade
Introduction to Literature	American Literature	British Literature	Introduction to World Lit.
Western Civilization	American History	Principles of American Democracy (1 sem.)	Statistics/Probability (1 sem., elective)
Algebra I	Plane and Solid Geometry	Amer. Democracy and the World (1 sem.)	Pre-calculus (1 sem., elective)
Astronomy/Geology	Biology	Algebra II and Trig.	Physics (elective)
P.E./Health	P.E./Health	Chemistry	French II
Band (elective)	Band (elective)	French I	Art and Music History
		Band (elective)	Band (elective)

Student C

9th Grade	10th Grade	11th Grade	12th Grade
Introduction to Literature	American Literature	British Literature	Introduction to World Literature
Western Civilization	American History	Principles of American Democracy (1 sem.)	Calculus AB (elective)
Plane and Solid Geometry	Algebra II and Trigonometry	Amer. Democracy and the World (1 sem.)	Physics (elective)
Astronomy/Geology	Biology	Statistics and Probability (1 semester)	Latin IV (elective)
Latin I	Latin II	Pre-calculus (1 sem.)	Computer Science (elective)
P.E./Health	P.E./Health	Chemistry	Painting and Drawing (elective)
		Latin III (elective)	
		Art and Music History	

them to begin work as soon as possible. They do not want to waste time on subjects they never expect to use. Such a narrow course of study has limitations which might present problems in the future if the original career goal does not work out. However, if a teenager has made up his mind that he will learn only what is important to him, we can waste our time and energy trying to force him to go beyond his self-imposed limits. If the original goal has to be scrapped, it is always possible, although it might be difficult, to return to school and learn something else or pursue another career.

The practical approach (or maybe it should be called pragmatic) even appeals to some educators within the school system, although for different reasons. Joe Clark, the notorious principal of Eastside High School in Paterson, New Jersey, battled to establish disciplinary standards in his high school so even a mini-mal amount of education could take place. Despite the improved environment, test scores and other indicators of academic progress remained dismal. Mr. Clark attributed the problem to missing educational foundations. Mr. Clark and others place little hope in making up the void of a worthless elementary education and would rather see these students take a direct leap into the business world. "Clark would urge the present generation to acquire as much wealth (and the power that comes with it) as they can from work, entrepreneurship, and an orientation to the future...."[1] Clark recommends a course of study much more pragmatic than a liberal arts education. Courses in marketing, consumer and business math, and other trade and vocational classes would replace all but the minimal requirements in literature, language, arts, and history studies. This is essentially the same philosophy driving School-to-Work programs throughout the country. In my opinion, this strategy of using education as job training and appealing to the most self-serving motives should be used only in the most drastic cases since it can do more harm than good.

"James Madison High School"

Former Federal Secretary for Education William Bennett has promoted what he calls "James Madison High School." This is a model for high school courses of study which emphasizes the basic academic subjects while allowing choices that take individual needs into account. Bennett's concern has been the increasing percentage of courses consisting of physical education, health education, work experience, remedial math and English, and personal development which have displaced core academics. Samples of student schedules included in Bennett's recommendations are shown in the chart on the previous page.

Following Bennett's ideas, we would plan a course of study that remains somewhat traditional yet allows for emphasis on an educational area. For instance, for students interested in one of the scientific fields, the course of study would be weighted towards math and science; communication skills would have next priority; and history, philosophy, and the arts would be covered more superficially.

Traditional

The majority of home educators stick (to some extent) with traditional courses of study which include standard courses in math, language arts, history, and science, plus electives. (See the typically required courses for either a general or college preparatory education listed on the planning charts at the back of the book.) There is more security in conforming to standard expectations, especially when students plan to go on to college. Beyond that, such a course of study does provide a fairly balanced education. The questions home educators raise about the traditional course of study challenge the underlying assumption that "one size fits all." There are thousands of subjects that students could be studying, yet the traditional course of study limits the choices to a small handful. For example, biology and chemistry are the standard science courses, but there is little that makes either inherently better than geology, botany, oceanography, or most any other scientific topic. Algebra is justified for all students because of the logic and thinking skills it uses, yet some people question if there are not more practical ways of teaching those skills.

Concocting Your Own Course of Study

Many veteran home schoolers end up creating their own courses of study that draw from any number of the above-described approaches combined with their own ideas. For example, Robin Scarlata, in her book *What Your Child Needs To Know When* (Family Christian Press), describes her "Heart of Wisdom" approach which is sort of a unit study approach based upon the Bible, but which stresses strong language arts development

(shades of Charlotte Mason's ideas here). Some traditional texts round out the study, and teens are encouraged to incorporate development of practical life skills.

The beauty of home education is that we have the freedom to determine what is best for each of our children. We need not determine which, if any, of the above approaches is best for everyone, but only what works for our children.

College Preparatory

"College Prep" is not a distinctive educational approach, but rather a goal that influences whichever approach we select. If we choose to follow traditional methods of providing a high school education in preparation for college, the time to begin planning for college is at the beginning of ninth grade. There are important decisions to make in regard to course work that cannot be delayed until later. Maybe your child, like many others, has no idea whether or not he wants to attend college. As long as he appears to have the basic wherewithal to tackle college, plan as if he is going. There is more to be lost by not taking college preparatory courses than there is to be gained in relief by following a student's inclinations to take easier courses.

College preparatory course work does not consist only of those courses which are required for college. Students should also have room in their schedules for electives or outside activities where they have freedom to pursue a wide range of interests. (Outside activities are often an important factor in college admissions, since they demonstrate that the student is well-rounded.) However, if our child desires to attend one of the exclusive institutions such as Yale or Harvard, or a more specialized school such as MIT or Cal Tech, he had better plan his course work carefully and plan to work hard. Common requirements to enroll at such institutions are:

– four years of English

– four years of mathematics, including at least an introduction to calculus

– two to four years of science, with at least two lab courses

– three years of history or social science, including World and U.S. History, government, and economics

– three or more years of a foreign language, with a preference for intensive study of one language, rather than two or more languages studied briefly

– one year of course work in the fine arts

– two years of physical education

– electives

While these requirements are quite stringent, we find that competitive colleges across the nation are also tightening up their requirements, forcing college-bound high school students to take meatier courses than they have chosen in the past. In 1985, the California State University and University of California systems issued new preparation requirements which were fully implemented by 1990. These are called the "A through F" requirements. They are:

a. History: U.S. History - 1 year required by CSU; UC requires U.S. History and 1 year of World History.

b. English - 4 years required

c. Mathematics - 3 years required (although 4 years are recommended, particularly for UC); must include Geometry and Algebra 2.

d. Laboratory science - 1 year required by CSU; 2 years required by UC (3 years recommended). UC science courses should be from the areas of biology, chemistry, and physics.

e. Foreign Language - 2 years required (3 recommended)—at least two years of the same language.

f. College Preparatory Electives - 4 years required by CSU; 2 years required by UC since solids take up time that might be used for electives. CSU requires that 1 year be visual or performing arts. Other electives are selected from subjects such as advanced mathematics, social science, history, laboratory science, foreign language, and agriculture. Highly competitive colleges and majors require 4-5 years of advanced math, 3-4 years of lab science, and 3-4 years of foreign language.

(From *Planning Guide for Students and Parents 1994-95*, Huntington Beach Union High School District.)

Not all colleges are so rigorous in their requirements. Bible colleges are often less demanding in prerequisites, although that does not guarantee that the one you choose will be. Most Bible colleges require entrance exams (SAT or ACT), but some do not. Less prestigious colleges cannot afford to be as particular about the students they admit so the standards tend to be lower, corresponding to the prestige of the college. However, prestige and reputation do not guarantee the quality of the education provided, and some small colleges provide a better education than Ivy League institutions.

Assessing Our Options

Old ways are not necessarily better, but our present educational system is obviously missing something important. So much of the material is repeated over and over again from elementary grades through high school. Much time is wasted, and children's talents and gifts that fall outside a narrow academic range are ignored. We need to take a hard look at our course of study in terms of what is best for our teen.

Some home educators are using a traditional approach, but are substituting some unusual classes to better suit their students' needs. We can, assuming that we have the legal freedom to do so in our state, approach high school with a very independent attitude, pursuing subjects of our choosing and ignoring others. I was encouraged by an interview by television talk show host Phil Donahue with the Colfax family on his program. Their courses of study sounded very flexible and creative. Reed, the second eldest son, said that he never read a history textbook, but he felt he knew more history than his college classmates. His knowledge came from reading historical novels. The idea that much learning can take place outside textbooks came up repeatedly in the discussion. Following the Colfax's example, we could plan a course of study that includes much informal learning in some subjects along with some textbooks for other subjects. Other such options can be designed to fit your situation.

There is no ethically right or wrong choice to make. Rather, it is a choice based upon our best understanding of God's future direction for each of our children. There should be a balance in our curriculum to develop the various faculties of the mind and to explore subjects for which our teen shows an interest and an aptitude. It is not important that home educators all agree upon the best approach, but it is important that each of us think about the options and make some purposeful decisions in planning a course of study.

A Christian Course of Study

We might choose any of the above or still other ideas for planning courses of study, but I have come to some conclusions of my own about two particular areas we need to address as Christians.

My first concern is that any course of study should help our young people develop their abilities to reason and deal with philosophical issues. Challenges in both areas will arise no matter what occupations they pursue. I want to discuss ethical topics with them while I have my chance to provide input. If I skirt issues now because of their age or immaturity, I may never again have the opportunity to initiate such discussions once my children are out of high school. As our teenagers move on to their separate lives, we often lose opportunities for weighty discussions. Our children become involved in other pursuits that absorb more and more of their time, and rightly so. As young adults they will come under the influence of other adults and peers with strong opinions. If they have not had their ideas and thinking challenged before, how will they be able to defend their beliefs against strongly opinionated adults or friends?

I do not believe we have to examine every worthless idea or philosophy that comes along, but I want to establish the thinking skills and basic philosophical ideas that will guide my children in confronting unfamiliar ideas. It can be compared to warming up and then practicing weight training for the muscles. Someone who has never done any exercise does not begin by lifting two hundred pound barbells. He begins with small weights and works up as his muscles develop the ability to deal with the increased work. Similarly, we need to warm up our thinking "muscles" and train by using those muscles in the discussion of ideas—what we might term philosophy—with those who are at least somewhat like-minded. Then we will be better prepared to confront those who would seriously challenge our beliefs.

For example, some Christians would avoid any mention of evolution because it is a false teaching. However, if our children do not understand what evolutionists believe, they will not be able to refute evolution or even recognize its influence on what people believe about religion, science, history, philosophy, and so on. (See Chapter Five for further discussion.)

The second point I want to make is based upon my belief that God has gifted each child with special interests and talents for His purposes. I think we have an obligation to recognize and develop those interests and talents as much as we can so that we are cooperating with God's plan for our child rather than superimposing our own. I am not talking about fostering purely self-serving interests, but interests which relate to relationships and careers. If a child has a musical interest and ability, God can certainly use that to His glory. If a child has an interest in computers, engineering, and things mathematical, God probably has a plan for him that involves such things. While our culture tends to lop-sidedly value academic skills over mechanical, those children with mechanical skills will be the ones that keep all of our vital machinery operating, so we certainly should encourage those with mechanical inclinations. If a girl takes much pleasure in homemaking activities, that too is worth developing in spite of society's bias against such traditional roles.

At the same time, I do not believe God would have an entire family devote most of its energy to the development of a single talent of one family member at everyone else's expense. We see this happen occasionally with talented athletes who prepare for the Olympics, talented musicians who want to reach the pinnacle of fame or recognition, and even academically-talented students who want to attend one of the most exclusive universities. There is a danger of becoming unbalanced in pursuit of recognition or achievement, especially when a child is particularly gifted. We must pray carefully for God's timing and direction in developing such gifts so that they are used for His glory rather than the glory of any one person.

Too Much?

The problem many of us recognize is that we often are trying to provide too much. We want our children to have a practical education in math and language arts which they will use whatever their futures hold. We also want them to have a classical education so they are familiar with ideas and history. We cannot forget spiritual development—an education which influences all other aspects of life. We might also be interested in a vocational education—after all, we need to be practical in equipping our children with marketable skills. We might even want them to have a small business of their own to obtain hands-on experience. They really do need to stay in good physical condition throughout all of this, so we are concerned about physical education and conditioning. If we can squeeze it in, we might also want them to have some training in music or art. Can we really provide all this? Not if we want to do it all well!

Our dilemma is a new one brought on by the industrial and technological revolutions. In past centuries, there was less technologically-related knowledge in the math and sciences being taught. There was more time to devote to both the liberal arts and practical education. Today, if a student wants to pursue a

technological career, he needs to devote a large portion of his study time to math and science, leaving much less time for the other studies. If a student chooses a business major, he has to sacrifice some liberal arts and science study. We face more difficult choices as the body of knowledge continually increases. There are tradeoffs that have to be made. The question comes back to goals. What do we wish to accomplish? Even more importantly, what does God wish to accomplish in our child's life?

As parents, we are looking at the total picture in a way that school educators rarely do. We are intimately concerned with the future of our child, so all of these things do matter to us, whereas most teachers deal only with the short term, narrow purposes of the school.

Reality means we have only twenty-four hours in a day and our children require some rest from our efforts to mold them into ideal human beings. So we cannot do it all.

We (and our children) have to make some choices and recognize what is most important. We must then make conscious decisions about how we allocate our educational energies. I cannot decide for you which things are of highest priority. That will depend upon your personal beliefs and your child's interests and aptitudes.

Writing Down a Course of Study

Once we have determined our priorities and goals, we can begin to formulate a course of study.

A written course of study lists which subjects will be covered each year. This list is not as detailed as a scope and sequence which gives detailed goals for subjects in the order they will be covered. For instance, in our course of study under the subject of language, we might list as topics a review of grammar and development of expository writing skills. In the scope and sequence we would list details such as review of eight principal parts of speech, learning the steps for writing a research paper, learning to use the computer card catalog at the library, etc.

It is wise to first plan a tentative course of study for the high school years as a whole, then break it down into yearly courses of study. This will help us arrange studies so that we can meet educational goals in the time available. (The planning charts E and F can also help us determine which subjects to cover which years.)

Writing out the course of study is relatively easy, especially if we have already been writing out courses of study for elementary grades. However, for upper grade levels, it is helpful to add more detail than you would write out for younger grade levels. The Course of Study form (Chart A)at the back of the book requires one page for each subject, allowing for extra detail.

At a minimum, the high school course of study should list each subject title with a brief description of the course content. This can be done, using descriptions like the following. (These examples show both brief and more-involved descriptions. Use whatever is most practical for you.)

➲ Algebra I

Two semester course using Saxon's *Algebra 1* with accompanying test booklet. 10 credits

➲ Introduction to American Literature

A survey course of modern American Literature using Bob Jones University Press' text *American Literature for Christian Schools: Modern Tradition, 1865 to the Present.* Emphasis will be on analyzing plots, themes, viewpoints, and characterizations, while learning about many genres and authors. Vocabulary work will be derived from reading selections. The novel, *To Kill a Mockingbird* will be used as a supplemental study. Two semesters/10 credits

➲ Expository Writing

Skills in expository writing will be developed in a group class through a variety of assignments. Students will also learn how to critique both their own and each others' work for grammar and content. A research paper will be included. The *Basic English Revisited* handbook will be used as a reference tool. Two semesters/10 credits

Electives should also be included

➲ Home Economics

Nutrition and cooking will be studied as Mary plans and prepares meals for the family. She will prepare weekly menus, work within a budget, and consider nutritional balance. She will be responsible for preparing dinners three nights a week to practice cooking skills. She will also be responsible for cleanup. One semester/5 credits

➲ Auto Mechanics

Chris will learn basic engine mechanics as he works with his father to rebuild a car engine. He will refer to repair manuals for information. One semester/5 credits

An even better approach is to include the course title, credits, curriculum to be used, description, and standard (guidelines for evaluation). If you are using a traditional textbook, less description is necessary. Some examples appear on this and the next page.

Course of Study	
Course Title	Biology
Course Credits	10 credits (2 semesters)

Course Curriculum	*Biology for Christian Schools*, BJUP
	Biology for Christian Schools Laboratory Manual, BJUP
	
	Outside reading material will be assigned supplementally as it relates to the subject matter. Suggested reading will include:
	    The Lie: Evolution by Ken Ham
	    A Child is Born, by Lennart Nilsson

Course Description	This is a high school survey course touching on most of the major areas of the biological sciences. It emphasizes areas of biology that overlap Christian philosophy, morals, and ethics. Some areas of biological study are therefore dealt with here in greater depth than in many other high school biology courses, while other areas have been greatly reduced or eliminated. Areas of coverage will included (but are not limited to) the foundations of science, the scientific method, how science relates to Christianity, cytology, genetics, creation science, microbiology, botany, zoology, ecology, and human anatomy and physiology. Lab work will selected activities from the Laboratory Manual.
Course Standard	Daily work = accuracy (1 point), neatly produced with obvious effort employed (1 point), and presented on time (1 point) = 3 points/day Chapter Essay or Test = 30 points each Semester Lab and Write-up Notes = 50 points (based on accuracy, presentation, and effort) Semester Exam = 50 points Research project = 50 points based on quality of research, presentation, and timeliness

The total number of points possible in a course will depend upon the number of daily written assignments and chapter tests required. This sample allows flexibility to add or subtract assignments as the term progresses based upon changing needs of the student. As you can see, this model also places a premium on daily work, encouraging timeliness, neatness, and effort as well as accuracy. The total number of points earned divided by the total number of points possible then becomes the basis for the semester grade.

****

	Course of Study
Course Title	Writing (English requirement)
Course Credits	5 (1 semester)
Course Curriculum	*Writing With a Point* by Stephens and Harper (Educators Publishing Service) *Write Source* handbook for research paper information
Course Description	This is a group class in expository writing with some creative writing activity. Major emphasis will be on logical development, organization, essay writing, and the research paper.
Course Standard	completion of all assignments in timely and satisfactory manner = 50% research paper meets requirements = 30% improvement in individual goals (e.g., improved organization and support skills or improved creativity and originality) = 20%

More detail for the scope and sequence of each course might be necessary for your own benefit. If you are using a standard textbook as the publisher has planned, the table of contents usually provides the detail you need. If you are creating your own course, you must know what it is you plan to accomplish, then show how you will use the various resources to meet your goal. This might take less than a page or it might take a number of pages depending how complicated you make it. For example, if you use Saxon's Algebra I, the table of contents lists every topic covered within the book. Your goals are pre-established for you if you choose to use the book as the publisher intends. In this case it is not necessary to write out goals.

If you choose to create your own course, as we have sometimes done, then you need to write out your plan in more detail. For example, for our botany class, I made a rough outline of the topics to be covered, then created entire lesson plans for the course. The rough outline by itself was only a starting place. In this case, the lesson plans needed to be created at the very beginning so that I could budget time for the entire school year.

The lesson plan for the initial botany lesson for a once-a-week group class looked like this (all unlabeled book references refer to A Beka's *Biology* text.):

Opening discussion:
What makes a plant a plant? (tree, shrub, herb, flower?)
Definitions: p.5
Notes:
– *trees/shrubs = woody plants, live several years*
– *tree = single tall woody stem capable of standing erect without support*

– *shrub or bush = several low woody stems, branched near ground, stand erect without support*
– *herbaceous plants = any plant with soft stem*
– *vine = woody or herbaceous, long thin stem, grows, along ground or other support*
Flowers/fruits/seeds
– *general look at different types (Peterson's pp. xvi-xxxii)*
Roots
– *examine various types of actual roots*
– *identify taproot, fibrous, spreading*
– *ask: What would you plant to hold soil in place?*
 Assignments: *Review pp. 2-5*
Collect 6 different types of leaves, making one-word notes about why they are different
Read pp. 6-7 for next week

The course of study should be kept on file. In some states this is a legal requirement, while in others it is simply for your benefit.

Record Keeping

Planning must move beyond the general course of study to daily or weekly lesson planning. For this purpose, any lesson plan book can be used or you can design your own system. Some parents create separate lesson plans for each subject, each in a separate notebook. Some write their lesson plans directly into a teacher's lesson plan notebook. Some create all of their lesson plans for the year in the summer preceding that school year, while others create the daily lesson plans each week, working from their scope and sequence or course outline. Lesson plans are very specific about exactly what is to be accomplished each day. Students can obtain their assignments from your lesson plan book, you can copy their assignments onto assignment pages, they can derive their own lesson plans from a contract, or you can otherwise convey that information to them. The point is that our teens need to know what is expected from them each day. Some samples of daily lesson plans for individual classes appear on the following page. Similar information might appear under the proper headings in a lesson plan book covering all subjects.

Inexpensive plan books are available at teacher supply stores and from Bob Jones University Press and Rod and Staff. Other plan books have been designed for home educators. Fine Line Publishing offers *The Planner Plus* [$6.95] with 8 1/2" by 14" pages for recording information for two students plus planning pages and report card forms. *The Home Schooler's Journal* (FERG N US Services) [$7.95] is another inexpensive option. It expands beyond the typical plan book with field trip logs, check-off list for yearly requirements, and individual pages for library lists. A wide column allows for notes and recording of unusual activities. An unusual feature for families who don't always follow the typical school week is the list of initials along the column for each day so we can customize our school week. We simply fill in the circle of the appropriate initial each day. *The Homeschooler's High School Journal* [$9.95] from the same publisher, uses a very similar format, adding charts for tracking hours, a chart for recording credits earned, and pages to record the use of educational supplements such as real books.

The pages of a lesson plan book or organizer should actually become our records of work accomplished, which then saves the effort of duplicate recording (except the recording of grades onto a transcript).

Family Academy has designed a planning/record keeping book for high school called *High School Your Way* [$10]. It is intended for students who are taking charge of their own learning, and especially for those working with Family Academy's two-volume *Homeschooling the High Schooler* [$15 each or $25 for a single-volume that contains both books]. A student works with an advisor setting goals and planning course objectives. The student and advisor then sign a contract. Periodic evaluations help keep the student on target. Quite a few of these charts are included in the book along with daily lesson plan pages that can be used for recording what actually is accomplished each day. Step-by-step instructions guide both student and advisor as they use this book. Family Academy's books are comb bound, which means we cannot add pages, but if we have more than one child, it is much easier to maintain records within one book. To enable us to do this, Family Academy offers supplements which include extra goal pages, envelope, and album page ($.75 per supplement). If we order a supplement with the book, they will bind the supplement pages into the comb binding.

Also targeted at junior and senior high students is the *T.I.P.S. (Taking Initiative to be a Prepared Student) Planner* by Katherine S. Koonce (Common Sense Press) [$18]. The bulk of the book consists of spaces for students to write down "to-do's" for each day. There should be enough space for student assignments

here, although it is less than you would have in a typical plan book and there are no subject subdivisions. Helpful extras direct students to do some self assessment. Month-at-a-glance calendars, and reference helps (punctuation basics, editing marks, periodic table, a chart of the Dewey Decimal System, and a few other such things) are at the back of the book. This book will work for students in home schools or traditional schools.

T.I.P.S. Planner for Teachers, also by Katherine Koonce (Common Sense Press) [$18] can be used as a companion to the student version, but it works very well on its own for homeschooling parents. It is similar to your basic teacher planner, but it features Six-Week Check-Ups that help us take stock at regular intervals. It also features great attendance record forms divided into four quarters—nice for those who need to turn these in quarterly. It includes some of the same extras we find in the student book plus four pages each for Individual Academic Profiles and Field Trip Notes.

Cary Gibson (Cary Gibson's Curriculum and Counseling Services) publishes the *Complete Homeschool Planner* [Master Pack - $15; complete with binder - $25] as a Master Pack of forms (one of each) for us to copy as needed. While it is particularly suitable for home educators in California, those in other states will probably find it equally useful. Forms included are Purpose of Homeschooling, School Year Calendar (year-at-a-glance without dates), Monthly Calendar, Weekly Lessons, Monthly Progress, Goals, Attendance, Faculty Qualifications (CA requirement), Course of Study, Quarterly Progress Report, Grades, Field Trip Record, Lending/Borrowing Record, Reading Book List, Student Assignments, Student Weekly Record, Repeating Schedule, Scripture Memory Record, and High School Planning Record.. We can purchase these forms either as the Master Pack only or as a complete set with a binder, tabs, and a copy of the World Book *Typical Course of Study*. This is an excellent assortment of forms that will suit most families.

A basic teacher's plan book will suffice for most people, but more extensive organizers are available which help with organizing both home and school. Although organizers are not essential, many home educators have found them very helpful for getting started with record keeping and then also for keeping track of family and school activities that are strongly interrelated.

Noble Publishing Associate's *Home School Organizer* [$34.95] includes most planning and record keeping pages that we might need for our home school. The pages that most families use are preprinted, and there are reproducible master pages for more specialized forms. *The Noble Planner* (also from Noble Publishing Associates) deals more directly with time management by balancing the demands of work, family, hospitality, and household organization in an 8 1/2" by 5 1/2" format. This planner is more like a *Day Runner* organizer, focusing more on other activities than school itself.

Cherry Patterson's personal organizer called the *Personal Touch Planner* (Personal Touch Planners) is also more like a *Day Runner* than a typical teacher's planning book. It is specially designed to meet the organizational needs of Christian mothers at home. (Others certainly can use it by selecting the forms that meet their needs.) It covers just about every area of life most

Lesson Plan for BJUP's *Earth Science*

Day	Assignment Date	Assignment
1		– SEE PAGE TE10 TO DISCUSS NOTEBOOK REQUIREMENTS FOR GRADING. – Read p. 2-5 – Section Review Questions 1A-1 – Begin making flashcards for Terms on p. 24
2		– Discuss What Do You Think #1 on p. 24 – Read p. 5-13 – Section Review Questions 1A-2
3		– Discuss WDYT #2 – Ideas 1A – Read p. 13-16 – Section Review 1B-1 – Study for short quiz on the geocentric and heliocentric theories
4		– Quiz – Discuss WDYT #3 – Read p. 17-23 – Section Review 1B-2 – Ideas 1B
5		– Discuss WDYT #4 – Ideas 1C – Investigation 1C
6		– Review for Chapter 1 Test

The following lesson plans are for an American literature course using A *Beka's Beginnings of American* Literature plus numerous required writing assignments.

Day	Assignment Date	Pages	Activities	Done
1		Chapter 1: 2-5	Beginnings of American Literature. Read "Enjoying Poetry" and "Enjoying Art" on p. 23.	
2		6-9	Write an extended definition of what you think an American is.	
3		10-13	Write an essay describing America as you see it.	
4		14-17	What is the central thought of Daniel Webster's "Liberty and Union"?	
5		18-21	Write a patriotic poem or speech.	

Lesson plans for courses such as a Saxon Math text might be as simple as the following:

Day	Assignment Date	Advanced Math Assignments	Grade
1		Review Lesson A	
2		Review Lesson B	
3		Review Lesson C	
4		Review Lesson D	
5		Test 1	
6		Review Lesson E	
7		Review Lesson F	
8		Test 2	
9		Lesson 1	
10		Lesson 2	
11		Lesson 3	
12		Lesson 4	

moms encounter. We find here the "standard" forms for weekly, monthly, and yearly planning; "to-do" sheets; address lists; library loans; resource lists; curriculum shopping comparison. and goal planning. But it includes much more with forms for family information; medical permission; health records; checklists for picnics, beach trips, camping, or travel; correspondence records; gift ideas; comparison shopping; menu planning; grocery lists; family spiritual growth; quiet time; prayer requests and more. The complete binder includes either single or multiple copies of all 39 forms, a movable plastic marker to easily locate "today," and a plastic zip pouch with a few note and recipe cards, and hole reinforcers. The lightweight binder itself is padded, washable vinyl, but washable cloth covers are also available at extra cost. Packets of complete binder refills or masters for all forms are sold separately, although we are given permission to reproduce all forms in the master package for our own use. We can even purchase individual form masters if we wish. Customization can occur on several levels: we can purchase the complete binder, then select only those forms we intend to use and organize them in whatever manner suits our needs. We can purchase specialized forms (standard 8 1/2" x 5 1/2" three-hole punch) to use with other planners. We can select a cloth cover for a different look. Its compact-size makes this planner small and light enough to carry everywhere, while still functioning as far more than an ordinary calendar. This is a very efficient way to carry information for the mom-on-the go. [Prices: Deluxe package (binder, dividers, pages, masters, plastic accessories/cards) - $58; filler package with multiple copies of forms - $20; masters (one copy of each form) - $20; cloth covers -$20.] Personal Touch also has a new *Kids Planner* designed by Cherry Patterson's daughter, Cami [$17.50]. [Diane Eastman/C.D.]

Home School Helper (K.T. Productions) [$25] is yet another binder-organizer. This one has forms for attendance, weekly planning, quarterly test grades, yearly overview, yearly curriculum, report cards, field trips, weekly jobs, rotating menus, books read, books/videos lent, and health records, plus dividers, a section for us to insert support group calendar and mailing list, and large envelopes labeled for awards/certificates, art work, and unit study projects (possibly pictures of projects rather than projects themselves). There are six of each form, so the weekly planner is likely to be the only one we will need to copy for a long time. *Home School Helper* lacks the professional typography and graphics of some of the others, but it does have a unique combination of forms. The publisher also offers separate packets containing one of each form if we choose to photocopy our own [$11.85], or individual forms [$1 each] if we prefer to purchase extras.

The *Time Minder File-a-Plan* (Holly Hall Publications/Homeschool Press) [tentative retail price $24.95] is a unique solution to planning and record keeping which was developed by Marilyn Rockett, author of the original *Time Minder* record keeping system. Based on years of experience and research, Marilyn has come up with a colorful file system that includes pre-printed file divider cards and reproducible forms, plus extras for personal customizing. Sections are reserved for course of study, curriculum planning, evaluations, attendance, field trips, goals, lesson plans, library lending, medical/health records, sample work, projects, scheduling, transcripts, career/work planning, household plans, and more. Extra stickers allow us to designate categories of our own, and we can add any other forms we wish. An Easy Guide Index and a manual come with the system, explaining how to organize and keep our records to an efficient minimum. Numerous reproducible master forms fit within the different categories. This system puts it all together in one place—instructions on how to organize, a filing system that makes it happen, and the forms to make it easy.

School Forms for Home and Classroom (Sycamore Tree) has fewer forms, but they are more specialized and might be a useful supplement even to the large organizers. They include reproducible forms for school entry medical examination, curriculum listing, weekly lesson plans, weekly schedule, attendance chart, grade sheet, report cards, work contracts, and achievement and completion certificates. Their separate *Assignment Sheets For Home And School* has twelve different monthly, weekly, and daily assignment forms including charts for chores, extracurricular activities, and practical arts.

Because we sometimes find ourselves using only a few of the forms in the large organizers, it might be more practical to use reproducible masters for those forms, copying them as needed. Of course, this depends upon easy access to reasonably-priced photocopying or it becomes impractical. One other drawback to copying forms ourselves is that low-priced copying generally limits us to copying on one side of each page. Then we end up with twice as much paper as we might have had in the organizer to begin with.

Schools maintain cumulative records (also called cum files) for each student. This form, usually printed on heavy card stock, is used for recording yearly grades, attendance totals, standardized test scores, and other such information that might be passed on if a student enters another school. Bob Jones University Press sells such a form, called *Academic Record*, either individually [$1.95] or in packages of 25 [$6.95]. Shekinah Curriculum Cellar lists a cumulative file with medical form, sold individually [$2], and Sycamore Tree sells single copies of the *Christian Cumulative Record* [$1.95]. A more comprehensive cumulative record can be maintained in *Home Academy Record Book* (Fine Line Publishing) [$5.95]. This comb-bound book can hold records for 1 student for 5 years, 2 students for 2 years, or 3 to 5 students for 1 year. It includes pages for recording attendance and hours, daily grades, report cards, quarterly student profile reports, medical records, school expenses, home school telephone numbers and addresses. Forms are high quality, the kind that look impressive to school personnel.

For More Detailed Help

There are a number of resources I know of that will provide more specialized, detailed help for high school, although each is valuable in different situations.

○ **Homeschooling the High Schooler, Volumes 1 and 2** by
Diana McAlister and Candice Oneschak (Family Academy)
Vol. 1 - $15; Vol. 2 - $ 15; both volumes - $25

While these two books complement each other, they can be used separately. The first volume addresses goal setting, covering the various factors that help form a plan as well as the nuts and bolts of completing high school requirements and getting into college. Extensive information on Advanced Placement, SAT, and ACT tests is very helpful. The highlight of this book is the idea of contracts between home schooling teens and their parents or teachers. McAlister and Oneschak deal with both traditional and nontraditional approaches to completing course requirements, demonstrating with numerous examples how courses can be constructed and completed. This is great for the parent or teen who wants to break free from textbook dependency, but wonders how to put together a course of their own and document it.

Volume 2 helps us construct our own courses using our choice of traditional or nontraditional resources. Extensive chapters on English, math, science, and social studies outline the minimum core of topics to be covered through the high school years, then expand under the headings "Non-Core Electives" and "College Prep. Electives" to show what other course requirements will be necessary or optional depending upon the goal. For each area, they describe and provide addresses for a variety of resources that we might use. Fine arts, foreign languages, health, physical education, and occupational education get briefer attention at the end of the book.

A third book from the same authors and publisher is *High School Your Way* [$10]. This is a record keeping book with contract pages and lesson plan pages, which is described earlier in this chapter. It works best with the two volumes described above, especially if we choose to create course contracts.

○ **Senior High: A Home-Designed Form+U+la (second
edition)** by Barbara Shelton (Homeschool Seminars and
Publications) $24.95

Barb Shelton has been assisting home educators for many years through her writing and seminars. Her animated personality is obvious in her writing style. We can just hear her exclaiming, emphasizing, and joking as we read through her material. *Senior High* is fun to read, but it is a lot more than that. It is a manual full of "stuff" to read, "stuff" to use, and "stuff" that will help you make it through those intimidating high school years. The book is divided into eight sections: Reinforcement for the Fainthearted, Requirements for Graduation and Promotion, Record-Keeping System, Potpourri of Curriculum Supplements, Grading Guidelines and Portfolios, Personalizing All This Stuff, Lifestyle of Learning Applications, and Resource Section. The "how to" receives much attention while curriculum recommendations are minimal yet sufficient to get us started in most subjects. Barb provides a smorgasbord of convenient charts for record keeping (including charts for logging hours) to use as is, or to use as springboards for our own ideas. About one-fourth of the book is the "Potpourri" section, where Barb shares practical teaching, learning, and motivation tips plus helpful forms.

Among the many gems in this book are assignment check-off sheets for numerous courses that give us great ideas for structuring our own courses.

Barb walks us through all of this in great detail, without slipping into school-at-home mentality. This manual shows how to take the sum total of all the student's learning experiences—via books and real life—and not only get the most educational value out of them, but also document them and translate them into a form and language to which the academic segments of our society can relate. She does express her particular philosophy of education, all the while steering us gently throughout the book toward seeking God's direction for each of our children. If you need help figuring out and recording hours, working with formal as well as nontraditional grading systems, creating a sharp-looking transcript and diploma, or meeting requirements in real-life ways, you need this book.

○ **The High School Handbook [6th Edition]** by Mary
Schofield (Christian Home Educators Press) $19.97

This expanded sixth edition of Mary's book is useful for anyone educating teens. For those living in California, there is also a valuable companion "California Supplement" with details about driver's education/training, work permits, community and California State college/university admission, and other state requirements. Mary covers some of the general information that also appears in my book, but she does an exceptional job on how to put together courses, write course descriptions, and assign credits. She doesn't stick with only the basic academic courses, but also covers alternative and elective courses such as auto mechanics, Christian missions, and animal husbandry. She provides plenty of reproducible forms with examples plus straightforward explanations without a lot of editorializing. The sample course outline forms are intended to serve as examples for us to create our own. While in this *Curriculum Manual* I concentrate on why we make various choices and review the possible options, Mary concentrates more on the practical end of how we actually do it.

Contracts

Contracts help clarify educational goals and standards for the benefit of both parent/teacher and student. They can also be a motivational tool.

In a contract, course requirements are spelled out (in as much detail as you need). You can set contracts up as pass/fail or graded courses, although colleges prefer graded courses so that the grade point average can be calculated. Standards can be specified for earning various grades, or the contract can be written for achieving a certain grade.

If a teen views a particular class as something just to get through and has no concern for earning an "A," then he might contract for a course that would deserve only a "B" or "C." Most of us would prefer that our teens aim for "straight A's," but, realistically, some will do only what they have to. (Make sure that your teen understands the importance of high grades for college entry and/or scholarships if he or she intends to go to college!)

Then teens either complete the contract and receive the specified credit or fail to complete the contract and do not receive credit. Parents and students work together to create a contract, agreeing in advance to the requirements and standards for completion of a course. Both parties sign the contract. (Contracts might also be created between a teacher other than mom and a student.)

Suggestions for creating contracts vary, sometimes reflecting the legal requirements within various states. Chart F at the back of this book shows what such a contract might look like. Family Academy's *Homeschooling the High Schooler, Volume 1* and Barbara Shelton's *Senior High: A Home-Designed Form+U+la* both offer instructions and examples for contracts.

Your contract might be very similar to the Course of Study as shown in the examples in this chapter. However, it would be wise to spell out requirements in more detail so that students know exactly what will be expected of them, including the specific points upon which they will be evaluated.

Many parents are concerned about their ability to educate their teens, because their teens do not listen or respond well to them. While this is a problem that needs addressing, it might not be solved immediately. In the meantime, I have recommended to numerous parents that they work with contracts, so that the contract becomes the intermediary and enforcer rather than the parent.

Unit Values or Credits

If we choose a nontraditional course of study, applying unit values or credits is tricky when the overall course content is not similar to what is being done by other schools. Still, whether we choose to use nontraditional or traditional courses, assigning unit values makes things look professional. If a course is too unusual, it is sometimes better to add an addendum to the transcript or create a portfolio explaining the course than to attempt to make it look like typical courses.

An addendum describes the course in some detail, as well as course standards, so that someone could easily ascertain the scope and quality of the course. (Information from a full-page course of study description might be sufficient.)

A portfolio is more involved. For example, if a teen studied veterinary care and medicine to fulfill the life science requirement, the portfolio might contain a record of books read, written reports, the student's written description of work with a veterinarian, photographs of the student working with animals, and a letter of confirmation from the veterinarian.

Unit or credit values are given to completed courses and vary from state to state. The number of credits assigned is not affected by the grade earned by the student. California high schools gen-erally assign five units to each semester class. Thus a full year math course would have a value of ten units. However, many states and most colleges assign units differently. Most common in high schools is one unit or credit per year-long course. A one semester course would have a value of one-half unit. Colleges and universities will often look at the total unit value of classes which meet basic requirements, such as math, language, science, and history. For example, the Bob Jones University *Bulletin* reads: "Applicants should have received a high school certificate and have at least 16-18 acceptable units of secondary work. (A unit is defined as five 45-minute periods each week for 36 weeks.)" (1988-89 *Bulletin,* Bob Jones University, p. 14.)

Some home schoolers keep track of hours for courses, either because they are required to or because they wish to. However, we encounter difficulties when we try to equate hours of home schooling with classroom schooling, since the time is used so differently. In classrooms, a tremendous amount of time is wasted on school business, classroom control/discipline, repetition for students who need extra attention, passing out and collecting papers, and other non-learning type activity. On the other hand, most schools assign homework outside the classroom hours. Of that total number of hours, it is likely that a significant number are spent daydreaming, fidgeting, or otherwise tuning out what is going on. Trying to figure out how many of those hours would be equivalent to home study that is dedicated to learning is almost impossible. Consequently, if you are not required to keep track of hours, I recommend setting goals of what is to be accomplished and/or learned rather than measuring hours spent. A "goal orientation" also motivates students to accomplish goals rather than "serve time." We can assign unit values to courses whether we count hours or meet goals.

If we list classes completed on a transcript, colleges are likely to infer unit values even if we do not provide that information. If we are going to bother creating a transcript, we might as well complete it thoroughly and assign unit values.[2]

Meeting Requirements

Junior high students do not usually need documentation of their educational history, although I hear of occasional exceptions. Some junior highs are assigning unit values to classes and creating transcripts just as for high school. Some private schools request transcripts of junior high work. If you have a transcript (list of classes and grades) for elementary and junior high work, that is fine, but if not, do not worry. Public high schools will generally accept freshman students without transcripts, although they might require testing. Many private high schools require en-

---

2   College units differ from high school units. A college unit, also known as a semester or Carnegie unit, is 15 hours in class. However, an hour means 50 minutes. A semester unit is worth more than a quarter unit. Quarter units are converted to semester units by multiplying the number of quarter units by 2/3. In reverse, semester units are converted to quarter units by multiplying the number of semester units by 3/2.

trance examinations, and they can determine a student's eligibility based upon these test scores alone.

Most of us worry about requirements for high school graduation. Actually, students can "graduate" in a number of ways. We can use GED testing, junior college class completion and other means than the traditional transcript/diploma route. Our primary concern should be for what our son or daughter needs to go on to the next step for college or career, since that might well dictate how we choose to "graduate" him or her from high school.

I realize that some parents are preparing their daughters to be wives and mothers, so they are placing less stress on academics. However, in such cases, those daughters are likely to home educate their own children, so they must be equipped educationally to teach their own sons and daughters.

It is very difficult to envision a situation where we should not be aiming for academic breadth and excellence. As I discussed earlier, unless there is an obvious reason for students not to go to college, we should plan as if we are preparing them for college entry. We need not follow a traditional approach for college preparation, but many of us will choose to do so. Included at the back of the book are Planning Charts D and E for both college bound and non-college bound students, designed for those who prefer following traditional guidelines.

Requirements for college and university entry have been tightening up over the past few years. After the academic laxity of the '60s and '70s produced a generation of college graduates sorely lacking in basic skills, college administrators have resurrected academic guidelines from earlier years. The most obvious of these is the foreign language requirement—two years of the same language and sometimes three. For many years, either one year of foreign language or one year of fine arts had been required by California universities. As I mentioned earlier in discussing a college preparatory course of study, the University of California system is the front runner in the return to more stringent requirements with the "A through F requirements" that were phased in through the early 1990s.

These requirements are typical of what students find at the better universities. However, there are extreme variations in the academic requirements of institutions of higher learning. They range from some Bible colleges who ask for nothing more than a signed statement of faith to schools such as Massachusetts Institute of Technology that have very stringent requirements.

If there is a particular college or university that your child has set his sights upon, it is vital that you check out that institution's requirements as your child begins high school, not during the junior or senior year of high school. If the goal is college, but the choices are many, there is more leeway in meeting preparatory requirements. However, we must also recognize that certain career goals in themselves influence preparatory requirements. If a student plans to be an engineer, he will be required to take many math classes in college. He must have foundational classes completed before college or he will not be able to complete all the required college classes within the typical four years. An extra semester or two of college might be a costly way to make up for poor high school planning. This situation holds true particularly for scientific fields.

Often we cannot predict the future direction for our teens, and it is difficult to decide when they are fourteen or fifteen whether or not they will be "college material." In Chapter Seven, I discuss alternatives to the traditional four-year, on-campus pursuit of degrees. As long as we are open to alternative methods for obtaining a college education or other avenues for career preparation, we actually have a great deal of flexibility in determining the high school course of study.

While college preparation should be a primary concern if our teens are college-bound, we might also need to be concerned about state requirements for high school graduation. Some states require home schoolers to meet the same requirements for graduation as public school students. For instance, students in California are required to study economics for one semester, although there is no effective enforcement of this for private schools. Other states require the study of state history. Also, some students will be working under independent study or school service programs which will set their own requirements for students, incorporating extras such as Bible courses.

If we are the one providing the high school diploma or other evidence of completion, it might be up to us to determine if requirements have been fulfilled. In practice, we only become answerable for credits we have granted our child for high school course work when our child applies to a college. If we say that they have taken a particular course, implying competency in that area, we will lose credibility when our child is unable to pass a basic placement examination in that subject.

If our child has acquired equivalent knowledge by creative learning alternatives, we should not be afraid to list it as a completed course, but we must be wary of presenting a false picture of his academic history.

Do not panic because of the courses we are discussing for college preparation. Many of us will not be able to teach all of these subjects at home. Do not lower your sights because of your inadequacies. There are many alternatives available for covering subjects we are unable to teach ourselves as we will discuss later. There are also many colleges and universities who will be more concerned with the student's academic potential than with his educational history. The less rigid a student is about which college he wants to attend and how quickly he wants to get through, the more possible solutions there will be for getting into college.

Students who do not plan to go on to college need not be overly concerned about meeting requirements other than those needed to "graduate" from high school. That might mean learning what is needed to pass the GED test, meeting requirements of a correspondence course or independent study program, or meeting particular requirements imposed by our state.

Testing for High School Completion

The GED is always an alternative for high school completion, although minimum age restrictions make it impractical in some states. Even if we are able to graduate our own son or daughter, some of us are more comfortable with outside affirmation of successful completion of high school through the General Educational Development (GED) or, in California, the Proficiency Examination. These are tests administered by the State. A certificate awarded for passing either test is, by law, equivalent to a high school diploma. (Note: GED scoring minimums have been raised slightly beginning January 1997. To pass, test takers must now score a minimum of 40 out of 100 points on each section plus an average score of 45.)

Minimum ages for taking the tests apply in different states. In all but California, only one test, the GED, is offered. Usually a minimum age is set with no maximum age. The minimum age established by the General Educational Development Testing Service is sixteen. However, some states have set the minimum age for testing within those states at older levels, with some allowing no testing option for early graduation from high school before ages eighteen or nineteen. There are also special qualifications in many states. Some states allow testing before the state's specified age, yet will not grant a certificate until the graduation date if the student had progressed with his class!

This situation is a real hindrance to home educators in some states since many of our teens complete high school requirements much earlier than their age mates. Students who wish to go on to college appear to have fewer problems in these situations, since there are several ways of continuing higher education without formal recognition of high school graduation. Some junior colleges will allow students to begin college courses without the GED certificate, but will withhold college credits until they receive a copy of the GED certificate.

While college students might be able to continue their studies before they "graduate" from high school, those who want to enter a career or business field might be refused the right to take the GED test to demonstrate their proficiency in high school subjects until they are eighteen, sometimes blocking them from pursuing jobs and careers. However, some states make exceptions on GED age requirements if an employer requests that a prospective employee be allowed to take the test.

From reading the requirements and exceptions for each state, it seems that exceptions are most commonly made for those entering the military, those who are pregnant, or those in penal institutions! There are a few other possibilities for exceptions, but early graduation is strongly discouraged by GED age requirements in most states. (This situation is an interesting contrast to most European countries which graduate their young people at age sixteen.)

Information about GED requirements might be found in the educational codes of your state (at the library) or write to GED Testing Service.

Whether or not the local Department of Education looks favorably upon home education has nothing to do with a person's right to take these tests as long as he or she is of legal age and follows proper procedures. When special permission is required from local superintendents, it might be a different matter. Check with your local Department of Education or high school for information pamphlets about these tests. (In California, booklets on the tests are available at most public libraries.)

The GED includes five tested areas: math, writing skills, social studies, science, and interpretation of literature and the arts. The math test covers arithmetic (50%), algebra (30%), and geometry (20%). However, knowing how to apply basic mathematical processes is more important than having in-depth knowledge of algebra and geometry. The writing skills test is in two sections: part one covers sentence structure, usage, and mechanics with multiple choice questions; part two requires applicants to write an essay.

Social studies, science, and literature/arts tests do not rely on particular knowledge from these subject areas, but on the ability to analyze and apply information provided from these subject areas on the test, abstract reasoning and problem solving, and general reading comprehension.

GED test preparation helps are available from many sources. Steck-Vaughn publishes both *Steck-Vaughn Complete GED Preparation* (order #9893X) [$10.98] and a six-book GED preparation series, *Steck-Vaughn GED* that concentrates more fully on each area of the GED test. (The six area books are on writing - #73619, essays - #73627, science - #73651, social studies - #7366x, math - #73643, and literature and the arts - #73635 [$11.93 each].) There are also companion exercise books for all six books.

Barron's publishes *GED - General Examination* [$14.95] as well as the similar *GED - Canadian Edition* [$18.95 Canadian]. Look for similar titles in the library.

Remedial students wanting to study for the GED should check out the catalog from Contemporary Books, Inc. Contemporary offers GED preparation resources for the complete test or for specific test areas. Their materials are written for older learners or ESL students who have poor educational backgrounds and/or learning difficulties.

The GED tests used in all states are written by the same people to the same specifications, so the test is essentially the same across the country, although there are alternate forms. Each state then sets its own standards on passing scores and age requirements.

Whether students graduate with a transcript or by taking GED or Proficiency tests might or might not matter to colleges or universities. Remember that colleges are seeking bright, capable students, and they might interpret a GED certificate earner as being a low caliber student. At junior or community colleges, which are easy to get into, it probably makes no difference whether students come with a traditional transcript and diploma or a GED certificate. However, with the GED schools are still likely to request transcripts of work completed in high school, even if incomplete. (At junior college, students must make up missing college prep requirements before going on to four-year colleges.) More selective schools will look twice at GED certificates. Here it is important that SAT or ACT test scores paint a positive picture, and that the reasons for obtaining the GED certificate be fully explained. Sometimes it is possible (and advisable) to rely only upon the SAT or ACT test score and skip the GED.

Some employers also look askance at GED certificates because they know it is the method high school dropouts use to go back and graduate from high school. They often view it as evidence of a second class education. If a student graduated early from high school, and used the GED as the means to do so, that should be explained to employers, letting them know the student was ahead of schedule in his studies rather than a dropout who took the GED only to graduate. Your teen should let the skeptical employer know that he is getting an eager, bright employee who will be an asset to his business.

For any of these tests mentioned, we need to plan ahead. Tests are administered a limited number of times a year in various locations. Students need to apply well in advance of the testing date to take the tests. They cannot decide to take a test "next week." Check at least six months ahead for dates and locations. Public libraries are a good source for information on schedules and applications.

Grading

To Grade or Not To Grade?

Before high school, grading might be optional unless you work under legal requirements, a correspondence school, umbrella program, or other "system" that requires grading. Ideally, we should set our own goals for each of our children, perhaps referring to a published Scope and Sequence for an idea of what others consider appropriate goals for each subject and grade level. Oftentimes, we will have additional goals that deal with character issues, career possibilities, learning skills, hobbies, or world view education. We should clearly identify our goals, then have some sort of check-off or record-keeping system that helps us record our progress toward these goals rather than focusing upon grades earned for a class.

Teresa Moon's book, *How Do You Know They Know What They Know?* (Grove Publishing) [$14.95], is one of the most thorough resources available for helping us through some of these steps. She shows us how to diagnose what our students already know, figure out what they need to learn, make a plan for accomplishing our goals, and evaluate progress and accomplishments. Teresa presents a number of options for each of these steps, with instructions, sample forms, and examples. Reproducible forms are included in the appendix. While some forms are specific to earlier grade levels, many, such as the public speaking evaluation, junior and senior high writing assignments, essay format, and writing critique are ideal for upper grades.

Robin Scarlata's *What Your Child Needs To Know When* (Family Christian Press) ($19.95) includes checklists and progress forms covering typical requirements for math, language arts, science, and social studies for up through eighth grade as well as character training. The latest edition of this book also deals extensively with goal setting and purpose.

At high school level, grades become much more important. If you want to create something at least close to a traditional transcript, grades are a must. However, it is possible to prepare a portfolio with student samples along with documentation of other kinds about what a student has accomplished through the high school years, without including grades. Check with potential colleges, the armed services, or wherever else your student might consider going after high school for their policy in regard to grades or alternative methods of evaluation and documentation. (Teresa Moon's book, *How Do You Know They Know What They Know?* (Grove Publishing) [$14.95] provides instructions for portfolios and other alternative methods of evaluation.)

If You Choose to Grade...

Grades can be determined either objectively or subjectively. Objective grading means there are certain standards against which we measure our student's performance. Students might earn a specified number of points per assignment or test, with points deducted for incorrect or incomplete work. They might receive a percentage grade reflecting numbers of right answers. Or they might receive letter grades for each assignment or test. Our personal interpretation or feelings have little to do with the such grades.

Subjective grading is the opposite. Grades are determined by our overall evaluation of the student's performance, rather than specific right and wrong answers. We have to use subjective grading for some subjects or assignments such as creative writing, sewing, woodworking, and art. Although there might be some objective criteria involved, most of the grade will be based on our overall impression of competence, skill, or accomplishment.

I have tried both types of grading (when we have used grades) and have come to the conclusion that subjective grading can be just as valid in the long run, while it requires much less record keeping. By the end of a semester or school year, I have a very good idea of how well my sons know different subjects. I can assign a grade based on an overall evaluation.

For some parents, subjective grades would be identical to those figured out objectively by recording scores or grades for lessons and tests. However, some parents have difficulty realistically assessing their teen's progress. Also, most parents lack the confidence and experience to grade subjectively, or they prefer to validate their grading system with an objective grading system. And, while subjective grading might be fine for junior high, it might not be for high school. Validation is very important for high school students applying to competitive colleges., and even some not-so-competitive colleges. Many colleges want to know your standards and methods for determining grades so that they can judge how valid they might be.

Another reason one might choose an objective grading system is so that the student knows what is expected and how adequately he is meeting the standard as he progresses through a course. If a student knows that he must score a 93% or higher on his next test to maintain an "A" in a course, or that an "A" essay includes five well-developed paragraphs with a strong introduction and conclusion and no more than one grammatical error, he has a very clear idea of how hard he must work.

Choose subjective or objective grading or a combination of the two depending upon a student's grade level, any educational or legal accountability requirements under which you work, and future college entry requirements.

Course Work

There are two aspects of grading to think about. The first is everyday grading of course work. The second is final course grades and transcript preparation.

I did not believe in using a grading system when our children were in elementary grades. If they did not complete an assignment properly, I returned it to them for correction or completion. My rationale was that in real life, if we do not do something correctly the first time, we must go back and fix it. We cannot leave things undone or done incorrectly. So if it took my children three tries to do schoolwork correctly, they did it three times. The end result was always an "A" paper. I saw no point in giving them straight "A's," so I assigned no grades during the year. However, at the end of the year, I did record a grade that reflected their overall mastery of the subject matter along with their attitude and effort.

I realized the pitfalls of this system after a number of years of home schooling. We had done no multiple choice work up until that time. Answers were mostly sentence writing, oral discussion, or mathematical answers that were either right or wrong. We began that year using a vocabulary workbook that featured multiple choice answers. The first assignments were turned in with several errors. We went over the assignments and reviewed how to use the dictionary to determine correct answers. One of my sons turned in the second assignment with almost 50% wrong. He obviously had not even bothered to look at the dictionary. His attitude had become, "If I don't guess right the first time, I'm down to only one out of three choices for my next try." I caught on to what had happened and immediately changed tactics. From then on, all assignments were graded the first time they were handed in. Then they were handed back for necessary corrections. The grade would not change, but the work would still be done correctly. This approach has worked with the subjects that lend themselves to objective grading.

Grading can be done daily, weekly, or at wider intervals—whatever best fits the type of work being done. Weekly grades should be the most that are necessary to determine an overall grade for course work. With daily grades, grade computation becomes cumbersome, and they are unlikely to provide a more accurate reflection of overall performance.

If we choose to use subjective grading methods, we should make evaluations throughout the semester rather than waiting till the end, so that we do not forget earlier performance levels. Doing well the last few weeks of a semester does not compensate for four months of lackadaisical work. At the same time, reduced effort in the last few weeks should not undermine three months or more worth of quality effort at the beginning of the semester.

Final Grades

When we assign grades, we have to be honest. If we give our child an "A" he should have done superior work, at a level of excellence that is significantly above average. A "B" means above average; the student has done more than just complete assignments. A "C" reflects student work that meets but does not exceed the requirements. A "D" should be given when the student does inadequate or below average work. An "F" indicates that the student fell significantly short of the requirements.

We cannot fall into the trap many schools have of inflating grades in an attempt to make the student, school, or teacher look better. High school grades are used to determine a student's grade point average. The grade point average is used in conjunction with SAT or ACT scores by colleges for admissions eligibility. Because colleges often doubt a parent's ability to objectively grade his or her own child, they are sometimes skeptical of home school grade point averages. However, if they do consider a homeschooler's grades, colleges are likely to ask what criteria were used for grading, or how work was objectively evaluated. Do not grade your child on what you know he could do if he just tried a little harder, but upon what he is actually doing. We are not being honest with him if we tell him he is doing well, when he is putting out a minimal effort.

We should have a plan for assigning grades prepared before school begins. For subjective grading, we must have some standards of accomplishment, even though we might not measure achievement numerically. For instance, our teen can be studying math independently, checking his own answers after each lesson, determining where he made errors, and seeking help as needed. We can check occasionally to see if he is making a significant number of errors, and check also to find out how well he is figuring out why errors occurred. Since he is essentially teaching himself, objective grading would be unfair since he may not be aware that he does not understand a concept until after he does the exercises. A student's ability to work independently and correct his own errors should be included in our evaluation. It certainly can be more difficult for us to assign grades in such learning situations, and subjective grading might be most practical, at least for daily work. We might use periodic tests to establish some objective grades, then combine those with the subjective grades.

Objective grading systems are set up before school starts. School teachers write out grading systems for the coming school year, showing the relative value of various assignments and how final grades will be determined. For example, semester examinations might each count for 25% of the final course grade (2 x 25% = 50%), while weekly quizzes are each worth 2% (25 quizzes x 2% = 50%). If everything were done perfectly the student would have 100%. Usually a point system is used. A possible course grading value system might be as follows:

⊃ Government and Economics

chapter reviews -	10 points each (18 reviews)	=180
chapter tests -	40 points each (8 tests)	=320
newspaper assignments -		
	5 points each (4 assignments)	= 20
semester tests -	40 points each (2 tests)	= 80

Total possible 600 points

Course grades are based upon the percentage of points earned out of the total possible. For example, if a student earned 450 points out of the 600 possible, his grade for the course would be determined by dividing 450 by 600, which would be .75 or

75%. (Equivalent to a low C on most grade scales.) If you need to provide grades halfway through the year, for the end of the first semester, use the number of points for assignments already completed rather than the total points for the entire year.

The most common grade equivalent scale seems to be the following:

93-100% =	A
85-92% =	B
75-84% =	C
70-74% =	D
Below 70% =	F

However, the following grade scale is becoming increasingly common:

90-100% =	A
80-89% =	B
70-79% =	C
60-69% =	D
Below 60% =	F

You can see why it is important to identify the grading scale used! Colleges seem to have no preferences regarding grading systems, but it is vital that you indicate what system is used on the transcript.

Some courses need to be graded by standards. For instance, a typing course might have a standard to be reached such as being able to type forty words per minute with no more than two errors. A grading system would be set up for standards above and below forty words per minute.

Recording Grades

Report cards are the standard reporting form for recording grades, although they were designed as a tool for reporting to parents more than anything else. Since we, the parents, record the grades in the first place, the only purpose for the report card then is to show the student or an outside party how well the student has performed. If necessary for such a purpose, report card forms are available from Bob Jones University Press (singly [$1.95] or in groups of 25 [$6.95]), Educational Support Foundation (personalized in sets of 10 with reproducible master for $12), and Sycamore Tree. Sycamore Tree sells sets of reproducible forms packaged as *School Forms for Home and Classroom* [$4.95]. Within this set are three different report cards for preschool-kindergarten, grades 1-8, and grades 9-12. The high school form includes a grading system key, space for quarterly and final grades, conduct and attendance grades, and comments. In addition there are forms for lesson plans, medical records, work contracts, completion certificates, curriculum planning, and scheduling.

A more useful form for long range record keeping is the cumulative record. The cumulative record might be a single form or papers kept in a file. When it is a single form, it is usually printed on heavy card stock and is used for recording yearly grades, attendance totals, standardized test scores, and other such information that might be passed on if a student enters another school. Usually there are spaces for recording data directly on the file. This is a permanent file from which we draw information for completing a transcript. Even if we create a transcript, we probably also need a cumulative file. The transcript is a more concise form that can be sent to colleges or others to show a student's high school history. The cumulative file will contain more extensive information. Bob Jones University Press sells such a cumulative file form, called Academic Record, either individually or in packages of 25. Shekinah Curriculum Cellar and Sycamore Tree both sell cumulative record forms individually.

Transcripts

A transcript is simply a list of classes taken, grades earned, and unit values. Final course grades are entered on a transcript form such as the one I have included at the back of the book (Chart C) or on a custom designed form such as the one in the *Personalized School Documents* line from Educational Support Foundation. Correspondence schools and independent study programs should provide transcripts for students who have completed high school work under their direction. Otherwise, it is up to us. (See "Creating Transcripts" in Chapter Seven.) A copy of the transcript is required for the admission process at most colleges and universities. The final grade point average should also be shown.

Grade points are determined as follows:

A = 4 points
B = 3 points
C = 2 points
D = 1 point

To determine the grade point average, total the grade points earned, then divide by the number of courses taken (not counting physical education.) For example:

Student <u>Jane Jones</u>

Subject	Grade	Grade Points
Algebra I	B	3
Geometry	A	4
Algebra II	A	4
English I	B	3
English II	C	2
English III	B	3
English IV	B	3
U.S. History	A	4
World History	A	4
Government	B	3
Biology	A	4
Physics	B	3
Spanish I	A	4
Spanish II	A	4
Music	B	3

Total 51

51 divided by 15 courses = 3.4 grade point average

Honors and Advanced Placement courses are valued at 5 grade points for an "A" and one additional grade point for each of the other letter grades.

For more help with transcripts, check out *Mentoring Your Teen* (Education PLUS+). A complete review appears in Chapter

Four. The section of *Mentoring Your Teen* dealing with transcripts, "How to keep records that will open doors of opportunity," is also available separately from the complete seminar for $12.

What About Diplomas?

What is a high school graduate? Is it someone with a fancy certificate or is it someone who has completed the standard requirements for high school completion? Sometimes we intimidate ourselves with questions such as, "How can my child graduate from high school without being enrolled in a regular school?" We must recognize that graduation is not the ceremony and recognition but the completion of certain requirements. If we are operating as a private school and are so recognized by the state, we are generally free to recognize such completion ourselves, just as any other school may do. The only exception, according to research from the National Center for Home Education, is Rhode Island, which will not allow anyone outside the recognized school system to issue diplomas. Students in that state can take the GED or work under an accredited program to surmount this difficulty if they truly need a diploma.

In some states, home educators are not allowed to call themselves private schools, and they might run into trouble if they issue their own diplomas. The safest alternative for those who want an acceptable diploma is to enroll the student in a correspondence course such as Pensacola or Christian Liberty Academy (or others listed under correspondence courses) that will issue a diploma upon completion of course work.

The technicalities of issuing a diploma are actually no big deal. The biggest problem I see is getting one of those nice certificates to fill out.

That has been solved by a number of sources. Alpha Omega sells blank diplomas. Berg Christian Enterprises has standard certificate forms that they can imprint with your school name[3] (When requesting information, tell them you are a home educator so they can send appropriate samples.) Home School Legal Defense Association offers an impressive diploma in a burgundy, *leatherette* case, embossed in gold with the "lamp of knowledge" [$20]. We fill in the information ourselves. Educa-

tional Support Foundation offers a personalized diploma, with all information typeset in calligraphic style [$12]. A padded presentation binder is optional. Fine Line Publishing sells an inexpensive, framed high school diploma for $6.95, to be filled in by parents.

In general, I think we are overly concerned about diplomas. After all, how often does anybody ask to see a diploma? Hardly anyone other than the military services ever does. (And the military services often want to see both transcript and diploma.) They instead ask what level of education has been completed by potential employees, students, etc. Unless a declared high school graduate is quite illiterate, I doubt that an employer would ever ask to see proof of graduation. Colleges rarely ask to see diplomas, but they do ask if students have graduated from high school and they do ask for transcripts. Even so, some home schoolers have been admitted to colleges without transcripts.

As we mentioned earlier when we discussed goals, we need to consider our son's or daughter's future goals in making decisions about graduation methods. If he or she is likely to pursue a career that will require four years of high school, documented by a credible transcript from a recognized school, think carefully before choosing home education. Enrollment in correspondence courses will serve in most cases to provide a credible transcript.

The Bottom Line

We do not have to do things as they have always been done in the past. Our transcript does not have to be exactly like one traditional schools would issue. The essential thing when making up our own transcripts and diplomas is to back them up with credible documentation and explanation.

Caps and Gowns?

After figuring out how to "graduate" your child, you might wish to celebrate in a more traditional way. For those who want to provide their graduate with a graduation celebration, a reasonable source for caps and gowns to rent or buy is Collegiate Cap and Gown Company. You can purchase one cap and gown set with no problems. Then create a diploma using one of the sources mentioned above, and the only thing missing is a mob of classmates to share the celebration. The missing "mob celebration" can be replaced by a "coming out" party with relatives and friends of all ages or other creative ideas.

3   Berg sells a variety of certificate forms, in either stock (no personalized imprint) or printed format. Personalized imprinting is expensive, so you might consider ordering a variety of their certificates for elementary and high school level, since the imprint cost per certificate, when all are printed with the same school name, drops dramatically.

Heading for College

"But, if I teach my teenager at home he won't be able to go to college!" This fear confronts many of us facing the decision whether or not to home educate our high schoolers. Actually, home educated students can and do go to college. Despite our fears, home schoolers have been accepted at hundreds of colleges and universities of all types. By and large, they have performed so successfully at college that some institutions are actively recruiting home schoolers. What many people expected to be a handicap in college entry is turning out to be a benefit.

Some of us are very concerned about keeping the proper records, creating an acceptable transcript, completing the set requirements, and so on. There is certainly comfort in knowing we are giving colleges the paper work they require in the form to which they are accustomed. While following the rules is more comfortable, it is not the only way to do things. The choice of whether to do things "according to the book" or not depends on where a student intends to go next as well as upon our level of confidence.

Some institutions are very particular about courses and requirements—this is more likely to be true of highly competitive universities and colleges and of state-run institutions. Since more and more home educated students are applying to competitive colleges, the need for detailed information about procedures, records, and requirements has become crucial. Since space is limited in this book, I felt it was necessary to have a separate book addressing "high-level" college preparation. Diane Eastman is in the process of writing that book (the title will probably be *Preparing for College: A Handbook for Homeschooling Parents*), and we will publish it as soon as it is available. That book will delve deeper into SAT I, SAT II, and ACT testing, NCAA requirements, Honors and Advance Placement courses, the application process, scholarships and financing.

While many institutions seem to be very particular about entry requirements, most seem to allow for a small percentage of applicants who are nontraditional. They are looking for the "unusual" student with promise—an apt description for many home schoolers.

If your son or daughter has his or her heart set upon one institution, it is always best to check out that institution's requirements (and its flexibility regarding those requirements) as early in the high school years as possible. If students are open to a number of options, even willing to go to junior or community college before going on to a four-year institution, they have much more freedom since it is almost always possible to find

somewhere that they will be accepted with even the most unusual educational history.

Also, if parents don't mind defending their course of study and methods to college authorities then they might be freer to choose more unusual methods and resources than the person who fears confrontations or challenges. It's always safer to educate a child in a manner that looks like "what everyone else is doing." But if parents lack confidence either in what they are doing or in defending it to others, then perhaps it would be best to stick with traditional ways of planning course work and keeping records.

The bottom line for most homeschoolers, is that most colleges rely heavily upon SAT I or ACT test scores while also requiring a transcript. A few require the GED or some other evidence of "graduation." However, as long as the SAT or ACT test scores are good, home educated students are generally being accepted wherever they apply. Competitive colleges often require SAT II test results in addition to the basic tests.

At present, what we find is a frequently-changing, wide range of expectations from colleges regarding home educated applicants. Hillsdale, a competitive, highly-regarded private college, provides a very brief list of requirements for home school applicants. They tell us:

> Students applying for admission to Hillsdale College who have been homeschooled must:
>
> **Submit the results of either the ACT or SAT.
>
> **Submit an official transcript from a homeschooling guild or association; or detailed course description, proficiency level, and textbooks used.
>
> **Submit a letter of academic recommendation from the primary educator. Other letters of recommendation are optional.
>
> **It is recommended that the student submit a list of extra-curricular activities. This could include any employment, philanthropic efforts, or other civic involvement. (1996 publication)

On the other extreme, we hear reports of colleges (most frequently state-run institutions) asking for very specific course requirements and submission of results from two or more tests. Some institutions are rejecting applicants who graduated from high school with a GED, and I have even heard that one university is refusing to accept any applicants from "independent study programs," even including homeschool programs run by the State Department of Education.

Our freedom to choose how to proceed might well depend also upon our son's or daughter's preferences. They might be so intent upon a particular goal, they are unwilling to take any risks

The Spiritual Dangers of College

Many of us struggle with the idea of sending our children off to college, where who knows what might happen, after we have invested so much time and energy to educate them in "the way they should go." It is a fact that many Christian young people lose their faith at college. I am certain this is much more often true at secular colleges, but it does happen even at Christian colleges.

So, do we keep our children at home until they get a job or get married? Some say, "That's not a bad idea." Those who feel this way should consider local opportunities and look at suggested resources for doing college at home.

Meanwhile, many of us are willing to let our children venture away to college, yet we still harbor concerns about their spiritual well-being.

My first suggestion is that you make sure that you have spent time with them studying world views (see Chapter Five), discussing challenging faith issues, and ensuring that their spiritual roots are deep.

My second suggestion is that you pray about where they should or should not go, and ask them to pray about this decision.

If you decide to let them attend college, encourage your teens to get in touch with Christian clubs on campus. Through such groups, they should be able to find support for maintaining their faith and information about which classes and teachers to choose or avoid.

If you decide to send your children to college, make sure they are "armed and ready."

---

in regard to documentation of their high school course work. We must be sensitive to their feelings since this is their future.

With those thoughts in mind, let us move on to discuss college selection, testing, transcript options, nontraditional alternatives for college, and financial aid.

College Selection and Admissions Processes

The first place to start is with one or more of the reference books/computer programs that help us identify colleges and universities that suit our needs—philosophical approach, location, majors available, size, cost, etc. Such resources help us come up with a list of possibilities. I also strongly recommend that you try to talk to people who have attended institutions in which you are interested; there is nothing like the insider's perspective.

Some of the most popular resources for college selection come from The College Board. *The College Handbook 1997* [$21.95] (updated yearly) is a directory to 3,300 two-and four-year colleges (public and private). It lists admission requirements, costs, financial aid, majors, student activities, enrollment

figures, and more. A guidance section helps with planning and provides checklists and work sheets.

The College Board has many other publications such as the *Index of Majors and Graduate Degrees* and *College Costs and Financial Aid Handbook*. *Index of Majors and Graduate Degrees* [$17] lists 600 fields of study showing which are offered at 2,900 colleges and universities. *College Costs* [$16.95] explains costs of various colleges and universities, how to apply for financial aid, specific data from more than 3,200 institutions, and state-by-state information on grants and student loans. *College Costs* also features an index of colleges that award scholarships in sports, academics, and the arts. The College Board offers a special package deal of $39 for *The College Handbook, Index of Majors and Graduate Degrees*, and *College Costs and Financial Aid Handbook*. *The College Explorer* computer software [$125] helps students match their needs with appropriate colleges. It contains the same type of information found in the *College Handbook*, but it does the searching for you.

America Online offers access to some College Board resources, including the complete text of *The College Handbook*. (This is really a great service, so use it to check out possible colleges.) In addition, you can communicate with other subscribers and with a College Board consultant online to ask your college-related questions.

Peterson's publishes many books which help with selecting a college and determining admission requirements. Some of their titles are: *Peterson's Four-Year Colleges 1998* [$24.95] and *Peterson's Two-Year Colleges 1998* [$21.95] (both books are updated each year); *Peterson's Competitive Colleges 1997-98* [$16.95]; six different regional guides to colleges for the Middle Atlantic States, Midwest, New England, New York, South, and West [$17.95 each]; and *Choose a Christian College* [$14.95].

Another very useful book for college admissions is *A Student's Guide to College Admissions: Everything Your Guidance Counselor Has No Time to Tell You*, by Harlow G. Unger (Facts on File) [paperback ISBN # 0-8160-3199-1 - $10.95; hardcover ISBN # 0-8160-3198-3 - $24.95]. Unger lays out step-by-step guidelines and adds advice based upon his experience. The guidelines are available elsewhere, but the advice alone is worth the cost of the book. Unger puts us inside the minds of admissions officers so we can understand what they are looking for and how they evaluate applications. Students who want to go to the most prestigious schools will find this book especially useful since Unger gives them special attention.

Of special interest to home educators is Cafi Cohen's book titled, *"And What About College?": How homeschooling leads to admissions to the best colleges and universities* (Holt Associates, Inc.) [$18.95]. Cohen begins by encouraging home educators with the good news about home schoolers' success both in college admissions and performance. She compares different homeschool approaches (traditional, unit studies, etc.); covers guidelines for college preparation, record keeping, and transcripts; then addresses college selection and the application process in detail. This book is full of how-to's, examples, contact addresses, and wise advice.

Since Christians are often looking for different things than non-Christians when selecting colleges, it is helpful to consult publications which share that Christian perspective. An excellent starting place is *The Summit Ministries Guide to Choosing a College* by Dr. Ronald Nash and Jeff Baldwin (Summit Ministries) [$9.95]. Nash and Baldwin consider the "college or not" question, supporting other choices such as apprenticeship and entrepreneurship. Assuming the choice is in favor of college, they then address selection, preparation, admissions process, and other basic issues. What sets this book apart is the stress placed on understanding world views and the role they play in college selection and attendance. The authors caution students against accepting colleges' claims of being Christian while they exhibit no commitment to any sort of orthodoxy. A substantial part of the book addresses contrary world views, including liberal theology and other "variations of Christianity" students will encounter at colleges. Although there are no recommended college lists in this book because problems can crop up or disappear quickly with the hiring or firing of only one or two professors, the authors occasionally name a few in examples of problems to guard against.

For more assistance in choosing a Christian source for higher education, *Choose a Christian College* (Peterson's) [$14.95] has information about eighty-four Christian colleges and universities belonging to the Christian College Coalition.

Clearly, all Christian colleges are not equivalent, and home educators are often far more particular than other Christians in college selection. They tend to ask even more challenging questions than are answered within most college selection guides. Those wondering what those questions might be, or those wrestling with the difficulty of finding a suitable college should read *The Quest for Authentic Higher Learning* (Canon Press) [$6]. This booklet actually consists of two essays by Douglas Wilson and Roy Atwood. The first essay, "Classical Learning and the Christian College," deals with the idea of a classical education, its relation to orthodox Christianity, and how poorly most Christian colleges address both. Whether or not you are a proponent of the classical approach, this is stimulating and valuable reading. The second essay, "A College Guide for Christian Families," shifts to a more practical-application level to address issues such as how to determine your calling and who has the final say (Atwood says the father should), as well as more common questions such as "Where should you live?", "Which colleges have the right degree programs and courses?", and so on. I highly recommend this booklet.

While it might not be possible for most of us to visit all of the colleges and universities in which we are interested, a great way to make personal contact is at college fairs. While they vary in size, college fairs typically will bring 20 to 100+ representatives of colleges to an exhibit hall where they will set up tables, hand out catalogs and/or brochures, talk about their admissions policies and special programs, and answer questions. Usually, such fairs include workshops on financial aid and other college-admission related topics. Some fairs feature only Christian colleges, while others are all inclusive. I have learned more about the "real" requirements at college fairs than from catalogs. Often, college representatives at fairs will explain to you the special procedures that they use for unusual applicants, special programs available for motivated students, or other appealing options that you are likely to miss in a catalog.

The best source for information about college fairs is the National Association for College Admissions Counseling. They can let you know when a college fair is due in your area. Typically, they occur in the springtime, but some take place in the fall.

Plan Ahead

You can run into problems with college admissions. To avoid problems check with potential colleges as early as possible, so course work can be planned to meet entrance requirements.

Find out not just their standard requirements, but how willing they are to deal with a student with an unusual educational history.

Many home educators choose to take a very different approach to education—following a child's interests rather than a typical program, skipping testing and grading or constructing educational programs vastly different from those of traditional schools. Some schools will be more willing to deal with this than others. If your teen has his heart set on a particular college, find out ahead of time if they will evaluate an unusual educational history with an open mind.

Some careers might require a traditional education. One family enrolled their student in a public high school, largely because their son wants to go to medical school. They think his chances of making it through the highly competitive enrollment process for medical school will improve if he has a traditional education and transcript. The situation right now is too unpredictable to know whether or not this is true.

Do not give up on home educating high schoolers just because people say they won't be able to get into college. It just is not true. As I mentioned previously, a number of colleges and universities are actively recruiting home educated students. Among those soliciting home educated students are Biola University, Bob Jones University, Boston University, Houston Baptist University, Oral Roberts University, and Western Baptist College. Biola has a nontraditional honors program that is very open to homeschoolers. Houston Baptist, Oral Roberts, and Bob Jones University offer pre-med programs seldom found on Christian college campuses. ORU offers pre-law, and both ORU and Houston Baptist offer double majors. Boston University offers more than 250 fields of major and minor concentration, plus "... the opportunity to seek cross-disciplinary studies that do not fall into conventional departmental divisions." Oral Roberts University offers a wide range of majors as well as the above-mentioned pre-med and pre-law and other pre-professional programs. They are also offering an automatic $1500 per year scholarship to any home educated student. And these are only a few examples of what is available.

Time Off Before College?

Before we plunge on, we need to stop and consider whether or not all teens should go directly from high school to college. Many of us are afraid to allow "time off" after high school, probably fearing that our sons or daughters will find other pursuits which will replace their educational ambitions. While this is possible, it can also be a waste of time, money, and energy for a student to attend college if he does not want to be there.

For some young people, it might be better to work for a while, spend some time exploring career possibilities by trying different jobs, or take some lightweight classes while working part-time. Another option might be a short-term mission experience or intensive spiritual training such as that offered through the Discipleship Training Schools of Youth With A Mission. A better understanding of God's purpose for their lives can help teens determine whether college is the way to get there, and if so, what they should study in college. A student who begins college with determination and goals is likely to make much better use of his opportunities than a reluctant student.

SAT I, SAT II, and ACT Tests for College

Most colleges and universities require either the SAT I (Scholastic Aptitude Test; see SAT Program for address and phone number) or ACT (ACT Assessment) for admission. The SAT I or ACT score is correlated with a student's grade point average (See Chapter 6 for information about determining grade point averages) to provide a ratio called the Eligibility Index which is then used to determine which students will be accepted. Following is a section of one Eligibility Index.[1] Note that with higher SAT[2] or ACT scores the grade point average needed is lower and vice versa.

Grade Point Average	ACT Score	SAT Score (combined)
3.29	12	570
3.20	17	840
3.10	22	1070
3.00	28	1270
2.90	33	1490
2.82	36	1600

In this index, students with G.P.A.'s below 2.82 probably need not bother applying.

Although some colleges prefer scores from one of the tests, both tests are widely accepted. A college's catalog indicates which test it prefers or requires for its applicants. When in doubt, take both tests. Applications for either test are available from high school or college counseling offices, and you do not need to show any identification or school affiliation evidence to obtain them.

Both the SAT I and the PSAT have been revised in recent years. New versions have lengthier reading passages with reading comprehension questions that stress critical thinking. They use "paired passages," reading selections representing contrasting viewpoints on a topic, followed by analytical questions. Vocabulary words are presented in context rather than in isolation. Sentence completions and analogies are retained, but antonyms have been dropped. Math questions still include multiple choice and quantitative comparisons, but additional problems require students to come up with their own answers which they enter on grids. Calculators are now allowed for the math sections.

SAT I is part of a broader SAT Program which also includes subject area tests, collectively called SAT II. SAT I, subtitled "Reasoning Test," covers both math and language skills, although it requires no actual composition. SAT II: Subject Tests are what were formerly called the Achievement Tests. These one-hour tests are offered in the areas of writing, literature, foreign languages, history, mathematics, sciences, and English as a second language. These, too, have been rewritten to better reflect current teaching methods and course content. For example, history tests have become more multicultural and less "European-based." SAT I is the basic test, and SAT II tests are required only as specified by the various colleges.

If we are not registered through a school, does that mean our child cannot get into college? Definitely not! It makes it a little easier to register for college entrance tests when we have a school ID number and a separate school address where results are to be sent, but the lack of either item is not a major problem.

Both the SAT and ACT testing offices say anyone can take their college entrance tests. No school affiliation is required although an identification card with a photograph is. (ID cards are also required for GED or Proficiency testing so you might need to obtain one for both purposes.) Driver's licenses will suffice. Or, ID cards can be made by the parent. Type information neatly on a wallet size card—school name, city and state, school year, e.g., 1997-98, student's name, student's signature. Take a picture in one of those cheap picture booths or get a passport photo if you do not have one of the appropriate size. Put it together neatly and get it laminated. If you do not want to make your own ID card,

---

1   This index is for University of California Santa Barbara, a moderately competitive institution. The Index for less competitive colleges is much more lenient. For example, the California State University will accept just about any score with GPAs 3.0 or higher. With a 2.0 GPA, scores of 30 on the ACT or 1300 on the SAT I are required. With a 2.5 GPA, scores of 20 on the ACT or 900 on the SAT I are required. More competitive colleges would move the other direction, requiring higher scores.

2   The mean (average) SAT score is 1016 for combined math and language scores according to the College Board online information available in August 1997.

they are available from the Department of Motor Vehicles in California and probably in other states. You need only present a certified copy of your birth certificate to get one, but allow a few months for the DMV or other government office to process it and mail the card to you.

SAT I and ACT tests are offered at various sites—usually high school or adult education campuses, and usually on Saturdays. The tests are given every few months, but students must apply to take the tests well in advance, so, again, planning is a must.

SAT II: Subject Tests are also required by some colleges, and the procedure for taking them is similar to that for SAT I and ACT tests. Subject tests are most commonly required for English, and quite frequently for math. Students entering a scientific or mathematical field at a university such as MIT or Cal Tech will certainly need to take subject tests in one or more areas of science.

The best way to obtain application forms for these tests is from a local public or private high school, a junior or community college, or the college which the student plans to attend. Otherwise, write to the SAT Program.

Test Preparation

I highly recommend that students prepare for tests by practicing on sample tests that are included in most test preparation books. The library usually has one or two books for SAT I preparation, and others are available from bookstores, directly from publishers, and from some home school sources. Some publishers and catalogs list numerous test preparation books. It might be wise to request one or more of these catalogs so that you know what is available. (You can also find some of their catalogs online.) Those with the most such resources are The College Board, Arco, Peterson's, and Barron's. (Barron's publishes preparation aids for the SAT I and ACT tests along with helps for the CLEP and Advanced Placement examinations.)

Numerous computer test preparation programs are available. For the most part they duplicate material available less expensively in book form, but if the computer provides the necessary incentive for a student to study well, then the extra expense is defensible.

There are definitely some strategies test takers can benefit from. Practicing test taking with sample tests available in many of the books and computer programs is probably the single most important thing to do. Learning the extra little tricks shared by some authors will also help, but it is easy to go overboard and spend too much time on test strategies.

Some of the books and computer programs available include:

For SAT I Preparation -

We have used a number of test preparation books over the years, and I have found that all of them we have used have errors. Keep this in mind as you correct practice tests, and be willing to consider challenges posed by your teens. My favorites thus far are *Princeton Review, Cracking the SAT & PSAT, 8 Real SATs*, and *SAT Preparation Course for the Christian Student*. I would

recommend a combination of all three for best results. However, you might have easy access to other test prep books, any of which should be adequate.

Note: While many resources use SAT in their name, SAT is a registered trademark of the College Entrance Examination Board which is not associated with any of these companies except the College Board.

➲ **Cliffs SAT Preparation Guide** (Cliffs Notes) $19.98

This book differs from most of the hefty test preparation books in its diminutive size. It claims to be concise, yet complete. It teaches strategy while also providing some basic information students should master to help improve their scores (e.g., lists of prefixes and suffixes, math formulas). There are two complete practice tests in the book with answer keys and explanations. There are also some helps for analyzing test results. This book is sold on its own but is also packaged with *Cliffs StudyWare for the SAT*, a computer program also from Cliffs Notes. The computer program is available for IBM, Apple II, and Macintosh machines. *Studyware* features questions and explanations for both correct and incorrect answers, four practice tests, and strategy helps. The beauty of such programs is that they help automatically diagnose areas of difficulty. The drawback is that students will not be taking the actual test on the computer, so the practice experience differs from the actual test. Using the practice tests in the companion book help overcome this problem.(S)

➲ **8 Real SATs** (The College Board) $16.95

This 578-page book includes 8 eight actual versions of the SAT I along with test preparation information. In my opinion, this is the best resource for test-taking practice.

➲ **Preparation for the SAT and PSAT** (Arco Books) $12.95; with software - $24.95

The 1997 edition includes full-length practice tests, explanations of answers, review helps, and test-taking strategies (ISBN 0028610709). *Preparation for the SAT and PSAT, 1997, with Study Planning Software* features the book and a CD-ROM for test preparation (ISBN: 0028610792).

➲ **14 Days to Higher SAT I Scores, Third Edition** (Barron's) $16.95

Students who are strong auditory learners will appreciate this method of test preparation. Two 90-minute audio tapes describe the SAT I, suggesting test-taking strategies. Along with the tapes comes a paperback book with mini-tests and one full-length test with answers.

➲ **How to Prepare for the SAT I, 19th Edition** (Barron's) $12.95

This is one of the standard works for test preparation. It packs a huge amount of information into 688 pages and also includes tear out pages with more than 200 vocabulary flash cards printed on heavy card stock. The book is divided into five parts: Get Acquainted with SAT I; Pinpoint Your Trouble Spots; Tactics, Strategies, Practice: Verbal and Math; Test Yourself; and Organize Your Admissions Game Plan. The second section includes a diagnostic test with answer key and self-evaluation tools. The third part helps students with test-taking tactics, practice exercises, long-range strategies to improve in knowledge areas, and almost 120 pages of basic words with their definitions and parts of speech. Eight model SAT I tests are included with answer keys and explanations of answers for each. The final section on admissions is rather brief in comparison to the whole book, but it has some of the best essay-writing tips I have seen.

○ Pass Key to SAT I, Second Edition (Barron's) $6.95

This is a compact version of *How to Prepare for the SAT I*. It includes two model tests, answers, and explanations.

○ Princeton Review: Cracking the SAT & PSAT, (Random House, Inc.) $18

I recommend this book, even if you also use something like *Real SATs*, because it not only teaches you how the test works, but it helps you get inside the test creators' minds and understand the design of the test and how to increase your chances of getting correct answers even when you don't know the answers for certain. This is valuable information that will certainly help students increase their test scores. Part One begins with basic principles of how the SAT works. Since the PSAT is an adaptation of the SAT, the same principles apply to both tests. Part Two addresses the verbal sections, Part Three the math sections. Both sections include strategies, explanations of how the test functions, and practice problems. Answers are in Part Six. Part Four is a brief section on what to actually do right before taking the SAT. Part Five is a vocabulary study section which students should begin months before their actual test date. Parts Seven and Eight are a practice diagnostic test and answers with explanations. An appendix deals with specifics of the PSAT, and the last section discusses the present and future of computerized versions of college tests. You should also purchase *8 Real SATs* for actual practice taking real tests. This review is of the 1996 edition. There are also 1997 and 1998 editions available which should not be significantly different.

Cracking the SAT & PSAT with Sample Tests on Computer Disk OR *on CD-ROM*, a book/computer disk or book/CD-ROM version offers computerized versions of practice tests that are computer scored and analyzed [$29.95 each].

○ SAT Cram Course (Arco Books) $8

At 144 pages, this one is a fraction of the size of most other prep books, but I guess that's the point of a cram course—there is less of it, so it goes faster.

○ SAT Math Review [videos] (Chalk Dust Co.) $125 for videos plus *8 Real SATs* book

Five, high-quality video tapes offer more than 10 hours of concentrated review and preparation for the math portion of the SAT I. Tapes are broken down under the headings "Arithmetic, Part 1," "Arithmetic, Part 2," "Algebra," "Geometry," and "Other Topics, Quantitative Comparisons, and Grid-Ins." However, students really should go through all of the tapes no matter

what their strengths and weaknesses since test-taking strategy tips are intermixed with review throughout the tapes. Host Dana Mosely reviews some basic concepts on topics such as fractions, decimals, algebraic operations, probability, percents, and geometry then shifts to sample problems in formats students are likely to encounter on the test. The review is not intended to substitute for skipped or failed courses but to serve as a refresher, thus the focus is primarily on practice in solving problems as they are likely to appear on the test. Mosely shares test-taking strategies, identifying clearly those strategies which might be different from the way a student would expect to tackle such problems in the classroom. He also spends significant time on two peculiar math sections of the SAT, "Quantitative Comparisons" and "Grid-In" answers to questions.

At the beginning of the tapes, Mosely tells us that he believes, as do many others, that the SAT is more a test of a student's SAT test taking skills than it is of mathematical skills. That is not to say that mathematical knowledge is irrelevant, but that knowing how the test works is bound to make a big difference in a student's score.

Students should practice taking sample tests to apply what they learn on these tapes so Chalk Dust includes a copy of the book *8 Real SATs* (published by The College Board). See the review of *8 Real SATs* in this section. Tapes are available only as a complete set.

○ SAT I Computer Study Program, Third Edition (Barron's) $24.95

Computer programs available for Macintosh, DOS, and Windows make studying for the SAT I much easier. There are four complete, model SAT I tests in the program. Students take the tests in either a learning or a testing mode. In learning mode, students are not timed and the program immediately lets them know if they answer incorrectly, giving them another chance. In testing mode, students are timed and the test is scored. Even better, incorrect answers are evaluated and grouped to highlight areas of difficulty for study. An instruction booklet is included.

○ SAT I IN-A-FLASH Flash Cards (IN-A-FLASH) $19.95

A sturdy, cardboard case holds two decks of cards for helping students prepare for math and verbal sections of the SAT I. A unique feature of these flash cards is the use of cartoon picture clues to associate word meanings and key math concepts. This works especially well for the verbal flash cards. For example, the card for the word "desecrate" depicts a man kicking over a tombstone. The reverse of the card has the definition, pronunciation key, and part of speech, but, in addition, it has lists of similar and dissimilar words, a sample analogy, and a sample sentence. These features help students get a better grasp of the meaning and usage of the word which will be required by the test. There are only 33 of these cards, but, if students study the similar and dissimilar words on each (which are drawn from words that appear most frequently on the test), the total number of words studied exceeds 500. There are 8 cards with reading passages, then 15 cards with questions relating to the reading passages that work on skills such as understanding connotations, identifying uncommon meanings of words, and reading between the lines.

The math cards also feature cartoon illustrations, although they might not be as necessary or helpful if students already know what phrases like "prime number" and "slope of a line" mean but are fuzzy on how to perform math calculations. That's where the information on the reverse of the cards comes in. Definitions and basic formulas are given followed by two or three examples or applications. There are 50 math cards addressing key topics from arithmetic, algebra I, and geometry.

Students should work through both the math and verbal decks for review. Then they should take a practice test from one of the other resources. They should identify what concepts they had trouble with on the test, then go back and pull out the appropriate cards for additional practice and review. *IN-A-FLASH* cards should be especially helpful for visual learners who work well with picture clues, but they are also a refreshing change of pace from the hefty book-based review courses.(S)

➲ IN-A-FLASH Two Practice SAT Exams (IN-A-FLASH) $14.95

This book differs from other test prep books in that coaching tips and explanations appear next to each question for the first sample test. This allows students to learn strategy and immediately apply it to a problem rather than absorbing lots of ideas then tackling an entire exam. The second test is then used as a practice exam. Answers are at the back of the book.

➲ SAT I Workbooks (Barron's)

Barron's offers two separate workbooks covering the mathematics [$12.95] and verbal [$11.95] parts of the SAT I respectively. Students who need significant review and practice in either area are more likely to find the help they need here than in one comprehensive book. The *New Math Workbook for SAT I* is 352 pages, while the *Verbal Workbook for Sat I* is 304 pages.

➲ SAT Preparation Course for the Christian Student by
James P. Stobaugh (For Such A Time As This Ministries) $65; with 9th-10th grade supplement - $73

This SAT prep course is quite different from any other. A primary difference is that it was designed to help inculcate a Christian world view in the student. Each day's lesson is introduced with Scripture reading and application. Students are encouraged to use a supplemental devotional plan included in the appendix. Since vocabulary knowledge plays a crucial role in SAT success, students are told to select books to read from a recommended reading list in the binder, then read 30 to 50 pages a day, making note cards with definitions of unfamiliar words to study and review daily. Test taking tips appear throughout the lessons, but are not as extensive as we find in books such as the *Princeton Review*. Practice problems representative of the various types found on the test are included in lessons in what appears to be a random fashion, i.e. a few math problems one day, then sentence completion and some math problems another. Correct answers are given with complete analysis in the answer key following the lessons. A few puzzlers from Mindtrap Games, Inc. challenge students to

develop thinking skills. There are daily lessons for 26 weeks, designed for independent study. These could be completed in half a year or, if time permits, spread out over a longer time period. A Ninth/Tenth Grade Supplement offers one lesson per week at a slightly easier level. Personally, I would rely on something like *Princeton Review* for test taking strategies and view this course as a broader language arts/Bible study curricula (there is enough work in language arts in here that it could be equivalent to a year-long language course) that reinforces test preparation. You might spot test taking strategies of Stobaugh's that differ from those in *Princeton Review*, especially his advice not to guess at any answers. Stobaugh includes two copies of SAT I's from the College Board that include answers for practice test taking. The course is presented in a three-ring binder and is not consumable, so we might use it with more than one student, but not at the same time.

➲ SAT Success, 5th Edition (Peterson's) $14.95

A CD-ROM comes bundled into this SAT prep book. The book includes three different study plans (depending upon how much time students have for test preparation); lots of practice material including a diagnostic test and a practice SAT; test-taking tips; and a light, upbeat presentation. A software program for IBM compatible computers (3.5" drive) includes a diagnostic test plus customized study plans. Between the book and the CD-ROM there are a total of five full-length sample tests.

➲ SAT Verbal [computer program for DOS, Windows, or Macintosh] (Smartek Software) $69.95

This interactive, multimedia CD-ROM program offers five different formats for improving verbal skills using 400 words most frequently used on the SAT test. Flashcards introduce students to the words. Multiple choice questions offer students the opportunity to hear and/or read definitions and explanations for each word. Column Matching and Laser Review are two drill games for students to work on definitions. The SAT Review is the most challenging option. It features reading passages from which are drawn analogy, sentence completion, and reading comprehension questions. Students can review their errors, and scores are analyzed by the computer showing a predicted verbal score. They can also compare scores to the average incoming freshman's score at various colleges and universities. The variety of learning methods incorporated into the program make it appealing to all types of learners. An added bonus is a video section of test-taking tips. Smartek guarantees at least a 100 point gain after a minimum of 20 hours of study if a student's initial SAT I verbal score is between 300 and 650.

The program is easy to install and operate, although you will probably want to consult the instruction booklet occasionally. *SAT Verbal* comes packaged with a supplementary book, *Tooth and Nail - A Novel Approach to the New SAT*. The book uses a story format to help students improve vocabulary and reading comprehension skills.

➲ The Test-Taking Advantage (National Association of Secondary School Principals) $44.95

Have you looked at SAT preparation books? Have you tried to "read" one? It's not impossible, but the reader needs to be motivated and persistent. I immediately thought of my oldest son when I heard about this game, since he is a "right-brain," creative, hands-on learner rather than a book-oriented learner. In fact, when I asked for field test volunteers, my eldest was first to volunteer, even though he did not need to prepare for taking the SAT. This is not the type of game you will pull out to share with friends for a friendly evening; it is too much of a learning tool for most people to consider it fun. However, it offers an entirely new option for SAT test preparation that is likely to be more appealing and effective for many learners.

The Test-Taking Advantage does much of what those big books do, but the game format breaks up the information into smaller doses. (Those who can manage larger doses can skip the game board and use the cards and the 182-page manual that comes with the game. The manual is designed much like the "big books" with strategy lessons, sample test, and answer key.) Using the game approach, students move playing pieces on the board to colored squares which correspond to question categories (shades of *Trivial Pursuit*). There are ten categories—algebra, geometry, arithmetic, sentence correction, usage, strategy, antonyms, analogy, reading comprehension, and sentence completion. For each category there are about sixty question cards. On the reverse of each card is the correct answer, as well as explanation and strategy helps. Some cards direct players to the manual for more information about a strategy or skill. All players write their answers down before anyone reveals his own. The player whose turn it is shares his answer first. If he is incorrect, other players can move ahead if they have the correct answer. A wrong answer results in a minimal penalty, reflecting the similar penalty on the actual test. While it is more fun to have more than one player, a single player can still play alone to challenge his own knowledge.

My eldest son summed up his reaction: "It's always more fun to learn with a game. I remember things better when I learn this way."

The price of the game being what it is, consider buying it with another family with teens, then plan some "SAT-game days" together. Of course, if you have more than one teen reaching SAT-testing age in the next few years, you will probably want to have your own game on hand all the time.

The game was updated for SAT I in September of 1994. Additional cards plus guide are available for $9.95.

For ACT Preparation -

➲ ACT Computer Study Program, 2nd edition [Computer programs available for Macintosh or IBM compatibles] (Barron's) $24.95

I have not seen this program myself, but it is reasonably priced enough to take a chance on if you want to use the computer for ACT preparation.

➲ ACT IN-A-FLASH Flash Card Deck (IN-A-FLASH) $19.95

See the review for *SAT I IN-A-FLASH Flash Card Deck*. I did not review the ACT version, but the concept is the same as for SAT I.(S)

➲ ACT Cram Course (Arco Books) $7

This is a much briefer prep course than most of the others, but it should serve well for those who need a condensed version (ISBN 0671847732).

➲ How to Prepare for the American College Testing Program, Tenth Edition (Barron's) $12.95

This 576-page book is one of the most popular ACT preparation books. It includes a diagnostic test and four complete model tests plus answers and explanations. It also features extensive review, practice exercises, and test-taking strategy tips.

➲ ACT: American College Testing Program, 1997 (Arco Books) $13.95

This seems to be Arco's newest, comprehensive ACT test preparation book, but I was not able to review it for this edition (ISBN 0028610717). *ACT: American College Testing Program, 1997, with Study Planning Software* combines the book with a CD-ROM (ISBN 0028610814) [$24.95].

For SAT II: Subject Tests (formerly called Achievement Tests) Preparation

The College Board produces a 95-page booklet, *Taking the SAT II: Subject Tests* which describes the content of all 21 subject tests and features sample questions. Booklets are supplied free to schools or they are available for $4 each.

➲ The Official Guide to SAT II: Subject Tests (The College Board) $15

There are full-length practice tests for nine subjects (Writing, Literature, American History, World History, Math I, Math IIC, Biology, Chemistry, and Physics) plus answer keys. In addition, there are mini-tests for French, German, Italian, Latin, Modern Hebrew, and Spanish. It also describes the five SAT II: Language Tests with Listening.

➲ SAT II study guides (Barron's) $11.95-$12.95 for book-only guides; $16.95-$18.95 for books with audio cassettes

Subject-specific study guides are offered for American History/Social Studies, Biology, Chemistry, Mathematics Level I, Mathematics Level IIC, Physics, and Writing. Books with 60-minute audio cassettes are offered for French, Japanese, and Spanish.

Other Test Prep Sources

Test preparation classes are offered by public and private colleges, and by private businesses. Many of these classes will guarantee a higher test score to their students.

Creating Transcripts

Colleges usually require a transcript along with test scores, and all private schools make up transcripts for their students. If you work under some sort of umbrella program, they will generally issue the transcript. If we consider our home school a private school, we should make up our own. Generally, colleges are not very concerned about whether students are coming from accredited schools or not, so we should not be afraid to give our school the same status as other private schools. In fact, home schoolers have done so well at colleges across the country, that presenting them as homeschooled students for admission actually works to their advantage in many cases. There is a transcript form to use in the Appendix of this book (Chart F), or you might be able to obtain a form from another source or make up your own. We can add additional documentation if we think it will help. (See Chapter Six for more information about completing transcripts.)

If the format of the typical transcript does not suit your home school history, you might do as the Colfax family did when their sons applied to Harvard. They prepared transcripts listing subject areas rather than classes. They listed books and materials used and included a portfolio of pictures and descriptions of learning projects. The Colfax's approach worked because colleges really want to know what subject matter the student has studied and what level of proficiency he has achieved.

It is a little harder to evaluate unconventional transcripts, so some admissions offices might give us a hard time over such a transcript. This is particularly true of state institutions and others that do not like to spend the extra time needed to evaluate unusual transcripts. Again, this is a reminder that we need to check with institutions ahead of time to find out their requirements and the amount of flexibility they allow.

In some cases colleges have not required transcripts from home educated students, perhaps assuming that a transcript prepared by a parent will be overly optimistic. Instead they have relied heavily on test scores.

Can We Avoid This Hassle?

Teens can skip all of the diploma, transcript, and testing problems by accumulating college credits without graduating from high school. They can then use those credits as educational history documentation for four-year colleges or universities.

Junior or community colleges are one possible means of doing this. Junior colleges are usually much less stringent on entry requirements; SAT and ACT tests often are not required until a student applies to a four-year institution. And many times, they are not even required at the point of transfer. In some states, anyone can attend junior college as long as they can do the work. High school graduation is not necessarily a requirement. Placement tests in basic subjects are usually required to ensure that students will be able to do the work. (Check admission requirements in your state.)

Once a student has completed one to four semesters at junior college (depending on the future college he wishes to attend), he may apply to any four-year college. High school transcripts and diplomas are sometimes irrelevant at this point since the student has already demonstrated that he is able to do college work. Most frequently, if a student has complete two years (four semesters) at a junior college, the high school record is of minor importance to four-year colleges. However, the four-year colleges will look very carefully at junior college records of transfer student applicants.

Junior colleges also might help home educated students make the transition from home to the school environment with less pressure because course work is sometimes less demanding than at four-year institutions. Typically, junior colleges offer lower student-to-teacher ratios for general education classes than do some of the large four-year institutions. This means students might receive more individual attention at the local junior college than at the expensive four-year institution.

Another alternative for acquiring college credits is college correspondence courses. Teens can remain at home and accumulate college credits by enrolling in college correspondence courses. The University of California Extension Independent Study Program offers courses without any application process, other than filling out a short informational form—no high school graduation requirements. These are available at the same prices to students in any state, and in Canada at only $7 extra. Course prices appear to average about $250-300 each plus the cost of textbooks. Students have one year to complete each course. Many of the courses easily transfer to other colleges.

Some of the well-known schools offering college level correspondence courses include the University of California and the University of Nebraska-Lincoln. *Bear's Guide to Earning College Degrees Nontraditionally* (reviewed on the next page) describes many other such options.

Oral Roberts University offers a core of college freshman classes via correspondence. These courses are transferable to other institutions and are not just usable at ORU. The purpose is to allow home educated students to make a gradual transition into college by completing work at home for the first year. There is also a significant savings over the cost of completing these same courses on campus.

Some students need more assistance than is offered by some of the correspondence courses. Others want to complete their college degree through a single institution. An excellent option for Christian young people is *Liberty University's School of Lifelong Learning*. They offer accredited degrees, almost entirely through home study. Most courses are offered by video cassette. Six to twelve hours (two or four courses) are normally required in residence and that requirement can be fulfilled during summer and selected holiday seasons. Bachelor's degrees are offered in church ministries, business administration, and psychology. The Master's is available in counseling and religion. Faculty are regularly available by telephone via a toll free number. While residential students must have accepted Jesus Christ as their savior, external students are not required to have done so. Liberty's chancellor is Dr. Jerry Falwell, and the dean is Mr. Jay Spencer.

Testing for Credit

Still another alternative is testing for credit. This is done by obtaining college level, or possibly challenging high school level, textbooks in particular fields of interest (for which tests are available) and studying them thoroughly. Two types of testing programs are available: Advanced Placement for high school students and CLEP or ACTPEP testing available to anyone.

Advanced Placement (AP) tests are offered to high school students only. They complete their study of AP course materials for a subject, then take the test in the spring. Students can take these tests as early as their sophomore year of high school. By passing the tests, they can receive simultaneous credit for high school and college. Course materials and tests are offered in art, biology, chemistry, computer science, economics (micro or macroeconomics), English (language and composition or literature and composition), French, German, government and politics, history (U.S. or European), Latin, mathematics (Calculus AB or Calculus BC), music theory, physics, psychology, and Spanish. Most colleges accept AP credits, but you should check to be certain. *Advanced Placement Course Description* booklets [$8 each] for each subject provide general information about the AP Program, examiner's expectations for that subject, sample questions, and a list of colleges who grant credits for AP exams. *Student Guides to AP Courses* are available for European History, English courses, mathematics courses, and U.S. History [$10 each]. These *Guides* include discussion of the benefits of AP courses and exams, exam descriptions and sample questions, and explanation of the scoring process. Multiple choice sections of previous examinations with Free-Response Scoring Guides are available for some of the exams. A free, 4-page *Advanced Placement Program Fact Sheet* outlines the program; provides details for when, how, and where tests are offered; and lists publications, addresses, and phone numbers. Information is updated every year. For information write to the College Board, Advanced Placement Program.

The other type of testing is available to anyone and qualifies only for college credit. The two most widely recognized college credit testing programs are:

➲ College-Level Examination Program (CLEP)

CLEP offers college credit-by-examination testing in 5 general and 29 specific subject areas. CLEP testing credit is accepted at more than 2800 colleges and universities. Tests are offered at most college campuses by preregistration. The College Board will provide us with two free booklets that are very informative: *CLEP Information for Candidates and Registration Form* and *CLEP Colleges*.

➲ American College Testing Program Proficiency Examination Program (ACTPEP)

ACTPEP offers 43 tests with the majority emphasizing occupational subjects such as health and business. They are accepted by over 800 colleges and universities, and are offered at over 160 national test sites.

Many colleges will allow limited numbers of credits for passing certain standardized tests. In California, the maximum number of units from CLEP testing which can be transferred to an accredited university is forty-four units. It is very important that students check directly with colleges or universities about their acceptance of such credits. Do not rely on catalog information which can often be inaccurate. The tests are challenging, but students can study for as long as they need before applying to take the tests. (Jonathan Lindvall relates that he took some of these tests and found them not as difficult as he expected.) This approach allows students to study at their own pace. They can choose which subjects interest them most, and they work under the guidance of their parents (or another adult selected by the parents) rather than under an unknown professor at a distant university.

The College Board, sponsor of the CLEP testing program, has published *The Official Study Guide for the CLEP Examinations* [$18]. It provides advice on how to determine which colleges will grant CLEP credits, decide which tests to take, prepare for the tests, and interpret test scores. The book also contains complete descriptions of each CLEP examination (general as well as subject exams) with sample questions and answers and recommended resources to help you study for the examination. While sample questions are given, no complete tests are included for practice. Look for other CLEP manuals in bookstores and libraries or check Barron's catalog.

One other source for credit by examination is:

➲ Ohio University Course Credit by Examination (Ohio University)

But Can We Get Degrees This Way?

Junior college, correspondence, and testing credits can be used to build an educational history to present to four-year institutions, but some might wish to use unconventional methods for all of their college work. Jonathan Lindvall and a few other home education leaders are suggesting this route as the better way to get a college education. Lindvall describes his views in his audio presentation, *Post-Secondary Education, Homeschooling College* (Bold Parenting) [$5.95]. He encourages the use of CLEP tests and correspondence study, using The University of the State of New York or Thomas Edison State College (both described below) as the source for the actual degree.

Information on other programs is available in books such as:

➲ Bears' Guide to Earning College Degrees Nontraditionally, 12th Edition by John Bear, Ph.D. and Mariah Bear, M.A. (C & B Publishing) $27.95

John Bear is also the author of a similar book reviewed below, entitled *College Degrees by Mail*. However, this volume is much more comprehensive. The present twelfth edition, co-authored by John Bear's daughter, is even more extensive and international in content than previous editions. It contains 336 pages, jam-packed with both data and commentary. The book is updated very frequently to keep it up-to-date. This book concentrates on academic degree granting institutions rather than vocational institutions, so you will need to check another source for vocational programs.

Bear begins by explaining nontraditional education as well as providing definitions and explanations of some of the basic terms we encounter along the degree path such as colleges, universities, degrees, transcripts, the various types of degrees (associate, bachelor's, master's, and doctorate), and accreditation. Those who are considering seeking a degree through a fairly obscure institution should appreciate the lists of state and foreign agencies which oversee educational institutions and lists of accrediting agencies. Among both lists are sources for inquiring about the reputation and history of institutions. Bear also provides a helpful list of questions to aid us in our detective work as we check them out.

A chapter on equivalency examinations shows us how to take tests to obtain college credit. There is also a chapter listing more than 100 U.S. institutions which offer correspondence courses which are accepted by almost all universities or colleges, as well as a number of such institutions in other countries. Credit for learning experiences, credit by learning contract, and credit for foreign academic experience are three more alternatives for racking up credits which Bear explains.

The heart of the book is the section which describes the degree-granting institutions. Information is supplied about fields in which degrees are offered, year the institution was established, degrees offered (bachelor's, master's, doctorate, and/or law), accreditation status, whether it requires student residency (short or long term) or non-residency, legal status, and approximate tuition costs. All data entries are followed by a paragraph of commentary about each institution.

Following this is a brief chapter on sources for high school diplomas/degrees. Two individual chapters are devoted to law and medical schools. You can find out about diploma mills and read through the sixteen pages listing those recognized as such. (Bear does not provide addresses for any of these, and no known diploma mills are listed in the section describing credible institutions.)

The purpose of this book is to demonstrate that there are many ways to get degrees, oftentimes at much lower cost and in much less time than with traditional attendance at a college or university. Home schoolers who want to take charge of college education just as they have the earlier years, will find this book a valuable resource for doing just that.

⊃ **College Degrees by Mail and Modem, 1998** by John Bear, Ph.D. (Ten Speed Press) $12.95

Dr. Bear describes different approaches for getting degrees such as correspondence study, online courses, credit for life experience, equivalency exams, intensive study, and degree mills. Bear's book is useful for eliminating programs that do not have credibility in the marketplace. Of those remaining, he has selected 100 of the best schools offering degrees entirely through home study.

⊃ **College Online: How to Take College Courses without Leaving Home** by James P. Duffy (John Wiley and Sons) $14.95

Many home schoolers will be interested in online courses as an alternative to on-campus or traditional correspondence classes for college. This book discusses the pros and cons of online learning, then presents hundreds of courses already available this way, including some options for completing a complete degree program online. Published in 1997, information is as up-to-date as is possible.

⊃ **How to Earn a College Degree Without Going to College** by James P. Duffy (John Wiley and Sons) $15.95

Essentially, this is an abridged and much less expensive version of *Bears' Guide*. It discusses external degree programs and how they work, as well as credit for work experience, accreditation, testing for credit, electronic classes, and the validity of alternative methods for obtaining degrees. It provides the details for colleges which offer external bachelors degree programs and briefer information on institutions that offer correspondence classes which might be applied to such degree programs. It is not intended to cover masters or advanced degree programs. All programs listed in the book are accredited. This book includes an important detail: the minimum age or educational requirements for students entering their programs. Some institutions admit only adult students, some admit only students who have already completed some college credits, and most require at least a high school diploma or GED. Nevertheless, there are many opportunities available to home school graduates that deserve investigation.(S)

⊃ **The Independent Study Catalog: A Guide to Over 10,000 Correspondence Courses, Sixth Edition** (Peterson's) $16.95

Although similar in some ways to *Bear's Guide*, this book is more comprehensive in some ways and less in others. It focuses on particular courses rather than institutions, although it does specifically list 100 different schools. It includes four which offer high school diplomas as well as numerous institutions which offer accredited high school courses although they do not grant high school diplomas themselves. College courses are the main emphasis, although listed courses are sometimes offered by institutions that offer courses but no external degree program. These distinctions are important, because credits earned for either high school or college courses from schools not offering degrees, must be transferred to another institution which combines accumulated credits for the student to grant the degree. In the case of high school credits, the general assumption is that you are working under an accredited school which will be granting a diploma. At the college level, the units might be transferred to any number of colleges, but you must ascertain ahead of time that the credits will be accepted by the institution which will ultimately grant the degree. *The Independent Study Catalog* narrows its listings to include only institutions accredited by widely recognized accrediting bodies (with two noted exceptions). These institutions must also accept and support the "published Standards of the Independent Study Division of the National University Continuing Education Association (NUCEA)." Because of these restrictions, apparently, a few options of significant interest to home educators are missing. At the college level, the University of the State of New York Regents College program, described below, and all but four Christian Colleges or Universities are missing. However, the number of institutions offering high school courses in addition to college courses seems to have increased dramatically since the last edition of this book.

The value of this book is for locating specific courses which can be taken to apply towards degrees. Courses are listed by title, number, and unit value, at both lower and upper division levels for each institution. An index of subject areas helps us easily locate sources for courses of interest. This book supplements *Bear's Guide* which gives better descriptions of the institutions themselves. (This book was developed with the National University Continuing Education Association. It can also be ordered from the University of California.)

➲ One Year to a College Degree by Lynette Long and Eileen Herschberger (Huntington House Publishers) $10.99

Bear's Guide to Earning College Degrees Non-Traditionally does a great job of putting us in touch with institutions which offer nontraditional options, even though this is sometimes only one part of a strategy toward earning a degree. *One Year to a College Degree* gives us step-by-step directions for pulling it all together when we use nontraditional methods. Even though the title describes one of the author's successful conquest of a degree in a year, most students will take a little longer. That discouraging realization does not diminish the value of this book one bit. The authors take an in-depth look at all of the methods for putting together the requirements for a degree from an accredited institution. They cover many of the same areas as Bear, but they go

much further. They share case histories, how-to's, worksheets, tips on the right order in which to seek different sources of credits, and recommended resources.

➲ Peterson' Distance Learning (Peterson's) $24.95

Peterson's Distance Learning is similar in concept to *Bear's Guide*, although it is more tightly focused on accredited institutions. It covers more than 1,200 degree and certificate programs from more than 750 accredited institutions (both private and public). It provides data on each institution about media/technology used to provide courses, student services, how to apply, typical costs, contact numbers for applying, and individual courses offered. Both two-year and four-year schools in the U.S. and Canada are included. At the back of the book are over 100 pages of expanded data provided by institutions plus indexes for locating particular courses and programs.(S)

➲ Virtual College by Pam Dixon (Peterson's) $9.95

Virtual College should be your starting point when considering any kind of distance learning whether it be book-based correspondence, video tape, audio tape, online or any combination of such methods. Pam Dixon tells us how distance courses work, how to check them out, how to know what type of accreditation to look for (assuming we agree with her that we want only a properly-accredited course), how to choose among our options, what it costs, what a "virtual classroom" is really like, tips for making distance learning work, and how to locate options. After reading this book, you will be "armed and ready" for guides like *The Independent Study Catalog, Distance Learning,* and *Bear's Guide to Earning College Degrees Non-Traditionally.*(S)

Once we begin to read books such as those listed above, we become aware that there are many ways to get a college degree without following the traditional route. To adventurous home schoolers, earning a college degree just might present another challenge to their ingenuity.

No Regrets

The Swann family with their ten children has become something of an idealized picture of what home education can be. The eldest daughter, Alexandra, completed all regular course work for a masters degree by the age of 16. Her younger brothers and sisters are following in her footsteps, all using correspondence courses from Calvert, American School, Brigham Young University, and others. Their secret seems to be the family attitude toward education—education is highly valued and given priority in the schedule. Year round schooling and extreme dedication on mom's (Joyce Swann) part are also significant factors. However, the Swanns do not consider what they have accomplished to be due to innate genius, but something attainable by others willing to invest the effort.

They chose accredited correspondence courses because they thought that they would provide a better assurance of college entry and because of the time and energy saved with preplanned course work. Calvert School, although not Christian, provided a solid academic grounding. American School, although weaker academically, allowed them to rapidly complete high school courses. Challenging college courses provided the knowledge and skills for Alexandra and at least a few of her siblings to move on to careers after completing their education.

The Swann's story is as much about family relationships as it is about education. The family members learned to work together for the good of all, enjoying the company of each other, and developing strength of character through the challenges they faced.

We do not need all home educated students to get masters degrees in their teen years, but we can all benefit from the inspiration of this family who chose a better way. You can read their story in Alexandra Swann's book, *No Regrets* [Cygnet Press] ($16.95).

At the same time, be aware that when we try using alternative methods for obtaining college credits we can run into trouble. The biggest problem is receiving credit toward a degree. All credits are not transferable to all institutions. Most institutions will accept only very limited numbers of credits from correspondence, independent study, or CLEP testing. However, there are several exceptions to this. Two institutions will grant degrees from credits accumulated strictly through other institutions and testing:

➲ The University of the State of New York

Regents College

(Author's note: This type of degree program is often called an external degree program. External degrees are those earned by study and experience outside the classroom.)

This fully-accredited university does not offer any actual classes of its own, although it does maintain a database of over 7000 courses and examinations "at a distance" which are offered by other sources. It evaluates transfer credits, including an unlimited number of correspondence courses, life experience which has been evaluated as college level, standardized tests (again unlimited), learning contracts, and so forth. Their informational brochure and catalog are very informative on all aspects of this approach. For $135, we can get a credit evaluation without paying the full enrollment fee. That money is also deductible for the enrollment fee if we do enroll.

➲ Thomas Edison State College

Thomas Edison State College offers adults the opportunity to complete associate or baccalaureate degrees no matter where they live. Adult learners complete degrees through a combination of methods most convenient to them, including testing, portfolio assessment, learning acquired at work or in the military, Guided Study courses at home, transfer of credit and other options. Thomas Edison's program is fully accredited.

Some external degree programs offer credit for life or work experience. An assumption made by such programs is that the individual has three to five years of life or work experience, thus these programs do not fit most teenagers. However, they might make sense as a long range tool for obtaining a degree through a combination of work and education.

For help in pursuing alternatives such as CLEP credits, pursuing degrees through the above institutions, or even just getting a jump start on accumulating college credits while still in high school, you might want to consult Dr. Douglas Batson through Essential Education. He is a nationally certified career counselor with a great deal of experience in alternative college education. He can help high school students determine how to "test out" of college classes, accumulating credits and saving a great deal of money. He will also assist those who would like to pursue their entire education through correspondence courses or other alternatives to the traditional college education. For a $99 consultation fee, he can "typically save a high school student $10,000 in college tuition costs and one academic year."

Financial Aid

There are an unbelievable number of sources for financial aid in the form of grants, scholarships, loans, and work/study programs. College financial counselors say tuition fees might have very little to do with the final choice of a college because of the help available. Sixty-seven percent of the students enrolled in college have some sort of financial aid. However, my understanding of the way things operate is this: families fill out a financial aid questionnaire. The questionnaire information is used to determine (according to a formula) what amount the family can be expected to pay towards their child's education. The child is then eligible for help covering any costs beyond that. Unfortunately, what many middle income families I know have been told is that they should be able to pay more than they actually are able. One person summed it up, "They expect you to take out a second mortgage on your home if you have any equity at all." Loans seem to be an assumed part of the package, which should pose problems for Christians who are trying to live debt free.

I might add that I think student loans are extremely dangerous for young people themselves. The assumption is that they will repay the loans as soon as they are out of college and start working. However, this is also the time when most of them are getting married. Beginning a marriage with debts is unwise and might even be the cause of forcing the wife to work outside the home. The consequences if she becomes pregnant or if anything else strains the budget are enormous. So, I personally recommend never taking out loans for college.

I highly recommend a new book by Gordon Wadsworth, titled *Debt Free College* (Financial Aid Information Services) [$19.95]. The purpose of this book is "to help students graduate from an institution of higher learning without the entrapment of financial bondage." Advocating the same financial principles regarding debt as those advanced by Larry Burkett, Wadsworth offers detailed advice (including the current impact of tax codes) on how to get a college education without going into debt. He discusses numerous financing options including "service cancelable programs" where college is financed in return for a promise of a period of service after graduation. Families can also receive a free financial analysis showing the EFC (expected family contribution) that they will encounter as their son or daughter applies to college. Wadsworth also covers some valuable finance basics on money management for young adults.

Scholarships are, obviously, much better financing tools for those who can qualify. Academic and talent scholarships are familiar to most of us. You might also find scholarships based on financial need. Do not forget to check out special scholarships from parents' employers, organizational affiliations, special interest groups, clubs, trades, and industries. These might be likelier options for middle income families that do not qualify for need-based scholarships.

Books on financial sources must be updated constantly, so look for the most current editions. The following are possible resources, although I have not reviewed each of them.

➲ **Free Money for College** by Laurie Blum (Facts on File) paperback ISBN#0-8160-3498-2 - $14.95; hardcover ISBN# 0-8160-3497-4 -$27.95

More than 1,000 grants and scholarships are listed, along with the source's or grant's restrictions, the amount of money given, and application deadlines. Six categories are used for identifying possible special sources of financial aid: state, area of study, grants for women, grants for ethnic students, grants for handicapped students, and miscellaneous.

➲ **College Money Handbook 1998** (Peterson's) $26.95

This guide, updated yearly, helps parents and students understand the financial aid process and explains the sources of financing available, including scholarships, athletic and merit awards, special aid, tuition plans, and grants. It also identifies colleges offering specialized scholarships for athletics, academics, or other factors. It comes with a computer disk, *Access Advisor*, that runs on Windows or Macintosh systems. The program helps families predetermine how much they will be expected to pay and what sort of options are likely to be available to them. Check out other Peterson's titles such as *Winning Money for College* [$12.95] which covers non-need scholarships and *Scholarships, Grants, and Prizes* which lists financial assistance available from private sources and tells how to successfully apply for it; .

➲ **The Scholarship Book** by Daniel J. Cassidy (Prentice-Hall) $32.95

This single volume is a comprehensive directory of private-sector scholarships, grants, loans, internships, and contest prizes for college students. It contains much of the same information that financial aid research services look through, including both well-known and obscure sources.

More Sources for Financial Assistance

I refer you to the library, local high schools, junior colleges, and colleges themselves for more resources. Check also with organizations with which you are affiliated, including employers, for special scholarships.

Investing in assistance from a financial aid/scholarship service might be well worth the money for many families. Find out about local services through high school counselors.

National Merit Scholarship Program

One program home schoolers often miss out on is the National Merit Scholarship Program. The first step by which students enter the competition for Merit Scholarships is taking the PSAT/NMSQT (Preliminary Scholastic Aptitude Test/National Merit Scholarship Qualifying Test). The test is administered by the SAT program, but offered only through local high schools. You must contact a local high school and make arrangements for your child to be tested along with their students. The test is given in October each year, and a student must take it in the junior year in order to participate in the Merit Program. Some students take it simply for practice for the SAT (it is very similar), while others are trying to qualify for the scholarship competition. If the PSAT/NMSQT was missed, there is a possibility of alternative arrangements for entering the program, but contact with NMSC must be made by March 1, following the October test that was missed.

The SAT I test, which is given a number of times each year, is one of the requirements for advancing in the competition.

Test inquiries or requests for the *PSAT/NMSQT Student Bulletin* (information) should be directed to:

PSAT/NMSQT
P.O. Box 24700
Oakland, CA 94623-1700
(609) 683-0449 east coast
(510) 653-5595 west coast

Questions about the *National Merit Scholarship Program* should be directed to:

National Merit Scholarship Corporation
1560 Sherman Avenue, Suite 200
Evanston, Il 60201-4897
(708) 866-5100

PSAT/NMSQT Preparation

The College Board publishes *TestSkills*, a book to be used by teachers to prepare students for the PSAT/NMSQT [$40]. One complete sample test is included. A free *PSAT/NMSQT Student Bulletin* also explains the test, but in a much more limited fashion. In most cases, using any SAT I preparation book will accomplish the same task as using a specialized PSAT/NMSQT guide. *Cracking the System: Revolutionary Techniques for Scoring High on the PSAT and SAT* and *Princeton Review: Cracking the SAT & PSAT* cover PSAT test preparation alongside SAT preparation. IN-A-FLASH offers the *PSAT IN-A-FLASH Flash Card Deck* which is similar to the SAT and ACT decks described earlier.

Options

Knowing how to get our teens into college is one thing, but we still have to figure out how to cover some of the challenging subjects required for college entry. How do we teach our teens a foreign language when we never studied one ourselves? How do we present science lab classes when we don't know a butane burner from a pipette? How do we teach our budding engineer calculus when our math education stopped with survival math? It certainly looks intimidating when we look at college requirements and consider our inadequacies. But we need not stop there. We have lots of help available to us if we just know where to look.

Correspondence Schools

The most obvious place to go for help is a correspondence course that provides books, teaching information, answer keys, and record keeping for us. At the high school level, enrollment in these schools sometimes provides bureaucratic benefits. They know how to complete transcripts and have such forms readily available. They can alert us to essentials we might overlook. and they might help with nitpicky details such as college entrance exams that request a high school code number, a number which correspondence schools generally provide to us.

The correspondence courses that have consultants available might be especially helpful. Many homeschoolers need someone they can turn to for both educational and technical assistance.

Because of the individual needs of each student, we must be cautious in choosing a correspondence course, or indeed, whether to use one at all. We must check out the textbooks and materials used to see if they are appropriate for our teen, judging to the best of our ability. We must look also at the rate at which work must be completed. Might it be more than our teen can handle? Rigid requirements are the most common cause of complaints I hear about correspondence courses. We also need to be concerned with turnaround time on tests and papers. If it takes a long time to receive feedback on how well a student has mastered a lesson, it can create problems in determining whether or not to move ahead on schedule.

The following correspondence courses are listed for your information, but this does not imply unconditional recommendation. All programs will provide free information upon request.

○ A Beka Correspondence School

This heavily-academic program uses A Beka texts for kindergarten through twelfth grade. A Beka prefers that home schoolers enroll in this program rather than buy their books and work independently, but they do not pressure home schoolers to enroll. The teaching methods are traditional with little hands-on

activity. This is a good program for students who have performed well in traditional schools with high academic standards. The cost is approximately $550.

○ A Beka Video Courses

A Beka offers home school video courses in addition to their well-known textbook line. We owe A Beka thanks for being the first to make the plunge into video for home educators. They realized that many of us lack the time, confidence, or ability to teach, so they brought the classroom teacher to our homes to help us out.

A Beka video courses are of actual school classes with teachers presenting lessons to the children. Our students watch the videos then complete assignments in their A Beka texts. Complete programs are available for kindergarten through high school. Elementary courses come only as complete programs, but we can select individual junior and senior high classes. The Jaffé Strings video program is available as an elective course for students who want to learn to play stringed instruments.

Two basic plans are offered—credit or noncredit. For an entire program, the cost for grades 7 and 8 is $830 for the credit plan and $775 for the noncredit plan; for grades 9-12, the cost is $920 for the credit plan and $865 for the noncredit plan. ($90 of each price is a refundable deposit on the videos.) Individual courses for grades 7-12 are $325 each ($55 of which is a deposit). Full tuition is required for each student completing each video course. Credits are not issued for individual courses unless A Beka receives a letter from the child's school stating that they will accept the credit. The cost for credit then increases by $20. The refund policy is very forbidding. "Once the course has begun, there are no refunds for the video program.. If all items are returned unused..., your money will be refunded, less a $100 processing charge."

Video tapes are shipped back and forth and remain the property of A Beka. Tapes are sent in groups and must be used on a fairly rigid schedule. All courses must be completed in nine months. In the credit option, student work and tests are sent in and an evaluation report is issued periodically. Work is evaluated every nine weeks for grades 4-12. Permanent school records are maintained for each student.

Courses require a minimal amount of supervision. Kindergarten videos run about 2 1/2 hours a day, with an extra half hour to an hour of seat work and interaction. For elementary grades, videos run 3 to 3 1/2 hours per day, but combined with seatwork and studying school time should take a total of 5 to 6 hours a day. High school videos are each about 45 minutes long, with homework time varying by class. Even for older students, this is a lot of passive viewing. I found myself nodding off fifteen minutes into the third tape I was reviewing in a single session. And I was motivated to watch them! I urge you to break up the sit time with moving around and talking time.

I have heard mixed reactions from those who have used the video courses—some thought they were great, others thought they were awful—but none of these people were using more than one or two of the video courses a year and all were working at junior high/high school level. I decided to get samples of a number of the different video courses to come to my own conclusions. After watching them, I realized that some reactions are based on teacher presentation. Some of the video teachers keep the action moving, encourage student responses, keep the video audience in mind, and otherwise make the course more appealing. Some of them are just boring. I also find it unsettling to watch the typical classroom humiliation that occurs when some students are unable to answer questions, especially when they are being recorded. (I have not seen anything really abusive on these tapes, but I guess I have become more sensitive to the issue through our years of homeschooling.)

Tape quality is an important issue, especially for children who will be watching three or four hours of these every day. Production is fairly low-quality. A single camera was placed in the back of each classroom. Most of the time it is focused upon the teacher, with occasional panning to show students at the chalkboard or responding into a microphone, or to show an overhead or visual aid. A Beka failed to take full advantage of the video media by inserting additional film footage or animated graphics as School of Tomorrow has done. (But, then they were the first to even tackle video!) Tapes are recorded on standard long play (also called extended play) tape which reduces the quality, no matter how good the original production. It also makes them unplayable on some video players. (I see no warnings of this incompatibility in their catalog.)

Considering that A Beka is the first to make all subjects at all grade levels available on video, they deserve credit for taking that first step. However, if they want to remain competitive in the video-course market, they will need to take better advantage of the video media and improve the overall quality.

➲ The Academy of Home Education

The Academy is a "service organization" for high-school-age home schoolers, sponsored by Bob Jones University. It functions more like a school service or umbrella program than like a correspondence school. It requires use of all BJUP materials. Self-reported grades are turned in at the end of each semester, and students are required to take a standardized achievement test each year. Telephone consultation assistance is available. High school age home schoolers, whether or not enrolled in AHE, may participate in the Quill Club for young writers. For a small fee, Quill Club members can submit an essay, poem, or short story for critique and evaluation. The cost of Academy enrollment is $115 application fee (which includes the costs of testing), $130 annual administration fee, plus the cost of BJUP curricula or resources for electives. A formal transcript and diploma are provided. and students can participate in an on-campus graduation ceremony each summer.

➲ American School

This secular, accredited high school correspondence course has been in business since 1897. It provides two main educational services by correspondence study: a diploma program for those young people and adults who do not attend traditional high school and wish to complete their secondary education and earn the American School diploma; and an independent study program for those students who, while remaining regularly enrolled in their local high schools, take classes with American School with the approval of a local school official in order to make up credits, or for enrichment and acceleration. They offer a very wide range of courses, and students may enroll in one or more courses. While the cost is higher for a single year ($379) than some of the other correspondence schools listed, the cost drops dramatically for two-, three-, or four-year enrollments ($579, $779, and $979 respectively), making the long-term cost lower than most other correspondence schools. Students may also enroll for single courses if they so desire. Payment can be made on a monthly basis, if necessary.

➲ Bridgestone Academy formerly Alpha Omega Institute

This correspondence course is open to students in grades K-12. The Academy uses the Alpha Omega LifePac curriculum (which is reviewed in Chapter Nine) to study math, language arts, science, and social studies. (Electives and Bible courses are available at extra cost.) Services included with enrollment include placement and prescription of which levels of LifePacs are needed for each subject, academic assistance, report cards, transcripts, permanent records, support to parents, annual achievement testing, and eighth and twelfth grade diplomas. High school students must earn 10 of their 21 credits with the Academy to receive their high school diploma. There is a $75 registration fee, with a $25 discount on registration for each additional student. (The registration fee jumps to $100 in August or September, so register early.) Annual tuition is $420 for the first student and $396 for each additional student from the same family. Electives for high school are $105 per subject. Students have up to twelve months to complete the curriculum, but if they finish early, they can go ahead and enroll for the next level (paying again as if it were a new school year). Students may enroll at anytime during the school year, although enrollment must be for a minimum of a full semester.

➲ Calvert School

Calvert offers academic courses for grades K-8 with all materials supplied for each course. Calvert's strength is in their coverage of geography, history, mythology, poetry, and literature, and the teacher's manuals. Teacher's manuals provide clear, concise instruction for the novice teacher. Even though Calvert makes no such claim, their teacher's manuals effectively teach us how to teach. Many of the Calvert courses are very good, although a few of the secular textbooks are mediocre. This is not a Christian school and some of the texts contain evolutionary concepts. However, we are welcome to supplement or substitute lessons reflecting our own beliefs and philosophies for the Calvert lessons.

Since subject studies are integrated to some extent, mixing of grade levels is not allowed. These courses are, for the most part, prepackaged curricula for each grade level, although Calvert allows enrollment in individual subjects at the eighth grade level only. This arrangement restricts the amount of individualizing that we can do before eighth grade. However, the complete curriculum is a good choice for missionaries or others who have great difficulty rounding up all the necessary materials.

We may enroll our teen and work with him or her independently, or we may elect to include the optional Advisory Teaching Service (ATS) for grades one through eight. With the ATS, tests are sent to Calvert for review and grading by a professional teacher/advisor, who also makes comments and suggestions. Only with the ATS will Calvert issue a certificate of completion for courses. Tuition for grades 7-8 is $515 per year; the ATS for grades 7-8 is $260. Individual courses for eighth grade are $125 per subject, and ATS is $85 per subject.

Calvert also offers enrichment courses: *Beginning French*; *Spanish* (see foreign languages); *Discovering Art*, an art appreciation course for grades 4-8 [$200]; and *Algebra I* can be taken by eighth graders who pass the placement test [$130; advisory service is $90; if the course is substituted for eighth grade math within the full grade level curriculum, the tuition for the complete curriculum increases to $525 and the ATS to $265]. Enrichment courses are available to those not enrolled in Calvert. Use of enrichment courses for group classes is priced differently. Call for details.

➲ Cambridge Academy

Cambridge Academy offers secular correspondence courses for grades 6-12. The Academy is accredited by the Distance Education and Training Council. It is currently undergoing evaluation by the Southern Association of Schools and Colleges and hopes to have SASC accreditation by the end of 1997. Two options are available: enrollment for a complete academic year or purchase of individual course material to be used for self-teaching.

The complete academic year option includes all necessary texts and study guides, a toll-free tutoring service, student testing, test grading, record keeping, and transcript. Textbooks are purchased by the student, but they can be returned at the end of the course for remuneration. The cost is $100 per credit plus books and $65 for pre-test and evaluation. (There are additional charges for the physics lab video tapes and Destinos materials.) Individual course costs and services follow the same fee structure; students receive only a course transcript rather than a comprehensive one.

For grades 6-8, students are assigned courses in language arts, math, science, and social studies. At high school level, they can choose from general education or college prep courses. To graduate from Cambridge Academy, students must complete four courses in language arts, three in social studies, three in math, three in science, and eleven electives. Students who have already begun high school at home or another school can have their prior work evaluated for credit. That transcript evaluation and the results of a Math and English Skills Evaluation Test will determine initial placement of a student. The student and parent, working with the Guidance Department, then determine the student's course of study.

Cambridge also has an external electives program for high school and a portfolio assessment program for middle school students. With the guidance of the Electives Program Counselor, students may choose subjects or activities of interest to them, develop their own learning program, complete it, and receive credit for their work. Examples of possible subjects or activities are drama, computer programming, art, and sign language.

Students use secular textbooks in conjunction with study guides prepared by the academy staff. Via an 800 tutoring line, the student works with a degreed instructor. Instructors are available between 8 a.m. and 5 p.m. on working days. Students complete and mail in tests which use a combination of true/false, multiple choice, essay, and other types of responses. Graded tests are returned to the student with answer information. Proctored final exams are given in each subject at the end of each semester's work.

Overall, the course of study aims toward college preparation, making it a more challenging program than those offered by American School or ICS. Math courses range from Basic Math Review up through Algebra II/Trigonometry, with Calculus due to be added sometime in the future. Science options include General Science, Everyday Biology, Life Science, Earth Science, Technology, Chemistry, and Physics. Physics lab is presented on video tape, but other courses do not yet include comprehensive lab components. Cambridge personnel are presently working on biology and chemistry lab programs. The Biology course text presents evolution in a single chapter at the end, and students are allowed to skip this chapter; they are not tested on information in this chapter. Social studies options are Early American History, U.S. History, Global Studies, Civil and Criminal Justice, and American Government/Economics. (Global Studies essentially replaces the traditional requirement for World History.) Language arts options are Grammar and Composition (I and II), American Literature, English Literature, College Vocabulary, or Creative Writing. Electives are Spanish, Business Law, Typing, Computer Awareness, Accounting (I and II), Fundamental Map Skills, and Basic Consumer Economics. Resources include texts from Amsco, Glencoe/Macmillan/McGraw-Hill, Globe Fearon, South-Western Publishing, Steck-Vaughn, Random House, Saxon, and Holt, Rinehart, and Winston. The Spanish course uses the *Destinos* materials reviewed under foreign language.

Although the courses are secular and reflect the typical problems of such courses, Cambridge does offer an inexpensive, accredited option for high school. Cambridge also says, "...we recognize each family's responsibility to train their children in the faith of their choice, and we support your efforts to include spiritual and moral values in your child's education."(SE)

➲ Christian Liberty Academy

Christian Liberty Academy (CLA) offers courses for kindergarten through twelfth grades with a program very similar to Christian schools, although they place a stronger emphasis on developing a thoroughly Christian world view. They have chosen an assortment of textbooks from various publishers as well as some of their own. The textbooks and program reflect a traditional approach to education using primarily workbooks and reading. Examples of texts used at high school level are Saxon's algebra series, *God and Government*, BJUP *Earth Science*, BJUP *Physics*, and *Economics in One Lesson*, along with Christian Liberty Press publications such as *Applications of Grammar, The Mayflower Pilgrims,* and *Streams of Civilization*. Each course comes with the needed instructions or teacher's manual, and CLA has written their own, simplified teacher's manuals and answer keys to be used in place of some of the huge volumes offered by many publishers. Although lab work for high school science courses is not required, students are encouraged to do whatever they can practically accomplish with equipment available to them at home using experiments described in the texts. Students who need lab courses for college entry are encouraged to take those courses at community or junior colleges.

CLA offers options of either purchasing only books through them, with no record keeping or enrollment (The Family Plan) [$255 for grades 7-8; $295 for grades 9-12], or full enrollment in the correspondence program [$315 for grades 7-8; $355 for grades 9-12]. This program is academically sound, but does not meet the needs of learners who require hands-on activity. In the past, people have had trouble with the amount of work required, but the program has been changed slightly—requiring less work and offering more flexibility and discretion to parents. CLA has shown a commendable responsiveness to the needs of home educators. They have done well in their effort to offer good materials at an affordable price.

⊃ Clonlara School Home Based Education Program

Clonlara School is a fully functioning private day school with an extension program to assist home educators. It aims to "create an environment where children and parents are free to guide their own learning. Close team effort with student and parent [is] encouraged and developed."

Clonlara truly believes that parents should be directing home education, so they leave most of the day-to-day schooling in parents' hands. Clonlara has no grade levels. Parents are free to choose any method of education with whatever resources they choose., but Contact Teachers can help them make choices. Families can use real-life activities, library books, student-designed projects, or traditional texts. Clonlara actually encourages staying away from textbooks as much as possible, but they will support you if that is your choice. Clonlara is non-sectarian, but Christian textbooks and resources are available through their Resource area. Standardized testing is recognized as a necessary evil in some states, so Clonlara makes them available to those who need them, but they do not require them from all students. They supply guidelines for what is typically covered in various subjects and assign a support teacher who offers guidance and assistance as needed. They keep cumulative files on students, handle legal and technical details, and issue report cards and transcripts. For high school, an accredited transcript is issued based upon Carnegie credit hours. For example, if a student is studying life science, he might accumulate hours by working

with the vet, caring for his own animals, or reading about and researching related topics. Clonlara will support students who follow traditional or nontraditional courses of study, including support through the process of college application and entry. They have established a credible reputation in educational circles.

Taking this philosophy of education onto the information highway, Clonlara offers Compuhigh. Compuhigh consists of selected classes offered on-line. Students access classes and class mentors through any online server. Class discussions and work are accomplished using e-mail and the world wide web. With mentors as guides, students can post messages on computer bulletin boards for all to read, participate in ongoing discussions with mentors and other students and take part in interactive lessons designed to be challenging and interesting. At present, Algebra I and II, American Government, Collaborative Writing, Computer Networking, Earth Science, Geometry, Independent Study, World Geography, American History, and Think About It are the course offerings. Courses are open only to those enrolled in Clonlara and the fee is $50 per course.

If you want the freedom to do school your way, but you also want the assurance of assistance from an organization with 30 years of experience, Clonlara fills the bill. Tuition is based upon the number of students enrolled per family.(S)

⊃ Covenant Home Curriculum

Covenant offers courses for grades K-12. They use an assortment of Christian and secular texts, with some alternatives offered so that courses can be better tailored to the individual needs of the student. The "tailored course" option makes Covenant a more flexible choice than some other correspondence courses. Covenant has their own diagnostic test that can be used to properly place children in math and English. The basic texts reflect a traditional, academic approach to education, although other options are available. Bob Jones University Press books are the mainstays of the science and history courses for junior and senior high. *Saxon Math* or alternatives from Amsco are used for math. An assortment of resources for language arts offers broad and thorough coverage of literature, grammar, vocabulary, and composition. Among Covenant's selections we find such quality resources as *Basic English Revisited, Vocabulary from Classical Roots*, and *Sketches from Church History*. In addition, students read classical literature, and *Classic Critiques* (unique "pamphlet" study guides to classical literature) come with Covenant programs. Foreign language, art, music, and other subjects are treated as electives. Test sets are available for most of the resources Covenant provides, not just the basics.

Underlying many of the courses is a strong Christian worldview from the Reformed perspective. At the younger level, this is evidenced by use of the *Westminster Shorter Catechism* and at the older level by *Sketches from Church History*. The Christian Reconstructionist viewpoint might be encountered by students at the upper levels who choose to study *The Institutes of Biblical Law* by R.J. Rushdoony and *God and Government* by Gary De-Mar.

Covenant offers two plans for high school, plus the availability of some courses individually. (Check with them for details.) Plan A is the high-intensity four years of solid academics listed in their course inventory catalog. Plan B allows for stretching out science and math courses for students who find these subjects difficult. Both plans are college preparatory. With both plans, "grade-auditing and tutorial" may be purchased so that transcripts will be issued. Grading is emphasized. The *Covenant Home Curriculum Preceptor* covers the basics of grading, scheduling, and record keeping. *Course Blueprints* for grades 11 and 12 are detailed lesson plans and teaching instructions for each course, varying in length from a few pages to book-length. These are extremely helpful, especially for the parent new to home education. (As I read through some of the *Course Blueprints*, I couldn't help but get excited about many of their courses, since the lesson plans and discussion questions sounded so interesting!) At junior high level through tenth grade, the optional *Day By Day* daily lesson plan guides offer similar assistance. I recommend the *Day by Day*, especially to new home educators, as long as the child is working primarily within a single grade level.

Covenant's program has been used successfully by families who prefer that all materials be provided through one source, yet who also want Christian materials with more flexibility than is offered by programs such as Christian Liberty Academy and A Beka. The *Day By Day* lesson plan guides and *Course Blueprints* also make Covenant's program easy for the parent with little experience.

The *Course Inventory Catalog* and the *Classical Approach Video* ($9.50 each or $15.95 for both, refundable upon curriculum purchase) explain the philosophy and details of Covenant's program. Standard course enrollment fee for grades 7-8 is $430; for grades 9-12 it is $545. Tailored course enrollment is $456 for grades 7-8 and $580 for grades 9-12. The tutorial fee and grade auditing is $145 for grade 7-8 and $160 per year for grades 9-12. Diagnostic tests are $24.50 and *Day by Day* scheduling is $32.

➲ Home Study International

Home Study International has been around since 1909. They offer accredited correspondence courses for kindergarten through high school, as well as post-secondary level. All students may enroll for individual courses or the complete program. Each course comes with study guides, exams, and support from their certified teachers. At junior high and high school levels, the school carries primary responsibility for the student's instruction with parents acting as supervisors. Tests must be administered by an unrelated adult who has been approved by HSI. Bible courses reflect Seventh Day Adventist doctrine, but they are optional. Some texts are from secular publishers, however, the science/health program for grades K-8 is creation-based. Junior high students study Bible, English, math, science/health, social studies/history, and reading. High school courses of study are typical for general education and college prep students, with some electives. The cost depends upon the number of classes: for grades 7 and 8 five classes cost $885 plus shipping; for high school, the cost of 5 units is $1460 plus the cost of supplies for each class (averaging $60-$80 with a few costing less and some costing more) and shipping.

➲ ICS Newport/Pacific High School

ICS (International Correspondence Schools) has been providing post-secondary vocational and high school correspondence courses for a long time, but in the last few years they have become more involved with home education through their Newport/Pacific High School. The program is accredited by the Distance Education and Training Council. The complete course for all of high school (tuition fee of $649) covers 16 core subjects, plus either 5 or 6 electives. Other payment plans allow us to spread out payments at slightly higher cost. Students may enroll ONLY for the entire program.

One feature of the program that I appreciate is that we are free to structure it in whatever manner we choose as far as order and timing. Parents and/or students can get educational assistance toll free. Tel-Test is an interesting testing option offered by ICS; students call in and take their tests over the telephone by pushing buttons on the telephone keypad. The alternative, called Exam Express, is a mail-in option with immediate grading (within 24 hours of receipt) and return of results.

The curriculum itself is strictly secular, striving to be philosophically neutral while not acknowledging God. However, what we end up with is the basic secular humanist approach. For example, in the Politics and People course, we are subtly told to look to government for solutions. Addressing the issue of world hunger and the role of the Secretary of Agriculture, the text offers a choice of four solutions, all having government buying, selling, or giving away money. The civics course rationalizes the need for a national debt and advocates ideas such as the periodic revision of the Constitution. While there is nothing significantly different from typical high school courses, I have trouble recommending a steady dose of this mindset. Nevertheless, I know that for some families, this will be an acceptable option because of cost and accreditation.

Another factor that makes ICS appealing for some students is that it is generally less demanding than other correspondence courses. Courses require students to complete and return only the multiple choice exams, most of which are not extremely challenging.

The various courses use a mixture of resources, but rely heavily on those from Amsco. Although the books are pedestrian, they accomplish the task. On the other hand, the electives offered by ICS Newport/Pacific are more interesting than those typically available to high schoolers. They include classes such as accounting, introduction to animal sciences, and introduction to interior design.

The core curriculum is not college preparatory at this time. It is divided into six areas. The first area is English, within which students complete four courses which will suffice for college. The second area is math, but the courses are General Math I, Consumer Math, and General Math II; college prep math courses are electives. Science is the third area, and it includes General Science, Systems of the Body, and Nutrition; again, not college prep level courses. Social Studies is fourth, with U.S. History,

Civics, and World History—sufficient for college prep. Fifth is arts and humanities with the two most troublesome classes, Politics and People, and Human Relations. A fitness class satisfies the last area of health and physical education. Remember that it will be necessary to choose an additional five electives, but those electives might be science and math courses. No foreign language courses are offered, which might present problems for those who are college bound.

I expect that this program will appeal most to those who want an inexpensive program that requires students to be accountable to someone other than parents. It is also, at least at the present time, most practical for those who do not plan to go on to college, since many college prep classes are treated as electives, are missing altogether, or are not of high enough caliber for college preparation.(SE)

➲ Keystone National High School

Keystone is a non-sectarian correspondence school, accredited by the Distance Education and Training Council and licensed by the State Board of Private Licensed Schools in Pennsylvania. They offer only grades 9 through 12. Students may enroll in entire grade-level programs ($750 a year) or selected courses ($150 each). Students may transfer into the program mid-high school, but their previously earned credits must be evaluated and "verified." Keystone offers both college prep and general ed/career programs. Keystone issues transcripts and diplomas for students who enroll in the complete program. Those transferring in late, must complete a minimum of 5 credits with Keystone. Enrollment is open year round, and students have a full calendar year to complete each course. Extensions are available for an additional fee. An Advisory Teaching Service is included with the cost of each course, and teachers may be contacted by mail, phone, fax, or e-mail. Each course also includes a learning guide, textbook(s), and workbooks if applicable.

All diploma program students are required to complete Skills for Success, a self-image and career planning course. 21 units are required for graduation; in addition to Skills for Success, these must include the following number of courses in each subject: math-3, science-3, art/music-1, English-4, social science-4, and health-1, plus 4 electives. Elective choices are fairly limited as are even some of the basic course choices. Refresher Math, Consumer Math, Algebra I, Geometry, and Algebra II comprise math offerings. Four English courses leave no other options. These courses are all built around Holt's *Elements of Literature* textbooks, incorporating grammar and writing skills in conjunction with the study of literature. Science options are Earth Science, Life Science, Biology, Physical Science, Chemistry, and Physics which gives students significant choice. Holt and Amsco texts are used for these courses. As far as I know, all are solidly evolutionary in perspective. This is very much the case with the Biology course where evolution is incorporated throughout the course as a foundational concept. As of January 1, 1998, Keystone will offer a lab component for their Biology course, with lab kits for other courses still in the works. Social Science options are Civics, World History, American History, Geography, and American Government. Your own state's requirements will

dictate which of these you must take in many cases. The required Health course uses a Holt text that reflects much of what is taught in government schools—sex ed, self-esteem, suicide, drugs, and decision making. Electives might be any of the above that do not meet basic requirements or Driver's Education, Sociology, Economics, or Psychology. (Note: Economics is required in some states.) Texts for the above courses come primarily from Holt, Amsco, Prentice-Hall, and Merrill. Spanish I and II, and possibly French and German, will be offered beginning January 1, 1998.

Keystone plans to add additional courses and services as they grow—more higher level math, Saxon math as an option, a Speech course, Internet research course, SAT and ACT support services, and online services for lesson responses and tests.

Some of the pluses for Keystone are more than 20 years of experience in the correspondence school business, availability of experienced teachers for help when needed, and personal comments and feedback on tests. Tests do include some multiple choice work, but they also require essay responses that give a better picture of student skills and knowledge.

Drawbacks primarily have to do with the lack of foreign language and advanced mathematics courses, and with world view problems within courses. Keystone is presently reviewing their courses to consider adding exercises "that would allow students to engage and challenge the view points expressed in the text books" that come with their courses.

Overall, Keystone seems to be a step above ICS/Newport Pacific in college prep coverage and quality of testing of students, but about equivalent in course content for comparable courses. Watch for expansion and improvements over the next few years.(SE)

➲ Landmark's Freedom Baptist Curriculum

Landmark offers a complete curriculum for grades K-12. Students can enroll in the complete program or purchase individual courses. There are three basic plans: Plan A provides all materials, record keeping, testing, report cards, and diplomas for $450 per year for the first child, $325 for the second and third, and $300 for each child thereafter. Plan B is placement and achievement testing which can be "purchased" alone or in conjunction with the other plans as specified. Plan C provides the course basics for any one course for $35. LFBC allows parents to purchase materials to use as they wish, but they encourage home schooling families to work under the auspices of some oversight organization for accountability. All prices include shipping and handling costs.

The curriculum is fairly strong academically, although there are no advanced math, chemistry, or physics courses offered. There are six core subjects at all levels: Bible, math, English, history, science, and literature. Electives offered are penmanship, typing, home economics, shop, personal development, and principles of music.

LFBC believes that it is parents' responsibility to pass on knowledge, wisdom, and values to their children, so the curriculum is strongly oriented toward a Judeo-Christian value system. Most people would describe the philosophy as very conservative. History shuns modern social studies, choosing to concentrate on history and geography. English takes a back-to-basics approach with parts of speech, diagramming, research papers, essays, and compositions. Science relies on a literal reading of the book of Genesis, with one high school course titled "Scientific Creationism." Bible courses use the KJV with an entire high school course titled "The Inspiration of Scripture," primarily an apologetic for the KJV as opposed to other (especially modern) translations. High school math options include two years of algebra, geometry, and business math. History includes U.S. and world history, Baptist history, culture wars, current issues, and government/economics. Science includes physical science, biology, health/dynamic living, and scientific creationism. There are no labs with science courses. The courses are uneven in quality, both graphically and in content. For example, the print quality of the literature readings is quite poor and the Geometry course had numerous irritations in layout, typos, and even the approach taken to present the subject. I have reviewed some of the LFBC courses elsewhere in this book in case you want to use selected courses. They are upgrading the curriculum at a fairly rapid pace, so watch for continual improvements.

➲ McGuffey Academy International

McGuffey Academy is a K-12 Christian correspondence school accredited by the Accrediting Commission International for Schools, Colleges, and Theological Seminaries. Curriculum is drawn from Alpha Omega, Basic Education, A Beka, Saxon, and others. Students can begin at the appropriate level in each subject area and work at their own pace until they complete their work. Tuition for junior high is $400 per year. High school includes five basic courses for $450 per year. Extra courses are $100 each. Electives include business courses, foreign languages, art, and home economics. Most student workbooks are covered by tuition costs, but some texts are extra.

➲ Montgomery Institute

The Montgomery Institute was founded to assist families who want to implement the Principle Approach. They offer three options: Option 1 - for $10 year you can obtain book service membership and obtain any of their more than 800 books and audio cassettes at discount prices; Option 2 - associate members pay $75 and receive book service membership, free admission to the annual Biblical World View conference (held in Idaho) and regional workshop, and the monthly newsletter; Option 3 - the Extension Study Program functions as a correspondence course. The required parent training program, taken through correspondence, costs $150. Tuition for the first child is $200, $100 for the second, and $75 for each additional child. As part of the training program you receive essential and valuable resources such as The *1828 American Dictionary of the English Language, The Christian History of the Constitution of the United States,* and *Teaching and Learning America's Christian History and Government*, along with a number of audio cassettes and study guides. Those enrolled receive the same benefits as do those in Option 2 as well as consultation and curriculum selection assistance, teacher notebooks for each grade level you will be teaching (detailed how-to's and lesson plans), achievement tests (plus

scoring and recommendations), annual certificate of completion and or/ final diploma, and the newsletter "Renewing Your Mind" by Paul Jehle. They will also connect you with any others in your area to form a support group. Among the texts used for junior and senior high are *Ray's Arithmetic; Saxon Math; Harvey's Grammar; Introductory Logic* by Douglas Wilson; *McGuffey Readers; Basic Chemistry* from BJUP; *Streams of Civilization;* Clarence Carson's *Basic American Government; Economics: Principles and Policy from a Christian Perspective; Basic History of the United States;* and *How Great Thou ART*, as well as a number of Principle Approach oriented resources.

➲ North Dakota Division of Independent Study

This school offers complete, accredited high school programs with a wide variety of class options to accommodate different learners' abilities and interests. For example, math classes include general mathematics, consumer mathematics, and precalculus as well as the more standard courses. Classes such as child development, etiquette, agriculture, accounting, business law, engines, electricity, aerospace, and welding stretch beyond the typical correspondence offerings. The cost is much higher than for ICS Newport/Pacific or Covenant, but lower than Home Study International averaging about $100 per course per semester. Students can enroll in as many courses as they choose, but they are required to be under the supervision of a credentialed teacher who receives materials and supervises tests.(SE)

➲ Oral Roberts University College Program

Oral Roberts is not offering high school correspondence courses, but rather a jump start on college. They offer only thirteen courses including Reading and Writing in the Liberal Arts, Introduction to College Mathematics, College Algebra, Introduction to Humanities, Principles of Biology and Laboratory, and Christian Faith and Ministry. These are mainly college freshman courses which can be completed at home. There are no prerequisites for most of the courses (such as high school graduation), but ORU expects that these courses would be taken after completion of the typically required college prep courses, rather than substituted for high school courses. For example, students should have completed at least two years of high school math and two years of science, including at least one lab. Also, to enroll in the higher-level courses being offered in English and math, students must pass a proficiency examination. (There is a $15 proctor's fee to take the exam.) ORU offers these courses as a transition program for home schoolers, hoping of course, that students will choose to complete their education at ORU. Students can complete the courses at their own pace, at a cost significantly lower than if they studied on campus. Courses cost $55 per credit hour (most are 3-hour courses making the cost $165 each) plus the cost of textbooks. Since ORU is accredited, the units are transferable to other institutions. I have heard from one parent that the courses are more challenging than "on campus" versions of the same courses, so don't expect to use them for easy college credit.

➲ Seton Home Study School

Seton Home Study School offers correspondence courses for elementary grades through high school for full or partial enrollment. They offer a traditional, Catholic education at a reasonable cost, using an assortment of Catholic, BJUP, Saxon, and other textbooks to provide a quality education. Secular course alternatives can replace Catholic course offerings at the high school level. Examples of some of the texts used are *Warriner's Grammar and Composition*, Saxon's math series, *Biology for Christian Schools, American Government and Economics in Christian Perspective, Adventures in Appreciation*, and the *Baltimore Catechism*. Because their primary desire is to be of service, Seton offers a wide variety of individual courses (partial enrollment) on subjects ranging from business education and computers through basic academic subjects. At the high school level, students might wish to enroll in a complete course or only in Latin, chemistry, higher math, or another specific course. Seton is one of the few private programs which allows single subject enrollment for high school. Of special interest are Catholic religion courses open for partial enrollment also to elementary students (up through eighth grade). Help is available by telephone if necessary. The cost for grades 1-8 is $495. The cost for high school is $545. Prices include application, registration, shipping, and textbooks. Single courses are $125 with costs for additional courses decreasing. They offer significant discounts for additional children in the family. Credit card and/or payment plans are available. Textbooks are used on loan unless we choose to purchase them. Seton has both new and used texts available for many courses. Contact them or check their website for more information.

➲ Summit Christian Academy

Summit is accredited by the National Coalition of Alternative Community Schools. Programs are offered for prekindergarten through twelfth grades. Upon enrollment, diagnostic testing is required for grades 3-12, ensuring proper placement in the curriculum. They use Alpha Omega, Bob Jones University Press, A Beka Book, Saxon, and Keyboard Enterprises Video Math for core subjects. (Alpha Omega is distributed from their warehouse, but other materials may be used with their approval.) They encourage multi-sensory learning and allow some flexibility in designing your program. Summit also offers their students credit for work-study programs. They can provide academic, general, or vocational diplomas for graduating high schoolers. Their toll-free telephone number allows parents to consult with the school when necessary. Enrollment is $30 per student, testing is $35. Tuition and curriculum costs depend upon the grade level and subjects taken. Discounts are given on tuition for additional children in the family. A payment plan is available. Students take the WRAT test and five subject tests when they enroll. See both "Testing Services" and "Diagnostic Testing" for information about Summit's testing services.

➲ Tree of Life School

Based in New Brunswick, Canada, this school serves home educators in both Canada and the U.S. who are interested in the classical approach to education. This is a home-based service provided by experienced home educators, Mike and Debbie Flewelling. They offer monitored and unmonitored enrollment. Monitored students submit tests, essays, and reports to Tree of Life for evaluation and comments. They provide texts and course outlines, placement assistance, a transcript and certificate of graduation for students who complete at least 30 high school credits through them. The basic tuition fee is $225 for grades 7-8 and $350 for grades 9-12 with materials costing an additional $300 to $600. Unmonitored students receive placement assistance plus course texts and outlines for $135 tuition plus between $300 and $600 for the course materials. Grades 1 through 12 are offered. Enrollment for single high school courses is $50 per course (plus materials). Emphasis is on both Christian world view and the classical approach. Students begin study of Latin in fourth and fifth grades. (They have already studied French the first three years and continue studying and using that language through at least eight grade.) Greek is added at 7th grade and Latin grammar at 8th. High school students can start from the beginning or continue with French, Greek, or Latin. Chronological history studies have 7th graders studying ancient Rome and 8th graders studying the Middle Ages and broader world history. At high school level, students are required to take both logic and rhetoric in addition to a challenging schedule of 5 English credits, 4 math credits, 4 science credits, 3 Bible credits, 4 foreign language credits, 5 history credits, and 2 "life and technology" credits. Real books are incorporated into the curriculum. Some adjustments can be made to the above high school requirements, and some will be necessary for U.S. students to meet requirements of each of their states.

➲ University of Nebraska-Lincoln

The University of Nebraska-Lincoln high school course is accredited by the North Central Association of Colleges and Schools and the Nebraska Department of Education. They offer both general education and college prep courses of study with a wide variety of class selections including advanced math, French, Latin, Spanish, chemistry, and physics. Many electives are offered such as agriculture, horticulture, drawing, typing, business, accounting, computer science, and driver education. Students may enroll in selected courses or complete degree programs. University of Nebraska-Lincoln is non-sectarian, so it reflects the typical content problems we would expect, but it has also added required courses in either "Ethnic Studies and Human Relations" (based on values clarification) or "Multicultural Literature" and "Career Planning" that many home educators will either object to or find unnecessary. On-site teachers or an academic advisor can be reached via phone, mail, fax, or e-mail. Student work is graded and returned within two days. Courses are offered as one-semester or 1/2 unit courses, so it requires two courses to complete a full course unit in most cases. The cost per 1/2 unit course is $86 for residents and $90 for nonresidents, plus the cost of texts, syllabi, and other materials. Some courses, especially science courses, cost significantly more because of the materials required.

The University of Nebraska-Lincoln is developing online courses, although only four are offered at present: "Global Perspectives," "Environmental Chemistry," "Advanced Composition," and "Informal Geometry." Cost is about the same, but the format allows online interaction and research not available through the traditional courses. Check for current offerings.(S)

➲ The Westbridge Academy

Westbridge Academy is a college preparatory school service that functions as a correspondence school, but without the rigid limitations common to most. Geared for academically accelerated students, Westbridge helps parents individualize their curriculum and timing to suit each learner. Instead of a prescribed curriculum, goals are set for three levels: Foundations for Learning (approx. grades pre-k to 3), Intermediate Studies (approx. grades 4-6), and Advanced Studies (approx. grades 7-12). Those goals include a Judeo-Christian and classical orientation that stresses the foundations of western civilization. While Westbridge is a Christian organization, they will accept non-Christian students. Upon enrollment, students take placement tests and produce writing and grammar samples for evaluation. Individual consultations are scheduled to develop customized academic plans. (It is unlikely that any two students would be using identical books in this program!) Westbridge offers some of their own specially-designed courses along with evaluation, counseling, record keeping, transcript, and college application services. Students may work at different grade levels in various subjects. Credit may be given for alternative learning experiences. The staff of Westbridge Academy includes Kathleen and Mark Julicher of Castle Heights Press and Robert and Kathleen Kustusch of Lightsource Editing Service. Tuition is $600 per year per student with discounts available for more than one student in the family. Book costs are in addition to tuition costs. Books are ordered by families directly from suppliers, although Rainbow Re-Source acts as their official supplier.

Courses Without Correspondence

➲ HomeQuest Curriculum [computer programs for IBM compatibles or Macintosh] (HomeQuest) Tomorrow's Promise - $225 per subject per grade level (monthly rental plan also available); Lifetime Library - about $650 for the complete program

HomeQuest primarily uses programs from the Jostens Company for grades K-8. The newest version of the Jostens program, *Tomorrow's Promise*, is the core of reading, math, and language arts instruction with history and social studies integrated within those subject areas. *Jostens Learning Comprehensive Assessment Test (JCAT)* is a series of computerized tests used for placement. Objectives for the tests and the curriculum are drawn from the major standardized tests used nationwide.

Tomorrow's Promise moves beyond simple recall answers into challenging application and analysis questions. Additionally, the language arts program walks students through actual writing assignments, although screen boxes sometimes impose limits on sentence or paragraph length that seem unrealistic. This is intended to be comprehensive subject area coverage for all areas, although I haven't seen the scope and sequence to verify this. All lessons present instruction, practice, and testing. Lessons vary in form of presentation, but typically, students read through instructional material, practice answering questions then take a test on that material, with tests closely resembling the practice material and format. We need a sound card in our computer since parts of the programs are presented auditorially. *Tomorrow's Promise* software has been created for greater learning efficiency than many other programs I have seen that move slowly between questions or get bogged down while cute little animated characters provide unnecessary diversion.

While *Tomorrow's Promise* lessons appear to be comprehensive, parents must understand that children cannot learn only through these programs. *HomeQuest* frees the parent from having to assign, teach, check, and record grades for text and workbook lessons, a major appeal for overloaded moms. However, children require interaction to learn to read well, discuss course content, ask questions, explore topics not covered in the curriculum, and cover other aspects of learning that cannot be handled by the computer (or only by workbooks for that matter). Teacher's Guides for each subject area and each level offer general suggestions for some activities that might be used to accomplish these goals.

HomeQuest sells *Lifetime Library* for use at junior and senior high levels. Although this is not a comprehensive curriculum like *Tomorrow's Promise*, it features 47 CD-ROMs (23 gigabytes of information!) and will provide a major part of your core subjects. Math 1 and 2 programs within *Lifetime Library* cover basic math skills typically taught at even younger levels to ensure a solid foundation for moving on to higher math. Math programs continue through pre-algebra, Algebra Part 1 and Part 2. Concepts covered within the Algebra program are fairly comprehensive for Algebra I and cover many concepts for Algebra II. Lots of word problems and practical applications are included in keeping with the NCTM Standards. Writing programs cover grammar, sentence structure, paragraph organization, and style. However, the exercises are limited to simple answers that can be evaluated by computer rather than true writing exercises. Reading programs concentrate heavily on real-life situations (interpreting want ads, reading advertisements, reading monthly statements), but they also direct study of literature and literary analysis. As with *Tomorrow's Promise,* although to a lesser degree, some social studies and science learning occurs within the reading programs. Programs function smoothly with pretests, instruction, tests, grading, record keeping, and online help nicely integrated. Programs move quickly from question to question as well as from one section to another. Illustrations, sound, and video clips are used throughout the programs which makes it much more interesting for students doing a significant amount of work with *Lifetime Library*. System requirements are higher than for many programs: a 486 66MHz or faster CPU with 8 MB RAM, VGA monitor operating in 256 color mode or better, 2x or better CD-ROM drive, Sound Blaster or compatible audio board, Windows 95, and 15 MB minimum hard drive space.

Both *Tomorrow's Promise* and *Lifetime Library* suffer from the same limitations as do many workbooks. Some skills are taught as isolated bits of information, and it is expected that somehow they will come together into a coherent whole. While such exercises can be useful, they cannot adequately serve as a complete curriculum on their own. Recognizing such limitations, *Tomorrow's Promise* solves part of the problem by building into the program integrated activities that require students to research a topic on the Internet, then use that information in activities that stretch across other subject areas. *HomeQuest* itself recognizes possible deficiencies, as evidenced by their sponsorship of Masters Academy, a private umbrella school which suggests 1 1/2 hours of computer-assisted study per day accompanied by an additional 1 to 2 hours of non-computer activity. Masters Academy might be especially useful at high school level since the curriculum is not complete on its own, and it is difficult to identify to what it will be equivalent. Masters Academy will be familiar with the program and can easily help you round out the rest of the curriculum.

Programs are sold through a network marketing organization, and your representative should be available to offer you assistance if you need it.(S)

⊃ HomeSat

Those concerned about covering high school math, science, and foreign language should check out *HomeSat*, BJUP's satellite presentation of such classes as Algebra II, Advanced Math, Biology, Chemistry, Physics, and Spanish I. (Courses offered differ from year to year. See the "previously-aired" classes on video option described at the end of this review if they are not offering classes you need at this time.) BJUP has tried to make the courses as accessible as possible by offering a reasonably priced satellite dish, which we can either have installed or install ourselves. Courses are sent over the satellite, and we record them on our VCR for use at appropriate times. We can record and watch as many courses as we please, but we register for courses by paying $39/month for the first course, $20/month for the second, $15/month for the third, and $10/month for each additional class. No additional fee is required for additional students in your own family. Enrolled students receive quizzes, tests, and handouts for each course. (Photocopy the quizzes, tests, and handouts for other students.) Answer keys come with courses, and parents check and grade student work. We also need to purchase the BJUP texts for each course. Parent preparation and participation is extremely minimal, a boon to parents who need their older students to accomplish much of their work independently.

The courses themselves differ from all the other video options I have reviewed. They were set up as live, video-linked courses for private schools. Special devices allow students at sites around the country (generally small Christian schools) to respond to the teacher's live presentation. Thus, the teacher pauses for responses from students at classrooms off-site. There are no actual students on screen. The presentation takes advantage of the video format to include graphics and demonstrations that would not be feasible in the normal classroom environment. Even with the responses, class presentations move at a good pace. Courses are transmitted via satellite each evening. We record selected classes with our VCR, then use the tapes at the most convenient time with our students. Tapes are ours to keep. Nothing is sent back to BJU, neither tapes nor student work.

HomeSat has accumulated videos of classes from the 1996-97 school year, and they are now available as complete classes on Super Long Play (SLP) video tapes, with one week's worth of classes on each tape. The previously-aired classes available are Algebra 1, Algebra 2, Advanced Math, Biology, Chemistry, French 1, Physical Science, Physics, Spanish 1, and Spanish 2. As with the satellite courses, the tapes come with handouts, quizzes, tests, and answer keys. The cost of textbooks is extra. Costs are $400 for the first course, $350 for the second, and $300 for each additional class.

⊃ Sonlight Curriculum-International Home Schoolers Curriculum

While Sonlight is not a correspondence course, it is designed like some such courses with a teacher's manual that outlines lessons for each day using specific pages within the materials provided. However, there is no option for sending in work for grading or record keeping.

Sonlight offers a complete, eclectic, literature-based program integrated around historical themes for kindergarten through ninth grade. (Most levels are designated by years rather than grade levels.) World history is taught in grades K-2 and years 5-6. American history is taught in grades 3, 4, and 7. "God's Kingdom Worldwide from Christ to the Present" is the topic for year 8, and "20th Century World History" is the theme in year 9. Year 10, with "American Government" the planned topic, might be released just prior to the next edition of this manual.

Sonlight stresses subject matter over grade level. Because it is a literature (rather than textbook) based program, parents with more than one child are often able to use one year's selection of history, read-aloud, and science books with all their children. In fact, from the fifth year up, Sonlight manuals are specifically designated for use by students in a range of grades. (This is why designations shift from "grade" to "year.") The fifth-year manual, for example is designed for use in any grade from fifth through ninth. The eighth year program is designed for students at any level from eighth through twelfth. While some of the eighth and ninth year materials can be used in tenth through twelfth grades, there are not yet enough separate teacher's manuals for all of those levels. You can use the courses at different levels by substituting the appropriate math and language arts materials your student needs, while using the history and science program from just one level. The seventh year resources are a case in point; they incorporate the BJUP American Republic text, typically used for eighth grade, with lots of literature, then add serious scientific studies in earth science, astronomy, and oceanography. These resources and lessons could easily be used for eighth graders, and the science and most of the historical literature might be suitable for ninth graders. Bible study resources for eighth grade tackle apologetics and basic beliefs. Coupled with the historical study of the church at that level, they comprise a heavy duty grounding in faith that might serve well for older students.

Sonlight also offers mix-and-match loose-leaf teacher's manuals for each subject in every grade. Subjects include Basic (history, readers, read-alouds, and Bible), Language Arts (phonics-oriented reading in early grades, handwriting, dictation, spelling, grammar, vocabulary, creative writing), Science, and Math. All manuals include week-by-week lesson guides with record-keeping calendars, and thorough instructions. Sonlight emphasizes only those activities that have clear educational purposes; make-work projects and crafts are nonexistent. Though parent-child interaction is required at certain times, little time is required for lesson preparation. I am impressed also with the weekly writing assignments built into the curriculum, as this area is lacking in so many other programs.

Sonlight Curriculum features quality literature, a few textbooks and workbooks (e.g., *Saxon Math, Rules of the Game, Wordly Wise*), many Usborne titles, a huge assortment of literature, historical fiction, topical fiction, and hands-on science. The educational philosophy stresses the use of real books as much as possible. Subjects include language arts (reading, writing, spelling, etc.), history, geography, math, science, and Bible (including Christian and missionary biographies). Supplemental materials are available for critical thinking, foreign language (*Power-Glide* only), art, music, geography, physical education, Bible study, typing, and creation/evolution.

Sonlight sells complete curriculum packages for each subject in every grade; it also permits you to purchase any individual items out of the complete packages. The Sonlight science program includes basic science supplies. On its Basic curriculum packages (history, readers, and read-alouds), Sonlight offers an eight-week "use it; if you don't like it, return your program for a complete refund" guarantee. Customers who purchase a complete Basic program have the opportunity to purchase science, math, language arts, and enrichment materials (physical education, art, music, foreign language, etc.) at a 10% discount. Prices for the Basic curricula (ranging from about $300 to $425, depending on the grade) reflect a 7% discount from list and include shipping anywhere in the world. Much of the curriculum is nonconsumable, so we can reuse a large percentage of each level with other children. Many of the books used in the curriculum are ones that I would personally be purchasing to build our family library, so, from this perspective, the cost is actually even more reasonable. We save even more if we teach children from the same resources whenever practical even though they might be at different grade levels.

Sonlight is proving to be an excellent option for families that want assistance putting together a "pick and choose" program, but who lack the experience to do it on their own. You really should read through Sonlight's catalog before determining which levels or resources to use. Send $2 for their catalog which includes a $2 coupon towards your first order of $25 or more.

Online Learning

Online options are expanding quickly, so the best way to get the most up-to-date information is to go online and check out what is available. To get you started, I want to mention a few options already available.

➲ Escondido Tutorial Service

Fritz Hinrichs and other teachers working with him offer tutorial classes online for Geometry; the Great Books (see full description in Chapter Thirteen); Shakespeare; Logic; Greek; Latin; Constitutional Law; Saxon texts for *Algebra 1/2, Algebra 1, Algebra 2, Advanced Mathematics, Calculus,* and *Physics;* and Rhetoric. All classes are not offered every year, so check for available classes each school year. Hinrichs is one of the leading pioneers in developing computerized learning options that take the most advantage of technology while remaining practical. He uses cutting edge technology as soon as it becomes practical and reasonably priced. Consequently, don't be surprised if he changes the presentation media from time to time. At this time, he uses CU-Seeme, Real Video, and Netmeeting to bring computer instruction close to what students encounter in a classroom. They can watch what he writes as he writes it and hear his verbal explanations. Students can respond by speaking into the microphones on their computers. Additional books, software, and/or videos are often used with these courses. Students complete assignments from the classes, and are required to participate to some extent in online discussions. However, testing and homework supervision is generally done by parents. Most classes require a once-a-week online meeting of from one to two hours. Most classes run two semesters and cost $105 per semester with additional charges for books, software, and videos. Check their website for current information.

➲ North Dakota Division of Independent Study

This division of the North Dakota Department of Public Instruction was established to provide distance education courses to students in grades 7-12. It is regionally accredited and is a member of the Independent Study Division of the National University Continuing Education Association (NUCEA). While most courses are offered as traditional correspondence courses, they are offering increasing numbers of courses online. Present online courses are Developmental English, Global Politics, Internet Research and Writing, Knowing About Art, Geography, Local History, and Russian. Sample lessons from each course can be viewed at their web site. For online courses, students read from texts and online lessons, then complete and send in assignments. Cost is around $100 per course plus texts and materials. To enroll, students must have the signature of the administrator of "their local, state approved school."(SE)

➲ Regina Coeli Academy (Institute for Study of the Liberal Arts and Sciences)

See the review of Scholars' Online Academy and Regina Coeli Academy. Both academies function similarly, although Regina Coeli is unequivocally Catholic in its purpose and presentation. Courses from both academies can be combined for a comprehensive course of study. Regina Coeli offers a four-year theology sequence based on the Catechism of the Roman Catholic Church. Alongside the theology course offerings is the presentation of a four-year Scholastic Philosophy series.

➲ **Scholars' Online Academy (SOLA) and Regina Coeli Academy (RCA)** (Institute for Study of the Liberal Arts and Sciences)

SOLA and RCA are private (though not state-accredited) schools chartered in the State of Louisiana under the nonprofit educational corporation of ISLAS. SOLA (non-sectarian) and RCA (Catholic) combine faculty and courses to offer a complete, college prep, Christian classical approach to education via online computer technology. Students may enroll full-time or part-time using any combination of classes from SOLA or RCA. Students interact with the professor and classmates in weekly or bi-weekly live conferences, the private World-Wide-Web "bulletin board" conference center, and private e-mail.

Students read and discuss original literary, historical, and philosophical works or study from textbooks selected for integration with professionally-prepared supplementary material on the World Wide Web. Students enrolled in the school's Integrated Writing Program prepare essays to be read by the entire faculty across all disciplines.

The rigor of the college preparatory courses affords students who are diligent in their studies the opportunity to gain college credits through university departmental testing, AP, and CLEP tests. Evidence of the rigorous level of study required in SOLA and RCA is the selection of texts such as the UCSMP high school math texts which are more difficult and wider ranging than most, and the selection of college texts or original works used in the study of Greek, Latin, philosophy, physics, English, government, and history.

Of special interest is ISLAS' presentation of various science and humanity courses taught from a Christian perspective. Students are taken through the study of philosophy beginning with an introductory course preparing them for the vocabulary and method of more advanced courses in Thomism, which many view as the Christian perfection of classical philosophy. History and literature are taught with genuine respect for Christendom as the cornerstone of western civilization.

In the biology class, the instructor counters Darwinism with discussion of the nature and limitations of scientific theory and arguments from intelligent design and creation, while requiring students to understand how evolution theory is currently used to unify and integrate basic biological concepts. Secular texts are used. Lab work is included although it doesn't require extensive equipment and resources. (More intensive criticism of Darwinism is undertaken at the philosophical level in Philosophy I and II.)

The cost ranges from $300 - $350 per course for the academic year (September - May) plus the cost of books or other learning materials. The Writing Program is open to full or part-time students and costs $125 per course per student. Summer courses include the following: "Molding Your Prose and Molding Your Argument" (English composition), "Mythos and Logos" (Introduction to mythology as pre-philosophy), and "Laid-Back Latin." The 10-week summer enrichment courses

are $150 each. The summer program serves primarily to orient younger students considering enrollment in college preparatory classes. Enrollment in at least one summer enrichment course is recommended before enrolling in the college preparatory program.

Independent Study Courses through Universities

Some colleges also offer high school correspondence courses, often called independent study, but do not offer diplomas. Usually the local school district has to give students permission to enroll, which might present a problem in some areas.

The University of California Extension, the University of Missouri, and the University of Alabama, are among institutions offering courses for high school students unable to complete all of their educational requirements in a regular classroom setting.

University of Missouri courses cost $84 per half unit course. The home school or another educational institution or school service grants students credit for these courses, and is the diploma grantor. Courses are available to students all over the world.

University of Alabama courses cost $75 per 1/2 unit course for high school courses.

For a list of other colleges and universities offering correspondence courses, we can order *The Independent Study Catalog* (Peterson's).

Correspondence Telecourses

Television can be useful! In some areas of the country school districts and colleges broadcast telecourses on educational channels (UHF or cable). Courses are offered at all different levels, but complete courses are available for college subjects. In our area, about twenty courses are offered each semester, mostly on cable channels. Students enroll by mail, with no high school graduation requirement. They watch the course, read the accompanying textbook, send in the required paper work (usually minimal), then either send in a final test or report to a testing site for the final exam. These courses are for college credit but can also be used without enrollment for high school work. Typical courses are American History, Business, Astronomy, Biology, Freehand Drawing, and Child Development. We used the Biology course to help us with our lower level biology studies. The videos depicted things so well that they were better than most lab work that we could have done. Of course you do have to be on guard for course content since these courses reflect the secular viewpoint. Check your television guide or write to your educational channel for complete listings.

School Services

School services usually have no campuses. They are similar to correspondence courses in that they serve students all over the country (and beyond our borders), but they allow families to choose materials, usually with their assistance. Often there is quite a bit of choice involved. Depending on the service, they might keep records, evaluate student work, and (usually) provide testing. School services can vary dramatically in what they offer, so check carefully to know what you are paying for.

The following school services provide enrollment throughout the country:

➲ Hewitt Research Foundation Child Development Center

This center is a school service originally founded to implement the philosophy of Dr. Raymond Moore, but Dr. Moore is no longer associated with it. Programs are open to both junior and senior high students. Hewitt provides testing, evaluation, textbook recommendations, and record keeping services as well as phone counseling on their toll-free line. Textbook costs are in addition to registration costs. The basic family registration is $25. Enrollment in seventh or eight grade programs costs $179, which includes an individualized curriculum guide (with curriculum recommendations), two hours of phone counseling, a written evaluation, and two PASS tests. (PASS tests are standardized tests created by Hewitt.) High school enrollment costs $356, which includes telephone consultation services (including curriculum recommendations), four written evaluations, and a transcript. Junior high students can take high school courses and receive "credit in escrow" for $85 per course, which allows them to use the course credit after completing ninth grade with Hewitt. Single course enrollment costs $85, and it includes book recommendation, phone counseling, written evaluation, and a transcript. Most courses come with a syllabus that guides the student through the course. In keeping with their philosophy of education, Hewitt offers high school students the opportunity to obtain credit for such studies or activities as woodworking, drama, photography, volunteer experience, and work experience. They also offer Honors history courses as an option. Hewitt is unusual in their ability to assist children with learning difficulties. They can help with assessment and tailoring of a program to suit each child. A Special Needs Package enrolls students, ages 3-21, and includes initial evaluation, written and phone assistance with curriculum and educational programs, and two written evaluations.

Hewitt recommends and sells learning materials and books from many publishers, but the cost of resources is not included in the enrollment services.

➲ Moore Foundation Curriculum Programs

Dr. and Mrs. Raymond Moore's Moore Foundation now offers membership plus a number of service options.

Moore Foundation Associates (MFA), for families who do not need special services, requires a minimum purchase of materials or donation of $100 and provides an enrollment card which shows that the family is identified with and attached to the Moore Foundation. MFA membership is prerequisite to enrollment in all other programs. MFA members may enroll in any Moore Foundation service programs, as long as there is space.

There are four service options available. Start Up (SU) is for families who want only initial counseling and curriculum planning. Moore Foundation Independent Study Program (MFISP) offers families ongoing services beyond MFA enrollment. The MFISP provides record keeping, evaluations, and certificate of completion or transcript. Moore Academy Full Service Program (MAFSP) is a limited (in enrollment numbers) plan in which those who need more extensive accountability receive more extensive service that includes maintenance of a cumulative record folder, processing of requests for past school records, customized curricula, telephone or letter counseling, an initial evaluation, two progress evaluations, and certificate of completion or transcript. Specialized Full Service Program (SFSP) is for children who might be "...learning-delayed, learning-different, talented & gifted, handicapped or otherwise in need of special counsel, special materials and perhaps teacher analysis of psychological tests." All programs except Start Up are available for both elementary and secondary students. Start Up is available for grades K-8. Cost varies according to the program.

➲ Sycamore Tree

Sycamore Tree offers full record keeping, field trips (if you live in the area), educational guidance, supervision, testing, student body cards, 60-80 pages of enrichment learning material every month, diplomas, transcripts and more for kindergarten through twelfth grade. They will assist you in developing an individualized program for each child. They also will grant work experience credit, a feature that should be of interest to many high school students. Courses taken at a community college or other high school or college will apply toward graduation requirements. Guidance is available by phone or mail. A credentialed teacher is on staff during all office hours. Enrollment entitles you to a 10 percent discount on curricula and materials ordered through Sycamore Tree. They recommend materials from a very wide range of publishers, including both traditional and informal learning materials. Students transferring mid-high school into the Sycamore program must have units from an accredited school or from a home school umbrella/independent study program for prior high school work. This is an especially good option for isolated families. There is a $50 enrollment fee for each child. Tuition is $450 per year for the entire family ($400 if paid by September 10).

➲ Advanced Training Institute International

The Institute, under the leadership of Bill Gothard, offers a program for home schooling based upon the Bible, *Wisdom Booklets,* other materials from the Institute, and your own selected textbooks for communicating academic skills. Apprenticeship for older students is another important part of the ATI program. (The term apprenticeship is used very loosely to describe a variety of work and training programs.) ATI is a unique program that requires familiarity with the Institute and its teaching methods and principles. Their goals stress life training rather than academic training. Families are discouraged from using very many traditional academic texts or workbooks. There is a strong emphasis on parental accountability. The entire family is enrolled in the program together, attends a two-day training seminar, commits to establishing daily family Scripture reading times led by the father, and agrees to several other guidelines. *Wisdom Booklets* provide the foundation for Scripturally-based unit studies that are excellent. ATI is not a correspondence course, although the Institute provides forms and booklets to help with scheduling, planning, and record keeping. Write to the Institute for more information.

Independent Study Programs[1]

Independent study programs are offered by both public and private schools and also by school services.

Public School Independent Study Programs

You may be able to enroll your teen in an independent study program through your local public junior or senior high school. Aside from the question of whether or not we should really have anything at all to do with the public school system, in many states we have the right to enroll our child in such programs. Generally, students are required to use the public school texts, although they might be permitted to use Christian texts on their own time at their own expense in addition to their required texts. Such programs are available in many states for elementary grades, but independent study programs at the junior/senior high school level are still quite rare. Enrolling in such a program will make it much easier to get a traditional diploma and transcript, although the tradeoff value (being under the authority of the public school system) is debatable.

Private Day School Independent Study Programs

Some private Christian schools are offering independent study programs for junior and senior high. This option is attractive since we get the assurance of the traditional transcript and diploma, without having to accept non-Christian philosophy, textbooks, and methodology. Participation in selected activities of the school can be a valuable bonus.

Other Independent Study Programs

There are hundreds of independent study programs across the country that offer services to local home educators. These programs vary tremendously in services offered, requirements,

and expertise of the administrators. Check with your local home school group for possibilities.

Part-Time School

Public school

More and more home schoolers are considering part-time school as an option. In some states students may enroll in their local public high school for selected classes. We again face the question of whether or not we want our children to have any involvement with the public school system. However, we may wish to have them take driver's education to avoid having to purchase private lessons (if it is possible in your state). We might also think that the situation is safe enough to enroll teens in science lab or foreign language classes.

Many schools have not dealt with home schoolers who wish to enroll part-time, so they do not know what to tell you. Before approaching a school, check the law in your state to determine your rights.

On the other hand, if schools really do not want your part-time student on campus, they can make things so miserable that you do not want to exercise your right to that option. They might also require extras that you do not want. For instance, driver's education is frequently offered as a combination class with health education. The health education class usually is heavy on sex education which most of us would rather handle on our own. Schools have the right to split the class for your convenience or require that your student take both parts.

Private school

Few private schools have had part-time students, so our children might be "guinea pigs." If this option interests you, approach your private school with a positive attitude and a willingness to try it on an experimental basis. The school will make money by enrolling your child, so unless it is disruptive, they should be open to the idea.

Support Group Schools

Part-time schools organized by home schoolers for home schoolers are becoming more and more common. In many states home schoolers are joining together and hiring teachers to offer classes for the more difficult subjects. Students usually attend school only two or three hours a week per class, then work at home on lesson assignments. The fact that fellow students are also home schooled makes the environment comfortable. Usually there is a tuition fee for such classes. Parents still maintain overall control, yet they have someone to whom they can turn to fill in for their weaknesses in different subject areas. This ap-

---

1   The terms "Independent Study Program" and "School Service" are often used interchangeably and inconsistently. What services are being offered is of more importance to you than how a program identifies itself.

proach has been very successful, and we should see many more such schools open in the future.

A problem that has arisen in these types of classes occurs sometimes when students spend most of one or two days together in a school-like atmosphere. Typical peer pressure problems quickly crop up, and teens begin to act much like teens who attend traditional schools. This does not always happen, but it has happened often enough to alert us to potential problems. Keys to preventing problems might be increased adult "participation" (more than one teacher/advisor with a large group of teens) and some relationship and attitude guidelines when students enroll.

Adult Education and ROP

Adult education is sometimes available to older teenagers, whether or not they have graduated from high school. A minimum age of sixteen is common, and teens might have to be accompanied by an adult. Adult education classes range from the basics in reading, writing, and math to vocational and trade subjects. Elective type classes in the arts, foreign languages, computers, cooking, and other subjects are also offered.

ROP, or Regional Occupational Programs are a form of adult education that is open to teens sixteen and older. (Programs might function under different names in different states.) Classes are designed to train students in marketable skills. Accounting, animal care, banking, business machines, cosmetology, electronics, fashion merchandising, legal secretary, photography, and welding are among the typical subjects offered by such programs. Students need permission from school officials to attend these classes since they work closely with the public school system.

New School-to-Work programs are producing more and more such options, all funded to some extent by the government.

Junior College or Community College

Most states have junior or community college systems. Some of these systems are even open to students who have not graduated from high school. In California, any student capable of doing the work (judged by placement tests) is legally able to attend junior college, although high school students require special permission. Some parents are teaching the classes they can handle at home and sending students to the junior college for more difficult classes such as math, science lab, foreign language, and computer. They are not even bothering to try to cover those subjects at home on the high school level. This method saves time in the educational process, and credits are accumulated that cost much less at junior college than they would at a four-year college.

There are some cautions here. Junior or community college is not necessarily a good option. Some teens are not able to work at the pace necessary for college classes. The pressure can be very stressful for students who are accustomed to working on loose time schedules and even for disciplined students who are just too young.

Additionally, junior college might be no better (or possibly worse) than sending our child to the public high school. Many teenagers, at ages fifteen, sixteen, or seventeen, are too easily influenced by teachers, professors, and other students who hold opposing beliefs. It makes no sense to guard our children at home for many years, then rush them off to a secular junior college to battle ideas on a level too mature for them. Even for the mature student, we should be cautious about the types of classes they take. They are still very impressionable, no matter how strong they are in their faith. Most college campuses are also a culture in themselves, and our son or daughter needs to be mature enough to handle the social environment.

Early Graduation

Some teens are graduating from high school at age sixteen or seventeen (sometimes even earlier) by taking either the General Educational Development (GED) or High School Proficiency Examination. (The Proficiency Examination is available only in California.) They are covering basic courses at home and saving others such as lab classes and foreign language that are not tested by the GED to take at college. However, GED restrictions in many states preclude testing for early graduation. Some states will allow students to take the GED before the minimum age with special permission, but generally that special permission is very difficult to get. Check with an adult education center or GED Testing Service (address in the Appendix) for information about your state.

Students who can graduate early through testing are then able to enroll in junior or community colleges, or even four-year institutions at younger ages as high school graduates. The same cautions mentioned above apply since diplomas or certificates do not provide spiritual protection.

Compulsory education laws in each state require that students attend school until a specified age. If they graduate before they have passed the age for compulsory attendance, they will need to continue their education in some manner.

Tutors

Hiring a tutor might be a viable option for one or two classes. Even better would be for two or more families to jointly hire a tutor, essentially designing their own private class. For example, we and four other families hired a tutor to help us with Spanish. The tutor came for one hour, one day a week, and we worked with our children on our own throughout the rest of the week. This system worked very well for us, giving us just the amount of help we needed to be successful.

Cross Teaching

This option is free! All of us have different strengths and weaknesses. If we can share our strengths, we can overcome our weaknesses. If one parent is good in science, he or she can teach a science class for a group of students, while another parent whose strength is in writing takes a turn providing writing instruction. The tradeoff does not always have to be in teaching skills. One mother might be willing to babysit in exchange for your teaching skills. Another might be willing to trade housework labor. Be creative in drawing upon the talents of other home educators in your area.

Getting a Head Start on College

As mentioned previously, home educated high schoolers can start piling up college credits through Advanced Placement test and CLEP or ACTPEP tests as well as junior colleges, telecourses, and college level correspondence courses. Such tests and courses are often challenging, but bright students should be able to handle them. Even though the courses are secular, by having students study at home, parents have the opportunity to counter objectionable content with the Christian viewpoint.

Some students might want to take GED or Proficiency Examinations before taking college level correspondence courses partly to eliminate any enrollment problems and partly to give them confidence in their ability to move beyond high school level work. Many more study options are available once students have the GED or high school equivalency certificates and fewer questions arise about a student's educational history.

Summary

Home educators are using all of the above options and creating new ones of their own. The key to overcoming hurdles is to keep an open mind about ways of meeting our goals. Just because something has not been tried before does not mean that we should not try it ourselves. Bureaucratic officials are usually the worst to deal with when we want to do something out of the ordinary, but confidence and a positive, friendly attitude can open many doors and enlist enthusiastic cooperation.

There certainly can be some risk involved when we choose to operate outside traditional channels, but the track record of home educated students already is proving that unconventional methods can produce outstanding results.

Reviews

Under my recommendations, I describe individual items that are worth your attention—some briefly, some more completely. Those with fuller descriptions are usually materials that I have been able to review more thoroughly than others. However, descriptions of materials from the major Christian publishers—A Beka, Bob Jones University Press, Alpha Omega, Christian Liberty Press, School of Tomorrow, and Rod and Staff—are sometimes briefer because I have included general information about their materials in the following chapter, "Major Publishers." I suggest that you read through this section before investigating the specific recommendations.

Major Publishers

Information about individual items from each publisher can be found under subject headings. By including only selected publishers here I am not implying their superiority over others, but it reflects the fact that they publish numerous items, all or most of which reflect the same general worldview and philosophy of education.

A Beka

A Beka offers materials for pre-kindergarten through 12th grade, including supplementary materials. A Beka also offers enrollment in their own A Beka Correspondence School (book or video/book options), but they will sell materials to individuals without enrollment.

A Beka's philosophy is conservative, Christian, and patriotic. Their approach to education is traditional with an emphasis on drill, repetition, and memorization. All material is written from a Christian perspective. Although this is very evident in the science and history books, it seems to be tacked on in math and some of the language arts. Conservatism and patriotism are most evident in reading/literature and history.

A Beka will sell teacher's guides/curriculum, teacher's editions (which sometimes serve as answer keys), separate answer keys, and texts at retail prices to individuals. Individual subject area curriculum guides lay out lesson plans and offer teaching suggestions, usually most appropriate for the classroom. A Beka is unusual in that they often separate answer keys (sometimes the teacher's editions, sometimes separate keys) from teaching information (usually found in teacher's guides/curriculum).

The organization of teacher material is not the same for all courses which creates some confusion. In some instances we will want both teacher's edition and teacher's guide/curriculum, but teacher's guide/curriculum volumes often are not useful for home educators.

The math and language worktexts include most instruction on new concepts. We need teacher's editions (answer keys) for these when the material gets too difficult to correct without them. The need for teacher's books varies text by text at high school level, so read the information under each subject heading.

A Beka's math and grammar are both challenging. Junior high mathematics worktexts are good in that they constantly review concepts already learned, but they also address topics that are well beyond the typical junior high curriculum. High school math texts should be "taught" rather than used for independent learning.

The grammar goes into great detail, and while it is not exciting, it gives children a thorough knowledge of the subject. Writing needs more attention than is given in the language worktexts alone, so either use ideas from the teacher's guides or use ideas from supplements for composition.

Science books are excellent. However, on junior high levels there is excessive emphasis on detail and memorization, so use tests and assignments with discretion. Junior high texts, *Matter and Motion* and *Science: Order and Reality*, are excellent for general science background. The high school *Biology* text is well-written and practical for home educators. *Chemistry* and *Physics* are much more difficult to use.

History books are good at junior/senior high levels, although A Beka's history books are quite subjective compared to most others. The perspective throughout the books is Protestant, anti-Catholic, conservative, patriotic, and opposed to the New World Order. Newest editions of these texts feature larger print and less content than the earlier editions. Since the older books were too difficult for some students, some will view this as a plus while others will see it as a minus. One of A Beka's weaknesses, evident in the history texts, is a lopsided emphasis on detail recall. It is easy enough to challenge our students with only the appropriate questions, so this does not present a major problem.

We can use history and some science books without Teacher's Guides unless we want answers to text exercises which are found in the Guides.

A Beka books are paperback. Worktexts used in many subjects are definitely not reusable.

A Beka materials can be ordered directly from A Beka, and they accept orders using MasterCard, Visa, or Discover.

A Beka also has courses on video cassette. See the description under "Correspondence Courses."

Alpha Omega

Alpha Omega materials are unlike typical school textbooks in several ways. Children are placed at the appropriate starting point in each subject area in the program, and they work sequentially through a number of workbooks, called LifePacs, as they master the material in each. LifePacs have been reprinted in full color (and are now called LifePac Gold) up through tenth grade level. These small workbooks contain instruction, information, questions (with blanks), and tests. Alpha Omega includes a variety of questions to encourage deeper thinking rather than simple recall of factual information. The curriculum is based on the mastery learning approach. Children must pass tests as they complete each section of a workbook before proceeding to the next. Tests check on student mastery of current subject matter and also review previously mastered material.

Students can work at their proper levels in all subjects rather than being regimented into a single grade level for all subjects.

Alpha Omega offers full curriculum for grades K-12, including Bible. LifePacs consist of ten booklets for each subject each year. Subject areas are: Bible, Math, Language Arts (English), Science, and Social Studies for the elementary grades, with typical high school courses and electives offered for high school.

Only five of the LifePacs require the use of supplementary books to complete the courses. Biblical perspectives are incorporated throughout the material.

Unlike School of Tomorrow, Alpha Omega emphasizes that this material should not be as a means of having students work entirely on their own, but that parents need to be involved, supplementing with activities and other interactive ideas from the teachers' manuals to ensure an effective program. Even though the LifePacs enable children to work more independently than most curricula designed for classroom use, parental involvement is essential for providing the complete learning experience intended by the publisher. Unfortunately, there is a tendency among home educators to ignore the teachers' manuals and allow children to use the material completely on their own. Because this happens so frequently, I recommend that LifePacs be used with older learners (junior and senior high) who are independent, self-motivated, and need less hands-on experience to learn well. However, if parents plan to use the material as designed by the publisher, then it will work with learners who need more parental interaction.

The LifePac approach can be a real boon to parents with many children, widely spaced in age, or to parents who feel inadequate to help their children in particular subjects. (Caution: High school math is not one of Alpha Omega's strengths, so if parents are also weak in this area, it might be wiser to choose a different math program.)

Materials are available through correspondence courses, through home school suppliers, or by direct order.

Direct ordering: You may order directly from the publisher. A Starter Kit is available to help you, which includes diagnostic testing materials, placement and ordering information.

Diagnostic tests are also available separately for use in placing your child correctly in this material. The diagnostic tests might be useful as a general testing tool for others as explained in the section of this book about testing.

A new option for grades 7 through 9 is the computer CD-ROM *Switched-On Schoolhouse* version of the LifePacs. Eventually, all grade levels will be available in this format. The CD-ROM will run on Windows 3.1 or Windows 95 computers with a sound card. Bible, Math, Language Arts, Science, and History/Geography can be purchased individually [$49.95 each] or as a complete grade level "set" [$249.95]. The programs follow the general format of the LifePacs, although they are not identical. Color illustrations and sound are included. Students read through a section of the material on the screen, hit "next" and answer the questions. Incorrect answers are immediately identified, although students are not allowed to correct them until later on. Students can scan the "text" material to figure out what the correct answer should be. Once students have answered all questions correctly, they take a quiz. Some written responses are required in the exercises, and parents/teachers must score these themselves. Quizzes are scored by the computer, although parent/teacher override is permitted.

Bob Jones University Press (BJUP)

Bob Jones University Press tries to be very helpful to home educators in providing information over their toll-free phone lines and in offering the opportunity to talk directly with textbook authors.

Their philosophy is conservative and Christian. Educationally, they seem to have balanced their curriculum with teaching methods that suit most learning styles, although much of the necessary information to properly teach to all the learning styles is contained in the teacher's editions, not in student books.

BJUP offers mostly hardbound student texts with the separate teacher's editions bound in three-ring binders. New teacher's editions are in a revised format—spiral binding with a hardback cover. The pages will not rip out of these as they might from the binders, plus they have rigidity for easier handling because of the hardback cover. Some reproduced student pages within Teacher's Editions are printed in black and white, even though student books themselves are printed in color. Teacher's editions contain material that often is essential to proper use of the texts. BJUP has been writing abridged, home school teacher's editions for a number of their texts. These are less expensive and more practical for home school use. Sometimes the teacher's editions contain the student text without answers so that a separate text is unnecessary. Cost might be higher than other publishers if we purchase the large teacher's editions for all subjects. Quality and durability are good.

Families with only one or two grade levels to teach generally find that they can make use of BJUP texts and teacher's editions more easily than families with more grade levels to teach. Because it takes so much time to wade through the enormous amounts of material in the teacher's editions, families sometimes use only the texts or workbooks, thereby eliminating essential parts of many courses. Check my descriptions of individual courses and/or the BJUP catalog to determine when teacher's editions are essential and the format for each. If they are essential for a course, then determine if you have time to use the material properly.

Textbook material is colorful and well presented. It also has strong Biblical material incorporated throughout in a very effective manner.

The Bible curriculum for junior and senior high school is well written, purposeful, and easy to use, even without the teacher's editions.

BJUP math encourages children to think and analyze through well designed word problems, but requires more one-on-one presentation than do many other math programs. At high school level, the teacher's familiarity with math topics is assumed, making BJUP higher math difficult for many home educating parents to teach without lengthier explanations.

Upper level history texts are outstanding. They are well-written, Christian in content, and have worthwhile discussion and assignment questions.

Junior high science *(Life* and *Earth Science)* and ninth grade *Basic Science* are good texts that will work well in the home school. Higher level texts assume the classroom environment for lab work and are increasingly difficult to use. However, BJUP is trying to remedy that situation with new Science Supplements for *Basic Science, Biology, Chemistry*, and *Physics* that help us select the most appropriate labs to use for greatest learning value and how to substitute less expensive or easier-to-find alternatives for hard-to-obtain or expensive equipment.

In keeping with the computer age, BJUP sells *AskIt* test-generation software for IBM or Macintosh computers. *AskIt* helps us create and edit test questions, setting them up in a database. Or, if we do not want to write questions ourselves, we can purchase the computerized test banks designed specifically to accompany various BJUP textbooks. (Book form test banks are already available for a number of textbooks.) We can select test questions, then print out tests and answer keys. For multiple choice and true-false questions we can even set it up so students take their test on the computer, which also scores the test. The *AskIt* program serves as the master program, and we then purchase the computer data disks as needed. Data disks presently are available for *Family Living, Heritage Studies* (history) for grades 4-12, *Literature* for grades 7-12, science for grades 4-6, *Life Science, Earth Science,* and *Biology. AskIt* is fairly unsophisticated and difficult to use compared to other programs. (A little more user-friendliness would be appreciated.)

If you are interested in using BJUP texts, you might also want to consider using *Education PLUS* by Inge and Ronald Cannon, an interdisciplinary curriculum built around biblical themes. It uses BJUP texts as resource material for history, science, literature, and health, selecting and rearranging portions of the texts to fit the *Education PLUS* program. This approach truly allows the parent to be in control of the curriculum. See the complete review in Chapter Ten.

Christian Liberty Press

Christian Liberty Academy was one of the pioneers in home education. They offer educational assistance through their home education program at extremely low cost because they view their role as one of ministry. To keep the cost of home education as affordable as possible, they have begun publishing many of their own books. Some of these books are reprints from the last century, but many are newly written. The quality of the reprints used to vary considerably, but in the last few years CLP has improved print and page size as well as rewritten most of those that were poorer in quality. All CLP books are inexpensive. Some of them are tremendous bargains.

CLP has published their own literature books for grades 7 to 9. These are shorter and less comprehensive than literature texts from A Beka or BJUP for junior high level. They include a mixture of historical and modern reading selections with an emphasis on character building and spiritual growth. CLP has put together a very inexpensive reading kit for remedial instruction that incorporates their books along with others. Their spelling series includes books for junior high level. Their *Applications of Grammar* books are written for junior and senior high. The *Studying God's Word* series is suggested up through seventh grade, but these books are so good that I would recommend them even to older students, perhaps starting with books F, G, or H. History books are an eclectic assortment of reprints and newly written books that can be used at various levels from second through eighth or ninth grade. *Streams of Civilization* deserves special mention here as a unique and well-designed, two-volume history text. Some supplementary books are also offered including: biographies of Robert E. Lee, Stonewall Jackson, Charles Spurgeon, and George Washington; two good books on the Pilgrims; the new *Exciting World of Creative Writing*, and, an interesting little book entitled *Training Children in Godliness*. Many textbooks have teacher's manuals written by CLP staff for minimal cost. They are very brief, containing answer keys and teaching suggestions. If you are not satisfied with CLP books, they may be returned within thirty days of shipment; however, you will be charged a ten percent restocking charge.

See also the description of Christian Liberty Academy's correspondence school, which uses a mixture of CLP books with those from other publishers.

Christian Light

Christian Light publishes a Mennonite version of Alpha Omega's materials reflecting Anabaptist doctrine. There are five strands of workbooks called *Lightunits*: Bible, language arts, math, science, and social studies. Each strand has ten *Lightunits* in each grade level.

Christian Light has its own hardcover texts with matching *Lightunits* for high school literature, as well as for a number of elementary subjects and grade levels.

Christian Light incorporates materials from other publishers at the upper levels, primarily for high school electives. Elective courses include keyboarding, accounting, practical record keeping, computer literacy, electricity, agriculture, woodworking, art, home economics, Spanish, consumer math, practical math, Greek, carpentry, small engines, and Christian ethics.

Canadian social studies is covered in an elementary unit study and in a set of four special *Lightunits* used typically at seventh grade level. Also available is a broad line of supplementary books and resources, including science kits.

Three ordering/service options are offered: <u>Curriculum and Materials</u> - no enrollment fee; <u>Training Without Services</u> -receive a one-week parent training program by mail for $75; or, <u>Full Program</u> - for $100 receive parent training, a one-year subscription to *LightLines*, plus one year of CLE assistance and record keeping that can lead to a CLE diploma. To maintain Full Program status, the fee is $50 for each subsequent year. Only Full Program customers may purchase achievement tests.

Landmark's Freedom Baptist Curriculum

Landmark's Freedom Baptist Curriculum (LFBC) is conservative, fundamentalist Christian in approach. The format is similar to Alpha Omega's and School of Tomorrow's in that learning is primarily through worktexts used, for the most part, by students working independently. Students read course material, then answer questions with written responses. Questions vary from matching and fill-in-the-blank to short essays. Courses are prepackaged as complete units with worktext(s), quizzes, tests, and answer keys. Most packages are priced the same for simplicity's sake, even though some courses are bulkier than others. Students may enroll for complete grade levels or for individual courses. LFBC has been a ministry of Landmark Baptist Church for eight years, although the curriculum has been around much longer. It has been going through numerous changes and will continue to do so as they rewrite, revise, and upgrade courses. Because courses vary in quality, I have reviewed a number of them individually under the various subject headings. Watch for future revisions and improvements. The scope and sequence varies somewhat from other Christian publishers. For example, high school science includes four courses: physical science, biology, health and dynamic biblical living, and scientific creationism. Neither chemistry nor physics is offered. Math courses offered for high school are two years of algebra, geometry, and business math. Electives are penmanship, typing, home economics, shop, personal development, Christian heritage, and principles of music, with more being created.

Rod and Staff

Rod and Staff is a Mennonite publishing company that is very cooperative with home schoolers. Their curriculum relies heavily on Biblical material in all subjects. Among the distinctives of the Mennonite philosophy are nonresistance and separation, including the belief that the church should not involve itself in government, and this is reflected in their texts.

The Mennonite philosophy is also one that emphasizes hard work and diligence, and this is very evident throughout the material. Learning occurs via reading, lectures, and memorization rather than through experimentation and discovery.

There is much busywork and extra material in Rod and Staff textbooks since they were designed for classroom use, so we should not be using everything in every book. If we know our goals and use curriculum as a tool, we can use Rod and Staff effectively by choosing how much of the material to have our child use.

Rod and Staff has few texts beyond junior high level at this time. They offer Reading for grades 7 and 8, English for 7 and 8, Spelling for 7, Math for 7 and 8, History for 7, Music for 7, and Science for 7-9.

The *Building Christian English* series, *Spelling By Sound and Structure*, and science texts for seventh and eighth grades are excellent, traditional curricula. Science books have excellent content, but they present science experiments to illustrate what has been taught rather than as a means of discovery learning.

School of Tomorrow (Formerly known as A.C.E.)

School of Tomorrow materials are designed for independent work. They use the mastery learning approach, where students read material, fill in the blanks, then test themselves on each section. They must pass each quiz before moving on to the next level. For the most part, no lesson preparation or presentation by the parent is necessary. Children work through individual worktexts, called PACEs (12 per course, per year, although the rate can be varied to suit each child).

School of Tomorrow diagnostic tests are important for determining placement of our child in the material. They will identify learning gaps and levels of mastery. The tests are also useful to those who are not using their material. (See "Diagnostic Tests" under "Testing.") These tests are shorter than the CAT, Iowa, or Stanford tests and are not timed.

Once children have been placed at the proper level in each subject area, they work sequentially through the worktexts as they master the material in each one. Students might be working at different levels in different subjects according to their individual abilities and needs. These small workbooks contain instruction, information, questions (with blanks), and tests. Some high school science courses include lab worksheets. As I already mentioned, children take tests as they complete each section of a worktext before proceeding to the next. Tests generally cover only what has recently been studied, rather than all course content previously covered.

School of Tomorrow has materials for grades K-12, most of it printed in full color. Subjects are covered under general headings of Math, Language Arts (English), Word Building (spelling and vocabulary) for grades 1-9 only, Science, and Social Studies. Electives are also available in Bible, business, computer literacy, economics, typing, art, literature, music, speech, government, health, French, and Spanish. Because School of Tomorrow views acquiring biblical wisdom as a major educational goal, they have built in "wisdom lessons" in various formats throughout their curricula.

Word Building reinforces phonics, then works on vocabulary and etymology at upper levels. Word Building tests are now available on CD-ROM, which makes it much easier for students to complete the Word Building PACEs independently. At eighth grade level, School of Tomorrow social studies shifts from a strong emphasis on the "social" end along with church and Bible history in the early grades (e.g., the first half of the seventh grade level is entirely devoted to careers) to stronger history coverage up through high school. Supplemental books are required or recommended with a number of courses, more so at the upper levels than in the early elementary grades. Although School of Tomorrow material moves very slowly at the primary levels, the difficulty curve rises quickly once we move past the elementary grades.

School of Tomorrow's biggest weakness is that the material relies heavily upon simple recall rather than deeper thinking. Students can scan for the correct answer (which should be discouraged by parents) without having to really think about the material. There is little to encourage deeper thinking. About fifth grade level, more thinking and application skills are required. However, thinking skills are better developed at upper levels as students are sometimes required to analyze and respond to material they are studying. Nevertheless, the basic methodology remains the same through high school level.

School of Tomorrow makes no bones about the fact that this approach is a deliberate choice reflecting their philosophy of education. School of Tomorrow believes in moving from simple to complex, from concrete to abstract as students mature. They view memorization and recall learning as the appropriate sort of concrete learning essential as a foundation for the future. While Perfect Paulas tend to respond best to this approach, others, particularly Competent Carls, might become frustrated because it is limiting in some ways.

It is important for me to point out that PACEs for science courses are printed in a reusable format with removable Activity Pacs. The Activity Pacs in the center of each PACE have all questions and review quizzes, plus the PACE test. These are removed from the PACEs, with the remainder of the PACE functioning as a textbook. New Activity Pacs can then be purchased instead of having to replace the entire PACE. This was a very considerate, money-saving format for School of Tomorrow to offer.

While no lesson preparation is required with School of Tomorrow PACEs, parents should use preparation time to develop activities that correlate with lessons to enhance the curriculum. Because students work independently for the most part, this curriculum best suits the older child who has developed independent learning skills, although high school materials do require increased parent presentation and interaction as compared to the younger level materials.

School of Tomorrow has developed both video and computer courses that drastically change the nature of their offerings, particularly for high school. I will start with the video courses. While many other video courses rely on talking heads, School of Tomorrow video instructors appear on specially designed sets. They intermix their presentations with graphics, film footage, animation, diagrams, demonstrations, and all of the other visually interesting things that can be done with video better than a book. Even when the video instructors are the focus, they skillfully use their voices to maintain interest and highlight important points.

School of Tomorrow has concentrated on high school math and science for their first complete video courses. Since these are commonly the most difficult for home educators to teach, they have done us a tremendous service. Available thus far are *Algebra I, Algebra II, Geometry, Physical Science, Biology, Chemistry, Physics*, and *Spanish I*.

All of the School of Tomorrow video courses are based on their PACE curriculum, with much of the dialogue taken verbatim from the texts, with the exception of the Spanish course. However, there are some helpful, expanded explanations on the videos, in some cases up to 10% more than is contained in the PACEs. The film footage, graphics, and other visual enhancements are the key differences, because they transform dry text into something far more engaging.

School of Tomorrow originally had only PACEs (workbooks) to accompany their videos. At this point, PACEs are available for all video courses, but computer disks (used with the computer-based CVI option) will eventually be available as an alternative for most of the high school math and science PACEs. Geometry is the exception. (CVI will be described shortly.)

The computer video interactive (CVI) courses combine computer software and videos for complete courses. Computer software puts student exercises and tests from the PACEs on the computer. For most courses, it seems to be an either/or situation —use the PACEs or the computer disks. There seems to be some confusion still as to whether *Physical Science* and *Physics* can be totally independent of the PACEs. Present CVI versions of courses are being improved to allow students to more easily search for review information, but until that correction is made, having PACEs makes information review much easier. (*Biology can be done without PACEs, but we found it much more convenient to have them available.*)

To go the computer route, we need to purchase the special all-in-one computer/video player (called Multimedia CVI System) from School of Tomorrow, as well as the software and videos. For those who already own an IBM type computer, a CVI Conversion Kit can be purchased to adapt your computer to the CVI environment. Software consists of either 12 or 24 disks (depending on the course), and it acts as the master controller, transforming the videos and software into an integrated course.

The software and video are inserted into the Multimedia CVI System. A simple command starts the software that signals the computer to change to video mode at appropriate moments. The course switches back and forth from video to software automatically. The software also provides feedback on student responses, on-line help, lesson summary, tracking of student progress, computerized testing, scoring, and reporting. It will also take a student back through material he has not mastered. The videos are the most expensive part of the program (aside from the Multimedia CVI System or CVI Conversion Kit), but they can be reused by many students. The software is less expensive, but can be used by only one student because the interaction overwrites the data stored on the disks. School of Tomorrow offers two rental options: videos only ($239.80 per course, broken down into quarterly rentals of $59.95 each) or rental packages that include PACEs and Score Keys ($299.80 per course or $74.95 per quarter). Note that rental costs are the same for all video courses even though the purchase prices vary. Video rentals are shipped in four groups per course. We have a generous 120 days to get through them. A $75 refundable deposit per course is required; rental fees are non-refundable. However, we order by quarters, so if we do not like a course, we must only pay for the one quarter. While A Beka requires separate rental fees for each student watching their videos, School of Tomorrow allows us to have two or more of our children watch them at no extra cost.

CVI courses have a few quirks that are primarily the result of the limitations of the format. Students respond via fill-in-the-blank questions on the screen, but each blank requires a specific answer. At present the computer programs are extremely specific about correct answers agreeing in spelling, capitalization, and hyphenation, with few synonyms accepted. (The exact word, spelling, etc. can be found in the PACE or in the on-screen summary, but it is difficult to recall this type of detail strictly from the video presentation.) School of Tomorrow tells me they are trying to decrease the computer's sensitivity, but there are limits to what can be done. If students miss too many questions, the program kicks them back to the beginning. However, if the teacher thinks that student responses should have been acceptable, she can override the computer and allow the student to proceed. A question-by-question override is also available on both Self tests and PACE tests. The videos (particularly science) move too quickly for careful notetaking, so students will generally use a function key to access summary information. While some might complain about this, it should be viewed as a plus since it forces students to go through the information, usually at least twice.

See reviews of individual courses under the various subject headings.

While I applaud School of Tomorrow's CVI courses, I look forward to their plans to convert them to CD-ROM in the future which will make them easier to use and more affordable.

School of Tomorrow has also developed the *Videophonics* reading program which was designed for older students.

Unit Studies and Comprehensive Programs

Unit study is a term that describes the grouping of learning activities around a theme. It might be a brief study around a theme in a single subject area, such as a study of flight that includes reading a biography of the Wright brothers, learning about flight dynamics, visiting an airport, and studying about the role of airplanes in World War I. The unit study might broaden to a year-long study of a topic, or even further to integrate science, literature, history, language arts and other subjects. Creating a worldview unit study as suggested in Chapter Five is another example.

We can create simple unit studies very easily, but complex, integrated unit studies take a great deal of time. There have been a number of integrated unit studies for the elementary market (*KONOS, The Weaver, The Classics,* etc.) for many years, but, until fairly recently, *The Weaver* was the only publisher who fully developed the idea for high school level. However, the Weaver's high school unit studies piggyback on the elementary curriculum. As the number of home educated teens mushrooms, options are also expanding. We are already seeing a great deal of curriculum development in this area and should see much more over the next few years.

○ Beyond Five In A Row by Becky Jane Lambert (Five In A Row Publishing) $24.95

Some of you might be familiar with the original *Five In A Row* literature-based unit studies for younger children. These were authored by Jane Lambert. Becky Jane Lambert, her daughter has developed the first in a series of studies for older students. This excellent, one-semester course is suggested for ages 8-12, but might easily stretch to include junior high students. Four books—*The Boxcar Children, Thomas A. Edison - Young Inventor, Homer Price*, and *Betsy Ross - Designer of Our Flag*—are the foundation for the unit studies. They are really written for the younger age levels, but activities in *Beyond Five In A Row* can take students to challenging levels. While this probably isn't the best resource to use if you are teaching *only* a junior high student, it might work well to combine studies for children ranging from third grade up through junior high. You can focus on the same topics, assigning more challenging research, writing, and activities to the older students. Subject areas covered include literature, some language arts, history, composition, science, and fine arts. A *Christian Character Bible Supplement* [$9.95], also by Becky Jane Lambert, stretches to include Bible-based character study that might comprise your Bible course.

Lessons are set up so that we read a chapter from the book, then work through our choice of the suggested activities which vary greatly from day to day. Quite a bit of historical and scientific information is included within the book, but we will defi-nitely want older students to be using additional resources to expand their study. Many such resources are suggested in the lessons. Lessons often include "Internet Connection" activities for students to do research at a particular site or sites on a topic related to the study. Most of the lessons include an essay question, so students who complete all of these plus the other suggested writing assignments will do a great deal of composition work. Occasional "Career Paths" sections help students consider career possibilities and offer suggestions for further research and/or experience in the field. Timelines are recommended as a means of helping students understand chronological relationships between people and events. A list of all topics covered (a form of scope and sequence) is located at the back of the book; this will help you for both planning and tracking your accomplishments.

Volume 2 along with another Bible Supplement is due out in December of 1997, and at least two more volumes are due in 1998.

○ Blessed is the Man [revised edition] by Lynda Coats (Small Ventures) $54.95

Lynda Coats, the original author of *Far Above Rubies*, has also authored this similar program for young men. *Blessed is the Man* offers a true alternative to traditional curriculum in both purpose and design. It comes as loose-leaf pages to put into a large, embossed binder. Designed for the high school years, its purpose is to train up young men to "assume the role of husband, father, and priest to his family." Based on Psalm 1, this program consists of nine units designed to reflect themes from different verses within that psalm. Students work from lists of activities within each unit. Activities are divided under the headings: Bible and Christian Character, Cultural Studies, Reading and Literature, Composition, Mathematics and Personal Finance, Science, Health and Physical Fitness, Practical Arts, and Creative Arts. Activities are briefly described, so we are left on our own to figure out how to do and to what extent to carry each. For example, one cultural studies activity reads: "Study the life of Charles Darwin, who was the father of the theory of evolution." Some activities direct students to particular books or resources: "Read Usborne's *The Greeks*, looking at the role religion and mythology played in their society, culture, and government." Lynda Coats describes a point system to be used to determine when enough work has been accumulated to be equivalent to a course credit. Consequently, she assigns a suggested point value to each activity. However, actual credit earned must be determined by parents. Record keeping forms for this purpose are included at the back of the book.

Students can complete their history, government, economics, language arts, science, health, and fine arts credits through this program. They will also accumulate many elective credits as they study home management, industrial arts, accounting and bookkeeping, home and family living, and practical agriculture. They will need to use other texts for their math, and if they are college bound, they will need to take whatever lab science and foreign language classes might be required.

Some suggested resources, such as some of the Usborne books, sometimes seem too low-level for high school, but others such as *The Messianic Character of American Education* are very high level. Students do not do all activities, so the actual choices make this program either more or less challenging. Also, the amount of work applied to each activity might vary tremendously, so parents should require appropriate levels and depths on activities.

Essential resources will be a Bible, concordance, dictionary, encyclopedia (a local library might do), a hymnbook, and a grammar handbook. A list of other suggested resources includes such items as field guides, general history texts, guide for writing term papers, poetry anthology, world almanac, and classical music. Many other resources will be required for activities. Some of these will be available at the library. However, many are not widely available at libraries but are available through Christian bookstores and homeschool distributors.

While young men are directed to study agriculture, machinery, and family finances, most of the study could also be used by young ladies. (But they would not get the emphasis on a woman's household skills, health care, and other elements that are included in the *Far Above Rubies* study.)

The program addresses psychology, mythology, theology, church government, abortion, evolution, the occult, and numerous other topics from a Christian perspective (although even Christians have differing opinions on some of these). Students can do much of their study independently, but parents need to be involved in choosing activities and resources as well as in discussion and evaluation, especially when it touches on controversial areas. Of course, parents are free to have their children skip areas with which they disagree, or else present alternate viewpoints.

This second edition is greatly expanded from the original with far more activities to choose from. (Those with the first edition will be able to purchase the updated sections.) The new edition also has a more polished look than the earlier one.

⊃ Creation Science: A Study Guide to Creation! by Felice
Gerwitz and Jill Whitlock (Media Angels Science) $16.95

This is one of a series of unit study guides from Media Angels, a team of two authors, teacher Felice Gerwitz and geologist Jill Whitlock, both of whom are also home schooling moms. The companion volumes are *Creation Anatomy, Creation Astronomy*, and *Creation Geology* [$18.95 each]. Each study should take about six to eight weeks to complete. The guides are set up for multi-grade teaching with activities divided into levels for K-3, 4-8, and 9-12. Activities for each level are further divided under the headings of Reading List, Vocabulary/Spelling List, Vocabulary/Spelling/Grammar Ideas, Language Arts Ideas, Math Reinforcements, Science Activities and Experiments, Geography/History Ideas, and Art/Music Ideas. Science receives

the most attention, with a good deal of background information for the teacher included in a "Teaching Outline" section in each book. (Read through this section in each book before you begin to teach the unit.) Lots of extras are included: bibliography of videos, books, computer resources; materials list; field trip guide; science experiment copy pages; and reproducible activity pages. At junior and senior high school level, you might use the four books to create a quite extensive Creation Science course. Coverage of other subjects is spotty, so you will probably want to add other resources to ensure sufficient attention to the other subject areas, or else consider the activities in these studies as supplements to your core curriculum. Activity instructions are fairly well spelled out; they are not just a list or outline of suggestions. The suggested reading list includes titles that are referenced within some of the activities. (Suggested books include titles from both secular and Christian sources.) You will need to plan ahead to determine which activities to do and what resources you will need. All studies are presented from the young-earth perspective and rely on a literal interpretation of the Bible.

A separate *Geology and Creation Science Hands-On Experiment and Activity Pack* [$12.95] features reproducible pages of activities and experiments with step-by-step instructions, questions, games, puzzles, a glossary, and more. It serves as a companion to both the main book and the *Geology* book. Experiments are most appropriate for the elementary grades up through junior high since they do not require any mathematical analysis.

⊃ Education PLUS: Patterning Learning Upon Scripture by
Inge and Ronald Jay Cannon (Education PLUS+) $149

This is actually an interdisciplinary study rather than a unit study, as the Cannons describe it: "It is true that interdisciplinary study is built from units. Interdisciplinary study, however, enables the 'whole' to be greater than the sum of its parts." In contrast to unit study where activities and learning often relate to the same topic, but rarely to each other, interdisciplinary study includes discussion of the interrelationships between subject areas and activities. There is an underlying theme to the curriculum; volume 1 centers around and is titled *Genesis 1-11*. Proceeding in Scriptural order, each week has a title/theme with key concepts for each day that serve as foundations for other studies. For example, week 1's topic is "The Beginning." The key concept for day 1 is "Genesis is foundational—to the rest of Scripture and to the development of faith." The parent/teacher prepares and presents lessons using a variety of resources. There is time when the entire family, all age levels, works together, then time when various ages separate to work at their appropriate grade levels. Lessons are outlined for four days per week, for 22 weeks. The publisher tells me that most families prefer to used each week's outline over a two-week period.

Volumes of *The Preacher's Outline and Sermon Bible (TPO)* are used throughout all of the studies and the required volume that coordinates with *Genesis 1-11* comes with that volume. On day 1 we begin with Scripture reading and singing the "hymn of the week." We continue with readings from *TPO* and other sources as well as discussions about the book of Genesis itself, the author of Genesis, and "prehistoric man." Next, we perform research on "how sociologists believe written communication began," then get into Scripture study using a Concordance and other tools.

Following these foundational daily lessons are subject area assignments divided into four levels: up through age 7, ages 8-12, ages 13-18, and "quantum" for ages 16 and up. Subject areas covered are language arts/literature, history, sciences, business/economics, government/law, mathematics, and fine arts. All subjects are not covered every day. Subject area assignments are a variety of textbook readings, reading from other resources, discussions, research, and hands-on activities, with most related to the general theme of the day or week. For example, science studies related to "The Beginning" for ages 8-12 include researching, "What does it mean to *evolve*? How do the words *evolution* and *evolve* relate? (See *Life Science*, BJUP, pp. 81-87.)" For ages 13-18, one assignment is, "*Natural revelation* involves those things that we can observe and therefore know. Work through Chapter 1, 'Science and the Bible' (*Basic Science*, BJUP, pp. 1-19) to understand the limitations of science."

Some of the required information is provided within the curriculum. We are frequently directed to textbooks and other resources. Some assignments do leave it to the parent to figure out how to present a concept; e.g., "Study the nutrition pyramid. How many categories of foods on it come from plant life?" You will need to develop an extensive home library as a ready source for such information as you use *Education PLUS* (as described below).

Many assignments from level to level address closely related or identical topics, but at more challenging levels, so your children might be studying the same ideas, each at his or her own level, simplifying the teacher's task. Textbook assignments do not necessarily follow the textbook's order of presentation, but are selected as they address specific topics. Math and language arts will need separate, sequential coverage, although language arts does receive extensive coverage in this program. *Genesis 1-11* includes orientation information for parents plus an excellent supplement for teaching literature.

While there are some hands-on activities, especially at the lowest level, this is primarily book-based study. We can find some resources at the library, but it will be necessary to purchase quite a few. Among those required for all volumes of *Education PLUS* are the complete sets of BJUP history, science and literature textbooks for high school level; the above mentioned *Preacher's Outline and Sermon Bible* (additional volumes come with each volume of *Education PLUS*); *Strong's Concordance*; *Major Bible Themes* by Lewis Sperry Chafer; *Encyclopedia of Bible Truths for School Subjects*; *Etiquette PLUS: Polishing Life's Useful Skills*; *God, Man, and Law: The Biblical Prinicples* by Herbert W. Titus; *The Timetables of History*; a hymnbook; a dictionary; a thesaurus; a grammar handbook; and *Best Books for Kindergarten through High School*. Another list of 22 books, mostly creation-science oriented titles, is required for teaching *Volume 1, Genesis 1-11*. Still more books are listed as optional for the complete series and for the *Genesis 1-11* volume. Although this requires a large financial investment, having a library

at your fingertips makes teaching much easier. To make it easier to get started in the program with a smaller initial investment, Education PLUS+ will provide you with a list of the books, showing which are needed for the first six weeks of the study and which are needed for the different grade levels.

Education PLUS combines the benefits of unit study with the convenience of textbooks in an unusual fashion. I expect that the inexperienced home educator might find this a little overwhelming since you still have to make a number of decisions about what to do with each child. But home educators seeking a Biblically-based, unified program should check this out. An *Orientation Kit* [$6] includes orientation pages and the first 37 lesson pages of *Genesis 1-11* plus a 60-minute audio cassette with answers to frequently asked questions. I highly recommend that you review the *Orientation Kit* first to become familiar with the program. Seven additional volumes are planned, with the next three titled *Genesis 12-50, Exodus,* and the *Life of Christ.* The development process should take about a year for each volume, so you will be able to continue through these using one per year. At high school level, you might wish to condense studies to complete two volumes per year when there are enough volumes available.

⊃ Far Above Rubies by Linda Coats and Robin Scarlata (Family Christian Press) $54.95; Companion - $25.95; Lesson Plans - $25.95 each book; set of the basic book, Companion, and Vol.1 of the Lesson Plans -$95; sample - $5

Far Above Rubies is a unit study covering four years of high school that was written specifically to train young girls to become godly women as described in Proverbs 31. According to the publisher, the "main emphasis of this unit is to prepare daughters for the life calling of wife and mother." Girls can prepare for college also with this curriculum, but the overall thrust is on a far more practical level. The authors set aside the traditional high school scope and sequence in favor of one based on the Bible and the practical needs of future wives, mothers, and homemakers. Young women are trained to care for their families' needs (nutrition, clothing, health, gardening, etc.) as well as to function in the community with skills in such areas as communication, math, bookkeeping, home business, typing, and finances. They are encouraged to prepare for or begin a business of their own as they work through the curriculum, but particularly in the fourteenth unit. Besides practical preparation, they learn creative arts so that they can create a pleasing home environment.

The philosophy of the curriculum promotes some viewpoints with which all Christian might not agree, but we can easily omit these topics or address them in other ways. For example, a number of recommendations buttress the idea that children are an unqualified gift from the Lord and that all contraception is a rejection of God's blessing. Another example, although less controversial, is an emphasis on teaching America's Christian History. Other distinctives relate to lifestyle such as an emphasis on gardening, farming, canning, and other such activities that might not be available to all families.

The curriculum (using a variety of the suggested resources and activities) can be considered complete for a general education, but college-bound students must supplement with other courses, especially for math and science. Students maintain subject notebooks, a journal, a geography notebook, and an art portfolio for their daily work. A system for assigning credit is outlined in the curriculum, with values assigned to each activity.

The entire study is divided into 20 units. Students should complete five per year for each of the four years of high school on a normal schedule. Each unit lists activities under the headings Bible, Cultural Studies, Reading and Literature, Composition, Math and Personal Economics, Science, Health and Physical Fitness, Practical Arts, and Creative and Performing Arts. The activities themselves are described briefly, leaving much room for interpretation and little specific direction for how to tackle each. For example, a science activity for the first unit says, "Learn about atoms and molecules." We are left to decide what it is that should be learned about atoms and molecules. Will it include atomic particles, electric charges, valences, chemical reactions, and other such topics? The suggested credit for the activity indicates that it should take about an hour and a half, so the intent must be much more superficial. Leaving it open to personal interpretation is not a problem for parents and students who have a firm grasp on what their goals are, but it might be for others.

The *Far Above Rubies Lesson Plans* are intended to make it easier to select and organize learning activities. There will eventually be four volumes, one for every five units of the primary book. Thus far, the first three volumes are ready. *Lesson Plans, Volume One* describes the structure of lessons throughout the program, then covers the first five units. For each subtopic under each unit, it charts the different activities that fulfill various parts of the lesson structure. Each of these sections includes a brief timeline, a form for recording individual plans, a form for listing resources to be used (with many recommendations listed on the form itself), and an assignment sheet. There are also additional activities described, following the same format is in the main book, but generally with more detailed descriptions for each. What I had hoped for, but find still lacking in the *Lesson Plans* are more details on how to teach or cover the learning activities described in the primary book. Nevertheless, the *Lesson Plans* are very useful. I would recommend that only experienced home schoolers who are used to searching out information and creating their own lessons use the primary book by itself; most home educators should also invest in at least the first volume of the *Lesson Plans*.

Students who are preparing for college will need to work at a more challenging level in the sciences than is required by the curriculum (although a student could take any of the topics addressed to a deep level of study on her own). The authors recommend a separate math curriculum, even though much practical math is included. Students who can complete the math activities in addition to algebra and geometry will be in great shape compared to students who only take the typical school courses.

I applaud the creation of such a curriculum that places the development of a Christian world view and godly character above traditional academic achievements. It will not appeal to every-

one, but it will meet the needs of many home educated young women.

The *Far Above Rubies Companion* provides some great information on philosophies of education, teaching tips, lesson planning how-to's, record keeping instructions and forms, and descriptions of many of the books suggested within the various units so that we can decide which ones we wish to use. The teaching tips explain the philosophy behind the curriculum as well as suggestions for the various subject areas, but the record keeping is probably the feature that will seem most important to potential users. If you want to use the curriculum's record keeping system, you really need the *Companion*. The *Lesson Plans* volumes also include more detailed lesson planning and record keeping charts that will help you compile information that is summarized in *Companion*. Both of these extras complement each other as well as the primary book.

Family Christian Press sells packages of some of the recommended books for each unit at discounted prices, a convenience for many families. If you have not actually seen the curriculum, first order the sample to see for yourself if this appeals to you. The *Far Above Rubies Catalog* is lengthy and descriptive by itself and might give you enough information to make your decision A similar program for young men called *Listen, My Son* is reviewed further on.

There are currently over 100 *Far Above Rubies* users exchanging ideas, tips, and web sites online. To subscribe to this free service, contact Robin Scarlata at Rscarlata@aol.com. A *Far Above Rubies* web page is under construction.

⮌ Genesis One by Rebecca L. Avery (The Weaver) $40

This six-week course, ideal for students in grades 4 through 10, but also adaptable for grades 11 and 12, uses the book of Genesis as the foundational theme for lessons covering creation science while incorporating natural science, social studies, and language arts. Lessons are designed to be presented by a teacher. Teaching illustrations, including some in full-color, are at the back of the binder. Children complete reproducible activity sheets and participate in activities including experiments with chemicals from the Chemistry Kit which you must also purchase for use with this course. (The Chemistry Kit is available from The Weaver [$45].)

As an example of how the course works, lesson 2-1 begins from Genesis 1:3-5 with a study of the creation of light and related Bible passages. Students then study the movement of light via waves and rays. They draw an illustration, and if the teacher chooses to use the optional activity, they research the light spectrum. Throughout the course, students are introduced to chemistry, geology, biology, and other scientific areas. Most lessons seem most appropriate for junior high in terms of fitting into the typical scope and sequence for science study. Lessons are laid out with fairly detailed instructions for teachers which saves lesson preparation time.

➲ In The Beginning, God!: From Creation to the Middle
Ages (Fountain of Truth Publishing) Volume I - $49.95;
Volumes II and III - $59.95 each

Students from primary grades through high school can participate in this unit study curriculum. Volumes I through III in a projected four-volume series are available at this time. Each is a one-year program designed especially for home educators. They follow each other chronologically: Volume I covers creation to the Renaissance. Volume II, "For God So Loved the World," studies various regions with special emphasis on Asia, Africa, and the Orient; cultures; governments; geography; wildlife; technology; weather; and other topics. Volume III, "God Bless America," studies American history from exploration through the revolution. For science it covers anatomy, wildlife, geology and weather. Volume IV, "Blessed to Be a Blessing," will continue American history up through the present day. Science topics featured are horticulture, veterinary science, physics, electricity, disease prevention, and the senses.

The curriculum is being developed through actual use by home schoolers in Christian Cottage Schools. Units were "initially taught to groups of 10-12 children ranging in level from kindergarten to eighth grade." Typically, teachers stretch it to fit such a span by teaching to the oldest student and adapting it down for younger children. Younger students do more hands-on activities and less book work, while older students do more book work and fewer hands-on activities.

Overall, hands-on, experiential learning plays an important role in this curriculum as it does in *KONOS*. The curriculum does not try to offer instructions and expanded information for most subjects as comprehensive as we find in the *Weaver, KONOS,* or other more extensive unit studies. Instead, it features activities and studies designed around the theme, buttressed by the use of texts and other resource materials. Three days a week are identified as "book days." On book days, students work primarily through workbooks, texts, and other learning materials, with unit study activity taking a 30 to 90 minute slot. One day is set aside for intensive unit study activity such as a project, art, field trip, or event. The fifth day is "writing day" for discussing, creating, and rewriting.

The publisher recommends that we purchase one history text and one science text for the year. These are used as resource books from which we make assignments, read aloud, and draw information depending upon the topic and the ages and needs of children. While we might be able to manage very well with only one text for history and science, we might need two if we are teaching a very wide age span (e.g. a first grader and a tenth grader).

A set of encyclopedias such as World Book would be extremely useful. Topical books and literature can be found at the library, although some families will find it easier to invest in books of their own.

Each volume should take a year, but the publisher suggests that families cycle through the four volumes twice, covering a total of eight years.

Lists of annotated recommendations at the beginning help us identify which books will be most useful. Each unit also includes annotated lists of books, videos, and other resources. Each unit's activities are broken down into four levels—primary, elementary, intermediate, and advanced—so that we can identify main points of study, vocabulary words, and daily activities appropriate for different learners. (The main points of study also serve as an aid for test preparation.) Typically, for the three "book days," there is one activity provided, with instructions added for the various levels when necessary. The activity for the fourth day of each week does not seem any more comprehensive than do the first three days' activities, which leaves us to determine what else we might do as a field trip, event, project, etc. for the rest of the day. The fifth day's "writing assignment" is often extensive. For example, on the tenth day of the "Roots and Relations" unit, students make stone soup, write up family recipes, and make a padded, fabric cover for a previously begun project, a Family Heritage Book.

Subjects covered in Volume I are Bible, astronomy, life science, physical science, geography, government, history, creative writing, literature, home economics, music, and art. However, you would not be able to consider life science coverage as a complete course in itself if you want to use this with high schoolers. Taken together with the other science courses you cover a year's worth of science. For high school credit you need to use a text or comprehensive course in any one of the science subjects, although you might extend completion of any one course over a few years. You might also have a student completing two different science courses such as biology and chemistry over two to three years. You would then enhance those subject studies with the appropriate unit study lessons, while not relying exclusively on the unit study.

History coverage in Vol. I is selective, which is fine for elementary grades but inadequate for junior and senior high students. (The publisher expects that *In the Beginning, God!* will be serving as a supplement to most junior and senior high studies rather than as the main course, so it is not intended to be comprehensive for the upper grades in all subjects.) The units are arranged to cover "history and the story of creation simultaneously," so emphasis shifts back and forth between the two subjects in alternate units. The publisher suggests two additional options for arranging the units, depending upon your purpose; one option arranges units in a chronological approach and the other arranges them according to the seasons. Because history coverage is selective rather than comprehensive, supplementing with a text for continuous, thorough coverage for older students makes sense. However, you should not require students to read an entire textbook and also complete all of the unit study activities. Use texts as a resource to fill the historical gaps or flesh out a topic.

The overall approach of *In The Beginning, God!* is user-friendly. The authors have provided great activities balanced with textbooks and other easy-to-use resources so that the work involved is manageable. Suggestions for scheduling and some basic teaching tips are especially helpful to those who worry about how much is enough of each subject. I consider this an excellent way for families to try unit studies without the numerous choices and work involved in the more comprehensive resources.

Volume II, *For God So Loved the World*, is especially strong in geography and social studies—enough for ninth grade level. It is arranged by geographical units: Mediterranean Region, Western Europe, Eastern Europe, African Safari, Southwest Asia, Central Asia, The Orient, and Oceania. Information on countries is up-to-date, more current than in most textbooks. This second volume is even better than the first. It has about 100 more pages and proportionately more content in almost all areas.

Volume III, *God Bless America*, studies North America, Central America, South America, explorers, missionaries to the new world, early settlers, and the establishment of the United States of America. Even more polished than Volume II, it offers quite a bit of background information and teacher helps to make it easier to prepare lessons. It retains the strong emphasis on activities and hands-on learning characteristic of the entire curriculum.

⊃ The JUBILEE! Curriculum (Earthly Treasures)

Watch for this new unit study curriculum. I was able to review only a preliminary copy of one unit, so you will need to contact the publisher for final details.

Thirty-five units should be available over the next few years. Each unit will feature a single theme (e.g., *Astronomy*) and cover social studies, language arts, science, art, music, and drama for grades K-12, and math for K-8. Each unit might take from one to six months to complete, depending upon how thoroughly you investigate each topic. Most families will reuse units every three years or so, going deeper each time around.

Activities direct students to "learn," "read," "define," "research," "observe," "make," "write," and "compare" in relation to the topics, with some background information provided within the guide. Complete information on most topics is to be gleaned from recommended resource books. (Earthly Treasures has an extensive catalog of real books and other resources that are ideal for unit study.) It will be up to parents to determine how much writing, discussion, or other forms of "output" are used.

In columns next to the activities are indications of appropriate grade levels for introducing, reinforcing, and expecting mastery of each topics. Objectives are drawn from five of the most widely used standardized tests. A section of Bible verses to accompany lessons is at the back of each unit. Approximate time required to complete each activity is indicated for high school level activities. Charts for recording time are at the back of the binder.

Earthly Treasures also will be offering four curriculum frameworks for math, science, social studies, and language arts. These list detailed objectives and grade levels, again based on standardized tests, for all grade levels. The frameworks can be used to create our own unit studies, checking off objectives as they are met. This is very helpful for those of us worried that we might miss something when we jump into unit studies.

⊃ KONOS History of the World (KONOS) Year One with Teacher's/Parent Guide and Map/Timeline packet -$150;

Year Two with Teacher's/Parent Guide and Map-Timeline packet - $150

KONOS for senior high is somewhat different from the younger-level volumes. The principle difference is that it is written directly to the student rather than the parent. Each volume covers Bible, history, English, and art for a full school year. As with other *KONOS* volumes, students are not expected to do all activities, but they should work with parents to select those necessary to provide sufficient work in each subject area and to cover the main topics adequately.

The beginning section of *Year One* teaches students how to study and how to use this curriculum. (*Year Two* repeats the same information in case students are starting there.) Each lesson follows the same basic format. It begins with the "Lesson Focus" listing the main ideas to be learned. Bible study is next, with passages to read, study, and memorize. Students keep a journal for their Bible studies. A Map/Timeline packet designed for each volume of *KONOS History of the World* includes full-color, self-sticking figures that students cut out and place on the timeline as they study each civilization and/or time period. These timeline figures are very individualized. (Interpreting the details of the figures themselves serves as a review or study prompt. For example, why is Diogenes pictured inside a barrel?) Students construct a large map with the pages included in the packet. They continue to mark and use the map throughout their studies. Vocabulary words for each lesson are to be written on 3" x 5" cards, then studied and reviewed. A number of other resources are used for study, a few of which are used so frequently that students should own them. In addition to basic study tools and reference works, students should get *Streams of Civilization* (published by Christian Liberty Press) and *A Picturesque Tale of Progress* (Books 1-4). The latter is out of print, but worth trying to obtain through a book search service. *The Book of Life* set is also used frequently, but easy access to a set should be adequate. The other recommended books are worth owning, but are not quite as essential. You might have or be able to obtain others that will substitute for those listed.

A number of activities are described within each lesson, although students are not required to do them all. Some are marked with symbols indicating that they are writing, art, or map activities. A mortarboard indicates advanced activities that college-bound students should tackle. Some videos are also recommended. Record keeping boxes are placed next to each activity so that students can note which assignments are to be done when and the time actually spent on each. Students also maintain a notebook in a three-ring binder that will include their journal, book lists, weekly schedules, essay questions, English reports, and tests. Evaluation questions at the end of each section help both student and parents assess progress. There are very few questions that require exact or predictable answers, but those answers are found in the Teacher's Guide portion of the course. Students are told how to create and maintain a portfolio of their work that can be used to validate their high school studies for high school graduation or college entry.

The entire curriculum is oriented toward developing a Christian world view with a deep understanding of the impact of philosophy and religion throughout history. Students do a great deal of reading, and there are numerous opportunities to write stories, essays, and papers. However, learning is still balanced with activities for various learning styles, a feature that has helped make the elementary level *KONOS* curriculum so popular with home educators. For hands-on learners, this higher level of *KONOS* still stresses experiential learning with activities such as visiting a rock quarry or stone cutter when studying the pyramids, presenting a monologue about "your life as Abraham or Sarah," or making a shofar (Jewish ram's horn) from papier-mâché.

All subject areas to not receive equal coverage. In *Year One*, ancient history coverage is comprehensive from the time of Abraham's departure from Ur up to pre-Rome (the Celts and Etruscans), and this is used as the organizing theme throughout the year. English activities stress literature, vocabulary, and writing with detailed lessons on various forms of writing incorporated into the different sections. Art is an ideal combination of history, appreciation, and expression. Bible coverage is extensive, particularly in the historical study of the Hebrews. Study for these subjects will be time consuming, so the authors recommend that students tackle only a few additional subjects such as math and science. *Year Two* adds an introductory Latin course equivalent to about 1/2 unit of credit.

Although the format of the curriculum is not traditional, the level of learning is quite challenging. This is definitely a high school curriculum and it might even be too challenging for some ninth graders. Parents should assist students as they make decisions about resources and assignments. While students can do much of the study on their own, discussion is really a vital part of the program. Parents should read the primary books that students are reading, then plan 2-4 hours per week for some great discussions.

Eventually, there will be volumes covering all of world history; thus far we have the first two. *Year One: The Ancient World* covers Mesopotamia, the Egyptians, the Indus Valley, the Hebrews and Their Neighbors, the Greeks, and the Foundations of Rome. (The Hebrews and their neighbors receive far more attention here than they do in most history studies.) *Year Two* covers Rome to Pre-Renaissance. *Year Two: The Medieval World*, is even better than *History of the World, Year One*. Though arranged in the same format, it covers Rome, the Byzantines, Moslems, Vikings, Charlemagne, the early Church, Medieval times, and China to the present day.

The curriculum stresses both content and acquiring the tools of learning. This idea of equipping teens with the tools of learning so they become independent learners is a feature that sets *KONOS* apart from many other programs. To create independent learners, each week's unit begins with five or six bulleted objectives each student is to accomplish by the end of the week, then it presents about six evaluation questions that parents can use to judge whether or not objectives have been met. This design trains students to begin each week with specific objectives in mind instead of aimlessly reading through whatever is set before them. Also, weekly lesson plan sheets are provided so that each week's schedule can be mapped out jointly by parent and student at the beginning of the week. Further, students are encouraged to research and write on an incredible number of topics, giving them continual practice in both areas.

The authors feel that students' world views are shaped by studying the historical context of ideas and philosophies and relating that to present day events. Consequently, students are asked to complete activities such as comparing the merits of multinational armies such as the one that existed in Rome prior to its fall to the present-day United Nations armies. Early church history, church fathers, and development of doctrine also receive far more attention than in other programs. The reading list for *Year Two* is challenging as it includes Shakespeare's *Julius Caesar*, Augustine's *City of God*, Dante's *Inferno*, Chaucer's *Canterbury Tales*, *Black Arrow*, *Beowulf*, *The Good Earth*, and *Quo Vadis?*. Rigorous academics are balanced by *KONOS'* characteristic hands-on activities such as designing their own coat-of-arms, sewing a Medieval tapestry, and surveying land as the ancient Romans did.

Each student must have his own book since he does record keeping on lesson pages. The Teacher's (or Parent) Guide is included with each volume, although you might want to pull it out and put it into its own binder.

○ Lessons from History - three volumes by Gail Schultz
(Hillside Academy) $19.95 each

Lessons from History are essentially unit study outlines that the author recommends for grades K-9. My judgment is that they will better suit up through eighth grade. Three volumes cover three different eras: *1400's to 1700's*, *1800's*, and *1900's*. At the front of each volume is a scope and sequence chart for covering history, social studies and science, geography, Bible, and the arts. Key people, events, or movements anchor each week's study. For example, the *1800's* volume's beginning lessons are on the American revolution, the Louisiana Purchase, the Lewis and Clark Expedition, and Robert Fulton. Lesson outlines for the week provide background information (e.g., a biographical overview), suggested books to read, related areas of study, projects, and discussion questions. Obviously, we need to adapt any of these to suit the ages of our learners. Recommended books vary in difficulty, although most seem to be children's titles. (I might look for related titles in the adult sections for mature junior high students.) Since each week's lesson outline is only a few pages long, this is clearly not a comprehensive, self-contained curriculum. It serves as a framework and outline for us to create our own lessons. Suggestions at the front of the book tell us how to put together weekly lessons, including language arts and field trips. At the end of each book are pictures that can be used to create a time line (instructions provided also). There is a distinctive Christian flavor throughout the books, although it is not always obviously stated. For example, the lesson on cowboys raises questions about character, responsibility, and family. However, sometimes it is obvious, such as in the questions about Louis Braille that require students to refer to Scripture verses. The books are well-organized and presented as well as nicely illustrated with appropriate clip art. Those who like unit studies but also like to have a great deal of control over the form it takes will find these books to be excellent resources.

➲ Listen, My Son (Linda Bullock) $54.95

In a similar vein to that of *Far Above Rubies*, this is a Bible-based curriculum for young men based on Proverbs 3. While it is focused more toward home businesses and apprenticeships than toward college, it can be the core of a college prep program. Linda tells us, "It is intended to help train young men in godly character, Christian family life, and practical skills while providing a balanced high school education in other areas such as history and science." While traditional academics are covered, practical knowledge for being a Christian father is stressed—knowledge such as home maintenance, being a home schooling father, godly relationships, and business leadership.

The program is divided into sixteen units, four per year, with each unit designed around a few verses from Proverbs 3. The curriculum is addressed directly to the student, although parents will need to be involved in making choices, securing resources, and overseeing work. Bible, English, history, science, and some electives are covered, but we need to select separate math textbooks. A number of supplemental resources will be necessary. Some textbooks might be used, but "real books" are the primary tools. The Bible is a major resource, but it is used along with others such as *Christian Manhood* and *Disciplines of a Godly Man*. Language arts might include *Wordsmith, Writing With a Point, Vocabulary from Classical Roots*, and numerous writing assignments. History (or social studies) is covered through such resources as biographies, historical fiction, *America: The First 350 Years, God and Government, Quest of a Hemisphere, Streams of Civilization*, stories about missionaries, and Wallbuilders resources. Science includes a study of biology as well as more general studies in topics such as geology, earth science, physics, and ecology. Recommended science resources might be Usborne books or others such as *Weather and the Bible* or *Pyramid Explorer's Kit*. Practical science such as electricity and agriculture is stressed. Students who want to prepare for college will need to use more in-depth science courses in line with college requirements (keeping in mind that colleges are often open to unusual science studies if they are challenging). A starter package [$66] of the essential books for the first unit includes *Wordsmith* and its Teacher's Guide; *Gaining Favor with God and Man; Gray's Anatomy Coloring Book; Young Man, Be Strong; It's All About Attitude* (audio tapes by Josh Harris); and *Education and the Founding Fathers*. It is probably a good idea to purchase this to begin, then take your time to more carefully select resources for future units.

All of this is presented in outline format rather than as complete lesson plans. Linda lists suggested numbers of points to be earned for completing each assignment, although we need to adjust these depending upon how in-depth each student chooses to pursue each assignment. Teens are not expected to complete every assignment, but to choose (with parental assistance) those most appropriate for their interests and educational goals.

You will need to purchase a number of books for the program, but these, for the most part, are valuable additions to a library rather than consumable textbooks.

A few supplemental tools will make using *Listen, My Son* easier. *Record Keeping for High School* [$19.95] was designed as a record keeping system for this and similar unit studies, although it might be used for other courses of study. It comes in a three-ring binder and will suffice for all four years of high school for one student. *LMS Lesson Planning Guide* [$10] has pages for lesson plans for one year. A special package offer [$75] includes the curriculum plus the *Record Keeping* and *Lesson Planning* books.

Rather than a course for the novice home schooler, *Listen, My Son* is for those with some home schooling experience, particularly in using or creating unit studies. As with *Far Above Rubies*, I applaud this effort to create a course of study for high school that addresses God's purposes for life. A *LMS Sample Unit* [$5] provides basic questions and answers about the program sample pages from the *Record Keeping* and *Lesson Planning* books, plus the complete first unit of *Listen, My Son*.

➲ The Noah Plan: An Educational Program in the Principle Approach (Foundation for American Christian Education) $60 per level; subject guides - $25 each

The Noah Plan is presented in two volumes—one for K-8 and one for high school. Each is a large, three-ring binder with two audio cassette tapes. Each presents a complete curriculum using the Principle Approach. I reviewed the K-8 curriculum but not the high school since it was not yet in print. Review details pertain only to the K-8 volume.

Based upon years of application in both traditional school and home school settings, this curriculum is the most complete resource for those wanting to go that route. It includes a "seminar" for teachers at the beginning of the binder; in the past, it has been necessary for those interested in this methodology to *attend* seminars to learn how to teach this way. This seminar teaches the foundational principles and how they are translated into the "Four R" method: research, reason, relate, and record. Divided into nine lessons, the seminar requires teachers to do additional reading, reflection, and writing as they learn. The two audio cassettes are used with this part of *The Noah Plan*.

The seminar is followed by the "Guidelines." The Guidelines introduce the actual curriculum with an overview of subjects to be studied and reproducible forms to be used. Next are guidelines for each grade, including a suggested schedule (geared toward traditional classrooms), a classroom constitution (agreement between student and teacher about attitude, getting work done, etc.), student supply list, a sample weekly goal sheet, and subject overviews. The subject overviews are the most helpful part for homeschoolers; they lay out the purpose and goals, principles to be taught, key definition, quarter-by-quarter topics to be covered, grading standards, notebook standards, texts, and recommended resources.

The Guidelines should be used in conjunction with the subject Curriculum Guides also published by F.A.C.E. Guides for Art, Literature, English grammar and Composition, History and Geography, and Reading will all be available during the 1997-98 school year. Math and Science, Classical and Modern Languages, the Fine and Performing Arts, and Bible will eventually be published. These guides get even more specific with about what and how to teach for grades K-8, and some helps for high school level. They include a teaching plan, model lesson plans, teaching methods, a sample student notebooks or records (as for art), and lists of resources required. I was able to review the *Reading Curriculum Guide*, written by Martha Barnes Shirley and the *StoneBridge Art Guide*, written by Wendy Giancoli and Elizabeth Youmans.

The *Reading Curriculum Guide* is quite extensive in scope. It outlines a reading curriculum that teaches intensive phonics and that uses the Bible for reading material. (Children's versions of the Bible are used for the early grades.) It includes explanation of the rationale and organization of the curriculum; charts for each grade level showing purpose, objectives, scope and sequence, definitions, suggested teacher and student resources, and specific skills to be developed within sub-areas of reading (through eighth grade level, with a Reading with Reason enrichment course provided for high school); "Foundations for Teaching Reading"—teaching principles; extensive how-to-teach information; and an appendix of recommended resources, reading lists for children, and reproducible forms.

The *StoneBridge Art Guide* differs some from the *Reading Curriculum Guide* since it was developed for a once-a-week art class at StoneBridge School. Time limitations and the nature of art study demand a slightly different application of the 4R methodology (less notebook work being the most obvious). Homeschooling parents might choose to expand the lessons given more time. The *Guide* presents the rationale for an art curriculum built upon biblical principles of art. It then translates the ideas into application through scope and sequence for grades K-8, sample lesson plans, background information for teaching, suggested projects, and timeline and illustrations showing how artists fit the model of Christianity's westward movement. Articles at the end of the book provide additional background for the teacher on art plus the basics of the Principle Approach.

The Noah Plan follows a challenging scope and sequence incorporating foreign language instruction throughout all grade levels in French, Latin, and Greek; research papers in the elementary grades; and other high level, challenging, academic goals.

The course of study for grades 7-8 in *The Noah Plan* is as follows: Bible study is a comprehensive overview of the Bible establishing God's purpose and plan while examining the principles (of the Principle Approach) in Scripture; math is studied with Saxon's *Math 87, Algebra 1/2*, and/or *Ray's New Higher Arithmetic*; reading lessons are taught from the Bible plus other fiction and non-fiction sources; seventh graders study modern history, eighth graders take a "rudiments" course where they focus on the seven key principles and how they relate to history and government; geography is studied in seventh grade; English includes literature, grammar, and composition skills; physical science and human physiology and anatomy comprise science courses; Latin is studied using the Jenney *Latin* series; art, music, drama, P.E., and computer literacy round out the course of study.

In all subjects, students create their own notebooks as they "four R" each subject. In addition to the subject *Curriculum Guides*, you will need to get a number of other resources such as the *American Dictionary of the English Language*, the "red

books" by Verna Hall and Rosalie Slater, *A Family Program for Reading Aloud*, and subject textbooks (but not for all subjects). Many of the books you acquire in the process of teaching this program will be the foundation of an excellent library.

The Noah Plan needs to be taught by the teacher, as is true with any Principle Approach program. The teacher must first absorb the material, which means that for many of us parents, we are finally getting a real education. The curriculum is challenging and requires a great deal of time, but it produces excellent results for those who put in the effort in both character development and test scores. (Students attending StoneBridge School, the pilot school for this program, average more than 1300 on their SATs.)

⊃ Remembering God's Awesome Acts by Susan Mortimer (Susan Mortimer) teacher's manual and one student notebook - $35; additional student notebooks - $20 each

More limited in scope than most resources reviewed in this section, this unit study focuses primarily upon Bible and history while also providing some coverage in art, writing, speech, drama, geography, social studies, linguistics, anthropology, and archaeology. The eight units in the study deal with creation, man, the fall, the flood, the dispersion, God's chosen people, Egypt, and the Exodus. Each unit integrates Bible study with historical/cultural studies as the foundation. History and social studies cover historical data about the Sumerians, Babylonians, and Egyptians in a somewhat random fashion, but religious beliefs are highlighted and often examined in great depth. Lessons at the beginning of the book coupled with these on non-Christian belief systems and mythology provide a strong introduction to world views upon which we can continue to build through the high school years.

From history and Bible-based lessons, the course branches out to activities in the other subject areas, all still related to the primary theme of each unit. Brief instructions for each lesson are given in the teacher's manual, but most of each lesson is derived from and requires the student notebook. The pages in the student notebook serve as sources of information and activity pages/worksheets that become a "permanent" notebook when the course is complete. These heavily-illustrated pages offer a great deal of variety and visual interest. Each student will need his or her own notebook.

The course is suggested for grades 5 and up. While some of the content is introductory level, much of it is challenging enough for junior high and, possibly, even the beginning of high school. However, even when the content is challenging, many of the activities seem a little young for junior high students. There is good bit of cut-and-paste, coloring, puzzles, filling in the blanks with words from a word bank, and other such activities more typical of the elementary grades.

Three subject areas deserve special mention. Drawing exercises interspersed throughout the book teach basic shapes, shading, drawing from life, drawing faces, and perspective, although instruction on each of these skills is very limited. Linguistics receive a great deal of attention in the unit on the dispersion from Babel. Students are exposed to a number of different languages and dialects (e.g., Turkish, Waroni [Ecuador], Vietnamese). Languages are approached in the context of country studies drawing on the book *Operation World.* (See review in Chapter Five.) You might expand this section beyond those countries for which studies are provided, following the models used for those lessons. Speech and drama activities require students to present orally before groups. To make this easier for them to do, scripts for Bible stories/teachings that use "object lessons" are provided within the teacher's manual. You, the parent/teacher, first presents each lesson to your student(s), then they are to familiarize themselves with the script and props and present the lesson to a Sunday School class, a backyard Bible study, or other appropriate audience. This is a wonderful way for our children to learn the value and basic skills of public speaking.

While this study includes sufficient Bible study, you will probably want to use it in conjunction with a text or other resources for more thorough history coverage. For other subject areas it is supplemental. Lesson preparation is fairly minimal, but you must look over lessons ahead of time in case you need to gather any books or materials. Lesson presentation time will vary from day to day; you can often expand or contract lessons as you choose. Students will complete parts of most lessons on their own. The NIV Bible is used; using other versions will require minor adaptation on some activity pages.

➲ Rebirth and Reformation by Vivian Doublestein (The Master's Academy of Fine Arts) $35; art activities kit - $18

Vivian Doublestein offers classes through the Master's Academy of Fine Arts where students meet one day per week. Since everyone cannot participate in the classes, she decided to put together a unit study curriculum to reflect her teaching methodology and her interest in the fine arts. The first volume, packaged in a three-ring binder, focuses primarily on the Medieval/Renaissance period although it begins with the fall of Rome and ends with the Renaissance without really getting into the Reformation. The study is not age-graded, and it is open-ended enough to work with all ages. You might spend up to two years to complete the study, depending upon which activities you choose to use. Study is divided into four main sections: The Church; Medieval Life; Barbarians, Explorers and Merchants; and The Renaissance. Each section has a number of subsections. For example "The Church" includes sections such as "Art and Architecture of the Roman Catholic Church," "Monasticism," "Education," and "The Crusades. Each of these subsections begins with a historical overview, followed by a list of activities for Bible, reading, writing, science, geography, math, arts, and field trips. We need to consult other sources for information in most cases. For example, reading suggestions might be biographies or finding information on a particular topic. A musical tape with appropriate selections is included. An appendix has a bibliography plus instructions for a medieval feast complete with "Mummer's Play." Reproducible planning and record keeping sheets are at the end of the book. A Christian worldview is evident throughout the study (including a reference to Francis Schaeffer's *How Should We Then Live?*). The study seems to take a nonjudgmental position on Catholic theology, pointing out the meaning of the

liturgy and the support and encouragement of music and the arts that occurred within the Catholic church.

You will be surprised at the physical appearance of this resource; even though it is only $35, it is printed with many full-page illustrations on high quality paper. Many pages even have full color borders that give it a "medieval manuscript" look. Considering that it also includes an audio tape, the price is unbelievable.

History By the Book!: Historically Based Arts Activities is an optional, companion art kit for the Medieval/Renaissance period. It includes complete supplies for six projects; all you'll need to find at home are glue, tape, scissors, pencil, and containers for water and paint as you work. The six projects are a Byzantine cross, a triptych, a tile mosaic, stained glass simulation with tissue paper, tapestry (created on burlap with yarn), and a plaster fresco. Complete instructions are included. These activities are most appropriate for younger children, but you might want to stretch your teens to try more complex versions of each project.

➲ Robinson Self-Teaching Home School Curriculum, version 2.0 [computer program for IBM or Macintosh computers] (Oregon Institute of Science and Medicine and Althouse Press) $195

When Laurelee Robinson, home schooling mother of six, died suddenly, her husband, Dr. Arthur Robinson, determined to continue home schooling. The children, ages 17 months through 12 years at that time, worked with their father to devise a plan whereby they could home educate themselves. Dr. Robinson reports that during the past nine years he has spent less than 15 minutes a day teaching his children. What the Robinsons developed out of necessity, presents an option for many families who lack the time or expertise to provide more traditional learning opportunities. The program is fairly simple. The children learn to read using a phonetic method. Once children are able to read, they are introduced to a vast array of good books to read for history, science, and literature. Many of these books are classics, some are college level texts, some are nonfiction books, and some are old encyclopedias. Children receive no specific instruction in grammar or spelling unless they have unusual difficulties. Dr. Robinson explains how his children learned grammar and spelling, albeit more slowly, through exposure to good literature and their daily writing. He corrects grammar and spelling within those writing assignments, occasionally providing direct instruction when necessary. Vocabulary activities suffice for most children to reinforce spelling skills. The Saxon math series from level 5/4 up through Calculus covers mathematics instruction. The children, from age ten and up, each write an essay per day. According to Dr. Robinson's plan, children focus on only three primary tasks: math, writing, and reading. The reading consists of the books featured on the CD-ROMs which are to be read in the recommended order. The children essentially teach themselves, achieving high levels of academic competence with very minimal parental input and supervision.

The Robinsons spend five hours per day, six days per week, twelve months per year with occasional days off for special activities. As you might expect from such a schedule, the older

Robinson children are tackling college curriculum ahead of schedule and taking advanced placement exams to secure college credit for those courses.

The *Robinson Self-Teaching Curriculum* is a philosophy of education as much as a curriculum. Dr. Robinson believes that children do not need the direct instruction that is the mainstay of the traditional classroom. In fact, he recommends requiring children to work independently with direct instruction used only when essential. He views reading as the primary source of learning, so once children are able to read, they acquire knowledge of history, geography, literature, science, etc. through reading on their own. Dr. Robinson believes that science, also, should be approached in a different manner. He suggests descriptive science books for students until they have completed calculus. After they know calculus, he recommends they study physics and chemistry, followed by biology. Of course, this means that students should be finishing calculus much earlier than normal to allow time for study of the sciences before college entry.

The *Robinson Self-Teaching Curriculum* consists of 22 CD-ROMs (in a nifty case that makes each disk easily accessible) that contain 600 dpi image copies of more than 230 books, the 30,000-page 1911 *Encyclopedia Britannica*, the 400,000-word 1913 *Webster's Dictionary* (these last two resources include special on-screen reading software), 6000-word vocabulary flashcard system, 2000 historic illustrations, progress exams for some of the books, and vocabulary/comprehension quizzes for some of the literature. We install the foundational programs on our hard drive, then access the various disks as needed. The program is easy to install and operate. Printing with older equipment and/or ink jet printers might be significantly slower than on newer, more-powerful computers with laser printers.

We can print out copies of the 230+ books as needed, and, since they are facsimile images, they look just like the originals. (The drawback here is that we can't search for words, select paragraphs, or otherwise play with the text in facsimile copies.) The books themselves form the core of a valuable library and are worth the cost of the program if for no other reason than to have access to such books. Some of the titles in the curriculum are the *McGuffey Reader* series, Josephine Pollard's *George Washington* and *Life of Christopher Columbus*, *Just So Stories*, the *Five Little Peppers* series, *Tom Sawyer*, *Heidi*, *The Swiss Family Robinson*, *The Hound of the Baskervilles*, *Do and Dare* by Horatio Alger, *Two Years Before the Mast*, *Little Women*, *Little Men*, *Don Quixote*, *The Life of George Washington*, *The Spy*, *Up from Slavery*, *Circulation of the Blood* by William Harvey, *Faraday's Lectures*, *The Prince* by Machiavelli, *Julius Caesar* by Shakespeare, *The Personal Memoirs of U.S. Grant*, *The Autobiography of Theodore Roosevelt*, *The Federalist Papers*, *Institutes of the Christian Religion* by Calvin, *Cicero's Orations*, *The Law* by Bastiat, *The Wealth of Nations*, *Paradise Lost*, *The Mechanical Universe*, *Statistical Mechanics*, and *Chemical Principles*. The last few books and others on the CD-ROMs are complete college-level science texts that Dr. Robinson recommends be used for physics and chemistry. The only thing missing to follow the program Dr. Robinson outlines are the Saxon math books. Those are easily available, but the Oregon Institute of Science and Medicine sells them at discounted prices to users of their curriculum.

Dr. Robinson's philosophy is reflected by the choices of reading material as well as his statements in the introductory matter. Christianity, free markets, and limited government are the most obvious beliefs I could identify.

The curriculum does not claim to parallel that of government schools (or most other schools of any type). It does not include health, driver's ed, art, music, foreign language, physical education, speech, drama, and electives. You are probably required by your state law to include some of these subjects, you might find them required for college entry, or you might believe that they are essential to your children's educations, so add to the curriculum whatever you feel is necessary. Keep in mind that students who score very high on their PSAT and SAT tests as did the two eldest Robinson children will usually be recruited by colleges even if they are lacking some of the usual credits.

On the first CD-ROM in the set, Dr. Robinson outlines the course of study, and includes articles about teaching the various subject areas, creating a study environment, and other helpful insights. This present version 2.0 has been greatly expanded from the first version to serve as a more thorough course of study based upon feedback Dr. Robinson has received from many families who used the first version. Parents can follow Dr. Robinson's recommendations or adapt the ideas and resources as they wish.

I am thoroughly convinced of the value of reading worthwhile books as a major component of our home schooling, and this is a very affordable way to obtain more than 120,000 pages to build a library. Dr. Robinson's approach to homeschooling offers a model that most of us can glean from even if we do not follow it exactly. It also suggests a much broader realm of possibilities for many families who are reluctant to home school or who consider it beyond their capabilities. While such an independent, reading-based approach to education might present problems for auditory (hearing) and kinesthetic (hands-on) learners, the Robinsons have proven it successful with their own children.

➲ **Training Our Daughters to Be Keepers at Home** by Mrs. Craig (Ann) Ward (Smiling Heart Press) $74.95

This is a truly ambitious, seven-year curriculum that covers many essential and other useful and interesting skills a homemaker needs to know. The primary areas covered are godly womanhood, sewing, cooking/baking, gardening, finances/stewardship, serving others, and fiber arts. Examples of other topics covered more briefly are herbs, caring for the elderly, women's health, and raising animals. The price is so reasonable for this 601-page curriculum that you need not feel compelled to use everything in the book; you will still get your money's worth if you pick and choose from the lessons.

The program is intended to fill about 90 minutes per day, five days a week for 36 weeks per year. There is some book work but much more actual practice of various skills. This course is not to be an afterthought to your daughter's "real" school, but an integral part of her education. The suggested age for starting is

11, thus finishing the material by high school graduation. If your daughter is older, you could spend longer each day or choose to delete some of the projects. Many of us with older daughters have probably already started teaching some of these skills already, perhaps in a more haphazard manner. If so, there will be some things we can skip in the curriculum. Whether or not we have already done this type of learning projects, both mother and daughter should appreciate having these well-organized lessons to follow.

Scripture is studied in each of the seven years using a variety of sources. The basic skills of sewing, cooking, and gardening receive extensive treatment, well beyond the basics. For example, later gardening projects include the cultivation of berry vines and fruit trees. Sewing instruction is practical rather than decorative, geared toward developing skills for our daughters to be able to create their own wardrobes.

While we need to purchase other resources for some lessons, much detailed information is included within the curriculum. Most prominent are numerous reprints from Oregon State University. Among the numerous books we need to purchase or borrow for the course are *The Pursuit of Holiness, The New Seed-Starter's Handbook, What the Bible Says About Child Training, How to Manage Your Money, The Way Home*, and *Natural Remedies*. These are intended to be foundational books for your daughter's library rather than temporary-use textbooks. Mrs. Ward includes addresses for ordering the books as well as suggested outlets for obtaining other resources inexpensively.

Handwork units include knitting, crocheting, braiding rugs, and embroidering. Under home management, our daughters learn finances, hospitality, and celebrations, health issues (with a refreshing emphasis on herbs), childrearing, grief, and animal husbandry. Some "pioneer" skills such as basketry and soap and candle making round out the curriculum, but by no means exhaust it. Obviously, many of these skills can save a family quite a bit of money, but others such as flower arrangement and greeting card making are more enhancements of family life. I appreciated the emphasis on having things that are simple and beautiful in our lives.

There are a few, very minor problems in the book. Some of the sewing instructions and projects should be arranged with basic instruction preceding projects, and some of the patterns (pp. 14-15) are difficult to decipher. While there is something for everyone in this program, there are also things that some will find annoying. For instance, some will be put off by the "girls shouldn't wear pants" attitude or the discussion about laughter and sobriety. Others might disagree with the natural approach to health and medicine. At the same time, these might be the very things that attract others. Overall, none of this should pose a problem because there is so much to choose from that if we used even half of it we would have a great curriculum.

My daughter was intrigued with the variety of projects. I was inspired by the author's commitment to provide our daughters with the means to manage a home successfully as a woman of God. And I appreciated Mrs. Ward's demonstration of how we can live simply and well on one income.

The latest edition is cloth bound (burgundy with gold imprint) for durability with a lay-flat, sewn binding and full-color dust jacket. Those who purchase the book, can receive free annual updates of information and resources and their availability. Smiling Heart offers a money back guarantee if books are returned in good condition within two weeks of receipt.[Kath Courtney/C.D.]

➲ TRISMS $100 each for Volumes I and II

TRISMS stands for *Time Related Integrated Studies for Mastering Skills*. "Time related" refers to the chronological approach of the study which covers the history of the world (early civilizations to the present). I appreciate the chronological approach for upper levels, since some children (especially if they have been working in non-chronological unit studies up until this point) still need to get the overview of how events and ideas influence each other in time.

"Integrated" refers to the integration of language arts, history, science, geography, and culture-studies. *TRISMS* Volume I gives an overview of world history. It includes a Bible and church history timeline to show how these events fit into the scope of history. Math is not included, although some references are made to mathematical discoveries and accomplishments in history. Biographies, historical fiction, and nonfiction books are primary sources of learning rather than textbooks. *TRISMS I* lesson plans are provided, with daily topics (not every subject every day) listed under the headings "science," "inventions," "explorers," and "language." Language encompasses all language arts skills. The language arts section includes assignments, some worksheets, and answer keys. Six forms are used frequently throughout the program: Scientists Questionnaire, Inventions, Explorers Questionnaire, Interviewing a Story Character, Book Report, and Compare and Contrast. The forms combine fill-in-the-blank activity with lengthier writing challenges. Students maintain separate notebooks on science, inventions, and explorers, as well their own time line and a language arts folder. For those who like to monitor student assimilation of knowledge, quizzes are provided for every three weeks. Parts of the program (lesson plans, notebooks, and forms) seem highly structured, but, since we choose our own resources for most topics, there is room for a good deal of personalization. Of course, we can also substitute, add, or skip topics if we choose.

The program is for middle school students through senior high although it can be adapted for younger students. Volume I is most appropriate for junior high, while *TRISMS II* stretches into the higher grade levels. Volume I includes 37 lessons that can be used for either one or two years. The suggested reading alone might take up to two years. There are supplemental activities within the program if needed, but we might want to add other resources, especially if we are stretching it to two years. At junior high level, consider beefing it up with *Daily Grams* for more grammar practice and/or *Writing Strands* for more comprehensive development of writing skills.

TRISMS Volume II directs an in-depth "civilizations"-oriented study of world history, but it divides the study into 34 lessons, traveling from the beginning of history up into the Middle

Ages. (*TRISMS* Volume III will continue with the Renaissance up to modern times.) The emphasis here is on the humanities, art, music, architecture, science, and civilizations, although students also develop composition skills through activities centered around the literature they are reading. Literature readings draw from writings of the civilizations or time periods studied. Many actual readings—especially poetry and excerpts from classical literature—are included in the curriculum, although we still need to borrow or buy other resource books.

A new supplement, *Reading through the Ages*, [$15] can be used on its own or alongside all the *TRISMS* volumes. It contains annotated lists of recommended books for children to read which are arranged chronologically. A key is used to indicate reading level, page count, and whether the book is historical fiction or biography.

Reproducible map and activity pages are packaged separately from the basic comb-bound volume. Student packs with copies of all forms needed for the year for each volume are $25 for Volume I and $30 for Volume II. *Volume II Questionnaire Answer Keys* [$35] contains answers for architecture, art, and civilization questionnaires, which you will probably want to invest in as a time saver for the teacher.

Students from *TRISMS I* can continue to build their same notebook as they work through *TRISMS II*. This curriculum improves with each new edition. Parents do need to put some effort into planning and preparation, but *TRISMS* offers a stimulating alternative to traditional curriculum, especially for less-than-enthusiastic students.

⊃ Unit Study Guides by Amanda Bennett (Holly Hall Publications/Homeschool Press) $13.99 each; Unit Study Journal - $7.99

Amanda Bennett has authored a number of science-based *Unit Study Guides*. The first four, titled *Oceans, Space, Flight,* and *Trains* were written for grades K-8, so they are not the primary focus of this review. The seven newest titles stretch to cover grades K-12. Titles are *Computers, Home, Gardens, Electricity, Olympics,* and *Baseball.* While there are plenty of recommended activities and resources for the younger ones, those for high school level are plentiful enough to create worthwhile unit studies for teens. All *Unit Study Guides* follow the same format: an introduction, a detailed outline of topics to be addressed, related job opportunities, reference resources with addresses and phone numbers, spelling and vocabulary lists, key subject words for library research, activity resources and ideas, field trip suggestions, questions, and an expanded outline with space for notes. We create our own unit studies following the outline and using the recommended resources, activities, and field trips. There are no preplanned schedules or lesson plans, so these work best for moms who want ideas and inspiration rather than for moms who want to know what to do and when to do it. *Computers* covers three broad areas concerning computers: their history, how they work, and how we use them. *Computers* can be expanded into a hands-on study of various applications or programming, although how far you extend the study is up to you. *Home* covers the history of homes, architecture, construction (lots of detail provided within the *Guide*), purchasing a home (mortgages, insurance, etc.), moving into a home, basic home operating systems (lighting, wall outlets, heating, plumbing, appliances, etc.), and maintenance and upkeep. *Baseball* is likely to be a popular volume. *Baseball* covers the history of the game, how the game is played, science in baseball (e.g., studying the aerodynamics of a thrown ball), the Major Leagues, players, awards, math in baseball, softball, equipment collectibles, and baseball art and music. The four other titles follow the same format as those described here.

A separate *Unit Study Journal* can be used to record information about each study. Since the *Journal* is designed for all ages, some of the layout seems a little young for teens to use. However, the *Journal* works well as a tool for mom to use, especially if the study involves more than one child.

⊃ The Weaver, 7-12 Supplements *Weaver* volumes - $135 each; *Supplement* volumes - $30-$50 each; *On Eagle's Wings* - $20

[Important note: The Weaver will be going out of business as of November 30, 1997. At this point, we expect that the materials will be published by another company, but we do not know who that will be. Send a SASE to Grove Publishing for further information.]

Those who enjoy the unit study approach used by *The Weaver* can extend those studies all the way through high school by using the *Supplements* to each Weaver volume. First, I will describe *The Weaver* volumes, then the *Supplements*. There are five volumes to *The Weaver Curriculum*, and each comes in a large three-ring binder. Any of the five volumes can be used for any number of students, with information in the basic volumes geared to grades 1-6. Each volume should take one year to complete. Each chapter is divided into subject areas, and each subject area is divided into grade levels. This makes it easy to organize our own lesson plans according to the learning level of each teen. Bible, music, health and safety, and art are offered as group lessons rather than on individual grade levels, although much of this material will be too young for teens. Many language arts activities are included. We must still add our own math program since math is not covered in *The Weaver*.

The Weaver provides much information within the program itself, although a great deal of learning relies on outside sources.

In *Volume I,* (covering Genesis 1:11-50) topics are local state history and geography, history and geography of 24 other states, ancient history of Sumeria, and introduction to Egyptian history. In *Volume II* (covering Exodus and the Books of the Law), topics are ancient history of the Egyptians and Hebrews, early American History, American Government and the Constitution. *Volume Three* (Joshua, Judges, Ruth, and I Samuel through verse 10) covers exploration and navigation, espionage and communication, recording of history, fortifications, music, thinking skills, United States history from 1789-1860, time, social structures and the family, and service. *Volume Four* (the period of the Kings and Prophets) covers spiritual giants; civil war; the wisdom of Solomon (includes an introduction to biology); the temple; ancient civilizations of Assyria, Babylon, Persia and Greece; and introduction to the Roman Empire. Volume Five (the Life of Christ) addresses topics such as covenants, government, the deity of Jesus, customs of worship, men and women of faith, both world and American history from 1865 to the present, astronomy, reproduction, cells, agriculture, stewardship, and geology.

The *Supplements*, one for each volume, add study outlines for social studies and science for grades 7 through 12, that build upon the sixth-grade activities in the basic *Weaver* volume. Activities for social studies and science are further broken down into three levels: grades 7-8, grades 9-10, and grades 11-12. Students need to do a great deal of research in outside sources at all three levels. The *Supplements* serve as study guides although they do provide some information.

The 11th-12th grade level includes suggested readings from *The Great Books of the Western World*. While *The Great Books* are highly recommended, they are not absolutely essential.

The *Supplements* do not claim to be complete in themselves. The separate book, *On Eagle's Wings*, describes what is necessary to provide a complete curriculum, as well as detailed objectives for each subject at each grade level from grades 7-12.

It is recommended that students read 20 books per year, so a list of recommended books is included at the front of each *Supplement*. A significant amount of language arts is covered through vocabulary and writing assignments such as research reports and essays.

Clarence Carson's *A Basic History of the United States* is referenced frequently enough to make it fairly essential. Occasionally mentioned reference books, such as some from Milliken and Usborne, might be substituted for with other resources. The combination of resource recommendations, especially if you use Carson's books and the *Great Books*, surpasses any textbook presentation. However, even though science lessons dig deep, the publisher recommends that we obtain a separate science text for chemistry, physics, biology, etc. For chemistry and physics, it is recommended that we follow the text because those topics build concept on concept in a logical progression. In biology and most other sciences, this is less true, so we can use the text as a reference book to accompany topics as they arise within *The Weaver*.

Essentially, the *Supplements* are providing coverage of social studies and science, with plenty of opportunity for practicing language arts. Since there is little chronological continuity in history studies (aside from Bible study) in the basic *Weaver* volumes, that situation also exists at the upper levels. However, many students will encounter no problems jumping back and forth between world history, U.S. History, government, economics, and geography. The coverage of all of these topics is extremely in-depth, even if somewhat scattered.

Within each chapter and topic study are objectives followed by suggested activities. Study, research, and report writing dominate these activities, but there are also science experiments and some drawing and simple construction projects. Questions within each section help us evaluate how well students have assimilated knowledge. Most activities seem more challenging than standard school fare.

The content of the studies can be adapted to suit the needs of individual students; all students need not do all of the reports that are suggested, and we might choose between two activities if both are meeting the same objective. The *Supplements* range up to about 800 pages, so there is a great deal of material here to work with; the problem is more likely to be too much material than not enough. Although I have not used the *Supplements*, I suspect that those teaching only teens will be relying primarily on the *Supplement* with only occasional reference to *The Weaver* itself. Foreign language and other elective courses must be selected separately. *On Eagle's Wings* shows how *The Weaver* equates as credit equivalents for meeting basic high school requirements, and an assignment of credits accompanies each *Supplement*.

➲ Zane Publishing's Home Library (Zane Publishing)

Zane Publishing sells hundreds of educational CD-ROMs, primarily through Amway distributors. These CDs cover all subject areas and all grade levels, but they are written for the secular market. Although the educational and production quality of the CDs is excellent, they lack the balance of a Christian world view. To solve that problem, Zane has published *Christian Home Learning Guides* (a single 342-page book) by Marshall Foster and Ron Ball [$45]. Intended to be a companion to the Zane CD-ROMs, this book is also valuable on its own. It is arranged in sections. The first section provides the overarching discussion about a Biblical worldview and why it is essential for Godly education. Part Two teaches about geography, history (broken into a number of different eras), and government. Within each of the "history" sections we find a list of related CD-ROMs, a historical overview from a Biblical Christian perspective, analysis of the pertinent CD-ROMs, review questions (answers are at the back of the book), related Scriptures, and a suggested reading list. The overviews also feature biographies of exemplary people or focus on key ideas. Part Three follows this same format, addressing the areas of art, literature, music, science, and myths and legends. Parts Four and Five do not correlate with the CD-ROMs; instead, the fourth section features biographies of Christian leaders, and the fifth section discusses preparation for college and life. The appendices following these five main sections are a valuable collection of historical documents, including the U.S. Constitution and the Westminster Shorter Catechism.

If you are interested in the Zane CD-ROMs, this is the best way to find out which ones are worthwhile. The reviews tell us the strengths and weaknesses of each and suggest areas that need balance or correction. Even if you invest in only a few or none of the CD-ROMs, the book is a valuable introduction to world view thinking and application in various subject areas.

CHAPTER ELEVEN

Bible Resources for Junior and Senior High

We hope that by this time, our children are very familiar with the Bible. They should understand basic doctrine and be ready to investigate the Bible more deeply. Rather than choosing a curriculum, we could use any of the many Bible study materials from our local Christian book store. For example, choose from among the hundreds of study aids one or two resources for studying a particular book of the Bible. Or do a topical study with a few tools such as a Concordance and an Expository Dictionary. A commentary set is also very useful. (Most single-volume commentaries on the entire Bible will frustrate you, so look for a good buy on a more comprehensive set.)

You can purchase all of these very reasonably from Great Christian Books, Christian Book Distributors (CBD), or, sometimes, from your local Christian bookstore. If you need help, most smaller distributors and local stores will answer questions and help you find resources that support your theological perspective or address a particular issue or topic.

Home educating families tend to be even more strong minded about their religious beliefs than they are about their educational beliefs. It is impossible to recommend Bible study materials that are in total agreement with all of our readers' convictions. Those included in this chapter agree on the divine inspiration of the Bible, salvation through Jesus Christ, as well as many other doctrinal areas.

Bible curriculum or study material should never be a substitute for individual Bible reading. God speaks to each of us through Scripture according to our present spiritual condition and need. No curriculum can even pretend to provide such individually-tailored lessons, although it can still be helpful.

Bible Curriculum

⮞ A Beka High School Bible Curriculum

Although I list the high school level titles here, I have found the A Beka Bible curriculum too classroom oriented for use in most home schools.

– *Joshua and Judges* - Teacher's Kit IV [8th grade level], includes Teacher's Guide, Student Study Outline and Review Questions - $39.95

– *Kings of Israel: Israel's United Kingdom* - Teacher's Kit [9th grade level], includes Teacher's Guide, Student Study Outline, and Review Questions - $34.85

– *Israel's Divided Kingdom* - Teacher's Kit [9th grade level] -$34.85

– *Genesis - First Things* - Teacher's Kit [Grades 11-12], includes Student Worktext and Teacher's Guide - $11.95

– *New Testament Survey* - Teacher's Kit [Grades 11-12], includes Student Worktext and Teacher's Guide - $18.90

– *Bible Doctrines for Today* - Teacher Kit [10th grade level], includes student book with teacher's guide, test book, and answer key - $30.95

⮞ Bob Jones University Press' Secondary Level Bible Study Curriculum [for grades 7 through 12] student worktexts - $10 each; teacher's editions - $42 each

Start at the first book in the series, regardless of age, because of the sequence of the study. These worktexts are excellent and can be used either with or without Teacher's Editions. Teacher's Editions are helpful, but there is plenty of material to work with without them. Most lessons open with a story to illustrate the theme, then study the Scripture from which the lesson is drawn. Memory work is included. Wall charts, test packets, and answer keys to test packets are available for some of these books, although I don't think homeschoolers need them. Check the BJUP catalog for options.

Level A: New Testament, Learning from the Life of Christ

Level B: Old Testament, Portraits from the Old Testament

Level C: New Testament, Lessons from the Early Church

Level D: Old Testament, Themes from the Old Testament

Level E: New Testament, Directions for Early Christians

Level F: Patterns for Christian Living

⮞ Daring Deliverers: Lessons on Leadership from the Book of Judges by Dr. Ollie E. Gibbs (Association of Christian Schools International) student book - $10.95; teacher's edition - $39.99

This one-semester study of key people in the book of Judges, focuses on godly leadership qualities. A student book and teacher's edition comprise a course that is suggested for students in grades 7-9, but which might be stretched to include both younger and older children. Lots of practical application and thought-provoking questions make this an intriguing study. Although it was written for classroom use, it will work well for homeschoolers. It does not assume a previous familiarity with Judges but includes an overview of the key events and themes so that students understand the context. Lessons are guided from the teacher's edition, so it does require some teaching, interaction, and discussion. Some group activities are suggested, but these are not crucial. The student book is also essential for much of the course content. Almost 100 blackline masters at the back of the teacher's edition are designed to be used or reproduced to serve as visual aids, worksheets, lesson outlines for notes, a ministry gifts survey, tests, and quizzes. The NKJV is used, but you can easily substitute another version of the Bible.

⊃ GENESIS, Finding Our Roots by Dr. Ruth Beechick (Education Services) $17.50

This unusual book defies classification. It is primarily a unit-study-style theological study, but it also covers a good deal of science, history, geography, literature, art, and linguistics. It consists of six units, all based on the book of Genesis, plus appendices. The six units are entitled, "God's Book of Creation," "Book of Adam," "Book of Noah," "Book of the Sons of Noah," "Book of Shem," and "Book of Terah." Each unit begins with Scripture and Scripture study. Following next are a series of topical studies. For example, in the first unit on creation some of the topics addressed are dragons, "day," the origin of the week, and creation myths. Short readings from other sources are often included, such as selections from two unbiblical "creation" myths. A final section offers suggestions for further study: correlated readings that fit in directly with the study (primarily from *Adam and His Kin* by Ruth Beechick and *The Genesis Record* by Henry Morris), science text topics to look for to expand knowledge, other topical areas for further reading, and writing assignments. Questions and activities are interspersed throughout each unit; they vary in difficulty from simple to challenging so we can select those that are appropriate for each of our children. Some will require outside reading and research and will clearly be best suited for older students. The KJV is used throughout, although we can substitute another version if we prefer. The perspective is that of a literal interpretation of the Bible, supporting a young earth. There might be areas where you might hold a different viewpoint. Some might be major (e.g., the age of the earth and length of each of the days of creation) and some might be less crucial (e.g., in talking about the writing of Chapter 1 of the book of Genesis, she states that God either wrote the words Himself or told Adam the words to write). Throughout the study, Dr. Beechick brings out the importance of developing a biblical Christian worldview.

This is a hardcover book, only about 112 pages in length, so it should take less than a semester to complete. It should work best for family Bible study time, perhaps led by Dad, with Mom then incorporating much of the extended topical studies into school time. The book is heavily illustrated and nicely formatted.

⊃ Landmark's Freedom Baptist Curriculum $35 per course

Landmark publishes a distinctive Baptist curriculum that covers the fundamentals of faith. The courses are presented in worktexts (called study guides), with weekly quizzes, quarterly tests, and answer keys included. Of particular interest to some will be the Bible course number B160, "The Inspiration of the Scriptures." This course presents the case for the King James Version as the most reliable Bible translation.

⊃ Teaching the Law by Paul A. Goedecke (New Testament Christian School/ order from Landmark Distributors) $25

Based upon the Principle Approach, this course is written for junior high students. However, both the content and academic level are also appropriate for high school students or even adults. Originally written as a classroom course, the book easily adapts for home school use. Students can read and study independently and answer the questions (many of them essay) at the end of each chapter. However, the content of the course is such that I highly recommend that a parent (preferably the father) spend time discussing each topic. The course begins with a brief overview and chronology of the Old Testament, and a study of law and its purpose. Then each of the following chapters is devoted to each of the Ten Commandments. The lessons are solidly based on Scripture and include definitions (incorporating study of Hebrew and Greek meanings), points to ponder (key ideas), case law applications, historical examples, and related verses. These last three areas are all drawn directly from Scripture, sometimes with elaboration. Questions at the end of chapters are presented as examinations, although some will find them more useful as a tool for reinforcing lesson content. If you choose to use them as exams, a parent must spend significant discussion time emphasizing and drawing out the key points that will be tested. This course raises a much higher standard for Bible study for junior high level. The course should take one semester to complete. Because the course is published by a small school, it is not a polished product; there are numerous typographical errors which I hope can be corrected with their next printing. In spite of these deficiencies, this is an excellent course.

⊃ Precept Upon Precept (Precept Ministries)

These are a series of Bible study workbooks that are "...designed to teach people of any background or educational level the inductive method of study which gives people the skills and, thus, the ability to go straight to the Word of God." Books are available in two formats for most titles: *Precept Upon Precept* books [$18 each] should take about five hours of study per week; *In & Out* [about $12.75 each] should take only one to two hours per week and are an easier type of course. Both types of books were written for use along with a weekly, hour-long presentation in a class setting. Sets of either audio or video tapes are offered for sale or rental to be used with the books especially if no class is available. The sets of audio tapes rent for a very reasonable price, and one or another of these presentation tools seems necessary to fully benefit from the courses. Titles in the series are *Genesis (Parts 1 and 2), Judges, Daniel, Habakkuk, John (Part 1 and 2), Romans (Parts 1-4), Philippians, Colossians, I Thessalonians, II Thessalonians, James, I John, II Timothy, Hebrews (Parts 1 and 2), I Peter, II Peter, Sermon on the Mount, Spiritual Gifts, Covenant*, and *Marriage without Regrets*. There are a few studies directed specifically to teens: *Daniels for the 1990's* and *The Mask of Hypocrisy Melts in the Flames of Suffering* (study in I Peter). Younger level materials (for ages 9-12 and for ages 7-8) are also available on a few of the above topics, but in different formats more appropriate for younger learners. These books are called *Line Upon Line* [$8.50 each] and include the titles *The Book of*

Genesis and *The Gospel of John.* Using these will help include younger students in family study of these books of the Bible.

A companion volume is also available that teaches the basics of the *Precept Upon Precept* study methods. This book, *How to Study Your Bible Precept Upon Precept* [$8.99], should be used to learn how to use the Precept materials.

All teaching is nondenominational, following a basic Christian statement of faith.

➲ Pro Series Bible Curriculum (Positive Action for Christ) student books - $8.35 - $10.20 each; teacher editions - $29 - $36.50 each

Although this curriculum is written for the classroom, almost everything is easily adaptable for the home school. This is a "meaty," Bible-based curriculum with a strong emphasis on character development.

Since the teaching comes primarily from the teacher's manual, this is not an independent study curriculum, but one that requires teacher/parent involvement. However, a minimal amount of lesson preparation is required because the teacher's manuals are well-designed.

An important feature of the curriculum is that it recognizes various levels of thinking skills and goes beyond simple recall of facts to develop understanding and application of knowledge. It also recognizes that teens are at different levels of spiritual growth. This fact has prompted the publisher to offer a number of choices for the junior high level so that we can select that which best fits our teen's need. The original junior high material assumes a more mature Christian walk. Since those materials are similar in format and challenge level to those for grades 9-12, I will discuss them first.

The original junior and senior high level books (grades 7-12) are challenging studies for students who are interested in spiritual growth. *Dynamic Christian Living* (suggested for seventh grade) is the foundation for the remaining levels. (Start here if in doubt.) *The God-Man* is designed to bring eighth-grade students to a deeper knowledge of the person of Jesus Christ through a study of the book of John. Alternatives that are less challenging for junior high students are *Wise Up!* and *Route 66,* which I will discuss just a little later.

The Inner Man (ninth grade) confronts students with the need to develop inner character rather than rely on the outward appearances of Christianity. *The Christian Adventure* (tenth grade), based on *Pilgrim's Progress,* is an exciting study of the application of the classic allegory in our lives. *Behold Your God* (eleventh grade) is designed to help students develop depth in their personal relationship with God. Twelfth graders study the principles of life as laid out in the book of Proverbs in a study called *Proverbs. Changes: Transforming Principles from the Beatitudes,* is an alternative to *The Inner Man* (less challenging level) for ninth grade level which also addresses internal spiritual changes through study of Matthew 5:1-10. These studies are all dependent upon presentation from the teacher's manuals. A separate student book contains study questions plus reading material (e.g., the text of *Pilgrim's Progress* is contained in the student book, *The Christian Adventure.*) Student books are

designed to be written in, so they are not reusable. The "high school" level studies should even be useful on an adult level. These are not simple, fill-in-the-blanks materials, but challenging, growth-provoking studies.

Wise Up! and *Route 66,* alternative courses for junior high level, both assume a lower level of spiritual maturity (probably a more realistic viewpoint) than the above courses. They assume that the teenager is struggling with typical issues—salvation, friends, obedience to parents, self-control, decision making, etc. The student books have written exercises, but most of them direct the student to Scripture rather than provide entertaining busy work. *Wise Up!* is subtitled "Wisdom in Proverbs." Scripture study here ranges far beyond Proverbs, but it centers around "getting wisdom" in all areas of life. *Route 66* (of which I have only seen a preview) looks like a Bible survey course with an emphasis on understanding God's relationship with man throughout history. It moves chronologically from Genesis to Revelation, even covering the minor prophets. Either of these courses is easier than those described above, yet they are still spiritually challenging.

All courses are designed to take a full school year, so for grades 7-9 we would choose one of the two options. Teacher preparation and presentation time is essential to each course. Both the teacher's manual and student book are required for each study.

➲ The Story of God and His People Series (Christian Schools International) text: softcover - $19.30, hardcover - $12.50; workbook - $7.95; teacher edition - $46.90

The curriculum authors of this series recognize that there are different purposes for Bible courses in church and in school. The authors have defined their purpose in writing Bible curriculum for schools, as that of imparting knowledge and equipping students for lives of service in the world, in contrast to the church's tasks of proclaiming the good news of salvation and calling people to faith, worship, and service. Thus we have a curriculum that assumes that children have already heard the gospel message, and that the school's task is to help equip these children for a Christian life.

This Bible curriculum is for preschool through eighth grades. Of all the Bible curricula designed for schools, this series is one of the best. The underlying and guiding theme throughout the series is the Bible and the story of God and His relationship with man. It deals with the Bible as a total picture rather than isolating Bible stories and incidents. Teachers are encouraged to use visual aids and activities to help children better understand what they are studying.

The Teacher's Guides are essential for all levels. While the thematic approach is the same throughout the series, there are different authors for the different levels, so the levels vary in lesson presentation and format. While there are student texts for sixth through eighth grades, a significant part of the teaching originates in the Teacher's Guides. Lesson plans are clearly laid out and very easy to use. Some supplemental materials are needed for lesson presentation.

For sixth through eighth grades there are both a student text and workbook. Both are not necessary. The student text provides reading material and questions. There is not enough room in the text for written answers, so they would need to be done in a separate notebook, or students can use the student workbook which has the identical questions with space for answers. The student text is reprinted in the Teacher's Guide, so it would also be possible for us to read and present the lesson from the Teacher's Guide, then have our child work in the student workbook on his own. Alternatively, students could do most of their work independently from the student text with only a short discussion of essential material from the Teacher's Guide. Bible reading and memory work (NIV or KJV) are both important parts of the curriculum.

Because a chronological approach has been used to keep the Biblical story in context, it is important to choose the proper level for our children according to topic rather than grade level. Sixth grade reviews the Old Testament through Ecclesiastes. Seventh grade overlaps sixth grade by beginning with 1 Samuel, then going up through the gospels. Eighth grade reviews the gospels and covers through Revelation.

➲ Studying God's Word (Christian Liberty Press) student books - $7 each; teacher's manuals - $1.95 each

Although this series (books A through H) is designated only for use up through seventh grade, the books do not show grade levels, and we might use some from the end of the series beyond seventh grade. They are particularly useful for students who have not done any significant amount of Bible study.

Book E covers from Genesis to Ruth, Book F covers 1 Samuel to Malachi, Book G covers the message and ministry of Jesus Christ, and Book H studies the Book of Acts. In future books, CLP plans to continue the series through the New Testament. Books of the Bible are taught chronologically rather than in the order they appear in the Bible. For instance, when studying through the books of Kings, lessons from other biblical books that correlate are inserted in their proper places. I almost hate to list this series under "curriculum" because the emphasis is on the Bible more than in typical curricula. Lessons reinforce Bible knowledge rather than developing slightly connected topics as do many so-called Bible curriculum lessons. The historical books are given more attention because the goal is to get the overview of God's plan. The Scripture passage(s), lesson goal, and a memory verse are listed at the beginning of each lesson along with a small timeline to help us place events in context. This is followed by background and explanatory information, then questions that require both recall and thinking. Thought questions prompt students to apply Scripture to their lives. Supplemental exercise (crosswords, word searches, mazes, etc.) are included after many of the lessons. Constant references to a time line help students to keep the "big picture" in sight. Unit tests are also in the student book.

CLP sells very inexpensive and very brief Teacher's Manuals for all levels. The few pages of introduction are essential reading. The remainder is your answer key. While they might be "too young" for some students, Books E through H are interestingly-written, solid Bible study for students who need to build a foundation.

Other Resources for Bible Study and Spiritual Growth

➲ American Student's Package [computer program] (Christian Technologies Inc.) $75

On a single CD-ROM for Windows we get complete copies of the Bible in two versions—KJV and Webster's 1833 update of the KJV, *Noah Webster's 1828 Dictionary, Strong's Greek and Hebrew Definitions*, and *Nave's Topical Index*. By January 1998, *American Quotations* by William Federer, with over 4,000 quotes, will also be included. (See the separate review of *Noah Webster's 1828 Dictionary* under Principle Approach.) Easy-to-use, it allows us to view both versions of the Bible simultaneously on a split screen, add additional Bible versions, and pull up the dictionary or other helps to aid in our study. *Strong's Greek and Hebrew Definitions* allow us to quickly pull up the Strong's number, pronunciation, and definition. *Nave's Topical Index* offers additional information on topics with cross references to other appearances of a word. *Webster's Dictionary* is particularly helpful for Bible study since it often defines words with biblical references. I like this program for homeschool students and parents because it has good basic features and takes little effort to figure out. Combining the *Webster's Dictionary* with Bible study tools is especially appropriate for home educators, many of whom would want the *Dictionary* for other purposes (e.g., Principle Approach research, access to definitions of some archaic words, biblical definitions, etc.). The Bible study part of the program offers more extensive features than does the dictionary. We can set searches for words and phrases. The program features "full Boolean and/or/not logic" which allows us to fine tune those searches. We can copy and print from the program. A number of users can maintain unique sets of notes within the study screens, and they can also combine, search, chain, and export them. Additional modules such as *Everyone in the Bible, The Life and Times of Jesus the Messiah, Greek and Hebrew Transliteration*, and other versions of the Bible can be added. A separate CD-ROM called the *General CD-ROM* contains a dozen Bible translations, the resources mentioned in the last sentence, plus the *Greek and Hebrew Definitions* for $150.

➲ A Blueprint for Thinking [video/audio tapes] by R.C. Sproul (Ligonier Ministries) video - $30; audio - $12; study guide - $4

In five 30-minute messages, Dr. R.C. Sproul addresses the most important questions of all: "How do I know what is true?", "What is real?", "Who is God?", "What is man?", and "What is right and wrong?". While Sproul uses the correct vocabulary ("epistemology," "metaphysics," etc.) he explains the meanings of terms in language and with illustrations clear enough for teens to understand. This series bridges the gap between basic Bible study and seminary training, dealing with crucial issues in a manner that is accessible to older teens and adults. Sproul uses numerous illustrations and stories that enliven his presentations and bring the issues down to a level where we can see what this has to do with everyday living. The visual impact of the video presentations is undeniably stronger than the audio, but the audio tapes don't miss anything essential as far as I can tell. The study guide is excellent. For each of the five sections there are relevant quotations, pre-listening questions to alert listeners to key points, discussion questions, personal response questions, lesson summaries, and an outline of the tape lecture. This series can be foundational for a study of world views and Christian living.

○ Choosing My Religion [video or audio course] (Ligonier Ministries) video tapes - $30; audio tapes - $12; student guide - $4; leader guide - $5

Challenge teens to think through their religious beliefs, guided by Dr. R.C. Sproul, with this video- or audio-based course. Two video (or three audio) cassettes together contain five, thirty-minute presentations by Sproul. The first section deals with absolute truth, logic, the existence of God, the nature of Jesus, and the concept of worldview. Part two gets into sin and redemption. The third part tackles salvation and the judgment. Part four deals with the Christian walk. The final presentation emphasizes God's holiness and the Christian's commitment to follow God in all areas of life. The concept of worldviews, although introduced in the first section, is a theme throughout the series. He speaks dramatically to a live audience against a visually interesting stage set. Otherwise, these weighty topics might cause some teens to nod off. The tapes are accompanied by both leader and student guides. The two guides are identical, but the leader's has three additional pages describing the course design along with six- to eight-page Bible study supplements. The course is best used in an interactive situation (e.g., parent and teen or larger group). Each video section sets the stage with an entertaining essay to read aloud. Questions are posed for students to consider as they view the video. The Bible study can be used or not as time allows, but it takes students deeper into the issues. A section on worldview follows, with the theological issues translated into real life applications. This section will prompt a great deal of discussion. The topics covered are vital for teens to study, but be sensitive to their maturity levels and spiritual states in choosing when to use *Choosing My Religion*. Sproul's doctrinal position is reformed Protestant and affirms the inerrancy of Scripture.

○ Christian Ethics for YOUth: A Study of Wisdom from the Book of Proverbs by Wilmer Bechtels (Speedy Spanish) $9.95; tests and answer key - $2.25; workbook - $6.95

This book is written directly to teens. The author has designed the book so that teens can do about one lesson per day. (They might choose to take longer, especially if they do the companion workbook exercises.) Each lesson hits a topic addressed in Proverbs by interweaving the point of the lesson with a story illustration. It might seem too "preachy" to some teens, but this will depend very much on their spiritual status and background. The few lessons that I had time to read were very effective; the stories evoke an emotional reaction (effective for conveying a message), and the instruction is solidly based on Scripture. At the back of the book is a section entitled "Topical Proverbs," which, as you might guess, lists individual proverbs under topical headings.

The companion workbook has two pages per lesson with vocabulary work and questions (true-false, sentence-response, short essay) that often lead students to the Bible for answers. The content seems appropriate for mature junior high students as well as those in high school. Unit Tests with an answer key are optional, but they help create a complete course that should be good for one-half credit.

○ The Complete Book of Bible Literacy by Mark D. Taylor (Tyndale House Publishers) $10.99

Want to make up your own Bible Trivia game? Need to know if a popular quotation really comes from the Bible? Fuzzy on church history? Looking for connections between the Bible, Christianity and the fine arts? You'll find it all in this one concise volume. You can pull questions from a number of topically organized quizzes (primarily multiple choice). Sections of the book on Bible quotations, key events and people of both Old and New Testament, church history, church life and theology, and the Bible, Christianity and fine arts are arranged alphabetically under names, phrases, or other key words. Even though the book is close to 400 pages, it doesn't begin to compare with separate books you might find devoted to any one of these topics alone. Yet, it makes a decent quick reference, especially for teens and younger students who might easily be overwhelmed with larger reference tools. The book also features a helpful timeline of church history from 100 B.C. up to the present. Theologically, the book is mildly biased toward "conservative" Protestantism, but Taylor tries to be evenhanded in his treatment of Catholicism while clearly labeling the more unorthodox beliefs of the LDS church, Christian Science, and Jehovah's Witnesses.

○ Discover Your Children's Gifts by Don and Katie Fortune (Revell/Chosen Books) $14.99

Subtitled "A parent's handbook to recognize and develop your children's God-given gifts," this book has many applications for home educating families. It features tests for identifying spiritual gifts using seven key words or categories to describe each type of person. There are four different tests for preschoolers, primaries, juniors, and teenagers. (The teen test works fairly well for adults, also, but there is an adult test in the Fortunes' book, *Discover Your God-Given Gifts*.) The seven categories used are perceiver, server, teacher, exhorter, giver, administrator, and compassion person. Far more than just a book for identifying which gifts each person has, this is also a child-training book. While it doesn't address the various ages and stages specifically, it discusses emotions, communication skills, self-image, approach to life, imaginative capacity, behavior, discipline, personal habits, friendships, relationships, intellectual ability, school performance, leadership skills, interests, sports, and more, all from a Christian perspective. The Fortunes tell us what to expect and suggest specific strategies for dealing with these areas. Another section of the book deals with parenting, overcoming problems that arise when our parenting style conflicts with our children's gifts, home atmosphere, ministering to our children, teaching and working with other children, and preparing our children for college, careers, and marriage. Parents of teens are likely to find the section on how different careers suit the various gifts very helpful. The section on marriage partners is useful for both parents and older teens. At the back of the book is a 13-week study guide for those who want to teach or study the book with a group.

⮩ **Discovering The Bible [video course]** (Vision Video) $59.95

Vision Video worked with Christian History Institute, publishers of the highly-regarded *Christian History* magazine, to produce this excellent video-based study about the Bible. Two video tapes together have four 30-minute video presentations. The four sections are titled, "Getting Acquainted" (an overview), "The Old Testament," "The New Testament," and "Preservation, Circulation, and Influence." The videos come boxed with a 32-page, colorful, illustrated summary of each of the four sections. This booklet, essentially, reflects information on the videos. A Leader's Guide presents complete lesson plans for presenting the videos, guiding discussion, working with student handouts, and directing related Bible study. It also includes further background information for the teacher. Unlike most study guides that accompany videos, this one seems to be well-thought out. Another booklet of Student Handouts and Worksheets can be reproduced to use with students with each lesson. The entire course can be presented as four lengthy lessons, or each lesson can be split so that we watch the video one time and use the activities, discussion, and Bible study another time. The boxed set also includes sample issues of Christian History Institute's *Glimpses* publications and an authentic piece of papyrus. The *Glimpses* are on the topics "Constantine Tischendorf," "The Canon," "Jerome," "The Middle Ages," "William Tyndale," and "The English Bible." *Discovering the Bible's* presentation is non-denominational Protestant. It covers issues such as authenticity, historicity, organization, the canon, transmission, conflicts, and impact of the Bible. Animations, film clips, reenactments, interviews, and many other film techniques are used to maintain interest, although it does move a little slowly at times. Students will probably most enjoy the fourth segment that incorporates lengthy clips from films about Wycliffe, Tyndale, and Luther. While the course emphasizes that the Bible is the inspired Word of God, it does not delve into deeper questions of inerrancy. Consequently, it functions best as either an introduction to the Bible or a survey course for those who already are somewhat familiar rather than as an in-depth study. It should be ideal for junior and senior high students, but I highly recommend that teachers familiarize themselves with the support materials and the videos ahead of time so they can interject discussion or activities if the video moves too slowly through some of the sections. This also works well as a family course led by dad or for use in Sunday School classes. Vision Video offers extra support materials including videos (e.g., *John Wycliffe: The Morning Star* and *God's Outlaw: The Story of William Tyndale*) and issues of *Christian History* magazine. See also the review of a possible follow-up series from Vision Video, *The Trial and Testimony of the Early Church.*

⮩ **Every Thought Captive** by Richard L. Pratt, Jr. (P & R Publishing Co.) $7.99

This is a concise statement of the tenets of Christianity (based upon the teaching of Cornelius Van Til) that is written in simple, straightforward language, rather than in theological vocabulary. The second half of the book is a foundation in apologetics—defending the faith. The author takes issue with apologetic approaches commonly used by Campus Crusade for Christ and other organizations that rely on rational persuasion and presents what he thinks is a more Biblical approach based upon recognition of the truth of the Bible and man's spiritual need. The other basic approach is presented in *Know Why You Believe,* described below. Our teens should have some knowledge of how to defend their belief, and they might not pick this up anywhere else.

⮩ **Everyday Life in Bible Times** by Arthur W. Klinck and Erich H. Kiehl (Concordia Publishing House) $8.99

The whole family will enjoy this book on life in Bible times. The authors examine occupations, agriculture, vineyards and orchards, food and drink, homes and their furnishings, trades carried on in both homes and shops, arts and sciences, travel, trade, commerce, social customs, and family life. Instead of brief dictionary-style entries, each topic is allotted enough space to include details that will hold the interest of both children and adults. It is interesting enough to read straight through or you can use it as a reference book. If you read it straight through, you can use the discussion questions as the end of each chapter. Either way, you might want to try some of the research and hands-on activities also found at the ends of chapters. (Order item #222540.)

⮩ **exeGeses Bible Series** by Herb Jahn (exeGeses Bibles) $70; Aramaic $30, CD-ROM - $100; Home School Special: all three -$100

[Note from Cathy: I don't usually review Bible translations here, but this one is such a handy study tool, that I thought it deserved attention.]

With all of the "dumbing down" of Scripture and the new versions purported to be more meaningful, relevant, and contemporary—not to mention gender-neutral and politically correct—it is refreshing to discover the Exegeses series of Bibles—all literal translations and transliterations of the Holy Word of God. (Transliteration is the direct rendering of alphabetic letters from one language to another.) Herb Jahn, the exegete, invested more than twelve years of research to complete these works. He presents us with direct translations revealing shades of meaning lost in the original KJV translation, such as "priestal scribings" instead of "Scriptures" when a different word than is commonly translated as "Scriptures" was used in the original. In *The exeGeses Bible*, all names are also transliterated (e.g., "Jesus" is spelled "Yah Shua.")

We no longer need to be experts in Aramaic, Hebrew, or Hellene (Bible Greek) to discover the literal meanings of the words used, because we can now read what the Scriptures actually say. This can drastically cut research time, possibly revolutionizing your Bible study. It helps the Scriptures come alive with the sense and flow of the original languages.

The exeGeses Bible series consists of three major works: *The exeGeses Parallel Bible*—two Bibles side-by-side. In the left column, the *exeGeses Ready Research Bible*, with the exegeses inserted at the points of occurrence, transforms the authorized KJV into a literal translation and transliteration. In the right column, *The exeGeses Companion Bible*, presents the same exegeses in an easier-to-read format. It also has a Lexicon keyed to Strong's Concordance that includes expanded explanations and definitions of key words.

The second major work is *The Aramaic New Covenant*—a literal translation and transliteration directly from the Aramaic language our Lord spoke. The third major work is *The exeGeses Bibles* CD-ROM (for UNIX, DOS, Windows, or Macintosh) which contains all the above plus a 5,000-page interlinear of the Aramaic New Covenant. Those looking for portability should put *The exeGeses Parallel Bible* first on their list, those looking for at-home study tools should consider the CD-ROM or the printed *Aramaic New Covenant*. [Bob Rico/C.D.]

➲ Exploring Ethics, Exploring Apologetics, and Exploring Faith and Discipleship (Christian Schools International) student books - $14.40 each; teacher guides - $8.75 each

These three books are written for students studying at the upper levels of high school. It is important that they first be familiar with the Bible as a foundation for getting into the deep application and life issues encountered in these books. Each book is a collection of articles, essays, and book excerpts, followed by discussion questions. The Teacher Guide for each is vital, for in it is background information on the author, the written work, and the topic, as well as additional discussion questions. These books can be used for a religion class, for part of a literature class, and for part of a worldview class.

I suggest beginning with either *Exploring Faith and Discipleship* or *Exploring Apologetics*, then concluding with *Exploring Ethics*. *Faith and Discipleship* helps young people to think through the reality of their faith by confronting challenges. *Apologetics* begins with an overview of worldviews, then deals with major challenges such as the exclusivity of Christianity, the question of evil, miracles, the nature of Jesus, the hypocrisy of some Christians, Christianity's relevance to life, Christianity as a force for oppression, and Christianity as a crutch for the weak. Once these foundational questions have been addressed, it's time to tackle ethical issues in the third book. *Ethics* is divided into three major sections: defining morality, making moral choices, and exploring issues. The last section is further broken down into the following issues: work, human sexuality, earthkeeping, wealth/poverty, racism/bigotry, medical ethics, and peace.

The articles in all three books are from a range of Christian and non-Christian writers so that students have a chance to hear the challenges in the challengers' own words. This can be unsettling, but there is a strong affirmation of the truth of Christianity throughout. This is the kind of reading our young people need to

encounter and discuss within a secure environment such as our homes, so that they will not have their faith dismantled when they encounter challenges on their own.

➲ A Family Guide to the Biblical Holidays by Linda Pierce and Robin Scarlata (Family Christian Press) $29.95

This 600+ page volume is an activity-based approach to learning about Biblical holidays that is designed for the entire family. It can be used as a home school curriculum for an entire year or only for certain seasons (instructions for these options is included). It also includes instructions for use in Bible study groups, church groups, Sunday or Sabbath schools, and co-op groups. There is a special home school section at the back of the book that outlines nine thematic unit studies incorporating activities for literature, writing, history, geography, art, science, and the use of library resources.

The first section of the book is overview, background, and historical study of the Hebrew roots of the feasts. This section also includes crafts and activities that might be used for any one or more of the feasts. Next, are sections on each of the feasts: Passover, Unleavened Bread, First Fruits, Weeks, Trumpets, the Day of Atonement, Tabernacles, Hanukkah, and Purim. Sabbath celebration is then presented as a weekly feast.

Each of the Biblical feasts from the Old Testament is examined for historical and spiritual significance. Original Jewish customs are described. Charts are used for such things as comparing aspects of each feast's observance in one column with the Messianic significance in a second column. Next, are extensive suggestions and instructions for conducting your own celebration of the feast, including recipes. Reproducible activity pages are appropriate for elementary grade children. As part of your curriculum, this will primarily be a Bible curriculum, serving supplementally for all other subject areas. This is wonderful for whole family participation or even combining with other families to share the celebrations.

➲ For the Layman, A Survey of the Old Testament by Ken Levy (For the Layman) $35; binders without audio tapes - $12

This survey course on the Old Testament consists of six hours of lecture presented on four audio tapes plus a three-ring binder workbook with detailed outline worksheets, charts, a final exam, and answer key. It can be used as an individual or group study, although it lends itself best to individual study since there are no discussion questions provided. Ken Levy's presentation is well-organized and clearly presented. The course stresses the continuity of the Old Testament. Levy introduces the study with historical background information covering such points as the contrast between the Hebrew scriptures and the Old Testament accepted by the early church. He ties together the various books of the Old Testament with a historical timeline and cross references from studies of some of the books so that we can clearly see the relationships. There are some blanks to fill in as we proceed through each study. Answers are at the back of the book. We should take time to read through each section of Scripture as it is studied, which means that the study will take much longer than the time spent listening to tapes and filling in the workbook. In fact, Levy encourages us to use the study to supplement our Scripture reading, not to replace it. If you use the study as a family, you should purchase extra binders for each person. This course is an excellent foundational course that I would recommend for students in junior and senior high. Levy plans to develop future courses on the New Testament, church history, theology, and other topics.

⊃ **Great Christian Hymn Writers** by Jane Stuart Smith and Betty Carlson (Crossway) $11.99

Almost 50 hymn writers are spotlighted in brief inspirational biographies. Students also learn some history as they read about these people who have lived during the past four centuries. You might consider this also as part of your music education.

⊃ **The Holiness of God** [audio or video series or book] by R.C. Sproul (Ligonier Ministries) video series - $30; audio series - $12; book - $8.95; study guide -$4

Your choice of either audio or video presentations is divided into six, 30-minute presentations. The study guide is divided into six lessons corresponding to the tapes plus a summary lesson. The study guide offers an outline of each presentation, serious Bible study questions, "Think about it" questions that take us into a deeper understanding of what the Bible says, and application questions. To take the lessons yet deeper, we are referred to pages in the full-length book of the same title by Sproul. The presentations are titled "The Importance of Holiness," "The Trauma of Holiness," "Holiness and Justice," "The Insanity of Luther," "The Meaning of Holiness," and "The Holiness of God." This is a terrific study for both teens and parents, but keep in mind that it is directed at the professing Christian rather than the unsaved.

⊃ **Know Why You Believe** by Paul Little (Inter Varsity Press) $8.99

This is one of the most popular books about apologetics. It uses a rational approach to deal with questions and arguments. It is concise and easy to understand.

⊃ **The Master Christian Library, Version 5** [CD-ROM] (AGES Software) $59.95

AGES has used the Adobe Acrobat® system to create a searchable library of over 330+ works primarily for Bible study, church history, and theology. The KJV and AS Bibles are included as well as a few less-common translations such as Darby's, *Young's Literal Bible Translation*, and a Spanish version. Among the commentaries are Clarke's six-volume set, Calvin's *Commentary on Hebrews*, and Matthew Henry's *Concise Whole Bible Commentary*. Reference and theological works include a Bible dictionary, word studies as well as specialized works such as Chesterton's *Heretics, Enchiridion* by Augustine, and the *Augsburg Confessions* by Melanchthon. Bible studies, maps, and works by Bunyan, Calvin (the complete *Institutes*), Luther, Moody, Finney, Spurgeon, Wesley, and many others reflect a fairly broad Protestant representation. Of particular interest to

me was the inclusion of Thomas Aquinas' *Summa Theologica,* the ten-volume *Ante-Nicene Fathers,* plus the 28-volumes of the *Nicene* and *Post Nicene Fathers*; I haven't seen the Church Fathers on any other CDs, yet they are required sources for serious Bible study.

The CD will run on either Macintosh or Windows (3.1 or 95) systems. The Acrobat program allows for single- or multi-volume searches by words, stems, or more complex strings. We can have a number of books open at a time, and a "librarian" in a sidebar makes it easy to move to a new resource. This is not as sophisticated as some programs in search capabilities, but the number and quality of resources on this single CD is outstanding.

⊃ **More Than Conquerors** John Woodbrigde (Moody Press) $29.99

Consult this 360-page book by John Woodbridge for short, captivating biographies of great Christian men and women. This book contains a total of 57 intriguing biographies, with two to five pages devoted to each. Unlike other biographies, the role of faith is revealed in each person's life. Every biography includes illustrations, photographs, timelines, and recommendations for further reading about that person. The biographies are arranged under categories of Mission (e.g., Hudson Taylor, Brother Andrew), Politics and Public Life (e.g., Robert E. Lee, Woodrow Wilson), Writers (e.g., Harriet Beecher Stowe, C.S. Lewis), Evangelism (e.g., D.L. Moody, Billy Graham), Preachers (e.g., Charles Spurgeon, E.V. Hill), Sports and Entertainment (e.g., Cliff Richards, Eric Liddell), Reformers (e.g., Chuck Colson, William Booth), Student Work (e.g., John Mott, Bill Bright), Thinkers (e.g., George Washington Carver, Henry Schaefer III), and Industry and Commerce (e.g., J.C. Penney, Cyrus McCormick). These biographies show how Christianity in action can make a difference in the world.

⊃ **Real Manna** by Rich Jeffus (Visual Manna) $9.95

This book contains black-and-white drawings intended to teach spiritual truths in home Bible study or Sunday School. It would also be appropriate for older students to use independently. The author suggests using these drawings and accompanying Bible verses as a method of study which combats the images of the world with which we are constantly bombarded. The drawings convey spiritual truth without the need for words and are, supposedly, easier to remember. Mr. Jeffus gives permission to reproduce any of the drawings for the purpose of spiritual teaching. There is enough variety of level and subject matter that the book can be used with children from preschool through high school. One or two drawings would be too intense for small children because they show demons or skeletons or deal with more mature subjects such as abortion.

There is actually quite a bit of text interspersed throughout the book and many of the drawings are quite clever and expressive. One of my favorites illustrated John 4:14 ("...but whoever drinks of the water that I give him shall never thirst"), and shows a little girl struggling up to a drinking fountain that is coming out of a Bible. Perhaps the greatest contribution of *Real Manna* would be as an inspiration; after studying a few of the drawings, it would be a worthwhile assignment to create your own "Visual Manna" of spiritual truths.[Kath Courtney/C.D.]

➲ Seven Devotional Tools (MEMLOK) $4

How do we move our teens beyond head knowledge into deep relationship with God? I personally think that meaningful prayer and worship play a major role. But focusing those activities and investing them with meaning can be a challenge. *Seven Devotional Tools* provides practical strategies for developing that deep relationship. *Seven Devotional Tools* is not a heavy-duty curriculum, but more of an idea resource that should be used with all of the teens and adults in your family. It works sort of like story starters that some of us use to encourage younger children to start writing. The seven tools are presented with brief explanation and helpful activity suggestions (some mental, some active, some written). The tools can be summarized as examining our hearts, focusing our worship, supporting our brothers, stating our desires, writing our thoughts, using our minds, and building our bridges. For example, there is a reproducible Daily Journal sheet to encourage us to focus more clearly on a Scripture passage, what it says to us, and what our response should be. (We fit seven days on one page, so we're not talking about lengthy writing here.) Other reproducible sheets are for intercessory prayer schedules, personal prayer diary, meditation on Scripture, and "Ambassador Praying" (some intriguing ideas here!). An extra sheet is included that describes fifty ministry ideas and discussion questions for using *Seven Devotional Tools* in group settings. The set of devotional tools is quite inexpensive, but might turn out to be one of your most fruitful investments.

➲ Tabletalk (Ligonier Ministries) $18 per year

Tabletalk is a monthly "magazine" that features daily, in-depth Bible studies, thought-provoking articles, and a read-through-the-Bible-in-a-year program. Pages are dated for Monday through Friday study, and we can begin at any month of the year. The theological perspective is Reformed Protestant—Calvin is frequently quoted. Although *Tabletalk* is primarily written for an adult audience of believers, it has a universal appeal that should make it appropriate for high schoolers who want to grow in their faith and their walk.

➲ Tracking Your Walk: The Young Person's Prayer Diary (YWAM Publishing) $12.99

One of the best ways for anyone to truly understand God's faithfulness is to keep a prayer journal or spiritual diary, where he or she records prayer requests and the results of each. I have always liked YWAM's *Personal Prayer Diary-Daily Planner*, but now they have created a new version that especially appeals to young people (ages 9 to 14). Simple instructions for using it also cover the basics of salvation and spiritual growth. The book is set up for one year, with monthly calendars (to be filled in with current dates by the user) and journaling pages. A few lines for "prayer priorities" show up every few pages. Each month two countries or people groups are featured with a brief description and prayer needs. "Facts and Prayer Points" data on these countries is included at the back. This helps teens, who can easily be-come self-centered, to focus at least some of their prayer requests outside themselves. Scripture memory verses are provided, approximately one for every ten days. Some teens might also want to use one of the two Bible memory plans at the back of the book. One takes them through the New Testament and Psalms in a year, while the other takes them through the entire Bible.

➲ The Trial and Testimony of the Early Church (Vision Video) $79.95

Similar in format to Vision Video's *Discovering The Bible* video course, this course has six segments rather than four. The Teacher's Guide has detailed lesson plans, teaching, tips, background information for presentation before viewing each segment, discussion questions (with suggested answers), biblical applications, Bible study lessons that connect with each segment, and creative activities. The activities (e.g., debate) are designed for older Sunday School type groups so they might not work well in family settings. The six segments of this course are "Foundations," "Spread," "Accusation," "Persecution," "Testimony," and "Transition." "Foundations" begins with Jesus Christ, the apostles, Paul, and the birth of the Christian church. "Spread" examines how the Gospel was transferred throughout the Roman Empire and beyond. "Accusation" deals with the reasons for resistance to the growth of Christianity. "Persecution" investigates attempts to destroy the faith. "Testimony" focuses on two early martyrs, Polycarp and Perpetua, who were representative of so many others who died for their faith even though they could have easily avoided that fate. "Transition" examines the political and cultural ascendance of Christianity under Constantine with both good and bad consequences. The course includes a companion book that adds a great deal more background information with text and beautiful full-color photos of art, artifacts and archeological sites. We also receive an issue of *Christian History* magazine subtitled, *Persecution in the Early Church*, copies of *Glimpses* (Christian History Institute papers that focus on single topics), and three pocket classics (little booklets containing original writings from early Christians leaders). I encountered a few instances on the videos where I would question the slant of the presentation. For example, in Foundations we are given the impression that Paul was trying to decide how to make the gospel acceptable, an idea with little Scriptural support. You might use any such instances to do further investigation for yourself. You might use this course with your family or a group.

➲ Welcome to the Catholic Church [CD-ROM] version 2.0 (Harmony Media Inc.) $79.95

Catholic homeschoolers will find this CD-ROM a valuable resource for Church history, doctrine and theology, Church documents, and lives of the saints. This is a smoothly functioning, beautifully designed program with 80,000 links between topics, a huge index, and excellent search capability so that we can pick a topic and quickly view different sources that address that topic. It includes over 1500 illustrations, and Gregorian chant plays in the background through many sections of the program. All texts carry the Imprimatur, making this a dependable source for information. Extensive footnoting and hypertexts to sources or references make it easy to research and identify the origin of information.

The home page features six main sections: Divine Revelation, Church Teaching, Mass and Sacraments, Prayer and Spirituality, Saints and History, and Church Organization. A number of books, including multi-volume series, plus major documents are included as sources. They are the Revised Standard and New American versions of the Bible, Catholic Edition; documents of Vatican II; *The Sources of Catholic Dogma* by Henry Denziger; *The Catholic Catechism* by Fr. John Hardon, S.J. (copyright 1975); *The Way of the Lord Jesus* by Dr. Germain Grisez (3-volume work on the Church's moral teaching); *My Daily Bread* by Fr. Anthony Paone, S.J. (daily meditation guide); *Ceremonies of the Modern Roman Rite* by Peter J. Elliot; *The Sacraments and Their Celebration* by Fr. Nicholas Halligan, O.P.; *The Catholic Encyclopedic Dictionary of Biblical Terms; A Summary of Catholic History* by Fr. Newman Eberhardt, C.M. (2-volume survey of world church history); *Introduction to Spirituality* and *Church of God* by Louis Bouyer; *Writings of Early Church Fathers* (single volume collection); *The Lives of the Saints for Every Day of the Year* (3-volumes); and hundreds of Encyclicals (1853-present) and other modern Church pronouncements.

While the obvious appeal is to Catholic homeschoolers, it is also a valuable tool for Protestants seeking broader coverage of church history or knowledge about Catholic doctrine.

The CD-ROM will run on Windows or Macintosh systems.

➲ **What the Bible Is All About for Young Explorers** by Frances Blankenbaker (Regal Books) hardcover - $14.99; paperback - $9.99

Here is an overview of the Bible geared for upper elementary and junior high, but still interesting to adults. Maps, charts, plenty of illustrations, background information, chapter summaries, and archeological information provide an excellent introduction for Bible study.

➲ **WORDsearch Bible Study software for Windows** [CD-ROM programs for IBM compatibles] (NavPress Software) Classic Library - $49.95; Life Application Library - $149.95; Youth Worker's Library - $179.95; Discipleship Library - $249.95; Comprehensive Library - $1499.95

Teens can get into serious Bible study with *WORDsearch* software. It comes on CD-ROMs, requires 12 Mb of RAM, and features an easy-to-use Windows 95 layout.

This is an extremely powerful Bible study/search program. Full texts of the Bible are available in KJV, NIV, NKJV, NRSV, NASB, NJB, NAB (New American Bible with revised NT), *Living, The Message, New Living Translation,* or *God's Word to the Nations.*

We can purchase the Classics Library with some programs, then add modules by receiving codes to unlock programs. It includes *WORDsearch,* the KJV Bible, maps, *Nave's Topical Bible, Strong's Greek and Hebrew Dictionary, Torrey's Treasury of Scripture Knowledge,* and the Legacy Library 1 (Torrey's *Topical Textbook, Matthew Henry's Concise Commentary, Easton's*

Bible Dictionary, Hitchcock's Dictionary of Bible Names, and Foxe's *Book of Martyrs*).

The Life Application Library package adds the NIV and Living Bibles; *Life application Notes, Outlines, and Topics; The Holman Bible Dictionary;* and one other translation or book of your choice.

The Youth Worker's Library builds on the *Life Application Library,* substituting *The Message* for the *Living Bible,* dropping the *Holman Bible Dictionary,* and adding LESSONmaker *4 Youth Meeting Kits and* Youthworker's *Encyclopedia.*

The Discipleship Library keeps all components of the *Life Application Library* except the *Living Bible,* then adds *LESSONmaker 4 Adult Lesson Kits,* A.T. Robertson's *Word Pictures, Teacher's Commentary,* and our choice of two other translations or books.

The Comprehensive Library includes all components listed plus others for a total of over 100 study tools.

These programs conform to the STEP standard for Bible software which means that other Bible study products using the same standard can read these books, and *WORDsearch* and *LESSONmaker* can read tools from other companies that conform to the STEP standard.

From the Bible text we can easily search by word or phrase, using tools such as Strong's. We can copy maps or text into other word processing or graphics programs. We can create our own outlines and add comments to personalize the program.

The Classics Library is a good starting point for most families. This is a superior product, recommended for anyone who would like a faster way to study the Scriptures.

➲ **Youthwalk magazine and Family Walk magazine** (Walk Thru the Bible Ministries, Inc.) $18 for 12 issues

Youthwalk magazine is designed for teens, while *Family Walk* is for the whole family. These excellent little monthly magazines are divided into weekly topics. Each topic is presented in segments that include stories, Scripture search, and practical application. Some topics in *Family Walk* (marriage, dating) are appropriate for teens or adults, but most are appropriate for the entire family.

Bible Memory

Since there are a limited number of resources for Bible memory, I include all those I am aware of that are practical for the home school. Bible memory courses choose verses from the thousands of possibilities, to work toward a predetermined goal. Thus there is inevitably doctrinal bias in any program. The following recommendations have tried to maintain a nondenominational appeal in their verse choices, by addressing topics of common Protestant belief.

➲ **MEMLOK/PC Memlok Bible Memory System** MEMLOK book version - $49.95; PC Memlok - $59.95

MEMLOK's memory program uses visual cues and is available in New International, King James, New King James, and

New American Standard versions of the Bible. There are a few features that set this apart from other programs.

Visual clues on memory verse cards illustrate beginning or key words of verses to act as memory cues. Some of the clues are silly, some stretch for the connection, some are great, but the overall idea is that by establishing a visual connection for each verse, the verses (with references) are recalled much more easily. Verses are arranged under 48 topics, with over 700 verses on 550 cards (the size of a business card) included. We learn the verses under whichever topic we choose. The verses are stored in the clear, plastic cardholders for review. Summary cards are provided for verses about each topic. There's enough memory work here to last a family for twelve years.

The visual clues are all incorporated onto one summary card, providing another memory device to recall related verses. The entire family can share one *MEMLOK* book (an 8 1/2" X 11" spiral notebook) by having each member choose a different topic to work on or by keeping memory verse cards in a central location in the home. The program should take only five to ten minutes a day, and long term retention of verses should be greater than with other programs because of the review system. Accountability is stressed. There is a Completion Record sheet to be initialed by whoever hears us recite the verses, but we must make our own arrangements for that person to check on our progress.

PC Memlok offers a computerized version of the basic *MEMLOK* with enhancements. The program comes on 3 floppy disks that run on Windows 3.1 and higher systems. One Bible translation of your choice is included. Automatic review ensures that review takes place. A number of users can be working on the same verses at the same time, with progress of each tracked by the computer. We can print out pages as needed. One program feature allows us to attach personal notes; another provides a practice pad for self-testing; and yet another lets the user erase portions of verses to learn a phrase at a time. If you have a suitable computer, this version makes the most sense for families with more than one program user.

We can also use MEMLOK techniques to learn the names of the books of the Bible. *Say the Books* [$8] is a 96-page book that teaches creative memory techniques that can be used by all ages. One memorable picture illustrates each book for the Old Testament, and a running story line helps us keep them in order. To help us remember the books of the New Testament, *Say the Books* features a house with associations for the various rooms.

○ Scripture Memory Fellowship International (SMFI)

This organization, with many, many years of experience, offers Scripture memory programs for preschoolers through adults, along with awards to be earned as memory students progress. They provide each "student" with a memory book which the memorizer selects according to grade level or previous experience in memorizing God's Word. For the most part, verses are in King James Version and are all arranged topically. You are enrolled as a family, one person, a church class, or a neighborhood group. You also select your supervisor who encourages you and helps keep track of progress. You may either purchase the memory books outright or enroll with rewards which you select from

their list contained in the *SMF Memorizer*. These incentives (rewards) are primarily Christian books—selections for all ages and a variety of interests. They suggest that Fall is the best time to enroll but enrollments are welcomed at any time of the year. Each September a new list of rewards is available. The enrollment fee is kept to a minimum and represents about one-third of their actual cost; the remainder is subsidized by supporters of the ministry. No one is turned away.

Church History

Church history is a sadly neglected area of education. Some history textbooks incorporate church history, but most simply ignore it. However, there are some interesting books available on the topic. The best way to find good resources is to check your church library or local Christian bookstore. The following suggestions are simply a few that I have encountered, rather than a selection of "the best."

○ Baptist History course H150 (Landmark's Freedom Baptist Curriculum $35

This year-long course in Baptist history is broken down into weekly segments. It consists of a worktext "study guide," answer key, and tests. Each weekly lesson follows the same format: three to four pages of reading with comprehension and essay questions. It covers distinctive Baptist doctrines and examines church history in light of these. It follows the history and development of the Baptist church, developments and controversies within the church, and important ideas and people from the early church down to the present day. The presentation is quite thorough.[Valerie Thorpe]

○ Church History in Plain Language by Bruce L. Shelley (Word Publishing) $14.99

Most church histories lean strongly to either Protestant or Catholic sentiments, slighting one side or the other in coverage or offering one-sided explanations of events. Shelley's 510-page book, on the other hand, is the most evenhanded, concise church history book I have come across. He divides the study into eight time periods from the time of Jesus and the apostles up through the present day. This makes it easy to coordinate study of the book with broader history studies. Despite its size, this is a fast moving, fairly easy-to-read book. Shelley often uses narrative or biographical approaches to keep the writing lively. Footnotes are rather sketchy, which makes it difficult to verify information. However, Shelley does include a list for suggested reading at the end of each chapter, and it is fairly safe to assume that these are likely to be the sources upon which he has relied. Interestingly, there are three indices at the end of the book rather than one. They provide listings under the headings of characters, movements, and events. I would recommend this book to high school students and adults.

➲ The Church in History by B.K. Kuiper (Christian Schools International) $15.95; teacher's guide - $15.95

This 412-page book covers the history of the Church from its beginnings to recent times. The author appears to be writing from a Reformed Christian perspective, but he takes a very even-handed approach to differences between denominations. Even Catholicism is treated fairly, although changes within the Catholic Church over the past few decades are not dealt with adequately. The original edition of this book was written in 1951, and it has been updated periodically, but there are occasional areas that need further updating. Questions are posed at the end of each chapter. Also available from CSI is a *Guide for Teaching Church History* by Dale Cooper and John Vander Lugt [$14.85]. This *Guide* was not written specifically for *The Church in History* although it is cross referenced to that book throughout. It is actually an outline with commentary that can form the foundation for study of church history on its own or with other resource books. It succinctly outlines events and provides commentary and references from other books. Suggestions for student discussion and activities are included. Both books should be used in the last years of high school. The *Guide* actually seems more appropriate for college level study. *The Church in History* may be used without the *Guide for Teaching Church History*. (There is no answer key to text questions in the *Guide*.) The *Guide* is most appropriate for those studying Church history in a group setting.

➲ A History of Christianity in the United States and Canada by Mark A. Noll (Wm. B. Eerdmans Publishing Co.) softcover edition - $30

While this book is not intended to be a typical church history book, it certainly covers the topic. Read the complete description under "American History" in Chapter Fourteen.

➲ Perspectives on the World Christian Movement edited by Ralph D. Winter and Steven D. Hawthorne (William Carey Library) $16.95

This is a collection of scholarly articles about Christianity through history. One article of special interest is a mini-history course of God's movement through history, somewhat similar to the Old Testament story told through the Bible. This book is for parents to digest and pass on to children. It provides information lacking even in church history texts. (Prices are discounted when ordering directly through the William Carey Library.)

➲ Reformation Overview [video course] (Vision Video) $79.95

Six half-hour video presentations are the foundation for this study of key figures and ideas of the Reformation. The six segments are titled John Wycliffe, John Hus, Martin Luther, The Swiss Reformation (focusing on Zwingli and Calvin), The Anabaptists, and William Tyndale. Two video tapes each feature three of the segments. Videos are excellent quality, integrating extensive footage from professional dramatic films about the lives of the key figures. Videos are accompanied by an extensive Leader's Guide. The Guide includes pre-viewing background information, discussion questions, and optional Bible study lessons. Reproducible student worksheets (four per video segment) are to be used with the Bible study lessons. Complete lessons should take up at least two complete sessions.

Also included are a copy of *Christian History* magazine that focuses on John Wycliffe and seven different copies of *Glimpses*, briefer studies on key people.

The viewpoint throughout is clearly Protestant. The inclusion of film footage of dramatized reenactments is certainly more interesting to watch, but it does allows a great deal of bias to creep in (e.g., evil, hatchet-faced Catholics contrasted with humble, kindly looking Protestants; dialogue conveyed with tones of voice that prejudice the audience). Throughout the presentations, key issues of contention between Protestants and Catholics arise, with the Protestant defense brought to the fore. A helpful chart in the back of the Leader's Guide contrasts Protestant and Catholic positions. The entire course is well-designed, easy to use, and certain to provoke serious discussion and learning experiences.

➲ Sketches from Church History: An Illustrated Account of 20 Centuries of Christ's Power (Banner of Truth) $17.95

Of all the church history books I have looked at, this seems to be one of the easiest to use because of its format. The text is broken up into manageable chunks rather than overwhelming chapters. Frequent illustrations add visual variety. Topically, it sticks with Christianity aside from a brief look at Islam (beginnings of the religion and the Crusades). Another plus for *Sketches from Church History* is that we can select a section from the middle of the book that might be pertinent to other topics being studied, without having to read the entire book straight through. Consequently, it works well as part of a unit study approach. I suggest using it as a supplement to world history studies, reading appropriate sections as they tie in chronologically and geographically. There will be some overlap, but *Sketches* covers much material that is skipped or glossed over even in Christian history texts. At the same time, *Sketches* is not a comprehensive study of church history such as we find in Latourette's well-regarded, two-volume set, *A History of Christianity*. (Latourette is great, but overwhelming for the typical high school student.) Its scope is limited geographically to Britain, Europe, and America. It also covers church history only up through the nineteenth century. The viewpoint is nondenominational Protestant with a "Reformed bent," expressing a strongly negative view of the Catholic church. Although it was written for adults rather than as a high school text, it is very readable for the average high school student.

Comparative Religions

I want to teach my children about other religions and their teachings myself. I do not want them introduced to false doctrines by a teacher who believes that all theologies have equal validity, so I want to cover "comparative religions" at home. I expect many other home schoolers agree, yet most of us are not familiar with all religions and belief systems. We can find many helpful resources at our local Christian bookstores and from mail order sources, but I also have reviewed some possibilities in Chapter Five, under "Philosophy, Religion, and Apologetics."

Bible History

⮌ Bible Land History and Geography (Rod and Staff)

Baker's Bible Atlas is the primary book for this course, but the *Bible Land History and Geography Study Guide* and *Outline Map Supplement* take us through lessons to actually learn the information. Lessons in the *Study Guide* rely on research done in both the Bible and *Baker's Bible Atlas*. Some information is found in the *Study Guide*, but it is primarily a workbook with a variety of exercises—fill-in-the-blanks, crossword puzzles, matchings, completing charts, etc. The *Outline Map Supplement* is a 27-page booklet of maps (non-reproducible) correlated with the lessons. The *Study Guide* and *Map Supplement* were written to correlate with the 1973 edition of the *Baker's Bible Atlas*, but there are only a few minor discrepancies if we use the newer 1981 edition. While this course is recommended for grades 7 to 10, anyone older who is willing to do the workbook exercises will find it worthwhile.

⮌ That the World May Know [video series] (Focus on the Family) $140 (sold as two sets of four tapes at $70 each)

This series of eight video tapes, sold in sets of two tapes each, features Bible teacher Ray Vander Laan on site in Israel. He presents historical Bible studies at the actual sites where events took place. We learn geography and history along with our study of the Bible, but Vander Laan always brings each lesson back to practical application_what does this mean for us? Beautiful photography and computer graphics make the videos entertaining to watch. There are 27 lessons and each presentation is about a half hour long. Discussion questions for each segment reinforce the lessons. These are especially suitable for teens and adults.

Mathematics

High school math poses the biggest hurdle for many home educators both because it is required and because it is many a parent's weakest subject. Some of us have never studied algebra or geometry. How can we possibly teach these subjects to our children? Admittedly, the task is challenging, but there is more help available than most of us realize.

Broadening Our Horizons

Frequently, our first instinct is to turn to correspondence courses, but they do have their drawbacks. Most correspondence courses have parents check daily work and send in only tests for grading. The biggest problem is the time lag between sending back exams and receiving the results. It is wasteful for students to keep working ahead without knowing if they have completed the last time period's lessons correctly, since repeating mistakes just reinforces them. Some correspondence courses do allow us to get in touch with a teacher right away if we encounter difficulties, but I think that many times students do not realize that they have a problem with a mathematical concept until they receive their tests.

The big need we face in high school math courses is for immediate feedback and help. Tutoring services can be a worthwhile investment, especially if we can work out a deal where we use the tutor on a consultation basis as needed. A "mathematically minded" friend who is supportive of our home education endeavors might be willing to tutor at no charge. A high school student already proficient in algebra or geometry might also be willing to provide tutorial help. If no tutor is available, it's up to us parents. However, teaching high school math does not have to be formidable for inexperienced parents because of the helpful resources available to us.

The Saxon math series has been overwhelmingly popular with home educators because it is easy for both parents and students to use and understand. New topics come in small doses with plenty of explanation (most of the time). Students can work fairly independently. Parents can study up on new concepts without having to wade through too much material. Some other math programs are equally easy to use. But traditional math courses aren't the only solutions.

Video Helps

Video can be a helpful alternative for some of us. A Beka offers complete classes on video, with students working in textbooks on the side. We can rely on the experienced video instructor to present the information, and we just have to oversee our child's understanding and completion of his assignments. All A Beka textbooks are now available as video courses. School of Tomorrow also offers algebra and geometry courses on video or in computer video interactive versions.

Other video options, such as the complete courses from Keyboard Enterprises and Chalk Dust Productions and the supplementary Video Tutor, are well worth investigating. (See reviews.)

Individual Needs

It is also important to recognize our child's learning style, aptitude, maturity, and potential before plunging into math courses. If he has a horrible experience with his first introduction to algebra, he might decide that math is something he cannot grasp, which in turn might limit his future educational choices. The problem might lie with the textbook, his preparation in earlier math courses, or his maturity rather than with his potential. Some home educators have found that waiting until age fifteen to study algebra instead of the traditional freshman age of fourteen made the difference between success and failure.

Learning Styles

By the teen years, most students have overcome the most serious limitations of their learning styles as they apply to math. Wiggly Willys, who cringed at the sight of pages of math problems to be worked, might still not enjoy using workbooks, but are now able to work in them when necessary. Perfect Paulas need to still be on guard against their tendency to learn by rote without thinking through the reasons for doing things. Competent Carls will usually find math one of their favorite subjects. Sociable Sues will probably continue to struggle through the principles, rules, and theorems of math that need to be mastered.

Many math programs for junior and senior high do not allow for the great variations in learning styles evident in elementary math programs. We often have to look further to find materials to meet special learning style needs. Most programs assume that teens can think abstractly, and that they no longer need work with concrete materials, which is not always true.

Wiggly Willys are most likely to need concrete experiences to learn math. Their entire curriculum cannot be concrete work. There must be some paper and pencil activity accompanying any hands-on work. These learners work best with a text or resources that use real-life situations and practical application of math concepts. Abstract texts that deal only with math theory are more difficult for them to understand. Wiggly Willys often do better with geometry (but not with the formal proofs) than with algebra, yet they need some foundation in algebra to be able to solve geometry problems. Keeping in mind occupational and educational goals, consider using practical math texts such as the business, consumer, and career texts listed below. *Career Math* (Houghton

Mifflin/McDougal Littell) is especially good. *Discovering Geometry* and the *Key to Geometry* series (both from Key Curriculum Press) should appeal to Wiggly Willys more than other geometry texts. Cornerstone's *Principles from Patterns: Algebra I* and *Math-U-See* build in manipulative activity throughout the programs, making them especially helpful for hands-on learners. *AIMS* activities are also great supplements for these learners. In addition, their need for drill and review of basic math skills can often best be met by using games.

Perfect Paulas need texts such as the Saxon series, that teach concepts from several different angles to ensure understanding. Look for good word and application problems in whatever you choose.

Competent Carls might be able to move ahead into college level texts. For geometry, consider using Harold R. Jacobs' *Geometry* (W.H. Freeman), which has a heavy emphasis on thinking skills and logic rather than hands-on learning. Also, look for texts that have solution keys to help students work independently.

Sociable Sues will probably want to understand how math concepts will be used in life situations before continuing into higher math. The shift toward inclusion of more life applications in newer texts should appeal to these learners.

Maturity

Abstract thinking skills are slower to develop in some students (particularly boys) than in others. This does not have anything to do with their long-range potential in math, but it has much to do with how quickly they move into abstract math topics. Some students need to wait until they are fifteen or sixteen to take algebra. They can take introductory courses in algebra and geometry, business or consumer math, or pursue more interesting books about mathematics such as Harold Jacob's *Mathematics, a Human Endeavor* (Freeman). Jacob's book can be "browsed" through rather than used as a text. This is an inviting way to let teens explore math without killing their interest. (Initial chapters of Jacob's book are much easier than later chapters, so caution students to choose something they can understand.)

Goals and Recommendations for Junior High

Goals

Junior high is a time for consolidating basic math skills and knowledge before progressing on to the more difficult subjects of algebra and geometry. Below is a typical scope and sequence covering seventh and eighth grades.

– Review of all previous material

– Read and convert exponents

– Define and find "mean," "median," and "mode"

– Use distance formula

– Calculate volume of given geometric solids

– Construct and interpret graphs

– Convert numbers from one system of measurement to another

– Read and write numbers written in expanded notation and/or scientific notation form

– Solve basic equations using any of the four basic operations

– Define and calculate the square root of given numbers

Math For Life by Janet Rhodes Lathan (Alpha Plus) approx. $25

Most students, even at junior and senior high level still benefit from hands-on and experiential math learning, even though those methods are largely absent from some of the most commonly used texts. We can create our own program, but that is very difficult in the upper grades. Probably, the most practical approach is to supplement a standard text, substituting or adding other types of learning activities as needed. Math expert, Janet Lathan, has condensed some of the most essential information into a book called *Math For Life*. It is a scope and sequence, a guide to either putting together your own math program or supplementing, and a reference for recommended resources. Her scope and sequence is in accord with the new math standards, stressing practical applications along with an understanding and use of math in real life situations rather than memorization of rules. The scope and sequence is divided into broad levels—readiness (ages 4-9), primary (ages 7-14), and intermediate (ages 12-16)—rather than grade levels. She groups concepts under various headings rather than the typical lists that we find in many publishers' scope and sequences. For example, for the intermediate level, skills are described at length under the headings: Number Sense; Spatial Sense; Measurement and Error Analysis; Problem Solving, Mathematical Models, and Logic; Problem Solving Strategies; Symbolic Representation; and Using Math-Context and Connections. Following the scope and sequence, Janet teaches us how to incorporate manipulatives into our math program, including supplementing the math curriculum we have already purchased. Next, she provides lists of math concepts by levels along with specific resources for tackling them. *Math For Life* makes it much easier for us to understand how, when, and what to use for hands-on math teaching. If you have Wiggly Willys, you need this resource. If you have other types of learners, you can still pull ideas from *Math For Life* to make math much more fun and easy to understand.

The Lathan family operates Alpha Plus, a business dedicated to math resources. You can purchase most everything Janet recommends from them, but I appreciate the fact that Janet has included a list of resources and publishers for us if we care to purchase items directly from the publishers or from other distributors.

– Understand and apply the Pythagorean theorem

– Learn properties of positive and negative numbers

– Begin learning about algebraic equations

However, you need to be aware that the NCTM Standards (National Council of Teachers of Mathematics Standards which are the primary source of math standards being adopted nationwide) aim at having students complete Algebra 1 by the end of eighth grade. This acceleration of math is beginning to show up as more challenging math concepts in new junior high textbooks.

Reviewing Arithmetic Skills

Some students have gaps in their arithmetic knowledge, and it is vital that those be plugged before going on to high school math topics. Students with learning difficulties, who might need materials written at a lower reading level or with simpler explanations, should see the recommendations at the end of this mathematics section under "Remedial Math."

Those who simply need to review some topics can use a resource such as *Arithmetic Skills Worktext* (Amsco) [$14.53; answer key $3.10]. This worktext provides explanations, examples, and practice problems for all of the basic arithmetic functions with whole numbers, fractions, decimals, and percents, as well as measurement, ratios, basic statistics, and graphs. The last four sections are more typical of high school level material, covering topics such as salary and commission, budgets, installment buying, checking accounts, and beginning algebra (solving both simple and two-step equations). There are plenty of word problems to practice applications, and a review quiz follows each section. A separate, inexpensive answer key is also available. The emphasis throughout is upon mastering basic math skills that everyone needs to acquire rather than upon preparation for advanced math study. Note: this is not a prealgebra course since it does not cover the material typically found in such courses.(S)

Those who need more extensive review in fractions, decimals, and percents should consider the *Key to ...* series (Key Curriculum Press) for each of those topics.

Moving beyond computation skills into applications challenges many students. *Math Word Problems* by Anita Harnadek (Critical Thinking Books and Software) [$29.95] offers almost 300 pages of word problems on whole numbers, fractions, decimals, and percent. Examples of applications include interest calculation, determining area and volume, computing averages, and figuring late payment penalties. Pages are reproducible, so one book can be used with all children in one family from upper elementary grades through junior high level.(S)

Seventh Grade Recommendations

➲ Algebra 1/2 (Saxon) home study kit - $49.95; solutions manual - $25

This hardbound text is recommended as an eighth grade text, but it consists heavily of review for those who have been through A Beka, BJUP, or any other good math program. Use after completing *Math 76, Math 87* or another good sixth or seventh grade program. The Saxon series provides leeway so that we can stretch out math lessons if our child is struggling, or advance him into *Algebra 1* even though he is working at eighth grade level in other subjects. Plenty of review, a steady, spiral learning process, thought-provoking word problems, and clear instruction make this one of the top recommendations. As is typical of the Saxon books, the level of difficulty rises sharply toward the end of the text. Saxon sells home educators a package containing a student edition, answer key, and tests. This is the 1990 revised edition of this book. The content has been slightly expanded with the addition of geometry fundamentals and application problems working with percents and ratios. Flaws in the older edition are minor, so if you can find a used copy, go ahead and get it. Saxon has resisted the rush to adopt the new math standards, so there are a few things missing in Saxon's series that are included in most new math courses. The most obvious is calculator instruction. While students can use calculators to solve problems when it is appropriate, they are not instructed to do so. Also missing is practice in graph analysis.(S)[1]

[Notes: There is typically a great deal of review in most junior high level math texts. Saxon effectively eliminated much wasted time in their original math series, allowing students to actually skip a year. However, some schools needed a text for that "extra year," so Saxon wrote *Math 87*. It is not necessary to use that book, although it can be useful for those needing more review. The spiraling method means that small amounts of new material are taught in each lesson while constantly reviewing previous material. There is a constant building process, but a simultaneous strengthening of the foundation.]

➲ Basic Mathematics 1 (first edition) (A Beka) $15.15; teacher key - $19.40

This worktext follows A Beka's traditional approach like the books for younger levels. You need to buy the student worktext and the teacher key. The method is similar to that of younger levels with introduction of new concepts using explanation, examples, and practice followed by review of previously learned material. There are more word and application problems in this text than in those for younger grades, but the format is not as colorful and print is small. Topics include review of previous math concepts, metric measurements and conversions, consumer math topics such as checkbook maintenance and computation of interest, a significant amount of both plane and solid geometry,

---

1   Throughout this book, I use (S) to indicate that a resource is secular in nature rather than Christian. (SE) indicates that it is secular and also might require some caution or "editing" for objectionable or untrue content.

an introduction to trigonometry plus assorted topics such as recording bowling scores and meter reading and analysis. This text is unusual in that it covers consumer math and practical topics that are often neglected in basic texts (unless students cover them in high school consumer math courses). It also goes far beyond typical seventh grade level with the geometry and trigonometry. I do find this book useful to broaden math application understanding rather than just reviewing (as happens in too many seventh grade level math books). Choose which topics to cover according to each child's needs. A Test and Quiz Book [$6.05] and companion answer key [$8.60] are also available. For students who need to speed up computation skills, they offer *Rapid Calculation Drills 7-8* [$8.90].(Watch for a revised edition of this book in the near future.)

➲ Exploring Mathematics Grade 7 (ScottForesman/Addison Wesley) student text - $39.48; teacher's edition - $112.98

ScottForesman's *Exploring Mathematics* was designed for government schools and correlates with the new math standards. Student books are colorful with an appealing variety of activities. Student texts are hard cover. Teacher's editions are large, spiral-bound volumes with hard backs and soft front covers. They include reduced pictures of student pages on the appropriate teaching pages. Answers are overwritten on the pictures of the student pages. Lessons are clearly presented in the teacher's edition but they do require some preparation time. Parts of each lesson are designed for teacher presentation and interaction, so parents need to be involved on a regular basis. Numerous group activities are included which you will need to adapt to your situation.

Manipulatives and pictures are frequently used to teach or illustrate concepts, but students are still required to do a good deal of paper and pencil work. Practical application, mathematical thinking, and word problems receive a great deal of attention, one of the positive reflections of the new math standards. Calculators are used frequently throughout the book, and while they have selected the TI-108 to work with, you can use whatever you might choose. A student handbook section at the back of the book explains how to determine what order of operations is used by your calculator and some basics about how calculators work..

This program moves beyond most others for seventh grade with the inclusion of many algebra, geometry, and number theory concepts typically taught at high school level. Much of it is on the level of most eighth grade programs (e.g., BJUP's *Pre-Algebra*). Curiously, it also reviews such topics as fractions and decimals at contrastingly lower levels such as comparing values of fractions without common denominators. Skill review pages at the back of the student book can be used for students who need more foundational review. Supplemental workbooks are available for reteaching, practice, and enrichment which might be useful to help adjust the speed of the program to suit each child.

All students need a compass, straight edge, and protractor. You might also need cubes (*Base Ten Block*® units should be suitable for most activities) and a spinner.

An "extra" found in the teacher's edition for most lessons is a "problem of the day." Problems of the day are intended to be presented from a separate flip-chart book, but we can present most

of them ourselves by simply copying them on to a white board. Answers/solutions are in the teacher's edition. The *Problem Solving and Critical Thinking Workbook* [$9.85] pages are correlated with lessons within the teachers' edition. These should be helpful for those looking for extra thinking skills work. Answers are shown in the teacher's edition.

Throughout the program, topics are presented sequentially with limited review. While topics taught within each chapter are reviewed throughout that chapter, topics from prior chapters are reviewed only in cumulative reviews at the end of each chapter and occasional brief skill reviews inserted sporadically at the end of lessons. For example, while students are studying geometry, they do not review percentage problems taught a little while earlier. There are two pages each for review, enrichment, or practice at the end of each chapter from which we could pull problems to use for review while students are working in future chapters. The teacher's edition offers brief "warm-up reviews" in the margins of each lesson, but these usually pertain only to topics taught within that chapter. The lack of regular review on all previously-taught topics might be a problem for some students who need to keep their skills sharp with more frequent practice.

Overall, this program is more appealing than some others because of appearance, the variety of activities and exercises, and the real-life applications. But it does move quickly into some challenging concepts, and the speed and lack of continual review might pose a problem for some students.(S)

➲ Fundamentals of Math by Hal C. Oberholzer II (Bob Jones University Press) $27; teacher's edition - $39

This new BJUP math text, intended for seventh grade, reflects the new math standards' emphases on applications, interpretation of graphs, and facility with rounding numbers and estimating, but it is balanced with solid review of foundational arithmetic skills. The two-volume teacher's edition provides lesson introductions and enhancements that should be presented by the teacher, but most of the time the key ideas are already covered within the student's textbook lesson. This means that most of the time, but not always, students can work independently through the text on their own. Occasionally, a key concept or piece of information only appears in the teacher's edition and must be presented to the student by some means. Each chapter is introduced with an inspiring biographical sketch on figures such as Charles Babbage, inventor of the analytical engine, forerunner to the computer, and Charles Lindbergh, praised for his perseverance and courage in both his aviation feats and later inventions.

Unlike Saxon's program, this text addresses a separate topic within each chapter. Cumulative review occurs only at the end of each of the fifteen chapters. Arithmetic basics are reviewed in the first two chapters, decimals and scientific notation are covered in chapters 3 and 4, geometry is introduced in chapter 5, and extensive work with fractions takes up the next 3 chapters. Remaining chapters tackle equations, ratios/proportion/percent, application of percent, integers, perimeter/area/volume, measurement, sets, and statistics. The chapter on using percent features consumer applications such as sales tax, discounts, sale prices, simple interest, and commission. Chapters are broken down into subsections (about 8 to 9 subsections per chapter). Each subsection includes exercises for students to complete, but questions pertain only to the topic taught in that section. A quiz for each section appears in the margin of the teacher's edition. The quiz might be copied onto paper or a whiteboard or chalkboard for the student. Answers are given next to the questions. The student text has both a chapter review and a cumulative review at the end of each chapter. Another end-of-chapter feature is lessons for solving word problems.

The level of difficulty is approximately equal to Saxon's *Math 87* and slightly more difficult than *Math 76*, although the content differs slightly, with the aforementioned emphases on graphs, estimation, and applications in the BJUP text being the most obvious.

◗ **Math 76** (Saxon) home study kit - $47.95

This hardbound math text is advertised as being appropriate for bright sixth graders or average seventh graders, but many seventh graders will be ready for *Algebra 1/2*. It reviews all math concepts that have been learned in a spiraling method of constant review. Progression is on the slow side. Children who have been working in A Beka or Bob Jones University Press math programs should be ready for this in sixth grade. Topics covered include decimal numbers and money; fractions; measurements including area, perimeter, and volume; place value; types of numbers; solids; percents; ratios; unit conversions; probabilities; angles; and coordinate points. Saxon sells a homeschool packet of *Math 76* with a student edition of the text, an answer key, and tests.(S)

◗ **Math 87** (Saxon) home study kit - $48.95

If students move through the Saxon series at an average pace, they are ready to move on to *Algebra 1* in eighth grade. Some students are ready to do so, while others are not. Saxon has created a text to fit that in-between period for those who need it. It reviews much of the same material that is in *Math 76* and *Algebra 1/2*, adding very little new material. If students skip this book, they will not be lacking any topics that are necessary before going on to algebra or other high school math courses. The format is the same as other Saxon texts.(S)

◗ **Math-U-See Basic Algebra and Geometry** by Steven Demme (Math-U-See) teacher manual - $25; videotape set - $60; student book - $15; basic manipulatives - $30; algebra inserts - $15

Steve Demme's *Math-U-See* combines the hands-on approach of manipulatives with the spiral learning techniques used by Saxon. Students learn new concepts through concrete, experiential methods, then practice and review those concepts continually. The methodology is heavily dependent upon manipulatives in the earlier levels. In *Basic Algebra and Geometry*, manipulatives are still used, but not as much as in earlier levels. For example, manipulatives are used to demonstrate basic equations, including the use of unknowns and negative quantities. They are also used to show such topics as the distributive property, factoring, and pythagorean theorem. But manipulatives sometimes become too cumbersome, and the paper and pencil (or whiteboard)

approach works better. Demme tries to present concepts simply and clearly, avoiding dense-sounding mathematical abstractions common to so many textbooks. Although the videos are very basic (single camera focused on Demme with a whiteboard against a white wall), Demme's presentation is enthusiastic and engaging. Although he is actually teaching the lessons to a class, we don't see or hear the students except for occasional moments when we can barely hear their answers.

This program differs from others in a number of ways. It teaches algebra and geometry, covering material that typically is taught in grades 7-10. (Some topics typically covered in junior high are covered in *Math-U-See's* "Advanced" level, so some review of that level or study of those topics on the side might be necessary for students new to *Math-U-See*.) The program consists of 3 videos (7 1/2 hours of instruction), a teacher's manual and the manipulatives. Instruction is via the video tape. Demme teaches one major new topic at a time in the video lesson. Students should practice working with the concept while watching the video or after a parent/teacher presentation. Then they complete practice problems (which were presented on the video) and four lessons in the workbook. Each lesson includes practice on the new concept along with review of previously-learned concepts. The teacher's manual includes solutions, answer keys, and instructions as well as one set of student worksheets. The worksheets are not reproducible, so only one student can complete the set that comes in the teacher's manual. We need to purchase additional student worksheets if we have more than one student. Demme tries to combine algebra and geometry rather than treat them as two separate, unrelated topics. In the first four lessons, he teaches some foundational algebra concepts (e.g. order of operations, distributive property, working with fractions in equations). Then he tackles basic geometry concepts in lessons 5-9. In the tenth lesson, he shows how algebra and geometry come together in a study of Cartesian coordinates. From there, he continues to teach and integrate various topics covered within traditional Algebra 1 and geometry courses. Coverage of both subjects is not as complete or intensive as in some of the other separate Algebra 1 and geometry courses I have reviewed. For example, he deals only with regular polygons when teaching about interior and exterior angles or pentagons, hexagons, etc. He teaches simple geometric proofs, but no algebraic or more complex geometric proofs. The quadratic formula is not taught until *Algebra II*. Most of the presentations are easy to follow, but I did not find adequate explanations of symbols used for correspondence, congruence, and similarity. On the other hand, the program does introduce transformational geometry at the very end, a topic often left for Algebra 2.

Algebra II will be available from Math-U-See by the end of 1997 [prices will be $50 for videos; student text - $15; teacher's manual - $25] with *Trigonometry* due sometime in 1998. Because of the different sequence of instruction, it makes sense to stick with this program through *Algebra II* to cover high school math requirements. Students should easily be able to move on to other higher-level math courses after completing the two courses.

↪ Moving with Math, Level D for Grades 7-8 (Math Teachers Press -MTP) Home School Student Set: consumable - $56.95; reproducible - $76.95; teacher guides - $49.95; manipulatives sold separately by MTP

This program incorporates hands-on activity into a complete math curriculum. It is one of the few such programs for students who still need extensive manipulative (hands-on) work at this level. There are three essential components to this program: *Skill Builders, Moving with Math* workbooks, and *Math Capsules*. (All of these plus Home School Instructions are included in the Home School Set in either consumable or reproducible formats.) *Capsules* is the diagnostic tool that will help determine which concepts your child needs to learn. The program is set up as a diagnostic/prescriptive approach, so after you determine the objectives, you then assign appropriate exercises. There are five *Moving with Math* workbooks covering numeration and problem solving with whole numbers; problem solving with fractions and decimals; problem solving with percent; geometry and measurement; and pre-algebra. *Skill Builders* is one large book containing instructions for manipulative activities and reproducible work sheets that rely more on use of manipulatives than do exercises in the workbooks. Reproducible review work sheets are included in *Math Capsules* to ensure that students continually review previously learned concepts.

Optional teacher guides for each book lay out daily lesson plans integrating *Skill Builders* with the workbooks. The teacher guides contain step-by-step instructions on how to use manipulatives and also include many games. The program can be taught without the teacher guides by determining from the diagnostic tools and the objectives which concepts your child needs to learn in what order. Teacher guides remove the need for determining the order and number of lessons to use. However, the trade-off is that we are then no longer individualizing the program. The inexpensive answer keys for each workbook are needed, unless you buy the teacher guides which contain the answer keys.

Moving With Math: An Overview for Home School is a video which describes the role of manipulatives and shows students at various levels using manipulatives. The video is available for rent, purchase, or it is free to home school groups or to those with orders over $125. Manipulatives you will need: either *Base 10 Blocks* (the expensive 1000's cube is unnecessary) or *Cuisenaire® Rods* (cut squares 10 cm. by 10 cm. from poster board to use in place of 100's squares that come with Base 10 sets); fraction bars; and a geoboard (easily made with a twelve inch square piece of wood, with nails arranged a few inches apart in five rows of five nails). Manipulatives are available from MTP, Creative Teaching Associates, Creative Publications, Builder Books, Shekinah, and other sources. MTP also offers an *Intermediate Introductory Calculator Kit* [$27.95] for grades 5-9. The kit includes a calculator and instruction manual. This Texas Instrument calculator performs computations with fractions. Calculator activities which emphasize estimation, checking answers, and looking for patterns are integrated throughout the Level D Teacher Guides, but we can use calculator lessons as we wish if we don't have the teacher guides.(S)

↪ Principles from Patterns: Algebra I (Cornerstone Curriculum Project)

This program is designed to follow immediately after Cornerstone's Level 6 of *Making Math Meaningful*. Even though it teaches algebra topics, because it uses manipulatives (*Unifix Cubes* and heavy graph paper cut into shapes resembling *Base Ten* or *Mortensen* materials), teens who are not mature enough in their abstract thinking for other *Algebra 1* texts should be successful with this course. It also covers pre-algebra topics. See description under "Algebra."

Eighth Grade Recommendations

↪ Algebra 1/2 (Saxon)
See review above.

↪ Algebra 1 (Saxon) home study kit - $49.95; solutions manual - $25

This is the most widely used algebra text among home educators. The spiraling method of presentation and constant review help students work fairly independently. A few of the explanations are more complicated than they need to be, but overall, the book is fairly easy for students to work through on their own. Interestingly, I have yet to find a text that does a better job with distance/rate/time problems than does this one, even though I know that students still struggle with them in Saxon.

If students have used *Math 76* and *Algebra 1/2*, they might be ready for this book in eighth grade. Very bright children might feel that the normal progression is too slow. Although many eighth graders will have no problem with this book, there are many who will not be developmentally mature enough to begin algebra for another year or two. If you feel that your child is not ready for *Algebra 1* at eighth grade level, either academically or developmentally, alternatives might be to use Saxon's *Math 87*, a consumer math program such as A Beka's *Consumer Mathematics* or Barron's *Essential Math*, or a specialized topic study such as one or more of the *Key to...* series at eighth grade level, before continuing with algebra. Or you might have your child begin *Algebra 1* in eighth grade, but move at a slower pace, taking a year and a half or two to complete it. In most situations, you can give credit for high school algebra for this course, even if it is taken early. The 1990 revised edition has more geometry included than does the previous edition. Working through the Saxon series, students do not take a separate geometry course, but learn geometry throughout the algebra series. However, because the geometry has been added to the original book, we find sporadic doses of geometry. It is not introduced incrementally as are algebra topics. Explanation of geometry topics is fairly brief, and does not begin to compare with the quality of presentation in such texts as *Discovering Geometry*. (Some home educators skip the geometry in Saxon and substitute a separate geometry course.) Saxon has resisted the rush to adopt the new math standards, so there are a few things missing in Saxon's series that are included in most new math courses. The most obvious is calculator instruction. While students can use calculators to solve problems when it is appropriate, they are not instructed to do so. Also missing is practice in graph analysis. Saxon sells home educators a package containing a student edition, answer key, and tests.(S)

○ Saxon Algebra 1 [video series] (Teaching Tape Technology) $399.95

Teaching Tape Technology presents Saxon's *Algebra 1* text on a series of eleven, two-hour video tapes created especially for small Christian schools and homeschools, but useful in a broad range of settings. Teacher Page Singleton presents each lesson following the book's format, using sample and practice problems directly from the text. Problems are worked step-by-step on a whiteboard. At the end of each lesson she directs students to complete all of the problems in the text. She presents the lessons very clearly but with no digressions or enhancements. Having a video instructor will make the Saxon text much more usable for students who prefer "being taught" to working independently through the lessons. Tapes are resalable, so you can easily recoup part of your investment. Or you might consider sharing the cost and the tapes with another family or two, watching the tapes together or adjusting your schedules so that one student completes the first tape before the next student is ready to begin.

○ Applying Numbers 8 (Rod and Staff) $15.40; teacher manual - $18.45; tests/worksheets booklet - $1.65

This text reviews basic operations, while also addressing applications of math skills. Students also learn ratio and proportion, plane and solid geometry, signed numbers, graphs, tables, statistics, percent, profit and loss, and other business math. The text introduces algebra and simple equations. A separate booklet contains worksheets (including some business and checkbook forms) and tests. You need all three components for the course.

○ Basic Mathematics II (second edition) (A Beka) $18.50; teacher key - $23.50; test/quiz book - $6.05; key for test/quiz book -$8.60; solution key -$20

The second edition of this book sticks with A Beka's traditional approach to math. It relies on rules and procedures rather than conceptual understanding. It reviews basic math, ratios, decimals, and percent. It continues work with measurement and the metric system. It introduces algebra, geometry, trigonometry, and scientific notation. There is an entire chapter on graphs, statistics, and probability, topics which increasingly appear on standardized tests. Another chapter on "business math" might better be titled "consumer math" since it covers income (including withholding deductions), sales tax, budgeting, checkbook maintenance, borrowing, installment buying, savings/interest, stocks, and insurance. This sort of practical application relating to money is great for junior high students who are questioning the value of math in real life. Some of the other topics are generally taught in high school level texts, so be cautious about overwhelming students with work that is too advanced. For example, algebra proceeds through solving equations and graphing lines, typical Algebra 1 topics.

Texts for pre-algebra vary greatly in what they cover, but one topic that I think should be covered is missing: calculators. While I am not an advocate of calculator use in the early grades, I believe that junior high students should have access to calcula-

tors as they start working with concepts like square root more extensively. This text spends quite a bit of time teaching students how to use square root tables and calculate square root without mechanical assistance; while it is good for students to understand what the calculator is doing, it does not make sense for students to spend much time performing such calculations since derivation of square roots in real life is almost always performed with calculators or computors.

The text itself is a worktext, with instruction and problems set up such that students should be able to work independently. Word problems and review exercises appear in most lessons. This text should work well for the self-motivated independent learner who grasps math concepts easily. You will need both the student worktext and the teacher's key. A Test and Quiz Book and companion answer key are available, and there is also a solution key for those who need extra help.

○ Exploring Mathematics Grade 8 (ScottForesman/Addison Wesley) student text - $39.48; teacher's edition - $112.98

See the review under "Seventh Grade Recommendations." Grade 8 reviews fractions and decimals in the first two chapters, then moves quickly on to algebraic equations; graphing equations and inequalities; ratio, proportion, and percent—much of it presented in algebraic terms; consumer math; measurements and conversions; geometry (constructions and measurement at a high school level); rational and irrational numbers; scientific notation; square roots; statistics (working with graphs and data); probability; and mathematical reasoning (venn diagrams and logic). I am even more concerned with the speed at which new concepts are taught at this level than in Grade 7. For example, the first lesson on line equations and graphing seems to expect students to figure out the meaning of mathematical terms in relation to a graph without adequate explanation. Many algebra and geometry concepts are definitely beyond those covered in other texts for eighth grade. I suspect they are striving to prepare students to go on into ScottForesman's UCSMP *Algebra*, but this course is more advanced than need be for even that challenging algebra course. Nevertheless, it should be a good course for students ready for challenging work who love to see how math is used in real life.(S)

○ Pre-Algebra by Hal C. Oberholzer II (Bob Jones University Press) $27; teacher's edition - $39; test packet - $7; test packet answer key -$4

You will need the hardbound student text and the two-volume teacher's edition for BJUP's pre-algebra course. This text was written by the same author who wrote their *Fundamentals of Math* for seventh grade, so it follows a similar format. However, it does not spend much time on review but moves quickly into algebraic expressions and equations. After additional work with decimals and integers, it moves on into number theory, rational and irrational numbers, equations and inequalities, ratio/proportion/percent, percent applications, geometry, area, volume, statistics and probability, square roots and special triangles, and graphing and functions. Some topics sound similar to those introduced at the seventh grade level, but they delve deeper. For example, some geometry topics in this book (e.g., volume of pyramids and cones, identifying the measurement of an angle in an irregular polygon) are generally covered within high school geometry courses. This text is actually slightly more difficult than Saxon's *Algebra 1/2*, also considered an eighth grade text. BJUP's text spends more time on practical application, word problems, consumer math, geometry, and graphing coordinates. It also introduces functions and trigonometric ratios. You need not complete all of these topics if a student is struggling to get through the course! Themes such as flowers, animals, and the solar system thread through each chapter via photos and captions. These are intended to help illustrate mathematical concepts or tie in to biblical principles, but some are such a stretch that they serve as no more than window dressing. Chapters are prefaced with a brief Bible story illustrating some mathematical relationship to a Bible truth. Each chapter ends with a word problem strategy lesson, a consumer math lesson, an optional "mind boggler" problem, and chapter review problems. Save the mind bogglers for students who need the extra challenge. Brief daily reviews are provided in the margin of the teacher's edition, but these draw only from topics covered in the previous chapter rather than all chapters to that point. You should also purchase the Test Packet which includes chapter quizzes and tests as well as three cumulative tests. As with *Fundamentals of Math*, students should be able to do most, but not all, of their work independently through this text, and lesson preparation time is minimal.

⊃ Prealgebra [video course] (Chalk Dust) $304 for prepaid orders of complete package of 10 tapes, text, and solutions guide

Ten video tapes, a worktext, and a solutions manual comprise a prealgebra course fairly similar in content to Saxon's *Algebra 1/2*. The worktext is *Prealgebra*, second edition, by D. Franklin Wright (Houghton Mifflin Co.). This is a 750+ page, paperback book that includes instruction, exercises, tests, charts, tables, and answer keys. Dana Mosely, the video teacher, generally follows the worktext lessons in order of presentation, although he often adds his own ideas about learning strategies to the lessons. He covers the main concepts, then works out sample problems on a chalkboard. Video presentations are very professional and include computer graphic illustrations. After watching the video, students complete margin problems and exercises in their worktext. Cumulative reviews begin to appear in chapter two. Chapter tests follow each chapter. Answers to all margin problems, cumulative reviews, and chapter tests are provided at the back of the book. However, there are answers for only odd-numbered exercise problems. Typically, there are 75 or more exercise problems per section, so students should have sufficient practice if they complete only the odd-numbered ones. However, most parents should be able to perform the math to check answers on the even-numbered problems if they decide to have their students complete those also. Parents might want to remove the answer keys from the back of the book and keep them elsewhere. The text first reviews basic math skills and concepts thoroughly before moving on to topics such as exponents, solving equations, polynomials, square roots, geometry, statistics, and measurement. It includes many word problems and practical applica-

tions. It introduces the scientific calculator in the first chapter. Dana Mosely teaches students the basics of how to use the calculator, but he doesn't use one in the video presentation every time the text lesson does. Mosely stresses the need for students to understand the mathematical concepts instead of expecting the calculator to do the math for them. The differences between this text and Saxon's *Algebra 1/2* are that this one uses the calculator, features more word problems, spends more time on graphs and statistics, and has a consumable worktext rather than a hardcover book. Mosely's presentation of the lessons makes it much easier for visual and auditory students to grasp lessons. It also provides students with two different approaches so they can compare both video and text presentations to make sure they understand a concept.

The solutions manual is useful, but some students might need to consult it so infrequently as to make it unnecessary. This would be especially true if a parent is strong in math and can help a student through any troublesome problems.(S)

Extras and Supplements

Games such as *Monopoly, Pinochle, Mastermind*, and many others make excellent supplements for developing mathematical thinking and proficiency. Some math games such as the *24 Game*, described below, can be used with younger children also, but work well at higher levels.

⊃ AIMS Education Foundation

The *AIMS Education Foundation* publishes a number of books for upper elementary and junior high levels that integrate math and science in fun learning activities [$16.95 each]. Choose books by topics: aerodynamics, the human body, floating and sinking, geology, and other science areas. Science offers the questions in these activities, while mathematics provides the language needed to arrive at conclusions. The integration of math and science provides a more real-world approach to teaching and learning both areas. Activities are time consuming so you probably should plan to use these about one day per week. Most activities lend themselves to groups better than individuals, although they can be used either way. These are terrific!(S)

⊃ Algebra Word Problems (Critical Thinking Books and Software) $7.95 each

Eleven separate books of 28 pages each concentrate on different aspects of basic algebra, a good deal of it at the pre-algebra level. Answer keys are found in the front of each book. However, there is a *Teacher's Manual and Detailed Solutions* book [$10.95] covering all eleven of the books. I highly recommend it to parents who are not sharp on their algebra skills.

It is probably best to start with the first two books, then choose from among titles that work on topics presenting difficulties for each student. The first book, *How to Solve Algebra Word Problems*, walks the student through strategies to translate word problems into mathematical forms, helps them identify what the problem is asking for, and teaches them to identify what steps are needed. Students are taught to check their solutions, taking time to think about the reasonableness (or unreasonableness) of their answers. The second book, *Warm-Up*, has students practice translating word problems into math statements in various situations. E.g. "When Cheryl is twice as old as she was four years ago, she will be one year younger than Bill is now," or "A room is three feet longer than it is wide. What is its area in terms of its width?"

Topic-specific titles that junior high students might tackle are *Ages and Coins; Mixtures* (e.g., "To have a mixture of 5% sand, 95% topsoil, how much sand must be added to twenty yards of topsoil?); *Formulas, Rectangles, D=rt;* and *Percents and Work Rates*. Problems increase in difficulty from beginning to the end of each book, so junior high students might be able to do some of the problems now, and some when they are at high school level. The same is true of *Fun Time* and the three books, *Miscellaneous A-1, B-1, and C-1* . (*Fun Time* has some math tricks junior highers should love.)

The books are reproducible, with a number of problems per page. Depending upon the student, you might use one problem at a time or groups of problems; there are no set lessons.

These are great supplements, especially for those time/rate/distance problems (in *Formulas, Rectangles, D=rt*) that are a stumbling stone for so many.(S)

⊃ Baseball Math (Good Year Books) $9.95

Design a better baseball stadium! Calculate how far your favorite team travels. This real-life math and problem solving book for baseball fanatics has a variety of different problems and projects that will help your player sharpen his thinking skills while learning more about his favorite game. Since it is recommended for grades 4-8, some of the problems will be too easy for most students, but if you have a student working below grade level in math, this book should work well.(S) [VT]

⊃ Bible Math Labs by John Block (Bible Math Labs) $15

If you're trying to answer your child's questions about, "What are we ever going to need this math for?", you should try *Bible Math Labs*. The title might be boring, but the book itself is anything but. John Block uses biblical events as springboards into practical applications. The story of the loaves and fishes helps us explore fractions and decimals. We figure out what actual part of the five loaves and two fish each of 5000 men would have received without divine intervention. Students learn about terminating and repeating decimals in the process, then go on to a discussion of decimals that neither terminate nor repeat such as pi. Some of the math will be review, but some of it will stretch into high school level topics, preparing them for future studies. (You might use this book with high schoolers, tying in lessons with topics they are studying for reinforcement.) Among math skills addressed in this book are measurement, conversion of units, scale and ratio, rates, exponents, percents, two and three dimensional shapes, volume, calculating costs, averaging, interest, discounts, using formulas, gathering and interpreting data, and more. Answers are at the back of the book. Lessons are designed to be taught rather than used for independent study, although, working through some of them will certainly be an individual exercise. You need purchase only one book, then you will probably want to reproduce some of the pages with blank charts, although that isn't essential since these can easily be drawn on paper. This book should be fun for parents and children to explore together. Block also publishes the bi-monthly *Math Labs Newsletter,* that offers still more math applications [$10/year].

⊃ Cranium Crackers: Critical Thinking Activities for Mathematics, Book 3 (Critical Thinking Books and Software) $19.95

Book 3 in this series is suggested for grades 7-8 but can be used by students above and below level because it is not age-graded. Critical thinking is truly the most important goal of this book, with mathematics being the vehicle. The purpose is to stretch children beyond rote levels of learning, into a wide range of ways of thinking about and applying math skills. There are problems dealing with logic and numbers, and even some that deal with organizational and analytical skills that do not include any numbers. "Book 3 assumes reasonable facility with the four basic operations using integers, fractions, and decimals. A working knowledge of percents and simple areas is also assumed." There is a great deal of variety from lesson to lesson. So much so, that few lessons bear resemblance to each other. The student workbook is reproducible. The teacher's manual/answer key is included at the back of the book.(S)

⊃ Football Math (Good Year) $9.95

Similar to *Baseball Math*, reviewed above, this book uses story problems and situations with a football theme. Students work with math concepts such as percents, ratios, and averages, sharpening their basic arithmetic skills while learning how to apply them. An answer key is at the back of the book.

⊃ Math Life-Skills series (Curriculum Associates, Inc.) $3.95 each; teacher guide - $3.95 each

Three books comprise this series of activity workbooks on consumer math. All are appropriate for junior high level but lack the depth that would make them suitable for high school level. *The Check is in the Mail* teaches students how to write checks and deposit slips, including how to write out numbers with words. They also learn how to maintain a check register and balance a statement as well as review some basic math skills. While the basics are covered, one of the more challenging skills—balancing the checkbook against the statement—is covered superficially without adequate instruction and no practice. Nevertheless, this is a good place to start.

Making Wise Buys has lots more math practice with rounding, multiplying decimals, working with discounts (percents), computing taxes and tips, and other everyday math applications. These are applied to comparison shopping, budgeting, installment buying, saving, planning a party, and taking a trip. As with the first book, the level is strictly junior high; for example, installment buying is presented simplistically without addressing it in terms of interest charges.

A Share of the Market introduces students to the stock market with basics about the origins and functioning of the market plus explanations for interpreting stock listings in the newspaper. Students get lots of math practice with paper and pencil as well as with a calculator. A stock market game at the end of the book has students select and track some phony stocks with information provided in the book. A second version of the game, directed from the teacher guide, challenges students to use real stocks selected from the newspaper. This book might stretch up into high school level.

All three books are dependent upon the teacher guides for each. Blackline masters and vital information is included there but not in the student books.(S)

➲ Mathematical Reasoning through Verbal Analysis, Book 2 (Critical Thinking Books and Software) student book - $20.95; teacher's manual - $12.95

Book 2 is targeted for students in grades 4-8, but it can be used by older and younger students since it is not age-graded. (Students working below level would probably do better in Critical Thinking Books' *Cranium Crackers: Critical Thinking Activities for Mathematics* series.) The verbal analysis, an essential aspect of the book, occurs through discussion, so the parent/teacher must plan time to interact with students for these lessons. A group class would be even better. Lessons are challenging, combining visual/spatial skills, logic, math, and verbal skills. An underlying goal is preparation for the thinking skills necessary for abstract high school-level math. There are six categories of lessons: number and numeration, geometry, operations, measurement, relations, and tables and graphs. Although actual mathematical knowledge reflects what is typically taught in grades 4-8, the lessons are challenging and best address the needs of average to above average students. Both the reproducible student workbook (283 pages) and the teacher's manual (183 pages) are necessary. The teacher's manual is essential for the discussions as well as for an answer key.(S)

➲ Mathematics Projects by Phil Schlemmer (Prentice Hall) $21.95

This is the fourth book in the "Learning on Your Own!" series that began with *Research Skills Projects* (see Chapter Three). It is not necessary to use other books in the series, but *Research Skills* lays a foundation for independent study if students have not already developed such skills. *Mathematics Projects* is written for "gifted or motivated" students in upper elementary through high school. It is a supplement to your basic program which should improve problem solving skills. There are a variety of indoor and outdoor projects that require a great deal of math (e.g. mathematical treasure hunt, tree mapping, and land surveying). The term "project" is very apt in this book, since projects are time consuming. For example, a project on simple equations should take about seven hours. While problem-solving skills are the main object, they are taught against a background of other mathematical skills. Other topics addressed are fractions, decimals, equations, geometry, measurement, ratios, proportions, and working with formulas. Algebra and geometry actually receive quite a bit of attention. While some basic instruction is provided within the book, the author assumes the teacher's familiarity with those topics. Parents using this book really should have a basic understanding of them or they might find it difficult to use many of the lessons. Another potential problem is the classroom design of the lessons. One lesson incorporates a

game that will require a bit of adaptation for the home school. Many of the projects would be much more fun tackled within a group than alone. Consider setting up a group class once a week to tackle some of these.(S)

➲ O! Euclid (Ampersand Press) $9.95

Introduce geometry to junior high and high school students with *O! Euclid* and they will be ahead on definitions and characteristics of many geometric shapes before they get into a serious geometry course. Instructions for four different versions of the game are included, but the first two are probably the ones that home schoolers will play. The first version leaves cards with pictures of fourteen geometric shapes visible while players try to construct those shapes from partial pieces shown on the remaining cards. The second variation is more challenging. Players have to recognize pieces belonging to the shapes as well as the name. To win, they also have to answer a question about the shape. (Questions vary in difficulty, so we can choose one appropriate for each player.) Knowing some basic geometry terms such as "congruence" and "vertex" help when playing the second variation. (We found ourselves devising a few rule clarifications while playing the second version, so the rules can use a little more fine tuning.)

The thing that makes this game effective is that it requires players to make either intuitive or rational judgments about which shapes each card belongs to. For instance, if a player has the bottom half of a triangle, he must identify what type of angle will be necessary to complete the top half. Other shapes such as the pentagon, octagon and trapezoid also help develop this sort of mathematical insight.(S)

➲ Operations (Learning Enrichment Games) $7.95

This double-size card deck comes with a small-print, 46-page booklet describing 15 different games that can be played with the cards. The deck includes cards for numbers 0-12, the four basic functions, fraction and decimal cards, and wild cards (x, y, and z). Different cards are used for the various games, with choices sometimes made to adjust the level of difficulty. Just about all ages can play these games at one level or another. Most of the games help develop thinking/logic skills as well as review math facts.(S)

➲ The Quarter Mile Math Game [computer program for IBM type or Apple II computers] (Barnum Software) $50 for single-subject area programs or cross-section program; $185 for set of five complete programs

Math drill in either drag racing or "wild" riderless, running horses format offers a new twist to the challenge of mastering math facts. The version of the program I reviewed, simply titled *The Quarter Mile*, is the one I judge the most likely choice for home schoolers. It contains a cross section of topics taken from the other five *Quarter Mile* programs described below. With this program, students practice the four functions, fraction functions, fraction reduction, least common multiples, greatest common factors, decimal functions, square numbers, exponents, percents, equations, percent/decimal/fraction conversions, rounding, estimation, and more. The first topics introduce students to keyboarding skills (number and alphabet) if they have not yet mastered those. During each race, problems appear one at at time, presented randomly from a pool of problems for each topic. Correct answers increase the player's speed and cause a new problem to appear. Incorrect answers leave the problem on the screen for three tries; then the program gives the correct answer. After each race, the dragster or horse gets an elapsed time. Once the student has raced five times, five elapsed average times are posted; students are then racing against the top five times from then on. More than one player can record scores so that a competition can ensue. Colorful graphics show the car or horse racing while a player answers the problem on the screen. Incorrect answers leave the problem on the screen for three tries, while correct answers increase the player's car's or horse's speed and cause a new problem to appear. The program can be run from floppy or hard drive and records can be saved to the game disk itself or separate disks.

If we want more practice in a single subject area or we want to focus on older level concepts, we can purchase the other versions of *The Quarter Mile: Whole Numbers!, Fractions!, Decimals & Percents!, Integers & Equations!,* or *Estimation and Math Tricks!* Alternatively, we can purchase the other five programs together as the *Value Set!* for a savings over individual program prices. The overall product line is appropriate for grades K-9. *Whole Numbers!* is for the younger audience. *Fractions!* and *Decimals & Percents!* should be used whenever students study those concepts. *Integers and Equations!* is appropriate for grades 5-9. *Estimation and Math Tricks!* is for grades 3-9.

A demo disk for $3 shows a cross section of topics that are fully functional, but the program will load only seven times. The cost of the demo can be applied to purchase.

Home schoolers can participate in Barnum Software's international *Quarter Mile* tournaments. Call for information on this competition or for details about a Macintosh version in development.(S)

⊃ Scratch Your Brain Where It Itches (Critical Thinking Books and Software) $9.95 each

There are five books thus far in this new series, two of which (at least partially) target the junior high student. The books are subtitled "Math Games, Tricks, and Quick Activities," which accurately summarizes the content of these math supplements. *Book C-1* (for grades 7-9) covers mathematical thinking working with number concepts, logic, visual puzzles, and arithmetic skills. *Book D-1* is based upon basic algebra. Some of these problems will need to wait until students have had basic algebra; some require either a graphing calculator or graphing software. *C-1* appears to be more fun, while *D-1* is more challenging. Books are reproducible and answer keys are at the end of each book.(S)

⊃ The Skills Bank Home Tutor (SkillsBank Corporation) $299 for all five modules

The Skills Bank Home Tutor (for IBM compatible and Apple II machines) has five modules, including one on mathematics. This software mimics the design of very expensive classroom programs which provide tutoring, testing, evaluation, and progress recording. However, it is much less expensive. The total cost for all five modules at this writing is $299 plus shipping (or $87.50 per module). Student access disks are necessary for each person who will be using the program. Five such disks come with the purchase of all five modules. (Only one with each individual module; we get two student disks if we buy two modules, and so on.) Each student disk allows <u>five</u> students to use any of the modules. That means that 25 students will have access when all five modules are purchased. It still sounds like a lot of money, but families might share the five lesson disks/modules. ("You take language arts this month, while I take math.")

The programs themselves are easy to use, uncluttered, but also unexciting. The documentation could use a little work, but it is fairly easy to figure out. Students can begin work wherever they need to. Programs cover all basic concepts within the selected subject areas for the elementary grades up through junior high and some high school.

The math program covers computation, concepts, word problems, and an introduction to geometry and algebra. I take issue with the way they teach the order of operations at the top level, but other than that, instruction seems sound and worthwhile. This is a good tool for junior highers to make sure their skills are sharp before going on to high school math. (See descriptions of other modules under subject headings.)(S)

⊃ Solutions: Applying Problem-Solving Skills in Math

(Curriculum Associates, Inc.) $4.95 each; teacher guides - $3.95 each

The *Solutions* series is a great supplement to stretch mathematical thinking skills. These are particularly useful if you are using a traditional program that stresses mastery of math facts, but which might be short on thinking and application skills (e.g. A Beka). There are eight books in the series (Levels 3-8 and A-B). Levels 3-8 progress in difficulty. Average junior high students should probably work in levels 7-8, and remedial students should begin at lower levels. Levels A and B are best for senior high and above. All books follow the same lesson sequence, but increasing in difficulty at each level. Each starts with an assessment. In keeping with the emphasis on mathematical thinking, there are sections on interpreting and restating problems, tracking down data from outside sources such as encyclopedias to determine an answer, selecting problem-solving strategies, solving non-routine problems (sometimes you have to work backwards to get to the answer), using calculators, identifying extraneous data, using graphs/charts/maps, and estimating. All of this is packed into a workbook of about 30 pages. This series better reflects the type of problems students encounter on standardized tests than do some math programs, so they might be especially useful for those preparing their children for testing. The one teacher guide that I received for review also has a page of open-ended problems that don't appear in the student book; these, too, are commonly seen on new tests. Teachers guides include answers plus guidance for using each section.(S)

➲ **Stock Exchange game** (Creative Teaching Associates) $16.95

Junior high students practice fraction/decimal conversions, applying those skills to buying and selling stocks. The game is a very good simulation of the stock market, with students reading and interpreting stock information just as it appears in newspapers. Play money, share cards, and a game board are used as students learn about appreciation and depreciation of stocks, dividends, and market fluctuations. While *Stock Exchange* is my favorite for junior high level, you might also want to check out *Big Deal, Bank Account, Budget*, and *Discount*.(S)

➲ **True Math game** (Aristoplay) $25

Suggested for ages 10 and up, this game is sort of a trivial pursuit focused on math related topics. The unusual game board includes features that enhance game playing fun—"chaos spaces" from which players can jump across the board, "binary boosts" that give players an extra turn, and challenge opportunities where players can "bet" on another player's knowledge. Question cards are divided into two types: true/false and genius. The board and cards have question categories: numbers, money, size and scale, geometry, logical thinking, and random access. Questions do not drill students on basic math facts, although they will have to apply those skills to answer some of the questions—e.g., "Of the 16 billion coins made in the U.S. each year, about 3/4 are pennies. That's about 12 billion pennies annually. True or false?" Some of the questions require logical guesses—e.g., "A dozen medium eggs weigh about what a basketball does. True or false?" Some are likely to require pure guesswork from most players—e.g., "Americans eat about 74 acres of pizza each day. True or false?" (Questions correspond to the new national math standards which stress mathematical thinking over computation skills.) Certainly, those with more math background and more general knowledge will have an advantage, but the game includes enough "random" features to allow less knowledgeable players to win. There are 300 cards with 900 questions in all, which means that you might use up the questions rather quickly. Of course, you can then make up your own questions or pass the game on to another family. We might also hope that Aristoplay will develop supplemental card decks before long.(S)

➲ **24 Game Single Digits** (Item #3397) (Suntex International, Inc.) $19.95 each

This is one of those deceptively simple ideas that accomplishes much more than one might guess. There are 192, 4" x 4" cards. Each has four single-digit numbers. The challenge is to combine those four numbers using addition, subtraction, multiplication, and division to make a total of 24. Since the cards are divided into three groups, from easy to difficult, children as young as eight (approximately) can play using the easy cards, while adults will find some of the difficult ones very challenging. Teens will find this a fun way to beef up their math computation skills. The beauty of such a game is the amount of mental math that takes place to find the correct solution. Games can be played in groups or solo. To add another dimension to the game, there are sleeves that cover either one or two of the numbers. The challenge then is to determine what the missing number or numbers might be. Want to make it even more difficult? Use two sleeves with one number covered in each, then find a single number that will satisfy both. (A hint for new players: read the second page of the instructions which suggests common patterns to look for.) This game has proven so popular that there are *24 Challenge* games across the country.

There are also four even more challenging editions: *Fractions* (Item #3497), *Decimals* (#3597), *Exponents* (#3697), and *Algebra* (#3797). The *Fractions Edition* is suggested for ages 11 and up. As with the *Single Digit* edition, there are three levels of difficulty, but I think everyone will want to start at the easiest level to figure out how to play. The cards have from one to three fractions per card as well as single-digit numbers. Otherwise, play is just like that for the *Single-Digit* game. Those who need easier levels can work with the "Primer" editions: *Add/Subtract Primer* (#3197), *Multiply/Divide Primer* (#3297), and *Fractions Primer* (#3427) (although the first two will be too easy for most junior and senior high students). *Decimals* (#3597), *Exponents* (#3697), and *Algebra* (#3797) are challenging games for students at least junior high level or older. These, too, offer three levels of difficulty, and I think most adults would struggle with the second and third levels. For example: given the four terms: 4, 3, 7, and $2(x+y)$, add, subtract, multiply, or divide using all four terms to come up with x and y values that produce an answer of 24. When you are working at learning the subject already, it is not as difficult as it looks at first. Also, hints for common patterns help us out a bit. Highly recommended.

High School Level

Most states require two years of high school mathematics, but requirements are being raised by both colleges and local school districts. For college-bound students, three or four years of math are recommended, including two years of algebra, geometry, and, possibly, other courses in higher math. Students aiming for careers in engineering or some science fields are strongly urged to take precalculus and/or calculus in high school so they will have time to take the math needed in college.

Students who are certain that they will not go to college can satisfy the requirement with practical math, pre-algebra, and other general math courses. Of course, they can still tackle algebra and geometry, but they might also consider general math, consumer math, business math, or career math depending on their areas of interest. Some of these courses are as challenging as algebra and geometry, but apply directly to work skills that these students might use as soon as they graduate from high school. The choice is not necessarily between "dumbbell math" and "real math," although there are business and consumer math texts for students who are working below level. (See specific recommendations later in this chapter.)

If high school students do not get the math they need in high school, they might be able to make it up at a junior college, but it might set back their college graduation a semester or two.

In states that allow students to attend junior college while still in high school, students might be able to take algebra, geometry, or other courses that parents are not capable of overseeing at junior colleges. However, students are expected to be able to handle college level studies, so this is not an option for all students.

Sequence of Math Courses

One problem that seems to arise frequently for home educators has to do with the sequence of math courses. The Saxon series is the primary cause. Because Saxon has integrated geometry with algebra across a span of three years/textbooks, students who wish to use Saxon are obligated to take three years of algebra to cover the required geometry course work. Those students who prefer to only take two years of high school math need to switch midstream if they want to cover geometry. (In my opinion, geometry seems to be far more useful than advanced algebra in terms of general life applications, making it a more vital course than a second year of algebra.) Another reason for following the traditional algebra-geometry sequence is testing. Students who plan to take the PSAT in their junior year should definitely cover geometry before taking that test since it is assumed that they have already done so.

Saxon's *Algebra 1* (or *Algebra 1* and *2*) can be used, followed by a geometry text from another publisher. We might wish to skip geometry content in Saxon if we will be covering it from another text. Some people choose to substitute another geometry course for the geometry content in Saxon simply because geometry is the weakest link in Saxon's books. This can be accomplished by skipping geometry within the Saxon books, and speeding up the course work to compensate. A different geometry text can be used between books or, in some cases, simultaneously.

Of course, choosing another publisher for both algebra and geometry is another possibility, and many such options are listed below.

New Approaches to Teaching High School Math

New directions in math education are likely to greatly change our traditional high school math scope and sequence over the next decade. The new mathematics standards encourage integration of algebra, geometry, trigonometry, statistics, probability, and discrete mathematics. They also recommend that calculators and other technology be used to perform complicated arithmetical calculations as an essential part of any program, freeing students to develop better thinking and application skills. Inductive skills (discovery learning methods) are also being emphasized as a means of developing thinking skills and understanding concepts. While many of these ideas are laudable, the down side of the new standards is decreased emphasis on mechanical computation skills and drill.

We are also beginning to see a shift toward "embedded academics" as part of the School-to-Work agenda of Goals 2000. This means that academic learning takes place within the context of job situations. Students learn the skills they need to perform a particular job. To facilitate this approach, schools are creating applied math courses such as "Algebra for Business."

This means that in the future we might no longer have courses labeled with the familiar titles of algebra, geometry, etc. Instead, we might have these career-oriented courses and/or courses with "generic" names which will include all areas of mathematics instruction, at increasing levels of difficulty each year.

The Saxon math series integrates high school math topics to some extent. However, the Saxon series is not designed to reflect the new math standards, as we can see by looking at the choice of topics covered and the methodology.

Colleges and universities will generally accept integrated math courses in lieu of traditional courses as long as the students have learned the necessary algebra and geometry. (Note: NCAA standards for those wanting to participate in college sports pose the most problems with unusual courses.)

There are some texts that do a good job of both implementing the new standards and teaching the subject matter. Recommended texts that reflect these changes are:

⊃ **Career Mathematics** (Houghton Mifflin/McDougal Littell)

See review under "Consumer, Business, and Career Mathematics." While this book is not a typical course purposely designed to meet the new standards, it actually does a better job than most texts that were so designed.(S)

⊃ **Discovering Geometry** (Key Curriculum Press)

See review under geometry recommendations. There is strong integration of algebra, hands-on activity, and thinking skills—excellent implementation of the new standards.

⊃ **For All Practical Purposes: Introduction to Contemporary Mathematics** (W.H. Freeman and Co.)

This college-level text might be used by home schoolers either in conjunction with or following a second-year algebra course. See the review under "Consumer, Business, and Career Mathematics."(S)

⊃ **Intermediate Algebra, Sixth Edition** by Miller, Lial, and Hornsby (ScottForesman/Addison Wesley)

See review under algebra recommendations. This is sold as a college-level text, but it can be used for high school.

⊃ **UCSMP courses**

See reviews of algebra and geometry UCSMP courses which are leaders in the move to the NCTM Standards.

Tuning in to Mathematical Thinking

⊃ **Critical Thinking Activities for Mathematics, Book 4**
(Critical Thinking Books and Software) $19.95

Book 4 in this series is suggested for grades 9-12. Critical thinking is truly the most important goal of this book, with mathematics being the vehicle. The purpose is to stretch students beyond rote levels of learning, into a wide range of ways of thinking about and applying math skills. There are problems dealing with logic and numbers, and even some that deal with organizational and analytical skills that do not include any numbers. "Book 4 is intended for the high school general-mathematics student. The arithmetic here expects general facility with the four basic operations on integers, fractions, and decimals, along with the ability to work reasonably well with percents and areas. No college preparatory mathematics knowledge is expected, but some problems demand fairly complex reasoning about arith-metic." There is a great deal of variety from lesson to lesson. So much so, that few lessons bear resemblance to each other. The student workbook is reproducible and the teacher's manual/answer key is included at the back of the book.(S)

⮑ Mathematics, a Human Endeavor by Harold Jacobs (W.H. Freeman and Co.) $53.95; workbook - $12.95; instructor's manual - $13.95

This is not a complete math program. Instead, it is a book about math that introduces a variety of topics in interesting contexts. Learn about inductive reasoning, deductive reasoning, functions and graphs, logarithms, polygons, mathematical curves, permutations, probability, statistics, and more with billiard balls, optical illusions, satellites, and other interesting applications. Cartoons, mathematical history tidbits, and a friendly writing style make this book inviting to read. Students can choose whatever topics they wish to explore rather than going through chapters in order.(S)

⮑ How to Lie with Statistics by Darrell Huff (W.W. Norton and Company) $5

See the review in Chapter Eighteen under "Thinking Skills." It is important to get a realistic view of how statistics are actually used before deciding to devote much study time to the topic. This book very entertainingly exposes the misuses of statistics. Watch for some objectionable subject matter, such as discussions about the Kinsey Report.(SE)

⮑ Solutions: Applying Problem-Solving Skills in Math (Curriculum Associates, Inc.) $4.95 each; teacher guides - $3.95 each

See the review under "Extras and Supplements" for junior high math. The *Solutions* series makes a great supplement to stretch mathematical thinking skills. Levels A and B are best for senior high and above, although lower levels will help students working below level or having difficulty with math application and thinking skills.(S)

Algebra

Algebra does not have to be a fearsome undertaking. Algebra is actually an easy way of performing mathematical problem solving, once we learn the "shorthand." Some students are intimidated if they begin algebra too soon, that is, before they are able to mentally manipulate a number of abstract concepts simultaneously.

Sometimes students are overwhelmed by the number of strange concepts they encounter in algebra, especially when they are not given any explanation as to why or how they can use these things in real life. Watch out for algebra programs that provide no examples or applications of its usefulness. If you can and will provide such information yourself, choose whatever program you want to use. If not, make sure the program provides that information.

An excellent supplement to use for any higher math topics is *When Are We Ever Gonna Have to Use This?* (Dale Seymour) [$10.95]. Author Hal Saunders interviewed people from 100 different occupations, then came up with application word problems that these people encountered all the time. Problems are arranged by occupation and math content, so that we can identify problems to fit current math topics being studied. The book is written for grades 7-12, and there are three levels of difficulty so that we can choose appropriate problems. An answer key is included, as well as a useful poster showing in chart form the 100 occupations and 71 kinds of math required. Parents should choose problems from the book as needed rather than expecting a child to use the book independently.(S)

Also, consider *Career Mathematics* (Houghton Mifflin) as another source for practical application of algebra, geometry, and trigonometry.

The biggest differences in algebra programs are in the methods of presentation. Some use manipulatives. Some books break concepts down into small bites (increments), while others provide a "meal" at a sitting. Also, explanations in some books are clearer than others.

I have found that explanations in most first-year algebra books are sufficient on their own, but the same is not true for second-year algebra. It is very helpful to pick up a second textbook, possibly from a used book or thrift store, simply to have for an alternative explanation of a concept that is hard to understand. Perhaps an even more practical way to tackle second-year algebra is to select one of the intermediate algebra texts written for college students. Since they are designed for use by students who do much of their work independently, they generally have better explanations of concepts.

Algebra Resource Recommendations

(Arranged in approximate order of increasing difficulty)

⮑ Basic Algebra (Educational Design, Inc.) $10.95

This is a very basic, introductory algebra worktext that covers the bare essentials. This book is for those who need a more gradual introduction to Algebra (perhaps a step in between Saxon's *Algebra 1/2* and *Algebra 1* for review and reinforcement). This book will take only a few months to complete, so it will not be a full year's math course. There is no practical application included; you simply follow instructions and learn the mechanics. Large print and few problems per page reduce the intimidation level tremendously. You will also want to order the answer key, but it is very inexpensive.(S)

➲ Flip-Chip Algebra (Flip-Chip Enterprises, order from Creative Home Teaching) Algebra with basic manipulatives - $42; basic manipulative kit - $6.50; extension kit - $5

Flip-Chip Algebra is for hands-on learners who want more than an introductory algebra course. In 567 pages, *Flip-Chip Algebra* covers the primary Algebra I concepts and actually a bit more as it tackles imaginary numbers and an introduction to functions. It does all of this without abandoning the use of manipulatives. The authors stress that they want students to understand algebra rather than memorize rules. (*Math-U-See* is similar in concept.) It covers positive and negative numbers, symbols and order of operations, multiplication and division of fractions, properties, expressions, equations, powers and roots, polynomials, factoring polynomials, quadratic equations, rules and graphs, systems of equations, and rational expressions. Imaginary numbers are covered under quadratic equations, and functions are introduced in a few places throughout the book, then dealt with again in the appendix. Students use manipulatives made from colored mat board which represent positive and negative numbers plus "x" and "y" variables. The *Extension Kit* adds extra manipulatives (xy rectangles, xy right triangles, (x-y) squared, and y-squared squares]. These come with a few pages of illustrated teaching suggestions for tackling more challenging factoring and multiplication of polynomials and the Pythagorean Theorem. (I recommend that you buy this kit also.) The manipulatives are used constantly, although transfer to the strictly numeric representation is also taught. The methods are not unique, although I have never previously seen such a clear explanation of how reciprocals work or such extensive work with factoring polynomials with manipulatives. In each lesson, a concept is taught showing illustrations of manipulative use, then transferring the concept to the normal mathematical symbols. Students then work with the manipulatives to complete the problems in the exercises at the end of each lesson. Answers are found at the back of the book. Students who do not need such extensive hands-on work might get bogged down with the manipulatives, and they might sometimes do better absorbing lessons from the book without actually using the manipulatives.

The program is not as comprehensive as Saxon's *Algebra I*, lacking such topics as least common multiples and greatest common factors, percents, set theory, scientific notation, square root tables, inequalities, graphing inequalities, and word problems. Some of these might be viewed as review topics, but others are more essential to a complete algebra course. Students who need a complete Algebra I course should either use *Flip-Chip Algebra* as a supplement to another text, selecting the hands-on lessons to use as needed, or supplement *Flip-Chip Algebra* with resources like *Algebra Word Problems* (Critical Thinking Books and Software) and selected lessons from another algebra text to cover inequalities, set theory, and scientific notation. Occasionally, explanations seem too cursory to me, relying too much on the manipulative presentation while neglecting the verbal explanation. Because of this, I suggest that you do have another algebra text handy for reference if you need it.

Many parents who are afraid to teach algebra because they don't understand it, will find this course a refreshingly easy method.(S)

➲ Algebra Essentials (Merrill) student book #0675054915 - $35.67; teacher edition #0675054923 - $44.10

This is an alternative for those looking for an easier algebra course, but not something as easy as Educational Design's *Basic Algebra*. This text covers most, but not all, of the content of a typical algebra course, yet it moves more slowly and does not require as much work. Print on the pages is larger and less overwhelming than in most algebra texts, yet it has the appearance of a standard text.(S)

➲ Key to Algebra (Key Curriculum Press) Books 1-10 - $2.10 each; answer books - $2.40 each; tests -$13.50

This series has been expanded from seven to ten workbooks. Where previously it was considered sufficient only as an introductory course, it now is equivalent to a complete first year algebra course, although it is less difficult than most. Titles of each book indicate topics covered: *Operations on Integers; Variables, Terms and Expressions; Equations; Polynomials; Rational Numbers; Multiplying and Dividing Rational Expressions; Adding and Subtracting Rational Expressions; Graphs; Systems of Equations*; and, *Square Roots and Quadratic Equations*.

The worktext format provides instruction, examples, and room for problem solving, all within each workbook. Word problems help students understand life applications for algebra. As in the *Key to Geometry* series, much of the time students "discover" mathematical principles through problem solving activities with presentation of the rules following. This is in contrast to most algebra programs which teach rules first, with application practice following. Review takes place at the end of each book. Reproducible tests are available. Answers and Notes come in three separate books: one covering Books 1-4, one for Books 5-7, and one for Books 8-10. Like the other *Key* series, the books are black and white, consumable workbooks. They have large print and fewer exercises per page than most standard textbooks, so they are unintimidating.

Because they are easy to use and understand, these books are especially good for both students and parents who are weak in math. While *Key to Algebra* can be a full first year algebra course, it can also be used for review or as a gentle introduction, possibly using only the first seven books before a student begins a rigorous algebra course. Students who plan to take Algebra II should choose a more rigorous course.(S)

➲ Algebra I [video course] (second edition) (The Teaching Company) $199.95; extra student workbooks - $10 each

Four extended-play videos, two outlines, and a workbook comprise a course that should be considered supplemental. The very engaging presenter, Dr. Monica Neagoy, a teacher at Georgetown University, does an excellent job of teaching using a white board, models (geometric models, rods, squares, etc.), and computer graphics to enhance the presentation. She explains at the beginning of the course that it is designed to reflect the new math standards' focus on applications, mathematical thinking, and conceptual understanding. She includes extensive use of a graphing calculator (required for the course) and real life applications. Presentations are enlivened with historical anecdotes and other stories about the origins and applications of math. The course includes a workbook, but it does not have nearly as much practice as is contained in traditional courses. The course includes 30 lessons, each 30 minutes in length, for a total of 15 hours of teaching. It breezes quickly through some foundational concepts for Algebra I, then addresses topics like slope/intercept and linear functions. However, it introduces the language and use of functions early on, which is usually reserved for Algebra 2; the entire course seems to address topics found in both algebra courses. Consequently, it must be used as a supplement for Algebra I, and possibly, also for Algebra 2. [Note: this is quite different in format from Teaching Company's *Algebra II* course.](S)

⊃ Principles from Patterns: Algebra I (Cornerstone Curriculum Project) $45; Unifix cubes - $10

This program is designed to follow immediately after Cornerstone's Level 6 of *Making Math Meaningful*. However, students working in other publishers' math series can use this course for a high school algebra course. It covers pre-algebra topics (positive and negative numbers, radicals, exponents, order of operations, etc.), as well as equations, polynomials, factoring, Pythagorean Theorem, and the quadratic formula—the basic topics covered in first-year algebra courses. However, coverage is less comprehensive than we find in most other courses.

The newest edition is bound in a lay-flat binding. An answer key is included in the book. Additional copies may be purchased at half price.

Principles from Patterns incorporates the use of manipulatives (*Unifix Cubes* and heavy graph paper cut into shapes resembling *Base Ten* or *Mortensen* materials) which make it much easier to grasp some of the abstract concepts. Some unique techniques are used, as well as the rectangle building technique featured by *Mortensen*. *Unifix Cubes* (sold separately by Cornerstone) are used in conjunction with grid paper included within the binder. However, *Lego* bricks can be substituted. The heavy graph paper which is included works well as a manipulative, but you might want to substitute Nasco's *Algebra Models* which function the same way and are easier to handle. Teens who need concrete learning experiences will particularly benefit from the teaching methods used here. Those who function well on an abstract level should also benefit with better understanding of concepts, although they might be able to shortcut through some of the hands-on activities.

Inductive teaching methods are frequently used, which lead learners to discover concepts themselves rather than just memorize rules and study examples.

Topics are covered in a progressive fashion, working toward mastery of each concept, rather than the scattered approach we encounter in the Saxon texts. At the end of each unit is a review lesson to ensure retention and understanding of previously-learned concepts. Many word problems within each unit help students understand the practical application of concepts.

Unlike the previous *Making Math Meaningful* courses, this one does not offer a script ("Say this," "Do this"), but speaks directly to the learner. Because of this, many students will be able to work independently.

⊃ Algebra I [video course] (Chalk Dust Co.) $339 for prepaid orders for complete package of 11 tapes, text, and solutions guide ($359 when components are purchased separately or are billed for later payment); starter package - $109

The first of Chalk Dust's productions was their *Algebra II* course. I was very impressed with this course, so I was not surprised to find their *Algebra I* course of equal caliber. The course is presented via text and video. Dana Mosely presents each lesson on video, correlating with the *Elementary Algebra* text from D.C. Heath and Co. by Larson and Hostetler. He teaches concepts and works through samples of each type of problem. Students then complete the exercises at the end of each section. Since there are typically about 100 problems for each section, we can assign only the odd problems to our students and still have plenty of practice. The primary reason for doing so is that answers to all odd-numbered problems are found at the back of the book and in the optional *Student Solutions Guide*. Parents confident in their own math skills might feel free to require students to do other problems that they will then check themselves. Mid-chapter quizzes and chapter tests are included in the text, and answers for all quiz and test problems are found both at the back of the book and in the *Student Solutions Guide*.

The text is designed to be taught so it does not function well on its own for home schooling students. However, combined with the video presentations it makes an excellent course. The text serves as a backup to the video lessons and a source for practice problems, quizzes, tests, and answers. I recommend that students review the text lesson after watching the video and before tackling the problems. The *Student Solutions Guide* should be especially helpful for families where parents have weak math backgrounds since it outlines each step in solving all the problems for which answers are provided in the book. The text contains numerous practical application problems and a stronger emphasis on conceptual understanding than we find in Saxon's *Algebra 1*. However, it does not cover quite as much territory as Saxon's text. Since the Heath text is not trying to incorporate geometry, it has less geometry; but it does have algebraic applications in geometry. It does not teach proofs, but it does feature optional lessons and exercises for using a graphing calculator. (Saxon offers occasional tips for using a non-graphing scientific calculator.) The Heath text teaches a wider variety of "formula" problems in contrast to Saxon's heavy emphasis on time/rate/distance problems. Although the book's appendix adds a section on statistics, this is not included on video.

Overall, the course is equivalent to most other Algebra I courses, although I expect that most students will find it less challenging than Saxon's. The starter kit will get you going with a smaller initial investment; it includes both the text and the *Student Solutions Guide* plus the first video.(S)

⊃ Algebra I and Algebra II [Computer Video Interactive course] (ACE School of Tomorrow) $450 for videos (purchase) for each course; $106.67 for computer disks; PACEs with answer keys - $64 for each course. School of Tomorrow offers two rental options: videos only ($239.80 per course, broken down into quarterly rentals of $59.95 each) or rental packages that include PACEs and Score Keys

($299.80 per course or $74.95 per quarter). Video rentals are shipped in four groups.

[*Algebra I* has just been released in a revised edition. It is available in PACEs and videos, with the computer disks due out in 1998. *Algebra II* is already available in all three media.]

The computer video interactive (CVI) courses combine computer software and videos for complete courses. Originally, School of Tomorrow had only PACEs for these courses. The videos now present the lesson material, doing a much better job than the PACEs by themselves. Computer software puts student exercises and tests from the PACEs on the computer. However, the videos are the crucial part of these courses, and they work very well if we choose to skip the computer and use only the PACEs (one for each video). The videos and computer disks help students to work independently, a must for some home schoolers.

To go the computer route, we need to purchase the special conversion kit from School of Tomorrow that will allow you to use your present computer and VCR player, as well as the software and videos. Software consists of twelve disks, which are essentially computerized versions of the PACEs. However, the software also acts as the master controller, transforming the videos and software into an integrated course. The software and video are inserted into the computer and VCR. A simple command starts the software, which signals the computer to change to video mode at appropriate moments. The course switches back and forth from video to software automatically. The software also provides feedback on student responses, on-line help, lesson summary, tracking of student progress, computerized testing, scoring, and reporting. It will also take a student back through material he has not mastered. The videos are the most expensive part of the program, but they can be reused by many students. Rental options make the video presentations affordable. The software is much less expensive, but can be used by only one student because the interaction overwrites the data stored on the disks.

The latest version of *Algebra I* features high-quality videos that correspond directly with the new PACEs. Explanations of concepts are expanded from the earlier version, and the PACE layout has been improved with less clutter and better organization.

Algebra II, already in an updated, improved version also offers a very effective way for home schooling students to learn this subject. The video presentations are professional, with clear explanations of algebraic concepts, better than those in most textbooks. Students learn concepts from videos, then do exercises in PACEs. Dialogue on the videos corresponds to text in the PACEs. Computer software allows students to input answers on the keyboard, working through the interactive format described above.

The scope and sequence of School of Tomorrow's algebra courses is slightly slower than most others. This factor, combined with the easy-to-understand presentations, should make learning algebra possible for many more students. The slower scope and sequence is not a major problem, but rather something to be aware of when going on to another publisher's material. The methodology is very traditional; for example, *Algebra II* begins with definitions and vocabulary to be memorized, probably the most boring part of the course. Even though the methodology lacks excitement, the course gets high ratings for doing a solid job with a challenging subject. Short character sketches add both a biblical base and interest to the *Algebra II* course.

Introductory Algebra, Sixth Edition by Miller, Lial, and Hornsby (ScottForesman/Addison Wesley) student worktext - $43.95; teacher's edition - $43.95

This worktext is designed for college students although the material is equivalent to a typical high school Algebra I course. It concentrates review of fractions, decimals, and percents into a single chapter at the beginning, then quickly moves into algebra. There are both margin problems accompanying the lessons, and pages of exercise problems. There are plenty of word problems, but it could use more practical-application explanations. There are helpful extras—cautions, step-by-step summaries for problem solving, and rules highlighted in contrasting boxes so they are easy to spot. Each section lists the section objectives and cross references the tape, solution manual, or computer program for students to consult for extra help.

In keeping with the new math standards, the use of calculators is encouraged on selected problems which are marked with a calculator symbol. Basic instruction for calculators is included (both for simple arithmetic calculators and for scientific calculators). The number of problems where calculators are suggested is a fairly small percentage of the whole, so students should not become overly dependent upon calculators.

A nifty feature is the use of contrasting blue pages at the end of each chapter which summarize key terms and give capsule reviews of key concepts. These are followed by review exercises and tests. Reviews are cumulative of all material covered thus far. A mid-term and a final test are included. Answers to odd problems, all answers to reviews and tests, and a solution key to selected problems are in the back of the book, so it is possible to use only the student book. A number of supplemental items are available: *Study Guide* -$15.54; *Instructor's Testing Manual* - $7.40, *Student's Solution Manual* - $13.69, *Instructor's Solution Manual* - $7.40 (we need both Solution Manuals to have solutions to all problems), and a computer test generator for IBM or Macintosh $80.29.(S)

Algebra on Video Tape by Leonard Firebaugh (Keyboard Enterprises) $49.95, $69.95, or $89.95 per Phase

This set of videos with accompanying work sheets and answer keys, comprises a complete first year algebra course and then some. Presentation is definitely not exciting, but it moves along at a steady pace without wasting time. Firebaugh uses a white board to demonstrate problem solving, explaining concepts clearly as he goes. (Although Firebaugh appears very stiff and forbidding at the very beginning, he soon loosens up and appears more natural.)

Each video lesson presentation (145 in all) takes about fifteen minutes, then students practice on work sheets for about 30-45 minutes. Answer keys showing full solutions are included as well as tests. About 800 pages of work sheets, solutions, and tests come with the course. No parent preparation or participation is necessary. Students can work independently through all course work.

The complete course consists of three groups of tapes, listed on the order form as Phase One, Phase Two, and Phase Three. One benefit of the "phase arrangement" is that we can purchase Phase One, try it out, then decide whether to invest in the complete program. A more important benefit is that we can use only Phases One and Two for a slower student who does not intend to pursue algebra any further. The material covered in the first two parts will still be sufficient for a first year algebra course. Students who complete all three Phases will have covered some coordinate geometry along with many Algebra II concepts.

The cost varies according to different quality options for each Phase—choices of best, better, or good quality reproduction tapes. The best quality are recorded on six separate tapes per phase; the better quality also fills six tapes, but reproduction quality is not as high; and, good quality consists of two tapes of lesser quality recording. (Compare these to taping on your VCR at varying speeds.) Even the most expensive choice is only about the same as A Beka's cost for rental of their course, and we keep the videos rather than returning them. Other options are much less expensive. We do not have to watch all of the classroom interaction that is part of the A Beka course, which saves time. Overall, I see this as a time- and money-effective solution, although it lacks polish.

Firebaugh is working on Geometry and Algebra II courses. Contact Keyboard Enterprises for information about when they will be available.

⊃ Elementary Algebra by Harold Jacobs (W.H. Freeman) $42.95; Instructor's Guide - $10.95

This is an atypical algebra text. It invites students to explore algebra concepts in a friendlier environment than other texts. Cartoons, interesting and creative applications, puzzles, and even poetry capture the interest of students who struggle with abstract mathematics. Jacobs always provides reasons for learning and using what is taught in each lesson. Four exercise sets are at the end of each lesson, with problems ranging from simple computation, through word and application problems, to challenging thought problems. By assigning appropriate problems, the text can be used with students of varying capabilities. Answers to questions from one of the sets from each lesson are in the back of the student text, so that students can see if they are getting the correct answers. The inexpensive teacher's guide is the source for the rest of the answers.(S)

⊃ Algebra 1 and Algebra 2 (Saxon) home study kits: Algebra 1 - $49.95; Algebra 2 - $50.95; solutions manuals for either text - $25 each

This is an excellent series. (Saxon also offers *Algebra 1/2*, a pre-algebra course which can be used for remedial or review work before taking algebra.) *Algebra 1* and *Algebra 2* are designed to be used sequentially, a different approach than commonly found in high schools. Most high schools teach one course in algebra, then geometry, then return to algebra. The Saxon series teaches geometry within all algebra courses. A student planning to take only one year each of algebra and geometry

could use Saxon's *Algebra 1* (possibly skipping over geometry instruction and problems), then switch to another publisher for geometry.

The geometry content within these texts is the weakest part of Saxon's approach. Originally, very little geometry was found in the first two books. *Advanced Mathematics* provided the bulk of the coverage, which was insufficient. Geometry was then added to *Algebra 1* and *2*, but it is scattered and presented very briefly in both books. (By the time students have completed second or third editions of both books they will have studied about one semester's worth of geometry. They complete their geometry requirement with the Advanced Mathematics book.) Because of this problem, I have often suggested using a different geometry text and skipping geometry exercises and instruction within Saxon. This can be done after *Algebra 1* or *2*, as well as after *Advanced Mathematics* (a less recommended option); or geometry might also be studied simultaneously. However, a third edition of *Advanced Mathematics* is due in 1998, and the publisher tells me that geometry will receive more complete treatment in the new edition. I still have reservations about the methods used to teach geometry in Saxon in the first two books, even if they do a better job in the third. So, while I expect that geometry coverage will improve, it remains to be seen whether or not this compares well with use of an alternate text.

Algebra 2 covers standard second-year algebra topics, although the inclusion of a significant amount of trigonometry is unusual. Right triangle trigonometry basics are introduced and practiced in many lessons.

Saxon has resisted the rush to adopt the new math standards, so there are a few things missing in Saxon's series that are included in most new math courses. Calculator instruction is presented within a single chapter in *Algebra 2,* in contrast to integrated calculator use throughout most texts covering the same material. (Graphing calculator use will be taught in the new third edition of *Advanced Mathematics*.) While students can use calculators to solve problems when it is appropriate, they are not instructed to do so. Also missing is practice in graph analysis. These texts are strong on skills but weak on applications—"How do we use this?"—another area that is emphasized in the new math standards.

The Saxon texts continually review concepts, requiring thinking and understanding by the student, yet they allow students to work independently most of the time. Lessons introduce bite-size concepts that are fairly easy to deal with. Explanation is included with each lesson, although a few of the explanations seem to make things sound more difficult than they really are.

Saxon sells home educators a package containing a teacher's edition (identical to the student text, but with an answer key in the back) and tests with an answer key. These texts can be used independently by good math students, although many students will need occasional help as they progress beyond the first few chapters. Parents can review or learn along with the students, or they can find someone capable of tutoring when necessary. These texts are the easiest that I have found for independent work.(S)

⊃ **Algebra I, An Integrated Approach** by Isidore Dressler (Amsco) $18.33 for paperback; $25 for hardcover; teacher's manual with answers -$13.20; answer key only - $4.10

This book is written for the average student and can be used for independent learning. Instruction is fairly brief, followed by model problems, then exercises. This is a solid algebra course in topic coverage. In fact, it includes a good bit of geometry and trigonometry in addition to advanced algebra concepts. However, it was designed to be used as a supplement or review book, so instruction is a little more cursory than we find in some texts. (My impression is that intensive study of the model problems is sufficient to help students grasp concepts without more extensive instruction.) The book is available in hardbound or paperback editions (each more than 580 pages), and a separate, inexpensive answer key is available. Seven different versions of a final exam are also included in the book, although there are no chapter tests.

If students enjoy Dressler's presentations, they should consider continuing with one or more of his other math books: *Modern Algebra Two, Algebra Two and Trigonometry*, and *Trigonometry*. Advanced students can jump to the *Algebra Two and Trigonometry* course, but others should probably tackle *Modern Algebra Two* as the continuation.(S)

⊃ **Algebra I, Landmark's Freedom Baptist Curriculum Course M145**

(Landmark's Freedom Baptist Curriculum) $35 for complete course without solutions manual; solutions manual - $25

Landmark's *Algebra I* course is strongly academic, but suitable for independent study. It teaches math theory and vocabulary, as well as applications and skills more comprehensively than we find in Saxon. It lays a solid foundation necessary for higher math studies. It does require more work and study than some other programs, but clear explanations enable students to do it on their own, especially with the help of the optional solutions manual. It reviews basic arithmetic skills quickly at the beginning, then proceeds to cover all basic Algebra I course material up through fairly extensive coverage of quadratic equations. It introduces functions and graphing of quadratic equations at the end, topics usually reserved for Algebra II. The presentation lacks polish; we can easily spot where some revisions have been made to the course. While there are some word problems, it is a very theory-based approach with no hands-on work and little application practice. The course includes two student worktexts (called study guides), answer keys, weekly quizzes and answers, and quarterly tests and answer keys.

⊃ **Algebra II, Landmark's Freedom Baptist Curriculum Course M155**

(Landmark's Freedom Baptist Curriculum) $35 for complete course without solutions manual; solutions manual - $25

Algebra II is similar in format to *Algebra I*. However, I am concerned that it might be too difficult for many students without a teacher present because it covers some challenging topics too quickly. Some topics for which coverage seems too brief are slope, graphing, parabolas, and determinants.

⊃ **Algebra II [video course]** (The Teaching Company) $199.95; extra student workbooks - $10 each

Like most of The Teaching Company's high school courses, this one consists of four extended-play videos, two outlines, and a workbook. High school math teacher Dr. Murray H. Siegel presents a very traditional *Algebra II* course which is quite a contrast to The Teaching Company's unconventional *Algebra I* course. Dr. Siegel uses a white board, flip chart, and computer graphics to enhance lessons. The course follows a progression similar to that of a number of standard textbooks, covering such topics as factoring, linear equations, graphing linear equations and inequalities, solving systems of equations, quadratic functions, imaginary numbers, square roots, cube roots, exponential functions, logarithmic functions, matrices and determinants, and sequences and series. The final presentation is an introduction to trigonometry. Although Dr. Siegel uses real-life applications and explanations for "why we need to know some of this stuff," he concentrates on the tools and skills of algebra rather than taking the new math approach. He does not teach with calculators (although students SHOULD be using calculators for some work at this level) or focus on concepts and theory, typical new math approaches. The video course itself is only fifteen hours, and the workbook lacks the amount of practice we find in texts, so Dr. Siegel directs students to consult a text for additional problems for each section of the tape. The course is not designed to stand alone, but it is to be used as an adjunct to a standard course. Consequently, it will work best for students who use it in conjunction with a text to cover concepts more fully and to get adequate practice with problem solving. In spite of the limited length, this is a solid course, and I expect it will work well for students who just need a teacher to present the lessons.(S)

⊃ **Essentials of Algebra II [videotapes and companion text]** videos by Dana Mosely (Chalk Dust Company) $250 for the set of ten tapes or $25 for individual tapes; Intermediate Algebra -$64; Student's Solutions Guide - $20; prepaid orders for a textbook, and tape set include the solutions guide at no extra charge

Professor Dana Mosely is your teacher in this series of ten video tapes covering a complete Algebra II course. The tapes vary in length since they are broken down into segments covering various topics, but there is a total of about 22 hours of video viewing. Mosely uses a chalkboard with occasional video animations to illustrate concepts or graphically explain an algebraic process. High production quality and skillful presentation combine to make a top notch video course. Mosely's many years of teaching experience are obvious as he clarifies commonly confusing issues. He keeps the presentation moving at just the right pace, although students can always rewind and review if they don't catch it first time around. Students watch the presentation, then practice problem solving from the textbook. Mosely closely follows the lesson outlines of the textbook, *Intermediate Algebra: Graphs and Functions* (D.C. Heath). This is a 1994 edition, written to conform to the new math standards. One of the most obvious influences of the math standards is that each chapter in the book and, consequently, each tape contain lessons on the use of scientific and graphing calculators. Video lessons actually show the calculator and its screen so that students can use their own calculators and follow along performing operations. Many Algebra I concepts are reviewed at length, a boon for students who have taken geometry after Algebra I. The scope and sequence is less advanced than some other Algebra II courses; while it covers functions at length, it does not even introduce trigonometry. Chapters are broken down into segments (corresponding to tape segments) with practice problems following each segment. Answers to odd-numbered problems are found at the back of the book. Midway through each chapter is a quiz to check on progress. Chapter reviews allow students to verify their understanding before taking the chapter tests, which are also contained in the text. Odd-numbered answers are provided for chapter reviews, but all answers are provided for mid-chapter and end-of-chapter tests. Theoretically, we could use nothing but the text book. However, instruction within the text is cursory, and the video instruction is superb. Unless a parent is very familiar with Algebra II, he or she will probably have difficulty figuring out procedures in some of the lessons using only the text. We are also missing even-numbered answers to exercises and reviews. I recommend that you purchase the *Student Solutions Guide* which has detailed solutions for the odd-numbered problems and all mid-chapter and end-chapter quizzes. It is possible to get the complete solution guide (which covers all of the problems) directly from the publisher, but there are so many problems that we should be able to manage with the combination of text and *Student Solutions Guide*.

Theoretically, *Essentials of Algebra* can be used other Algebra II texts by cross referencing topics, but this would require too much extra time to be practical for most families. *Intermediate Algebra* and the solution manual can both be purchased from Chalk Dust Company or from D.C. Heath.

Compare the cost of these tapes to the rental of School of Tomorrow's tapes for their course or to the correspondence "loan" costs of A Beka's video course! And the tapes are yours to share or sell when you are through. I highly recommend this course.

Chalk Dust Company also publishes *Algebra I, Geometry, Precalculus, Trigonometry, College Algebra*, and *SAT Math Review*; with Calculus I, Physics, General Math, GED Math Review, and Statistics scheduled for the future. Chalk Dust offers a 30-day money back guarantee plus a one-year tape replacement guarantee.(S)

⊃ **Algebra 1 and Algebra 2** (Bob Jones University Press) student books - $28 each; teacher's editions - $39 each; solutions manual for Algebra 1 - $36; TestBank for Algebra 1 - $16

BJUP recommends these texts only to those parents who have an excellent knowledge of algebra themselves, although I think that parents working along with their students should be able to figure things out. It would be wise to find someone you can consult if you encounter problems or feel there is not enough explanation. Lessons are designed to be taught rather than for independent learning, so it is necessary to consult the teacher manual rather than just hand students the textbook. As with most textbooks, *Algebra 1* appears easier to use than *Algebra 2*. Each lesson covers a larger chunk of material than in the Saxon books.

Lessons are introduced with practical applications whenever possible. *Algebra 1* is planned for ninth grade level. We can use only the first ten chapters and still provide a solid course. The last three chapters can be covered by bright students, however, the topics in these chapters (rational expressions, rational equations, and quadratic functions) are covered again in *Algebra 2. Algebra 2* is suggested for eleventh grade level, and geometry is a prerequisite. Standard topics are covered, as well as trigonometry, matrices and determinants, and probability, although these latter chapters can be skipped if necessary. Purchase both student and teacher's editions. The teacher's editions contain a copy of the student text with most answers, the remaining answers in an answer key, and lesson presentation information. A TestBank is available for *Algebra 1*.

⊃ **Algebra I and Algebra II** (A Beka) $15.65 and $16.45 respectively; solution keys - $48.60 each

Similar to BJUP in that they are recommended only to parents with strong math background, these texts are designed to be used for ninth and tenth grades. For *Algebra I* and *Algebra II* you will need to order a student text and the solution key. The teacher's edition is not necessary; the minimal amount of instructional information there is simply a restatement of information already in the student text. The solution key contains the answers and demonstrates how to reach them. Each lesson introduces quite a bit of information—more than Saxon, but with less explanation. Instruction is fairly easy to follow for those with a strong math background. The solution keys are a big help, since we can always check the process followed to solve the problem.

⊃ **Algebra I or Algebra II Video Courses** (A Beka)

A Beka adds another option for algebra courses by offering instruction on video. The videos are of actual classrooms. They are not edited, but include everything that occurs in the classroom. Our students learn by watching the teacher instruct the class, and by listening to interaction between students and teacher. Students work in the A Beka *Algebra I* and *II* texts at home and send in work as they would for any correspondence course. Even though the videos are rented rather than purchased, the cost is significant, and the time required is the same as in a traditional day school. Despite these drawbacks, this might be a practical alternative for parents without a solid math background

The gentleman presenting the *Algebra I* video course seems to be a very organized teacher in the traditional mode. He explains concepts using an overhead projector and a chalkboard. Students answer questions and solve problems at the board. The teacher keeps the class moving at a good clip. In the sample tape I viewed, students already had their work on the board, and he moved quickly from student to student with little time wasted.

⊃ **Algebra, 1998 edition** (ScottForesman/Addison Wesley) $42; student text packaged with calculator - $61.98; teacher's edition - $60.23; solution manual -$26.04

The University of Chicago School Mathematics Project (UCSMP) math program consists of six texts teaching integrated mathematics. The first book in the series, a pre-algebra text, is titled *Transition Mathematics*. This *Algebra* text is second in the series. This is probably the best and most comprehensive of the new math programs based on the new math standards. It stresses four "dimensions of understanding": skills, properties and relationships, applications, and representation of mathematical concepts. Rather than teach concepts in a theoretical manner, it presents concepts in contexts, using illustrations or other means of showing how they might be used. Each lesson presents a concept within the textbook, including explanations that students can understand without a teacher's presentation. Sample problems are shown. A set of questions concentrates on the new concept, then another set of problems reviews previously-learned concepts. The final group of problems are for "exploration." Occasionally, these questions will require outside research in a dictionary, encyclopedia, or other reference works. There are also optional projects that can be pursued selectively, depending on time and the needs of each student.

The organization is quite different from traditional texts. Since mathematical thinking is a major goal, some concepts that are saved for higher levels in traditional programs are integrated in early *Algebra* lessons. In keeping with the new math standards, students must use a scientific calculator with the text, and a graphing calculator would be even better. (An appendix offers lessons in using scientific calculators.) Other reflections of the standards are the inclusion of numerous problems which students must answer with written explanations to demonstrate both understanding and their ability to explain the concept to others, much work on interpretation of graphs and charts (questions using these skills show up with increasing frequency on standardized tests), thoroughly developed treatment of the graphing of equations and inequalities (beyond what we find in most Algebra I texts), the integration of geometry (e.g., Pythagorean Theorem, volume of solids), and the inclusion of a chapter on functions (usually reserved for higher levels).

There are self-tests and review tests following each chapter, and these might be sufficient for tracking student progress. Selected answers to exercises and reviews are found at the end of the student text. An *Assessment Sourcebook* ($69.90) contains more thorough tests, but it is probably too expensive for most home educators.

We really do need the teacher edition, which is far more than an answer key. Some lesson preparation is necessary, although students can do much of each lesson independently. Parents with weak math backgrounds should go through the text with their teens so that they are able to be involved when necessary.

At almost 900 pages, there seems to be more here than the average student can complete in a single school year, although the teacher's guide indicates that average students should be able to complete 12 of the 13 chapters. The teacher's guide suggests that we use the text at whatever grade level is appropriate for each student, anywhere from seventh grade through tenth grade according to their charts showing suggested sequences for using their series of math texts. Even though this text is classroom-designed and suggests some group activities, it should work well for home educators. You can follow with the next UCSMP texts, *Geometry; Advanced Algebra; Functions, Statistics, and Trigonometry*; and *Precalculus and Discrete Mathematics*.(S)

⮌ **Intermediate Algebra, Sixth Edition** by Miller, Lial, and Hornsby (ScottForesman/Addison Wesley) $43.96; instructor's manual - $43.96; solution manuals: instructor's - $21.56, student's -$15.95

My frustration with the quality of high school texts for the second year of algebra has led me to look at some college textbooks as options. This text looks like a practical alternative to high school texts. Instructions for independent study are included. Key definitions and rules are conveniently placed for reference.

It is designed to cover the content of second-year high school algebra courses, as preparation for college math. While it does not include trigonometry, it covers all typical topics covered in second year algebra. This newest edition has been updated to try to adhere to the NCTM guidelines, which means that they have added more concept development, writing activity, and algebra integrated with some geometry applications. Instructions for the use of scientific calculators is very helpful.

I find the introductions to new concepts easier to understand in this text than in most others. Practical applications are clearly explained at the beginning, and concept presentations are written in understandable language. Bright yellow boxes caution students about common errors to avoid. Answers to selected exercises (usually all odd-numbered problems) are at the back of the student text. The *Student's Solutions Manual* shows half of the problems worked out, corresponding to those for which answers are provided in the back of the textbook. The *Instructor's Solutions Manual* has all problems worked out.(S)

⮌ **Advanced Algebra, 1998 edition** (ScottForesman/Addison Wesley) $45; text packaged with calculator - $64.98; teacher's edition - $63.24; solution manual -$27.69

The University of Chicago School Mathematics Project (UCSMP) developed a series of texts based on the new math standards. Their *Algebra* text is reviewed elsewhere in this chapter. This text would follow algebra and geometry (in their sequence), serving as an Algebra II course. However, the scope and sequence is advanced beyond some other second-year algebra courses, including Saxon's. (Remember that *Algebra II* is the second in Saxon's high school series, so we must compare this text partially to Saxon's *Algebra II* and partially to Saxon's *Advanced Math*.) It is similar in design to the UCSMP *Algebra* course, incorporating practical application, mathematical thinking, and challenging skills. A scientific calculator is required, although a graphing calculator would be even better. Topics addressed are functions, variations and graphs, linear relations, matrices, systems, quadratic functions, powers, inverses and radicals, exponential and logarithmic functions, trigonometry, polynomial functions, quadratic relations, and probability. Explanations are better than in most texts at this level, so most students can work on their own. However, they should have a knowledgeable adult available for consultation if needed. We need both the student text and the teacher's edition.(S)

⮩ **Algebra the Easy Way. third edition** by Douglas Downing (Barron's) $12.95

This is a <u>really</u> different approach to algebra. It is written as an adventure novel! The characters learn about algebra, why it is used and how it works as the story unfolds. Part of the rationale is that algebra is simply a shorthand way of writing mathematical situations; we should all appreciate short cuts and know how to use them. Rules are simply stated with technical terms pointed out, but not emphasized. In 289 pages, the author covers concepts from both Algebra I and II, so coverage is rather hurried. Concepts are presented in a different order than in most algebra programs, which makes it difficult to switch to another Algebra II course. Exercises for practice are included. I love the approach for its creativity. However, it might move too quickly for those who have difficulty with math, and it might also be too incomplete for those who need a thorough math foundation to go on to higher math. It should be useful for review purposes and for students who would benefit from the more "user friendly" approach. It should satisfy the general ed high school algebra requirement. There is a sequel from the same author, *Calculus the Easy Way*, covered below. Other books in the "Made Easy" series are by different authors and lack the creativity of Downing's books.(S)

⮩ **College Algebra** (Chalk Dust Co.) $314 for prepaid orders for complete package of 10 tapes, text, and solutions guide ($334 when components are purchased separately or are billed for later payment); starter package - $109

College Algebra stands apart from Chalk Dust's other math courses, although we might use it after *Algebra II* or, in exceptional cases, instead of *Algebra II*. The complete program includes ten video tapes, the *College Algebra* textbook by Larson, Hostetler, and Hodgkins (published by D.C. Heath), and a study guide. The text follows the same format as do Larson's *Elementary Algebra* and *Intermediate Algebra*. Mid-chapter and Chapter End tests are included in the text. Answers to all odd-numbered exercise problems plus all answers to quizzes and tests are included at the back of the text. A solutions guide is also available from Chalk Dust which shows step-by-step solutions for the same problems for which answers are provided in the text.

The course reviews much of the material covered in Algebra II but takes it to a deeper level in most instances and at a more rapid pace. For example, in the section on graphing equations, we encounter new types of equations and graphs. In the study of functions, we encounter more complex functions than previously. This book also seems to use more word problems and applications of math than does *Algebra II*. It might be possible for outstanding Algebra I students to skip Algebra II and move directly into this text, but for most students it should follow an Algebra II course. Some students will be able to skip the first tape and first section of the book which review fundamental concepts of algebra. In comparison to Saxon's math series, the content of *College Algebra* is somewhat equivalent to Saxon's *Advanced Math*. However, Saxon includes trigonometry while this program does not. (Chalk Dust offers a separate *Trigonometry* course.) On the other hand, this course covers statistics and prob-

ability which receive little attention in Saxon, and it also presents more coverage on conic sections. The use of a graphing calculator is highly recommended, although the course can be completed without one. An unusual feature is an "Index of Applications" showing on which page we can find a particular math application such as "Projected revenue," "Purchasing power of the dollar," or "Compound interest." Although the course is titled *College Algebra*, it is only a little more challenging than *Algebra II*. While the text claims to be appropriate for science and engineering students, it should be coupled with a trigonometry course before students can tackle calculus. College-bound students who do not need calculus and trigonometry will have a very solid math background if they continue algebra studies through this course. With the combination of video and textbook presentations, students should be able to work independently through most lessons. The solution guide will be especially helpful for students who lack someone to consult when they have difficulty. The starter package will get you going with a smaller initial investment; it includes both the text and the *Student Solutions Guide* plus the first video.

Chalk Dust also offers a *SAT Math Review* course which should be of interest to college-bound students.(S)

Algebra Supplements

⮩ **Algebra Magic Tricks, Books 1 and 2** (Critical Thinking Books and Software) $14.95 each

These two books of algebra tricks by Ronald Edwards are great for those intrigued by the numerical tricks performed by magicians. The first book has 20 magic tricks, while the second has 15. They use algebraic analysis to show how the tricks work. Activity sheets guide the student through the process with hints and questions. Eventually, students might even begin to design their own. The algebra is simple enough to be used by beginning algebra students. It's amazing how much algebra students will learn when it is presented in a context such as this.(S)

⮩ **Algebra Word Problems** (Critical Thinking Books and Software) $7.95 each

Eleven separate books of 28 pages each concentrate on different aspects of basic algebra. Answer keys are found in the front of each book. However, there is a *Teacher's Manual and Detailed Solutions* book [$10.95] covering all eleven of the books. I highly recommend it to parents who are not sharp on their algebra skills.

In most cases, it is best to start with the first two books, then choose from among titles that work on topics presenting difficulties for each student. Students who generally have little problem with word problems, but who get stumped with one particular type, can skip the first two books. The first book, *How to Solve Algebra Word Problems*, walks the student through strategies to translate word problems into mathematical forms, helps them identify what the problem is asking for, and teaches them to identify what steps are needed. Students are taught to check their solutions, taking time to think about the reasonableness (or unreasonableness) of their answer. The second book, *Warm-Up*, has students practice translating word problems into math statements in various situations. For example, "When Cheryl is twice as old as she was four years ago, she will be one year younger than Bill is now." or "A room is three feet longer than it is wide. What is its area in terms of its width?"

Other titles in the series are *Ages and Coins; Mixtures* (e.g., "To have a mixture of 5% sand, 95% topsoil, how much sand must be added to twenty yards of topsoil?); *Formulas, Rectangles, D=rt;* and *Percents and Work Rates; Miscellaneous A-1; Miscellaneous B-1; Miscellaneous C-1; Fun Time, and Diophantine Problems* (such problems have only integers for answers, but might have more than one answer to a problem). Problems increase in difficulty from beginning to the end of each book, so younger students might be able to do some of the problems now and some later. Problems do not involve trigonometry or algebra higher than high school level.

The books are reproducible, with a number of problems per page. Depending upon the student, you might use one problem at a time or groups of problems; there are no set lessons.

These are great supplements, especially for those time/rate/distance problems (in *Formulas, Rectangles, D=rt*) that are a stumbling stone for so many.(S)

➲ Video Tutor, Algebra I (Video Tutor, Inc.) about $30 per tape or $150 for the set of six

This set of six videos is designed to supplement a first-year algebra course or as a refresher course. The videos vary in length from 30 to 103 minutes. They cover all first-year algebra topics including variables, equations, radicals, square roots, graphing lines, and solving quadratic equations by both factoring and using the quadratic formula.

Explanations are brief, assuming that the student has encountered instruction elsewhere. However, John Hall, the video instructor offers problem-solving tips which he has gleaned from his years of actual teaching experience. Hall does the teaching from a white board, as does Firebaugh in *The Basics of Algebra on Video Tape.* However, Hall is more expressive and lively and, consequently, more engaging to watch. (Keep in mind that Firebaugh's course is complete, while this course is for supplement or review.)

Small booklets with some practice problems (and answer keys) accompany each tape.

Video Tutor also has videos for other junior and senior high math topics with presentations similar to those in the *Algebra I* series. Titles are *Percents, Decimals, Fractions, Pre-Algebra, Basic Word Problems, Basic Number Concepts* (pre-algebra level), and *Basic Geometry.*(S)

Hands-On Help for Algebra

Many teens still need experience with concrete materials to understand mathematical concepts. Concrete materials used for math, such as *Cuisenaire® Rods, Base Ten Blocks, Mortensen* materials, and others are called manipulatives. Teens rarely need an entire program built around the use of manipulatives, yet they

often benefit from introduction of new concepts with them. For instance, factoring polynomials is much simpler when first experienced with manipulatives. Algebra programs that incorporate the use of manipulatives are *Math-U-See* and *Principles from Patterns* and *Math-U-See.* Manipulatives can also be purchased for use as supplements.

Mortensen Math has an entire strand of workbooks on algebra to use with their manipulatives. (There are five different strands in the total program: Arithmetic, Problem Solving, Measurement, Algebra, and Calculus.) *Mortensen* uses good visual/hands-on techniques for understanding algebra, which are based on simple, but powerful counting concepts and building rectangles. However, this is a supplement or an introductory program, not a complete program. For more extensive coverage of algebra course concepts, students should also work in the upper levels of the Problem Solving and Calculus strands. *Mortensen* is great on techniques which are explained well in their *Algebra Level 1 Guidebook* and other manuals, or their Introductory Video. However, the Mortensen workbooks are uneven in quality and content.

Other tools that work on the same principle are available. Nasco's *Algebra Models* is much less expensive than Mortensen products, although it is not as comprehensive. *Algebra Models* includes an instruction booklet with manipulatives that can be used to demonstrate algebraic concepts using both positive and negative numbers. In addition, a teacher presentation package is available which includes 14 blackline masters with problems, a 15-page teacher introduction, and answer key. A video introduction to *Algebra Models* is also available at no cost, if we return it within 30 days. (Otherwise, it sells for $19.95.)

Cuisenaire® Rods and *Base Ten Blocks* can be used for upper-level math concepts, but most books explaining how to use them concentrate on elementary grades. Either product could be used with Mortensen instruction manuals or ideas from *Algebra Models.* *Cuisenaire®* does not include hundreds squares found in other products, although they are necessary for working with large numbers and algebra. You can make your own hundreds squares by cutting 10 cm. x 10 cm. squares from poster or mat board.

Geometry

We have three basic directions to go with geometry. We can provide an introduction to geometry and leave it at that. We can offer a college preparatory geometry course that includes formal proofs. Or, we can choose a course that does not include formal proofs, but that still provides adequate preparation for college math.

Some secular publishers have recognized that formal proofs (proofs written in two columns of mathematical language) are the downfall of many a geometry student and have come up with alternatives that disguise proofs by asking questions that require plain English answers rather than mathematically stated proofs. While proofs themselves are helpful in logical thinking, there is no evidence that formal writing of proofs is essential to understanding and applying geometrical knowledge. (However, they really are a much more efficient way to say what you want to say in geometry!) The alternative—informal proofs—is becoming increasingly popular in textbooks. Generally, students who are mathematically-minded will prefer the conciseness of formal proofs, while students who are more language-oriented will find informal proofs more comfortable.

Geometry Resources

(Arranged in approximate order of increasing difficulty)

⊃ Key to Geometry (Key Curriculum Press) books 1-6 - $2.10 each; books 7-8 - $6.90 each; answer books - $2.40 each

No prerequisite knowledge of algebra is required. The series of eight booklets provides a basic introduction to geometry. It is not equivalent to a typical high school geometry course. It might be used as a substitute for a non-college bound student or as an introductory course for a student who needs to mature before getting into geometry. One booklet looks manageable to a student who might be overwhelmed by a two-inch-thick hardback text. However, multiply this booklet eight times and there is still a decent amount of learning taking place.

Construction with compass and straight edge, combined with inductive reasoning, are the primary learning tools. Proofs and theorems are lacking, but students can build a beginning foundation without them. The publisher is very conscientious about stating clearly that this is not a full geometry course, but schools <u>are</u> using them with students who need a simpler course. Home schoolers should be able to do the same. Just be cautious about misrepresenting it as a college prep course. (List it as Introductory Geometry on the transcript.)

The books have large print, so students go through these very quickly (ten pages a day is reasonable). They are largely self-instructional. Books One through Six have only 55 pages each, while Book Seven has 154 and Book Eight has 138. The entire course should take about twelve weeks, so you will need to do something else for the rest of the year. Also, consider using this course as a geometry supplement for Saxon's *Algebra I* and *II*.(S)

⊃ Informal Geometry (Addison-Wesley) student edition #0201-25314-3; teacher edition #0201-25315-1

Prerequisite: Algebra I. This text is easier than many others reviewed here since it does not use formal proofs. Instead, it uses language such as, "How can we know?" (informal proofs). It is similar to Houghton Mifflin's *Basic Geometry* in that it uses larger print and less work on a page (593 pages altogether), but it uses more real life applications than the Houghton Mifflin text. Purchase both the student and teacher's editions.(S)

⊃ Basic Geometry, 1995 copyright (Houghton Mifflin/McDougal Littell) student text - $40.65

Prerequisite: Algebra I. This text is a step down from traditional geometry texts since it does not place as much emphasis on proofs as do traditional texts. Theorems and proofs are covered, but they are not as intimidating here. Even though the book has 558 pages, the print is larger than many other texts, with less work on a page—two more factors that make this text easier. You need to buy a student textbook and the solution key.(S)

⊃ Informal Geometry (Merrill) student book #0675058546 - $36.92; teacher edition #0675058554 - $46.82

Prerequisite: Pre-algebra. While similar to Addison-Wesley's *Informal Geometry*, this text focuses on reaching a wider range of students. It also takes more of a discovery approach to learning. Constructions are used throughout the text as tools for discovering geometric concepts. Calculator and computer (Logo) problems are integrated throughout the text. Short chapters prevent students from feeling overwhelmed. All concepts usually taught

in traditional geometry courses, except formal proofs, are included. Buy the student book and the *Teacher Annotated Edition*.(S)

⊃ Geometry (School of Tomorrow) $450 for videos (purchase); $106.67 for computer disks; PACEs with answer keys - $64. School of Tomorrow offers two rental options: videos only ($239.80 per course, broken down into quarterly rentals of $59.95 each) or rental packages that include PACEs and Score Keys ($299.80 per course or $74.95 per quarter). Video rentals are shipped in four groups.

Geometry is one of the video-based courses developed by School of Tomorrow. It will not be computer video interactive because of the nature of the subject. Students are required to draw constructions and to learn to handle geometric equipment such as the compass, protractor, and straight edge. In the PACEs, students create their own handbook of definitions, postulates, theorems, etc. in pull-out sections in the center of each PACE. This is an excellent feature that helps students learn and remember foundational information, while also providing a handy reference tool. Geometry concepts are presented on the videos with graphics and film footage. Periodically, the video instructs students to stop and complete work in their PACEs and handbooks. There are 12 PACEs and 12 videos for the course. This is a "proofs"-based course. It teaches constructions, along with postulates and theorems, from the very beginning. Students solve problems using proofs beginning in the first PACE, although the concept is presented gradually as "explanations and reasons." Content is challenging, equivalent to average high school level geometry courses. It lacks sufficient application explanations and word problems in the early parts of the course, but adds more toward the end. To add interest, short character-trait scenarios and math facts are interspersed throughout each video.

○ **Geometry [video]** (The Teaching Company) $199.95; extra workbooks - $10 each

Four extended-play video tapes are the mainstay of this geometry course. Teacher James Noggle presents a very traditional approach to geometry using an easel and a blackboard. He begins with definitions and quickly moves into logic and proofs which he uses throughout the course. Videos contain 30 lessons. Along with the video tapes, we receive two booklets outlining each lesson and listing definitions, abbreviations, theorems, and postulates. We also get a workbook that contains both student work pages and answer key. The workbook has only 67 pages of actual problem solving, so it is not comparable to the amount of work students would do in a textbook. Workbooks are not reproducible, so you will need to buy extras for additional students. The videos cover a comprehensive geometry course including an introduction to trigonometry, but there is not enough practice for a stand-alone course. Another problem is that there is no index to easily find previously-covered concepts. Consequently, I view this as a supplement for the student using a traditional geometry text who can benefit from a teacher's presentation. The presentation is straightforward and well organized, and it also includes some practical application.(S)

○ **Discovering Geometry: An Inductive Approach, 2nd edition** (Key Curriculum Press) student book - $41.17; teacher's guide and answer key - $29.95; teacher's resource book - $49.95; quizzes, tests and exams - $59.95

Here is a truly different approach to teaching geometry. This is a complete, college-preparatory course, but it is more interesting and inviting than any other text I have seen. The first thing students encounter in the book is art—geometric art. The art leads students into their first investigations about lines and shapes. Investigations by students help them discover postulates and theorems by inductive reasoning. Many investigations involve students in activities, including making and working with models. Word problems are imaginative. Real life applications are more true-to-life than in other texts. Formal proofs are taught only in the last three chapters, after students have mastered concepts and understand relationships between theorems. (However, students are applying deductive reasoning and working with informal proofs much earlier.) The only negatives with this book are in the word problems—constant role reversal and a few others that refer to wizards and dragons. (These word problems are presented in a comical rather than serious way.) You need the hardback student text and the *Teacher's Guide and Answer Key*. The *Teacher's Guide* includes a section that will help you plan which chapters of the text to use, tailoring the course to be more academic or less, according to the needs of each student. Extra geometry investigations are included for ambitious students. A separate book of quizzes, tests, and exams is available, but it might not be worth the cost for a single student. Using the chapter reviews for testing might be sufficient.

Discovering Geometry works best when presented by a teacher or parent and when two or more students work through activities together, but it can be used by students working independently.

Geometer's Sketchpad [$169.95 for single user version] is a computer program (either Macintosh or Windows versions) that comes with a 248-page guide and reference manual. This program can be used in conjunction with *Discovering Geometry* or other geometry courses. We tried to review the Windows version and encountered quite a few problems. The program was originally designed for Macintosh, so we asked if problems were peculiar to the Windows version. The publisher tells us that they have had very few users encounter problems, and they found our experience unique. We ran out of time to pursue this and overcome our problems, although the folks at Key Curriculum seem to be extremely helpful. Consequently, all I can tell you is that this program sounds like it should be very useful, especially for situations where a group class is impossible. Students can create numerous constructions quickly on the computer and compare results, whereas it would be too time consuming to do many of them manually. This is not an easy program to use, even if it works properly. Expect to spend some time becoming familiar with it and exploring possibilities. It should be worth the effort.(SE)

○ **Geometry for Decision Making** (South-Western Educational Publishing) $57.95; teacher's edition - $92.95

I view this text as being similar to *Discovering Geometry* in topical content, yet it uses different methodology. It, too, combines inductive and deductive reasoning, but it relies much less on discovery learning through construction activities. Construction work with a compass begins in Chapter Six, and is used less extensively throughout the book. Discovery activities are included in each chapter, and often full explanation is provided with the activity. (*Discovering Geometry* does not always immediately restate discovered concepts as does this text.) This text teaches formal proofs earlier, although it also teaches informal proofs. Trigonometry is introduced at the end of the book. There is a similar amount of real life application problems. Plentiful illustrations make concepts fairly easy to understand. The format is uncluttered but has variety and color. This is actually a fairly traditional geometry course, enhanced with more activities, life application, and an easy-to-use format.

The student text contains answers to the odd-numbered problems, plus chapter tests and a cumulative review that might serve as a final test. The teacher's edition has answers overprinted on pages identical to the student text, as well as lots of extra teaching helps. Student text ISBN 0538602937; Teacher's Edition ISBN 0538602961.(S)

○ **Geometry [video course]** (Chalk Dust) $349 for complete package of 11 tapes, text, and solutions guide

Following the same format as on their *Algebra 1* and *2* courses, Chalk Dust presents geometry on 11 video tapes to be used in conjunction with the D.C. Heath text, *Geometry: An Integrated Approach*, by Larson, Boswell, and Stiff. Teacher Dana Mosely presents each lesson, following the scope and sequence of the text. Students then do the exercises for each chapter. Answers for all "Guided Practice" and mid-chapter self-test problems, plus the odd-numbered exercise, end of chapter, and cumulative review problems are at the back of the student book;

these should provide sufficient practice and evaluation problems for which we have answers. The Solutions Manual provides step-by-step solutions to the same problems. The approach aligns with the new math standards (reflecting some of the best aspects of those standards), combining conceptual learning and computational skills while teaching with both construction activity and traditional proofs. Proofs are introduced in the second chapter, then used throughout the text, although the stress on logic is not at the level we encounter in Harold Jacobs' *Geometry* text. Construction activity is used throughout the book, and some inductive methods similiar to those in *Discovering Geometry* show up in "Special Projects," "Chapter Explorations," and "Lesson Investigations" in the text. The text also features some optional computer and calculator activities. The projects, explorations, investigations, and computer and calculator activities are presented only in the text, not on the video. However, I highly recommend that students tackle as many of the projects, explorations, and investigations as they are able. A computer drawing program is necessary for the computer activities and a graphing calculator for the calculator activities. Neither is crucial to the course. The text is heavily illustrated with lots of practical application: e.g., why does a "baby gate" not have a bi-driectionally rigid framework while a bridge using a similar parallelogram structure is rigid (p. 282). Some of this carries over to the videos, but the video presentations focus primarily on key concepts and skills. Algebra is applied within geometry lessons, and some "mixed reviews" in the text offer opportunity for problem solving practice on algebra problems to help students retain skills. The video presentation by Dana Mosely is excellent. Dana uses a chalkboard, visual aids, and computer animations to present concepts as clearly as possible. While the text is fairly good on its own, its explanations of some concepts are perfunctory. Dana expands the lessons wherever necessary; for example, the book's presentation on slope is very brief, while Dana uses visual aids for a much lenghtier, more complete teaching of the topic. With the other Chalk Dust courses, the text can play a less significant role. In this course, I think students should watch the video, then go through the text lesson, picking up on some of the activities that are omitted on the tapes, then do the exercises. The course covers typical content including a brief introduction of trigonometry. The book is divided into 13 chapters with a number of sections (6 or 7) per chapter; each of these sections is presented as a video lesson to correspond to the text presentation. (The chapters are condensed onto 11 tapes instead of 13 to keep the cost down.) After lesson 13 in the text, are seven "Excursions in Geometry," extra short lessons that are optional. Most of these are very interesting and not overly challenging, so consider using them if you have time. They deal with topics such as Platonic and Archimedean solids, topology and Mobius strips, and fractal geometry.

Overall, I think this course will be great for home schoolers. It includes some of the elements I like so much from *Discovering Geometry* (application, inductive thinking, construction activity, and interesting presentation), and it can be used by students working independently (while *Discovering Geometry* really needs a teacher).(S)

⮑ Geometry For All Practical Purposes [second edition] by Harold R. Jacobs (W.H. Freeman) $42.95; instructor's guide - $15.95

Jacobs has managed to write a user-friendly geometry text that is heavy on logic, deductive reasoning, and proofs. He uses entertaining illustrations (including cartoons), as well as practical application explanations and engaging word problems.

He spends the entire first unit (nine chapters) on logic. Many people cite the value of geometry as being the development of logical thinking skills. Jacobs takes this idea seriously, ensuring that students are truly tuned in to logical thinking before tackling geometry topics. Given the foundation in logic, students then immediately begin work with proofs, which continues throughout the text. Topic arrangement is different than I have seen in most texts. For instance, work with circles follows introductory lessons on trigonometry. (The trigonometry is introduced as a natural progression in the study of triangles, so this is not really an outlandish arrangement.) Even if the arrangement is unusual, there is a clear continuity to topics, building one upon another.

Construction activities (using straight edge and compass) are very minimal. Because of this and the emphasis on logic, I recommend this text for abstract thinkers rather than hands-on learners. Very reasonably-priced instructor's guide and test masters are also available.(S)

⮑ Advanced Mathematics, second edition (Saxon) home study kit - $53.95; solutions manual - $25

This highly recommended text is one of the easiest to work with, as are other Saxon math books. This is designed to be a one-year course, although it could easily be spread out longer if desired. Saxon sells a package to home educators containing a teacher's edition (identical to student text, but with the answer key in the back) and tests. A Solutions Manual is also available. Geometric proofs are taught, along with trigonometry, logarithms, infinite series, conic sections, matrices, and determinants. This text moves even more into the theoretical math realm than do earlier Saxon texts. By the time students complete Saxon's *Advanced Mathematics*, they should be on a par with students who have completed pre-calculus work. The publisher tells me that a third edition is due in 1998. Geometry instruction will be improved, and there will be new lessons on functions, graphs of functions, statistics, and use of a graphing calculator.(SE)

⮑ Geometry (Bob Jones University Press) $28; teacher's edition - $39; test packet - $7; test packet answer key -$4

This text is recommended by BJUP only for students whose parents have a knowledge of geometry. They say, "This teacher's manual assumes that the person teaching geometry has been trained in mathematics. If you have not been, you will need to work diligently to develop the confidence you need to stimulate enthusiasm for the subject" (Teacher's Edition, p. iv). In spite of that warning, I think that a number of home schooling families can manage to tackle this course. However, it would be wise to have someone knowledgeable to consult if you hit a roadblock. This text has a traditional rules-oriented presentation of formal proofs, with strong emphasis on development of deductive thinking skills and logic which continues throughout the text. Life applications are included throughout the text. Constructions are taught beginning in Chapter Four, and are used frequently throughout the lessons. However, when they are introduced, connections are rarely made to geometric principles that each construction demonstrates. (This deficiency seems to make the course far less interesting than those that make those connections.) Topic coverage is similar to other challenging geometry courses that include an introduction to trigonometry. The final chapter also covers graphing of figures such as parabolas and ellipses, typically found in Algebra II courses. However, students need not complete the last two chapters of this book in geometry since the topics will be covered again in Algebra II. Exercises cover only topics taught within each section, and chapter reviews cover only material from each chapter. A test packet includes chapter tests, two midterms, and two final exams, which will be more comprehensive. You might want to create more cumulative review by selecting problems from earlier chapters for review. Purchase both student and teacher's editions. The teacher's edition contains the lesson presentation ideas with even-numbered problem answers first, followed by student pages with some answers overprinted in red and odd-numbered problem answers at the back. There is also a section called "Lab Experiments," which describes rather-involved, hands-on activities that we can use if we so desire.

⊃ Plane Geometry and Analytical Geometry (A Beka)

A Beka offers two geometry texts. *Plane Geometry* [$16.50], a one-year course, uses traditional methods, including formal proofs. The emphasis is on logical, systematic thinking skills. The course is primarily theoretical rather than practical. (An example of a more practical course would be *Discovering Geometry*.) Order the student text and the solution key, which demonstrates solutions to problems. A *Student Test Booklet* and *Student Quiz Booklet* are also available. This text is equivalent to the typical high school geometry course.

Analytical Geometry [$14.25] can be either a semester or one-year course. The latter book is recommended only for parents with good math knowledge and students who plan to major in math-related fields. (A Beka recommends using *Analytical Geometry* one semester and their *Trigonometry with Tables* the other semester.) A solution key for selected problems is available as well as a student test/quiz booklet.

Geometry Supplements

⊃ Geometric Constructions by Daniel, Sarah, and Kathleen Julicher (Castle Heights Press) $9.95

This inexpensive little book by homeschooled kids can supplement any geometry course after students have learned some construction techniques. Techniques required are all demonstrated at the front of the book. There are eight story problems which are quite lengthy—about a page each, plus an accompanying map on which the student works through the various constructions to solve the problem. For example, in problem 3, "You are the captain of the USS Swift Shark, a submarine. While en route to the secret submarine base, your ship's computer fails and deletes the secret location of the base. You must get there with critical information before the enemy destroys Rockcliff Harbor. The only way there is by following a set of coded instructions sent from the base...." By constructing an angle bisector, perpendiculars, a circle, and a tangent we locate the secret base on the map. Only a straight edge and compass are required. Art work is not professional, yet it should appeal to most teens. An answer key is included.

⊃ Geometry and Trigonometry for Calculus - A Self-Teaching Guide by Peter H. Selby (John Wiley and Sons) $17.95

If you have decided to skip a formal geometry course for your student, opting instead for a math program that skips formal proofs and constructions, this text can be very helpful as a reference text for your student. Provided that the student has complete Algebra II (such as Saxon's) and is planning to go on through calculus, it will serve as a complete review of plane and analytic geometry as well as trigonometry and trigonometric analysis. Straightforward in its approach, this programmed study systematically deals with the subject in such a way that students can easily find the areas where they need further study. The author follows each principle with easy-to-follow examples. Frequent reviews, practice exercises, and self-tests reinforce the learned material. Nonetheless, this text was written for adults as a college reference text and will probably be too tedious to be used as the primary high school geometry course of study.(S)

⊃ Geometry Tutorial [on-line class] Fritz Heinrichs (Escondido Tutorial Service) $105

Fritz Hinrichs offers this geometry tutorial that serves as an excellent adjunct to Saxon's high school math series which is deficient in geometry. The tutorial uses Euclid's *Elements* and the *Geometer's Sketchpad* software (Key Curriculum Press). It emphasizes geometric proofs and an appreciation of the historical development of mathematics as well as its influence on Western philosophy. Students use the software to create and manipulate geometric constructions on the computer. The class is presented over the internet. Check with ETS for requirements to participate.

⊃ Scratch Your Brain Where It Itches, Book E-1 Geometry (Critical Thinking Books and Software) $9.95

The subtitle of the "Scratch Your Brain" series is "Math Games, Tricks and Quick Activities." This one tackles geometry with visual puzzles, hands-on activities, and inductive learning. Many of the activities are very similar to those used in the *Discovering Geometry* textbook; these are the type of activities that make that text so effective. A number of the activities suggest that we can use geometry software if we choose, but all can be done with a straight edge and compass. Activity pages are reproducible and the answer key is at the back of the book. This is a good supplement for a traditional geometry program. Pull out the inductive learning activities before those concepts are actually taught in your text so that students really do discover the principles on their own.(S)

➲ **UCSMP Geometry** ScottForesman student text - $41.55; student text with TI-30 Challenger Calculator - $59.10; teacher's edition - $56.07; solution manual - $25.04

The UCSMP series probably reflects the NCTM Standards better than any other high school math series. Algebra is integrated throughout the course. Technological tools are vital to the course. Real world applications show students why they need to learn geometry. And, lessons are designed to motivate learners with different interests and abilities. As you might imagine, the result is a 900+ page text. While the text covers topics found in other geometry courses (including a brief introduction to trigonometry), it tackles them in a different sequence and, frequently, with different methods.

Students must use a scientific calculator with this course. A graphing calculator and geometric drawing programs for the computer are highly recommended—some lessons seem to rely on the use of drawing programs! Recommended drawing programs are *GeoExplorer* (ScottForesman), *The Geometric Supposer, Geometer's Sketchpad* (Key Curriculum Press), *Cabri,* and *Geodraw*. The first three are available for both Macintosh and IBM compatible platforms, while the last two are only for Macintosh and IBM compatibles respectively. (Lessons are keyed to the *GeoExplorer.*) Students do learn how to do traditional constructions with compass and straight edge as well as how to use a protractor, but such constructions and drawings take a back seat to learning through study and the application of logic combined with the use of electronic tools. (Students who have used previous UCSMP texts will have already used compass and straight edge constructions.) The course also introduces logical symbols early on and teaches two-column proofs. This is in keeping with the NCTM Standards that stress mathematical thinking and the importance of student familiarity with technology.

The teacher's edition (two volumes) suggests schedules for completing each chapter for either a "full course" or "minimal course" approach. This seems to translate into simply taking more days to finish each chapter, with a comment to the effect that slower students will not finish all chapters. However, some of the most important concepts, such as triangle similarity and properties of circles are in the last two chapters. Consequently, it seems to me that all students should complete the text, although parents might decide that there are sections within some chapters that they might skip.

Questions at the end of each section include review questions on previous lesson material. End of chapter "Progress Self-Tests" and "Chapter Reviews" cover preceding lessons within that chapter. End of chapter summaries highlight key points. Student books feature an appendix with theorems, postulates, formulas, glossary, selected answers to a few problems from each lesson, all answers to Progress Self-Tests, and answers to odd-numbered Chapter Review problems. The teacher's edition includes slightly reduced reproductions of student pages surrounded by teaching information and tips. Answers are overprinted in red on student pages. The teacher's edition is essential. An Assessment Sourcebook [$66.76] offers multiple forms of tests, but I suspect that most home educators will use Chapter Reviews as their primary means of assessment. The So-

lution Manual might be useful for more complete explanations of answers.

The course is not intended for independent study; instruction is necessary. Also, since the text was designed for classroom use, some activities are suggested for cooperative groups. Decide which of these are essential and a parent can be the other half of a "group" if necessary.

While this course is very comprehensive, that feature also means that it will be challenging to cover it all. And you might not wish to. For example, when exploring a particular characteristic of triangles, students are taught the same concept using computer drawing program, construction tools, and drawing tools (protractor). While all of this is useful, you might not have the equipment and time to cover all three methods. Also, optional activities are suggested in the teacher's edition, and you can use discretion as to which of these to use.

My biggest concern is practicality because of the time required to figure out which parts of lessons to use as well as for lesson presentation itself. Those looking for a text reflecting the NCTM standards and who have the time to teach it properly should find this an excellent course.(S)

Hands-On Help for Geometry

Drawing tools such as protractors and compasses incorporate hands-on work into most geometry courses. Because of this, many hands-on learners prefer geometry over algebra and other math courses. Take advantage of this natural preference to use drawing as a learning tool.

Some students will appreciate three-dimensional, visualization tools such as the *D-Stix* sets from Nasco. *Mira™* is an interesting tool that acts somewhat like a mirror. It can be used for introduction of geometric concepts or for higher level study with the supplementary books *Mira Math Activities for Elementary Schools* (for grades 3-8) or *Mira Math Activities for High School*. Still more advanced activities using the *Mira* are in *Geometry: Constructions and Transformations* by Iris M. Dayoub and Johnny W. Lott. (The *Mira* tool and books are available from Nasco.) The *Image Reflector™* [$3.95] from Cuisenaire is almost identical to *Mira*. Cuisenaire offers the companion book *Geometric Constructions and Investigations with a Mira* [$14.95].

Trigonometry and Higher Math Recommendations

(Arranged in approximate order of increasing difficulty)

➲ **Trigonometry with Tables** (A Beka) $14.25

This book is a one-semester course that can be combined with A Beka's *Analytical Geometry* for a full-year math course. A solution key (for selected problems), answer key, test/quiz booklet, and teacher guide/curriculum are available. Recommended only for parents with an excellent knowledge of trigonometry.

⮩ Trigonometry: A Graphing Approach (Chalk Dust) $314 for prepaid orders for complete course with books; tapes $25 each; text - $64; solution guide -$20

Trigonometry: A Graphing Approach is a combination text book and video course that covers both trigonometry, and some analytic geometry. This is a well thought out course, and both the coverage and quality of the materials is very high. The videos are similar in quality to the other Chalk Dust courses. The book is published by D. C. Heath and Co., who also produces a number of supplements for the course. Among them are the *Study And Solutions Guide* which contains worked out solutions to the odd numbered problems, a valuable resource when parents are not very familiar with the subject; *Instructor's Guide; Computerized Testing Software*; and preprinted tests. You probably will not need these last three items, but D.C. Heath offers one more you might consider. *Graphing Technology Guide* (item #0-669-34226-2) contains instructions on how to use several brands of graphing calculators. This highlights one of the unique aspects of the course. It emphasizes the use of graphing calculators to demonstrate various equations. Graphing calculators are referenced throughout the text and demonstrated throughout the video as well. Although these calculators can be somewhat expensive, they can be worth their weight in gold in demonstrating equations. Although a computer screen would be better in general for graphing equations due to its higher resolution, they are obviously more expensive and less portable. (Heath also offers inexpensive graphing software for both IBM PC and Macintosh computers called *BestGrapher,* which I have not reviewed. However, there are many programs available for graphing for both computers if that one is not to your liking.)

The videos are simple but well done. They are just a simple camera shot of an instructor going over the material, working out problems and graphing. The video also has shots of a calculator displaying the graphs. Although useful to back up what the student is seeing on his or her own calculator, some high quality computer graphics would be an improvement. The instructor is good at explaining, and fairly animated, so he keeps the subject matter interesting; more sophisticated viewers might long for a more multi-media presentation, however.

The textbook is very professionally produced, well-organized with excellent text and pictures and odd-numbered answers to problems in the back. It has problem sets at the end of each section and chapter, as well as cumulative tests for several chapters.

Although I still prefer the Saxon program's constant review, this book is an excellent traditional textbook.[Michael Courtney]

⮩ Advanced Math (Bob Jones University Press) $20; teacher's edition - $39

This text should be used after a second year algebra course. It covers trigonometry, advanced algebra, and pre-calculus. As with other BJUP math texts, this is designed for classroom use by a teacher familiar with math concepts.

⮩ Advanced Mathematical Concepts (Merrill) student edition #0028243145 - $45; teacher edition #0028243153 - $59.28. This is a topical course, rather than a sequential one. It is

organized into five units: 1) Relations, Functions, and Graphs; 2) Trigonometry; 3) Advanced Functions and Graphing; 4) Discrete Mathematics; and 5) Introduction to Calculus. It also has up-to-date instruction in the use of calculators. Purchase the student edition and the *Teacher's Guide and Solutions Manual*.(S)

⮩ Advanced Mathematics (Saxon)

See description under Geometry above.

⮩ Advanced Mathematics: Precalculus Course with Discrete Mathematics and Data Analysis, ©1994 (Houghton Mifflin/McDougal Littell) $48.99

This text covers precalculus, plus some probability and statistics topics usually covered in calculus. Use of the calculator and computer are strongly recommended. Purchase the student's edition and the teacher's manual which contains solutions.(S)

⮩ Functions/Trigonometry (Alpha Omega)

This LifePac course was designed for independent work. While I have not reviewed this course, I have heard from a number of home educators that LifePac high school math courses are sometimes difficult to understand. I suggest purchasing one LifePac to try before buying the entire course.

⮩ Prof. E. McSquared's Expanded Intergalactic Version! Calculus Primer by Swann and Johnson (Everyday Learning Corporation) $20

This introduction to calculus covers some of what is taught in Saxon's *Advanced Mathematics* and other precalculus courses, but it goes further into functions than they do. The major sections of the book are Functions, Limits, and Derivatives—all calculus fundamentals. The book's format is quite different from anything else as you might guess from the title. Lively cartoons illustrate the principles in a creative and humorous way. Students who have completed three years of high school math (equivalent to two years of algebra and one of geometry) can use this as an introduction to calculus to demystify the subject. The book also serves as a calculus text for non-math/science students who still want to know something about the subject. Instruction, exercises, answers, selected solutions, and extra mathematical "excursions" are all included in the single volume. The approach is very user-friendly—ideal for self-directed learners.

Check out the *Graphing Calculator Lab Manual* (Everyday Learning Corporation) reviewed below. It is recommended for use along with this "text."(S)[Valerie Thorpe/C.D.]

⮩ Precalculus With Limits [video course] (Chalk Dust) $564

This course consists of 20 VHS tapes, a textbook, solutions manual, and a text for learning how to use a graphing calculator. There are twice as many tapes for this course as for most other Chalk Dust courses because of the complexity of the material. Dana Mosely, the video teacher, follows the same format as in the other courses, following along with lessons in the text, expanding explanations and working out sample problems. The text used is *Precalculus With Limits, A Graphing Approach*, 2nd edition by Larson, Hostetler, and Edwards. It is a one-semester course at the college level. There are eighty lessons prepared, but due to the fact that some lessons are somewhat longer (with lessons ranging in length from 20 to almost 80 minutes) and some are more challenging, realistically count on 95-100 lessons for the average student. If you add days for homework, review, tests, and such, you should consider completing this course in two semesters which makes more sense for the typical student.

Due to the video format, time for student questions isn't built into the course. Students should stop and review the presentation and consult the book when they have trouble with a concept. Technical support is also available by phone if students get stuck. To think concepts through, students really do need to stop the video occasionally and try to solve example problems. For this reason, consider that some sessions might take up to double the lecture time to complete. Students then work through problems in the text. Answers to odd-numbered problems are at the back of the text, and solutions to odd-numbered problems are in the solutions manual. Completing only odd-numbered problems (approx. 45-65 problems per lesson for which answers and solutions are available) should be sufficient practice for most students. Be sure to also plan in "lesson time" for students to check the problems and redo incorrect answers. Answers to all test problems (even and odd) for all chapters and cumulative tests are in the student solutions manual.

A graphing calculator is both necessary and standard equipment to complete this course, and the recommended graphing calculators are the Texas Instruments TI-82 or the TI-83. (Appendix B shows step-by-step instructions for different types of graphs for 13 different calculators including the TI-85, TI-92, and others.) Parents educated before the "new math" may find the idea of utilizing graphing calculators to learn calculus distasteful; however, success with calculus and physics in college does require adeptness in the use of graphing calculators. In fact, many colleges, including community colleges, require a one-unit computer class that is designed to coincide with each specific advanced math course in addition to the use of graphing calculators to solve upper level math. As it happens, in our own community college district, all students of college algebra and advanced math courses are required to become proficient in the TI-85 scientific graphing calculator, and thus this study was reviewed using the TI-85 to see if it was feasible to use a graphing calculator other than the primary ones recommended. Chalkdust makes use of a graphing technology guide explaining how to use the differrent models of calculators from Texas Instruments, Casio, Sharp and Hewlett Packard. Of course, each calculator manufacturer also provides its own guidebook. Obviously it would be easiest to just use the recommended calculators; however, the cost of these particular calculators (approximately $80) makes one think twice about whether to purchase a calculator that will be used in subsequent classes or a calculator which might be used only for one year. It would be wise to consult with math departments of the colleges you are considering before making a purchase.

It is recommended that if your student does not have experience in the use of graphing calculators that he become acquainted with its use using the manufacturer's guide before he takes the course. After two weeks of daily drills, the student should have a working knowledge of the calculator enough to begin the course, but it will be very challenging, indeed, and it is also recommended that he have access to a user of the same model to assist him if he runs into basic problems.

Following some very good review lessons, this course covers functions and their graphs (including exponential, logarithmic, and trigonometric functions); analytic trigonometry; solving systems of equations and inequalities; matrices and determinants; sequences, probability and statistics; two- and three-dimensional analytic geometry; limits and introduction to calculus. A highlight of this book is that problems at the end of each chapter provide both business and scientific applications which is often lacking in other texts. This feature makes the course practical and gives vision to the students to keep them going in what could be a character-challenging subject.

The video course is thorough, well-prepared, and well-presented. It will require students to be conscientious and self-motivated, but that should not be a problem for most students who have advanced to this level in math while home schooling. This course will most certainly prepare any student to take calculus for math/science majors at the college level. A student should not consider taking an "AP" high school calculus course following this but a college level calculus course.[Diane Eastman/C.D.](S)

⮑ Pre-Calculus Mathematics (Merrill) student book #0675049784 - $43.31; Teacher Guide and Solution Manual #0675049792 - $25.19

This is Merrill's more challenging precalculus course. The publisher says that the sequence is very similar to that of college calculus courses. It covers advanced algebra and trigonometry, second-degree relations, transcendental functions, vectors, matrices, analytic geometry, and an introduction to limits, derivatives, and integrals. Applications are included, so the course is not just theory. Purchase the student edition and the *Teacher Guide and Solutions Manual.*

Calculus I should be available Fall of 1998.(S)

⮑ Calculus with Trigonometry and Analytic Geometry by John Saxon and Frank Wang (Saxon) home study kit - $67; solution manual - $25

Following the incremental method used in previous books, many students can learn calculus on their own. This is a challenging course, comparable to other Advanced Placement courses; students should be able to pass the AP test or the CLEP test after completing this course. At the beginning of the course, students review mathematical concepts required for calculus. They should have already completed *Algebra 1, Algebra 2*, and *Advanced Mathematics* in the Saxon series or through precalculus in other texts. Instruction on new concepts begins with applications or conceptual explanations and ends with proofs, the opposite of the approach used in some other calculus books. Numerous applications in physics, chemistry, engineering, and business are used throughout the text. Explanations are easy to understand, so most students should be able to work independently. However, they should have someone they can consult in case they encounter a concept that they have trouble understanding. Another alternative is to pick up another calculus text for comparison. Try a used book store or other inexpensive source. It is a good idea to purchase the *Solution Manual* to have handy in case a student is stumped by occasional problems.

Each new concept is presented in increments, then reviewed in later lessons. Each lesson also includes constant review of previously learned concepts, which means that there is usually space for only a minimal amount of practice with the new concept within that lesson. This should not be a major problem since concepts are reviewed and expanded upon in later lessons. Since concepts are often spread across a number of non-sequential lessons, it can sometimes be difficult to review or even locate a particular topic, although the index will usually help us locate the range of pages to search. While any student who has mastered *Advanced Mathematics* should be able to use this text, those who are planning to major in mathematics might prefer or benefit more from a calculus course which is more theory-based. For future engineers or others who will use calculus in applications, this should be a great option. There appear to be only a few topics missing from this course that are typically covered in first-year college calculus courses: partial derivatives, infinite series, and solid geometry. These topics might be picked up in a future class, but it might be wise to cover them from that alternate textbook if students plan to take the AP and skip that first college course.

The student text and answer key to "homework" problems are packaged together for home educators at the same price as the student book by itself. The *Solution Manual* is extra.(S)[Michael Courtney/C.D.]

➲ Calculus The Easy Way, third edition (Barron's) $12.95

Calculus is taught through a fantasy story—a unique and engaging approach. All math should be this fun! Practice exercises, tests, and answers are included in one book. This is not as comprehensive as other calculus books, but any high school student who gets this far is already ahead. Highly recommended as an introduction, supplement or a course for "fun."(S)

Supplements for Advanced Math

➲ Graphing Calculator Lab Manual (Everyday Learning Corporation) $16.95

Once you get past Algebra II (and even in some Algebra II classes), a graphing calculator is extremely valuable, if not required. Graphing calculators differ from scientific calculators because they display graphs of functions on their miniature screens and they can be programmed. Such calculators come with their own instructions which are essential to even figure out basic operations. However, anyone who plans to use one of these calculators should have more practice and familiarity with them. Everyday Learning Corporation offers this manual to familiarize students with the Casio 7700G or TI-81 or TI-82 calculators and their use in precalculus. The book is printed in a "reversible format"—start from one side of the book for the Casio lessons, or flip the book over and start from the other end for the Texas Instruments lessons. The book can be used with any precalculus course that does not already include significant work with a graphing calculator (e.g., *Prof. E. McSquared's Expanded Inter-*

galactic Version! Calculus Primer), and I recommend it particularly to those who will be continuing on to calculus. Each lesson poses a situation, then walks through the steps for using the calculator. This is followed by additional problems for students to attempt on their own. Solutions are at the end of the section for each calculator.(S)

➲ The Trig Explorer [CD-ROM for IBM compatible or Macintosh computers] (Cognitive Technologies Corporation) $49.95 for progam and workbook; CD-ROM alone - $39.95

The Trig Explorer is a CD-ROM software supplement to most trigonometry courses. The installation of the Windows version, which also runs under Windows 95 and includes an uninstallation program, went smoothly. The program uses a number of animation and sound sequences for the computer illustrations that require Apple Computer's Video for Windows; the installation program automatically installed the latest version and deleted older versions.

The animation sequences often include narration. The narration does more than simply read the text printed on the screen, so it is a help. The program starts up with a well done opening animation sequence, which you can thankfully skip over once you've seen it. The program uses a number of examples, both new and familiar, to illustrate trigonometry. Familiar ones include latitude and longitude on the earth's surface; less familiar ones would the technique Eratosthenes used to measure the circumference of the earth back in the third century B.C.

There were a number of small glitches in the program. None were major, but some of the animation sequences did not work as obviously intended. Another minor problem was inconsistency in the use of significant digits in calculations. For instance, Eratosthenes' technique to measure the earth's circumference relied on knowing how far apart two cities were. This was measured by foot, and found to be 5,000 stadia. This number is obviously approximate, even to Eratosthenes, yet subsequent calculations treat it as a number good to the nearest stadia. It is remarkable that even with such primitive methods, Eratosthenes was able to arrive at the correct circumference to within 15% of the current scientific value. (Note: the manual addresses this issue, mentioning an alternative historical viewpoint.)

The program has exercises to complete which, using the computer's capabilities, vary from session to session. The program does not ever say "wrong" if you enter an incorrect answer but does print a large "right" for correct ones. Incorrect answers have the correct answer shown worked out.

The program is, in general, well done and well executed with only a few minor annoyances. The user interface is not standard windows fare but was fairly simple to follow. It took me a while to figure out how to end the program, and I eventually found it in with a control panel for settings for sound and music. The program can play music in the background while you work, which some will like and others not. It, like many programs, does not transition well between music sequences, with sudden starting and stopping of the music, especially when there is a sound sequence that goes with the current lesson. The "smoothness" of the music will depend greatly upon your system, but turn it off if it's a problem. Turning off the music also increases the program's speed.

Overall, the program is a positive addition to a trigonometry course, allowing the student to study some examples and work out additional problems that differ from the way his own book handles the subject.[Michael Courtney]

The program also comes bundled with a home school workbook (which the publisher tells me was previously considered the teacher's manual). Assuming this is the same book as before, I suggest getting the bundle rather than the CD-ROM on its own.(S)

Consumer, Business, and Career Math

Some students are not going to study algebra or geometry at home. Whether it is because they do not plan to attend college or other reasons is not important. Consumer, survival, career, or business math are all options worth considering. Business math texts are generally written for college classes, so check a college bookstore for options. Also, some high school and college correspondence courses include business math in their offerings.

➲ Applications of Mathematics (Merrill) student book #0675057175 - $38.55; teacher edition #0675057183 - $44.95

High school students who have a shaky math background would do better to use this text than to jump into algebra. This text is similar to consumer math texts in that it covers many basic math applications such as interpreting transit system schedules and tax tables, applying percentage to sales, and using measurements. Most of the book would be repetitious for students who learned seventh and eighth grade math. It begins to stretch to new concepts in some of the geometry lessons, some of the work with graphs, probability, statistics (depending upon which curriculum has been used), patterns, and functions (very simple), and plotting on the coordinate plane. Algebra is introduced as solving open sentences—most pre-algebra students will have already covered this material. This is definitely remedial level.

Students who need concrete applications for understanding will find plenty of real-life situations used as the foundations for each lesson. Each new topic is introduced with an application situation. Examples and instruction follow, then students do the exercises. Exercises include computation, word, and mental math problems. Both chapter and cumulative reviews are included at the end of each chapter along with a chapter test. (Answers are in the Teacher Annotated Edition.) A Basic Skills Appendix, forty-one pages long, explains and provides review exercises for skills that should have been mastered, such as place value, estimation, division, decimal operations, factoring, and fractions. Students who have not learned these concepts must do so before they can go on. After completing the book, students might be able to go on to algebra. Some students will need to pursue a more practical math education by using texts such as *Ca-*

reer Mathematics (published by Houghton Mifflin) or one of the many business or practical math texts from other publishers.

The Teacher Annotated Edition contains answer keys, teaching information, and a copy of the student text with answers.(S)

➲ Applied Mathematics (A Beka) $17.50; solution key - $34.65; test/quiz book - $7.95; text/quiz key - $8.95

This new A Beka math text is a little more challenging than A Beka's *Consumer Mathematics*. It covers personal finances, bookkeeping and accounting, business formulas, investments, taxes, and banking. Concepts from arithmetic, algebra, and geometry are incorporated into problem solving strategies, although not at a deep level. The student edition and solution key are the most useful components, although a teacher's edition and test booklet are also available. The text can be used as either a one-semester or full-year course. Recommended for grades 10-12. (A Beka recommends their *Using the Personal Computer* text as a second-semester course.)

➲ Career Mathematics, ©1989 (Houghton Mifflin/McDougal Littell) $39.03

Prerequisite: Algebra I or introductory algebra. This is a challenging text based entirely on applications. Part One reviews measurements, fractions, decimals, and percent. Part Two applies algebra to such topics as ratios and proportions, electrical and horsepower formulas, and begins working with geometry, while teaching about machines, mechanical advantage, gears and pulleys, car transmissions, etc. Part Three covers plane and solid geometry in construction, machinery, and manufacturing operations. Part Four provides study through occupational simulations of building a house and publishing a book. Part Five examines trigonometry and statistics through topics such as navigation, data analysis, and graphing. A parent using this text should have some familiarity with geometry since the instruction provided is rather scanty. It is helpful, but not necessary, for students to take a geometry course first, but an introductory course such as *Key to Geometry* would be ideal.

➲ Consumer Math (Bob Jones University Press) $28; teacher's edition - $39; student activity book - $12; activity book teacher edition - $16; test packet - $7; test answer key -$4

Listed as an alternative to Algebra at ninth grade level, this text provides a general review of math and basic algebra (covered in pre-algebra courses) in addition to practical life applications of mathematics such as doing taxes, budgeting, buying a house, etc. Purchase both student and teacher editions.

➲ Consumer Mathematics (A Beka) $14.60

This text is recommended for non college-bound students. Purchase student and teacher editions. A *Skill Workbook* is also available. This is a very practical text, appropriate for any level. It covers topics similar to *Essential Mathematics* above. (A revised edition is due out in 1998.)

➲ Mathematics for Everyday Living series (Meridian Creative Group) $19.95 each; $17 each when 6 or more are purchased; $3.50 for solutions manual for each book

A series of eight workbooks covers some very practical aspects of consumer math. The beauty of this series is that you can focus on particular areas without having to purchase a comprehensive course. Titles in the series all stand alone and vary in level of difficulty, reflecting the more complex nature of some of the topics. Titles all begin identically as *The Mathematics of...*, with the eight completions of the titles being *Buying, Saving, Borrowing, Insurance, Taxes, Investment, Statistics*, and *Inflation and Depreciation*. As you would expect, lessons draw heavily upon practical application and word problems. Reflecting a higher level of mathematical thinking than we find in some other consumer math books, this series includes formulas that apply to the various applications. Even though some of the topics are covered within other basic math texts, this series goes beyond others in scope and detail. For example, the first book, *Buying*, is divided into five sections: Unit Prices, Markup, Discounts, Utility Bills, and Spotlight on the Pharmacist. The first three sections cover topics which students have likely encountered (or are likely to) in junior high math texts, but the extensive use of formulas will probably be less familiar. The discussion of utility bills includes very detailed lessons about short and long-distance telephone carriers and rate computation. "Spotlight on the Pharmacist" begins with an overview of that career, then continues with practical math applications a pharmacist will probably encounter. *The Mathematics of Investment,* the other title from the series which I reviewed, is a primer for investing in stocks, bonds, and mutual funds suitable even for adults. It spotlights "Financial Management" as a career in the last section. In all books, solutions to "Try One!" exercises and odd-numbered problems are included in the workbook. The Solutions Guide for each book covers all the problems. Students can work through these books independently, and they should be suitable for both junior and senior high students as long as they are already familiar with simple formulas and how to manipulate numbers/letters on both sides of an equation. The only drawback to these books is the cost, although we do get a discount if we purchase six or more volumes.(S)

➲ For All Practical Purposes: Introduction to Contemporary Mathematics [Second Edition] (W.H. Freeman and Co.) $59.95

This college level text, designed to meet the new standards, might be used by home schoolers either in conjunction with or following a second-year algebra course. The emphasis throughout is the practical usage of math, but at higher levels than is covered in other books reviewed here such as *Career Mathematics.* Algebra and geometry topics are developed through applications—e.g., historical anecdotes, examples, and real world problems. Answers to odd-numbered problems are in the back of the book. The instructor's guide contains teaching strategies and other teaching helps, as well as answers to even-numbered problems.(S)

Remedial Math

There are a number of options for remediating poor math skills. We can always choose a lower level text and have our child review areas of weakness, speeding through until they are up to level. However, some students either are far behind or simply unable to complete typical high school level math, so we need to consider other solutions. Programs such as *Mastering Mathematics* or *Developmental Mathematics* (reviewed in the *Elementary* volume of this book) can be used to cover basic math topics from the elementary grades without grade level stigma attached to the books. The *Key to...* series of books on fractions, decimals, percents, geometry, and algebra also can be very useful. The *Key to...* books use large print and an uncluttered format, incorporating drawing and visual helps for the learner who has trouble with abstract presentations. The geometry course is strictly introductory, and remedial students might be able to use only part of the algebra series, but both are options used by other schools for students who cannot complete standard courses.

Some resources have been designed expressly for adult learners or teens who are lacking functional math skills.

➲ Number Sense (Contemporary Books, Inc.) $7.66 each

For grades 4 and up. This is a series of ten, sixty-four page workbooks designed for remedial, special, and adult education. (Parents lacking the basics can go back and learn through these books.) Instruction is brief and clear, and lessons are presented in a highly visual format. When a more thorough introduction, alternative presentation, or manipulative activity is needed, the *Teacher's Resource Guide* (covering all books) is very useful. Topics covered include whole numbers (addition, subtraction, multiplication, division), decimals, fractions, and ratios/proportions/percents. Relevant life-skills applications are presented in each lesson. This is not a complete program like A Beka or BJUP that would be used to begin instructing younger children. Some concepts are not taught directly—I cannot find where measurement or money are ever taught specifically (see *Real Numbers* books for help with these topics), although both are incorporated into word problems. This series could work well with children who have delayed beginning formal academics until they are older or with children who have a poor math background and need to review. They can move very quickly through these books, covering most of the basic topics that are learned in first through sixth grades. Diagnostic placement and mastery tests are available, as well as a separate answer key. Students can work independently unless they need further instruction on a concept.(S)

➲ Real Numbers: Developing Thinking Skills in Math (Contemporary Books, Inc.) $8.86 each

This series has six titles: *Estimation 1: Whole Numbers and Decimals; Estimation 2: Fractions and Percents; Tables, Graphs and Data Interpretation; Measurement; Algebra Basics;* and *Geometry Basics*. These eighty-page books cover topics quickly, but they use illustrations and drawing activities throughout to aid visual and kinesthetic learners who struggle with the abstract presentations of most math textbooks. Abundant life applications demonstrate the purpose of learning the concepts. What is lacking are explanations of mathematical logic. For instance, formulas for solid geometry volume are given, but explanations of why those formulas work are not. This is not to be taken as a negative comment. Because many remedial students just do not have the time or capacity to work through the logic, it might be a good choice to present information in this way. These books also lack the depth of typical course content in all areas. I can see these books being most useful for the student who has been removed from school in the middle of high school and who has been failing math courses for a few years. They will help that student become mathematically literate, but will not equip him for college. Answers are in the back of the book and there is no teacher's guide since they are designed for independent work.(S)

⮑ Number Power (Contemporary Books, Inc.) $11.20 each

This series of eight books designed for older learners moves beyond the level of *Real Numbers*, with the goal of equipping students to pass the GED examination. The first and second books cover addition, subtraction, multiplication, division, fractions, decimals, and percents. The third and fourth books cover algebra and geometry respectively. Book Five teaches graphs, tables, schedules, and maps. Book Six concentrates on word problems, applying all previously learned math skills. Book Seven is entitled *Problem Solving and Test-Taking Strategies*. The last book assumes that these students will probably be weak in calculation skills, so it teaches the use of calculators. Each workbook is self-contained, including both instruction and practice, with answers in the back.(S)

Language Arts

Junior High Remediation

By junior high, we hope that our children are reading well and have already mastered basic composition and grammar skills. Unfortunately, these are areas in which our students sometimes fall short, either because of learning difficulties, lack of cooperation on the part of our children, or neglect on our part. It really is necessary that reading and writing skills be at least at their current grade level before students advance to high school work, otherwise they will not be equipped with the tools of learning necessary for further progress. If any of these areas pose problems at junior high level, NOW is the time to correct them.

Remedial Reading

For several reasons, junior high students might still have a deficiency in reading skills. Many of us are in situations where we have hoped that our child would outgrow his problems as he matured. Sometimes, the problems persist, and both we and our child have become very discouraged. If our child still has reading problems at junior high level, <u>we might need a professional evaluation</u>. There might be a vision problem, a learning disability, or an emotional problem. Whatever the reason, it needs to be identified and dealt with.

Some students have simply never deciphered the phonics code. They probably learned to read by sight at younger levels and have relied on sight method crutches which become very inadequate at older levels. Many people unconsciously decipher phonics principles on their own as they read, whether or not they have actually been taught phonics; but many do not. For those who need a phonics foundation, use a remedial program rather than one designed for young children. These students already feel "dumb" and giving them childish materials validates their feelings. (Keep in mind that there is a small percentage of the population that might not be able to learn phonics. This is the point where a professional evaluation is even more vital.)

Professor Phonics-EduCare has a simple-to-use remedial program in a single book, *Sound Track to Reading* (Professor Phonics-EduCare) [student book alone - $12; with teacher's manual - $15]. This is a good resource for those with minor problems who need to review or solidify phonetic concepts.

For those who need thorough, basic phonics instruction, the people who originally published *Sing, Spell, Read, and Write* (International Learning Systems) have put together a program for older students called *Winning* [$175]. The content is very similar to the younger level program, but everything has been rewritten to appeal to pre-teens through adults. The program uses multi-sensory learning methods. There are six cassette tapes, four consumable student workbooks, two card games, four in-

structor's manuals, and a carrying case. Instead of the cute little songs of *Sing, Spell, Read, and Write*, they use catchy rap, blues, country, and swing style songs to teach phonetic concepts. Games and workbooks provide reinforcement and writing practice. Both art work and stories reflect the interests of teens and adults.

Discover Intensive Phonics by Charlotte Lockhart (Communication through Language Development, representatives) is a complete phonics program that can be used with all ages. There are no readers or other content that is age specific. With the book version of the course [$105], much of the learning takes place in one-on-one instruction at a chalkboard (or whiteboard, etc.) This is a serious, no frills approach, but it works well for students who want to learn to read and spell quickly. If the one-on-one teaching intimidates us, or if we feel we lack the phonics background to present phonics on our own, consider investing in the new K-3 CD-ROM computer courseware version, which is suitable for learners of all ages. This software will run on Windows, DOS, or Macintosh systems and it features 75 interactive lessons on two CD-ROMs. It begins with letters and sounds and continues up through decoding multi-syllable words. You will need sound capability on your computer since lessons are all presented auditorially. Colorfully illustrated stories on the CDs provide reading practice as students progress. I have only one complaint about the pronunciation on the CDs; letter sounds are often pronounced with an "uh" sound following rather than the briefer sounds that letters actually make.(S)

Some students understand and use phonics, but read so slowly that their comprehension is limited. Unless there is a vision problem or learning disability, students need to spend more time practicing reading to increase their speed. Comprehension also might be poor simply because students have never learned to think about what they read. Comprehension activity workbooks are easily available from teacher supply stores and sources such as Builder Books and Shekinah Curriculum Cellar listed in the Appendix.

The Amsco Language Arts Catalog lists a number of resources that will be useful for developing comprehension skills. *High Marks: Stories That Make Good Reading* (Amsco) [$8.06; answer key - $2.25] features twenty-two short stories from authors such as Leo Tolstoy, O. Henry, H.G. Wells, and Nathaniel Hawthorne as well as some from less well-known authors. While some of these are similar or even identical to stories found in anthologies, because they are printed in a large type style in a smaller book, the reading seems less intimidating. Stories are also short enough to keep the interest of reluctant readers. Each story is followed by questions covering main idea, fact recall, word meanings, plus a variety of other reading skills.(S)

Amsco also publishes a series of three books in the same type of format entitled, *The Reader as Detective* [$9.06 each; answer keys - $2.05 each]. Book I has a readability level of grades 5-7; Book II, grades 6-8; and Book III, grades 7-9. Reading selections are "high-interest and suspenseful," again, to involve the reluctant reader. Stories are interrupted sometimes once, sometimes more frequently, to challenge the reader to analyze the clues in the story thus far and answer some questions. The denouement of each story follows a challenge to the reader to figure it out for himself. The idea works something like the *Encyclopedia Brown* books (popular with younger readers), but at a more advanced level. Questions with each story have to do with factual recall, inferences, and understanding word meanings. Examples of stories are "The Adventure of the Red-Headed League" (Doyle), "A Retrieved Reformation" (O. Henry), "The Disappearing Man" (Asimov), and "The Tiger's Heart" (Kjelgaard). All of the Amsco books have inexpensive answer keys available. Check their catalog for other titles.(S)

Even if you use one of the resources mentioned above, one of the most effective ways to increase comprehension is to have the student read a selection of his choice out loud, and at the conclusion ask him questions about both details and meaning.

Reading skills are so vital to all other academic studies that it might be better to spend a few months on nothing other than reading to bring those skills up to a satisfactory level. Students can catch up in other subjects later, since their improved reading skills will enable them to work more quickly and with more retention than before.

Reading non-fiction becomes increasingly important for older students. Sometimes they need help developing those skills. *Strategies for Reading Nonfiction: Comprehension and Study Activities, Grades 4-8* (Spring Street Press) [$15.95] is a specialized resource for non-fiction reading skills. There are over 40 reproducible activities that can be used with a wide range of non-fiction books, be they textbooks or topical books. Students learn how to read with purpose, identifying what type of information they should be looking for before they begin. They practice taking notes and summarizing what they have read. They think about and analyze information. And, since new words are often crucial to new knowledge, vocabulary activities are included. The activity pages follow various formats, most of them functioning as organization maps to help students. The graphical/visual creativity makes it easier and more appealing to work on these activity pages than doing the same things with blank paper. Simple instructions (and objectives) are on the back of each activity page, and most students will be able to figure out how to use these on their own. This is a resource for all students, not just those who need remedial help.(S)

For those students who continue to be deficient in reading skills, consider using *Reading for Survival in Today's Society* (Good Year Books) [$14.95]. This book is aimed at teens who might soon be entering the job market, even if only for part-time employment. The authors set the tone of the book with a story of a phone company customer who has been paying the "date" on his phone bill rather than the amount due. All exercises are centered around common experiences such as getting a social security card, selecting a job, figuring out the best route, comparing advertisements, completing order forms, making budgets, maintaining a checkbook register, reading instructions for assembling products, and locating information. Explanations, samples, exercises, and blank forms walk the student through each activity. Activities go deeper than simply reading and filling in blanks, by raising thought-provoking situations such as "Dealing with a Difficult Customer." Much of this book would be worthwhile for the average student, but there are some activities and exercises that will seem insultingly easy to him or her.

Remediating Handwriting and Spelling

If our teenagers still have abominable handwriting, it is tempting to just let them use the computer and give up on efforts to improve handwriting. However, there are going to be times when they will need to be able to take notes or communicate without the aid of a computer or typewriter. If they cannot write important information quickly and legibly, they are going to be handicapped. Spelling presents the same sort of problem. Poor spellers are in the same boat as sloppy writers since they have trouble deciphering what they have written.

Often, the two deficiencies go hand in hand. Putting these students into typical texts where they practice more of the same in the same ways is not very helpful. One resource written particularly for these students is *Writing Skills for the Adolescent* by Diana King (Educators Publishing Service) [$7.10]. The author covers handwriting, grammar, spelling, typing, and composition instruction methods for dyslexic and dysgraphic students. She offers strategies that work from her experience with many struggling students.(S)

Cursive Writing Skills (also by Diana King from Educators Publishing Service) [$6.35], in editions for right-handers and left-handers, should be used along with *Writing Skills for the Adolescent*.(S)

Remediating Composition Skills

Some students are still unable to write a coherent paragraph by junior high. This sometimes occurs because of learning disabilities that, like reading problems, need to be professionally diagnosed. More often this occurs because students have not been taught and have not practiced writing. The process is dependent to a large degree upon the teacher, and many of us doubt our ability to teach our children to write since our own writing skills are poor. We must overcome our inadequacies and establish a writing discipline for our students. There are resources (see below) that will help with the first part, but the discipline is up to us. We must have our children writing frequently. However, lengthy writing assignments can be discouraging to poor writers, so it is much better to have many small assignments rather than a few lengthy ones.

A crucial factor in stimulating writing skills is our reaction. If students write papers that we simply check off and toss in the

What Should Our Children Read?

Much of what passes for "teen literature" today is garbage. Help is at hand for sorting out what our teens should and should not be reading.

Reading Between the Lines: A Christian Guide to Literature by Gene Edward Veith, Jr. (Crossway Books) $13.99

Many of us have recognized problems in popular literature and have set restrictive guidelines. Yet, often our hold on those guidelines is shaky. *Reading Between the Lines* will help.

For example, I have been told by many home educators that they allow their children to read only books that are true. But we overlook an important aspect of literature when we do this. When an author writes a biography about a person who lived a century or more in the past, and there is little first hand information about him or her (such as diaries, eye-witness reports, letters to friends, etc.), we must ask ourselves how much of that biography will be true and how much is manufactured to fill in the blanks of the author's knowledge. Do such biographies constitute truth any more than do stories that are written about fictional characters but based upon real-life events? The only written work that is wholly true is the Bible. Everything else has the possibility of containing untruth. If we do not want to restrict our children's reading to only the Bible, we must wrestle with the issue of what is acceptable.

Reading Between the Lines helps us to sort through the different factors relating to our Christian faith, literary value, and enjoyment when choosing reading material. Mr. Veith, a university instructor, loves literature, and because of this he promotes guidelines that some of us might feel are too liberal. However, as you read this book, you will probably do some rethinking about your view of literature. Even with the area of fantasy, which seems to be one of the biggest problem areas, he does an excellent job of explaining how to differentiate between that which is worthwhile and that which is not.

For those of us with a poor literary background, this book provides an excellent mini-course in literature. Veith piques our interest by quoting from various authors, and whetting our appetites for "the whole story." You are likely to find yourself making a list of books that you need to read. Some of us might find ourselves overwhelmed if we try to read this entire book straight through. I recommend taking a leisurely approach, reading those sections that are most pertinent to our concerns first and others as we find the time or need.

Read for Your Life by Gladys Hunt and Barbara Hampton (Zondervan Publishing House) $12.99

See the lengthier review in Chapter Five under "Literature." This book helps Christian teens (and parents) set guidelines for suitable literature, then provides annotated descriptions of over 300 books with recommendations that often include cautions or philosophical observations.

---

trash, we communicate to them that their writing is worthless. If we discuss their writing, with both praise and constructive criticism, have them rewrite to improve it, then "publish" their final result by passing it around for others to see (when it is merited), we send the message that their writing is of value and interest to others. It is obvious which message will stimulate them to writing excellence. This is the kind of approach that can never come from a textbook.

If language arts skills are up to par we can then move on to more challenging goals.

Language Arts Goals

Approximately <u>6th</u> through <u>8th</u> grade levels

– Read widely at challenging levels with comprehension
– Develop a love for reading
– Use plural possessives and contractions
– Recognize and write compound sentences
– Identify and write topic sentences
– Write outlines
– Apply proper word usage in writing and speech

– Write using correct punctuation including quotation marks, indentation, colon, and semicolons
– Write compositions, dialogue, simple poetry, short research papers, book reports
– Write business and friendly letters
– Write with unity and coherence
– Proofread and edit their own work
– Use dictionary to locate word origins, dictionary spellings (pronunciations), usages
– Recognize and diagram basic parts of speech: subject, verb, adjectives, adverbs, prepositions, conjunctions*
– Recognize prepositional phrases
– Recognize appositives and direct address
– Recognize helping and linking verbs
– Identify predicate adjective and predicate nominative/noun
– Diagram predicate adjective and predicate nominative*
– Diagram more complicated sentences*
– Understand use of italics
– Recognize and use simple similes and metaphors
– Use a thesaurus or the *Synonym Finder*
– Take notes from printed and oral material
– Use card catalog, or the modern computer equivalent, and other reference materials

– Organize information from reference materials for reports

– Write research paper including bibliography (7th-8th grade)

– Give oral reports

– Participate in discussions

– Give oral presentations in front of a group, with attention given to body movements, voice, enunciation, speed, eye contact, and effectiveness of presentation

* or use *Winston Grammar* or other methods for identifying parts of speech

High School Goals

Model Curriculum Standards, Grades Nine through Twelve, first edition (California Department of Education publication now out of print) summed up well what they call the prerequisites for high school language arts work with the following:

> Students who are most likely to succeed in this [high school] curriculum are: (1) those who have acquired a core of knowledge about people, ideas, and literature which equips them to take on more sophisticated materials; (2) those who have learned to listen and speak in a variety of situations and are thus able to engage in discussions of central literary issues; (3) those who have written about topics that have meaning to them and are thus prepared to express their convictions with greater clarity; and (4) those who have acquired basic reading and study skills.

Although these are described as skills students need as they begin high school, we can see that they also describe or imply goals for the high school years.

The first area has to do with the idea of cultural literacy that was discussed earlier in this book. This comes primarily from reading. There is simply no adequate substitute. Students who have read widely have a foundation upon which to build additional knowledge. Those with a limited foundation read and discuss with limited understanding. A good example that comes to mind is a column that runs in our county newspaper once a week. A reporter stations himself at some public location and asks passersby a current events or opinion question such as: "Should the United States help to support Israel financially?" The answers usually reflect total ignorance of the background of the situation. Typical answers sound like, "The people are poor so we should share with those who have less than we do." Or, "The countries that are closer to Israel should be helping them." The scary thing is that answers rarely sound any more well informed than this! To help our children become culturally literate, our language arts curricula should include extensive reading over a broad range of subject areas.

The second area—listening and speaking—also is not covered by a textbook. Instead we must interact with our children. Then they must interact with other people. They need to practice listening carefully to what someone is saying. They need to practice clearly expressing their own thoughts both one-on-one and in front of a group. We need to see that they have opportunity to practice speaking beyond specifying their daily needs. (That also means we have to practice being good listeners.) Public speaking opportunities must be arranged whether in front of a small group of home schoolers, our family and friends, or a more varied

group. Public speaking only becomes easier with plenty of experience. If we provide the opportunities for experience in less threatening situations at younger ages, public speaking will come more easily later on.

The third area is the ability to express oneself in written form. This includes both the proper use of the English language (grammar, spelling, and vocabulary) and composition skills.

Many students (and parents) have trouble comprehending a reason for learning grammar and parts of speech. It is generally acknowledged that a knowledge of grammar does not clearly correlate to excellence in writing, so learning grammar to write well should not be your only rationale for grammar instruction.

What has been recognized is that students who read a great deal usually write well. This is because they are familiar with how written language should sound. Students who do not read much, usually do not write well. So, if we wish to improve our child's writing skills, one of the most important things we should do is encourage them to read from a broad selection of well-written books.

Even though there is little direct correlation between technical grammar knowledge and good writing, grammar provides the common vocabulary for discussing writing. We can encourage our child to write more colorful sentences by using descriptive adjectives and adverbs if he understands what adjectives and adverbs are and which words they describe. We can also do this by asking questions such as, "How did the boy run?," but grammar vocabulary provides a much more efficient way of doing this. Additionally, grammatical knowledge will help to "fine tune" writing for those who go on to do much writing later in life.

We have also found that knowledge of English grammar is essential for learning a foreign language beyond a conversational level. We need a common vocabulary of grammatical definitions to learn corresponding parts of speech in the new language. The application of grammar concepts in a foreign language also provides both a reinforcement of and incentive for further learning of English. As an extra bonus, knowledge of a foreign language often results in improved English vocabulary.

I would like to digress a moment to mention two resources for teachers regarding grammar instruction. Both are based on the Principle Approach but are useful for anyone who wants to understand what grammar encompasses and the purposes for learning it. Most students will already be beyond the grammar lessons themselves as outlined in these books, but the principles are instructive for student and teacher alike. The first resource is *English Grammar: An Overview of the Subject of Grammatical Syntax* by Estrid Kieffer Wilson (Landmark Distributors).

Estrid Kieffer Wilson was one of the first people, if not the first person, to apply the Principle Approach to grammar. The results of her studies and application are contained in this 46-page book. Wilson provides the background for grammar, dividing it into four sections. In this book she concentrates on the single section of "syntax," which she defines as "the true mode of constructing sentences, or the agreement and government of words, and their arrangement in proper order." Syntax then includes both "analysis (parsing) and synthesis (rules of construction)." Wilson defines the other three areas, showing the breakdown into the various aspects of what we generally teach under the headings of grammar and English. Rather than offering detailed lessons or even lesson plans, Wilson demonstrates how diagramming and the use of questions are used to teach syntax. This book is intended to be a teacher resource for parents to understand the principles of grammar and the essentials for teaching some parts of that very large topic. Teachers can create their own lessons from the ideas presented, although it is more likely to serve as a "shell" within which teachers will use other grammar books. Anyone teaching grammar or English can benefit from Wilson's clear explanations and suggestions.

The second resource is *A Guide to Teaching Grammar Using The Principle Approach* by Dorothy E. Robbins (The Rebuilders of the Foundations of America's Christian Heritage) [$12]. This 33-page book is a teacher's resource for understanding how to apply the Principle Approach to grammar instruction. The first section of the book explains the rationale for this approach. This is followed by specifics about the teaching of grammar itself, expressed in terms of principles rather than comprehensive explanations. The author suggests Rod and Staff's *Building Christian English* as a source for comprehensive instruction, although Rod and Staff's English series continues only through eighth grade level.

We move now beyond grammar to spelling and vocabulary. Spelling and vocabulary can be combined as one subject, included in other language arts activities, or dealt with individually. The majority of students profit most from vocabulary work at high school level. Spelling of common words should be mastered by high school level, and dictionary skills should be adequate for looking up the more difficult words. If a student spells well, let him concentrate on vocabulary rather than spelling.

Composition skills can be divided into creative, experiential, and expository writing, although dividing lines are not always clear. Creative writing consists of all of those "fun ideas"—imaginary newspapers, "The Day I Turned into a Piece of Chewing Gum," and other nonsense—along with short stories, poetry, and other fictional writing. Students write about and from their own experiences in experiential writing. Expository writing includes reports, essays, themes, and research papers—the types of writing that most of us find least enjoyable. Most basic textbooks deal with all these types of writing, and many supplementary books specialize in particular areas.

The fourth area of prerequisites according to *Model Curriculum Standards* deals with reading and study skills. Study skills have already been discussed in Chapter Three. Reading skills should be good enough that we need not devote school time to reading instruction. The study of literature is different from reading instruction and should begin in junior high if not before. Students will spend time studying literature in depth, becoming familiar with renowned authors of both past and present.

What we have just discussed are the areas that *Model Curriculum Standards'* authors say are prerequisite to high school level work, yet most of our students are working on developing some of these skills as they enter high school, so do not be alarmed if your child has not mastered <u>all</u> of these goals before high school—he is probably about where most other students are. However, if he is weak in a number of language arts areas,

these should receive attention before other subjects since language art skills are necessary for success in other areas of study.

A Summary of Goals

To sum up our goals at high school level—for the majority of students, the most important goal is improvement in writing and communication skills. Grammar, spelling, and vocabulary may be learned or reviewed depending upon prior knowledge. Literature should be studied. All of these aspects of language arts should be balanced to complete the English requirement. Three years of English are required by many states for graduation, although most colleges and universities require four. While English courses might concentrate on one area or another from year to year, over the high school years all of the above areas need to be addressed.

Language Arts Tools

Regardless of which curriculum is used, there are a few basic tools all students need.

Dictionary: Do not buy a children's dictionary unless you must because of a problem such as a severe learning disability. Purchasing the most comprehensive dictionary you can afford is essential to avoid the frustration of being unable to locate a word simply because it has not been included—a problem typical of student dictionaries and highly abridged editions. Webster's original *American Dictionary of the English Language* (Foundation for American Christian Education) is useful for looking up definitions of archaic words or some words that we encounter in British Literature. The definitions often include Scripture references and biblical references.

Grammar Handbook: There are many choices, and it does not matter much which we choose. The *Write Source* versions, BJUP Handbook, or others will all do the job. The object is to have an easy-to-use reference for grammatical details rather than trying to sort through a textbook.

Thesaurus: Stretching to find just the right word is a hallmark of a good writer. It is expected that writers will consult a thesaurus rather than have all of the possibilities on the tips of their tongues. I particularly like the *Synonym Finder* by J.I. Rodale (Warner Books) and other thesauruses that include figures of speech and slang expressions.

Computer: Writing is probably the best excuse for purchasing a computer for your home school. Most of the drill exercises that are available for other subjects can be duplicated with workbooks, but nothing competes with the computer's value as a word processor. If we truly want our teens to write prolifically and work through the writing process—planning, organizing, writing, and revising—the best encouragement we can give them is a tool that eliminates the busy work. (Computers are also becoming very important as a research tool.)

Evaluating Student Writing

Many parents question their own ability to evaluate their teen's writing because they do not feel that they know how to write well themselves. It is very difficult to identify problems if we do not have a good grasp of the mechanics of writing. We can enlist the help of a friend who is more proficient than we are to either work with our teen individually or, even better, with a group class. Group classes are wonderful for motivation and stimulation of ideas, especially as children get older. The students in a group class can act as co-editors to help with improving and polishing written pieces. They also serve as an audience for sharing and encouraging.

In situations where group classes are not possible and no help seems to be available, we can take advantage of long distance help. Lightsource Editing Service, a ministry of the Kustusch family, is a business that enrolls families for $25 per year, then edits all work for $1 per page editing fee. No grades are issued, but helpful suggestions for improvement are included. I have a feeling that the Kustusch family is likely to be overwhelmed with response since their charges are so reasonable.

Christian Liberty Press also offers writing evaluation services through CLASS for students in grades 4-12. This is not the open-ended service of Lightsource. Instead, students prepare three specific writing projects (persuasive essay, descriptive report or letter, and book report) according to guidelines provided by CLASS. Students submit these for review and evaluation, receiving feedback within three to four weeks. The cost is $14.95.

A specialized evaluating service is offered by The National Writing Institute. Parents who want assistance with correcting and evaluating their students' composition from *Writing Strands* can sign up for this unique service. Parents send in first and second drafts of student papers from the assignments, and National Writing Institute "corrects" and evaluates them, commenting and making suggestions. Contact The National Writing Institute for details.

An even better strategy is for parents to sharpen their own evaluating skills. National Writing Institute's *Evaluating Writing* [$19.95] is designed to do just that. Author Dave Marks shows keen insight into the problems both parents and children face. In one section, he describes common writing problems and how to correct them. Read straight through that section for a valuable mini-writing course. Next, he presents numerous samples of student writing along with evaluation comments and suggested conversations so that we truly understand how to approach the process. Many examples are from *Writing Strands* lessons, so they will be especially useful to those using that series. Examples come from writers at all levels so we get a good idea of what we might expect, although Marks emphasizes the individuality of each child and impossibility of setting identical goals for all. An appendix suggests "rules" for writing the various drafts of writing assignments and also includes lists of spelling rules and commonly misused words.

Combined Grammar and Composition Resources for 7th and 8th Grades

Basic texts

➲ Applications of Grammar, Books 1 and 2 [revised edition, 1996] (Christian Liberty Press) $7.95 each; answer key - $6.95 each; test packet - $3.95 each

Books 1 and 2 in this series are designated for grades 7 and 8, although you might use them at different levels since there are no grade level designations. These books primarily focus upon grammar (both parts of speech and usage), but attention is also given to composition and dictionary skills. Diagramming is also taught.

Book 1, subtitled *Basics for Communicating Effectively,* is quite comprehensive; students with little grammatical knowledge can start here. Instruction begins with the basics, but it continues on through complex concepts appropriate for this level. Complete explanations of concepts are presented with examples so students can work independently. Each lesson is followed by a variety of exercises. Composition instruction focuses mostly upon sentence structure, with paragraph writing addressed fairly briefly in the last section. One 200 to 400-word paragraph is the lengthiest writing assignment in the book, so you will probably want your student to tackle additional writing projects outside of this book.

Book 2, subtitled *Structure for Communicating Effectively,* advances the grammar lessons to topics typically addressed at high school level. This book features very useful charts for grammatical concepts, and grammar rules are numbered so that you might use this as a grammar reference book as you might use *Learning Grammar through Writing*. I was surprised at the thoroughness of this book. It includes concepts such as conjunctive adverbs and phrases classified according to six different forms, that are not typical for this level. But these are clearly explained with examples and charts when appropriate. Units in Book 2 cover parts of speech and syntax, phrases, clauses, diagramming, sentence writing (complex structures), vocabulary building (suffixes, prefixes, troublesome words), agreement (noun/verb, pronoun/antecedent, person/ gender, and number), verb conjugations, punctuation, and composition. Composition lessons focus on problem areas rather than organization and structure. Students are given two writing assignments at the end of the book (150 and 200 words each), but, aside from this, they are not doing any significant amount of composition.

These books are less overwhelming than A Beka's grammar books, but topic coverage is fairly comparable. These offer more explanation and examples in a format that is spread out with more "white space" per page, which is less intimidating for students. Christian content is evident throughout the books from the introduction through most of the lessons. A glossary and index are helpful for reference. Students will need a good, unabridged dictionary for a number of the lessons in Book 1. Answer keys are very helpful but test packets are optional.

Building Christian English 7 and 8 (Rod and Staff) Grade 7: pupil book - $15.80; teacher's manual - $21.85; tests - $1.10; worksheets - $3.65. Grade 8: pupil book - $15.00; teacher's manual - $20.85; tests - $1.10; worksheets - $2.50

Building Securely is the subtitle for the seventh grade book. This is a hardback student text with heavy emphasis on grammar and godly character. Rod and Staff covers grammatical concepts by eighth grade that other publishers spread out through high school, so this text is more difficult than others for seventh grade. It is too detailed for the needs of some students and has extra busywork that should be used only as needed. Using the exercises selectively helps overcome any problems this presents.

Preparing for Usefulness, the subtitle for the eighth grade book, accurately reflects the shift from grammar to application at this level. Remaining elements of grammar are covered, but, more importantly, students work with many forms of written communication. A newly revised edition should be out as we go to print. While the previous edition relied on the *Rod and Staff English Handbook*, the new edition does not. (Prices are for the new edition.)

Teacher's manuals, worksheets, and test booklets are available for both seventh and eighth grade texts.

I appreciate the fact that Rod and Staff is one of the rare publishers who recognizes that grammar skills can be mastered in much less than twelve years.

Comprehensive Composition (Design-A-Study) $14

This is a teacher's resource book for writing instruction for grades 1-12. The author's goal was to provide a vehicle for writing instruction based upon integration of writing assignments with other subjects being studied rather than depending upon textbook composition topics. The author provides thorough instruction in skills with some sample topics to get students started. Students then can apply the skills to other topics being studied.

The writing process is developed throughout the book with general guidelines provided for what should be expected at different levels. Specific guidelines are given for various types of writing (essays, descriptive writing, writing a news story, etc.).

One section of the book deals with elements of style and grammar in sentence construction. Another chapter is a grammar reference source. Although it does not cover the parts of speech, it does cover capitalization and punctuation. The book is not intended to be used in strict sequence but in the order best for each learning situation.

One of the most valuable parts of the book is the final section of sample lessons. In each sample, the assignment topic is given and we are shown how the lesson was presented or how the student worked to develop his composition. Then we read the final (and sometimes intermediate) results.

This has to be one of the most concise, yet comprehensive books for teaching the writing process available to home educators. Material for early grades is rather limited, but from middle elementary through high school level it should be excellent.

Kathryn Stout has a 60-minute audio tape, *How to Teach Composition,* will also help you learn how to teach and evaluate composition skills [$4.50].

Elements of Writing

(Holt, Rinehart and Winston) First Course (Grade 7) and Second Course (Grade 8) student books - $43.25 and $43.25 respectively; teacher's editions - $71.75 each

When Harcourt Brace Jovanovich merged with Holt, Rinehart and Winston the long-enduring Warriner series for composition and grammar were rewritten. It seems that only the *Warriner's High School Handbook* remains from the earlier series. The new series, entitled *Elements of Writing*, incorporates John Warriner's approach to grammar with the composition lessons of Dr. James L. Kinneavy. The result is a series that emphasizes composition instruction, with grammatical instruction presented within that context. Literary models are included within each text as learning tools. This helps students learn both grammar and composition skills within the context of actual usage, which helps with motivation and retention of information. Writing assignments are defined more by process than topic, which gives students much more room to individualize their writing than do assignments found in some other texts.

Grammar is also presented separately in the second part of the book. It can serve as a handbook (particularly when used in conjunction with exercises in the first part of the book), and it also has exercises, diagnostic tests, review/posttests, and writing assignments.

Following the grammar section are chapters on speaking, listening, library/media, dictionary, vocabulary, letters and forms, and studying and test taking. An appendix covers diagramming.

The format is colorful, and, in keeping with educational trends, the content strives for multiculturalism with writing selections and illustrations reflecting diverse cultures and ethnic groups.

There is quite a bit of overlap in content from year to year in each, although some new topics are presented in each text. Various types of writing activities would be the most prominent difference between the First and Second Course texts. Consider using a single text over a two-year period rather than buying separate ones for each year, since there is plenty of material in any one book. (The Second Course book is 972 pages!)

The Annotated Teacher's Editions feature large reproductions of the student pages surrounded by teaching suggestions and helps. Most parents will want the teacher's editions for help with the exercises.(SE)

English 7 and 8 (Houghton Mifflin/McDougal Littell)[1990 editions] pupil editions - $37.08 each; teacher's editions - $79.77 each; skills practice books - $12.66 each; teacher's editions for skills practice books - $17.67 each

These practical and comprehensive texts do an especially good job of developing writing skills, the focus of the first half of each book. Writing instruction encompasses the writing process, paragraph development, and various types of writing such as narrative, descriptive, explanatory, persuasive, report, and (in the eighth grade) research. Grammar coverage is also fairly comprehensive, taking up most of the second half. Lessons are designed so that we can jump back and forth between composition and grammar lessons. Both parts of speech and usage are taught, with instruction followed by exercises and writing assignments to practice applying the concepts. Diagramming is taught very briefly; only in the teacher's edition is it suggested to teachers that they actually have students do any diagramming, and then it is only suggested for advanced students. Instead, students are taught to use underlining, arrows, and notations to identify parts of speech and/or functions. Lessons on the history of language, speaking and listening skills, using the library and reference works, dictionary and spelling skills, study skills, and test-taking skills round out this language arts program.

I have the same reservations about content that I have about so many other texts. The politically-correct examples clearly intend to influence the way students feel and think about various issues. For example, a persuasive writing example tries to influence the audience to believe that a vacant school should be turned into a teen center rather than sold to a private business. It uses invalid supporting details that imply that a teen center can create equivalent jobs and tax revenue the same as a business. Ecology, evolution, whales, and other such issues make frequent appearances.

The teacher's edition is useful primarily as an answer key, although it does include helpful teaching ideas such as how to present lessons for average, slow, or advanced students. Also of interest to home educators might be the *Skills Practice Book*, a workbook of exercises to reinforce text lessons. A companion teacher's edition serves as the answer key.(SE)

⊃ English PACEs 1073-1084 for grade 7 and 1085-1096 for grade 8 (School of Tomorrow) 12 Paces - $48; answer keys - $16 for each level

12 PACEs per grade level are used for instruction in grammar and composition. Each PACE features a character quality as its theme, with a "Wisdom" study in the center of each booklet and a related Scripture verse to be memorized. Grammar receives the most attention via sentence completion, fill-in-the-blank, matching, and brief response exercises. Diagramming is taught. Students need more composition practice than they receive within the PACEs at this level.

⊃ Grammar and Composition 1 and 2 (A Beka) $12.45 each

In these worktexts for seventh and eighth grades the emphasis is more on grammar than writing. If students have been using A Beka until seventh grade, they have had a lot of grammar already. We might choose to use only one of these books or switch to BJUP or another publisher to put less emphasis on grammar. (If they are really having problems with grammar, consider *Winston Grammar*.) When using these texts, be sure to have students do extra composition work. The teacher's edition is a copy of the student worktext with answers (your answer key). The *Teacher's Curriculum Guide for English 7* gives daily lesson plans correlating grammar, literature, vocabulary and spelling from A Beka books.

⊃ Learning Language Arts through Literature (Common Sense Press) Gray Book $16

The *Gray Book* (for grades 7-9) has twenty-five lessons. Lessons vary as to the amount of time each will take, but the entire book should take about one school year to complete. This language arts course is based upon ideas from Ruth Beechick's books. Literary passages from books such as the *Bible, The Black Arrow, A Little Princess, A Tale of Two Cities, Moby Dick*, and *White Fang* are the foundation for study each week. Students practice taking the passages by dictation. Using the passage as a springboard, they study and apply grammar, spelling, vocabulary, and writing skills. The method is "whole language" in that all language skills are taught in relationship to one another. Lessons are also keyed to *Learning Grammar through Writing* for those who wish to use that book as a grammar reference/text, although other grammar books can be used instead. Large-print copies of the literary passages, called Student Editing Models, are also included in the back of each book to make it easier for students to either copy or correct their work.

A section at the beginning of the book provides specific teaching methods for each of the language arts areas, plus suggestions for including younger children and for multi-level teaching. The bibliography at the end of the book can also serve as a reading list.

Some students might need more in-depth work in particular language arts areas than is provided here, so you might use other materials to round out your curriculum. Even though the *Learning Language Arts through Literature* lacks the review and repetition we find in most other language courses, the effectiveness of the methods used here should help children to learn better without frequent repetition. The scope and sequence is a little unusual, but the Skill Index at the back of the book lists the goals of each lesson so that we can identify each skill area covered. All of the concepts covered in typical language arts programs for junior high receive attention, and writing skills are well developed. In addition to instruction in mechanics and composition, the lessons are also designed to provoke an interest in good literature that will take children beyond the small literary excerpts included in the lessons. Lessons are presented by the teacher, and students maintain their work in a notebook. Since the book is self-contained and non-consumable, the cost is very reasonable.

The books are written by Christian home educators and reflect Christian attitudes, although religious perspectives are not dealt with in studying every literary selection. For instance, a selection from *White Fang* by Jack London does not deal with London's atheistic philosophy. However, excerpts such as those from the Bible and the work of Francis Schaeffer do provide Scriptural lessons.

⊃ Understanding Writing : A Christ-centered, Mastery-oriented English Language and Composition Curriculum for Grades 1-12 by Susan Bradrick (Bradrick Family Enterprises) $65

In *Understanding Writing* Susan Bradrick has successfully combined the teaching of language and composition skills in a format that adapts easily to multi-level teaching and is totally Christ-centered in philosophy. This is an approach to writing that places equal emphasis on development of skills and development of godly character.

It is comprehensive, covering those skills generally taught in English courses. Two resources, *Easy Grammar* and *Easy Writing,* are incorporated into the program at junior high level to develop grammar and writing skills. Also, the author recommends that we have a grammar handbook available for reference for all levels. (A Beka *Grammar and Composition* worktexts *II* and *IV* might also be used with *Understanding Writing*, but you should skip the writing instruction and assignments in those texts since both are covered thoroughly in *Understanding Writing*.)

This one-inch-thick book is divided into three parts. The first part, "Rethinking Writing," discusses "...the theory behind an effective approach for studying English composition." The second part, "Understanding the Basic Elements of Writing," covers "...the elements of content, style, and mechanics essential for effective writing and gives examples of each. The third part, "Teaching the Basic Elements of Writing," "...provides detailed lessons for teaching your child to master the content, style, and mechanical skills of effective, God-honoring written communication."

Although Part III is divided into twelve levels, they need not necessarily correlate to grade levels. All older students really need to begin at the second level, proceeding at whatever pace is comfortable for each student. Most will move through the lessons more quickly than younger students. They might be able to skip some lessons on mechanical skills, but they should not skip any of the writing practice. Children of varying skill levels can easily be instructed at the same time upon a new concept, then work at their ability level in their individual writing time. (The Bradricks have used this method successfully with their nine children.) Each child maintains an "English notebook" (folder or three-ring binder containing drafts of written work rather than copied exercises), so there is no need to purchase student books other than dictionaries or thesauruses.

Students working in Levels 7-12 should be able to do much of their work independently. A well-motivated student who begins *Understanding Writing* in grades 9-12 should be able to read through the curriculum on his own, completing necessary exercises, and learning at his own pace.

For students working under a parent/teacher, lessons are structured in units with daily assignments which include a balance of discussion and writing time that varies according to a child's level. While most lessons require no parent preparation time, the few that do, state this clearly at the beginning of the lesson.

Children write about personal experiences and observations rather than fiction until the high school level where they branch out into creative and expository writing. Suggested topics are included in the Appendix. Because the thrust of this curriculum is mastery of God-honoring communication, most composition assignments are to be written for a specific reader. They are also to be actually delivered (usually in letter form) to that individual so that a habit of skillful, genuine communication is the result of the student's writing study.

A reproducible "Composition Planning and Evaluation Sheet" is used to help students think through their composition before they begin, then provide key areas for parents to address in their evaluations. (These sheets are also available from the publisher in pads of fifty, three-hole-punched sheets.)

Understanding Writing is well-structured with clear goals yet it retains flexibility enough for multi-level teaching. The only complaint I hear about *Understanding Writing* is that it is difficult to jump into the program with older students, but if you start at the second level, and move as quickly as the student desires, it should work fine.

⮑ Wordsmith: A Creative Writing Course for Young People
by Janie B. Cheaney (Common Sense Press) $13; teacher's guide - $4

Junior high tends to be a transition time for many students, particularly in the area of language arts. However, most courses for this level simply repeat what has already been taught, instead of stretching students in new directions.

Wordsmith skillfully fills the gap between elementary and high school learning. It can be used with children as young as ten or eleven, and with high school students whose writing skills are undeveloped.

Wordsmith assumes that the student knows basic grammar. It moves on from there to work with grammar through written applications. For example, one assignment has them come up with vivid action verbs to replace weak verbs accompanied by adverbs. The goal is to sharpen writing skills by choosing words carefully for the best effect.

After working on grammar, they tackle sentence construction, again with the goal of writing more interesting yet concise sentences. Once grammar and sentence structure are under control, they can apply those skills to composition writing.

Although *Wordsmith* does not teach all the different forms of writing such as reports, research papers, etc., it covers techniques that can be applied in almost any writing situation. Lessons work on skills such as describing people, narrowing the topic, and writing dialogue. At the end, students write their own short story. Helps on proofreading and editing are included.

The student book may be written in, or it can be used as a reusable text by doing the brief activities in a notebook. Lesson organization is clear and well-designed. Some teaching, primarily in the form of discussion and evaluation, is required, although students will do much of the work on their own. The author's humorous touches scattered throughout the book add special appeal.

A bright, motivated student might be able to work through the book in a semester or less, although most students should need a year or more.

Parents who lack confidence in their ability to teach students how to write will appreciate the inexpensive teacher's guide. It includes answers, lesson plans, teaching suggestions, and ideas for expanding lessons. Parents with strong writing skills will probably be able to manage without it.

Other books attempt to meet the same goals, but the presentation here is better than anything similar at this level. Consider supplementing with *Writing with a Point, Creative Writing and the Essay for the Beginner,* or *Practicing the Writing Process 2: The Essay* for further development of essay writing skills.

⊃ Writing a Step Above: A Strategy for Improving Reading, Writing, and Listening Skills by Connie Schenkelberg (Schenkelberg Home Enterprises) $19.95

This ungraded manual can be used with students in junior and senior high (and perhaps even earlier). It contains teacher instructions, daily lesson plans, reproducible worksheets, and an answer key. Lessons need to be presented by the teacher, although this will not require much time. It combines sentence patterns (using various parts of speech by name) and sentence combining to improve student composition skills. It begins with a review of the basics—nouns and verbs—then continues through all parts of speech, including the seldom-covered nominative absolute. Students learn to identify various parts of speech then diagram sentences as a tool for learning to write more complex and interesting sentences. Connie allows us to skip the diagramming if we choose, but I suspect that this is really a key to the value of these lessons. As students see the expanding, logical connections between words demonstrated in diagrams, they reinforce understanding of syntax. It should take one year to complete this course. Students who already know diagramming, can still be challenged to construct sentences according to the various patterns studied. These exercises will teach them to write in sentence patterns and combinations that they might never have tried before. The actual composition work is limited, so you will want to translate skills students learn here into lengthier composition assignments such as essays, creative writing, etc.(S)

⊃ Writing and Grammar 7 and 8 (Bob Jones University Press) teacher's editions - $36 each; student worktexts - $12 each; TestBank - $16 each

Seventh and eighth grade BJUP language courses should be used as parts one and two of a series. The teacher's editions are essential for a complete program. There is enough material in either course for about half of the school year, since it is expected that the English course will also include the study of literature. The student workbooks serve as practice and reinforcement rather than as the primary source of instruction. There is a good balance of grammar and composition, but lessons do seem to jump from topic to topic, sometimes with insufficient coverage. BJUP's labels for word functions include a few not encountered in other programs with which I am familiar (e.g., isolates), but they should be easy enough for students new to BJUP to understand. These books are much stronger than A Beka's *Language* in writing instruction, although they lack creativity and originality. A writing assignment is included with each chapter (about one for every two weeks), and thorough instruction is provided for completing those assignments. BJUP emphasizes all aspects of the writing process including the publication or sharing of completed assignments as a motivational incentive. Home teachers will need to create an audience for written pieces, whether it is family, group classes, friends, or relatives. Christian themes flow through each course, helping to provide a rationale to students for learning language skills. An audio cassette accompanies the seventh grade text, and while it is not absolutely essential, it is very helpful.

⊃ Writing for 100 Days: A Student-Centered Approach to Composition and Creative Writing by Gabriel Arquilevich (Fairview Publishing) $15

Individual lessons for 100 days address four areas: composition, fiction, poetry, and writing in action. Assuming the student has a foundation in basic grammar and composition, this book goes on to tackle elements that produce excellent writing. Composition lessons focus on skills such as word economy, word choice, use of dialect and slang, transitions, sentence variety, use of parentheses and dashes, tone, and organization. The strategy is often humorous; sometimes students are instructed to produce a negative example, then a positive example. In each lesson, instruction is followed by an exercise. When appropriate, answers to the exercise are provided at the back of the book. The fiction section walks students through the actual writing of a story. Poetry addresses selected forms such as haiku, limericks, sonnets, and free verse. "Writing in action" lessons tackle a variety of real-life applications such as business letters, writing news reports, conducting an interview, writing a television commercial, technical writing, and travel writing. For fun, a few "word" games are added. A list of additional assignments is provided at the end of the book, but I think students will find some of the activities worthwhile enough to tackle more than once. Of course, we are free to expand, skip, or repeat lessons as we choose. Ideally, these lessons should be done in a group (even two students will do!). However, they can be used by a lone student working independently as long as there is a parent/tutor to evaluate the work; a single student will also miss the described opportunities to interact with another student on some of the pieces. Overall, this book offers a well-balanced combination of skills instruction, motivation, and practice.(S)

⊃ Writing for Success: A Comprehensive Guide to Improved Creative Writing Skills by Alexandra and Francesca Swann (Cygnet Press) $29.95

Alexandra and Francesca Swann have written a writing program specifically for independent study students. It is suitable for either junior or senior high level, depending upon students' prior knowledge and experience. The book begins with a review of grammar basics: nouns, verbs, adjectives, sentence patterns, punctuation, types of sentences, etc. Students with a solid background can skip ahead to composition skills such as writing with topic sentences, avoiding shifts in person or time, and various types of descriptive writing. Next, the book deals with narrative writing, short stories, cause and effect paragraphs, letter writing, essays, and titles. All of this is interspersed with skill lessons on topics such as comma usage, writing with quotations, numbers and abbreviations, and word usage problems. The lessons are each concise and to the point. While they are not creative like those in *Wordsmith*, they are comprehensive and easy-to-follow. Examples and practice exercises are included within each lesson, and there are also periodic Self-Check Tests. As students tackle lessons on writing skills, they are assigned numerous writing projects. Answer keys are included whenever appropriate. This is a very practical solution for covering a wide range of language skills.

Grammar for Junior High Level

⊃ **Amsco School Publications** (Amsco)

Amsco has a Language Arts catalog listing many resources appropriate for junior high through adult learners. Their books work well for home education because most of them are designed for independent learning, generally in a worktext format. They are inexpensively priced, and, instead of costly teacher's editions, Amsco sells very low priced answer keys. Available titles cover a wide range of topics. Examples: *Essentials of English, Laugh Your Way through Grammar* (lower, upper, or remedial levels), and *English Alive*.(S)

⊃ **Basic Language Principles with Latin Background**

(Educators Publishing Service) $7.15

With this book, students review basic English grammar with beginning instruction in Latin. It jumps around too much to be used as a basic Latin course, but serves as a thorough introduction. It helps students to see how knowledge of grammar is used in learning foreign languages.(S)

⊃ **Beginner's Writers Manual: Spelling Checker, Grammar Rules, and Suggested Topics** (Laguna Beach Educational Books) $14.95

This ambitious little book contains quite a bit of information for the student of writing. The majority of the volume is a spelling list of 7000 words, organized by the first *two* letters in the word. This shortens dramatically the number of words in each subheading, so that the student has many fewer words to look through, making the list much quicker to use than a dictionary. The list is followed by a discussion of spelling rules, with a quick linguistics lesson on spelling phonetically.

The rest of the book gives useful information for the writer, such as common abbreviations (an excellent list), brief grammatical rules, and examples of various types of writing. The writing process is explained simply enough for junior high, and perhaps even younger, students. Finally, there is a resource of story starters and literary terms for the teacher, and all this is contained in a little over 100 pages.

Of course, there are some writing topics that are not included, but the real advantage to this book is the simplicity of the explanations. It won't replace the spell checker on your word processor, but it covers a whole lot more.(S)[Kath Courtney]

⊃ **Caught'ya!: Grammar with a Giggle** by Jane Bell Kiester (Maupin House Publishing) $14.95

Grammar review can be truly customized using Jane Kiester's ideas from *Caught'ya!* The teacher uses a story (already written by someone else or invented) as the primary vehicle for review. It helps if the story is funny or takes unexpected twists and turns. Each day the teacher writes a few sentences on the board, leaving out all capitalization and punctuation. Students copy the sentences, putting in proper capitalization and punctua-

tion. Vocabulary words can be incorporated. Stories and/or sentences can be adapted to review whatever grammatical skills students need. *Caught'ya* outlines the methodology and includes three sample stories—one each for grades 3-5, grades 6-8, and grades 9-11. Since the book is not written for Christian audiences, you might want to find or make up your own stories rather than use these. (I suggest using stories with which your children are not familiar to maintain their interest in "What happens next?") However, the stories will give you excellent models with which to work.

This method is truly fun, and it works well across fairly wide age spans at junior/senior high levels. We used this method very successfully for one year with our boys when they ranged from ages 11-16. There is also a sequel with more stories titled *Caught'ya Again!*, but it suffers from content problems.(SE)

⊃ **Easy Grammar** (ISHA Enterprises) Original - $24.95; Plus - $28.95; book of student pages only - $11.95

We now have two options for the popular *Easy Grammar: Easy Grammar Original* and *Easy Grammar Plus*. Both books are identical in instruction and exercise pages. *Easy Grammar Plus* adds to the *Original* with reviews, tests, cumulative reviews and cumulative tests. ISHA Enterprises tells me that junior high students are most likely to need the *Plus* version, and high school students probably will not require as much reviewing and testing and, consequently, should get the *Original* version. However, the extra cost to have the reviews and tests available might make the *Plus* version more appealing.

Easy Grammar is one, very large book (505 pages in the *Original* and 682 in *Plus*) of bare bones instruction on grammar plus exercise pages. Answer key and reproducible student pages are both included in the book, or we can buy the big book plus separate books of student pages if photocopying is a problem. One key difference from other approaches is the presentation of prepositions and prepositional phrases first to eliminate confusion in identifying subjects, objects, indirect objects, and objects of prepositions. We tried this idea with our youngest, and it worked well. It gets a bit boring to do nothing but *Easy Grammar* work sheets, so use these as a supplement to other things. It is not age graded, so it can be used for many years and grade levels.(S)

⊃ **Editor in Chief series** (Critical Thinking Books and Software)

Book A1 - $12.95; Book B1 - $14.95; Book C1 - $16.95; set of all three - $39.95

Children can improve their spelling, punctuation, and grammar skills in context with the brief exercises in *Editor in Chief*. A reading selection is accompanied by a picture and a caption. The problem is to identify errors and make proper corrections. An editing checklist is at the front of each book to alert students to types of errors they should watch for. A substantial "Guide to Grammar, Usage, and Punctuation" is at the back of each book for handy reference. Extensive answer keys identify and explain errors (helpful for us parents who will have trouble finding some of them ourselves). There are 33 lessons per book which works out to about one per school week in a normal school schedule. Book A1 is recommended for students working at 4th through

6th grade levels. Book B1 is recommended for those working at 6th through 8th grade levels. Book C1 is recommended for eighth grade level and above.(S)

⮌ **English Fun Stuff** by Frode Jensen (Wordsmiths) $11

See the review under "Grammar and Composition Resources for High School."

⮌ **General Punctuation** by Frode Jensen (Wordsmiths) $11

Students learn more than 60 punctuation rules and practice applying them in exercises drawn from the Lewis and Clark expedition. The rules cover everything from commas and periods through brackets, hyphens, and dashes, as well as capitalization and the use of italics. The exercises are numerous lengthy paragraphs which students correct, noting the rule that applies in each instance. This consumable worktext is written for students junior high level and older. They can use this for initial learning, practice, or reinforcement. Students can work through this book on their own, requesting help if they do not understand something. *General Punctuation* supplements writing-based, whole language approaches very well by systematically covering punctuation skills. A reference chart of rules with their numbers should be photocopied and kept close at hand while students complete the exercises.

Author Frode Jensen says, "*General Punctuation* includes all the rules and should follow *Major Punctuation. General Punctuation* is laid out a bit differently from *Major Punctuation* in that the rule book comes first and then all the exercises follow. The learning curve is a bit steep to begin with, but it tapers off quickly, especially if the student has already learned the five rules covered in *Major Punctuation.*"

⮌ **The Grammar Key** by Robert L. Conklin (The Grammar Key) instructor's manual - $19.95; student workbook - $19.95; computer program - $59.95; video - $29.95

Students who are weak in grammar can catch up on all they should have learned about parts of speech and syntax with this super-efficient course. Choose the book, video, or computer version—all follow the same presentation and lesson design. The beauty of this program is simplicity, consistency, and efficiency. Conklin introduces parts of speech along with their sentence functions, using key questions to help with identification. Key questions are repeated and memorized as are lists of helping verbs, linking verbs, determiners, pronouns, etc. Students mark sentences with labels, arrows, circling, and underlining. Although diagramming is presented within the instruction for each topic, students are never required to diagram sentences themselves (a plus or a minus, depending upon how you view diagramming). Lessons build continually so knowledge is integrated rather than taught in isolation. The course begins with noun recognition and continues through verbals (infinitives, participles, and gerunds). With *The Grammar Key*, we no longer need to have students use book after book covering essentially the same grammar material, since this one resource can be used with students from the middle elementary grades through high school.

The instructor's manual presents the lessons in such a fashion that students can read it on their own. After the instruction, students shift to the workbook to complete exercises. Periodically they encounter "Writing Practice" assignments which have them identify the sentence elements that they have studied thus far within their own short compositions. The exercise answers are found in the instructor's manual. Lessons are not intended to encompass all areas of grammar (e.g., no verb tenses or subject-verb agreement lessons), although there are some helpful mnemonic (memory-assisting) devices for capitalization and commas at the end of the instructor's manual. This means that you still need to cover some usage and mechanics as well as writing instruction elsewhere. (*The Grammar Key Mechanics* is in the works.) *The Grammar Key* essentials are summarized on a large, folded reference card which students can use for quick reference as needed. These three components—instructor's manual, student workbook, reference card—can stand alone, although you may substitute computer or video options. (The reference card comes with the instructor's manual, the student workbook, or the computer program.)

The computer program runs on either Macintosh or Windows systems. The program won't dazzle you with speed and sophistication, but it does a straightforward job of presenting both the instructional material (from the instructor's manual) and student exercises. The program requires at least eight hours of work to cover all of the topics, but this should be spread out so that students have time to absorb and apply the information as well as time to complete the other written assignments from the workbook. The computer monitors student progress, with the capability of tracking unlimited students from the same program. The publisher asks only that purchasers buy a program for each computer that will be used. The program does not allow students to progress to the next level until they pass the present level, so students cannot skip ahead even if they have previously mastered topics. Occasionally, the program is hypersensitive to placement of the sentence tags, rejecting appropriate answers if they are not placed just so, but the program signals clearly when all of the correct labels are in place. If the computer seems to be rejecting a tag that the student feels is correct, he should try it twice in case the computer is not registering it. The computer program allows for a more independent-study approach than the books since it monitors and tracks progress, but students should also have the student workbook since it has more practice sentences than the program and includes the writing activities which the program lacks. In fact, students are directed by the computer program to complete corresponding sections in their workbooks.

The eighty-minute video serves as a tutorial although it is not as comprehensive as the instructor's manual. Students who learn better via audio or multi-media presentations might find this option better than the instructor's manual, but I recommend that those purchasing the video also purchase an instructor's manual for complete course information. Whatever the case, students still will need the workbooks to complete their exercises.

The Grammar Key is a practical solution for students who need to either learn or review parts of speech in an efficient fashion.

⇨ **Grammar Songs - Learning with Music** by Katherine Troxel (Audio Memory) $19.95

This is grammar instruction through music—appealing for junior high level and below. The songs are not too "young" for junior high as is true for so many other cassette instructional materials. The songs, professionally recorded on cassette tape, teach parts of speech, punctuation, sentence structure, capitalization, Greek and Latin suffixes and prefixes, and more. The basic set includes a seventy-two page student workbook and a teacher's guide that helps us coordinate the tape and workbook with a few extra activities. This really helps as a supplement, particularly for parts of speech, regardless of what other approach we use.

⇨ **The Great Editing Adventure Series, Volumes 1 and 2** (Common Sense Press) $14 each; student workbooks - $9 each

Escape the drudgery of endless workbook grammar review by switching to *The Great Editing Adventure Series*. If our children have already been studying grammar for a few years, and they have a handle on the basics of punctuation, spelling, and grammar, these books will provide plenty of material to review, reinforce, and stretch their learning. In each book there are 90 lessons, appropriate for grades 4-8, so each provides either a year of lessons for every other day, or a half-year of daily lessons. The lessons are derived from three complete short stories. For each lesson, we write a few sentences from the story (in order) on a chalk or white board. However, the sentences contain grammatical (usage, parts of speech, capitalization, punctuation, etc.), structural (letter writing and addressing envelopes) and spelling errors that children must spot, vocabulary words with which they need to become familiar, and words for which they must discover synonyms. The authors have covered language arts concepts typical for grades 4-6. (The books function as review material for grades 7-8.) Everything needed to present each lesson is contained within each book, although students will need to have a dictionary and thesaurus handy. Answers as well as explanations are provided right here, so we can actually teach or re-teach a concept that poses problems for a student without having to go elsewhere for assistance. We might wish to purchase the student books which already have each day's sentences written out with space for students to write their corrected versions.

The stories themselves are entertaining as we might guess from their titles: "Incredible Kooky Inventions," "The Adventures of a Sheep Named Bill," and "Around the World with the Roaming Detectives." Take a break from grammar texts for a while and see if this isn't at least as effective and a lot more fun.

⇨ **Great Explorations in Editing Series** (Common Sense Press) $14; student book - $9

Those already familiar with *Great Editing Adventures* will find this a very similar resource for older students. There are two stories presented as only a few sentences per day. Parents/teachers can copy these onto a blackboard or whiteboard using only the teacher's book, or students can work directly in the student book. Story portions are written with various spelling and grammatical errors which students must identify and correct. They

also must be able to define circled vocabulary words. Each lesson will take only a few minutes per day. Since many junior and senior high students already have a fairly solid foundation in spelling and grammar, this is a great way to review and drill without using a comprehensive program. It might also be used as a complement to a comprehensive grammar or spelling program. Skills covered are at the "teaching" level for students in grades 7 to 9, and at review level for older students. Volume 1 in the series is available.

⇨ **Harvey's Revised English Grammar** (Mott Media) $16.99; answer key - $5.99

While this book can be used in junior high, it is a comprehensive grammar text which can also be used through high school. It is a revised edition of a nineteenth century text, which is evident in some of the subject matter and vocabulary as well as the style of presentation. The book is divided into four parts: orthography (study of letters, syllables, sounds, and spelling), etymology (meaning parts of speech, tense, number, mode, and other attributes of words as they are used in sentences), syntax (study of punctuation plus the study of sentences, their elements, and the relationships of parts), and prosody (study of accent, quality and tone of language as well as technical aspects of poetry). *Harvey's* goes beyond any grammar texts commonly used today, particularly in the fourth section. An answer key is available.

⇨ **Jensen's Grammar, Parts 1, 2, 3, and Review** (Wordsmiths) $11 each

Jensen's Grammar books are straightforward grammar workbooks that move at a fairly quick pace. They present a great deal of grammatical vocabulary within each lesson. This means students must work harder to learn definitions, but it also helps them better understand what they are learning. Students who have been studying in challenging grammar programs like those from A Beka or Rod and Staff should have no trouble working with these books. However, those with weak grammar backgrounds might be overwhelmed with the amount of material covered if too much of it seems new to them. While some students will be able to use these books independently for learning each lesson, in most cases it will be best for the parent/teacher to go over the lessons and examples with the student. Each lesson consists of one page of instruction and one page of exercises. There is an answer key in the back, but many exercises include at least a few items where student answers will vary and must be evaluated by the teacher. In Books 2 and 3, this is true of the last five items of almost every lesson. Concepts are reviewed throughout the book. Five tests each review all topics from the beginning of the book up through the current lesson, to again ensure that students retain what they have learned.

Part 1 covers parts of speech and word functions (with a handy reference chart), punctuation, and sentence structure. However, it concentrates heavily upon nouns, verbs, adjectives, adverbs, and prepositions. All of these topics are covered in detail such as we might find at college level. Students do many exercises where they construct sentences to "formulas," which requires that they develop a comfortable familiarity with definitions and functions. Part 2 continues to build on the lessons in

Part 1, although there is more emphasis on sentence patterns and formula writing than previously. More complicated structures and usage are covered along with topics such as appositives and internal sentence punctuation. The format is similar to that of Part 1. Part 3 completes the series with verbals, parallelism, and other challenging topics.

These books are recommended for high school level, although some junior high students will be able to use them. It should take about one year to complete all three books. It is unnecessary to study grammar again, but review might be helpful. *Jensen's Grammar, Review,* soon to be published, should serve that purpose.

See also the reviews of other Wordsmith language arts resources, *Major Punctuation* and *General Punctuation.*

◐ **A Journey through Grammar Land, Parts 1, 2, 3, and 4** (Wordsmiths) $15 each

Parts 1, 2, 3, and 4 are available with at least one more book scheduled.

Wordsmiths' workbooks, written by Christian teacher Frode Jensen, are designed to work in either homeschool or regular school settings. They are entirely self-contained. They can be used as consumable workbooks, or students can write answers in notebooks to preserve the books for other students.

The author has designed the *Grammar Land* books to be used for grades 5-7, although any older student lacking a foundation in grammar should probably begin with this series. The books are well designed for independent study. "These books are in allegory format and tell the story of how Tank, a young fellow with grammar and writing problems, travels through *Grammar Land* meeting all sorts of folks and learning about the language in the process." The first half of the book is the story (with illustrations); the second half is the exercises, called scrolls within the story. As students read through the story, they are actually receiving grammatical instruction. Every so often, the character is assigned to work on a particular scroll (exercise), which is a signal to the student to do that exercise. Helpful notes, definitions, and examples are scattered through the exercise section. Examinations are included.

Part 1 covers subjects, predicates, nouns, rules for noun plurals, inflectional and derivational suffixes, pronouns (person, case, gender, and number), antecedents, possessive nouns and pronouns, reflexive and indefinite pronouns, and punctuation. Part 2 reviews and expands upon the previously covered topics, with an emphasis on verbs (complete predicates, action verbs, linking verbs, verb tenses, etc.). Part 3 deals with adjectives and adverbs. Part 4 covers prepositions, prepositional phrases, conjunctions, compound sentences, and punctuation relating to all of these topics. Concepts are reviewed periodically to ensure retention of knowledge. An answer key is at the back of each book along with very brief notes for teachers. Since *Grammar Land* can be used independently by students, no teacher preparation time for the lessons is necessary, but it is helpful if parents take a few minutes to read the page found in the middle of each book (a strange location) which explains how to use the book. Students should be able to complete one or more books a year, depending upon what type of schedule is established.

The *Grammar Land* books should appeal to students who respond better to the story format and the unusual presentation, as well as those who prefer to work independently. Some students will find the pace too slow because of the interjection of the story.

◐ **Learning English with the Bible: A Systematic Approach to Bible-Based English Grammar** (AMG Publishers) $7.99; answer key - $4.99

This is a complete study of parts of speech using Scripture. Use with the *Diagramming Guide* below. This is a good tool for concentrating study of parts of speech rather than spreading it out over many years. It is most appropriate for upper elementary grades through high school. A companion answer key is also available.

◐ **Learning English with the Bible: Diagramming Guide** (AMG Publishers) $6.99

This is a complete course for diagramming. It accompanies *Learning English with the Bible* above. The text includes answers. Sentences from Scripture are used for the exercises and examples. Purchase the English grammar book and answer key plus the diagramming book as a set for $17.99.

◐ **Major Punctuation** by Frode Jensen (Wordsmiths) $11

While *General Punctuation* (reviewed above) covers the wide range of punctuation skills, this book focuses on five basic rules that Jensen says account for 75-90% of punctuation errors commonly committed by students. The rules deal with such issues as combining independent clauses, the use of semi-colons, and coordinating and adverbial conjunctions. Jensen uses symbols and patterns for sentence types, teaches with examples, then provides plenty of practice in a consumable worktext. Practice exercises use material drawn from classical literature. Students should be able to work through the exercises independently for the most part. Recommended for grades 7 and above.

◐ **Practice Exercises in Basic English 7 or 8** (Continental Press) $5.95 each

This small workbook covers basic skills except diagramming. Use this with *Easy Grammar* or *Winston Grammar* plus a writing supplement for a "minimalist" approach.(S)

◐ **Rules of the Game** (Educators Publishing Service) $7.15 each; answer keys - $2.45 each

This is a series of three, softbound workbooks that teach grammar by the inductive method. That means that rather than telling students a "rule" and following it with exercises, students are led to discover a general principle or definition for themselves. In actuality, the amount of discovery is quite minimal, but it still is a more interesting way to introduce grammar concepts. Once the concept has been presented, students practice with a variety of exercises. Like *Easy Grammar,* this is a more concise means of learning grammar, and it can be used with children of widely varying ages—from about fifth grade through high school. Book 1 covers nouns, pronouns, subjects, verbs, capitalization, punctuation, sentences, contractions, possessives, adjectives, adverbs, prepositions, interjections, conjunctions, compounds, and subject/verb agreement.

Book 2 briefly reviews the above, then continues with direct and indirect objects, linking verbs, predicate nouns and adjectives, appositives, objects of prepositions, prepositional phrases, and punctuation.

Book 3 works on dependent clauses, complex and compound-complex sentences, and verbals, while also supplying comprehensive application exercises for all previously learned grammatical elements. These inexpensive books are not reproducible, so purchase one for each student. Answer keys are also available at minimal cost.(S)

⊃ Skills Bank Home Tutor [for IBM and Apple II type machines] (SkillsBank Corporation)

See the description of the entire program where it first appears under math resources for junior high. The language module will help students with capitalization, grammar (including usage), punctuation, and spelling. While it is not comprehensive in all areas, it covers a lot of territory. Within each of the four areas listed, there are from eighteen to twenty-two topics covered at varying levels of difficulty. Instruction is included with guided practice, quizzes, and on-line help. Student progress is tracked on each student's access disk, so we can see which topics have been covered and which of those have been mastered.(S)

⊃ Winston Grammar by Paul Erwin (Precious Memories Educational Resources) Basic - $40; Advanced - $35; Supplemental Workbook and key - $17.50; extra Student Packet - $12.50

This is a hands-on approach for learning parts of speech, some usage concepts, and sentence structure. Students use Clue Cards as well as worksheets which they mark with arrows, lines, and symbols to identify sentence components. Good for most students, it is especially recommended for those who have had difficulty with traditional methods. It is more fun than diagramming and accomplishes the same purpose. There are two kits, Basic and Advanced. The Basic level covers all parts of speech, noun functions, prepositional phrases, and modifiers. The Supplemental Workbook is optional. It has more practice sentences (with subject matter drawn from U.S. history and geography). The Advanced level offers additional lessons on pronouns as well as verbals, clauses, and sentence types. However, *Winston Grammar* is not designed to offer complete coverage of all grammar topics that typically are taught in textbooks. The teacher's manual for each level has lesson plans and answer keys.

Composition Resources for Junior High

⊃ Amsco School Publications (Amsco)

Amsco has a Language Arts catalog listing many resources appropriate for junior high through adult learners. Their books work well for home education because they are designed for independent learning, generally in a worktext format. They are inexpensively priced, and instead of costly teacher's editions, they sell very low priced answer keys. Available titles cover a wide range of topics. Examples: *Writing About Amusing Things* (good for paragraph development), *Writing Logically, Fifteen Steps to Better Writing*, and *Writing the Research Paper.*(S)

⊃ Confidence in Writing by Ed Reynolds and Marcia Mixdorf (Harcourt Brace and Company) $30

This resource is ideal for high school level, but advanced junior high students should be able to use it. The complexity of both the ideas and the writing assignments might be too challenging for the average junior high student. See the complete review under high school level.

⊃ Creative Writing (A Beka) $7.10

Use this creative writing workbook to round out A Beka's *Language* series. This is best used on younger levels, but if students have done no writing, it is a good place to begin.

⊃ Creative Writing and the Essay for the Beginner by Dorothy E. Robbins (The Rebuilders of the Foundations of America's Christian Heritage) $12

Dorothy Robbins applies the Principle Approach to essay writing in such a way that it will work for those following that methodology in all areas as well as for those who are not. The seven principles of the Principle Approach are described in relation to the essay so that we understand the purpose behind the presentation. Robbins adds a brief historical background on essays so that we see the principles applied through history. Essay instruction itself emphasizes planning, form, and creative expression. Instruction includes various aspects of essay writing such as audience, appropriate choice of words, and various styles. Examples used are from modern, classical, and historical writings. Writing assignments are "meaty," worthwhile topics like the following example: "You will be writing an essay using the argumentative type of discourse to refute one or more of the twelve 'counterfeit principles' listed. Write this in the third person, singular, using 'one' and nouns rather than first or second person pronouns.... Use the Biblical principles to help you refute the unbiblical ones." The student might then choose a "counterfeit principle" such as "The Bible is a combination of myth and history book, written by men." or "The world is continually improving." Expect only a reasonable mastery of the concepts from students if they have had little experience in essay writing previously. These lessons set a high standard to which our students must aspire, but one which might take some time to achieve.

⊃ Critical Thinking Activities to Improve Writing Skills: Arguments A-1 by Michael Baker (Critical Thinking Books and Software) $10.95

This reproducible writing activity book poses sixteen different problems in the form of people looking for advice or solutions to problems of their own. Students are then taught how to analyze each problem and present possible solutions. In the process they develop a variety of writing skills such as outlining, organizing, letter writing, and paragraph development. Students are also working on critical thinking skills, reading skills (e.g., comprehension, inferences, identifying fact and opinion), and understanding the importance of proper grammar for clarity in writing. Lessons are designed for cooperative group learning, but they will adapt fairly well for use between a parent and child as long as the parent presents each lesson and participates in discussion. These lessons are actually quite fun, so I recommend trying to get a few junior high level students to work through them together.

There are three other books in the series, but because of their content and design, I find them less useful for home schoolers.(S)

➲ Easy Writing (ISHA Enterprises) $20.95

From the author of *Easy Grammar* comes a new approach to teaching writing. This is not a comprehensive writing program, but one that concentrates on sentence structure. Children learn how to write more interesting sentences by using conjunctions, subordinate clauses, participial phrases, and other more complex structures. Each unit within the book is divided into an easier level and a more difficult level. Some children instinctively construct interesting sentences, but many do not. This book will help those children (and parents) who have difficulty writing sentences more interesting than "The boy chased the dog." Student work sheets are reproducible, so one book will serve for more than one child.

➲ EZ Writer by Gerald R. Wheeler, Ed.D. and Vance Socash (Wheeler Applied Research) $39.95

EZ Writer helps students improve their expository writing skills with a systematic approach to sentence and paragraph writing. Training students to automatically write more creative and complex sentences and paragraphs than do most unskilled writers is the basic goal of the program. The system asks students to write numerous five-sentence paragraphs, each containing five different types of specified sentences. I won't reveal the "key" for the five different sentences since that's the heart of this program, but it has much to do with various parts of speech. This is a great tool for helping students see how learning parts of speech can translate into improved writing skills. Instruction begins with a 70-minute video tape covering the basic principles of the program. The video periodically tells the student to stop the tape and do some actual writing. This breaks up the passive time for those who have difficulty just sitting and watching. The video overlaps the first seven pages of the student book. Once finished with the video, students continue on through the book. A brief, 10-page teacher's guide offers parents guidelines for using the course. A tear-off pad of "Scrubbers" is included. Scrubbers are half-page sheets for students to evaluate and improve their own work. It features check off boxes next to 11 key things to recheck to "scrub their writing clean." The program urges students to substitute synonyms for over-worked words, but fails to recommend a thesaurus as a valuable tool for that purpose, something we can easily remedy ourselves. Towards the end of the book we find examples and suggestions for tackling academic reports, both those that can be contained within five sentences and lenghtier pieces. A Book 2 from *EZ Writer* plans to continue with

techniques for writing persuasive paragraphs, media copy, and dialogue. Appendices assist students with capitalization and punctuation rules, lists of adverbs, prepositions, and pronouns, and a four-step strategy summary. While *EZ Writer* focuses upon only one part of your language arts program, it is an excellent tool for developing and refining writing skills. *EZ Writer* might be used with students as young as fourth or fifth grades with lots of teacher assistance, but junior and senior high students should be able to go through most of it on their own.(S)

➲ From Heart to Page: Journaling Through TheYear For Young Writers by Michelle Van Loon (Michelle Van Loon) $4.25

Often, our problem with getting children to write stems from a lack of ideas. Michelle Van Loon promotes the use of daily journaling to establish the habit and discipline of writing, but she makes it easy by suggesting writing prompts for each day. She has arranged the prompts by seasons, with fewer for summer than for the other seasons. She leaves every fifth day (typically Friday) a "free writing" day. The prompts themselves are good for all ages and are wide-ranging; they deal with events, experiences, observations, feelings, spiritual issues, and more. These are not directed writing lessons to be evaluated, but prompts to encourage our children to establish regular writing habits. Journals become personal records rather than documentation of learning. Children who write every day will undoubtedly improve their skills, and those skills can be developed and evaluated using other resources and methods. A few examples will help you "get the flavor" of this booklet: "Describe your perfect autumn day. Start with the first thing you'd like to do after breakfast and tell how you'd fill your day." "Do you have any siblings? What do you like best about each of them? What causes your biggest conflicts?"

➲ Newspaper Workshop by Howard Decker (Globe Fearon Educational Publisher) $12.95; teacher's resource manual - $7.95

Students learn how a newspaper is written, then work through fun writing activities that include proofreading and copyediting. Also purchase the teacher's manual.(S)

➲ The Paragraph System for Successful Writing by Caulean Vesey (Royal Fireworks Press) $9.99

This is a handbook for junior and senior high students, which helps them develop skills in organizing their writing. Since well-constructed paragraphs are the key, most of the book works on different methods for structuring paragraphs, depending upon their purposes. Models for different strategies are used, with examples provided. After basic paragraph development is mastered, lengthier types of writing are tackled. There are actually very few assignments in the book, so it is up to the student or parent to determine what, when, and how students will apply lessons.

The author assumes that students are in traditional schools and are doing the types of writing assignments that are typical of schools. Thus, most lessons are structured with those assignments in mind. There are strategies for writing book reports, various types of essays (especially in answer to essay test questions), short reports, and assignments for other subject areas. Lessons on using dialog and anecdotes equip students with skills to make their writing more interesting.

The author's approach stresses discipline, structure, and organization throughout. A clue to the tone of the book is the introductory chapter on penmanship, which stresses a very neat, traditional style, with attention to details. The strategies can seem a little complicated at first to those who are not used to analyzing paragraph construction, but they should be especially effective with students who are concerned about detail, enjoy analyzing their writing, and appreciate pre-planned formats. A little effort put into practicing these skills will pay off in the future, particularly for students who will be encountering the myriad of writing assignments typical of high school and college.(S)

➲ Practicing the Writing Process 1: The Paragraph
(Educational Design) $10.95

This workbook on writing skills emphasizes paragraph-writing technique. It contains a few sections that some might find objectionable, particularly a writing example about a dance performance that is used throughout the book. It is recommended for grades four through high school, but it was originally designed for remedial teaching for older students. Students can work independently through this book to develop and improve writing skills.(SE)

➲ Practicing the Writing Process 2: The Essay (Educational Design) $10.95

Many students have difficulty developing their essay writing skills, either because the topic is not covered at all or it is not covered well enough. Junior and senior high students can use this book to develop and sharpen those skills. The book is suitable for either independent or group work. However, the writing exercises do require evaluation and/or assistance from a parent/teacher.

Lessons offer thorough treatment of the skills required for writing essays that are both structurally sound and interesting to read. Lessons are organized according to the writing process with sections on prewriting, writing, revising, and editing. A section on constructing good sentences helps students avoid common mistakes. The emphasis throughout the first five sections is upon writing personal essays, so the sixth section teaches students how to write expository and persuasive essays. Especially valuable for home educated students who rarely experience writing under the same time constraints as do classroom students is the final lesson, "How to Write Under Pressure." Lessons use plenty of examples and practice exercises, with lengthier writing assignments as they progress.

This book differs from *Wordsmith* in that it concentrates more on essay writing and less on grammar and structural elements. *Writing with a Point* emphasizes creative elements and organization around the central thesis, with less time spent on the overall writing process. While *Practicing the Writing Process 2* works well on its own, you might find it useful to combine it with other resources depending upon each student's needs.(S)

➲ Practicing the Writing Process 4: The Writing Test
(Educational Design) $11.95

The main topic in this book is essay writing, with an eye toward the types of essays found on tests. The persuasive essay gets the most attention since it seems to be the most commonly-tested form. Other types are comparison/contrast, problem/solution, how-to, and descriptive. Instructions are interspersed with numerous examples of student essays of varying quality. Weak essays are used for rewriting and improvement practice, while excellent essays are analyzed to figure out why they "work." The authors have done an excellent job of presenting the material in interesting lesson formats, mixing instruction and practice. Many of the sample essays and writing prompts (test questions) concern school issues, but none should be impossible for home schoolers to deal with. Most are quite similar to the types of prompts I have seen on tests. Evaluation checklists help students edit their own work, although working with another student or a parent might be even better. After students have completed the lessons, assign your own essay topics or select some from literature or history textbooks.

In addition to essay-writing skills, there is a section on sentence construction, usage, and mechanics. It covers the basics: subject-verb agreement, pronoun cases, spelling rules, punctuation, capitalization, etc. This section is followed by a series of practice tests on these concepts. This book is usable for junior high level, but when complemented by the study of literature, makes a complete high school course.(S)

➲ Report Writing: Formula for Success (Continental Press) $6.75

This is a concise book on how to do a research report, written in a very easy-to-read format. It is perfect for the reluctant researcher.(S)

➲ Skills Bank Home Tutor [for IBM and Apple II type machines] (SkillsBank Corporation)

See the description of the entire program where it first appears under math resources for junior high. The writing module covers language mechanics (e.g., letter writing, error identification, quotations, comma usage), language usage (parts of speech in usage), sentence structure (syntax, patterns, construction, combinations), and paragraphs (organization and coherence). There are actually up to twelve separate topics addressed within each of the four described areas. Working through this module will help sharpen writing skills for students in preparation for high school level writing assignments, although students do no actual writing of their own.(S)

➲ WIN Program by Dr. Les Simonson (Elijah Company) *Level II* - $20, *Essay Handbook* - $10

The WIN program consists of a series of books with general grade level designations. *Level II* comes in a comb-bound book and is suggested for grades 3-5 but appropriate for any age beginning writer. *The Essay Handbook,* for grades 6 through high school, is a lengthy book also in comb-bound format. All of the WIN books use a "formula" approach to writing. There are designated lines and/or boxes for conveying specific information.

Wordy writers have to learn to be concise. While the idea of writing to a formula is somewhat constricting, it does teach the importance of organization and planning very well. There are key elements essential to stories and other forms of writing, and none will be omitted if students work through these lessons. The presentation of the WIN Program makes it very easy for the inexperienced parent to successfully teach her (or his) children to write.

Level II will stand alone and it makes an excellent introductory writing course. It is suggested for grades 3-5. There are no grade level indications, and content is not necessarily "young," so I see no problem with students even up through high school working with *Level II*. It works with four basic story elements: setting, story problem, action-solution, and conclusion. Instruction covers both mechanics and style, although it is by no means a grammar course. Students work through a number of models/forms, studying examples and gradually building upon basic skills. They write on the forms (reproduced from the originals provided in the book), working within controlled boxes. Although the boxes are limiting, they teach discipline and organization. In the appendices are additional exercises and helps for lively story starters and dialogue, lists of more colorful synonyms for commonly-used words, an editing chart, reproducible forms, plus guides for capitalization and punctuation. While it might be possible to work through all of this in a year, it will probably take a few years to bring students up to the advanced levels of writing demonstrated here. *Level II* is a good resource to use for a group writing class.

The Essay Handbook focuses on this particular writing form, which is so essential as students progress into high school and college. Dr. Simonson wrote this user-friendly book to make the essay writing process simpler for students to understand and easier for teachers to teach. The result is a formula-approach to essay writing that helps students develop a thorough understanding of the elements of a good essay. The emphasis is on organization, reasoning, and logical presentation rather than style. (Check out *Writing with a Point* [Educators Publishing Service] or lessons in *Level II* to work on style.) The essay-writing process is tackled in four steps: outlining, planning (expanding upon notes), rough draft, and final draft. Reproducible worksheets for each step walk students through with explicit instructions. Samples are provided. The Appendix includes instructions, sample, and forms for writing an eleven-sentence essay—a great way to introduce students to the concepts taught in this book without overwhelming them.

⊃ Write Source 2000 Language Series (Great Source)
handbook - $11.75; SourceBooks student editions - $10.95 each; teacher editions - $14.95 each

Write Source 2000 Language Series is a three-year middle school writing program. The authors have centered almost exclusively on teaching the writing process, and they have certainly produced a product of superior quality and ease of use. There are several components of the program, ranging in price from quite expensive to very inexpensive, and luckily for home schoolers, it is the inexpensive parts that are of the most interest. This comprehensive writing program centers around a student handbook called *Write Source 2000*. A student assignment book is also necessary, and there are three optional resources for the teacher. Because the names of some of the components are similar, the catalog can be confusing at first. Let's take a look at each of the five books separately.

The central item, the *Write Source 2000* handbook, is a one-time purchase which can be used in sixth through eighth grades. Among the topics covered in the handbook are paragraphs and essays, writing various types of essays, creative writing, usage, and an almanac. Do not depend upon the handbook for basic grammar instruction since it is designed for grammatical reference rather than as a teaching tool. A large section of the handbook details the writing process itself, from brainstorming to revising. *Write Source 2000* is colorful and non-threatening, with humorous illustrations. Three student *SourceBooks* (one for each grade level) contain the actual writing activities. These books are consumable and have more of a workbook approach than the high school program, but many assignments require writing at least a paragraph. Each *SourceBook* has some grammar review, vocabulary work, and study techniques, in addition to the writing assignments. The work in the *SourceBook* is keyed to the *Write Source 2000* handbook for easy reference and professional samples of the type of writing being taught. (A caution is in order about a few of the samples. Some of the topics depict school life that might be unfamiliar to home schoolers, and others focus on "current events," such as the Live Aid Concert. However, these are minor inconveniences compared to the worth of this program.)

The teacher-support material is optional to varying degrees. The *Language Series Program Guide* ($125) contains daily activities, thematic units, overview, objectives, and information on assessment. A separate *Program Guide* is needed for each grade level. The *Program Guide* is geared to the traditional classroom, and most home school teachers will have little need of this material. There is a teacher's guide to the *Write Source 2000* handbook ($14.95), also geared to the classroom, but so inexpensive that it is probably worth investing in. It has start-up activities, mini-lessons, and reviews, and is a one-time purchase also. A teacher's edition of each *SourceBook* is also available, and this will be useful to most parents, providing answers for the grammar and usage workshops.

Write Source 2000 provides new learning experiences in each grade, but also recycles enough activities that students who use the program for three years will be able to refine their writing. *Write Source 2000 Language Series* is designed to be used for three years, and there is also a high school version, called Writers INC. (See high school section.) However, a student can enter at any point and still get value from using the program. Even if you already have a writing program that your students are happy with, consider buying the handbook for their reference.(SE)[Kath Courtney]

⊃ Writing for Life, Books 1 and 2 (Globe Fearon Educational Publisher) $7.95 each; teacher's manuals - $4.50 each

These books are for the desperate parent who is concerned about his or her child's ability to write well enough to function. They are written for the student writing at a very low level because of poor educational background, physical reasons, etc. The purpose is to develop functional skills. Students can work independently through the books because of the worktext format. However, most students who will need this type of book will also need supervision and interaction. In Book 1, students begin by writing complete sentences, then paragraphs. Next they learn how to write telephone messages and notes as well as how to take notes about something they have read. Letters, addressing envelopes, writing invitations, directions, and thank-you notes are covered in the next section. Assuming that most students are in school, the next section covers class schedules, computerized test response forms, other school forms, and taking notes. The last section deals with life: bank accounts, ordering by mail, and writing business letters. Book 2 helps students develop writing skills essential for work and dealing with businesses, including writing a resumé.

Examples and exercises help students to break down tasks into manageable chunks before they tackle a task in its entirety. There is space for all work to be done in the books.(S)

➲ Writing Poetry (Curriculum Associates) $6.95

Writing Poetry is a tool for introducing and developing poetry appreciation and writing skills. It begins with activities to develop awareness of what poetry is and helps tune students into sensory words and feelings which play a major part in poetry. The next section works on rhyming, followed by synonyms and antonyms. Students are then introduced to free verse, then the idea of painting pictures with words. (This middle section of the book is good for developing similar skills to use with any type of writing!) Students begin to search for just the right word to convey their meaning, while also learning how to use similes, metaphors, personification, hyperbole, and alliteration. Exercises that help students change general statements to specific sharpen their skills. Toward the end, various poetic forms are taught, including haiku, tercet, cinquain, limerick, quatrain, and narrative. The lessons do not get into meter, accent, and other more advanced poetic conventions.

This self-contained book has the answers to pertinent exercises in the back. Instruction and examples are provided, followed by activities or lines for writing exercises. Most junior high and all senior high students should be able to work through this book independently. There is a strong leaning toward feelings and emotions within the book (as is appropriate for poetry), but some students will find this type of study very uncomfortable and/or exceedingly difficult because of their personalities.(S)

➲ Writing Step by Step: Developing Paragraphs by Asking Questions by Mary Lou Ward (Builder Books) $8.95

Mary Lou Ward has developed some terrific ideas for helping children to see how simple the writing process can become with some "maps" to help them organize their ideas. She gives some basic questions for writers to ask themselves to get started with ideas, then shows how to string the ideas together with connective words to create a paragraph very simply. There are three sections in the book, one geared for lower grades, one for upper grades, and the last containing reproducible "maps" for students to use for writing projects. In the upper grades, students learn how to write a basic paragraph and organize their thoughts. Later

they learn four other types of writing: explaining steps in a process, comparison and contrast, problem/cause, and cause/effect. Use this resource if your child is not yet able to write an orderly paragraph or has trouble organizing ideas.

➲ Writing Strands, Levels 5 through 7, Creating Fiction, Writing Exposition, and Reading Strands (National Writing Institute) Levels 5 and 6 - $20.95 each; Level 7, Creating Fiction, Writing Exposition, or Reading Strands - $22.95 each

This is a great way to teach writing in the home school, especially for the parent with little writing experience. Lots of creative ideas, laid out step-by-step for (primarily) independent student work, set these books apart from others. Lessons are broken up into daily assignments to keep students from becoming overwhelmed. The strands (types of writing) within the books at these levels are argumentative, creative, explanatory, and report. (Developing skills in these areas will be important for high school level work.) Level numbers do not correspond to grade levels; Level 5 might be used in ninth grade, or it might be used earlier if a student has already completed Level 4. Levels 6 and 7 are best for high school. *Writing Strands* is a good supplement to *Learning Language Arts through Literature* or *Understanding Writing*.

After Level 7, students might want to tackle *Creating Fiction* or *Writing Exposition*. According to the author, *Creating Fiction* is "a fairly sophisticated creative writing book. It contains the creative writing assignments I have created for my son and used in my high school and college creative writing classes. It contains not just the assignments but the best of the papers and writings those assignments have produced. It is a program designed to teach a student to write short fiction." The lessons are well-developed, but some home educators will have problems with some of the content. For example, one of the first writing assignments asks students to write descriptions of a cheerleader from six different points of view including those of two older men in the stands and her boyfriend. This and other assignments and examples create an overall tone quite different from that of the other *Writing Strands* books. At the end of the book is information about how to submit pieces to magazines that publish young writers.(S)

Writing Exposition is an advanced course in expository writing. Thirteen lessons each tackle different writing assignments. Some of these are quite inventive, and many are very challenging for the average high schooler. Assignments include writing a "suspenseful" piece, creating a library manual, writing about (and exploring) abstract ideas, evaluating books by their covers, writing an argumentative piece about cultural stability, writing an argumentative piece on role models, writing a comparison and contrast piece, analyzing conversations for the use and reactions to the word "I," writing a reaction paper, writing with bias, writing a propaganda piece and an analysis of how propaganda works, writing a research paper, and writing about magazine evaluation. Lessons vary on how much step-by-step help is offered. "Notes" page(s) follow each lesson which help students with the collection and organization of information. The last of the book is appendices. These include student writing samples from the above exercises, two-pages of instructions on writing expository papers, helps for the SAT II writing test, essay prompts and sample essays, tips for taking essay exams, and a section on "Writing Problems and How to Avoid Them." Lessons might be used in any order, so you might select those that seem most appropriate for a student, perhaps using the different lessons over more than a single school year.

For extra help in developing good creative writing skills, check out the National Writing Institute's *Reading Strands* [$22.95]. It teaches parents how to use a Socratic method of instruction that can be used with children ages 4-18. Many of the sections that teach parents how to help children analyze what they are reading can be of great value as we are teaching writing. *Reading Strands* helps students develop reading interpretation skills, which in turn helps them think more about plot, characterization, motivation, etc. and how to translate those elements into interesting stories of their own.(S)

⊃ **Writing to God's Glory: A Comprehensive Creative Writing Course from Crayon to Quill** by Jill Bond (Holly Hall Publications/Homeschool Press) 39.99

Jill Bond translates her wealth of experience as a published author into a valuable resource for parents and teachers who want to stimulate and guide their own, sometimes reluctant, budding authors. This 300-page book is divided into two primary sections: a teacher's guide and student pages.

An introductory section of about 50 pages "teaches the teacher" with specific guidelines for teaching this program as well as more universal writing instruction guidelines under headings such as, "Grading and Other Forms of Torture," "Kevorkian Teaching Techniques" (which tend to kill off budding authors), and "Light, Salt, and Red Marks" (the proper use of encouragement and red pens). As you might guess from these headings, Jill uses a humorous approach throughout the book. Within this initial section, we also find "Action Learning," ten terrific, pre-writing activities that develop skills such as observation, characterization, identifying shades of meaning, and use of the five senses.

The remainder of the teacher's guide and the section containing the student pages are both organized into five divisions: Writing Well (the writing process or mechanics of building a story), Craftsmen Exercises (work with grammar), Outlet Journal (preparing and sending pieces for publication), Ideas (worksheets and a checklist for planning stories), and Favorites (favorite quotes, story ideas, fun words, examples, and more). Writing Well and the Craftsmen Exercises form the bulk of the activities.

Throughout the book, rather than tackle all types of writing, Jill focuses on story writing. However, she observes that the skills for writing an interesting story transfer readily to writing interesting essays and reports. Writing Well lessons alert students to techniques for describing setting, developing characters, outlining plots, identifying conflicts, ensuring that a story has a conclusion, and developing style. It also stresses a "Christian" approach to writing in purpose, content, and presentation.

The Craftsmen Exercises are not a primary teaching tool for grammar, but, through creative exercises, they help students understand how grammar rules apply to their actual writing.

Parents and children can actually learn to write together through *Writing to God's Glory*. It can be used with children of all ages if we adjust the activities in keeping with the ages and abilities of the writers. (We'll skip some activities with younger children.) We can use most of the activities in whatever order we please, although, if students are tackling a complete story, they should first work through the lessons on character development, plot, etc. in the Writing Well and Ideas sections.

The teacher needs to invest time reading the first section, then looking through lessons to select those most appropriate. Once those steps are accomplished, lesson preparation time is minimal. We need to reproduce the student pages, which students should maintain in a three-ring binder, divided into the five sections reflecting the organization of the book. Lessons are presented by the teacher, then students spend varying amounts of time completing their writing assignments. Some of the activities are very brief, but those who actually write stories will obviously invest much more time.

This is an inspiring, user-friendly approach with tremendous flexibility and Godly purpose.

⊃ **Written and Illustrated by...** by David Melton (Landmark Editions, Inc.) $15.95

Landmark Editions is the publisher of books which are written and illustrated by children. Every year they sponsor a contest to select such books for publication. *Written and Illustrated by...* is a teaching manual for helping children write, illustrate, assemble, and bind their own books. It has lesson plans, illustrations, and suggestions for working with all grade levels. Whether or not children choose to enter the contest, they can still learn to expand their creativity with the practical ideas provided here. To obtain a copy of the current Rules and Guidelines, send a self-addressed, business-sized envelope, stamped with $.64 postage to The National Written and Illustrated by... Awards Contest for Students at Landmark's address, listed in the appendix.(S)

Listening Skills

⊃ **Communicate** by Rebecca L. Avery (The Weaver)

See the review under "Grammar and Composition Resources for High School."

⊃ **Learning To Listen** (Educators Publishing Service) $5.55; teacher's manual - $4.15; cassette - $5.35

Suggested for grades 7-9, this book deals with the broader communication process rather than writing alone. This 48-page workbook takes students through eight basic listening skills: following directions, following a sequence, using context clues, using different skills for different subjects, finding topics and main ideas, listening for details, listening to make inferences, and taking notes while listening. The teacher's manual contains the "scripts" for the listening assignments, each of which will take no longer than three minutes to read. If preferred, there is a cassette tape of the selections that students may listen to so that they can work independently. Listening assignments are followed by workbook exercises.(S)

Grammar and Composition Resources for High School

Most high school students should have already acquired a mastery of basic grammar, so their energies should be directed toward improving composition skills. A poor knowledge of grammar can be corrected by reviewing material in any upper level English text or using any of the non-age-graded materials listed above such as *Easy Grammar, Rules of the Game,* and *Exploring Truths.*

Rather than having high school students do a complete grammar program, it might be just as effective to use only reference sources for grammar skills. The basics should have been mastered, so a reference book could be used for areas that present problems, either while writing or for correction afterwards. *Writers Inc* (Great Source) might serve well as a handbook. (See commentary below.) *BJUP's English Handbook* and many college level grammar handbooks are quite similar to each other, and most any will work well at high school level. Another resource, which you might have been using on a younger level is *Learning Grammar through Writing* (Educators Publishing Service) [$7.95], which presents the rules of grammar and composition listed with reference numbers. The teacher can use this to mark students' writing with reference numbers for the student to identify and correct errors.

Many students will need only a minimal amount of review to retain grammatical knowledge. *Daily Grams* (ISHA Enterprises) [$16.95] is ideal for such review.

⊃ Applications of Grammar, Books 3, 4 and 5 (Christian Liberty Press) $7.95; teacher's edition - $6.95; test booklet - $3.95

Books 3-5 in this series are designated for grade 9-11, although you might use them at different levels since there are no grade level designations. These are wide-ranging books, covering grammar, spelling, vocabulary, and composition. If students have been using serious grammar resources up to this point, they can switch to this series at ninth grade, but students with poor backgrounds in grammar will need more coverage of the basics before they can use these books. Grammatical instruction is the strongest aspect; they cover parts of speech and usage at increasingly difficult levels. Most of it is conventional, although the idea of topic sentences having both a topic and a "clew" uses an uncommon definition for clew. Grammar lessons typically follow the same format: brief instruction, examples, and practice exercises. Diagramming is not taught. Spelling and vocabulary words are presented as lists for students to study on their own. Sometimes a single fill-in-the-blank exercise or writing assignment accompanies a list, but there are no other specific guidelines or activities given. Writing assignments often instruct students to research a topic about which they will write. Instruction for the writing process is minimal, so we should use another resource or other writing activities to better cover the subject.

These books are less intensive than A Beka's grammar books, but they do provide good coverage of grammar, and they are very inexpensive. The teacher's editions have answers and occasional teacher notes or explanations that we should share with students. Other than that, students can work through their books on their own. I found nothing distinctively Christian about the content; the books could be used in any traditional school. Books 1 and 2 for seventh and eighth grades have been totally revised and differ dramatically from Books 3, 4, and 5. (Note: Book 3 should be revised in 1998, with other books due to be revised in 1999 or later. See the review of Books 1 and 2 which have already been revised.)

⊃ Basics of Systematic Grammar (Bob Jones University Press) $8; teacher's manual - $6

This 64-page booklet is for independent use by students who reach high school with little or no knowledge of English grammar. It covers parts of speech and basic functions in sentences. Programmed-learning is the instructional method.

⊃ Comprehensive Composition (Design-A-Study) $14

See the description under recommendations for junior high.

⊃ Confidence in Writing by Ed Reynolds and Marcia Mixdorf (Harcourt Brace and Company) $30

Confidence in Writing is one of the best comprehensive writing texts for home schoolers at the high school level. It fits the independent learning mode of most home educated teens since it speaks directly to the student rather than relying on a "classroom with teacher" setting as does the excellent *Writing: Process to Product*. It covers the writing process from brainstorming and writing paragraphs through essay writing, while stretching beyond the mechanics to the "heart" of writing. Assignments range from creative through expository, but always stressing audience, point of view, purpose, and other elements that produce interesting writing. It uses numerous examples, from rough drafts to final versions, so that students can learn how to take their own initial efforts and improve them with more vivid or purposeful language. A section on summary writing covers an important but oft-neglected area with simple but effective strategies. Lessons are presented with instruction combined with examples, then followed by assignments. The assignments are specifically focused on particular aspects of the writing process, but students are also given nine "Standards for Judging Writing" (pp. 14.-15) by which they are expected to continually evaluate their own writing. The last quarter of the book is a reference handbook that includes capitalization and punctuation rules along with sentence structure concepts and common writing problems and their solutions.

Two omissions prevent me from giving this resource an unqualified recommendation. The first omission is research-based writing. I would prefer to see some instruction on footnotes, endnotes, and bibliographies since I believe that high school students should be learning to draw information from recognized sources rather than relying only upon their personal experiences and opinions. However, this lack can be supplemented with inexpensive resources such as *Report Writing* from Continental

Press. The other lack is more significant for Christian home educators—the lack of a Christian viewpoint modifying the content. While there are only a few mildly troubling examples used within the book (e.g., description of a Viet Cong soldier being blown up and a gang shooting), most of the writing examples reflect the world as encountered by the typical public school student (should we expect anything else?) and lack the morally uplifting character that many of us prefer.

The pluses—comprehensive coverage of the writing process, interesting presentation, format appropriate for independent work, and the fact that we need purchase only the one book—make this an excellent choice for home educators.(SE)

➲ Creative Writing (A Beka) $7.10

This fairly easy book can be used for grades 7-10 as a supplement. It is recommended for those with little experience in creative writing.

➲ Driving It Home (Twain Publishers) $45

A video and text team up for this narrowly focused presentation about improving writing skills. The key idea is that good writing uses strong rather than weak verbs. The approximately 30-minute video features dramatized vignettes and a passionate presentation by Paul LeRoux to illustrate the contrast between active, to-the-point writing and passive, wordy writing. The 43-page textbook repeats the ideas, using different language and illustrations. Exercises referred to in the video are at the back of the text along with the answers, so you will need both components. I suggest watching the video, working through the exercises, then going back through the text at a more leisurely pace to reinforce the lessons. *Driving It Home* was designed for the business world, as evidenced by the examples and references to bosses and co-workers, but it should work well for homeschoolers in both junior and senior high. It does not assume prior student mastery of grammar, so it might be especially useful for the student who has a weak academic background and needs some real-life application for motivation. Also see the review of *Enough About Grammar* from the same publisher.(S)

➲ Easy Writing (ISHA Enterprises)

See description under seventh and eighth grades.

➲ Elements of Writing (Holt, Rinehart and Winston) *Third Course* (Grade 9), *Fourth Course* (Grade 10), *Fifth Course* (Grade 11), and *Complete Course* (Grade 12). Pupils editions cost $53, $53, $55.75, and $55.75 respectively; teacher's editions cost $91, $91, $94.50, and $102 respectively.

When Harcourt Brace Jovanovich merged with Holt, Rinehart and Winston the well-regarded Warriner's English Composition and Grammar series was revised. The new series is entitled *Elements of Writing*. It is co-authored by John Warriner and Dr. James L. Kinneavy, who strengthens the composition aspects of the series. The books are updated in appearance with color and illustrations. The composition instruction is the heart of the book, with the grammatical instruction cross referenced through composition lessons and used as reference material. Literary models are included within each text as learning tools. This helps students learn both grammar and composition skills within the context of actual usage, which helps with motivation and retention of information. Writing assignments are defined more by process than topic, which gives students much more room to individualize their writing than do the assignments found in many other texts.

Grammar is presented separately in the second part of the book. It can serve as a handbook (particularly when used in conjunction with exercises in the first part of the book), but it also has exercises, diagnostic tests, review/posttests, and writing assignments. No diagramming is in the *Complete Course* book, but it is included in an appendix in the *Second Course* (eighth grade level). I haven't been able to determine whether or not it is in the other high school level books, but most students should have studied diagramming as much as they need by high school level.

Following the grammar section are chapters on topics such as speech, debate, library/media, dictionary, vocabulary, letters and forms, and studying and test taking. (Topics vary slightly from text to text.)

There is quite a bit of overlap in content from year to year in each text, although some new topics are presented at each level. Various types of writing activities would be the most prominent difference. Consider using a single text over a two- or three-year period rather than buying separate ones for each year, since there is plenty of material in any one book. (The *Complete Course*/12th grade book is 1154 pages! There is enough in this one book to cover a number of years of instruction.)

Annotated Teacher's Editions feature large reproductions of the student pages surrounded by teaching instructions. They also have answers to exercises. Parents will probably want both student and teacher editions, although parents who are strong in grammar should be able to manage without the teacher's book.(S)

➲ English Fun Stuff by Frode Jensen (Wordsmiths) $11

See the review "Grammar and Composition Resources for High School."

This new book by Mr. Jensen is full of games, activities and a few worksheets to spice up a language arts program. It is a resource book, rather than a textbook, but it can be used many times in the years from junior high through high school. Its low price makes it an excellent value. The author's slant shows the influence of the traditional classroom (he suggests "filling up the time" at the end of the period with some of the activities), but most activities can very easily be used in the home. Some are small group activities and some are for individuals. Jensen shows how to apply various games to other subject areas, such as to help reinforce science vocabulary. Many of the sections are quite imaginative, and there is great variety in the types of games. One group of puzzles are lists of proverbs, both scriptural and folk wisdom, rewritten in exaggerated language. The trick is to put them back into everyday speech. For example, "the promptest feathered biped seizes the annelid," becomes the very familiar "the early bird catches the worm." One of these a day could be used to spark interest at the beginning of class. Other types of puzzles range from logic problems to cryptograms of quotes from Shakespeare (including instructions to make your own cryptograms). The directions for the games are easy to follow. The least interesting sections are those that are the most traditional (the worksheets), but even some of these are quite imaginative. Our family tried out several of the games, outside of our school time, and had fun with all of them.[Kath Courtney]

⮌ **English 9, 10, 11, and 12: Writing and Grammar** (Bob Jones University Press) student worktexts - $12 each; teacher's editions - $36 each; TestBanks - $16 each

BJUP balances grammatical skills with their end goal of purposeful and effective communication by providing instruction, practice, review, and practical application throughout their English courses. Motivational themes trail through each course, with stories about the impact of writing as well as other "communication" experiences.

All levels review basic grammar. Levels 9 through 11 each introduce a few new grammatical concepts. There is a strong emphasis on writing skills throughout all levels. Grade nine covers a wide variety of basic writing skills, concentrating on good description and organization. Grade ten works on outlining, writing, and revising. Students write a story in this course. Grade eleven teaches more types of writing, including persuasive writing and the research paper. Grade twelve helps students learn to use the power of the written word in formats such as literary criticism, essays, interviews, letters, tracts, resumes, and letters to the editor.

While there are student worktexts for each grade, the teacher's editions contain essential parts of the courses for each level. The teacher's editions also organize presentation of each lesson, which, if taken just from the worktext, might seem haphazard. Students also need the English Handbook (BJUP) to use at all levels. TestBanks are available for each level.

Lessons contain material for about half of the school year, assuming that the other half of English class will be devoted to the study of literature. Lessons for literature and writing/grammar can be alternated in sections, but they will not work well if alternated day by day. Alternatively, a semester can be allocated for each.

⮌ **English** (Houghton Mifflin/McDougal Littell) [1989 editions] student books: 9th grade - $39.54, grades 10-12 - $41.31 each; teachers editions: 9th grade - 86.46, grades 10-12 - $86.46 each

There are separate texts for grades 9 through 12. This English series does an outstanding job of developing writing skills, moving beyond the mechanics of the writing process into mood, voice, tone, and other elements of style. Plenty of examples help to illustrate ideas clearly, and the examples in the ninth grade book I reviewed seem to lean less toward political correctness than do those in the junior high books. Grammar is taught separately in the last third of the book. Grammar instruction is fairly straightforward. Writing practice activities that link grammar with writing appear periodically throughout the grammar chapters. Diagramming is covered superficially in a small section. Additional chapters in the ninth grade book address vocabulary development, speaking and listening, library skills, test taking,

study skills, and spelling rules. A Writer's Handbook at the end of the book features writing prompts, organizing strategies for writing, and a dictionary of common usage problems. Books for grades 10-12 follow the same format.

This McDougal, Littell *English* series (there are other series that teach English from the same publisher, but they have different titles) is a good solution for those who want a complete English course in one book. Students can work independently through the much of the text, even though developing writing skills always requires interaction and feedback from time to time. Parents might want to set up a schedule that intermixes units on grammar and writing rather than concentrating heavily on writing first and grammar last. This also balances time needed for interaction on writing assignments with independent work on grammar activities.

The primary value of the teacher's edition will be as an answer key, although there are also some tips on teaching and evaluating writing.(S)

⮌ **English I-IV courses for grades 9-12** (School of Tomorrow) 12 Paces - $48; answer keys - $16 for each level

12 PACEs per grade level are used for instruction in grammar, literature, vocabulary, and composition. Each PACE features a character quality as its theme, with a "Wisdom" study in the center of each booklet and a related Scripture verse to be memorized. Grammar, including diagramming, receives the most attention in *English I*, with little time spent on composition. The balance shifts to more composition and less grammar through each level. Students learn to write essays, short stories, and term papers. Literature is incorporated throughout each level, with students assigned books to read. Questions regarding the books are found in the PACEs. *English I* uses *Swiss Family Robinson* and *Twice Freed*. *English II* requires students to read *The Hiding Place* and *God's Tribesman*. *English III* assigns excerpts from *The Oregon Trail* and the entire book of *In His Steps*. *English IV* incorporates *Macbeth*, *The Rime of the Ancient Mariner,* and *Silas Marner*.

⮌ **English Handbook** (BJUP) $26

This basic handbook for grades 9-12 is to be used with all levels of *BJUP's Writing and Grammar.*

⮌ **Enough About Grammar: What Really Matters and What Really Doesn't** by Joe Floren (Twain Productions) $30, student workbook - $17; answer key - $10

This funny and common-sense guide to grammar is aimed at adults in the workplace. Consequently, it is great for high school students who want to know what is really useful for the "real world." An example will give you a sense of the author's approach: In discussing poets' frequent violations of grammatical rules, he says,

Grammarians, sore as anything about poets' ignoring the rules, asked the government to tax them. The King responded by forcing every rhyme-maker to buy a Poetic License (the cost varying with the weight of the poem). So that solved that. However, pretty soon English peasants and other illiterate folks unable to read the

Rules of Grammar also began to take shortcuts in usage. Fearing that if the government clamped down, the people would revolt and storm the Bastille (which, as a precaution, had been located in France), grammarians decided just to let it ride. The true point in this false history is that everyday usage over the centuries has knocked the corners off textbook English.

Many other examples use "work place language"—employees, staff, job descriptions, corporate expenditures, etc.

This book presents the rules that matter, while encouraging the reader to get beyond the idea of just writing correctly. Its goal is to strengthen writing by using clauses with active verbs. The author also tells how to place these clauses within sentences so that they produce the greatest effect. Capitalization, punctuation, abbreviations, and spelling all receive special attention.

The book itself is a hefty, 200+ page hard cover resource. Also available is a consumable exercise workbook for students plus accompanying answer key. Exercises help students practice and review concepts presented in *Enough About Grammar* using only sentences from the Bible and hymns. The workbook is, therefore, more serious in tone than the book itself. There are numerous examples in the main book, but exercises are important to ensure that students actually understand and can apply the lessons.[Valerie Thorpe/C.D.]

⮕ The Exciting World of Creative Writing by Ruth E. McDaniel (Christian Liberty Press) $6.95

This really is an "exciting" book about creative writing. Author Ruth McDaniel has written many short stories which I have read and thoroughly enjoyed. She is an ideal person to create a book to help others follow in her footsteps. Consequently, this is a practical, meaty, interesting resource rather than a school exercise-oriented book, although, it does have a few exercises to review grammar and sentence construction essentials early in the book. Use these or not according to the language skills of each student. The bulk of the book is creative writing lessons for prose and poetry, with major concentration on short stories. McDaniel includes numerous inspiring and instructive examples, so we get the feeling, "This isn't so difficult!" She offers solid advice for figuring out what to say and how to say it for the greatest effectiveness. McDaniel views writing as a means of conveying the Gospel and Christian principles through stories that show rather than preach God's message. This perspective and guiding purpose is very evident throughout the lessons. At the end are proofreading and evaluating guidelines, then information on critiques and copyrights, because students who complete this course are likely to be writing publishable pieces. Although the publisher recommends it for grades 7-9, I think that it is appropriate for all high school students and even aspiring adult authors. Students can complete some of the writing exercises within the book itself, but they will also need a separate notebook for lengthier writing assignments. [A suggestion for your consideration: A number of excerpts are from the CLP literature book, *Exploring Christian Literature*, or from authors represented therein, so it might be interesting to correlate use of the two resources.]

⮕ Format Writing by Frode Jensen (Wordsmiths) $11

This is probably the most comprehensive tool for teaching expository writing at the lowest price. The content is divided up into four major sections: paragraph writing, essay writing, the principle of condensation, and major papers. These are the major writing skills that should be developed in junior and senior high school. (Actually, paragraph writing should already be mastered before high school, although it rarely seems to happen.) For paragraph writing, students are taught to work with a seven-sentence format that begins with a topic sentence and ends with a conclusion. They write seven different types of paragraphs: example, classification, definition, process, analogy, cause-and-effect, and comparison. The number of each type of paragraph that students produce will depend upon the time available to the teacher. Sufficient practice at this stage prepares students for the next section—the five paragraph essay. Students follow the format described in the book, writing seven different types of essays just as they do with paragraphs. The section on the principle of condensation teaches students to sort through research information to identify the essentials. They can then transfer the crucial points into their own papers without wasting both their own time and their readers'. Students practice précis writing (condensing and summarizing) with samples within *Format Writing* as well as others the teacher assigns. This is an important skill, largely neglected or treated very briefly in most high school courses. The final section deals with major papers—reports or research papers of at least 1000-1200 words. Jensen teaches the traditional note card organizational method, supplemented with detailed instructions for title pages, citation methods (including CD-ROM or on-line citations), abbreviations, bibliographies, and appendices. Instructions for the various assignments are all quite detailed and there is an index at the back of the book, valuable features for both student and teacher. Jensen includes reproducible check-off forms at the end of the book for evaluating writing assignments. These are extremely useful since Jensen includes a point system and detailed instructions for evaluation that will teach parents with little writing background how to evaluate their teens' work. Sample schedules and scheduling tips also help the inexperienced teacher judge how many assignments to use and how long each should take. An answer key for the few exercises with predictable answers is included. This book should be suitable for junior high through college level, so you can use it across a wide span of age/skill levels.

A few final notes: *Format Writing* has distinctly Christian content. Also, while Jensen employs a formula approach to writing, it is not as strictly structured as the approach used in the *WIN Program*.

⮕ Getting Started in Journalism (National Textbook Company) $15.93 (order # 59527); teacher's guide - $11.33 (# 59535)

The focus here is on producing a school newspaper. Students learn how to put together a paper from the ground up, both writing and producing it. A discussion of ethics and legal restrictions is included.

➲ **Grammar and Composition 3 and 4** (A Beka) $12.45 each

Suggested for grades nine and ten, these worktexts offer a thorough review of grammar with some work on writing skills. Students who have been studying grammar every year will find these repetitious, but those who have neglected grammar for a few years will find them sufficiently comprehensive. Purchase student book and teacher's edition (your answer key). *Teacher's Curriculum Guides for English 9* and *10* correlate language, literature, spelling, and vocabulary, but this isn't essential. You can supplement with A Beka's *Creative Writing* (if a student has done little or no writing), *Writing Strands*, or similar resources for composition work.

➲ **Great Explorations in Editing Series** (Common Sense Press) $14; student book - $9

See the review under "Composition Extras and Alternatives for Junior High."

➲ **Handbook of Grammar and Composition plus Workbooks A and B** (A Beka) handbook - $12.95; workbooks - $10.95 each

Workbook A is for 11th grade and *Workbook B* is for 12th, while the *Handbook* is used for both. The *Workbooks* have a strong writing emphasis with grammar review and application, although they are not as interesting as McDougal Littell or BJUP. Purchase student books plus teacher editions (answer keys).

➲ **Harbrace College Handbook** (Harcourt Brace and Company) $32

This classic handbook for grammar and writing skills is now in its eleventh edition. It is a handy, compact size, easy to use, yet comprehensive. In fact, I pull my eighth edition *Harbrace College Handbook* off my shelf for reference more than any of the other grammatical reference books I own. The new edition contains revised and updated examples and exercises. Newer topics addressed are word processing and how to avoid sexist language. There are also instructor's manuals and instructor's editions as well as workbooks to accompany the *Handbook*.(S)

➲ **How to Write Clearly** by Michel Lipman and Russell Joyner (International Society for General Semantics) $4

This short, 14-page book is an excellent tool for students (or others) who need to polish their writing skills. Examples and exercises work on editing for clear communication. Students work on developing a readable style with good sentence structure and effective word choices. Short exercises often feature poorly written samples for rewriting practice. Samples of effective rewrites are provided in the back of the book. Students can work through this book on their own if desired. Be aware that it is written at an adult level in terms of both content and vocabulary. This is a very inexpensive little book that makes an excellent supplement for any upper level writing course.(S)

➲ **An Introduction to Christian Writing** by Ethel Herr (Cathedral Builders Press) $12

Many home educated children envision careers as writers, but they do not know how to go beyond the basic writing instruc-

tion offered in their curriculum. Ethel Herr has written this book to help aspiring writers move from amateur to professional. Although the book is written for an adult audience, serious young writers should find it easy to read and work with. Herr has woven together two strands involved in becoming a writer. She has done this by dividing the book into eleven, two-part lessons. "Part One of each lesson deals with the writer, his person, relationships, attitudes, market study, preparation, and work habits. Part Two gives specific instruction in writing skill areas." Herr includes numerous examples, checklists, and work sheets along with assignments for applying what she is teaching throughout the lessons. Herr has narrowed the focus of her book to Christian writing, that is, writing intended for the Christian market in book, magazine, devotional, or other formats. Because of that focus, she repeatedly stresses the need for a close relationship with God. Excellent content backed up by spiritual principles makes this a valuable book for aspiring Christian writers.

➲ **Journalism Today!** (National Textbook Company) $46.59 (order #59756); teacher's manual - $39.95 (#59780); student workbook - $16.73 (#59764); teacher's edition for workbook - $32.66 (#59772)

This text is written at a higher level than *Getting Started in Journalism*. The assumption is that students are working on their high school newspaper, where they will practice many of the skills they learn. Students learn about writing, interviews, newspaper production, ethics and responsibility, and careers. This is a hardbound student text. *The Journalism Today! Workbook* is a comprehensive workbook that covers the same basic topics, but in a different format which includes a "...large number of exercises, allowing flexibility in a variety of activity contexts." It can be used as a supplement to the hardbound text or another text, as well as on its own.(S)

➲ **Language Arts** (Alpha Omega LifePacs) 9th grade - $50.95; 10th grade - $48.95; 11th grade - $51.95; 12th grade - $42.95

The LifePacs include grammar, spelling, composition, literature, and practical application. These may be repetitive on grammar or other skills that have been mastered previously, but you can choose the LifePacs that meet your child's needs by examining the scope and sequence from Alpha Omega which describes the content of each LifePac before you buy. Ninth grade level includes study of the play, *The Miracle Worker*, and the novel, *Twenty Thousand Leagues Under the Sea*. Tenth grade level studies *In His Steps*; eleventh grade level studies the play, *Our Town*, and the novel *The Old Man and the Sea*; and twelfth grade level studies *Hamlet*. It would be possible to use only the single LifePacs which cover each literary work without using the entire curriculum, but answer keys and teachers guides are designed to cover more than one LifePac, making it a bit more complicated to use in this way. It would be easier to use the entire curriculum, skipping previously mastered material. The high school language arts material from Alpha Omega is one of the publisher's strongest areas. Home schoolers generally have had quite favorable experience with it.

➲ Learning Language Arts through Literature (Common Sense Press) Gold Book $18

The *Gold Book,* written by Dr. Greg Strayer for high school level, varies significantly from other levels in this series. It is written in units rather than as individual lessons, with students reading entire pieces of American literature rather than small excerpts. Students read from *Great American Short Stories, The Mentor Book of Major American Poets, The Red Badge of Courage,* and *The Old Man and the Sea.* (These books are available through Family Learning Center.) A Bible and a concordance are required. Students study the elements of fiction and poetry as well as how to analyze them. Writing assignments range from simple answers to essays, with significant attention given to essay writing. Discussion is an essential part of the learning process, so parents should also read the literature so that they can lead the discussion. This is an excellent college preparatory class.

➲ Look It Up (Globe Fearon Educational Publisher) $7.95; annotated teacher's edition - $8.95

Although I have not personally reviewed this workbook, it appears to be a worthwhile tool for improving reference skills using such reference works as a thesaurus, almanac, encyclo- pedia, atlas, reader's guide, and dictionary.(S)

➲ Major Punctuation by Frode Jensen (Wordsmiths)

See review under resources for junior high grammar.

➲ Practicing the Writing Process 2: The Essay (Educational Design) $10.95

See the complete review under junior high composition resources. This book is a very useful tool for those high school students who need help developing essay writing skills.(S)

➲ Practicing the Writing Process 4: The Writing Test (Educational Design) $11.95

See the complete review under junior high composition resources. This is one of the most practical resources for honing essay-writing skills for testing. It should be used in freshman or sophomore years so that skills are in place before students take crucial tests.(S)

➲ WIN Program by Dr. Les Simonson (Elijah Company) *Level II* - $20, *Essay Handbook* - $10

See the review under Junior High level.

➲ Within Reach: A Guide to Successful Writing by Anna Ingalls and Dan Moody (Allyn and Bacon) $34

I was of two minds in reviewing this resource. I really liked the layout—it combines thorough instruction and practice in writing with grammar instruction in the most common areas with which people have problems. On the other hand, it was written for a secular, college-level audience and includes numerous examples and references that are offensive (e.g., a hike to a water fall where the writer discovers his "oneness with god"). On balance, I decided to include it because I believe that it will be particularly effective for both students who have weak grammar

Young Writers' Institutes

The Young Writers' Institute is a terrific opportunity for fledgling writers (grades 3-12), or even reluctant writers, to attend a one-day workshop with an outstanding Christian author learning about "real" writing. Two of the following authors are present at each event: Sigmund Brouwer, author of the *Winds of Light* and *CyberQuest* series; Bill Myers, creator of *McGee and Me* and *Wally MacDoogle*; Nancy Rue, author of Focus on the Family's *Christian Heritage* series; Dave and Neta Jackson, authors of the *TrailBlazer, Secret Adventure,* and *Hero Tales* series; or Bob Elmer, author of the *Young Underground* and *Adventure from Down Under* series. The focus is on creative writing, with children separated into two different grade groupings. In a keynote session adress, both authors introduce themselves and share from their own experiences. Each author teaches three hands-on activity based workshops designed to teach the fundamentals of creative writing in a fun, exciting way. Special workshops for parents help them learn how to motivate their children. Parents are welcome at all workshops and are responsible for their children throughout the event.

A local site administrator works with the YWI office and a regional or state home school group to put on the Institute, with YWI bearing all of the costs. The YWI has already visited cities across the country and in Canada. Contact them for information about events in your area or about hosting one yourself.

backgrounds and those who have had little prior writing experience. Although it was written for the college classroom, it should work fairly well for home educators. A student can do much of this independently, although interaction with the teacher will be necessary every so often. The worktext layout is easy to use. A companion instructor's manual offers important instructions for using the program, pointing out that teachers should feel free to assign lessons or parts of lessons according to each student's needs. This will be especially true with the grammar lessons. Detailed lesson plans are included for the first four units (20+ lessons). After that, you should be comfortable selecting appropriate activities from lessons, especially with lists in the instructor's manual that identify key concepts within each lesson. The book includes examples (sometimes including both correct and incorrect ones), workpages for both composition and grammar skill practice, writing assignments, and writing checklists for self evaluation. In addition to basic "how to teach the course" information, the instructor's manual has reproducible quizzes and proofreading essays for students to tackle, as well as answer keys. The grammatical vocabulary has been simplified to some extent, which might be confusing to the student with a decent grammatical background, but helpful to the student without. For example, participles are referred to as "-ing adjectives" (although it does appear that their accurate name is mentioned once). The student who already does well in grammar should probably be concentrating on the writing itself rather than the grammar lessons, so this might be no problem at all.

Instruction begins with paragraph writing, which can remain at the single-paragraph level for some time or quickly be expanded to multi-paragraph writing. Students tackle narration, writing instructions, descriptions, comparison/contrast, classification, cause and effect analysis, and short essays. While the topics sound like those found in many other courses, they are taught at fairly sophisticated levels here in keeping with the fact that the intended audience is college students. Because of this, I would most likely recommend *Within Reach* to students in tenth grade or above.

Be prepared for some hassle when ordering the instructor's manual. The publisher won't give out a price for it because they expect to give it free to teachers adopting the text for an entire class. Using it with only one student did not compute. Maybe you can get it free!(SE)

⊃ Wordsmith Craftsman by Janie Cheaney (Common Sense Press) $14

Designed for high school students, *Wordsmith Craftsman* can be used after completion of *Wordsmith: A Creative Writing Course for Young People* or any other courses that have built up a basic foundation in grammar, mechanics, and composition. High school students who have done a great deal of grammar but little composition should probably complete the *Creative Writing Course* before jumping into *Wordsmith Craftsman*.

This book is divided into three parts which might be used over a span of anywhere from one to four years depending upon the student. Part One draws students into the writing process with practical, everyday writing tasks like note taking, outlining, summarizing, personal letters, business letters, and even business reports (althought the last topic is addressed very briefly). Part Two gets more technical with exercises on paragraph writing (narrative, descriptive, persuasive, and expository), word usage, and style. Part Three concentrates on essay writing. Cheaney does an excellent job of pointing out different organizational strategies you might use to construct different types of essays. Plentiful examples help students visualize their goals. Cheaney's emphasis on style encourages students to move beyond mechanical correctness to excellence in communication skills. The book is written for a student to work through independently, receiving feedback and encouragement from a parent/teacher as needed. Students should work through the lessons at a pace slow enough to allow time for them to practice and master the various skills. A ninth or tenth grader should not expect to complete the book in one year, while an eleventh of twelfth grader might.

⊃ Writers INC Language Series (Great Source) handbook - $12.50; Sourcebook student edition - $10.50 each; teacher editions - $14.95 each

Writers INC Language Series is an impressive four-year high school writing program. The authors have centered almost exclusively on teaching the writing process, and they have certainly produced a product of superior quality and ease of use. The program consists of five components which coordinate over the course of four years to teach and refine student writing. This comprehensive writing program centers around a student hand-

book called *Writers INC*. A student assignment book is also necessary, and there are three optional resources for the teacher. Because the names of some of the components are similar, the catalog can be confusing at first. Let's take a look at each of the five books separately.

The central part of Writers INC Language Series is a truly excellent student handbook, called *Writers INC*. The handbook is a one-time purchase which can be used all through high school (and beyond), and contains a wealth of information. It includes short directions for various types of writing (with examples), an MLA stylebook, a dictionary of literary terms and an almanac. A creative parent could build a writing program just with this one handbook, but why invest the time when the people at Write Source have provided such great materials for use in conjunction with *Writers INC*? Student *SourceBooks* (one for each grade level) contain the actual writing activities, workshops, and units. The *SourceBooks* are not workbooks; each lesson is an actual writing assignment, not just "filling in the blanks." The workshops are on the technical aspects of writing, and the units each cover a practical aspect of writing such as business letters or summaries. The work in the *SourceBook* is keyed to the *Writers INC* handbook, and both contain student and professional samples of whatever type of writing is being taught. The student samples have obviously been written by real students, but they are nonetheless well-written. (A caution is in order about a few of the samples. There is some mild swearing in the professional samples, and some of the topics reflect some modern culture: AIDS, divorce, school life. The handbook has a section (which you might or might not wish to use) on using words that give equal treatment to both sexes, such as replacing "the best *man* for the job" with "the best *person*" and "*fireman*" with "*firefighter.*" These are minor inconveniences compared to the worth of this program.)

The teacher-support material is optional to varying degrees. *The Language Series Program Guide* ($140) is a three-ring binder containing management forms, learning strategies, an answer key, and information on assessment. A separate *Program Guide* is needed for each year of high school. The *Program Guide* is geared to the traditional classroom, and most home schoolers will have little need for most of the material. There is a teacher's guide to the *Writers INC* handbook ($14.95), with information on how to use the handbook, teaching strategies, start-up activities and reviews. This is also geared to the classroom, but so inexpensive that it is probably worth buying, as it is a one-time purchase also. Teacher's editions of each *SourceBook* are also available, and again, these would probably be useful to most parents, providing answers for some of the workshops. (If you purchase the *Program Guide*, you do not need the teacher's edition of the *SourceBook*.)

The Write Source approaches in writing what the Saxon books do for math study. Each year of the program has the same writing framework, with personal, subject, creative, reflective, and academic writing. (I'd like to see a bit more academic writing, but overall, it is a well-balanced selection, with a wide variety to keep interest up.) Each year the workshops repeat some techniques, delving deeper each time. The student actually has the opportunity to refine his writing from year to year. Each

SourceBook also adds a few new aspects of writing each year; for example, the twelfth grade book adds impromptu writing, for those inevitable college essay tests.

The Writers INC Language Series is designed to be used for four years, and there is also a middle school version, called *Write Source 2000*. (See junior high section.) However, a student can enter at any point and still get value from using the program. Because the handbook services all grades, and because of the repetition of the types of writing, it would be fairly easy to use the *Write Source* with two or more students in different grades. Even if you already have a writing program that your students are happy with, consider buying the handbook for their reference.(SE)[Kath Courtney]

⮑ Writing for Life Books 1 and 2 (Globe Fearon Educational Publisher)

See the review under junior high level.

⮑ Writing for 100 Days: A Student-Centered Approach to Composition and Creative Writing by Gabriel Arquilevich (Fairview Publishing) $15

See the review under junior high level. This book is even better for high school level.

⮑ Writing for Success: A Comprehensive Guide to Improved Creative Writing Skills by Alexandra and Francesca Swann (Cygnet Press) $29.95

See the review under Junior High resources. High schoolers can review grammar basics and develop their writing skills with this program. It is ideal for those with minimal writing experience, but is also helpful for those with a moderate amount of experience. The latter can skip to appropriate lessons rather than completing all of them.

⮑ Writing: Process to Product, 1991 edition (Houghton Mifflin/McDougal Littell) student book - $24.72; teacher's manual - $18.15

This book has great content, but it takes some work to figure out how to use it. It is an ungraded student "text" with a teacher's manual that is absolutely necessary. The author's goal was to provide a writing program with instruction in all facets of writing, including editing and revision, so that, as the teacher, he would have to spend less time instructing and could spend more time serving as final editor. He also wanted to provide a program that could be individualized to meet the needs of writers with varying degrees of skill. The book is designed to be used in a classroom, with peer group brainstorming and editing as an essential part of the process. If you can round up two or more teens to work together through this book, great. If not, consider getting involved in the writing process yourself and have your teen help evaluate your work. (If your skills are weak, you might then wish to have another person whom you can consult for final editing comments.) Even if you serve as teacher with one student, you can easily adapt lessons to fit your situation. Instructions are very clear with lots of examples. I particularly appreciate the numerous checklists of points to consider for evaluation—some for the

student as he writes, some for the peer or teacher evaluator. Parents with poor writing skills often avoid teaching writing because they are not equipped to properly evaluate assignments. This book will help those of us in that situation.

The text is divided into three sections which can be used as desired. The first section teaches the writing process itself, then provides twenty-one different writing assignments such as narrative paragraphs, autobiographical essays, reviews, and business letters. The second works on content and organization, while the third section deals with style. The teacher's manual tells how to use the text and provides evaluation information and forms, activity ideas, and an answer key to the few discussion questions scattered through the text.

⮑ Writing with a Point by Jeanne B. Stephens and Ann Harper (Educators Publishing Service) $7.95

This is my favorite resource for developing essay writing skills. It covers gathering and organizing ideas as do other books, but it stresses the importance of communicating in such as way that people want to read it. It teaches writers how to grab the reader with the first sentence, then use description and other tools to maintain interest throughout the piece. This is a self-contained workbook with instruction supported by examples, then followed by a variety of writing exercises. Some of these exercises might be done aloud. This book lends itself well to a small group class where students might toss ideas back and forth. Lessons build upon one another, so you should use this book from cover to cover.(S)

Spelling and Vocabulary
Recommendations for Junior and Senior High

⮑ Basic Goals in Spelling N and G [7th and 8th grades] (Macmillan/McGraw-Hill—School Division) $15.56 each; teacher's editions - $42.72 each

This is a solid spelling program that uses a phonetic approach. The worktext format allows students to work independently. Teacher's editions are necessary as answer keys.(S)

⮑ Building Spelling Skills, Book 6 (Christian Liberty Press) $7; answer key $1.95

Book 6 in this series, although suggested for sixth graders, might be useful for many junior high students. It reviews the basic spelling rules that students most likely encountered in the early elementary years. This is a good time to review, because most students have forgotten that there are patterns to help them figure out the spelling of unfamiliar words, even if they use that knowledge without realizing it. Review does not take students back to one-syllable words but introduces challenging words. Suffixes and prefixes (including Latin and Greek prefixes) are also addressed in depth. Spelling rule coverage is not as thorough as that found in *The Writing Road to Reading* and other resources decribed here that are dedicated specifically to spelling rules. However, this book should be very useful for the student who either never learned the rules or does not use them when needed.

⇨ Building Spelling Skills, Book 7 (Christian Liberty Press) $7; answer key $1.95

Book 7 is obviously more difficult than Book 6 with its smaller, more abundant print. Suffixes and prefixes are the organizing themes for all lessons, but vocabulary development is the overall emphasis. Students become familiar with many new and challenging words. Since spelling is practiced rather than taught in this book, students lacking spelling skills (rule familiarity) should use Book 6 first. Book 7 can also be used with students at older grade levels. Typical of words in the lessons are infringement, ingenious, befriend, psychic, infirmary, apologize, and noticeable. Examples of some of the more challenging words: prerequisite, antediluvian, expatriate, ostentatious, and recapitulate.

⇨ The Childs Spelling System: The Rules (Educators Publishing Service) $4.75

This can be used as a reference tool just as *Learning Grammar through Writing* can be used for grammar. When a student misspells a word, direct them to the rule, identified by its code.(S)

⇨ Demonic Mnemonics: 800 Spelling Tricks for 800 Tricky Words (Fearon Teacher Aids) $9.99

This slim paperback is a compendium of mnemonic tricks to help the student remember how to spell those "sticklers" that are most commonly misspelled. Each trick is based on one of eight different links. A well-known example is the famous "A rat in the house might eat the ice cream" to spell *arithmetic*, using the first letters of each word in the memorized sentence. Another type of link has to do with meaning: to remember the silent *c* in *muscle*, memorize "If you have *muscles*, then you are *muscular*," where the letter *c* is sounded.

Demonic Mnemonics is not a book you will want to sit down and study, but it is rather an excellent reference book to be used when you run across troublesome words. The author encourages you to be creative; if one of your "sticklers" isn't included, go ahead and make up your own. At the end of the book, a list of twelve simple spelling rules is included to help with the most cnmmon errors.

Capitalizing on the meaning of *demonic* as "extremely difficult," the author has filled the book with humorous pictures of rotund "demons" with enormous noses (complete with horns, forked tails and wings). Sometimes these creatures illustrate one of the mnemonics. Although clearly intended for humor, the idea of these cartoons might bother some. A possible way to use the book might be to have the teacher write out the mnemonic on a white board for the student, and have the student keep track of the tricks in a notebook, drawing his own illustrations.(SE)[Kath Courtney]

⇨ English from the Roots Up: Help for Reading, Writing, Spelling and S.A.T. Scores by Joegil Lundquist (Literacy Unlimited) $23.95; flash cards - $15

This book presents lessons for children to learn the roots of the English language that are found in the Greek and Latin languages. The goal is similar to that of *Vocabulary from Classical Roots* (from Educators Publishing Service). This book uses more interactive, teacher-directed teaching methods, while *Vocabulary from Classical Roots* is a workbook approach. However, older students might be able to use the book independently. In this approach, index cards, a file box, and a good dictionary are the primary tools for learning vocabulary. Actual teaching information provided is brief but loaded with activity suggestions. The teacher is on her own to implement the ideas, although preprinted flash cards are available which will save a great deal of preparation time (highly recommended). Examples of activity ideas: for the root "graph"—a number of related words are presented with accompanying ideas—"Telegraph—Let someone present a research report on Thomas Edison's early days as a telegrapher. Let someone do a report on Morse code and give a demonstration of it." or—"Lithograph—Discuss the process of lithography and talk about Currier and Ives. Their lithographs are still used every year as Christmas cards. Make potato or linoleum block prints." These activity ideas could be turned into great unit studies. This resource will be especially suited to the creative teacher who prefers general guidelines rather than detailed lesson plans.

⇨ Instant Spelling Power by Norman Lewis (Amsco) $9.13

Junior and senior high students who never learned the basic spelling rules can learn them efficiently with this worktext. It is designed for independent study; it does not even use spelling quizzes. Students work through a variety of exercises in each lesson related to a particular spelling rule or group of phonograms that produce the same sound. The written exercises are designed to reinforce learning rather than to "quiz" students, so no answer key is required. Students are encouraged to see, say, and write each word they are studying, although the key strategy is memorizing the way each word looks to build up a visual memory. Overall, the approach is sound, but I would question the decision to print the word lists with words divided into syllables; if the goal is to build up a visual memory then the words should appear the same as they appear in print. I might also challenge the author's assertion in the introduction that "Good spellers are made, not born." It seems to me that some people lack the ability to develop a dependable visual memory, even though they have tried to do so. This is often a problem with those who have learning disabilities. Consequently, *Instant Spelling Power* is likely to work for students who lack instruction, but it is unlikely to be the solution for students who struggle with spelling because of a visual problem or functional learning disability like dyslexia. One other criticism applies to the actual content: Unit 34 teaches changing "y" to "i" before adding "-er" or "-est" to adjectives. But it uses acceptable, but non-preferred spellings of some words as examples (e.g. shy, shier, shiest rather than the preferred shyer, shyest). Nevertheless, this is a cost effective method for covering spelling basics.(S)

➲ PICKTWO (Tah Dah, Inc.) $15.95

PICKTWO is a simple but effective way to learn while having fun. It has 180 plastic letter tiles that are used to play a variety of games, from simple to very challenging. Young children can use the letters as a movable alphabet to spell their names and simple words. As they progress they can play games such as "Spelling Countdown" where they make as many words from a group of letters as they can. It gets more challenging when they start to create their own crosswords. When they are ready for a tough challenge, they play under a time limit, creating ever-expanding and changing crosswords. The game includes a score pad (for Countdown and Crossword games), a timer, and instructions.(S)

➲ A Prescriptive Spelling Program, Books One, Two, or Three (McGraw Hill) student editions - $7.95 ; teacher editions - $8.15

These books review spelling rules and apply them to spelling lists. They are recommended for students who have had difficulty in spelling. Reading levels of the three books are grade levels 3.5, 4.5, and 5.5 respectively. (Ordering numbers for the student books are 45065058, 45065059, and 45065060 respectively. Numbers for accompanying teacher editions are 45065069, 45065070, and 45065071 respectively.) If you have a teen with significant spelling problems because he or she was never properly taught, this series reteaches the spelling rules that should have been learned.(S)

➲ Riverside Spelling 7 and 8, 1988 editions (McDougal Littell/Houghton Mifflin) student texts: hardcover - $23.46 each OR consumable workbook - $14.16 each; teacher's editions - $60.09 each

Spelling books for grades 7 and 8 review spelling rules and cover advanced word studies, dictionary usage, word usage, vocabulary, and word origins. The inductive approach used in these texts works particularly well since it forces students to analyze words for common elements to come to an understanding of the rules. I liked these best of everything we tried at this level. Pages of both hardcover and softbound student books are identical, but students can write in the softbound workbook. You will probably want the teacher's edition as an answer key since some answers are not obvious.(S)

➲ Rummy Roots Card Game (Eternal Hearts) $10.95

Rummy Roots is a card game that offers an alternative to book approaches for studying Greek and Latin roots. It is exceptionally well designed for learning purposes, because it includes instructions for four different games using a card deck of Greek and Latin roots plus English meanings. The first game helps us learn the meanings of the roots with a "Go Fish" type game. (Lists and glossaries for this and other games are included so we need not have a dictionary at hand.) Once we are somewhat familiar with root meanings, we move on to the next game of combining two roots to make an English word. The method of play is different, plus it includes the use of "bonus" and "stump" cards for fun. Players are supposed to say the meanings of their words, but we added that step after we played the game first just figuring out how to combine roots. (Take time to make sure players know

the meanings of the roots before moving on to higher levels.) The third game allows players to make words combining up to three roots. Stump cards are now used to challenge players on word definitions. The fourth game adds yet another dimension of difficulty.

Some educational games are so busy teaching that they forget that games are supposed to be fun. *Rummy Roots* avoided that mistake by adding enough game elements, especially once we get past the introductory game.

Rummy Roots teaches "...42 Greek and Latin Roots, 193 Vocabulary words, and the knowledge to decipher half of over 2000 other words." The publisher says the game is for players ages 8 to adult, but younger players will probably need to play mostly at the first two levels. Do not be in a hurry to push them on to levels where they might become frustrated. I think this game is ideal for junior high and high school students, although younger ones can be included.

More Roots, a second game from Eternal Hearts [$10.95], teaches an additional 42 new Greek and Latin Roots using the same methods as *Rummy Roots*.

➲ Scholastic Aptitude Vocabulary by Joseph R. Orgel (Educators Publishing Service) $6.80; answer key - $2.45

This 128-page book is recommended for eleventh and twelfth grade students preparing for college entrance. It lists one thousand words that show up frequently on versions of the SAT and gives meanings, related forms, synonyms, and antonyms. Four specimens of vocabulary examinations are included along with twenty vocabulary mastery drill tests. You will want to also purchase the answer key.(S)

➲ Spell-N-Meld (Learning Enrichment Games) $7.95

Junior high seems an ideal time to use *Spell-N-Meld*. This double-size card deck comes with a small-print, 38-page instruction book, with directions for fifteen different games. While younger children can play at least some of the games, the level of thinking required for many of them seems to be older. Some of the games compare to *Boggle* and similar, more expensive games that have limited playing options. These games can be used to work on alphabetizing, phonics, vowel/consonant recognition, and parts of speech, as well as spelling. Some games can be played by a single player, while most require two or more. This is an excellent tool for improving spelling skills as well as other language art skills because of both design and flexibility. Hands-on learners as well as those who learn well in social situations such as game playing are particularly likely to benefit from this resource.

➲ Spelling Boosters: Easy to Use Enhancement Exercises for *The Writing Road to Reading* by Wanda Sanseri (Back Home Industries) $12.95

If you are also teaching younger children, this book will be a good investment. It is an idea book rather than an instruction manual or course. Many of the ideas are for younger children, but there are still quite a few for older students. I see this resource as particularly useful for teens who are tired of workbooks, yet who still need to spend a little time improving spelling skills. Although it was designed to reinforce phonics and spelling as taught in *The Writing Road to Reading*, almost everything here is useful for those who have not used that method. Suggested activities help children improve spelling, writing, and vocabulary skills, and there are even a number of ideas for working with Latin and Greek roots.

⮞ Spelling by Sound and Structure 7 (Rod and Staff) $17.80 for both pupil and teacher books

The seventh grade student book is hardbound as is the teacher's edition. The teacher's edition has the student pages printed on the left-hand pages and teaching information/answers on the right-hand pages. It might be possible to work only from the teacher's edition, but since the books are so inexpensive, I suggest getting both books. Although the title at this level is still *Spelling by Sound and Structure*, the emphasis switches from sound and structure to Latin word elements—roots, prefixes, and suffixes. The content is challenging, but the lessons are quite interesting and thought-provoking. "Old English Dialects," "Abstract and Concrete Meanings," "First Bible Accounts in English," and "Old English Place Names" are typical of the side studies we find in various lessons. Consider using this text with students beyond seventh-grade level because of the quality content.

⮞ Spelling Power, third edition by Beverly L. Adams-Gordon (Castlemoyle Media) $49.95

Originally designed to teach spelling to an older student with spelling problems, this very comprehensive spelling program uses a base list of about 5,000 frequently used words. (A list of the 12,000 most frequently used and misspelled words is included as a separate section. It codes each word showing when it should be taught, by grade level and in correlation with *Spelling Power*.) These words are broken down into groups with common elements. Diagnostic tests place the students at the proper beginning point in the list. Then each student progresses at his own rate, studying only those words with which he is having trouble. Frequently used words are reviewed periodically to insure retention. A ten-step study process is used for each group of words to be learned. Parental/teacher involvement is essential, although we can note daily activities on the study sheet for students to do on their own. Once you have used this system for a while, both parent and child should become familiar enough with the process that students do much of their work independently. The "Quick-Start Introduction" at the beginning of the book walks you through placement and instructions for using the program. The interaction required between teacher and child actually makes this program more ideal for homeschoolers than for the regular classroom.

Reproducible study, test, dictionary, and record keeping forms and a whole section of game and activity ideas are included. You can successfully use this one book to teach all of your children throughout their school years. The *Spelling Power Activity Task Cards*, reviewed next, make teaching this program much easier. [Valerie Thorpe/C.D.]

⮞ Spelling Power Activity Task Cards by Beverly Adams-Gordon (Castlemoyle Books) $29.95

The author of *Spelling Power* has created a set of 365 color-coded, 4" x 6" *Activity Task Cards* that can be used along with *Spelling Power* or any other phonic-based spelling program. More than 360 brightly-colored cards are filed in a sturdy box for easy use. Cards are divided into five categories: drill activities, skill builders, writing prompters, dictionary skills, and homonyms and more. Within each category, cards are further color coded into four categories responding to age/skill level groupings covering all grade levels. Activities designed for auditory, visual, kinesthetic, and tactile learning modalities provide learning opportunities for all children. Examples of a few of the activities are games, dot-to-dots, painting, puzzle making, as well as a variety of writing activities. Most activities can be done by a single student although a few require a partner. The *Activity Task Cards* come with a very helpful teacher's manual. The manual tells us how to use the *Activity Task Cards*, offers suggestions for making our own letter tiles, cross references to *Spelling Power* lessons, and includes answers for the appropriate cards. Cards can be used as supplements to lessons or sometimes in place of lessons. If you are using *Spelling Power,* I highly recommend this set as both a time saver and lesson enhancer. For those using other programs, it will help supplement lessons through all grade levels.

⮞ Spelling, Vocabulary and Poetry 6 (A Beka) $7.65

Level 6 is considered sixth grade level by A Beka, but it compares with seventh and eighth grade levels of others. The advanced level of difficulty is characteristic of all levels of A Beka spelling. The revised edition is colorful and includes more exercises and activities on usage, pronunciation, and word analysis than did the old edition. However, the basic method is still "teach, practice, and test" on the words themselves rather than working through exercises as in most spelling workbooks.

⮞ A Spelling Workbook by Mildred B. Plunkett (Educators Publishing Service) $10.90

This book is helpful for students struggling with spelling. Students who cannot spell well by high school sometimes have a related difficulty with reading. This book seeks to help by emphasizing spelling rules and generalizations, providing phonetic drills, and working on syllabication. Using such methods helps students improve spelling and phonics skills, both essential for good spelling.(S)

⮞ Spelling Workout G and H [7th and 8th grades] (Modern Curriculum Press) student books - $6.25 each; teacher's editions - $5.65 each

These spelling workbooks include words frequently found in texts for science, social studies, and math at these grade levels. A teacher's edition is available for each grade level and includes an answer key.(S)

⊃ Think Speak and Write Better! [computer program]
(Smartek Software) single volume - $49.95 each; 2 volumes
or more - $39.95 each (suggested retail is $64.95 each) call
for current special prices and volume discounts

Think Speak and Write Better! is an efficient and effective
vocabulary and spelling program for junior high through adult
levels. It runs on either Macintosh or IBM compatible computers
from a CD-ROM or floppy drive. The CD version has built in
sound, while the floppy version comes with audio cassettes that
we must coordinate. I suspect that coordinating the two would be
so much hassle that most people would use the floppies without
sound. I strongly recommend the CD version over the floppy if
you want sound. There are ten different levels, each a separate
CD or disk that you purchase. On each level, there are from 9 to
13 groups of 20 words each that are the "core words" studied.
One of the advantages of this program is that it teaches via the
three learning modalities: seeing, hearing, and doing.

Words are introduced with closely related synonyms, then
used in exercises with four "common misconceptions"—words
or meanings which people commonly confuse. The result is
about 1400 words with which students become familiar at each
level. There are five learning modes for each word group. The
first mode is "multiple choice with audio discussions." One word
from the word list is highlighted and five options are listed to the
right from which to choose the meaning. We hear the word used
in a sentence, then select the answer. Once the proper word has
been selected, we hear and view the "audio discussion." We can
read the screen while listening to an expanded definition, word
origin and history, and usage information. The audio pronunciations are very helpful, although they are not always accurate.
(Probably this is a problem with computer voices, but it is not
nearly as bad as the manufactured computer voices we hear from
places such as telephone directory assistance.) The next mode is
"flashcards." Here, a phrase or sentence uses the synonym identified with a list word in the multiple choice lesson. We are given
a short time to answer mentally, then the list word appears on the
flashcard. The next mode is "column matching," then the fourth
mode is "sentence completion." To complete sentences, we must
fill in the blank with the correctly spelled word from the list. The
list is not displayed unless we call it up on the screen. If the spelling is close but not perfect, we get another chance. If it is too far
off, the properly-spelled word is displayed to the right on screen.
The "laser review" mode is a multiple choice game where we
shoot the correct synonym.

The down side to these programs is that words are presented
with only one meaning throughout all the different exercises,
while, in reality words often have a number of meanings. Additionally, the selected meaning in the program is sometimes not a
common usage of the word. I found this to be a significant problem in Volume A, but less so at upper levels.

The program allows tremendous flexibility to enter and leave
at any time and to access audio discussions or helps. Sound effects and excellent graphics make it visually and auditorially interesting. The program also tracks and records scores in the
appropriate modes. Learners can select whichever modes are
most effective for them or use all of them. Words are based on the
research of linguist Johnson O'Connor for developing effective

vocabulary improvement programs. We find a mix of
commonly-used and challenging words from levels A through J.
Volume A "contains the most common words and Volume J contains words unknown to 90% of adults." (Volume A is titled
Word Adventure, and has additional graphics to appeal to
younger learners. I don't like Volume A as well as the upper levels for reasons mentioned above.) I recommend that if your teen
needs a great deal of vocabulary and spelling work, you begin
with a lower level volume such as Volumes B or C. If he or she is
an average student choose from Volumes C through G. If he or
she is brilliant or very advanced, choose Volumes H through
J.(S)

⊃ Visual Vocabulary (Little River Press) $18

Visual Vocabulary is a book of flash cards for practicing vocabulary words commonly found on the SAT I. The book contains 150 cut-out cards, each 3 1/2" by 5 1/2". On one side of each
card are the vocabulary word and a picture to illustrate the word.
On the reverse are the phonetic pronunciation, part of speech,
definition, and a sentence that conveys the word's meaning. Pictures are often humorous but almost always helpful, even though
they sometimes stretch to convey the meaning. This is a great
tool for visual learners. Junior highers who read voraciously
might find these to be on the appropriate level, but otherwise use
them with high school students, especially those preparing for
college entry.

⊃ Vocabulary from Classical Roots Books A-E (Educators
Publishing Service) each level-student book - $7.15; teacher's
guide - $4.15

This vocabulary workbook series can be used for junior and
senior high. Each book is written at an increasingly difficult
level. Words with similar roots are grouped thematically for ease
of study. A variety of exercises including work with synonyms,
antonyms, analogies, and sentence completion helps students
develop full understanding. Two unusual extras are included.
Literary, historical and geographic references help develop cultural literacy. And suggestions for extended writing activities
help students to apply new vocabulary. Books D and E add exercises for testing vocabulary within the context of short articles.
One student, who has used earlier levels of this series, pointed
out that Book E contains creeping elements of political correctness, even though they are subtle and sporadic rather than obvious and pervasive.

Students with some exposure to Greek and/or Latin will immediately recognize the derivation of words from those languages. Other students without prior knowledge of those
languages will develop some familiarity with Greek and Latin
simply by using these workbooks.

A *Teachers' Guide and Answer Key* for each level has teaching suggestions, exercise answers, and glossaries of some of the
literary and historical references.(S)

⊃ Vocabulary for Christian Schools (Bob Jones University
Press) worktexts - $8 each; teacher's editions - $9 each

Levels A through F for grades 7 through 12. You will need
both the worktext and teacher's edition for answers. There are

only 15 fairly brief lessons per book, so, little time is required compared to books like *Wordly Wise*. At the same time, this means that students receive minimal practice actually working with the vocabulary words. According to the BJUP catalog new words are taught "...primarily through context. Students learn about word parts (prefixes, roots, and suffixes), word families, synonyms, antonyms, homonyms, and methods of word formation. The study of word parts helps students learn spelling as well as meaning. Some lessons also contain helpful spelling principles." *Books A* through *C* concentrate on Latin word parts along with more common vocabulary topics. *Book D* teaches Greek word parts; *Book E* covers words originating from French along with some Greek and Latin words; and, *Book F* broadens to cover words from many languages. Many lessons are designed around one or more word parts (all vocabulary words derived from them), while others might center around topics such as synonyms, antonyms, a particular subject, or a literary selection. Lessons sometimes crossover to include grammar and writing skills. The format is more interesting than that of many vocabulary workbooks because of the background information and application in the lessons. Christian content is another plus.

⊃ Vocabulary for College 1989 editions (Holt, Rinehart and Winston) $15.25 each; teacher's manuals - $6.25 each; tests - $6.75 each

These are basic vocabulary books used by many schools. Books A through D are appropriate for grades 9-12. Tests and teacher's manuals are available.(S)

⊃ Vocabulary: Latin I and Latin II; Greek I (Wordsmiths) $11 each

In the first two books, vocabulary lessons are based on Latin roots, suffixes, and prefixes. Knowledge of those word elements enables students to define an enormous number of words beyond those with which they are already familiar. In some ways, it is like understanding the phonics code for knowing how to pronounce words; this is the vocabulary code which helps us decode meanings for a significant part of the English language which has been derived from Latin. The third book, *Greek I*, follows the same format, but uses Greek roots, suffixes, and prefixes.

These workbooks are written by a Christian teacher and designed to work in either homeschool or regular school settings. They are entirely self-contained—instructions, tests, and answer keys are all included as is appropriate in each case. They can be used as consumable workbooks, or students can write answers in notebooks to preserve the books for other students.

A chart in the front of each book lists the roots, suffixes, and prefixes to be covered within that book along with their meanings. Each lesson has four parts, one to be assigned for each day. All four parts work with the same group of words, but attacking them in a different manner each time so that students absorb the meanings of the parts. These lessons are challenging, requiring students to work from the list of meanings, while searching for shades and relations of meaning. However the books are designed so that students can do most of their work independently. Teacher involvement is required for weekly testing. After completing each lesson, the teacher gives a quiz on this week's words

as well as a few review words. A sample test (covering lessons 1-9 is included at the back of the book. (An answer key in the back of the book will help with exercises, but the tests are up to us.) It is vital that parents first read through "Hints and Tips" and "Notes to the Teacher," then work through the first lesson (all four parts) with their student to make sure they understand how to do them. This series is recommended for grades seven and up.

⊃ Vocabulary/Spelling/Poetry I, II, and III [for grades 7, 8, and 9] (A Beka) student books - $6.95 each; teacher editions - $11.10 each

This new, colorful edition from A Beka has exercises and practice for both spelling and vocabulary built into the student book. Vocabulary is the major emphasis throughout the series. Spelling rules are reviewed throughout the lessons, with some commonly misspelled words keyed to applicable spelling rules. All three levels are correlated with other A Beka language arts curricula for each level, but they also work very well used on their own. Word lists in all levels are quite challenging. Excellent poetry from authors such as Longfellow, Scott, and Tennyson is included for appreciation. The teacher edition has answers, lesson presentation information, and other helps. A quiz booklet and an answer key to the quiz booklet are also available.

⊃ Vocabulary, Spelling, and Poetry IV through VI [Levels 10 -12] (A Beka) student books - $8.30 each; teacher editions - $11.15 each

These books follow the format of levels I-III. Content in these three levels shifts to an emphasis on vocabulary from great literature and general reading. Word analysis exercises teach students to utilize knowledge of Greek and Latin roots, suffixes, and prefixes. Spelling rules are reinforced. Verbal analogies develop logic skills. The level of difficulty is very advanced. Teacher editions provide necessary information for lesson presentation as well as answer keys. A student quiz booklet and accompanying answer key are available for Level IV.

⊃ Vocabulary Workshop 1994 edition by Doris Bain Thompson (Holt, Rinehart and Winston) student books - $15.25 each; assessment booklets - $4.75 each; answer key -$10.50

This is a series to improve vocabulary, typical of those used in schools. It is not exciting, but it is effective. Six volumes are available for junior high and high school levels, with the final volume called the *Complete Course*. There is a test booklet for each book and a teacher's answer key for all levels.(S)

⊃ Vocabu-Lit, Book 1, 2, 3, or 4 (Perfection Learning) student books - $6.95 for softcover, $12.15 for hardcover; teacher edition $12.95

All books are appropriate for sixth through ninth grades. Choose the book with literary excerpts that appeal to you the most. (Titles are listed in the *Perfection Language Arts Catalog* but sample titles included in the various books are *Johnny Tremain, The Phantom Tollbooth, A Wrinkle in Time, Black Beauty, The Red Pony, The Call of the Wild*, Kennedy's *Inaugural Address, Life with Father, The Prince and the Pauper*, and *Silent*

Spring.) These books use a different approach to vocabulary. Start with a short literary excerpt with ten key words to be studied in bold print. Students then do dictionary work, synonym/antonym application, analogies, a crossword puzzle, and fill in the blanks of sentences guided by context clues. A glossary is provided at the end of each book. Student books are available either in softcover (can be written in) or hardcover. Teacher's editions contain the answers.(S)

➲ WORDpak vocabulary series [three books]: Spectrum, Rangefinder, and Lexicon (Perfection Learning) student books - $6.95 for softcover, $12.15 for hardcover; teacher edition $12.95

All three books are appropriate for grades 10-12. This series is almost identical in format to *Vocabu-Lit*, but reading selections are longer and more challenging. Examples of titles and excerpted titles contained in the various books are *The Declaration of Independence, The Deerslayer, Jane Eyre, The Red Badge of Courage, Tess of the d'Urbervilles, Billy Budd, Heart of Darkness*, and *Lord Jim*. All three *WORDpak* books are written at the same level of difficulty, so the choice is arbitrary. Student books are available either in softcover (can be written in) or hardcover. Teacher's editions contain the answers.(S)

➲ Wordly Wise, Book Four (Educators Publishing Service) $6.35; answer key - $4.75

The *Wordly Wise* series is my favorite overall vocabulary series because it addresses vocabulary through a number of avenues to establish better understanding. Students use one list of words through four or five different types of exercises to become familiar with the word's usage in different contexts. Exercises include definitions, recognition of proper usage, word origins, prefixes and suffixes, synonym substitution, and crossword puzzles. The answer key is relatively inexpensive. The *Wordly Wise* series is popular with home educators because they are effective, reasonably priced, and easy to get.(S)

➲ Words to the Wise: Using Latin roots to build English vocabulary by Caroline Owens (Classical Connection Resources) $19.95

Vocabulary study is structured around Latin roots in this 20-lesson course for junior or senior high students. It is very easy to use. Latin roots and their meanings are given at the beginning of each lesson. Some lessons focus on Latin abbreviations such as "e.g." and "N.B." or Latin phrases such as "magnum opus" or "sine qua non." The first exercise in most lessons requires students to identify and define the root of an English word, then provide the English meaning of the entire word. Other exercises are fill-in-the-blank, identifying synonyms or antonyms, and matching columns. Each lesson includes a list of the key words, a few other words derived from the same roots, and the definitions of each word. Students can do most of the exercises drawing on information provided within the book itself, but they will occasionally need to use a dictionary. The course might be only moderately useful if students simply look through the book to find definitions to fill in for the questions rather than checking a real dictionary. Likewise, consulting a dictionary will help famil-

iarize them with methods of identifying roots and derivations on their own. Yet, this won't happen without a purposeful effort to do more than complete the exercises. Two separate booklets come with the main book. One is an answer key. The other has two pre-tests, one of which is used as a pre-test and the other as a post-test. Sixteen crossword puzzles and four tests are also found in this same book. The crosswords will require some of that extra dictionary work students need, so be sure they work on these also. The level of difficulty of the vocabulary words varies from simple to challenging—e.g. militant, erupted, disparity, subversive, and perfidious. However, the stress is not necessarily on mastering many difficult vocabulary words but upon becoming familiar with roots that will open the door to much broader vocabulary mastery. This makes the books suitable for a wide age range, depending more upon whether or not a student has had previous exposure to a study of Latin roots.(S)

Literature

The following literature anthologies and readers are for approximately seventh and eighth grade levels:

➲ A Christian's Treasury of Stories and Songs, Poems and Prayers... compiled and edited by Lissa Roche (Crossway Books) $25

This 560-page book is an anthology of uplifting prose and poetry, all from a Christian perspective. It is divided into sections: meditations, poems/songs/ballads, stories for young readers, and stories for older readers. Unlike most anthologies that are primarily stories, 263 pages are devoted to the first two sections. Meditations are quotes of varying lengths, written by well-known people, arranged by topics such as work, thankfulness, truth and understanding, and overcoming adversity. The other three sections are divided into similar categories. Representative authors are Wordsworth, Shakespeare, Erasmus, Dante Alighieri, Ben Jonson, Jonathan Edwards, Martin Luther King, Jr., T.S. Eliot, Emily Dickinson, C.S. Lewis, George Macdonald, Laura Ingalls Wilder, Leo Politi, Ray Bradbury, John Bunyan, Lloyd C. Douglas, and Dorothy Sayers. This should be a family resource which older students use selectively.

➲ Enjoying Christian Literature (Christian Liberty Press) $7; answer key - $1.50

This collection of short stories and poetry is designed for seventh grade level. Selections are intended to be spiritually uplifting and character building. The subject matter is far-ranging, with a mixture of historical and modern selections. Examples of some of the well-known authors are C.H. Spurgeon, McGuffey, A.L. Tennyson, and Patrick Henry. The introduction to the book outlines the importance of identifying plot, characters, theme, setting, mood, life applications lessons (or the moral of the story), as well as evaluating the unity or flow of each story or poem. Questions following each selection help to some extent, but general questions posed in the introduction, should be addressed as is appropriate with each reading assignment. This means that the parent/teacher should also read the story or poem, then be prepared to discuss the questions provided with the story as well as raise the additional questions that help students understand the items listed above.

⊃ **Excursions in Literature** (Bob Jones University Press) $27; teacher's manual - $36; TestBank - $16; AskIt -$14

This eighth-grade-level text covers a variety of themes portraying a Christian's journey through life, including choices he must face. It continues the character emphasis of the seventh grade book. Content areas are titled Choices, Friends, Viewpoints, Adventures, Discoveries, and Heroes and Villains. Students are introduced to story analysis in the text. Excerpts from *Pilgrims Progress* serve as a theme throughout the book. The novel *Wine of Morning* is studied in the final unit. A video cassette of the story is also available. Lessons in the teacher's edition follow a format of overview, objectives, potential problems (e.g., objections to authors portraying animals as having human qualities), introductory discussion, the reading, analysis, application, and additional activities. Suggestions for journal writing are given.

I strongly recommend getting the teacher's edition which contains lesson plans plus all the commentary. You might also want to use the TestBank (softbound book) or TestBank Data Disk (computerized version which requires the *AskIt* program).

⊃ **Explorations in Literature** (Bob Jones University Press) $27; teacher's manual - $36; Activity Sheets - $8; answer key to activity sheets - $3; TestBank - $16; AskIt - $14

The seventh-grade-level text covers a wide variety of themes while emphasizing character. Literary analysis and enjoyment is taught from a Christian perspective, although literary selections are not all by Christian authors. One of the main purposes seems to be helping students to progress beyond simply reading for pleasure to the point where they enjoy reading for inspiration and wisdom. Content sections are titled Courage, Nature and Man, Generosity, Our Land, Humility, and Family. All teaching material and commentary is contained in the teacher's edition, which I recommend that you purchase. There are student activity sheets and a separate answer key which are optional but useful. Although discussion questions appear in the teacher's edition, written activities are in the activity sheets, along with vocabulary and thinking activities and writing assignments. A TestBank (softbound book) or *AskIt* computer disk will save time on test preparation if you wish to test your student.

⊃ **Exploring Christian Literature** (Christian Liberty Press) $7; answer key - $1.50

This is a delightful and inspiring collection of stories and poems whose purpose is to build faith and Christian character. It features a mixture of widely recognizable selections, such as Kilmer's poem "Trees," excerpts from Shakespeare's plays and Robinson Crusoe, and Jonathan Edwards' "Sinners in the Hands of an Angry God." In addition, there are exceptional works by lesser known authors, many of them contemporary. Comprehension questions accompany some of the selections, which often will develop into discussions of significant issues. The book is suggested for ninth grade, but is appropriate for any teenager.

⊃ **Language Arts** (Alpha Omega LifePacs)

See description under "Grammar and Composition Materials for High School." Ninth-grade-level includes study of the play, *The Miracle Worker*, and the novel, *Twenty Thousand Leagues Under the Sea*. Tenth grade level studies *In His Steps*. Eleventh grade level studies the play, *Our Town*, and the novel *The Old Man and the Sea*; and twelfth grade level studies *Hamlet*.

⊃ **Moore-McGuffey Readers 3 and 4** (The Moore Foundation)

These readers cover a wide range of reading skill levels. Most eighth graders will still be in the third reader. Stories are morally uplifting and emphasize positive character development.

⊃ **Of People** (A Beka) $14.95

Reading selections all reflect different aspects of character—most of them positive. They are followed by information about authors, discussion questions, and speed reading charts. Questions are much more thought-provoking than those found in younger level A Beka readers.

⊃ **Of Places** (A Beka) $14.95

Selections are from renowned authors with different settings as the themes. It is recommended for eighth grade level but appropriate for many seventh graders. See comments on *Of People* above.

⊃ **Original Mott McGuffey Reader, Third Reader and Fourth Reader** (Mott Media) $16.99; $26.99 respectively

These readers have some archaic expressions and stories but excellent content. The third level is appropriate for many eighth graders.

⊃ **Our Heritage** (Pathway Publishing)

The Pathway readers are anthologies that clearly want to influence the character and beliefs of students. Coming from a Mennonite publisher, they teach Mennonite doctrine ("Sola Scriptura," Anabaptist, pacifist) and reflect an agrarian lifestyle. The philosophy and theology in these books comes across strongly in stories about or touching upon conscientious objectors, persecution of Anabaptists, criticism of Catholics and other Protestants, and other topics. A few Bible-based stories are scattered through the collection. The eighth grade reader, *Our Heritage,* honors the heritage and culture of the Mennonites as you can easily tell from the unit titles: Our Heritage, True Values, People Who Served, Thinking of Others, Nature's Wonders, In Olden Days, The Way of Love, and Home on the Farm. A few selections are from recognized authors such as Longfellow, Kipling, and Tennyson, but most are from lesser known or unknown authors. Stories and poems are followed by "Thinking It Over" questions and, usually, a few vocabulary words. Questions require both recall and deeper thinking/analysis. The reading workbook features additional questions regarding each story and poem, intermixed with occasional research, writing, and vocabulary activities. At least some of the questions should be used for discussion, not just answered in the workbook. The workbook is optional since the reader contains sufficient questions and vocabulary work by itself. The vocabulary workbook, *Working with Words*, introduces words that will be used in each of the stories and poems in advance of their appearance in the reader. Exercises in this book work on roots, derivatives, suffixes, prefixes, spelling rules, and grammar in addition to vocabulary. Of the two workbooks, *Working with Words* seems the most useful.

➲ Seeking True Values (Pathway Publishing)

See the review of *Our Heritage* above. The layout and philosophy of the reader and workbooks is the same. Stories in the seventh grade reader, *Seeking True Values*, stress godly character through stories and poems from many unknown and little-known authors as well as a few recognizable names such as Longfellow and Bunyan.

➲ Studying Christian Literature (Christian Liberty Press) $7; answer key - $1.50

This is CLP's new eighth grade reader. The format is very similar to *Enjoying Christian Literature*, but it has more "preachy" content—much of it would make great sermon material. In addition to stressing Christian character and action, certain selections promote a strong patriotic stance. One piece advocates self-sufficiency and responsibility rather than dependence upon the government. There are fewer fiction pieces than non-fiction. Representative titles are "What Constitutes Value?" by S.R. Whately, "Character of Columbus" by Washington Irving, "Washington's Farewell Address," and "Paul Revere's Ride" by H.W. Longfellow. There is no separate teacher manual, since the introductory section explains how to use the book to analyze literature as well as the ideas presented. Only a few of the selections include questions, so we need to develop our own from the instructions and sample questions in the introduction.

➲ A Time to Gather (Rod and Staff)

This seventh-grade-level reader includes stories, poetry (including selections of both from the Bible), and composition themes. Vocabulary lists and exercises follow each lesson. The inexpensive teacher's guide contains answers as well as teaching suggestions.

➲ A Time of Peace (Rod and Staff)

This eighth grade reader is the newest volume in Rod and Staff's reading series. It includes narratives, Bible prose and poetry, English poems, and essays for a total of 60 selections. According to the publisher, "The selections have been chosen on the basis of both Scriptural integrity and academic merit." Many selections are about "faith in action." Godly character building is a primary goal throughout. Questions (written and discussion) follow each selection. The teacher's manual contains teaching tips and answers.

Teaching Literature with "Real Books"

Good literature should be an essential part of the curriculum. Students at this level should primarily be reading full length books rather than anthologies, although anthologies are useful for introducing more variety into students' reading and providing discussion ideas. Discussion and oral reading should take place from time to time, especially when students are doing most of their work independently.

Best Books for kindergarten through high school (Bob Jones University Press) [$9.95] is a compilation of annotated listings of recommended fiction, arranged by levels. Books have been chosen for literary merit and propriety for Christian children. For junior and senior high levels, there are additional listings of worthwhile literature that requires some discussion because of questionable elements. (Those elements are described for us.) Another section lists biographies and autobiographies. At the end are excellent guidelines for choosing books. (Read this section first.)

Great Books of the Christian Tradition by Terry W. Glaspey (Harvest House) [$8.99] is a valuable tool for determining which of the "Great Books" we would like our teens to read. He focuses first on "Christian classics" with a sort of worldview introduction explaining why we should be reading the recommended books. Listed books are not all theological or spiritual, but have risen out of the Christian worldview. Recommendations are given with explanation of why the work is important and what version might be best, or what parts are most important. For instance, in recommending that we read the early Church Fathers, Glaspey mentions the translation to look for and highlights a few writers on which to concentrate for a start. Glaspey recommends three of Martin Luther's works plus two biographies written about Luther. We find Shakespeare, Jonathan Swift, George MacDonald, Leo Tolstoy, G.K. Chesterton, C.S. Lewis, Paul Johnson, Chuck Colson, and other authors up through the present day among the recommendations. Authors represent the broad range of Christian thinking through the ages. In the second half of the book, Glaspey expands to "Other Books Which Have Shaped Our World." He explains the impact of authors reflecting non-Christian worldviews and the importance of understanding "secular thought." In truth, not all authors included under this heading are non-Christians, so the distinction between sections might be based upon the content of particular works more than the authors themselves, although I cannot find any explanation for this. In this section we encounter authors such as Homer, Plato, Machiavelli, Voltaire, Hobbes, Marx, John Locke, Herman Melville, Nietzsche, Jack London, Herman Hesse, Aldous Huxley, Saul Bellow, and Kurt Vonnegut. Following this is a shorter section recommending books for young readers. A section titled "How to Make Use of This Reading List" is especially valuable for identifying starting points. Lists like Glaspey's "Ten Books Which Every Christian Ought to Know" and "Ten of My Favorite Novels" are great for parents and teens. However, do not expect all teens to be able to tackle all of Glaspey's recommendations, since some of them are "heavy reading." The final extensive list of modern novels that are great for discussion groups might be used as the source for a significant part of your high school literature curriculum.

Those interested in a classical approach to literature, should check out *Let the Authors Speak: A Guide to Worthy Books Based on Historical Setting* by Carolyn Hatcher (Old Pinnacle Publishing) [$18.95]. Hatcher uses the first half of the book explaining the rationale for using real books for learning and for literature, basing her ideas upon those of Charlotte Mason, Susan Schaeffer Macaulay, Marva Collins, and others. The second half lists books, first by historical setting (time period, location), then by author. A supplemental section lists myths/legends, fantasy, folk tales, fables, and allegories by time period. Few recommendations of drama and poetry are listed, and few 20th century titles appear since most have not yet had time to establish themselves as classics. Brief comments accompany each entry. Hatcher works from a Judeo-Christian world view and and leans toward a western-civilization background, which is reflected in the lists. However, all books listed are not necessarily Christian.

Suggested Books for Junior High

Following are some titles that appear on numerous recommended lists:

Adam of the Road by Elizabeth Janet Gray
The Adventures of Sherlock Holmes by A. C. Doyle
All Creatures Great and Small and other titles by James Herriot
America's Robert E. Lee by H. Comager
The Bronze Bow by Elizabeth George Speare
Call of the Wild by Jack London
Danger to Windward by Armstrong Sperry
Island of the Blue Dolphins by Scott O'Dell
Ivanhoe by Sir Walter Scott
Johnny Tremain by Esther Forbes
Julie of the Wolves by Jean Craighead George
Kidnapped by R. L. Stevenson
Kim by R. Kipling
The King's Beard by Leonard Wibberley
Life on the Mississippi by Mark Twain
The Pearl by John Steinbeck
The Red Badge of Courage by Stephen Crane
Rip Van Winkle and the Legend of Sleepy Hollow by Washington Irving
Sounder by William H. Armstrong
Tom Sawyer by Mark Twain
Twenty Thousand Leagues Under the Sea by Jules Verne
Where the Red Fern Grows by Wilson Rawls
A Wrinkle in Time by Madeleine L'Engle

The library is a good source for all of these books, and many distributors carry broad selections of classical literature.

Junior High Supplements and Study Guides

To challenge students to read beyond the surface meaning, you might wish to use one of the following books as an aid to studying novels:

➲ Amsco Literature Series (Amsco)

For those who want to study full-length selections, the Amsco Literature Series offers reasonably priced assistance. Unabridged editions of books are available that have large, readable type. In the Reader's Guide Editions of these books, the text of the book is first, followed by "...explanations, questions, and activities to bring out the details of plot, characterization, theme, style, and vocabulary." Included are questions of all types, which vary depending upon the book being studied. For example, background information and questions for *Hamlet* and *The Scarlet Letter* are very different because of the nature of each work. Representative titles: *Great Expectations, Hamlet, Jane Eyre, The Red Badge of Courage, The Odyssey, The Scarlet Letter,* and *Treasure Island.* (Shakespeare volumes also provide vocabulary assistance on facing pages within the text, making them much easier to use.) Separate answer keys are available and recommended. In reading through the study guide section for *The Scarlet Letter*, we did encounter some content problems. Whoever wrote this, clearly considers God, Satan, witchcraft, etc. as superstitions. This colors the explanations and questions. While such a point of view presents problems when studying literature, it can also be a vehicle for examining world view assumptions. E.g., What can we determine about the commentator's beliefs about God and man? Does this reflect agreement with the author of the book we are studying? Parents who lack the background to discern such problems or the time to deal with them, might better stick with the study guides coming from Christian publishers.(SE)

➲ Bookshelf Collection from the Reading Skills Discovery Series: 5th-8th grade levels (Common Sense Press) $14

Alternatives to book reports are provided for 16 books. For each book, there are discussion questions and activity suggestions, as well as a synopsis of the story for parents. Discussion questions range from factual recall through higher level thinking. Some of the 16 books are *Little House in the Big Woods, Railway Children, Mr. Popper's Penguins, Heidi, Anne of Green Gables,* and *King of the Wind.*

➲ Inside Stories, Book 4 and Book 5 (Dandy Lion) $12.95 each

Each of these books covers ten novels, with questions that take students from basic comprehension levels through higher levels of thinking. Each book is studied through a number of lessons with questions for discussion following every few chapters. Conclusion and summary discussion questions stretch students' thinking, and activities take them beyond the boundaries of the novel itself. For example, after studying *Across Five Aprils*, a novel of the Civil War, students are directed to research two political figures mentioned in the book and present it as either a first-person speech or autobiographical paper. Novels such as *Johnny Tremain, Bridge to Terabithia, The Witch of Blackbird Pond, Sing Down the Moon,* and *Wrinkle in Time* are studied in Book 4, suggested for grades 6-7. In Book 5 for grades 7-8, novels such as *The Incredible Journey, The Pearl, Across Five Aprils, The Grey King, Jonathon Livingston Seagull,* and *A Swiftly Tilting Planet* are included. Use discretion about novels that you choose for study. All are not worthwhile reading for Christian students.(SE)

⮑ Literature Units (Teacher Created Materials) $7.95 each

Teacher Created Materials offers comprehensive studies of popular fiction as unit studies. Each unit or book covers one novel. Student activity pages are reproducible. Units are available in three levels, Primary, Intermediate and Challenging. Challenging level units will meet the needs of some junior high students. Among the popular fiction books for which units are written are *The Incredible Journey, Where the Red Fern Grows, Julie of the Wolves, Old Yeller, Anne of Green Gables, Bridge to Terabithia, The Hobbit,* and *Book of Greek Myths* (by the D'Aulaires). The literature units include sample lesson plans, with prereading activities, vocabulary and short answer quizzes. The novels are broken down into chapter groupings for study. Along with reading the novel, the unit suggests other learning experiences, inspired by the subject of the book. In the case of *The Incredible Journey,* this included such topics as glaciers, caring for pets, and beaver dams. Activities range across the curriculum (whole language approach) including writing, vocabulary, geography, art, music, math, science, social studies, thinking skills, and practical arts like cooking. Quizzes and answer keys are included within the intermediate and challenging units. There seems to be a good balance of recall, research and creativity. At the end of *The Incredible Journey* unit, students are asked to write an essay on the novel. I particularly liked one of the tests in which students had to write about quotes from the book, thus demonstrating their understanding of the plot and characterization. Many activities are designed for classroom use, so we will need to either adapt or skip them. We also need to exercise discernment in selecting which books and which activities within each unit study to use since books are selected for and activities are designed primarily for the public school.(SE)[Kath Courtney/C.D.]

⮑ Progeny Press Study Guides for Literature (Progeny Press) middle school level home editions - $6.99 each

At present a number of study guides in a much larger series from Progeny Press are geared for junior high levels. They are for the books *The Lion, The Witch and the Wardrobe; The Magician's Nephew; The Hiding Place; The Indian in the Cupboard; Carry On, Mr. Bowditch; Shiloh; Johnny Tremain; The Bronze Bow; Bridge to Terabithia; Island of the Blue Dolphins; Amos Fortune, Free Man; The Sign of the Beaver;* and *The Secret Garden.* (*The Lion, The Witch and the Wardrobe* study guide will actually suit learners down to fourth grade level.) *The Hiding Place Study Guide* includes an additional study of the short story *The Power of Light* by Isaac Bashevis Singer which relates very closely to the themes of *The Hiding Place.* These study guides, although written by different authors, all come from a Christian perspective. Thus, we find questions that refer us to Scripture such as "Read through I Corinthians 12:12-27. How does this passage reflect the importance of each individual within a church or family?" (from *The Hiding Place Study Guide*).

The study guides deal with both literature as art and literature as a reflection or source of ideas. So there are studies of vocabulary, literary terms, plot, etc. as well as studies about the characters, events, and ideas presented.

The format varies from one study guide to another, but with many common characteristics. A synopsis and some background is first. Ideas for pre-reading (and sometimes mid- and post-reading) activities are next. Then studies are divided up to cover groups of chapters at a time. Each study section has vocabulary activities along with comprehension, analysis, personal application, and thought questions. A lengthier writing assignment completes each section. A variety of vocabulary activities are used within each guide, so the studies maintain a higher level of interest than those which use the same format for every lesson. Questions go well beyond the recall level, asking students to infer meanings, identify symbolism, draw analogies, and apply principles to their own lives. Students can work through the study guides independently, although discussion enhances any literature study. Answer keys are found at the back of each book, so each *Study Guide* is self-contained aside from the novel itself. The novels are available from Progeny Press if you need a source.

⮑ Responding to Literature: Writing and Thinking Activities, Grades 4-8 (Spring Street Press) $15.95

75 reproducible worksheets can be used with any books children read to integrate reading, writing, and thinking activities. The key areas addressed are plot, character, setting, and literary forms with subtopics such as mood, theme, historical fiction, biography, autobiography, plays, folk tales, mysteries, poetry, vocabulary, judgments, and analyzing an author's purpose. A variety of approaches is used to tackle each area so that we can select one that best meets each child's learning style needs. For example, to identify and describe the plot one child might write a news report. Another child will write a ballad that retells the story. Still another child might write and illustrate a postcard to a friend concerning the story. Since the book is geared for grades 4-8, there is a range of difficulty evident in the activities. Since the activities can be used along with any books, we are not limited to a prescribed or even recommended reading list. At the end of the book are eight reproducible reading record sheets—some like book report forms and others designed for recording number of pages read, books read, or student evaluations of books read. This is an ideal resource for home educators because of the tremendous flexibility.(S)

⮑ Total Language Plus (Blakey Publications) regular guides - $16.95; advanced guides - $18.95 each; Set 1 - $65.80; Set 2 - $81

Total Language Plus "...covers reading, comprehension, spelling, grammar, vocabulary, writing, listening, and analytical and critical thinking with a Christian perspective." Each volume is a student workbook that accompanies a novel. Students read sections of the novel each week, answer comprehension questions, and tackle writing topics. The week's study also includes vocabulary work consisting of four lessons working with words drawn from the reading and four activities for a list of spelling words also drawn from the reading. Grammar worksheet activities include dictation exercises, and grammatical work with the dictated material that serves to review rather than teach grammar. Students create their own glossary toward the back of the book by entering definitions and parts of speech labels for their vocabulary words each week. Vocabulary review tests and an answer key are both at the back of the book. At the front of each book are projects, drawing, and writing activities, as well as critical thinking questions and a puzzle. These activities, with the exception of the critical thinking, are not tied directly to any one chapter so we can use them when, if, and how we wish. We can select more activities to turn our study into an in-depth unit study, or choose fewer and stick to the basics. The activities are presented as suggestions, rather than as fully-developed plans, so they will require independent research and work beyond what is presented here.

The number of lessons in the various volumes of *Total Language Plus* ranges from five to eight, so some books are likely to take longer to study than others. Generally, a volume should take from 9 to 10 weeks to complete. (Plan to complete one per quarter.) If impatient students want to read through the novel quickly, rather than spread it out, they can do so covering the comprehension and critical thinking questions as they go, and working through the remainder of each week's lessons on a slower schedule. The only supplementary items needed are the novel and the small teacher's manual which serves for all volumes in the series. We might substitute the new audio cassette of a *Total Language Plus Workshop* for the teacher's manual. The cassette explains how the curriculum was designed and offers suggestions for its use.

Lessons dealing with grammar, writing, and spelling rules are application and review oriented rather than instructional. A basic understanding is assumed. For example, since spelling words are selected from the chapter, there are no common patterns or spelling rules being covered. I view *Total Language Plus* primarily as a resource for studying novels, and secondarily for expanding vocabulary and spelling skills. Its effectiveness in developing broader writing skills is dependent upon our selection of assignments from the front of the book, as well as upon our work with our children on the writing process within those assignments.

Books have been selected to meet the needs of various age levels and interests. The catalog features very complete descriptions of each study guide as well as a synopsis of each novel. Available titles are *Anne of Green Gables; The Bronze Bow; Caddie Woodlawn; Carry On Mr. Bowditch; My Side of the Mountain; The Cricket in Times Square; The Giver; The Light in the Forest; The Lion, the Witch, and the Wardrobe; A Wrinkle in Time; Johnny Tremain; Julie of the Wolves; The Witch of Blackbird Pond; The High King; The Trumpeter of Krakow; The Wheel on the School; Where the Red Fern Grows; Words by*

Heart; The Call of the Wild; The Scarlet Letter; The Hiding Place; The Swiss Family Robinson; The Yearling; and *Rifles for Watie.* Some of these titles might be appropriate for students as young as fifth grade, while others will be suitable through the high school years. Additional, more-challenging study guides for *Jane Eyre, Oliver Twist,* and *The Scarlet Letter* are designed for advanced high school students. *Total Language Plus* might serve as a supplement or a primary learning tool depending upon the needs of each student. Purchasing Set 1 or Set 2 saves money: Set 1 is your choice of four guides plus the tape or teacher's manual; Set 2 adds to Set 1 four novels.

You might want to work on reading comprehension with one of the following:

➲ Reading for Comprehension H and I (Continental Press) $6.75 each

Half-page, interesting stories are followed by multiple choice questions in these workbooks for junior high level.(S)

➲ Reasoning and Reading, Level 1 and Level 2 (Educators Publishing Service) $9.30 each; teacher's guide - $5.35 each

Level 1 is recommended for grades 6-7 and Level 2 for grades 8-9. These 160-page workbooks help students understand and evaluate what they read.(S)

➲ Skills Bank Home Tutor [for IBM and Apple II type machines] (SkillsBank Corporation)

See the description of the entire program where it first appears under math resources for junior high. The reading module in this program will still be useful at junior high level. It has three sections: reading comprehension, vocabulary building, and word knowledge. The most difficult sections within each area address topics such as hyperbole, personification, Latin and Greek roots, and suffixes that form nouns and adjectives. This is a good way to review reading skills before moving on to more difficult literature.(S)

High School Level Literature

We can use literature texts from Christian publishers—which I do recommend—but some of us might want to construct our own literature programs, and all of us should be encouraging our teens to read many full-length books in addition to any anthologies they might be using.

Among core literature recommendations recommended for students in public high school are (listing does not imply recommendation):

The Adventures of Huckleberry Finn and other works by Mark Twain

The Aeneid of Virgil by Virgil

Alice's Adventures in Wonderland by Lewis Carroll

All the King's Men by Robert Penn Warren

Anna Karenina, War and Peace, and other works by Leo Tolstoy

Anne Frank: The Diary of A Young Girl by Anne Frank

Anne of Green Gables and other titles by Lucy Maud Montgomery

Billy Budd, Moby Dick, and other works by Herman Melville
Brave New World by Aldous Huxley
Canterbury Tales by Geoffrey Chaucer
"The Charge of the Light Brigade" and other works by Alfred
    Lord Tennyson
The Chosen by Chaim Potok
Christy by Catherine Marshall
Pride and Prejudice by Jane Austen
David Copperfield, Great Expectations, A Tale of Two Cities,
    and other works by Charles Dickens
The Death of Socrates and other works by Plato
"The Devil and Daniel Webster" and other works by Stephen
    Vincent Benet
Don Quixote by Miguel de Cervantes
The Good Earth by Pearl Buck
*The Grapes of Wrath, The Pearl, The Red Pony, Of Mice and
    Men*, and other works by John Steinbeck
The Great Gatsby by F. Scott Fitzgerald
Gulliver's Travels and other works by Jonathan Swift
*Hamlet, Henry V, Macbeth, Midsummer Night's Dream,
    Othello, Merchant of Venice*, and other works by William
    Shakespeare
"The Hollow Men" and other works by T.S. Eliot
The Hound of the Baskervilles and other works by Sir Arthur
    Conan Doyle
Jane Eyre by Charlotte Bronte
"The Legend of Sleepy Hollow" and other works by Washing-
    ton Irving
Light in the Forest by Conrad Richter
Little Women by Louisa May Alcott
A Man for All Seasons by Robert Bolt
Martian Chronicles and other works by Ray Bradbury
Men of Iron by Howard Pyle
The Miracle Worker by William Gibson*The Miracle Worker*
    by William Gibson
1984 and *Animal Farm* by George Orwell
The Odyssey and *The Iliad* by Homer
Oedipus the King, Antigone, and other works by Sophocles
"Ozymandias" and other works by Percy Bysshe Shelley
Perelandra, Out of the Silent Planet, and other works by C.S.
    Lewis
"The Pit and the Pendulum" and other works by Edgar Allen
    Poe
Pygmalion by George Bernard Shaw
"The Road Not Taken" and other works by Robert Frost
Robinson Crusoe by Daniel Defoe
The Scarlet Letter by Nathaniel Hawthorne
To Kill a Mockingbird by Harper Lee
Treasure Island, Kidnapped, and other works by Robert Louis
    Stevenson
The Trilogy of the Ring by J. R. Tolkein
*Twenty Thousand Leagues Under the Sea, Around the World in
    Eighty Days*, and other works by Jules Verne
Uncle Tom's Cabin by Harriet Beecher Stowe
Wuthering Heights by Emily Bronte
The Yearling, Cross Creek, and other works by Marjorie K.
    Rawlings

I would add to the above (or use instead):
The Divine Comedy by Dante
The Great Divorce, Screwtape Letters, and *Mere Christianity*
    by C.S. Lewis
In His Steps by Charles M. Sheldon
The Marquis' Secret and other works by George MacDonald
    (updated versions)
Paradise Lost by John Milton
Pilgrims' Progress by John Bunyan
The Spy and other works by James Fenimore Cooper

Also look for top-quality fiction from Christian authors such as Frank Peretti, Bodie Thoene, and Stephen Lawhead. Christian publishers are making a determined effort to publish more such fiction, so look for new titles from them over the next few years.

Ideally, students should be reading full-length books in both British and American literature along with other classical literature such as some of the titles listed above. Critical thinking skills can be developed in discussing and reporting on what they read. It is often helpful to have Christian literature textbooks to help as we study secular literature. Themes that might sound objectionable in themselves, can be used to illustrate the results of evil or immorality.

Books on Tape

Auditory students might need or enjoy taped versions of good books. There are a number of sources for such tapes, although you must be aware, as for books, that there are abridged editions that drastically alter the originals.

➲ Blackstone Audio Books

Those seeking unabridged books on tape need to check out Blackstone's extensive catalog. They sell and rent only unabridged books along with selected plays, speeches, and special programs. Their catalog is so large that tapes are categorized under headings like "Literature of the 20th Century," "Literature" (i.e., classics), "Children's," "Non-fiction," "Politics," and "Religion." Prices depend upon the length of each work. For example, *Robinson Crusoe* is produced on eight 1 1/2 hour cassettes, sells for $56.95, and rents for 30 days at $12.95. *Little Women* fills fifteen 1 1/2 hour cassettes, sells for $95.95, and rents for 45 days at $15.95. Send for their free catalog.

➲ Children's Classics Library and Family Classics Library
[audio tapes] (Newport Publishers) $39.95 each set

There are forty audio cassette tapes in each of these sets. The *Children's Classics* set is only slightly younger in content than the *Family Classics*. All tapes are recorded with sound effects and a variety of voices. All presentations are abridgements, although some are extremely short presentations—some little more than plot summaries—and others are much lengthier. Among titles in the *Children's Classics Library* are *The Adventures of Huckleberry Finn* - 6, *Gulliver's Travels* - 4, *The Legend of Sleepy Hollow* - 2, *The Wind in the Willows* -6, *Peter Pan* - 1, *Fiction and Fantasy* - 1, *Sleeping Beauty* - 1. (Numbers following titles indicate the number of tapes for each presentation.) Among *Family Classics Library* titles are *The Pickwick Papers* - 1, *Les Miserables* - 6, *The Call of the Wild* -1, *The Count of Monte Cristo* - 1, *A Tale of Two Cities* - 9, *A Christman Carol* -3, *Great Expectations* - 5, and *The Scarlet Letter* - 4. Quality varies from presentation to presentation. For example, *Gulliver's Travels* was hard to understand and the use of speeded-up and slowed-down voices for tiny people and giants did not work well. The retelling of *Little Red Riding Hood* on the *Fiction and Fantasy Tape* featured a distressing combination of professional and amateur reading voices. On the other hand, *A Tale of Two Cities* and *The Count of Monte Cristo* are both quite good. Most of the tapes, with the exception of a few single tapes (e.g., fairy tales, Aesop's Fables, Nursery Rhymes), are for an audience at least in their teens rather than for younger children, partly because of the vocabulary level and partly because of length and children's attention span. The value of these tapes for homeschoolers is exposure to stories that might not be read in their original versions. (I'm not recommending such substitutions as a major part of a literature program, but only as a supplement to expand familiarity and possibly stimulate interest in the original version.) Although the quality and age appropriateness vary greatly from tape to tape, if we consider either set as an investment for the entire family they are a bargain.(S)

Resources for Using "Real Books"—High School Level

⮑ Amsco Literature Series (Amsco)

See the review of these guides under "Junior High Supplements and Study Guides" in the junior high section.

⮑ Brightest Heaven of Invention: A Christian Guide to Six Shakespeare Plays by Peter J. Leithart (Canon Press) $15.50

Many Christians shy away from Shakespeare because of concerns about witches, ghosts, murders, and other elements that occur in his plays. Peter Leithart presents these studies of six of Shakespeare's plays from a Christian point of view. He shows how these possibly objectionable elements are used to illustrate eternal truths in keeping with Scripture. Actually, this is only a minor aspect of Leithart's book. It is really a guide for exploring the beauty and depth of each of the six plays selected from the three primary types of dramas penned by Shakespeare. From the historical plays, he covers *Henry V* and *Julius Caesar*; from the tragedies, *Hamlet* and *Macbeth*; and from the comedies, *The Taming of the Shrew* and *Much Ado About Nothing*. Each study begins with background for that particular play. This is far more than the superficial treatment typical of must study guides. It gets into philosophy, history, culture, and other significant factors. Leithart suggests that students familiarize themselves with each play by first reading a simplified version or viewing a film version. (Leithart discusses which films are suitable for this purpose.) Then students read a portion of the play, read through Leithart's discussion of that section, and answer ten review and ten thought questions. Thought questions might be used for ei-

ther discussion or written work. After the study of each play there are suggestions of ten possible topics for lengthier writing assignments. High school students can work through this book independently, but it would make a wonderful resource to be used in a group class where students could practice reciting lines dramatically, sharpen each others' understanding, and share ideas.

⮑ The Courtship of Miles Standish, Teacher Guide and Poem developed by Elizabeth L. Youmans (Foundation for American Christian Education) $13

This syllabus was developed to be used as part of the American Christian History Literature course of study which will soon be available from F.A.C.E. However, it can also be used as a stand-alone study of poetry and Longfellow's poem, "The Courtship of Miles Standish." Principle Approach methodology and background are integral to the study. The key principles are incorporated into this guide in the historical background leading up to the writing of this poem. As with other Principle Approach study, students are expected to use the notebook method. This guide explains how to apply the Principle Approach in the study of literature, but does not cover all aspects of teaching with that methodology. The study incorporates, reading, reasoning, writing, oral presentation, and drama. Line notes add specific commentary for understanding the poem. Students are directed to particular lines to answer questions, which teaches them to respond directly to the text instead of offering fuzzy, emotional explanations as we commonly encounter in questions in modern literature studies. The guide features line references that exemplify external and internal characterizations that should be extremely helpful to the teacher who might offer suggestions to students of which lines to examine. Subjects for oral presentations, written compositions, art projects, and dramatization are suggested. The complete text of the poem is included in the second half of the book.

⮑ Progeny Press Study Guides for Literature (Progeny Press) high school level home editions - $8.99 each

See the review of these guides under "Junior High Supplements and Study Guides" in the junior high section. There are a number of study guides for novels and plays for high school level: *The Red Badge of Courage, The Yearling, Heart of Darkness, Jane Eyre, The Merchant of Venice, Romeo and Juliet, Hamlet, Out of the Silent Planet, To Kill a Mockingbird, A Day No Pigs Would Die, The Scarlet Letter, The Adventures of Huckleberry Finn,* and *Perelandra.* The novels and plays themselves are also available from Progeny Press if you need a source.

⮑ Shakespeare: The Writing Company Catalog (The Writing Company)

This is a great catalog of literature resources, the majority of them for studying Shakespeare. They carry books (numerous versions of Shakespeare's plays), videos, audio cassettes, posters, games, T-shirts, study guides, activity books, computer software, dramatic production aids, and more. A smattering of resources for literature other than Shakespeare is included. If you're interested in studying Shakespeare, you have got to check out this catalog.(S)

➲ Sundance Catalog (Sundance Publishing)

The *Sundance Secondary Catalog* features reading, literature, and writing resources, but I include it here because it lists numerous pieces of classical literature in book, audio, and video formats. Audio cassettes include some abridged and some unabridged versions.(S)

➲ Total Language Plus (Blakey Publications) $18.95 each

Total Language Plus is developing a series of high school-level study guides for selected American and British Literature. The guides available thus far are for *Jane Eyre, Scarlet Letter,* and *Oliver Twist.* Like the younger level guides reviewed under literature for junior high, these guides cover "...reading, comprehension, spelling, grammar, vocabulary, writing, listening, and analytical and critical thinking with a Christian perspective," although the format differs somewhat from the previous levels. Each volume is a student workbook that accompanies a novel. Students read chapters of the novel each week and answer comprehension questions. The week's study also includes vocabulary work consisting of four lessons working with words that have been drawn from the reading. There are also four activities for a list of spelling words drawn from the reading. Grammar worksheet activities include dictation exercises, and grammatical work with the dictated material that serves to review rather than teach grammar. Students create their own glossary toward the back of the book by entering definitions and parts of speech labels for their vocabulary words each week, then writing sentences using their new words. Vocabulary review tests and an answer key are both at the back of the book. Additions at this level are extensive writing activities and oral readings. I am particularly impressed with the quality of the writing activities. They teach and stress organization and planning, while offering students ideas about the main points they might wish to include. This seems to be a challenging area for many students, and many parents are unsure about how to develop these writing skills. *Total Language Plus's* writing assignments should provide a significant part of your composition instruction.

The number of lessons in the various volumes of *Total Language Plus* varies since some books are likely to take longer to study than others. (*Jane Eyre* should take about seven weeks to complete.) If impatient students want to read through the novel quickly, rather than spread it over the time it takes to complete the accompanying lessons, they can do so covering the comprehension and thinking questions as they go, and working through the remainder of each week's lessons on a slower schedule. The only supplementary items needed are the small teacher's manual which serves for all volumes in the series and the novel. We might substitute the new audio cassette of a *Total Language Plus Workshop* for the teacher's manual.

The level of the vocabulary and spelling in these advanced-level guides is quite challenging, so this is definitely high school level study. The amount of both vocabulary and spelling practice is appropriate for high schoolers, although students might need to work on additional vocabulary words that are at a less challenging level. Since spelling words are selected from the chapter, there are no common patterns or spelling rules being covered. *Total Language Plus* for high school serves primarily as a re-

Reading the Great Books

Great Books Tutorial (Escondido Tutorial Service)

The Great Books, writings from the most influential writers from ancient days up through modern times, are a wonderful source of learning and literature. However, high schoolers definitely need some help in tackling many of the Great Book authors. Enter Fritz Hinrichs, a Christian familiar with many of these works who offers his services as a tutor via modern technology using internet-based video-conferencing. Hinrichs studied philosophy using the Great Books at St. John s College in Annapolis, Maryland and also studied at Westminster Seminary in Escondido, California. He says that this background convinced him that the best method for developing discerning Christian minds is the study of western history accompanied by the attempt to bring all thoughts captive to Christ. Students "meet" with Hinrichs in a weekly on-line class to discuss the assigned reading for the week. Hinrichs leads the discussion as they read excerpts and answer questions to explore the literature.

Hinrichs has divided a chronological study of the Great Books into a six year sequence. The first year begins with the ancient Greeks. The second year moves from Greece to the ancient Romans. The third year broadens to encompass Church fathers, Dante, Shakespeare, Chaucer, and Spenser. The fourth year begins with Machiavelli, then moves into the Renaissance and Reformation eras. The fifth year explores the Enlightenment and French and American Revolutions, while also covering some of the philosophic foundations of liberalism. The sixth year tackles some of the philosophers who have reshaped history—Hegel, Marx, Nietzsche, and Freud as well as writings by Tocqueville, Husserl, Lincoln, and C.S. Lewis.

Any student capable of contributing to and benefiting from the discussion is welcome to enroll. There are writing assignments and an essay exam which are critiqued by Hinrichs, but actual grading is left to the parent. All classes are not offered every year, so check for current classes. The cost is $105 per semester per student. For online classes, Hinrichs uses internet-based video conferencing where students can see on their screens in real time what Hinrichs writes on the whiteboard as they hear him speak and watch his live video. Students are able to contribute to the class discussion by using the microphones on their computers. Online students may also download the Real Player from http://www.real.com in order to watch the class recordings if they have to miss a tutorial. See the ETS Web site for more details.

source for studying novels and developing writing skills, and secondarily for expanding vocabulary and spelling skills.

Senior High Literature Textbooks

I suggest selecting literature anthologies that relate to historical periods that you are studying rather than whatever text is typically used at a particular grade level. This approach enhances both literature and history studies if we make connections between them. This usually means that we use parts of different literature books over a few years rather than completing one before beginning another.

General Literature

○ Elements of Literature (Bob Jones University Press) $27; teacher's edition - $36; TestBank - $16; AskIt - $14; *Great Expectations* - $9.46; teacher's edition for book -$23

Suggested for tenth grade, this text teaches students literary analysis at a more challenging level than the ninth grade level *Fundamentals of Literature* from BJUP. It delves into topics such as themes, allusions, symbolism, irony, as well as teaching more about the forms of literature—fiction, poetry, biography, drama, etc. Shakespeare's *Romeo and Juliet* is included for study within the text. Study of *Great Expectations* by Charles Dickens is an optional part of the course. There are separate teacher's editions for the basic student text and for *Great Expectations*, both of which include reproductions of the student text pages as well as teaching information and helps. Time factors will probably limit us to covering either *Romeo and Juliet* or *Great Expectations*, so plan accordingly. A TestBank or AskIt disk are also available.

○ Fundamentals of Literature (Bob Jones University Press) $27; teacher's edition - $36; TestBank - $16; AskIt - $14

Suggested for grade nine, this textbook is the foundation for the study of literature. It studies conflict, character, theme, structure, point of view, and moral tone through both traditional and contemporary selections. The drama *Cyrano De Bergerac* is included for study in the text, with a videocassette also available. Interpretation and evaluation from a Christian point of view are a major emphasis. Reading selections are not necessarily Christian, since interpretation and evaluation can be truly taught only by studying examples written from more than one perspective. The teacher's edition contains reproductions of the student text pages as well as questions and helps for discussion and analysis. While it might be possible to work strictly from the teacher's edition, covering answers when necessary, it is probably more practical for both teacher and student to have a text during discussions. A TestBank to accompany this text is available in both softbound book and computer disk formats.

○ How to Read the Bible as Literature (and Get More Out of It) by Leland Ryken (Zondervan Publishing House) $14.99

Many people have the idea that a book discussing the Bible as literature will take a very humanistic approach which reduces the Bible to simply another piece of literature. Mr. Ryken's book is as far from this as possible; always, he operates from a Christian perspective with great reverence for and belief in the truth of the Bible. He is not trying to replace a theological or historical interpretation, but to enhance the Bible by looking also at its literary side.

How to Read the Bible as Literature shows the difference between expository writing and literary writing: literature presents an experience, rather than telling about the experience. The story of the Good Samaritan is an excellent example. Jesus did not define the word "neighbor" (expository writing); instead, He gave us a picture of what a neighbor is (literary writing). Literature involves the reader intellectually, emotionally, and imaginatively. Mr. Ryken shows that literary language, such as similes, metaphors, and personification, is used even in the most expository parts of the Bible (think of the Church as a body).

The author provides excellent analysis of narratives and poetry as literary genres, so you don't have to be trained in literary criticism to understand his points. He constantly uses examples from Scripture. Among the topics he discusses are how to chart the progress of a story; how elements like setting, characterization, and structure add to the truth of the passage; and how parallelism in biblical poetry reinforces the meaning. Some extensive examples for applying the techniques are given in later chapters.

This is a fascinating book for any person looking to enhance his or her understanding of Scripture. It is an excellent home school resource for the parent who is preparing or leading Bible study. The book could be used as a text for a high school class on the Bible as Literature. This might be interesting for a student who has had years of traditional Bible study. A small group approach comes to mind as a possibility. Marginal notes serve as an outline to the text, and there are good references for further reading listed for each chapter. There are no assignments included, but it would be easy to develop some. A student could write an essay on the use of parallelism in a Psalm, or compare and contrast characters such as David, Saul, and Jonathan.

○ Library of the Future, Fourth Edition [CD-ROM for Windows and DOS systems] (World Library) $59.95 (suggested retail)

A single compact disc contains the complete text of "over 5,000 historical, classical, and cultural titles." If you have always wanted to own a set of the Great Books, but couldn't find the space or money, this is the most practical alternative I have found. In fact, I think it will be even more useful than the actual books since we can search through the disc for information on topics much faster than we could ever search through the books. Included are titles from philosophers, historians, poets, playwrights, scientists, and authors of fiction. A sampling of authors and/or titles we find: Aeschylus, Aesop, Alcott, Aristophanes, Augustine, Francis Bacon, Baum (*The Wizard of Oz*), Robert Browning, William Cullen Bryant, Lewis Carroll, Chaucer, Cicero, Confucius, Charles Darwin, Defoe, Arthur Conan

Doyle, Hawthorne, Hobbes, Homer, Hume, Ibsen, Irving, Kipling, Milton, Nietzsche,Thomas Paine, Pound, Shakespeare, Tennyson, Twain, and Wilde. In addition, there are historical documents (the *Constitution, Emancipation Proclamation, Monroe Doctrine*), plus religious documents (the Bible, Book of Mormon, Upanishads). One interesting piece of modern non-fiction is included—Phillip Johnson's *Darwin on Trial.* We can print out hard copy of any of these as needed. This is a fantastic resource for literature, history, and world view studies.

○ Norton Anthologies (W.W. Norton and Co.) $35-$40

There are a number of anthologies published by Norton including *Norton Anthology of English Literature, Norton Anthology of American Literature (two volumes), Norton Anthology of Literature by Women, Norton Anthology of Poetry,* and others. These books emphasize classical selections unlike most anthologies written for high school students. Commentary is included, although it is written at college/adult level. Various editions of these books have been printed over many years, so it is fairly easy to find them in used book stores at fantastic prices.(S)

○ Perspectives of Life in Literature (Christian Light Publications) text - $22.95; student materials - $10; teacher materials - $17

This Christian Life course uses the 611-page *Perspectives of Life in Literature* text, a teacher's guidebook, two student LightUnit workbooks, and two test booklets. Answers to exercises, and tests are in the teacher's guidebook.

The course can be used by students working independently, although a parent really must read the selections so that she can evaluate subjective answers and writing assignments, as well as be prepared to discuss them. The LightUnits outline detailed, daily lesson plans. The text features a wide range of literary selections: poetry, short stories, allegories (including the complete *Pilgrim's Progress*), and biographies. Each story is preceded by vocabulary exercises and followed by comprehension, interpretation, and application exercises as well as one on literary techniques (theme, symbolism, etc.) and a writing assignment. Reading selections are by authors such as Nathaniel Hawthorne, Leo Tolstoy, Robert Browning, John Bunyan, William Shakespeare (brief selections), Edwin Markham, Fanny Crosby, John Milton, George Macdonald, and lesser known authors. Selections from the Bible are also included. The text is divided into five units, four of which focus upon literary forms: the short story, poetry, biography, and allegory. A fifth unit focuses on the theme, "Reflections for the victorious life," instead of a single form.

The final sentence of the introduction to the text summarizes the overall approach of this course: "The best reason for studying literature is to find, in the lives and writings of others, patterns to help our lives conform more nearly to the life of 'him that is true' (1 John 5:20)." Suggested for grades 9 and 10, the course might easily be used for students a grade level below or above.

○ Perspectives of Truth in Literature (Christian Light Publications) text - $22.95; student materials - $10; teacher's materials - $5; teacher's guidebook - $12

Short stories, poetry, and essays comprise this anthology suggested for twelfth grade level. The Teacher's Guidebook is the answer key and guide for the text. The Teacher's Materials are needed only if you choose to use the Student Materials. Student Materials consist of a study guide and tests.

This course stands alone and does not require LightUnits as does *Perspective of Life.* The theme "truth" is used throughout the text, but particularly in the first unit. Remaining units are organized according to literary form: short stories, poetry, and essays. Literary works are from the Bible; well-known authors such as John Greenleaf Whittier, Victor Hugo, Robert Louis Stevenson, Edgar Allen Poe, Nathaniel Hawthorne, Thomas àKempis, and Ray Bradbury; and many less familiar authors.

Questions at the end of each selection deal with content, ideas, and literary elements. Instruction on literary technique and writing skills follows most of the selection in units other than that on poetry. Occasional writing assignments or written activities are part of the literary technique sections, but the bulk of writing assignments are in the "Writing for Skill" sections. These require students to tackle different forms of writing, generally on topics other than literary analysis. The text actually provides a well-rounded language arts program with the variety of activities provided.

○ Themes in Literature (A Beka) $14.95

Character qualities such as courage, joy, justice, and humility are the themes of selections in this ninth grade text. It features authors such as Tolstoy, Hawthorne, and Chaucer. Included in the student text are information on authors and literary devices, vocabulary lists, and discussion questions.

○ Working with Poetry (Educators Publishing Service) $8.70

This book is designed for eleventh and twelfth grade students who lack experience reading poetry. According to the catalog description, students analyze a variety of poems, focusing on words, images, rhythm, and rhetorical devices.(S)

American Literature

○ American Literature (Bob Jones University Press) $28; teacher's edition - $39; TestBank - $16; AskIt -$14

Suggested for grade eleven, this text covers American literature from the colonial period up through this century. Representative authors are William Bradford, Benjamin Franklin, Nathaniel Hawthorne, Henry David Thoreau, Herman Melville, Samuel Clemens, Thornton Wilder, and Bruce Catton. Selections are organized by historical literary periods, while addressing some of the philosophical movements that influenced literature. There is significant discussion of the world views reflected by authors and their works. Background information, analytical help, discussion suggestions, and a reproduction of the student text are in the two-volume, spiral-bound teacher's edition. I highly recommend purchasing the teacher's edition and a student text, so that both teacher and student have easy access to the text for discussions. A TestBank and AskIt disk are also available.

○ The American Literature Critical Thinking Course by James P. Stobaugh (For Such A Time As This Ministries) $35

American literature, critical thinking, and world views are twined together in this heavy-duty, year-long course for Christian home schoolers. Bloom's Taxonomy of Thinking Skills is introduced at the beginning of the book, albeit with little explanation. However, questions throughout the course develop all the different levels of thinking skills. World views are introduced in the second week, then applied through all the lessons to the reading selections. Students are required to do very extensive reading including complete versions of books such as *The Scarlet Letter, The Adventures of Huckleberry Finn, Billy Budd, Ethan Frome, A Farewell to Arms*, and *The Unvanquished;* they also read speeches and writings such as "Sinners in the Hands of An Angry God"; poems by Emerson, Frost, and Auden; and plays such as *The Little Foxes* and *The Glass Menagerie*. While these readings are the primary focus of each week's lesson, it is strongly suggested that students read (from an extended reading list included in the course) quite a few more books. Occasionally, one book or reading is studied for two weeks, but in most cases, each book or reading is to be read before each week's lesson. The lesson then focuses on critical thinking and "challenge" questions, with responses taking the form of essays and reports. Lessons vary in format with some including background on the author or setting, recall questions, vocabulary words, and Biblical applications. An answer key is included, although some responses will be so subjective that you might well differ in your judgment of acceptable responses from those provided by Mr. Stobaugh. Ideally, parents should be reading through the selections so that they can readily discuss them, but if that is not possible, the course will still function well for students working independently. For some, the reading requirements might be excessive, especially if they have been assigned other books to read for other courses, as I would expect. So you might have to use some judgment about how quickly to progress through the material.

○ Beginnings of American Literature (second edition) (A Beka) $14; teacher guide - $14.65; curriculum - $20; test book - $3.95; answer key -$7.80

Suggested for first semester of eleventh grade, this book studies various genres of American literature. Themes for the various units are patriotism, humor and legends, the short story, devotional verse, spiritual life (sermons), early accounts of life in the colonies, early works by American authors, and early poets. Within this text is the entire book of *The Scarlet Letter*. Many of the selections in this book use archaic or unusual expressions, and "translations" or explanations are found at the bottom of the pages where they appear. Most readings include a brief biographical sketch of each author and questions to be used for discussion and/or writing assignments. At the end of each unit are some challenging composition questions and identification exercises. You will need the teacher guide for more complete lesson presentation on topics such as plot and characterization.

Answers to textbook questions are contained in the separate teacher guide which integrates A Beka's literature, grammar, and vocabulary/spelling. A single test booklet and answer key as well as the Curriculum cover both this text and the second semester text, *The Literature of the American People*.

○ Great Books Guides by Karen Maddry (McJake Enterprises) $18.95 each

This is a planned series of study guides for both American and British classic literature, with selections drawn from recommended reading lists for college-bound students. The first four guides in the series are now available for *The Adventures of Huckleberry Finn, The Scarlet Letter, The Great Gatsby,* and *The Crucible*. Designed for high school students, the guides include in-depth literary study, vocabulary, writing, and enrichment activities. Literary terms are defined or explained, an element missing in most other "novel study guides." Questions for each chapter or act (of plays) can be used for discussion or writing assignments. Included after the chapter questions are separate lists of questions/assignments. Critical thinking questions challenge students' thinking with questions such as, "What aspects of American life and beliefs are criticized in the novel?" Creative writing project ideas suggest a number of possible lengthy writing activities. In keeping with the author's suggestion that college-bound students should write a five-paragraph literary analysis, expository writing assignments are suggested for that purpose. The detailed check list for the five-paragraph analysis will help students understand what is required and will also help them check their own work before turning it in. (Parents should also use the check lists for their evaluation.) A reading comprehension test will help students focus on important aspects of the literatary piece, and it will also be useful if students are reading independently and parents need to ensure that they are actually reading the book or play. The unit test should be used for all students. An answer key for all questions is at the back of the book. Enrichment activities are included; in the *Huckleberry Finn* study they feature such activities as "Dress as Huck Finn and tell one incident from the book...." and "Bake a Mississippi Mud Cake" using the recipe that is included.

This series of guides should offer solid, college-prep level American and British literature study for high school students that is more comprehensive than that found in anthologies or most other "novel" study guides on the market. However, consider that all titles recommended for college prep students might not be literary works that you wish your children to read and make your choices accordingly. Future guides are planned for *Death of a Salesman, The Old Man and the Sea, The Snows of Kilimanjaro, Canterbury Tales, Beowulf, Idylls of the King, Macbeth, Hamlet, Julius Caesar, 1984, Animal Farm,* and *Brave New World*.(S)

○ The Literature of the American People (A Beka) $14; teacher guide - $14.65; curriculum - $20; test book - $3.95; answer key to test book - $7.80

Suggested for second semester of eleventh grade, it is intended that we use this book with *Beginnings of American Literature* which is reviewed above. Nineteenth and twentieth century American authors are studied by periods in literature, topics, and genres. The format is essentially the same as for *Beginnings of American Literature,* except it adds an overview of early American literature complete with timeline at the beginning of the book, then updates the timeline and overview for the different time periods throughout the book. The eleventh grade language arts curriculum integrates both literature volumes with A Beka's grammar and vocabulary/spelling for eleventh grade. You probably don't need it for that purpose, but you might want it since it contains answers to textbook questions. A single test booklet and answer key cover both literature volumes.

British Literature

◌ British Literature (Bob Jones University Press) $28; teacher's edition - $39

Suggested for twelfth grade, this course includes a hardback student text and a two-volume teacher's edition. The teacher's edition is highly recommended. The student text is reprinted within the teacher's edition. Even though answers appear in the bottom border section along with teaching notes, some families will prefer to purchase only the teacher's edition. This book covers eight literary periods from Old English to Modern. Selections are often chosen to illustrate philosophical and cultural issues from various perspectives. Religious developments receive far more attention here than they do in other British Literature texts. Representative authors include John Wycliffe, Geoffrey Chaucer, Thomas More, Shakespeare, Ben Jonson, William Wordsworth, and Robert Browning. The play *Macbeth* is also included for study. Discussion questions follow each selection, and, while some might be used as writing assignments, discussion should be the primary method of helping students assimilate the material. No tests or quizzes are included in the student text or teacher's edition, but a TestBank and AskIt disk are available. Teachers are expected to pick reading selections that are best for their students, so there is more within this course than we can reasonably expect to cover in a year.

◌ The English Literature Critical Thinking Course, Volume One by James P. Stobaugh (For Such A Time As This Ministries) $35

This course can be combined with Stobaugh's *The SAT Preparation Course For the Christian Student* to comprise a one-year program, or it can be used on its own as either a one-semester or one-year program. This is both a literary study guide and a course in developing critical thinking skills, particularly in regard to discerning worldviews and their impact. Presented in three-ring binder format, this volume begins with the narrative Anglo-Saxon poem, *The Seafarer,* and continues with ballads, poetry, sonnets, and tales, up through Shakespeare and the King James translation of the Bible. Students are encouraged to read complete writings, although they are not always required to do so for the study. Writing plays a major role; Stobaugh suggests that students write for one hour per day. He provides basic instruction in essay writing at the beginning of the course, then numerous writing assignments of varying length throughout the lessons. Stobaugh addresses literary elements through brief instruction

and analytical questions. Even though worldview and faith issues come up frequently throughout the lessons, each lesson also includes one or more "Biblical Application" assignments. A "Partial Solution Manual" is at the book. The actual reading material is not included; students will need to use their library for some writings. Stobaugh recommends the purchase of Norton's *Anthology of English Literature, Vol. 1* as a source for many of the readings. (This is a volume that I recommend as part of a basic library.) Plan ahead to make sure you have the necessary literary pieces on hand before you begin the pertinent lessons. Students can complete most coursework independently, but a parent should be reading the literature to carry on worthwhile discussion.

◌ Introduction to English Literature (A Beka) $14

Suggested for first semester of twelfth grade, this text covers the development of English literature from the Anglo-Saxons through the Puritans. Both *Macbeth* and *Pilgrim's Progress* are included for study. Background information is included in the student text.

◌ The Literature of England (A Beka) $14

Suggested for second semester of twelfth grade. Use with *Introduction* listed above. Selections from the Restoration through the twentieth century are chosen to reflect the spiritual state of England through those periods. Selections are from Dickens, Defoe, Boswell, Tennyson and others.

◌ The Play's the Thing [game] (Aristoplay) $30

If you choose to have your students read Shakespeare's plays *Hamlet, Romeo and Juliet,* or *Julius Caesar,* you can follow up with this game to reinforce learning, and, perhaps, make some literary points that were not covered previously. The game includes a game board, instruction booklet, and a variety of game cards (for characters, plots, scenes, etc.). Players move around the board, answering questions and collecting and losing cards until they have completed sets. When each set is completed, depending upon which version of the game you choose, the player reads a short scene (dramatically we hope), or—for "serious drama students"—acting it out from memory. Because there are variations, the instructions take some time to figure out. We separate the cards, using only those from one of the plays, unless we have read more than one play and wish to combine them. The variety in play, and the fact that it can actually be three separate games for the three plays, keeps the game interesting for repeated use. As far as educational games go, it is excellent. However, don't expect this to be a monopoly-type game that they want to play over and over again for years.(S)

◌ Shakespeare Interdisciplinary Unit (Teacher Created Materials) $14.95

Create unit studies for junior or senior high students based upon Shakespeare's plays *Romeo and Juliet, Much Ado About Nothing,* or *Richard III.* An introductory section covers general topics such as the author, the world of Shakespeare, the theater, Elizabethan times and clothing, and the history of the English language. Next are sections devoted to each of the three plays.

Each of these sections includes lesson plans that concentrate primarily on language arts activities. Following these sections are suggestions for extending any of the unit studies into math, science, social studies, arts and crafts, and life skills. The book was written for classroom use, so some adaptation is needed for home schoolers. It would be most useful if you have a small group of students who can do activities together and act out parts of the plays. There are some content problems which we need to work around. For example, astrology is treated as a harmless belief, and witchcraft is treated as a form of discrimination. I was also bothered by the historical inaccuracy of describing King James I as a religious man, supposedly, because he instigated the production of the King James Version of the Bible. Problems aside, there are many useful activities, reproducible work pages, and fun ideas for exploring Shakespeare.(SE)

➲ Shakespeare Parallel Texts (Perfection Learning) paperback - $8.60 or hardcover - $13.80 each; answer key - $5.95

Perfection has published Shakespeare's plays of *Hamlet, Julius Caesar, King Lear, Macbeth, The Merchant of Venice, A Midsummer Night's Dream, Othello, Romeo and Juliet*, and *The Taming of the Shrew* in parallel editions. On one page is the original version of the play and on the opposite page is a line-by-line paraphrase. Each book contains a supplement with study questions, vocabulary work, and further activities. If you are reluctant to study Shakespeare with your children because you do not understand it, this is your key to success. One inexpensive answer key covers all nine books. There are also companion *Reading Guides* [$6.50 each] to some of the *Parallel Texts(Julius Caesar, Macbeth,* and *Romeo and Juliet)*. The *Reading Guides* include extension activities, personal journal topics, writing activities, and reading questions. Teacher editions to the *Reading Guides* are $11.95 each.(S)

World Literature

➲ Backgrounds to World Literature (A Beka) $14

This book is suggested for first semester of tenth grade. It includes an introduction to literary devices and uses art masterpieces for illustrations. It tackles various themes such as character development in short stories or plots in suspense stories. It draws from world literature, although there is a predominance of British authors. Purchase only the student text.

➲ Masterpieces from World Literature (A Beka) $14

Suggested for second semester of tenth grade. Use this book with *Backgrounds* listed above. *Masterpieces* presents selections in historical order with commentary on the time period and its effect on literature. It begins with the Ancient East, then travels through Classical Greece, Imperial Rome, the Middle Ages, and the Reformation and Renaissance up through the Modern Age. A test booklet and answer key also available. (See mention of use of this text as part of world view studies in Chapter Five.)

➲ World Literature Activities Kit (Prentice Hall) $27.95

The *World Literature Activities Kit* is a resource for teachers of secondary students with short (worksheet) activities and projects. A student who actually read all the works necessary to complete the book would be extremely well-read in the field of comparative literature. There are many clever activities to choose among; for example, the student can be a travel agent preparing for the First Crusade, or must compare the *Odyssey* with *El Cid,* two epics spaced 3000 years apart. Each section includes a variety of learning activities, from geography to reasoning to literary analysis, and it would be possible to spend months on a single section.

The downside of the program is that it reflects a decidedly global and valueless worldview. Some excellent classics are included in the readings, such as Forester's *A Passage to India*, but also some authors who are objectionable to Christians, such as Camus, Colette, and the dadaists. A large amount of teacher preparation is required also, because the individual teacher has to make the actual reading selection. There is an extensive bibliography at the end of each section, but it is unclear whether this is a student reading list or a teacher resource list. However, a parent who loves literature could use the book selectively, and as there are so many activities available (and by no means are all of them questionable), she could easily find a year's worth of acceptable reading and activities.(SE)[Kath Courtney]

Speech and Debate

What good does it do if our teens recognize the importance of communication, yet their only experience is in written communication? Most of our communication is oral, not written!

The lack of a group class should not deter us from helping our teens develop speech skills. We can involve the entire family in speech activities, with each family member offering something on his or her level. An older teen might present an original speech about a current event. A junior high student might present his own entertaining version of a radio commercial. A younger child could present a dramatic reading of a poem, while a still younger child could "show and tell." Ideally, Mom and Dad also get involved. Plan opportunities for oral presentations and speeches as often as possible. Our teens need to practice making oral presentations to more than just their family members. I strongly recommend getting together with other home educators to provide settings for frequent oral presentations, possibly as a group class.

Many of us need guidelines and ideas for training our children in the skills for oral presentations. Bob Jones University Press publishes the only Christian speech text with which I am familiar. Most secular speech texts will also be suitable. The principles of effective speech have not changed, so we can save by purchasing older, used textbooks from second-hand book or thrift stores.

➲ Speech and Interpersonal Communication by Dave Marks (National Writing Institute) $17.95

In this book, Dave Marks addresses some sophisticated communication skills for group speaking, listening, and personal conversations, most of which are omitted in speech classes. Students learn about the art of conversation, physical posture, eye contact, reinforcing a speaker's message, introductions, interviews, understanding others' points of view, how to disagree, and how to defuse potential arguments. The goal is both effective communication and improved relationships. These very practical skills apply in daily life, not just public presentations. I recommend this book for high school students. You might want to spread out the lessons over a year or more, or else revisit them as students mature and develop their communication skills. Exercises within each section direct students to apply the various skills and techniques. However, some exercises tell students to use negative techniques which are likely to make others uncomfortable or angry. While Marks cautions the student about these situations and suggests revealing the purpose of exercises afterwards, I would recommend forewarning your "victim" and asking him or her to cooperate with the exercise, or else practice only the positive techniques.(S)

➲ Debate Video Set (Home School Legal Defense Association) $20

Two videos introduce students to the principles and reality of formal debate. These videos should be used in conjunction with *An Introduction to Argumentation and Debate* by Christy Farris (reviewed below). The book offers a comprehensive explanation of how debates function and how to prepare for them. The first video is a 45-minute presentation by debate coach Deborah Haffey on the principles of debate theory. The second tape is an actual debate, enhanced with commentary by Deborah Haffey. Students who want to participate in the national debate tournament sponsored by HSLDA should view these tapes and use the companion text to prepare.

➲ From Playpen to Podium: How to Give Your Children the Communication Advantage in Every Area of Life by Dr. Jeff Myers (Noble Publishing) $12.95

Jeff Myers, a popular speaker at home education conferences and worldview "camps" around the country, has already demonstrated his outstanding mastery of speaking and communication skills, so he is well-equipped to share his knowledge and experience with parents. He does that in this very practical book for Christian parents that actually stretches beyond communication skills into learning motivation, teaching our children to be observant, developing a sense of purpose in our children, developing creativity, and other areas. Emphasizing the importance of early training, he shares ideas for parents to actually begin with children at the "playpen" stage. About half of the book focuses on why and how we should work on these areas with our children. This information is interspersed with numerous, but brief, activities and suggestions. Further on, three separate groups of "Project Pages" offer detailed activity ideas that we can do with our children/families. Once beyond the early years, Myers makes the book easy to use by breaking up some of this information into

three separate age groups: ages 3-7, ages 8-12, and ages 13 and up. Projects progress from storytelling and puppets, through memory games and telephone skills, up to persuasive speeches and creating an advertising campaign.

➲ An Introduction to Argumentation and Debate by Christy Farris (Home School Legal Defense Association) $10

Christy Farris, experienced debater and daughter of Michael Farris (who has also has been involved in numerous debates of all types), has written an 83-page text for formal debaters. The most valuable aspect of this book for homeschoolers is that Christy clearly explains how formal, cross-examination debates are structured. She briefly covers the issue of why students should participate in debates, then quickly moves into the "meat" of debates: logic, fallacies, evidence, how to use evidence, research, and citations of sources. Students next learn how to construct and present both affirmative and negative cases; this is very thoroughly presented, dealing with timing and strategy. Since such debates are done in teams of two, speaker's must divide up responsibilities, making the best use of each one's talents. Christy suggests ways of doing this, adds tips about presentation and delivery, then concludes with practical tips on what to bring to the debate, how to use time wisely, and how judging is done. Although some logic is covered in this book, it really is specifically targeted to those participating in formal debates such as those sponsored by state homeschooling organizations and Home School Legal Defense Association. It appears that a national debate tournament each fall will become a home schooling highlight, so think about spending the previous school year developing debating skills in prepartion for that tournament. You should also view the two-video tapes on debate from HSLDA. (See Debate Video Set review.)

➲ National Textbook Company

The English and Communication Arts catalog from National Textbook Company has a number of resources for speech, drama, and debate. Some titles are *Contemporary Speech, Getting Started in Public Speaking, Getting Started in Debate, Basic Debate, Strategic Debate, Coaching and Directing Forensics, The Book of Scenes for Acting Practice, Stagecraft, Theatre and Drama,* and *The Dynamics of Acting.* Get their catalog for descriptions of these and other specialized resources.

➲ Principles and Types of Speech Communication (ScottForesman/Addison Wesley) $28.76; teacher resource manual - $7.60; test bank - $7.60

This comprehensive speech text is in its thirteenth edition. It teaches a broad range of speech skills as well as critical thinking and listening skills which help develop better speaking skills. It includes many sample speeches for example and inspiration.(S)

➲ Speech for Christian Schools (Bob Jones University Press) student text: hardbound - $27 or softcover - $20; teacher's edition -$36

Recommended for tenth through twelfth grade, this text covers the basic topics that we encounter in secular speech texts, but with a Christian perspective. There is also strong emphasis on the areas of debate, dramatic interpretation, broadcasting, and drama with some scripts included in the text. Speech skills are presented with many practice assignments to help students develop communication skills as a means of both glorifying God and benefiting others.

➲ Speech for Effective Communication (Harcourt Brace and Company) $57.25

This high-school-level, hardcover textbook covers all major speech communication topics.

History/Social Studies/Geography

Foundations

Who wants to learn something that's boring? History had to be the most boring subject of all for many of us since we used "dry as dust" textbooks, memorizing names and dates and regurgitating them for tests. But history doesn't have to be like that. In fact, it can even be fun, as many home educators have already discovered. Thanks are due, at least partially, to the inspiration of such men as Richard "Little Bear" Wheeler (Mantle Ministries) and Marshall Foster (Mayflower Institute) and women such as Belinda Beth Ballenger (Noah Webster Educational Foundation). They have a talent for creating an excitement and enthusiasm for history that we missed when we were in school. Surprisingly, they accomplish this by teaching more historical facts rather than substituting entertainment for factual information. The true facts about history are eye-opening and thought-provoking, even to children. We also have some excellent (truth and fact-filled) history books and teaching aids available to us. For many of us parents, it is like discovering a brand new subject that we never knew existed. It certainly bears little resemblance to what we were presented in school.

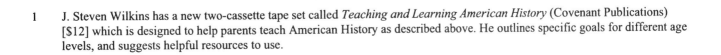

Many of us who have been able to teach our children at home for the elementary grades have had opportunities to try some of these ideas and materials, and we have discovered that our children learned a great deal and enjoyed history.[1] There are certainly some home educators who never quite got into this sort of history in earlier years and missed out on the fun. There are many more just beginning home schooling, possibly facing the task of undoing the last six to eight years of history as taught in the school system. The task for both is much more difficult. They must provide both the "foundation" and the "building" in a much shorter time span.

Our children need a historical foundation beginning with the Bible. Laid out in the Bible is the motivation for all that has happened since the beginning of creation. Man acts according to his

heart as evidenced by stories throughout the Bible. The historical truth of the Bible provides crucial information about the development of cultures and societies. For instance, the story of the Tower of Babel explains why and how men were scattered throughout the world, and how each group began speaking an individual language. All of history ties in to the Bible, either factually or motivationally. I recommend to you a resource previously reviewed in Chapter Five, *What in the World's Going On Here?* (Diana Waring -History Alive!). Diana Waring's presentation helps us understand a biblical view of history.

A second layer of that historical foundation should consist of a chronological overview of history. Students must have some idea of the sequence of events to be able to form a coherent picture. For instance, an understanding of the Enlightenment and the changes it produced in the philosophies of entire nations is dependent upon an acquaintance with the general time frame of those events.

A third foundational layer consists of basic geographical knowledge. We cannot refer to third world countries without some idea of where those countries might be located. We cannot conceive of the difficulties of exploration without knowledge of geographical barriers.

A fourth layer should consist of cultural awareness. We need not spend undue amounts of time studying obscure African tribes to ward off charges of racism, yet our children do need to understand some of the basic differences in social structures, philosophy, and beliefs of cultures other than our own.

The public school system has placed a lopsided emphasis on the fourth layer, with little emphasis on the second and third layers, and total rejection of the first. We must reverse their approach to provide a satisfactory foundation.

Upon such a foundation, we can then erect a building. That building will be constructed of details—the color of history that makes it come alive.

---

1   J. Steven Wilkins has a new two-cassette tape set called *Teaching and Learning American History* (Covenant Publications) [$12] which is designed to help parents teach American History as described above. He outlines specific goals for different age levels, and suggests helpful resources to use.

Avoiding Name-Date Syndrome

If you were given a list of names and dates to commit to memory with no additional information about the people or events represented by those names and dates, you would find it difficult to retain such information for very long (unless you are a whiz at mnemonic devices or other such memory tools). The list does not connect to anything else you know, and there is nothing of interest in the bald information itself to cause you to reserve a corner of your memory for it.

When we teach history, we too easily fall into the "name-date syndrome," assuming that if our children know all the recognizable names and dates, they know history. Yet, those names and dates rarely find a lasting home in children's memory banks beyond the upcoming test.

Going beyond names and dates and providing our children with the stories of history is what makes it come alive. Our children become "acquainted" with many of the important players and dramas from past ages through biographies, historical novels, well-written textbooks, Richard "Little Bear" Wheeler's presentations, movies, etc. Rather than relying solely upon textbooks, we draw upon other interesting resources that have drawn our children into the stories of history in a more personal way. It is similar to the feeling that we have toward a main character after watching a movie. We feel as if we have come to know the character more intimately because we became momentarily involved in his or her life.

At junior and senior high levels, we should not be always repeating factual information, but rather we should be building upon information that is already there, linking threads of history together. Our children should already have basic knowledge to which they can "hook" new knowledge. Unfortunately, for some junior high students this will be a time of laying foundations rather than adding on to their building; and it is important that we take time to cover foundational concepts if that has not yet been done.

When our children have had poor history instruction through the elementary grades, we have a tendency to want to rush them through material to bring them up to date. Yet, in these cases, it is more profitable to concentrate on basic ideas than a wealth of information. There is no point sowing more information if there is no soil in which the seeds can take root.

Avoiding Common Historical Mythology

Christian history texts seem very radical when compared to textbooks used in government schools. However, most of them still accept the common interpretations of history. They fail to identify how far we have strayed from the Constitution and from Common or Natural Law. They ignore manipulation behind the scenes by powerful, wealthy individuals. They tend to paint the United Nations in impotent terms and downplay the idea of One World Government. We need to broaden both our own and our children's understanding of history by using other resources that tackle these vital issues. This is especially important as we are now in the midst of a culminating effort to install the New World Order before the end of the decade. Resources along this line are written at the adult level, so they will be more challenging to use with average high school students. Sometimes it is better for parents to read a book, then summarize it and discuss the issues raised with their teens.

Why Learn History?

Even if our teens have a foundation for historical knowledge, they will not correlate information to it if they do not believe that the information is of value to them. Most teenagers will not naively accept our statement that something is important to learn without some evidence to support it. But, do we really believe that history studies are important for any reason other than that this is one of the subjects we have to teach? If we do not see the value, our children will sense our lack of conviction.

Yet, there are excellent reasons for studying history, especially for Christians. The Bible repeatedly talks about the importance of remembering and learning from what has gone before. Our own country was founded upon Christian principles, although our founding fathers took care to make sure we would have neither a government controlled by any one church nor churches controlled by the government. They had seen the abuses when either institution controlled the other throughout centuries past. They decided upon a republican form of government, having studied all preexisting governing systems because of their desire to avoid the mistakes of others. They based it upon Christian principles because of their knowledge of history. Our present day legislators generally do not know history as well as our founding fathers did, and we are suffering the consequences of their ignorance. A thorough knowledge of how our government operates is more than ever necessary for Christians in an increasingly hostile society.

As Christians, we are also instructed to share the Gospel of Jesus Christ to the ends of the earth. Yet, to approach another person in total ignorance of his cultural background is presumptuous and, possibly, foolish. We might be so offensive in our approach that the door is slammed shut before we can even begin to share. We need to know about other people's beliefs, or we will have difficulty contrasting them with the truth. We gain that knowledge through studies of other cultures and philosophies.

Economics

Economics is tightly linked with history and government, so it makes sense to integrate the study of all these subjects. Understanding the driving force of economics upon events is crucial to real understanding of history. Beyond that, our children should have a basic grasp of economics (particularly free market economics since it is seldom taught in colleges) before they leave home. They are likely to face indoctrination with false economic ideologies from most other sources, particularly colleges. An economics course of one or two semesters (or a course integrated with other studies) should provide them with enough information to identify major differences in economic philosophies. Even though economics is not a universal requirement for graduation, and is seldom a college entry prerequisite, I urge you to make it part of your course of study.

Unusual History Resources

I have come across some valuable resources for history and related topics that don't fit into any of the organizational groupings for other resources. Because I would hate for them to escape your notice, they have their own section here.

◑ Evaluating Books—What Would Thomas Jefferson Think About This? (Bluestocking Press) $8.95

The typical public school education in government, history, economics, and law that most of us have endured was usually an indoctrination into a quasi-socialist point of view. Rarely were we taught about natural law, free market economics, and limited government. Numerous books can help both us and our children learn what we need to know, but it can be difficult to identify those books. Richard J. Maybury offers such assistance in *Evaluating Books: What Would Thomas Jefferson Think About This?*. *Evaluating Books* is a perfect follow-up to Maybury's previous books, *Whatever Happened to Penny Candy?* and *Whatever Happened to Justice?*. *The book basically has two parts—one for "positive indicators" and one for "negative indicators." Under each heading are a number of topics such as the Great Depression, child labor laws, unions, quality of life, and isolationism. As an example, on the topic of isolationism we first find the statist viewpoint stated, "Isolationism is bad." The other side of the story is summarized in a few paragraphs explaining the views of the founding fathers on the subject. This is accompanied by a single quote from George Washington and three from Jefferson. Last is a bibliography of recommended reading on the topic, with indications of appropriate age levels. (Most recommended books will be for students high-school age and older, with a few for younger students.) Ultimately, this is more than a "book guide" because it teaches basic principles of economics and government in bite-size nuggets, with examples to take it beyond theory. Although it lacks a Christian perspective, this book relies on the same Judeo-Christian foundations that influenced the thinking of our founding fathers.(S)*

◑ Foundations of Liberty (Liberty Bookstore/East Moline Christian School) 1-4 titles - $2 each; 5-9 titles - $1.80 each; 10 or more titles - $1.50 each

We can expand coverage of government, law, economics, the judicial system, history, and philosophy with the *Foundations of Liberty* booklets. These are topical study booklets, containing "...64 to 80 pages [The two samples I reviewed contained 78 and 102 pages, so these figures appear to underrepresent the actual size of the booklets.] of selected writings that will expose your students to a variety of authors who expound on the freedom philosophy. The booklets are compilations of writings that build a better understanding of Biblical Law, limited constitutional gov-

ernment, the right of private property and the free market system. It is designed for the casual as well as the more serious reader and serves as an excellent source to enhance the conservative viewpoint."

There are 26 booklets (back issues) available at present. New topics are continually being developed and published. Send for their order form for a complete list of topics so that you can select topics/booklets that interest you or fit in with current studies.

Published titles are *George Washington, Abraham Lincoln, Not Yours to Give, Our First Thanksgiving, Work Ethics, Public Education—Its Philosophy, Sex Education in the Public Schools, Perestroika—Freedom or Web of Entrapment, A New World Order, The Free World—Mesmerized by the Bear, Take Pride in America, Abortion is Unconstitutional, America's Problem is a Spiritual Problem, Thomas Jefferson, James Madison, Douglas MacArthur, Patriotic Poems, Poems that Build Character, Freedom, Creation or Evolution, America Founded on Biblical Principles, The Supreme Court, Tuition Tax Credits, Faith of our Fathers*, and *The Keys to Success.*

Writings within each booklet consist of reprints of articles by well-known and lesser-known authors as well as an occasional piece by an East Moline Christian School student. They vary in reading level difficulty from average to challenging. Unless the topic is of particular interest, most readers are likely to select readings from each booklet, rather than read from cover to cover. Booklets can be used as sources for students to develop their own topical papers, as source material for subject area studies, or, for self-motivated students, as interesting reading material.

◑ History Flash Card Sets (Veritas Press) $19.95 per set of cards; audio tapes - $6.95 each; sets of cards and a tape -$24.95

Five different sets of 32 cards each cover history in five chronological time periods: *Old Testament/Ancient Egypt; New Testament/Greece & Rome; Middle Ages, Renaissance & Reformation; Explorers to 1815; and 1815 to the Present.* The 5" x 8" cards are printed in full color. A reproduction of a well-known piece of artwork or, occasionally, a photograph depicts the key event or person discussed on each card. On the reverse are the date and a brief summary of the event or topic. At the bottom of the card is a list of resources, including page numbers, where the topic is discussed at length. Using this information, following through the card deck, we can actually construct our own chronological history course using a number of resources like the *Greenleaf Guides, Streams of Civilization, The Church in History*, and the *Kingfisher Illustrated History of the World.* Color coding and numbering systems also help students categorize and organize the cards.

The cards were designed for students in the elementary grades, but those without a solid, chronological knowledge of history should find this an easy way to pull it all together. If a student reviews through the cards, he can identify those topics with which he is not familiar, then focus study in those directions.

Companion audio tapes feature a lilting recitation of the key names, dates, and events set to music; this presentation enhances learning for some students. The tapes are only about 10 to 15 minutes long, with the identical song on the reverse. The phrasing is awkward, although the singing is quite lovely. Tapes are optional.

The perspective of the cards is Reformed Protestant. Students will have a much stronger exposure to church history than they will encounter in most textbooks if they work through all series of the cards. I don't view these as substitutes for good history courses, but they make an excellent supplement or a useful review tool in a number of situations.

⊃ **Perspective: The Time Line Game** (The Branch Office, Inc.) $30

Many home educators choose to use real books rather than textbooks for history, but they often wonder if they are paying too little attention to names and dates. While there are a few dates with which everyone should be familiar, most of the time the important issue is when events happened in relation to other events. For example, it is important to know that the French Revolution took place after the American Revolution, and that Plato and Aristotle lived before Jesus Christ. We don't have to return to the textbooks to remedy a deficit in this area, because there is a great alternative—*Perspective: The Time Line Game*. In fact, even if we are using textbooks, we can still cement in some of those names and dates with this game rather than written exercises.

Perspective uses a large game board divided into four, color-coded eras: Ancient (the beginning of time -477 AD), Middle (477-1589), Modern (1589-1901), and 20th Century. There are two decks of cards designated average or more challenging. The cards feature a person and/or event on one side and the year on the reverse. The cards are color-coded to match the four eras on the board. We might have cards such as blue, ancient-era cards on Stonehenge and the Great Wall of China, and yellow modern-era cards on Bell's patenting of the telephone and the beginning of building the Taj Mahal. Each player is dealt six cards, then players take turns laying their cards on the board in chronological order. Opposing players can challenge their placement, at which time, cards are turned over to check the dates. Benefits and penalties result from challenges. This keeps all players engaged in the game through each turn.

We can customize the game in a number of ways. We can select only those cards from a narrow time frame that we are studying. We can select easy or more challenging cards to use. We can make up cards of our own to include other information. Although the game is recommended for ages 12 through adult, we might allow a younger student (or Dad if he's just getting involved in history studies) to use a reference book, establishing a time limit for looking things up. Two or more players can play, and games should take about one half hour, so this is the type of game you can play as part of school or for family time. The only negative is that the game draws information from sources based

on secular humanist assumptions such as evolution, and all religious figures receive equal time. You might want to eliminate, edit, or substitute for the cards referring to the Ice Age, Neanderthal man, the beginning of formation of the Grand Canyon, and the first signs of different life forms. I would probably add some cards for biblical and church history.

I love the way this game makes us think about events in relation to one another, something rarely encouraged in textbooks. I can see this game fitting in with just about any home school approach to history.(SE)

High School Requirements

States require up to three years of history/social sciences for high school graduation. This should include:

1. United States History and Geography
2. World History, Culture, and Geography
3. American Government, Civics, and Economics[2]

College entry requirements for history/social studies vary considerably. For instance, the California State University system requires only one year of U.S. History. Biola University, a Christian university in California, requires two years of social studies with no specific courses listed. Many college catalogs list a vague social studies requirement, assuming that whatever the states' school systems have set as graduation requirements will be adequate to meet the college's desire that students be prepared for further study in the history/social studies area.

In states where we have freedom to set our own course of study, we then have plenty of choice in history/social studies. I personally feel that we should be covering all of the above areas at high school level for two reasons: the topics should be covered when students are mature enough to understand the philosophical ideas that motivate history, government, and economics (they are not mature enough in elementary grades); and this may be the last or only chance for our children to study these topics from a Christian, patriotic, conservative, free-market perspective (or whatever your personal viewpoint happens to be).

World History Resources
(listed in approximate order of increasing difficulty)

⊃ Greenleaf Books history resources: Famous Men and Greenleaf Guides (Greenleaf Press)
Greenleaf Guide to Old Testament History

---

2   In California and many other states, one semester of economics is required. It can be covered as a one semester course (the other semester can usually be spent on U.S. government and civics), or economics can be incorporated into both world and U.S. history studies, especially via a unit study approach.

by Rob and Cyndy Shearer $10.95

The Old Testament is the perfect place to start teaching history since it truly starts at the beginning. Many of us shy away from such a study because of the difficulties we might encounter, but the Shearers have made it much easier with this Guide. It covers Genesis, Exodus, Numbers, Deuteronomy, Joshua, and most of Judges. This *Guide* differs from the others in that it is based upon Bible reading and discussion rather than readings from an assortment of books. (Either *The Children's Bible Atlas* or *The Cultural Atlas of the Bible* is recommended as a visual tool, but nothing else is necessary.) We read through sections of Scripture with our children, then use the *Guide's* questions to lead a discussion. The Shearers also suggest using Charlotte Mason's narration" technique where children relate back in their own words what has just been read. The questions generally focus on who, what, where, when, why, and how" for historical understanding rather than as theology lessons. Background information is included whenever it is useful. The Shearers also offer practical tips for dealing with the difficult passages like Tamar and Judah. You can tell from the suggestions that they have used all of this with their own family of seven children. This is not like your typical Bible study material that uses stories or incidents to teach spiritual truths or doctrine. But even though this is not the primary focus, children will, indeed, learn foundational spiritual truths. Young children can easily answer most of the questions if they learn to listen carefully, but there are a few questions that will challenge older children to think more deeply. Adults will also enjoy the study, because most will find they have missed many interesting details in their previous readings. It should take a full school year to complete the book.

Famous Men of Greece, Famous Men of Rome, Famous Men of the Renaissance and Reformation, and *Famous Men of the Middle Ages* edited and updated by Rob and Cyndy Shearer $15.95 each

Instead of dry textbooks, children can learn about ancient history through biographical sketches of influential figures in the *Famous Men* books. Stories often build one upon another and are presented in chronological order. The effect is like reading a good storybook. Although some of these are written at fairly young reading levels, junior and senior high students will still enjoy most of the content. Some, such as *Renaissance and Reformation*, are best for high school students. The accompanying *Guides*, available for most of the *Famous Men* books, can be used to challenge their thinking and research at the appropriate levels. The Greenleaf materials can form the foundation for studies of these areas, even at high school level, if we skip some of the activities and supplement with age-appropriate resources.

Guides that might be used for junior or senior high are *The Greenleaf Guide to Famous Men of Greece*, The *Greenleaf Guide to Famous Men of Rome, The Greenleaf Guide to Famous Men of the Middle Ages and The Greenleaf Guide to Famous Men of the Renaissance and Reformation [$7.95 each].* (There is also a *Greenleaf Guide to Ancient Egypt*, but the level is probably too young to use with most teens.) The *Middle Ages* guide seems the easiest to use with older students. I also expect that the *Ren-*

aissance and Reformation Guide will also best suit older students with its unusual selection of biographies that addresses philosophical and spiritual defects that require a certain amount of maturity to understand. We meet famous men like Petrarch, Leonardo da Vinci, Erasmus, and some of the standard Reformation leaders, but we also encounter characters such as Lorenzo d' Medici, Cesare Borgia, Niccolo Machiavelli, Albrecht Durer, and representatives of the Anabaptist movement. The result is a richer picture of the period than we typically encounter.

The *Guides* turn the reading into unit studies with activities, discussion questions, geography (including map building projects), and vocabulary for each chapter of each book. Biblical standards are used as the measuring rod when discussing the lives of the famous men. Chronological summaries of people and events are at the end of each book. Project work is optional for the most part, with more emphasis on reading and discussion. Frequently, lessons refer to the supplemental resources (available individually or in Greenleaf "packages") for further research and reading on Greece, Rome, or the Middle Ages.

The *Ancient Greece Study Package* includes *Famous Men, The Greenleaf Guide, The Greeks* (an Usborne book), and *Children's Homer. The Ancient Rome Study Package* includes *Famous Men, The Greenleaf Guide, City,* and *The Romans* (an Usborne book). *The Middle Ages Study Package* includes *Famous Men, The Greenleaf Guide, Castle, Cathedral*, and *Cultural Atlas of the Middle Ages.*

Of particular note in the *Greenleaf Guide to Famous Men of the Middle Ages* are the "worldview" comparison charts. On one chart we compare creation and end-of-the-world stories from Teutonic mythology and the Bible. Greek myths are compared against the other two belief systems as we consider characteristics of God and the gods, what they value, who they honor, what they honor, and man's purpose for living. Another chart compares beliefs of Islam with Christianity. Discussion questions in all of the guides cover names, dates, and events, but they go much further than textbooks in dealing with character issues and Biblical principles.

⮑ Creation to Canaan (Rod and Staff) student text - $10.80; workbook - $4.80; teacher's workbook manual -$7.30; test booklet - $1.10

This book is designated for seventh grade level, but it can be used for younger or older students (up through eighth grade). Black-and-white photos, maps, and illustrations help children visualize people, places, and events. The Rod and Staff catalog describes the intent of this text well: "A conviction has been growing that we need history books centered on God's dealing with His people, presenting for our students to idealize heroes of faith rather than military heroes. Teachers using this book will guide the minds of their pupils to a better understanding of God's unfolding plan for mankind rather than follow man's pursuits and achievements."

The text covers history from creation through the conquest and settlement of Canaan. The time period overlaps that of most world history courses, but the emphasis is upon a time period that is usually breezed over elsewhere. The philosophical approach taken by the authors helps children develop a "God's eye" view of history—to begin to understand that history is the outworking of God's plan rather than a collection of random events. Discussion/study questions follow each chapter.

The accompanying workbook has space for writing answers to discussion/study questions (assuming we want students to write rather than discuss), along with additional exercises. Many activities require Bible research. The Teacher's Workbook Manual has the answers for all questions. Tests are available separately.

⊃ **World Studies** (BJUP) student text: softcover - $21, hardcover - $28; teacher's edition - $39; activity sheets - $8; activity sheets answer key - $3

Suggested for seventh grade, this textbook covers world history at an introductory level. It is well illustrated and has worthwhile questions, but it lacks the vibrancy of "real books." The emphasis on foreign cultures is stronger than it is in the BJUP tenth-grade-level *World History*. The student text, which is available in either softcover or hardback, can be used alone. Excellent comprehension and discussion questions are included, although answers are in the teacher's edition. As with some BJUP books, the student text is also contained in the teacher's edition so we can buy only the teacher's edition if we prefer. Student activity sheets come in a softbound book and there is a separate answer key for these. A *TestBank* (softbound book) [$16] as well as the *AskIt* software [$14] containing a variety of types of test questions for us to use are also available.

⊃ **The History of the World in Christian Perspective** (A Beka) student text - $16.95; teacher's edition - $24.95; test booklet -$4.95; key -$8.60; quiz booklet - $4.35; key $8.60; *World Atlas and Geography Studies* -$6.15; key - $9.05; maps and time lines - $22.65

History of the World begins with creation and continues through the late twentieth century. Reflecting A Beka's Christian (Protestant), patriotic, conservative stance, this text teaches history with purposeful intent. This text is a condensed version of A Beka's previous two-volume history for the junior high years. Consequently, it serves as an overview rather than an in-depth study. (Students will cover material more deeply at high school level.) Full-color illustrations and an interesting format enhance the text.

World Atlas and Geography Studies of the Eastern Hemisphere should be used along with the text although it is not absolutely essential. The *World Atlas* is the first of two supplemental geography books, with the second covering *Western Hemisphere* at eighth grade level. (See reviews under "Geography.") It has numerous map activities and related questions. A teacher's edition with answers is available.

Additional, but optional, materials are a test booklet, quiz booklet, teacher keys for both items, and a Display Maps and Time Lines set. The teacher's edition is similar to the student text, but with answers.

⊃ **Christ the King, Lord of History** by Anne W. Carroll (Tan Books and Publishers, Inc.) $24

Catholics, especially, will appreciate this Christ-centered presentation of world history. Anne Carroll uses stories, quotes, and original sources to present a lively, interesting history that is quite different than most. She uses church history as the focal point, while covering the broad expanse of events. The first few chapters draw heavily upon the Bible with chapters titled "Abraham," "Moses," and "The Kingdom of Israel." Carroll occasionally presents as fact, details that remain unproven, especially in these early chapters; e.g., "Earlier than about 3000 B.C., we have no written historical records because writing had not been invented." Students should be made aware of this, so that they do not accept all statements as proven fact. (This is true of other texts, also.) She presents history from the Catholic perspective, including events ignored by most Protestant texts, and contradicting Protestant viewpoints on others. Review questions at the end of each chapter generally require fairly complex answers rather than simple recall of facts. Project suggestions are excellent, but don't ask students to tackle more than one per chapter! This text is more interesting than most available for junior high level. I would also recommend it as a counterbalance and enhancement to be read alongside other texts in which the Protestant view dominates.

⊃ **Ancient History, A Literature Approach** by Rea Berg (Beautiful Feet Books) $12.95; literature pack - $62.95; jumbo literature pack for senior high -$157.95

This study has been designed for junior and senior high students but includes literature recommendations for younger students so they can be studying the same time period. Using a literature-based approach, Rea Berg covers ancient history, focusing primarily on Egypt, Greece, and Rome. Unlike most Beautiful Feet guides, this one relies also on a textbook for more comprehensive coverage. *Streams of Civilization, Volume I* (Christian Liberty Press) serves as this background text. It provides a much broader scope, encompassing time from creation up through the Middle Ages. This ensures that students at the higher grade levels are covering all they should for a solid historical foundation. The text itself comes with chapter tests, and there are also tests with answer keys on each major period within the guide. Primary literature and resource selections for the course include the Bible; a Bible atlas; *Pyramid* by Macauley; *Tales of Ancient Egypt* by Green; *Pharoahs of Ancient Egypt* by Payne; *The Golden Goblet* by McGraw; *The Greeks, A Great Adventure* by Asimov; D'Aulaires *Book of Greek Myths*; *The Children's Homer* by Colum; *The Bronze Bow* by Speare; *Augustus Caesar's World* by Foster; *City* by Macaulay, Shakespeare's *Julius Caesar*; Shakespeare's *Antony and Cleopatra*; and *Quo Vadis?* by Sienkiewicz. Other recommended literature is also listed in the guide. Many of these books are available through Beautiful Feet Books. Seven essential books are offered as the *Ancient History Literature Pack* with the others also included in the Jumbo Pack.

Daily lesson plans tell us what parts of each book are to be read each day; provide study and discussion questions (not for all lessons); and describe writing, research, and notebook activities. Students maintain a notebook where they record results of research and reading, and where they paste and draw maps and pictures, illustrations, newspaper articles, and other information related to each topic they study. The study can easily be stretched to include younger children as you read through some of the books together.

While this study is not as reflective of the Principle Approach as is the study done in Berg's *Literature Approach to Medieval History*, it does utilize that approach to learning to some extent. However, the study does not require a prior familiarity with the Principle Approach.

⊃ **A Literature Approach to U.S. and World History** by Rea Berg (Beautiful Feet Books) $13.95; literature pack - $169.95

U.S. and world history are combined in this senior-high level course that covers the time period from the Civil War to the 1970s. Following the format of other Beautiful Feet study guides, this one uses a number of "real" books as the foundation, providing activities to be used for each chapter or group of chapters as students read through each book. Activities include reading, composition, discussion, vocabulary work, drawing, geography, and research. Students can easily fulfill their history and language arts requirements for two years through this study. Study is divided into four units: The Civil War Era; Post-Reconstruction to the Great War; the Great Depression, WWII, and The Korean War; and the Civil Rights Era up through the 1970s. Among the books used in the study are *A Basic History of the United States* by Clarence Carson; *Abraham Lincoln's World; Uncle Tom's Cabin; Across Five Aprils; Rifles for Watie; The Red Badge of Courage; Harriet Beecher Stowe and the Beecher Preachers; Sojourner Truth, Ain't I A Woman?; Virginia's General: Robert E. Lee and the Civil War; A History of US: An Age of Extremes; The Jungle; Bully For You, Teddy Roosevelt!; Big Annie of Calumet; Stalin: Russia's Man of Steel; The Yanks Are Coming* OR *America At War: World War I; All Quiet on the Western Front; In Flanders Fields; A History of US: War, Peace and all that Jazz; Roll of Thunder, Hear My Cry; To Kill A Mockingbird; The Korean War!; House of Sixty Fathers; The Cay; The Trapp Family Singers; The Hiding Place; Anne Frank: The Diary of a Young Girl; The Story of D-Day; The Vietnam War: How the United States Became Involved;* and *Profiles in Courage.* Three volumes from the *History of US* series are used, but that series has been criticized for its liberal leanings and omissions. The study guide turns such problems into learning lessons by pointing out the biases and directing us to resources (books, web sites, etc.) with contrasting viewpoints. The *History of US* is included in spite of its problems because it is one of the few well-written sources on U.S. History for junior and senior high level.

Many other books and a few videos are also recommended; they can be used as substitutes for or in addition to the other resources. Parents will need to participate in and direct the study to some extent. Teacher notes at the end of the guide help parents do that even if they don't have time to read through all of the books.(SE)

⊃ **Social Studies LifePacs** (Alpha Omega) 700 level - 7th grade $41.95 for complete set

This level introduces social studies concepts: history, geography, anthropology, sociology, economics, and political science for both the United States and the world. Although this is a more boring approach, it covers the material fairly thoroughly. It is recommended for parents with little time for direct instruction and for children who work well independently.

⊃ **The Story of Liberty** by Charles C. Coffin (Maranatha Publications, Inc.) $14.95 each book

Reprinted from an original 1879 manuscript, this book takes a unique approach to history, by tracing the "story of liberty." It begins with King John and the story of the Magna Charta, jumps over to the story of John Wycliffe (spelled Wicklif in this book) and the beginnings of spiritual liberty, and continues on through the stories of such vital contributors to the cause of liberty as Guttenberg and Sir Thomas More. Along the way, we also encounter those who battled to "withhold liberty"—various popes, kings, queens, and their emissaries. *The Story of Liberty* ends with the planting of the seeds of liberty in the New World by the Pilgrims. The story continues in the next volume, *Sweet Land of Liberty.* The author, Charles Coffin, writes to a student audience (junior or senior high), using stories written in the present-tense. This lends an air of immediacy and life to the stories that we lose in most retellings of history. Conversational dialogues also add interest as do numerous black-and-white illustrations. (Adults will find this fascinating reading as well. There is nothing childish about it.) Coffin strongly denounces the Catholic church, particularly the abuses of the popes and others who set themselves up as spiritual leaders. Reformation leaders are heroic figures in contrast to them. Although this book does not cover historical events in the same fashion as other history books, the coverage is quite comprehensive. Students who have already studied a survey course in world history will find this an interesting book to enlarge their thinking and understanding, even if it comes from a very opinionated perspective.

A companion *Study Guide*, authored by Steve C. Dawson, introduces the study with basics from the Principle Approach. The *Study Guide* then refers back to the principles periodically, with a final examination of essay writing based entirely upon them. The chapter-by-chapter study questions are both factual and inferential, with frequent directions to students to reference Scripture for answers. Some questions seem too easy for high school students, while others will challenge their thinking. Additional activities, such as video viewing or supplementary reading, are suggested, along with the creation of a timeline. We can use this *Study Guide* in its entirety or use only the chapter questions if we prefer. An answer key comes with the *Study Guide*.

⊃ **World History course H140** (Landmark's Freedom Baptist Curriculum) $35

World history is taught through two worktexts with separate answer keys, weekly quizzes and quarterly tests. Lessons are broken down into weekly units, each with a two-page reading portion, exercises (including fill-in-the-blank), short essays,

Scripture writing, and application of biblical principles. Each semester, students complete a longer report, one on "Moses" and one on "Salvation by Grace vs. Salvation by Works." These reports are broken down into a few assignments to make them easier to handle. The viewpoint is thoroughly Christian. In fact, so much time is spent on Scripture that the history itself is rather briefly presented. I find that the information is often so sketchy that it is difficult to answer the questions. It also ends at World War II. You might want to have another world history text for more complete information. However, this is a junior high level course, and much of this is covered in greater detail at high school level. (LFBC is working on a new high-school-level world history course at this time.) The scriptural teaching is specifically Baptist. For example, infant baptism and non-immersion baptism are refuted. Scriptural principles play a major role in every lesson. For instance, in a lesson comparing the American Revolution with others, students look up and record a number of verses from Proverbs 29 about principles of good government. They then write a short essay about how these principles might prevent revolutions from occurring. The course is well laid out and easy to use, although it would appeal most to workbook-oriented students who do not mind a great deal of written work.[Valerie Thorpe/C.D.]

⮥ Streams of Civilization Volumes 1 and 2 (Christian Liberty Press) student text - $18.95 and $19.95 each; teacher's guide for Vol. 1 - $4.95; test booklets - $3.50 each; answer key for Vol. 2 - $4.95; timeline - $14.95

Christian Liberty has updated and reprinted a notable, two-volume history text that was out of print for a number of years. This is a Christian text that recognizes the importance of religious and philosophical views throughout history. Volume 1 is much easier reading than Volume 2. In Volume 1, coverage of history is broad, yet not as in-depth in either content or the handling of ideas as other high school texts such as those from BJUP. However, it offers more comprehensive coverage of ancient history than does BJUP *World History*. It can be used at either junior or senior high level, since the reading level is not difficult. A teacher's guide for Volume 1 offers overview, objectives, teaching strategies, project ideas, and assessment and evaluation suggestions.

Volume 2, subtitled "Cultures in Conflict Since the Reformation," covers modern history (16th century through the present). Although it is a World History text, it is centered around Euro-American considerations, treating many issues primarily from a "Western" viewpoint. As I already mentioned, this book is more challenging than Volume 1. Church history, philosophy, and theology are integrated into historical coverage more than we find in most history texts from Christian publishers. This makes it a good choice for those who want to emphasize the Biblical Christian worldview in their coursework. Streams of Civilization is written from the Reformed Protestant theological perspective as well as a conservative political position, and it offers strong opinions based upon the presuppositional ideas inherent to both. Questions and projects at the end of each chapter are excellent.

Black-and-white or two-color illustrations are numerous. At the end of each chapter is a list of suggested projects which range from discussion questions through building projects. For instance, among the options for chapter eleven in the first volume are writing a detailed report on one of the key figures of the chapter, comparing Mohammed and the founding of Islam with Joseph Smith and the founding of Mormonism, and making a cut-away model of a donjon. A list of key vocabulary/concept words is also found at the end of each chapter. Separate test packets are available for both volumes, and an answer key is available for Volume 2 rather than a teacher's guide.

Streams of Civilization Historical Charts is a packet of timeline charts covering both volumes. Printed on heavy duty paper, the timelines are illustrated with key figures and events under the typical categories plus church history and intellectual history.

⮥ A Literature Approach to Medieval History
by Rea C. Berg (Beautiful Feet Books) Study Guide - $12.95; Literature Pack for grades 5-7 - $48.95; Jumbo Literature Pack for grades 8-9 - $169.95

This Study Guide for literature-based history study is subtitled, "A One Year Course with Study Notes for Grades 6/7 and 8/9." Rea Berg combines the Principle Approach with the study of good literature to create a unique approach for studying the medieval period. Although the course is designed for one year, we might take two years to truly benefit from the wealth of material. Author Rea Berg states, "The main purpose and goal in this course is to acquaint the student with the progression of religious and civil liberties, through some of the best classic literature known to Western civilization." Essential for either level is *The Story of Liberty* by Charles Coffin. Also recommended but not essential are *Teaching and Learning America's Christian History* by Rosalie Slater and *The Christian History of the Constitution* by Verna Hall. The latter two books are available from other sources (such as Foundation for American Christian Education) and *The Story of Liberty* is available through Beautiful Feet. While these books serve as the background and highlight the principles, literature is the primary learning tool. Recommended literature is divided into two lists, one for the lower level and one for the upper. The 124 Study Guide lessons (some requiring much more than a single day) concentrate on *Ivanhoe, The Talisman, Scottish Chiefs, Joan of Arc, Henry VIII*, and *Westward Ho!* with lesser attention directed toward the other books. The remaining books can be read in historical order without study guide assistance. Even though the bulk of the literature lessons are working at the upper level, younger students can read books in the Literature Pack—*The Door in the Wall, Otto of the Silver Hand, Castle, Cathedral, Spy for the Night Riders, Adam of the Road, The Hawk that Dare Not Fly by Day*, and *The Morning Star of the Reformation*. The Study Guide is actually best suited to the older learner, but sixth and seventh grade siblings can benefit from the background and principles of the three essential books, while reading literature on their own level. A *Medieval History Time Line* from Beautiful Feet Books covers the same period as the Study Guide, making a wonderful hands-on/visual supplement. The *8-9 Jumbo Literature Pack* includes the *Study*

Guide, Time Line, and ten other books including those mentioned above for the upper level.

⊃ World History [1994 edition] (Bob Jones University Press) $28; teacher's edition - $39; student activity book - $12; teacher's edition for activity book - $13

This is one of BJUP's best books. Suggested for tenth grade, this book studies world history from Christian and patriotic perspectives. It cautions against placing our faith in governmental solutions, although, in my opinion, it sometimes treats some of the evils of government too benignly. It includes politics, economics, geography, the arts, and science, dealing with more abstract facets of history rather than primarily upon wars and conquests as we generally see in younger level history books. Even so, the general organization, as we find in just about every textbook, follows history through a succession of wars and conquests. The new edition adds periodic section reviews to highlight key points to remember. At the end of each chapter are vocabulary terms, map activities, factual recall questions, and thought-provoking questions. I particularly like the last group of questions since they relate biblical principles to history and raise world view issues. For example, one question states: "Arius taught that Christ did not always exist but that He was created by God the Father." It then asks, "How does John 1:1-4 show this teaching to be false?"

The 1994 edition is very similar to the previous edition in content, with the major changes occurring in the last few chapters (covering the dissolution of the Soviet Empire and recent history). Some of the chapter questions have been improved; some of the previous editions' questions were too broad, so they have been replaced with more tightly-focused questions. Illustrations have been changed: some are in full-color rather than black-and-white, and some new ones replace others.

The teacher's edition has student pages without color, but with teaching notes and answers. Those who don't mind students having access to the answers, might find this usable without purchasing a separate student edition. While lack of color is not a vital issue, it does make a great deal of difference in terms of the value of the illustrations. I recommend that you purchase separate student and teacher editions. The student activities manual and a companion teacher's edition have just been released. A test packet [$7] and companion answer key [$4] or the *AskIt* computer software [$14] are also available.

⊃ World History and Cultures in Christian Perspective, 2nd edition (A Beka) $20.95; teacher guide - $20; test/map book - $6.05; test book answer key -$8.60; quiz book - $4.35; quiz book answer key - $8.60

This 1997 edition of A Beka's *World History* text combines fact and opinion in a format that features larger print than the first edition and colorful illustrations (including full-color maps). Taking a more subjective approach than do most history texts, this one is strongly Protestant, anti-Catholic, capitalistic, patriotic, and anti-United Nations. Church history and religious issues receive a great deal of attention throughout the text. A test

booklet and answer key are also available. The test booklet includes map project pages which you really should use. The student text includes frequent groups of fact-based and identification questions throughout each chapter. At the end of each chapter are short answer and discussion questions as well as map work assignments to be used with the pages in the test booklet. The teacher's guide includes answers to text questions, suggestions for supplementary materials, a list of objectives, and chapter overviews.

⊃ Modern Times: From the Twenties to the Nineties Paul Johnson (HarperCollins Publishers) $20

Serious history students must have this book! Johnson uses Einstein's Theory of Relativity and its impact on society in mid-1919 as a dividing line, ushering in "modern times." While this is not a Christian book, a key theme is the abandonment of moral absolutes and the results. Johnson traces this theme through the Russian Revolution, rise of Hitler and the Third Reich, expansion of Communism, changes in Europe, and the moral decline and simultaneous dependency upon government-based solutions in the United States. While that theme is evident, the book can still be viewed on a simpler level as a valuable history resource.

The historical information is loaded with details that enlarge our understanding, yet at the same time will overwhelm many readers. Because Johnson builds his presentation, it is really not practical to use the book as a reference, picking and choosing scattered sections to read. However, there are some sections that you might feel that you can skip while maintaining overall understanding. I suspect that this book will most often be read by adults who will excerpt information to share with their teens, but if your teen is seriously interested in history, I highly recommend that you make this book a part of his library.

World History Extras

⊃ By Jove (Aristoplay) $25

Before playing the game, we "meet" the mythological characters by reading the included storybook, *By Jove Stories.* Then we allow our children to experience for themselves the capriciousness of the so-called gods that were worshipped by ancient civilizations as they play this board game. Children learn about classical mythology characters such as Hercules, Ulysses, and Achilles while also learning about the religious beliefs that spawned them. For ages ten to adult.(S)

⊃ Catholic World History Timeline and Guide, Volumes I-III (Marcia Neill) $15 each volume

Most timelines represent world history from a Protestant view, leaving out early church fathers and other people and events that receive attention in Catholic history texts. These three timeline volumes include most figures you find in other timelines plus those of especial interest to Catholics. Brightly-colored, heavy-duty paper is cut into strips to mount on the wall. The 125 figures in Volume I are created in an old-fashioned engraved style and labeled with names or events plus biblical references and/or dates. Patterns for additional stick figures are supplied. The books include instructions for constructing the timeline and using it as a teaching tool. Each volume includes charts showing the people or events, date of location on timeline, and a brief summary of the "contribution" of the event or person. Volume I covers creation through 200 A.D., Volume II covers 200 A.D. through 1500 A.D., and Volume III covers 1500 A.D. through the present. (Vol. I is available now, with the next two volumes due before 1998.)

⮑ The Great Christian Revolution by Otto Scott (The Reformer) $14.95

"It was Christianity alone that brought intellectual and spiritual hope, an end to human sacrifice, and the recognition of individual rights to the world. No other religion ever created a church that limited governments. That limitation enabled the free Christians of Europe to clear the land of great forests, to tame the wild beasts and wild tribes, to develop better methods of agriculture and manufacture, to build cities, to create cultures that were diverse but united in a single faith, to erect the largest, richest, and most polyglot civilization the world has ever known." This statement from the publisher's brochure is the essence of this unusual exposition of history. The book opens with the period of the Renaissance and the Reformation, identifying what needed to be reformed. It recalls the enthusiasm for paganism (idealization of the ancient Greek and Roman cultures) and the contrast with the calls to reform sounded by Luther, followed by Calvin and others. Yet, this is not a history of the church so much as a broader history demonstrating the inextricable links between the beliefs of people and the forms of government. To keep it manageable, the story is limited to tracing the Reformation, primarily through Calvin and Geneva, then into England from the reign of the Tudors, through the Protestant Protectorate under Cromwell (The Great Christian Revolution), and ending with the Restoration of the Monarchy. The Epilogue establishes the connection between these events, particularly the Revolution, and their influence on America. Scott tells us, "...all the liberties men now have come from Christianity, from its lessons about the individual and the State; God and His Covenant." Scott writes history as if he is telling a story, retaining a narrative flavor as he describes such events as the behind-the-scenes machinations of Cranmer and Cromwell during the reign of England's Henry VIII. Otto Scott is a superb historian, and this is evident in the detail and depth of characterization he provides. This book was written with home schooling parents in mind; the content and vocabulary both make this evident even though Scott deals with the sexual perversions of rulers and cultures since they were often significant factors (but not in an objectionable manner). While adults should read the book, I also recommend it to mature teens who really want to understand history rather than just get through the books.

⮑ Hanged on a Twisted Cross [video] (Vision Video) $24.95

This is an excellent video for studying World War II, the Holocaust, the role of the Church in relation to government, and issues of pacifism and legitimate warfare. Bonhoeffer was a liberal Christian minister and theologian in Germany during the Nazi era. Although he wrote and spoke in defense of pacifism, as the Nazis began to murder the Jews, Bonhoeffer realized that defense of innocent victims overruled the ideals of pacifism. He eventually became involved in political conspiracies against Hitler and the Nazi regime. He said, "Christians in Germany face the terrible alternative of willing the defeat of their nation in order that civilization may survive, or willing the victory of their nation and thereby destroying civilization. I know which of these alternatives I must choose...." Bonhoeffer was arrested after failed attempts by the conspirators to assassinate Hitler. In prison he ministered to both other prisoners and the guards. Out of his life experiences, even through his years in prison, he spoke and wrote from a religious and philosophical perspective about Christianity, government, ethics, and personal responsibility. He was hanged at a Nazi concentration camp only three weeks before Hitler committed suicide. This 120-minute biographical video uses photographs and film footage (particularly from WWII) to use the life of Bonhoeffer as a window into the soul of the Church in Germany and the choices made to accommodate or confront evil. It is also a history lesson that forces us to think about challenging issues such as pacifism and war.

⮑ Knights and Castles game (Aristoplay) $25

Knights and Castles is an excellent game for teaching and reviewing the era of the Middle Ages and about knights and royalty. Each player has three knights-in-training to move. As they travel around the board, they advance from the rank of page to full knight, sometimes by rolling the die and sometimes by answering questions. Questions deal with topics like knights, armor, tournaments, culture, castle architecture, and a little history. It helps to know some of this information ahead of time, but players can learn as they play because explanations are provided with the answers. Although suggested for ages six and up, the games is really best for older players who have some background knowledge. The high-quality art work is typical of Aristoplay; the game is both a good learning tool and fun to play over and over.(S)

⮑ Never Give In: The Extraordinary Character of Winston Churchill by Stephen Mansfield (Holly Hall Publications/Highland Books) $14.99

For anyone interested in a foundational work on the life of Winston Churchill. Mansfield does an excellent job of introducing the reader to Churchill's family and early life as well as some of his experiences in the Boer War and the first and second World Wars. Mansfield's primary motivation in writing the book is to give the reader a powerful picture of Churchill's character and his religious convictions. This is a must read for anyone studying Churchill's life or interested in learning more about the man behind the scenes. This book is part of a leadership and biographical series edited by best selling author George Grant. The series currently includes Teddy Roosevelt, C.S. Lewis, Patrick Henry, and Robert E. Lee as well as Winston Churchill.[Josh Duffy]

➲ Picture the Middle Ages (Golden Owl Publishing) $24.95

Children learn to picture the Middle Ages by participating in this extensive, activity-based unit study. Designed to be used for grade levels 4-8, this resource book is loaded with such a variety of activities that it is hard to do it justice. Twelve chapters divide studies into key areas such as "The Town: Craftsmen and Guilds," "The Monastery: Monks and Nuns," and "Making Costumes and Armor." The entire study is based upon the imaginary medieval world called Higginswold, created at the Higgins Armory Museum in Worcester, Massachusetts. A huge fold-out picture of Higginswold is included, as well as a timeline; patterns for costumes, shields, helmets, and breastplates; maps, illustrations of coats of arms, banners, and guild signs; and recipes. Students study literature, the arts, and history, including the oft-neglected church history. The vocabulary and writing assignments, together with supplemental reading are extensive enough to replace other language arts curricula. Of course, we are free to pick and choose from among the wealth of options. The authors suggest allowing five to eight weeks to complete the study. It is designed to culminate in a Medieval Festival, complete with tournaments (academic), games, a play, a feast, and a fair. The unit study will work best with a group. It might be worth forming a special group for this purpose even if you don't already have one. There is still plenty to do if a group is not possible.

If you want to extend the study even further, additional resources are listed for each chapter. Among these are some of the *Jackdaw Portfolios of Historical Documents*. (See separate review.)

➲ World History: The Fertile Crescent to the American Revolution [video course] (The Teaching Company) $199.95; extra workbooks - $10 each

I was skeptical about even reviewing this course, since secular treatments of history generally leave much to be desired. But I have to say that The Teaching Company has done a terrific job with this course. "SuperStar" teacher Lin Thompson is also an actor, so he dresses in costume and takes on various historical characters to walk us through a survey of world history. This is not a complete course. There are four, extended-play videos with a total of 30 lessons, each of which is 30 minutes in length. This should work out to about one lesson per week, and it should be used as a supplement to your study of world history. It might be more frequent if you are completing all of world history in one year since this course only goes up to the American Revolution, leaving some of your book study unaccompanied by anything from this course. Of course, if you want to spread world history out over two years, then the videos can be used once per week or less. Surprisingly, religion plays a prominent role throughout this series. The perspective is nonjudgmental, but the presentation of Christianity seems quite accurate. It even has Martin Luther explaining salvation by faith rather than works. Still, Zoroaster and other religious leaders along with their teachings are presented such that disciples of those belief systems would be unlikely to feel challenged.

The lessons tackle broad historical periods such as early Egypt, Ancient Rome, Chinese dynasties, and the Protestant Reformation. In the amount of time available, Thompson often focuses on a single character giving us a sort of "slice of life" view of the time period. Still, he does an excellent job of tying together major events in story format. In fact, the appeal of this course lies in the fact that Thompson tells stories rather than just lecturing.

Two booklets contain outlines for all of the lessons. They also present two essay questions per lesson. However, the essay questions are identical to those found in the accompanying Study Workbook for the course. The Study Workbook has 10 "comprehensive" questions plus the two essay questions. Generally, the comprehensive questions ask who, what, where, why, and how type questions that require more than a simple answer. The essay questions sometimes require fairly significant research. For example, one question asks, "What was the new teaching of Luther, and how did it differ from the Catholic Church?" Frequently, there is little difference between the two types of questions, so you might use some for written assignments and others for oral discussion. Suggested answers and key points to look for in those answers are in the last half of the Study Workbook. This book is not reproducible and we need to purchase a separate book for each student.(S)

American History and Government Resources

[See also "Studying the U.S. Constitution and Law."]

➲ America: Land That I Love (A Beka Book) $16.95; Teacher Edition - $24.95; Student Test and Study Booklet -$4.95; Quiz Booklet - $4.35; teacher keys - $8.60 each; Geography Studies of the Western Hemisphere - $6.95; teacher key for Geography Studies -$9.05; Civics Activity Book - $8.75

A Beka has written this new eighth-grade text for American history probably because so many other schools and publishers cover that topic at eighth grade level. A Beka has an excellent American History text for the elementary grades as well as one for high school, so this was not an essential addition. They condensed their previous two-year coverage of world history over grades seven and eight into a single seventh grade text to make way for this new book. Nevertheless, they have done a commendable job. This text is up-to-date (1994), and it includes more coverage of women, Indians, and minority groups than we find in earlier editions of A Beka texts. At the same time, it strongly reflects A Beka's bold patriotic, conservative, Christian (Protestant) position. Unlike most textbooks, this one is obviously opinionated. Some might see this as a negative, but as long as these positions align closely with yours, this actually makes the book far more interesting than one that strives to be neutral.

The reading level is appropriate for junior high. The book is over 500 pages long, but the print is fairly large and there are numerous full-color illustrations.

Questions in this text are a big improvement over older editions; they are a mix of factual recall, map reading, and thought questions. Within each chapter are periodic "check ups" with factual questions and identifications. Chapter reviews have more extensive questions, map work, and thought questions. Between check ups and chapter reviews there are enough questions that using the quiz or test booklets might be optional. However, you might still want to use them for mid-term and final tests.

The teacher's edition has answers to text questions. Support materials include *World Atlas and Geography Studies of the Western Hemisphere*, a quiz booklet, a Student Test and Study Booklet, teacher's keys to accompany each of these, and a *Civics Activity Book*. The *Civics Activity Book* is fairly superficial, so you might want to skip it and cover government much more extensively using A Beka's high school text for American government or another resource at a later date. Maps, time lines, and flashcards for states and capitals are also available.

➲ American Adventures, True Stories from America's Past, Part 1 and Part 2 by Morrie Greenberg (Brooke-Richards Press) $9.95 each

In each of these two books, fifteen high-interest stories from American history are used for special, self-contained lessons or to supplement a comprehensive history study. Johnny Appleseed, the Orphan Train, and the Camels of the Old West are three of the topics in Part 1, and Theodore Roosevelt, John Ponzi (of the infamous "Ponzi Scheme"), and Rosa Parks are three topics featured in Part 2. Stories are short—about three pages, followed by activities. Activities are grouped into three areas: writing/journal (short writing activities, vocabulary exercises), discussion (good discussion questions and thought-provoking challenges to defend both sides of an issue), and cooperative group (further research and presentation). A timeline and short summary of "What Else Was Happening?" put each story in focus. The books were not written for Christian audiences, so don't expect to hear the "whole story" such as Johnny Appleseed and his gospel preaching. You'll also have to deal with such "perspective" problems as an exercise that asks students to identify "four most important qualities you think a U.S. President should have" from only these eight traits: intelligent, experienced, inspiring, logical, reasonable, caring, healthy, and energetic. Suggested for ages 10-15.(SE)

➲ American Government in Christian Perspective, 2nd edition (A Beka) $16.45; teacher's guide - $20; test/quiz book - $4; test/quiz book answer key - $8.60

This one-semester course in government is intended to be complemented with A Beka's new *World Geography,* another one-semester course. (The *World Geography* text is due December of 1997.) American history is prerequisite although this provides quite a bit of review. Students might study government later than ninth grade so that they are able to first take a U.S. History course. This text presents a conservative, free enterprise, Christian, patriotic perspective, contrasting our government with other governmental systems. The text leans too strongly towards the "America can do no wrong" outlook, but any differences of opinion we might hold should merely provide extra discussion material. It also advocates participation in govern-

ment by Christians. Groups of six questions appear frequently throughout each chapter. These primarily focus on vocabulary and factual recall. At the end of each chapter are essay, short-answer, and thought/discussion questions that stretch student thinking. These questions should be sufficient for evaluating a student's grasp of the content, but a Student Test/Review Booklet and accompanying answer key are also available. This 1997 edition is a revision of the earlier book, *American Government and Economics*. Much of the original content and organization of the original remains, but it has been rewritten in a larger typeface and edited down in size, making this a much easier-to-read, less-challenging text than the first edition. The teacher's guide includes answers for the text questions and lesson plans.

➲ American Government for Christian Schools (Bob Jones University Press) $28; teacher's edition - $39; test packet - $7; answer key - $4

This text, like A Beka's, teaches about our government by interrelating history, including the influences of Christianity. It also incorporates an introduction to economics, comparing different economic systems, while promoting the free enterprise system. The student edition contains both content and application/discussion questions. Student text pages are reprinted in the teacher's edition which also has objectives, annotations to the text, answers to questions in the student text, and suggested activities in the margins. Instructions for a mock Congress and a mock trial are included, and both activities would be great to do if you can gather a group. The student book can be used on its own if we do not need the answer key in the teacher's edition and prefer to have our students work independently. Alternatively, students could read the text from the teacher's edition rather than purchasing the student text, although they would then have access to answers to questions. If you choose to use the test packet and its companion answer key, you might find that you have plenty of questions and answers and, consequently, might feel more comfortable skipping the teacher's edition.

This book has been written for twelfth grade students, but may be used with younger students who have developed their thinking skills and have a good background in American history. A *TestBank* (softbound book) [$16] and an *AskIt* test bank data disk [$14] are available. BJUP also has a separate economics text.

➲ United States Government (Landmark's Freedom Baptist Curriculum) $35

This easy-to-use worktext is an excellent resource for teaching twelfth-grade students about the form and function of the U.S. federal government. It covers the Declaration of Independence, Constitution, Bill of Rights, the branches of government, and more. Each section goes in depth, discussing not only basic ideas but also the Founding Fathers intentions based on an abundance of quotes. A great deal of time is spent discussing Constitutional amendments and resulting issues such as freedom of religion and expression, the right to bear arms, due process, and jury nullification. Throughout the text, the true nature of the federal government and its relationship to the states and their citizens is examined. Each chapter contains questions in essay, short answer, and fill-in-the-blank formats. Quizzes, exams, and answer keys are included. This course is intended for one semester followed by LFBC's *Economics* course for the second semester.

⊃ **American History Explorer [CD-ROM computer program]** (Parsons Technology) $29

Children ages 11 and up can supplement U.S. history studies with this computer program. Designed for IBM compatible computers running Windows, it uses a "point and click" graphical interface to present material covering the Age of Discovery up through the Civil War and Westward Expansion. Sight and sound combine in slide shows, maps, a time line, pictures (including some 3D images), primary documents, articles, six video clips, and a game that will be especially helpful for students who prefer multisensory learning. There are over 1300 articles and 85 primary documents which comprise the most important information. Articles are hyperlinked to the time line, maps, and images. The 92 maps can be edited and the game quizzes students on the who, what, where, when of history. This is strictly supplementary since much information is summarized rather than presented in detail. You will need a mouse, sound card, 256-color VGA display running on a 386 or better computer.

⊃ **The American Republic** (BJUP) $28; teacher's edition - $39; student activity book - $12; teacher's edition for activity book - $13

Written for eighth grade students, this book is an introduction to United States history. If your teen has already studied United States history at an elementary or junior high level, and if he or she is mature enough to handle the deeper philosophical questions, you can skip to the BJUP eleventh-grade-level *United States History* which is more interesting. The eighth-grade text does have good discussion questions, and the student activity book greatly enhances the text. While it includes some fill-in-the-blank questions, it also features construction of graphs and charts, map work, and other more analytical, thought-provoking activities. For example, one assignment is to write war memos as an American commander summarizing the details of a battle. Then, assuming the role of a historian, the student is to describe the significance of the battle. You will want the teacher's edition for the student activity book. The teacher's edition of the text itself, contains the student pages without answers, so we might purchase the teacher's edition for the text along with both the student activity book and its teachers' edition. Optional items are an *AskIt* test bank data disk [$14] and a softbound *TestBank* book [$16].

⊃ **America's God and Country Encyclopedia of Quotations** by William J. Federer (AGC, Inc.) $19.99

Students who are writing term papers or researching topics related to history, government, law, and even current events will find this 864-page volume invaluable. It is a collection of quotations, usually with brief explanatory or background information. Quotations come from influential people such as our Founding Fathers, philosophers, statesmen, scientists, and preachers, as well as from court decisions, newspaper reports, Congress, personal letters, and various public documents. Naturally, the quotations are selective. In this case they were chosen to document the role of Christianity primarily in America's history but also, to a lesser extent, in world history. For instance, the quotes from Charles Darwin reflect his doubts and criticisms of his own theory of evolution, rather than a defense of that theory. The book is indexed by subject and also by entry title, with entries themselves arranged alphabetically. It is fully footnoted for use in research documentation. This book makes a great addition to the family library for everyone to use.

⊃ **Ancient Rome: How It Affects You Today** by Richard J. Maybury (Bluestocking Press) $8.95

This "Uncle Eric" book follows Maybury's *Are You Liberal? Conservative? or Confused?* While it is not necessary to read the other Uncle Eric books first, it is helpful to read the entire series since the ideas presented in each book are interconnected. Government is the main topic in *Ancient Rome* even though economics gets considerable attention. The focus is upon the ancient Roman Empire model of a strong central government since that model has been adopted by so many societies since Rome. Maybury takes us on a brief tour through historical events, highlighting "Roman" governmental systems in action. Ultimately, the subject is the government of the U.S., our gradual shift to the Roman model, and the economic consequences we should expect from what Maybury calls the "Roman disease." He repeats the limited government theme that is foundational to all of the Uncle Eric books. As with the other books in this series, Maybury uses a series of letters from Uncle Eric to convey heavy concepts in easily-digestible chunks, appropriate for all teens. Maybury writes from a philosophical basis that is consistent with the principles of America's founders: limited government, free markets, and higher law principles. Since he does not write from a biblical perspective, we need to add that dimension ourselves. (Read this in conjunction with your studies of U.S. Government.) Resources such as Jehle's tapes on the Constitution would enlarge the picture presented by Maybury.

⊃ **Basic American Government** by Clarence B. Carson (American Textbook Committee) $32.95

Clarence Carson, known to many home educators for his American History series, has tackled American Government, a subject inevitably made dull by most textbooks. Carson brings life to his subject by putting it in context, dealing with the people and ideas that formed our government rather than treating us to lists of lifeless facts. Carson tackles topics others shy away from. I was particularly pleased to see that he deals with the definition of our form of government as a republic rather than a democracy. He credits the Judeo-Christian view of man as the reason for that choice by our founding fathers. Carson frequently addresses the expansion of federal power at the expense of the states' rights. One such instance is in relation to the 17th amendment which provided for direct election of senators. He shows how this was a dramatic shift from the selection of senators by state legislatures, which moved our country away from the intended form of republicanism and toward democracy.

The entire book is 592 pages, but the actual text is only 480 pages. A glossary, notes, documents, and an index comprise the rest. Still, this is a hefty book for some high schoolers—slow going at times, but, for the most part, very interesting reading. It is arranged in four sections: Introduction and Examination of American Government, Background of Political Thought and Practice, American Government in the 19th Century, and Leviathon: American Government in the 20th Century. That last section title should give you a clear idea of Carson's views of government! The arrangement makes it possible to use the book in sections. You might do the introduction, then use the second section in conjunction with world history studies. The last two sections could be studied in conjunction with U.S. History. Thus, reading the book could be spread out over a couple of years. There are no questions or quizzes with the book, but I suggest that parents and teens read the book together and discuss it. Carson makes little attempt to hide his opinions, and the book is all the more interesting for it. This is one of the few books I would put on the "must read" list.

⊃ **A Basic History of the United States** by Clarence B. Carson (American Textbook Committee) individual volumes - $9-$16 each; set - $46.50; teacher's guide - $8

This series of six books is written at college/adult level, so it is appropriate for very mature students and might be most useful as a reference tool. Carson presents a conservative's view of United States history from 1607 to the present. The role of religion in history is discussed yet this is not an obviously Christian series until we reach the sixth book. Carson writes in a more entertaining literary style than is generally found in history texts. He also includes much background information to enhance understanding of events. This really is more comprehensive and accurate (at least from my point of view) history than you will find in other textbooks. The sixth book, written after the other five to bring the series up to the present, is especially interesting since it is less objective than the others. Carson introduces worldview conflicts in the second chapter, "The Philosophic and Religious Divide." The viewpoint is clearly conservative, constitutional, and Christian as he continues with chapters such as "The Debacle of the Welfare State," "Conservatives and Liberals...," "The Collapse of Communism," and "Political Gridlock III-Clinton's Tailspin." A teacher's guide contains summaries, points to emphasize, discussion questions, lists of people and terms to identify, and activity suggestions that can be used at the teacher's discretion.

⊃ **The Challenge of Godly Government** (The Committee for Biblical Principles in Government) $5.95

See review under "Law and Government" in Chapter Five.

⊃ **Christ and the Americas** by Anne W. Carroll (Tan Books and Publishers, Inc.) $24

This paperback text is a good general survey U.S. history text for junior high and high school students. Though it has a decid-

edly Catholic leaning it is more thorough and accurate than the average history text. Although Carroll's *Christ the King, Lord of History* (world history text) focuses very heavily on church history, *Christ in the Americas* includes church history but doesn't let it dominate the text. Carroll uses stories and anecdotes which make for interesting reading. She also offers analytical commentary throughout the text rather than presenting bare facts. This is especially helpful in discussions of policy issues such as common schools, the New Deal, and Great Society programs. The text begins with early Indian civilizations and continues up through the Clinton administration (albeit briefly). Protestants might also use this text alongside another to get a more complete perspective. Essay/discussion questions and project suggestions follow each chapter. Project suggestions include research, reports, creative writing projects, art, and drama.

⊃ **The Christian and Politics** [audio tapes] by Paul Jehle (Heritage Institute Ministries, available through Landmark Distributors) $20

On this set of six audio tapes, Paul Jehle outlines a biblically-based approach to political involvement for Christians. He traces American history to the present, and makes a connection between the form of government and the spread of the gospel.

⊃ **The Civil War** by Pat Wesolowski (D.P. & K. Productions) $18

Ages 9 and up can participate in this unit study on the Civil War. Organized around major battles of the war, the study involves children in activities from history, geography, literature, language arts, speech, journalism, economics, art, home economics, and music. Historical background information is included, although further research will be essential. Right at the beginning, we are challenged to dig into the true history surrounding the war with questions and answers that blow holes in some common beliefs. The author refers us to the book *Facts the Historians Leave Out* as a source about causes of the war. A key part of the study is production of a newsletter (weekly or less frequent depending upon the size of your group). Ideally, the study works best with more than one family, although it can be done with a single family. The more children involved, the more side issues can be developed in individual articles for the newsletter, which expands learning exposure for all. It also means that you have more bodies to participate in reenactments, debates, or other activities you might choose to do. Small group or large, there are plenty of activities to choose from beyond the newsletter. Suggestions and background information are given for geography (blackline map masters included), creating a time line, literature, vocabulary, and economics/statistics. One chapter focuses upon key people and interesting facts. A brief chapter on "Crafts, Cooking, Music & Movies" describes some hands-on activities and supplementary resources. There is an extensive section of reproducible "Puzzles, Games, Codes and More." Suggestions for field trips and activities such as a library scavenger hunt are next, followed by 100 "Quiz Bowl" questions that might be used in a competition, and a book and periodical bibliography. The author used this study with other families, meeting once a week, but you could select from the suggested activities and/or design a different schedule to suit your needs.

⊃ **Critical Thinking in United States History series** by Kevin O'Reilly (Critical Thinking Books and Software) student books - $21.95 each; teacher's guides - $15.95 each

History textbooks tend to be rather bland in their presentations, rarely exposing students to conflicting viewpoints or interpretations. Consequently, most students rarely are exposed to the idea that there are numerous ways to interpret historical events. Because they have not been trained to examine conflicting viewpoints, they are in a weak position when they are challenged on issues of historical interpretation (e.g. "Was the American Revolution in keeping with Biblical precepts?", "Were the southern states within their rights to secede from the Union?").

This series of four books can be used along with almost any history course to train students in critical analysis. (Along the way they will also learn a significant amount of history.) Unit One of each book is dedicated to teaching critical thinking skills themselves: evaluating sources, logical fallacies, cause and effect, etc. From that point on, lessons revolve around selected topics such as "Did Pocahontas Really Rescue Captain John Smith?", "What Caused the Salem Witch Hysteria?" and "Should the Government Role be Laissez-faire or the General Welfare State?" Students are provided with background and relevant information, quotes from mostly primary and secondary sources, maps and charts when appropriate, and worksheets. Teachers may photocopy student pages for single classroom use, so one student book will suffice for two or more students that you might be teaching. Occasional outside research might be helpful. Students can work through these lessons on their own, but some discussion time is essential. (The teacher's guides help us guide discussion.) The ideal way to use these books is in a group setting. If you lack a group, a parent-student discussion will do. In spite of the "classroom design," the books are suitable for home schoolers.

A major concern with any critical thinking course is the author's point of view and his evenhandedness in his presentation. Kevin O'Reilly, author of this series, does a fairly good job with that delicate task. He treats the Salem witch trials far more open-mindedly than others, presenting numerous possible explanations, including the idea that witchcraft was a reality in Salem. I have trouble with his treatment of the Great Depression when students are presented a worksheet with ten proposals; eight of the proposals are dependent upon government action, one is to institute communism, and only one suggests a private solution, in this case private charity to help the poor survive. All in all though, he does a credible job.

The four volumes in the series are *Colonies to Constitution, New Republic to Civil War, Reconstruction to Progressivism,* and *Spanish-American War to Vietnam War.* You can begin this series with mature junior high students, tying in lessons as they correlate with your other history studies. The books can also be used on their own for a separate group class. Lessons vary in the amount of time required; many lessons will require two or more

class sessions. The lessons are both interesting and challenging. Even if students feel stretched mentally, I expect they will enjoy such lessons far more than reading textbooks.(S)

⊃ **Electing America's Leaders: Participating in the Political Process to Elect Quality Leaders** by Jessica Hulcy (KONOS) $15

See review under "Law and Government" in Chapter Five.

⊃ **Fighting for Liberty and Virtue** by Marvin Olasky (Regnery Publishing, Inc.) $24.95

Marvin Olasky has authored another book which I recommend, *The Tragedy of American Compassion,* and he also serves as the editor for *World* magazine, another of my favorite resources. Consequently, I eagerly anticipated reading *Fighting for Liberty and Virtue,* a book that addresses the revolutionary period of American history by dealing with the "connections between morality and freedom, virtue and economic prosperity, good values and good government." This book exceeded my expectations. Olasky masterfully intertwines historical events with behind-the-scenes motivations and philosophical movements to paint a complex picture of our country's beginnings. One of the key themes is the contrast between the decadence of England, particularly London, and the moral standards of the colonists, much of which came out of the two Great Awakenings. Olasky submits that the colonists were reluctant to pay continually higher taxes to England, knowing that much of the money would go to support England's decadence. To make his case, he describes immoral lifestyles that were rampant in England and that were transmitted through her representatives and admirers to the colonies. (He writes to an adult audience, so parents must use discretion about having their teens read this book and should probably read the book themselves first.) Olasky describes some of our Founding Fathers from philosophical, moral, and economic perspectives which helps us see them as "real people" instead of as the caricatures that we encounter in most history texts. Another major focus of the book is the Constitution, its origins, the controversies surrounding it, and problems of interpretation and application which erupted from the very beginning. Olasky's bottom-line message is a call for limited government that does not inhibit the practice of religion. He ends with the statement, "Those who desire small government and those who yearn for holy government must hang together, or we will all hang separately." While I highly recommend this book, because of content and reading level, it is for mature teens.

⊃ **Free Indeed: Heroes of Black Christian History** by Mark Sidwell (Bob Jones University Press) $8

The focus here is upon black Christians in America rather than the typical black heroes. The book opens with a brief history of the black church in America, then presents biographies of thirteen men who demonstrate the work of salvation in their lives. Each story is as much a spiritual journey as a historical one. The book is geared to reading levels for junior and senior high students. Excellent discussion questions center around religious issues more than history so you might use this as part of Bible study and history. The companion teacher resource materials [$7] include "project ideas, illustrations for bulletin boards, a unit test, and other materials helpful in using *Free Indeed*."

⮑ **God, Man, and Law: The Biblical Principles** by Herbert W. Titus (Advanced Training Institute International) $25

See review under "Law and Government" in Chapter Five.

⮑ **A History of Christianity in the United States and Canada** by Mark A. Noll (Wm. B. Eerdmans Publishing Co.) softcover edition - $30

Since Christianity has played such a key role in the history of both the U.S. and Canada, author Mark Noll has written a history text that focuses on that topic. Since both countries are closely intertwined historically, he expanded coverage beyond just the United States. Mexico receives brief mentions occasionally, but otherwise has not been included. Noll states in the introduction that for purposes of definition in this book, "...the church consists of all who name the name of Jesus Christ." Because of this, Mormons, Jehovah's Witnesses, Catholics, Seventh Day Adventists, Pentecostals, Presbyterians, and Baptists are all lumped together as Christians with no distinctions made as to what it truly means to be a Christian. While this manner of treatment will offend some, the overall content of the book is valuable for understanding the changes that have taken place in the more private realm of religion as well as in the public arena due to the influence of Christianity.

What appeals to me about this book is that Noll tries to balance different aspects of people and situations, rather than trying to arrive at some conveniently simplified description. He tells about figures such as Christopher Columbus, showing the strength of courage and spiritual convictions, while also demonstrating that he was sometimes driven by less lofty motivation. Use this book as a reference tool or as an adjunct to history studies.

⮑ **A History of US** by Joy Hakim (Oxford University Press) $10.95 each; $99.95 for the set

This ten-volume U.S. history has garnered lots of attention—good and bad. I had written a fairly lengthy review pointing out the positives and negatives. However, the publisher refused to acknowledge the inaccuracies and biases I cited. They threatened a libel suit in response to my review. Since I'm not inclined to spend my time and energy fighting a libel suit, I've decided to omit the review and just let you know why.(SE)

⮑ **Kaw Valley Films [videos]** (Kaw Valley Video Sales and Rentals) $10 annual membership fee; $19.95 per video: rental program available

Among videos in Kaw Valley's catalog are some pertaining to U.S. history. One is entitled *"We Proceeded On..." The Expedition of Lewis and Clark 1804-1806*. This 32-minute video tracks the expedition from the confluence of the Missouri and Mississippi Rivers all the way to the Pacific Coast then back. It capsulizes the hardships of the expedition and their discoveries with enough information to make it interesting without being

overwhelming. Members of the expedition and the Indians they met and traveled with are introduced, and we are given biographical insight into the nature of the two strong leaders, Lewis and Clark, who planned and executed this expedition so magnificently. I am told that this is the same video shown at the Fort Clatsop National Park on the Oregon Coast, which was built by the expedition. (If you have seen other such videos at national parks you have an idea of the professional quality.)

Likewise *Gettysburg: 1863* is shown at the Gettysburg Visitor's Center. This film describes the events leading up to this fateful battle, then the battle itself. It depicts the battle with a topographical map, arrows, and other markings, then fills in the story about the key generals, the status of the war, and the consequences, both immediate and long term.

Another video, *The History of American Railroads* makes a great supplement as you study the period of the westward movement. This 80-minute video is divided into four sections so that you can easily insert segments into your studies at the appropriate times.

The 1880s video is like viewing newspaper headlines about key events of that era—snippets about all kinds of unrelated topics. Interesting but superficial. These are high-quality videos that appeal to all ages.

While I reviewed only these few videos, you should check out others in their catalog such as *Oregon Trail, Pony Express, The Mississippi River*, and *Shiloh*. A $10 annual membership fee allows you to purchase videos at $19.95 each or participate in their rental program.

⮑ **A Nation Adrift: A Chronicle of America's Providential Heritage [video]** (Proactive) $19.95

This ninety-minute video presentation begins like some others that discuss America's Christian history. However, the scope is broader while the purpose is more specific than in other presentations. On one hand, I might describe it as a super-condensed overview of United States history very professionally presented with an assortment of illustrations, film footage, quotations, and reenactments. Teens will enjoy watching this video, especially as it moves into more modern history with actual film footage. In terms of coverage, it's so condensed that we jump from Amelia Earhart to the bombing of Pearl Harbor. However, the point is to trace the path from our country's origins to its present state, highlighting major events, rather than to cover all the details. A Christian, conservative viewpoint is clearly evident, but it takes on a stronger political tone as Margaret Sanger and her work with eugenics and the founding of Planned Parenthood is followed by the introduction of Roger Baldwin, founder of the ACLU. As the presentation gallops through the 60s and 70s, the message becomes even more clear: that America has lost its spiritual foundation and has rejected God and his law. The video offers a counterpoint with references to some of the major revivals in America and the drastic changes that took place in society (albeit relatively short-lived) as the result. Be aware that towards the end, footage illustrating an abortion and footage of some homosexual activity (hugging, kissing, lewd dancing) are included.

The message at the end is a wake-up call for Christians to renew their faith and be politically involved.

➲ To Pledge Allegiance: A New World in View by Gary DeMar and Fred Douglas Young (American Vision) $16.95

This book is the first of seven planned in the "To Pledge Allegiance" study of U.S. History. Most history texts deal briefly with the period of exploration, then jump into the colonial era. This series, instead, dedicates the entire first volume on historical background information and the explorations that were crucial to our country's foundations. The idea of worldviews in conflict is introduced at the beginning of Chapter 1 and is a central theme of the study. In describing the foundational principle of the series, the publisher says, "Nations and individuals either serve God or some idol.... Their allegiance explains both their actions and the results of their actions." While various worldviews are contrasted, the Biblical Christian worldview, emphasizing God's providence, is clearly presented as truth.

Although the book is heavily illustrated in color, it is best suited for students sixth grade and above rather than younger levels. Sidebars on most pages add essential and fascinating detail; do not skip these! The writing style is very engaging with occasional dashes of humor most evident in titles for the sidebars and some of the subsections. The content is excellent. Rather than a dry recitation of names and dates, it tackles the motivational issues related to beliefs and values that drive men to either noble or despicable deeds. Touchy issues such as the conflict between Cortes and Montezuma are treated fairly without whitewashing the failings of the explorers. Each chapter is followed by a few questions, best used for discussion. (You will need to determine acceptable answers on your own from the text, which means that a parent needs to read along with the student.) A separate study guide has lesson plans plus test questions and answers.

The second volume in the series will be out by the end of 1997. It will be about double the size of the first and will sell for $19.95. I expect that this series will prove very popular with homeschoolers.

➲ The Patriot's Handbook: A Citizenship Primer for a New Generation of Americans by George Grant (Holly Hall Publications/Highland Books) 14.99

Following a long-standing tradition popular in earlier eras, George Grant has compiled a collection of readings that are foundational for understanding what the United States is all about. Documents, speeches, articles, poems, court decisions, essays, and biographies are each preceded by an introduction written by Grant. The book is arranged in four sections: early settlement, independence, expansion, and the modern era. Some examples of readings from the modern era are the "Seneca Falls Declaration," a seminal piece on women's rights by Elizabeth Cady Stanton; "The Pledge of Allegiance;" The "Atlanta Exposition Address" by Booker T. Washington promoting freedom for self-advancement by Blacks; William Jennings Bryan's "Cross of Gold Speech" about the question of adhering to the gold standard; "Cuba to Columbia," a poem by Will Carleton about the Spanish-American War; Woodrow Wilson's "Fourteen

Points" speech; the *Brown V. Board of Education of Topeka* Supreme Court decision written by Justice Earl Warren; John F. Kennedy's Inaugural Address; modern amendments to the Constitution; and biographies of the presidents from 1822 to the present. Each of the other three sections is similar in its breadth of content.

I suggest using this book alongside other resources you might be using for U.S. history, selecting appropriate readings for each time period as it's being studied. While all the readings do not all reflect a common worldview, they all contribute to a better understanding of major ideas and forces that have shaped our country, and the majority of the readings are meant to inspire an attitude of patriotism.

➲ The Rewriting of America's History By Catherine Millard (Christian Publications) $13.99

We must understand our country's history and heritage if we are to understand our form of government and how it was intended to function. However, our country's history is being rewritten, most often to remove any indications of our Judeo-Christian heritage. Catherine Millard documents numerous examples of the revision of historical records at national monuments, memorials, national parks, churches, colleges, the Library of Congress, and other places where we might learn about our heritage. Some of it occurs as books and documents mysteriously "disappear"; some seems to be more obvious attempts to hide the truth. Millard has done a fantastic amount of research to document her findings, which she embellishes with photos, quotations, stories, and pictures. Millard's presentation is alarming, but at the same time it is extremely informative—we learn the truth about our heritage so that we then understand why the disappearance of its evidence is so important. The book is divided into three main sections: "Where Have We Come From?"(our country's origins and the founding fathers), "19th Century Heroes Who Built upon the Foundation," and "Where Are We Going?". This last section documents stories such as that of the Liberty Bell which was removed from Independence Hall and from its historic base which included the words of Leviticus 25:10. The Liberty Bell is at present housed across the street and is now interpreted as "a symbol of world freedom." This is fascinating reading for teens and parents. Use it in conjunction with your United States history and U.S. government studies.

Millard has authored another book titled *Great American Statesmen and Heroes* [$13.99]. *Great American Statemen and Heroes* overlaps the content of the first book to some extent, but it focuses on 39 key men and women, expanding biographical background information and primary source quotations for each. Millard's goal is to prove the Christian focus of these people rather than to build biographical sketches. Consequently, she selects quotations from their own diaries, letters, and speeches along with information conveyed by their own relatives and friends to make her case. Among the 39 are Christopher Columbus, Captain John Smith, Roger Williams, William Penn, Samuel Adams, Thomas Jefferson, Benjamin Franklin, George Mason, John Jay, Marcus Whitman, Andrew Jackson, Abraham Lincoln, and many other "statesmen and heroes." Use this book as an adjunct to your U.S. history studies or assign if for independent reading.

⊃ Social Studies LifePacs (Alpha Omega) 800 level - 8th grade $41.95 for complete set

United States history is covered in greater depth in this Life-Pac course than at previous levels.

⊃ Sweet Land of Liberty by Charles C. Coffin (Maranatha Publications, Inc.) $14.95

Sweet Land of Liberty follows Coffin's previous volume, *The Story of Liberty*, although it is not necessary to read the first volume before the second. The organizing theme is liberty, and the author traces the growth of that idea through the early history of our country. This book covers the settlement of America and the Colonial period up to the Revolutionary War. Originally written in 1881, the book has a perspective and flavor unlike modern history books; it seems more like a series of stories than a narrative. Coffin's writing style is very engaging and easy to read. I found his treatment of the Salem witch trials to be typical of his approach. He deals with the context in which they occurred, describing the popular beliefs and common fears that contributed to such a miscarriage of justice. He also addresses history in terms of personalities and motivations, frequently using dialogue to convey information as well as the more subtle nuances of events. The book is heavily illustrated with black-and-white drawings. It should appeal to both teens and parents.

⊃ Teaching and Learning American History [audio cassettes] by J. Steven Wilkins (Covenant Publications) $12

J. Steven Wilkins, the gentleman who presents the excellent tape series, *America: The First 350 Years*, has produced a two-hour intensive seminar that equips parents to teach American history. The seminar is both philosophical and extremely practical. Wilkins talks about the reasons for learning and teaching an accurate view of history that balances the misinformation prevalent in most textbooks. He tells us how to do it and what resources to use, offering brief evaluations of resources for various age levels, elementary through adult. He even comments on some of the Christian history textbooks I have reviewed in this manual, both negatively and positively. This seminar is not meant to replace history books, but it will help us choose wisely which of them we wish to use. Wilkins' bibliography of recommended reading sometimes promotes a single viewpoint, but he points out in this seminar that in these cases the other viewpoint has dominated almost exclusively, and the issue needs correction and/or balance. Older high school students should listen to the seminar themselves.

⊃ The Truth Behind the Declaration of Independence [video] (R.A.C.E.) $20; transcript - $5

Reclaiming America's Christian Ethics (R.A.C.E.) was founded to verify America's Christian foundation and to advocate a restoration of that biblical morality that shaped our country. Hosted by Vaughn Shatzer, vice president of R.A.C.E., this video reviews the early days of our country and the men who helped formulate our Constitutional Republican form of government. Part of the purpose is to demonstrate the widely held Christian beliefs of our Founding Fathers about both government and personal morality. The video continues tracing historical threads of government, education, and religion through our history up to the present. Much of this is similar to presentations by David Barton and others. However, this video continues where Barton leaves off in addressing concerns about our government in the 1990s. Shatzer outlines a litany of modern-day violations of the very charges made against King George of England in the Declaration of Independence. (A copy of the Declaration of Independence also comes with the video.) He demonstrates how our present government has turned the Constitution on its head and undermined the biblical foundation that was essential to our country's existence. Within this context, Shatzer addresses two key issues: absolute truth and the redefinition of our form of government as a democracy. The purpose of the video is to educate Christians and urge them to become involved in reclaiming our country and returning it to its Constitutional foundation. The video itself is mostly of Shatzer speaking, but it includes occasional illustrations. Since it is about 80 minutes long and is mostly "talking heads," I suggest viewing it in two or more sessions. The printed transcript in booklet form includes footnotes. So much information is covered in the video, I expect that you will find the transcript a valuable tool for reviewing key concepts without searching through the video.

⊃ U.S. History, course H145 (Landmark's Freedom Baptist Curriculum) $35

This is a well balanced U.S. history course, suggested for ninth grade, that is written from a conservative, Christian viewpoint. The book begins with an explanation of some worldviews with regard to history and civilization and maintains a clear and open-minded approach throughout. It covers early exploration up till modern times. It includes an extensive overview of the Constitution and the Bill of Rights—more than we typically find in a U.S. History course. The text does an excellent job of presenting the facts along with contrasting points of view. Each chapter includes a section of questions, both short answer and essay, based on subject matter, vocabulary, and Scripture. Quizzes, quarterly tests, and answer keys are all included.

⊃ United States History: Heritage of Freedom [second edition] (A Beka) $20.95; teacher guide - $20; test book - $6.05; test key - $8.60; quiz book -$4.35; quiz key - $8.60

Suggested for eleventh grade, this study of United States history features a conservative, patriotic viewpoint, strongly promoting the benefits of capitalism. You need the student text which has many full-color illustrations, and I strongly recommend that you also get the teacher guide which contains the answers. Quiz and test booklets are optional.

Lessons include review questions scattered throughout each unit plus an extensive chapter review with identification, definitions, geographical identification, map skills, and some excellent discussion/essay questions. The teacher guide suggests weekly current events assignments (great idea). It also has pop quizzes, valuable "teacher notes" that expand upon the textbook material, and answers to all of the section and chapter questions, including the discussion/essay questions. Study of the Constitution is integrated with various chapters via instructions from the teacher guide. The text of the Constitution and a chart breaking it into sections with accompanying study questions is found in the student text. This study is fairly basic and would not be equivalent to a government class, but it is a worthwhile enhancement to the study of U.S. history.

This text makes no pretensions of neutrality; it is clearly anti-Catholic and anti-Communist. It promotes a Protestant viewpoint, criticizing secularism, existentialism, and other rejections of God. The philosophy of government is inconsistent. It reflects modern conservative thought which leans toward government intervention in some places (e.g., commerce and education) but comes down hard on government social programs such as the Great Society.

There is also a video course which uses this text. The video class I reviewed spent much time covering student homework and responses. It highlighted one of the major drawbacks of this approach—all the time that is wasted when students give incorrect responses and the teacher tries to elicit the correct answer from other students. I suspect that it does more harm than good for our students to listen through incorrect responses unless they are used to expand on a common point of confusion. On the plus side, the teacher does emphasize A Beka's providential view of history and urge the students to make connections between cause and effect.

⊃ Unit Study Adventures series by Amanda Bennett (Holly Hall Publications/Homeschool Press) $13.99 each

Although there are other titles in this series that might fit under U.S. history studies—*Pioneers, Elections,* and *Thanksgiving*—most students will have already covered pioneers and Thanksgiving well enough by junior high and should be ready to tackle more advanced topics like elections. These guides can be used for grades K-8 by requiring student reading, research, and presentations at appropriate levels. These guides feature detailed outlines, both a condensed one in the front of the book and an expanded "working outline" with space to fill in our own details regarding resources and teaching plans. Each guide shares the same organizational structure which includes lists of recommended resources for both reference and reading; spelling/vocabulary lists (at two levels); subject word list; activities; writing ideas; recommendations for games, videos, and software; "room decoration" ideas and resources (with addresses); internet resource addresses; field trips; and lists of questions (answer key included). These are narrowly focused unit studies that we develop ourselves by searching out information from the recommended topics and resources and preparing our own lessons. Guides are approximately 130-140 pages each and include minimal Christian content with the exception of *Thanksgiving* which is thoroughly Christian in its treatment. Recommended books are available at the library and through home school distributors. No prices are listed by some of the recommended resources, so it is difficult to determine which will be affordable. This informa-

tion would be especially useful on the government agency publications whose prices can range from free to outrageous. Plan to spend at least a few months on any of these unit studies.

⊃ The United States at War [audio cassettes] (Knowledge Products) $17.95 per two-tape set

Twelve, two-cassette sets serve as supplements to U.S. history studies. The tapes are not simply accounts of the various wars, but they provide an in-depth look at the economic, political, and social forces that were at work. Various actors portray historical figures, quoting from their speeches and writings to give us firsthand information. The "acting" is intermixed with a well-paced narration. The presentation is very well done, yet the tapes assume that the listener has a decent historical background for understanding the details presented here. Because of this, the tapes are best for older students who have already studied American history or as a follow-up or supplement to such studies. The content strives for historical accuracy rather than promoting a viewpoint as we encounter on tapes such as *America: The First 350 Years* or those from Mantle Ministries. Tapes sets are *The American Revolution* (Parts 1 and 2), *The War of 1812/The Mexican War, The Civil War* (Parts 1 and 2), *The Spanish American War, World War I* (Parts 1 and 2), *World War II* (Parts 1 and 2), and *The Korean War/The Vietnam War* (Parts 1 and 2). We can select one or more of the sets, and they are not dependent upon one another except for the two part sets. Bluestocking Press offers savings on quantity purchases of the Knowledge Products tapes.(S)

⊃ United States History, 2nd edition (Bob Jones University Press) $28; teacher's edition - $39; map packet - $6; student activity book - $12; teacher's edition for activity book - $13; test packet - $7; test packet answer key -$4; TestBank - $16; AskIt disk - $14

Suggested for eleventh grade, this is another outstanding text from BJUP. It offers an excellent, balanced treatment of history (at least from the conservative, Protestant viewpoint) through the Bush administration, including the role of religion. Rather than simply presenting information, this text looks deeper into philosophies and ideas out of which arise the issues and events of history. The perspective is less extremely conservative/patriotic than A Beka's texts, yet it is still unquestionably conservative in outlook. The teacher's edition comes in two, spiral-bound books, with student pages reproduced in only two colors. It is not essential to have the teacher's edition if we read the text and keep up with our student. However, it is helpful for answers, activity ideas (many only practical for the classroom), and occasional "additional background." One of the strongest features differentiating this text from A Beka's is the excellent, thought-provoking discussion questions which are included in the student text. The student text is one, large, hardbound book. A test packet and companion answer key, *AskIt* test bank data disk, or a *TestBank* in book form are also available. You need only one of these options.

The student activity book is optional, but it does help to reinforce learning through a variety of activities. Among the activities are fill-in-the-blank questions, short essay questions, map work, writing news articles, crossword puzzles, and some more analytical activities such as defending a particular point of view. You will want to purchase the teacher's edition for the Student Activity book as an answer key. The map packet is also very useful.

⮑ **U.S. History through Children's Literature from the Colonial Period to World War II** by Wanda J. Miller (Teacher Ideas Press) $25

This is a resource book for teachers who want to use a real book approach for teaching U.S. history to students in grade 4 through 8. It is divided into nine topical areas: Native Americans, Exploration, American Revolution and the Constitution, Slavery and the Civil War, Pioneer Life and Westward Expansion, Immigration, Industrial Revolution, World War I, and World War II. Each topical section features detailed studies for about six or seven books. The first study is supposed to be for an entire class, while the rest of the studies are supposed to be completed in small groups. Even so, the studies can easily be adapted with little effort for home school use with one or a few students. Selected books are briefly summarized, approximate grade level is indicated, and biographical information on the author is given. Next, are activity suggestions which include such things as map work, writing assignments, additional research, creation of posters, and role-playing. Discussion questions, which follow next, are easier or more difficult reflecting the suggested grade levels for each book. Last are a list of vocabulary words with definitions and the page number of the book where each word appears. At the end of each unit, following these studies, is an annotated bibliography of books and other resources on the topic plus an "End-of-Unit Celebration." The Celebration involves foods representative of the topic (recipes included) and other activities and research projects. These tend to be more large-group oriented than are those following individual book studies. A final chapter includes a "Literature Response Guide" which seems too much concerned with feelings and personal reactions rather than historical fact. You can use it or not as you please. The entire book is written for government schools, but it does present books that represent a variety of viewpoints. Consider this a supplement to enhance your U.S. history studies since it does not offer comprehensive coverage of even those topics under discussion. Choose whichever of the books to study that are appropriate and appealing; you need not go in order or complete all of them. I especially recommend this resource to parents who also have younger children with whom they can utilize the studies of some of the younger level books.(SE)

Primary Source Documents

⮑ **American Freedom Library [CD-ROM]** (National Center for Constitutional Studies/produced by Western Standard Publishing) $99.95

This is one of the most comprehensive CD-ROM collections, especially of those featuring documents, books, and magazines relating to American history and contemporary political and social issues. Use it as a companion to government, Constitution, and U.S. history studies. It features 11 collections: *Documents and Histories of American Freedom; Classics of Western Civilization; The Constitution Reference Collection; The Founding Fathers; The Presidential Papers; U.S. Congress; The Supreme Court; National Party Platforms; Today's Issues, Traditional Values; How to Win an Election; Public Policy Organizations;* and *Quotes.*

Examples of the content within collections: *Classics of Western Civilization* includes the KJV Bible, the works of Shakespeare, and 19 classic political and economic works such as Plato's *Republic, Leviathan* by Hobbes, and *The Roots of American Order* by Russell Kirk; *U.S. Congress* includes articles on the structure of Congress and how it functions, member directories of the House and Senate, House committees directory, committee jurisdiction, House rules, House *Ethics Manual*, FAQs about the U.S. Senate Chamber, *Historical Almanac of the U.S. Senate* by Robert J. Dole, History of the United States Senate, and a glossary of Senate terms. Among the other collections are Woodrow Wilson's five-volume *History of the American People,* De Toqueville's *Democracy in America*, the *Federalist Papers,* the *Autobiography of Benjamin Franklin,* Supreme Court decisions, periodicals and public policy papers from organizations such as Heritage Foundation and National Review, and contact information for over 300 public policy organizations.

The program is quite sophisticated, but once you have learned how to use its many features (it should not take long to master basic functions), you should find it fast and easy to use. It has excellent search, print, and copy features. Maneuvering is made more efficient with backtrack and trail features plus the "layered" table of contents with hyperlinks. Both students and parents should find this program an excellent tool for information and research, as well as a source for hard-to-find writings.

System requirements: IBM compatible computer, 386 or better (486 or better recommended); Windows 3.1 or higher; CD-ROM 2x or faster.

If price makes you hesitate, consider sending $7.95 shipping and handling fee for a locked version of the program. You will be allowed free access to one entire collection, then you can choose to pay for access to selected additional collections.

⮑ **The Anti-Federalist Papers and the Constitutional Convention Debates** (National Center for Constitutional Studies) $7.99

This book is an edited version of these source documents that should be read in conjunction with *The Federalist Papers* for an accurate understanding of the controversy surrounding the foundation of our government. The arguments are primarily those against a strong central government. This is fascinating reading since so many of the concerns of our forefathers accurately identified the very problems we confront in our federal government today.

➲ **A Documentary History of the United States** edited by Richard Heffner (Back Home Industries) $7.99

Although I have not reviewed it myself, this resource sounds like a useful compilation of some of the most crucial documents we might want our children to read and study. Back Home lists some of the collected documents as Thomas Paine's *Common Sense*, the *Declaration of Independence*, the Roe v. Wade decision, and Ronald Reagan's "Inaugural Address."

➲ **The Federalist Papers** (National Center for Constitutional Studies) $6.99

Alexander Hamilton, James Madison, and John Jay contributed the major arguments in favor of a strong federal government. *The Federalist Papers* are those original writings, and they are a vital resource for understanding why our government was established in the form that it was. Also read *The Anti-Federalist Papers* to understand the opposing view. (Both books are also available through Back Home Industries.)

➲ **CD Sourcebook of American History** [computer program] (Western Standard Publishing) $29.95

Western Standard Publishing offers the *CD Sourcebook of American History* which includes some of the most influential historical books represented by over 1000 documents (most in excerpted form) and hundreds of VGA images. Some of the documents and books found on the CD are *The Mayflower Compact, The Declaration of Independence, Ponce de Leon in Florida* by George Bancroft, *John Locke and the Fundamental Constitutions of Carolina* by H.R. Fox Bourne, Bancroft's six-volume *History of the United States, Democracy in America* by d'Tocqueville, and the ten-volume *Great Epochs in American History. CD Sourcebook of American History* runs on Macintosh and Windows platforms. The programs can either be installed on the hard drive or run from the CD. Powerful but complex search features should expedite research for those who master search procedures. Information can be copied into separate files as needed. While some elementary students will use this program, the primary audience is likely to be high school and above. The wealth of information accessed with the search feature could save hours of library research for term-paper writers. One of the most important reasons to have such programs is to have access to more accurate historical information than is provided in modern texts.

Also see the review of *American Freedom Library* from the same publisher which is a much larger collection of such documents and books.

➲ **Jackdaw Portfolios of Historical Documents and Study Guides** (Golden Owl Publishing Company) Portfolio and Guide sets - $37 to $39

More than 65 different Portfolios and Study Guides cover historical topics under the broad headings U.S. History; World History; Ancient, Cultural, and Religious History; Government, Law, and Civil Rights; Labor and Industry; and Rebellion and War. Examples of specific titles are: *American Revolution, California Gold Rush, Reconstruction, Slavery in the U.S., Colum-*

bus and the Age of Explorers, Russian Revolution, Magna Carta, Martin Luther, The New Deal, The Depression, French Revolution, and *The Holocaust*. Portfolios contain from eight to eighteen historical source documents which are facsimiles of originals. Transcripts are included since some of these are difficult to read. Four to eight Broadsheets expand upon selected topics, tying in the source documents. Notes for each portfolio include background on each document, suggested books to read, thought questions, plus assorted extras depending upon the topic (such as a list of places to visit). Reading level is fairly high, so use these selectively with younger readers.

The Study Guides help us fully utilize the portfolio material, serving as reproducible activity guides. Many activities involve writing, primarily relying upon the source documents and broadsheets for selected information. In addition to writing, are projects such as determining the best route to California during the time of the Gold Rush. Activities range from simple questions to involved research/projects. Some reproducible vocabulary worksheets are included.

Guides are dependent upon the Portfolios, referring to them for information, so they may not be purchased separately. Both Portfolios and Study Guides are intended for use with a wide range of age groups. I see junior high and high school levels as the ideal time to use these resources, because by then students have accumulated background historical knowledge and they have also matured in their thinking enough to deal with issues and controversies in context.(SE)

➲ **The Primary Source Document Series** (Perfection Learning) $15.15 - $19.95 each

The series includes seven separate, softcover volumes, each with 10 to 15 source documents. A study guide comes with each book. In addition to each document, we get a brief summary of its origins and thought-provoking questions. Topics are: Volume 1—*Pre-revolutionary America*; Volume 2—*The Founding Period*; Volume 3—*Expanding America*; Volume 4—*Modern America* (liberal ideas are heavily represented); Volume 5—*American Court Cases*; Volume 6—*Early American Speeches*; and, Volume 7—*Modern American Speeches* (weighted towards humanistic ideas and Democratic influence). The documents from earlier periods and court cases make interesting reading and serve as excellent supplements to history studies.(S)

Geography

The best way to teach geography is to travel, referring to maps as we go. Since travel is too expensive for most of us, the easiest way to teach geography is to continually refer to maps, globes, or historical atlases as we study history or read other books with actual geographical settings. Other materials can serve as supplements.

Workbooks, atlases, and other materials are available from Nystrom Publishers, Hammond Inc., American Map Corporation, Geography Matters, A Beka, and Bob Jones University

Press. Hammond sells map skills workbooks, a Bible atlas, the "History through Maps" series, computer-generated atlases, historical atlases, maps, and charts.

Current periodicals such as *National Geographic Magazine* (SE) are wonderful, in spite of their evolutionary outlook. National Geographic maps that come with some issues are superb, often providing much more information than just the geographical locations. Many of these maps actually teach history, science, geology, sociology, and other topics. These should be filed and used as needed rather than left in the magazines. Some thrift stores bind and sell old *National Geographic* maps. This is a very inexpensive way to get some of these maps.

Write to any of the publishers noted above for more information about other geography teaching materials.

Most students will prefer games far above textbooks for geography studies, so I also include reviews of some excellent geography games.

Geography Resources

⮑ **Exploring Your World - The Adventure of Geography** (National Geographic Society) $40

This beautiful geographical reference work covering physical and human geography, and earth sciences, also comes with a map. The articles are arranged encyclopedically, and every page has charts, maps, and photographs to illustrate the topics. The love for geography can come alive if this book is used in conjunction with a general outline of geography. Those participating in unit studies or interested in writing their own curriculum should seriously consider using this resource. On the basis of the exhaustive number of topics addressed, the number of pages (608), and the reading level of this book, consider it junior high or high school material if you are going to use it as a supplemental text. As a reference book, every good library should consider this work, keeping in mind, however, that there may be references to evolutionary ideas. (regular edition - ISBN 0-87044-726-2) (SE)[Diane Eastman]

⮑ **Geography** (BJUP) $28; teacher's edition - $39; map packet - $6, TestBank - $16; AskIt disk - $14

Although titled *Geography*, this appears to be more of a social studies course since it includes much more than geographic information. Actually, this makes the course more interesting than if it dealt only with geography. A missionary and spiritual context raises it above the level of typical, secular social studies texts. This is a large, 616-page book, written for ninth grade level, with an accompanying map packet that should also be used. The teacher's edition is helpful, and we can choose either the softbound *TestBank* book or the *AskIt* computer disk for help with creating tests.

⮑ **Geography Studies and Projects - Western Hemisphere** (A Beka) $6.95; teacher key - $9.05

This geography worktext was designed to be used with A Beka's *America: Land That I Love*, but it can also be used on its own or along with other resources. A similar volume, *World Atlas and Geography Studies of the Eastern Hemisphere*, is used for seventh grade level. Be aware that A Beka divides studies by hemispheres, an unusual approach not found in very many other texts. If you are using a comprehensive world history text, purchase both A Beka geography books and use the lessons in them in the order that corresponds to your text.

The first part of the book consists of maps and data on the countries of the western hemisphere. However, the U.S. is divided into sections and given more attention than South America, for which there is a single map and minimal information about each country. Students will need to refer to these maps as well as historical maps, such as those in *America: Land That I Love*, to complete the "geography projects" in the second half of the book. These projects are fill-in-the-blank exercises and map marking. Although this is not an exciting way to learn geography, the format is colorful and students have to search out information and do some analysis to figure out some of the answers. It's just the right amount of geography work for most students.

⮑ **Mapping the World by Heart Lite** by David Smith (Tom Snyder Productions) $59.95

Would you like your children to be able to draw a map of the entire world, including latitude and longitude markings without copying or referring to another map? David Smith's methods are designed to enable children to do just that. This geography curriculum is recommended for grades 5-12, although it fits most appropriately in upper elementary and junior high levels. I suggest using it either by incorporating it into United States and world history studies in junior high levels or else as a concentrated course just before starting U.S. and World history study at high school level.

It uses an assortment of activities to develop map skills, but the most important are the actual map-drawing activities. Besides properly locating and identifying places, children learn geographical knowledge that includes map reading skills, i.e., directions, symbols, topographical maps (great activities for learning how to make these!), the various types of map projections, the earth's rotation/seasons, dimensions, and more.

This ungraded program comes in a nicely designed three-ring binder. It can be used as a one-year program or it can be used as a supplement over a number of years, perhaps studying continents in conjunction with history topics. Lessons are well-designed and easy-to-follow. Great illustrations and layout make it especially easy to use.

Lessons need to be presented by the parent/teacher, but after the presentation students do much of the work on their own using reproducible work sheets from the binder. With the binder we get two sets of 9 double-sided 11" x 15" region maps to be used by students for initial work. We also get two sets of projection maps (three different types drawn on grids) and blank, 11" x 17" grids (reproducible) for students to use for their final map which will be done from memory. Additional maps are available in sets, although they are quite expensive. (The classroom edition of the program includes 30 of each map.)

There are lots of extras included in the program that we can use or not as we please—games, activity ideas, mnemonics, addresses for resources, and instructions for putting on a "World's Fair."

This method of learning geography has proven to be much more effective and less painful than traditional methods (even though it isn't as comprehensive as some of the textbooks) since it involves a variety of activities that interest and challenge students.(S)

Physical Geography by Arnold Guyot (American Christian History Institute) $8

This is a reprint of the 1885 edition of this book. It serves as a companion to the section on teaching geography in James Rose's *A Guide to American Christian Education* (American Christian History Institute). It is also quoted and referred to in *Teaching and Learning America's Christian History,* although it is not required for that book. I am not knowledgeable enough to critique the geographic content of the book, and I assume it is accurate, although there are certainly more recent discoveries that would shed more light on some topics (such as earthquakes and plate tectonics.) When Guyot ventures away from geographical facts, the content of the book becomes debatable. I am bothered by Guyot's approach to The Human Family—the white Caucasian is held up as the ideal with every other race as inferior. He also makes a few generalizations about continents and historical movements that I consider to be more philosophical than factual. When reading Guyot, we must keep in mind the time period and culture from which he wrote, since some of his ideas seem out of step with contemporary thought.

This is a heavy-duty geography textbook. It is not very readable alone but would serve better as a source book. According to the publisher, this edition is the only textbook on physical geography written by a dedicated Christian and creation scientist in the twentieth century from the viewpoint that the earth and its geography are God's handiwork. A supplement, *Physical Geography Maps* (American Christian History Institute) [$10], includes 36 maps with instructions and a sample full-color map.

Providential Geography: A Stage for Men and Nations -Year One by Daniel R. Eby (Patria Ministries) $12 each

See the complete review under the review of *Homeschool Teaching Packets* in Chapter Six.

Social Studies PACEs 1097-1108 (School of Tomorrow) 12 Paces - $48; answer keys - $16

World Geography is the topic for this series of PACEs. A Christian world view is evident from the first lessons about creation, the flood, and possible explanations for changes in the earth and the atmosphere. Like the other PACEs, emphasis is on factual recall, although occasionally a question is preceded by the word "think," indicating that the answer requires more than simple recall. Numerous map activities occasionally stretch students into more analytical responses. PACEs are generously illustrated in full color. The content is geared for junior or senior high students.

The PACEs are designed with removable Activity Pacs in the center. The rest of each PACE containing the text material is re-usable, so you only need to purchase another set of Activity Pacs for another student.

Student Ocean Challenge $90 a year subscription fee to enroll your "school"

Families who like alternative learning methods will love the Student Ocean Challenge. This program has been around since 1982. Each school year it offers a different "adventure"—school classes get involved vicariously in a fantastic ocean-oriented adventure (although one year it was a dog sled trek). They track the route of participants, learn about their background, study the ocean, geography, history, and other science topics using math, language arts, and computer technology. A computer and modem are required as students receive e-mail fleet reports, and communicate with ocean experts. Unit study material and supplemental visuals are also delivered via e-mail. The heart of each year's program is a teacher's guide that helps the teacher lead students through related learning activities. For 1997-98, students participate in the OceanEXPO. OceanEXPO tracks 45 sailboats from 17 nations as they circumnavigate the globe. This event commemorates the 500th anniversary of Portuguese exploration and celebrates the opening of EXPO '98 in Lisbon, Portugal.

"Through an interactive online project...students become explorers in their own right, as e-mailed fleet reports combine with monthly study units featuring geography and cultures, science, and sailing. Woven throughout the program are suggestions for the integration of art, music, history, language arts, mathematics and the Internet."

A new theme/adventure is usually selected for each year although The OceanEXPO began in January of 1997 and continues through May of 1998. Materials for the next school year are sent out as early as the preceding Spring.

A subscription includes one Teacher's Resource Guide, bi-weekly e-mail updates with news from the fleet, and one e-mail address with unlimited interaction. Schools outside the USA can participate for an additional $10 to cover increased mailing costs. Extra teacher's guides are $25 each, and an additional e-mail address is also $25. This should be a good resource to share as a group with a few other families.(SE)

Where in the World (Aristoplay) $32

There's more than meets the eye with this game since it can be played four different ways. In addition, players of different skill levels can play together by selecting easier or more difficult questions. Play can be concentrated on one geographical region being studied if desired. Along with geography, players learn some economic and cultural information. At the top level, current events are incorporated into game play. I recommend it because of its educational value, quality construction, and flexibility of use for players eight years old to adult.(S)

World Atlas and Geography Studies of the Eastern Hemisphere (A Beka) $6.15; key $9.05

This geography study is meant to accompany A Beka's seventh grade textbook, although it can be used on its own. It follows the same format as *Geography Studies and Projects -Western Hemisphere* which is reviewed above.

⊃ World Geography (A Beka)

This one semester course is due in December of 1997. It is intended to complement the new edition of *American Government*, also a one-semester course. This will be a high school level text.

Studying the U.S. Constitution and Law

This topic should be part of a U.S. History or U.S. Government class if you don't study it as a class of its own.

⊃ Civics Activity Book (A Beka) $8.75

This Civics workbook is designated for use with *America: Land I Love*, A Beka's eighth grade text. However, it is a curious mix of activities that sometimes seem more appropriate for younger age levels. The book is divided into three levels of government: federal, state, and local. For each section, students search out and fill in basic data such as the name of our president, his cabinet members, and local officials, as well as the state population figure, names of local attractions, and pictures of the state flower and tree. The first section on the federal government includes an introductory course on the Constitution. The text of the Constitution and the Amendments is in the textbook, and students really should read the full text rather than just the summary. The *Civics* book includes some excellent charts that help us sort out many of the details regarding the form and function of our national government, but more commentary would be helpful. Curiously, the state and local sections do not cover details about government except to list the names of officials. Activities are similar to typical fourth-grade state notebook projects (information gathering and regurgitation). This is strictly an introduction to the topic and should be used in conjunction with the American history text.

⊃ Constitutional Law for Christian Students by Michael P. Farris, Esq. (Home School Legal Defense Association) $20; teacher's manual - $5

Serious students at the junior and senior levels of high school will develop a much better understanding of the present state of Constitutional law from reading this book. It contains actual text of Supreme Court decisions that have helped to shape law into its present form, along with the original texts of the foundational documents of our government. Commentary by Mr. Farris prior to each document guides students in their reading to key points in each decision. Study questions which can be used either for written work or discussion help to enlarge understanding.

The first unit discusses the "Historical Background of the Constitution." Farris uses an interesting analogy, comparing the Declaration of Independence and the Constitution to a present-day corporation's articles of incorporation and by-laws respec-

tively. Other related documents such as The Articles of Confederation and The Bill of Rights are included in the discussion.

Unit II addresses "The Constitution as Higher Law," covering the roles of state and federal constitutions and the establishment of the principle of judicial review. Unit III deals with executive and legislative branches and limits to their constitutional authority. Unit IV tackles the thorny problem of the judicial branch acting as lawmaker, and also the proper limitations on the scope of judicial activity. Unit V covers religion-related constitutional issues, which should be of special interest to Christian students. Unit VI (added to the 1995 edition) addresses some of the most recent decisions regarding property rights, unionism, and government rights.

While the commentary is very readable, some of the justices' writing takes perseverance to unravel, so make sure your teen is able to work at this level. This book is also suggested for all adults. The accompanying, inexpensive teacher's handbook is recommended.

⊃ The Declaration of Independence: Our Nation's Charter [video series] (CEBA) $75 for the series

Five videos, varying in length from 35 to 40 minutes each, comprise this series dealing with the role of the Declaration of Independence in the interpretation of our Constitution. The premise of this series, advanced through discussion, and recorded presentations before live audiences, is that the Declaration of Independence is part of our nation's "organic law." The Declaration itself outlines the principles upon which our country was founded and recognizes the Creator as the source of natural law from which all law must flow. The Constitution is dependent upon the Declaration for an understanding of how it should be interpreted. The five videos build this case, ending with a call that we require legislators and government officials to abide by both documents. Other related subjects, such as the effects of relativism upon schools and families, are interjected. At the end the question is raised as to whether or not we should try to restore our nation as "Christian America," but the concept is briefly discussed and rejected.

To create the videos, host Robert Mateer interviewed a number of godly, knowledgeable men including, author/teacher Professor Ronald Nash, columnist and attorney Doug Bandow, Dr. Larry Arnn (Claremont Institute), Dr. Charles Wolff (of F.A.C.E.), and attorneys Robert Cannada, Sam Casey, Douglas Kmiec, and Herb Titus. Some of the film is from presentations by these and other speakers at a conference on the Declaration of Independence. Many of the speakers repeat and reinforce the same concepts, so the series sometimes seems to move too slowly. Because of the nature of the presentation it is really geared for adult audiences interested in the topic rather than general audiences. Consequently, I would not recommend it for the average home schooled teen. Instead, for teens and general audiences, I would recommend that you contact CEBA to find out if they have completed work on an abridged presentation on this topic.

The ideas presented here are absolutely crucial, offering concrete steps for actually turning our country around and restoring it to a solid foundation.

When you order the set of videos you also receive free your choice of two books, either *Cease Fire on the Family* by Douglas Kmiec or *Mere Creatures of the State* by William Bentley Ball, plus a subscription to the semi-annual journal *Christian Perspective*.

⊃ Elementary Catechism on the Constitution of the United States- for the use of schools by Arthur J. Stansbury and William H. Huff (William H. Huff) $15 for one; $25 for two

In 1993, William Huff edited and published this edition of Stansbury's *Catechism on the Constitution* which was originally written in 1828. He has added some quotes and comments along with copies of a few key documents, including, of course, the Constitution. Stansbury's format was traditional question and answer, although most answers are too lengthy for students to memorize verbatim. Some questions and answers are purely factual, others are interpretive, but taken together they hit many of the key points. Huff's notes bring out some major problems in our country that have resulted from ignoring and/or disobeying the Constitution such as the Federal Reserve Bank's control of the money supply, federal abuse of Constitutional taxing powers, and federal usurpation of States' rights. Use this book to supplement study about government and the Constitution for junior and senior high students. Mr. Huff also offers other related information and resources.

⊃ The Five Thousand Year Leap by W. Cleon Skousen (National Center for Constitutional Studies) softbound - $13.95; hardbound - $16.95; curriculum guide - $19.95: curriculum guide with softbound text - $29.95; 12 audio tapes - $99.95; 7 video tapes - $149.95

The Five Thousand Year Leap of the title refers to the tremendous progress made by our country in its brief historical lifetime. That leap was made possible by what Skousen identifies as 28 great ideas recognized by our founding fathers and incorporated into our form of government. Those familiar with the Principle Approach will see some overlap in the identification of principles here, although, since the curriculum is intended for use in all schools, the Biblical base is not stressed in discussions of the common belief of our Founding Fathers in natural law and a Creator. Although space prohibits listing all of the principles, some of them are "The only reliable basis for sound government and just human relations is Natural Law," "A free people cannot survive under a republican constitution unless they remain virtuous and morally strong," "A free society cannot survive as a republic without a broad program of general education," and " The United States has a manifest destiny to be an example and a blessing to the entire human race." (The third principle I've listed, regarding education, does not specifically affirm taxpayer-funded schools in the textbook, but I don't have the tape presentation of that lesson to know if that holds true there also. Nevertheless, the wording might lead one to think that government has a compelling interest in education, which I and many others would dispute, even though this is probably not the author's belief since he and the publishers of this book strongly support private schools. You might find this and other ideas in this presentation worthy of further discussion.)

Skousen describes the careful construction of our Constitution with its system of checks and balances, asserting that the basic concepts are as valid today as they were when written. Skousen quotes Founding Fathers, earlier thinkers, and source documents to prove his thesis. Unlike many other works on such topics, this book is very readable for high school students.

This book can be used as part of a course in government, this study being part one, taking one semester. Part two would be based on Skousen's book *The Making of America*. The curriculum guide is not yet available for that study.

To successfully use the curriculum guide, you need either the audio or video tapes. (The audio is taken from the video, so content is identical.) Tapes are dependent upon the book; students are frequently told to turn to certain pages in the book during each lecture. Lectures, presented by Earl Taylor, Jr., expand on the book's content with additional background, commentary, and examples. The videos are basically single-camera taping of Mr. Taylor's lectures, so, while it might be easier to maintain student interest with the videos than the audio tapes, they won't miss any content with audio tapes. The curriculum guide explains in a few pages how the course works and suggested scheduling, then provides "lesson objectives" for each presentation. The objectives are actually key questions that might be used for written work or discussion. Page numbers are shown for where each question is addressed in the text. Tape presentations on the one tape I reviewed ran from 18 to 33 minutes each and are probably representative of other lesson lengths. There are fill-in-the-blank and short answer quizzes for each chapter plus two exams. The quiz questions are identical to those on the exams. The course works best with a group but can be used for independent study.(S)

⊃ Gospel of Liberty [video and study guide] (Vision Video) video - $19.95; study guide - $9.95

This 37-minute video, alone or in combination with the study guide, can be used as an introduction to study of the first amendment to the Constitution. The video, focused on the Great Awakening in Virginia and itinerant preachers George Whitfield and Samuel Davies, dramatizes the challenge faced by the State-established Anglican Church as the Great Awakening brought Protestant preachers from other denominations into their domain. The vital issue of the roles of government and church were brought into focus and became the subject of heated debate. An actor portraying Thomas Jefferson narrates the story, filmed on location at colonial Williamsburg. The video can stand alone, or it can be followed by readings, discussions, and activities from the 32-page study guide. This is extremely useful for helping young people understand the difference between an established church exclusively supported by all taxpayers, and governmental recognition and encouragement of religion—issues vital for understanding the real meaning of the first amendment. The production quality of the video is excellent, and the story moves along quickly enough to easily maintain the interest of junior and senior high students.

➲ Institute on the Constitution [video or audio seminar] by
John Eidsmoe (audio tape seminar available from John
Eidsmoe; video seminar available from John Eidsmoe or
Plymouth Rock Foundation) videos - $65; audio - $35

John Eidsmoe, well-known Constitutional lawyer, author,
and professor, presents a twelve-part seminar on the Constitution. It is presented on three video tapes or six audio tapes with a
companion booklet. Eidsmoe ranges wide in the first few tapes to
present the history and a brief study of the law and government
background that contributed to the creation of our Constitution.
Then he proceeds through overviews of the various sections of
the Constitution. The last two sections confront the two primary
problems we face in regard to the Constitution; Eidsmoe titles
these sections: "The Crisis of the Constitution: From Biblical
Absolutes to Evolutionary Humanism" and "Reclaiming the
Constitution: A Victory Plan for Restoring Our Constitutional
Heritage." Accompanying either set of tapes is a study guide
with detailed outlines of all of the lectures plus study questions.
Eidsmoe's legal background is evident as he draws from court
cases, laws, and legal documents to make his points. While Eidsmoe is not as dynamic as Paul Jehle, his presentations are loaded
with valuable information. Eidsmoe also has a dry sense of humor that lightens things up now and then. Like Jehle and others,
Eidsmoe works from a clear understanding of the biblical principles underlying our government.

➲ The Land of Fair Play (Christian Liberty Press) $8; answer
key - $3; tests - $2

The Land of Fair Play is an in-depth civics textbook, expanded and updated from a pre-World War II text. It explains the
origins of our form of government and analyzes how it functions.
It also addresses state and local government. It does so in fairly
simple language, which is easier to read and comprehend than
most high school civics texts.

Because of its origin, it still retains concepts that seem outdated. The section about local government is the best example
with overly simplistic descriptions of government services and
significant attention given to villages. Appendices have been
added to this latest edition. Highlights here are a discussion of
types of government (attacking the myth that the U.S. is a democracy) and an overview of the Christian origins of our government.

Questions, both written and discussion, are provided for
each section. Clip art illustrations are mixed with presidential
portraits, graphs and charts, all in black-and-white. An answer
key and tests are available separately.

Philosophical statements are scattered through the book, but
appear particularly in the appendices; they endorse proper interpretation of the Constitution, support for the right to bear arms,
and the correct interpretation and application of the term "separation of church and state."

➲ The Making of America: The Substance and Meaning of
the Constitution by W. Cleon Skousen (National Center for
Constitutional Studies) $26.95

Recommended for advanced students in grades 10-12, this
book includes some U.S. history and biographies, even though
primary emphasis is on the Constitution. This is actually one of
the most thorough analyses of the Constitution available. It is
written from a conservative, Christian perspective, although it is
not overtly Christian in content. Check out other books from the
National Center for Constitutional Studies, such as biographies
of George Washington, Benjamin Franklin and Thomas Jefferson and *Soldiers, Statesmen, and Heroes*, which is about the first
seven presidents. I don't recommend the original NCCS tapes
and study guide workbook that were designed to be used with
this book. The tapes are boring, and the workbook emphasizes
simple recall of facts already covered in the book. Watch for the
new curriculum guide and tapes which should be a much better
option. The new course is intended to be used as part two of a
government class that follows part one using *The Five Thousand
Year Leap* curriculum.

➲ A More Perfect Union: America Becomes A Nation
[video tape] (National Center for Constitutional Studies)
$19.95

Brigham Young University created this professional, dramatized story of the Constitution, centered around the character of
James Madison. It portrays the people and motivations that
brought that document into existence in a quality production almost at a level that we might find on television. Actually, the
content is better than most television productions, even though
the acting is occasionally mediocre and the story is drawn out a
little too much towards the end. As we might expect, the film
takes small liberties to flesh out the story. While the general presentation is historically faithful, there are minor misrepresentations, such as the implication that Madison favored democracy,
and that because of this he resisted the one vote per state compro-
mise. The script does include some significant quotes such as
Franklin's plea for prayer to solve the Constitutional Convention's deadlock. I recommend using this video as a part of a study
on the Constitution since the story format is likely to hold the attention of many teens more easily than a book on the subject.

➲ Our Living Constitution Then and Now (Good Apple)
$13.99

This 164-page book offers a thorough study of the historical
and literal facts about the Constitution, and a briefer look at modern applications. The publisher recommends it for students in
grades 5 to 8, but it is also appropriate for high school level. It
covers the entire text of the Constitution, The Bill of Rights, and
the remaining amendments, arranging them in two-column fashion with the original text on the left and a "translation" on the
right. Interspersed at various points are explanations, activity
pages, and research assignments. With younger students, we
might cover selected sections and activities, saving more challenging assignments for older students (e.g., "In the space below
cite several examples in today's world where Congress has exer-

cised implied power. Look in newspapers and magazines for additional ideas," or "What is the main essential in a writ of habeas corpus?"). While the perspective is secular, it seems well-balanced. We can use the trivia game found toward the end of the book to "quiz" students on their knowledge. The book is reproducible and an answer key is at the back. Consider planning a semester-long course using this book along with *You, Your Child, and the Constitution* for the Christian perspective.

○ **An Overview of Constitutional Law audio cassettes** by Paul W. Jehle (Heritage Institute Ministries, available through Landmark Distributors) $20

We must understand how government should function under our Constitution if we want to know how to respond to the political issues bombarding us these days. Paul Jehle, an advocate of the Principle Approach, presents the best explanation of the Constitution I have heard or read in this series of five audio tapes. He outlines the spheres of jurisdiction and their limitations as originally intended, then goes on to explain the Constitution, the amendments, and their application and interpretation through Supreme Court decisions. From this foundation, Jehle shows how and why we have strayed far from the original boundaries of the Constitution. We learn why some of the amendments are in direct conflict with the original intent of the Constitution's authors and why some Supreme Court decisions overstepped Constitutional boundaries.

A topic such as this usually invites yawns, but Jehle is a dynamic speaker who brings us face to face with Constitutional issues, not just as theory, but as life issues touching each one of us. I highly recommend this tape series.

○ **Reclaiming the American Dream by Reconstructing the American Republic** by Tom Rose (American Enterprise Publications) $6.95

When studying government and the Constitution, it is easy to conclude that the U.S. Government has run seriously afoul of Constitutional restrictions and boundaries. Many people question how to repair "this breach in the walls." One of the most interesting answers is a biblically-based solution called interposition. In this 44-page booklet, Tom Rose explains interposition as "lawful representatives interposing themselves between the people and a higher level of government which they consider to be in error...." He goes on to explain the biblical and historical roots and applications of this strategy as well as how the concept is being resurrected as a modern-day solution. This is thought-provoking reading and makes great discussion material.

○ **The Story of the Constitution** (Christian Liberty Press) $4.95

This paperback edition is a reprint of a 1937 book, but with a few additions and updates. The first and most interesting section is the background information, followed by brief biographies of the signers, then the text of the Constitution and amendments. Next is an alphabetical analysis of the Constitution (similar to a concordance), then a few interesting writings such as Washington's "Farewell Address." Last is a section of random questions

and answers to pass on interesting tidbits of information such as the number of lawyers who were members of the Constitutional Convention. This book was designed to be used with *The Land of Fair Play* (a CLP book) for a complete civics class.

○ **Two Good and Noble Men [video]** (National Center for Constitutional Studies) $19.95

This 53-minute video is a fictional drama of a debate between Benjamin Franklin and Patrick Henry. Patrick Henry visits Benjamin Franklin before the Constitutional Convention takes place, and they enter into debate over the Articles of Confederation versus their replacement by a stronger federal government. Franklin advances the cause of federalism while Henry defends maintenance of power by individual states. Both present their arguments in an entertaining format. Franklin's sister hosts Henry as a guest in their home. She offers him food, and Franklin uses Henry's need to eat as an excuse to bend his ear without immediate response. Once Henry finishes eating, he tackles Franklin's argument and the debate begins. Humorous touches throughout the drama make the contrived setting entertaining as well as informative. The acting is excellent, although there is a great deal of shouting back and forth and both men passionately present their thoughts. I would use this video after students have already been introduced to the basic issues addressed by the Constitutional Convention. At that point, they should know enough to catch more of the subtleties than if they watched it without any prior knowledge.

○ **The United States Constitution [audio tapes]** (Knowledge Products) $17.95 per two-tape set

Four sets of two audio cassette tapes each tell the fascinating story of our Constitution. Actors portray characters such as Jefferson, Madison, George Mason and other key figures to dramatize their writings and speeches. We hear their own words, interspersed with narration. I particularly like the tapes on the "Bill of Rights and Additional Amendments"—the explanations and background is excellent. The amendments are dealt with in historical context so that we understand the passions that gave them birth. We can use the tapes as we reach the various time periods or topics in our history studies. For example, when we study the Civil War, we can listen to the section about the fourteenth through sixteenth amendments that arose from the issue of slavery. There are four sets available in this series: "The Constitutional Convention at Philadelphia," "The Ratification Debates," "The Text of the U.S. Constitution," and "The Bill of Rights and Additional Amendments." We can select one or more of the sets, and they are not dependent upon one another.(S)

○ **Whatever Happened to Justice? [from the "Uncle Eric" series]** by Richard J. Maybury (Bluestocking Press) $14.95

Richard Maybury, author of *Whatever Happened to Penny Candy?,* has done even better with *Whatever Happened to Justice?* Written for a slightly older audience (ages fourteen and up), it discusses how our justice system has changed from a reliance upon common law to a reliance on political law. He shows how the abandonment of common law has left us with a fickle system that reacts to pressure as much as to any more important factor of law.

Maybury has a gift for translating what sounds like tedious information into very personalized examples. He follows the *Penny Candy* format where Uncle Eric is writing letters to nephew or niece Chris (could be male or female). Each letter is reasonably brief, so students will not be overwhelmed with too much information at once.

Some "chapter" titles are "Two Kinds of Law," "The Lawless West," "Instability, Nuremberg, and Abortion," "Competing for Privilege," "The Constitution: Highest Law of the Land?," and "Are Lawyers and Judges Corrupt?" Final letters address "unsolved problems" such as risk, capital punishment, the environment, and poverty. *Whatever Happened to Justice?* covers issues of government and law that are not addressed in any other textbooks.

Use this book as an introduction and/or supplement to American history or government studies. It will not take much time to read through, although it might generate lengthy discussions. No matter what else you use, this book is a must!(S)

➲ **You Decide! Applying the Bill of Rights to Real Cases** by George Bundy Smith and Alene L. Smith (Critical Thinking Books and Software) student book - $21.95; teacher's manual - $18.95

Students in grades seven and up will learn more about the meaning and application of the first eight amendments to the Constitution through these interactive activities. The reproducible student book includes readings for background understanding on the Constitution, Bill of Rights, and court decisions. There are brief comprehension questions and vocabulary exercises. Each lesson includes a number of activities—discussion topics and debate topics are often specified, but many questions might also be used for written assignments. This study works best with a group of students; obviously a debate with one student is not feasible. The teacher's manual is essential; it explains how to use the activities and offers suggested answers to questions. The authors take a fairly evenhanded approach by advancing arguments for more than one interpretation or position, but there are so many controversies surrounding the Bill of Rights, that you might easily find still more arguments to consider in other sources. This is not as challenging or comprehensive in its presentation of court decisions as Michael Farris' *Constitutional Law for Christian Students*, but it is easier to teach and understand.(S)

➲ **You, Your Child, and the Constitution** by Dorothy E. Robbins (The Rebuilders of the Foundations of America's Christian Heritage) $20

This is one of the best Christian-oriented resources I have seen for teaching the Constitution to students in junior high or the early years of high school. The author takes care to translate concepts into practical applications. Since Dorothy Robbins teaches and writes about the Principle Approach, it is not surprising to see the depth of this study that derives from research into scriptural principles and history. Robbins takes us through the Pream-

ble in detail to clarify the intent of the document writers. For the body of the Constitution, she selects key topics and principles such as the proper roles of the three branches of government. Her approach leans strongly toward limited government and sticking to the original intent. For example, she begins a section about the Constitution and Property by saying, "One of the most misunderstood concepts is that of property. The second most misunderstood concept is liberty. The following assignment is designed to teach children the Biblical principle of property.... the purpose for civil government is to protect it [property]." She also makes scriptural connections throughout because Scripture strongly influenced the document. Each section includes questions for discussion, research, and writing—we make our own choices about how to use the questions. (Many of the questions are purposely geared for younger children.) The only point I would contest (and this is a very minor quibble) is a remark within the "Pledge to the Constitution" on the opening page which says that the Constitution is intended to guarantee "those God-given rights enumerated in the Bill of Rights." The Bill of Rights was not intended to list only those rights "owned" by citizens, but to spell out the fact that any authority not specifically delegated to the Federal government remained with states or individuals.

This resource is more limited in scope than *Our Living Constitution*, but the two books together should make an excellent course for junior high or ninth grade .

➲ **Are You Liberal? Conservative? or Confused?** [from the "Uncle Eric" series] by Richard J. Maybury (Bluestocking Press) $9.95

Follow *Whatever Happened to Justice* with this book. Those who haven't read the previous Uncle Eric books can still understand Maybury's message here, but they will benefit far more if they have first read the others. Using the same letter-format of earlier books, Maybury tackles political labels and what they represent. From conservatives and liberals to Nazis and Communists, he shows how they all believe in state control to varying degrees. (He does a great job describing the difference between socialism and communism, two "isms" people generally lump together as one.) He proposes a new label, juris naturalis (natural law), to describe those who prefer as little government control as possible and proceeds to argue the case for this position. As always, Maybury translates concepts that confuse many adults into language clear enough for teens to understand. Since Maybury does not write from a biblical perspective, his idea of juris naturalis extends only as far as "freedom" issues and does not address Christian viewpoints of how individuals should function under our government. Paul Jehle's *An Overview of Constitutional Law* (audio tape set) would add the missing dimension.(S)

America's Christian History—The "So What?" Question

Numerous people are speaking and writing about America's Christian History. The thrust of many of these messages is to convince us that the large majority of our Founding Fathers were Christian and that they set up a Christian form of government. We can argue about who really qualifies to be considered a Founding Father and about which of them were truly Christians. However, the evidence is clear that most of them claimed to be Christians and that they founded a governmental system largely reflective of Judeo-Christian beliefs. We can also argue about whether the system was derived from the Bible, reflected a cultural acceptance of biblical principles, or resulted from observations of other governments and men themselves. But we do know that we have a governmental system that presupposes a citizenry that abides by biblical principles. In his *Commentaries on the Law,* published in 1879, Sir William Blackstone said,

> The doctrines thus delivered we call the revealed or divine law, and they are to be found only in the holy scriptures...[and] are found upon comparison to be really part of the original law of nature. Upon these two foundations, the law of nature and the law of revelation, depend all human laws; that is to say, no human laws should be suffered to contradict these.

The question remaining at the end of many books and presentations is "So what?" What do we do with this information? What impact should it have on anyone, other than "I never learned that before!" I believe that most such authors and presenters do have an agenda—something they hope to accomplish by sharing the information. I am concerned that those agendas are not clearly communicated to audiences so that they can decide for themselves whether they wish to participate.

I see two major agendas behind the movement. Communicators concerned with the first agenda use this knowledge to teach the principles themselves to students so that they can understand how both our government and individuals should function They encourage participation in the governmental process, but always keeping in mind that politics and government cannot solve the problems of sinful man. They tend to promote the idea of a very limited federal government.

Communicators of the second agenda often fail to recognize the problem of government assuming authority in areas over which it should have no jurisdiction. Some of these advocates just want to ensure that government authority is used to enforce their own agenda. Rather than reclaiming the freedom intended by our Founding Fathers, they would dictate the policies of a still-coercive government. Some of them tend to view the Constitution as an evolutionary document which can be reshaped to promote Christian ideas. Although I believe promoters of the second agenda are well-intentioned, I disagree strongly with them.

My primary concerns have to do with their view of the role of government and the amount of personal freedom that should be allowed. The Constitution's authors recognized the dangers of a large centralized government, so they purposely designed a cumbersome system that would allow the federal government to accomplish as little as possible. They believed that citizens should have as much freedom as possible, but citizens were also expected to assume responsibility for themselves.

Over the years, the Constitution has come to be ignored and distorted by legislators who view the government as the ultimate parent of all citizens. The government has involved itself in feeding, clothing, housing, educating, and licensing citizens—roles alien to our Founding Fathers' view of government responsibility. Those promoting the second agenda would scale back government provisions for citizens, but they largely want to keep the controls that are in place. Rather than getting government out of education altogether, they would have government fund private religious schools (which would then be controlled by the government). Rather than eradicating government sponsorship of anti-Christian programs, they would ensure equal funding of Christian programs.

I realize that these are vast oversimplifications of peoples' positions, but home schoolers need to be aware that there are political agendas at work here. I do not want home educators to be "used" to further political strategies that amount to little more than power struggles, especially if they are unaware of a speaker or writer's position.

Having said this, I turn now to reviews of resources for teaching America's Christian history. Remember that many of the following resources were not created to provide comprehensive coverage of a topic but more often resulted from determination by Christians to set aright the falsehoods that have been taught for so many years. Remember that they do not strive to be "fair" but to counterbalance the revisionist history that prevails. Because they often present controversial ideas or viewpoints, I suggest using them as sources for discussion. Most of these resources should be used to supplement basic United States history studies.

A number of publishers, organizations, and distributors specialize in America's Christian history materials and have many other resources available in addition to those reviewed here. Among these sources are American Christian History Institute, Foundation for American Christian Education, Landmark Distributors, and the Mayflower Institute.

➲ **America, The First 350 Years [audio tapes with study guide]** by J. Steven Wilkins (Covenant Publications) $69.95

This is a more in-depth study than either *The Light and the Glory* or *The American Covenant,* yet it is very easy to understand because of the excellent presentation. The set comes with 16, ninety-minute cassette tapes (with two lectures per tape), a three-ring binder notebook, and a study guide that can also be inserted into the binder. Mr. Wilkins' goal is to teach the truth about American history—to correct the misinformation that has been taught as fact in the schools and the media. He covers selected historic events and ideas from colonization through the Civil

War, with an underlying theme of how far our country has strayed from its original ideals and the need to resurrect those ideals. He does have some strong theological leanings (e.g., postmillenialism) that you might or might not agree with, but these play a minor part in the presentation. Mr. Wilkins is speaking to an adult audience, yet the tapes could be used with junior high or high school students. Ideally, this should be used as a family study with older children. (Younger children will probably have too short an attention span to listen through the tapes.) The notebook clearly outlines each presentation with the key ideas noted. Documentation of quotations and bibliographies are included. The notebook itself can be used as a refresher course for review. The study guide has a page of discussion questions (which could also be writing assignments) for each tape. This set would also work well with an adult study group. Components can be purchased separately or as a set. The price is very reasonable for so many tapes.

⮑ **The American Covenant, The Untold Story** by Marshall Foster and Mary Elaine Swanson (The Mayflower Institute) $11; audio seminar - $32; video - $20

This book is about America's Christian history and also relates to the Principle Approach. It has workbook exercises and can be used alone or with two other Principle Approach volumes, Teaching *and Learning America's Christian History and* The *Christian History of the Constitution of the United States of America (published* by Foundation for American Christian Education, but also available through American Christian History Institute and others). *The American Covenant* presents the key events which shaped America's history, emphasizing the Christian character of our founding fathers as well as the biblical principles which were an intrinsic part of our country's history. This book is probably the easiest to work with of all those available that address America's Christian history.

The American Covenant Audio Seminar—an eight hour seminar on eight cassette tapes—dramatically enhances the information in the book.

The American Covenant Movie is a video tour of ten of America's great monuments, which provide a backdrop to Marshall Foster's presentation on the forgotten roots of our country.

⮑ **America's Christian History** by Jean S. Smithies (Intrepid Books) $12.95 each

This is a series of eight books written for grades 1-8, but also usable on older levels. The language and vocabulary are purposely on a higher level than today's textbooks written for those grades. Mrs. Smithies has made the Principle Approach very accessible with these books. They are thought provoking without being overwhelming. This is not a typical U.S. history course since it concentrates on particular points to illustrate principles.

Intrepid also offers other history-related books plus shorter studies for the junior/senior high level.

⮑ **America's Christian History: The Untold Story** [book or audio presentation] by Gary DeMar (American Vision) $10.95; tape - $6.95

Gary DeMar presents the case for describing America as a Christian nation based upon a wealth of historical evidence. He traces that evidence from the founding of the first colonies, through written works, the establishment of Christian universities, national pronouncements, physical evidence, and the lives of our presidents. He also investigates the Christian foundations of a number of the states. He deals with the controversy over the Treaty of Tripoli, the idea of Separation of Church and State, and misrepresentations about Jefferson, Washington, John Adams, and Lincoln. The new, expanded edition (which should be in print by the time you read this) also covers Thanksgiving, theocracy and democracy, and Christopher Columbus and the Flat Earth Myth. DeMar's longtime involvement in studying the issue enables him to define his terms and address the arguments clearly and persuasively. His use of numerous quotes and footnotes make this an excellent resource for researching topics without becoming overwhelmed.

The audio tape is a dramatized presentation of events similar to those in the book, although it does not follow the book's outline. This is a highly professional presentation that is both entertaining and informative. It makes an excellent introduction for teens who might be reluctant to begin with a book. Highly recommended.

⮑ **America's Godly Heritage** [video] (WallBuilders) $19.95

David Barton sets forth the beliefs of many of the famous Founding Fathers concerning the proper role of biblical principles in education, government, and the public affairs of our nation. Excerpts from court cases show that for 160 years Christian principles were upheld. Graphics show the degeneration in America since rejecting the founders' beliefs. Barton's rapid-fire delivery and use of visual aids combine for an excellent presentation loaded with information.

Barton and WallBuilders offer many videos, books, cassettes, video transcripts, and other resources, all relating to America's Christian history.

⮑ **America's Providential History** by Mark A. Beliles and Stephen K. McDowell (Providence Foundation) $15.95

Beliles and McDowell have rewritten much of the material from Rosalie Slater, Verna Hall, Arnold Guyot, and others, into a very readable book. The theme, that God in His providence directs both individuals and nations, is prominent. It begins with an overview of geography and ancient history to lay groundwork for presenting the theme in the context of American history, economics, and foreign affairs. There is an extensive section on education in America, including the basics of how to apply the Principle Approach. The final chapters describe the "apostasy and decline" of America and a plan for the "reformation" of our country. The authors present a strong call to action and Christian political involvement. This book has a purposeful message with which readers might agree or disagree, but it is nevertheless valuable as a balancing source for the presentation of American history. It is best used as a parent resource book, although teens should use it for research and selected readings. (The book is 296-pages, softbound, with large print and black-and-white illustrations.)

● The Christian History of the American Revolution by Verna M. Hall (Foundation for American Christian Education) $42

This volume provides the biblical background of the American Revolution by comparing the liberty of the Gospel with American political liberty. It contains an essay by Rosalie J. Slater entitled "The Education of John Quincy Adams" that is both a model and an inspiration to home educators.

● The Christian History of the Constitution of the United States of America, Volume I and Volume II, subtitled Christian Self-Government with Union (Foundation for American Christian Education) $40 each

These books by Verna Hall provide the primary source references that help to form the philosophical foundation for the Principle Approach. They also lay out the basic principles. They are rather confusing to use on their own and work best as source books in conjunction with other books from F.A.C.E. These are beautiful, hardbound volumes as are the other books from Foundation for American Christian Education.

● God and Government (three volumes)—I: A Biblical and Historical Study; II: Issues in Biblical Perspective; and III: Restoration of the Republic by Gary DeMar (American Vision) $12.95 per volume or $32.95 for three-volume set

This three-volume series was written to help Christians develop a Biblical world view and an understanding of the Christian foundations of our country. Begin with *Volume 1* and use the books in sequence. (It is not necessary to use all volumes.) Written for junior high level or above, *God and Government* works well as a supplement to history, government, and Bible study. DeMar quotes widely from both Scripture and historical documents to provide evidence for his assertions. Essay-type questions for discussion or writing are at the end of each chapter, with answers (lengthy explanations) provided in the book. Questions direct students to Scripture as they compose their answers, but the book's answers go far beyond what most students are likely to come up with. Because of this, it is probably best to use the questions for discussion based upon reading and analyzing the Scripture references along with DeMar's "answers." (There is no separate teacher edition or answer key.) DeMar's theological perspective (largely Reformed Protestant) is quite evident throughout the books, and parents should be involved with both reading and discussion as teens tackle crucial theological issues.

● Keys to Good Government [video] (WallBuilders) $19.95

This is another of David Barton's video presentations relating to America's Christian history. This presentation focuses on our form of government and the basis on which it was founded. Barton explains the difference between a republic (our form of government) and a democracy (a form rejected by our Founding Fathers). He then goes on to prove that the character, both public and private, of public officials was considered a paramount issue. Some states had religious requirements for office holders, and many people felt that those who failed to exhibit Christian character in their private lives were unfit for public office. The main point is that if we are not ruled by men of Christian character, we will have problems such as those we face today. This is a wake up call for Christians to get involved in the political process.

● The Light and the Glory by Peter Marshall and David Manuel (Baker Book House) $11.99

If you have teens who have already taken secular history courses in school, this is a great book to introduce them to a different viewpoint for studying early American history. It tells the stories of famous men in our country's early history, including in those stories the often-ignored influence of God in their lives. This is the history that most of us never learned! A Study Guide workbook is also available. Follow this book with the sequel *From Sea to Shining Sea* [$11.99], which covers the period from the Constitutional Convention up to pre-Civil War times. No study guide is available for the second book. (Prices are for paperback editions.)

● The Mayflower Institute

The Institute offers seminars featuring Marshall Foster on topics relating to America's Christian history. Many of these are available on audio and/or video cassette. See the review of *The American Covenant* above. Write for their brochure of available titles and descriptions.

● Noah Webster Educational Foundation [audio tapes] $7 each

The Noah Webster Educational Foundation was founded by Belinda Beth Ballenger, a master teacher of the Principle Approach who studied under Verna Hall, Rosalie Slater, and James Rose. She is best known for relating America's Christian History through storytelling. Her well-researched stories are available on tapes for both younger and older audiences. Titles for older audiences are *Pocahontas - An Indian Princess, Christopher Columbus, Footprints of the Pilgrims, George Washington's Garden, No Way Out and the American Spy, The Fall of an Uncommon Man,* and *Liberty, the Gift of God.*

NWEF also offers a program called "The Little Red School House" which utilizes "circuit-riding teachers" to support home school groups and classroom teachers (K-12) by offering dramatic storytelling sessions in American History and instruction on the Principle Approach.[Diane Wheeler/C.D.]

● Story of America's Liberty [video] (American Portrait Films) $19.95

This is an educational documentary on America's Christian heritage. The key idea in this video is that America was founded on Christian principles and with a recognition of God's providence in the challenges faced by our founding fathers. There was recognition that they were dependent upon God's continued blessing to survive, an important truth seemingly lost in modern America. Video footage of historical sights, documents, paintings, statues, etc., provide evidence along with quotations from original writings. While junior high students will learn much from this video, I think that senior high students will benefit most, especially if they take time to discuss the people, events, and ideas presented.

➲ Study Guide to the Christian History of the Constitution of the United States of America, Volume II by Mary-Elaine Swanson (American Christian History Institute) Study Guide - $8; answer key - $8; *Civics* audio cassette - $5

The purpose of the *Study Guide* is to focus on materials in Volume II of *Christian History of the Constitution* by Verna Hall (see above) which tells how and where our Founders discovered and developed the seeds of American unity and union. The principles underlying the choices of our Founding Fathers are stressed, demonstrating their reliance upon a Christian world view. The *Guide* may be used by adults or mature high school students. The use of a notebook as outlined in *The Principle Approach* (by Slater) is strongly recommended. You should also purchase the *Answer Key to Study Guide to the Christian History of the Constitution, Volume II.*

For more help, the *Civics* audio cassette tape by Swanson walks us through the steps of teaching with the *Study Guide*. The tape should make the teaching process easier and save us time.

American History: In Addition to Textbooks
History Games

➲ Hail to the Chief: The Presidential Election Game (Aristoplay) $25

This game reviews American history and helps students understand how our electoral system works. This is a high-quality game with a full-color game board. Questions assume a basic knowledge of United States history. We are a game-playing family, and we have had lots of opportunities to compare various games related to U.S. history. We have found ourselves comparing them all to *Hail to the Chief* because it stands at the top of the list. Some other games can be played by younger players and some cover different topics, so there is never a straight across comparison. But *Hail to the Chief* offers the best combination of questions and playing appeal. While it is recommended for ages 10 and up, two levels of questions allow knowledgeable and less-knowledgeable players to compete fairly. In an unusual setup, the game actually offers two types of play. President questions (personal questions about presidents or events during their administrations) are answered in phase one as players move around the outside edge of the board. When enough points are accumulated, players move to the U.S. map on the inside answering history and geography questions to accumulate enough

points (delegates) to win the election. Great family game. (*Hail to the Chief* was updated in 1995.)(S)

➲ Made for Trade: A Game of Early American Life (Aristoplay) $25

Learn about the history, culture, trades, and economy of colonial America with this outstanding game for ages eight to adult, with four different levels of play.(S)

State History

Some states require students at junior and senior high levels to study state history, so I am including reviews of a few appropriate state history resources I've found. Check with your state or regional home school organization to determine if you have such a requirement in your state and what resource recommendations they might have. Usually, there will be one or two resources that are consistently recommended.

➲ History in Light of the Cross for Arkansas, Minnesota, Missouri, Oklahoma, or Texas (State Histories) student text - $12-$14; teacher's guide - $7; workbook - $7

For each of the above mentioned states, State Histories publishes a junior/senior high state history course that consists of a student text, workbook, and teacher's guide. (They also publish state history studies for the elementary grades for Oklahoma, Colorado, Missouri, Texas, and Arkansas.) These are not polished publications, but comb-bound books printed in black-and-white of about 100-120 pages each. You can see "Principle Approach" influences in the courses: they teach God's providential hand throughout history, they discuss the "westward movement of Christianity," and they require students to create a notebook—all elements common to Principle Approach, although the totality of the work required is not as extensive as we often find in P.A. resources. Content is similar to most state history texts, focusing on geography, development, government, resources, and each state's role in the various wars. However, the biblical Christian viewpoint is prominent in creation/evolution statements, discussions of missionary activity, biographical sketches, etc. Some maps, illustrations, and diagrams enhance the text. The workbooks have completion, matching, true/false, and essay questions, plus an occasional puzzle or activity page. The teacher's guides have quizzes and exams, answer keys, resource lists, field trip ideas, course grading information, notebook instructions, and brief lesson plans. Watch for development of texts for other states' histories from this publisher. The elementary level state history worktexts from State Histories are very similar in content to the high school level books, so you might easily have a younger and older student both working through the same topics in state history at the same time, but doing workbook/worktext activities that are age-appropriate for each [$6 each]. A guide for New Mexico should be ready soon.

➲ Modern Hawaiian History by Dr. Ann Rayson (The Bess Press) hardcover - $34.95; softcover - $19.95; workbook - $7.95; answer key -$9.95

This high school level text is written for students who already have an understanding of U.S. and world history plus a grasp of the basics of economics. It covers the period from the overthrow of the monarchy to the present. Appendices cover early Hawaiian culture, the monarchy, geography, the language, and factual data, so if students have not studied Hawaiian history at an earlier level, this will still provide comprehensive coverage. This book is more readable than most such texts since it is written often in story form rather than as straightforward presentation of the facts. It deals in personalities and conflicts, presenting an unvarnished picture of Hawaii's history. Religion and its influence are not adequately addressed, but aside from that, it does a good job. The workbook follows a somewhat similar format for each chapter. First are quite a few fill-in-the-blank questions first, followed by a vocabulary activity, discussion or essay questions, and suggestions for enrichment activities such as research, reports, interviews, debates, and drawing. You will probably want the answer key to check workbook answers.(SE)

Genealogical Study

➲ Family Treasures version 3.0 [computer program] (Family Technologies) $49.95

Requirements: IBM compatible computer running Windows 3.1 or higher on 386 or faster system with 4MB RAM, a mouse, and 4MB available hard disk memory.

Family Treasures is a program for building a treasury "...of your family's most precious mementos; the history, stories and pictures which make your family truly unique." We can create "...any number of family databases with up to a million members and families each." This program is easy for adults to install and use. Even better, it is a wonderful tool for teaching our children about their family history. The program accommodates detailed information on family members, including lengthy biographies. We can also scan in photos or pictures (assuming we have a scanner). A Family History book can be automatically printed with pictures and biographies included. We can also record a sound clip for each family member (if we have a sound card). We can build our family tree, studying our ancestors in conjunction with each historical era. This is a wonderful, ongoing project to incorporate into our home education. We can work at it sporadically or consistently as best suits our schedule. We can display information as a family tree, as a time line, by families, or for individuals. Parents or older children will need to do the basic installation, then make decisions among the various options. At that point younger children can get involved in data entry. They will also need some assistance accessing information once the family history has been created.

We can share information with those outside our immediate family by providing printouts or sending them data disks. (They need the *Family Treasures* program to read your disk, unless you are sending only sections entered as text files.)

Current Events

The study of current events is essential for informed citizens. Skip the television news reports that are more entertainment than information. Instead read newspapers, news magazines, or weekly publications from God's World Publications.[3]

I believe the newspaper should be an important resource in our curriculum. Teenagers should be studying and analyzing past events, contrasting these with current events from the news. Editorial pages help point up controversial issues if we have trouble identifying them ourselves. While teens are learning historical, geographical, and cultural information through current issues and events, they are also developing and sharpening their thinking skills.

News magazines can also be helpful, but there are better resources available than *Time* and *U.S. News and World Report*. God's World publishes elementary level *God's World News* at five age/grade levels from prekindergarten through ninth grade. The "senior" edition of *God's World News* is written for grades 7 through 9. Teacher's Helper sheets that come with individual orders of *God's World News* give in-depth study ideas for current news topics. These publications are great for younger grade levels, but the most useful of all is *WORLD* magazine, which also comes from God's World Publications. *World* is great for teens and adults, and it covers news events with insightful commentary from a biblical Christian perspective. As far as I'm concerned, every Christian family should subscribe to *World*.

Missionary and evangelistic outreaches also provide wonderful incentives for cultural studies. Supporting a missionary organization and reading their newsletters or magazines gives us a much better picture of particular cultures than we could ever get from textbooks.

Bob Jones University Press brings us up to date in the areas of both science and history with *Current Events for Christian Schools*. There are a Teacher's Resource Guide and Student Activity manual, both updated yearly with the latest developments [teacher's resource guide - $12; student activities -$8]. Text, maps, and charts illustrate many topics. *Current Events* concentrates on topics already covered within the BJUP history and science texts to bring them up to date (similar to encyclopedia year books), so it does not include current events in the same manner as the other resources listed here.

---

3   *God's World News* is published every week through the school year, while *WORLD* magazine is published weekly throughout the year.

For current events from a broader and more comprehensive perspective, check out the *National Public-policy Resource Theme-packets*. These are an unusual resource that can do a great job of turning our older students on to learning. C. Bernard Schriver, an educational and public affairs consultant, has researched many current event topics, summarized background information for us, compiled articles, and suggested activities for student involvement. Schriver says, "Analysis includes contemporary application of the principles of traditional American concepts of individual rights, private property, free markets, and limited Constitutional government." While Schriver's conservative philosophy is usually evident in the analytic material, the articles and other material he includes present a range of viewpoints to encourage thinking.

Some previous topics of *Theme-packets* are "Bi-partisan Commission on Entitlement and Tax Reform," "Clarence Thomas Speaks Out - Two Speeches," "Flat-Rate Tax: An Idea Whose Time Has Come," "Equal Protection For Economic Liberty," "Affirmative Action: An Idea Whose Time Has Gone," "Will Whitewater Be Clinton's Watergate?," "Combatting Terrorism at Home and Abroad," "Religion and the Public Square," "Term Limits -Limited Prospects in Near Future," "America's News Media -Reporting or Distorting the News?," "Balanced-Budget Amendment–Can Victory Be Snatched from the Jaws of Defeat?", "Social Security's Future," and "Gun-Control or Criminal-Control." There are four *Theme-packets* on free-market economics and eight in a Constitutional series entitled "Beyond the Bicentennial/America's Third Century."

Packet prices are $10 each plus postage. We can "subscribe" and receive nine packets for the school year, mailed monthly as they are compiled. However, the cost ($100) might be prohibitive for many families. They can instead purchase only the packets that seem most pertinent to their studies. Another alternative is sharing the cost of the series through a support group or with other families.

The value of these packets lies in the fact that Schriver does the research that most of us do not have time and money to do. He pulls together information and presents it within a context that stimulates students to examine issues on a deeper level than occurs when they simply read through textbooks. Consider using some of these as supplements to history, government, and economics courses or as part of worldview studies.

Mr. Schriver has a free catalog which clearly describes the packets so we can easily identify those most useful for our studies if we choose to purchase them individually.

Test Taking Skills for Social Studies

➲ Mastering Social Studies Skills (Amsco) $13.33 softbound or $19.60 hardcover; answer key - $2.05

This unusual book is not a social studies course, but a resource which teaches some basics of social studies while primar-

ily teaching test-taking skills. The social studies content consists primarily of geography—map reading, latitude and longitude, climate zones, time zones, and the various types of maps. Test-taking skills are not limited to the social studies area, just as most social studies tests do not usually test social studies knowledge as much as they do reading and thinking skills.

These test-taking skills include reading; writing; use of reference tools; reading tables, charts, and graphs; and interpreting photographs, drawings, and cartoons (editorial or political).

Of particular interest to me is the writing section where the book helps students understand the difference between a single sentence answer and a paragraph answer to a question. It shows them how to expand on a brief answer, an important skill to develop for essay questions.

Junior or senior high students who have had little exposure to standardized tests or those who have weak backgrounds in social studies will benefit from this book. It is in worktext format, with many practice exercises on the above topics. I reviewed the softcover edition, but it is also available as a hardback book. Inexpensive answer keys are available.(SE-watch cartoon section particularly for subtle biases.)

Economics

While it might seem a little unusual to follow history resources with economics, my reason for doing so is that many states require one semester each of government and economics, so the two courses are often offered in the same school year, sometimes within the same textbook.

Introductory Economics

➲ Whatever Happened to Penny Candy? [from the "Uncle Eric" series] by Richard J. Maybury (Bluestocking Press) $9.95

For the economically illiterate, begin with the book *Whatever Happened to Penny Candy?*, a simple, entertaining introduction to economics. *Penny Candy* introduces the economic facts of life where they touch us most—continuing increases in the cost of things. The book is written as a series of letters from fictional Uncle Eric to Chris, who could be either his niece or nephew. Uncle Eric explains simply the economic facts of life, adding interesting historical tidbits along the way. Doses of economic theory in each letter are just enough to prod thinking without overload. The author has also included an excellent annotated bibliography with suggestions for where to go next to learn more about economics. A complete study guide is available which includes an economic timeline.

Consider following this book with Richard Maybury's *The Money Mystery: The Hidden Force Affecting Your Career, Business and Investments* and, possibly, *The Clipper Ship Strategy.* (See the review under "More Challenging Resources for Economics.")

Canadians can order a twenty-page supplement to *Penny Candy* that explains the differences between American and Canadian monetary and economic history, which will help Canadian students better understand and apply the principles taught. Order the supplement from Rudiger Krause, WT Educational Services, 12563 Carrs Landing Rd., Winfield, B.C., Canada V4V 1A1, phone (250) 766-0568.(S)

➲ Biblical Economics in Comics (Vic Lockman) $9

Biblical Economics in Comics teaches economic principles in story form with great comic illustrations. As children learn principles of economics, they also find out how government intervention makes a mess of things. At the end, Lockman includes a biblical view of government and economics. Teens and adults will best understand Lockman's views while younger children may simply perceive the book as entertainment.

➲ Financial Study for Teenagers (Crown Ministries) $15; leaders' guide - $10

This Christian financial study was designed for use in small groups of teens ages 13 to 19. However, it will work well with a parent and one teen. There are a few pages of material to read with each lesson, Scripture to memorize, discussion questions, written activities, and a prayer log. The entire course is as much or more about biblical attitudes toward money, life purposes, and relationships as it is about finances. Money is viewed as a "primary competitor with Christ for the lordship of our lives." So it begins with basic spiritual principles, then tackles topics such as debt, financial counsel, honesty, giving, work, saving, and relationships and responsibilities. Students learn practical knowledge and skills such as maintaining a checkbook, creating a budget, writing a resumé, and creating a personal financial statement. As a practical demonstration of our dependence upon God, each student maintains a prayer log in the back of his or her book. The high-quality artwork throughout the student book deserves a mention because it visually enhances the course. We need both the student book (separate student books for each student) and the leader's guide. There is also an optional audio tape for leaders which offers tips on how to lead the study [$6]. This would be a great study for dad to lead.

➲ Get a Grip on Your Money: A Young Adult Study in Christian Financial Management by Larry Burkett (Christian Financial Concepts) student book - $7.50; teacher's edition - $9.50

High school students will find Burkett's approach to personal economics much easier to understand than most textbook presentations. Topics covered from a Biblical perspective are choosing a career, looking for work, resumés, job interviews, budgets, record keeping, checking accounts, loans and credit cards, coping with budget busters, insurance, buying a car, and buying a first home. The student text has reproducible forms/work sheets in the back. A student can work independently, and the thirteen lessons should take about one hour each to complete. As far as I can tell, the Teacher's Guide is not essential for students studying independently, but it is very useful for class instruction with suggestions for presentations, discussions, and

activities. There are quizzes in the student book, but the answer key is found in the back of the student book. Cartoon illustrations that make the book user-friendly, practical illustrations, and solid teaching make this the best resource I have seen for covering these topics with teens.

➲ Money, Banking, and Usury (Vic Lockman) $4

Vic Lockman teaches how banks use fractional reserves to enrich themselves, and how the government creates money. He also covers the subject of debt, including scriptural injunctions against debt. He uses his trademark cartoon presentation format. This book should be understandable for most junior high students and is appropriate for anyone older.

More Challenging Resources for Economics

While regular texts offer adequate coverage of economics, there are far more interesting resources available. I rarely make explicit recommendations, but I think it is quite difficult for most home schooling parents to figure out what to use for economics if they choose not to use a standard text, so I'm making an exception here.

Recommended economics course: Start with *Whatever Happened to Penny Candy?* Next, read Hazlitt's *Economics in One Lesson.* Follow that book with CEBA's *Economics, Freedom & Values* video course, then tackle Clarence Carson's *Basic Economics.* Select other resources such as *The Myth of the Robber Barons, A Bankers' Confession,* and/or Larry Burkett's *The Coming Economic Earthquake* as supplements. You'll need to create your own written assignments and tests.

➲ American Government (BJUP)

This text, reviewed previously, also covers economics. Note that BJUP also has a separate *Economics* text reviewed below.

➲ A Banker's Confession by Gary Sanseri (Back Home Industries) $9.95; study guide - $2.50

This is an easy-reading book about debt, thrift, and wise use of resources from a Christian perspective. Sanseri offers practical suggestions for Christians trying to live by biblical principles in a world which has rejected them. His use of history and stories helps to illustrate and explain his reasoning. Sanseri, a banker by profession, also advocates prepayment of home mortgages, demonstrating mathematically the huge financial savings that can result. This is an excellent book for older students who will soon be involved in the treacherous financial marketplace. I recommend it also to college students and adults. A companion study guide with questions to reinforce and expand ideas in the book is also available.

➲ Basic Economics by Clarence Carson (American Textbook Committee) $16

Some students might want to go beyond the basic introduction to economics that is presented in government and economics texts from A Beka and BJUP. Carson's book draws very much upon history and government for an understanding of economics and, again, reflects a conservative, Christian philosophy, but with a strong emphasis on free enterprise and private property rights. It is recommended only for very capable students or else as a resource text for selected readings. An extensive study guide is included within the book itself.

⮱ The Clipper Ship Strategy by Richard Maybury
(Bluestocking Press) $15.95

The Clipper Ship Strategy, another in the "Uncle Eric" series, should follow *Whatever Happened to Penny Candy?* and *The Money Mystery*. This book covers practical business economics: how to determine what type of businesses to pursue, how to structure those businesses, where to keep your assets, what type of assets to keep, how to develop a dependable customer base, how to keep your business afloat and even prosper when others are going bankrupt, how to identify the best locations for businesses and customers, and much more. Recognizing that our government daily increases its intrusion into the economic functioning of our country, Maybury suggests ways to protect ourselves from the dangers of that intrusion. As Maybury says, just as we might try to protect ourselves from Godzilla on the loose in downtown Tokyo, we must develop a plan to protect ourselves from a Godzilla-like government that might at any moment do something to wreak havoc in our lives and businesses. Written in Maybury's easy-to-understand style, mature teens should be able to handle the reading level. They will need some life experience and motivation to handle the content—possibly their own experience in some sort of business. While Maybury's "lessons" are valuable for everyone, I especially recommend this book to potential entrepreneurs and businessmen. I would make it required reading for them if I could. (Those who might be employees can also find out how to select a career and/or company to work for that is likely to remain economically healthy!) Maybury also includes numerous references to articles that enhance our understanding of the topic. You might not agree with all of Maybury's suggestions, but after reading it, I expect you will know more about the way business *really* works than many business college graduates.(S)

⮱ Economics, Freedom & Values: A Christian View of
Fundamental Economic Issues [video course] (CEBA)
$100 for videos plus study guide; individual videos - $18
each

Seven video tapes, each about 45 minutes long, provide a philosophical grounding in free market economics based on Christian principles. Videos are primarily footage of Dr. Ronald Nash teaching a special class at Liberty University. Nash speaks passionately about the market, capitalism versus socialism, welfare, liberation theology, and human nature, translating dry economic issues into real life decisions. Interviews with others are interspersed throughout the videos, and the entire video on welfare dependence is a lengthy interview with Dr. Walter William. This particular video interview is one of the best summations of the devastating consequences of the welfare state to the poor. Videos are accompanied by a study guide that includes readings

that expand upon each lesson plus discussion questions. I suggest going through the discussion questions first then assigning the readings immediately after watching each video.

I have only one complaint about this program. In both of the last two videos Nash refers to our system as democratic capitalism. I know that he is not the only person using this term, but I dislike the term because it seems highly inaccurate. Democracy implies people voting directly about every issue. Capitalism has nothing to do with who gets to vote, and it certainly doesn't rely upon a majority voting for one expenditure or investment or another. The brochure for the course also describes "...the combination of democracy and our capitalistic economy (free enterprise) [as] the philosophical foundation upon which the practical solutions to almost all political-economic problems and issues must be based." I find this troubling since we live in a constitutional republic rather than a democracy. In spite of that one quibble, I highly recommend this series to be used as a component of your economics course, whether you are already using a textbook or are creating your own course. This series should take about 10 hours including video, readings, and discussion. When you order the complete set, you receive a free subscription to the semiannual journal, *Christian Perspectives.*

⮱ Economics in One Lesson by Henry Hazlitt (Random
House) $10

Although this book was first printed in 1946, it has been reprinted regularly over the intervening years, attesting to its value. The newest edition, published in 1982, has three additional chapters. If students read this book and no others on economics, they would be prepared to deal with practical economic issues. Instead of presenting dry economic theory, Hazlitt explains economic principles through stories and real-life illustrations. Despite the time elapsed since the original writing, the material is not out of date—we can pick up today's paper and find articles illustrating some of the same economic missteps Hazlitt has described. His philosophy is pro-free market and favors limited-government intervention, although he is not a purist. One of the key themes of this book is to look beyond short-term interests to long-term consequences. Economic policies and decisions, according to Hazlitt, must be made with an eye to the long-term, which requires a deeper level of analysis of economic policy than we commonly see. Some of the issues addressed are public works, taxes and their effect on production, tariffs, government bailouts of industry, government price-fixing, minimum wage laws, and inflation. A chapter on rent control was added to the 1979 edition. Although the issues are specialized, together they illustrate a fairly broad view of economics. The second to last chapter, entitled "The Lesson Restated," sums up economic principles. A final chapter, also added in 1979, is "The Lesson after Thirty Years." Hazlitt examines economic policy changes that occurred between 1946 and 1979, and reviews the downward path that the U.S. as well as other countries have followed.

Students should probably be working at junior and senior levels of high school before tackling this book. At that point they should have enough historical background as well as life experience to understand the issues addressed. Students might also need a separate reference book for definitions or fuller explanations of some topics, but otherwise this book serves as the foundation for a topnotch economics course. (ISBN#51754823-2)(S)

⊃ Economics (School of Tomorrow) $57.60 for entire U.S. Civics/Economics course

Economics is half of the one year course in U.S. Civics and Economics. Six of the twelve PACEs cover each subject area, with two answer keys also for each subject. It covers various economic philosophies, emphasizing free-market theory. Biblical principles are also addressed. The book *Economics in One Lesson* is also used as an essential part of the course. You can order it from School of Tomorrow or purchase it on your own. It is also possible for you to order only the PACEs and keys (numbers 3133-3138, 3333, and 3336) for economics.

⊃ Economics for Christian Schools (Bob Jones University Press) $28; teacher's edition - $39; student activity book - $12; teacher edition to activity book - $13; TestBank - $16; AskIt disk - $14

BJUP's new economics text is designed for use at twelfth grade level. It deals with economics in business, government, the marketplace, and the home. The ideas taught reflect free-market philosophy and Christian values, although students do learn about conflicting ideas. Students are introduced to many key people in economics on both philosophical and practical levels through brief biographical sketches. Brief sketches on different countries help us understand global implications of any country's economic policies and choices. Chapter reviews include terms (definitions), content questions, and excellent application questions. The teacher's edition is useful to home schoolers as an answer key, but it also contains margin notes, objectives, activity suggestions including an interesting stock market project, supplementary ideas, a resource directory, and a bibliography. A student activities book, accompanying teacher's edition, *TestBank* (softbound book), and *AskIt* disk are also available.

⊃ Economics: Principles and Policy from a Christian Perspective, Second Edition by Tom Rose (American Enterprise Publications) $22.95; instructor's manual - $8.95

This is a basic economics course from a Christian perspective, written at a challenging level. The book is hardcover and 380 pages long. It focuses on microeconomics—beginning with individual consumers and producers, then moves on to individual markets and the economy. It includes chapters on the Bible and economics; economics and political science; the distribution of income; business organization; supply, demand, and prices. The instructor's manual provides teaching helps and answers to the textbook questions. Recommended for grades 11 or 12.

⊃ Economics: The American Economy from a Christian Perspective by Tom Rose (American Enterprise Publications) $22.95; instructor's manual - $8.95

This is a companion text to the above book, *Economics: Principles and Policy*. It shifts from microeconomics into mac-

roeconomics discussing such topics as labor unions, taxes, public policy, money, the banking system, fiscal policy, international trade, and economic development. It continually brings the issues back to consideration of the biblical viewpoint. The teacher's manual provides teaching helps and answers to the textbook questions.

Also check out AEP's *Free Enterprise Economics* [$2], an 18-page pamphlet that concisely explains free enterprise economics.

⊃ Economics: Work and Prosperity (A Beka) $16.45; teacher guide - $24.65; test book - $3.75; quiz book - $3.95; answer keys to test and quiz books - $8.60 each

This text by the late Dr. Russell Kirk, one of the leading conservative writers in the United States, seems less like a textbook than other A Beka books, probably because it is so well written. Dr. Kirk uses our daily encounters with economics (at the grocery store, the shopping mall, etc.) to illustrate principles. As we would expect from this author, he explains and defends the free enterprise system. Competition, supply and demand, and government influence upon economics are also covered. Discussion questions are interspersed where appropriate rather than at the end of each chapter. The questions are dramatically different from those found in most A Beka texts—they are interesting and relevant. The book is listed in the catalog as a one-semester course for twelfth grade level, but the reading level is appropriate for most high schoolers. The limiting factor is that students must have the familiarity with modern history that is necessary for full comprehension. Consider using this text with A Beka's new *American Government* text since each is a one-semester course.

⊃ Financial Freedom audio cassettes by Jonathan Lindvall (Bold Christian Living) 3-tape album - $17; individual audio tapes - $6 each; videos - $25 each

This three-tape album addresses topics that fall under the "economics" heading even though they are not covered in traditional courses. On the first tape, "Financial Freedom Part One: DEBTLESSNESS," Lindvall discusses the Bible's position on debt, including mortgages, and how we should deal with it. The other two tapes are "Financial Freedom Part Two: SELF-EMPLOYMENT" and "Financial Freedom Part Three: SELF-SUFFICIENCY." Personal experiences, biblical directives, and practical motivations lead Lindvall to recommend self-employment as a preferable means for Christians to earn a living, although he admits that there are times when it is neither possible nor practical. He discusses the tension between the desires for security and freedom. These tapes, especially "DEBTLESSNESS," are a must for parents and teens alike.[Josh Duffy/CD]

⊃ Government and Economics (A Beka)

See description earlier in this chapter. The viewpoint is Christian and supports the free market.

⊃ **The Great Economic Thinkers** [audio cassettes]
(Knowledge Products, available through Bluestocking Press)
$17.95 per two-tape set
    See review in Chapter Five under "Economics."

⊃ **Larry Burkett books**
    The Coming Economic Earthquake (Moody Press) [$11.99],
Surviving the 90's Economy (Moody Press) [$3.99], *Investing
for the Future* (Chariot Victor Publishing) [hardcover -$17.99;
paperback - $10.99], and other books by Larry Burkett offer a
Christian outlook upon our shaky economic situation. The contents of many of Burkett's books overlap each other, so it is not
necessary to read all of them. Teens can choose topics that are of
most interest.
    The Coming Economic Earthquake predicts a rather dismal
economic future based upon factors such as the deficit, financial
shortcomings on state and local levels, the savings and loan collapse, personal debt, social security's likely shortfall, stock market cycles, and foreign loans. He suggests strategies for
Christians such as becoming debt free and changing investments. The book includes a very practical list of helpful resources.
    Surviving the 90's Economy reviews many of the causes of
economic decline mentioned above plus others. Then Burkett offers broader coverage of solutions and strategies for government,
business, and family to manage in tough times.
    Investing for the Future focuses in on investment strategy.
While it reviews some common Burkett themes such as becoming debt free, it goes much further in personal financial planning.
Of particular interest to teens should be his suggestions for the
first "financial season of life" where he addresses situations
faced by young couples. (Parents should be interested in the specific advice Burkett offers.)
    Teens interested in financial careers will find any of these
books very helpful as a Christian balance to the typical education
in economics and financial planning.

⊃ **The Money Mystery: The Hidden Force Affecting Your
Career, Business and Investments** by Richard Maybury
(Bluestocking Press) $8.95
    As in *Whatever Happened to Penny Candy?*, Richard May-
bury uses the same format of "Uncle Eric" writing letters to
"Chris" to explain how money supply and control works. While
Penny Candy introduces economic basics, this book focuses on
narrower aspects of economics that few people recognize yet under which everyone suffers. Maybury addresses inflation, paper
money, the gold supply, interest rates, and "velocity" with real-
life examples such as the Carter Administration's runaway inflation and the run on the dollar that resulted from the U.S. freeze of

Iranian assets in retaliation for the Ayatollah Khomeini's seizure
of the American embassy and 52 hostages. While the concept
level is a large step beyond *Penny Candy*, the presentation is still
at a level that most older teens can understand. While I might use
Penny Candy in Junior High, I would probably save this book
until the last few years of high school. The book is actually directed at older students and adults as one might guess from Maybury's inclusion of recommendations of where to keep your
economic assets at the end of the book. (Note: My recommendation of this book does not include an endorsement of Maybury's
investment strategies.)(S)

⊃ **The Myth of the Robber Barons** by Burton W. Folsom, Jr.
(Young America's Foundation) $9.95
    This is a great book. The author divides entrepreneurs into
the two categories of market and political entrepreneurs. Political entrepreneurs depend on the government for financial backing, political favors, real estate bargains, etc., while market
entrepreneurs rely on the free market to accomplish their ends.
The author shoots down the traditional lumping together of nine-
teenth- and twentieth-century capitalists under the description
"robber barons" by pointing out the differences in approach between an honest businessman and a businessman who uses the
government to "steal" from others. Presented in biographical
story fashion, the book makes interesting reading, although the
closing chapter (where the author attempts to sum things up) is
superfluous. Key figures featured in the book are Cornelius Van-
derbilt, James J. Hill, The Scrantons, Charles Schwab, John D.
Rockefeller, and Andrew Mellon. My thanks to Anne Beams, a
terrific historian and economist from San Diego, for bringing
this book to my attention.

⊃ **Principles of Economics** by Paul A. Goedecke, M.A.
(available through Landmark Distributors) about $25
    Paul Goedecke tackles the subject of economics from the
Principle Approach. He begins with a biblical view of economics, then reviews the history of economic thought. In the next
section he covers microeconomics topics we typically find in
economics texts. In the final section he discusses the relationship
between government and the economy. I reviewed a preliminary
version of this book, so there might be some changes. However,
Goedecke's approach always returns the issue to the biblical
principles involved. Thus we find a condemnation of government creation of fiat money as a power issue which denies the
sovereignty of God. Goedecke explains the difference between
charging interest on money used for investment and interest on
loans to the legitimately poor which is prohibited in Scripture.
This is not nearly as intimidating as it sounds; although it covers
a lot of territory, it moves quickly and is very interesting.

Science

Junior High Science: Preparing for High School

Students should have a solid foundation in basic science concepts when they enter ninth grade. Generally these concepts are presented within the categories of life, physical, and earth science plus general science skills. The following are the most important concepts that should have been covered:

– scientific method

> Scientific method means an understanding of the principles of how to study science—how to ask questions, how to pose possible answers, how to test those answers, how to record and interpret the results, and how to pose follow-up questions. Scientific method is essentially logical thinking and recording of information. It need not be any more difficult than doing an experiment with seed growth under different conditions, recording results, and suggesting reasons for the recorded results.

– classification

– environments/ecosystems

– water cycle

– weather/climate/atmosphere

– plants (characteristics, reproduction, growth)

– animals (characteristics, reproduction, growth)

– human body (including health topics if not covered separately)

– geology (land forms, rocks, minerals, erosion, and movement)

– solar system

– simple machines

– basic physical forces (e.g., gravity, motion, friction)

– magnetism

– electricity

– heat energy/solar energy

– states of matter

– atomic structure (introduction)

– applications of physics in technology

– important scientists through history

If one or more of the above areas are weak, choose materials or activities that will help fill the learning gap so that students will be prepared for high school science.

Personalized Science Curriculum

At the high school level, the question of what topics to cover is easier to answer than for elementary and junior high levels. (See "Meeting Requirements" under "High School Level" later in this chapter.) However, I have been encouraging parents of children in the elementary grades and, sometimes, junior high to avoid science textbooks and to, instead, opt for real books, experiments, and field trips on topics of their choosing. This avoids the mile wide, inch deep coverage typical of most textbooks. Our children get to focus on subjects in which they are interested each year (as much as possible) rather than studying whatever comes next in the textbook. More hands-on activity combined with experiments and observation results in better knowledge and comprehension of topics covered. This approach becomes a form of unit study with the unit centering around a science topic and sometimes including activities in other areas of the curriculum. This approach CAN be used for high school subjects, often resulting in far more interesting and worthwhile courses, but it requires much more work on the part of parents.

At whatever level, if you follow this approach, you are then faced with the problem, "If I don't use a text, how will I know if I'm covering what I need to?" There are two great resources to help you answer that question.

➲ Teaching Science and Having Fun! by Felice Gerwitz (Media Angels Science) $12.95

Felice Gerwitz outlines topics that need to be covered at various grade levels (K-3, 4-8, 9-12) in general terms rather than the specifics Kathryn Stout offers in *Science Scope*. Felice shows us how to create a topical study or comprehensive unit study based upon a science topic. She stresses the importance of knowing and applying scientific method at all grade levels, emphasizing the vital role that experiments play in learning scientific method. Because of this, Felice offers extensive suggestions for creating lab activities for high school level science, including lots of budget-conscious substitutes. She adds resource lists with commentary so that we can find other resources to flesh out our courses. *Teaching Science and Having Fun!* addresses the big picture (Why teach science? How do we teach children of differing ages? What topics do we cover?) and problem areas (What kind of microscope should I buy? How can I create a chemistry lab at home?) rather than attempting to offer complete course outlines. This is a very inspiring, practical, and helpful resource for teaching science to children of all ages.

➲ Science Scope by Kathryn Stout (Design-A-Study) $15

Even if we are willing to abandon the textbook approach, many of us feel insecure determining at what level our child should be working on a science topic. Does making a model of the body systems equally satisfy learning needs of both a seven-year-old and a fifteen-year-old? Probably not. Kathryn Stout's *Science Scope* helps us identify appropriate activities for different age groups within each science area. This is an extremely useful resource. Divided into four main areas—general science, life science, earth science, and physical science—it takes specific topics under each heading, then suggests methods to use with students at primary, intermediate, junior, and senior high levels. It offers more detail in this area than does *Teaching Science and Having Fun!* Science *Scope makes* it easier to select appropriate resources for whatever topic is chosen for study.

Science and the Principle Approach

Science can also be taught using the Principle Approach. Students create notebooks as they "4 R" the subject. (See the Principle Approach description in Chapter 6.) The methodology for this approach is described in James Rose's *A Guide to American Christian Education for the Home and School*, and it is outlined in even more detail in Daniel and Susan Eby's *Natural Science for Home Schooling Families: A Principle Approach Guide for the American Christian Curriculum* (Patria Ministries) [$15]. As with other such guides by various authors, this one begins with an overview of the Principle Approach. How-

Science Fair Projects

The Complete Handbook of Science Fair Projects by Julianne Blair Bochinski (John Wiley and Sons) $14.95

Part I of this 206-page book discusses science fairs and projects, how to select a topic and get started with your research, the important elements in choosing and conducting an appropriate experiment, proper display, and elements of judging.

Part II presents 50 award-winning science fair projects that are all within the realm of possibility for junior high and high school students. The appendices list sample science subject areas to assist students in creating their own topics to research, a comprehensive list of scientific supply companies by geographic location, and a list of the International Science and Engineering Fair Affiliates by state.

This book provides a realistic and wholly achievable challenge for parents who might consider having their students concentrate on several high quality science experiments over their homeschooling science career. This will allow the student to experience the entire lab experience from creating a worthwhile experiment using the scientific method, all the way through writing up the conclusions and presenting these conclusions for others to evaluate and appreciate.

International Science and Engineering Fair

For information about the International Science and Engineering Fair (mentioned above) and its affiliates who also host numerous state and local competitions, contact Science Service, the national, nonprofit organizing host.

The Complete Science Fair Handbook by Anthony D. Fredericks and Isaac Asimov (Good Year Book) $9.95

Everything we need to put on a science fair is included here. Instructions are given for teachers, parents, and students. There are tips on how to make your science fair a success, timetables for planning, suggestions for projects by grade levels, chapters on conducting research and the scientific method, ideas for presenting and displaying projects, criteria and forms for judging, and more. Even if there is no science fair, students can work on science projects on their own using guidelines and ideas from this book.

Science Fair Project Handbook by Felice Gerwitz (Media Angels Science) $5

This 26-page booklet is a guide for those who intend to compete in science fairs beyond your local home school group. It alerts us to the requirements for fairs run by groups such as the ISEF so that students can follow the proper guidelines for competition. The booklet covers choosing a project, planning, finding information, the display, the written presentation (when appropriate), and resources for further information. Given, the size of the booklet, information is limited. Felice recommends books like *The Complete Handbook of Science Fair Projects* for those who need more specifics.

A Science Project (A Beka) $6.95

This is a resource book offering step-by-step explanation of scientific investigation, research papers, presentations, and science fair exhibits. Recommended for grades 7 - 12 for projects.

The Ultimate Science Project Notebook (Castle Heights Press) $9.95

Subtitled "Ideas for Truly Great Science Projects," the goal of this little, thirty-four page book is to help students come up with truly interesting projects that stimulate real learning. A secondary goal is to offer unusual ideas that have not been done hundreds of times before. There are forty-five project ideas described here. Some of the ideas have to do with electronics. (Some of these require building your own radio frequency detector or light meter.) A few of the ideas: using the light meter to test the reflectivity of light off of plant leaves which would be related to productivity of the plant in areas with limited light exposure; determining the bursting strength of chip packages, ketchup packets, or hot sauce bags; designing an energy 'clean' house; and a comparison of hacksaw blade construction and durability.

Basic science project information and a planning chart are included, although this information presented here is less extensive than that found in other books. You will want this book for the ideas and perhaps another one for more help on organization and presentation.

ever, most of the book outlines a course of study for natural science for grades K-12 which is based upon the six days of creation. The general order is (day 1) physics and chemistry, (day 2) meteorology and oceanography, (day 3) geology and botany, (day 4) astronomy, (day 5) zoology, and (day 6) zoology, human anatomy and physiology. This progression is used in a spiraling fashion throughout the school years. For grades 7-9, it is suggested that students begin the study again (this then being the fourth cycle following the suggested progression). At seventh grade level they would cover chemistry, physics, meteorology and oceanography; at eighth they cover geology, botany, and astronomy; and at ninth, they cover zoology, anatomy, and physiology. Chemistry, physics, and biology each receive a year's attention for the last three years. Outlines for each grade level are general, because they refer us to A Beka and BJUP science texts for the information itself. But the texts are used as resources from which teachers glean information. Chapters are selected and rearranged to suit our purposes. For example, at seventh grade we need both BJUP *Basic Science* and *Earth Science* as the primary resources. For eighth grade, we again need BJUP *Earth Science* as well as BJUP *Biology for Christian Schools*. Essentially, this is a unit study approach which can be used to teach children at various grade levels, covering the same material at whatever depth is appropriate for each. Additional books and resources for activities and experiments are also recommended. This book is only 109 pages long, but it offers a significantly different approach to teaching science which many of us might wish to explore.

Junior High, Recommended Texts

⮑ Earth Science [revised, second edition text and Teacher's Edition] (BJUP) $28; teacher's edition - $39; activity book - $12; teacher's edition for activity book - $18; test packet - $7/answer key - $4; TestBank - $16; AskIt disk -$14

This is a well-written book with interesting and worthwhile activities. However, the scope and sequence seems to be different from many other earth science texts with more emphasis on astronomy and less on topics such as oceanography than is typical. Purchase both the student text and the activity book for experiments and exercises. Since most of the experiments can be done at home, but not necessarily indoors, it is practical for home schoolers to use. Teacher's editions for both the text and the activity book are available. It is written for eighth grade level, but could be used for junior or senior high (although not as a college prep lab class). If the activities do not fit your needs or if you want super-comprehensive lab work already laid out for you, consider substituting lab activities from Science Labs-in-a-Box. You have a choice of testing instruments: *Test Bank*, test packet, or *AskIt* computer program.

⮑ Investigating God's Orderly World 1 (Rod and Staff) $14.15; teacher edition - $9.50; tests - $1.65

This is part one of a basic science course covering life, physical, and earth science topics. Unit topics include the definitions of science, astronomy, gravity, heat energy, weather, planet earth, life on earth, fire, parasitic diseases, food and digestion, and agriculture. Study and review exercises are included in the student book. Some experiments are described in the text. The teacher's guide suggests teaching methods, lists equipment needed, and serves as an answer key. Test booklets are also available. Like other Rod and Staff science books, it glorifies God as Creator, relating science to Scripture throughout. This text is suitable for grades 7-8.

⮑ Investigating God's Orderly World 2 (Rod and Staff) $14.15; teacher edition - $9.50; tests - $1.65

This is part two of a basic science course. Topics covered include light, sound, the body, behavior, work and machines, energy and engines, principles of chemistry, elements, electricity and magnetism, reproduction and heredity, and care of the body. Study and review exercises are included in the student book. Some experiments are described in the text. The teacher's guide suggests teaching methods, lists equipment needed, and serves as an answer key. Test booklets are also available. This text should be used for eighth grade or else following the first volume (*Investigating God's Orderly World*) to provide comprehensive coverage of science.

⮑ Life Science 1997 edition (Bob Jones University Press) $28; teacher's edition - $39; student activity book - $12; teacher edition for student activity book - $17; prepared slide set - $37.95

This book covers many topics also covered in high school biology but at less challenging levels, requiring less vocabulary mastery. BJUP's description reads: "Discusses science and its relationship to the Word of God, examining the attributes of life, classification, cells, and biblical creation. Deals with such subjects as the life processes of organisms, genetics, and biological evolution. Presents concepts in microbiology, plant biology, and zoology, including reproduction. Looks at ecosystems, interrelationships among organisms, and a biblical perspective of man's stewardship of the earth. Concludes with a discussion of the human body and its basic structure and function." Human reproduction is treated in a special chapter within the teacher's edition. In contrast to high school level texts, this book is heavily illustrated with over 500 color photos.

You should purchase the teacher's edition for the text which has reduced student pages with answers and marginal notes. It also helps you correlate the activities from the student activity book. The student activity book suggests many worthwhile activities to enhance the lessons. Most of these are practical for home schoolers, although they will require quite a few supplies. To help with lab work, you might want to use the dissecting kit and instructions available from either Nasco or BJUP, and you might want to purchase the prepared slide set with 9 prepared slides, 3 blank slides, and a storage box.

Another option for lab work is the Science Labs-in-a-Box. (See the description below.)

➲ Life Science Work-Text (Amsco) $12; answer key - $1.90

This life science book (order #N 567 W) is an easier option than the BJUP *Life Science*. First of all, it is a worktext with instruction, lab activities, and questions all in one book. Each unit begins with lab activity. These include such things as microscope work, dissecting, fairly simple chemistry experiments, plant activities, physical tests, and growing cultures. Most of these should pose little difficulty for home use, although they require the acquisition of a microscope, specimens, and a minimal amount of lab equipment. Questions and charts for data recording are included with the lab activities.

Instruction is not as comprehensive as in the BJUP text, although it will be sufficient for junior high and, in some cases, for senior high.

Topics range from cells through a wide range of plants and animals, the human body (studied by body systems as well as under other headings), reproduction, heredity, genetics, energy for living things, food production, ecology, and conservation.

The book is illustrated, primarily with black-and-white line drawings. It is softbound and printed on inexpensive paper, both of which keep the cost very reasonable. We will need the answer key which is also very inexpensive.

The emphasis on lab activity (and the fact that it is right there at the beginning of each unit) makes this a good choice for Wiggly Willys who need hands-on involvement.

Evolutionary content offers some problems throughout the book, and particularly in a discussion about dinosaurs. The dinosaur feature is one of a number of "Science, Technology and Society" features scattered throughout the book. These are the most likely to expose worldview clashes such as the evolution/creation debate, and they can either be omitted or used for discussion without detracting from the course.(SE)

➲ Matter and Motion in God's Universe [1994 edition] (A Beka) $14.50; teacher edition - $20; Curriculum with Lab Demonstrations - $20; test booklet - $4.90; activity booklet - $2.85; booklet answer keys - $8.60 each

(You should first read the review of *Science: Order and Reality* that appears below.) Since this is the sequel to *Science: Order and Reality*, use both books to provide a thorough introduction to various areas of science. While *Matter and Motion* seems to lack the humorous touches of *Order and Reality*, it is still an improvement over the previous edition, primarily because it has been simplified to keep students from being overwhelmed by too much detailed information. Like *Order and Reality*, questions are much improved with the inclusion of "Thought Provokers." While there are some experiments within the student text, the *Curriculum with Lab Demonstrations* covers much more. Topics covered in *Matter and Motion* include astronomy, motion, birds (including bird watching), magnetism, electricity, and creation versus evolution. You will want the teacher edition for the student text. You might also want to purchase the student test book-

let and/or the student quiz booklet and their accompanying answer keys.

This book is more than one hundred pages shorter than *Order and Reality* since it is intended to be used for only one semester. The second semester is set for use of A Beka's eighth-grade health text, *Let's Be Healthy*.

➲ Science: Order and Reality [1993 edition] (A Beka) $15.95; teacher edition - $24.20; test booklet - $4.10; quiz booklet -$4.35; booklet answer keys - $8.60 each

This book should be thought of as part one of a two-year science course for seventh and eighth grades. Part two is contained in the A Beka text, *Matter and Motion*. Reviews are of the revised editions, which differ significantly from the previous editions. Because the two books are closely related, I discuss common features here.

These books have been completely rewritten to make them more "user-friendly." The slightly larger format and larger type style make them easier to read. New illustrations, hands-on experiments, a colorful format, and touches of humor make the new *Science: Order and Reality* more appealing to the average seventh-grade student. (*Matter and Motion* is a little more sober in content.) A complaint about the earlier editions was that questions were almost exclusively of the rote-recall variety. Now, chapter reviews in both books include "Thought Provokers" as well as some recall-type questions.

The topics covered in both books have been revised and rearranged, so much so that it will not work to use a new edition of one text and an old edition of the other. Gone from the old edition of *Order and Reality* are the chapters on farming, radio, and television. Astronomy is still covered, but in a briefer and more accessible form in *Matter and Motion*. The extensive section on the human body has been dropped from *Matter and Motion*, and, instead, the subject is covered in a single chapter of *Order and Reality*. New material has been added; *Order and Reality* now has a chapter on insects with instructions for making a collection. Both books have chapters discussing creation versus evolution. Other chapter topics in *Order and Reality* are plants, atmosphere, weather, climate, physical science, cells, and classification. You will probably want to purchase the teacher edition for answers, and you might also want the student test and/or student quiz booklets and their accompanying answer keys.

The A Beka health text, *A Healthier You*, is intended to complete the science curriculum for seventh grade. It should take about eight weeks of the school year time allotted to science.

➲ Science LifePacs [700 - 7th grade level or 800 - 8th grade level] (Alpha Omega) $41.95 per grade level

Alpha Omega presents each year's program in ten LifePacs per subject. You also need the teacher handbook for each level which is usually sold separately. The teacher handbook contains basic instructions for using the curriculum, tests, discussion topics and questions, answers, and activities—all of which are important for a complete course. Topics covered in 700 for seventh grade are tools and methods of science, science careers, measurement and graphing, astronomy, the sun, the moon, the atmosphere, weather and climate, and the human body. Topics in 800 for eighth grade are science and society, the structure of matter, health and nutrition, energy, machines, balance in nature, and science and technology.

➲ Technology (Creative Learning Systems, Inc.)
See review under high school level "Technology."

Extras or Supplements

➲ AC/DC: The Exciting Electric Circuit Game (Ampersand Press) $9.95

Introduce the principles of electric circuitry with this game, and I guarantee students will understand it better than if they try to get it from a textbook. The circuitry concepts are fairly basic—series or parallel circuits, power sources, switches, wiring, fuses, and energy users. An extra sheet which sums up the basic information (titled "What You Always Wanted to Know about Electricity But Were Afraid to Ask") is included. Diagrams of workable and unworkable circuits also help us figure some of this out. "Shock" and "Short" cards are included to keep the play interesting, although neither is really explained.

Three, twelve- to thirteen-year-old boys figured out how to play the game in about ten minutes on their own and gave it a thumbs up for fun. That means the rules are easily decipherable, and the game playing aspect is strong enough that they will play it more than once—something I can't say about many educational games.

➲ AIMS Education Foundation Program $16.95 each

AIMS (Activities Integrating Math and Science) produces materials that integrate mathematics, science, and other disciplines through activity-oriented learning. Fun projects allow students to experience science in action, while they also learn about other subject areas.

For example, students use topographical maps (two-dimensional) to construct models (three-dimensional) of Mount St. Helens before and after the 1980 eruption. Through this activity students learn how to transfer information from two to three dimensions while learning about changes in the earth. Another example of an AIMS activity has to do with the amount of popped corn obtained from various brands of popping corn. As students proceed, they learn about ratio, volume, value-for-cost, etc.

Each AIMS book contains a thorough teacher text and reproducible student pages for activities, information, and recording data from the activities. Books are offered covering various grade levels, but our interest here is with the oldest level of books covering grades 5-9. There are books on topics such as aerodynamics, food, flight, mapping, and the human body. These are great for all students, but particularly good for students who struggle with both math and science, since the fun activities provide positive experiences in those subject areas as well as real life application of math and science skills.

Many activities are time consuming, so plan a special time each week (such as Friday afternoons), gather a group, and have some fun with math and science. (S)

➲ Circle of Learning Workbooks™ series by Debby Willett (Circle of Learning Workbooks) $5.95 and up

Debby Willett has developed eight books thus far in her series of workbooks designed to accompany titles from Usborne. She tells us, "My focus in these workbooks has been to take a secular book (Usborne) and present it as a tool from a Christian perspective that can be used in a variety of ways to enhance your homeschool teaching. For example, as a test bank over material studied; reinforcement of knowledge learned; documentation for those states that require it; comprehension checks; reinforcement of writing skills; and even in unit studies." Each workbook is about 25 to 30 pages long, and a separate answer key is included for each. Questioning methods are varied to appeal to different learning styles—multiple choice, fill-in-the-blank, true/false, complete sentence answers, and short essays. Questions address various levels of thinking from recall and comprehension up through more challenging comparison/contrast and drawing conclusions exercises. Students are often directed to compare biblical viewpoints with material presented in the Usborne books on topics such as evolution. These workbooks will be extremely helpful for those who like the "real book" approach but want more accountability for student learning. Titles of the eight workbooks presently available are followed by the companion Usborne book title in parentheses: *CLW Vikings (Who Were the Vikings?*—this one is probably too young for junior high and is the only non-science topic thus far), *CLW Earthquakes (Earthquakes & Volcanoes), CLW Weather (Weather & Climate), CLW Archaeology (Archaeology), CLW Scientists (Scientists), Seas (Seas & Oceans), CLW Inventors (Inventors),* and *CLW Explorers (Explorers).*

➲ Constellation Station game (Aristoplay) $25

Constellation Station is Aristoplay's solution for making the study of astronomy fun and interesting. The game consists of a colorful board, markers of various sizes, and cards with astronomical data for each of the constellations in the northern sky. Players move around the board, acquiring constellations by naming the star group and/or reciting facts about it, and paying rent when they land on a constellation "owned" by another player.

As in other Aristoplay games, *Constellation Station* offers play at various levels within the same game. The first two levels were not very interesting or challenging, and to progress to the other levels, students need to already have some knowledge of astronomy. The game would probably be best used in conjunction with a unit on astronomy. However, if you are willing to bend the rules to suit your family's needs, *Constellation Station* would be useful in several areas. Its most obvious use is in simply learning to recognize the shapes of the constellations. The accompanying cards contain both historical and astronomical data so the varying interests of different students can be accommodated.(S)[Kath Courtney]

⮑ Creative Learning Systems, Inc.

Their *Transtech* catalog features books, software, and kits for science topics. (See the description under "Sources for Materials.") Students interested in technology should check out their *Technology* textbook, *Collins CDT* (craft, design, and technology) series, or the *Design and Technology Video Series*.(S)

⮑ The Exploratorium Science Snackbook series (John Wiley and Sons) $10.95 each

The four titles in this series are *The Magic Wand and Other Bright Experiments on Light and Color, The Cheshire Cat and Other Eye-Popping Experiments on How We See the World, The Spinning Blackboard and Other Dynamic Experiments on Force and Motion,* and *The Cool Hot Rod and Other Electrifying Experiments on Energy and Matter.* The San Francisco Exploratorium is one of the world's best hands-on science museums for children. In this series, teachers have adapted Exploratorium exhibits and demonstrations for children to recreate at home. Topics range over the areas of chemistry, physics, and life science, but visual effects seem to be an important part of many activities. Each project has clear directions with illustrations of both the original Exploratorium exhibit and the homemade version. Scientific explanations follow each activity. I appreciate the fact that the explanations are easy to understand, using analogies to familiar phenomena and occasional illustrations. For those of an investigative bent, there are often follow-up activities under the heading "Etc."

These projects range from simple to very complicated—learning about air with a hair dryer and a ping pong ball on the easy end as compared to a gravity experiment using clear plastic, rigid-walled tube, rubber stoppers, copper tubing, vacuum tubing, vacuum pump, and clamps. Most materials for projects can be obtained at places such as hardware and toy stores, although you might have to obtain some items from sources listed in the book's resource guide, found in the back. Remember that these projects were designed by teachers for classroom use, so many are more complicated than what a single family might tackle at home. (Consider doing some of the more complicated or expensive projects with home school groups.) Some projects require some serious power tool usage for cutting wood to precise measurements or routing work, offering an excellent challenge for older students. Science concepts will be most easily understood by students at junior high level or older, although younger children can certainly begin to understand some scientific principles. With 96 experiments in the series, there are plenty of challenging projects for older students. Some of these projects might even provide "jumping off" ideas for science fair projects.

Check out the Exploratorium's online catalog at http://www.exploratorium.edu for other unusual science resources.(SE)

⮑ Facts, Not Fear: A Parent's Guide to Teaching Children About the Environment by Michael Sanera and Jane Shaw (Regnery Publishing, Inc.) $14.95

Christians tend to reject most environmental education resources because they embody animistic or pantheistic worldviews combined with pseudo-science. (Christians shouldn't be the only ones rejecting this nonsense!) Assuming that most young people have been exposed to quite a bit of environmental misinformation, Sanera and Shaw try to set the record straight. While acknowledging the reality of some environmental problems, they balance popularly-held concepts with scientific fact and logical analysis to put things into proper perspective. For example, they tackle global warning by examining the records of temperature change (acknowledging about .5 degree Celsius change over the past 100 years); discussing mathematical computer-generated models; pointing out questionable and unlikely assumptions within those models; addressing common questions; and suggesting activities, field trips, and additional reading. This is a resource book for parents to use with children of all ages, but it will be extremely helpful for teen research papers or projects. Since *Facts, Not Fear* was not intended for only Christian audiences, it does not address the spiritual worldview issues except for a brief mention that this is an issue to consider. Assuming that most children attend government schools, the authors frequently refer to texts used in those schools. They also provide two lists of "environmental" books—one list of books to avoid, and the other of books to add to your library.(S)

⮑ Hands-On Science! (Prentice Hall) $24.95

This science activity book differs from most others with its strong emphasis on practical application. It discusses current science issues without taking the extreme liberal position so prevalent in other non-Christian science books. While there are probably still a few points where Christians will take exception (e.g., lesson on genetic engineering), overall, the book is well-balanced. There are 112 activities, designated for various age groupings from fourth through eighth grades. The section headings reflect the content of the book accurately. Some of these headings are Creating an Atmosphere of Science-in-Action in the Classroom, Science for Living, Using the Process Approach in Science, Developing Scientific and Technological Literacy and Competency, Science/Societal Issues, and Personal Aspects of Science. Examples of some activities/experiments are identifying chemical food additives, tracking air pollution, and analyzing muscle fatigue. Some unusual materials are required (houseflies, copper tubing, petri dishes, heavy art paper) but nothing that is extremely difficult or expensive. The book assumes a classroom set up, with students working in groups, so they sometimes suggest resources such as "freezing units" and "hot plates" for which we can easily substitute freezers and stove tops. Detailed instructions are easy-to-follow, and activities are followed by analysis and discussion. Some reproducible student recording pages are included. Reluctant science students might be turned on when they experience these science activities that really relate to life.(S)

⊃ **The Human Body (#IF8754) (Instructional Fair) $10.95**

The Human Body is a reproducible book of work sheets, suggested for grades 5-8, but also useful for a low-level junior or senior high school course. It serves as a supplement for studying the human body, which reinforces learning through coloring, labeling, puzzles, and other activities. Most of the work sheets involve identification, but some also deal with function and purpose. Drawings are detailed, yet not cluttered, since they do not include everything that we would find in books for older levels. There are 100 different work sheet activities, and an answer key is in the back of the book.(S)

⊃ **Lyrical Life Science, Volumes 1 and 2 (Lyrical Learning)** each text, tape, and workbook set - $25.50; text and tape only - $19.95; additional workbooks - $5.95

Teacher Doug Eldon struggled to get his sixth graders to remember life science vocabulary and concepts until he hit upon the idea of putting the information to music. The result was a recording of eleven life science songs, professionally recorded with a variety of instruments by Bobby Horton, well-known for his historical ballads. Songs on Volume 1 of *Lyrical Life Science* pack an amazing amount of detail into lyrics set to popular tunes like "Dixie," "Clementine," and "Yankee Doodle." For example, "Oh Bacteria" is set to the tune of "Oh Susanna" and begins:

"Oh lacking any nucleus, you do have a cell wall
You live in water, air and soil and anywhere at all...."

The meter and phrasing occasionally leaves something to be desired, but you can't beat this approach for liveliness. You can't help laughing when you try to sing along to "Algae and fungi, lichen, moss and liverworts...." Topics Volume 1 addresses include scientific method, living things, invertebrates, coldblooded vertebrates, birds, classification, algae/fungi/nonvascular plants, vascular plants, protozoa, genetics, viruses, and bacteria.

Volume 2 - Mammals, Ecology, and Biomes, uses tunes like "Erie Canal," "The Yellow Rose of Texas," and "Irish Washerwoman" to teach about bats, carnivores, insectivores, pinnepeds, ecology, biomes toothless mammals, manatees, whales, dolphins, and single-family orders. You won't have to wade through evolutionary nonsense.

Along with each tape comes a textbook which expands upon the information summarized in the songs. The textbooks, about 100 pages each, are generously illustrated with line drawings and touches of humor. They include song lyrics and simple music. The corresponding workbook lessons offer matching, fill-in-the-blank, essay, and labeling exercises. Answer keys are at the back. Although originally written for sixth graders, the content reflects some of what we find in typical high school life science texts. Whatever level you choose to use these for, they remain supplements rather than comprehensive courses. While this approach is not for all students, it does offers a rare alternative for auditory learners when it comes to science.

⊃ **Physical Science Activities for Grades K-8 (Prentice Hall) $28.95**

Over 170 activities are presented in this 264-page book. The activities are generally quite simple and easy to do at home with minimal preparation. Junior high students with little background can learn basic principles of physical science through the experiments and activities. The first section of the book, called "Starter Ideas" is designed to arouse curiosity as well as to stimulate thinking. For example, the first activity is the challenge of separating intermixed salt and pepper. The remaining sections focus on topical areas of physical science: the nature of matter, energy, light, sound, simple machines, magnetism, static electricity, and current electricity. If we want to tie activities to topics in a textbook, there is a concepts/skills index at the front of the book so that we can easily locate an activity to demonstrate the concept being studied. Activity descriptions are very straightforward-a list of materials needed, procedure, and teacher information/explanation. Junior high students should be able to follow the instructions on their own for many of the activities.(S)

⊃ **Science Labs-in-a-Box (Science Labs-in-a-Box, Inc./Science Projects)** monthly cost for 1-2 students - $87.50-$97.50; cost decreases dramatically for additional students

Mike Bolinsky of Science Projects has created *Science-Labs-in-a-Box* to accompany Bob Jones University Press science texts (or texts from other publishers covering the same science topics) for elementary grades through junior and senior high. Thus far labs available for junior and senior high are Earth Science, Life Science, Physical Science, Biology, and Chemistry. Labs need not be used at the specified grade levels for the BJUP texts. The labs are the result of classes designed by Mike for hundreds of home schoolers in Texas. Students purchase and use the BJUP science textbooks or another appropriate text, then use the lab videos and experiments to complete each course. For Chemistry, a text is supplied with the materials. If you use the BJUP texts, Science Labs-in-a-Box will provide a list of reading assignments that follows along with their lab program. Students will get far more from this combination of lab and text study than they would in most any classroom. There are a total of 30-32 labs per course, divided into eight separate kits with four lab sessions each. There are eight to sixteen video tapes per course plus student handouts and lab equipment we use on a "rental" basis. The kits arrive one per month, covering four labs per kit.

The professionally-filmed videos show Mike presenting lessons to a class. This is not simply a "how to do lab work" approach, but a comprehensive, Christian approach to real science. Students perform numerous experiments and activities with the equipment. The high-quality equipment (valued at about $2000 per course) must be returned to Science Labs-in-a-Box, unless we choose to purchase items at discounted prices. Videos must also be returned. We are given permission to reproduce student handout pages as needed. A deposit is required to insure the return of equipment in good condition.

Each kit contains sufficient material for two students, but additional equipment kits can be "rented" for extra students at a lower price since you only need one set of videos. Kits are shipped and picked up by UPS with shipping costs prepaid by Science Labs-in-a-Box.

Yes, the labs are expensive, but it is unlikely that we can duplicate the experiences using such high quality equipment on our own for less. And if you form groups of student, the cost per student drops dramatically.

➲ TOPS Learning System (TOPS Learning Systems) $15 each

Individual books written in a structured activity-sheet format titled *Magnetism; Balancing; Electricity; Pendulums; Metric Measuring; More Metrics; Animal Survival; Green Thumbs: Radishes; Green Thumbs: Corn and Beans; The Earth, Moon and Sun;* and *The Planets and Stars* incorporate math and thinking skills for learning about scientific principles through activities. Activity instructions are simple to understand and easy to do successfully. The *Electricity* book provided the first successful electricity experiments I was able to do with my children after a number of previous attempts with other methods. Equipment needed is minimal and inexpensive. Activity sheets are reproducible so one book can be used for many children. Lessons can be used with children in grades 3-10. These activities will generally be too easy for the child with a good science background, but they will help children with little science background to overcome their fear that science is difficult.

TOPS also publishes 23 *Task Card* books, written for students in grades 7-12 [$8-$16 each]. These are available in an open-ended *Task Card* format. Choose those that relate most closely to the area(s) of science to be studied each year. Sample topics are *Graphing, Probability, Oxidation, Heat, Pressure, Electricity, Motion, Light, Sound,* and *Machines*. These task cards, like the activity sheets above, use simple materials and are reproducible for sharing among many students.

TOPS also will send their combination catalog/magazine to homeschoolers at no charge. You can read more about the products there, but every issue of the catalog also includes a couple of complete science lessons from the activity sheets or task cards so you can try before buying.

➲ Turning Kids On To Science in the home series by Dr. Tik Liem (Science Inquiry Enterprises) $15.50-$22.50 each

This series of four books features science experiments that are easy to do at home with minimal expense and difficulty. The activities range from simple to challenging, stretching across elementary through senior high grade levels in concepts covered. Each book focuses on different topics. The number of experiments in each book is indicated in parentheses. Book 1 is *Our Environment* (150); Book 2 is *Energy* (120); Book 3 is *Forces and Motion* (100); and Book 4 is *Living Things* (50). You should choose books that coincide with whatever subject area(s) you are addressing in science each year. Each experiment is clearly laid out with a list of materials needed, instructions, questions to ask, and explanations. One feature that makes this series stand out is that it presents experiments as "discrepant events"—something occurs that raises questions which provoke thought and analysis. This approach makes science experiments fun! Concepts illus-

trated range from simple (gravity and the speed of falling objects) to complex (e.g. torque, pendulums/frequencies, accelerated motion), so it will be up to us to choose those most appropriate for our students. While most instructions are easy to follow, a few seem confusing and might require some trial and error to do what is intended.(S)

➲ Unit Study Adventures series by Amanda Bennett (Holly Hall Publications/Homeschool Press) $13.99

The Unit Study Adventures guides were written for grades K-8, so they will stretch easily into the junior high years. These are not comprehensive unit studies such as *KONOS* or *Weaver* but guides that concentrate on single areas of science. Present science-oriented titles are *Baseball, Gardens, Computers, Home, Oceans,* and *Olympics*. Watch for new titles being added to this series. *Electricity, Space, Flight, and Trains* should be available soon (most of these are revisions of Amanda's very first editions). They feature detailed outlines, both a condensed one in the front of the book and an expanded "working outline" with space to fill in our own details regarding resources and teaching plans. Each guide shares the same organizational structure which includes lists of recommended resources for both reference and reading; spelling/vocabulary lists (at two levels); subject word list; activities; writing ideas; recommendations for games, videos, and software; "room decoration" ideas and resources (with addresses); internet resource addresses; field trips; and lists of questions (answer key included). We choose from among the topics, resources, and activities to create our own lesson plans. Guides are approximately 130-140 pages each, and some of them include Christian content (e.g., the *Oceans* outline begins with "History of the oceans in the Bible."). Recommended books are available at the library and through home school distributors. No prices are listed by some of the recommended resources, so it is difficult to determine which will be affordable. This information would be especially useful on the government agency publications whose prices can range from free to outrageous. Each book should take at least a few months to complete.

➲ The Usborne Illustrated Dictionary of Science - Physics, Chemistry and Biology Facts by Corinne Stockley, Chris Oxlade, and Jane Wertheim (Educational Development Corporation) $24.95

If you have extra money in your budget to splurge on science, take a look at this 384-page dictionary. It is full of beautifully drawn applications of scientific principles your student will certainly study in the standard high school and college-level sciences. It seems criminal that textbooks could not be as bright and fun to read, but this is the pattern that has made Usborne books so cherished, and this dictionary is no different. This book is no substitute for a good text, but it can enhance understanding by providing clear visual charts, tables, illustrations, and examples of difficult scientific concepts and symbolism in a very concise manner. ISBN 0-86020-989-X (SE)[Diane Eastman]

➲ The Weather Wizard's Cloud Book by Louis D. Rubin, Sr. and Jim Duncan (Algonquin Books of Chapel Hill) $8.95

For budding meteorologists this is an outstanding resource. It is written for all ages, rather than as a textbook for children. However, because the teaching is done with illustrations and the reader's own observations, it is practical for teens to use. A subtitle/description on the book's cover reads, "A unique way to predict the weather accurately and easily by reading the clouds," and this is the main thrust of the book. However, we do not merely memorize cloud shapes and colors, but go much deeper into cloud formation, thunder and lightning, hurricanes and other storms, and the effects of volcanic activity on weather. A brief chapter at the end tells how to build your own weather station.

I suggest using the companion book, The Weather Wizard's 5-Year Weather Diary [$13.95]. While it conveys some "how to's and definitions on observing weather, it is primarily a weather journal for recording observations, as well as data on wind, barometer reading, humidity, precipitation, temperature, and clouds. The page for each date has space for recording five years, so that comparisons and trends are readily seen. Setting up a weather station and the initial reading/study will take a significant amount of time (perhaps a few months), but ongoing observations will require much less, although on a daily basis. Consider using these resources as part of an earth science or general science course.(S)

About Microscopes

Laboratory work in the life sciences should include work with a microscope if at all possible. Cheap microscopes (most of those in the under $100 range) are just about useless. In most cases you will be better off with small magnifiers that magnify images ten to thirty times. Hand-held, pocket-size instruments will usually give you clearer views than you can get with cheap microscopes. (Nature's Workshop, Plus! sells a small 30x illuminating microscope—a pocket instrument that sells for less than ten dollars. This is a good alternative for those who do not want to invest in a "real" microscope, but it does only low-level magnification. You can find a similar instrument at Radio Shack.)

Microscopes, even in the fifty to hundred dollar range, usually are difficult or impossible to focus at high magnification. While they can be focused more easily at low magnification, preparing good slides is still a challenge. An exception is the Blister Microscope (General Science Service Co.). The Blister Microscope sells for $45.95. It comes with a 50x magnification lens (25x and 100x lens are also available for $9 each) that can be used to view both slides and thicker, opaque objects that cannot be viewed with a regular microscope. The microscope uses a more efficient appliance-size light bulb rather than the frustrating mirror setups common to lower priced microscopes. It plugs in rather than operating on batteries. Special blister slides make slide preparation much easier than traditional slides although regular slides may also be used. This microscope is made of heavy duty metal and is easy to focus and operate successfully. You still won't get the high magnification you get with more expensive microscopes, but you can view what you can with the

Blister Microscope, then look at magnified pictures of the items that need high magnification.

The Blister Microscope, together with a hand-held viewer such as the illuminating microscope (which can be used in the field since it is not dependent upon electricity), should provide for sufficient indoor and outdoor magnification activities, but you will lack high-level magnification.

Just a step up in price, but a major improvement in magnification is the Discovery microscope from LW Scientific, Inc. This microscope, priced at about $120, offers 40x, 100x, and 400x magnification with mirror illumination. It performs like standard microscopes, but is less expensive, largely because of its aluminum construction and less-expensive light source. However, it does have glass optics, which provide clearer viewing than do the plastic optics often found on less-expensive microscopes. The same company also offers the Explorer microscope for $199. It is "manufactured from heavy cast alloy and has a 110v tungsten illuminator." The Explorer model is most popular with home educators. All LW Scientific microscopes come with instruction booklets that include activity suggestions and lifetime warranties. LW Scientific also carries other microscopes.

Other sources for quality, standard microscopes are Nasco, Schoolmasters Science, Edmund Scientific, and Carolina Biological Supply. Nasco tells me that they are able and willing to special order even more microscopes than those described in their catalog. The people at Nature's Workshop, Plus! sound like they have already searched for microscopes with home schoolers' needs in mind. They describe their microscopes clearly so you can easily choose one to meet your needs. They, too, can order other microscopes than those described in their catalog.

For those unfamiliar with slide preparation, many of the sources listed under "For Labs," later in this chapter, sell prepared slides. While these can be very helpful, learning to prepare slides should be part of a biology lab.

One very inexpensive option that will provide viewing opportunities, but not the complete experience of operating a true microscope, is the Microslide Viewer (available from Nasco and Schoolmasters Science). Prepared strips of slides, called Microslides, are available to use with the Microslide Viewer, or an extra lens can be added to the top for viewing three-dimensional objects. Microslides are already enlarged pictures of objects, with the Viewer providing only a minimal increase in magnification. This can provide the high magnification viewing lacking when you use the Blister Microscope.

High School Level

If the student does not already have a good foundation in science, you might begin with basic science texts (seventh or eighth grade level) such as those listed above.

Meeting Requirements

The minimum high school graduation requirement for most states is two years of science including physical science and life science. Many colleges require one or two lab sciences, and some require three years of science, with at least two of those being lab courses. Which courses actually fulfill requirements is rather vague, depending primarily on college admission requirements. For non-college bound students, a general science course and a life science course are usually satisfactory. Keep in mind that students who graduate by taking the GED or Proficiency Examination need only be concerned about college entrance requirements and their personal educational needs.

For college preparation, courses should usually be biology and chemistry or physics. However, it should be acceptable to substitute classes such as botany or zoology for biology. Similarly, we should be able to use other equally challenging courses that would come under physical or life science headings as long as they include enough laboratory experience. Students preparing for science majors need be most concerned about taking the proper classes, and those seeking acceptance at competitive colleges or universities should find out what courses will best enhance their chance of being accepted.

If our teen plans to finish high school at home and go directly from there to a competitive four-year college or university, he had better plan to do as much science as possible at home rather than settle for the bare minimum. If science is difficult for whatever reason, check out video courses such as those from School of Tomorrow or A Beka (all A Beka and School of Tomorrow high school science courses are available on video), correspondence courses such as chemistry courses from Seton or the North Dakota Division of Independent Study, part-time school, or other options discussed in Chapter Eight.

The laboratory aspect of many high school science courses seems to pose the most problems. Laboratory classes are not required by some states for high school graduation but are often required by colleges for admission. It is important to check with potential colleges for their policies.

Those who plan to spend some time at junior college or enroll in a less-selective college, usually have more leeway in science preparation. Some home schoolers purposely skip science lab classes at home and take them at junior colleges.

For Lab Work

➲ **Lab Science: The How, Why, What, Who, 'n' Where Book** Written and compiled by Barb Edtl Shelton (Homeschool Seminars & Publications) $11.95

This unusual book concentrates on one of the most challenging tasks of home schooling for high school. In her friendly, no-pressure style, Shelton combines tips from science experts with practical experience and recommendations of a number of home schoolers to broaden both our options and confidence for tackling lab science. She presents a variety of approaches, explaining that there is no one "right way" to do it. She answers the question, "Why do lab science even if you don't have to?" Lots of ideas and samples, some frameworks and course outlines give us some solid "what to do's." Excerpts from works by Mary Schofield (*The High School Handbook*), Kathleen Julicher (Castle Heights

Press), Diana McAlister (*Homeschool the High Schooler*), Ted Wade (*The Home School Manual*), and others provide a variety of specialized commentary. In one section, Shelton includes reproducible sheets for teacher and student such as Class Content Plan/Framework, Lab Science Check-Off Sheet, Grading Criteria and Course Assessment, Lab Experiment Record, Microscope Sketch, collection record pages, Scientist Interview, and God's View of Science Word Study. At the end of the book is a "where to find it" resource address section. Even if we choose to use a fairly standard course based on a text or program, Shelton's book will help us organize and manage the lab end of it. If we choose to create our own courses, it should be even more useful.

You can order individual laboratory kits, dissecting materials, and other lab supplies to do experiments from the following sources:

➲ **American Science and Surplus**

American Science and Surplus has a lot of surplus science-type items at fantastically low prices. However, stock changes constantly, and you never know what they have from month to month. Catalogs are published about six times a year (showing a cover price of $1.00) and provide detailed descriptions of their weird and variable products. They usually have motors, mechanical and electrical devices, educational science kits, and books; supplies for teaching, art activities, offices, and hobbies; plus many other items that defy classification (e.g., diagonal mirrors for telescopes, dental tools, foldup stereo optic viewers, and bicycle seats). Some of these items should suggest science projects to the invention-minded.

➲ **Blue Spruce Biological Supply**

Blue Spruce offers two basic dissection kits that includes ten specimens (earthworm, frog, starfish, grasshopper, perch, clam, crayfish, squid, dogfish shark, and pig) in either "plain or deluxe" (smaller or larger) sizes [$10 or $18]. We can also buy individual specimens of the above or other items such as sheep brains or cow eyes. In addition they sell dissecting tool kits, pans, and numerous other science supplies.

➲ **Bob Jones University Press**

The BJUP catalog lists scientific supplies, with quantities appropriate for home educators. The list includes a dissecting kit similar to that available from Nasco. BJUP also publishes two *Laboratory Manual Supplements*, one for *Basic Science and Biology* and the other for *Chemistry and Physics* [$8 each]. In these books, they chart out which of the experiments in the respective lab manuals are practical for homeschoolers and which are essential. They also suggest practical lab setups and equipment for homeschoolers taking into account safety and cost issues. These are extremely helpful.

➲ **Carolina Biological Supply Company**

This is a source for science kits (including individual kits for lab experiments), living and preserved specimens, multimedia, books, microscopes, apparatus, and much more. They carry just about anything you might want for science. Their huge, comprehensive catalog is free when requested by a teacher on school stationery. Otherwise, the catalog price is $17.95 (postpaid). The catalog includes a coupon worth $17.95 on any purchase of $25 or more. Carolina Biological Supply also has free specialty catalogs for elementary science, 5-12 mathematics, and books and multimedia.

⊃ Edmund Scientific Company

Edmund's has a variety of science equipment, including microscopes and laboratory supplies.

⊃ Fischertechnik (available through Timberdoodle)

This is a big line of mechanical and electrical construction kits that can even work with computers (robotics). They are more complicated and more expensive than *LEGO*, but very intriguing and very well built. In our experience, *Fischertechnik* constructions hold together better than *LEGO* constructions.

⊃ Frey Scientific

This is an economical source for equipment and supplies.

⊃ Home Training Tools

Home Training Tools offers science equipment and supplies for home schools. They can supply chemicals in small quantities. Their catalog includes microscopes, slides, dissecting equipment and specimens, science resource books, chemicals, lab equipment, and other resources. Items are arranged in the catalog under topical headings (e.g., biology, chemistry, physics) making it easy to find what we need. Request a free catalog.(S)

⊃ LEGO (LEGO Dacta)

LEGO makes educational Technic sets that come with teacher's guides and individual lessons on mechanical principles such as levers, pulleys, gear ratios, and rack and pinion steering. They also sell computerized sets for Macintosh, Apple IIE and GS, and MS-DOS machines. These are reasonably priced and make terrific teaching tools for some physics principles. There are some *LEGO* kits in stores labeled as Technic sets, but stores rarely carry the educational sets with teaching materials. Write to *LEGO Dacta* for information on educational sets or order from one of the suppliers shown in the Appendix.

⊃ Nasco

Request their free science catalog. They have a large selection of just about everything you could possibly need, and their prices are very reasonable. For biology, they offer a complete dissecting kit with tools, "creatures," and instructions.

⊃ Nature's Workshop, Plus!

Nature's Workshop and Ruark's Home & School Accessories have been combined into one larger company that carries lab equipment, microscopes, prepared slides along with a broader line of resources for home education.

⊃ The Science Projects Store (Science Projects, Inc.)

Science Projects will provide almost any science material and equipment at very competitive prices without a minimum purchase requirement. (They will even ship a single test tube if we are willing to pay the freight!) They have a free price list, but call to confirm availability, lead time, and pricing, especially on unusual items.

⊃ Tobin's Lab

Tobin's Lab puts out a great catalog especially for home schoolers. Structured to reflect the days of creation, the catalog includes everything for science but textbooks. They carry many topical science books (including creation science), videos, equipment, kits, chemicals, posters, puzzles, and dissection specimens. They ask that you send six stamps to cover postage costs for their free catalog.

Achieving Competence in Science (Amsco) $6.33; answer key - $4.75

Achieving Competence in Science does not fit into any of the categories I am using. I envision this unusual book fitting two possible purposes. This first might be to provide an overview of science subjects for the student who has put little time into studying traditional high school science topics, yet needs that information for test taking, meeting requirements, or personal benefit. The second purpose might be to assist the parent who will be teaching junior and senior high science, yet lacks background knowledge.

There are three chapters on earth science, three on life science, two on physical sciences, one on energy sources and issues, and a final chapter on interactions of science, technology, and society.

Throughout the book are helps for learning "process skills," such as interpreting data in a table, designing a controlled experiment, and designing an observation procedure.

Vocabulary terms are emphasized in the text (also with a glossary at the end), an important part of the knowledge required for test taking. The reading level is fine for average high school students.

Each chapter presents the information with illustrations, followed by multiple choice questions. The presentation seems just right for the purposes of this book—not so much detail as to be overwhelming, yet enough to develop understanding. Process skills instruction also includes multiple choice questions. At the end of the book is a comprehensive, seventy-question practice test, similar in format to standardized tests.

This book is very inexpensive, yet it is almost 200 pages long.

Evolution is given a brief nod of approval, but is not a significant theme throughout the book.(SE)

Recommended Texts and Resources

General Science

➲ Basic Science Text plus Activity Edition (Bob Jones University Press) student text - $28; teacher's edition - $39; student activity book - $12; teacher's edition for activity book - $15; Test Packet - $7/answer key - $4; TestBank - $16; Supplement - $8

This is an excellent text for physical science, but it should be preceded by BJUP's eighth grade *Earth Science* for astronomy, meteorology, geology, and oceanography to ensure broader science coverage. (But do not skip it just because you can't use *Earth Science*.) If students need to meet their physical science requirement, but do not need chemistry or physics, this course will suffice. (Students who will be taking more science in college should try to take at least one of either chemistry or physics.) This course covers both chemistry and physics at introductory levels. Teacher's editions for the text and the activity book are available. A *TestBank* (softbound book) or test packet are also available. BJUP also publishes the *Basic Science and Biology for Christian Schools Laboratory Manual Supplement* [$8] for home schools and small schools which assists home schoolers in selecting lab experiments form the BJUP lab manual to get the most lab value with minimal cost and complexity. The *Supplement* suggests simple substitutions for more extensive classroom type equipment and supplies where appropriate.

➲ Earth Science (Science Workshop Series), Books 1, 2, and 3 (Globe Fearon Educational Publisher) $11.95 each; teacher's editions - $16.95 each

This is a remedial science course for students who are not college bound. The three worktexts contain instruction, work pages, and experiments/activities. Topics in Book 1 (*Geology*) are an introduction to scientific methods, studying the Earth, rocks and minerals, erosion and weathering, building up the Earth, and fossils. Book 2 (*Oceans and Atmosphere*) covers the hydrosphere, atmosphere, weather, ocean currents, pollution, hurricanes, and tornadoes. Book 3 (*The Universe*) discusses space exploration, the solar system, the Earth's motion, stars, satellites, and exploration.

The activities do not require school lab setups, so they are practical for home educators.

The teacher's editions for each book contain teaching strategies, answers, and review tests.(SE)

➲ Physical Science (Science Workshop Series), Books 1, 2, and 3 (Globe Fearon Educational Publisher) $11.95 each; teacher's editions - $16.95 each

As with the *Chemistry* series from the Science Workshop which is described later, these comprise a simpler course than typical high school textbooks, although you can still grant credit for an introductory high school physical science lab course. This particular series combines chemistry and physics topics, fulfilling the physical science requirement of most high schools, but not meeting the requirements of most four-year colleges. The format is worktext with instruction, work pages, and easy-to-do experiments, all within each book.

Topics in Book 1 (*Matter and Energy*) are introduction to scientific methods, states of matter, atoms and elements, motion, and simple machines. Book 2 (*Chemical Changes*) covers heat, compounds, mixtures, solutions, acids and bases, and chemical reactions. Book 3 (*Electricity and Magnetism*) includes sound, light, electricity, magnetism, energy, nuclear power, and conservation.

The teacher's editions for each book contain answers, teaching strategies, and a test.(SE)

➲ Physical Science [Computer Video Interactive course] (School of Tomorrow) $550-video set; $106.67-computer disks; $64-PACEs plus answer keys. School of Tomorrow offers two rental options: videos only ($239.80 per course, broken down into quarterly rentals of $59.95 each) or rental package that include PACEs and Score Keys ($299.80 per course or $74.95 per quarter). Video rentals are shipped in four groups.

See the general description of the computer video interactive (CVI) courses under the reviews of Major Publishers in Chapter Nine as well as the reviews of School of Tomorrow's *Algebra I* and *Biology* courses. This course functions in the same manner, covering physical science with 24 videos, 24 computer disks, 12 PACEs, and a lab record.

Physical Science is covered with 24 videos, 24 computer disks, 12 PACEs, and a lab record. Videos are the key element of this course, providing instruction as well as well-chosen film footage (National Geographic quality) to illustrate topics. These are interesting to watch. They coordinate with either the PACEs or computer-based learning. The PACEs are intended to be optional, but they will be almost essential unless School of Tomorrow makes the computerized help screens more easily accessible. Students complete separate lab records as they watch experiments and demonstrations, although they do not actually do lab work themselves.

Topics covered are essentially an introduction to chemistry and physics, but the content is challenging. For example, chemical bonds and valence structures are addressed.

Videos can be used with PACEs minus the computer disks, with the major loss being the convenience and appeal of computer interaction and record keeping.

Some might choose to use PACEs by themselves, and this is adequate, although unexciting. While short stories and biblical applications are interspersed throughout the PACEs, the videos feature clips explaining and emphasizing character development and include short, fascinating facts relating to science. Both the PACEs and the videos present a biblical perspective on science topics.

➲ Science LifePacs [900 - 9th grade level: General Science] (Alpha Omega) $41.95

This ninth grade level material includes ten LifePacs and a teacher handbook. Students work independently through Life-Pacs for most of the course, while important discussion and activity is directed by the parent using the teacher handbook. Topics within the "General Science" LifePacs are: atomic energy, volume, mass, density, physical and historical geology, body health, astronomy, oceanography, science and the future, and scientific applications.

➲ Science of the Physical Creation, 1996 edition (A Beka) $22.90; teacher guide - $20; student lab manual - $11.60; teacher lab key - $20.20; test book - $6.05; quiz book - $4.35; test book key - $8.60; quiz book key -$8.60

Designed for ninth graders, this course introduces students to high school level chemistry with a combination of text, lab activities, research paper, and project. Major areas of science covered are meteorology and oceanography, chemistry, geology, and physics. At the beginning of the text, students learn how mathematics, scientific method, and measurement are used in science. The Biblical Christian worldview is obvious throughout this text, most particularly in a lengthy section concerning the fossil record. Although this is an "introductory" text, the content is in-depth. The text includes section review questions with occasional paper-and-pencil activities. The teacher guide has an overview of the course, explanation and instructions for the science project, instructions for writing an abstract, answers to the text questions, daily lesson plans (detailed), and additional teacher notes to expand upon lessons. If you do not wish to use this as a lab course, you can work with these two components, possibly adding quiz or test booklets. The Lab Manual assumes that you have a classroom laboratory setup. Although the experiments are worthwhile, it will be too difficult for most home educators to set up the necessary labs on their own. However, chapter reviews are also found in the student's Lab Manual, with answers in the Teacher Lab Key. The quiz and/or test booklets should provide adequate assessment of student knowledge, even if you choose to skip the Lab Manual. Since experiments and activities are a great way to learn science, consider using one or more of the books reviewed here that offer easy-to-use lab activities on some of topics covered in this course.

Extras

➲ Boy Scout Merit Badge booklets (Boy Scouts of America Supply Division) less than $2.40 each

Round out or specialize in different areas of science with the Boy Scout Merit Badge Booklets. Each booklet is about 70 pages and offers an outline of merit badge requirements that can serve as at least a partial course outline. The bulk of each booklet is information, project instructions, resources, and career information related to the topic. Examples of some of the general science titles are *Animal Science, Astronomy, Aviation, Bird Study, Energy, Electronics, Geology, Mammal Study, Oceanography, Soil and Water Conservation, Space Exploration,* and *Weather.*

You can often find these books in your local library, but they are very inexpensive to purchase.

➲ Cooking and Science: The Kitchen Science Workbook by Joseph Julicher (Castle Heights Press) $9.95

This book of ten cooking experiments teaches science concepts. Titles of some of the experiments will give you an idea of what this covers: "Divinity: A Study in Boiling Points," "Southern Pecan Pie: A Study in Colloid Formation." Some of this gets a little dangerous (e.g., deep fat frying) so plan to do these with older students. Each experiment has background information, pre-lab, in-lab, and post-lab sections. Step-by-step instructions are given, and questions guide the learning activities. Students will need to do a little outside research on some of the questions, but most of the learning will occur through the experiments themselves. An answer key is at the back of the book. One book can be used by the entire family, since no writing is done in the book.

➲ Discover Nature at the Seashore: Things to Know and Things to Do by Elizabeth P. Lawlor (Stackpole Books) $14.95

This is the book I wished I had when we made our numerous field trips down to the Bolsa Chica saltwater marsh in past years. It is divided into three sections: The Rocky Shore, The Salt Marsh and the Mud Flats, and The Beach. This book is much more than a field guide. It does not attempt to be comprehensive, leaving that for the field guides. However, it provides in-depth information on each topic along with activities. Some of these activities can get quite involved, so choose which to do according to your needs. Data charts within the book can be used with the activities, but it would be better to keep a separate notebook.

As I mentioned, the book strives for depth rather than breadth as evidenced by the six chapters within The Rocky Shore section. Chapters cover the six topics of barnacles, sea stars, slipper limpets, blue mussels, seaweeds, and periwinkles. Within those limited topics, related and associated species are discussed.

Activities can be used with younger children also, so this is a good book for whole-family studies. The book works well as part of a self-designed life science course, although it will be a valuable supplement to textbook studies.(SE-evolutionary assumptions at the very beginning)

➲ The Everyday Science Sourcebook - Ideas for Teaching in the Elementary and Middle School by Lawrence F. Lowery (Dale Seymour Publications) $19.95

This 438-page teacher resource book can be very useful for the parent who wants to take advantage of the flexibility of homeschooling by drafting his or her own laboratory experiments. The author charts the developmental stages of acquiring scientific knowledge from K-12. Grades 6 through 9 should be at the stage of acquiring inferential knowledge, i.e., making generalizations, evaluating information, making predictions and theorizing. By Grades 9 through 12, the student should be ready to apply gained knowledge, using it to identify examples, create, construct, grow, raise, collect and invent. Since this book attempts to demonstrate to teachers of K-9 students how they can create lessons and lesson plans that take the student through his or her different phases of learning, the book will be most useful to parent-teachers who plan to do just that. A secondary use is for the ever-inquiring high school student who is fully into designing his own science experiments (of the Colfax family or science fair variety). ISBN 0-86651-260-8 (S)[Diane Eastman]

⮑ Krill (Ampersand Press) $9.95

If students are studying marine life, this is a helpful way to understand interactions and their food chains. It will actually be more useful with younger students, since teens will quickly tire of the narrow focus of the game. Purchase it primarily for use with elementary students, but do pull it out for older students for a relief from book learning.

⮑ Suburban Nature Guide: How to Discover and Identify the Wildlife in Your Backyard by David Mohrhardt and Richard E. Schinkel (Stackpole Books) $16.95

Many of us who live in the suburbs lack easy access to the wilds of nature. If you live in the eastern United States (east of the Mississippi River), you will find this guide a wonderful way to begin nature studies without leaving home. It includes sections on mammals, birds, reptiles and amphibians, insects, spiders, trees and shrubs, vines, flowers, grasses, ferns, mosses, fungi, and the interesting category of "creatures in moist places." If you cannot find examples from one category, you certainly will find them from others. In case you need to attract wildlife, an appendix tells how to construct bird houses and feeders.

The reason I particularly like this book is that most of us cannot afford to have guides on hand for every one of the above categories. There are a number of species that are common to many areas, and by showing and describing those that we are most likely to encounter, this book has summarized information from a number of guides into one. Fleas, silverfish, cockroaches, toads, sparrows (many kinds), squirrels, snails, yellow jackets, mulberry trees, yarrow, bermuda grass, and lichen are a sampling of the more common living things we can learn about in this book. In addition to descriptive information, there is a good deal about habitats and habits.

Even though we live on the West coast, the majority of the living things described in this book can also be found here. In fact, this book helped me identify the stinkhorn (it smells as bad as it sounds) my son discovered growing under our apricot tree.(S)

⮑ Turning Kids On To Science in the home series by Dr. Tik Liem (Science Inquiry Enterprises) $15.50-$22.50 each

See the review under Junior High "Extras or Supplements."

Biology

⮑ The Anatomy and Physiology Coloring Book (ScottForesman/Addison Wesley) $16.40

If you are studying the human body, this book is extremely useful. It is a coloring book, but with enough detail for a serious anatomy student, plus explanations of functions. Much of this will be beyond typical high school students, but we can use as much or as little as we please. (For less detail, check out Instructional Fair's The Human Body.(S)

⮑ Biological Science course B135 (Landmark's Freedom Baptist Curriculum) $35

This course covers the plant and animal kingdoms and the human body. It consists of a worktext, weekly quizzes, quarterly tests, and answer keys. Each lesson in the worktext contains a two-page reading portion, comprehension questions, words to define, and a short paper that might involve further research. Several special projects are suggested. There are few pictures or diagrams and no color. Since there are no lab activities, those would need to be added to fulfill requirements for a lab course. Curiously, while the course is published by a Christian publisher it lacks any significant evidence of this until lessons on the human body. Overall, this is a comprehensive non-lab course, unexciting, but fairly easy to use. [Valerie Thorpe]

⮑ Biology [Computer Video Interactive course] (School of Tomorrow) videos - $550; computer disks - $106.67; PACEs plus answer keys - $64. School of Tomorrow offers two rental options: videos only ($239.80 per course, broken down into quarterly rentals of $59.95 each) or rental package that include PACEs and Score Keys ($299.80 per course or $74.95 per quarter). Video rentals are shipped in four groups.

See description of the computer video interactive courses under School of Tomorrow's review in Chapter Nine under Major Publishers as well as the review of the Algebra I course. This course functions in the same manner, covering biology, but there are two videos and two computer disks per PACE (24 of each all together). The videos, alone, change the nature of this course significantly from a "PACEs only" course. The videos are very professionally done and are interesting to watch. Unlike A Beka videos, they are of specially planned presentations with supplemental film footage, rather than videos of classes in progress. The addition of the computer dimension of the course coordinates video viewing with student feedback. It is also intended to replace the PACEs. However, questions posed on the computer must be answered exactly as they were presented on the video—exact spelling and capitalization. Yet the videos go too quickly for students to take such exacting notes. There is a summary feature where students can review the information, but the present version forces the student to go through all of the information until he arrives at what he needs, and it does not have a search feature. This defect should be fixed in future versions. We found it almost essential to have the PACE handy to figure out the required answers in a timely manner. If students miss too many questions (even before completing the exercises), the program kicks them back to the beginning. If you don't have PACEs to refer to, reviewing the lesson presentation will be essential for most students, but, at the same time, it will be very time-consuming to go through it over and over. (School of Tomorrow is adjusting the programs so that more synonyms will be accepted as answers, which will help some.)

Course questions and tests rely on repetition rather than deep thinking and analysis for learning. This is my biggest complaint. Students spend much time looking for the exact words required, rather than pondering concepts. For most students, this is not a major problem, but seriously inquisitive minds might find it too restrictive. The course is not as challenging as A Beka or Bob Jones courses, but my judgment is that, if they use the videos, students will actually learn what is presented better than they might in more challenging courses because the presentation is so much more interesting. Character trait clips also add interest and biblical applications to the course.

Excellent lab presentations are included. Students are shown both actual and microscopic views of dissections, so they actually see more than they are likely to when doing their own dissections. Although the students do no actual lab work, they fill in reports documenting their understanding of experiments they watch on video.

The catalog says that all material covered in the standard PACEs is covered with the addition of ten percent added academic information under the computer version. This course is one of School of Tomorrow's best. The catch is the price, but the rental option makes the cost comparable to A Beka's video course, and more than one student can view the videos for the same price.

➲ Biology (Bob Jones University Press) student text - $30; teacher's edition - $39; lab manual - $12; teacher's edition for lab manual - $27; dissection video - $49.95; test packet - $7; test packet answer key - $4; TestBank - $16; AskIt disk - $14; supplement - $7

Although this is a challenging course to use, it should still be suitable for home schoolers. The teacher's edition comes in two volumes which have hard backs and spiral binding. In the teacher's edition, student pages identical in size and format to the student textbook pages are reprinted on larger pages surrounded by teaching notes and answers to exercises (at the bottom of the pages). Some parents might choose to purchase only the teacher's edition, covering up answers as students complete the exercises. Each chapter includes thought questions that should be used for discussion rather than written activity. The text is vocabulary-laden, so use your best judgment as to how much to require students to master. Read the introductory teacher's information, since it offers excellent advice as to how to use the material presented. One feature that makes the text more flexible is the separation of some material into boxes and "Facets of Biology" sections which are optional depending upon your time, goals, and interests. The text is very colorful, although the language is often very dry. Sections on the philosophical and religious aspects of biology are certainly more interesting than the vocabulary and data oriented sections such as the "Microstructure of a bone." Arrangement of topics is fairly traditional, beginning at the cellular level and ending with man. Significant attention is given to the creation/evolution controversy, and the Biblical Christian worldview is evident throughout the text. Interestingly, this text spends less time on botany than does the A Beka text; it should take about two and a half weeks to cover the

bulk of the instruction on botany here, while A Beka dedicates almost a third of the book to botany. It appears that BJUP spends much more time on cytology (cells) and microbiology than does A Beka.

A companion Lab Manual and its teacher's edition contain numerous experiments and activities to accompany the various chapters of the text. It is possible to use the text without a lab, although lab work makes it more interesting and fulfills lab requirements for either graduation or college preparation. Because the lab work is classroom oriented, BJUP has published Basic Science and Biology for Christian Schools Laboratory Manual Supplement which will assist home schoolers or small Christian schools in selecting and adapting experiments and lab work from the course lab manuals to get the most lab value with minimal cost and complexity. (Note that both the Basic Science and Biology courses are covered within the single Supplement.) The Supplement does strongly recommend the purchase of a microscope, the largest investment you will need to make to "construct" your lab.

Other options might be to use Science Labs-in-a-Box for serious labs designed to accompany this text, use Experiences in Biology (Castle Heights Press), create our own labs using dissection sets and other activities, and/or view BJUP's Biology Dissection Video. A test packet and companion answer key, a TestBank, and an AskIt test disk are available, but any one of these options will suffice for testing purposes.

➲ The Biology Coloring Book by Robert D. Griffin (ScottForesman) $12

This 233-page coloring book was designed for students in college biology courses, but it will be a valuable tool for high school level students also. It covers basic processes and structures of plant and animal life in detail. [order #0-06-460307-5](S)

➲ Biology Dissection Video (Bob Jones University Press) $49.95

If you don't want to do dissecting yourself, but your son or daughter still needs to know what dissecting is all about, the Biology Dissection Video is a great solution. It also fills the bill if your students want to perform dissections, but you want a professional teacher to lead them. Dr. Tom Coss demonstrates dissections of the earthworm, frog, crayfish, and perch. He tells where to cut, then shows clearly how to do it. Dissection manuals and instructions frequently are too general in cutting instructions, which presents great difficulty for the inexperienced. Following Dr. Coss's instructions and example makes it much easier. The video uses magnification to closely examine some parts of the creatures, something we are unlikely to do in the middle of a dissection, but a worthwhile sidetrack. All in all, watching the video alone might be at least as productive as performing the dissections yourself. This video can supplement any biology course.

⮑ Biology: God's Living Creation (A Beka) $24.05; lab manual - $12.20; teacher edition for lab manual - $20.20; test book - $5.55; quiz book - $3.95; answer keys for test or quiz book - $7.80 each

This is an excellent text that differs from most others. It is unusual in that it proceeds from the "whole" to the "part," the opposite of other texts. For instance, botany study introduces types of trees and plants, moves on to parts of stems and flowers, then into cellular structure, whereas other texts begin with cellular structure and work up toward complete organisms. While the idea of such an organizational structure is appealing, it creates a few problems since understanding of structures is often crucial to understanding larger organisms. We ended up changing the order in which we studied the chapters back to something more akin to the order found in other texts.

A revised edition of this text is due early 1998, and it will have a separate teacher guide. There is none for the present edition of the text.

A Field and Laboratory Manual provides instructions for twenty-seven labs and three projects, but many are difficult to do at home. For lab work, consider using a dissecting kit with instruction manual from Nasco or BJUP, or use Castle Heights Press' *Experiments in Biology*.

This course is also available on video, but it was one of the most boring of the A Beka courses I have seen. The teacher wastes a lot of time waiting for students' responses, and the entire class moves too slowly. I suggest passing on the videos and using the A Beka textbook as described above. For those who are still interested, lab work is demonstrated on the tape, although students are not required to do any lab work other than the written portion. Some parents purchase dissecting specimens and have their students do the lab work in conjunction with the class presentations.

⮑ Boy Scout Merit Badge booklets (Boy Scouts of America Supply Division) less than $2.40 each

Boy Scout Merit Badge booklets were designed to help Scouts learn more about specialized topics, often with an eye to giving them a taste of possible future career or study interests. A list of most of the available books can be found under "electives." However, there are a few related to the biological sciences that you might wish to use as supplements to personalize biology courses. Possible titles are *Animal Science, Bird Study, Environmental Science* (a great study), *Fish and Wildlife Management, Insect Study, Mammal Study, Nature, Reptile and Amphibian Study*, and *Veterinary Medicine*.

⮑ Designs in the Living World by Lester, Englin, and Howe (SimBioSys Publishers) text chapters 1-13 - $30; text chapters 14-16 and lab manual - $25

This biology course is unabashedly Christian, comparing evolutionary versus creation viewpoints throughout, as well as contrasting different interpretations and theories among Chris-

tian creationist scientists. It was originally designed for a college class but is being adapted for homeschool use. The present edition is usable, but could stand a few improvements. It comes in two parts, both of which are necessary. Chapters 1-13 are in one package, while chapters 14-16 are in a separate package along with the lab manual. These are unbound pages, three-hole-punched for insertion in your own binders. The pages are printed in black-and-white with few illustrations. The need for illustrations is met by the requirement that students purchase *A Photographic Atlas for the Biology Laboratory*, third edition, by Van De Graff and Crawley (Morton Publishing Co.) [$20]. Contact information comes with the course. This course also differs from others in that it is less comprehensive. It emphasizes foundational information, but spends less time on specialized areas such as botany, microbiology, and zoology than do most other texts.

Design and order are the theme of this course. So it begins with an introduction to chemistry, since chemical design underlies physical form and function. It does not assume prior knowledge of chemistry. From there the course works from the molecular stage up through cells, life processes, genetics, reproduction, DNA/RNA/genetic coding, ecosystems and interrelationships, the origin of life, and the history of life (theories and evidence), ending with classifications and study of different life forms.

No questions or quizzes are included in the text pages. The lab manual includes numerous questions beyond the actual lab work, although parents will need to construct other means of comprehensive assessment.

The lab activities are serious lab work. Students work with a microscope, participate in online genetic investigations, dissect a fetal pig, and more. The lab manual is in the process of being revamped to make it easier for home schoolers to use, but, in the meantime, you will find some of the activities difficult to impossible to do at home, but many that are excellent and practical if you take the time to get the proper equipment and perform them. One important element missing from the lab manual is a list of supplies for each activity. This means we have to read through and determine what is needed on our own. Supply lists are being added to SymBioSys' web site.

Work on a teacher's manual is in progress, and this will provide additional help as well as answers. Meanwhile SimBioSys operates a free web site for support.

Although there are a few things lacking in this course at the moment, it looks like a promising and practical, high-quality biology course that will be especially appealing to Christians.

⮑ Experiences in Biology by Kathleen Julicher (Castle Heights Press, Inc.) $24.95

While biology lab experiments are much easier to do at home than chemistry experiments, lab manuals that accompany textbooks still assume that we have access to a wide array of lab supplies. Kathleen Julicher recognized that this is a problem shared by both home educators and small schools, so she developed lab experiments that are practical for schools with limited supplies.

In this book, she offers thirty investigations from five biological areas: zoology, human anatomy and physiology, cellular biology, botany, and ecology. Students or parents choose about 12 to 15 experiments to do; they cannot do all of them since some, like the fetal pig, are lengthy. The investigations include a number of dissections with illustrations and instructions, work with a microscope, lab experiments, and field study. Materials needed for each investigation are conveniently listed at the front of the book. Students follow scientific method to describe the investigation, record information, analyze results, and state conclusions, all in a notebook they maintain or in the optional *Student Activity Notebook* [$9.95]. They also make drawings as a means of recording information.

In the back of this book, is a description of the fundamental requirements of a biology class (very useful to home educators who are designing their own classes), information on record keeping (notebooks and reports), instructions for lab drawings (with a reproducible form to use), instructions on microscope usage (with a work sheet for identifying parts of the microscope), plus a detailed explanation of scientific method.

Experiences in Biology is designed so that a family must purchase only a single copy. They are free to make copies of the necessary pages for the family. Answers are included. Space for recording information is somewhat limited on the pages within the book, so I recommend obtaining the *Student Activity Notebook* ($9.95) for each student. The *Student Activity Notebook* is so well laid out, that it actually makes the experiments and recording of information appear easier than if students work solely from the primary *Experiments in Biology* book.

Castle Heights Press has made arrangements with The Science Projects Store to offer the materials needed for dissection [$30] and microscopic work [$50]. Contact the store directly for information.

⊃ Science LifePacs 1000 - 10th grade level: Biology (Alpha Omega LifePacs) $41.95

LifePacs were designed to be used independently by students for most of the course work, but they do require some teacher interaction as directed by the teacher handbook. You will need to purchase the ten LifePacs for level 1000 and the teacher handbook. Lab experiment materials are available at significant extra cost. The Lab Kit for Biology (#SR1001 - $250) must be ordered from Sempco, Inc. You will probably also need Sempco's Core Kit of basic lab equipment (#SR0501 - $395). Some chemistry-type experiments are included which require chemicals, test tubes, beakers, and other apparatus. Obviously, the cost of the lab equipment will make this course impractical for many home educators. You might consider purchasing the LifePacs, determining which experiments are crucial, then find inexpensive and or practical ways to do them. However, since experiments are built into the body of each lesson it is difficult to do this. Unfortunately, the experiments do not correlate with those in *Experiences in Biology for Small Schools*, so there's no help there. Required materials are listed in the teacher's handbooks, so you can put together your own lab equipment. Check the sources under " For Lab Work" for information about materials you might

wish to order. You might decide that Alpha Omega's laboratory kit is a worthwhile investment to save you time and energy.

The course itself is challenging for high school level biology; it covers more chemistry than others and includes more difficult vocabulary. It covers taxonomy, chemical aspects of biology, microbiology, cells, plants, human anatomy and physiology, genetics, cell division and reproduction, ecology/pollution/energy, and principles and applications of biology. It has less coverage on animal anatomy and physiology than do most other courses, and requires a very minimal amount of animal dissection (a chicken leg was all that I spotted). Nevertheless, there are more activities and experiments than we find in some other courses, and students are required to write numerous essay answers ranging from a few sentences to multiple paragraphs. At the teacher's discretion, students are also assigned a number of written reports. The Christian viewpoint is very evident throughout the course.

⊃ Schick Anatomy Atlas (American Map Corporation) $29.95

For those studying the human body, this is an excellent reference resource. Thirty, full-color anatomy charts are each overlaid with transparent identifying overlays as we see in college physiology books. Teens (and younger children) will find these fascinating to look at aside from their studies. It is an excellent investment and well worth the cost. (Order number 1448-2)

⊃ StudyWare for Biology [Computer program for IBM or Macintosh machines] (Cliffs Notes) $19.98 suggested retail

This program can be used to supplement a biology course. It is designed for review rather than instruction. Questions are posed on the screen, with multiple choice answers. Both correct and incorrect answers are explained. An on-line glossary, hints, and illustrations are easily accessible.(S)

⊃ Reviewing Biology (Amsco) $5.60; answer key - $1.95

Students who want to take New York State Regents Exams or other achievement tests can use this book to review all the key concepts of biology. It reviews at two levels of difficulty, marking with asterisks those topics that are beyond a typical high school biology course, such as biological structure formulas (learned from chemistry). A brief chapter on evolution will prepare students with information to fit the biases they will encounter on tests, especially important for students who have studied only from Christian texts.

Since this book is intended for review, it covers each topic very succinctly, followed by multiple choice questions. A glossary is included. Almost half of the book is sample tests (New York State Regents Exams). The inexpensive answer key is also necessary.(SE)

Chemistry

While A Beka, BJUP, and Alpha Omega all offer chemistry courses, it can be difficult to set up a laboratory at home if you are trying to follow their lab instructions. Alpha Omega is easier than the others if you purchase the lab equipment from Sempco, Inc., but the kits are quite expensive. Accredited courses such as those available from the North Dakota Division of Independent Study, University of Nebraska-Lincoln, and American School are options that might be of interest. Seton's chemistry course described below might also be an excellent alternative since the course is designed for home educators and the cost is very reasonable. You might also wish to check with private schools, junior colleges, public high schools, etc., for opportunities to enroll your child in chemistry with a good lab program and save yourself the hassle of doing it at home.

⊃ **Basic Chemistry** (Bob Jones University Press) student text - $28; teacher's edition - $41; lab manual - $12; teacher's edition for lab manual - $15; supplement - $8

This course really requires a knowledgeable teacher. Instruction must be presented from the teacher's edition, and it assumes teacher familiarity with the subject. Even with a qualified teacher, homeschoolers will generally find the lab impractical for home purposes since it assumes classroom equipment and resources. However, the situation is slightly improved with BJUP's *Chemistry and Physics for Christian Schools Laboratory Manual Supplement* which helps home schoolers select and adapt activities from the lab manuals for each course. (Both courses are covered within the single *Supplement.*) While the *Supplement* suggests less expensive or less dangerous substitutions where appropriate, the cost and challenge of setting up a chemistry lab is still formidable. This is probably one of the more difficult BJUP courses for home schoolers to adapt for home use.

⊃ **Building Blocks of the Universe** by Isaac Asimov (Abelard-Schuman, out of print)

This out-of-print book is a wonderful introduction to the study of chemistry if you can find a copy. (Check used book stores.) Asimov introduces twenty-three of the most common elements, teaching basic chemical principles without the mathematical explanations for valences and bonding. It is more of a "get acquainted" approach, telling about characteristics and uses of each element. For every element, there is an unusual or interesting association, such as neon gas and neon lights. *Building Blocks* is a good book for preventing "chemistry-phobia" right from the beginning. Read this before beginning a chemistry course.(SE)

⊃ **The Camelot General Chemistry Primer** (Kenndon, Krastins & Gould) $17.95

This is a lighthearted but not lightweight book written by an experienced chemistry tutor. Serious chemistry and outrageous puns and cartoons combine to make a unique worktext. The story theme is medieval alchemy, and the main characters are a dragon and a fairie, but these are just for fun and have no occultic overtones. Some parents will be reassured to know that the foreword for this book was written by Dr. Duane Gish, a well-known creation-scientist with the Institute for Creation Research.

The material covered is supposed to be equivalent to a high school honors chemistry course or a little more than the first semester of a three-semester college general chemistry series. This course is too involved for non-science majors, but it does cover material required for science majors. However, it is not as comprehensive as most other texts in its treatment of elements. While students can use it as a stand-alone course, it would be best if they are able to meet occasionally with someone who knows chemistry to ask questions and go over exercises, midterm, and final. Because this challenging course is designed for self-study, it really is essential that the student be self-motivated to do it.

As with any serious chemistry course, the content requires a great deal of study, but the author tries to balance the "mind-numbing" aspects with levity through cartoons and humor. The author's background involved tutoring chemistry students, so he has become familiar with the types of problems most students are likely to encounter. Consequently, he has tried to address such issues within the book to keep confusion and puzzlement to a minimal level. Chemistry problems are included in the book, with answers following a page or two later. This helps students determine whether or not they are grasping the material as they go along. Interspersed are "profiles" of various elements. In one page, the author introduces an element, then comments on its nature, discovery, and use. Unfortunately, because of its brevity, these profiles tend to dissolve into vagueness. However, the reader should not expect his curiosity to be satisfied by so brief a discussion, but should be inspired to look for more information elsewhere. Challenging vocabulary and a great deal of math (algebra) remind us that this is not a course for average students.

The biggest concern has to do with organization. The first chapter covers dimensional analysis. The text is broken up and sometimes crowded with cartoons and puns, occasionally making it difficult to follow the concepts. Since dimensional analysis is the foundation of the book and chemistry in general, this is a major detraction. A notebook-insert glossary and log-table insert are included for ready reference.

Ten chapter examinations, a midterm and a final are available in the separate *Teaching Guide and Assessment Battery*. This is not a teacher's manual, but primarily a source for exams (which are thorough and challenging) and answer keys with suggestions for grading and scoring the entire course. It does include a description of the course philosophy and learning objectives. No lab activity is included.

This book was the first attempt to create a user-friendly, yet high-caliber chemistry course for independent study, so, while it has some faults, it deserves serious consideration. [Craig Roberts/Valerie Thorpe/C.D.]

⊃ **Chemistry [video course]** (The Teaching Company) $199.95; extra student workbooks - $10

This is a supplementary chemistry course presented on four, extended-play VHS tapes, with two lesson outline booklets and a student workbook. There are a total of 30 lessons, each 30 minutes long. Master teacher Frank Cardulla explains at the beginning of the course that the emphasis will be on problem solving rather than all chemistry concepts. Mr. Cardulla claims that "chemistry is the easiest class in school" because the mathematical thinking and manipulation centers around just a few basic models. If students learn how to perform the mathematical manipulations, chemistry becomes a much easier course. Consequently, Mr. Cardulla focuses on setting up and solving various types of problems encountered in chemistry such as converting between systems of measurement, solving mole problems, empirical formulas, balancing chemical equations, and solving equilibrium problems. He uses a flip chart and chalk board to talk and work through problems. It's a very "chatty" approach compared to most chemistry courses, probably because it is intended to defuse many of the fears students have about the subject. Students should use it alongside a complete course. They should watch the first lesson at the very beginning of their chemistry study, then watch the following lessons as each concept comes up. Students might skip around in the lessons to match up with what they are being taught in their primary textbook. Two booklets that come with the tapes outline each lesson. A student workbook has 62 pages of chemistry problems. Answers are in the last half of the book. Application problems in the workbook help students test their grasp of the various skills and concepts. The workbook is not reproducible, so you need to buy extras for additional students.(S)

⊃ Chemistry [video course] (School of Tomorrow) $12
PACEs - $48; answer keys - $16; videos: purchased - $550
OR rented - $59.95 per quarter

School of Tomorrow offers three options for studying chemistry: PACES only, a combination of videos and PACEs, or a combination of videos with computer software (CVI). This course is vocabulary intensive and requires a familiarity with algebra for math computations. Content is similar to other high school chemistry courses. Lab demonstrations for which students complete lab data worksheets are only presented on the videos; students using only PACEs will not be able to view labs and, thus, will not be able to complete the lab worksheets. Students read through text material in the PACEs or view each video segment, then complete the questions either in PACEs or on the computer screen if they are working with the software. Periodic tests cover content only within the PACE in which students are working. There are no comprehensive, cumulative tests. Famous scientists and historical scientific events are interwoven with the text from time to time to make it more interesting. Each PACE includes a "Teen Life Principles" reading that focuses on character qualities. Although there is little to no connection with chemistry in these readings, questions from them are included in some of the tests. (They deal with issues like dating principles, the value of Bible meditation, and wise decision making. You might choose to skip these, especially if you disagree with any of the content.) The 24 videos for the course are very professionally done, incorporating computer graphics, lab experiments, film footage of real-life chemistry applications, and even some

dramatization. The narration sticks fairly closely to the wording of the PACEs themselves, so students can follow along and/or review in the PACEs if they choose. PACEs also include charts students will need for reference as they go through the course. When the videos are combined with the computer software, students do not need the PACEs except for the reference charts. The computer presents questions, records and evaluates answers, retaining a record of student progress and scoring. The video presentation is adequate although less interesting than the *Physical Science* course—the presenter could be a little livelier. I think the course seems less interesting than some other School of Tomorrow courses largely because so much time is spent on vocabulary and definitions.

⊃ Chemistry [correspondence course] (North Dakota Division of Independent Study)

It takes two, one-semester courses to comprise a complete high school chemistry course. The same textbook, *Basic Chemistry* by Seese and Daub, is used for both parts. Laboratory experiments are included, and students need to order the lab kits for each semester. As of this writing, the Lab Kit for Chemistry I costs $83.50; the Lab Kit for Chemistry II is $76. Out-of-state students pay a little less than $50 for enrollment in each course, plus the cost of the text ($48), study guides for each semester ($15 each), plus the lab kits.

⊃ Chemistry [correspondence course] (Seton Home Study Program) $125 includes registration, tuition, text, and syllabus

Seton offers a chemistry correspondence course. The course includes the A Beka *Chemistry* text, lesson plans, tests, and lab experiments. The lesson plans were written to correlate with the textbook, and the lab experiments are appropriate for home study. Household items are used for lab work, with the exception of just a few chemicals that you will need to order. (Seton provides assistance in locating chemicals if you need it.) The course is very reasonable in cost and offers a fairly easy method for providing a comprehensive lab class.

Seton also offers the Castle Heights *Experiments in Chemistry* as a supplementary option for lab work. (It can provide all lab work if we choose to use it for that purpose.)

⊃ Chemistry: Precision and Design (A Beka Book) $24.90;
teacher edition - $35.20; solution key - $31.50; lab videos - $150 each

A Beka's *Chemistry* text assumes that there is a teacher for the course. Consequently it is quite difficult for most home educators to use. The lab work also assumes a complete school lab set up. If you choose to use A Beka's course, the teacher's edition contains the complete student text plus teaching notes. Answers are contained in a separate solution key. Two videos of lab demonstrations might substitute for actual lab work, although they are very expensive. Castle Heights' *Experiences in Chemistry* might also offer a more practical lab approach.

The entire course is also available through A Beka's Video Home School in one of two options: Basic Chemistry which requires General Science and Algebra I as prerequisites, or College Prep Chemistry which requires Algebra I and Algebra II. In the video course, the teacher really cares about his subject and tries to stimulate his students to think about and analyze what they read and hear. This course would benefit much from the inclusion of graphics, but given A Beka's limited approach with the video, the teacher does a decent job with the class.

⊃ Chemistry—Science Workshop Series—Books 1, 2, and 3 (Globe Fearon Educational Publisher) $11.95 each; teacher's editions - $16.95 each

This is a chemistry course including laboratory work that is practical for home schoolers who do not need a rigorous chemistry course. (It is written as a remedial course.) The books have shorter reading passages in a worktext format requiring brief responses. Lots of diagrams and photographs are included along with many activities. The first book is introductory—many students will have already covered the content in elementary school or junior high. Topics in Book 1 (*Atoms and Elements*): introduction to scientific methods; states of matter; atoms and elements; and compounds. You might want to skip Book 1 and begin with Book 2. Book 2 (*Mixtures and Solutions*) covers mixtures, solutions, acids and bases, pollution, toxic waste, and acid rain. Book 3 (*Reactions*) covers matter, chemical reactions, metals, oxidation, and reduction. Older editions of this series covered slightly more difficult content, so use them if you can find them.

This course does not compare with typical high school chemistry courses in scope or depth, although you could grant high school credit for it as an introductory course. College preparatory students will usually need a more challenging course depending which college they plan to attend and what studies they will be pursuing. The experiments in these books can be done easily at home and will satisfy the need for a lab class.

The teacher's editions for each book contain answers, teaching strategies, and tests.(SE)

⊃ ElementO (Lewis Educational Games) $31.95

Monopoly fans will love *ElementO*. *ElementO* imitates *Monopoly* with a sturdy, colorful game board, moving pieces, "money" (two forms, called protons and neutrons), opportunities to acquire monopolies (of element groups), "hazard" cards, and a similar manner of play. However, the accumulation of protons in order to win only occurs as students move around the board, becoming familiar with the Periodic Table and individual elements. The elemental groups are color coded, so students begin to learn about their relationships to one another. No prior knowledge is required. In fact, this game is an excellent tool for introducing students to chemistry without overwhelming them. The game is suggested for players ages ten to adult. While ten-year-olds are able to play, junior and senior high students will be in better positions to use the knowledge. The instructions are quite involved, and we found them unclear or incomplete in a few situations where we ended up making up our own rules. You must read through the instructions completely before beginning and clarify how you will deal with situations that don't seem to be covered in the rules before actually starting to play. While this might be a lit-

tle frustrating for some, we enjoyed the freedom to "play it our way." An option for reduced playing time or various ways you might end the game are offered, otherwise the game might last days like Monopoly games. This game is truly instructional, but it also meets the "playability test"—it is fun to more than once.

⊃ Experiences in Chemistry by Kathleen Julicher (Castle Heights Press, Inc.) $24.95

"This uncomplicated chemistry laboratory manual was written for the small school with modest resources," according to the author. The experiments described in this book have been tested in both regular and home schools and cover the breadth of topics typical of high school chemistry courses. Although experiments are not written to correlate with any particular textbook, the topics are common enough that we should be able to correlate them with any text we choose. Experiments are arranged under the general topic headings of density, kinetic energy and molecular motion, chemical reactions, and types of reactions.

Introductory information about basic goals for high school chemistry knowledge, safety rules, and chart making are found in the front of the book, while in the back are lists of supplies and sources plus a description of scientific method.

Experiments are well organized. Materials needed are listed in a box at the top of the page. Background information and the purpose is explained. Step-by-step procedure is followed by questions about the experiment itself and about related topics. Some questions direct students to do outside research that will expand their understanding. The author has frequently inserted information about "real life" situations where the chemistry knowledge can be observed or applied, which makes learning more interesting to many students. Observation charts for recording data are also included with most experiments. Families are free to copy all necessary pages from the book for their students, but there is also a *Student Activity Notebook* ($9.95) in which students can record their work. An answer key is included in *Experiments in Chemistry*.

Parents who have had chemistry before should not find this book too difficult, but parents without any background knowledge might have some trouble. (Familiarity with lab procedures is helpful especially when we have to make substitutions or figure out alternative methods to use.) Overall, I think that most parents will find this book a very practical tool for helping them create chemistry lab courses. Most will also want to get a *Student Activity Notebook* for each student because it keeps all their questions and answers, data recording, observations, etc. in one place.

Castle Heights has made arrangements with the Science Projects Store so that they have the supplies for creating your own chemistry lab. Complete equipment costs $100 and chemicals are $30.

⊃ Exploring Creation with Chemistry by Dr. Jay L. Wile (Apologia Educational Ministries) $90 OR $45 per semester

The author's premise in this book is that chemistry is hard because it is told in the form of a formula instead of a story. So, he has told a story to teach chemistry. The chatty style improves the communication of concepts in many instances, but it also slows the pace somewhat. Chemistry is tedious, and this is a tedious book in some ways. It must be read, and there is a great deal of reading, lots of tests, quizzes, and exams. There is not much provision for lecture from a teacher (a relief for many parents)—the author leads the student through the study and exercises so that minimal parent/teacher involvement is needed.

The one-year course comes in a three-ring binder and can be purchased one semester at a time if that better suits your budget. It covers essentially the same content as most chemistry high school courses.

The primary goal in a high school chemistry course seems to be to prepare the student for college chemistry. The secondary goal is to teach the student methods of rigorous examination to use in other subjects. A third goal is to introduce students to some real world applications not addressed in other subject areas. It does a fairly good job of meeting these goals with a few exceptions. It lacks a little on the lab end in preparing for college chemistry classes and could use more practical applications.

The author assumes a good background in algebra and arithmetic, so he does not spend a great deal of space reviewing all the math concepts needed in the course. The answers to the tests present all of the math, so a student whose math skills are not quite as good as they should be can figure out what he doesn't understand. This marvelous idea is so rare and so welcome.

An index, glossary, and appendix which includes the periodic chart, math laws and tables, physical constants, and other helps make it easy for students to locate information they need quickly.

Of particular note, the section on catalysts includes some great diagrams and excellent dialogue that explains concepts very clearly. Another plus is the teaching methodology. Concepts are taught, then students are guided through practice exercises before they are turned lose on their own.

This course includes lab activity so that this can be considered a college-prep lab science course. The lab exercises are very good; they are exacting in detail, achieving a great deal of precision with minimal equipment. I commend the author on his ingenuity. However, students will need to be cautioned about danger when performing some of the experiments, and they will need instruction about how to dispose of dangerous byproducts. For the future college student, there is very little introduction of standard chemistry lab equipment. This lack of familiarity will probably hurt later.

On the down side, chemicals are introduced by formula but not by common name, and vice versa. This is annoying and discourages the student. Some reference to discovery, manufacture, and use of some of these chemicals would be greatly appreciated and make the subject more real.

Dr. Wile offers free question and answer service to those who purchase the curriculum. Students or parents can contact him via e-mail, phone, fax, or snail mail and receive a response within one business day. There is also a money-back guarantee on the program.[Craig Roberts]

⊃ **Friendly Chemistry** by Joey and Lisa Hajda (Hideaway Ventures) book plus 11 manipulatives - $75; parent's guide with video - $30; all of these - $100

A hefty book comes packaged with a number of card decks, charts, score sheet pad, colored fuzzy "balls," winks, game playing pieces, and a Doo-Wop Board™—a wooden board with cups arranged for learning about atomic valences. Students learn chemistry vocabulary as well as about structures, ions, forming compounds, formulas, reactions, equations, and more. The book includes fairly extensive explanations of these basic concepts plus some problems to be solved and an answer key.

This is not a comprehensive, in-depth course, although students using this course will be exposed to all topics typically taught in a public high school chemistry course. The text part of this book is only about 250 pages of widely-spaced text as compared to the typical 300-400 pages of dense type found in other textbooks. The goal of the course is to lay a foundation so that students are prepared for a freshman college level chemistry course, yet to keep it from being overwhelming. Consequently, you can consider it a complete course, although it won't be as challenging as courses such as BJUP's or A Beka's.

Those who want to teach a more challenging course, might introduce chemistry to their children with this "kit" at least a few years before they are actually ready to tackle a challenging course. They can master vocabulary and basic concepts ahead of time, which will them allow them to progress more easily and quickly through a course. Some of the games use a mixture of familiar formats such as Element Bingo, war (with the periodic table and a card deck), and a board game to work on atomic families. But some are more straightforward in requiring students to demonstrate knowledge. A certain amount of basic knowledge, which is covered in the book, is essential before students can even play the games. So you should use them as reinforcement/drill/practice tools to be used along with instruction. However, the hands-on, visual approach to learning that takes place with some of the games and activities will certainly make it easier for many students to grasp concepts, particularly valence structures.

A lab guide and a parent's guide are just being completed at this time. The parent's guide comes with a two-hour video. The guide will feature week-by-week lesson plans. The forthcoming lab guide will give complete instructions for performing basic lab activities to correlate with concepts taught in the textbook.

⊃ **Reviewing Chemistry** (Amsco) $5.60; answer key - $1.95

Students who want to take New York State Regents Exams or other achievement tests can use this book to review all the key concepts of chemistry. It reviews at two levels of difficulty, marking with asterisks those topics that are beyond a typical high school chemistry course. Even the lower level of review assumes solid knowledge of algebraic equations used in chemistry.

Since this book is intended for review, it covers each topic very succinctly, followed by multiple choice questions. A glossary is included. About one-third of the book is sample tests (New York State Regents Exams). The inexpensive answer key is also necessary.(S)

➲ Science LifePacs [1100 - 11th grade level: Chemistry] (Alpha Omega) $38.95

This is a challenging chemistry course, covering a significant amount of organic chemistry. Algebra I is prerequisite. Quite a lot of lab work is required throughout the lessons. The Lab Kit designed to use with the LifePacs (#SR1101 - $295) must be ordered from Sempco, Inc. You will probably also need the Core Kit with basic lab equipment (#SR0501 - $395), also available from Sempco, Inc. (The Core Kit can also be used with other lab courses.) You might buy the LifePacs and their companion teacher handbook first, then make a list of necessary chemicals and equipment in order of priority. Then make your purchases from sources such as those listed under "For Lab Work." However, this will be very time consuming. The experiments themselves are incorporated into the lessons and are essential for completing the course, so most of them need to be done one way or another. However, if you choose to skip some of them (especially some of the more dangerous ones), the answer key does describe what the results should have been. You can use that information to discuss the experiment with your son or daughter, then go on with the lesson.

➲ StudyWare for Chemistry [Computer program for IBM or Macintosh machines] (Cliffs Notes) $19.98 suggested retail

This program can be used to supplement any chemistry course. It covers topics such as scientific notation, atomic structure, the periodic table, acids and bases, orbital structures, electrochemistry, nuclear chemistry, quantum theory, biological chemistry, and organic chemistry. It is designed for review rather than instruction. Questions are posed on the screen, with multiple choice answers. Both correct and incorrect answers are explained. An on-line glossary, hints, graphs, and figures are easily accessible.(S)

Physics

➲ Conceptual Physics, 8th edition by Paul Hewitt (ScottForesman/Addison Wesley) $58.80; instructor's manual - $25.56; study guide - $11.95; lab manual -(price to be determined); Test Bank - $25.56

[Note: I have reviewed the 1985 and 1993 editions. The new 1998 edition should not have changed significantly. Prices are for the latest edition.] This award winning physics text keeps popping up as the most recommended textbook. The Colfax's write in *Homeschooling for Excellence*, that this book "...was less comprehensive than we would have liked but more accessible than anything else we could locate" (p.89). It is written as a college text, but can be used at high school level. It does not require a background in higher math for understanding, although some algebra is required. Hewitt writes about physics in clear, non-mathematical language understandable to those lacking science background. (Parents might even read the book and adapt the information to fit all ages.) Each chapter has a section called "Home Activities," which describes fairly simple lab/experiment activities which can easily be done at home without fancy equipment. Using these activities can make this a complete lab

course. A new lab manual will offer more challenging lab activities. Topics covered are mechanics, properties of matter, heat, sound, electricity and magnetism, atomic and nuclear physics, and relativity and astrophysics. This course is adequate for non-science majors, but insufficient for physics majors and those who will major in other areas of science because it is not based on the use of calculus. The publisher tells us that the text can be used for Advanced Placement Physics B.

I originally reviewed and recommended the 1985 edition. The 1993 edition has at least one significant change. It includes an additional paragraph and cartoon drawing explaining that "facts are revisable data." This is a significant philosophical statement that denies the existence of absolutes—a philosophical statement that essentially denies God. While this is a serious error, it is the only one that I am aware of thus far in the revised edition. I still recommend the book, but be sure to correct this misinformation and watch for other problems.

It is an expensive book, but it is hardcover and 650 pages long. You will want the instructor's manual as an answer key. I haven't seen the lab manual, but it is not necessary if you use the "Home Activities" to create your own lab. (Order through the publisher's high school division, not the college division, even though the book is advertised as a college textbook.)(SE)

➲ Exploring Creation with Physics by Dr. Jay L. Wile (Apologia Educational Ministries) $90 or $45 each semester

[Note: This course came too late for in-depth review for accuracy.] Dr. Wile's new physics course follows the same format as his *Exploring Creation with Chemistry* course. It comes in two, three-ring binders and can be used for independent study. It includes some lab activities, although these are fairly simple for a high school lab course. Lab experiments seem to be designed to illustrate principles more than to provide opportunities for serious scientific work. Math is applied in only a few experiments, and because Dr. Wile is trying to have students use easy-to-obtain household items, measurements and accuracy will not be as precise as they would be in a formal lab situation. However, this is still a math-based course, much more so than *Conceptual Physics*. It requires the use of algebra and trigonometry. Mathematical symbols are used frequently, although Dr. Wile seems to explain these before using them. A glossary, index, and appendix are included at the back of the second-semester volume. As with the chemistry course, practice problems and examples help students verify their understanding as they work through the lessons. There is a test at the end of each chapter, but no cumulative tests or finals. Answer keys with full explanations are included. Students can also contact Dr. Wile if they have problems or questions about the course. This course will satisfy most college entry requirements for a physics course with lab.

➲ Physics for Christian Schools (Bob Jones University Press) student text - $21; teacher's edition - $39; lab manual - $12; teacher's edition for lab manual - $14; TestBank - $16

This is a twelfth-grade-level text with an accompanying *Physics Lab Manual*. We need not purchase a student text since the teacher's edition includes teacher's instructions and answer key plus a complete, bound copy of the student text. If you intend to do the labs designed for the course, you need both the student lab manual and its teacher's edition. You will also probably want to use *Chemistry and Physics for Christian Schools Laboratory Manual Supplement* [$8] which charts key experiments and offers practical substitutions for home schoolers. It includes complete lists of supplies and sources, including two kits that alone might provide the bulk of your lab equipment for less than $100.

Like most physics texts, this one draws on logic and math learned in high school math courses, so algebra I and II as well as geometry and some trigonometry are prerequisites. It combines both conceptual (as in the *Conceptual Physics* text) and mathematical approaches to physics. The course actually uses a great deal of higher level mathematics, so the teacher should also be familiar with the math involved. This text differs slightly from Saxon's *Physics*, using a traditional outline approach unlike Saxon, and including the Christian perspective. The book is well-written, illustrated, and includes interesting historical biographies and other sidebar discussions. This text is useful for the teacher/parent who is familiar with physics and higher math, who can work closely with the student, and who will work to develop lab experiences at home. (BJUP offers a wide range of science lab equipment and supplies. Contact them for more information.)[Michael Courtney/C.D.]

⊃ Physics (School of Tomorrow) videos - $550; computer disks - $106.67; PACEs plus answer keys - $64. School of Tomorrow offers two rental options: videos only ($239.80 per course, broken down into quarterly rentals of $59.95 each) or rental package that include PACEs and Score Keys ($299.80 per course or $74.95 per quarter). Video rentals are shipped in four groups.

Prerequisites: Algebra 1 and 2 and Geometry. The *Physics* course is one of the new CVI (computer video interactive) courses from School of Tomorrow. (See the general CVI description under the review of School of Tomorrow in Chapter Nine under Major Publishers plus the reviews of the *Algebra I* and *Biology* courses.) *Physics* has two videos and two computer disks per PACE like *Biology*. The PACEs are not necessary with the CVI course, but, until School of Tomorrow makes searching for information easier, most students will appreciate having the PACEs. The *Physics* videos feature pictures and graphic demonstrations, although they are not quite as interesting as the *Physical Science* and *Biology* video courses. Also, the videos demonstrate laboratory experiments, but students complete a lab record without actually doing lab work themselves just as in the *Biology* and *Physical Science* courses. The course teaches challenging, high-level physics. Math is integrated throughout. However, it tends to leave students at the lower levels of thinking. Students are not challenged to analyze and hypothesize as they are in most physics classes. Because of this, the course will be suitable for some learners, but not all—especially not for the Competent Carls who thrive on opportunities to do independent, imaginative thinking. Nevertheless, since this is one of the few courses that does not assume that a physics teacher is on hand to explain things, it will probably be one of the easiest ways for

homeschoolers to cover physics at home if they do not have a physicist in the family.

The course can be used without videos or without the computer. The PACEs contain all instructional material and can be used on their own, so we choose between the PACEs or the videos for the lesson presentation. The videos can be paired with the PACEs rather than the computer, but the videos do not stand alone.

⊃ Physics: An Incremental Development (Saxon) home study kit - $61.95; solution manual - $25

Saxon has created a physics text that should be suitable for a wide range of students from average to gifted. Even better, students should be able to do most of their studying independently; the text does not require a teacher with prior knowledge of physics. However, there should be someone with physics knowledge available for consultation or further explanation if needed. The text is challenging and comprehensive enough to prepare students for the Advanced Placement test. Although it appears that only *Algebra 1* and *Algebra 2* are prerequisite, some knowledge of trigonometry ahead of time would be helpful. (Students learn trigonometry in *Advanced Mathematics*.) The trigonometry and calculus that students will need is covered within the *Physics* book, but it would be better if students already had a broader understanding of those subjects.

Saxon uses the same incremental approach that he uses in his math series, which might bother students who prefer comprehensive coverage of one topic at a time. Nevertheless, this text is comprehensive, well-written, and easy-to-use. Explanations are clear, and there are plenty of practical applications to which students can relate. Five "curveball questions" at the end of each chapter force students to think through concepts and applications. Solutions follow immediately after these questions, but I would urge students to wrestle with these on their own before looking at the solutions. The only significant problem is the lack of lab activity.

This course would be best for all students who want to use it only for high school credit, and for non-engineering/science majors who want to test out of a college first-year physics course. Engineering/science majors should take a calculus-based course for physics.

The home study kit includes an answer key to the problem sets for the same cost as the student book by itself. You should also purchase the solution manual.[Michael Courtney/C.D.]

⊃ Physics: The Foundational Science (A Beka) $24.90; solution key - $31.50; teacher's guide - $15.75; lab manual - $12.20; teacher edition for lab manual - $15.75; test book -$6.05; quiz book - $4.35; answer keys to quiz and test books - $8.95 each; video demonstrations - $150

Prerequisites are Algebra I and II. This text from A Beka should work for home educated students. It moves from the familiar—matter, energy, solids, liquids, gases, and mechanics—to the less familiar concepts—thermodynamics, wave phenomena, light, electricity and magnetism, quantum theory, special relativity, and electronics. For better understanding, practical examples are given and ideas are related to everyday experiences. The harmony between the Bible and science is repeatedly demonstrated. The text can be adapted for students of varying ability by choosing from various options within the text. Video tape lab demonstrations will help with lab work but they are very expensive. A teacher's guide, solution key, test packet, and quiz booklet are available as well as a lab manual and accompanying teacher's guide, which I have not reviewed.

➲ Reviewing Physics (Amsco) $7.27; answer key - $1.95

Students who want to take New York State Regents Exams or other achievement tests can use this book to review all the key concepts of physics. It covers mechanics, energy, electricity and magnetism, waves, and "modern physics," with optional units on motion in a plane, internal energy, electromagnetic applications, geometric optics, nuclear energy, and solid state physics. The math required to understand concepts as presented in this book is at least through precalculus. Since this book is intended for review, it covers each topic very succinctly, followed by multiple choice questions. A summary of equations, reference charts, and a glossary are included. About one-third of the book is sample tests (New York State Regents Exams). The inexpensive answer key is also necessary.(S)

➲ Science LifePacs [1200 - 12th grade level: Physics] (Alpha Omega) $38.95

Prerequisite: Algebra I. Designed for independent work, the course consists of ten LifePacs, teacher handbook, and answer key. LifePac topics include: kinematics, dynamics, work and energy, introduction to waves, light, static electricity, current electricity, magnetism, and atomic and nuclear physics. This course does not have to be used as a lab course, but it is strongly recommended. Sempco, Inc. sells a lab kit designed to accompany the LifePacs (#SR1201 -$395). You also probably need Sempco's Core Kit (#SR0501 - $395). The kits are very expensive, and you might find that you can construct enough experiments of your own with household equipment at a lower cost.

Technology

Technology often fits under "physics," but, since some resources actually serve as complete high school level courses, and since technology is increasingly being emphasized in the new educational goals, it is fitting that it get a separate category here.

➲ Electronic Kits International (EKI) HOMEMC1 - $79.95; HOMEKITS - $59.95

The basic Electronics Discovery Kit (HOMEMC1) is a self-teaching course for learning basic electronics for IBM compatible or Macintosh computers. It includes software, lab book, a solderless circuit board, and electronic components. The course is broken down into lessons on individual areas of electronics with quizzes on each section. Lessons are presented via text and visual aids on 14 computer disks (there is no textbook), which makes it far more interesting and easier than textbook-based courses. The lab book covers many of the same concepts as the software, but also shows step-by step assembly of circuits on the

solderless circuit board. Students get lab experience on the computer and by building actual electronic devices; they complete a lesson, then do the "lab work" on the board. The course comes in a three-ring binder which holds disks and installation instructions. The computer disks are designed to be used by an entire class and to record each student's progress separately.

We can purchase the basic course then create our own electronic experiments, but EKI has put together electronic kits for putting newly-attained knowledge into practice. The kits come as a set (HOMEKITS)—5 kits plus a three-ring binder holding 5 disks with instructions for building the kits. Kits reinforce and expand upon the lessons in HOMEMC1. For example, once students have learned about resistors, they should be able to build the "LED Blinker Kit"—a light circuit with a resistor in it. With the first five kits students build alarms, blinkers, and lights—projects both teens and adults like to build.

Additional courses are available; HOMEMC2, Digital Magic [$99.95], features 14 disks covering topics such as digital electronics, integrated circuits, logic circuits, and logic gates. HOMEMETER [$129.95] features 8 disks covering such things as analog and digital meters, checking continuity, and measuring voltage and current. This kit includes both a digital multimeter and an analog multimeter. Both of these kits come with the required electronic components.

HOMECH3 [$15.95] is actually three, game-like review courses which challenge the student's mastery of electronics topics they have already studied. It includes 3 disks titled "Resistor Color Code Challenge," "Ohm's Law Challenge," and "Multimeter Challenge." Check the EKI catalog for other electronics resources.

➲ Technology (Creative Learning Systems, Inc.)

I lack the time and the expertise to review this book personally, but I am certain that many home educators will love the idea of studying technology rather than the traditional science courses. The book and accompanying materials were developed by Brad and Terry Thode. Thus, course components are referred to as the Thodes' course. The catalog description says, "...it is filled with exercises and activities that challenge students and help them develop higher-level thinking skills. More than 73 design briefs give students the opportunity to plan, build,, and test their solutions to real problems—the same kinds of problems they'll confront in the workplace.... Throughout the text, technology is integrated with other subjects such as math, science, and language arts." Some home schoolers might be interested in the software (Mac Hypercard) with interactive lessons. The book is suggested for grades 7-12 and should cost less than $50.(S)

➲ Creative Learning Systems, Inc.

Their Transtech catalog features books, software, videos, and kits on technology. (See the catalog description under "Sources for Materials.")(S)

Botany

Botany is not a required subject, but it is life science. Students who do not need to have biology, might consider botany as a substitute. Anyone wishing to study botany should probably first gather catalogs from suppliers such as those listed under "For Lab Work," or from Lifetime Books or other distributors with a broad line of products, then sort through for resources they might wish to use. Those who are concerned about providing courses more like those in schools can look for botany textbooks from used or college book stores. (These books tend to be uniformly gray and boring in appearance.) While texts can be useful for background information and detailed explanations, field guides and field study usually provide the most effective and interesting learning. We also found the Boy Scout merit badge booklet for botany very helpful, especially since we used the merit badge outline as part of our course. (Unfortunately, the botany merit badge has been discontinued, so the merit badge booklet is out of print.) There are a few other plant-related merit badge booklets that might be of interest: *Forestry, Gardening*, and *Plant Science*.(Check your phone book for the nearest Boy Scouts of America store.)

In searching for effective botany resources, I was frustrated by the almost universal inclusion of evolutionary theory throughout the books. Evolution is used to explain and identify plant groups by showing how they supposedly all are descendants from simpler life forms. I have not found any botany textbook that is not based upon evolution. (Let me know if you find one.) Even the children's books are loaded with it, so we have to watch content most of the time. Some resources that I would recommend to you are:

⊃ **The Book of Forest and Thicket: Trees, Shrubs, and Wildflowers of Eastern North America** by John Eastman (Stackpole Books) $16.95

"It is one thing to recognize a plant or animal. It is another to know where to look for it, to become familiar with its way of life, to achieve a sense of its links to other organisms and its existence as a community dweller." This introductory statement highlights the difference between this guide and so many other field guides. Identifying plants is better done with a field guide, but for those who want to know more, this is a wonderful book.

A description of each plant is given along with alternate names, and a listing of close relatives. Next is a section on each plant called "Lifestyles." This is where it gets interesting. We learn about the plant's habits, likes, dislikes, and peculiarities. "Associates" describes plants, animals, and other insects that are typically in the surrounding environment. "Lore" delves into man's use of the plant and its history, as well as folkloric uses and associations.

This book will add a dimension to botanical studies which appeals to learners who want to know more than just the basic information and want to truly understand nature. (Note that it is specific to Eastern North America rather than a comprehensive book.)(S)

⊃ **Peterson's Field Guides** (Houghton Mifflin/McDougal Littell) $12-$19

These guides are for those willing to first familiarize themselves with botanical vocabulary. To use the guides, we follow a key which classifies plants according to structural characteristics such as the number of petals and their arrangement, the number of stamens, placement of the ovary, etc. While illustrations of these features are provided in the books, some knowledge is necessary to use them properly. On the other hand, these books can be much more efficient to use than others such as the Audobon that require us to look through many pages to try to find a matching picture. Peterson's Field Guides titles for botany are *Pacific States Wildflowers, Southwest and Texas Wildflowers, Eastern and Central Edible Wildplants, Mushrooms, Ferns, Eastern Trees, Western Trees, Trees and Shrubs, Eastern Forests, Rocky Mountain Wildflowers, Wildflowers of Northeastern/Northcentral North America*, and *Medicinal Plants*.(S)

Health

Note: Also see "Sex Education" in Chapter Eighteen, "Beyond the Three R's."

I include a review of an herbology course since this topic is of tremendous interest to many home educators. Since the review was written by someone much more knowledgeable about the subject than I, I cannot vouch for it personally. However, it sounds like one of the few such options that does not conflict with Christian philosophy.

⊃ **Be Your Own Doctor Herbal Course** David Christopher (The School of Natural Healing) $100

This correspondence course for teens through adults is "a structured course of studies, to train Herbalists in the prudent, safe, and effective use of herbs, within the confines of natural healing. ...the school concentrates on teaching wholistic principles, which, when applied correctly can deal with all diseases." While other courses teach the treatment of symptoms, this course teaches causes of illness and treatment programs. It covers the fundamentals of herbology, internal cleansing, herbal home health care, and the story of Dr. John Christopher. The course consists of audio and video tapes, books, study guide, and test. This is a beginning herbal course that takes a "big picture" approach. Those who want to pursue details and background research will need to take follow-up courses such as the "Master Herbalist Study Program" and "Midwifery." Phone tutorials are also available. The presenter acknowledges God and the Bible, but is silent on Jesus Christ, so, while it is not a truly Christian course, it is not New Age as are so many others.(SE)[Diane Wheeler]

⊃ **Dynamic Biblical Living course S156** (Landmark's Freedom Baptist Curriculum) $35

Dynamic Biblical Living is sold as the second semester of a year-long, eleventh-grade course, with the first semester being LFBC's *Health* course. Neither course can be taken alone; students must take both. It includes a worktext, quizzes, tests, and answer keys. Students also need a KJV Bible. This conservative Christian course covers Bible reading, preparing the heart, living what you read, Biblical meditation, applying thinking skills, and Bible principles. There is leeway for individual thinking in the worktext answers, so students are not just parroting back information. [Valerie Thorpe/C.D.]

➲ Health course S155 (Landmark's Freedom Baptist Curriculum) $35

Thoroughly based on biblical principles, this course covers anatomy and physiology in relation to health. From that foundation, it moves on to discussion of germs, nutrition, hygiene, exercise, weight, sleep/energy/fatigue, alcohol, tobacco, and drugs. The last six weeks focus on relationships, moral purity, human reproduction (carefully skirting details of sexual intercourse), and mental attitudes. Some topics are covered more thoroughly than others. For example, the lesson on hygiene is very detailed, but a lesson that is supposed to cover germs and diseases, barely mentions germs and says nothing about diseases. Each lesson is followed by numerous activities: matching, fill-in-the-blanks, short-answer questions, completing lists of key points, writing and memorizing Bible verses, essays, and reports. Students are required to do a significant amount of research and writing throughout this course, so, while coverage of some topics seems scant, this might well be compensated for in the research assignments. The viewpoint is very conservative—tobacco, alcohol, and sex outside of marriage are wrong. Modesty in dress is stressed, including comments that shorts and mini-skirts are improper attire for young ladies. Single dating is discouraged, and group activities encouraged. STDs and AIDS are covered fairly briefly—what we do and don't know about means of AIDS transmission could probably use more attention since this is a great concern for many young people. Quizzes, exams, and answer keys come with the worktext. This is intended to be used a one-semester course, used for the first half of eleventh grade, followed by LFBC's *Dynamic Biblical Living* course.

➲ Health for Christian Schools (Bob Jones University Press)
$28; teacher's edition - $39; testbank - $16; AskIt - $14; Blackline Masters - $14

This text can be used for one or more years from 7th through 12th grades, depending upon requirements in your state and when you wish to teach the various topics. Bob Jones University Press' philosophy is evident throughout this text: alcohol and tobacco should never be used, sexual activity outside of marriage is wrong, etc. Aside from these positions, the book takes a "middle of the road" (for want of a better way of describing it) Christian approach to topics. For example, the issue of global warming is presented but accompanied by the caution that there is no actual proof it is happening. Traditional medicine is the standard with no mentions of herbology or chiropractic services. Steady dating is viewed as a final step before engagement rather than a desirable activity for most teens. Even though many home educating families might prefer that dating be eliminated apart from an actual courtship situation (and occur there only within

proscribed limits), the BJUP *Health* textbook's position actually is more conservative than that of most Christian churches. I appreciate the fact that, in keeping with their statement that sexual activity outside of marriage is forbidden, the authors then spend only minimal time addressing issues related to sexual activity—no how-to's, brief descriptions of sexually transmitted diseases, bare mentions of AIDS (a little extra information on AIDS and STDs is in the Appendix), and no mention of homosexuality. For those who want more information on such topics as well as other information appropriate for older students, a softbound book of 236 blackline masters is available. We can copy out whichever pages we choose. Additional information on sex education can also be found in the teacher's edition.

Scripture references are referenced and quoted throughout the text to identify biblical positions on different issues. General topics covered are the human body systems, mental and emotional health, social health, nutrition, exercise, safety, first aid, diseases, personal hygiene, environment and health, drugs, alcohol, tobacco, and growth and development. The presentation is often banal, spending time on such topics as how to wash your hair and answering questions like "What is an accident?" Too often, it repeats the obvious. I assume that this is just in case a teen has never heard some of this before, but it does get boring. Occasionally the content gets into a "meaty" topic, but parents will need to spend time on supplementary discussion and activities if they want students to enjoy the class. Some suggestions are included in the teacher's edition, but I suspect that current events and personal experiences will provide the best opportunities for such discussions and activities.

Frequent "Section Reviews" offer questions that can be used to assess student comprehension as you go through each chapter. At the end of each chapter are vocabulary terms, content questions (which might be used as tests), and application questions which stretch into some worthwhile activities.

You should purchase both a student text and a teacher's edition. The teacher's edition contains much of the lesson presentation, teaching hints, and answers printed in a border surrounding a reduced picture of each student text page. Pictures are only in black-and-white in the teacher's edition, while they are full color in the student text. If you don't mind your student having access to the answers, you might get away with purchasing only the teacher's edition. If you want test questions in addition to the content questions at the end of the chapters, a softbound *Test-Bank* as well as the *AskIt* test bank data disk are available.

➲ A Healthier You (A Beka)
$12.15; teacher edition - $17.30; test and study book - $4.90; answer key to test/study book - $8.60

This health text is designed to complement science studies at seventh grade level. It should take anywhere form 9 to 18 weeks to complete. Unlike secular texts, this one focuses on both inner and outer health. Topics include emotional changes, self-control, attitudes, courtesy, posture, grooming and appearance, drugs (with a strong stand against drugs, alcohol, and cigarettes), and spiritual fitness. You really don't need the teacher edition. A student review and test booklet plus an accompanying answer key might be useful for those who want to test their students.

↪ **Let's Be Healthy** (A Beka) $14.05: teacher edition - $20.05; review and test book - $4.90; quiz book - $3.75; answer keys to review/test book and quiz book - $8.60 each

Topics in this health text (suggested for grades 8-10) include nutrition, diets, food abuse problems, AIDS, and first aid. AIDS education covers the crucial information without describing deviant sexual practices, condoms, and other elements deemed essential in public school AIDS education programs. This is a 9-18 week course, designed to supplement science (ideally at eighth grade level). Discussion and written questions are in the student text. The teacher edition includes presentation information and answers to the student text questions. Extras: Student Review and Test Booklet and accompanying teacher key; Student Quiz Booklet and accompanying teacher key.

↪ **Foodworks and Sportworks** (Addison Wesley) $9.95 each

These are two separate books, originally from the Ontario Science Center. Each is a combination of information and experiments. *Foodworks* has over 100 activities plus all kinds of information—some interesting, some disgusting—about food. Perfect for junior high kids! *Sportworks* will help teens identify their basic body shape, learn how to react intelligently when someone mentions "lats, pecs, and delts," understand the dynamics of movement in different sports, and much more. More than fifty activities are scattered through the book. Both books have humorous text and lots of funny illustrations. These are books that teens will enjoy reading and using. I expect that they will learn and remember more practical information from these books than they will from textbooks.(S)

↪ **Total Health: Choices for a Winning Lifestyle** by Susan Boe (RiversEdge Publishing Co.) hard cover - $27.95; softbound - $22.95; test and quiz book - $14.90; Parent Connection - $11.95

Up until now, there has been no comprehensive health curricula written specifically for Christian day schools <u>and</u> home schoolers. This 464-page book is definitely written from a Christian perspective. The emphasis on spiritual motivation based on our relationship with God plays a major role throughout the book. Since *Total Health* was written for either Christian day schools or home schools, there are two different teacher's editions available, although we want the one for home schools. The *Test and Quiz Book* includes fairly brief teaching instructions plus quizzes, tests, and answer keys. The textbook covers all of the topics addressed in other texts, although the amount of time devoted to many of them is very different. For example, human reproduction is covered very briefly <u>without</u> full details or illustrations. Instead of spending pages and pages describing various types of drugs, it discusses drugs and drug abuse in a more general fashion in less than three pages. For many home educators, this approach makes far more sense, since we spend more time on positive health and nutrition issues and less time on the negative issues that seem to require so much attention in public

schools. Also, while other texts address physical, mental, and social health, *Total Health* adds a section on spiritual health. Social health deals with personal care, first aid, attitudes, responsibility, and relationships, including dating. Although very conservative in approach (encouragement to group date and avoid sexual activity of all kinds), the author treats dating as acceptable. Treatment of topics such as health, fitness, and nutrition is generally mainstream (no discussion of homeopathy, herbology, alternative medicine, etc.). While this course might not be as radical in some of its positions as many home educators are, it does seem to be the most comprehensive, conservative alternative designed for home education. The layout makes it very easy to use. Chapter reviews offer excellent discussion questions and activity suggestions so that parents have a natural opportunity to expand topics or shape the course as they choose.

The teacher's edition [$34.95] features chapter outlines, suggested course plans, vocabulary exercises, worksheets, transparency masters, activity suggestions, and discussion questions.

There is a new supplement for parents of teens studying *Total Health—The Parent Connection*, but I've not reviewed it.

Creation Science

Our beliefs about the origin of life play a major part in our world view if we think through the implications of our beliefs. It is vital that we work with our teens to help them explore the ramifications of a belief in evolution as well as a belief in biblical creation.

Study of the creation versus evolution controversy is addressed by some resources reviewed in Chapter Five such as the *Understanding the Times* curriculum as well as by others in that chapter listed under "Science." However, some of the resources listed below will be more easily available to some of us, and will do a good job of exploring world view implications of evolutionary doctrine. *Evolution Conspiracy* (Jeremiah Films) and *The Genesis Solution* (Films for Christ) are two such examples. (See the descriptions below.)

Master Books is one of the best sources for creation science resources. (Write for their catalog for complete listings.) One of their best books is *Origins: Creation or Evolution* [$9.95] which compares the two models of how our world began. Written for teens and classroom use, this is an easy and effective resource to use. A companion video and video teacher's guide are also available.

Master Books has many other books written for all age levels, and among those you should consider are *Fossils: Key to the Present* [$5.95], *Origin of Life* [$5.95], and the three-volume set, *The Modern Creation Trilogy* [$34.95] by Dr. Henry Morris. The Trilogy volumes are subtitled "Scripture and Creation," "Science and Creation," and "Society and Creation." The set also comes with a free CD-ROM which runs on a system with Windows 3.1 or 95. The CD-ROM is STEP compatible and includes the QuickVerse Library Book Viewer.

Master Books publishes most of the resources that come out of the Institute for Creation Research. However, you might want to contact ICR directly for information on their museum and other resources. They have an extensive catalog of products including most Master Books publications. (Their address is in the appendix.)

➲ Ancient Man-Created or Evolved [video] (Bridgestone Multimedia) $14.95

This is one of four videos by Roger Oakland covering the creation vs. evolution controversy. Oakland exposes the flaws of all of the supposed evolutionary "links" between man and apes. Then he demolishes the idea that man has evolved from a primitive state toward increasing perfection. He primarily uses archeological findings to demonstrate that advanced civilizations were in place far earlier than is commonly realized. Oakland does present scientific evidence for his statements, but the overall orientation is not as strong scientifically as *A Scientist Looks at Creation*. Although the video is of a presentation by Oakland at a church, the use of illustrations and color slides throughout are a great enhancement. The video is 58 minutes long and is appropriate for all except young children.

➲ Answers in Genesis video series (Master Books) $19.95 each or $199.95 for set of 12

A series of twelve videos features Ken Ham and Gary Parker addressing a wide array of topics related to creation and evolution. Only the first video, *What Really Happened to the Dinosaurs?*, is for younger children. The rest are for teens through adults. The videos address topics such as the book of Genesis and history, *Life Before Birth*, evolutionary beliefs and their influence on society, world view conflicts, genetics, and the evidence against evolution, *Fossils and the Flood*, and *Creation Evangelism*. See the full review of one tape in the series, *Facts and Bias: Creation vs. Evolution—Two World Views in Conflict in Chapter Five*.

➲ The Case for Creation [video] (Films for Christ) $29

This 45-minute video, hosted by Dr. D. James Kennedy, challenges the primacy that has been given to the theory of evolution, especially in the classroom. The video demonstrates the lack of evidence to support evolution. Kennedy uses the same logic that was used by the defense in the Scopes trial, that is, that we should be able to discuss all of the evidence and weigh conflicting theories to choose which we believe to be right or wrong. Interviews with scientific authorities, both Christian and non-Christian, are used to add weight to this argument and also to buttress the creationist view. I suggest using this video as an introduction to the creation/evolution controversy with teens.

➲ Creation and Time by Dr. Hugh Ross (NavPress) $12

For those who really want to explore the various viewpoints on creation science, I suggest Dr. Ross' book *Creation and Time*. Dr. Ross believes in creation, but he rejects a belief in a young earth. He presents his explanation of the agreement between biblical truth and science, even though it is not universally accepted in Christian circles. His position conflicts with that of major groups such as the Institute for Creation Research, but it deserves

attention. He gets into fairly deep scientific explanations which I don't have the knowledge to evaluate. I recommend this book primarily to parents with a science background.

➲ Creation and Time: A Report on the Progressive Creationist Book by Hugh Ross by Mark Van Bebber and Paul S. Taylor (Films for Christ/Eden Communications) $6.99

As I mentioned in the review of the original book, Hugh Ross' *Creation and Time* has been rejected by many Christians. If you are interested in both sides of the story, read this critique.

➲ Creation Science: A Study Guide to Creation! by Felice Gerwitz and Jill Whitlock (Media Angels Science) $16.95

This is one of a series of unit study guides from Media Angels that teach creation science in conjunction with language arts, math, history, and geography. See the review in Chapter Ten.

➲ Death of the Dinosaur [video] (Bridgestone Multimedia) $14.95

This 30-minute video is the fourth from the Roger Oakland series. I have not reviewed it, but recommend it based on the quality of two other videos in the series. The catalog describes it: "Examine the mystery of dinosaur extinction by evaluating the observable evidence and comparing it with two opposite world views-creation or evolution."

➲ The Education Debate Video by John Mackay (Creation Research) $25

ustralian creation-scientist, John Mackay, debates three professors and the chaplain from the University of Saskatchewan, Canada. Mackay comes to the debate loaded with evidence and overheads, while his opponents, representing the fields of geology, education, veterinary science, and religion, repeat "evolutionary slogans" about the validity of the fossil record and evidence for evolution based upon changes within species rather than between species. While the professors' positions are interesting, the chaplain's is disturbing. He presents what he claims to be the mainline Protestant belief that Genesis cannot be taken literally, that the stories are mythological, and that Christians should believe evolution because it is good science. He also claims that only narrow, fundamentalist Christians support creationism. This is an eye-opening, two-hour debate that is guaranteed to generate questions, reactions, and conversations.

➲ The Evidence for Creation [video] (Bridgestone Multimedia) $14.95

This is one of the four videos by Roger Oakland covering the creation vs. evolution controversy. Here Oakland looks at the biblical story of the creation and the flood, comparing this with the evolutionary or uniformity model. He uses color illustrations and photographs to show changes that have occurred on our planet. Especially interesting are the evidences of tropical plants that used to grow in what are now very cold regions. Similar problems with the remains of life forms found in unlikely places are also used to build the case for the creation model. A primary theme is the atmospheric changes and resulting geological changes following the flood. The video is 61 minutes long and is appropriate for all except young children.

○ Evolution Conspiracy [video] (Jeremiah Films) $19.95

This video goes beyond the debate over creation/evolution into worldview applications. It explores the development of evolutionary thought, discusses evolutionists' claims for mutational and transitional forms in light of the fossil record, and demonstrates the theological ideas implicit in evolutionary theory (showing also the links to New Age beliefs). The presentation is tightly organized, making it easy to follow the line of reasoning throughout. I highly recommend this video. (This video is available only for "home-use/private exhibition." It is not licensed for public showings.)

○ Evolution-Fact or Fiction [video] (Bridgestone Multimedia) $14.95

This is another of the four creation/evolution videos featuring Roger Oakland. It appears to differ from *The Evidence for Creation* in concentrating on the origin of the earth rather than the flood. I have not viewed it, but I recommend it based upon the quality of two other videos in the series.

○ Fossil Evidence of Creation [video] (American Portrait Films) $19.95

This 27-minute video focuses on fossils and dinosaurs to challenge evolutionary assumptions about the age of the earth and explanations for the disappearance of dinosaurs. What makes this presentation better than most is that it includes interviews with evolutionists defending their conclusions. However, their statements are contrasted with evidence presented by Dr. Andrew Snelling, supported by Dr. Gary Parker, and Dr. Steven Austin. They explore the fossil record, examining fossils found in the strata as well as questions about the formation of strata itself. They present an interesting hypothesis about the strata that deals with the time it takes for formation of many layers. The entire presentation is very well done and should easily hold the attention of teens and adults.

○ The Genesis Solution (Films for Christ) $29

This video makes an excellent lead-in to the study of creation versus evolution. Speaker Ken Ham's theme here is how foundational a belief in either creation or evolution is to the rest of a person's worldview. He shows the importance of the book of Genesis for understanding all of Scripture as well as God's relationship with and plan for man.

Ken Ham, a native Australian, is a talented speaker who skillfully lightens the presentation with humor. Animation is very effectively intermixed with Ham's presentation, making the presentation even more entertaining and also visually memorable.

If you have to pick just one film on creation and evolution, the choice might be between this film and *The Evolution Conspiracy*.

Viewing restrictions apply to this video. It is sold at two prices; the lower price allows viewing only within homes, not in larger gatherings such as churches or schools. The more expensive price licenses viewing in larger settings. Those who purchase originally for home viewing may pay the difference for licensing for larger group viewing at a later date.

Both book and video versions of *The Genesis Solution* are also available from Master Books.

○ The Grand Canyon Catastrophe: New Evidence of the Genesis Flood [video] (American Portrait Films) $19.95

Doctors Andrew Snelling, John Morris, Duane Gish, and Steven Austin present a scientific case for the formation of the Grand Canyon as the result of a flood rather than a slow, gradual process. This outstanding presentation draws on scientific observations from the Mt. St. Helens eruption, Grand Coulee, and other geological events. Comments from evolutionists present their position, but creationists present their counter-arguments. The creationists pose some credible theories about how the Grand Canyon was actually formed that deserve serious consideration. The presentation is 27 minutes long and is suitable for junior high level and up.

○ The Illustrated Origins Answer Book
by Paul S. Taylor (Films for Christ/Eden Communications) videos - $29 each or $149 for the series; book - $10.99

Films for Christ rents or sells a film/video series entitled *Origins: How the World Came to Be*. The videos are excellent, but since there are six videos in the series, home educators might prefer to purchase only one or two from the series to start.

The Illustrated Origins Answer Book follows the sequence of the videos, presenting the same information, so if you use only selected films, you can fill in with the book. The six topics are "Origins of the Universe," "The Earth, a Young Planet?," "The Origin of Life," "The Origin of Species," "The Origin of Mankind," and "The Fossil Record." Both book and videos present a more scientifically-based, in-depth look at the issues than we find in many other resources. Science plays the starring role, proving the validity of the evidence for creation and undermining evolution.

The book has space to provide even more research information than do the films. The first half of the book is a presentation of the topics, while the second half is references—definitions, bibliographical information, scientific explanations, and quotations. Those who want to really understand the scientific discussion of origins will appreciate either or both resources.

○ In the Beginning [video] (American Portrait Films) $19.95

Six creation scientists from different well-known laboratories and pursuing different areas of specialization make a case for a young earth by focusing on plate tectonics and floods. While the presentation is theoretical in nature, it offers convincing evidence to counter "millions of years" theories in the formation of present-day continents, mountains, and other geographic features. It repeats some footage from *The Grand Canyon Catastrophe* (also available from American Portrait Films) regarding flooding and strata deposits. Interesting content, beautiful film footage, on-site presentations, and animated graphics make this 27-minute presentation excellent for high school student through adult audiences.

⮑ The Real Roots [video] (Creation Research) $25

This 35-minute video tackles the question of how so many different races came to be. Host John Mackay presents a case for the biblical account, asserting that all races are descended from Noah. He makes his case from a practical, common sense perspective rather than by appealing to scientific proof. The video includes interviews with people from different cultures, some re-telling their own culture's stories about the Tower of Babel, the Flood, and other Genesis stories. Mackay also interviews some scientists. Although some alternate ideas are mentioned, they are briefly refuted. The video should appeal to junior and senior students.[Josh Duffy]

⮑ A Scientist Looks at Creation (American Portrait Films) $19.95

Dr. Robert Gange presents scientific evidence for creation in this two-part video. He relies largely on astronomical evidence, but does delve into other areas of science and mathematics to prove his point. He believes that the earth was created as recorded in the Bible, yet, unlike many creation scientists, he believes that creation took place billions of years ago. This video spends most of the time building the scientific evidence and much less time on the religious implications. At the end of part two, Dr. Gange simplifies the implications of the evidence into two basic philosophic choices—materialism or theism. He suggests that scientists are continually making new discoveries about the origin of the universe which are forcing them to arrive at the same place Christian theologians have been for centuries. The video incorporates illustrations and film clips with Gange's presentation so that it maintains the visual interest of the audience. Science topics are quite advanced, so use this video with older students.

⮑ The Search for the Origin of Life [video course] (Creation Research) $120

Five, 25-minute videos and a text/workbook comprise this creation science course designed for 11th and 12th graders who have already studied cellular biology and evolution theory. Australian scientist and teacher, John Mackay, presents a scientific discussion about creation and evolution, while trying to avoid scientific jargon as much as possible. His lively presentation makes it easier for students to understand the sometimes challenging concepts he presents. The videos are titled *Spontaneous Generation 1850 AD - 2000 AD; RNA, DNA, and the Origin of Proteins; The Origin of Coded Information; What Mutations Do;* and *How to Recognize a Creation.* Students should first watch a video presentation, then study the text material (from the combination text/workbook) which repeats much of what was presented on the video. Then they should tackle the workbook questions. The basic course should take five, one-hour sessions. An additional historical supplement that examines the history of science, famous scientists, and ideas is in the second half of the book. Working through this study material and questions might take another 5-10 hours. While I recommend this course to you, I also urge you to stick with the suggested guidelines for grade level and prerequisites.

⮑ Unlocking the Mysteries of Creation (Creation Resource Foundation) $22.95

Because of its comprehensiveness, one of the very best creation science books is *Unlocking the Mysteries of Creation* by Dennis Petersen. This is an outstanding book for all ages. It includes thorough discussion of creation, bringing in history and science. It incorporates scripture, science, and interesting information in a nicely illustrated format. We can pick and choose information to read as we adapt to the ages of our children.

⮑ The World of Living Fossils (Creation Research) $25

John Mackay, Australian creation-scientist, examines the fossil evidence for creation, contrasting it with the teachings of evolutionists. One of the main points of this 45-minute video is that there is no evidence in the fossil record of interspecies change over time. If the evolutionary explanation of the fossil record is true, and it tells us that the bottom layers represent periods in ancient history when life was in early stages of evolution, we should find simpler life forms there which increase in complexity through the higher layers of a fossil column. Mackay shows that there is no evidence of this, but, instead, shows evidence to the contrary. Since the fossil record is one of the primary weapons in the evolutionist's arsenal, this is a useful video to counter their arguments.

CSA Creation Resource Library

The CSA Creation Resource Library, operated by Mrs. Ellen Myers, is a lending library for videos, audio tapes, and books on creation and evolution. Out-of-area borrowers are asked to cover return postage and to include $3 for postage/handling when returning borrowed materials. (Checks should be made out to Mrs. Ellen Myers.

Videos and books are available for children through adults, while all audio tapes are for adults. Numerous videos are recommended for teens. Videos feature many different speakers including such notables as Dr. Henry Morris, Ken Ham, and Dr. Richard Bliss. Some videos are featured as courses so that we can set up a regular program. Some videos reviewed in this book are available: *Evolution Conspiracy, The Genesis Solution,* and *Gods of the New Age.* They include audio and video tapes on a broader range of topics (hundreds of items listed!), so send a legal-size SASE for their free catalog.

Foreign Language

Foreign language should be of importance to us as Christians, since knowledge of other languages permits us to communicate with more people. With the huge influx of immigrants from other countries into the United States, almost all of us have opportunities to share with people who speak other languages. We cannot foretell what languages we might need to learn in our lifetime, but the study of one foreign language makes it easier for us to learn others. This is especially true for related languages such as the Romance languages—Latin, Spanish, French, and Italian.

Study of foreign language provides many students with their first real need to use the grammar vocabulary they have been accumulating over the years. Grammatical knowledge from the study of English helps us understand similar constructions in other languages. Thus, foreign language study indirectly becomes a reinforcement tool for English grammar.

Most states require one year of foreign language for high school graduation, although no such requirement is reflected in GED tests. (The State of California requires one year of study in either foreign language or visual/ performing arts—a choice that reflects the low priority that both subjects have in California schools.) A minimum of two years of study in one foreign language, and sometimes three, is preferred by most universities, and this is the requirement with which we should be concerned.

We might find it quite difficult to teach our child a foreign language if we have not already studied that language ourselves. Libraries offer tapes on many languages, so we can experiment with a few to see what seems most interesting. Then we will have to find a text or materials to work with. If we feel that we are just not able to teach a foreign language ourselves or we find that we don't have the time or inclination, we need to consider other options such as audio or video courses, group classes, community college, tutoring, or trading skills with another home schooler.

Linguistics

Developing an appreciation for languages in all their diversity can inspire someone to actually learn one or more languages. Brenda Cox approached me at a home school conference and offered me a copy of her book, *Who Talks Funny?* (Linnet Books) [$25] to review. Her book turned out to be a delightful introduction to languages with all their similarities and contrasts. Subtitled, "A Book About Languages for Kids," it probably works best as a family read aloud book, understandable for children about age seven or eight and older (although teens can certainly read it on their own). It works in conjunction with social studies as Brenda covers the history of languages, their geographical origins, and the connection between language and politics, religion, and culture. As you might expect, it also deals with a broad range

of language arts as it compares grammar, syntax, alphabets, sounds, intonation, writing, and vocabulary for languages from around the world, often in a humorous fashion. In the appendix are greetings and selected words from many languages, and a bibliography of language resources. Although the book is not written as a Christian book, mentions of missionary work with languages combined with the overall content make it an especially good book to awaken our children to the value of language study for communicating the gospel to the entire world.

Sources for Foreign Language Materials

[Note: The reviews presented here lopsidedly reflect my familiarity with Latin and Spanish.]

Miscellaneous

➲ Calvert School French and Spanish Level 1 of either language - $110, Level 2 - $120; Advisory Teaching Service (see description in the Calvert School description in Chapter Eight) for any of the language courses is $80 per student. If more than one student enrolls in the same course, we pay a reduced "group course" fee of $35 for additional students (they receive supplies and workbooks, but no audio tapes).

Calvert offers correspondence courses for grades seven and eight in French and Spanish. These courses are conversational rather than grammatical, although some grammar is covered, especially in Level 2. The courses include audio tapes, workbooks, and supplies. *Beginning French,* Levels 1 and 2, or *Spanish* Levels 1 or 2 can be used with students in grades 4-8.

➲ Language Now! [Computer programs for Windows and Macintosh platforms] (Transparent Language) Master Program Package: $129; individual literature selections are about $15-35 each

Language Now! is a fantastic supplement for high school (or higher level) language study. Students learn by working through common words and "survival phrases" then reading actual literature in the language they are studying. It includes some basic instruction. Even though they do not present material as is done in more traditional courses, the basic programs do provide so much help that a very dedicated student could possibly teach himself by simply working through a number of reading selections. (I recommend a more grammatical approach for efficient learning of the basics.) This works especially well with the literary selections as each piece appears on screen surrounded by windows offering various forms of assistance. One window shows the translation of the highlighted word; another shows the meaning of the phrase; another the meaning of the sentence; still another provides grammatical explanation of the highlighted word. Comments, notes, and information about root words appear on various screens, depending upon the language and the type of computer. Even if we do not know the language, we can begin reading by glancing back and forth from text to translation. But that is not really the purpose. Ideally, students who have begun the study of a language can read through a selection, reinforcing and expanding their vocabulary and grammar. Selected literature is written at adult levels, and this is obvious in the level of reading/translation difficulty. This means that students should probably be well into a first year of language study (high school level) before beginning *Language Now!*, and they should be proficient readers of adult-level books.

We need to purchase the Master Program Package for French, Spanish, Latin, German, Italian, Portuguese, Swedish, Dutch, or Russian. This is the basic program which is required for reading any of the *Language Now!* titles, and even if you have students studying two different languages, you will only need one Master Program. Each Master Program comes with four titles (e.g., Spanish titles are *The Most Common Words in Spanish, Survival Phrases in Spanish, A Spanish Adventure with Andres,* and *Spain: A Personal Tour.*) All of these are presented as an "immersion" program for language learning. Students listen, speak, play games, and participate in interactive dialogues where their speech can be compared to that of native speakers. Native speakers provide pronunciation of every word and sentence. Some full-motion video clips are also included. With the CD-ROM, we also get a clearly written User's Guide and an extensive catalog of other available titles.

Earlier versions of these programs included much higher-level literature, but present selections are geared more toward the adult traveler, so if you have read about these programs in the past, keep in mind that the newest versions are a bit different. The higher-level literature is still available through the Transparent Language catalog.

Language Now! is super easy to use. It takes only a couple of minutes to insert a CD-ROM, find a selection, and start reading. A user-supplied microphone (highly recommended) is used to record your own voice and compare it to the native reader, and your computer must have a sound card.

Transparent Language also offers *WordAce!*, electronic, bilingual dictionaries and verb conjugators for Spanish, French, German, Italian, Portuguese, Swedish, Dutch, Danish, Norwegian, and Finnish. These are available on CD-ROM for Windows or Macintosh platforms. Included in the program are dictionary/thesaurus, verb conjugator, spell checker, translator, and two games to practice foreign synonyms (expands vocabulary) and verb conjugations. The best way to utilize *WordAce!* is to install it permanently on your hard drive so you always have quick access. Regular price is $99, but they often run deeply discounted specials.

Grammar Pro! is another add-on that serves as both a tutorial and reference for the selected language. It integrates seamlessly with *Language Now!*. Quizzes are included on the CD-ROM.

For those interested in Latin, the beginnings of the *Cambridge Latin* course are included in the Latin program. It appears to me that we will still need the texts and workbooks, but the program should be helpful with translations for parents without Latin background.

Transparent Language also produces *Power Chinese* and *Power Japanese* [$159 each], courses designed for business people and professionals, but still useful for anyone wishing to learn those languages. These CD-ROM Windows courses combine graphics, entertaining dialogues, and memory techniques with basic vocabulary and grammar instruction. According to the publisher, each course is approximately equivalent to one year of college level study.(S)

⊃ The Learnables—French, German, Spanish, Russian, Chinese, Japanese, Hebrew, Czech, or English
(International Linguistics Corporation) entire set - $175;
Book One with five tapes - $45

This unusual approach uses picture books (no text with the pictures) and cassettes to build up vocabulary and teach sentence structure from repeated usage. The same books are used with each language. You get four books with twenty-one audio cassettes. (We can also purchase Book One with five tapes to begin instead of the entire set.) Tapes begin with words and short phrases whose meanings are obvious from the pictures. Translation is not given. If you are in doubt, repetition of a word in another picture will likely clear things up for you. Sentences become more complex as do the pictures. This approach is certainly more enjoyable than typical programs of either the textbook variety or the records that have you simply repeat the foreign language phrases after the speaker. You have to think about what is happening in the pictures to understand the meaning.

Basic Structures supplements *The Learnables* to provide some (albeit not as extensive as other programs) reading and writing practice. *Basic Structures* (available in French, Spanish, German, Hebrew, and Russian) consists of one book and four cassettes that combine listening, reading, and writing activities. Begin using *Basic Structures* after completion of Book 1 of *The Learnables*.

An intermediate *Learnables* program in German has four more books with five cassettes to accompany each, so students can pursue German studies to a higher level of proficiency which includes reading German. The *Spanish Language Series, French Language Series*, and *German Language Series* (published by International Linguistics) also provide intermediate study programs which include reading practice.

Grammar is not taught directly in any of these programs, but students acquire grammatical knowledge from actually using the language. At elementary and junior high levels this does not present a problem, but it does for high school where formal grammar is often required.(S)

➲ **National Textbook Company**

Their catalog lists hundreds of language resources for a number of languages—more than I have seen in any other catalog. They have both conversational and grammatical instruction materials for all ages. In addition, there are many supplemental items that will be helpful with other courses we might use. The primary languages they provide for are Spanish, French, German, and Italian, but they also have materials for Latin, Russian, Japanese, Chinese, Korean, Greek, Hebrew, and Portuguese.

➲ **North Dakota Division of Independent Study—Foreign Language Courses**

Accredited high-school-level courses are available in French, German, Latin, Norwegian, Russian, and Spanish. Two years of every language except Russian are offered. Most courses come with audio and/or video cassettes. Computer-assisted Spanish I and II courses are available for those with Macintosh computers. Prices vary greatly depending upon the materials required, so consult their catalog for complete information.(S)

➲ **Vis-Ed Vocabulary Cards** (Vis-Ed) $9.95

Vocabulary Cards for French, German, Spanish (choose the bilingual Spanish-English edition rather than the classical Spanish edition), Greek (both classical and biblical), Hebrew (biblical), Italian, Latin, and Russian. Each, very inexpensive set includes about 1,000 flash cards (1 1/2"x 3 1/2" each) and a study guide containing simple instructions and a mini-dictionary, all packaged in a sturdy box. Extra helps, such as the principal parts of irregular verbs, are shown on the cards. Many words (in the Spanish set reviewed) have related forms which appear as nouns, verbs, and adjectives, so all are shown on the cards. For instance, the noun "el calor" (heat) has an adjectival form—"caluroso/a" which is also on the card. The foreign language is printed in black on one side, and the English equivalent is printed on the reverse in green. Use these cards to review and expand vocabulary for any of the above languages. As with the *Think Spanish (French,* etc.) sets, the cards could also be used with a game board.

➲ **VocabuLearn [audio tape with book]** (Penton Overseas, Inc.) $10.95 each

The *VocabuLearn* series includes *Beginners French, Spanish, Italian,* or *German.* For each language, we have two tapes available as Series 1 and Series 2, and each tape is packaged with a booklet that has a complete transcript of the tape with a few additional notes. Each 30-minute audio cassette features over 250 commonly used words and phrases from the selected languages, presented bilingually with the English translation. Lessons are set to upbeat music. These are very easy to listen to because of both the music and the high-quality presentation. This is definitely junior high/high school level rather than younger because of its grammatical focus. Lessons are divided up into ten presentations focusing on singular nouns, plural nouns, adjectives, adverbs, conjunctions, numbers, etc. Series 2 of each language presents all new content without repeating lessons from Series 1.

These tapes will work well alongside most foreign language programs for reinforcement. They might also offer students using a text-only course an opportunity to hear the spoken language.(S)

French

➲ **French I and II** (Bob Jones University Press) student texts - $28 each; teacher's editions - $36 each; student activities manual - $11; teacher's edition for activity manual - $14; audio cassettes - $60

The *French I* course teaches both grammar and conversation so that students actually practice using the language. Grammatical explanations are provided within the text, so students can work independently for much of their study. However, conversational practice and oral drill should be done for effective learning. Since this text is designed for Christian students, "...dialogues and readings center on events in the life of an American missionary and his family in France." Folk songs, Christian choruses, and Bible memory verses—all in French—help to reinforce learning. The catalog tells us that the course "targets an intermediate-low to intermediate-mid level of proficiency." Course components are the hardbound student text; spiral bound teacher's edition which includes notes and answers; nine audio cassettes; softbound, consumable student activity manual; and teacher's edition of the student activity manual, which includes a tapescript of the cassettes.

French II expands comprehension skills for both spoken and written French. Components similar to those for *French I* are available for the course.

➲ **French 1 (Nouveaux Chemins) and 2 (Langue et Louange)** (A Beka) French 1 components: student text - $30.30, teacher guide - $23.10, vocabulary manual - $13.60, vocabulary teacher edition - $21.90, Pronunciation/Scripture cassette - $8.95, vocabulary cassette set -$17.90, exercise book - $6.75, tests book - $3.75, answer key to tests - $8.60; French 2: student text - $29.20, teacher guide - $23.10, vocabulary manual - $18.45; vocabulary teacher guide - $20.05, test book - $4.60, key to test book - $8.60

A Beka offers two years of instruction in the French language. The course includes Bible memory verses in French, Christian reading material, missionary emphasis, grammatical foundations, and strong vocabulary development. Grammatical and conversational instruction are blended. There are more components for *French 1* than for *French 2.* The basics are the student text and student vocabulary book. In addition, there are teacher's guides for both of these books, a pronunciation/Scripture cassette, two vocabulary cassette tapes, *Oral Mastery Exercises,* and a student test booklet with separate answer key. For French 2, there are the two student books and accompanying teacher editions, plus a test book and answer key. Both of these courses are available on video through A Beka's Video School.

➲ Think French, Levels I and II (Vis-Ed) $18.95 each

The concept is the same as *Think Spanish*, reviewed below under "Spanish."

German

➲ Praktisches Deutsch - Grundstufe
, Grundstufe II, and Mittelstufe I
(distributed by Bob Jones
University Press) student worktexts -
$14 and $16; cassettes for each level
- $59.95 per set

BJUP offers the only German language program written from the Christian perspective that I know of. This is a three-year program that uses the total immersion approach. Student worktexts are entirely in German. Vocabulary is learned through association, description, and illustrations. Students also complete written exercises for reinforcement. The subject matter sounds interesting: German history, art, literature, travel, amusement, politics, and religion. The textbook authors assume a teacher's knowledge of German, so it will be difficult to use if the parent/teacher lacks that knowledge. Audio cassette sets are available for the two textbooks, which will help with pronunciation. Instruction, practice, and exercises are all contained in the worktext. No teacher's edition is available. *Praktishes Deutsch: Mittelstuff I* [$10.15] has review tables, and advanced grammar instruction in a worktext format. This book should be used at the beginning of the second year. Purchase a German-English dictionary from another source for reference.

➲ Think German, Levels I and II (Vis-Ed) $18.95 each

The concept is the same as *Think Spanish*, reviewed below under "Spanish."

Also check out German materials from Transparent Language, International Linguistics Corporation, and Penton Overseas which are mentioned under "Miscellaneous."

Greek

➲ Basic Greek in 30 Minutes a Day by Jim Found (Bethany House) $15.99

Because this book relies heavily on cognates (words that sound very similar to familiar English words), learning is simplified. A parent with no background in Greek should be able to teach from this book (or learn Greek for him or herself).

➲ Greek (Alpha Omega LifePacs) $38.95

This is a one-year course, with supplemental materials including *Greek Manual, Textus Receptus, and Lexicon.*

➲ A Greek Alphabetarion [book, audio tape, and computer program] (Trivium Pursuit) $12; audio tape - $5

These materials serve as an introduction to the study of Greek. The book teaches letter identification, formation, sound,

and articulation, as well as relationships to the letters of our alphabet. Learners are encouraged to practice writing as they learn. Charts are used to help organize the information and make it easier to learn. A set of Greek letter cards (to be copied from the book) can be used for learning activities and games. Historical and linguistic background information, as well as a lesson on numerical values of the Greek letters, are also included. The audio tape gives us auditory input of the same information. Greek Flash Cards add another tool to make it easier to learn the language. All of these components can work together to provide multisensory learning for greater effectiveness. Continue with Trivium Pursuit's *Homeschool Greek* after completing this course.

➲ Greek Tutor [CD-ROM] (Parsons Technology) $49

Multimedia technology really works in this introductory Greek program for IBM compatible computers running Windows 3.1 or Windows 95. The program begins with the alphabet and sounds of the letters, then continues through 28 "chapters" covering such topics as syllables and accents, personal pronouns, aorist and future passives, subjunctive verbs, and clause types. Each of the chapters is divided into four lesson sections: learn, drill, exercise, and review. If you have sound capability (highly recommended), you can hear pronunciations of letters, words, and phrases. Spelling and reading exercises enhance learning. Button bars allow the student to access lesson maps to get an overview of where the lesson is going or evaluate how much he or she has accomplished. The button bar also allows quick access to the index of topics. Everything is self-paced; exercises and practice are untimed. Along with the program we also get a very large stack of flash cards for both grammar and vocabulary, so students can also practice off the computer. A Greek TrueType font is installed on your computer upon installation of the program. The font can be used from within a word processing program such as Microsoft Word for Windows to type in actual Greek letters. I really appreciate this program's extra features that allow quick and easy movement between lessons, easy access to lookup features, repetition, and a logical, clear organization. On top of that, the program installed very quickly and easily on my computer. (Parsons also offers *Hebrew Tutor.*)

➲ Hey, Andrew!! Teach me some Greek! by Karen Mohs (Greek 'n' Stuff) Reader - $9.95; book or full answer key for each level: Level One - $12.95 each, Level Two - $15.95 each, Level Three - $18.95 each, Level Four - $18.95 each; abbreviated answer keys - $3 per level; quiz and exam packet for each level - $4.50 each

This is a Christian program for teaching Greek to children of all ages. Although this program is designed to begin using it with younger children, we can still start with teens. Skip the Reader and Level One with older students and begin with Level Two.

Plan to move quickly through Levels Two and Three, then concentrate on Level Four.

Level Two reviews all of the letters that were taught in Level One. By page 37 (out of 162 pages), students are learning words through a variety of exercises. They work with flashcard recognition for both letters and words. (Vocabulary words are repeated and reviewed from book to book, but a few words used for letter or word recognition don't repeat in every book.)

Level Three condenses presentation of letters and sounds to 10 pages, then concentrates on vocabulary for the remaining 187 pages. While the earlier levels basically use a memorization and drill approach, this level begins to introduce some grammar. Since it is designed for early- to mid-elementary grades it does not assume that students have even learned English grammar. For example, simple verb conjugations are introduced, but without any labels referring to person, number, or tense. By the end of the book, students are translating sentences in their workbooks. At the back of the book are an alphabet chart, glossary, declension charts for second declension masculine and neuter nouns, a conjugation chart for present active indicative verbs, and flash card pages.

Level Four begins with a review of the alphabet (6 pages), vocabulary (10 pages), and Greek grammatical principles (16 pages, now with English grammatical terminology introduced.) The Greek article is taught in all three persons and both numbers. Short and long vowels, diphthongs, breathings, iota subscripts, and syllable names and length are introduced in preparation for the general rules of Greek accent, followed by the special rules for noun and verb accent. Word order and punctuation are discussed. All four feminine declensions are presented. Additional vocabulary is interspersed throughout this 170 page workbook, again with varied activities and sentence translation practice. At the back of the book are Greek-English and English-Greek glossaries, 32 flash card pages, Flash Card Tips, and charts for the alphabet, articles, conjugations, declensions and accent rules.

Level Five should be available by the time this book is in print. It will cover masculine first declension nouns, adjectives of the first and second declensions, prepositions, and more vocabulary.

Answer keys are separate for each level and are available in two formats: one is a complete student book with answers while the other is answers only. Workbooks are consumable and we need one for each student. Quiz and exam packets with answer keys are available for each level, although these are optional.

Overall, this is an easy-to-use program for parents who have no background in Greek. We should be able to use the books with children spanning a number of grade levels.

➲ Homeschool Greek, Volumes I (Trivium Pursuit) $60

This is a self-contained Greek course for students ages thirteen and up. It assumes that students are familiar with the symbols and sounds of the Greek alphabet. (The *Greek Alphabetarion* provides the necessary groundwork.) Students need not have prior instruction in English grammar, although it will certainly be helpful. The course is designed for independent self-teaching. Instruction on a topic is followed immediately by questions. Answers are found just below the questions for immediate feedback. Students are instructed to use a covering page to hide answers until they are ready to check their own responses. They can write their answers or do them orally, except on the examinations. Comprehensive Review and Diagnostic Examinations periodically assess student progress. Greek instruction is correlated with English grammar and diagramming. Because of this, some of the course will seem repetitive to students who already know English grammar, however, the review will not hurt anyone, and the application will reinforce their knowledge. Actually, those with no prior grammar knowledge might be overwhelmed with the grammar since they are learning so much new material at the same time. I suspect that most students will have at least some grammar background and will find it a practical reinforcement and application of their English grammar lessons. The course has a strong Christian perspective, evidenced by its subtitle, "A Thorough Self-Teaching Grammar of Biblical Greek." Parents need not know Greek, both because this is a self-taught course and because author Harvey Bluedorn encourages students to write or call with any problems. Students create and maintain a reference notebook as they learn. The Volume I course, *Mostly Nouns and Such,* consists of a 250-page, plastic comb-bound textbook, a 65-page Greek reader, vocabulary cards, and two audio tapes. Volume II, *Mostly Verbs and Such,* should be available in 1998. The course appears to be very practical and easy-to-use.

Hebrew

➲ The First Hebrew Primer (EKS Publishing Co.) $29.95

As I mentioned earlier, I am not familiar with Hebrew, so I cannot review such resources well. However, EKS Publishing Co. has a broad line of materials for learning Hebrew that will take us from beginning letter recognition to being able to read the Bible in Hebrew. See the review for *Teach Yourself to Read Hebrew,* which should be used before the Primer. *The First Hebrew Primer* "...is designed to bring beginners as quickly as possible to the skills needed for reading the Bible in the original Hebrew. A complete course of 30 lessons presents vocabulary, grammar, exercises, stories, biblical quotes, the entire Book of Ruth, spelling charts, verb charts, and many more devices to help you learn this ancient language." While this is the principle book, there are also a teacher's guide [$8.95], answer key [$9.95], and flash cards [3 individual sets at $8.95 each or a master set for $25.95].

In their brochure, EKS lists other resources for learning Hebrew which you should investigate.

➲ Hebrew Tutor [CD-ROM] (Parsons Technology) $49

Hebrew Tutor follows the same format as *Greek Tutor.* See the review above.

⊃ **Hooked on Hebrew: A Multimedia Learning Course for the Beginner [CD-ROM]** (Bridgestone Multimedia Group) $49.95

In this flashy, multimedia presentation of beginning Hebrew, high quality graphics and sound combine with elementary instruction in letter and sound recognition, plus work with basic vocabulary. Quizzes help learners check themselves. A great deal of variety in presentation (plus extras like photos of Jerusalem and Tel Aviv) allows the user to track off different directions. Actually, this does get to be confusing at times, because we can easily lose track of where we need to go next. While the graphics and sound are generally an enhancement, they also slow the program down significantly as we listen to or watch introductory material before being able to access one or more sections. There don't seem to be any shortcuts in many such instances. We ran this program on two different computers, both up-to-date systems. In both cases, we had problems with inconsistent sound—sound didn't function at all on detail screens such as the sounds of the letters on one computer, and on the other, it said something to the effect that there needed to be a Hebrew letter in a box where this wasn't any sort of option. Problems were different on both computers which we found inexplicable. Still, if you can get this to function properly, the program offers a pleasant introduction to the study of Hebrew. This course might even be used with children in the elementary grades.

⊃ **Teach Yourself to Read Hebrew** by Ethelyn Simon and Joseph Anderson (EKS Publishing Co.) book - $9.95; book with tape set - $31.95

Five audio cassettes and a 104-page book comprise this introductory course for adults that should also work well for teens. Tapes pronounce the sounds for each exercise, using the Sephardic pronunciation. The course is designed to teach letter forms, recognition, and pronunciation of sounds sufficient for reading Hebrew. This course should be followed by *The First Hebrew Primer* from EKS.

Latin

⊃ **Artes Latinae** by Waldo Sweet (Bolchazy-Carducci Publishers) Level I package - $306; Phase I package - $101

Rome

While Bolchazy-Carducci publishes many classical language materials, the most interesting to home educators is *Artes Latinae*. This is a programmed Latin course for independent learning. It includes texts, readers, reference notebooks, teacher's manuals, test booklets, cassettes, and optional audiovisual materials for Levels 1 and 2. Students first become familiar with pronunciation and the sound of the language in sentences. Later, they look at sentence elements and develop vocabulary. Knowledge builds in small increments that are constantly repeated for reinforcement—the essential description of the programmed method. It does teach Latin grammar, but in an unusual way. I have some concern about the methodology beyond the pro-

grammed method itself. For instance, in Book One, before nominative and accusative cases are named, students are told to identify subjects and objects by endings of "s" or "m"—a fact which will not hold true with plurals and other declensions. Later, the proper terms and other endings are introduced, but I personally find this confusing. Proper grammar is taught as the program progresses, on a "need to know" basis. The program moves slowly (at least through the first half of Book One) with much repetition, although students can zoom ahead through this at whatever rate is comfortable for them. Coordinating the teacher's manual and other materials with the textbook is also quite confusing, but we really do need all the extras except the audiovisual materials, which are recommended but not essential.

My opinion has been influenced by our experience using it with one of our children, which certainly is limited exposure. Many knowledgeable people do not share my misgivings about *Artes Latinae*. I have also solicited reactions from a number of people using the program. The majority of them are very pleased with the program, so I feel that it is important to balance my misgivings with the fact that I am in the minority.

Components of the program for Level I are two student texts, a Unit Test Booklet, Graded Reader, Reference Notebook, Teacher's Manual (which covers both student texts), teacher edition of the Graded Reader, Teacher Guide for Unit Tests, two filmstrip sets (five filmstrips in each), and 15 audio drill cassettes. We can purchase the entire Level I or only the essentials for the first part of the course, which are packaged as Phase I. The Level II package is $303 and Phase 1 of Level II is $112.

Artes Latinae is also available on CD-ROM for IBM compatible computers. [Level I - $273; Level II - $283] The CD-ROM package for each level includes disks, readers, reference notebooks, manuals, and test booklets. The computer version is very much like the book version, but includes sound and the convenience of computerized presentation and tracking of student work.(S)

⊃ **Basic Language Principles with Latin Background** (Educators Publishing Service) $7.15

This small book combines English grammar review with a beginning course in Latin. Students improve their understanding of English grammar and learn the basics of Latin grammar and some Latin vocabulary. This is especially appropriate for use with junior high students.(S)

⊃ **Cambridge Latin Course [third edition]** (Cambridge University Press) Unit I: student book #343798 - $21.95, teacher's manual #348536 - $15.95, workbook #348544 - $7.95; Unit II - student #34381X - $23.95, teacher's manual #348552 - $16.95, workbook #348560 - $7.95; cassette for Units I-II #249139 - $22.95; Unit III - student #343828 - $33.95, teacher's manual #348579 - $22.95, workbook #348587 - $8.95, cassette #249147 - $22.95; Unit IV - student #343801 - $42.95, teacher's manual #348595 - $34.95, workbook #348609 - $10.95

This Latin program is a three- or four-year course. The third edition consists of Units 1, 2, 3, and 4. To begin at junior high level, use Units 1 and 2 each for an entire year. To begin at high school level, plan to cover both Units 1 and 2 in one year. Units 3 and 4 each will take a year. This program assumes teacher familiarity with Latin. It provides cultural background information and teaching hints in the teacher manual. Grammatical information and a Latin-English dictionary are included in the third edition student text. Translation work is from Latin to English, but not the reverse. A student workbook is available for each unit. Answer keys to both student textbooks and workbooks are available separately from North American Cambridge Classics Projects (NACCP) Resource Center [text answer keys range in price from $4.50-$9; workbook answer keys are $2.30-$2.60 each]. Although this program is challenging, it is also interesting because of the historical tidbits and use of a story format for much of the student work. Pronunciation is covered on an optional cassette (for Units I and II) rather than in the text. Filmstrips are also available, but not essential. Grammar is incorporated from the beginning. Cambridge also offers a Latin grammar and Latin readers. NACCP has an extensive list of supplements including books, slides, and software programs. They carry *Transparent Language* (see the review elsewhere in this chapter) which features modules with the complete *Cambridge Latin* course for units 1-3 (unit four in production).(S)

⊃ Ecce Romani (ScottForesman)

This lavishly-illustrated, full-color Latin course is one of the few designed especially for intermediate students. It is not as challenging as some other high school courses, yet it is quite comprehensive—equivalent to two and a half years of Latin. It should work with bright fifth or sixth graders, junior high, and high school students. Rather than stories of Caesar's wars, the story of an upper class Roman family is carried through the series. Cultural tidbits also make the text interesting. You might want to get all of the components: student's text or texts, teacher's guide, Language Activity Book, and Activity Book teacher's edition for each level. The text assumes the teacher's familiarity with Latin, but not to the extent of most other programs. The teacher's guide is easy to read and very helpful. It has translations of readings, answers to exercises, teaching instructions, plus explanations of cultural resource materials, unusual constructions, and new concepts. The teacher's edition for the Language Activity Book is essentially a student edition with answers. The student text contains both a Latin-English glossary and an English-Latin glossary. Student texts are available in two different formats: paperback and hardbound. Paperback versions are divided into five student books: Level IA, IB, IIA, IIB, and III [$14.28 each]. IA and IB are equivalent to a high school Latin I course, so they should be spread out over two years for most younger students. IIA and IIB are equivalent to Latin II, and III is equivalent to a semester of Latin III. The hardcover editions are contained within only three books reflecting the three years and are numbered I, II, and III [$39.36 for I and II and $30.53 for III]. The same teacher's guides are used with either version, and they are contained in three books for the three years: I [$38.61], II [$38.61], and III [$14.71]. There are four Language Activity Books, two each for the first two years, but none for the third.

They are IA and IB [$5.64 each], and IIA and IIB [$5.61 each]. Separate teacher's guides for the activity books are required [$14.43 each]. Test masters are also available for each of the three levels [$14.28 each]. Two other simple Latin readers, *The Romans Speak for Themselves* (2 volumes), can also be used for supplemental readings to accompany the cultural topics in *Ecce Romani*. Send for their catalog for more complete information.(S)

⊃ The Jenney Latin Program—First Year Latin, Second Year Latin, Third Year Latin, Fourth Year Latin [1987 edition] (Prentice-Hall, School Division) (prices are shown for two editions for each component as 1987 price/1990 price) First Year: student book - $47.47/47.47, workbook - $20.97/11.47, teacher's guide - $33.97/176.47; Second Year: student book - $48.97/48.97, workbook - $20.97/11.47, teacher's guide - $26.47/176.47; Third Year: student - $52.47/52.47, teacher's guide - $24.97/24.97; Fourth Year: student - $52.47/52.47, teacher's guide - $24.97/24.97

Many newer Latin programs have moved away from the classical approach by using fictional stories about children and everyday situations rather than the classical writings, and by de-emphasizing grammar, instead using a more conversational approach. The Jenney series has been updated so that it is more interestingly written than our old, classical high school Latin texts from the 1940s and '50s. (There is a 1990 edition, with the previous update having been published in 1987.) However, it still uses classical writings and a strong grammatical approach. Colored pictures, cultural background, and famous Latin quotations are intermixed with solid grammatical study. The student text is hardcover, and a workbook is also available for the first two years. The Teacher's Resource Guide has answers for both text and workbook, teaching suggestions, additional exercise practice, composition work, and tests. This is a high school course and assumes that students already have a good foundation in English grammar and understand grammatical vocabulary. We tried a number of Latin programs, but I wish that we had started with the Jenney series.

The Teacher's Resource Guides for the first two years of the newer 1990 edition cost $176.47 each, while the Teacher's Resource Guides for the first two years of the 1987 editions are around $30 each. The price difference is largely because of the inclusion in the newer version of cassette tapes and "tapescripts" which are not essential. Since there is no option to purchase only what we need as an answer key for the 1990 edition, I suggest trying to purchase the 1987 edition to save money. If the 1987 series is phased out before you complete all four years, you should be able to easily transition to the 1990 editions.(S)

⊃ Latin Grammar Book 1 by Douglas Wilson (Canon Press) $20, answer key - $8

Wilson has written a traditional Latin program especially for Christian private and home school students in grades six and above. It consists of a worktext designed for independent study and an answer key. It is similar to *Jenney Latin* in grammatical instruction methodology, but it lacks the frills and includes more drill. The worktext provides instruction and exercises in a straightforward manner. There are no tests and no classroom busywork. It is assumed that the student already has a basic knowledge of English grammar, but brief review is included. Lessons have students translate from Latin into English and the reverse, review pronunciation and grammar, practice conjugation and declension memorization chants, and translate short reading passages. The teaching method is traditional/grammatically-based rather than conversational. In Book 1, students study through the fourth conjugation verbs (six tenses each), through fifth declension nouns, through third declension adjectives, and through pronouns. A Latin to English glossary is included at the back of the student book. I would recommend that students get a Latin-English/English-Latin dictionary for easier reference, particularly if they intend to continue study beyond this book. The course requires a significant amount of study and memorization, but the reward is improved knowledge of English grammar, expanded vocabulary, and the world of learning that is open to those who know Latin. Since the books are paperback and the contents more streamlined than classroom-designed material, the cost is much less than for other programs.

⊃ The Latin Road to English Grammar by Barbara Beers (Schola Publications) $129 per level for Volumes I and II (complete sets); extra text - $24; extra worksheets/tests - $9.95; posters $13.95

Forget direct comparisons to other Latin programs; this one is really different. It combines instruction in English grammar with Latin, eliminating the need to use anything else for those subjects in most situations. Volumes I and II are available at present, with the final unit, Volume III, due by the end of 1997. The author states that students as young as fourth grade level have successfully worked through Volume I, although it will be more appropriate for most students who are at fifth grade level or beyond. It should work well with students beginning at junior or senior high levels.

Some of Barbara Beers' experience comes from teaching *The Writing Road to Reading*, so we find that methodology repeated as children compile their own notebooks of everything they are learning. They create ten sections in their binders for vocabulary, pronunciation, definitions, grammar, cases/declensions, conjugations, text work (answers to text questions/exercises), work sheets, word study, and tests. Even though information is presented in the student text, children record it in their notebooks to enhance learning and provide a ready-reference tool.

New concepts seem to come at us as if from a shotgun in this program. For example, in Chapter 1, children briefly review the eight principal parts of speech (nine if you separate articles from adjectives). In the next day's lesson, they are working with syntax, covering subjects, predicates, direct and indirect objects, linking verbs, predicate adjectives, and predicate nominatives. Latin syntax structures are presented immediately following the English syntax. While much of this is introduced superficially—as material for a student to copy into his notebook for now—it accumulates quickly. I think that most students will be

more successful in this program if they have already studied basic grammar. Treating the English grammar coverage here as review and application seems the most practical. (This means that we might use one grammar text at upper elementary or a higher level before beginning this course.) There are plans for 140 daily lessons. If we take extra time where needed, it will definitely take a year to get through Volume I.

English grammar is usually taught simultaneously with the Latin as structural similarities are noted. This method is very efficient. It is also a positive motivator for students to see that this grammar knowledge does serve an immediate purpose. Coverage of English grammar in Volume I includes parts of speech, syntax, gender, number, voice, mood, tense, person, principle parts of verbs (stressed more in Latin than in English), types of sentences, prefixes, adjective/noun agreement, and subject/verb agreement. Latin instruction encompasses all of the above plus case, stems, distinctions in ablative case usage, enclitics, and word particles while teaching through the second declension nouns and first conjugation verbs (six tenses). Volume II continues with all of the above, working through the third declension nouns and adjectives, pronouns, demonstrative adjectives, and third conjugation verbs. Students continue to drill and build upon all they have learned in the first volume. All three volumes are supposed to provide a Latin course equivalent to two years of standard courses, so the progression on Latin is slower here. (Certainly, that is appropriate for pre-high school students.) When coupled with the in-depth coverage of English grammar, the program is moving at a pace that should be appropriate for most students, but possibly too quick for some.

The program for each level comes as a Curriculum Set with additional textbooks, worksheets, and tests available separately. The set includes the teacher's binder, an audio cassette tape, flash cards, and a student textbook. The teacher's binder has daily lesson plans and teaching directions, section separators for the teacher to construct her own notebook similar to the students', answer keys, charts to be used with lesson presentation (and posted for reference), and reproducible tests and map. On the audio cassette, Barbara pronounces the Latin sounds and the words pertinent to the various lessons. (The pronunciation method she has chosen differs from that of all the other Latin resources I have examined. She is using what she describes as Church Latin or Italian pronunciation.) The flash cards are printed on heavy card stock, and they are color coded to identify parts of speech as well as gender of nouns. (These cards are great for drilling declension and conjugation endings as well as vocabulary.) The first half of each student book is the text which has instruction and exercises. (No writing in the book in this section.) Reading practice material in Latin, such as The Lord's Prayer, the Pledge of Allegiance, and the song, "O Come All Ye Faithful," is incorporated into the student texts. Latin/English and English/Latin glossaries are in the middle. Perforated, tear-out worksheets comprise the last half of the book. We can reuse the text part of a student book, purchasing only replacement worksheets for subsequent students to save money.

The program is designed to be taught, rather than for independent study. Some lesson preparation is necessary, especially the compilation of the teacher's own notebook. According to the author, those without Latin background can teach this course, but I suspect that those teachers without a solid English grammar background might be the ones who have difficulty. Parents who have an adequate grammar background, as well as the time to teach this course properly, should find it an excellent tool for building a thorough, solid foundation in both English grammar and Latin.

⊃ The Phenomenon of Language (ScottForesman) $12.38; teacher's manual - $12.30

This book is not a Latin course in itself, but rather an introduction to study of languages with Latin used as the example. Concepts learned here apply to English and many other foreign languages. Prior knowledge of a foreign language by the teacher is unnecessary. The book is in worktext format with good cartoon illustrations and interesting information tucked in here and there to keep students' attention. This would be great to use in junior high or early high school to overcome foreign language phobia. For non-college bound students, it might be enough in itself. You should purchase the teacher's manual, but minimal lesson preparation time is necessary. Students can work independently, although parent/teacher interaction is highly recommended.(S)

⊃ Latin (Seton Home Study School) $105 if this is the only Seton course taken

Seton offers a Latin correspondence course using the Henle *Latin* series from Loyola University Press. This is a strong traditional course. Cost includes use of materials on loan; purchasing the books is optional.

⊃ Wheelock's Latin by Frederic M. Wheelock and Richard A. Lafleur (HarperCollins/HarperCollins College Outline) $17; workbook - $14

This paperback text (ISBN 0064671798) is in its fifth edition, with the most recent revision in 1995. I received a few rave recommendations for this Latin text that prompted me to review it. It probably has not been too well known because it was written for college and adult students and it only covers a little more than does a typical first year high school Latin course with no subsequent volumes. (It should be easy enough to switch to another traditional Latin program to continue on from *Wheelock*.) While it covers five noun declensions and four conjugations as does Wilson's *Latin Grammar*, it is far more comprehensive in treatment with copious explanations, practice exercises, translations, and word etymologies. (An answer key is in the back of the book.) It is probably more comparable to *Jenney Latin* in scope.

The reading level is obviously higher than most high school programs, including *Jenney Latin,* as evidenced by the following typical explanatory paragraph: "The personal *agent by whom* the action of a passive verb is performed is indicated by **ab** and the "ablative of agent"; the *means by which* the action is accomplished is indicated by the "ablative of means" without a preposition, as you have already learned in Ch. 14."

The text is proudly humanistic; the foreword tells us that "Frederic Wheelock set about to create a Latin text that would give students something to think about, a humanistic diet to nurture them both linguistically and philosophically." Consequently, parents must ensure that the philosophic influence of this text is used in a worldview context to consider the ideas presented, weighing them against biblical Christianity. The text is being used with at least one online course where I expect that this will happen, but it will be more challenging to ensure the necessary discussion if students use the text for true independent study. The price makes this a very appealing option.(S)

While there are a good number of practice exercises and translations in the text, the companion *Workbook for Wheelock's Latin, third edition,* by Paul T. Comeau and Richard A. Lafleur (ISBN 0062734717) is very helpful. The additional practice exercises will help focus student practice in grammar and vocabulary. The workbook does not include an answer key, and I have been unable to determine whether or not one exists, even though I expect that it must.(S)

Consider also supplementing with *Latin Stories* by Anne H. Groton and James M. May (Bolchazy-Carducci Publishers), which was designed to accompany *Wheelock's Latin*. At the beginning of each reading, it tells us what grammatical knowledge is assumed and to which *Wheelock* chapter the reading correlates.(S)

Sign Language

Note: most major colleges and universities will not accept sign language in lieu of a foreign language.

⊃ Say It by Signing (Audio-Forum) $44.50

This course on video cassette for learning sign language can be used by learners of all ages.

⊃ Sign Language for Everyone [videos and book] by Cathy Rice (Bill Rice Ranch, Inc.- found alphabetically under Bill Rice) $54.95 for the set; book only - $18; videos only - $39.95

Two 2-hour videos teach over 600 signs of American Sign Language. This is the only introductory signing course that I know of that also teaches signs for witnessing. The signs are taught in groups with logical associations so that they are easily remembered. A 170-page, hardback book comes with the videos, making it easier to review and practice what we have watched on video. The course is appropriate for all ages.

⊃ Modern Signs Press

Modern Signs Press offers a wide variety of sign language materials. A new publication, *Signing Exact English,* [$29.95 in softbound edition] is the "largest single collection of English signed vocabulary." Signing Exact English is itself a sign system "that matches signs with the English language." It differs significantly from American Sign Language. The book includes basics about sign language, sign systems, and deafness as well as more than 4,400 words, numbers, contractions, prefixes, and suffixes.

Spanish

⊃ Breaking Out of Beginner's Spanish by Joseph J. Keenan (University of Texas Press) $14.95 (paperback edition)

Breaking Out of Beginner's Spanish is an excellent supplement for the intermediate Spanish student. Keenan's purpose in writing the book is to help the student become truly fluent in Spanish, using words with their connotative meanings and polite slang as it is used by native speakers. He is a journalist who has lived and worked in Mexico for over ten years. Because he is a native speaker of English and has had to go through this exact process of learning to sound less like a "gringo," he understands the pitfalls in achieving Spanish fluency. In fact, he understands these problems much better than a native Spanish speaker would. His explanations are clear and much more practical than the typical Spanish textbook.

Breaking Out is not a a textbook, and it will not take the place of a good Spanish text. There is no practice work included, other than Keenan's encouragement to get out there and use your Spanish. But it will help you to sound less like your only contact with Spanish has been the pages of a high school text. Also, this book is far too detailed to be helpful to the first year Spanish student. Only after the student has mastered the major tenses and has some familiarity with the subjunctive would Keenan's explanations begin to make sense. The style of writing and vocabulary used is definitely for the older student.

The only caution that needs to be given for Christian parents using *Breaking Out of Beginner's Spanish* with their teens is that Keenan includes a chapter called "Invective and Obscenity." He addresses the fear that it seems he is therefore encouraging students to swear (which he is not), because he believes that there is more danger in not knowing some information on the topic. For example, there are (as in English) seemingly innocent words which have come to have strong sexual implications in Spanish, and it is important to know to avoid these words. As these terms are all collected into one chapter, it is easy enough to avoid this information, if you prefer. If you do read it, or your teen does, be sure that you understand that Keenan gives the English translations without pulling any punches. One redeeming point might be that the chapter definitely centers on obscenities rather than blasphemies.

The rest of this book is so helpful that I hope you won't be put off by that one questionable chapter. Keenan's explanation of the subjunctive mood is clearer than any I have seen in a traditional textbook. In fact, it made the subjunctive so interesting that I wanted to go out and find someone to use it on. Another chapter discusses the connotative meanings of sixty-four different verbs. Other topics covered are different levels of formality in greetings, the history of the Spanish language, and that old nemesis of the Spanish student: the differences between *ser* and *estar*, *saber* and *conocer*, *traer* and *llevar*. If all this makes *Breaking Out of Beginner's Spanish* sound like an enormous, dry tome that only a linguist could love, be assured that it is not. The book is around two hundred pages long, with chapters short enough to be swallowed in one sitting. A good way to use it would be to assign a chapter a week to be read, and when finished, review it as a resource in preparing compositions or have it handy when doing translations. I think you'll want to keep it handy with your dictionary as long as someone is studying Spanish.(SE)[Kath Courtney] (Cathy's note: consider using this along with *Transparent Language* and an advanced grammar workbook to make a third year Spanish course. I like *More Practical Spanish Grammar* by Marcial Prado, although it appears to be out of print. Another, newer title by the same author, *Advanced Spanish Grammar: A Self-Teaching Guide* should serve the same purpose. Both books are from John Wiley and Sons.)

⊃ Curso Primero: Workbook for a First Course in Spanish (Amsco) $13.46; answer key - $2.30

Parents who have a reasonable grasp of Spanish might want to use this inexpensive tool for teaching Spanish. Instruction is cursory, reflecting the book's design to be used as a supplement to another form of instruction. There is strong emphasis on grammar throughout, taking students through present tense verbs, nouns, articles, adjectives, "to be," numbers, time, preterite tense, and pronouns. Optional chapters cover commands, present participles with estar, position of object pronouns, and future tense. Grouped vocabulary words, relating to such topics as school, home, and food, can be used to extend vocabulary before actually getting to the exercises in those chapters at the end of the book.

Reading and listening practice exercises are included at the end, requiring assistance from someone familiar with proper pronunciation and at least the basics of Spanish.

Students using this book can develop a solid grasp of Spanish grammar, as well as good reading and writing ability. However, I do not recommend this book to parents with no Spanish background, because they will find it difficult to determine important points of each lesson and fill in meanings for words whose definitions have not yet been taught.

Verb charts and vocabulary lists (English-Spanish and Spanish-English) are at the back of the book. An inexpensive answer key is available.

Second and third courses in the same format are also available from Amsco.(S)

⊃ Destinos: An Introduction to Spanish (Houghton Mifflin/McDougal Littell) Textbook - $43.95; Workbook/Study Guide (2 books, Part I and Part II) - $17.25 each; audio cassettes (Part I and Part II) - $46.86 each set; videoscript - $26.79; audioscript - $18.90. For videos, contact Annenberg/CPB Project, (800) LEARNER. Videos (individual viewing version, Parts I and II) $199 each set; videos (group viewing, Parts I and II) - $699 for both parts or $389 per part

Destinos is a video-based Spanish course offered on educational television stations, as a telecourse through local colleges, as an elective from Cambridge Academy, and to individuals. The videos use a "soap opera" format, following a single story through the entire series. The story revolves around the search for dying Don Fernando's child by his first wife, whom he thought had died in a bombing raid. Raquel Rodriquez, a lawyer from Los Angeles, is hired to investigate. Only Spanish is spoken, but beginning lessons are slower with more limited vocabulary than later lessons. We are not expected to understand all that we hear, but to pick up the gist of the story. At the end of each lesson, Raquel summarizes and reviews some vocabulary. The story takes place all around the world, so we hear the variations in spoken Spanish typical of various countries.

Contact your local public broadcasting station to find out if they plan to air the series. Otherwise, purchase the video cassettes. Videos are priced for individual use or for group use ("public performance" as they call it). The individual version has more lessons per tape with a total of 14 tapes, while the public performance version has fewer lessons per tape on a total of 26 tapes. Video production is top quality.

Some people might watch the videos, learning what they can through this "conversational" approach alone. But the complete course delves into grammar and linguistics. The basic course consists of the videos, a hardback student text (one book for the entire course), two *Workbook/Study Guides*, and audio cassettes. The course is divided into two parts, equivalent to Spanish I and II. On our PBS station, they air the videos in four parts, breaking both Spanish I and II in half again. You might find (as I have) that the first two parts (Spanish I) are aired far more frequently than the last two.

Prior to viewing each video lesson, the textbook prepares students with review and viewing tips. After viewing the lesson, students answer questions from the text which are designed for reinforcement and practice rather than testing. Vocabulary and grammar instruction follows, then listening and writing activities. The audio cassettes are used throughout both the text and the *Workbook/Study Guide*. The workbook takes lessons further than does the text (especially in grammar) and includes some guided writing activities and self-tests. Answer keys for both text and workbook are at the end of each book.

The entire *Destinos* is equivalent to two years of high school Spanish. The course is very comprehensive, combining both conversational and grammatical approaches for thorough coverage. It would be difficult to eliminate any of the course components without leaving a big gap in course content. The cost for such a multimedia course is kept very reasonable by private foundation funding. There are extra components that are optional: *High School Study Guides* (unnecessary), audioscript (useful, but not essential), and videoscript (again, useful, but not essential).

Since the course was designed primarily for independent learners, home schoolers should find it easier to work with than many classroom-designed courses. Overall, the cost is very reasonable for such a high-quality course. Obviously, the course is not Christian, but the producers seem to have taken pains to keep the content unobjectionable.(S)

➲ ¡Habla! [video course] (Penton Overseas Inc.) Spanish Video Course $59.95 each

This two-volume Spanish video course is useful as a supplement to a Spanish program that lacks conversational practice with native speakers (programs such as your typical textbook being taught or "supervised" by a home schooling parent who has never studied the language). In each volume, the course consists of two videos (4 1/2 to 5 hours of viewing), a 90-minute audio tape and a 350+ page Study Guide (mostly for reference, rather than actually working in, and printed in a very unattractive typeface). The Study Guide does not take the place of a textbook because the emphasis is on memorizing phrases and sentences rather than understanding grammatical concepts. Volume One is for basic to intermediate levels, while Volume Two is for intermediate to advanced levels.

I reviewed only Volume One, but Volume Two follows the same format, covering more advanced language usage. As a supplement, this video course has several aspects to recommend it. Each unit on the video starts with basic sentences, giving the student the opportunity to repeat what he hears; there is no reading in this part. Then each sentence is broken into words or phrases; this time the student sees the words on the screen while he hears and repeats. Finally, the conversation is repeated at close to normal speed, with the student again repeating after the Spanish speaker. Notes given in English on the video and in the book address special issues, such as formality of greetings and differences between words with similar meanings. The audio tape gives further opportunity to practice memorization and pronunciation, but it should be used as a supplement to the video tapes.

Pronunciation on the video and audio tapes is excellent. In the middle portion of each unit, the student has a close-up of the speaker's face and can see *how* the words are pronounced as well as hear them. The notes give good examples of the pronunciation of the various Spanish vowels. Also, the authors suggest that you make an audio recording of each session, so the student is able to compare his pronunciation with that of native speakers.

One drawback could be that the course is geared toward the adult learner. All the speakers on the video are adults, and some of the vocabulary would not be very useful to most home school students (e.g., *ashtray, embassy*). Also, Penton includes a note that their extended play videos "may" require occasional adjustments to the tracking. I tried the video in two different VCR's, and had nearly constant trouble with both; if the sound was clear, the picture was not, and vice versa. This problem was more of an annoyance than a serious deterrent; however, it is something that should be considered.(S)[Kath Courtney]

➲ SPANISH Say Hello [audio course] (WordMate) $39.95

This program, consisting of four audio cassettes and a 175-page book, is a non-grammatical approach to Spanish using the "bilingual-dichotic method." You must study the vocabulary using stereo headphones because the words are given simultaneously in Spanish and in English (Spanish in the right ear and the English translation in the left). The rationale is that the different and proper side of the brain will respond to each language. At the same time, you read the spoken words in both Spanish and English. Each list of ten to fifteen words is repeated three times, in different order each time, and it takes less than five minutes to study each list. Each list is usually linked morphologically also, for easier memory; for example, the months of the year are given together, various foods are grouped, and common ailments make up another list. There are also dialogs to listen to and repeat, but these are read only in Spanish.

Because the grammar is presented in short overviews and in the introduction, and there is no comprehensive study of grammar included, WordMate's *SPANISH Say Hello* tapes would be most helpful for the third or fourth year student, who already has a grasp of the grammatical concepts. The real benefit is in reinforcing the vocabulary in an easy and relaxed manner. You can lie on the couch, close your eyes, and listen to the lists. Also, there is a slight emphasis on words and phrases that would be useful for traveling in a Hispanic country. Some words are going to be useful only to adults (e.g. "insurance" or "I'd like to rent a car"). Two lists included the words for "cigarette" and various alcoholic beverages, but these could be easily skipped. The Spanish vocabulary tends towards that of Spain, rather than Latin America, but the pronunciation is not obviously one accent.

The publisher claims that the program is very effective, but we found some interesting reactions among our "field testers." I, personally, found it helpful and not at all confusing. Well, it sounds strange at first, but I quickly "tuned out" the sound of the English, which is the goal. Several phrases have stayed with me, despite the fact that I am not doing the full program, testing myself after each list. What I don't know is how long the learning will actually last. My son found it confusing at first, but came to like it once he was used to it. My daughter (who has learning disabilities) hated it. She could barely listen to a full list. She said it made her head hurt. Reversing the headphones (suggested for lefties) was worse. She could not adapt to it.

My husband was not bothered by the simultaneous presentation of two languages; he found it interesting. His question was how effective the system would be, which, of course, we can't know.(S)[Kath Courtney]

[Cathy's note: We had a few others test this program, and found a curious thing—another girl with learning disabilities also found it impossible to listen to, while others didn't. There might be some "brain-scrambling" problem causing the learning disability, which also interferes with this dual form of presentation. WordMate has a money back guarantee, so you can always return it if it should not work for your students. The publisher tells me that it is better for students with average to below-average short term memory rather than those with excellent short term memory. *JAPANESE Say Hello* [$49.95] is also available.]

➲ **Logos Language Institute Spanish [plus introductory study of 20 other languages]** (Logos Language Institute) Introductory Packet - $15; levels - $17.10 each; complete package - approx. $100 (these are discounted prices for home schoolers)

Logos assumes that their students are studying independently. They provide everything we need to learn to speak a basic conversational level Spanish. There are six books with a cassette tape accompanying each book. An *Introductory Study Packet* is the first book. This book provides us with a pronunciation key, everyday phrases to use for basic communication and witnessing, and key Scriptures. The intent is to get us "up and running" with some immediately usable Spanish. The other five books are the actual course. They are called *In Depth Study Packets,* Levels One through Five. The five levels correspond approximately to two years of high school Spanish. I would use the *Introductory Study Packet* if starting with younger students who are weak in grammar, but skip straight to Level One if beginning with older students.

The people at Logos view foreign languages through "missionary eyes." Much Christian vocabulary is included in keeping with the purposes of the Institute. The Institute advances no particular denomination. The Spanish study does include some Catholic words since a majority of Spanish speaking people are Catholic. Tapes alternate male and female speakers saying the words and phrases to be repeated, first at slow speed, then a little faster. Books include grammar instruction, sample sentences, fill-in-the-blank exercises, speaking exercises, and a little bit of cultural background information. The emphasis is on practical usage of Spanish rather than translation. Students need a basic knowledge of grammatical vocabulary—nouns, adjectives, gender, etc. (The level one book includes a brief review of English grammar.) This is a terrific way to reinforce grammar learned in English studies, as students see how they can apply grammar knowledge. Upper elementary grades or junior high would be a good time to start this program, although it is appropriate for all ages in content. Students should also buy a Spanish/English dictionary.

➲ **Spanish ABC book and tape** (Speedy Spanish) $7.95

This book and tape set introduces the Spanish letters and sounds—very helpful for use along with any Spanish course that does not provide this help on audio tape.

➲ **Spanish 1** (Bob Jones University Press) $28; teacher's edition - $36; student activities manual - $11; teacher's edition for activity manual - $14; audio cassettes - $84

BJUP's Spanish course can be taught by non-Spanish-speaking teachers since all of the grammar sections are explained in English, but it will be challenging. It includes some Christian vocabulary lacking in other texts (with a Protestant and missionary emphasis), but otherwise covers essentially the same material as other Spanish 1 courses. However, as taught from the teacher's edition, the course uses an inductive, immersion approach. The teacher is instructed to speak only Spanish as much as possible and to use pictures or context, rather than translations to teach meaning and sentence constructions. Students are encouraged to figure out meaning from usage and applications, rather than memorizing vocabulary and rules. Nevertheless, there is a solid grammatical foundation and the rules are covered. If the teacher is not fluent in Spanish, she can teach from the text, using whatever suggestions from the teacher's edition are workable. Teachers who are not fluent should be working as hard as the student to learn the language or they are likely to have problems further on in the course. Because of the intended immersion approach, we might encounter potential problems for those without Spanish background. For example, pronunciation instruction appears throughout the book, rather than at the beginning, but we are using pronunciation skills in the early lessons which have not yet been formally taught. The audio tapes are essential, whether we teach it as an immersion course or not, especially for learning pronunciation. Vocabulary reflects Latin American usage rather than Peninsular or European Spanish. Course essentials are the student text, the set of 12 audio cassettes, student activity manual, and teacher's editions for both the text and manual. After looking at many Spanish programs, this one looks very good, but only for parents who already have some knowledge of Spanish.

➲ **Spanish 2** (Bob Jones University Press) $28; teacher's edition - $36; student activities manual - $11; teacher's edition for activity manual - $14; audio cassettes - $44

Spanish 2 follows the same format as *Spanish 1*, using excerpts from Spanish literature and cultural studies of Latin American countries.

➲ **Spanish I** (Alpha Omega LifePacs) $83.70

This is a one-year course with 30 audio cassette tapes (3 for each of the 10 LifePacs) that are essential to the course.

➲ **Spanish I [video course]** (School of Tomorrow) 12 Activity Pacs - $33.60; 4 answer keys - $16; videos: purchased - $550 for the set OR rented - $59.95 per quarter

School of Tomorrow's new *Spanish 1* course is one of the best methods for studying that language. It consists of 25 videos, twelve Activity Pacs, and four scoring keys. The video presentation is outstanding. Two fluent Spanish speakers truly teach the lessons. Unlike most School of Tomorrow video courses, this one is absolutely dependent on the video presentation—primary instruction comes from the videos with practice and reinforcement activities found in the Activity Pacs. The videos also make use of technological enhancements such as graphics for vocabulary and superimposition of images of other scenes and places as new vocabulary is introduced. They also vary the "stage setting," sometimes bringing in additional "actors" to present new vocabulary. Students hear Spanish so much on these tapes that it greatly enhances their pronunciation and listening skills; they will get far more auditory exposure with this course than they will get with most other courses available to home educators. Careful attention to pronunciation, common and uncommon usage, geographical variations, and other details of actual language usage make this course especially practical. It combines both conversational and grammatical approaches so that students are

quickly able to use short Spanish phrases yet develop long term understanding of how the language functions. Like most Spanish 1 courses, it covers typical topics like food, relationships, clothing, calendar terms, numbers, etc. Geographical and cultural information on Spanish speaking countries as well as occasional Bible verses, biblical proverbs, and wisdom principles are scattered throughout the course. "Witnessing" vocabulary is also addressed in one lesson. Students complete exercises and tests in their Activity Pacs, although both are usually dependent upon video presentation of exercise and test questions to some extent. (One of the videos contains <u>only</u> test presentation material.) The presentation is a well-balanced mix of vocabulary, written work, translations, listening, reading, and other activities, although all of these are not used in every lesson.

The only things lacking are a dictionary and an index. Ideally, students should be compiling notes of their own as they go through the course, but I expect most will not. Even if they do, a Spanish/English dictionary and a grammar handbook with grammatical summaries and conjugation charts will be extremely helpful for quick reference.

Although only *Spanish 1* is available at this time, students should easily be able to go into other Spanish 2 courses until School of Tomorrow completes their own Spanish 2.

➲ **Spanish I, Por Todo El Mundo and Spanish II, Mas Que Vencedores** (A Beka) Spanish I: student text - $30.30, teacher guide - $23.10, vocabulary manual - $13.60, vocabulary teacher edition - $16.10, Pronunciation/Scripture cassette - $9.95, vocabulary cassette - $9.95, test book - $4.05, answer key to tests - $8.60; Spanish II: student text - $31.50, teacher guide - $23.10, vocabulary manual - $15.20; vocabulary teacher edition - $18.40, test book - $4.05, key to test book - $8.60

This is a fairly traditional, grammatical approach to learning Spanish, yet there is a strong emphasis on Christian witnessing. You will need to buy a student text, teacher's guide, *Vocabulary Manual*, and teacher's edition to the *Vocabulary Manual* for each course. Two coordinated cassette tapes are also needed for *Spanish I*. The student test booklet is optional. *Spanish II* is similar, but it does not have cassette tapes.

Courses are also on video cassette through the A Beka Video School. In the *Spanish I* videos, the teacher keeps the course moving at a rapid pace, with students participating in much oral vocabulary drill. The sample I viewed, was from fairly early in the course, and the speed of the teacher's pronunciation is bound to be baffling to students who have not heard much spoken Spanish. However, she does slow things down periodically, to ensure that students are catching correct pronunciations. She calls on students to translate and converse at the microphone, an experience that appears to be extremely uncomfortable for some students. On the plus side, I have heard positive feedback from a few families who have used the entire course.

➲ **Spanish 1 for Homeschoolers** (Debbie Cleveland) $29.95

Teacher Debbie Cleveland has put together a self-teaching course in Spanish that is very similar to what students would actually get in a classroom. It is almost as complete as other Spanish 1 courses, but it does not address the use of "gustar," and vocabulary is not as comprehensive. It combines conversational and grammatical approaches; grammatical coverage of the concepts it teaches is thorough. I was impressed with the practical usage details Debbie provides that help us understand the idiosyncrasies of the language. She has designed the course to reflect Mexican and South American Spanish rather than Castilian, so it mentions but does not teach "vosotros." The course text is about 100 pages long, presented in a three-ring binder. It comes with an audio cassette tape that is absolutely essential to the course. Instructions clearly indicate to students when they are to listen to the tape. Exercises and tests are included within the course. A 16-page answer key is at the back of the binder. The course is not fancy, but it is very practical and easy to use. Students can work on their own, but parents should correct their tests and check on their progress.

My only negative comment (other a few typographical errors) is that I would like to see this course "beefed up" just a bit more to be equivalent to others. *Spanish II* should be available by Fall of 1998.(S)

⊃ Speedy Spanish books - $12.95 each; tapes for Level I - $32.95, Level II tapes - $40.95; Primer books and tapes set - $19.95; tests - $1.50 per level; answer key for tests - $1.50 per level

This conversational Spanish course, written by a Christian family, can be used with all ages, although it is best suited for younger learners who need to be taught with a conversational approach. It is not equivalent to high school courses, although Levels I and II combined come close. Components are the *Elementary Spanish Book* and a set of four, ninety-minute cassette tapes. One book is needed for each student since many activities and exercises are done in the book. One set of tapes will do for all. I was particularly impressed by the creativity and variety of the program. Each of the thirty-six lessons is set up to take one week of study. New vocabulary words and practice sentences are studied while listening to a cassette tape. Match-up exercises in the book have children identify Spanish and English words and phrases that mean the same thing. Children can check their own answers by listening to the tape. Bible verses and short worship and praise songs are taught in Spanish. (The songs are in the book and on the tape.) At the end of each lesson, children practice vocabulary with a lotto-type game called Quiz-nish. Vocabulary cards are included at the back of the book, to be cut out and used for study and for Quiz-nish. The variety of activities is bound to prove interesting to children and encourage learning. The only things lacking in this program are professional polish and grammatical instruction (although declension charts are pro-

vided). However, it is intended as an introductory course rather than a complete grammatical course. Even so, many grammatical concepts are picked up through usage. The program's authors believe that children should have fun with the language and learn to speak it correctly, then learn the whys and wherefores later when they get into more formal language study.

Speedy Spanish, Book 2 comes with five, ninety-minute cassettes. It teaches more complicated sentence structure while continuing to build vocabulary. Declension charts are provided in the back of the book, and a pronunciation chart is in the front. Development of a biblical/Christian Spanish vocabulary is stressed throughout, in lessons and songs as before. It is recommended that students obtain and read a Spanish Bible.

The inclusion of games, songs, and flash cards make the material appropriate for use with young children, although you might eliminate one or more of these elements with an older learner. High school level tests and answer keys are available for both levels with five tests for each.

⊃ Think Spanish, Levels I and II (Vis-Ed) $18.95 each

Here is an inexpensive supplement for any Spanish course. Level I contains 400 flash cards and a cassette tape. 200 of the cards, called Concept Cards, have cartoon-type pictures with a question in Spanish on one side. The answer, also in Spanish, is on the reverse. A featured vocabulary word heads the reverse of the card (e.g., a noun with its article). Irregular words show the regular form beneath so you can find them in a dictionary, if necessary. The cartoon situations provide clues to the sentences, but they are not entirely self-explanatory. You need to have a beginning Spanish vocabulary to start using these cards or you will be frustratedly looking up 90% of the words. The cassette tape is over an hour long and features native Spanish speakers reciting the sentences from the concept cards to help with pronunciation. The other 200 cards deal with grammatical constructions, with questions on one side, and answers on the reverse. They are designed for practice in usage with an emphasis on verb forms. I would suggest that you not begin using *Think Spanish* until you have studied Spanish for at least three months and have a foundation. (Suggestion: The concept cards could later be used along with a game board—answer correctly and move ahead.) Level I covers the content of one year of high school Spanish or one semester of a college course. Level II covers a second-year high school course or second semester college course.(S)

Also check out Spanish materials from Transparent Language, International Linguistics Corporation, and Penton Overseas which are mentioned under "Miscellaneous."

CHAPTER SEVENTEEN

Visual and Performing Arts

Visual or performing arts courses are optional in most situations. However, this does not mean that we should ignore education in the fine arts. Christians have largely neglected the arts in recent centuries, and we seem only recently to be rediscovering the use of God-given talents for artistic expression. Francis Schaeffer might well have been the most influential force in the Christian "rediscovery of art," and he does a masterful job of helping us understand the tremendous impact the arts have on life and how they serve as a reflection of our society in his book *How Should We Then Live?* (Crossway). That perspective is crucial as we involve ourselves in the arts as creators or enjoyers, because, as we think with "God's mind" about the arts we gain discernment and understanding the true sources of pleasure, beauty, and talent.

With this in mind, we can discuss the purpose of including the arts in our curriculum. Objectives for studying the arts might include:

– how social, political, economic and technological events have influenced the development of artistic styles
– how art can be used as a means of nonverbal communication
– how to use art to express concepts
– how dance, drama, music, and visual arts are expressed in different cultures and in history
– interrelationships between art and other subject areas
– art as a reflection of the ideals and values of cultures
– learning self-expression through the arts
– learning to make aesthetic judgments of various art forms
– study of particular art forms to achieve skill
– preparation for a career in one of the visual or performing arts.

If those objectives sound too philosophical, perhaps it is easier to think of art study in terms of the three categories of technique (or methods), history, and appreciation.

Rarely do schools address the arts in an integrated fashion. Instead, they break the arts down into discrete units—music, band, drama, visual arts, choir, etc. We need not maintain these dividing lines in home schooling, but it might be difficult to visualize any other approach without some assistance. Among art textbooks, the series that does the best job of integration is Laura Chapman's *Discover Art*, and in particular, the two junior high texts *A World of Images* and *Art: Images and Ideas*.

Art

You should plan to use an assortment of the materials reviewed here along with others to meet whichever of the above objectives you choose. You need not purchase everything since you might want to just touch on some topics rather than do in-depth study. Check your local library as well as college libraries to which you have access for books on art history, art prints, and artists' biographies.

➲ Adventures in Art (Cornerstone Curriculum Project) Gallery 1 = $60; Galleries 2 and 3 - $55 each; portfolio - $30

Adventures in Art stands on its own, but it also is the perfect complement to programs that focus on hands-on art activities. Author, David Quine has carefully gathered top quality prints of famous art works that illustrate how art reflects ideas. This is a wonderful tool for teaching about art from a Biblical Christian worldview.

There are three levels (or galleries) for the series. When we order the first set (or first "gallery") we receive the *Comprehensive Study Guide* that is to be used with all three galleries. The *Study Guide* provides detailed instructions for teaching and guiding discussion with our children as we study each print. Material has been written on a level to use with children as young as first grade as well as up through high school. Galleries two and three do not include the *Study Guide*. The *Comprehensive Study Guide* outlines schedules that might be used for younger and older age groups. Younger children are not likely to fully understand the philosophical implications of the study that older children can apprehend, so adjust your lessons accordingly. If you use (or have used) these with children in the early elementary grades, go back through the lessons again in high school. You might also use some of the individual art works to supplement other studies, particularly history. The portfolio is a specially-designed binder that will hold and protect all but one or two of the larger prints.

Those familiar with Francis Schaeffer's book *How Should We Then Live?* will spot Schaeffer's theme that philosophy and ideas are reflected in art. Charlotte Mason's ideas (popularized in the book *For the Children's Sake*) also are foundational.

Classical Composers and the Christian World View is a music program, also from Cornerstone Curriculum Project, that serves as a companion to *Adventures in Art*. (See review under "Music.")

➲ Art Extension Press sets of 100 prints: junior - $20, folio - $135; or folio prints for $1.75 each

This company offers prints of the world's masterpieces for study in either junior (3" x 4") or folio (7" x 9") sizes, grouped by levels (primary, intermediate, and upper). The levels seem to be somewhat arbitrary—there is not a great difference in the text or subject matter from primary to upper. I suggest starting with the primary print set with children of all ages. *Learning More About Pictures,* by Royal Bailey Farnum [$12.50], is the "teacher's manual" for art studies based upon the prints. It provides an outline of art history and commentary on the 100 prints offered. Purchase the book and one or more of the sets of prints. These are great for those of us who have little art background. Special subject groupings of art prints are also offered.(S)

⊃ **Art History and Appreciation Activities Kit** (Prentice Hall) $89.95

"Ready-to-Use Lessons, Slides and Projects for Secondary Students" reads the subtitle for this resource. It is a 368-page, spiral-bound book that includes 40 slides in plastic pocket pages. The book is divided into sections reflecting art periods and cultures: the Beginnings of Art; Asia; Mycenae and Greece; Rome and Byzantium; Africa and Islam; Middle Ages, Romanesque, and Gothic; Renaissance; Baroque; Romanticism, Realism, and Impressionism; Traditional Art of the Americas; Modern Art; and Contemporary Art. We get an overview of an "area," then lessons focusing on paintings, sculpture, architecture, etc., through slides, background information, and projects. The 88 different projects are an important part of the curriculum, because they teach art history as well as art technique and appreciation. Projects are truly multimedia—a plus in terms of learning experience, but a possible hindrance in home situations. However, each project is followed by "Further Suggestions." Some of these function well as simpler, alternative projects for those that are too overwhelming. Directions for projects are detailed enough for non-artist teachers. In fact, throughout the book, it seems that everything is provided so that the teacher need not do extensive research to present lessons. The real preparation work will be determining how much of each lesson to use and obtaining art materials. Some student pages (project instructions, timelines, work sheets, etc.) are reproducible, but otherwise all student information is contained in the single book. There is a significant amount of crossover into history and religions since art is a strong reflection of both; however, the presentation here is totally nonjudgmental. All types of art are presented without any moral reflections. Teachers will need to use their own judgment about what to skip or add. Correlating art study with world view studies (see Chapter 5) can make the study of art much more relevant. Because this book largely follows a historical progression, it should be easy to tie those studies together.(SE)

⊃ **Art Smart** (Prentice Hall) $79.95

In many ways this program is similar in approach to Laura Chapman's *A World of Images* and *Art: Images and Ideas.*. Art history and appreciation are taught through illustration and activity, but in one large book rather than smaller grade level books. Children do projects that mimic art works representative of different time periods and types of expression. Painting, architecture, sculpture, and other types of art expression are included. *Art Smart* divides activities chronologically so that you can easily integrate art with history. Unit headings are Stone Age, Egyptian,

Greek and Roman, Middle Ages, Renaissance, Post-Renaissance, Pre-through Post Impressionism, Modern Art (then breaking away from chronology), Art of the Middle East, Far East, and Africa. Activities vary in difficulty and can be easily tailored to children's ages so the program can be used with all ages. Forty color slides of museum art works come with the book. Content is definitely secular, written from the viewpoint that art is a reflection of differing values which are all equally valid. But the book is a teacher resource manual, not something you hand the children, so screening content is fairly easy. *Art Smart* is similar in format to the *Art History and Appreciation Activities Kit* reviewed above, although it is "younger" in approach.(SE)

⊃ **Audio-Visual Drawing Program—Drawing Textbook, and other book and video titles** by Bruce McIntyre (Audio-Visual Drawing Program)

Bruce McIntyre, a former Disney illustrator, has been teaching drawing (including a nationally broadcast telecourse) for many, many years. He presents techniques of drawing in a simple manner that anyone can comprehend. His goal is artistic literacy—the skill of being able to sketch out an idea quickly because you know the principles of drawing. The books are as easy to understand and apply as his telecourses. My favorite is *Drawing Textbook*, available as a single book [$8] or as a *Self-Study Course* [$99]. *Drawing Textbook* includes 222 drawing exercises covering the seven elements of drawing. In the *Self-Study Course* there are 37 booklets with 222 exercise divided up into six exercises per book. Instruction is more expanded than in the *Drawing Textbook* with extra rules of drawing plus worksheets. McIntyre has also written books on special drawing topics: *Drawing in 3-Dimensions, Cute Animals, Flowers and Trees, Scenery, Things for Sports, Water Vehicles, Land Vehicles,* and *Art Elements* [$5 each]. Telecourses designed for elementary grades (but not childish) are for sale, and your local educational station might be showing McIntyre's older level *Freehand Sketching* program. All of McIntyre's resources are excellent for both aspiring artists and those who simply want to acquire basic skills. Send for free descriptive, illustrated catalog.(S)

⊃ **The Big Book of Cartooning, Books I and II** (Vic Lockman) Book I - $15; Book II - $8

Students interested in drawing cartoons can learn from a Christian cartoonist. Step-by-step lessons with examples make it easy for just about anyone to be successful. Topics taught in *Book I* include faces, figures, hands and feet, animals, scenery, perspective, layout, lettering, inking, and special effects. *Book II* is on animals, and it expands to cover many types of living creatures including dogs, horses, elephants, insects, birds, and sea creatures.

⊃ **Calligraphy Kit** (Walter Foster Publishing, Inc.) $15.95

The *Calligraphy Kit* includes a 32-page book for beginners along with three calligraphy pens, a guideline sheet, a practice pad, and calligraphy paper.

⊃ Davis Publications

Davis sells many excellent art books, including some of the most popular art history textbooks. Write for their catalog to get full descriptions. A number of Davis Publications books are reviewed below—some actual curricula, while others are likely to be of general interest.

⊃ Discovering Art History, third edition by Brommer (Davis Publications) $44.50; teacher's edition - $55.50

Brommer concentrates on relationships among art, culture, religion, and society throughout history in this text for high school through adult levels. There are over 800 illustrations, plus a significant number of examples from non-Western art. Expensive sets of art prints and slides are designed to accompany the course, but they will be too expensive for homeschoolers. Nevertheless, this book should be a good resource for making the connection between art and other subject areas.(S)

⊃ Drawing on the Right Side of the Brain by Betty Edwards (Jeremy P. Tarcher, Inc.) $15.95 paperback; $23.95 hardcover

Betty Edwards helps adults and older children develop an artistic eye by teaching us to look at things as they truly are—in terms of line, angle, positive/negative space, etc.—rather than through our preconceived ideas of what particular things look like. (Think of how the majority of children represent any tree with a lollipop shape.) This book is big on theory and philosophy, some of which you will have to weigh for yourself, deciding whether or not it is useful. Right brain/left brain theory receives much attention, including some exercises to help those dominated by the left brain hemisphere develop artistic abilities, which are localized in the right brain. The book is written on an adult level, but activity ideas can be presented to any age group. Lessons quickly advance in difficulty getting into perspective, mathematical proportions in the human body, and methods of cross-hatching to achieve shading. An extra chapter on handwriting has been added to the latest edition. Edwards emphasizes the value of consistent, legible handwriting, both as a message about the writer to the reader and as an art form in itself. She gives some excellent ideas and exercises to help us recognize and improve upon our sloppy handwriting habits. Because of the quick pace of Drawing on the Right Side of the Brain, teens and adults with at least some minimal drawing experience will benefit most from it.(SE)

⊃ Drawing with Children by Mona Brookes (Jeremy P. Tarcher, Inc.) paperback - $15.95; hardcover - $24.95

Mona Brookes has helped many people discover that art is not only for those who feel they were born with talent, but that anyone can "do art" with just a few lessons. The first few chapters of the book deal with attitudes and preparation. She gives specific instructions about materials. Expensive art supplies are not necessary—just begin with a pen, then move on to felt pens and colored pencils. If we want to experiment with pastels and watercolors, simple instructions are supplied. Parents can use the book as a guide to work with children as young as three or four,

or anyone able to read the book can use it as a self-teaching tool. Teens should be able to use it independently, but most would receive much more motivation from working with someone else. Lessons begin with the five elements of shape. Next we draw from two-dimensional pictures, then from still life (three-dimensional). Instructions for drawing people are excellent without being overwhelming; she shows the general shapes that can represent body parts, their relationships, and some positions without getting into mathematical proportions. Mona Brookes gives a few specific assignments of things to draw, but for the most part it is up to us to draw what we wish utilizing the techniques that she has taught. Drawing with Children would be a good starting place for most younger children and for teens with little drawing experience.(S)

⊃ Drawing for Older Children and Teens by Mona Brookes (Jeremy P. Tarcher, Inc.) $13.95

Mona Brookes carries further her successful method of teaching drawing. There is a lot of material here. It might even be a little overwhelming for some. Beginners might prefer to start with the simpler ideas in Drawing with Children until they feel more confident. For those who are ready for something more, all the important principles of drawing are introduced.

A parent could use this book to set up a full year's art course for their high schooler. Teaching tips are included. One important feature of the book is its emphasis on acceptance and enjoyment as well as an absence of criticism. The message Mona Brookes conveys is, "Yes, you too can draw!"(S)[Valerie Thorpe]

⊃ Feed My Sheep by Barry Stebbing (How Great Thou ART) $39.95; with paints and brushes - $54.95

This is a combined art text and workbook for teaching drawing, color theory, art appreciation, perspective, portraiture, anatomy, lettering, painting, and more to students in grades 4 through 9. However, students beyond ninth grade (even adults!) without art experience should find this a valuable course. It contains more than 300 pages and includes a packet of seventeen heavyweight painting pages. For many of the lessons, students need only drawing pencils, a set of colored pencils, a kneaded eraser, a ruler, an extra-fine marker, sketch book, and poster board. Later lessons on painting use acrylic paints and brushes. A drawing board, triangle, and T-square are also helpful in later lessons, but not essential. Students learn primarily to draw realistic images but also some cartoon figures. Depending upon the age and ability of the student, it might take a number of years to complete this book. So the painting lessons might be delayed until later. If you want to tackle painting as soon as possible, purchase the book along with a set of acrylic paints and brushes. Otherwise, start with just the book and purchase paints later so they will be fresh when you want to use them.

Author Barry Stebbing's Christian perspective is evident throughout the course in Bible verses, lesson explanations, appreciation lessons, and even the choices of examples. The book is written to the student so he or she can work independently. However, younger students will probably need some assistance.

Instructions are thorough in almost all lessons, although every once in a while further explanation might be helpful. For example, an early lesson asks the student if he knows how to make a color wheel, then asks him to complete and copy one, although, at this point, he is not including the secondary colors in the color wheel. Secondary colors are taught only two pages later, so this is not a major issue, just a little confusing.

Art appreciation is incorporated into many of the lessons, and more-focused lessons direct students to the library to locate and copy artists' works or examples from particular periods. Students also research answers to questions posed about art history, styles, artists, etc.

Overall, this is a very comprehensive course. For parents who wish to maintain academic accountability, there are occasional quizzes on art theory and appreciation, with an answer key at the back of the book. This single volume offers a tremendous amount of art instruction at very low cost. Since students actually work in the book, you need to purchase separate books for each student.

⮑ History of Art for Young People, fifth edition by H.W. Janson and Anthony F. Janson (Harry N. Abrams, Inc.) $49.50

Francis Schaeffer's book *How Should We Then Live?* prompted me to use H.W. Janson's *History of Art* (also published by Harry N. Abrams, Inc.) as a primary resource for our world view studies. (See Chapter Five.) The adult level book is lengthy, heavily illustrated, and expensive. It has been around for many, many years (updated periodically), so older editions might be available through used book stores at lower prices. A more practical alternative for most of us will be the somewhat condensed version of the book entitled *History of Art for Young People*. The style of writing (and actual words) are essentially the same, although some portions of the text are rewritten, and others have been omitted. There are fewer illustrations, yet there are still more than 500, with almost half of those in full color!

Janson's books are valuable resources because he follows a historical outline. Information about art, architecture, and sculpture as well as religion, philosophy, science, and other subjects is skillfully intertwined. All of this, together with biographical information about key historical figures, provides a helpful background and expansion of ideas presented by Schaeffer in his book. In fact, the abundant illustrations in both books include most paintings, sculptures, and buildings referred to by Schaeffer in *How Should We Then Live?* Chronological Charts (time lines) are included in *History of Art for Young People*, showing links between political history, religion and literature, science and technology, architecture, sculpture, and painting. A glossary and index both help to make it easy to understand and locate information in the book.

Janson's books are not Christian, so they must be used with care. I recommend them to those who are knowledgeable about both the Bible and Bible history, and who are able to interpret historical events in Biblical context. For instance, if we are studying Greek sculpture (lots of naked bodies) we do have to consider the philosophical view of the Greeks. We need to dis-cuss why they glorified the human body, and we also need to discuss their pantheon of gods who seemed to differ from humans only in their immortality and power.

In terms of teaching world views, both of Janson's books provide visual proof of Schaeffer's assertion that art reflects man's spiritual status through the ages. We can see the progressive changes reflecting man's view of man and his purpose in life.

I recommend using *History of Art for Young People* as a read-together activity with discussion rather than for independent reading by teens. I also suggest incorporating readings with world history studies so that the history studies (hopefully from a Christian text) are fleshed out with the content of Janson's book, while the content of *History of Art* is balanced with the Christian perspective. Another option is to choose selected sections to read rather than trying to cover the entire book.(ISBN 0810941503)(SE)

⮑ How Great Thou ART, I and II by Barry Stebbing (How Great Thou ART) $13.95 each; Teacher's Manual - $7.95

A Christian artist created this drawing program for teens, which can be taught by an instructor or used for independent study. (Either way students each need a copy of the book.) It requires only a few "art" pencils (H and B type), a kneaded eraser, a ruler, and this book. Lessons follow an orderly progression, with the first lesson beginning with drawing lines; next, ellipses; then glasses and jars that are made from lines and ellipses; and so on. There are 68 actual lessons, but suggestions for many, many more based on the information taught. Students learn shading, texture, composition, shadows, foreshortening, nature studies, human anatomy, portraits, one-point perspective, and other topics. Some of these topics will require practice for mastery, so students should not be expected to zip through all of the lessons in a regular progression. Extra blank pages are provided for practice at the back of the book, and space for each lesson's assignment is provided adjacent to each lesson. Students are encouraged to draw from life and nature which helps develop observation skills. I appreciate the author's provision of examples of errors to avoid as well as plentiful examples of proper technique. Another bonus are Scripture verses or quotes from artists on each page.

The second volume is a continuation of the course. We need to spend another few dollars to purchase an extra fine black marker and a calligraphy marker pen. The course quickly reviews a few of the fundamentals from the first book, then takes students through numerous still-life lessons to practice composition skills, shadows, shading, and pencil control. Students then learn how to reproduce drawings on grids, changing the scale. Next are lessons on one- and two-point perspective. Then it introduces pen-and-ink drawing, followed by extensive lessons on anatomy, and final lessons on lettering, calligraphy, and creativity.

Both books are illustrated beautifully with sketches. In keeping with the nature of sketches, there is a loose creative feel, but with elements of beauty and grace. I am impressed with these books! They have a Christian perspective; they cover skills in a logical, comprehensive order; they provide clear instruction and evaluation; and they are inexpensive. While students can work through these books on their own, parents who prefer to be more involved in art lessons, can purchase the single-volume teacher's manual which covers both Volumes I and II. It adds background, suggestions, and tips for each lesson that go beyond what is provided in the lesson books.

Also from Barry Stebbing is *The Student's Guide to Keeping an ART Journal* [$12.95]. Stebbing explains in great detail and with many examples how to create an art journal. This practical and inspirational book is written for more serious drawing students, both teens and adults.

➲ Introduction to Art Course-correspondence course elective (ICS Newport/Pacific High School)

This is a course for non-artists, especially Perfect Paulas and Competent Carls who want to learn the rudiments of drawing even though they lack any greater artistic ambitions. It covers basic pencil drawing, shading, simple perspective, cast shadows, composition, and pen-and-ink drawing. Students practice drawing objects such as building or landscapes, but they do not get into proportions for figure drawing. The course includes all necessary materials: 3 unit-study booklets, one pad of paper, a roll of tape, India ink, a viewfinder, three pencils, an eraser, pen with three tips, and "Scantron" type test forms to send in. It appears that only one exam drawing is required. The course is practical for home educators, and even though it is secular, there are no nudes or modern art. It actually is a little "old-fashioned" in appearance. It should be good for those who need basic skills, but it lacks inspiration for serious artists.(S)[Valerie Thorpe]

➲ KidsArt (KidsArt)

KidsArt provides art instruction, appreciation, and activities for all ages and abilities in a booklet format. Each KidsArt brings you 16 pages of reproducible worksheets on a wide variety of art topics for $4 per booklet. The "Faces" unit, for instance, studies famous portraits (art history and appreciation), then gives instruction for drawing portraits. Next, it shows how to enlarge pictures using diagonal or square grids; activities include making "blockhead" portraits and clay sculptures. *KidsArt* also includes tips on art products, materials, and resources. Activity instructions are complete and easy-to-follow for even the least experienced non-artist. *KidsArt* also has a free catalog full of sample activities and art resources as well as unique arts and crafts items.(S)

➲ Mark Kistler's Draw Squad (Simon and Schuster) $16

Kistler, a student of Bruce McIntyre (see *Audio-Visual Drawing Program*), decided that he wanted to help spread the good news that everyone could learn how to draw by learning just a few basic techniques. He teaches the same basic ideas that McIntyre does, but his book has a "jazzier" format with some cartoon characters popping up occasionally to make things more interesting. Lessons are well laid out and easy to follow—a fourth or fifth grader can use it on his own, and the format is such that it appeals equally to adults. ISBN 0-671-65694-5.(S)

➲ Masters of Art series (Peter Bedrick Books) $22.50 each

At present, there are eight books in this series: *Michelangelo, Vincent Van Gogh, The Story of Sculpture, Picasso, Rembrandt and Seventeenth-Century Holland, The Impressionists, Leonardo Da Vinci,* and *Giotto and Medieval Art.* We were able to review *Rembrandt* and *Picasso. Rembrandt,* like all the books in this series, is presented in a beautiful, large-format, hardcover book, packed with detail and great illustrations. In this case, it covers religion, commerce, trends, and the culture of Holland in the 1600s. Coverage of art history is excellent, broadening to include works of other Dutch artists of the period such as Rubens and Vermeer while tracing the not always admirable life of Rembrandt. It also provides a background for approaching study of the American colonial period. *Picasso* covers the many innovative styles of an important figure in modern art. However, it is a little too worshipful and uncritical of this sometimes disturbing art. Also, reading about Picasso's life with a long succession of mistresses is not very edifying. While young children might benefit from these books to some extent (use discretion in which books you choose), the books are primarily aimed at a young adult to adult market.(SE)[Valerie Thorpe, C.D.]

➲ The National Gallery of Art

The National Gallery of Art's Publications Office sells books, art reproductions, and post cards at very low prices. They have a catalog available for $3.50.

The Resources Department of Education offers a library of audiovisual art materials, including slides with audio cassettes, videocassettes, and films. They have many resources, called Extension Programs, organized as topical studies. Some are historical, such as "700 Years of Art" and "The European Vision of America." Some are technical, such as "The Artist's Hand: Five Techniques of Painting." Others are narrow in scope, such as "Picasso and the Circus" and "The Treasures of Tutankhamun." The only cost for using these materials is return postage. Requests must be made three months in advance, so planning ahead is essential. Send for the free *Extension Programs Catalog* which describes programs, available formats, and borrowing procedures.(SE)

➲ University Prints

This company lists 7,500 fine art prints in their catalog. These very inexpensive prints, all 5 1/2" by 8", cost only $.08 (black and white) and $.18 (color) each. These would be suitable for study of art history more than technique since the detail is not usually fine enough to make out brush strokes. Prints are not just of paintings but also of sculptures, and some prints are of photographs of famous buildings. Prints can be purchased individually or in topical sets which are very affordable. For instance when you study about ancient Egypt, you might purchase the set of 66 prints entitled "A Visit to Ancient Egypt" for only $5. The Topic Study Sets brochure lists six pages of grade-level prints on hundreds of topics. Send for the free "Price List and Introduction" or send $3 for their very extensive 246-page catalog.(SE)

➲ Video Lending Library membership fee for homeschoolers $25 (yearly) or $45 lifetime (must mention you are a homeschooler for reduced price!)

Buy or rent art videos, choosing from more than 1200 titles. Homeschoolers who choose to rent videos get a special low membership fee. Video rental costs of $6 or $9 are on top of the membership fee. Rental videos can be kept for a full seven days. Most titles are about 60 minutes long. Among the topics are watercolor, Chinese brush painting, drawing, American artists, art history, pastels, acrylics, cartooning, art theory, calligraphy, ceramics, airbrush technique, and crafts. Request their free brochure so you can determine which topics are of interest, then I suggest calling for advice on appropriate videos before actually ordering.

➲ A World of Images and Art: Images and Ideas by Laura Chapman (Davis Publications) $37.50 each; teacher's resource binder - $54 each

Two books continue Laura Chapman's Discover Art series through junior high. (Elementary Level Discover Art books are titled Adventures in Art.) These books teach art history, appreciation, and techniques as related topics. For example, within a chapter on drawing, we examine representative samples from major international collections, learn about Leonardo da Vinci (art history) and see samples of his work, discuss ideas for drawing, learn drawing techniques, learn about drawing media, explore design concepts, look at samples of student work, and discuss related careers. Activity is a major part of each chapter, and supplementary or alternative activity ideas are provided. Written assignments (which can also be done orally) are suggested at the end of each chapter under the headings "Aesthetics and Criticism" and "Art History." There are many color and black-and-white illustrations within each chapter, so students can experience the variety of outcomes that might result from using one technique or variations on that technique.

These two books are different from earlier levels, primarily in format. In younger level Teacher's Editions, the student text pages are reproduced within teacher's pages and it was possible to purchase only the Teacher's Edition. The junior high books are much larger, hardbound books, and Teacher's Editions are separate binders. The Teacher's Editions are important to help us get the most out of each course. The seventh grade Teacher's Edition which I reviewed includes lesson plans, presentation methods, lots of background information, reproducible student pages (some hands-on activities, some written activities/study sheets), a lengthy bibliography, lists of print and audiovisual resources, a glossary, and a transparency for teaching color theory.

Chapter titles in the seventh grade book, entitled A World of Images, are Basic Art Concepts, Careers in Art, Design: The Language of Art, Seeing and Discussing Art, Art History before 1900, Art History: The Twentieth Century, Art: A Global View, Drawing, Painting, Printmaking, Graphic Design, Sculpture, and Crafts.

Chapter titles in the eighth grade book, entitled Art: Images and Ideas, are The Creative Process and Careers in Art, Design: The Language of Art, Aesthetic Perception and Art Criticism, Art: A World View, Early Art in North America, North American Art: Twentieth Century, Drawing, Painting, Printmaking, Graphic Design, Sculpture, and Crafts.

Even though some chapter titles are the same in both books, the content is different at each level. However, there is so much within each book that we might need two years to adequately cover just one.

The art history content can be useful for studying world views (see Chapter Five's discussion of teaching world views), although we will have to add commentary to the information presented.(SE)

➲ Young Masters Home Study Art Program (Gordon School of Art) $190; extra student art book - $15; extra supply packs - $7.50

John Gordon believes that everyone can learn to be an artist if they simply put the time and effort into it. He teaches art as a science, composed of numerous techniques that must be mastered in consecutive order. Gordon tells us that success in his program depends upon diligence, perseverance, and concentration rather than innate artistic ability. Students who have sloppy work habits, are careless, or who dislike following instructions exactly are not good candidates for the program, although tips for working with such students are included in the teacher's manual. Actually, this is also true for the parent or teacher who must work very closely with the student, studying the lessons and mastering the techniques in preparation for monitoring the student. (For simplicity's sake, I'll assume the teacher is the parent.) The parent must read through the teacher manual before beginning since the course is built upon principles that must be thoroughly understood. All students must begin with the Foundation Course (which is a combination of the first four levels as defined by Gordon). It consists of the teacher manual, a student art book, one set of some of the basic art supplies, and three professional-quality video tapes. The course is restricted for use by no more than 2 students (typically the parent and one child). Additional family members must each purchase their own student art books. We are not permitted to teach non-family members without special permission.

The Introductory video tape describes the program, shows examples of student work, and explains the principles upon which it is based. The other two videos provide lesson instructions. Students develop basic skills in pencil manipulation, line control, line quality, shading, and drawing on grids, while working with pencils, pens, crayons, and colored pencils.

Lesson plans, worksheets, and the worksheet demonstrations video coordinate for each lesson. Skills are broken down into minute steps, which might seem tedious at times, but are designed to develop technical proficiency needed for more challenging projects.

As soon as students demonstrate a minimal level of proficiency, they tackle projects under the direction of the parent using the project demonstrations video and accompanying worksheets. Projects throughout this level are all small grid drawings of increasing difficulty.

The course functions as a correspondence course. Two free mail evaluations are included with the program, which should be sufficient for a student who seems to be mastering the skills. Additional consultations are available for $12. Students must send in their work and have it approved to graduate from the program. No one who has not mastered the Foundation Course will be allowed to purchase higher levels. (Higher levels should eventually go all the way through Level 12—drawing and painting from life, but at present only the Foundation Course and Level 5 are offered.) The Foundation Course might take from four months to four years to complete depending upon the age and ability of the student.

This is not a Christian course, thus we see samples of student art on the introductory tape that we might not wish our children to draw. However, children are not asked to draw these particular pictures. Those that come with the course are not objectionable. Many of the project drawings are cartoonish, but inoffensive. In fact, Gordon tried to include a variety of types of drawing projects to appeal to everyone.

The program is as rigid as it sounds, but purposely so. Gordon believes that these are the very techniques learned by the great art masters. He rejects the self-expressive techniques taught in many art courses which lead us to believe that art is an inborn talent owned by few people. On the introductory tape, he shows samples from all of his students (at the time of taping) to buttress his claim that everyone willing to put forth the effort can learn the techniques.

The introductory video is available for one week for a $25 deposit, with $20 of that refundable. Since this is an expensive course, check it out for yourself before enrolling. Level 5 is also available.(S)

Telecourses

Some public television stations offer drawing courses that can be taken for college credit if desired. Some of these are excellent. Look for courses that give students "tools" for developing their own skills rather than courses that ask students to simply mimic the teacher. Check with your community college for information.

Music

Your local library might be an excellent source of tapes, records, and books on various musical styles, music history, and composers. Students should be encouraged to try playing at least one type of instrument and learn the rudiments of note reading, but don't force it if it is too painful for all involved.

Recommended resources

◌ Basic Library of the World's Greatest Music (World's Greatest Music, Inc.) $199 - specially discounted price for home educators

This is a broader, classical music appreciation resource than *Music and Moments with the Masters* since it includes works

from thirty-one different composers representing "nearly all the orchestral forms in the world of Classical Music." However, there are fewer selections on average per composer than in *MMWM*—selections are chosen to be representative of various musical forms rather than "biographical." Forty-six complete works are presented on sixteen cassettes which come packaged in a cassette album. An important part of the *Library* is the *Listener's Guide* which is included at no extra charge to home schoolers. In the *Listener's Guide* are well-written biographies; background information on the musical pieces; timetable charts of musical periods which also shows musical history in relation to other historical events; a dictionary of musical phrases; listening activities; extended activity suggestions in art, writing, dramatization, etc.; questions and answers; and puzzles. The biographies and musical background are the most useful parts of the *Listener's Guide*. Children are unlikely to pick up the *Listener's Guide* and read on their own, so it will require parental assistance to make full use of this resource. There are also workbooks for children available for the set.(S)

◌ Children Sing the Word, complete set - $49.95: Book 1 - $5; Book 2 - $25; Book 3 - $15; tape - $5; flashcards - $4; teacher's manual - $15

This is a Christian, Biblical approach to teaching music, written especially for home schooling families. The songs are from Scripture and the instruction is built upon Biblical precepts. The course consists of three books and a cassette tape. Optional Flash Cards and Teacher's Manual (containing teacher helps and answer keys) are available. The three books are distinctive in purpose, rather than a progression in teaching skills. Book 1 teaches singing and can be used with very young children through adults. The cassette tape contains recorded versions of the twelve songs. Book 1 also has drawings and brief histories of ancient musical instruments. Book 2 contains basic music theory—note reading, key signatures, and timing. Lessons use step-by-step instruction based upon Biblical precepts and are designed to build good habits for music study. A "practice keyboard," printed on heavy paper and eleven notes (white piano keys) long, is provided for children to practice beginning exercises. Book 3 completes the program with lessons for guitar and piano. Included in the lessons are staff writing practice, review, and daily practice schedules. The entire set is very reasonably priced and appears to be a practical method. As with many small companies, quality is improving with each new printing and revision. Also available are *The Children Sing the Word Primer for the Piano* [$10], *The Children Sing the Word Beginning Recorder Book of Scripture Songs* [$10], and an intermediate book entitled *The Dynamics of Music* [$5]. Children Sing the Word offers a 30% discount to children's ministries and missionaries.

⮑ Classical Composers and the Christian World View
developed by David Quine (Cornerstone Curriculum Project)
$30 for cassettes; $50 for CD's

   Classical Composers and the Christian World View is the
continuation of *Music and Moments with the Masters* (reviewed
below) and the companion to *Adventures in Art*. This program
includes six cassettes or CD's and an accompanying teacher's
manual that provides us with the dialogue to use with our children as we study each major period of music from the Baroque
Period to the Modern Period, showing how each composer fits
into each period. The emphasis of *Classical Composers and the
Christian World View*, as with *Adventures in Art*, is to show how
world views are reflected in music. The CD's are by far the most
practical choice for this course, since we listen to selections from
the various recordings for each lesson and it is much easier to locate tracks on CD's than on tapes. Lessons begin by listening to
the music, then discussing reactions. Selections are presented in
chronological sequence reflecting the development of musical
styles, and this is where shifting world views start to become evident. As students listen to each piece a second time, they identify
characteristics of classical music (tone, rhythm, melody, harmony, and dynamics), recording their "observations" on a summary chart (reproducible form in the book). After students have
become familiar with the first 18 selections, they move on to lessons on comparing and classifying composers (more charts included for our use). This is done largely from their music, but
there are brief biographies included for some of the major composers. (We are referred to Smith and Carlson's *The Gift of Music*
for more information.) Examples by these composers are on the
selected CD's or tapes, but listening to additional pieces is recommended, and cross references are made to the *Music and the
Masters* series for those who have those tapes. The final study
section is "Classical Composers and the Christian World View."
Here, Quine addresses the question, "What does philosophy
have to do with music?" For those who have Adventures in Art,
there is also a final lesson where we can integrate the art works
and the music to get a more complete world view perspective.
This is a fascinating study for older students that makes philosophy accessible to those who generally lean toward the affective
realm rather than the logical. When philosophical ideas are demonstrated through music (and art), it opens a whole new set of
ideas. Because this curriculum is as much about ideas as it is
about music, it is best for junior and senior high students who are
ready to work on this level. We can begin with the first sections,
listening to the tapes and analyzing the music itself, moving on
into the more worldview oriented lessons as our teens are ready.

⮑ Classical Music Start-Up Kit (published by Naxos, available
from Homestead Learning) $14.95

   This is an unbelievable bargain. You get two high-quality
CDs with mostly full-length recordings of classical pieces, each
accompanied by a 42-page study guide. We begin with the study
guide, reading the introduction, then starting our musical history
tour in chronological order. The first disk covers the years 1500
through 1825, while the second covers 1825-1945. We read
about a composer and about the selected piece of music before

listening to it. Often there is a detailed description of the piece
that we should read as we listen. Each piece is on a separate track,
so we can easily identify stopping and starting points. The written information is interestingly presented, and, although not
written from a Christian perspective, it frequently discusses
God, spiritual beliefs of the composers, and their spiritual experiences and inspiration. More detail for those with musical knowledge is provided in shaded boxes. Among the composers
represented are Palestrina, Vivaldi, Bach, Mozart, Beethoven,
Liszt, Sibelius, Mussorgsky, Mahler, Strauss, Stravinsky, and
Bartok. Teens can use the *Start-Up Kit* on their own, but it would
be fun to share the experience with others.(S)

⮑ Davidsons Music $20.95 for cassette and book for most
courses; Piano Course for Christians, preparatory and level 1
-$27 each, levels 2-5 - $17 each

   Those who want to learn to play the piano but cannot afford
lessons, should consider Davidsons' guaranteed, self-teaching
courses by Madonna Woods. Courses for playing by ear, by note
reading, or both are offered. Much of the music is oriented toward church and gospel. Courses for organ, guitar, electronic
keyboard, and a number of other instruments are offered, but the
bulk of the business concentrates on piano instruction and playing for different age and ability levels. Typical piano courses include a book, audio cassette, chord chart, keyboard decals (for
learning notes), and sound setups for playing the organ.

   Davidsons' newest release is the *Piano Course for Christians*. Six levels (labeled Preparatory and Levels 1-5) cover beginning through advanced material, teaching music theory and
technique particularly aimed at those who want to play in
church-type settings. However, students will be able to play any
type of piano music after completing the course. Instruction is set
up so that it can be used by an experienced teacher, inexperienced parent, or even by older students working on their own.
The typical home schooled teen can truly teach himself or herself
with this course. A book and one or two audio cassettes come
with each level. The first two levels (Preparatory and Level 1)
cover music fundamentals. Because this requires more explana-
tion/teaching, each of the first two levels have two cassettes.
Children begin playing familiar songs (hymns or tunes of a
Christian nature) almost from the very beginning. Madonna
Woods teaches the use of chords and other musical elements that
are essential to true musicianship. The difference is apparent in
Level 2. (Students who have already learned the fundamentals
through some other means can probably start in Level 2, skipping Preparatory and Level 1.) Courses are very reasonably
priced. If you have foregone piano lessons because of the cost,
here is your answer.

⮑ Focus on Composers (Teacher Created Materials) $11.95

   For a basic course in music appreciation for grade levels 4-8,
this has to be one of the most practical resources. Short biographies of composers, overviews of musical periods and styles, information about instruments and music theory, plus plenty of
activities combine in one book that should suit many families.
The first section tells how to use the lessons plus ideas for ex-

tending them. Reproducible composer research forms help students ferret out information for themselves. Brief sections on women in music and music up to the Middle Ages bring us up to the point where music is presented by periods or styles: Middle Ages, Renaissance, Baroque, Classical, Romantic, Modern, and Contemporary. The last section of the book pictures musical instruments by families, introduces basic musical terms, note values, and rhythm. Activities scattered throughout the book range from simple written answers to complicated projects such as making your own instruments. Choose activities most appropriate for the ages and interests of your children. Listening activities recommend musical pieces of a composer, a style, or a time period so that children get a full range of musical experience.(S)

⊃ The Gift of Music—Great Composers and Their
    Influence
    by Jane Stuart Smith and Betty Carlson
    (Crossway) $15.99
        This fascinating book examines great composers and their music from a Christian perspective. Detailed biographies of composers are written on an adult level.

⊃ God Made Music series (Praise Hymn) student books -
    $4.78 each; teacher's manuals - $10.98 each; mini-packets
    range from $21 to $24; music packets range from $28 to $53
        This Christian music curriculum is available for kindergarten through adult levels. The seventh grade book presents all needed material in one student book which can be used at upper elementary levels through high school. Interesting format and content make this series outstanding, although it might be overwhelming for non-musicians to jump in at the upper level. We can purchase Music Mini-packets for each level which include student workbook, teacher's manual, and *We Sing Music* cassette. Complete packets add additional cassettes of classical music recordings.

⊃ Great Christian Hymn Writers by Jane Stuart Smith and
    Betty Carlson (Crossway) $11.99
        See the review in Chapter Eleven.

⊃ Homespun Tapes, Ltd.
        Homespun offers hundreds of instructional video and audio tapes plus CDs for a wide variety of musical instruments. They offer lessons for country, bluegrass, folk and many other styles. *Easy Gospel Guitar, Flatpick Country Guitar, 5-String Banjo, Learn To Play Autoharp,* and *Making and Playing Homemade Instruments* are just a few of the titles that might interest you. Homespun has lessons for guitar (acoustic and electric), fiddle, banjo, mandolin, autoharp, dulcimer, drums, keyboards, bass, synthesizer, harmonica, penny whistle, dobro, jaw harp, and musicianship. Vocal instruction (including yodeling) is also available. Tapes are for skill levels from beginning through advanced intermediate. Homespun also sells some books, strings, and small instruments.(S)

⊃ Keyboard Capers: Music Theory for Children (Elijah
    Company) $18.95
        The title almost does this book a disservice by designating it only for children. Somehow, with four years of piano and five years of violin plus assorted music classes in school, my music theory knowledge is pitiful. This book really covers the basics <u>and</u> the things that I have missed! It is recommended for children because the author presents the material in short lessons with visual aids and games that are designed for early-elementary-age children. There are a couple of little poems that are used, but the games are not cluttered with too many cutesy gimmicks. Most learning takes place with the visual aids and activities. If you are short on time, purchase the prepared visual aids sold by the publisher. For older students or adults, pick and choose the games that are useful and get right to the heart of the lesson. Lesson plan headings are the musical alphabet, orientation to the piano, musical notation, rhythm, intervals, note identification, music vocabulary, ear training, and major scales. The piano or keyboard is the primary teaching tool used with the book. A xylophone could be substituted, but an inexpensive electronic keyboard would be preferable. The basic knowledge of music learned is applicable to any other musical instrument and to singing.

⊃ Music and Moments with the Masters (Cornerstone
    Curriculum Project) Set 1 - $55 for cassettes, $75 for CD's;
    Sets 2, 3 and 4 - $45 each for cassettes, $65 for CD's
        Cornerstone sells four different sets of excellent quality recordings. Each set has eight cassette tapes covering four composers—two tapes per composer. There is a biographical tape that intersperses the composer's music with his story, and there is a tape of some of the composer's most popular pieces. Biographical tapes are so well done that they will appeal to all ages. The book, *A Gift of Music,* is included for background information. The first set features Bach, Handel, Haydn, and Mozart. Set two features Beethoven, Schubert, Verdi, and Mendelssohn. Schumann, Chopin, Wagner, and Grieg are in Set three. Strauss, Brahms, Tchaikovsky, and Dvorak are in Set four. This is a wonderful way to introduce your family to classical music if you don't know where to start. It has extra appeal since children can listen and learn entirely on their own. *Classical Composers and the Christian World View* is the continuation to *Music and Moments with the Masters.*(S)

⊃ Music Education in the Christian Home by Dr. Mary Ann
    Froehlich (Noble Publishing Associates) $12.95
        Dr. Froehlich has written this book based on her belief that music education is not an option but a scriptural command for Christians. She uses the first two chapters to buttress her statement by discussing music in Scripture and its practical application.

        Once we are convinced that we need to teach music, we then need to know how to go about it. Froehlich discusses the most popular methods of music education (for those of us who have no idea whether Suzuki is the best method or if there are any other possibilities).

The rest of the book is practical information that can be used whether or not we have chosen one of the methods that were discussed. The author assumes that at some point we will be choosing some type of lessons for our child. However, a well-rounded music education will go beyond the scope of what is learned in lessons from a single teacher. It is the parent's responsibility to work on a comprehensive plan for music education. A Music Education Checklist in the book will help us identify goals for music education. The author provides suggestions for meeting those goals. For example, listening is a major part of music education, so the author includes lists of musical examples from medieval times through modern. Since a book this size could not possibly provide us with all of the details that we need to actually teach music, a large proportion of the book consists of listings of music resources including books on education, history, reference, techniques, and theory. Those of us who like the integrated approach might use the timelines in the back of the book to tie musical history to other history-based studies.

The non-musician might find all of this intimidating, but he/she should just choose a starting place such as listening to some of the works by major composers. (Check if your library has tapes, records, or CD's for loan.)

It helps to work with a music teacher who includes parents in children's lessons as do Suzuki teachers. In this way we learn along with our children and get guidance on what we can do on our own.

➲ **Piano Discovery** (Jump! Music) $219; levels 2 and 3 software - $49.99 each

This is probably the most painless way to give your children piano lessons. It comes with a MIDI compatible piano, software for Level 1, cables, and a manual. It requires a computer with Windows 3.1 or 95, 8 MB RAM, a 2x CD-ROM drive or better, 100% Sound Blaster 16 compatible sound card, SVGA monitor, and at least 10 MB free disk space. Three levels of piano lessons take students from the very beginning to playing fairly simple, music with chords. You need to purchase the other two levels of software separately. This is a fantastic course for piano-lesson-averse students as well as for those who want to do it on their own at their own pace. CD-ROMs offer students their (or a supervisor's) choice of six options: School House, Practice Room, Jam Stage, MIDI Studio, Arcade, and Performance Hall. Total interaction ensures that learning is multisensory as students read, hear, and perform. The School House teaches a lesson. Students should then move to the Practice Room (also referred to as the Practice Bungalo) where they can hear a song played, practice it, play it along with "the teacher," or practice either right or left hand separately. The Arcade sets up three different games that help students practice their music theory knowledge and playing skills. The Jam Stage and MIDI Studio allow students to perform and record songs accompanied by an "orchestra." In the Performance Hall, students are accompanied by an orchestra as they play through their songs. Their performance is rated; they receive a standing ovation for a correct performance, but a newspaper review will let them know if it is less than perfect. If they pass, the computer displays a certificate which we should be able to print out. However, we could not get ours to print correctly for whatever reason. Musical pieces are an eclectic collection of children's songs, ditties, holiday tunes, classical adaptations, folk songs, patriotic and gospel tunes. Speed, timed by a metronome, can be adjusted to slower or faster speeds as needed. The multimedia quality is excellent, the entire program is easy to figure out and work through, and the layout is entertaining. Minor problems have to do with the way the program switches from one page of music to the next; in actuality, most pianists read ahead as they play which you can only do if the music is there ahead of time. An irritation for some students might be that if the student makes a mistake in the School House, the program sends the student back to only right or left hand practice after a student has already been playing a piece with both hands.

Watch for two new CD-ROM releases to be used with the Piano Discovery interface: *Piano Discovery Christmas Collection* ($19.99) and *Piano Discovery Gospel Collection* ($24.99).

➲ **Progressive Gospel Piano** by Leroy Shultz (Leroy Shultz) Level 1 - $9.10; Level 2 - $14.30; Level 3 - $17.55

This unusual course teaches beginning pianists how to quickly develop professional-sounding skills. Students must have taken piano lessons for at least a year so that they already know some basics. The three levels in this course combine book and audio tape instruction. There is one book per level, and books are spiral bound so that they lie flat. Level 1 has one 60-minute tape, level 2 has two tapes, and level 3 has three tapes. The first level rushes through music fundamentals, then teaches how to add passing tones, added tones, and neighboring tones to a simple line of music. Instruction on pedaling is included. Music theory is interspersed with very practical lessons centering around gospel tunes such as "Faith of Our Fathers," "Take My Life and Let It Be," and "Amazing Grace." Level 2 builds on level 1, adding topics such as more music reading (e.g., D.C. al Fine), timing, major scales, transpositions, syncopation, and some chords. Level 3 adds topics such as triplets, chord inversions, optional left-hand accompaniments, and improvisation. All of this is taught in the context of actual songs the student plays. Shultz covers the basic theory and techniques on the audio tape, pointing out and demonstrating new or problematic areas of each piece before the student tackles it. There are some theory exercises in the books, and answers are included at the back of each book. Music for many standard gospel songs is included throughout the course, but the words are missing. The course moves quickly, although the student should take as much time as is necessary at each step. Because success with such a course depends upon the student's zeal and dedication, it should work best for dedicated students who have learned the rudiments, but are anxious to produce more professional-sounding results. You might want to pay $5 extra for a vinyl cassette album that holds 2, 3, or all 6 audio tapes.

➲ Sounds of Praise Christian Music Studies by Debra Matula Levels O and AO kits - $25; extra student book - $12.50; Levels 1 and 2 kits - $35; extra student books - $17.50.

Debra, a home schooling mom and musician, searched for a comprehensive music course that taught about instruments, composers, hymn writers, and hymn histories, while also providing instruction in music theory. Not finding such a course, she decided to put it together herself. We now have Level 0 for grades K-2, Level AO (advanced O) to follow level O, Level 1 for third grade and up, and Level 2 for older students or after Level 1. Thus, most junior and senior high students would use Levels 1 and 2.

Each course consists of a student workbook, teacher's edition of the student book with answers, a teacher's guide that provides lesson outlines with background information, two cassette tapes, and a set of flashcards. Level 1 covers theory basics: recognition of the staff, notes, other musical symbols, time and key signatures, placement of instruments into families, and the orchestra. There is detailed study of selected instruments (harp, oboe, French horn, timpani, violin-bow, flute, and piano). The composers studied at this level are Handel, Mendlessohn, Tchaikovsky, and Mozart. Hymn writers include Fanny Crosby, Adelaide Pollard, George Stebbins, Ira Sankey, and Harriet Beecher Stowe. The stories behind eight hymns round out the study. Level 1 is the starting place for any student who has not already studied basic music theory and has little familiarity with instruments, no matter their grade level. Level 2 reviews Level 1, then adds advanced theory, additional instruments, composers (Vivaldi, Beethoven, and Bach), hymn writers (Watts, Adams, Bradbury, and Walford), and hymn histories. It includes tapes and flashcards.

This is an ambitious course, particularly Level 1. It touches on many topics that require significant time and attention. While it makes an ideal supplement for a child who is taking lessons for an instrument because they can see and apply what they are learning, it can be used with all children. Student materials are reproducible for family use only.

As with so many fledgling home businesses, the product is not polished. Tapes are compilations of professional recordings mixed with Debra's recordings. Hand lettering and uneven print quality are other marks of an amateur publisher. However, as with so many other such businesses, these problems are bound to be overcome with experience. The quality of the content more than makes up for any flaws in production.

➲ The Spiritual Lives of Great Composers by Patrick Kavanaugh (Zondervan Publishing House) $10.99

Twelve famous composers are profiled in this book: Handel, Bach, Haydn, Mozart, Beethoven, Schubert, Mendelssohn, Liszt, Wagner, Dvorak, Ives, and Stravinsky. Kavanaugh's approach is not that of a biographer, since there are already numerous such works available. Instead, he chose to concentrate on the spiritual aspects of their lives. Still, there is some biographical information which helps put their spirituality into perspective.

Kavanaugh draws on letters and other writings of the composers themselves as well as their friends and families. Such references are footnoted for those wishing to check it out for themselves. Kavanaugh introduces each composer with a brief vignette, then takes a few pages to relate the story of each composer. He ends with a short piece highlighting a key, positive character trait exhibited by each man and "Recommended Listening" suggestions to acquaint us with each composer's music. The writing style is lively and interesting, suitable for teens to read on their own, but even better enjoyed together as a family. Each section is short enough to be covered in a single sitting.

I found this book to be one of the most readable books about composers I have encountered. I also appreciate the balance it provides in contrast to popular modern images of some of the composers. Mozart is one of the best examples. He was made to look mentally unbalanced and amoral (at least) in the movie *Amadeus*, yet Kavanaugh introduces a deeply spiritual side of Mozart that most of us have never seen. He does not whitewash these men, yet he shows that they are much more than one-dimensional caricatures. Kavanaugh says that although the twelve composers "...come from a wide variety of backgrounds and beliefs....there is a surprising level of agreement on basic Christian beliefs."

➲ Theory Time by Heather Rathnau and Karen Wallace (Theory Time) student books - $7.95 each; teacher's editions - $17.95 each

Music theory books are offered for a primer level and for grades 1-12. Teens need not start at the primer level, but they might be wise to begin with a level 3 or 4 book if they are just starting their study of theory. Books review basic information up to a certain point, adding additional information of increasing difficulty at each level, so students might also jump from one level to a few levels higher for the next book. This is serious music theory study. For example, the seventh grade book covers "rhythm drill, drawing enharmonics, melodic/harmonic intervals, chromatic/diatonic half steps, double sharps & flats, simple/compound meter, conducting patterns, triplets, major keys, I, IV and V triads, relative minors, minor circle of fifths, pure minor scales & key signatures, major & minor thirds & triads." There are three teacher's editions, each covering a span of grade levels. The teacher's edition covering grades 1-6 includes reproductions of selected pages from the first three student books, answers, "ear training guides," and activity pages. The second and third teacher's editions cover grades 7-9 and 10-12 respectively, and both include complete copies of each of the student books with answers. Theory Time does not sell directly, but will direct you to a local or mail order distributor.(S)

Instruments to Rent or Buy

➲ New Creation Music

This Christian company offers violins, violas, cellos, wind and brass instruments, beginner drum kits, and recorders, plus instruction books, inspirational music for various instruments, and accessories. Instruments are available for rental, purchase, or on a rent-to-own basis. Operated by a homeschool family, New Creation will ship anywhere in the U.S.A. Request their free brochure for more information.

➲ Tretter Violins

If you need a violin, check prices from Tretter Violins before you do anything. They sell beginners' violins (all sizes) at very low prices. Even better, they have a buy-back policy that makes it cheaper to buy, then sell back the instrument than to rent one from another supplier. They also have a wide variety of quality violins for experienced players.

Drama

Drama can be difficult without a larger group, but support groups and community theaters offer possibilities. On the other hand, dramatic reading can be practiced with an audience of only one if that is all that is available. All of our teens should at least attempt to do some dramatic reading, even if their dramatic efforts never blossom any further.

Many of the poems and stories in literature books lend themselves to dramatic reading. Most literature books also contain at least one play script that can be used for practice. (With only a few family members, each person can take on more than one role, changing voices and mannerisms to fit the characters.)

Eternal Hearts has published an excellent book for those interested in putting together dramatic productions. It can be used as a foundation for anything from skits to serious productions. Bob Jones University Press offers packets containing scripts for five different plays that are consistent with biblical values and appropriate for high school level (see descriptions in the BJUP catalog). Don't forget that speech skills are essential to drama, so check out speech resources such as BJUP's *Speech for Christian Schools* which are reviewed under Language Arts.

➲ Drama Made Easy by Karena Krull (Eternal Hearts) $16.95

Drama Made Easy is a step-by-step manual for putting on a theatrical production. It is not a drama curriculum, even though it includes two short skits, but rather a manual for the director or producer of a play. Mrs. Krull includes most of the myriad of elements that go into even the simplest skits, and breaks down the process into manageable bits. Very few details of production, from earliest meetings to actual performance, are forgotten. She defines terms used in theater and walks the reader through putting on a production. Included are reproducible sheets for budgeting, auditions, and scheduling, and there are checklists for dress rehearsal and performance. In fact, the very completeness of the details included might seem intimidating to the beginner, but the friendly tone of the writing will quickly overcome this. In the case of a small production (e.g., Sunday School skit, at-home production for family and friends), it is easy to see that many of the tasks can be left out or consolidated. A theater production can be as simple or as complex as one wants, and *Drama Made Easy* gives the reader the know-how to choose which details are important for each production. Taking the time to read through the book will save even seasoned directors a big headache.

The second part of the manual includes two skits, suitable for Sunday School or school-age children; they are purposely on a fairly simple level for new directors or novice dramatists. Director's notes for scheduling and blocking are included; even an inexperienced director would be able to follow the notes and put on these productions. Teenagers or parents could follow the example of the Director's notes to produce another skit. *Drama Made Easy* will be especially helpful for families who are involved in church group activities where drama is commonly employed. Anyone who has always wanted to put on skits at church or as an outreach will find this book an invaluable resource that will enable them to jump right into the theater.[Kath Courtney]

Beyond the Three "R's"

Physical Education

Many teens would far rather read a good book than run around chasing balls. (I think we need a new term for sedentary book readers that parallels the idea of television couch potatoes.) This is not a problem endemic to home education, but rather one that is easier to ignore if there is no outside pressure to do otherwise. We parents have to think back to our high school days. If no one had forced some of us to "suit up" for gym class, would we have exercised on our own? Do we exercise now? Too many of us parents think of exercise as something only kids and jocks do. Some of us parents excuse our children's lack of exercise because we don't feel like doing it ourselves.

On the other extreme, we have parents who thrived on sports in school, and their biggest complaint about home education is that their teens can't play on the school team. A number of parents have rejected the opportunity to home school because they were not willing to forego the chance for their teens to participate in school sports.

Home educators need to find a practical middle ground for physical fitness. School sports cannot be the goal of a high school education, even for the teenager who is so incredibly gifted athletically that "we just know he'll get a sports scholarship that will pay for his college education." What if he ruins his knee in his senior year? What if he discovers that God has another call on his life that precludes sports? Fortunately, most home educators have seen that intellectual education should take precedence over physical education. I don't doubt that there are still a few extremist home schoolers who overdo sports activities, but "sports abuse" doesn't seem to be a widespread problem in home schooling. Lack of any sort of P.E. program is far more of an issue in home education.

Physical education is a requirement for most high school programs, but it plays a different role in terms of college entrance requirements—the issue that should concern us more than high school requirements. Colleges are looking for well-rounded individuals, those who participate in a variety of activities, including some that are physical. While there are college scholarships for those lucky few who are gifted with significant athletic prowess and skill (and many of these are more easily obtainable for women than for men), in most cases colleges are simply looking

for an appropriate involvement in physical fitness activities. Even if those activities occur outside the typical school setting, it usually presents no problem for college entry.

Aside from college requirements, physical fitness should be part of our curriculum because our bodies are temples of the Holy Spirit. If our lifelong outlook is to be of service in whatever area God calls us to, then maintaining our bodies well so that we are physically able to be of service is essential.

Most of us have no objections to physical fitness, but the problem for many of us is how to provide appropriate opportunities. As home schooling has grown, more and more areas are creating home school teams for various sports. Some of these are even allowed to play in regular school competitions. This satisfies those who want that level of involvement, but it doesn't help those who want something less competitive or less demanding. Interestingly, many home schoolers are rejecting intense team sports and competition on Biblical principle, and are instead seeking fitness activities that do not involve violence, antagonism toward opponents, unhealthy pride, or needless humiliation. Jonathan Lindvall has an audio tape, *Sports and Godly Families* (Bold Christian Living) [$6], in which he discusses his own struggle with the lure of competition and sports addiction. He examines the historical background of sports in relation to present attitudes, then contrasts that with what Scripture tells us. Lindvall does not claim to have all the answers on the subject, but he challenges our thinking on the issue.

For those of us who want physical fitness without the trappings and demands of team competition, we need to find more creative solutions. Some solutions others have found are gymnastics or dance classes, working along with exercise videos at home, jogging, horseback riding, swimming, playing tennis or other sports on a casual basis, participating in classes at the YMCA (at least three home school groups have set up special P.E. classes through local YMCA's), and working with *The President's Challenge Physical Fitness Program*. Which particular fitness activities are appropriate and/or appealing to our teen is for each of us to decide. Meanwhile, following are reviews of a few options that we might consider.

The President's Challenge Physical Fitness Program might be most useful as a motivating tool. Young people ages 6-17 can work towards achieving one of four awards: The Presidential Physical Fitness Award, which recognizes an outstanding level of physical fitness; The National Physical Fitness Award for achieving a basic yet challenging level of physical fitness; the Health Fitness Award for maintaining a healthy level of fitness; or The Participant Physical Fitness Award just for participating in the program. The first two awards are earned by meeting qualifying standards (according to age and sex) in five areas of fitness: curl-ups, shuttle run, v-sit or sit and reach, one-mile run, and pull-ups or flexed-arm hang. Emblems and/or certificates are the awards. I noted a restriction in the 1993-94 information packet that I had not seen in earlier packets: a certified physical education teacher/specialist must oversee instruction and testing to qualify students for the awards. If this is not possible for you, you might still want to use the program for the sake of fitness without awards. (Write for current information.)

Fitness at Home: A Physical Fitness Program for Home Schools offers yet another option, suitable for children ages 6 to 17. Similar in many ways to *The President's Challenge*, this program concentrates on a number of fitness exercises and activities, with a pre-test and a post-test. The particular exercises involved differ from *The President's Challenge*; they have tried to make the standards more realistic for the average student while still representing a significant fitness achievement. Participation patches and achievement certificates are offered in conjunction with the program. Tips on how to create pull-up bars and an inclined pull-up help us implement the program at home. Complete information, including cautions, is in the *Parent Manual*. Individual *Student Training Program* charts illustrate and describe exercises. The Christian rationale for fitness, along with related Bible verses also differentiate this program. Parent manuals are $4.75; Student Training Programs (one per child) are $2.95 each and include an award certificate to be filled in by the parent; and embroidered emblems are $2.25 each.

Logic and Thinking Skills

Developing thinking skills will primarily depend upon interaction between parent and child on various subjects, going beyond the obvious and encouraging deeper questions. For instance, we read an article on a controversial subject from the newspaper, then everyone comments about it. If everyone is well informed about the subject, the discussion can provide some lively debate. Becoming well informed does not occur overnight, but happens gradually as we and our children read newspapers, books, and magazines—accumulating a background of information. There are often reaction-provoking articles in the editorial section of the newspaper. This is a good place to start.

Thinking does not have to center around current events. If our children can take information that they have picked up somewhere and then apply it in a new way in a different situation, they are operating at the higher levels of thinking. If they can read an advertisement and identify the half-truths and propaganda, they are thinking critically.

Curriculum to teach thinking skills is not absolutely necessary if we are debating ideas and challenging opinions (but not arguing) as a normal part of our family interaction. But some of us are not comfortable with debates and discussions, and prefer not to stir up family emotions over current events. For the calmer folk, some of the thinking skills materials are more practical. Even the outspoken among us might prefer to use some of the materials just because they are fun.

Some high school students will want to take all of this to a deeper level by tackling a course in logic. They will encounter introductory logic in *Critical Thinking Skills*, *Elements of Clear Thinking*, and *Wff N' Proof*. Those who want more should check out *Introductory Logic for Christian Private and Home Schools*, R.C. Sproul's tape series of *Introductory Logic, Better Thinking and Reasoning*, or *Logic* by Gordon Clark.

➲ **Better Thinking and Reasoning** by Ron Tagliapietra (Bob Jones University Press) $1195

This great little book is easy to overlook among all of BJUP's other offerings, but it deserves your attention. This is a logic course, but author Ron Tagliapietra also explains how it can be used as a resource or supplement for other courses. Thus, students might use it alongside history, math, speech, science, or English studies; in conjunction with one or more additional resources to create a complete logic course; or as a special unit within any of the above mentioned courses, a world view study or some other option. Tagliapietra specifies which chapters of this book to use in each of these situations.

The book draws on scriptural truths and principles, oftentimes focusing on applications in apologetics. Because of this, I would also suggest the possibility of using it as an apologetics unit within Bible class. And, even though Tagliapietra mentions its use as part of a speech course, I think it should be of special interest to those preparing to participate in debate. Of all the logic resources I have reviewed, this one seems best suited to teach students how to make strong, logical arguments in debate. Because of this, I visualize a complete course that would consist of this book, the debate tapes and book from Home School Legal Defense Association (see "Speech" in Chapter 13), and *How to Lie with Statistics*.

The book focuses on definitions, truth (logical expressions and values), types of argument, and logical fallacies. Each chapter includes concepts with explanation and examples, applications, a summary, and questions. The content is very challenging in some of the chapters on expressions of truth statements, actually requiring students to do mathematical thinking and application. (Students must have studied both algebra 1 and geometry before starting this book.) Questions are excellent, requiring students to demonstrate a grasp of the principles taught, to actually apply them, and do additional reading or research. The last question in each chapter directs students to research a key person in the field of logic and write a paragraph about his background and ideas. A few times, students are directed to read from outside books. The only one that seemed to be recommended to be read in total was *How to Lie with Statistics*. Of course, parents can select which of the questions or assignments they require students to complete in any of these lessons.

➲ Critical Thinking Books and Software

Critical Thinking Books and Software specializes in supplemental book and software activities to sharpen thinking skills for better academic performance at all grade levels. Subject areas covered are mathematics, language arts, science, and social studies. Most of their books have reproducible student pages.

Two of their more basic books appropriate for teens are *Building Thinking Skills, Book 3—Figural*, and *Building Thinking Skills, Book 3—Verbal*. They are suggested for grades 7-12. Activities are fairly brief, but include a wide range of thinking skills. The *Figural* book has students identify figural similarities and differences; complete sequences; work on congruence, area, volume, and rotation; apply deductive reasoning; and more. *Verbal* teaches identification of verbal similarities and differences, sequencing, analogies, deductive reasoning, following directions, map skills, logic, cause and effect, flow charts, scheduling, analogies, and more. [Cost: student books - $23.95 each; teacher's manuals -$18.95 each.]

For high school students, I particularly like *Critical Thinking, Books One* [$18.95; teacher's manual - $9.95] and *Two* [$19.95; teacher's manual -$10.95]. This is a fun course in logic that will challenge parents too. Some of the exercises are silly, but effective. You can skip around to a certain extent, choosing lessons that are most interesting, easier, or more challenging. These books need to be used interactively, since they are not designed for independent work. You will also need the teacher's manuals for each book. We occasionally had trouble with the author's point of view as reflected in the phrasing of statements and/or questions. We sometimes used those to identify her world view, sometimes skipped them, and sometimes changed them. There isn't anything seriously objectionable on the surface, but attitudes and opinions can be subtle influencers.

The *Mind Benders* series consists of sets of smaller (28-30 page) books [$7.95 per book]. Each book is self-contained with brief teaching information and an answer key in the front. Students organize clues (some direct and some indirect) in grids to derive logical conclusions. For example, in the first lesson of book *B-1*, students are told, "Klare, Lemon, Morton, and Nelson are women who love their work (dress designer, florist, gardener, symphony conductor). From the clues below, match up each woman's name with her kind of work. 1.Klare is violently allergic to most plants. 2.Lemon and the florist are roommates. 3.Lemon likes only rock music. 4.The gardener, the dress designer, and Nelson are strangers." There is a chart (grid) on the page to help students chart the information in a logical format. Other lessons get much more complicated than this. One series of books, *B-1, B-2, B-3,* and *B-4* is designed for students in grades 6-10. *C-1, C-2,* and *C-3* are for grades 10-12.(SE)

Math Mind Benders [$7.95 each] use challenging numerical crossword puzzles to help develop reasoning and analytical skills. The student must examine the data given and look for possible patterns, reasonable assumptions, and possible inferences. It's like doing one of the *Mind Benders* above, then assigning nu-

merical values or other numerical derivatives to those answers. Students should tackle word-based logic problems before trying these. Detailed solutions are included at the back of each book in case we get stuck. There are two "Warm-Up" books for the elementary grades; Book A1 is suggested for grades 4-7, but I would start here for students who are new to this type of problem. Book B1 is for grades 7-10 and Book C1 for ninth grade and above.

A Case of Red Herrings: Solving Mysteries Through Critical Questioning, Books A-1, A-2, B-1, B-2 [$11.95 each] is a series of books for junior high students based on the game "20 Questions." Each page has a short paragraph that on the surface seems to be impossible or a contradiction. The teacher reads the paragraph and then answers questions that the students ask to determine a situation where the reading would make sense. The directions given are fairly loose, but the teacher, or a student leader, needs to read the answers first (provided in the back of the book) to help guide the questioning. In general, the paragraphs toward the beginning of each book are easier, but as it may take a leap of intuition to solve them, there is no real need to proceed in order. *A Case of Red Herrings* would be excellent to use as a game; it is a break from the traditional routine and best to use in a small group. Participants should be junior high age at least (although there is no upper limit), because some of the situations depend on considering alternate meanings of a word. For example, "likeness," can mean "a portrait" or "a similarity in appearance." One of the cases revolves around making this distinction. Some of the answers are more farfetched than others, and a student might come up with a solution that is different from the one in the book, but which works equally well. We had a lot of fun trying this out in our family. As the game does not depend on knowledge, but rather your ability to think creatively, it is a great way for less academically-oriented students to compete on an equal basis with those who are more academic.(S)[Kath Courtney]

Organizing Thinking: Graphic Organizers, Book II [$32.95] offers a totally different format for developing thinking skills. It covers the basic subject areas of math, writing, science, language arts, and social studies, as well as enrichment topics and problem solving. It uses graphic organizers such as Venn diagrams, flow charts, time lines, and others that provide visual organization structures for information. Each organizer is presented as a blank "chart" and also as a particular lesson, accompanied by a lesson plan and background information. We can try the sample lessons to become familiar with use of the organizer, then branch out on our own. Organizers are reproducible, and when there are predictable answers for sample lessons, they are entered in nonreproducible blue ink to serve as an answer key. The organizers are also available on computer disks for the Macintosh, so that either we or our students can adapt or write information on the original forms. *Book II* is suggested for grades 4-8, however, it might be used over an even wider age span. Since the lessons themselves address specific topics such as comparing and contrasting Abraham Lincoln and Frederick Douglass, we must choose lessons that relate to subject areas appropriate for our children. (Some topics are more general and thus easier to use with more students.) *Book II* is hefty (342 pages) with so many sample lessons to choose from that we can get a lot of mileage out of it without getting beyond the sample lessons.

Many of Critical Thinking Books are in series, and they are often sold as sets at discounted prices.(S)

⮕ The Elements of Clear Thinking (Educators Publishing Service) $7.15 each; teacher's keys - $1.25 each

The Elements of Clear Thinking is actually a series of three workbooks designed for high school level. The individual titles are: *Sound Reasoning*—how to distinguish between good and bad arguments, characteristics of deductive and inductive reasoning, pitfalls and fallacies, and identifying arguments; *Accurate Communication*—the use and misuse of language (slanted language, connotations, ambiguity, jargon, etc.); and *Critical Reading*—prereading, choosing reading rate to fit subject matter, organizational patterns. Here students also write a precis, a paraphrase, and evaluations. Choose one or all three titles. Teacher's keys are available for all three. One thing that I noticed, particularly in the first book, sets these apart from some of the other "logic" courses—the author introduces each formal logic principle or thinking skill, but always moves to practical application in typical situations such as conversations, advertising, or politics.(S)

⮕ An Introduction to Argumentation and Debate by Christy Farris (Home School Legal Defense Association)

See the review under "Speech" in Chapter 13. This text and the *Debate Video Set* are designed to prepare students for formal debate. Students who study logic often find debate a natural outlet for applying what they have learned.

⮕ Introductory Logic [audio tape series] by R.C. Sproul (Ligonier Ministries) $18 for set of 6 tapes; outline notes - $2

R.C. Sproul teaches an introductory logic class covering thinking fallacies and "truth tests" for evaluating statements and ideas. Sproul begins with common thinking fallacies such as *post hoc ergo propter hoc* (after this, therefore because of this), then addresses some of the basics of logic like the law of noncontradiction and syllogisms. Finally, he teaches how to use Venn diagrams and symbols to express relationships and logic. Sproul's purpose is theological—to equip Christians to both defend and explain their faith as a reasonable belief in contrast to other belief systems that are logically flawed. The course consists of six, 60-minute audio tapes with brief outline notes. Although the presentations were made before an older audience, mature teens should find it understandable. The use of Venn diagrams in particular transform abstract ideas into visual illustrations. This course should be a little easier than Douglas Wilson's, although not as extensive.

⮕ Introductory Logic, third edition by Douglas J. Wilson, updated by James Nance (Canon Press) student book - $15; solution key - $4

"Introductory" in the title of this book makes it sound easier than it is. But this is the real thing—a challenging course in logic for students who are serious thinkers. However, the presentation has been geared for students in junior high. The third edition of this book expands and clarifies explanations, making it easier to use than the previous editions. It consists of a worktext suitable for independent study and a solution key. Some of the topics covered are statements, consistency, contrariety, subimplication, syllogisms, counterexamples, and fallacies. From the topics, you can see that the content is beyond typical high school level material. While I think that some students will be overwhelmed by this, there are many logical thinkers who will benefit from this course. The authors are Christians, so interesting theological and world view applications pop up throughout the book. Two examples from the book are groups of sentences to be analyzed for the type of argument or fallacy represented: "If a ministry is of God, then it will succeed. The Mormon church is successful, and we can conclude that it is blessed by God (p. 70)" and "If a country is rebellious, it has many rulers. Argentina has had many rulers; it must be a rebellious country (p.70)."

⮕ Just Think® 6 or 7, Stretch Think® 3, or Think Quest® 4 (Thomas Geale Publications, Inc.) prices range from $15 to $45 per book

While these particular books in the publisher's series are designed to be used through junior high, because they were designed for gifted classes they can easily be used in high school also. These books develop thinking skills through a variety of creative methods. While all books include activities from almost every subject area, some place more emphasis on one area. *Just Think® 6* has a strong American History component, so consider using it the year that you study American History. *Just Think® 7* includes many activities that challenge students to consider current problems and issues. *Stretch Think® 3* seems to have more science-related topics than the others. I have not seen *Think Quest® 4*, but I am told that it has a special analysis component that should be interesting for high schoolers. One book can be used with any size group. Any pages that students need to use are reproducible. These are not workbooks, but teacher's manuals. The teacher must read through each activity before presenting it, but there are no extra teaching aids to prepare.(S)

⮕ Logic by Gordon H. Clark (The Trinity Foundation) book - $8.95; workbook - $11.95; answer key to workbook - $4.95

High school juniors and seniors should be able to tackle this logic book by prolific Christian thinker/author Dr. Gordon H. Clark. It is presented with plenty of story illustrations, including numerous references to philosophy and Christianity. In some ways, logic is foundational to study about apologetics, and this is reflected in Clark's approach when he deals with logic in relation to Biblical truths. The workbook and answer key should be helpful for students to evaluate their own understanding as they read through the book's chapters.

➲ Rex Games Inc.

Rex Games specializes in games that develop logic and thinking skills. I review two of them here: *Tangoes®* and *Word Trek®*. *Tangoes* [$11.95] uses traditional Chinese tangrams and puts two sets of colored, plastic tangram pieces in a case with a deck of cards. The cards and pieces are then used by solitary players, two opponents, or even groups to try to create the tangram design on each card as quickly as possible. This is a great game, but the case is really difficult to open. *Word Trek* [$11.95] has two card decks for a total of 216 word puzzles and solutions. Players—from two to as many as you like—work to transform a word into another word (e.g., "rock" to "salt") by changing one letter at a time while always creating actual words. For example, rock progresses through sock, sack, sank, sane, sale, and, finally, to salt. There are many ways to accomplish these transformations, but the trick is to use as few words as possible. *Tangoes* and *Word Trek* can be played by younger children, but you might want to give some hints to keep them from getting frustrated. Otherwise they are great for all teens and adults. Think about giving these to friends and family as gifts.(S)

➲ Wff N' Proof (Wff N' Proof Games) $33.50

Wff N' Proof makes logic games that can easily overwhelm the faint hearted. Their *Equations* game [$28] is probably easier to tackle than most of the others. *Propaganda* [$28] should also appeal to many home schoolers. *Propaganda* would actually be great to use in conjunction with *Critical Thinking, Books One* and *Two* (Critical Thinking Books and Software) as it applies many of the same propaganda techniques learned about in those books. There are a number of game variations described in the instruction manual, but they essentially involve identifying propaganda techniques used for the examples on the game cards such as the following: "My dictionary has three thousand pages, yours only two thousand. Mine must be right."

The original *Wff N' Proof* game itself is very difficult, dealing with serious logic, but if you have a student who needs a challenge, this is it.

➲ Critical Thinking Activities (Dale Seymour Publications) $13.95

The activities in this reproducible book hail from the field of mathematics and are divided into the three areas of patterns, imagery (not the new age type), and logic. Written for grades 7-12, the activities vary in difficulty to reflect that grade span. We can pick and choose appropriate activities by topic and difficulty level.

The patterns section goes far beyond "fill in the missing number" to include work with such topics as equations, charts, Venn diagrams, exponents, geometric formulas, and designs. Imagery has to do with developing visual skill in "seeing" accurately as well as predicting such things as how a shape will look from a different angle or when combined with another shape. Many activities here resemble those I have seen on intelligence tests. Geometry skills get some extra practice here. The logic section includes Venn diagrams, logic statements, deductive exercises, and even one word logic game. While almost all activities are related to math, the skills are transferable to other subject areas as well as to life situations.

There are 163 pages of activities, and the answer key is found at the end of the book.(S)

➲ How to Lie with Statistics by Darrell Huff (W. W. Norton and Company) $5

There is one last book that I would like to mention here, even though it might more properly belong under mathematics. *How to Lie with Statistics* is a small, paperback book that was originally written in 1954. It has been reprinted at least thirty-six times according to my copy of the book. The author introduces us to all of the shady ways that statistics can be interpreted to say whatever one desires. In a very humorous way, he talks about how advertisers carefully choose just the right numbers, and manipulate those numbers to enhance their products. Advertisers are not the only culprits targeted by Mr. Huff. Pollsters and politicians are equally exposed. While teens can read this on their own, it is the type of book that is fun when shared out loud. Watch out for a few references to the Kinsey sexual research. These can easily be skipped. Also, be aware that data has not been updated since the originally printing. Even so, the author's point still comes across clearly—we have to be alert and thinking logically when we evaluate information, such as that in advertisements and commercials, that has been designed to influence our behavior.

Use this as a supplement or introduction to statistics since it does not address the proper and legitimate use of statistics to a significant extent.

Electives

Typing

Typing is very important for each student to learn, whether it be learned on a typewriter or a computer keyboard. Typing courses can be taken in summer school or studied at home with a text from a used book store or college book store. If you have a computer, *Type!, Typing Tutor*, and other good programs, including free or inexpensive public domain programs are available.

Computer Literacy

Computer literacy is becoming a basic requirement, like it or not. College students are assumed to have access to a computer, with some colleges actually requiring it as part of enrollment. But computer literacy does not require that everyone know computer programming. For the general public, computer technology is moving in the direction of requiring less and less understanding of the computer's internal functioning, but more familiarity with applications such as using data bases, word processors, and other software. There will be those who are interested in computer programming, who will certainly need to study programming languages (e.g., Basic, Pascal, and Fortran) and electronics. Those interested in using the computer as a tool should be devoting time to learning about the applications, not the technology that makes the applications possible. For instance, a person interested in desktop publishing needs to study word processors, publishing software, graphic art software, printing, and other aspects of the field.

Another aspect of programming is the fact that it enhances your use of applications. Most major word processors (e.g., *Word Perfect* and *Microsoft Word*) include a programming capability that ranges from simple key substitutions to macros to full programmability. Also, there is quite a bit of specialized business software that exists in the form of spreadsheets for programs such as *Microsoft Excel* and *Lotus 1-2-3*. Learning programming can help in learning, maintaining, and fixing such programs in the business environment.

I would also add that programming can be a worthwhile course for anyone as a tool for teaching logic. Writing flow charts is a logical challenge which depends upon good thinking skills.

For the average student, I suggest the primary investment be in a decent word processing program. *Word Perfect* or Microsoft *Word* are best since they are industry standards. Students who are familiar with these programs graduate with a marketable skill! However, less expensive programs are acceptable as long as they allow a good amount of formatting control. Essential features to look for beyond the basics are automatic page numbering, columns, footnotes and/or endnotes, spell-checker, paragraph indentation, tabs, and choices of alignment.

Learning desktop publishing or basic accounting skills on the computer prepares students with marketable skills, but it is sometimes better to take a class for such programs. Local classes are usually available; check with your local computer bookstore or computer clubs. For independent, book-based courses consider the following resources, keeping in mind that book learning alone does not compare with actual hands-on experience.

➲ **The Big Book** (Computer Courseware Specialists) $90

One large binder and two floppies comprise a computer course for the new user or the computer illiterate to learn the basics of computer hardware and software. It begins with an explanation of the computer's primary components and how they work. The course is broken up into sections so that the student can choose which programs he or she needs to know and can ignore the rest. The software covered by the course includes Microsoft products: MS-DOS, Windows 95, Word, Excel, and Powerpoint. This course is designed for computers equipped with Windows 95 and Microsoft Office. Software programs to be used in the various exercises throughout the course are included on the disks. While instruction is quite extensive it is not comprehensive on every program. In many ways this "focus on the programs" approach is more practical than the "intro to computing" courses presented in most textbooks.

➲ **Computer Literacy** (School of Tomorrow) $64

12 PACEs and two answer keys comprise a one-year course in computer literacy. The first six PACEs are an introduction to computers, and the last six have the student working with *Microsoft Works*® as they learn word processing, data base manage-

ment, spreadsheets, and communications. You will need an IBM compatible computer and *Microsoft Works*® 1.0 to 1.5 OR 2.0. The last six PACEs are available in two different versions, depending upon which version of *Works* you have.

➲ **Introduction to Computers** correspondence course (ICS Newport/Pacific High School)

There are five booklets to this elective course, each a study unit on a particular area of computer use. The five topics are an introduction to computers, programs, data processing, communication with computers, and information systems. Essentially, it covers the basics of computers, software, and hardware, and common usages. The course is fairly easy to use, although in some cases, general information needs more detail or examples to familiarize the student with the topic. No actual computer use is required, but it would be a tremendous help if a student were able to apply what he is learning as he covers the various topics. (It would probably very boring to do such a course if one were not interested in computers and did not have access to one.) Students send in only the multiple-choice exams.(S)[Josh Duffy]

➲ **Using the Personal Computer** (A Beka) $13.95

This text teaches applications rather than programming. Students learn how to work with word processing, data bases, spreadsheets, and graphing. Fundamentals of typing are covered at the beginning for those lacking keyboard skills.

No computer program comes with the text. Instead students must work with programs to which they have access for their own computer. Lessons give general instructions such as "Center the title and use 12 point bold" since it would be impossible to provide instructions for particular key strokes to accomplish this within all of the different programs. For a student with no prior knowledge of any of the applications, this means that he will have to rely heavily upon the program manuals for chosen application programs. He will have to learn the basics of each program before he can work on the lessons.

Exercises include business, school, and home applications, using Christian hymns and Bible verses for some exercises.

Getting on the Internet

Going online poses a number of concerns for homeschooling parents. Primary among those concerns are the easy accessibility of pornographic or otherwise objectionable sites. Filtered access can help screen such sites, prohibiting their access from your computer. The Institute in Basic Life Principles now offers Internet access through CharacterLink™. Four different levels of access allow you to tailor service to your family's needs. To ensure "safe sites" CharacterLink allows access only to those sites which have been inspected and approved. They have more than 300 local access numbers and offer web-hosting and e-mail accounts (with ability to include attachments). Contact CharacterLink for more information.

⮌ Homeschool Guide to The Internet by Mark and Wendy Dinsmore (Holly Hall Publications/Homeschool Press) $14.99

This book is intended to follow the more basic *Homeschool Guide to the Online World* by the same authors, although it stands very well on its own. It covers how to get on the Internet, how to find things, what to use it for, and 250 more Internet addresses. Very similar in format to the first book, it also will suffer from that book's problem of becoming outdated quickly.

⮌ Homeschool Guide to the Online World by Mark and Wendy Dinsmore (Holly Hall Publications/Homeschool Press) $12.99

This book is divided into several sections. The first chapter provides answers to common questions about being and getting online including the origins of the World Wide Web, electronic mail, online services, and necessary computer equipment to access all of this. This chapter also has a brief discussion of whether or not using the Internet is either unsafe or unbiblical. The second chapter deals with four of the largest online services—America On Line (AOL), Compuserve, Prodigy, and eWorld—and the authors' experience and suggestions on each. The third chapter, which is the bulk of the book, contains over 140 Web site addresses categorized into sections such as Homeschooling, Christian Resources, Math, Reference, and Science. The authors note the problem of publishing lists of Web site addresses such as these that are bound to become out of date soon after publication, due to sites moving or changing, but it is nevertheless a good representative list of educational material available and should still be mostly correct. This book does not intend to give the reader a step-by-step guide to buying a computer, setting up the hardware and software, and making his first call to an online service. However, it does provide some reasonable general advice on buying a computer in several price ranges for both Windows and Macintosh versions. The book also has several useful appendices. The first lists software programs, called browsers, that help you navigate through the Internet. Another deals with some of the common shorthand used in chatrooms, forums, and electronic mail, and the emoticons such as the sideways smiley face :) that lets the reader know that you are kidding. Like all published books on the subject of the Internet, some of the information will be obsolete by the time you read it, but it is still a good inexpensive introduction to going online.[Michael Courtney]

⮌ Soaring Through the Internet (A Hands-on Text Book) by Donna Stoner (Forever His Publishing) $22.95

This book is intended to be a textbook for junior and senior high school students and for adults. It has questions and assignments at the end of the chapters. Some of the answers to the questions come from the text, while others must be worked out by sitting in front of a computer and using the Internet. The book attempts to make as few assumptions as possible about the reader's knowledge of computers, online services, and the Internet. It starts with basic computer equipment needed, a history of the Internet and the World Wide Web, then discusses service providers such as America On Line (AOL), Compuserve, and Prodigy.

It then leads the student step by step through the process of logging on to an online service, electronic mail, the World Wide Web, and many other topics. The book has a more complete discussion of some of the problems and dangers of "surfing the net" —pornography, unsavory newsgroups, and chatting with unsavory strangers—than others reviewed here. It discusses the problems, and includes several possible solutions.

The book's shortcomings are few, but the book could stand a more professional touch on the publication side. The typeface for most of the text is difficult to read, and the book uses too many different styles of type. There are a few small errors, and the book could really use an index. The mechanics of writing are sloppy and uneven, such as overuse of the phrase "a lot" and use of "I feel" instead of "I think." It uses some words incorrectly and the overly casual style of writing made it difficult for me to take the author seriously. On the plus side, the casual style might appeal to some and make it more approachable than many books about the Internet. Overall, however, the text is complete, has good exercises and tips, and is well organized. The authors also plan to provide updates to the book as various parts become outdated.[Michael Courtney]

⮌ The Student's Guide to Doing Research on the Internet by Dave and Mary Campbell (Addison-Wesley) $14.95

This book is divided into two main sections; the first teaches how to access the Internet, and the second tells us where and how to track down information for particular areas of inquiry. The authors are writing primarily to college students who might well have access to the Internet through campus systems. However, they also explain how those without free and/or convenient access can get connected. Step-by-step instructions walk us through some of the more complex connections we might encounter if we are using a free or campus-provided service. If we connect through a third party (e.g., Compuserve, AOL, Prodigy), the process is much simpler. The second half of the book is intended to be a research guide. It describes numerous Internet sites under broad categories such as humanities, computer science, education and general reference resources, geography and travel, and literature. Many destinations will interest those who are not doing research, but who are just searching for information. This is a resource book from which you select those sections that pertain to your situation. You will need to have a computer and some form of access available to really try it out and make sense of what you are reading or you will be lost in "computerese" by page 30. This book was published in July, 1995, but because of rapid changes in Internet services, information is quickly outdated.

Computer Software

There are hundreds of sources for educational software. Because of the lack of time and space, I have not tried to review all of the good software available.

In spite of my limitations, there are a few software sources that I want to let you know about.

Learning Services offers discounted educational software for a number of computers. They are selective in their offerings but still have a large selection of quality products. They also carry multimedia products (e.g., CD-ROM and laser disc players plus software). Send for their free catalog.

The Home Computer Market specializes in computers and software for home educators. Of especial interest is their *The Homeschooler's Computer Guide: A Resource for Choosing and Using Educational Software and Computers [$7]*. This resource guide also serves as a catalog. It is 110 pages in length and features about 250 software reviews by Dan and Tammy Kihlstadius who are also the software columnists for *Practical Homeschooling* magazine. This is probably the best single source for the most reviews of software products of interest to home educators. Dan and Tammy carefully screen programs for home educating families who desire products with educational value but without objectionable content. Most of the worthwhile products are sold by The Home Computer Market. Of course, you should then order those products from Home Computer Market to help support their work in sorting through the new products that come out and saving you money you might have spent on objectionable or worthless software. (Most of their products are discounted 25-35%.) The resource guide also features a number of articles to help you in selection and use of hardware and software, use of the internet, judging software's educational value, programs to avoid (a lengthy list!), and much more. Two super-useful charts will help you in software selection: the Software Planning Grid shows what software to use for different subjects for each grade level, and the Unit Study Guide suggests software programs to be used under a number of different possible unit study headings such as U.S. History, physical science, etc.

Magazines dealing with computer products for the home school market are getting scarce. We used to have two computer magazines for homeschoolers, but both are being absorbed (or reabsorbed) into other comprehensive home school magazines. *Homeschool PC* content will again appear within the pages of *Practical Homeschooling. Homeschool Computing's* staff will now be contributing to The *Teaching Home* magazine.

Accounting and Bookkeeping

⮌ Accounting (School of Tomorrow) $56

School of Tomorrow teaches basics of accounting with 12 PACEs and 2 answer keys. The course includes, "...introduction to assets, liabilities and capital, journalizing, ledger analysis, account management, balance sheet and income statement completion, accounting for sales and purchases, inventory control, tax preparation, and partnership and corporate accounting." This is a one-year course.

⮌ Accounting 1 (Christian Light Publications) $90 for essential materials; additional cost for optional materials

Century 21 Accounting is the basic text used for this course that covers both bookkeeping and principles of accounting. Optional business simulations provide application experience.

Homemaking

Homemaking encompasses far more than home economics. It has to do with heart attitudes and life purposes. Being a homemaker is a godly calling and potentially the most rewarding "career" of all.

The *Far Above Rubies* unit study curriculum recognizes the honor of the role of homemaker more than any other resource. So much so that they have developed an entire curriculum around the goal of training young women to be godly wives and mothers—keepers of their homes. (See the review under unit studies.)

Chris Ellyson of Georgia passed on a great suggestion for developing the less obvious homemaking skills—the things that make a home an inviting, comfortable place to be. She suggests reading Edith Schaeffer's book, *The Hidden Art of Homemaking* (Tyndale House Publishers) [$9.99], one chapter a month, and allowing our children to practice and embellish Mrs. Schaeffer's ideas in our own homes.

Home economics does deserve attention in terms of coursework, but home economics as taught in many textbooks is often not nearly as useful as practical experience under the supervision and instruction of mom or another mentor, with the use of real reference books. At home, we already have the tools and the motivation for learning the arts of homemaking. Planning menus, purchasing food, preparing it, then getting the family's reaction is eminently more practical than the limited experience we get in a class or from a book. We can acquire more information from a friend, the library or bookstore if needed. One book that I found to be an exception to the rule (although I am certain there are others) is Karey Swan's *Hearth and Home* (Singing Springs Productions) [$17]. At first, brief glance this appears to be a cookbook but it is far more than that. Yes, it has loads of recipes, but it also deals with nutrition, gardening, and soap making, plus educational philosophy, child training, and relationships. Spiritual wisdom, poetry, and quotes mix with the text for delightful reading as well as practical use. It makes a wonderful book for mothers and daughters to read, discuss, and use together. As far as the cooking and nutrition, Karey stresses real foods (i.e., whole grains, fresh produce) and less fat. But her recipes do not rely exclusively on "from scratch" products and methods. Recipes are accompanied by sidebar comments and helpful hints and alternatives. She frequently points out creative ways to make do and make use of what you have on hand. Ultimately, the message of the book is that the role of mothers and wives is to nurture their families and create appealing, loving homes. Home education becomes part of that "holistic" lifestyle for raising children in a Biblical Christian worldview.

Still, some of us don't feel equipped to operate as the Proverbs 31 woman; we need some assistance. There are times when it is worth looking for outside help. If mom does not know how to sew, perhaps a mentor could be found within the family, neighborhood or church. Adult education and college classes are available for more complicated sewing techniques such as pattern making and tailoring. Cake decorating or other specialty classes can also be fun and worthwhile. Work with the assets on hand for basic homemaking skills, then seek out sources for help with special needs or interests.

Driver's Education

Driver's education is conceded as a must because of state educational requirements and insurance rates. In addition, the certificate from driver's education will, in some states, enable teens to get their licenses at a younger age and at lower insurance rates. Driver's Education is also supposed to ensure that our young drivers are proficient in their knowledge of the rules of the road and the handling of their vehicles.

Before I go on, I need to make an important distinction between two terms: driver's education and driver's training. In California, and I think in most other states, driver's education describes the classroom portion of instruction while driver's training is the behind-the-wheel instruction. Both are required, but they are often available separately. In spite of these distinctions, the terms driver's education is generally used to mean both parts.

Unfortunately, parents are not always considered competent instructors, so in some states it is necessary to enroll under a recognized (certified, credentialed, etc.) instructor. Sometimes this is true for both driver's education and driver's training, but sometimes it is true for only one or the other. The situation varies from state to state, so it is important to check with your state homeschooling organization for the current status and requirements.

In the early days of home schooling, we could often enroll our students in public school driver's education courses for free. Summer school is the time to take driver's education at your public high school if available. Some home schoolers have run into problems such as refusal because of lack of space, or the requirement of taking health education at the same time. (Health education classes often include sex education or other material offered from a humanistic viewpoint.) With budget cuts in many states, this option is increasingly limited.

Most people are turning to private driving schools, which can be quite expensive. Some driving schools offer group discounts so consider gathering a group of teens who would like to take driver's education together. When I called about a half dozen driving schools to check costs when three teens took the class together, all but one offered a discount. Check the yellow pages for driving schools. They sometimes offer specials during "spring break" and summer vacation so you might save money by knowing about bargain times and planning ahead. If you request information, they often put you on a mailing list and send notices of special discounts.

As happens with other challenging areas of home education, other options are starting to appear.

Charles Taylor, an experienced driving instructor, has developed a parent-taught driver's education program that families in many states will be able to use. He is continually working with people in the various states to work out the technical or legal difficulties of getting the program recognized as a legitimate alternative. The program, *Help! My Teenager Wants to Drive!!!* (Published by Noble Publishing Associates; available through them or through Advanced Traffic Technologies, Inc.) [$59.50]

includes both classroom and behind-the-wheel training, with the latter part of the course probably more complete and thorough than what we get from most private driving programs. Material presented in the student workbook requires both reading and discussion. The much larger parent/teacher's manual includes a second section for each lesson presenting the behind-the-wheel training. The parent/teacher learns how to teach—everything is covered from technical detail to the teacher's attitude. (The teacher's attitude receives major attention since it is so crucial.) When I first heard about this program, I thought that it couldn't be as good as "professional training." But every challenge I could come up with was addressed. What about manual transmissions? What about cooperation from our teenagers? What if the parent is overly fearful about his or her child crashing? Everything has been taken into consideration. Taylor has even provided humorous illustrations and other reminders to "lighten up" when things get too tense.

Written tests conclude each lesson, with three versions provided so that students can retest if needed. Numerous situation diagrams help to illustrate problems. We record evaluations and remarks on Driver Training Log pages. We also keep track of hours since many states require specific numbers of hours of both behind-the-wheel and classroom training. Students receive a certificate of training on completion of the course for an additional $30. If parents wish, Advanced Traffic Technologies will monitor their driving for two years and, when appropriate, send safe driving awards as part of the $30 certification fee. A toll-free number is available for assistance if needed.

In addition, supplemental videos are available for rent to supplement each lesson. They even have some of those grizzly accident videos for teens who need to realize that driving is serious business. A computer program for IBM-compatibles is available that provides teens with opportunities to practice making driving decisions before going out on the road [$30 to purchasers of the basic program]. Inexpensive, magnetic "Student Driver" signs are available.

Help! My Teenager Wants to Drive!!! does lack coverage of some topics that are required in some states as part of driver's education, although Advanced Traffic Technologies has videos that can be used to cover them. The major missing topics are vehicle systems and maintenance, laws about licensing, laws pertaining to driving while intoxicated, driving motorcycles, pedestrian laws, and insurance. Aside from vehicle maintenance, the essentials on each of these topics should be covered in each state's booklet about vehicle codes.

This program should be an excellent alternative for many if not most home-educating families, but it is important to be aware of any state limitations on who may provide driving instruction. Advanced Traffic Technologies should also be able to help with such information.

Western Educational Associates (WEA) offers Californians drivers education "textbook" materials to students enrolled full-time in Western Christian Academy, a ministry of WEA, and to independent study programs. Students must do drivers education and drivers training under the private school (or ISP) in which they are enrolled as a full-time student in order for instructors to issue the DMV Completion forms. The main text is *Keys to Driving* from WEA, which is very similar in concept and methodology to the School of Tomorrow PACEs. It consists of six workbooks (or PACEs), titled Skill Pacs 1109-1114. Each PACE has text, an answer key, a practice test, and a final test.

Each activity and test requires a supervisor/parent to sign-off completion. There is much that the student can do on his own with this workbook-type system; however, this is not a self-teaching program. It requires a great deal of parent participation to ensure that students grasp all of the concepts.

Keys to Driving teaches that what makes a good driver is not how well a driver knows how to drive but how well a driver chooses to drive. Thus, this is a Bible-based program that appeals to the student's sense of personal responsibility and ethical/moral sense of right and wrong.

The PACEs are designed to fulfill the requirements set by the State of California for driver's education curriculum. The student will still be required to study and know the information in the California Driver handbook, DL 600, in order to pass the DMV written examination.

Tests and workbooks are sent back and forth for review to Western Christian Academy, which means that the course might take longer to complete. However, when students take private driver's education classes, they are required to sit in a "classroom" for 30 hours whether or not they are actually working all that time. An independent study course such as this allows us instead to tailor study time so that it is most convenient for the family.

While Western Christian Academy's course is designed for Californians, *Keys to Driving* can be used by students in other states as a curriculum if approved by the state's motor vehicle department. WEA does not offer the behind-the-wheel drivers training for this course, so that will have to be handled in some other way. Contact Western Educational Associates about enrollment or curriculum purchase.

We can opt for the same texts used in most classrooms, although they lack coverage of the Christian character issues. One of these is *Responsible Driving* (written by the American Automobile Association but available through Glencoe/McGraw-Hill). The comprehensive student text [hardcover #0026533480 -$29.47; softcover #0026533499 - $14.53] is colorfully-illustrated and written at a very easy reading level. It covers all the essentials plus extras such as shopping for a car, maintenance, troubleshooting, first aid, and emergency procedures for all sorts of situations (e.g., being alert for baby strollers and skateboarders). Comprehension "checkpoints" team up with chapter reviews (summaries of key points), projects (e.g., explain or demonstrate a topic, find out about something), cross-curriculum activities (tying driver's ed to math, science, etc.), chapter tests, and writing assignments for review and asseessment. The Study Guide [student edition #0026533529 - $8.88; teacher's edition #0026533642 - $11.35] is helpful. Tests are available in two versions (one will do) [version A is #0026533669 - $8.49]. While the annotated Teacher Wraparound Edition [#0026533510 - $43.71] includes actual students pages along with chapter objectives and suggested AAA re-

sources that might be of use, most of us will probably function just fine with only the student textbook.

Keystone National High School, a correspondence school, offers a driver's ed/training course that includes *Responsible Driving* as the primary text. Students may enroll in only this one course from Keystone for $140. A Learning Guide outlines lessons, which are primarily working through the text. Tests must be proctored by a parent, guardian or other responsible adult before being sent in. The Learning Guide also includes a section on actual driver training. A companion video works with the Guide to describe basics for behind-the-wheel training. There is far less assistance here for driver training than we find in resources like *Help! My Teenager Wants to Drive!!!*, but it should be adequate. A checklist helps us identify skills on which to work, but the checklist is very poorly designed for the actual record keeping that needs to be done. Still, this will serve as a comprehensive course. As with any course, however, it will still be necessary to determine whether or not it will satisfy your state's requirements. You will also need to check if Keystone can provide the necessary forms for your state. The reasons for choosing this course would be having outside accountability and prepared lesson plans and tests. If Keystone can provide the final paperwork signing off on the driver training, it might save the cost of paying for behind-the-wheel training from a private driving school that charges more.

Another textbook frequently used in schools is *Drive Right* (ScottForesman). In its ninth edition, this popular text is similar in many ways to *Sportsmanlike Driving*. The softbound edition of the student text is $15.99, the teacher's edition is $37.25, the *Skills and Applications Workbook* is $8.37, and its teacher's edition is $11.70. In addition, they offer an individual *Testbook* for only $3.87.

I saw that the University of Nebraska also offers a correspondence course for the classroom instruction for driver's education, but I have not had time to check it out. Contact them at (402) 472-2175 for more information.

Sources for Electives

Outside of the fundamental academics, there are many ways of enriching our curriculum that should be considered not only as options, but as essential to a well-rounded curriculum. Classes in arts and crafts, physical education, music, mechanical arts, and much more are available through many sources. Check not only curriculum suppliers, but also your parks and recreation department, museums, community colleges (including television courses), private lessons, tutors, and other home schoolers with special talents.

Christian Light Publications offers courses in woodworking, small engines, automotive services, carpentry, electricity, and agriculture. Check their catalog for more information on these and other options.

Excellent sources for do-it-yourself elective courses are the Boy Scout Merit Badge booklets (Boy Scouts of America Supply Division) [$2.40 each]. Though intended as an aid to Boy Scouts, Varsity Scouts, and qualified Explorers in meeting merit badge requirements, the Merit Badge booklets are of general interest and can often be found in school and public libraries or purchased at very reasonable cost at Boy Scout supply sources (check your yellow or white pages). The booklets, which are prepared under the supervision of experts in each respective field, are good enough to stand alone as introductions to a variety of topics. The booklets are generally up to 70 pages in length. Each booklet lays out the merit badge requirements which can serve as part or all of your course outline. The remainder of each booklet relates additional information on the topic, project ideas and instructions, related career information, and comprehensive bibliography for further study or information. In a few cases, this is all you will need, but in most cases you will probably want to combine the merit badge booklet with other books on the topic being studied. This is a great way to sample possible careers, one of the original motivations for the merit badges themselves.

Samples of the titles that might be used as electives are *American Business, American Labor, Archery, Architecture, Astronomy, Athletics, Atomic Energy, Auto Mechanics, Aviation, Backpacking, Basketry, Camping, Canoeing, Cinematography, Coin Collecting, Collections, Communications, Computers, Consumer Buying, Cooking, Cycling, Dentistry, Dog Care, Drafting, Electricity, Electronics, Emergency Preparedness, Energy, Engineering, Environmental Science, Family Life, Farm Mechanics, Fingerprinting, Fire Safety, First Aid, Fish and Wildlife Management, Fishing, Forestry, Gardening, Genealogy, Geology, Golf, Graphic Arts, Hiking, Home Repairs, Horsemanship, Indian Lore, Journalism, Landscape Architecture, Law, Leatherwork, Lifesaving, Medicine, Metalwork, Model Design and Building, Motorboating, Music and Bugling, Orienteering, Painting, Personal Fitness, Personal Management, Pets, Photography, Pioneering, Plumbing, Pottery, Public Health, Pulp and Paper, Radio, Railroading, Rifle Shooting, Rowing, Safety, Salesmanship, Sculpture, Shotgun Shooting, Skating, Skiing, Small-Boat Sailing, Soil and Water Conservation, Space Exploration, Sports, Stamp Collecting, Surveying, Swimming, Textiles, Theater, Traffic Safety, Truck Transportation, Waterskiing, Weather, Whitewater Wilderness Survival, Wood Carving,* and *Woodwork.*

There are other titles that are more specifically science oriented listed in the science chapter. These books are generally suitable for either girls or boys who might be interested in a topic. We have incorporated a number of merit badge booklets into our school over the years and found them very useful.(S)

Personal Development

In addition to the above-mentioned topics, there are a number of things that we should be doing that fall outside the area of standard curriculum, or at best are on the fringes.

An easily overlooked area is preparation for adulthood and increased responsibilities. While all of this is fairly obvious to some, others of us will wish to have some resources to draw upon.

Bob Jones University Press offers an eleventh- and twelfth-grade level text entitled *Family Living* [$28], that covers preparation for family life along with personal development. Included

topics are time management, grooming, friendship, dating, budgeting, and consumer education.

A similar book comes from A Beka—*Managing Your Life Under God* [$11.95]. Written for tenth through twelfth graders, this book covers relationships, sex and drugs, preparation for marriage, responsibilities, job success, safety, abortion, and evolution. Course content should take between nine and eighteen weeks to complete.

Another BJUP book is *Beauty and the Best*, by Beneth Peters Jones [$6.95], dealing with make-up, clothing, and etiquette for young women. The author also "...gives advice for developing the meek and quiet spirit of a godly woman."

Inge Cannon addresses all ages in *Etiquette PLUS: Polishing Life's Useful Skills* (Education PLUS+) [$13]. This book is divided into two parts: the first identifies seven primary character traits, then clusters related character traits around each. Inge then offers definitions and Scripture verses for each so that we understand the Biblical call to maintain personal character while extending ourselves to and for others. The second half of the book (see page 85 in *Etiquette PLUS*) consists of checklists of the "social graces" to concentrate on through seven age groups from three-year olds through adults. Checklists are cross-referenced with the character trait clusters. They cover such graces as putting toys away (for the young ones), table manners, personal correspondence, tipping, friendships, and conversation. There are no specific guidelines within the book itself for how to use it, so it will be up to each family to determine whether to use it as a part of family devotions, for individual lessons, or, perhaps, for an older child to read through on his or her own. However, you can get specific suggestions for implementation to expand the usefulness of the book by adding Inge's audio tape *Etiquette - Privilege or Panic?* [$5].

Oops, Your Manners Are Showing ((The Oops Group) [student workbook - $11.95; teacher's edition - $14.95; set - $26.90] is a Bible-based course for ages eight and up with step-by-step lesson plans that covers manners, courtesy, introductions, conversations, telephone etiquette, table manners, and table settings. The course works best for a group class since it includes interactive activities, games, team work, and food, but it includes instructions for adapting activities for individual families. (A preschool edition should be available by late fall of 1997.)

Wayne and Emily Hunter are the authors of *Man in Demand* and *Christian Charm* (Harvest House) [$7.99 each; teacher books - $9.99 each], Christian courses in personal development for young men and women. Physical development, relationships between the sexes, manners, personal hygiene, smoking, drinking, drugs, and other topics are discussed from a conservative, fundamental viewpoint. Because of the sensitive nature of the content, it is appropriate that *Man in Demand* be taught by the father and *Christian Charm* by the mother, although teens can read either book independently.

One Of The Few: Toward Christian Womanhood, by Donna R. Fisher (Hewitt Educational Resources) [$6.95] is a syllabus/textbook for a one-year course for high school girls in "Christian womanhood." Although suggested for eleventh and twelfth graders, it should also be appropriate for some ninth and *tenth graders. It is divided into four sections, to be used for the four quarters of a school year. The first section is "Every Wise Woman Builds Her House" which covers some of the basics about attitudes, priorities, goal setting, and responsibilities. The second section, "Physical and Social Foundations," has to do with nutrition, fitness, dress, modesty, deportment, and dating/courtship. Part three, "Management of Time, Resources, and Home Care," deals with both personal and family management. The fourth section, "The Ministry of the Home," trains young women in the basics of hospitality. Each section is presented in the form of a dialogue between an older woman and her teenage granddaughter Amber. Following the dialogue, are assignments for the quarter which include books to read and report on plus activities like studying an etiquette book, planning a strategy to incorporate what you learn, and charting your progress. Examples of other activities: establishing and charting daily prayer and Bible reading time, planning a week of menus, writing a research paper on dating/courtship, making a flower arrangement, and hosting a party. While this is not meant to be as extensive as Far Above Rubies, it covers a tremendous amount of territory. One Of The Few should work well as a supplement to* most courses of study, adding a vital dimension for young women.

Those who want God's very best, no matter how difficult it might be will be inspired by Paul Jehle's *Christian Discipline* seminar on eight audio tapes (Heritage Institute Ministries, available through Landmark Distributors) [$30]. Jehle describes the seminar with the following: "The topic believers need the most but want the least is discipline. Without it, we remain full of potential that is never fulfilled. With it, we can begin to see our lives practically transformed so that we become a model for others. Be inspired to embrace the cross, discipline, and yoke of GOD!" The titles of the eight sessions are "Bearing the Yoke of God," "Discipline and Faith," "The Discipline of Obedience," "The Discipline of the Mind," "Building Christian Character," "Practical Disciplined Manners," "Discipline of Pride and Vanity," and "Discipline of Time and Finances."

The transition from childhood to adulthood is fuzzy in our modern society. We no longer celebrate most of the "rites of passage" observed in other and older cultures. Jonathan Lindvall and others have suggested a return to such rites of passage to signal changes in life roles and responsibilities. Lindvall presents his ideas on an audio tape, *Rites of Passage: Bar-Mitzvah for Godly Young People* (Bold Christian Living) [$6], where he challenges us to think through the issues and consider new possibilities.

As teens look to their futures, the challenges facing them can seem discouraging and overwhelming. *How To Plan Your Life* by Jim Davidson (Pelican Publishing Company) [$14.95] offers very practical advice for "being successful." He addresses the question of what it means to be successful, writing as a Christian (although non-Christians will also find the book valuable). The book is full of wisdom. Even Davidson's short piece on acting versus reacting is worth the price of the book. But there are many more reasons to read this book such as his discussion about cause

and effect, and his ideas about service as a key to success. Topics he addresses are self-image, importance of goals, a personal inventory, the use of our minds, choices, healthful living, success, setting and achieving goals, careers or jobs, natural laws, true, long-lasting success, self-examination, spiritual life, the role of traditional families, free enterprise, planning for future security, time management, personal habits, communication skills, and life-long learning. *How To Plan Your Life* is a splendid book for older teens and adults.

LifeKeys: Discovering Who You Are, Why You're Here, What You Do Best (Bethany House Publishers) by Jane Kise, David Stark, and Sandra Krebs Hirsh [$14.99] crosses boundaries between personal development, outreach activities, and careers. It is a book about discovering personal gifts and talents, then identifying what God might have you do with them. It is directed to those college age and older, but it should fit home educated teens very well. It works from a number of directions, similar to Larry Burkett's Career Pathways. It helps a person identify their life gifts relating to the world of work, spiritual gifts, personality type (using the Myers-Briggs system), values, and passions. It suggests practical ways to put those discoveries to the test and into practice. For example, if a person thinks that he might have a gift of administration, he should test it by taking on a limited administrative task and see how well he handles it. Each of these tools for identifying gifts, personality, values, etc. works with the others to help a person focus in on areas for personal growth and development. Taken together they might well direct him or her to a career, role for church involvement, or other important life activity that makes the best use of the gifts and talents God has given.

Sex Education, Dating, and Preparation for Marriage

Everyone does not need a book to learn what they should know about relationships between the sexes, dating, sexually transmitted diseases, and so on. Ideally, these should be topics for ongoing discussion and learning, with the appropriate information passed on as the child matures. However, the ideal situation seldom exists, and many of us will want to rely on books to help us make sure that all of the important issues have been covered. Current issues, such as the AIDS epidemic, will require teaching that was not needed in the past. Following are reviews of resources that address these areas.

⊃ AIDS: What You Haven't Been Told [video] (Jeremiah Films) $19.95

This hour-long video offers a comprehensive and frightening overview of the AIDS crisis. Interviews with medical and political authorities as well as AIDS victims provide both statistical and personal information that is often glossed over by the popular media. The political issues linking the homosexual movement, AIDS research, and civil rights are explored, while exposing the dangers imposed upon our society by governmental fear of the power of homosexual organizations. The idea of safe sex is exposed as a fraud, while abstinence is promoted as the best defense. The film is Christian although most information is presented in a factual manner without being dependent upon belief in the Bible. Christians are urged to demonstrate a Christ-like attitude in helping to care for AIDS victims without accepting or approving of the sin involved in most cases. This film is used as part of the *Understanding the Times* course. Jeremiah Films also has a shorter version, *No Second Chance*, that is reviewed below.

⊃ Dating, Is It Worth the Risk? by Pastor Reb Bradley (Family Ministries) $5

In this 50-page book, Pastor Reb Bradley contrasts modern concepts of dating and courtship, explaining the pitfalls of dating from a biblical perspective. He examines point-by-point many of the problems which are fostered by modern dating, and he encourages both parents and teens to examine the issue more carefully. The book is intended as a guide for parents to help them better understand what is at stake and also as a book for teens to read and discuss. Because it deals with the sexual aspects of dating and marriage preparation, it is probably best for older teens. Ideally, parents and teens should read and discuss it together. Strong on biblical evidence and light on anecdotes, Bradley presents his arguments concisely, which means that this book is quicker reading than most others on this topic. It is especially valuable to give to loved ones who think you are "crazy" for implementing courtship with your children.

⊃ Facing the Facts: The Truth About Sex and You by Stan and Brenna Jones (NavPress) $10

This book is appropriate for an audience aged somewhere in the 11-14 year-old range, and especially for those recently removed from a "regular" school rather than longtime home schoolers. It deals with body changes, pregnancy, birth, saving sex for marriage, love and dating, petting, sexually transmitted diseases (without giving symptoms), condoms (emphasizing failures), peer pressure, incest, and homosexuality. Sex in marriage is presented as primarily for union rather than procreation. Unfortunately, the authors assume that dating is part of the picture, so they just add some cautions about waiting until you are ready to handle it. If your teens are going to date at age 16, they should read a book like this by the time they are 14, but it would be better to reject dating altogether. One wishes that all teenagers would not need to know so much so soon, but the book is nevertheless fairly gentle and positive in its presentation. [Valerie Thorpe/C.D.]

⊃ Her Hand in Marriage: Biblical Courtship in the Modern World by Douglas Wilson (Canon Press) $7.50

When I saw that George Grant ranked this book as his top choice on the subject of dating and courtship, I decided that I really had better review just one more book, even though I feel like I have overdosed on the subject. I thank Mr. Grant for that recommendation because I think this is one of the best treatments

of the subject for both parents and teens. It is both broader and narrower in scope than its counterparts. Wilson dismisses recreational dating as unbiblical without the recitation of pages and pages of horror stories we commonly encounter. He supports biblical courtship, allowing for dating within the context of a biblical courtship. The goal is marriage, but he allows for a breaking off of the courtship, a point others might dispute. Wilson cautions against dogmatism on the mechanics of biblical courtship, pointing out the crucial importance of heart attitudes rather than legalism. The breadth of this book is evidenced by his treatment of parenting principles largely ignored in other such books. Wilson explains how young women are under the authority and protection of fathers. That authority and protection is then handed over by the father to the daughter's husband. He points out that young men need to be raised differently, to understand their proper role in both courtship and marriage. He also stresses the importance of the trust children (especially daughters) should have in parents (especially fathers), and how this must be built up over years rather than expected to magically appear. This book stretches beyond the courtship process into marriage relationships, and parenting because, in the end, none of these are inseparable.

His Perfect Faithfulness: The Story of Our Courtship by Eric and Leslie Ludy (Family Foundations Publishing) $6.99

To date or not... a burning question in home schooling circles. Yet, the Ludy's challenge even that question with other, more important questions: "Is Jesus Christ the greatest love of your life?....Do you love Jesus more than your music? Or how about sports? What about your reputation? Do you adore Jesus more than every other thing in you life? Do your friends hold a tighter reign on your heart than the King of Kings? Does your passion for pleasure have a greater priority in your life than knowing that God is pleased with you?" (p.97) These penetrating questions form a backdrop as Eric and Leslie Ludy relate the story of their courtship, including the difficult life choices they encountered on their journey to adulthood. Leslie had to break away from traditional school, her friends, and activities, including dating when she realized that she was not living as God would have her do. Eric, too, came late to the idea of courtship. But the key to their story and their decisions was a desire for God's best and to live lives pleasing to Him. This is an easy-to-read and encouraging book, appropriate for both teens and parents. It should be especially appropriate for teen girls who worry about what happens to their social life if (or when) they homeschool.

⊃ Learning About Sex series (Concordia) $8.99 each

This is a series of books on sex education. Titles for older children include *Sex and the New You* by Richard Bimler, recommended for children eleven to fourteen; and, *Love, Sex, and God* by Bill Ameiss and Jane Graver, for ages fourteen to young adult. Concordia is a Lutheran publishing house and reflects that denomination's attitudes. In these books, strong stands against abortion and homosexuality are taken, while birth control (within marriage) and teen dating are treated as acceptable. Alcohol, drugs, AIDS, venereal diseases, and other related topics are covered in *Love, Sex, and God*, making this quite a comprehensive book. Generally, most Christians will have no trouble with the basic information presented. The format of each book is interesting and age appropriate. For parents who would rather retain more control than just handing their child a book, Concordia published *How to Talk Confidently with Your Child about Sex*, by Lenore Buth. The beginning of the book is more of a marriage manual than sex education, but the rest of the book covers essentially the same information that is in the books written for children. Here the writer is speaking directly to parents rather than children, so we would use this book to study a topic and then share with our child rather than reading it to him or her.

⊃ **Love, Dating and Sex: What Teens Want to Know** by George B. Eager (Mailbox Club Books) softcover - $10.95; hardcover - $16.95

If our teenager is ambivalent about his or her relationship with God, Biblical arguments for chastity hold little weight. This is unfortunately the situation we have with many of our sons and daughters. Most teenagers are not convinced solely by scriptural guidelines. Thus we have the "Just say no" campaign, designed to spread the message that chastity is a good choice purely from the self-centered viewpoint. What arguments will help these teens to buy the "Just say no" propaganda? There are a number of books available, but one of the best is *Love, Dating and Sex: What Teens Want to Know*. This book carries a clear message that sex before marriage brings nothing but grief. It teaches a pragmatic morality—there are good self-serving reasons for chastity as well as avoidance of drugs and alcohol. I would rather have my teens choose to do what is right because it is God's desire and pleasing to Him, but if that does not work, an appeal to their self interest is probably the next best argument. Mr. Eager does an excellent job of discussing the emotional aspects of dating and sexual relationships, and he speaks to teens on their wavelength. Although the author discusses sexually transmitted diseases, with brief descriptions of some of the most prevalent ones, this is not a clinical book on sexual functioning or a how-to manual. Mr. Eager deals with the underlying reasons why so many teens get into sexual relationships—feelings of inadequacy, desire to be accepted, pride, peer pressure, etc.—and sends a clear message of encouragement to stand strong and resist temptation. A modified version of the book is also available on audio cassette tapes, but the tapes are intended to be used along with the book. They contain missing words that teens identify while reading the book. (We can only order the tapes with the book.)

Since this book is 208 pages long, Mr. Eager has split some of the material up into separate books that some teens might be more likely to read. *Love and Dating* and *Understanding Your Sex Drive* [$7.95 each] both contain material from the original book along with some new material. *Peer Pressure* [$8.95] includes about four chapters from the original, but most of the content is new.

⊃ **No Second Chance** [video] (Jeremiah Films) $19.95

This thirty-minute video describes what AIDS is, how it is transmitted, and promotes abstinence as the only reasonable protection against the disease. It features interviews with AIDS victims to demonstrate the horrors of the disease. A nurse speaking to a classroom of teenagers serves as the film's vehicle for reinforcing key points and presenting the Biblical view of sexual behavior. The film also promotes a compassionate Christian attitude toward AIDS victims. *AIDS: What You Haven't Been Told*, a lengthier video from the same company, uses many of the same interviews and scenes to present a more comprehensive overview of the AIDS issue.

⊃ **Passion and Purity** by Elisabeth Elliot (Revell/Chosen Books) $8.99

This is an encouraging book for our older teens to read. Elisabeth Elliot, wife of slain missionary Jim Elliot, tells the story of their courtship and marriage. Both of them determined to make major life choices only when they were convinced of God's purpose for their lives. When they realized that they were interested in each other as marriage partners, they restrained themselves from showing physical affection, waiting for marriage. Even when they were certain that they were to marry each other, they waited for the Lord's timing. These are real people, living in a culture operating by totally different standards—they didn't even have a "home schooling" community to support them in choosing to live by a higher standard. It wasn't easy, as we learn from Elisabeth's journal entries as she shares the struggles they endured. The bottom line, is an encouraging message to trust God and allow Him to lead us in relationships, career, and life choices.

⊃ **Preparing for Adolescence** (Regal Books) paperback - $5.99 or $9.99; Growth Guide - $14.99; Family Tape Pack -$39.99

Many of us are already familiar with this classic book by Dr. James Dobson. Dr. Dobson, speaking to teens in a friendly, non-threatening tone, covers physical, emotional, and spiritual angles of physical (primarily sexual) development, boy-girl relationships, the sex act, grooming, and more. This book should be required reading for both parents and teens and probably even preteens. *A Growth Guide Workbook* for *Preparing for Adolescence* is available from the publisher. *The Family Tape Pack* is an eight-tape set, with two tapes directed toward parents only, and the other six aimed at both teens and parents. The audio tapes cover much, but not all, of the book's contents.

⊃ **Sex, Love, and Romance: Sex Education from the Bible** (A Beka) $5.25

This book, written for junior and senior high students, "...details God's plan concerning dating and marriage and the consequences of disobeying His moral commands in these areas." Unlike most secular sex education books, this one does not deal with physical details but with attitudes and standards. While it is "preachy" in tone, it is still a refreshing change from the humanistic view of sex education which, because of its moral depravity, spends most of its time teaching about birth control, safe-sex, and AIDS.

⊃ **The Shaping of a Christian Family** by Elisabeth Elliot
(Thomas Nelson Publishers) $15.99

The jacket of this book says, "More than a manual on raising children or a treatise on the biblical basis of family life, *The Shaping of a Christian Family* sheds light on the many facets of family living: homely joys and shared troubles, triumphs and tragedies, difficult choices and rich rewards.

Sound advice is woven around Mrs. Elliot's stories of her childhood and parenting. Her godly wisdom shines through every chapter. This book is the ideal "textbook" for a parenting class, even though it is too special a book to be thought of as a schoolbook.

Also, parents who were not raised in godly homes can draw on Mrs. Elliot's experience as a model for themselves to improve their own parenting skills.

⊃ **Biblical Roles of Husbands and Wives** [audio seminar] by Pastor Reb Bradley (Family Ministries) $13

Prepare young people for marriage with this study of Ephesians 5. As always, Pastor Bradley uses many personal examples and illustrations to present his message. This seminar is presented on two audio tapes and includes a complete outline in a syllabus. Also, see the review of *Preparing Your Children for Courtship and Marriage* under "Abolishing the Dating Custom" below.

Abolishing the Dating Custom

As teens become more aware of and interested in those of the opposite sex, we confront the issue of dating. Some home schooling families (and others) have decided that dating is an unbiblical concept, and, because of that conviction, they approach social activities in the teen and young adult years in a manner quite different from most families. While guidelines vary from family to family, most restrict boy-girl activities to group events. Single couple, boy-girl (or should we say man-woman?) relationships then are saved for the time when both are ready to consider marriage commitments. This approach helps teens to better understand the commitment of marriage, helps them avoid morally dangerous situations, prevents broken hearts over breakups, helps teens to maintain balanced relationships with a wider variety of people, and stabilizes groups because they aren't constantly being disrupted by changing loyalties within the group.

Jonathan Lindvall has been "thinking out loud" about dating and courtship for many years, but if you have not heard a recent tape, you were only in on "earlier stages of development." Mr. Lindvall's ministry, Bold Christian Living, offers tapes of his current presentations. Of particularly interest on the romance and dating issue is *Scriptural Romance*, a three-tape audio set [$17] with the subtitles, "Youthful Romance: The Problems with Dating," "Scriptural Betrothal: God's Design for Pre-marital Romance," and "Shamefaced Romance." Each of the tapes is also available individually [$6 each] and "Youthful Romance: The Problems with Dating" seems to be the most popular. Lind-

vall speaks to both parents and teens, but he emphasizes parental involvement as an essential part of marriage preparation. His ideas on betrothal are considered extremist by some, but they deserve careful consideration. Videos of many of Lindvall's presentations are available for $25 each. Lindvall also offers a tract, "Youthful Romance: Scriptural Patterns" [single copy is free and minimal charge for additional copies]. (Contact Bold Christian Living for a list of other tapes.)

John Holzmann, another home schooling father, has also dealt with the dating issue in his book, *Dating with Integrity* (Word Publishing)[$10.99]. Instead of recommending a prohibition against dating, he redefines it. The basic guideline he suggests is that everyone should treat everyone else (male or female) just as they would a biological brother or sister. For instance, he raises the question to a young man, "Would you hold hands with your biological brother or sister?" If not, don't do it with anyone. The same idea applies to conversations and all other activities. This guideline permits some single-couple, boy-girl activity, yet keeps it on a strictly-friends level.

Holzmann's ideas are especially suited for young people who attend college away from home. An important part of making this concept work is in communicating the idea behind it to those with whom a person associates, and this is even more difficult when no parents are on hand to oversee such things. If a young man or woman does not explain clearly what they are doing, since they will be operating in such an unusual way people (particularly those of the opposite sex) will probably not be able to understand the arms-distance approach and rejection of going-steady type commitments. While I find Holzmann's ideas quite practical, the problem I foresee is that introverts might have trouble communicating their relationship guidelines to others. Ideally, we should be establishing such guidelines within home school support groups in earlier years where young people will find it much easier to uphold such standards with group support. That experience might then enable them to continue on in the same way when they move beyond home school circles.

Of Knights and Fair Maidens by Jeff and Danielle Myers (Media Mailers) [$7.95] is probably closest to Holzmann's in principle. In telling the story of their courtship, Jeff and Danielle Myers share the biblical principles that guided their relationship. They also share some very practical advice and numerous lists of suggestions for activities you might participate in during a courtship, questions a guy might ask of a girl's father (at the beginning of a courtship), topics that a couple preparing for marriage need to discuss, and more. This book is shorter than most of the others, but also more practical in the "how-to" sense.

Paul Jehle has been teaching on this topic since the 70s, but he has finally put much of it into written format in his book *Dating vs. Courtship* (Plymouth Rock Foundation) [$10]. This book is written to both parents and teens. It reflects Jehle's Principle Approach background since it stresses Biblical principles throughout. Jehle goes further in depth scripturally than do the others, discussing issues such as the long term consequences in our relationships because of obedience or disobedience to God's laws. He delves into the historical realm and the introduction of dating in the United States after the Civil War. He explodes some

Accountability in Relationships

If considering a dating relationship we should stop and try to understand our motivations and the effect our choices may have on us and upon others. We must learn to set aside our own selfish desires and to put God first.

We need also consider our parents, dating partners, and even the person we might eventually marry. Accountability to our parents is the command of scripture, "Honor thy father and thy mother." Our parents are an authority over us and responsible for us to God so we must consider them in every important decision that we make. To our dating partners we are accountable because we are drawing them into an emotional and sometimes physical relationship through which they can be greatly harmed. This harm can be both in the immediate form of the "broken heart" and in the harm that can be done to all their future relationships. We are also accountable to the person we may eventually marry. For this person we must consider the consequences of making emotional commitments to others before them. We need also consider the effect that many short-term relationships might have on our marriage which should last the remainder of our lives.

These are the people to whom, according to Scripture, we are accountable for all our romantic relationships. If we cannot learn to put others first and to consider even these specific others before becoming involved in temporary and self-gratifying relationships, then we are not ready for any relationships. Our time would be better spent learning to put others first and making the Lord number one in our lives.

- Josh Duffy

---

of the myths about dating. He proposes team ministry as "God's alternative to dating." Jehle speaks from many years of working and developing relationships with teens, and that practical experience lends a great deal of credibility to his message. This book is the first of a series of three on family and relationships. The next one will address courtship and marriage, and the third will address family life and child training.

Still another resource on dating is an audio-tape series, *Preparing Your Children for Courtship and Marriage, From Toddlers to Teens* by Pastor Reb Bradley (Family Ministries) [$27]. In six, ninety-minute tapes Pastor Bradley instructs parents of children of all ages about romantic relationships, teaching children the sanctity of sex, sexual values, understanding true and false love, and choosing a mate. His goal is to instill in parents a "...biblical vision for preserving their children's sexual purity."

Like the previously mentioned resources, *Preparing Your Children* challenges many of the accepted notions about relationships, dating, and marriage, recommending Biblical guidelines in their place. Bradley's approach is broader than Lindvall's or Holzmann's, covering more background and related issues while spending less time specifically on the dating/courtship issue, although it receives plenty of attention. Bradley just approaches the courtship issue within the broader perspective of raising children to be what God intends them to be, and that includes being Godly husbands and wives. Tapes are actually directed at a multi-age church audience, so they are appropriate for teens to listen to on their own. However, I recommend listening as a family activity, followed by discussion. The accompanying twenty-page *Syllabus and Study Guide* can be used by older family members as seems appropriate.

Bradley's speaking style is professional and entertaining, a real plus when we want our teens to listen. Even so, since each tape (except for the last) is ninety minutes long, you might want to listen to half of each at a sitting so that you do not lose the interest of those who have a hard time just listening for such a lengthy period. Also check out other tapes and resources from Pastor Bradley (Family Ministries) such as *Bringing Your Children to an Early Maturity* (2-tape set with syllabus for $13), *Saving the Next Generation: Equipping Your Children as Warriors for Christ* (2-tape set with syllabus for $13), and *Dating, Is It Worth the Risk?*.

Josh Harris, son of Gregg Harris, has become a vigorous spokesman for the "no-dating" viewpoint. He speaks directly to teens out of Scripture and his own experience on his audio tape *I Kissed Dating Goodbye* (Noble Publishing Associates) [$6.95]. Josh advocates a position similar to those described above, although he seems to take a more open position than Lindvall on courtship and betrothal. The fact that Josh is in his early 20s puts him in the thick of the issue, wrestling with the practical problems when you choose a different path. This is probably the best tape to recommend specifically for teens, since they seem to be extra receptive to the ideas when presented by "one of their own."

Josh Harris has also written a book of the same title, *I Kissed Dating Goodbye* (Questar Publishers/Multnomah Books) [$8.99]. Josh discusses the pitfalls of dating without really getting into the courtship process. From a biblical basis, he addresses alternatives ways to have healthy social relationships without becoming romantically involved. Although not so logically presented as other books, this one uses lots of stories and examples making it easy reading compared to some of the others. Much of the discussion goes beyond dating issues into the basics of biblical relationships. Josh includes lots of practical advice on dating and relationships. This is an introductory book on the subject for teens who may have already dated, are confused on the issue, or need strength to hang on to their convictions. Great for parents, too.

Actually, all these resources represent only a portion of what's out there. Alan and Kathie Morrissey started a business called the Courtship Connection just so that they could provide such resources all in one place. Contact them for their free catalog.

Testing and Resources

Testing

There are two aspects of testing to consider—the everyday tests that reflect student mastery of material being studied at that time, and standardized tests that reflect the overall level of competence.

Mastery Testing

The first type of test is used widely in schools since teachers have few other means of ensuring that students are learning anything. They do not have time to read everything that students write, listen to oral reports, or participate in discussions with every student. At home, with constant interaction, we can use these other methods of evaluation. However, when children are working independently, as they usually are in high school, testing becomes more necessary. If we are home educating more than one child, we cannot possibly read everything that we assign, which makes it difficult for us to use interactive methods of evaluation all the time. Teens will figure out quickly that they know more about some subjects than we do. Some teens will gladly share their newfound knowledge, but others might take advantage of the situation to skim through lessons.

We must determine which subjects most need discussion and interaction, then read those assignments so that we can help our teens. Leave the cut-and-dry subjects that are more objective for our teens to study on their own, and use the tests that are available from the publishers to monitor progress if necessary.

Some students will have developed a love of learning and recognize its value. We will not need to check up on these students with frequent tests. Others need to know that someone is monitoring them regularly. Do what seems best in your situation.

Standardized Testing

Some of us give our children standardized tests without clear ideas of what we expect to learn from such testing. Many of us feel that this is a necessary part of education because "the schools do it." In some states it is required by law for home educated children to be tested periodically. Some of us want to demonstrate to skeptical relatives that we are indeed educating our children by sharing with them our children's standardized test results. A few of us, whether we admit it or not, want proof that our children are more intelligent than others. Then, there are those of us who want to find out if we are doing an adequate job as teachers.

Schools test children regularly for a number of reasons, most having little to do with the individual child, but more to do with statistics, politics, and money. We need not be concerned with testing for these purposes.

When the state demands standardized testing, there is little we can do but go along with the requirement. Skeptical relatives can be a definite problem, and sometimes good test results will relieve the pressure on us. But, more often, skeptical relatives are impressed with the results that they <u>see</u> in our children after a year or two of home education. All of us want to be proud of our children, but that is not adequate reason to submit them to standardized testing. The concern over our adequacy is legitimate. Usually we can tell how well our children are doing just because we are working so closely with them every day. But it can be difficult to step back and objectively examine what we are accomplishing.

A standardized test will <u>not</u> give you a total picture. It does not measure curiosity, creativity, social wisdom, attitudes, and the other intangibles that can be of utmost importance. A standardized test will tell us to some extent how well our child has mastered and retained basic subject matter, and how well he applies reading and thinking skills. However, the content of public school material might be quite different from what you are covering. So, standardized tests might not even be measuring the same academic content you are teaching.

"Gap Testing"

The most important reason for testing, and one which few of us identify, is to test for gaps in knowledge. If a child misses every problem having to do with fractions, but answers correctly every other math problem, there is a definite learning gap. Gap testing can be useful in the areas of math and language arts, but not for social studies and science. The first two areas are generally taught following, at least to some extent, a recognized scope and sequence. Social studies and science are seldom taught in any recognized and consistent order, although this is changing with the implementation of national standards. Testing for social studies and science often assesses reading and thinking skills as much or more so than subject matter content. Even the content-oriented questions can be problematical in that they might be testing information and concepts that we have not taught. Consequently, test results for social studies and science are not likely to be very helpful.

It is important that we receive a complete breakdown of standardized test results, showing what particular skill or skills within a subject area show weakness. A general score showing poor language usage is often of little value. More valuable would be a breakdown showing that most punctuation questions were answered incorrectly, while other skills were satisfactory. Standardized test results are returned to us in various forms—some providing only a minimal amount of information and others giving a thorough breakdown of subject areas. We must know what kind of result interpretation we will get from the testing before we send in our money. If we need a thorough breakdown of results, we must make sure that that is what we will receive.

Testing Services

Bob Jones University Press Testing Service offers a wide range of testing and evaluation materials. Achievement testing is available using either the *Iowa Test of Basic Skills* or the *Stanford Achievement Test*. Learning/school ability tests are available on their own or in combination with either of the above-mentioned tests. They also offer the *Metropolitan Math, Reading*, or *Language* diagnostic tests (which are nationally-standardized), *Personality Profiles*, writing evaluations, and a career/vocational guidance program, along with a variety of test preparation aids. For the Iowa and Stanford tests, results are given in terms of norm-referenced scores (scaled/standard scores, percentiles, grade equivalents, and stanines), objective-referenced scores (graphed skills ratings, skills measurement/evaluation), and ability/achievement comparison on combination tests. Achievement tests, learning/school ability tests, and diagnostic tests must be administered by either a state-certified teacher or someone with a four-year college degree. The other tests/evaluations *do not* have this requirement—any parent can use them. Request their *Information and Order Form* or contact the Testing Service at 800-845-5731 for more information.

Christian Liberty Academy Independent Achievement Testing Service offers *California Achievement Tests (CAT)* to both enrolled and non-enrolled families. Testing may be administered by parents. Student test form (answer sheet only) and grade equivalent results for individual subjects are returned to you. The cost is very reasonable and there are no restrictions on who can administer the test, making this a favorable alternative for many families.

For a small additional fee, Christian Liberty Academy will also use the test results to provide you with curriculum recommendations for the coming school year, if you so desire. Recommendations are not limited to materials used in CLA courses. While recommendations will be chosen to suit the obvious grade level placement, there is no avenue for evaluating learning styles, family situation, individual interests, or other factors that are important in curriculum selection. This service would probably be most appealing to those just beginning who need to start somewhere and feel unable to evaluate all of these other factors until they have had some experience. This service does help solve the major problem of grade level placement, and it will be likely to point out learning gaps from earlier years and recommend materials to fill in.

Covenant Home Curriculum offers an adapted version of the 1964 SAT test. (Older SAT tests were more challenging than present editions.) **Covenant Home Achievement Tests** evaluate English and math skills of students in grades K-12. Tests are hand-scored and provide results under general headings such as grammar, reading comprehension and spelling. Test scorers include some observation comments that might pinpoint specific problems. The English section of the test is tied to the Warriner English series, although it should adequately evaluate skills of students using other English programs. Tests are available to all home educators, and no credentials or degrees are required for those administering the tests.

McGuffey Testing Service is available to home schoolers in grades K-12 whether or not they are enrolled in McGuffey Academy. The *Stanford Achievement Test* is offered and may be administered by parents without special qualifications unless a certified teacher is required by your state. McGuffey Academy will hand-check each test and will send you a copy of the results along with an evaluation and letter that will help you to interpret the scores accurately. The results show a detailed breakdown of skills within subject areas.

Summit Christian Academy offers the *Iowa Basic Skills* test in the Spring for students in grades 3-8. They also offer the *Test of Achievement and Proficiency* for grades 9-12. Both tests are computer-scored with results sent to the parents. The cost is $35 for enrolled students and $40 for others.

Sycamore Tree offers the *Comprehensive Test of Basic Skills* for K-12. There are no restrictions on who can administer the test. Tests are scored professionally on May 15 and August 15, providing a very detailed and helpful breakdown. The rest of the year, tests are hand-scored and there is an extra $10 charge. Testing is free to families enrolled in Sycamore Tree.

Write to these organizations for information. Many of the independent study programs arrange standardized testing for those who desire it. In states requiring testing, contact your local support group for the best means of meeting those requirements.

Outside of these testing services (and others not listed), standardized tests such as the Iowa test are available only to qualified teachers, schools, and school services.

Diagnostic Testing

If we wish to identify gaps in learning, a shorter diagnostic test might do the job just as well as a standardized test, but with a lot less hassle. Most diagnostic tests can be administered by parents without strict guidelines. Diagnostic tests are available from Bob Jones University Press, Family Christian Academy, Summit Christian Academy, Alpha Omega [$10 a set], and School of Tomorrow for anyone who wishes to order.

Regarding the Alpha Omega and School of Tomorrow tests, use only the Math and English tests, since the others will not be useful for general purposes. These tests are parent-administered and graded, but they are not perfect. Since they were designed to place students in the publishers' curricula, they do ask some questions that pertain only to each particular curriculum. You should look for and cross out these questions before your child takes the test. The tests from Alpha Omega and School of Tomorrow also reflect each publisher's scope and sequence, which might differ from yours or that of the publisher whose material you wish to use. Use the results to (1) identify weak areas; (2) compare with your scope and sequence (what you plan to teach and when) to identify areas that should already have been mastered or are next to be taught; and (3) plan the child's course of study to either review or teach areas as needed.

Alpha Omega diagnostic tests in English and math are offered by Summit Christian Academy along with the more widely accepted *Wide Range Achievement Test*. This combination of tests is offered for diagnostic purposes for $35. Tests are teacher-graded, and results are sent to parents.

A more specific diagnostic tool for reading is *The Blumenfeld Oral Reading Assessment Test* (Paradigm) [$19.95, or $24.95 with Pronunciation tape]. This assessment is designed to analyze a person's ability to decode and pronounce words, progressing from very simple three-letter words to difficult multi-syllabic words. Easy administration instructions are on the audio tape as well as in the printed material that comes with the tests. Words are also pronounced on the tape for the parent/teacher if he or she needs it. There are 380 words on the test, arranged in increasing order of difficulty. There is also a post-test to use later on to check for improvement. Five copies of each test are included with the kit, and extras are available at reasonable cost from the publisher. While the test can be used with any age from beginning reader through adult, it will be especially useful for the parent who begins home schooling in the mid-elementary grades or later and suspects that her child might have difficulty with decoding or phonics. The test will help to identify whether reading problems are caused by lack of phonetic knowledge or lack of experience with words (vocabulary). It is not designed to identify learning disabilities or comprehension problems, although dyslexia problems might show up during test administration.

There are other diagnostic tests, but these are the most easily accessible to home educators.

Preparing Teens for Testing

There are many materials to help students do well on standardized tests. Familiarity with test-taking strategies will help them do their best. At least three publishers offer test prep materials for standardized tests. *Scoring High* series (McGraw Hill) [about $3-$10] and *On Target for Tests, Book C* [$3.95], for grades 7-9 (Continental Press) are both general test prep resources that cover multiple subjects within one book. Both include test-taking strategies. Curriculum Associates, Incorporated publishes their *Test Ready* series of test preparation books for math, Algebra I reading and vocabulary, language arts, science, and social studies [$5.95 each; teacher guides - $3.50 each]. Books range in size from about 30 to 40 pages each. Each book is broken down into 8 to 10 practice lessons which might be used over a period of about two weeks. Lessons are somewhat like brief practice tests. Most questions are multiple choice with little bubbles to fill in. The *Test Ready Plus Mathematics* includes one page of open-ended problems. *Test Ready Language Arts, Social Studies*, and *Science* all include some actual writing tasks. At the end of each book is a timed practice test with separate bubble answer sheet. *Test Ready Language Arts* and *Test Ready Reading & Vocabulary* reflect older style standardized tests which emphasize concrete knowledge and skills. Apparently, there is also a new *Test Ready Plus Reading* series that might reflect whole language methods. *Test Ready Mathematics* is fairly traditional in approach, focusing a great deal on basic computation skills while also including some problems from geometry, measurement, time, money, and graph interpretation. The newer *Test Ready Plus Mathematics* series reflects the new math standards, so we encounter data interpretation, numeration, geometry, number theory, pre-algebra, and measurement problems presented as word problems rather than mostly numerical problems as in the other math series. It is important to know what kind of test your child will be taking to select the correct math preparation series. *Test Ready Algebra I* reflects the content of most algebra courses used by home schoolers, although it might be a bit easier than what some students might have covered. Science and social studies series reflect typical government school textbooks in content, so you will encounter some of the same social engineering and philosophical assumptions in both places. They do require students to have concrete knowledge in both subject areas. Science and social studies books do not use only questions that rely upon reading skills like those we used to encounter on tests. (Some of these remain, but they are not the bulk of the practice lessons.) Unlike *On Target for Tests* and *Scoring High*, all of these books are primarily for practice with only minimal help as far as test-taking strategies. Teacher Guides are essential for instructions and answer keys. Books are available in all series for either grades 7 and 8, with Algebra 1 the only high school level book.(S)

Learning Difficulties/Disabilities

However we choose to label them, there are definitely home educated children who are having difficulty learning by traditional methods. For inexperienced parents, this can create an overwhelmingly frustrating situation. There is a strong temptation to put these children into the public school system so that they will get special education. Too often, the special education programs simply pass children ahead in subjects by giving them very, very easy work to do as a substitute for normal classroom activities. Rarely do schools take time to address the underlying causes of learning problems. This is because they do not have the necessary time to spend with each child to help overcome problems. It is a lot faster to use "band-aids."

There are a number of avenues that might lead to real help for those with learning disabilities. Although most disabilities are still present to some degree no matter what we do, there are things we can do to try to alleviate major problem areas. Two of the most successful strategies for helping those with learning disabilities are vision therapy and perceptual motor training.

A child's eyes must do more than just see words and numbers. They must send the proper information to the brain. Then the brain must send the proper response to be spoken or written or acted upon. There is much room for errors in transmission. If the eyes do not see well or do not send the proper message to the brain, the result often appears to be a learning disability. The first thing to check in most situations is visual functioning. This in not what we call 20/20 vision, but rather proper functioning in a variety of situations such as tracking words across a page, following from line to line, and focusing at close range for reading. Over the years, I have seen too many parents spend hundreds of dollars on full range disability testing and therapy, when the problem turned out to be one that could be solved with glasses or fairly simple vision therapy. More and more I am recommending to parents of children exhibiting learning difficulties that their first step should be to visit a developmental or behavioral optometrist for a thorough vision examination. The Optometric Extension Program Foundation, Inc. can give you a referral to a qualified optometrist in the U.S. or any of 35 other countries. Their brochure, *Does Your Child Have a Learning-related Vision Problem?*, includes the following checklist that might alert you to a vision problem.

- Holding a book very close (only 7 or 8 inches away).
- Child holds head at an extreme angle to the book when reading.
- Child covers one eye when reading.
- Child squints when doing near vision work.
- Constant poor posture when working close.
- The child moves his or her head back and forth while reading instead of moving only eyes.
- Poor attention span, drowsiness after prolonged work less than arm's length away.
- Homework requiring reading takes longer than it should.
- Child occasionally or persistently reports seeing blurring or double while reading or writing.
- Child reports blurring or doubling only when work is hard.
- Loses place when moving gaze from desk work to chalkboard, or when copying from text to notebook.
- Child must use a marker to keep their place when reading.
- Writing up or down hill, irregular letter or word spacing.
- Child reverses letter (b for d) or words (saw for was).
- Repeatedly omits "small" words.
- Rereads or skips words or lines unknowingly.
- Fails to recognize the same word in the next sentence.
- Misaligns digits in columns of numbers.
- Headaches after reading or near work.
- Burning or itching eyes after doing near vision work.
- Child blinks excessively when doing near work, but not otherwise.
- Rubs eyes during or after short periods of reading.

- Comprehension declines as reading continues.
- Child fails to visualize (can't describe what they have been reading about).
    (Reprinted with permission.)

Sometimes, the solution is glasses, but sometimes it is visual therapy. Visual therapy involves exercises to help improve eye function, which in turn can help the learning process.

Sometimes, "whole-body" therapy is necessary. If the message is properly perceived by the eyes, it may yet be lost in transmission by garbled transmission lines to the brain or hands. If the proper connections are not made by nerve cells, this too interferes with learning. Perceptual motor exercises are designed to help improve the connections within the nervous system so that messages promptly reach their proper destinations.

If some of this sounds like hocus-pocus to you, you are not alone. However, I have seen the results of a number of children working through both methods. While neither method can guarantee improvement for all children, in my unscientific observations, I would judge that a large proportion of those who faithfully follow a program of exercises (visual or perceptual motor or both) do achieve some measure of improvement.

Unfortunately, we often have trouble determining whether our child's learning difficulty is caused by a learning disability rather than other factors such as immaturity, laziness, or rebelliousness. This is the question facing many of us when we think that our child is functioning below level in one area or another. We don't want to shell out hundreds of dollars for a professional evaluation unless we are fairly certain there is a problem. And, even if we are looking for professional evaluation, many of us have no idea where to find an evaluator or what type of evaluator we need.

It is helpful to have some guidelines of symptoms to look for that indicate learning disability problems before rushing off to the professional. Some of the books described below provide such guidelines. Some of the problems we encounter are minor enough that we can deal with them ourselves with just a little guidance, such as is provided in most of the materials described here. Rosner's *Helping Children Overcome Learning Difficulties* (published by Walker, sold by BJUP), offers more specific help for working in each subject area to overcome a range of difficulties.

If you suspect that your child has a significant problem, you really should see a specialist. He or she is trained to identify things that we might easily miss. Also, because of their experience, specialists can often suggest the best methods to use to overcome problems. Some testing services that offer services to home educators are described under "Developmental Testing and Testing for Special Problems." You might ask other home educators for referrals to such services in your area.[1]

---

1   I am not an expert on learning disabilities, so I offer these recommendations to you, trusting that you will check them out yourself, asking questions about the programs, asking for references, and using discernment about what is best for your child.

Developing Your Child for Success by Kenneth A. Lane, O.D. (Learning Potentials Publishers, Inc.) $24.95; workbooks - $9.95 each or $47 for the set

Dr. Lane has written this book based upon years of work in vision therapy. In the first chapter, he explains the many factors involved in the reading process (in fairly technical language). Next, he explains how we can help children develop perceptual motor skills for reading success. The remainder of the book is divided into eight sections of activities, each focusing on a developmental area. Activities are arranged according to level of difficulty so that parents can begin at easy levels, then work up to more complex levels. A list of materials and equipment needed for the exercises is included. (The most expensive item is probably a small trampoline.)

The author does not recommend that this book be used as a substitute for professional evaluation. However, he outlines a very comprehensive program covering a multitude of activities that are generally recommended for overcoming various learning disabilities. Parents could work through the activities with their children without professional assistance.

Comprehensive explanations and illustrations of activities, and the fact that no special tools are required make this a practical resource. However, in this book there are few tools to help identify problem areas and no differentiation of therapy programs according to individual needs. Instead, all children should do all of the exercises. A book such as *How to Identify Your Child's Learning Problems and What to do About Them* might be useful in helping to pinpoint problem areas if you are unable to afford professional evaluation.

Dr. Lane has also developed a reasonably-priced diagnostic program. Parents can administer a developmental test to their child that Dr. Lane then grades, or he can screen children through diagnostic software.

Dr. Lane has also developed five workbooks that can be used as part of a total perceptual program to work on specific areas. Workbook titles are *Recognition of Reversals, Spelling Tracking, Visual Tracing, Visual Scanning*, and *Visual Memory.*

Dr. Lane offers even more assistance. He says, "To further help parents, I am also offering a daily lesson plan. Depending on the diagnosis from the computer screen or the developmental test battery, I can write out a daily lesson plan that will give them five activities to do a day for six months. These activities are taken from my workbooks and *Developing Your Child for Success*."

Helping Children Overcome Learning Difficulties by Jerome Rosner (BJUP) $18.95

Rosner offers help to both parents and teachers, assuming that they are functioning within traditional school settings. In spite of that limitation, his book is packed with helpful information. Strategies for both teachers and parents to use when dealing with learning disabled children go beyond teaching into relationships and life functioning.

He begins with discussions of the various forms of testing, explaining how they work. While he directs us to professionals for physical tests (vision and hearing), he gives instructions for doing perceptual testing ourselves. Part II has instructions for working on visual or auditory perceptual skills as well as general motor skills. Part III offers specific help for school subject areas—reading, arithmetic, spelling, and handwriting. At the end, Rosner offers preventive suggestions for preschool children.

All of the foregoing make this book more comprehensive than the others described here. However, Rosner does not emphasize large-muscle, perceptual motor exercises as do the others, relying instead on more specific, small-motor exercises in combination with teaching techniques.

How To Identify Your Child's Learning Problems And What To Do About Them by Duane A. Gagnon (Pioneer Productions) $12

"Do you suspect your child of having a learning problem but would like to know for sure? Do you have a child that has already been identified as having a learning difficulty, but you would like to have activities you can do with him/her at home that will help?.... Or would you just like some practical activities to do at home with your children to help develop their learning skills?" These are the questions the author poses to his readers.

He has written an easy-to-read tool for laymen (parents) who suspect their children can use help with a learning problem. Part one helps us evaluate strengths and weaknesses in both auditory (hearing) and visual (seeing) skills in nine areas: attention, analysis, synthesis, sequencing, short term memory, long term memory, comprehension, abstract reasoning, and expression.

Part two consists of methods and activities to help in areas that show weakness. These activities are NOT perceptual motor activities such as those found in Lane's book, but are instead school-like activities typically used by special education teachers. For example, to improve visual comprehension, show the child a picture of a person and have him indicate the various parts of the body and what they do. These activities can be useful, but if you identify a serious problem, consider both a professional evaluation and the use of perceptual motor therapy, vision therapy or some other means of alleviating the problem.

How to Teach Your Child to Read and Spell by Sheldon R. Rappaport, Ph.D. (Effective Educational Systems, Inc.) $19.50

Dr. Rappaport has tremendous faith in parents' abilities to diagnose and help their children overcome learning disabilities based on visual or auditory problems. That faith is evident in this do-it-yourself manual. He does advise consulting a professional when necessary, but he also helps us make preliminary diagnoses so we can figure out whom we need to consult.

He does not just leave us with an identified problem, but he shares strategies to overcome or correct the problem, as well as teaching methods to help a child develop compensating mechanisms. The diagnostic tests are low-pressure, requiring easily found items such as string or a penlight. (The most expensive item mentioned was a $60 light meter, but it is not essential in most situations.) Extensive visual and auditory skills checklists are provided to be used in conjunction with the simple tests.

The book covers visual skills (including the seven basic visual functions), environmental factors (lighting and posture), auditory functions and processing, readability levels, and reading performance. Since poor spelling is often a side effect of reading problems, there is a special section on spelling strategies and games. Much of the visual and auditory skill development is done through simple games described in the book. The games are excellent for all learners, not just those who have learning difficulties.

Dr. Rappaport directs parents to resources for further assistance, for example, he tells how to determine what type of vision specialist to consult along with an address for obtaining referrals.

This book differs from others reviewed here in that it provides in-depth help for both visual and auditory problems. Dr. Rappaport offers scientific explanations for visual and auditory functioning, although complete understanding is not necessary to apply everything else in the book. *How to Teach Your Child to Read and Spell* is quite comprehensive yet very readable for the average parent.(S)

⊃ Learning in Spite of Labels by Joyce M. Herzog (Greenleaf Press) $9.95

Home educators looking for help with their learning disabled children finally have something written just for them. Joyce Herzog, a learning disabilities specialist, shares encouragement and practical strategies based on her many years of experience. On top of that, this book is reader-friendly. Joyce keeps the message short-and-sweet and tells it in plain English instead of educational gobbledygook.

Rather than a step-by-step curriculum guide, this is a collection of ideas: things to think about, things to look for, and things to try. An unusual feature of the book is the chapter on dealing with depression. Teaching children with learning disabilities can be both tiring and discouraging at times, but this book can help you learn to maintain a positive outlook. The creative ideas in Chapter Seven will help you break away from classroom-type thinking, and the teaching tips in Chapter Eight will help you get past some major educational stumbling blocks.

Since children differ in their needs, you will have to decide which of the teaching tips might work for your child. However, the methods of encouragement and the Christian perspective presented here can be used with all children. [Valerie Thorpe]

⊃ Special Education: A Biblical Approach Edited by Joe P. Sutton (Published by Hidden Treasure Ministries, available through Bob Jones University Press) $19.95

Hidden Treasure Christian School is a rarity—a Christian school for students with moderate to severe disabilities. Through their experience they have a learned a great deal about dealing with children with special needs from a biblical perspective. That experience has been coupled with the expertise of other learning disabilities specialists to produce this book. Although the presentation assumes that most readers work from within a day school environment rather than a home school, it does acknowledge that part of the audience consists of home educators. The book is intended to primarily assist Christian schools to pro-

vide special education, but home educators can glean plenty of practical information. Rather than parrot public school policy for the Christian school environment, the authors integrate a biblical philosophy of special education throughout each section of the book.

Although there is a section on recognition and identification of problems, this book is not intended to be a diagnostic tool. We understand that better if we realize that the authors are addressing far more than learning disabilities. They cover all types of physical, emotional, and learning disabilities, including mental retardation.

The special education world has a vocabulary and structure of its own, and the authors translate that into everyday language. Individual education plans are described along with a sample form used by Hidden Treasure. Other sample forms for evaluating school work are also provided. Extensive appendices at the back of the book can steer us to resources and organizations for more help.

⊃ Smart but Feeling Dumb by Dr. Harold Levinson (Warner Books) $12.99

This intriguing book suggests that many learning disabilities are based upon inner ear problems. Dr. Levinson advocates use of temporary medical treatment to achieve a permanent cure. I know of one well-known learning disability practitioner who incorporates such medical treatment into his program with sometimes successful results. (The library call number for this hard-to-find book is 616.8553.)

⊃ 20/20 is Not Enough by Dr. Arthur S. Seiderman and Dr. Steven E. Marcus (Random House) $5.99

Experts often find that vision problems are at the root of learning difficulties or disabilities. Doctors Seiderman and Marcus believe that vision therapy can be of tremendous help to many struggling learners and also to those who are nearsighted. Through case histories, they discuss various vision problems, provide the medical explanation, and describe possible treatments. This is not intended to be a do-it-yourself manual, but rather a guide that will help us identify possible problems. (It provides checklists of possible symptoms of vision problems.)

In addition to vision problems that hinder education, the book deals with sports and vision, the work place and video display terminals, aging and vision, and the possibility of curing myopia (nearsightedness).

An appendix summarizes various vision research studies and lists bibliographical information both for the studies cited and for further related reading. (ISBN# 044921991-7)(S)

Allergies

One further problem that some parents have discovered at the root of their child's learning difficulties is allergies. If you have been puzzled by your child's ability to learn well and easily one day, and a seemingly contradictory inability to function the next, maybe allergies are the culprit. In her book, *The Impossible*

Child: A Guide for Caring Teachers and Parents/ In School At Home, Dr. Doris J. Rapp (The Practical Allergy Research Foundation) [$10.95] describes and gives examples of behavioral and appearance clues to help spot allergy-related problems. Next, she deals with possible environmental or food sources. Suggestions follow for teachers to deal with problems including behavioral problems (such as unresponsiveness in learning situations) that have been caused secondarily by allergy problems. A later section provides suggestions for parents to try to help alleviate problems under their control. Rapp points out that many children who have been labeled as learning disabled are in reality suffering from allergies. There are a number of methods of dealing with allergies that are discussed. A lengthy section of references will direct parents to sources for more information or assistance. Although written for teachers and parents in typical school settings, almost everything in this book will be equally applicable for home educators. *Is This Your Child?* [$12] is a newer book that covers much of the same information, but it is updated and concentrates less on the classroom environment.

The Practical Allergy Research Foundation carries other books by Rapp such as *Allergies and Your Family* [$10] and also provides helpful information such as a Multiple Food Elimination Diet that can be used to identify or eliminate possible food allergens.

Developmental Testing and Testing for Special Problems

Developmental tests help identify maturity levels and learning styles that in turn can guide us in determining methods for teaching each child. Tests for learning disabilities can help us identify specific problems. For developmental testing or testing for learning disabilities or handicaps, we refer you to the services below. These services will also be helpful in advising methods to overcome problems.

Linda Howe, M.A.. Linda has a Masters Degree in Education and is a learning disabilities and perceptual-motor consultant. She has completed advanced study and received special training in perceptual-motor development from Elizabeth Davies. Her methods are often very effective for children with dyslexia, dysgraphia, kinesthetic deficits, and other such problems. Linda Howe has had great success working with many home educated children, even those who have tried other methods that did not work. The cost is reasonable, $150 for the initial perceptual-motor evaluation which includes the remedial program. The prescribed program is done by parents with their child at home, with occasional re-evaluations and program adjustments at $55 each.

Dr. Ray Nadeau, Nadeau Testing and Treatment Clinics. The Nadeau Clinics offer developmental testing and brain wave testing for all ages. They use special brain wave testing equipment that can detect dysfunction in different areas of the brain. Then an exercise treatment program is designed and given to the parent to be used at home each day (for varying amounts of time depending on the child's needs). The Nadeau Clinics also give special discount prices to private schools and home school groups. (Non-sectarian organization)

National Academy for Child Development (NACD)/Robert J. Doman, Jr.. NACD is based in Utah, but has branches and Certified Consultants throughout the U.S. and Canada. They design individualized programs for children on a continuum from brain injured to gifted. In the programs, the parent assumes the role of primary "therapist" with NACD's training. They recognize that parents are the world's greatest experts on their own children. A six-hour audio tape series, "The Miracles of Child Development," [$50] explains the theory and philosophy behind individualized therapeutic programs. NACD has developed a worthy reputation over the years because of their tremendous success. Write or visit their web site for free information. (Non-sectarian organization)

National Institute for Learning Disabilities (NILD). Although the NILD is based in Virginia, they can refer you to educational therapists, usually through a local Christian school. NILD's purpose is to help Christian schools or organizations develop programs for students with special learning needs. They have trained classroom teachers in assessment and therapy to become educational therapists, who in turn work one-on-one with students. Some therapists will be limited to working with only students enrolled in their school, but others should be willing to work with home educators. NILD uses a variety of methods to help students overcome weaknesses rather than simply providing mechanisms students can use to compensate. Contact the national headquarters for referrals to local therapists. Qualified home educators (bachelor's degree, preferably in education) are invited to take NILD therapist training (with the Executive Director's approval), offered at a number of locations around the country. Request details, cost, and schedule information if you are interested.

Dr. Stanley Walters/Center for Children and Parents. They offer a full range of testing and interpretation plus follow-up services for those who need them. Many parents begin with the full Educational Check-up for their child, then have monitoring check-ups annually. Dr. Walters has a tremendous amount of experience and insight into methods and materials appropriate for different children as well as effective parenting techniques for those with difficult children. He is especially good at identifying potential problem areas and suggesting preventive measures. Dr. Walters has a number of publications that are very helpful for parenting/teaching. Some of the most highly recommended are *Implementing Positive Shaping in the Home, Temperamental Children—Diagnosis and Treatment,* and *Learning Theory for Parents and Teachers.* For information on publications write to Center for Children and Parents. (Non-sectarian organization)

Seriously "Challenged" Homeschoolers

Many children who are being educated at home have difficulties beyond the normal range of learning disabilities. Some are blind, deaf, crippled, have Down's Syndrome, and present parents with challenges beyond those facing most of us. An organization of their parents, called **NATHHAN**, works together for mutual support and encouragement. NATHHAN acts as the center of a support network to help unite these families and share information. They publish a quarterly newsletter. NATHHAN membership is $25 a year and includes a newsletter subscription. They also publish a Family Directory, and they operate a lending library for members. They have a national office and state coordinators, so contact the national office for information about the state support group nearest you. There appear to be about forty state groups (grown from just a couple of moms only a few years ago!).

Sources for Materials

Once you have decided what to use, you are ready to order textbooks and other resources. How on earth do you go about it?

It can seem very intimidating to contact publishers to order curriculum directly from them. While we can order directly in most cases, there are other ways to get these resources.

You can enroll in a correspondence course, independent study program, or school service as a means of obtaining textbooks without hassle. Generally, if purchasing books is your goal, this is a more costly way to get them. If the services offered (other than supply of textbooks) are helpful to you, then enrollment is worthwhile. On the other hand, if you are only using this method because you do not know how else to get the books, you will generally be wasting money.

There are several businesses set up especially to serve the home school community with materials. Others offer materials appropriate for home education although that is not their primary purpose. Some of each are listed below. All of these offer a free catalog or brochure of their materials unless otherwise indicated.

Codes are used to alert you that resources or companies are not Christian or present some potential problems. Even Christian companies carry materials from secular suppliers, most of which will present no problems at all. As is true throughout this book, (S) indicates a company that is secular in outlook rather than Christian. (SE) indicates that they are secular and also that they carry some items that are in conflict with Christian beliefs or morals.

Academic Distribution Services, Inc.

This Canadian mail order company carries the complete Alpha Omega line, Canadian social studies , French resources, and products from publishers like Cadron Creek, School of Tomorrow, Common Sense Press, ISHA Enterprises, Bob Jones University Press, Usborne, Saxon, National Writing Institute, Backyard Scientist, Trend, Mott Media, and Modern Curriculum Press. Their catalog is a combination of the Alpha Omega catalog and their own. They also carry math and science resources not listed in the catalog. Check to see if they have what you need for these areas.

Activity Resources Company, Inc.

This company offers only math materials, but they have searched out the best. They offer Cuisenaire® and Base Ten, plus many other books and materials appropriate for preschool through junior high levels.(S)

Alpha Omega

Alpha Omega, publisher of the LifePac curriculum, has developed a catalog of learning materials for home educators. While most items will supplement the LifePacs, some will replace them. Games, literature, hands-on helps, and supplementary books form the bulk of the catalog items. Resources for grades K-12 are included. Visa, MasterCard, and Discover cards are accepted. Their customer service personnel will try to help with curriculum selection decisions.

ATCO School Supply

ATCO has a walk-in store, open Tuesday through Saturday, and they also fulfill phone and mail orders. They carry thousands of items such as *Alpha Omega* language arts and science for high school, *Drive Right*, Saxon Math, *The High School Handbook, Understanding Writing*, and *Writing Strands,* plus some items not listed in their catalog. Their inventory ranges from traditional texts through creative learning materials, including many items reviewed in this book. Call, write, or fax for a free catalog. Credit cards are accepted.

Beautiful Feet Books

Beautiful Feet offers their own literature-approach study guides (such as *A Literature Approach to Medieval History*), time lines, and books for studying various historical periods. In addition, they offer a line of quality books including literature, history, and biographies. Send for free catalog. Visa and MasterCard accepted.

Bend Cornerstone Books

Bend Cornerstone Books' catalog features a broad selection of reprints of good literature and history with an emphasis on building Christian character. America's Christian history, courtship and dating, and life preparation books and resources are also well represented. Included in the catalog are resources from publishers such as Mantle Ministries; Christian Liberty Press; Family Christian Press (*Far Above Rubies, Celebrate the Feasts*, etc.); *Listen, My Son;* F.A.C.E.; and Rod and Staff. They also carry many of the books for *Far Above Rubies* although they are not listed in their catalog. While they carry *Easy Grammar,* and curriculum and parent help books for homeschooling, their catalog focuses more on the aforementioned areas than on reading, writing, and arithmetic. You can order 24 hours a day via voice mail or fax using MasterCard or Visa.

Blue Spruce Biological Supply, Inc.

Blue Spruce is a good source for science lab materials for elementary grades through high school. While they carry a few books, the bulk of their inventory consists of specimens (live and preserved), dissecting equipment, slides, and lab equipment. They are anxious to be of service to home educators and will send a special *Home School Science Catalog* free upon request.(S)

Bluestocking Press *(Educational Spectrums Catalog)*

Bluestocking Press carries a different line of materials than any of the other suppliers. They feature resources for an integrated approach to history, combining political history, economics, and law. Their primary emphasis is on U.S. History, but they do have a section on Ancient Rome and an Overview of World History section. History resources for pre-k through adult levels are arranged chronologically within the catalog and include fiction, nonfiction, primary source material, historical documents, facsimile newspapers, historical music, historical toy-making kits, audio history, and more. Also included are books on entrepreneurship. They sell their own unique publications *Special Report:The Home School Market Guide* [$150], *How to Stock a Home Library Inexpensively* [$14.95], and the Uncle Eric books. *The Home School Market Guide*, updated yearly, is extremely useful for those who would like to learn how, when, and where to sell to the home school market. Send $3 to cover first class shipping of their catalog for immediate delivery. Otherwise, they bulk mail catalogs only once each year in the Spring. Money back guarantee. MasterCard and Visa accepted.(S)

Bold Parenting Seminars

Jonathan Lindvall is a prolific speaker on many topics. You can hear him in person at conferences and seminars all around the country, but you can also order any of a number of his tapes (all in audio, some in video), including complete seminar sets. The *Bold Parenting Seminar* is presented on six audio cassettes. Examples of other topics, some available individually and some in sets, are *Youthful Romance, Dare to Shelter, Godly Fatherhood, Training Godly Teens, Psychology vs. Christianity, Television and Godly Families, Training Sons vs. Training Daughters*, and *Financial Freedom*.

BUDGEText

BUDGEText's *Home Education Text BookSource* catalog features new and used textbooks for grade K-12. They include texts, workbooks, and teacher's editions (although not all components for all courses) from both secular and Christian publishers. Among publishers represented in their catalog are Bob Jones University Press, A Beka Book, Harcourt Brace, McGraw-Hill, D.C. Heath, Riverside, Addison Wesley, Houghton Mifflin, ScottForesman, and many more. They carry new editions of BJUP and Saxon Math texts. The catalog has far more resources for high school subjects than do most others including texts for such courses as driver education, business, keyboarding, accounting, business law, cosmetology, architecture, drafting, child development, graphic arts, and auto repair. They have a 30-day return policy.

Builder Books

They sell a full line of carefully-selected educational materials for home education, including many items recommended in this manual such as those from Saxon, Progeny Press, Common Sense Press, Providence Project, Green Leaf Press, Write Source, Brown Paper School Books, and Aristoplay. Among their other products are *Spelling Power, Total Language Plus,*

Easy Grammar, How to Identify Your Child's Learning Problems, Wordsmith, Writing Strands, Winston Grammar, "Uncle Eric" books, *Far Above Rubies*, and *Listen, My Son*. This is a good source for those who need educationally-sound, cost-effective alternatives as well as the most effective traditional materials. Most prices are discounted. They ship most orders within 24 hours of receiving them. Toll free order line. Credit card orders accepted. Send for free catalog.

CSA Creation Resource Lending Library

CSA Creation Resource Lending Library offers audiovisuals on a freewill offering basis. Available resources include many video and audio tapes, primarily for creation science, but also for other topics. Some creation science titles are described in Chapter Five. Among their other offerings are the audio version of John Eidsmoe's *Institute on the Constitution,* and the video tape series *How Should We Then Live?* and *Understanding the Times* (all videos for the complete course). To order materials, write or come to the library. We can specify the name of the resource we want to borrow and the date we will need it ahead of time. They ask that we send at least $1.50 per video or $1 per audio tape to cover postage. Contributions above postage costs are used to enhance library and other CSA services. They ask that we order only tapes that we can use and return within 5 days.

Canadian Home Education Resources

The Baradoys, an experienced home schooling family, have carefully selected resources for their catalog reflecting a consideration for the needs of various learning styles and educational philosophies while being selective as far as content that is not objectionable to Christians. They carry items such as *Five in A Row, Remembering God's Awesome Acts, Pathway Readers, Far Above Rubies,* Progeny Press guides, *Easy Grammar*, Saxon math series, Richard Maybury books (*Whatever Happened to Penny Candy?*, etc.), *Training Our Daughters to be Keepers at Home*, Critical Thinking Books and Software, *Lego dacta* and *Technic* sets™, *The Learnables, World Book Encyclopedia*, and Canadian history and geography resources. All prices in their catalog are shown in Canadian dollars, and they offer a low price guarantee. They accept Visa, MasterCard, and COD orders by phone, mail, fax, or e-mail.

Children's Books

This is a source for children's reading books and homeschool curricula which have already been screened for ungodly content. The catalog lists all types of books—biographies, classics, educational, beginning reading, preschool, and fiction—along with a few games and flash card sets. They carry books from Troll, Dover, Usborne, and others, including Christian literature from publishers such as Mott, Bethany House, and Moody. Both reading levels and interest levels are listed under book descriptions. Curricula comes from publishers such as Christian Liberty, Alpha Omega, Saxon, and Common Sense Press. Literature is discounted 20-30%. Curricula is also discounted but at lower rates. Visa, Discover, and MasterCard are accepted. Send for free catalog.

Christian Book Distributors (CBD)

CBD is a discount source for Christian books, similar to Great Christian Books. Memberships are available but are not required for ordering. Non-members can remain on the mailing list and receive free the bi-monthly regular catalogs. Members also receive CBD's home school catalog, plus sale catalogs and newsletters (alternating months with the regular catalogs) offering special bargains. They carry over 5000 titles with discounts usually ranging between 20% and 75%. CBD also publishes special academic and family catalogs, available upon request. Memberships are $5 for U.S. and Canada, $8 for all other countries.

Christian Curriculum Cellar

Christian Curriculum Cellar sells used and new curriculum from A Beka, Bob Jones, and Alpha Omega along with items from other publishers such as Saxon, Mott Media, and Key Curriculum Project, and reprinted books from the 16th through the 19th centuries. They also serve as a reseller for materials we no longer need by giving us a credit for 30% of their selling price. Since the stock is ever-changing, call to see if they have what you want. A list of materials being accepted for trade-in credit is at the back of their catalog. Catalogs are free.

Creation's Child

They offer world and U.S. history time lines, books on America's Christian heritage, and more. Send SASE for free brochure.

Creative Home Teaching

Their catalog lists over 300 items, leaning towards creative, hands-on resources rather than traditional texts. They list many intriguing items not reviewed in my book, as well as resources such as Dale Seymour products, Key Curriculum products, Common Sense Press publications, *Discovery Scope*, Critical Thinking Books and Software, *Flip Chip Algebra, Art Lesson* Videos, and more. An unusual line that they carry is the Reflective Educational Perspectives Learning Style Assessment kits. Credit cards are accepted. Call or write for a free catalog.

Creative Kids Learning Co.

This Christian family business carries materials for all subject areas plus special education, with an emphasis on creative/alternative learning more than on textbooks. Among their offering are *Winston Grammar, Easy Grammar,* Usborne, Dover, Saxon math, *Learning Language Arts through Literature, Christian Charm, Man in Demand, Writing for 100 Days,* and *Knex* (including *Knex* science curriculum kits). Send $1 for price list and/or send $3 for *The Best Homeschool Catalog Ever!*

Creative Learning Systems, Inc.

Creative Learning Systems' *Transtech* catalog covers many science topics, but technology seems to be the favorite. They sell an assortment of books, software, and kits, as well as Fischertechnik, LEGO, Capsela, and LASY sets. Among their outstanding selection of books we find titles such as *Sportworks,*

David Macaulay's books, Usborne Books, and Eyewitness books. They also carry in-depth "modular courses" in aeronautics, electronics, pneumatics, structures, materials technology; *Technology* textbooks, and books and videos on design and technology. In addition, they have a number of CD-ROMs for science-related subjects such as architecture, gardening, and the human body. Visa and MasterCard accepted.(S)

The Eagle's Nest Educational Supplies

They carry a wide variety of texts and activity-oriented materials, promoting a practical approach to creative curriculum for all grade levels. Examples: Saxon Math, creation science books, Usborne science books, Greenleaf Press history, *Far Above Rubies* unit study materials, *Training Your Daughters to be Keepers at Home,* ISHA products, *Jensen's Grammar, Wordsmith, Understanding Writing,* and the *High School Handbook.* They offer a 30-day money-back guarantee. Catalogs are free and credit card orders are accepted. They maintain a store location in Escalon at 1357 Escalon Ave. Call ahead for hours.

The Elijah Company

The newest Elijah Company catalog (at 190+ pages) reflects a greatly expanded line of resources for all subject areas. This business, operated by a home schooling family, has selected quality materials that reflect their eclectic philosophy of home education. They describe various educational philosophies extensively at the front of their catalog to provide a better background for making your own selections. Excellent commentary on what and how to teach is sprinkled throughout the catalog. A large part of the catalog is devoted to history resources, listed by topic/time period. Their listing of science resources under topic headings is very helpful. Send for free catalog.

Excellence in Education

They describe their catalog as one "specifically designed to bring the joy of learning to your homeschool." Consequently, their catalog is heavy with games, videos, activity-oriented materials, light-weight workbooks, biographies, and math manipulatives. The most traditional curricula they carry are Mott Media books (*McGuffey Readers, Spencerian Penmanship, Ray's Arithmetic*). Visa, MasterCard, and American Express accepted. Send $1 for catalog. They also have a retail walk-in store; call for hours and directions.

Family Christian Academy

This company has a free 200-page catalog which lists a wide variety of resources and includes special unit study and Hebraic roots sections. They have seven walk-in stores with regular business hours, located in Nashville (main office), Knoxville, Chattanooga, Bristol, Orlando, Colorado Springs, and Dallas. Call for locations and hours. In addition, they offer testing services.

Family Learning Center

They are a retail source primarily for Common Sense Press but also for other products. They carry *Learning Language Arts through Literature, Learning Grammar through Writing, How to*

Home School, The Reading Skills Discovery Series Bookshelf Collection, Record Keeping Sheets, The Great Editing Adventure, and *Write Source* materials.

Farm Country General Store

In spite of its name, this catalog focuses primarily on home education resources, offering many at discounted prices. In addition to basics such as Saxon math, *Learning Language Arts through Literature*, and *Daily Grams*, they carry a wide variety of books and hands-on resources for all subjects. As a Christian company they have selected resources carefully, without limiting their product line to only Christian publishers. Unlike most other distributors, and in keeping with the name "General Store," they have a section of products for "health, nutrition, and home" that includes cookbooks and a few natural remedies, flour mills, and open-pollinated seeds. MasterCard and Visa are accepted.

Follett Home Education

Follett carries used and out-of-print editions of books from both Christian and non-sectarian publishers such as A Beka, Addison-Wesley, Amsco, BJUP, Glencoe, Harcourt Brace, Houghton Mifflin, Macmillan, McDougal Littel, Open Court, Riverside, Saxon, and ScottForesman. Their free brochure lists titles, year of publication, and prices of the most popular items for home educators but no other information, so you need to know what you are looking for. They carry some exercise books, workbooks, teacher guides, and answer keys. Because stock is always changing and they carry far more items than listed in the brochure, call to check on availability of particular titles.

Great Books and Gifts

They carry materials from many publishers reviewed in this book, such as Key Curriculum, Saxon, Cuisenaire, ISHA, Steck-Vaughn, Educational Insights, Common Sense Press, Educators Publishing Service, and Crossway, plus many items from small home school publishers. Credit card orders and layaway accepted. They also have a walk-in store with regular hours; call for directions.

Great Christian Books

A $5 yearly membership fee enables you to purchase Christian books at discount prices. (If you mention *Christian Home Educators' Curriculum Manual*, they will waive the membership fee!) GCB has more than 15,000 items from hundreds of publishers. While GCB is not exclusively a home education source, they continue to expand their line of homeschooling products. By the time this publication goes to press, GCB will have nearly 6000 homeschool-related products listed in their *Homeschool Discount Warehouse Catalog*, as well as Christian books, children's resources, music, Bibles, study helps, etc. in their monthly catalogs. They have some veteran homeschoolers on staff who have helped select GCB offerings. Enhanced descriptions as well as practical reviews from "noted experts" are appearing more frequently in catalogs. Complete satisfaction is guaranteed. Credit card orders are accepted. Request a free sample homeschool catalog.

Hearthside Homeschool Helps

Hearthside's homeschooling catalog specializes in KONOS materials and lots of "real books" in addition to ISHA Enterprises products, *Learning Language Arts through Literature,* the *Wordsmith* series, Key Curriculum products, Saxon math series, hands-on math products, and much more. On a few pages, they focus particularly on high school level. 33 pages of their catalog list products according to their correlation with each of the KONOS volumes. Visa, MasterCard, and Discover are accepted. Request a free catalog.

Heppner & Heppner Construction

Although their catalog is small, Heppner & Heppner Construction carries a selective line of carefully-tested (with their 13 children!) resources. They specialize in non-consumable, age- and subject-integrated materials which save us time, energy, and money. The Heppners will help you sort out your home school needs via their 800 telephone number. (They also offer workshops and seminars.) Resources are carefully screened to avoid content problems. Examples of what you will find in their catalog: books by Josh Harris, the Colfaxes, Mary Pride and Francis Schaeffer; Jr.-Sr. high resources for math, history, music, art, and creation science; high school at home guides; books on nontraditional learning alternatives for high school and college; Common Sense Press books; and Tops Learning System. A few prices are discounted, and free shipping and quantity discounts are available. Call for upcoming e-mail, website, and fax contact numbers.

Hewitt Research Foundation

Hewitt offers a continually growing array of products in addition to their school service and tests. Their illustrated, descriptive catalog features hundreds of items such as the Beautiful Feet Books "literature-based-history" packages, Audio Memory tapes, *Understanding Writing, Easy Grammar, Writing Strands,* and Saxon math. They have created syllabi for many of their courses, but they also sell these separately to those not enrolled in a program. The syllabi outline courses, often centered around a particular text but sometimes generic enough to allow you to select whatever resource you choose for a subject. For example, their *Ancient History Syllabus* for Honors history uses *Streams of Civilization, Volume One* along with library resources; the *Chemistry Syllabus* is used with *Exploring Creation with Chemistry* from Apologia Educational Ministries. A few syllabi stand on their own; *One of the Few: Toward Christian Womanhood* (reviewed in Chapter Eighteen) and *A Man for All Seasons* do not require a particular resource book. Check Hewitt's catalog for more information.

Home and Hearth

Home and Hearth services Canadian home educators through their mail order catalog. They carry about a thousand items including products from Master Books, Saxon, Aristoplay, Castle Heights, Educational Insights, Noble Publishing Associates, ISHA, and Common Sense Press, as well as resources for

Canadian social studies. New owners have expanded the product line with an emphasis on hands-on learning resources. Send for a free catalog. Phone orders are accepted.

The Home School Books and Supplies

This is a full-service bookstore that sells a full line of home education materials (over 18,000 items in stock), including A Beka, Alpha Omega, Modern Curriculum Press, Saxon, classic literature, software, and many other items listed in this book. They have access to thousands more items, so call to see if they can supply what you need. If you are in the Washington area, they have a store (with regular business hours) where you can browse through their huge selection. Send for free catalog. Overseas surface delivery at only 20% (most packages insured). Mail, call, or fax orders. Checks, Visa, Discover or MasterCard accepted.

The Home School Exchange

The Home School Exchange is a bimonthly newspaper that serves primarily as a clearinghouse for used materials and also as a source for some new resources. Subscribe for $6.50 per year and you can place 50 free words of classified advertising in every issue, and, of course, you have access to hundreds of ads placed by fellow subscribers.

Home School Resource Center

Debra Bell has been presenting home schooling seminars for years, helping thousands of parents educate their own children. The Home School Resource Center grew out of her work as a means of providing many of the resources Debra recommends. They carry a wide selection of books, tapes, CD-ROMs, and other resources, including tapes and handouts from some of Debra's seminars. The Resource Center catalog leans toward "real" books but does include some textbooks. They carry the hard-to-find Harold Jacob's *Elementary Algebra* and *Geometry For All Practical Purposes* books.

The Home Works

This Canadian distributor carries a diverse line that includes Saxon math, Alpha Omega products, *Learning Language Arts through Literature*, Alta Vista curriculum, math manipulatives, games, Usborne books, French resources, and Canadian social studies resources. They have a lowest price guarantee and accept Visa and MasterCard. Free catalog.

John Holt's Book and Music Store (Holt Associates)

They offer a magazine, books, games, tapes, and more for home educators via mail order or at their walk-in store. While items reflect a wide (primarily non-Christian) philosophical range, they tend to be very creative and unusual. They carry a number of titles that are difficult to find elsewhere. They accept telephone and fax orders using MasterCard or Visa.(S)

Landmark Distributors

They specialize in Principle Approach resources of all types, including just about everything related to the Principle Approach reviewed in this book, plus distinctively Christian books to enhance understanding of a biblical worldview in many academic disciplines. Their books cover biblical law, government, social commentary, and all areas of history (including extensive collections on the Civil War, Black History, and the American Revolution). Among their offerings are books by Reformed authors such as R.J. Rushdoony, George Grant, and Cornelius Van Til; *Greenleaf Guides;* Christian Liberty history books; biographies; historical novels; "Little Bear" Wheeler and David Barton video and audio tapes. They also carry selected items for most other subject areas. They accept Visa, MasterCard, and Discover cards.

Alan and Lori Harris of Landmark present seminars and book fairs on numerous topics, including many on various aspects of the Principle Approach.

Liberty Tree Review and Catalogue

Liberty Tree specializes in history, government, and economics from a free market, libertarian perspective. They carry a number of excellent books by authors such as Paul Johnson (*Modern Times, Intellectuals*), Richard Maybury (*Whatever Happened to Penny Candy?*), and Clarence Carson (*Basic American Government, A Basic History of the United States*), plus many titles that explore the above-mentioned areas in depth such as *Economics in One Lesson, The Whiskey Rebellion, The Character of John Adams*, and *James Madison on Religious Liberty*. Resources are primarily for adults, but some are for children. Send for a free catalog.

Library and Educational Services

Although they do not carry textbooks, they do offer many other children's books at discounted prices (at least 30% off of list price). Catalogs, published every 4-6 weeks, list books from Bethany House, Focus on the Family, and other publishers, and include biographies, classic literature, history, literature (primarily Christian), videos, and many other items for home schooling. They frequently add new items to the catalog, and they include coupon specials and occasional closeout sales. Catalogs are free.

Lifetime Books and Gifts (Bob and Tina Farewell)

Lifetime's 240-page catalog is titled *The Always Incomplete Resource Guide and Catalog. Resource Guide* is accurate because product descriptions are more detailed than in most catalogs and they include practical tips for using many items. Lifetime offers a huge variety of materials for home educators including good literature, biographies and history (listed under time periods), science and nature (with resources listed under the days of creation), unit study curricula, resources for special needs, a separate special needs brochure, and much more. Mrs. Farewell also offers a special book search service for out-of-print books such as old editions of *The Book of Life*. Send $3 for *The Always Incomplete Resource Guide and Catalog*. Credit card orders are accepted.

Lifetime Canada

Since 1994, Lifetime Canada has provided Canadians with a large selection of interesting educational books on topics such as Bible reference, educational helps, geography, history, language arts, literature, math, science, and unit studies. Prices are listed in Canadian dollars. Send $3 for their 130-page catalog.

Mission Resource Catalog (William Carey Library)

The William Carey Library specializes in missions resources. Their free catalog lists books and audio and video tapes for all ages. They sell everything at discounted prices since their goal is to get the resources out rather than making a profit. This is the most complete catalog for such resources I know of. They sell books such as *Operation World, Perspectives on the World Christian Movement,* and *You Can Change the World.*

The Moore Foundation (Dr. Raymond and Dorothy Moore)

They offer all of Dr. Raymond and Dorothy Moore's books, the Moore-McGuffey Readers, a newsletter—*The Moore Report International,* and a variety of materials that are in accord with their educational philosophy including *The Weaver, KONOS, Math-It, Winston Grammar,* Saxon math, Usborne books, and more. They plan to increase the number of resources offered, so send for a catalog for a complete list.

Nasco

Nasco has free catalogs for math, science, arts/crafts, and home economics. While they do not carry basic textbooks, they do offer what might be the broadest selection of supplemental materials. Catalogs are descriptive with color illustrations.

Rainbow Re-Source Center

Rainbow's *Retail Catalog* covers all subjects. This Christian family business has done a great job of selecting some of the best items for a variety of learning styles. Most prices are discounted, and the catalog is free. Visa and MasterCard orders accepted.

Shekinah Curriculum Cellar

Shekinah sells a full line of home education materials, books, and games, including many items recommended in this manual such as A Beka, *Spelling Power, Writing Strands, Easy Grammar,* Saxon math, history (reprints of classic editions), science kits, literature, Bible-based study guides for literature, and Usborne. They guarantee the lowest prices. Shekinah also has a store, albeit with limited shopping hours. If you are in the area, call for a recorded message about store hours. Catalogs are provided free of charge to groups. To request them, send Shekinah your group's name, address, and current membership number. Visa and MasterCard accepted. Individuals should send $1 to cover postage and handling for a catalog.

Sonlight Curriculum-International Home Schoolers Curriculum

Sonlight Curriculum is available to all homeschoolers. Even though they offer complete grade-level packages, we can purchase anything from a single book to the complete curriculum.

With its offer of free shipping anywhere in the world on orders over $100 ($5 flat shipping fee on orders under $100), Sonlight's selling prices reflect an effective discount worth up to 17% or more off retail for the complete curriculum. See the description under "Correspondence Schools" for a fuller description of the types of materials offered. Send $2 for catalog, refunded with first purchase of $25 or more.

Sycamore Tree

They offer Alpha Omega, Saxon, and Pathway curriculum, plus a huge selection of books, games, and toys (more than 3000 items from more than 200 publishers). Sycamore was the first home school supplier on the scene and has a long-standing reputation for dependability. They supply resources primarily through mail order, but their warehouse is open to walk-in customers the first and third Wednesday of every month.

Send $3 for their catalog, which includes a $3 certificate redeemable on your order. The catalog will be sent to you free if you mention *Christian Home Educators' Curriculum Manual.* Credit card orders accepted.

Teacher's Aid Co-op

Jack and Joyce Webb have come up with yet another unusual way to meet home educators' needs—through co-ops. They request that you form your own co-op of from eight to twenty homeschool families. They supply one set of catalogs plus order forms for more than fifty products/publishers. Orders are sent in only twice a year, in June and January. Then they are shipped to the leader's address in August and March respectively. Individual family orders are shrink-wrapped so that the co-op leader's job is easy. Typical of products/publishers listed are Addison Wesley, Good Apple, *Calculadder,* Greenleaf Press, Key Curriculum, Master Books, and Usborne. A number of Christian publishers are on the list. Co-op members receive 20% discounts plus free postage. Write for an information packet.

The Teaching Company

The Teaching Company produces a large number of video and audio courses, some of them designed specifically for high school students. Most of those for high schoolers are available only in video. Their Superstar Teachers series features some of the best teachers in the country teaching their specialties. I've reviewed a number of The Teaching Company courses, but I cannot review them all. The catalog gives fairly lengthy descriptions, but it does not usually indicate whether a course is a complete stand-alone course or a supplement. The majority of those I've reviewed are supplemental. Their catalog lists courses for high school and higher-level learning for math, science, history, philosophy, literature, the fine arts, and religion. The philosophical perspective is secular, but not always from any one consistent viewpoint since there are so many different presenters and they are hired to teach their areas of specialization. Sale catalogs frequently offer courses at discounts up to 50%.(S)

The Titus Woman's Homeschool Potpourri

Owner Jenny Sockey handles both new and used materials for home education. They will sell your used materials on consignment. (You get 50% of the selling price.) They carry many items reviewed in this book.

Window Tree Learning Project

One of the first Canadian sources for home education materials, Window Tree has developed a broad service. Their catalog includes textbooks, workbooks, resource books, reference materials, and manipulatives from many publishers. They feature items such as *Whatever Happened to Penny Candy, Greenleaf Guides, A Child's Story of Canada,* and other materials on Canadian history and geography. In British Columbia and Alberta, they offer testing, consultation, and workshops for parents.

Special sources

Schools often discard outdated or unneeded books. Keep your eyes open. Library book sales and thrift stores are often surprising sources for good materials. Encyclopedia sets, reference books, classic literature, and just about anything else can be found sooner or later at one of these sources.

There are a number of national magazines for home education. *Growing Without Schooling* has been around the longest. Although this is a substantial magazine, it retains it's newsletter look and contents, primarily featuring letters from home schoolers sharing their experiences. It leans toward the "unschooling philosophy," a reflection of its founder, John Holt.

The Teaching Home was the original Christian home schooling national magazine. It carries news, feature articles, columns, advertisements, letters to the editor, and teaching tips. This magazine is very encouraging, with personal input from other home educators. The perspective is distinctively Christian. More than forty state editions include a state newsletter in the center of the magazine. [$15 per year]

Homeschooling Today reflects Ruth Beechick's and Susan Schaeffer Macaulay's philosophies of education with lots of articles on learning from real life and real books. They have pull-out features with ready-to-use lessons including David Quine's wonderful art studies with full-color prints. The philosophy is Christian and the appeal is especially strong for parents of children from preschool up through the elementary grades.

Practical Homeschooling is Mary Pride's bi-monthly magazine (Home Life) [$19.95 for one year/$34.95 for two years]. It features columns, articles, ads, and lots of reviews, and it, too, reflects a Christian worldview. There tend to be more articles here than in the other magazines that appeal to veteran home schoolers. It also features articles and reviews on computer products.

Home School Digest, published by Wisdom's Gate [4 issues for $18], differs in format from the other magazines. Articles dominate the content, taking up at least two-thirds of the pages. They appear first, followed by ads, concentrated together in the last part of each issue. Articles by authors such as Jonathan Lind-

vall, Phil Lancaster, and Robin Scarlata offer both challenge and encouragement to Christian home educators. *Home School Digest* offers two subscriptions for the price of one to readers of the *Christian Home Educators' Curriculum Manuals.*

Home Education Magazine also has articles, reviews materials, and carries advertisements. They are non-sectarian but often distance themselves from Christian home schooling groups.[$20 for 6 issues]

c) **O.T. Studios** and **CTI** have been taping workshops at home school conventions for many years. They offer tapes from such events for many months afterwards. These tapes address just about every aspect of home education, although the quality varies from tape to tape because of the convention settings. Write to O.T. or CTI for catalogs of their home school tapes. You might also contact your state home school organization to see if they also have tapes available.

d) *Free for the Asking, The Resource Guide for Free Educational Materials and Programs* (Hirst) $17.95 This book by Pat Hirst tells us where to get all sorts of learning materials for elementary grades through high school including maps, posters, curriculum guides, lesson plans, coloring books, slide presentations, videos, and much more. For example, one listing reads: "**Exploring Maps Teachers Packet** contains two colorful 22" x 60" posters that feature illustrations of map development from 900 B.C. to present day, as well as map-related texts and a do-it-yourself timeline. The teaching guide includes four activity sheets (themes: location, navigation, information, and exploration), notes, questions, and glossary." Appropriate age levels and the source address follow. An index makes it easy to locate items related to an area of study.

Sources for special needs

While in this book I spend a minimal amount of time addressing special learning needs resulting from disabilities, physical handicaps, or (on the other extreme) giftedness, I realize that some children will need materials that are more challenging, move at a slower pace, or are designed to help overcome a particular handicap. Following are some useful sources. All offer free brochures or catalogs.

Braille Institute

The Braille Institute, a not-for profit organization located in southern California, provides programs and services free of charge to blind and visually-impaired persons of all ages. These free services include independent living classes, library services, visual aids consultations, career services, and an on-site store with a variety of devices helpful to those with sight loss. An assortment of informational brochures are available by calling their Orange County Center. Tours are available by appointment. Braille Institute has a toll free number providing complete blindness resource information nation wide.

Contemporary Books, Inc.

Contemporary offers books for adult learners who lack educational background or for ESL students. They emphasize math and language arts, although they do address a few other areas with a couple of items. The materials are designed to help students build basic skills (both life and educational) and/or help them pass the GED examination.(S)

Edmark Corporation

Edmark Corporation publishes and distributes software and print resources for preschool through tenth grade, as well as for special education.(S)

Educators Publishing Service

EPS offers materials for average students as well as for those above and below average. This is one of the best sources for materials for children with "minor" disabilities such as dyslexia and dysgraphia. Books range from general materials useful with all children to those addressing very specific needs, and they are very reasonably priced.(S)

Globe Fearon Educational Publishers

They have academic curricula for junior and senior high, written at elementary reading levels, covering all the basic subject areas, life and consumer skills, and health. They also sell material for adults who have learning difficulties.(S)

Gallaudet Bookstore Catalog

They offer materials for the hearing-impaired for all subjects.(S)

Phoenix Learning Resources

They offer *Programmed Reading*, plus a wide range of other materials for students with learning disabilities and for special education.

Tapes 'n Books for Gifted Education (GCT, Inc.)

They have a large catalog of materials for gifted learners.(SE)

Ordering

When ordering from publishers, it is a good idea to use school stationery for a more professional look. Some publishers will sell to us only if orders are written on school letterhead. To create school stationery/letterhead have either a typesetter or someone with a laser printer create a heading on a plain 8 1/2" by 11" piece of paper as you have seen on other business stationery. It need not be fancy, but it should look professional. It should include school name, address, and phone number. Then find a print shop to print professional looking stationery from your original. If you need only a few pieces of stationery, try to get them printed out on a laser printer rather than pay for a large quantity at a print

shop. One source for personalized school stationery is *Educational Support Foundation* which offers a stationery package that includes 20 preprinted sheets (plus a master for getting more printed locally), envelopes (unprinted), and second sheets [$22]. They also sell preprinted-custom labels, report cards, transcript forms, and diplomas.

A very few publishers have policies stating that they will not sell to individuals. Some say they will sell student texts but not teacher's editions or answer keys to individuals. Their concern is usually to prevent regular school students from getting teacher's editions for purposes of cheating. If you order on school letterhead or send a copy of a school affidavit or other proof that this is a "legitimate school," you will usually have no problem with any of the publishers that I have listed. If someone in the ordering department of a publisher tells you that you must have a letter of authorization from your school district or some other authorization that is difficult or impossible to obtain, do not give up. Recognize that they want to establish your legitimacy, then suggest other possibilities such as an order on letterhead, copy of an affidavit, or anything else that might reassure them. Usually, just sending the order on school letterhead without making prior inquiries raises no questions at all.

Some publishers charge extra fees for small orders. This means that it might be more economical for us to order their materials from one of the distributors that carry them (shown by the code letters at the end of appendix entries).

It is a good idea to order books for the fall well in advance—at least by early summer—to avoid back orders and long waits. Many publishers will offer an examination/return period, although they will ask for payment ahead of time. You can then return books that do not satisfy you. This can be a lot of trouble and the postage can be expensive, so do try to examine textbooks at conventions, other home schoolers' homes, Christian schools, or wherever else you have the opportunity so that you can avoid problems.

A few last thoughts before you order:

Costs vary greatly among publishers, yet the cost will still usually be far less than the cost of Christian school. Cost does not always guarantee the best quality. Paying more than is necessary to accomplish our goals is a waste of our resources. On the other hand, choosing the cheapest option might cost more if we have to buy something else to replace it because it did not suit our purposes.

Do not judge books solely by their appearance. Flashy graphics and color can sometimes be a cover-up for poor content, particularly with the secular publishers. If the appeal of color and pictures is important for the child, that is one thing, but the content needs to be worthwhile. Paperbacks will generally be less expensive but also less durable than hard backs. If it is very likely that books will be used by more than one child, purchase hardbacks whenever possible.

And finally, do not buy curriculum for children far ahead of schedule. It is impossible to tell what will be best for them a year or two from now.

Appendix A

Sources and Addresses

Sources for materials I have referred to in this manual are included here. If you are looking for a publisher with what sounds like a person's name in the title, it will be listed under the first letter of the first name. (E.g., David C. Cook is under "D") You can usually contact the publishers directly, but sometimes publishers would rather not sell to individuals. In these cases, they have distributors to sell us their products. In most cases you will pay the same price whether ordering from a distributor or a publisher.

I have referred you to a number of distributors who carry lines of products for home educators in the section titled "Sources." It can be very time consuming and expensive to write to every publisher and distributor who might have something of interest. I have tried to make things easier by providing a key to help you identify a distributor who might carry a number of the items in which you are interested. Then you can place one larger order, saving on shipping costs and hassles. In the key, I list again some of the sources described more fully under the "Sources for Materials" section. These particular sources were chosen because of the number of reviewed products that they carry, their established reputations, and their ability to fill orders from all over the country. (It also reflects their willingness to take time to go through this appendix and identify which items they sell.) Obviously it is difficult to keep track of who is selling which items, and that information changes from time to time. Because I do not indicate that an item is carried by a certain distributor, it does not preclude the possibility that they do indeed carry it. The best approach is to obtain catalogs from a number of these sources for reference.

I have included prices unless the publisher did not supply them for some reason, but I must caution you that prices change frequently, so you must check the actual price before ordering. You will also need to check the cost of shipping and tax on any order. Prices are supplied only so that you will have some idea what a product might cost, an important factor for many of us as we narrow down our choices.

I know that many home educating families operate on very limited budgets and are looking for bargains. However, if you seek information or advice about a product from a distributor who sells at full retail price, then you purchase the item from a discount source, you are taking unfair advantage of that distributor ("...for the worker is worthy of his support." Matt. 10:10).

ATCO ....A
BUILDER BOOKS ....B
ELIJAH COMPANY C
GREAT CHRISTIAN BOOKS....................................D
THE HOME SCHOOL BOOKS AND SUPPLIES ......E
LIFETIME BOOKS AND GIFTS ....F
RAINBOW RESOURCE CENTER ....G
SHEKINAH CURRICULUM CELLAR ....H
SYCAMORE TREE I

Reading the Codes

Code letters for each of these distributors appear in parentheses ( ). If that distributor carries only selected items from this publisher, the parentheses with code/s follows immediately after that item. Otherwise, the parentheses with code/s after the "—" at the end of the listing mean that all items from that publisher are carried by the indicated sources. When the listing says "some items," it means that the distributors either did not indicate which of the items they carry or that they carry some items from that publisher that are not named.

All of the publishers and sources listed will send a free catalog or brochure unless otherwise specified. SASE means self-addressed stamped envelope. This should be a business-size envelope with a $.32 stamp. Check for more complete details concerning distributors under "Sources for Materials."

Many publishers and sources have toll free telephone numbers. This means that they pay for the cost of our call. These numbers all have (800) or (888) as their area code prefix. If an (800) or (888) number is for orders only, please call the other number listed with other types of questions.

ACE School of Tomorrow
See School of Tomorrow.

ACH Study Groups
P.O. Box 905
Morgan Hill, CA 95037
(408) 779-3030
(408) 782-8901 FAX
e-mail: histbuff@garlic.com

ACT Assessment
P.O. Box 414
Iowa City, IA 52243
(319) 337-1270

ACTPEP
P.O. Box 4014
Iowa City, IA 52243
(319) 337-1387

AGC, Inc.
4999 Fyler Avenue
St. Louis, MO 63139
(800) 404-3263
(214) 341-9994 FAX
America's God and Country—(D,F)

AGES Software
1100 Jackson St. S.E.
P.O. Box 1926
Albany, OR 97321-0509

(800) 297-4307
(541) 917-0839 FAX
The Master Christian Library

AIMS Education Foundation
P.O. Box 8120
Fresno, CA 93747-8120
(209) 255-4094
(888) 733-2467
(209) 255-4094 FAX
web site: http://www.AIMSedu.org

AMG Publishers
P.O. Box 22000
6815 Shallowford Rd.
Chattanooga, TN 37421

(800) 251-7206
(800) 267-7171 FAX
Learning English with the Bible: A Systematic Approach to Bible-Based English Grammar, Learning English with the Bible: Diagramming Guide (F,I; some items-C)

A Beka Book Publications
Box 19100
Pensacola, FL 32523-9160
(800) 874-2352
(800) 874-3590 FAX—(H)

A Beka Book Correspondence/Video School
Box 18000
Pensacola, FL 32523-9160
(800) 874-3592
(800) 874-3593 FAX

Academic Distribution Services, Inc.
528 Carnarvon St.
New Westminster, BC V3L 1C4
Canada
(604) 524-9758
(800) 276-0078
e-mail: ads@intergate.bc.ca

The Academy of Home Education
1700 Wade Hampton Blvd.
Greenville, SC 29614
(888) 253-9833
(864) 242-5100, extension 2047
e-mail: ahe@bju.edu

Activity Resources
P.O. Box 4875
Hayward, CA 94540
(510) 782-1300
(510) 782-8172 FAX

Addison-Wesley
1 Jacob Way
Reading, MA 01867
(800) 447-2226
(617) 942-1117 FAX
High school math, *Cuisenaire*® (G,H,I), *Foodworks, Sportworks, The Student's Guide to Doing Research on the Internet.* Prices shown are list prices, but you might be able to purchase at school prices which are lower. (Some items-A,B,D,E)

Advanced Traffic Technologies, Inc.
4164 Austin Bluffs Parkway, #309
Colorado Springs, CO 80918
(719) 572-9394
(719) 572-9232 FAX
e-mail: advtraffic@aol.com
website: http://www.advtraffic.com
Help! My Teenager Wants to Drive!!!(A,C,F,H)

Advanced Training Institute International
Box 1
Oakbrook, IL 60522-3001
(630) 323-7073
God, Man, and Law: The Biblical Principles

Algonquin Books of Chapel Hill
division of Workman Publishing Company, Inc.

708 Broadway
New York, NY 10003
(800) 722-7202
The Weather Wizard's Cloud Book, The Weather Wizard's 5-Year Weather Diary

Allyn and Bacon
P.O. Box 10695
Des Moines, IA 50336-0695
(800) 666-9433
(515) 284-2607 FAX
e-mail: orderbkAB@aol.com
Within Reach: A Guide to Successful Writing

Alpha Omega
300 North McKemy Ave.
Chandler, AZ 85226-2618
(800) 622-3070
(602) 438-2702 FAX (D,E,I; some items-A,B,H)

Alpha Plus
Janet and Jim Lathan
P.O. Box 185
Chewsville, MD 21721
(301) 733-1456
Math For Life

American Christian History Institute
James Rose
P.O. Box 648
Palo Cedro, CA 96073
(530) 547-3535
(530) 547-4045 FAX
website: http://www.achipa.com
A Guide to American Christian Education for the Home and School, The Principle Approach(C or from Foundation for American Christian Education)

American Enterprise Publications
177 N. Spring Rd.
Mercer, PA 16137
(412) 748-3726
(412) 748-5373 FAX
Economics: Principles and Policy, Economics: The American Economy, Free Enterprise Economics, Reclaiming the American Dream by Reconstructing the American Republic

American Map Corporation
46-35 54th Road
Maspeth, NY 11378
(718) 784-0055
(718) 784-1216 FAX
(800) 432-6277
Schick Anatomy Atlas(G), maps, and atlases—(E; some items-B,G,H)

American Portrait Films
P.O. Box 19266
Cleveland, OH 44119
(800) 736-4567
(216) 531-8600
(216) 531-8355 FAX
e-mail: amport@ix.netcom.com
web site: http://www.amport.com
No Alibis, The Grand Canyon Catastrophe, The Silent Scream, Fossil Evidence of Creation, The Massacre of Innocence, The Right

to Kill, A Scientist Looks at Creation, plus many other videos on hot topics—(D; some items-B)

American School
2200 E. 170th
Lansing, IL 60438
(708) 418-2800

American Science and Surplus
3605 Howard St.
Skokie, IL 60076
(847) 982-0874
(800) 982-0881 FAX
e-mail: jarvis@sciplus.com
web site: http://www.sciplus.com

American Textbook Committee
51054 Highway 22
Wadley, AL 36276
(205) 395-4432
Basic American Government(B), *Basic Economics,* and *A Basic History of the United States*(B,G)— (C,E; some items-F; also available from Bluestocking Press)

American Vision
P.O. Box 724088
Atlanta, GA 31139
(800) 628-9460 credit card orders only
(770) 988-0555 other orders and inquiries
(770) 952-2587 FAX
God and Government, Biblical Worldview magazine, *To Pledge Allegiance: A New World in View*—(D; some items-C)

Ampersand Press
750 Lake St.
Port Townsend, WA 98368
(800) 624-4263 orders only
(360) 379-5187
(360) 379-0324 FAX
O! Euclid(G), *Krill, AC/DC*—(B,E)

Amsco School Publications, Inc.
315 Hudson St.
New York, NY 10013
(212) 886-6565 orders and customer service
(212) 886-6500 information
(800) 969-8398
Source for inexpensive textbooks, all subjects, primarily high school/college level. Send for free catalogs. The Educational List & Net Prices catalog is simply a title and price listing. Specific Mathematics, Language Arts, Science, Foreign Language, and Social Studies catalogs provide descriptive information. Titles reviewed: *Achieving Competence in Science, Curso Primero (Spanish), Algebra I, Algebra: An Introductory Course, Instant Spelling Power*(H), *Life Science Work-Text, Reviewing Biology, Reviewing Chemistry, Reviewing Physics, The Reader as Detective, High Marks, General Science,* and the Amsco Literature Series.—(some items-A,B,E,H)

Apologia Educational Ministries
Dr. Jay L. Wile
808 Country Club Lane
Anderson, IN 46011
(765) 649-4076 phone and fax

website: http://www.netusa1.net/~jlwile
Exploring Creation with Chemistry(B), *Exploring Creation with Physics*

Arco Books
Distributed by Macmillan
201 W. 103rd St.
Indianapolis, IN 46290
(800) 428-5331
(800) 882-8583 FAX
website: http://www.superlibrary.com
SAT Cram Course, ACT Cram Course, Preparation for the SAT and PSAT, ACT: American College Testing Program, 1997, Practice for Air Force Placement Tests, Practice for the Armed Forces Test-ASVAB, ASVAB Basics, Practice for Army Placement Tests

Aristoplay
450 S. Wagner Rd.
Ann Arbor, MI 48103
(888) 478-4263
(313) 995-4353
By Jove, Constellation Station, Hail to the Chief, Knights and Castles, Made for Trade, The Play's the Thing, True Math, Where in the World—(A,B,D,F,G,H;some items-C)

Art Extension Press
P.O. Box 389
Westport, CT 06881
(203) 256-9920

Association of Christian Schools International
P.O. Box 35097
Colorado Springs, CO 80935-3509
(800) 367-0798
e-mail: Fran_Burdick@ACSI.org
Daring Deliverers, Understanding the Times(B,G)—(some items-C,D,E,H)

ATCO School Supply, Inc.
425 East Sixth St. #105
Corona, CA 91719
(888) 246-ATCO orders only
(909) 272-2926
(909) 272-3457 FAX
e-mail: atco@atco1.com
website: http://www.atco1.com
The Camelot General Chemistry Primer

Audio-Forum
96 Broad St.
Guilford, CT 06437
(800) 243-1234
(203) 453-9774 FAX
e-mail: 74537.550@compuserve.com
website: http://agoralang.com/audioforum.html
Say it by Signing—(E)

Audio Memory Publishing
501 Cliff Dr.
Newport Beach, CA 92663-5810
(800) 365-SING
Grammar Songs—(A,B,D,F,G,H,I)

Audio-Visual Drawing Program
Bruce McIntyre
P.O. Box 186

Ridgecrest, CA 93556
(760) 375-2892—(C,F,G,H,I)

Back Home Industries
Gary and Wanda Sanseri
P.O. Box 22495
Milwaukie, OR 97269-2495
(503) 654-2300
A Documentary History of the United States, A Banker's Confession, Spelling Boosters, The Federalist Papers, The Anti-Federalist Papers—(D,F; some items-B,C,E,H)

Baker Book House
P.O. Box 6287
Grand Rapids, MI 49516-6287
(800) 877-2665
(616) 676-9185
(616) 676-9573 FAX
website: http://www.bakerbooks.com
When Skeptics Ask. Parent company for Revell/Chosen Books: *The Light and the Glory*(A,G,I), *From Sea to Shining Sea*(A,G,I), Study guides for *The Light and the Glory*(A,I), *Passion and Purity, Discover Your Children's Gifts*—(some items-B,C,D,E,F,H)

Banner of Truth
P.O. Box 621
Carlisle, PA 17013
(717) 249-5747
(717) 249-0604 FAX
e-mail: jbebanner of truth@compuserve.com
Sketches from Church History—(B,C,D,F,G)

Barnum Software
3450 Lake Shore Ave. Ste. 200
Oakland, CA 94610-2343
(800) 553-9155
(800) 553-9156 FAX
The Quarter Mile Math Games

Barron's
250 Wireless Blvd.
Hauppauge, NY 11788
(800) 645-3476 for orders only
(516) 434-3311
Algebra the Easy Way, Calculus the Easy Way, Essential Mathematics(H), *How to Prepare for the GED, ACT Computer Study Program, SAT II study guides, How to Prepare for the American College Testing Program, SAT I Computer Study Program, 14 Days to Higher SAT Scores, SAT I Workbooks, Pass Key to SAT I, How to Prepare for the SAT I,* and Spanish books—(some items-A,B,C,E,F,H,I)

Beautiful Feet Books
139 Main St.
Sandwich, MA 02563
(508) 833-8626
(800) 889-1978 orders only
Ancient History, Medieval History, A Literature Approach to U.S. and World History—(B,C,F,G,H; some items-D)

Bend Cornerstone Books
62570 Dixon Lp.
Bend, OR 97701-9360

(800) 487-5952
(541) 389-0898 FAX
e-mail: bcornerstone@juno.com

Berg Christian Enterprises
P.O. Box 66066
Portland, OR 97290
(503) 777-4101

The Bess Press
3565 Harding Ave.
Honolulu, HI 96816
(800) 910-BESS
(808) 734-7159
(808) 732-3627 FAX
e-mail: sales@besspress.com
web site: http://www.besspress.com
Modern Hawaiian History

Bethany House Publishers
11300 Hampshire Ave. S.
Minneapolis, MN 55438
(800) 328-6109 orders
(612) 829-2500
e-mail: cs@bethanyhouse.com
Basic Greek, Kingdom of the Cults, LifeKeys, The New Absolutes, Men and Women of Faith series—(D,E,F; some items-B,H)

Bethlehem Books
15605 County Road 15
Minto, ND 58261
(800) 757-6831
Designing Your Own Classical Curriculum—(B,F,G)

Bible Math Labs
John Block
HC 79, Box 46
Gothenburg, NE 69138
(308) 537-7538 (phone and fax)
e-mail: mathlabs@navix.net

Bill Rice Ranch, Inc.
627 Bill Rice Ranch Rd.
Murfreesboro, TN 37128
(615) 893-2767
Sign Language for Everyone. The book is published by Thomas Nelson Publishers and can also be obtained through them.—(A,F,G,I)

Biola University
Office of Admissions
13800 Biola Ave.
La Mirada, CA 90639
(800) OK-BIOLA
(562) 903-4752
e-mail: admissions@biola.edu
website: http://www.biola.edu

Blackstone Audio Books
P.O. Box 969
Ashland, OR 97520
(800) 729-2665
website: http://www.blackstoneaudio.com

Blakey Publications
P.O. Box 12622
Olympia, WA 98508
(360) 866-8775

e-mail: total.language.plus@juno.com
Total Language Plus—(B,E,G)

Blue Spruce Biological Supply
701 Park St.
Castle Rock, CO 80104
(800) 825-8522
(303) 688-3396 (in Denver area)
(303) 688-3428 FAX
e-mail: admin@bluebio.com
website: http://bluebio.com

Bluestocking Press
P.O. Box 2030
Shingle Springs, CA 95682
(800) 959-8586 orders only
(916) 621-1123
(916) 642-9222 FAX
How to Stock a Quality Home Library Inexpensively, Whatever Happened to Penny Candy?, The Money Mystery, Whatever Happened to Justice, The Clipper Ship Strategy, Evaluating Books: What Would Thomas Jefferson Think About This?, Are You Liberal? Conservative? or Confused?, Ancient Rome: How It Affects You Today, The E-Myth Revisited, Capitalism for Kids: Growing Up To Be Your Own Boss. The 8-book set of Uncle Eric books sells for $77.—(A,E,F; some items-C,B,D,G,H,I)

Bob Jones University Press
Greenville, SC 29614
(800) 845-5731
Textbooks for all subjects, *Better Thinking and Reasoning, Free Indeed*—(D)
For the HomeSat program call (800) 739-8199.

Bolchazy-Carducci Publishers
1000 Brown St., Unit 101
Wauconda, IL 60084
(847) 526-4344
Artes Latinae(C,F), *Latin Stories*

Bold Christian Living
Jonathan Lindvall
P.O. Box 820
Springville, CA 93265
(800) 454-6382 orders only
(209) 539-0500
e-mail: Lindvall@BoldChristianLiving.com
web site: http://www.BoldChristianLiving.com
Youthful Romance: The Problems with Dating; Sports and Godly Families; Post-Secondary Education, Homeschooling College; Financial Freedom; Bold Christian Youth Seminar; and many other audio tapes—(D,F; some items-C)

Boston University
Office of Admissions
121 Bay State Road
Boston, MA 02215
(617) 353-2300

Boy Scouts of America Supply Division
Direct Mail Center
P.O. Box 909
Pineville, NC 28134-0909
(800) 323-0732

merit badge booklets

Bradrick Family Enterprises
P.O. Box 2240
Port Orchard, WA 98366
(360) 249-2472
Understanding Writing—(A,B,D,E,F,G,H,I)

Braille Institute
Orange County Center
527 North Dale Ave.
Anaheim, CA 92801
(800) Bra-ille for referral information
(714) 821-5000

The Branch Office, Inc.
837 Sopris Ave.
Carbondale, CO 81623
(970) 963-9371 phone and FAX
e-mail: branch@rof.net.
Perspective: The Time Line Game—(G)

Bridgestone Academy
300 North McKemy Ave.
Chandler, AZ 85226-2618
(800) 682-7396
e-mail: bmgacad@bmgaop.com

Bridgestone Multimedia
300 North McKemy Ave.
Chandler, AZ 85226-2618
(800) 622-3070
Hooked on Hebrew; videos: *The Evidence for Creation, Evolution-Fact or Fiction, Ancient Man-Created or Evolved, Death of the Dinosaur*—(D,E)

Brooke-Richards Press
9420 Reseda Blvd., Ste. 511
Northridge, CA 91324
(818) 893-8126
(818) 349-2558 FAX
American Adventures—(A,B,E,F,I)

BUDGEText Home Education
P.O. Box 1487
Fayetteville, AR 72702-1487
(888) 888-2272
(501) 442-3064 FAX
e-mail: sales@homeschoolmall.com

Builder Books
P.O. Box 99
Riverside, WA 98849
(800) 260-5461 Orders only
(509) 826.5624 FAX
(509) 826-6021
e-mail: books@televar.com
Writing Step by Step(A,B,H)

C & B Publishing
P.O. Box 826
Benicia, CA 94510
(707) 747-5950
(800) 707-5567 orders only
(707) 745-2245 FAX
Bears' Guide to Earning College Degrees Nontraditionally(C,F,G)

CEBA
P.O. Box 11471
Lynchburg, VA 24506

(804) 582-2338
The Declaration of Independence: Our Nation's Charter; Economics, Freedom & Values: A Christian View of Fundamental Economic Issues

CLEP
P.O. Box 6601
Princeton, NJ 08541-6601
(609) 771-7865
(800) 323-7155
website: http://www.collegeboard.org
College credit by testing. *Official Study Guide for the CLEP Examinations.* Send for free booklets: *CLEP Colleges* and *Information for Candidates* (published by The College Board).

CSA Creation Resource Lending Library
8904 Masten
Overland Park, KS 66212
(913) 492-6545

CTI
1704 Valencia N.E.
Albuquerque, NM 87110
(505) 265-1177

Calvert School
Dept. 2CCM, 105 Tuscany Road
Baltimore, MD 21210-3098
(410) 243-6030
(410) 366-0674 FAX
e-mail: inquiry@calvertschool.org
website: http://www.calvertschool.org

Cambridge Academy
3300 S.W. 34th Ave., Ste. 102
Ocala, FL 34474
(352) 873-7750
(800) 881-2717

Cambridge University Press
110 Midland Ave.
Port Chester, NY 10573
(800) 872-7423
(914) 937-4712 FAX
Latin series. Order answer keys and other supplementary materials from North American Cambridge Classics Projects Resource Center.

Canadian Home Education Resources
7 Stanley Cr. S.W.
Calgary, AB T2S 1G1
Canada
(403) 243-9727 phone and fax; order line for Calgary area
(800) 345-2952 orders only
e-mail: cher@cadvision.com

Canon Press
P.O. Box 8741
Moscow, ID 83843
(800) 488-2034
website: http://www.moscow.com/Resources/Credenda/
Latin Primer, Latin Grammar, Introductory Logic, Classical Education and the Home School, The Quest for Authentic Higher Learning, Her Hand in Marriage—(B,D,F; some items-G)

Career Directions
108 Oak Park
Boerne, TX 78006
(888) 816-9191
(830) 816-9191
e-mail: careers@gvtc.com
Heading in The Right Direction

Carolina Biological Supply Company
2700 York Rd.
Burlington, NC 27215
(800) 334-5551
(800) 222-7112 FAX
e-mail: rknauff@carolina.com
website: http://www.carolina.com
Bob Knauff, at extension 6353, is their
home school contact person.

Cary Gibson's Curriculum and Counseling Services
440 Old Airport Rd.
Auburn, CA 95603
(916) 823-3164
Complete Homeschool Planner—(A,D)

Castle Heights Press, Inc.
Kathleen Julicher
2578 Alexander Farms Dr.
Marietta, GA 30064
(800) 763-7148
Experiences in Chemistry(G,I), *Experiences in Biology*(G,I), *Geometric Constructions, Cooking and Science, The Ultimate Science Project Notebook,* and *The Homework Assignment Book*—(F; some items-C,D)

Castlemoyle Media
6701 180th St. S.W.
Lynnwood, WA 98037
(425) 787-2714
Spelling Power, Spelling Power Activity Task Cards—(A,B,C,E,F,G,H)

Cathedral Builders Press
731 Lakefair Drive
Sunnyvale, CA 94089
(408) 734-4707
An Introduction to Christian Writing

Center for Applications of Psychological Type
2815 N.W. 13th St., Ste. 401
Gainesville, FL 32609
(800) 777-2278
People Types and Tiger Stripes and *Please Understand Me*

Center for Children and Parents
See Dr. Stanley Walters.

Chalk Dust Company
11 Sterling Court
Sugar Land, TX 77479
(800) 588-7564
(281) 265-2495
(281) 265-3197 FAX
Prealgebra, Algebra I, College Algebra, Essentials of Algebra II, Intermediate Algebra, Geometry, SAT Math Review(C), *Trigonometry: A Graphing Approach, Pre-Calculus with Limits*—(F)

CharacterLink™
Box One
Oak Brook, IL 60522-3001
(888) 330-8678

Chariot Victor Publishing
4050 Lee Vance View
Colorado Springs, CO 80918
(800) 437-4337
(719) 536-3280 FAX
How to Be Your Own Selfish Pig, Investing for the Future—(A,B,C,D,F,G,H)

Charlotte Mason Research and Supply Company
P.O. Box 936
Elkton, MD 21922-0936
Charlotte Mason Home Schooling series(C,D), *The Parents Review* magazine

Children Sing the Word
Box 183
Chesterville, OH 43317
(419) 768-3152
(419) 768-4135 FAX
e-mail: Wordsing@aol.com
website: http://members.aol.com/wordsing.htm

Children's Books
P.O. Box 239
Greer, SC 29652
(800) 344-3198
(864) 968-0391

Christian Book Distributors (CBD)
P.O. Box 7000
Peabody, MA 01961-7000
(978) 977-5000

Christian Curriculum Cellar
4460 S. Carpenter Rd.
Modesto, CA 95358
(209) 538-3632 1-4 p.m. PST, Tues.-Fri.

Christian Financial Concepts
P.O. Box 100
Gainesville, GA 30503
(800) 722-1976
Get a Grip on Your Money

Christian Home Educators Press
12440 Firestone Blvd., Ste. 1008
Norwalk, CA 90650
(562) 864-2432
The High School Handbook—(A,B,C,H,I)

Christian Liberty Academy/Christian Liberty Press
502 W. Euclid Ave.
Arlington Heights, IL 60004
(847) 259-4444
(847) 259-2941 FAX orders only
website: http://www.homeschools.org
—(some items-A,B,C,D,F,G,H)

Christian Life Workshops
See Noble Publishing Associates

Christian Light
P. O. Box 1212
Harrisonburg, VA 22801-1212

Perspectives of Life in Literature, Perspectives of Truth in Literature

Christian Publications
3825 Hartzdale Drive
Camp Hill, PA 17011
(800) 233-4443
The Rewriting of America's History(C), *Great American Statesmen and Heroes*—(A,D,F,G)

Christian Research Institute
P.O. Box 7000
Rancho Santa Margarita, CA 92688-2124
(888) 7000-CRI
(714) 858-6100
(714) 858-6111 FAX

Christian Schools International
3350 East Paris Avenue S.E.
Grand Rapids, MI 49512
(800) 635-8288
The Church in History, The Story of God and His People series, *Exploring Ethics, Exploring Faith and Discipleship, Exploring Apologetics*

Christian Technologies Inc.
4332 Brentwood
P.O. Box 2201
Independence, MO 64055
(816) 478-8320
(800) 366-8320
(800) 291-1578 FAX
website: http://www.idir.net/~cti
e-mail: cti@idir.net
American Student's Package, Noah Webster's 1828 Dictionary(A)

Christian Worldview Library
(UPS address) 700 E. 37th N.
Wichita, KS 67219
or (mail address) P.O. Box 546
Wichita, KS 67201
(316) 832-3319
e-mail: cwvl@southwind.net

Circle of Learning Workbooks™
P.O. Box 1252
Canyon, TX 79015
(806) 655-4245 phone and fax
e-mail: CLWbooks@aol.com
website: http://members.aol.com/CLWBooks/CLW.html
Send SASE—(E,I)

Classical Connection Resources
P.O. Box 161823
Austin, TX 78716-1823
(512) 440-8562
Words to the Wise

Cliffs Notes, Inc.
P.O. Box 80728
Lincoln, NE 68501
(800) 228-4078 orders and inquiries
(402) 423-9254 FAX
Test preparation and literature guides, *Cliffs StudyWare for the SAT*—(some items-G)

Clonlara School Home Based Education Program
1289 Jewett
Ann Arbor, MI 48104
(313) 769-4511
(313) 769-9629 FAX
e-mail: clonlara@delphi.com
website: http://www.clonlara.org

Cognitive Technologies Corporation
5009 Cloister Dr.
Rockville, MD 20852
(800) 335-0781
(301) 581-9652
(301) 581-9653 FAX
e-mail: cthc@cogtech.com
website: http://www.cogtech.com
The Trig Explorer

The College Board
45 Columbus Ave.
New York, NY 10023-6992
(212) 713-8165 customer service
website: http://www.collegeboard.org
Also distributed by the Macmillan Publishing Company.
The College Board publishes many books including *The College Handbook, Index of Majors and Graduate Degrees, College Costs and Financial Aid Handbook, College Explorer, Moving Ahead with CLEP, CLEP Colleges, The Official Handbook for the CLEP Examinations, The Official Guide to SAT II: Subject Tests, 8 Real SATs*(G), *Test-Skills*, test preparation books for SAT, ACT, PSAT/NMSQT, CLEP, plus some college preparation software. Most books may be ordered through local bookstores.

College Board, Advanced Placement Program
P.O. Box 6671
Princeton, NJ 08541-6671
(609) 771-7300
website: http://www.collegeboard.org

Collegiate Cap and Gown Company
901 Bob King Dr.
Arcola, IL 61910
(800) 553-3737
Write or call for the name of the distributor in your area.

The Committee for Biblical Principles in Government
P.O. Box 6031
Aloha, OR 97007-0031
(503) 357-9844
website: http://www.teleport.com/non-profit/committee/
The Challenge of Godly Government, The Challenge of Godly Justice

Common Sense Press
P.O. Box 1365
8786 Highway 21
Melrose, FL 32666
(904) 475-5757
(904) 475-6105 FAX
Bookshelf Collection, Learning Language Arts through Literature, The Great Editing Adventure, Great Explorations in Editing,

Wordsmith: A Creative Writing Course for Young People, Wordsmith Craftsman, T.I.P.S. Planners. Common Sense Press sells only to retailers. Orders should be placed through dealers. Refer to our key or call for dealers in your area.
—(A,B,D,E,F,G,H; some items-C,I)

Communication through Language Development
325 E. Delaware Rd.
Burbank, CA 91504
(818) 845-9602
Discover Intensive Phonics. Send SASE for more information.

Compact University
305 N. 500 W. Ste. C
Provo, UT 84601
(801) 373-2495
First-Hand History of America—(E)

CompuServe
(800) 848-8199

Computer Courseware Specialists
1103 C. S Limestone St.
Gaffney, SC 29340
(864) 489-7380
e-mail: llkmdd@pic-a-book.com
The Big Book

Concordia Publishing House
3558 South Jefferson Ave.
St. Louis, MO 63118
(800) 325-3040
website: http://www.cphmall.com
Considering a Church Career?, Everyday Life in Bible Times, Learning About Sex series(D,I)

The Constitutional Coalition
P.O. Box 37054
St. Louis, MO 63141
(314) 434-7028
Idols and Ideas

Contemporary Books, Inc.
order from National Textbook Company
Real Numbers, Number Sense, Number Power, plus GED preparation helps

Continental Press
Elizabethtown, PA 17022
(800) 233-0759
On Target for Tests, New Language Patterns and Usage, Practice Exercises in Basic English, Report Writing: Formula for Success—(A,B,H)

Cornerstone Curriculum Project
2006 Flat Creek
Richardson, TX 75080
(972) 235-5149
Building A Biblical World View, Let Us Highly Resolve(D,H), *Music and Moments with the Masters, Adventures in Art, Principles from Patterns: Algebra I, World Views of the Western World*—(F)

Courtship Connection
3731 Cecelia

Toledo, OH 43608
(419) 729-4594
e-mail: KMorris895@aol.com

Covenant Home Curriculum
17800 W. Capitol Dr.
Brookfield, WI 53045
(414) 781-2171
website: http://covenanthome.com

Covenant Publications
224 Auburn Ave.
Monroe, LA 71201
(318) 323-3061
America, The First 350 Years(G,H) and *Teaching and Learning American History.* Send a SASE for free brochure. They also carry cassettes (music) and books relating to America's history.—(B,C,D,F)

Creation Research
P.O. Box 281, Hartsville, TN 37074
(615) 374-3693
(615) 374-3045 FAX
The Education Debate Video, The Search for the Origin of Life, The Real Roots, The World of Living Fossils

Creation Resource Foundation
P.O. Box 570
El Dorado, CA 95623
(916) 626-4447
e-mail: creation@juno.com
website: http://www.creationresource.com
Unlocking the Mysteries of Creation—(A,B,C,D,E,F,G,H,I)

Creation Resource Library
Attn. Mrs. Ellen Myers
1429 N. Holyoke
Wichita, KS 67208
(316) 683-3610

Creation's Child
P.O. Box 3004 #44
Corvallis, Or 97339
(541) 758-3413—(D,E,F,H)

Creative Home Teaching
P.O. Box 152581
San Diego, CA 92195
(619) 263-8633 phone and FAX
Source for *Flip-Chip Algebra*

Creative Kids Learning Co.
Naomi and Lydia Strunk
964 Holland Rd.
Holland, PA 18966
(215) 355-5834

Creative Learning Systems, Inc.
16510 Via Esprillo
San Diego, CA 92127-1708
(800) 458-2880
(619) 675-7700
(619) 675-7707 FAX
website: http://www.clsinc.com
Technology

Creative Publications
1300 Villa St.
Mountain View, CA 94041

(800) 624-0822
(650) 988-1000
(650) 988-1111 FAX
Cuisenaire® Rods, Base 10 blocks, and other learning materials—(some items-D)

Creative Teaching Associates
P.O. Box 7766
Fresno, CA 93747
(800) 767-4282
(209) 291-6626
(209) 291-2953 FAX
e-mail: cta@psnw.com
website: http://www.mastercta.com
Stock Exchange and other educational games, AIMS Education Foundation materials—(some items-A,B,D,F,H,I; also available at teacher supply stores)

Critical Thinking Books and Software
P.O. Box 448
Pacific Grove, CA 93950
(800) 458-4849
(408) 393-3277 FAX
Critical Thinking Skills, Building Thinking Skills, Editor in Chief, Math Word Problems, Organizing Thinking, Mind Benders, Math Mind Benders, Critical Thinking Activities for Mathematics, Mathematical Reasoning through Verbal Analysis Book 2, Scratch Your Brain Where It Itches, Algebra Tricks, Algebra Word Problems, Critical Thinking in United States History series, and many other titles on thinking skills—(some items-B,C,D,F,G,H)

Crossway Books
Division of Good News Publishers
1300 Crescent Street
Wheaton, IL 60187
(630) 682-4300
(630) 682-4785 FAX
sales@goodnews-crossway.org
Mary Pride's Big Book of Home Learning; Schoolproof; Books Children Love; The Gift of Music; Great Christian Hymn Writers; The Great Evangelical Disaster; How Should We Then Live?; Reading Between the Lines; Recovering the Lost Tools of Learning; Turning Point; Freedom, Justice, and Hope; The Tragedy of American Compassion; World Proofing Your Kids; Postmodern Times; The Feminist Gospel; A Christian's Treasury of Stories and Songs, Poems and Prayers—(some items-A,B,C,D,E,F,G,H,I)

Crown Ministries
530 Crown Oak Centre Dr.
Longwood, FL 32750
(407) 331-6000
Financial Study for Teenagers

Crusade for Life
18030 Brookhurst St., #372
Fountain Valley, CA 92708
(714) 963-4753
A Christian Response to Euthanasia

Cuisenaire®-Dale Seymour Publications®
125 Greenbush Road South
Orangeburg, NY 10962

(800) 872-1100 or (800) 237-0338 orders
(800) 237-3142 customer service
(800) 551-RODS FAX
e-mail: info@awl.com
websites: http://www.cuisenaire.com/ OR http://www.awl.com/dsp/
Cuisenaire® Rods(A,I), *Critical Thinking Activities, When Are We Ever Gonna Have to Use This?, The Everyday Science Sourcebook, Geometric Constructions and Investigations with a Mira, Image Reflector,* plus many excellent resources for math and science—(some items-C,D,F,G,H)

Curriculum Associates, Inc.
153 Rangeway Rd.
P.O. Box 2001
N. Billerica, MA 01862-0901
(800) 225-0248
(800) 366-1158 FAX
website: http://www.cahomeschool.com
e-mail: sales@cahomeschool.com
Writing Poetry (also available through Hewitt Educational Resources), Math Life-Skills series, *Solutions: Applying Problem-Solving Skills in Math*

Cygnet Press
HC12, Box 7A
116 Hwy. 28
Anthony, NM 88021
(505) 874-9121
(505) 874-3306 FAX
No Regrets (available for $15.52, postpaid, from this address), *Writing for Success*(B,D)—(E,F)

DBLM Publications
503 West Henry Ave.
Tampa, FL 33604
(813) 238-6837
A School To Come Home To—(C,D,F)

D.C. Heath and Company/Great Source
Division of Houghton Mifflin
181 Ballardvale St.
Wilmington, MA 01887
(800) 334-3284
Write Source and related books(B,C,G,H), *Geometry: An Integrated Approach, Elementary Algebra, Intermediate Algebra, College Algebra, Trigonometry.* Order teacher editions on school letterhead or provide other evidence that you are a home school.—(some items-D,F)

D.P. & K. Productions
2201 High Road
Tallahassee, FL 32303
(850) 385-1958
(850) 385-7072 FAX
Information, Please!, The Civil War(C)—(D,F,G)

Dale Seymour Publications
see Cuisenaire-Dale Seymour Publications

Dandy Lion Publications
3563 Sueldo #L
San Luis Obispo, CA 93401
Inside Stories

Davidsons Music
6727 Metcalf
Shawnee Mission, KS 66204
(913) 262-4982
(913) 722-2980 FAX
Madonna Woods piano/organ courses—(D,I)

Davis Publications, Inc.
50 Portland St.
Worcester, MA 01608
(800) 533-2847
(508) 753-3834 FAX
e-mail: davispub@aol.com
website: http://www.davis-art.com
Discover Art series(B,H), *Discovering Art History,* and specialized art texts for high school level

Debbie Cleveland
3702 N.E. Green Rd.
Claremore, OK 74055
(918) 343-9803
Spanish 1 for Homeschoolers

Design-A-Study: Resources for Creating a Custom Curriculum
by Kathryn Stout
408 Victoria Ave.
Wilmington, DE 19804
(302) 998-3889 phone and FAX
website: http://www.designastudy.com
e-mail: kathryn@designastudy.com
Comprehensive Composition, Science Scope—(B,D,F,G,H)

Diana Waring - History Alive!
122 W. Grant
Spearfish, SD 57783
(605) 642-7583
website: http://www.dianawaring.com
e-mail: diana@dianawaring.com
What in the World's Going on Here?, Getting Off the Textbook Interstate: History Via the Scenic Route, Maps and Timeline Pack, Pictorial Timechart Set One: Ancient & Bible History, Pictorial Timechart Set Two: European & American History—(B,C,D,E,F,G)

Distance Education and Training Council
1601 18th St. N.W.
Washington, DC 20009
Formerly known as National Home Study Council

EKS Publishing Co.
1029 Solano Ave., Ste. A
Albany, CA 94706-1617
(510) 558-9200
(510) 558-9255 FAX
e-mail: eks@wenet.net
The First Hebrew Primer, Teach Yourself to Read Hebrew

The Eagle's Nest Educational Supplies
1539 Oakwood Dr.
Escalon, CA 95320
(209) 838-3193
(209) 838-6747 FAX

Eastgate Publishers
4137 Primavera Rd.
Santa Barbara, CA 93110
Psychoheresy, Prophets of Psychoheresy

EdiTS
P.O. Box 7234
San Diego, CA 92167
(800) 416-1666
(619) 222-1666

Edmark Corporation
P.O. Box 97021
Redmond, WA 98073-9721
(800) 362-2890

Edmund Scientific
101 E. Gloucester Pike
Barrington, NJ 08007-1380
(609) 573-6259 for product information
(609) 573-6250 or 547-3488 for ordering
(800) 728-6999 orders

Education Associates
P.O. Box 4290
Frankfort, KY 40604
(800) 626-2950
Project Discovery

Education PLUS+
P.O. Box 1350
Taylors, SC 29687
(864) 609-5411
(864) 609-5678 FAX
e-mail info@edplus.com; Web page:
http:\\www.edplus.com
Mentoring Your Teen, Genesis 1-11, Growing in Wisdom and Stature, Etiquette–Privilege or Panic?, Etiquette PLUS. Also a source for *The Independent Study Catalog*.

Education Services
8825 Blue Mountain Dr.
Golden, CO 80403
(800) 421-6645
GENESIS, Finding Our Roots(A,C,E,F,G,H,I)

Educational Design, Inc.
345 Hudson St.
New York, NY 10014-4502
(800) 221-9372
Practicing the Writing Process 1, 2, and *4; Basic Algebra*—(B; some items-A,H)

Educational Development Corporation
P.O. Box 470663
Tulsa, OK 74147-0663
(800) 475-4522
(918) 622-4522
(918) 665-7919 FAX
U.S. distributors for the Usborne books, including *The Usborne Illustrated Dictionary of Science–Physics, Chemistry and Biology Facts*—(some items-A,B,C,D,E,F,G,H,I)

Educational Support Foundation
1523 Moritz
Houston, TX 77055
(713) 870-9194

Educators Publishing Service
31 Smith Place
Cambridge, MA 02138
(800) 225-5750
(617) 497-7779 in MA
(617) 547-0412 FAX
website: http://www.epsbooks.com
Learning Grammar through Writing, The Childs Spelling System: The Rules, Basic Language Principles with Latin Background, Wordly Wise, Reasoning and Reading, Vocabulary from Classical Roots, Writing with a Point—(some items-A,B,C,D,E,F,G,H)

Effective Educational Systems, Inc.
164 Ridgecrest Rd.
Heber Springs, AR 72543
(501) 362-0860
(800) 308-8181
e-mail: eesinc@mail.snider.net
How to Teach Your Child to Read and Spell—(C,F)

Electronic Kits International, Inc. (EKI)
178 South State St.
Orem, UT 84058
(800) 453-1708

The Elijah Company
1053 Eldridge Loop
Crossville, TN 38558-0249
(615) 456-6284
(888) 2-ELIJAH orders only
(615) 707-1601 counseling and questions
(615) 456-6384 FAX
Why So Many Christians Are Going Home to School, Keyboard Capers, WIN Program
—(F; some items-H,I)

Escondido Tutorial Service
Fritz Hinrichs
2634 Bernardo Ave.
Escondido, CA 92029
(760) 746-0980
website: http://www.gbt.org
e-mail: gbt@gbt.org
Great Books Tutorial, Geometry Tutorial, on-line classes

Essential Education
Dr. Douglas Batson
13502 Gordon Ct.
Herndon, VA 20171
(703) 318-0226
e-mail: dbatson@dgs.dgsys.com
website: http://www2.dgsys.com/~dbatson

Eternal Hearts
P.O. Box 107
Colville, WA 99114
(509) 732-4147
Rummy Roots Card Game(G,I), *More Roots*(G), *Drama Made Easy*—(B,C,D,F,H; also from Back Home Industries)

Everyday Learning Corporation
P.O. Box 812960
Chicago, IL 60681
(800) 322-MATH
(312) 541-0210

Prof. E. McSquared's Expanded Intergalactic Version! Calculus Primer, Graphing Calculator Lab Manual—(A)

Excellence in Education
2670 S. Myrtle Ave. #107
Monrovia, CA 91016
(626) 821-0025

exeGeses Bibles
Herb Jahn
P.O. Box 1776
Orange, CA 92668
(800) 9-BIBLE-9

Exploratorium Mail Order Department
3601 Lyon Street
San Francisco, CA 94123
(415) 561-0393
website: http://www.exploratorium.edu
Exploratorium Science Snackbook

Facts on File, Inc.
11 Penn Plaza
New York, NY 10001
(800) 322-8755
(212) 967-8800
(800) 678-3633 FAX
But, What If I Don't Want to Go to College?; Free Money for College; various titles on careers; *A Student's Guide to College Admissions*—(some items-B,C,E,F,G)

Fairview Publishing
P.O. Box 746
Oak View, CA 93022
(805) 640-1924
e-mail: gabriel@fishnet.net
Writing for 100 Days—(B)

Family Academy Bookstore
10013-D Shoultes Rd. #56
Marysville, WA 98270
(360) 653-0917
(360) 653-8956 FAX
e-mail: FABookstore@juno.com
High School Your Way, Homeschooling the High Schooler—(B,C,E,F)

Family Christian Press/Family Christian Academy
487 Myatt Drive
Madison, TN 37115
(800) 788-0840 catalog orders only
(615) 860-3000 school and store (main office)
(615) 860-9788 FAX
(423) 588-2106 Knoxville store
(423) 968-7182 Bristol store
(423) 875-2686 Chattanooga store
(407) 671-3343 Orlando store
(719) 574-4222 Colorado Springs store
Dallas store - contact directory assistance
e-mail: FCAPub@aol.com
A Family Guide to the Biblical Holidays, Far Above Rubies(I), and *What Your Child Needs to Know When*—(B,C,F; some items-D,G,H). Also a school service, bookstore (with multiple locations), mail-order catalog service, testing service, and publisher of the *Family Christian Academy* newsletter.

Family Foundations Publishing
P.O. Box 320
Littleton, CO 80160
(303) 797-1139
His Perfect Faithfulness: The Story of Our Courtship (F andHeppner & Heppner Construction)

The Family Learning Center
221 Long Lake Rd.
Hawthorne, FL 32640
(352) 475-5869

Family Ministries
Pastor Reb Bradley
P.O. Box 1412
Fair Oaks, CA 95628
(916) 965-7873
(916) 966-7124 FAX
(800) 545-1729 orders only
Effective Parenting of Teens, Preparing Your Children for Courtship and Marriage, Saving the Next Generation, Biblical Roles of Husbands and Wives—(F)

Family Protection Ministries
Roy Hanson
910 Sunrise Ave., Ste. A1
Roseville, CA 95661
(916) 786-3523
Comparing World Views

Family Technologies
8872 Walker Rd.
Portland, NY 14769
(716) 792-9679
Family Treasures

Farm Country General Store
Rt. 2, Box 412
Metamora, IL 61548
(800) 551-FARM
(309) 367-2844 phone and FAX
e-mail: fcgs@mtco.com
http://www.outrig.com/farmcountry

Fearon Teacher Aids
A Division of Frank Schaffer Publications
23740 Hawthorne Blvd.
P.O. Box 2853
(800) 321-3106
(614) 876-0371
Demonic Mnemonics(E,H)

FERG N US Services
P.O. Box 578-D
Richlandtown, PA 18955-0578
(610) 282-0401
(610) 282-0402 FAX
The Home Schooler's Journal, The Homeschooler's High School Journal
(A,B,C,D,E,F,G,H)

Films for Christ/Eden Communications
1044 N. Gilbert Rd.
Gilbert, AZ 85234-3304
(800) 332-2261 orders only
(602) 497-8200
The Genesis Solution, The Case for Creation, Origins series, *Creation and Time: A Report on the Progressive Creationist Book by Hugh Ross,* and *The Illustrated Origins*

Answer Book. Videos are available for rental or purchase. Purchases can be made under one of two options: home-use only viewing versions are much less expensive but are restricted to normal use within the home; church-use licensing is more expensive but covers use with classes of all types at a single church or school. Home-use videos can be licensed for church use by paying the difference in cost at a later date.

Financial Aid Information Services
5830 Haterleigh, Ste. 130
Alpharetta, GA 30005
(770) 495-0040
(800) 791-9680 FAX
Debt Free College

Fine Line Publishing
1878 Lake Shore Dr.
Romeoville, IL 60446
(815) 293-0081
Home Academy Record Book, The Planner Plus, high school diplomas

Fitness at Home
1084 Yale Farm Rd.
Romulus, NY 14541—(D)

Five in a Row Publishing
14901 Pineview Dr.
Grandview, MO 64030-4509
(816) 331-5769
Beyond Five in a Row(B,D,E,F,H)

Focus on the Family
Colorado Springs, CO 80995
(800) 232-6459 for credit card orders only
(719) 531-5181 for orders and inquiries
Citizen magazine, *Fatal Addiction, The Way They Learn*(I), *That the World May Know*—(some items-C,D,E,F,G)

Follett Home Education
5563 South Archer Avenue
Chicago, IL 60638
(800) 554-5754
(800) 638-4424 FAX

For the Layman
128 S. Fairmont Ave.
Lodi, CA 95240
(209) 368-2955—(B,F,G,H)

For Such A Time As This Ministries
James P. Stobaugh
39 West Lancaster Ave.
Downington, PA 19335
(610) 873-3768
(610) 269-6588 FAX
e-mail: JPSTOBAUGH@aol.com
SAT Preparation Course for the Christian Student, For Such A Time As This... An American Literature Critical Thinking Course

Forever His Publishing
563 S. Carr St.
Lakewood, CO 80226
(888) 418-5338
(303) 984-2120
e-mail: donna026@ix.netcom.com

Soaring Through the Internet

Foundation For American Christian Education (F.A.C.E.)
P. O. Box 9588
Chesapeake, VA 23321
(800) 352-FACE
(757) 488-6601
http://www.face.net
The Noah Plan and information and materials on the Principle Approach—(some items-D,E,G)

Fountain of Truth Publishing
3560 W. Dawson Rd.
Sedalia, CO 80135
(303) 688-6626
In The Beginning, God!: From Creation to the Middle Ages, For God So Loved the World, God Bless America—(B,F)

W.H. Freeman
Order from VHPS
175 5th Ave.
New York, NY 10010
(800) 877-5351
For All Practical Purposes: Introduction to Contemporary Mathematics, Mathematics: A Human Endeavor, Elementary Algebra, Geometry For All Practical Purposes—(C,D,F)

Frey Scientific
905 Hickory Ln.
Mansfield, OH 44905
(800) 225-FREY
(419) 589-1522 FAX

GCT, Inc.
314-350 Weinacker Ave.
P.O. Box 6448
Mobile, AL 36660-0448
(800) 476-8711
(334)460-4540 FAX
e-mail: TapesBooks@aol.com
Tapes 'n Books for Gifted Education

Gallaudet Bookstore Catalog
800 Florida Avenue N.E.
Washington, DC 20002
(202) 651-5380

Gazelle Publications
11560 Red Bud Trail
Berrien Springs, MI 49103
(616) 471-4717 phone and FAX
(800) 650-5076
e-mail: tedw@imail.com
website: http://www.hoofprint.com
The Home School Manual—(A,B,C,D,E,F,G,H,I)

GED Testing Service
American Council on Education
One Dupont Circle, Suite 250
Washington, D.C. 20036
(800) 626-9433
(202) 939-9490

General Science Service Co.
221 N.W. 2nd St.
Elbow Lake, MN 56531

(218) 685-4846
Blister Microscope and supplies

Geography Matters
P.O. Box 15855
Evansville, IN 47716
(800) 426-4650
e-mail: geomatters@earth-
link.net—(D,F,G,H)

Globe Fearon Educational Publishers
P.O. Box 2649
Columbus, OH 43216
(800) 848-9500
*Newspaper Workshop, Writing for Life,
Look It Up, Get That Job!, Earth Science
Workshop, Chemistry Workshop, Physical
Science Workshop*—(some items-E)

God's World Publications
P. O. Box 2330
Asheville, NC 28802-2330
(800) 951-5437
(704) 253-1556 FAX
Weekly newspapers plus *World* magazine

Golden Owl Publishing/Jackdaw Publications
P.O. Box 503
Amawalk, NY 10501
(800) 789-0022 orders only
(914) 962-6911
(914) 962-0034 FAX
Picture the Middle Ages, Jackdaw Portfolios and *Study Guides*—(C,G)

Good Apple
A Division of Frank Schaffer Publications
23740 Hawthorne Blvd.
P.O. Box 2853
Torrance, CA 90509-2853
(800) 421-5565
(800) 837-7260 FAX
*Our Living Constitution Then and
Now*(G,I), *Getting Smarter*—(A,B,C,E,H)

Good Year Books
1900 East Lake Avenue
Glenview, IL 60025
(800) 628-4480, ext. 3038
The Complete Science Fair Handbook(A,B,I), *Reading for Survival in Today's Society*—(some items-H)

Gordon School of Art
P.O. Box 28208
Green Bay, WI 54324-8208
(800) 210-1220
e-mail: gordon@netnet.net.
website: http://www.newmasters.com
Young Masters Home Study Art Program

Gospel Light Publications
2300 Knoll Drive
Ventura, CA 93003
(800) 4GOSPEL
*Community Impact Seminar Series, Not
Worth Living?*—(D)

The Grammar Key
P.O. Box 33230
Tulsa, OK 74153

(800) 4800-KEY—(B)

Great Books and Gifts
9797 W. Colfax #3SS
Lakewood, CO 80215
(303) 274-0680
(303) 274-0288 FAX

Great Christian Books
P.O. Box 8000
229 S. Bridge St.
Eltkon, MD 21922-8000
(800) 775-5422
(410) 392-8842 FAX

Great Source
See D.C. Heath for ordering

Greek 'n' Stuff
P.O. Box 882
Moline, IL 61265-0882
(309) 796-2707
e-mail: timohs@earthlink.net
website: http://home.earthlink.net/~timohs/
Hey, Andrew!! Teach me some Greek!(I)

Greenleaf Press and Greenleaf Publishing
3761 Highway 109N., Unit D
Lebanon, TN 37087
(800) 311-1508 orders only
(615) 449-1617
(615) 449-4018 FAX
e-mail: greenleafp@aol.com
website: www.greenleafpress.com
Greenleaf Guides—(A,B,C,D,E,F,G,H)

Grove Publishing/Home Run Enterprises
16172 Huxley Circle
Westminster, CA 92683
(714) 841-1220
(714) 841-5584 FAX
website: http://www.jatec.com/grove
*Christian Home Educators' Curriculum
Manuals, Government Nannies, Teaching
World Views, Goals 2000 and School-to-
Work, Hot House Transplants, Learning
Styles*—(some items-A,B,C,D,E,F,G,H,I)

Hammond, Inc.
515 Valley St.
Maplewood, NJ 07040
(201) 763-6000
Map skills workbooks, Bible atlas, "history
through maps" series plus teachers
guides—(some items-I)

Harcourt Brace and Compnay
Order from Holt, Rinehart and Winston/Harcourt Brace and Company
Harcourt Brace and Company acquired
Holt, Rinehart and Winston in 1986. Holt,
Rinehart and Winston will specialize in the
materials for secondary schools, while HB
will specialize in elementary level resources. The imprint on upper level HB
books will change with future printings. Titles published originally by HB are *Elements of Writing*(A), *Speech for Effective
Communication, Confidence in Writing*, vocabulary workbooks for high school, *Harbrace College Handbook*.—(some
items-C,D)

Harmony Media, Inc.
683 Glatt Circle
Woodburn, OR 97071
(503) 982-7675
(888) 427-6334
(503) 982-7833 FAX
e-mail: harmonymed@aol.com
Welcome to the Catholic Church

HarperCollins Publishers
Direct Mail Department
1000 Keystone Industrial Park
Scranton, PA 18512-4621
(800) 331-3761
(800) 822-4090 FAX
*Intellectuals, Modern Times, Wheelock's
Latin, Workbook for Wheelock's
Latin*—(some items-D,E)

Harry N. Abrams, Inc.
100 Fifth Avenue
New York, NY 10011
(800) 345-1359 (ask for trade sales department)
(212) 206-7715
History of Art and *History of Art for Young
People*(G)—(C,F)

Harvest House Publishers
1075 Arrowsmith
Eugene, OR 97402
(800) 547-8979
(541) 343-0123
(541) 342-6410 FAX
*The Islamic Invasion, Great Books of the
Christian Tradition, Christian Charm, Man
in Demand*—(H)(some items -
A,C,D,E,F,G,I)

Hearthside Homeschool Helps
74 Lynn Dr.
Woodbury, NJ 08096
(609) 845-3681 phone and fax
e-mail: hearthside@juno.com

Heppner & Heppner Construction
Box 7, 305 Lake St. N.E.
Warroad, MN 56763-0007
(800) 257-1994
(218) 386-1994

Heritage Institute Ministries
P.O. Box 1353
Buzzards Bay, MA 02532
Heritage resources all sold through Landmark Distributors

**Hewitt Home Schooling Resources/Hewitt
Research Foundation**
P.O. Box 9
Washougal, WA 98671
(800) 348-1750
(360) 835-8708
(360) 835-8697 FAX
School service, and source for learning materials: *Studying Poetry, One Of The Few:
Toward Christian Womanhood*—(some
items-D)

Hideaway Ventures
HC 68 Box 20
Westerville, NE 68881

(800) 774-3447
e-mail: hideaway@juno.com
Friendly Chemistry(I)

Highland Books
See Holly Hall Publications which is the
parent company
*Never Give In, The Patriot's Hand-
book*—(D,F)

Hillside Academy
1804 Melody Lane
Burnsville, MN 55337
(612) 895-0220
Lessons from History—(A,B,F,G)

Hirst
P.O. Box 914
Marshall, VA 20116
(540) 364-3245
Free for the Asking

HIS Publishing Company
1732 NE 3 Avenue
Ft. Lauderdale, FL 33305
(954) 764-4567
(954) 768-9313 FAX
The Simplicity of Homeschooling(F)

The Hoffman Center
P.O. Box 231087
Montgomery, AL 36123
(334) 272-8846
The Education of James Madison—(F)

Holly Hall Publications
255 S. Bridge St.
P.O. Box 254
Elkton, MD 21922-0254
(888) 669-4693 wholesale orders
(410) 392-5554 customer service
(410) 392-0354 FAX
*Unit Study Guides, Writing to God's
Glory*—(A,D,E,F,H; some items-C,I). Parent
company for Highland Books, Full Quart
Press, and Homeschool Press.

**Holt Associates/John Holt's Book and Music
Store**
2269 Massachusetts Ave.
Cambridge, MA 02140
(617) 864-3100
(617) 864-9235 FAX
Growing Without Schooling magazine, *And
What About College?*(C)

**Holt, Rinehart and Winston/Harcourt Brace
and Company**
National Customer Service Center
6277 Sea Harbor Dr.
Orlando, FL 32827
(800) 225-5425 orders only
(800) 874-6418 FAX
(800) 544-6678 customer relations
(407) 826-5070 in Florida
*Vocabulary Workshop, Vocabulary for Col-
lege, Warriner's High School Handbook*(C),
Elements of Writing. Homeschoolers can
purchase teacher's editions and answer keys
and also purchase at discounted school
prices by supplying some proof that they are
indeed a home school (e.g., copy of your af-

fidavit, letter from school district, or letter
from home school organization).—(some
items-E)

Home and Hearth
2604 106 Ave. S.W.
Calgary, AB T2W 2J1, Canada
(403) 281-9644
(403) 281-5229 FAX

The Home Computer Market
P.O. Box 385377
Bloomington, MN 55438
(612) 844-0462
http://www.homecomputermarket.com
The Homeschooler's Computer Guide

Home Education Magazine
P.O. Box 1083
Tonasket, WA 98855
(800) 236-3278
e-mail: HomeEdMag@aol.com

Home Life
P.O. Box 1250
Fenton, MO 63026
(314) 343-7750
(800) 346-6322 orders only
e-mail: phscustsvc@aol.com
website: http://www.home-school.com
Practical Homeschooling magazine, source
for any of Mary Pride's books

The Home School Books and Supplies
104 S. West Ave.
Arlington, WA 98223
(360) 435-0376
(800) 788-1221 orders only
(360) 435-1028 FAX
http://www.thehomeschool.com

The Home School Exchange
P.O. Box 1378
Boerne, TX 78006
(800) 894-8247
(830) 336-3105 FAX
e-mail: HSXchange@aol.com
website: http://mem-
bers.aol.com/HSXchange/index.html

**Home School Legal Defense Association
(HSLDA)**
Box 3000
Purcellville, VA 20134
or 17333 Pickwick Dr.
Purcellville, VA 20132
(540) 338-5600
(540) 338-2733 FAX
website: http://www.hslda.org
Constitutional Law(C,D,F), *Where Do I
Draw the Line?*(D,F), *Debate Video Set, An
Introduction to Argumentation and Debate*,
information on home education, diplomas,
and legal protection

Home School Resource Center
1425 E. Chocolate Ave.
Hershey, PA 17033
(717) 533-1669
(800) 937-6311 orders only
website: http://www.hsrc.com
e-mail: hsrc@hsrc.com

Home Study International
P.O. Box 4437
Silver Spring, MD 20914-4437
(800) 782-4769
(301) 680-6570
e-mail: 74617.74@compuserve.com

Home Training Tools
2827 Buffalo Horn Dr.
Laurel, MT 59044
(800) 860-6272
(406) 628-6454 FAX

The Home Works
1760 Groves Rd., P.O. Box 340
Russell, Ontario K4R 1E1
(613) 445-3142
(613) 445-0587 FAX
e-mail: homework@magma.ca
website: http://www.home-
school.com/mall/how/how/html

HomeQuest
757 South Main
P.O. Box 887
Springville, UT 84663
(800) 511-0084
(801) 489-0222
(801) 489-9290 FAX
Tomorrow's Promise, Lifetime Library

Homeschool Press
Order through Holly Hall Publications
*Homeschool Guide to the Online World,
Time Minder File-a-Plan, Homeschool
Guide to The Internet*, Unit Study Adven-
tures series.—(E,F; some items-C,I)

Homeschool Seminars & Publications
182 No. Columbia Heights Rd.
Longview, WA 98632
(360) 577-1245
(360) 423-4912
BEShelton@aol.com
*Lab Science: The How, Why, What, Who, 'n'
Where Book; Senior High: A Home-
Designed Form+U+la*—(B,C,E,F)

Homeschooling Today magazine
P.O. Box 1608
Ft. Collins, CO 80522-1608
phone calls are handled by ProServices -
(954) 962-1930

Homespun Tapes, Ltd.
Box 694, Dept. CHE
Woodstock, NY 12498
(800) 338-2737
(914) 679-7832
(914) 246-5282 FAX

Homestead Learning
P.O. Box 604
Lionville, PA 19353
(610) 524-2046
Classical Music Start-Up Kit. They have a
catalog of homeschooling resources, most of
them for younger children.

Houghton Mifflin
See McDougal Littell/Houghton Mifflin

Houston Baptist University
Judie Smelser, Director, Office of Admissions
7502 Fondren Road
Houston, TX 77074-3298
(800) 969-3210
(281) 649-3211
(713) 649-3217 FAX

How Great Thou ART
10802 Bishopville Rd.
P.O. Box 211
Bishopville, MD 21813
(410) 352-3319
Feed My Sheep(B,F,G)

Huntington House Publishers
P.O. Box 53788
Lafayette, LA 70505
(800) 749-4009
One Year to a College Degree, In His Majesty's Service—(C,D,I)

ICS Newport/Pacific High School
925 Oak St.
Scranton, PA 18515
(800) 238-9525, extension 7512
website: http://www.icslearn.com

Ignatius Press
Distribution Center
P.O. Box 1339
Ft. Collins, CO 80522
(800) 651-1531 credit card orders only
(970) 221-3920 information or orders
(970) 221-3964 FAX
website: http://www.ignatius.com
Catholic Education: Homeward Bound

IN-A-FLASH
2400 Josephine St.
Pittsburgh, PA 15203
(412) 481-7281
SAT I IN-A-FLASH Flash Card Deck, ACT IN-A-FLASH Flash Card Deck, PSAT IN-A-FLASH Flash Card Deck

Institute for Creation Research
museum and offices:
10946 Woodside Avenue North
Santee, CA 92071
(619) 448-0900
orders:
P.O. Box 2667
El Cajon, CA 92021
(800) 628-7640
(619) 448-3469 FAX
website: http://www.icr.org

Institute for Study of the Liberal Arts and Sciences (ISLAS)
3 Nellis Terrace
Bedford, MA 01731
(781) 274-0004
(781) 274-9030 FAX
website: http://www.islas.org
e-mail: admissions@islas.org
Scholars' Online Academy (SOLA), Regina Coeli Academy (SOLA)

Instructional Fair
P.O. Box 1650

Grand Rapids, MI 49501
(800) 253-5469
The Human Body—(D,G,I)

International Learning Systems
1000 112th Circle North, Ste. 100
St. Petersburg, FL 33716
(800) 321-8322
(813) 576-8833
(813) 576-8832 FAX
Winning—(A,D,E,H)

International Linguistics Corporation
3505 East Red Bridge
Kansas City, MO 64137
(800) 237-1830
The Learnables—(B,D)

International Society for General Semantics
P.O. Box 728
Concord, CA 94522
(510) 798-0311
(510) 798-0312 FAX
e-mail: isgs@a.crl.com
website: http://www.crl.com/~isgs/isg-shome.html
How to Write Clearly, also available through Bluestocking Press

Inter-Varsity Christian Fellowship of the U.S.A.
P.O. Box 7895
Madison, WI 53707-7895
(800) 828-2100
e-mail: 2100ord@ivcf.org
website: http://www.ivcf.org/mmcp/
The Search, also available from Films for Christ.

InterVarsity Press
P.O. Box 1400
Downers Grove, IL 60515
(800) 843-9487
(630) 887-2500
(630) 887-2520 FAX
Know Why You Believe, Between Heaven & Hell, Reason in the Balance, The Universe Next Door, The Universe Upstairs, Darwin on Trial, Politics for the People, Defeating Darwinism—(some items-C,D,F)

Intrepid Books
P.O. Box 22614
Sacramento, CA 95822-0614
(916) 684-1530 phone and FAX
e-mail: intrepid@ips.net
America's Christian History: Christian Self-Government(A,B,F)

ISHA Enterprises, Inc.
P.O. Box 12520
Scottsdale, AZ 85267
(800) 641-6015
Easy Grammar(C), *Daily Grams*(C), and *Easy Writing*. Send SASE for free brochure.—(A,B,D,E,F,G,H,I)

Jeremiah Films
P.O. Box 1710
Hemet, CA 92546
(800) 828-2290
(909) 925-6460

(909) 652-5848 FAX
e-mail: jeremiah@pe.net
Gods of the New Age, The Evolution Conspiracy, The Pagan Invasion, and other videos—(some items-D)

Jeremy P. Tarcher, Inc./Putnam Publishers
200 Madison Ave.
New York, NY 10016
(800) 788-6262
(212) 951-8581
Drawing on the Right Side of the Brain(I), *Drawing with Children*(C,G,H), *In Their Own Way*(C,G)—(B,E,F)

JIST Works, Inc.
720 North Park Ave.
Indianapolis, IN 46202-3431
(800) 648-5478
(800) 547-8329 FAX

John Eidsmoe
2648 Pine Acres
Pike Road, AL 36064
(334) 270-1789
Institute on the Constitution, Christian Action for the 1990s, Current Issues in Biblical Perspective

John Wiley and Sons, Inc.
Distribution Center]
1 Wiley Dr.
Somerset, NJ 08875-1272
(800) 225-5945
(732) 469-4400
(732) 302-2300 FAX
How to Earn a College Degree Without Going to College(C,G), *Geometry and Trigonometry for Calculus, The Complete Handbook of Science Fair Projects, College Online, The Exploratorium Science Snackbook* series(A)—(some items-D,E)

Jump! Music
201 San Antonio Circle, Ste. 172
Mountain View, CA 94040
(650) 917-7460
(650) 917-7490 FAX
e-mail: info@jumpmusic.com
website: http://www.jumpmusic.com
Piano Discovery

June Whatley
10471 Pine Meadow Dr.
Tuscaloosa, AL 35405
(205) 345-3613
Will My Child Fit?—(F)

K.T. Productions
P.O. Box 1203
Menomonee Falls, WI 53051
(414) 251-3563
Home School Helper

Kaw Valley Video Sales and Rentals
15819 W. 127th Terrace
Olathe, KS 66062
(913) 791-3812 voice mail

Ken Fast Productions
531 1220 8th Ave. N.E.
Calgary, Alberta T2E 0S6, Canada

(403) 830-5548 business/cellular
(403) 277-7674 home/FAX
Dr. William Coulson on Education

Kenndon, Krastins & Gould
The Camelot General Chemistry Primer(A,H)

Key Curriculumm Press
P.O. Box 2304
Berkeley, CA 94702
(800) 338-7638
(800) 541-2442 FAX
Key To... math series (A,B,D,E,F,G,H,I and Activity Resources), *Discovering Geometry, Geometer's Sketchpad*

Keyboard Enterprises
5200 Heil, #32
Huntington Beach, CA 92649
(714) 840-8004
Algebra on Video Tape

Keystone National High School
School House Station
420 W. 5th St.
Bloomsburg, PA 17815
(717) 784-5220
(717) 784-2129 FAX
e-mail: kschool@mail.prolog.net
website: http://keystone.ptd.net

KidsArt
P.O. Box 274
Mt. Shasta, CA 96067
(916) 926-5076
website: http://www.kidsart.com
—(some items-I)

KidsWay, Inc.
5585 Peachtree Rd.
Chamblee, GA 30341
(888) KIDSWAY
Young Entrepreneur

Alfred A. Knopf
Knopf books are ordered through Random House—(some items-C,D,E,F,G)

Knowledge Products
P.O. Box 305151
Nashville, TN 37230
(800) 876-4332
The Giants of Political Thought, The Great Economic Thinkers, The Giants of Philosophy, The United States Constitution, The United States at War. Order from Bluestocking Press.

KONOS Character Curriculum
P.O. Box 250
Anna, TX 75409
(972) 924-2712
e-mail: info@konos.com
KONOS History of the World(I), *Electing America's Leaders*—(F)

LW Scientific, Inc.
4727 N. Royal Atlanta Dr., Ste. G
Tucker, GA 30084
(800) 726-7345
website: http://www.lw-scientific.com

Discovery and *Explorer* microscopes(E,F,I)

L'Abri Fellowship Foundation
1465 N.E. 12th Ave.
Rochester, MN 55906
(507) 282-3292

Laguna Beach Educational Books
245 Grandview
Laguna Beach, CA 92651
(714) 494-4225
Beginner's Writers Manual—(F,I)

Landmark Distributors
P.O. Box 849
Fillmore, CA 93016
(805) 524-3263
(805) 524-7222 FAX
e-mail: landmark@jps.net
website: http://www.jps.net/landmark
Creative Writing and the Essay for the Beginner; English Grammar; God, Man, and Law: The Biblical Principles; A Guide to Teaching Grammar Using The Principle Approach; Teaching the Law; Principles of Economics; The Christian and Politics; Christian Discipline

Landmark Edition, Inc.
P.O. Box 270169
Kansas City, MO 64127
(816) 241-4919
Written and Illustrated by...(G)

Landmark's Freedom Baptist Curriculum
2222 East Hinson Ave.
Haines City, FL 33844-4902
(800) 700-LFBC
(813) 421-2937

Learning Enrichment Games
111 Merrywood Lane, Valley View Estates
San Marcos, TX 78666
(512) 353-2833
Spell-N-Meld and *Operations*

Learning Potentials Publishers, Inc.
230 West Main St.
Lewisville, TX 75057
(972) 221-2564
(800) 437-7976
e-mail: klane@123go.com
Developing Your Child for Success—(B,F)

Learning Services
P.O. Box 10636
3895 E. 19th Ave.
Eugene, OR 97440-2636
(800) 877-WEST
(800) 877-EAST
(541) 744-2056 FAX

LEGO Dacta, mail order product information:
555 Taylor Road
Enfield, CT 06083
(800) 527-8339
OR
P.O. Box 1707
Pittsburg, KS 66762
(800) 362-4308

Ask for free brochure on the educational *Technic* sets. You may also request a list of LEGO dealers in your area. Educational *Technic* sets are available from Nasco and other distributors.

Leroy Shultz
P.O. Box 67222
Lincoln, NE 68506
(402) 489-3386
Progressive Gospel Piano

Lewis Educational Games
P.O. Box 727
Goddard, KS 67052
(800) 557-8777
ElementO(G)

Libertatis Causa
536 Crestridge Rd.
Omaha, NE 68154
(402) 333-6079
This business should be moving to Long Pine, NE in Spring of 1998.
Come Let Us Reason(C)

Liberty Bookstore/East Moline Christian School
900 46th Avenue
East Moline, IL 61244
(309) 796-1485
Foundations of Liberty

Liberty Tree Review and Catalogue
The Independent Institute
100 Swan Way
Oakland, CA 94621
(800) 927-8733

Liberty University
External Degree Program
1971 University Blvd.
Lynchburg, VA 24502
(800) 332-1883
(804) 582-2000

Library and Educational Services
8784 Valley View Dr.
P.O. Box 146
Berrien Springs, MI 49103
(616) 471-1400

Life Pathways
P.O. Box 1476
Gainesville, GA 30503
(770) 534-1000

Lifetime Books and Gifts
Bob and Tina Farewell
3900 Chalet Suzanne Ln.
Lake Wales, FL 33853-7763
(800) 377-0390 orders only
(941) 676-6311

Lifetime Canada
R.R. 6
Markdale, Ontario, Canada N0C 1H0
(519) 986-4686

Lightsource Editing Service
The Kustusch Family
6064 North Paulina

Chicago, IL 60660-2308
(773) 743-3625
e-mail: Editnow4u@aol.com

Ligonier Ministries
400 Technology Park, Ste. 150
Lake Mary, FL 32746
(800) 435-4343
Choosing My Religion, The Holiness of God, Battle for Our Minds, A Blueprint for Thinking, Introductory Logic, Tabletalk, Ultimate Issues, What Is Truth? —(some items-D)

Linda Bullock
444 Oriole Circle
Clarksville, TN 37043
(615) 647-3986
Listen, My Son—(B,C,F,G)

Linda Howe
4187 Bernardo Court
Chino, CA 91710
(909) 628-9441
Learning disabilities/perceptual-motor consultant

Linnet Books
2 Linsley St.
North Haven, CT 06473
(203) 239-2702
(203) 239-2568 FAX
Who Talks Funny?

Literacy Unlimited
P.O. Box 278
Medina, WA 98039-0278
(425) 454-5830
(425) 450-0141
e-mail: joegilkl@aol.com
English from the Roots Up(G,H): *Help for Reading, Writing, Spelling and S.A.T. Scores*—(A,B,C,D,E,F)

Little Brown and Company
3 Center Plaza
Boston, MA 02108
(617) 227-0730
(800) 759-0190
Source for Warner Books titles—*The Synonym Finder, Homeschooling for Excellence,* and *Smart But Feeling Dumb*—(some items -A,C,D,E,F,H)

Little River Press
P.O. Box 1756
Buford, GA 30515
(757) 865-8652
(770) 271-2967 FAX
Visual Vocabulary(B,F,H)

Logos Language Institute
P.O. Box 55
Belton, TX 76513
(800) 44L-OGOS
(254) 939-6343 FAX
Logos. Send for free brochure. A self-addressed, stamped envelope is appreciated.—(H)

Lowry House Publishers
P.O. Box 1014

Eugene, OR 97440-1014
(541) 686-2315
(541) 343-3158 FAX
website: http://home.aol.com/GTcatalog
Real Lives, The Teenage Liberation Handbook. Also available from Holt Associates.

Lyrical Learning
8008 Cardwell Hill
Corvallis, OR 97330
(541) 754-3579
(800) 761-0906
Lyrical Life Science(B,F,H)

Glencoe/McGraw-Hill
P.O. Box 544
Blacklick, OH 43004-0544
(800) 334-7344
Merrill publications, *Responsible Driving, Technology Education catalog,* vocational education books

Macmillan/McGraw-Hill—School Division
220 East Danieldale Rd.
DeSoto, TX 75115
(800) 442-9685
Basic Goals in Spelling (also sold by many teacher supply stores). Teacher's editions must be ordered on school letterhead or the order must be accompanied by an affidavit or other proof that the order is from a school. This address is for Macmillan and McGraw-Hill school books for grades K-8.

Mailbox Club Books
404 Eager Road
Valdosta, GA 31602
(800) 488-5226 orders only
(912) 244-6812
(912) 245-8977 FAX
e-mail: mailboxclb@aol.com
Love, Dating and Sex: What Teens Want to Know, Understanding Your Sex Drive, Peer Pressure, Love and Dating, supplemental audio cassettes

Manas Systems
P. O. Box 5153
Fullerton, CA 92635
(714) 870-4355
(714) 870-6970 FAX
Learning Patterns and Temperament Styles(B,F,G,H). Source for *Please Understand Me.*

Mantle Ministries
Richard "Little Bear" Wheeler
228 Still Ridge
Bulverde, TX 78163
(210) 438-3777
(210) 438-3370 FAX
e-mail: mantle3377@aol.com—(A,D,E,F; some items-B)

Maranatha Publications, Inc.
P.O. Box 1799
Gainesville, FL 32602
(352) 375-6000
The Story of Liberty, Story of Liberty Study Guide, Sweet Land of Liberty—(A,B,C,D,E,F,G; some items-H)

Marcia Neill
4790 Irvine Blvd., Ste. 170-286
Irvine, CA 92620
(714) 730-9114 phone and FAX
e-mail: SMAcademy@aol.com
Catholic World History Timeline and Guide

Master Book Publishers
P.O. Box 727
Green Forest, AR 72638
(800) 999-3777
Creation-science books for adults and children, including *Origins: Creation or Evolution*(B,H); *Men of Science, Men of God*(B,C,F,H,I); *Facts and Bias: Creation vs. Evolution—Two World Views in Conflict; Answers in Genesis; The Modern Creation Trilogy*—(F; some items-A,D,E,G)

The Master's Academy of Fine Arts/The Master's Press
3571 Baywater Trail
Snellville, GA 30278
(770) 978-6324
Rebirth and Reformation, History by the Book!

Math Teachers Press
5100 Gamble Dr., Ste. 375
Minneapolis, MN 55416
(800) 852-2435
(612) 545-6535
(612) 546-7502 FAX
Moving with Math. Tell them you are a home educator when you write or call so they give you correct ordering information.

Math-U-See
1378 River Road
Drumore, PA 17518
(717) 548-4946 FAX
from California, order from Math in Motion (address above).(B,H)

Maupin House Publishing
P.O. Box 90148
Gainesville, FL 32607
(800) 524-0634
(352) 373-5546 FAX
e-mail: jgraddy@maupinhouse.com
Caught'ya!, Caught'ya Again!

Mayflower Institute
P.O. Box 4673
Thousand Oaks, CA 91359
(805) 523-0072
Marshall Foster presents seminars on topics related to America's Christian history for which audio and video cassettes are available. The Institute publishes *The American Covenant, The Untold Story*(B,C,D,E) and sells this and other titles, including *Christian Home Learning Guides. The American Covenant* is also available from Foundation for American Christian Education and American Christian History Institute.

McDougal Littell/Houghton Mifflin
for orders from the Southwest, Southeast, and Pacific regions:
13400 Midway Rd.

Dallas, TX 75244
for orders from the Midwest and Northeast:
1900 S. Batavia
Geneva, IL 60134
from Canada:
1120 Birchmont Rd.
Scarborough, Ontario M1K 5G4
(800) 733-2828
(800) 733-2098 FAX from U.S.
(800) 268-2222 from Canada
Cultural Literacy(C), *Peterson's Field Guides*(C,I), foreign language and math texts, *Career Math, Basic Geometry, Advanced Mathematics: A Precalculus Course, Writing: Process to Product, English* series, and *Riverside Spelling.* (Some items-D,E,F) When ordering directly from the publisher, teacher's editions must be ordered on school letterhead or the order must be accompanied by an affidavit or other proof that the order is from a school. CAUTION: Their company policy varies from state to state, but in a number of states, your name and address will be forwarded to the local school district when you place an order for teacher's editions and/or answer keys. Since they cannot guarantee confidentiality, make sure this is not a problem for you before ordering. Supplying verification is not necessary when ordering from home school suppliers, although they generally cannot provide teacher's editions.

McGraw Hill
220 E. Danieldale Rd.
DeSoto, TX 75115
(800) 843-8855
Scoring High series(G,I), *Prescriptive Spelling*(H)

McGuffey Academy International and McGuffey Testing Service
P.O. Box 109
Lakemount, GA 30552
(706) 782-7709
Correspondence course and testing service

McJake Enterprises
110 Leckford Way
Cary, NC 27513
(919) 469-1229
e-mail: Karenncary@aol.com
website: http://members.aol.com/mmaddry/
Great Books Guides

Media Angels Science
16450 S. Tamiami Trail, Suite 3
Ft. Myers, FL 33908
e mail: whitlock@sprynet.com OR MediAngels@aol.com
website: http://www.noahzark.com
Creation Science: A Study Guide to Creation!, Creation Geology, Creation Astronomy, Creation Anatomy, Science Fair Project Handbook, Teaching Science and Having Fun!—(D,E,F,G,H,I; some items-A)

Media Mailers
P.O. Box 44
Great Bend, KS 67530
(888) 792-4445
Of Knights and Fair Maidens(A,D,F)

MEMLOK/PC Memlok Bible Memory System
Drake Mariani
420 E. Montwood Avenue
La Habra, CA 90631
(800) 373-1947
(714) 738-0949 phone and FAX
e-mail: memlok@pacbell.net
website: http://www.memlok.com
(A,B,C,D,G,H)

Meridian Creative Group
5178 Station Rd.
Erie, PA 16510-4636
(800) 695-9427
(814) 898-2612
(800) 530-9968 FAX
website: http://www.home.meridiancg.com
The Mathematics of Everyday Living series

Merrill Publishing Company
Order Merrill titles from Glencoe/McGraw-Hill.
Algebra Essentials, Informal Geometry, Advanced Mathematical Concepts, Pre-Calculus Mathematics, Applications of Mathematics. (Use ISBN numbers listed within each review.)—(some items-E)

Michelle Van Loon
2833 Lincolnshire Ct.
Waukesha, WI 53188
(414) 542-2998
e-mail: wvanloon@worldnet.att.net
From Heart to Page

Modern Curriculum Press
4350 Equity Dr.
P.O. Box 2649
Columbus, OH 43216
(800) 321-3106
(614) 771-7362 FAX
website: http://www.mcschool.com
Spelling Workout(A,B,D,H)

Modern Signs Press, Inc.
P.O. Box 1181
Los Alamitos, CA 90720
(562) 596-8548 regular phone or TDD for hearing impaired (same number)
(562) 795-6614 FAX
Signing Exact English

Montgomery Institute
P.O. Box 532
Boise, ID 83701
(208) 888-2315 phone and FAX

Moody Press
820 North LaSalle Drive
Chicago, IL 60610
(312) 329-2102
(312) 329-2144 FAX
The Coming Economic Earthquake, Finding the Career That Fits You, More Than Conquerors(B), *Seven Men Who Rule the World from the Grave*(A,B,C), *Surviving the 90's Economy, Your Career in Changing Times*—(D,F)

The Moore Foundation
Dr. Raymond and Dorothy Moore

Box 1
Camas, WA 98607
(360) 835-5500
(360) 835-5392 FAX
e-mail: moorefnd@pacifier.com
website: http://www.caslink.com/moore-foundation
Moore Foundation Curriculum Programs, Dr. Raymond and Dorothy Moore's books(C,D,I), the *Moore-McGuffey Readers*(B,D,I), *The Moore Report International*

Mortensen Math/V.J. Mortensen Company
P.O. Box 98
Hayden, ID 83835
(800) 475-8748
(208) 765-1974
(208) 667-9438 FAX
e-mail: request@mortensenmathdirect.com
website: http://www.mortensenmthdirect.com
Mortensen Math. Write or call for location of local distributors.

Mott Media
1000 East Huron
Milford, MI 48381
(800) 421-6645
(248) 685-8773
(248) 685-8776 FAX
Sower series biographies(A,B,C,G), *Original Mott McGuffey Readers*(A,I), *Harvey's Grammar*—(D,E,F,H)

Moving with Math
See Math Teachers Press.

Nadeau Testing and Treatment Clinic (Dr. Ray Nadeau)
11060 Artesia Blvd., Ste. D
Cerritos, CA 90703
(800) 462-READ

Nasco
901 Janesville Ave.
Fort Atkinson, WI 53538
(800) 558-9595

NATHHAN
Main Office
5383 Alpine Rd. S.E.
Olalla, WA 98359
(206) 857-4257
(206) 857-7764 FAX
newsletter/membership

National Academy for Child Development/N.A.C.D.
Robert J. Doman, Jr.
P.O. Box 380
Huntsville, UT 84317-0380
(801) 621-8606—(D)
website: www.nacd.org

National Association for College Admissions Counseling
1631 Prince St.
Alexandria, VA 22314-2818
(703) 836-2222
(703) 836-8015 FAX
website: http://www.nacac.com

National Association of Secondary School Principals
P.O. Box 3250
Reston, VA 20195-1250
(800) 253-7746
The Test-Taking Advantage

National Center for Constitutional Studies
HC 61 Box 1056
Malta, ID 83342
(800) 388-4512
American Freedom Library, The Five Thousand Year Leap; The Making of America: The Substance and Meaning of the Constitution; The Federalist Papers; Two Good and Noble Men; The Anti-Federalist Papers and the Constitutional Convention Debates; The Real Thomas Jefferson; The Real Benjamin Franklin; The Real George Washington; Soldiers, Statesmen, and Heroes; A More Perfect Union: America Becomes A Nation(A)—(some items-C,E)

National Gallery of Art
Department of Education Resources
Extension Programs Section
Washington, DC 20565
(202) 842-6263

National Geographic Magazine
P.O. Box 30661
Tampa, FL 33630
(800) 647-5463

National Geographic Society
Attn. Educational Services
P.O. Box 10597
Des Moines, IA 50340
(800) 368-2728
Special books for science, Exploring Your World-The Adventure of Geography

National Home Education Research Institute (NHERI)
P.O. Box 13939
Salem, OR 97309
(503) 364-1490
(503) 364-2827 FAX
e-mail: mail@nheri.org
website: http://www.nheri.org
Strengths of Their Home

National Homeschool Association
P.O. Box 290
Hartland, MI 48353-0290
(513) 772-9580 voice mail

National Institute for Learning Disabilities (NILD)
107 Seekel St.
Norfolk, VA 23505
(757) 423-8646
(757) 451-0970 FAX

National Public-policy Resource Theme-packets
1733 Lancaster Rd.
Manheim, PA 17545
(717) 665-3397

National Textbook Company
A Division of NTC Publishing Group

4255 W. Touhy Ave.
Lincolnwood, IL 60646-1975
(800) 323-4900
(847) 679-2494 FAX
Contemporary Books source, foreign language catalog, materials for debate, speech, drama, and journalism—(some items-E)

National Writing Institute
7946 Wright Road
Niles, MI 49120
(616) 684-5375
Speech and Interpersonal Communication, Writing Strands(C,I), *Writing Exposition, Reading Strands*—(A,B,D,E,F,G,H)

Nature's Workshop, Plus!
P.O. Box 220
Pittsboro, IN 46167-0220
(888) 393-5663

NavPress
P.O. Box 9099
Oxnard, CA 93031
(800) 366-7788
(800) 860-3109 FAX orders
Facing the Facts: The Truth About Sex and You, Creation and Time—(D,F)

NavPress Software
1934 Rutland Dr., Ste. 500
Austin, TX 78758
(800) 888-9898
Wordsearch—(D)

Nehemiah Institute
1323 No. 3rd St.
Aberdeen, SD 57401
(800) 948-3101
(605) 229-4090
PEERS Testing

New Creation Music
11475 Foxhaven Dr.
Chesterland, OH 44026
(800) 337-4798
(440) 729-8288
(440) 729-2902 FAX
e-mail: ncmc@newcreationmusic.com
website: http://www.newcreationmusic.com

New Society Publishers
P.O. Box 189
Gabriola Island, B.C. V0R 1X0, Canada
(604) 247-9737
Dumbing Us Down(C,F). Also available from Holt Associates.

Newport Publishers
100 North Lake Ave., Ste. 203
Pasadena, CA 91101-1883
(800) 579-5532
(626) 796-4027
(626) 796-7588 FAX
Children's Classics Library, Family Classics Library

Noah Webster Educational Foundation
Belinda Beth Ballenger
849 East Stanley
Livermore, CA 94550
(510) 447-5692

(510) 447-1828 FAX
George Washington Study Guide, audio tapes

Noble Publishing Associates
710 Northeast Cleveland, Ste. 170
Gresham, OR 97030
(800) 225-5259
(503) 667-5084
(503) 618-8866 FAX
e-mail: Noblebooks@aol.com
The Christian Family Complete Household Organizer, From Playpen to Podium, Noble Planner, Help! My Teenager Wants to Drive!!!(I), *I Kissed Dating Goodbye, Music Education in the Christian Home, Government Nannies*—(D,E; some items-A,B,C,G,H)

North American Cambridge Classics Projects (NACCP) Resource Center
P.O. Box 932
Amherst, MA 01004-0932
(413) 256-3564
Answer keys and supplements to Cambridge Latin course

North Dakota Division of Independent Study
State University Station
1510 12th Ave. N.
Box 5036
Fargo, ND 58105
(701) 231-6000
(701) 231-6052 FAX
(800) 529-1606
website: http://www.dis.dpi.state.nd.us/

W.W. Norton and Company
800 Keystone Industrial Park
Scranton, PA 18512
(800) 223-2584
How to Lie with Statistics, Norton Literary Anthologies

Nystrom
3333 Elston Ave.
Chicago, IL 60618
(800) 621-8086
(773) 463-1144
Maps, globes, atlases, science charts, models, and educational programs

O. T. Studios
Convention Dept.
11830 E. Washington Blvd.
Whittier, CA 90606
(562) 693-8173
Offers tapes of home schooling events. Write for list.

Ohio University Course Credit by Examination
Tupper Hall, Ohio University
Athens, OH 45701
(800) 444-2910

Old Pinnacle Publishing
1048 Old Pinnacle Rd.
Joelton, TN 37080
(615) 746-3342
e-mail: CarolynRH@aol.com
Let the Authors Speak—(A,B,C,E,F,G,H)

The Oops Group
P.O. Box 5868
Katy, TX 77491
(888) 749-OOPS
(281) 347-1244
(281) 347-1277 FAX
Oops, Your Manners Are Showing

Optometric Extension Program Foundation, Inc.
1921 E. Carnegie
Santa Ana, CA 92705
(949) 250-8070
(949) 250-8157 FAX

Oral Roberts University Home Education
7777 S. Lewis Ave.
Tulsa, OK 74171
(800) 678-8876
(918) 495-6621

Oregon Institute of Science and Medicine and Althouse Press
2251 Dick George Rd.
Cave Junction, OR 97523
(541) 592-4142
Robinson Self-Teaching Home School Curriculum—(F)

Oxford University Press
Customer Service Department
2001 Evans Road
Cary, NC 27513
(800) 451-7556
A History of US series(A,C,E,F,G)

P & R Publishing Co.
P.O. Box 817
Phillipsburg, NJ 08865
(800) 631-0094
Every Thought Captive—(D)

Paradigm
P.O. Box 45161
Boise, ID 83711
(208) 322-4440
The Blumenfeld Oral Reading Assessment Test(A,D,G)

Parsons Technology
1700 Progress Drive
P.O. Box 100
Hiawatha, IA 52233
(800) 644-6344
(319) 395-7449 FAX
website: http://www.quickverse.com
Greek Tutor(D), *Hebrew Tutor, American History Explorer*

Pathway Publishing
2580 N. 250 W.
Lagrange, IN 46761
In Canada: Pathway Publishers
R.R. 4
Aylmer, Ontario
N5H 1R3 Canada
Our Heritage, Seeking True Values(B,D,G,H,I,J)

Patria Ministries
3330 Beck Road at Waterloo
Rice, WA 99167

(509) 738-4308
(509) 738-4663 FAX
Natural Science for Home Schooling Families, Rudiments of America's Christian History and Government, Providential Geography: A Stage for Men and Nations, Home School Teaching Packets

Pelican Publishing Company
P.O. Box 3110
Gretna, LA 70054
(800) 843-1724
(888) 5PELICAN
How To Plan Your Life

Penton Overseas, Inc.
2470 Impala Dr.
Carlsbad, CA 92008-7226
(800) 748-5804
(760) 431-0060
(760) 431-8110 FAX
e-mail: penton@cts.com
http://www.pentonoverseas.com
VocabuLearn, ¡Habla!(G)

Perfection Learning
1000 North Second Ave.
Logan, IA 51546-1099
(800) 831-4190
Vocabu-Lit, WORDpak, Parallel Texts, Reading Guides, Primary Source Document series

Personal Touch Planners
Cherry Patterson
5814 Caribbean Circle
Stockton, CA 95210
(209) 476-9535
e-mail: ptplanners@aol.com

Peter Bedrick Books, Inc.
156 Fifth Ave.
New York, NY 10010
(212) 206-3738
(212) 206-3741 FAX
Master of Art series(E)

Peterson's
P.O. Box 2123
Princeton, NJ 08543
(800) 338-3282
(609) 243-9111
(609) 243-9150 FAX
Peterson's Handbook for College Admissions, Peterson's Guide to Four-Year Colleges, Peterson's Distance Learning, Peterson's Guide to Two-Year Colleges, Competitive Colleges, regional college guides, *Choose a Christian College, SAT Success, Independent Study Catalog, College Money Handbook, Virtual College, Winning Money for College*—(some items-C,F)

Phoenix Learning Resources
2349 Chaffee Dr.
St. Louis, MO 63146
(800) 221-1274 orders
(800) 526-6581 information

Pioneer Productions
P.O. Box 328

Young, AZ 85554-0328
How to Identify Your Child's Learning Problems and What to Do About Them(B,I)

Plymouth Rock Foundation
P.O. Box 577, Fisk Mill
Marlborough, NH 03455
(800) 210-1620
You may also order Plymouth Rock resources from Landmark Distributors.
Institute on the Constitution, Dating vs. Courtship(D,F)

Positive Action for Christ
P.O. Box 1948
Rocky Mount, NC 27802-1948
(800) 688-3008
(919) 977-2181 FAX
Pro Series Bible Curriculum

The Practical Allergy Research Foundation
P.O. Box 60
Buffalo, NY 14223-0060
(716) 875-0398
The Impossible Child, Is This Your Child?(F,I and Bluestocking Press)

Practical Homeschooling magazine
See Home Life

Praise Hymn, Inc.
P.O. Box 1325
Taylors, SC 29687
(800) 729-2821
(864) 322-8284 FAX
God Made Music series

Precept Ministries
P.O. Box 182218
Chattanooga, TN 37422-7218
(423) 894-3277
http://www.precept.org
Line Upon Line, Precept Upon Precept—(F,H)

Precious Memories Educational Resources
18403 N.E. 111th Ave.
Battle Ground, WA 98604
(360) 687-0282
Winston Grammar—(A,B,C,D,E,F,G,H,I)

Prentice-Hall School Division
P.O. Box 2649
Columbus, OH 43216
(800) 848-9500
website: http://www.phschool.com
Jenney Latin Program—(E)

Prentice Hall
Order Processing Center
P.O. Box 11071
Des Moines, IA 50336-1071
(800) 643-5506
(515) 284-2607 FAX
Art Smart(I), *Art History and Appreciation Activities Kit*(I), *Hands-On Science!*(A,I), *Physical Science Activities for Grades 2-8*(I), *World Literature Activities Kit, The Scholarship Book*(I)

President's Challenge Physical Fitness Program
Poplars Research Center
400 E. 7th St.
Bloomington, IN 47405
(800) 258-8146
(812) 855-8999 FAX
website: http://www.indiana.edu/~preschal

Proactive
5761 E. LaPalma, #299
Anaheim Hills, CA 92807
(714) 776-6084
(714) 776-6985 FAX
A Nation Adrift

Professor Phonics-EduCare
Susan M. Greve
4714 Hubble Rd.
Cincinnati, OH 45247
(513) 385-1717
(513) 662-6629 FAX
e-mail: sue@professorphonics.com
Professor Phonics—(B,D,H)

Progeny Press
200 Spring St.
Eau Claire, WI 54703-3225
(715) 833-5259
(715) 836-0105 FAX
e-mail: progeny@mgprogeny.com
website: http://www.mgprogeny.com
—(B,C,D,E,G,H; I carries non-fiction titles)

Providence Foundation
P.O. Box 6759
Charlottesville, VA 22906
(804) 978-4535
e-mail: provfdn@aol.com
website: http://www.providencefoundation.com
America's Providential History(A,B,C,G,H), *Liberating the Nations*—(D,E,F)

Questar Publishers/Multnomah Books
P.O. Box 1720
Sisters, OR 97759
(800) 929-0910
Deadline(F), *I Kissed Dating Goodbye*(C,D), *Reaching the Heart of Your Teen*

R.A.C.E.
1461 Lincoln Way East
Chambersburg, PA 17201
(800) 318-RACE
(717) 263-5645
The Truth Behind the Declaration of Independence

Rainbow Re-Source Center
8227 Ulah Rd.
Cambridge, IL 61238
(888) 841-3456 orders only
(309) 937-3385 phone hours M-F, 8:30 a.m.- 5 p.m. central time
(309) 937-2983 FAX
e-mail: rainbowres@aol.com

Random House
Distribution Center
400 Hahn Rd.

Westminster, MD 21157
(800) 793-2665 orders
(410) 848-1900
(800) 659-2436 FAX
website: http://www.randomhouse.com
20/20 Is Not Enough, Economics in One Lesson(A or Bluestocking Press), *Princeton Review: Cracking the SAT & PSAT, What Smart Students Know*—(some items-C,D,E,F,G)

The Rebuilders of the Foundations of America's Christian Heritage
11037 Erickson Way #79
Redding, CA 96003
(916) 241-1149
e-mail: der76@juno.com
You, Your Child and the Constitution(G); *Creative Writing and the Essay; Guide to Teaching Grammar Using the Principle Approach*—(F)

Reflective Educational Perspectives
M. Pelullo-Willis and V. Kindle-Hodson
1451 E. Main St. #200
Ventura, CA 93001
(805) 648-1739
website: http://www.redp.com
Learning Style System

The Reformer Library
P.O. Box 570
Windsor, NY 13865
(607) 655-1900
The Great Christian Revolution, Bringing in the Sheaves, Killer Angel—(D)

Regal Books
2300 Knoll Drive
Ventura, CA 93003
(805) 644-9721
(800) 4-GOSPEL orders only
Preparing for Adolescence(H,I), *What the Bible Is All About for Young Explorers*—(A,C,F)

Regnery Publishing, Inc.
1 Massachusetts Ave. N.W.
Washington, DC 20001
(202) 216-0612
Facts, Not Fear; Fighting for Liberty and Virtue

The Relaxed Home Schooler/Ambleside Educational Press
Mary Hood, Ph.D.
P.O. Box 2524
Cartersville, GA 30120
(770) 917-9141
The Relaxed Home School(C,D), *Countdown to Consistency: A Workbook for Home Educators*—(B,F,G,H)

The Re-Print Corporation
P.O. Box 830677
Birmingham, AL 35283-0677

Research and Education Foundation
Robert Morey
P.O. Box 250
Newport, PA 17074
(800) 41-TRUTH

Revell/Chosen Books
order from parent company, Baker Book House
Passion and Purity, Discover Your Children's Gifts—(C,D,F)

Rex Games Inc.
530 Howard St. Ste. 100
San Francisco, CA 94105-3007
(800) 542-6375
(415) 777-1013 FAX
Tangoes®, Word Trek®—(C,G)

RiversEdge Publishing Co.
P.O. Box 622
West Linn, OR 97068
(503) 557-1850
(503) 557-8662 FAX
Total Health(E,F,G)

Rod and Staff Publishers
P.O. Box 3, Hwy. 172
Crockett, KY 41413-0003—(some items-A,C,E,G,I)

Royal Fireworks Press
P.O. Box 399
Unionville, NY 10988
(914) 726-4444
(914) 726-3824 FAX
e-mail: rfpress@ny.frontiercomm.net
Want to Work?, The Paragraph System for Successful Writing

SAT Program
P.O. Box 6200
Princeton, NJ 08541-6200
(609) 771-7600 east coast, recorded information available 24 hours
(609) 882-4118 customer service
website: http://www.collegeboard.org
SAT I and II information. Receive applications quickest when requested by phone.

Saxon Math Series
Saxon Publishers
1320 West Lindsey
Norman, OK 73069
(405) 329-7071
(800) 284-7019
math texts, *Physics*—(A,B,C,D,E,F,G,H,I)

Schenkelberg Home Enterprises
13158 Quann Lane
Dale City, VA 22193
(703) 878-4280
e-mail: cmdrford@erols.com
Writing a Step Above

Schola Publications
1698 Market St. #162
Redding, CA 96001
(916) 275-2064
The Latin Road to English Grammar—(F,I)

The School of Natural Healing
P.O. Box 412
Springville, UT 84663
(801) 489-4254
Be Your Own Doctor Herbal Course

School of Tomorrow
P.O. Box 299000
Lewisville, TX 75029-9000
(800) 925-7777
Algebra 1, Algebra 2, Physical Science, Biology, Chemistry, Geometry, Spanish I

Schoolmasters Science
745 State Circle
P.O. Box 1941
Ann Arbor, MI 48106
(800) 521-2832

Science Inquiry Enterprises
14358 Village View Ln.
Chino Hills, CA 91709
(909) 590-4618
(909) 590-2881 FAX
Turning Kids On To Science in the Home

Science Labs-in-a-Box, Inc./Science Projects
13440 Floyd Rd., Ste. 7
Dallas, TX 75243
(972) 470-0395
(800) 687-5227 (Science Projects office which handles *Science Labs-in-a-Box*)
(972) 669-1518 FAX

Science Projects, Inc.
267 Hickerson St.
Cedar Hill, TX 75104
(800) 742-7805
The Science Projects Store

Science Service
1719 N Street, N.W.
Washington, DC 20036
(202) 785-2255
website: http://www.sciserv.org.com
International Science and Engineering Fair

ScottForesman-Addison Wesley
School Services
1 Jacob Way
Reading, MA 01867
(800) 552-2259
UCSMP Algebra, UCSMP Advanced Algebra, UCSMP Geometry, Informal Geometry, The Anatomy and Physiology Coloring Book(C), *The Biology Coloring Book*(A,C,G,I), *Exploring Mathematics, Introductory Algebra, The Phenomenon of Language*(B,G), *Ecce Romani*(G), *Principles and Types of Speech Communication, Conceptual Physics*(A or from Holt Associates)—(some items-E,F)
To order the algebra texts and answer keys at school prices, or answer key to *Conceptual Physics*, we must supply evidence that we are either a school or part of a school, or else have a credentialed teacher or school order for us. Ordering on school letterhead is usually sufficient.

Scripture Memory Fellowship International
Box 411551
St. Louis, MO 63141
(314) 569-0244
(314) 569-0025 FAX
e-mail: memorize@stlnet.com
website: http://www.scripture memory.com

Sempco, Inc.
attn. Mr. Ro
P.O. Box 3262
Nashua, NH 03061
(603) 889-1830
(603) 889-1766 FAX
lab kits for high school science, plus science modules

Seton Home Study School
1350 Progress Drive
Front Royal, VA 22630
(540) 636-9990
(540) 636-1602 FAX
e-mail: info@SetonHome.org
website: http://www.SetonHome.org

Shekinah Curriculum Cellar
101 Meador Rd.
Kilgore, TX 75662
(903) 643-2760
(903) 643-2796 FAX
website: www.shekinahcc.com
e-mail: customerservice@shekinahcc.com

SimBioSys
Route 1, Box 205
Hull, GA 30646
(706) 546-7469
(706) 245-4424 FAX
e-mail: llester@athens.net
website: http://www.emmanuel-college.edu/biology/designs
Designs in the Living World—(H)

Simon and Schuster
200 Old Tappan Road
Old Tappan, NJ 07675
(800) 223-2336 orders
(800) 223-2348 customer service
website: http://www.simonsays.com
Mark Kistler's Draw Squad, Mere Christianity, The Timetables of History—(some items-A,B,C,D,E,F,G)

Singing Springs Productions
7072 Singing Springs
Evergreen, CO 80439
(303) 670-0673
(303) 674-3431 FAX
e-mail: karey@hearth-n-home.com
website: http://hearth-n-home.com
Hearth and Home—(F)

SkillsBank Corporation
7104 Ambassador Rd.
Baltimore, MD 21244
(800) 42-TUTOR for demo disk (available only in MS-DOS format), fact kit (includes detailed description), or orders
(410) 265-8874 FAX
Skills Bank Home Tutor program. Send for free demo disk and fact kit.

Small Ventures
11023 Watterson Dr.
Dallas, TX 75228
(972) 681-1728
Blessed is the Man(B,D,E,F,H)

Smartek
7908 Convoy Ct.

San Diego, CA 92111
(800) 858-WORD
e-mail: Smartekinc@aol.com
website: http://www.WordSmart.com
Think Speak and Write Better!, Word Adventure, SAT Verbal

Smiling Heart Press
P.O. Box 208
Fossil, OR 97830
Training Our Daughters to Be Keepers at Home(B,C,D,E,F,H)

Sonlight Curriculum
8121 S. Grant Way
Littleton, CO 80122-2701
(303) 730-6292
(303) 795-8668 FAX
e-mail: sonlight@crsys.com
website: http://www.crsys.com/sonlight

Sounds Of Praise Christian Music Studies
Debra Matula
442 Pennsacola Rd.
Ebensburg, PA 15931-3600
(814) 472-7704

South-Western Educational Publishing
Order from:
ITP Distribution Center
P.O. Box 6904
Florence, KY 41022
(800) 824-5179
(800) 487-8488 FAX
Geometry for Decision Making(E)

Speedy Spanish
36107 S.E. Squaw Mountain Road
Estacada, OR 97023
Speedy Spanish and *Christian Ethics for YOUth*—(B,G,I)

Spring Street Press
2606 Spring Blvd.
Eugene, OR 97403
(541) 697-2181
Responding to Literature, Strategies for Reading Nonfiction—(B,G)

Stackpole Books
5067 Ritter Rd.
Mechanicsburg, PA 17055-6921
(717) 796-0411
(717) 796-0412 FAX
The Book of Forest and Thicket, Suburban Nature Guide, Discover Nature at the Seashore—(some items-C)

State Histories
Route 1, Box 160
Anadarko, OK 73005
(405) 247-2963
e-mail: achs@tanet.net
Arkansas, Minnesota, Oklahoma, or Texas *History in Light of the Cross*

Steck-Vaughn
P.O. Box 26015
Austin, TX 78755
(800) 531-5015
Steck-Vaughn GED, Steck-Vaughn Complete GED Preparation—(I)

Student Ocean Challenge
Mame Reynolds, Director
P.O. Box 631
Jamestown, RI 02835
(401) 423-3535
(401) 423-2877 FAX
e-mail: soc@wsii.com
website: www.bwsailing.com/SOC.html

Summit Christian Academy
2100 N. Highway 360, Ste. 503
Grand Prairie, TX 75050-1026
(800) 362-9180
(972) 602-8050
(972) 602-8243 FAX

Summit Ministries
P.O. Box 207
Manitou Springs, CO 80829
(719) 685-9103
e-mail: info@summit.org
http://www.christiananswers.net/summit/sumhome.html
Understanding the Times book(B,C,D,F)
and curriculum, *Lightbearer's Christian
Worldview Curriuclum, The Summit Ministries Guide to Choosing a College*(C,D,F)

Sundance Publishing
234 Taylor St.
P.O. Box 1326
Littleton, MA 01460
(800) 343-8204

Suntex International, Inc.
118 N. 3rd St.
Easton, PA 18042
(610) 253-5255
(610) 258-2180 FAX
e-mail: math24@aol.com
24 Game. The publisher does not accept direct orders. Order from B, F, G, or Dale
Seymour Publications.

Susan Mortimer
731 W. Camp Wisdom
Duncanville, TX 75116
(972) 780-1683
Remembering God's Awesome Acts(B,H)

Sycamore Tree
2179 Meyer Place
Costa Mesa, CA 92627
(714) 650-4466 for information
(800) 779-6750 credit card orders only
(714) 642-6750 credit card orders only
e-mail: sycamoretree@compuserve.com
website: http://www.sycamoretree.com
School service, publisher, and distributor

Tah Dah, Inc.
221 Bunn Dr.
Rockton, IL 61072
(815) 624-8337
(815) 624-8452 FAX
PICKTWO—(B,C,G)

Tan Books and Publishers, Inc.
P.O. Box 424
Rockford, IL 61105
(800) 437-5876
(815) 226-7770 FAX

website: http://www.tanbooks.com
*Christ the King, Lord of History, Christ and
the Americas*

Teacher Created Materials, Inc.
6421 Industry Way
Westminster, CA 92683
Send orders to:
P.O. Box 1040
Huntington Beach, CA 92647
(800) 662-4321
(800) 525-1254 FAX
Literature Units, *Focus on Composers*(G,I),
Shakespeare Interdisciplinary Unit—(A;
some items-D,H)

Teacher Ideas Press
P.O. Box 6633
Englewood, CO 80155-6633
(800) 237-6124
(303) 220-8843 FAX
website: http://www.lu.com
e-mail: lu-books@lu.com
U.S. History through Children's Literature

Teacher's Aid Co-op
613 Big Hill Road
Mooresburg, TN 37811

The Teaching Company
7405 Alban Station Court, Ste. A-107
Springfield, VA 22150-2318
(800) 832-2412
*Algebra I, Algebra II, How to Be a Super-
star Student, Chemistry, Geometry, World
History: The Fertile Crescent to the American Revolution*

The Teaching Home
P.O. Box 20219
Portland, OR 97294-0219
(503) 253-9633

Teaching Tape Technology
8648 Highway 11
Chelsea, AL 35043
(205) 678-9996
(205) 678-9993 FAX
e-mail: teach@vol.com
Saxon *Algebra 1* video series

Teen Missions International, Inc.
885 East Hall Road
Merrit Island, FL 32953
(407) 453-0350
e-mail: tmi@cape.net
website: http://www.tmi.org

Ten Speed Press
P.O. Box 7123
Berkeley, CA 94707
College Degrees by Mail and Modem(C),
The Three Boxes of Life

Theory Time
9207 Woodleigh Dr.
Houston, TX 77083
(281) 575-8101
(281) 933-3612 FAX
e-mail: Theorytm@flash.net

Thomas Edison State College
101 West State St.
Trenton, NJ 08608-1176
(609) 984-1150
website: http://www.tesc.edu

Thomas Geale Publications, Inc.
P.O. Box 370540
583 Sixth St.
Montara, CA 94037
(800) 554-5457
(650) 728-5219
(650) 728-0918 FAX
Just Think(G,H), *Think Quest,* and *Stretch
Think*(G,H)

Thomas Nelson Publishing
Nelson Place at Elm Hill Pike
P.O. Box 141000
Nashville, TN 37214
(800) 933-9673, ext. 2037
Psychological Seduction (out of print),*The
Shaping of a Christian Family, Evidence
That Demands a Verdict.* Parent company
of Word Publishing.—(D,F)

Timberdoodle
E. 1510 Spencer Lk.Rd.
Shelton, WA 98584
(360) 426-0672
e-mail: mailbox@timberdoodle.com
website: http://www.timberdoodle.com

The Titus Woman's Homeschool Potpourri
12815 N.E. 124th St., Ste. F
Kirkland, WA 98034
(425) 820-4626

Tobin's Lab
P.O. Box 6503
Glendale, AZ 95312-6503
Tobin's plans to move to Culpeper, Virginia
in Spring of 1998, so try their 800 number,
e-mail, or directory assistance for Culpeper.
(800) 522-4776 orders only
(602) 843-4265 orders
(602) 843-3520 Help Line - Mon-Fri. 8
a.m.-12 noon
e-mail: mike@tobinlab.com

Tom Snyder Productions
80 Coolidge Hill Rd.
Watertown, MA 02172
(800) 342-0236
(617) 926-6222 FAX
website: http://www.teachtsp.com
*Mapping the World by Heart
Lite*—(C,D,E,F,I)

TOPS Learning Systems
10970 S. Mulino Rd.
Canby, OR 97013
(888) 773-9755 orders
(503) 266-5200 FAX
customer service e-mail: tops@integrityon-
line.com
website: http://topscience.org
—(some items-G)

Transparent Language
22 Proctor Hill Road
Hollis, NH 03049

(800) 752-1767
(603) 465-2230
(603) 465-2779 FAX
Language Now!

Tree of Life School
RR #2
Lakeville, NB E0J 1S0, Canada
(506) 328-6781
(506) 328-9506 FAX
e-mail: treeofl@nbnet.nb.ca
OR write to:
106 Main St.
Ste. 518
Houlton, ME 04730-9001

Tretter Violins
13651 Hope St.
Garden Grove, CA 92843-3240
(800) 626-6228
(714) 534-6228
(714) 534-7966 FAX
e-mail: trettervio@aol.com

The Trinity Foundation
P.O. Box 1666
Hobbs, NM 88240
(505) 392-8584
(505) 392-7274 FAX
Logic—(D)

TRISMS
1203 S. Delaware Pl.
Tulsa, OK 74104
(918) 585-2778 or 491-6826
website: http://www.trisms.com
Reading through the Ages(F,G)

Trivium Pursuit
139 Colorado St., Ste. 168
Muscatine, IA 52761
(309) 537-3641 (call noon to 8 p.m. central time)
e-mail: trivium@muscanet.com
website: http://www.muscanet.com/~trivium
A Greek Alphabetarion, Homeschool Greek, and other classical language materials and thinking skills resources—(C), *Teaching The Trivium* newsletter

Twain Publishers
2120 Timberlane
Wheaton, IL 60187
(630) 665-9370
e-mail: twain@twainassociates.com
website: http://www.twainassociates.com/homeschool.html
Enough About Grammar, Driving It Home

Tyndale House Publishers
P.O. Box 80
Wheaton, IL 60189
(800) 323-9400
(708) 668-8300
(708) 669-8905 FAX
The Hidden Art of Homemaking(A,B,C,F,G), *The Complete Book of Bible Literacy*—(D,H)

U.S. Government Printing Office
Washington, D.C. 20402
(202) 512-1800

The Occupational Outlook Handbook

University of Alabama, College of Continuing Studies
Division of Distance Education
Box 870388
Tuscaloosa, AL 35487-0388
(205) 348-7642
(205) 348-9278
(800) 452-5971
(205) 348-0249 FAX
e-mail: disted@ccs.ua.edu
website: http://ualix.ua.edu/~disted/

University of California Extension
Center for Media and Independent Learning
2000 Center St. #400.
Berkeley, CA 94704
(510) 642-4124 high school and college information
High school and college distance learning courses plus *The Independent Study Catalog*

University of Missouri
Center for Independent Study
136 Clark Hall
Columbia, MO 65211
(573) 882-2491
(800) 609-3727
(573) 882-6808 FAX
website: http://indepstudy.ext.missouri.edu

University of Nebraska-Lincoln, Division of Continuing Studies
269 Clifford Hardin Nebraska Center for Continuing Education
Lincoln, NE 68583-9800
(402) 472-4321
(402) 472-1901 FAX
e-mail: unldde@unl.edu

University of Texas Press
P.O. Box 7819
Austin, TX 78713-7819
(800) 252-3206
(512) 471-7233
Breaking Out of Beginner's Spanish

The University of the State of New York
Regents College
7 Columbia Circle
Albany, NY 12203
(518) 464-8500

University Prints
P.O.Box 485
21 East St.
Winchester, MA 01890

VGM Career Horizons
A Division of NTC/Contemporary Publishing Company
4255 West Touhy Ave.
Lincolnwood, IL 60646-1975
(800) 323-4900

Veritas Press
19 Funk St.
Strasburg, PA 17579
(717) 687-5122
(717) 687-8477 FAX
e-mail: Veritasprs@aol.com

website: http://members.aol.com/Veritasprs
History Flash Card Sets—(F)

Vic Lockman
233 Rogue River Hwy., #360
Grants Pass, OR 97527
(800) 847-9312
Biblical Economics in Comics(C,G); *Big Book of Cartooning; Money, Banking, and Usury*—(B,D,E,F; some items -A,H)

Video Lending Library
5777 Azalea Dr.
Grants Pass, OR 97526
(541) 479-7140 phone or FAX

Video Tutor
2109 Herbertsville Rd.
Point Pleasant, NJ 08742
(800) 445-8334

Vis-Ed/Visual Education Association
P.O. Box 1666
581 W. Leffel Lane
Springfield, OH 45501
(800) 243-7070—(G)

Vision Video
P.O. Box 540
2030 Wentz Church Rd.
Worcester, PA 19490
(800) 523-0226
(610) 584-4610 FAX
website: http://www.gatewayfilms.com
e-mail: visionvide@aol.com
Discovering The Bible, The Trial and Testimony of the Early Church, Reformation Overview, Hanged on a Twisted Cross

Visual Manna
P.O. Box 553
Salem, MO 65560
(573) 729-2100
Real Manna(some items-D,F,G)

Walk Thru the Bible Ministries, Inc.
P.O. Box 80587
Atlanta, GA 30366
(800) 877-5539
Family Walk and *Youthwalk*

WallBuilders
P.O. Box 397
Aledo, TX 76008
(817) 441-6044
e-mail: wallbuil@flash.net
website: http://www.christian answers.net
America's Godly Heritage, Keys to Good Government—(some items-D,E,F,G)

Walter Foster Publishing, Inc.
23062 La Cadena Dr.
Laguna Hills, CA 92653
(800) 433-1046
(714) 380-7510
Calligraphy Kit—(F)

Dr. Stanley Walters/Center for Children and Parents
2509 Meadowgrove
Orange, CA 92867-2005
(714) 283-3390

(714) 637-1128

Warner Books
Order from Little Brown and Company.
The Synonym Finder(A,B,H), *Homeschooling for Excellence*(A,B,C,D,H), *Smart But Feeling Dumb*—(E,F)

The Weaver
Going out of business as of November 30, 1997. Products will probably be sold under another name by another publisher. No contact name or address is available at this time. Send a SASE to Grove Publishing for information after that date.
The Weaver 7-12 Supplements, On Eagle's Wings, Genesis One

The Westbridge Academy
1610 West Highland Ave., Box 228
Chicago, IL 60660-1206
(773) 743-3312

Western Baptist College
5000 Deer Park Dr. S.E.
Salem, OR 97301-9392
(800) 845-3005
(503) 375-7005

Western Educational Associates
P.O. Box 429
30128 Auberry Rd.
Prather, CA 93651
(209) 855-3324 orders
(209) 855-8783 Academy
(209) 855-6284 FAX
Western Christian Academy is a ministry of WEA

Western Standard Publishing
P.O. Box 990
Orem, UT 84059-0990
(801) 426-3500
American Freedom Library, CD Sourcebook of American History

Wff N'Proof Games
1490-GH South Blvd.
Ann Arbor, MI 48104
Wff N'Proof game, *Equations* game, *Propaganda* game—(D)

Wheeler Applied Research
38-221 Desert Greens Dr. W.
Palm Desert, CA 92260
(909) 594-4850
or (619) 773-5795
(619) 773-2674 FAX
EZ Writer

William B. Eerdmans Publishing Company
255 Jefferson Avenue S.E.
Grand Rapids, MI 49503
(800) 253-7521
(616) 459-4591
(616) 459-6540 FAX
e-mail: wbesales@eerdmans.com
A History of Christianity in the United States and Canada—(A,D,E,F)

William Carey Library
P.O. Box 40129

Pasadena, CA 91114
(626) 798-0819
(800) MISSION for orders
Perspectives on the World Christian Movement, Mission Resource Catalog

William H. Huff
12 Carroll St. #119
Westminster, MD 21157
(410) 374-4255
Elementary Catechism on the Constitution of the United States

Window Tree Learning Project
19866 24 Avenue
Langley, B.C.
V2Z 1Y5, Canada
(604) 533-3274
(604) 533-6781 FAX
e-mail: Llink@mortimer.com

Wisdom's Gate
P.O. Box 374
Covert, MI 49043
Home School Digest

Word Publishing
See Thomas Nelson Publishing, the parent company, for ordering address.
Barna Report newsletter, *Can Man Live Without God, Children at Risk, Church History in Plain Language, A Dance with Deception, Dating With Integrity, Don't Check Your Brains at the Door*(A,H), *The Index of Leading Spiritual Indicators, Right From Wrong*—(D,F)

WordMate
P.O. Box 992
Skokie, IL 60076-0992
(888) 967-3628
(847) 677-6186 FAX orders
e-mail: WordMate@aol.com
SPANISH Say Hello audio course—(D)

Wordsmiths
1355 Ferry Rd.
Grants Pass, OR 97526
(541) 476-3080
(541) 474-9756 FAX
e-mail: frodej@chatlink.com
website: http://www.jsgrammar.com
English Fun Stuff, Vocabulary: Latin, Vocabulary: Greek, A Journey through Grammar Land(I), *Jensen's Grammar*(I), *General Punctuation*(I), *Format Writing*—(B,D,E,G,H)

World Library, Inc.
P.O. Box 19625
Irvine, CA 92623
(800) 443-0238 for orders
(714) 424-5100
(714) 424-5115 FAX
Library of the Future

World's Greatest Music, Inc.
P.O. Box 352
Midlothian, VA 23113
(800) 414-8003
(804) 272-4250
(804) 330-5856 FAX

e-mail: amw-lee@webtv.net
http://www.amusicworld.com
Basic Library of the World's Greatest Music—(F)

Worldview Academy
P.O. Box 5032
Bryan, TX 77805
(409) 822-5045
e-mail: wvacad@txcyber.com
website: http://www.worldview.org

The Writing Company
10200 Jefferson Blvd., Room K2
P.O. Box 802
Culver City, CA 90232-0802
(800) 421-4246
(310) 839-2436
(310) 839-2249 FAX
(800) 944-5432 FAX
e-mail: access@WritingCo.com
website: http://writingco.com/shakespeare
Shakespeare: The Writing Company Catalog

Young America's Foundation
110 Elden St.
Herndon, VA 22070
(703) 318-9608
The Myth of the Robber Barons

Young Writers' Institutes
1425 E. Chocolate Ave.
Hershey, PA 17033
(717) 520-1303
e-mail YWIHERSHEY@aol.com

Youth With A Mission, North American Office
7085 Battlecreek Rd. S.E.
Salem, OR 97301
(503) 364-3837
website: http://www.YWAM.org

YWAM Publishing
P.O. Box 55787
Seattle, WA 98155
(800) 922-2143
(425) 771-1153
Tracking Your Walk(B,G), *Stepping Out, The GO Manual: Global Opportunities in Youth With A Mission*

Zane Publishing, Inc.
1950 Stemmons, Ste. 4044
Dallas, TX 75207-3109
(214) 800-6000
(214) 800-6090 FAX
website: http://www.zane.com
Christian Home Learning Guides

Zondervan Publishing House
5300 Patterson S.E.
Grand Rapids, MI 49530
(800) 727-1309
Another Gospel, Read for Your Life, How to Read the Bible as Literature, Operation World, The Spiritual Lives of Great Composers(I)—(some items-A,B, C,D,F,G,H)

Index

Course of Study

Course Title	
Course Credits	
Course Curriculum	
Course Description	
Course Standard	

Chart A

DAILY ACTIVITY LOG - INDEPENDENT STUDY

NAME   WEEK OF: 19

SUBJECT	ACTIVITIES
BIBLE	
MATH	
SCIENCE	
GRAMMAR	
VOCABULARY/SPELLING	
LITERATURE	
COMPOSITION	
HISTORY/GEOGRAPHY CIVICS/ECONOMICS CURRENT EVENTS	
FOREIGN LANGUAGE	
PHYSICAL EDUCATION	
FINE ARTS	
ELECTIVES	
WORK EXPERIENCE	

High School Transcript

School Name: Place of Birth:
School Address: Date of Birth:
                                                Previous School:
School Phone: Date of Entry:
Student Name: Graduated:
Parents or Guardians: Credits Earned:
Address: Grade Point Average:

Phone:

Class	Semester/Year	Grade	Grade Points	Credits

Outside Credits/Awards:

Grade Scale   **Grade Points**

A	93-100	4
B	85-92	3
C	75-84	2
D	70-74	1
F	Below 70	0

Test Scores:

Signed _____

Position _____

Date _____

Chart C

HIGH SCHOOL PLANNING CHART
COLLEGE PREPARATORY

Use this chart to plan the program for a college bound student. In the columns marked 9th, 10th, 11th, and 12th, mark in the year in which you plan to cover that subject. Although not specifically included in the chart, critical thinking skills and personal development are neceessary.

Subject	9TH	10TH	11TH	12TH	COMMENTS
BIBLE					4 years suggested
ENGLISH					4 years recommended - emphasize writing skills

MATHEMATICS
    Algebra
    Geometry
    Advanced Math
					Algebra and geometry are generally required. Advanced math is recommended. Taking a course in 12th grade will keep you in training for college math.

SOCIAL SCIENCES
    U.s. History
    World History
    American Government
    Economics
					3 years are required. Full year courses of U.S. and World history, one year combination of government and economics.

SCIENCE
    Biology
    Chemistry
    Physics
    Geology, Oceanography,
    or other
					Biology and chemistry usually required. Should include lab work.

FOREIGN LANGUAGE					Some colleges require 2 years of the same language.
DRIVER'S EDUCATION					Recommended for all students
PHYSICAL EDUCATION					2 years required

FINE ARTS
    Art, Music, Drama,
    Dance
					In spite of varying requirements, plan on 1 year of fine arts. (California allows the substitution of foreign language for fine arts.)

ELECTIVES
    Typing
    Computer
    Home Economics
    Woodshop
					A computer class is highly recommended. Typing skills are almost a necessity.

Chart D

HIGH SCHOOL PLANNING CHART
GENERAL EDUCATION

Use this chart to plan your high school program for a non-college bound student. In the columns marked 9th, 10th, 11th, and 12th, mark in the years in which you expect to cover that subject. Included are subjects covered in public schools.

SUBJECTS	9TH	10TH	11TH	12TH	COMMENTS
BIBLE					4 years suggested
ENGLISH					3 years required - emphasize writing skills
MATHEMATICS					2 years required - can be consumer or survival math, pre-algebra, algebra, geometry.
SCIENCE 　Life science 　Physical science					2 years required - labs are optional
SOCIAL SCIENCE 　World History 　U.s. History 　American 　Government/Civics 　Economics					3 years required - full year courses of U.S. and World histories plus 1 semenster each of govenment and economics.
FOREIGN LANGUAGE or FINE ARTS 　Art, Music, Drama					1 year of either is required
PHYSICAL EDUCATION					2 years required
DRIVER'S EDUCATION					strongly recommended
ELECTIVES 　Typing 　Computers 　Auto Mechanics 　Woodshop 　Electronics 　Home Economics					seek out future job-interest-related work experience Investigate apprenticeships.

Chart E

Contract

Student Name _____

Course Title: _____

Credit Fulfillment Value: _____

Grade Level: _____

School Year: _____

Course requirements:

Activity:	Completion Date	Points Possible	Points Earned

Credits earned _____

Grade earned _____

Course standard(s): _____

_____

_____

Date of completion: planned _____ actual _____

I agree to complete this course according to the standards agreed upon.

Signed: _____ (student)

I approve the course outline and standards.

Signed: _____ (teacher)

Total points possible: _____ Total points earned: _____

_____ has completed the above course meeting the standard for earning: (Grade earned)_____

Credits earned: _____

Signed: _____ (teacher)